SUPPLEMENT OF
BASIC DOCUMENTS TO
INTERNATIONAL ENVIRONMENTAL LAW AND WORLD ORDER

A PROBLEM-ORIENTED COURSEBOOK

By

Lakshman D. Guruswamy
Professor of Law
The University of Tulsa

Sir Geoffrey W.R. Palmer, PC, KCMG, AC
Professor of Law
Victoria University of Wellington and
The University of Iowa

Burns H. Weston
Bessie Dutton Murray Professor of Law
The University of Iowa

AMERICAN CASEBOOK SERIES®

WEST PUBLISHING CO.
ST. PAUL, MINN., 1994

TEXT IS PRINTED ON 10% POST
CONSUMER RECYCLED PAPER
 PRINTED WITH
SOY INK

Acknowledgments

We wish to express our appreciation and gratitude to three very special students at The University of Iowa College of Law who gave selflessly and tirelessly of themselves in the preparation of this collection: Sally A. Bullen, awarded a Master of Laws (LL.M.) Degree in International and Comparative Law in May 1994; Chunping Shen, a third-year law student; and Sara A. Peterson, also a third-year law student and highly valued research assistant to Professor Weston. Much deserving of thanks are Professor Weston's secretary, Beverly A. Heitt, and the staffs of The University of Iowa's Main Library and Law Library for their expert aid and comfort, likewise most gratefully acknowledged. Of course, per customary practice informed by the principles *jus cogens* and *erga omnes*, we alone assume full responsibility for any and all errors, of which we hope there are none or exceedingly few.

L.D.G.
G.W.R.P.
B.H.W.

May 1994

*

Table of Abbreviations

The following abbreviations are used in the headnotes and footnotes to the instruments included in this documentary supplement.

A	United Nations General Assembly
Add.	Addendum
A.J.I.L.	American Journal of International Law
Alb.	Albania
AMR/SCM	Document of the Session of the Special Consultative Meeting on Antarctic Mineral Resources
App.	Appendix
ASEAN	Association of South-East Asian Nations
ATSCM	Special Consultative Meeting of Antarctic Treaty Parties
Belg.	Belgium
Can.	Canada
C/E	Council of Europe
CONF, Conf	Conference
C.M.L.R.	Common Market Law Reports
Czech.	Czechoslovakia
Den.	Denmark
Doc.	Document
E	United Nations Economic and Social Council
ECE	Economic Commission for Europe
EEC	European Economic Community
FAO	Food and Agriculture Organisation of the United Nations
Fr.	France
G.A., GA	General Assembly
Ger.	Germany
IAEA	International Atomic Energy Agency
IAEA INFCIRC	International Atomic Energy Agency Information Circular
IAEA Leg. Ser.	International Atomic Energy Agency Legal Series
I.C.J.	Reports of Judgments, Advisory Opinions and Orders of the International Court of Justice
I.L.A.	International Law Association, Reports of Annual Conferences of the International Law Association
I.L.M.	International Legal Materials
IMCO	Inter-Governmental Maritime Consultative Organisation
IMO	International Maritime Organisation
Mtg.	Meeting
Neth.	Netherlands
N.Z.	New Zealand

No.	Number
O.A.S. Off. Rec.	Organisation of American States Official Records
O.A.S.T.S.	Organisation of American States Treaty Series
OAU	Organisation of African Unity
OEA/Ser.	Organizacion Estados Americanos Series (Organisation of American States Series)
O.E.C.D., OECD	Organisation for Economic Co-operation and Development
Off.	Official
O.J.E.C.	Official Journal of the European Communities
P.C.I.J.	Permanent Court of International Justice: Reports
Pt., pt.	Part
RES, Res.	Resolution
Rev.	Revision, Revised
S	United Nations Security Council
Ser.	Series
Sess.	Session
Stat.	U.S. Statutes at Large
Supp.	Supplement
T.I.A.S.	U.S. Treaties and Other International Acts Series
U.K.	United Kingdom
U.N., UN	United Nations
UNEP	United Nations Environment Programme
U.N. GAOR	United Nations General Assemble Official Record
U.N.J.Y.B.	United Nations Juridical Yearbook
U.N.R.I.A.A.	United Nations Reports of International Arbitral Awards
U.N.T.S.	United Nations Treaty Series
U.S.	United States
U.S.T.	U.S. Treaties
Y.B.I.L.C.	Yearbook of the International Law Commission
Y.B.U.N.	Yearbook of the United Nations

Table of Contents

ix

SUPPLEMENT OF BASIC DOCUMENTS TO

INTERNATIONAL ENVIRONMENT LAW AND WORLD ORDER

A PROBLEM-ORIENTED COURSEBOOK

*

1. CONSTITUTIVE/ORGANIC

A. GENERAL

1.1 CONSTITUTION OF THE UNITED STATES OF AMERICA. *Arts. I, II, III, V & Amendment X*

ARTICLE I

* * *

SECTION 8. The Congress shall have Power To lay and collect Taxes, Duties, Imposts and Excises, to pay the Debts and provide for the common Defence and general Welfare of the United States; but all Duties, Imposts and Excises shall be uniform throughout the United States;

To borrow Money on the credit of the United States;

To regulate Commerce with foreign Nations, and among the several States, and with the Indian Tribes;

To establish an uniform Rule of Naturalization, and uniform Laws on the subject of Bankruptcies throughout the United States;

To coin Money, regulate the Value thereof, and of foreign Coin, and fix the Standard of Weights and Measures;

To provide for the Punishment of counterfeiting the Securities and current Coin of the United States;

To establish Post Offices and post Roads;

To promote the Progress of Science and useful Arts, by securing for limited Times to Authors and Inventors the exclusive Right to their respective Writings and Discoveries;

To constitute Tribunals inferior to the supreme Court;

To define and punish Piracies and Felonies committed on the high Seas, and Offences against the Law of Nations;

To declare War, grant Letters of Marque and Reprisal, and make Rules concerning Captures on Land and Water;

To raise and support Armies, but no Appropriation of Money to that Use shall be for a longer Term than two Years;

To provide and maintain a Navy;

To make Rules for the Government and Regulation of the land and naval Forces;

To provide for calling forth the Militia to execute the Laws of the Union, suppress Insurrections and repel Invasions;

To provide for organizing, arming, and disciplining, the Militia, and for governing such Part of them as may be employed in the Service of the United States, reserving to the States respectively, the Appointment of the Officers, and the Authority of training the Militia according to the discipline prescribed by Congress;

To exercise exclusive Legislation in all Cases whatsoever, over such District (not exceeding ten Miles square) as may, by Cession of particular States, and the Acceptance of Congress, become the Seat of the Government of the United States, and to exercise like Authority over all Places purchased by the Consent of the Legislature of the State in which the Same shall be, for the Erection of Forts, Magazines, Arsenals, dock–Yards, and other needful Buildings;—And

To make all Laws which shall be necessary and proper for carrying into Execution the foregoing Powers, and all other Powers vested by this Constitution in the Government of the United States, or in any Department or Officer thereof.

SECTION 9.   The Migration or Importation of such Persons as any of the States now existing shall think proper to admit, shall not be prohibited by the Congress prior to the Year one thousand eight hundred and eight, but a Tax or duty may be imposed on such Importation, not exceeding ten dollars for each Person.

The Privilege of the Writ of Habeas Corpus shall not be suspended, unless when in Cases of Rebellion or Invasion the public Safety may require it.

No Bill of Attainder or ex post facto Law shall be passed.

No Capitation, or other direct, Tax shall be laid, unless in Proportion to the Census or Enumeration herein before directed to be taken.

No Tax or Duty shall be laid on Articles exported from any State.

No Preference shall be given by any Regulation of Commerce or Revenue to the Ports of one State over those of another; nor shall Vessels bound to, or from, one State, be obliged to enter, clear or pay Duties in another.

No Money shall be drawn from the Treasury, but in Consequence of Appropriations made by Law; and a regular Statement and Account of the Receipts and Expenditures of all public Money shall be published from time to time.

No Title of Nobility shall be granted by the United States: And no Person holding any Office of Profit or Trust under them, shall, without the Consent of the Congress, accept of any present, Emolument, Office, or Title, of any kind whatever, from any King, Prince or foreign State.

SECTION 10.   No State shall enter into any Treaty, Alliance, or Confederation; grant Letters of Marque and Reprisal; coin Money; emit Bills of Credit; make any Thing but gold and silver Coin a Tender in Payment of Debts; pass any Bill of Attainder, ex post facto Law, or Law impairing the Obligation of Contracts, or grant any Title of Nobility.

No State shall, without the Consent of the Congress, lay any Imposts or Duties on Imports or Exports, except what may be absolutely necessary for executing its inspection Laws: and the net Produce of all Duties and Imposts, laid by any State on Imports or Exports, shall be for the Use of the Treasury of the United States; and all such Laws shall be subject to the Revision and Control of the Congress.

No State shall, without the Consent of Congress, lay any Duty of Tonnage, keep Troops, or Ships of War in time of Peace, enter into any Agreement or Compact with another State, or with a foreign Power, or engage in War, unless actually invaded, or in such imminent Danger as will not admit of delay.

ARTICLE II

SECTION 1. The executive Power shall be vested in a President of the United States of America. He shall hold his Office during the Term of four Years. * * *

* * *

SECTION 2. The President shall be Commander in Chief of the Army and Navy of the United States, and of the Militia of the several States, when called into the actual Service of the United States; he may require the Opinion, in writing, of the principal Officer in each of the executive Departments, upon any Subject relating to the Duties of their respective Offices, and he shall have Power to grant Reprieves and Pardons for Offences against the United States, except in Cases of Impeachment.

He shall have Power, by and with the Advice and Consent of the Senate, to make Treaties, provided two thirds of the Senators present concur; and he shall nominate, and by and with the Advice and Consent of the Senate, shall appoint Ambassadors, other public Ministers and Consuls, Judges of the supreme Court, and all other Officers of the United States, whose Appointments are not herein otherwise provided for, and which shall be established by Law: but the Congress may by Law vest the Appointment of such inferior Officers, as they think proper, in the President alone, in the Courts of Law, or in the Heads of Departments.

The President shall have Power to fill up all Vacancies that may happen during the Recess of the Senate, by granting Commissions which shall expire at the End of their next Session.

SECTION 3. He shall * * * receive Ambassadors and other public Ministers.

* * *

ARTICLE III

SECTION 1. The judicial Power of the United States, shall be vested in one supreme Court, and in such inferior Courts as the Congress may from time to time ordain and establish. * * *

SECTION 2. The judicial Power shall extend to all Cases, in Law and Equity, arising under this Constitution, the Laws of the United States, and Treaties made, or which shall be made, under their Authority;—to all Cases affecting Ambassadors, other public ministers and Consuls;—to all Cases of admiralty and maritime Jurisdiction;—to Controversies to which the United States shall be a Party;—to Controversies between two or more States;—between a State and Citizens of another State;—between Citizens of different States;—between Citizens of the same State claiming Lands under Grants of different States, and between a State, or the Citizens thereof, and foreign States, Citizens or Subjects.

In all Cases affecting Ambassadors, other public Ministers and Consuls, and those in which a State shall be Party, the supreme Court shall have original Jurisdiction. In all the other Cases before mentioned, the supreme Court shall have appellate Jurisdiction, both as to Law and Fact, with such Exceptions, and under such Regulations as the Congress shall make.

* * *

SECTION 3. Treason against the United States, shall consist only in levying War against them, or in adhering to their Enemies, giving them Aid and Comfort. No Person shall be convicted of Treason unless on the Testimony of two Witnesses to the same overt Act, or on Confession in open Court.

The Congress shall have Power to declare the Punishment of Treason, but no Attainder of Treason shall work Corruption of Blood, or Forfeiture except during the Life of the Person attainted.

* * *

ARTICLE VI

This Constitution, and the Laws of the United States which shall be made in Pursuance thereof; and all Treaties made, or which shall be made, under the Authority of the United States, shall be the supreme Law of the Land; and the Judges in every State shall be bound thereby, any Thing in the Constitution or Laws of any State to the Contrary notwithstanding. * * *

* * *

AMENDMENT X

The powers not delegated to the United States by the Constitution, nor prohibited by it to the States, are reserved to the States respectively, or to the people.

* * *

1.2   CONSTITUTION OF THE INTERNATIONAL LABOR ORGANIZATION (WITHOUT ANNEX, BUT AS REVISED THROUGH 9 OCTOBER 1946). Concluded at Versailles, 28 June 1919. Entered into force, 10 January 1920. 15 U.N.T.S. 35, 49 Stat. 2712 & 3480, T.I.A.S. 1868, T.S. 874: *Arts. 1, 2, 22, 24–34, 37*

PREAMBLE

Whereas universal and lasting peace can be established only if it is based upon social justice;

And whereas conditions of labour exist involving such injustice, hardship and privation to large numbers of people as to produce unrest so great that the peace and harmony of the world are imperilled; and an improvement of those conditions is urgently required; as, for example, by the regulation of the hours of work, including the establishment of a maximum working day and week, the regulation of the labour supply, the prevention of unemployment, the provision of an adequate living wage, the protection of the worker against sickness, disease and injury arising out of his employment, the protection of children, young persons and women, provision for old age and injury, protection of the interests of workers when employed in countries other than their own, recognition of the principle of equal remuneration for work of equal value, recognition of the principle of freedom of association, the organisation of vocational and technical education and other measures;

Whereas also the failure of any nation to adopt humane conditions of labour is an obstacle in the way of other nations which desire to improve the conditions in their own countries;

The High Contracting Parties, moved by sentiments of justice and humanity as well as by the desire to secure the permanent peace of the world, and with a view to attaining the objectives set forth in this Preamble, agree to the following Constitution of the International Labour Organisation:

CHAPTER I—ORGANISATION

Article 1

1. A permanent organisation is hereby established for the promotion of the objects set forth in the Preamble to this Constitution and in the Declaration concerning the aims and purposes of the International Labour Organisation adopted at Philadelphia on 10 May 1944 the text of which is annexed to this Constitution.

2. The Members of the International Labour Organisation shall be the States which were Members of the Organisation on 1 November 1945, and such other States as may become Members in pursuance of the provisions of paragraphs 3 and 4 of this article.

3. Any original member of the United Nations and any State admitted to membership of the United Nations by a decision of the General Assembly in accordance with the provisions of the Charter may become a Member of the International Labour Organisation by communicating to the Director–General of the International Labour Office its formal acceptance of the obligations of the Constitution of the International Labour Organisation.

4. The General Conference of the International Labour Organisation may also admit Members to the Organisation by a vote concurred in by two-

thirds of the delegates attending the session, including two-thirds of the Government delegates present and voting. Such admission shall take effect on the communication to the Director–General of the International Labour Office by the government of the new Member of its formal acceptance of the obligations of the Constitution of the Organisation.

5. No Member of the International Labour Organisation may withdraw from the Organisation without giving notice of its intention so to do to the Director–General of the International Labour Office. Such notice shall take effect two years after the date of its reception by the Director–General, subject to the Member having at that time fulfilled all financial obligations arising out of its membership. When a Member has ratified any international labour Convention, such withdrawal shall not affect the continued validity for the period provided for in the Convention of all obligations arising thereunder or relating thereto.

6. In the event of any State having ceased to be a Member of the Organisation, its readmission to membership shall be governed by the provisions of paragraph 3 or paragraph 4 of this article as the case may be.

Article 2

The permanent organisation shall consist of—

(a) a General Conference of representatives of the Members;

(b) a Governing Body composed as described in article 7; and

(c) an International Labour Office controlled by the Governing Body.

* * *

Article 22

Each of the Members agrees to make an annual report to the International Labour Office on the measures which it has taken to give effect to the provisions of Conventions to which it is a party. These reports shall be made in such form and shall contain such particulars as the Governing Body may request.

* * *

Article 24

In the event of any representation being made to the International Labour Office by an industrial association of employers or of workers that any of the Members has failed to secure in any respect the effective observance within its jurisdiction of any Convention to which it is a party, the Governing Body may communicate this representation to the government against which it is made, and may invite that government to make such statement on the subject as it may think fit.

Article 25

If no statement is received within a reasonable time from the government in question, or if the statement when received is not deemed to be satisfactory by the Governing Body, the latter shall have the right to publish the representation and the statement, if any, made in reply to it.

Article 26

1. Any of the Members shall have the right to file a complaint with the International Labour Office if it is not satisfied that any other Member is securing the effective observance of any Convention which both have ratified in accordance with the foregoing articles.

2. The Governing Body may, if it thinks fit, before referring such a complaint to a Commission of Inquiry, as hereinafter provided for, communicate with the government in question in the manner described in article 24.

3. If the Governing Body does not think it necessary to communicate the complaint to the government in question, or if, when it has made such communication, no statement in reply has been received within a reasonable time which the Governing Body considers to be satisfactory, the Governing Body may appoint a Commission of Inquiry to consider the complaint and to report thereon.

4. The Governing Body may adopt the same procedure either of its own motion or on receipt of a complaint from a delegate to the Conference.

5. When any matter arising out of article 25 or 26 is being considered by the Governing Body, the government in question shall, if not already represented thereon, be entitled to send a representative to take part in the proceedings of the Governing Body while the matter is under consideration. Adequate notice of the date on which the matter will be considered shall be given to the government in question.

Article 27

The Members agree that, in the event of the reference of a complaint to a Commission of Inquiry under article 26, they will each, whether directly concerned in the complaint or not, place at the disposal of the Commission all the information in their possession which bears upon the subject-matter of the complaint.

Article 28

When the Commission of Inquiry has fully considered the complaint, it shall prepare a report embodying its findings on all questions of fact relevant to determining the issue between the parties and containing such recommendations as it may think proper as to the steps which should be taken to meet the complaint and the time within which they should be taken.

Article 29

1. The Director–General of the International Labour Office shall communicate the report of the Commission of Inquiry to the Governing Body and to each of the governments concerned in the complaint, and shall cause it to be published.

2. Each of these governments shall within three months inform the Director–General of the International Labour Office whether or not it accepts the recommendations contained in the report of the Commission; and if not, whether it proposes to refer the complaint to the International Court of Justice.

Article 30

In the event of any Member failing to take the action required by paragraphs 5*(b)*, 6*(b)* or 7*(b)*(i) of article 19 with regard to a Convention or Recommendation, any other Member shall be entitled to refer the matter to the Governing Body. In the event of the Governing Body finding that there has been such a failure, it shall report the matter to the Conference.

Article 31

The decision of the International Court of Justice in regard to a complaint or matter which has been referred to it in pursuance of article 29 shall be final.

Article 32

The International Court of Justice may affirm, vary or reverse any of the findings or recommendations of the Commission of Inquiry, if any.

Article 33

In the event of any Member failing to carry out within the time specified the recommendations, if any, contained in the report of the Commission of Inquiry, or in the decision of the International Court of Justice, as the case may be, the Governing Body may recommend to the Conference such action as it may deem wise and expedient to secure compliance therewith.

Article 34

The defaulting government may at any time inform the Governing Body that it has taken the steps necessary to comply with the recommendations of the Commission of Inquiry or with those in the decision of the International Court of Justice, as the case may be, and may request it to constitute a Commission of Inquiry to verify its contention. In this case the provisions of articles 27, 28, 29, 31 and 32 shall apply, and if the report of the Commission of Inquiry or the decision of the International Court of Justice is in favour of the defaulting government, the Governing Body shall forthwith recommend the discontinuance of any action taken in pursuance of article 33.

* * *

Article 37

1. Any question or dispute relating to the interpretation of this Constitution or of any subsequent Convention concluded by the Members in pursuance of the provisions of this Constitution shall be referred for decision to the International Court of Justice.

2. Notwithstanding the provisions of paragraph 1 of this article the Governing Body may make and submit to the Conference for approval rules providing for the appointment of a tribunal for the expeditious determination of any dispute or question relating to the interpretation of a Convention which may be referred thereto by the Governing Body or in accordance with the terms of the Convention. Any applicable judgement or advisory opinion of the International Court of Justice shall be binding upon any tribunal established in virtue of this paragraph. Any award made by such a tribunal shall be circulated to the Members of the Organisation and any observations which they may make thereon shall be brought before the Conference.

* * *

1.3 CHARTER OF THE UNITED NATIONS (AS AMENDED). Concluded at San Francisco, 26 June 1945. Entered into force, 24 October 1945. 1 U.N.T.S. xvi, 1976 Y.B.U.N. 1043, 59 Stat. 1031, T.S. 993

WE THE PEOPLES OF THE UNITED NATIONS DETERMINED

to save succeeding generations from the scourge of war, which twice in our life-time has brought untold sorrow to mankind, and

to reaffirm faith in fundamental human rights, in the dignity and worth of the human person, in the equal rights of men and women and of nations large and small, and

to establish conditions under which justice and respect for the obligations arising from treaties and other sources of international law can be maintained, and

to promote social progress and better standards of life in larger freedom,

AND FOR THESE ENDS

to practice tolerance and live together in peace with one another as good neighbours, and

to unite our strength to maintain international peace and security, and

to ensure, by the acceptance of principles and the institution of methods, that armed force shall not be used, save in the common interest, and

to employ international machinery for the promotion of the economic and social advancement of all peoples,

HAVE RESOLVED TO COMBINE OUR EFFORTS
TO ACCOMPLISH THESE AIMS

Accordingly, our respective Governments, through representatives assembled in the city of San Francisco, who have exhibited their full powers found to be in good and due form, have agreed to the present Charter of the United Nations and do hereby establish an international organization to be known as the United Nations.

CHAPTER I. PURPOSES AND PRINCIPLES

Article 1

The Purposes of the United Nations are:

1. To maintain international peace and security, and to that end: to take effective collective measures for the prevention and removal of threats to the peace, and for the suppression of acts of aggression or other breaches of the peace, and to bring about by peaceful means, and in conformity with the principles of justice and international law, adjustment or settlement of international disputes or situations which might lead to a breach of the peace;

2. To develop friendly relations among nations based on respect for the principle of equal rights and self-determination of peoples, and to take other appropriate measures to strengthen universal peace;

3. To achieve international co-operation in solving international problems of an economic, social, cultural, or humanitarian character, and in promoting and encouraging respect for human rights and for funda-

mental freedoms for all without distinction as to race, sex, language, or religion; and

4. To be a centre for harmonizing the actions of nations in the attainment of these common ends.

Article 2

The Organization and its Members, in pursuit of the Purposes stated in Article 1, shall act in accordance with the following Principles.

1. The Organization is based on the principle of the sovereign equality of all its Members.

2. All Members, in order to ensure to all of them the rights and benefits resulting from membership, shall fulfil in good faith the obligations assumed by them in accordance with the present Charter.

3. All Members shall settle their international disputes by peaceful means in such a manner that international peace and security, and justice, are not endangered.

4. All Members shall refrain in their international relations from the threat or use of force against the territorial integrity or political independence of any state, or in any other manner inconsistent with the Purposes of the United Nations.

5. All Members shall give the United Nations every assistance in any action it takes in accordance with the present Charter, and shall refrain from giving assistance to any state against which the United Nations is taking preventive or enforcement action.

6. The Organization shall ensure that states which are not Members of the United Nations act in accordance with these Principles so far as may be necessary for the maintenance of international peace and security.

7. Nothing contained in the present Charter shall authorize the United Nations to intervene in matters which are essentially within the domestic jurisdiction of any state or shall require the Members to submit such matters to settlement under the present Charter; but this principle shall not prejudice the application of enforcement measures under Chapter VII.

CHAPTER II.   MEMBERSHIP

Article 3

The original Members of the United Nations shall be the states which, having participated in the United Nations Conference on International Organization at San Francisco, or having previously signed the Declaration by United Nations of 1 January 1942, sign the present Charter and ratify it in accordance with Article 110.

Article 4

1. Membership in the United Nations is open to all other peace-loving states which accept the obligations contained in the present Charter and, in the judgment of the Organization, are able and willing to carry out these obligations.

2. The admission of any such state to membership in the United Nations will be effected by a decision of the General Assembly upon the recommendation of the Security Council.

Article 5

A Member of the United Nations against which preventive or enforcement action has been taken by the Security Council may be suspended from the exercise of the rights and privileges of membership by the General Assembly upon the recommendation of the Security Council. The exercise of these rights and privileges may be restored by the Security Council.

Article 6

A Member of the United Nations which has persistently violated the Principles contained in the present Charter may be expelled from the Organization by the General Assembly upon the recommendation of the Security Council.

CHAPTER III. ORGANS

Article 7

1. There are established as the principal organs of the United Nations: a General Assembly, a Security Council, an Economic and Social Council, a Trusteeship Council, an International Court of Justice, and a Secretariat.

2. Such subsidiary organs as may be found necessary may be established in accordance with the present Charter.

Article 8

The United Nations shall place no restrictions on the eligibility of men and women to participate in any capacity and under conditions of equality in its principal and subsidiary organs.

CHAPTER IV. THE GENERAL ASSEMBLY

Composition

Article 9

1. The General Assembly shall consist of all the Members of the United Nations.

2. Each Member shall have not more than five representatives in the General Assembly.

Function and powers

Article 10

The General Assembly may discuss any questions or any matters within the scope of the present Charter or relating to the powers and functions of any organs provided for in the present Charter, and, except as provided in Article 12, may make recommendations to the Members of the United Nations or to the Security Council or to both on any such questions or matters.

Article 11

1. The General Assembly may consider the general principles of co-operation in the maintenance of international peace and security, including the principles governing disarmament and the regulation of armaments, and

may make recommendations with regard to such principles to the Members or to the Security Council or to both.

2. The General Assembly may discuss any questions relating to the maintenance of international peace and security brought before it by any Member of the United Nations, or by the Security Council, or by a state which is not a Member of the United Nations in accordance with Article 35, paragraph 2, and, except as provided in Article 12, may make recommendations with regard to any such questions to the state or states concerned or to the Security Council or to both. Any such question on which action is necessary shall be referred to the Security Council by the General Assembly either before or after discussion.

3. The General Assembly may call the attention of the Security Council to situations which are likely to endanger international peace and security.

4. The powers of the General Assembly set forth in this Article shall not limit the general scope of Article 10.

Article 12

1. While the Security Council is exercising in respect of any dispute or situation the functions assigned to it in the present Charter, the General Assembly shall not make any recommendation with regard to that dispute or situation unless the Security Council so requests.

2. The Secretary–General, with the consent of the Security Council, shall notify the General Assembly at each session of any matters relative to the maintenance of international peace and security which are being dealt with by the Security Council and shall similarly notify the General Assembly, or the Members of the United Nations if the General Assembly is not in session, immediately the Security Council ceases to deal with such matters.

Article 13

1. The General Assembly shall initiate studies and make recommendations for the purpose of:

    a. Promoting international co-operation in the political field and encouraging the progressive development of international law and its codification;

    b. Promoting international co-operation in the economic, social, cultural, educational, and health fields, and assisting in the realization of human rights and fundamental freedoms for all without distinction as to race, sex, language, or religion.

2. The further responsibilities, functions and powers of the General Assembly with respect to matters mentioned in paragraph 1(b) above are set forth in Chapters IX and X.

Article 14

Subject to the provisions of Article 12, the General Assembly may recommend measures for the peaceful adjustment of any situation, regardless of origin, which it deems likely to impair the general welfare or friendly relations among nations, including situations resulting from a violation of the provisions of the present Charter setting forth the Purposes and Principles of the United Nations.

Article 15

1. The General Assembly shall receive and consider annual and special reports from the Security Council; these reports shall include an account of the measures that the Security Council has decided upon or taken to maintain international peace and security.

2. The General Assembly shall receive and consider reports from the other organs of the United Nations.

Article 16

The General Assembly shall perform such functions with respect to the international trusteeship system as are assigned to it under Chapters XII and XIII, including the approval of the trusteeship agreements for areas not designated as strategic.

Article 17

1. The General Assembly shall consider and approve the budget of the Organization.

2. The expenses of the Organization shall be borne by the Members as apportioned by the General Assembly.

3. The General Assembly shall consider and approve any financial and budgetary arrangements with specialized agencies referred to in Article 57 and shall examine the administrative budgets of such specialized agencies with a view to making recommendations to the agencies concerned.

Voting

Article 18

1. Each member of the General Assembly shall have one vote.

2. Decisions of the General Assembly on important questions shall be made by a two-thirds majority of the members present and voting. These questions shall include: recommendations with respect to the maintenance of international peace and security, the election of the non-permanent members of the Security Council, the election of members of the Economic and Social Council, the election of the members of the Trusteeship Council in accordance with paragraph 1(c) of Article 86, the admission of new Members to the United Nations, the suspension of the rights and privileges of membership, the expulsion of Members, questions relating to the operation of the trustee-ship system, and budgetary questions.

3. Decisions on other questions, including the determination of additional categories of questions to be decided by a two-thirds majority, shall be made by a majority of the members present and voting.

Article 19

A Member of the United Nations which is in arrears in the payment of its financial contributions to the Organization shall have no vote in the General Assembly if the amount of its arrears equals or exceeds the amount of the contributions due from it for the preceding two full years. The General Assembly may, nevertheless, permit such a member to vote if it is satisfied that the failure to pay is due to conditions beyond the control of the Member.

Procedure

Article 20

The General Assembly shall meet in regular annual sessions and in such special sessions as occasion may require. Special sessions shall be convoked by the Secretary–General at the request of the Security Council or of a majority of the Members of the United Nations.

Article 21

The General Assembly shall adopt its own rules of procedure. It shall elect its President for each session.

Article 22

The General Assembly may establish such subsidiary organs as it deems necessary for the performance of its functions.

CHAPTER V. THE SECURITY COUNCIL

Composition

Article 23 [1]

1. The Security Council shall consist of fifteen Members of the United Nations. The Republic of China, France, the Union of Soviet Socialist Republics, the United Kingdom of Great Britain and Northern Ireland, and the United States of America shall be permanent members of the Security Council. The General Assembly shall elect ten other Members of the United Nations to be non-permanent members of the Security Council, due regard being specially paid, in the first instance to contribution of Members of the United Nations to the maintenance of international peace and security and to the other purposes of the Organization, and also to equitable geographical distribution.

2. The non-permanent members of the Security Council shall be elected for a term of two years. In the first election of the non-permanent members after the increase of the membership of the Security Council from eleven to fifteen, two of the four additional members shall be chosen for a term of one year. A retiring member shall not be eligible for immediate re-election.

3. Each member of the Security Council shall have one representative.

Functions and powers

Article 24

1. In order to ensure prompt and effective action by the United Nations, its Members confer on the Security Council primary responsibility for the maintenance of international peace and security, and agree that in carrying out its duties under this responsibility the Security Council acts on their behalf.

2. In discharging these duties the Security Council shall act in accordance with the Purposes and Principles of the United Nations. The specific powers granted to the Security Council for the discharge of these duties are laid down in Chapters VI, VII, VIII, and XII.

---

1. Amended text of Article 23 which entered into force on 31 August 1965.

3. The Security Council shall submit annual and, when necessary, special reports to the General Assembly for its consideration.

Article 25

The members of the United Nations agree to accept and carry out the decisions of the Security Council in accordance with the present Charter.

Article 26

In order to promote the establishment and maintenance of international peace and security with the least diversion for armaments of the world's human and economic resources, the Security Council shall be responsible for formulating, with the assistance of the Military Staff Committee referred to in Article 47, plans to be submitted to the Members of the United Nations for the establishment of a system for the regulation of armaments.

Voting

Article 27 [2]

1. Each member of the Security Council shall have one vote.

2. Decisions of the Security Council on procedural matters shall be made by an affirmative vote of nine members.

3. Decisions of the Security Council on all other matters shall be made by an affirmative vote of nine members including the concurring votes of the permanent members; provided that, in decisions under Chapter VI, and under paragraph 3 of Article 52, a party to a dispute shall abstain from voting.

Procedure

Article 28

1. The Security Council shall be so organized as to be able to function continuously. Each member of the Security Council shall for this purpose be represented at all times at the seat of the Organization.

2. The Security Council shall hold periodic meetings at which each of its members may, if it so desires, be represented by a member of the government or by some other specially designated representative.

3. The Security Council may hold meetings at such places other than the seat of the Organization as in its judgment will best facilitate its work.

Article 29

The Security Council may establish such subsidiary organs as it deems necessary for the performance of its functions.

Article 30

The Security Council shall adopt its own rules of procedure, including the method of selecting its President.

Article 31

Any Member of the United Nations which is not a member of the Security Council may participate, without vote, in the discussion of any question

2. Amended text of Article 27 which entered into force on 31 August 1965.

brought before the Security Council whenever the latter considers that the interests of that Member are specially affected.

Article 32

Any Member of the United Nations which is not a member of the Security Council or any state which is not a Member of the United Nations, if it is a party to a dispute under consideration by the Security Council, shall be invited to participate, without vote, in the discussion relating to the dispute. The Security Council shall lay down such conditions as it deems just for the participation of a state which is not a Member of the United Nations.

CHAPTER VI.   PACIFIC SETTLEMENT OF DISPUTES

Article 33

1.   The parties to any dispute, the continuance of which is likely to endanger the maintenance of international peace and security, shall, first of all, seek a solution by negotiation, enquiry, mediation, conciliation, arbitration, judicial settlement, resort to regional agencies or arrangements, or other peaceful means of their own choice.

2.   The Security Council shall, when it deems necessary, call upon the parties to settle their dispute by such means.

Article 34

The Security Council may investigate any dispute, or any situation which might lead to international friction or give rise to a dispute, in order to determine whether the continuance of the dispute or situation is likely to endanger the maintenance of international peace and security.

Article 35

1.   Any Member of the United Nations may bring any dispute, or any situation of the nature referred to in Article 34, to the attention of the Security Council or of the General Assembly.

2.   A state which is not a Member of the United Nations may bring to the attention of the Security Council or of the General Assembly any dispute to which it is a party if it accepts in advance, for the purposes of the dispute, the obligations of pacific settlement provided in the present Charter.

3.   The proceedings of the General Assembly in respect of matters brought to its attention under this Article will be subject to the provisions of Articles 11 and 12.

Article 36

1.   The Security Council may, at any stage of a dispute of the nature referred to in Article 33 or of a situation of like nature, recommend appropriate procedures or methods of adjustment.

2.   The Security Council should take into consideration any procedures for the settlement of the dispute which have already been adopted by the parties.

3.   In making recommendations under this Article the Security Council should also take into consideration that legal disputes should as a general rule be referred by the parties to the International Court of Justice in accordance with the provisions of the Statute of the Court.

Article 37

1. Should the parties to a dispute of the nature referred to in Article 33 fail to settle it by the means indicated in that Article, they shall refer it to the Security Council.

2. If the Security Council deems that the continuance of the dispute is in fact likely to endanger the maintenance of international peace and security, it shall decide whether to take action under Article 36 or to recommend such terms of settlement as it may consider appropriate.

Article 38

Without prejudice to the provisions of Articles 33 to 37, the Security Council may, if all the parties to any dispute so request, make recommendations to the parties with a view to a pacific settlement of the dispute.

CHAPTER VII. ACTION WITH RESPECT TO THREATS TO THE PEACE, BREACHES OF THE PEACE, AND ACTS OF AGGRESSION

Article 39

The Security Council shall determine the existence of any threat to the peace, breach of the peace, or act of aggression and shall make recommendations, or decide what measures shall be taken in accordance with Articles 41 and 42, to maintain or restore international peace and security.

Article 40

In order to prevent an aggravation of the situation, the Security Council may, before making the recommendations or deciding upon the measures provided for in Article 39, call upon the parties concerned to comply with such provisional measures as it deems necessary or desirable. Such provisional measures shall be without prejudice to the rights, claims, or position of the parties concerned. The Security Council shall duly take account of failure to comply with such provisional measures.

Article 41

The Security Council may decide what measures not involving the use of armed force are to be employed to give effect to its decisions, and it may call upon the Members of the United Nations to apply such measures. These may include complete or partial interruption of economic relations and of rail, sea, air, postal, telegraphic, radio, and other means of communication, and the severance of diplomatic relations.

Article 42

Should the Security Council consider that measures provided for in Article 41 would be inadequate or have proved to be inadequate, it may take such action by air, sea, or land forces as may be necessary to maintain or restore international peace and security. Such action may include demonstrations, blockade, and other operations by air, sea, or land forces of Members of the United Nations.

Article 43

1. All Members of the United Nations, in order to contribute to the maintenance of international peace and security, undertake to make available to the Security Council, on its call and in accordance with a special agreement or agreements, armed forces, assistance, and facilities, including rights of

passage, necessary for the purpose of maintaining international peace and security.

2. Such agreement or agreements shall govern the numbers and types of forces, their degree of readiness and general location, and the nature of the facilities and assistance to be provided.

3. The agreement or agreements shall be negotiated as soon as possible on the initiative of the Security Council. They shall be concluded between the Security Council and Members or between the Security Council and groups of members and shall be subject to ratification by the signatory states in accordance with their respective constitutional processes.

Article 44

When the Security Council has decided to use force it shall, before calling upon a Member not represented on it to provide armed forces in fulfilment of the obligations assumed under Article 43, invite that Member, if the Member so desires, to participate in the decisions of the Security Council concerning the employment of contingents of that Member's armed forces.

Article 45

In order to enable the United Nations to take urgent military measures, Members shall hold immediately available national air-force contingents for combined international enforcement action. The strength and degree of readiness of these continents and plans for their combined action shall be determined, within the limits laid down in the special agreement or agreements referred to in Article 43, by the Security Council with the assistance of the Military Staff Committee.

Article 46

Plans for the application of armed force shall be made by the Security Council with the assistance of the Military Staff Committee.

Article 47

1. There shall be established a Military Staff Committee to advise and assist the Security Council on all questions relating to the Security Council's military requirements for the maintenance of international peace and security, the employment and command of forces placed at its disposal, the regulation of armaments, and possible disarmament.

2. The Military Staff Committee shall consist of the Chiefs of Staff of the permanent members of the Security Council or their representatives. Any Member of the United Nations not permanently represented on the Committee shall be invited by the Committee to be associated with it when the efficient discharge of the Committee's responsibilities requires the participation of that Member in its work.

3. The Military Staff Committee shall be responsible under the Security Council for the strategic direction of any armed forces placed at the disposal of the Security Council. Questions relating to the command of such forces shall be worked out subsequently.

4. The Military Staff Committee, with the authorization of the Security Council and after consultation with appropriate regional agencies, may establish regional subcommittees.

Article 48

1.   The action required to carry out the decisions of the Security Council for the maintenance of international peace and security shall be taken by all the Members of the United Nations or by some of them, as the Security Council may determine.

2.   Such decisions shall be carried out by the Members of the United Nations directly and through their action in the appropriate international agencies of which they are members.

Article 49

The Members of the United Nations shall join in affording mutual assistance in carrying out the measures decided upon by the Security Council.

Article 50

If preventive or enforcement measures against any state are taken by the Security Council, any other state, whether a Member of the United Nations or not, which finds itself confronted with special economic problems arising from the carrying out of those measures shall have the right to consult the Security Council with regard to a solution of those problems.

Article 51

Nothing in the present Charter shall impair the inherent right of individual or collective self-defence if an armed attack occurs against a Member of the United Nations, until the Security Council has taken measures necessary to maintain international peace and security.   Measures taken by Members in the exercise of this right of self-defence shall be immediately reported to the Security Council and shall not in any way affect the authority and responsibility of the Security Council under the present Charter to take at any time such action as it deems necessary in order to maintain or restore international peace and security.

CHAPTER VIII.   REGIONAL ARRANGEMENTS

Article 52

1.   Nothing in the present Charter precludes the existence of regional arrangements or agencies for dealing with such matters relating to the maintenance of international peace and security as are appropriate for regional action, provided that such arrangements or agencies and their activities are consistent with the Purposes and Principles of the United Nations.

2.   The Members of the United Nations entering into such arrangements or constituting such agencies shall make every effort to achieve pacific settlement of local disputes through such regional arrangements or by such regional agencies before referring them to the Security Council.

3.   The Security Council shall encourage the development of pacific settlement of local disputes through such regional arrangements or by such regional agencies either on the initiative of the states concerned or by reference from the Security Council.

4.   This Article in no way impairs the application of Articles 34 and 35.

Article 53

1. The Security Council shall, where appropriate, utilize such regional arrangements or agencies for enforcement action under its authority. But no enforcement action shall be taken under regional arrangements or by regional agencies without the authorization of the Security Council, with the exception of measures against any enemy state, as defined in paragraph 2 of this Article, provided for pursuant to Article 107 or in regional arrangements directed against renewal of aggressive policy on the part of any such state, until such time as the Organization may, on request of the Governments concerned, be charged with the responsibility for preventing further aggression by such a state.

2. The term enemy state as used in paragraph 1 of this Article applies to any state which during the Second World War has been an enemy of any signatory of the present Charter.

Article 54

The Security Council shall at all times be kept fully informed of activities undertaken or in contemplation under regional arrangements or by regional agencies for the maintenance of international peace and security.

Chapter IX.   INTERNATIONAL ECONOMIC AND SOCIAL CO–OPERATION

Article 55

With a view to the creation of conditions of stability and well-being which are necessary for peaceful and friendly relations among nations based on respect for the principle of equal rights and self-determination of peoples, the United Nations shall promote:

a. higher standards of living, full employment, and conditions of economic and social progress and development.

b. solutions of international economic, social, health, and related problems; and international cultural and educational co-operation; and

c. universal respect for, and observance of, human rights and fundamental freedoms for all without distinction as to race, sex, language, or religion.

Article 56

All Members pledge themselves to take joint and separate action in co-operation with the Organization for the achievement of the purposes set forth in Article 55.

Article 57

1. The various specialized agencies, established by intergovernmental agreement and having wide international responsibilities, as defined in their basic instruments, in economic, social, cultural, educational, health, and related fields, shall be brought into relationship with the United Nations in accordance with the provisions of Article 63.

2. Such agencies thus brought into relationship with the United Nations are hereinafter referred to as specialized agencies.

Article 58

The Organization shall make recommendations for the co-ordination of the policies and activities of the specialized agencies.

Article 59

The Organization shall, where appropriate, initiate negotiations among the states concerned for the creation of any new specialized agencies required for the accomplishment of the purposes set forth in Article 55.

Article 60

Responsibility for the discharge of functions of the Organization set forth in this Chapter shall be vested in the General Assembly and, under the authority of the General Assembly, in the Economic and Social Council, which shall have for this purpose the powers set forth in Chapter X.

CHAPTER X. THE ECONOMIC AND SOCIAL COUNCIL

Composition

Article 61 [3]

1. The Economic and Social Council shall consist of fifty-four Members of the United Nations elected by the General Assembly.

2. Subject to the provisions of paragraph 3, eighteen members of the Economic and Social Council shall be elected each year for a term of three years. A retiring member shall be eligible for immediate re-election.

3. At the first election after the increase in the membership of the Economic and Social Council from twenty-seven to fifty-four members, in addition to the members elected in place of the nine members whose terms of office expires at the end of that year, twenty-seven additional members shall be elected. Of these twenty-seven additional members, the term of office of nine members so elected shall expire at the end of one year, and of nine other members at the end of two years, in accordance with arrangements made by the General Assembly.

4. Each member of the Economic and Social Council shall have one representative.

Functions and powers

Article 62

1. The Economic and Social Council may make or initiate studies and reports with respect to international economic, social, cultural, educational, health, and related matters and may make recommendations with respect to any such matters of the General Assembly, to the Members of the United Nations, and to the specialized agencies concerned.

2. It may make recommendations for the purpose of promoting respect for, and observance of, human rights and fundamental freedoms for all.

3. It may prepare draft conventions for submission to the General Assembly, with respect to matters falling within its competence.

4. It may call, in accordance with the rules prescribed by the United Nations, international conferences on matters falling within its competence.

3. Amended text of Article 61, which came into force on 24 September 1973.

Article 63

1. The Economic and Social Council may enter into agreements with any of the agencies referred to in Article 57, defining the terms on which the agency concerned shall be brought into relationship with the United Nations. Such agreements shall be subject to approval by the General Assembly.

2. It may co-ordinate the activities of the specialized agencies through consultation with and recommendations to such agencies and through recommendations to the General Assembly and to the Members of the United Nations.

Article 64

1. The Economic and Social Council may take appropriate steps to obtain regular reports from the specialized agencies. It may make arrangements with the Members of the United Nations and with the specialized agencies to obtain reports on the steps taken to give effect to its own recommendations and to recommendations on matters falling within its competence made by the General Assembly.

2. It may communicate its observations on these reports to the General Assembly.

Article 65

The Economic and Social Council may furnish information to the Security Council and shall assist the Security Council upon its request.

Article 66

1. The Economic and Social Council shall perform such functions as fall within its competence in connexion with the carrying out of the recommendations of the General Assembly.

2. It may, with the approval of the General Assembly, perform services at the request of Members of the United Nations and at the request of specialized agencies.

3. It shall perform such other functions as are specified elsewhere in the present Charter or as may be assigned to it by the General Assembly.

Voting

Article 67

1. Each member of the Economic and Social Council shall have one vote.

2. Decisions of the Economic and Social Council shall be made by a majority of the members present and voting.

Procedure

Article 68

The Economic and Social Council shall set up commissions in economic and social fields and for the promotion of human rights, and such other commissions as may be required for the performance of its functions.

Article 69

The Economic and Social Council shall invite any Member of the United Nations to participate, without vote, in its deliberations on any matter of particular concern to that Member.

Article 70

The Economic and Social Council may make arrangements for representatives of the specialized agencies to participate, without vote, in its deliberations and in those of the commissions established by it, and for its representatives to participate in the deliberations of the specialized agencies.

Article 71

The Economic and Social Council may make suitable arrangements for consultation with non-governmental organizations which are concerned with matters within its competence. Such arrangements may be made with international organizations and, where appropriate, with national organizations after consultation with the Member of the United Nations concerned.

Article 72

1. The Economic and Social Council shall adopt its own rules of procedure, including the method of selecting its President.

2. The Economic and Social Council shall meet as required in accordance with its rules, which shall include provision for the convening of meetings on the request of a majority of its members.

CHAPTER XI. DECLARATION REGARDING NON–SELF–GOVERNING TERRITORIES

Article 73

Members of the United Nations which have or assume responsibilities for the administration of territories whose peoples have not yet attained a full measure of self-government recognize the principle that the interests of the inhabitants of these territories are paramount, and accept as a sacred trust the obligation to promote to the utmost, within the system of international peace and security established by the present Charter, the well-being of the inhabitants of these territories, and, to this end:

a. to ensure, with due respect for the culture of the peoples concerned, their political, economic, social, and educational advancement, their just treatment, and their protection against abuses;

b. to develop self-government, to take due account of the political aspirations of the peoples, and to assist them in the progressive development of their free political institutions, according to the particular circumstances of each territory and its peoples and their varying stages of advancement;

c. to further international peace and security;

d. to promote constructive measures of development, to encourage research, and to cooperate with one another and, when and where appropriate, with specialized international bodies with a view to the practical achievement of the social, economic, and scientific purposes set forth in this Article; and

e. to transmit regularly to the Secretary–General for information purposes, subject to such limitation as security and constitutional considerations may require, statistical and other information of a technical nature relating to economic, social, and educational conditions in the territories for which they are respectively responsible other than those territories to which Chapters XII and XIII apply.

Article 74

Members of the United Nations also agree that their policy in respect of the territories to which this Chapter applies, no less than in respect of their metropolitan areas, must be based on the general principle of good-neighbourliness, due account being taken of the interests and well-being of the rest of the world, in social, economic, and commercial matters.

CHAPTER XII. INTERNATIONAL TRUSTEESHIP SYSTEM

Article 75

The United Nations shall establish under its authority an international trusteeship system for the administration and supervision of such territories as may be placed thereunder by subsequent individual agreements. These territories are hereinafter referred to as trust territories.

Article 76

The basic objectives of the trusteeship system, in accordance with the Purposes of the United Nations laid down in Article 1 of the present Charter, shall be:

a. to further international peace and security;

b. to promote the political, economic, social, and educational advancement of the inhabitants of the trust territories, and their progressive development towards self-government or independence as may be appropriate to the particular circumstances of each territory and its peoples and the freely expressed wishes of the peoples concerned, and as may be provided by the terms of each trusteeship agreement;

c. to encourage respect for human rights and for fundamental freedoms for all without distinction as to race, sex, language, or religion, and to encourage recognition of the interdependence of the peoples of the world; and

d. to ensure equal treatment in social, economic, and commercial matters for all Members of the United nations and their nationals, and also equal treatment for the latter in the administration of justice, without prejudice to the attainment of the foregoing objectives and subject to the provisions of Article 80.

Article 77

1. The trusteeship system shall apply to such territories in the following categories as may be placed thereunder by means of trusteeship agreements:

a. territories now held under mandate;

b. territories which may be detached from enemy states as a result of the Second World War; and

c. territories voluntarily placed under the system by states responsible for their administration.

2. It will be a matter for subsequent agreement as to which territories in the foregoing categories will be brought under the trusteeship system and upon what terms.

Article 78

The trusteeship system shall not apply to territories which have become Members of the United Nations, relationship among which shall be based on respect for the principle of sovereign equality.

Article 79

The terms of trusteeship for each territory to be placed under the trusteeship system, including any alteration or amendment, shall be agreed upon by the states directly concerned, including the mandatory power in the case of territories held under mandate by a Member of the United Nations, and shall be approved as provided for in Articles 83 and 85.

Article 80

1. Except as may be agreed upon in individual trusteeship agreements, made under Articles 77, 79, and 81, placing each territory under the trusteeship system, and until such agreements have been concluded, nothing in this Chapter shall be construed in or of itself to alter in any manner the rights whatsoever of any states or any peoples or the terms of existing international instruments to which Members of the United Nations may respectively be parties.

2. Paragraph 1 of this Article shall not be interpreted as giving grounds for delay or postponement of the negotiation and conclusion of agreements for placing mandated and other territories under the trusteeship system as provided for in Article 77.

Article 81

The trusteeship agreement shall in each case include the terms under which the trust territory will be administered and designate the authority which will exercise the administration of the trust territory. Such authority, hereinafter called the administering authority, may be one or more states or the organization itself.

Article 82

There may be designated, in any trusteeship agreement, a strategic area or areas which may include part or all of the trust territory to which the agreement applies, without prejudice to any special agreement or agreements made under Article 43.

Article 83

1. All functions of the United Nations relating to strategic areas, including the approval of the terms of the trusteeship agreements and of their alterations or amendment, shall be exercised by the Security Council.

2. The basic objectives set forth in Article 76 shall be applicable to the people of each strategic area.

3. The Security Council shall, subject to the provisions of the trusteeship agreements and without prejudice to security considerations, avail itself of the assistance of the Trusteeship Council to perform those functions of the United Nations under the trusteeship system relating to political, economic, social, and educational matters in the strategic areas.

Article 84

It shall be the duty of the administering authority to ensure that the trust territory shall play its part in the maintenance of international peace and security. To this end the administering authority may make use of volunteer forces, facilities, and assistance from the trust territory in carrying out the obligations towards the Security Council undertaken in this regard by the administering authority, as well as for local defence and the maintenance of law and order within the trust territory.

Article 85

1. The functions of the United Nations with regard to trusteeship agreements for all areas not designated as strategic, including the approval of the terms of the trusteeship agreements and of their alteration or amendment, shall be exercised by the General Assembly.

2. The Trusteeship Council, operating under the authority of the General Assembly, shall assist the General Assembly in carrying out these functions.

CHAPTER XIII. THE TRUSTEESHIP COUNCIL

Composition

Article 86

1. The Trusteeship Council shall consist of the following Members of the United Nations:

    a. those Members administering trust territories;

    b. such of those Members mentioned by name in Article 23 as are not administering trust territories; and

    c. as many other Members elected for three-year terms by the General Assembly as may be necessary to ensure that the total number of members of the Trusteeship Council is equally divided between those Members of the United Nations which administer trust territories and those which do not.

2. Each member of the Trusteeship Council shall designate one specially qualified person to represent it therein.

Functions and powers

Article 87

The General Assembly and, under its authority, the Trusteeship Council, in carrying out their functions, may:

    a. consider reports submitted by the administering authority;

    b. accept petitions and examine them in consultation with the administering authority;

    c. provide for periodic visits to the respective trust territories at times agreed upon with the administering authority; and

    d. take these and other actions in conformity with the terms of the trusteeship agreements.

Article 88

The Trusteeship Council shall formulate a questionnaire on the political, economic, social, and educational advancement of the inhabitants of each trust territory, and the administering authority for each trust territory within the competence of the General Assembly shall make an annual report to the General Assembly upon the basis of such questionnaire.

Voting

Article 89

1. Each member of the Trusteeship Council shall have one vote.

2. Decisions of the Trusteeship Council shall be made by a majority of the members present and voting.

Procedure

Article 90

1. The Trusteeship Council shall adopt its own rules of procedure, including the method of selecting its President.

2. The Trusteeship Council shall meet as required in accordance with its rules, which shall include provision for the convening of meetings on the request of a majority of its members.

Article 91

The Trusteeship Council shall, when appropriate, avail itself of the assistance of the Economic and Social Council and of the specialized agencies in regard to matters with which they are respectively concerned.

CHAPTER XIV. THE INTERNATIONAL COURT OF JUSTICE

Article 92

The International Court of Justice shall be principle judicial organ of the United Nations. It shall function in accordance with the annexed Statute, which is based upon the Statute of the Permanent Court of International Justice and forms an integral part of the present Charter.

Article 93

1. All Members of the United Nations are ipso facto parties to the Statute of the International Court of Justice.

2. A state which is not a Member of the United Nations may become a party to the Statute of the International Court of Justice on conditions to be determined in each case by the General Assembly upon the recommendation of the Security Council.

Article 94

1. Each Member of the United Nations undertakes to comply with the decision of the International Court of Justice in any case to which it is a party.

2. If any party to a case fails to perform the obligations incumbent upon it under a judgment rendered by the Court, the other party may have recourse to the Security Council, which may, if it deems necessary, make recommendations or decide upon measures to be taken to give effect to the judgment.

Article 95

Nothing in the present Charter shall prevent members of the United Nations from entrusting the solution of their differences to other tribunals by virtue of agreements already in existence or which may be concluded in the future.

Article 96

1. The General Assembly or the Security Council may request the International Court of Justice to give an advisory opinion on any legal question.

2. Other organs of the United Nations and specialized agencies, which may at any time be so authorized by the General Assembly, may also request advisory opinions of the Court on legal questions arising within the scope of their activities.

CHAPTER XV. THE SECRETARIAT

Article 97

The Secretariat shall comprise a Secretary–General and such staff as the Organization may require. The Secretary–General shall be appointed by the General Assembly upon the recommendation of the Security Council. He shall be the chief administrative officer of the Organization.

Article 98

The Secretary–General shall act in that capacity in all meetings of the General Assembly, of the Security Council, of the Economic and Social Council, and of the Trusteeship Council, and shall perform such other functions as are entrusted to him by these organs. The Secretary–General shall make an annual report to the General Assembly on the work of the Organization.

Article 99

The Secretary–General may bring to the attention of the Security Council any matter which in his opinion may threaten the maintenance of international peace and security.

Article 100

1. In the performance of their duties the Secretary–General and the staff shall not seek or receive instructions from any government or from any other authority external to the Organization. They shall refrain from any action which might reflect on their position as international officials responsible only to the Organization.

2. Each Member of the United Nations undertakes to respect the exclusively international character of the responsibilities of the Secretary–General and the staff and not to seek to influence them in the discharge of their responsibilities.

Article 101

1. The staff shall be appointed by the Secretary–General under regulations established by the General Assembly.

2. Appropriate staffs shall be permanently assigned to the Economic and Social Council, the Trusteeship Council, and, as required, to other organs of the United Nations. These staffs shall form a part of the Secretariat.

3. The paramount consideration in the employment of the staff and in the determination of the conditions of service shall be the necessity of securing the highest standards of efficiency, competence, and integrity. Due regard shall be paid to the importance of recruiting the staff on as wide a geographical basis as possible.

CHAPTER XVI. MISCELLANEOUS PROVISIONS
Article 102

1. Every treaty and every international agreement entered into by any Member of the United Nations after the present Charter comes into force shall as soon as possible be registered with the Secretariat and published by it.

2. No party to any such treaty or international agreement which has not been registered in accordance with the provisions of paragraph 1 of this Article may invoke that treaty or agreement before an organ of the United Nations.

Article 103

In the event of a conflict between the obligations of the Members of the United Nations under the present Charter and their obligations under any other international agreement, their obligations under the present Charter shall prevail.

Article 104

The Organization shall enjoy in the territory of each of its Members such legal capacity as may be necessary for the exercise of its functions and the fulfilment of its purposes.

Article 105

1. The Organization shall enjoy in the territory of each of its Members such privileges and immunities as are necessary for the fulfilment of its purposes.

2. Representatives of the Members of the United Nations and officials of the Organization shall similarly enjoy such privileges and immunities as are necessary for the independent exercise of their functions in connexion with the Organization.

3. The General Assembly may make recommendations with a view to determining the details of the application of paragraphs 1 and 2 of this Article or may propose conventions to the Members of the United Nations for this purpose.

CHAPTER XVII. TRANSITIONAL SECURITY ARRANGEMENTS
Article 106

Pending the coming into force of such special agreements referred to in Article 43 as in the opinion of the Security Council enable it to begin the exercise of its responsibilities under Article 42, the parties to the Four–Nation Declaration, signed at Moscow, 30 October 1943, and France, shall, in accordance with the provisions of paragraph 5 of that Declaration, consult with one another and as occasion requires with other Members of the United Nations with a view to such joint action on behalf of the Organization as may be necessary for the purpose of maintaining international peace and security.

Article 107

Nothing in the present Charter shall invalidate or preclude action, in relation to any state which during the Second World War has been an enemy of any signatory to the present Charter, taken or authorized as a result of that war by the Governments having responsibility for such action.

CHAPTER XVIII.   AMENDMENTS

Article 108

Amendments to the present Charter shall come into force for all Members of the United Nations when they have been adopted by a vote of two thirds of the members of the General Assembly and ratified in accordance with their respective constitutional processes by two thirds of the Members of the United Nations, including all the permanent members of the Security Council.

Article 109 [4]

1.   A General Conference of the Members of the United Nations for the purpose of reviewing the present Charter may be held at a date and place to be fixed by a two-thirds vote of the members of the General Assembly and by a vote of any nine members of the Security Council.   Each Member of the United Nations shall have one vote in the conference.

2.   Any alteration of the present Charter recommended by a two-thirds vote of the conference shall take effect when ratified in accordance with their respective constitutional processes by two thirds of the Members of the United Nations including all the permanent members of the Security Council.

3.   If such a conference has not been held before the tenth annual session of the General Assembly following the coming into force of the present Charter, the proposal to call such a conference shall be placed on the agenda of that session of the General Assembly, and the conference shall be held if so decided by a majority vote of the members of the General Assembly and by a vote of any seven members of the Security Council.

CHAPTER XIX.   RATIFICATION AND SIGNATURE

Article 110

1.   The present Charter shall be ratified by the signatory states in accordance with their respective constitutional processes.

2.   The ratifications shall be deposited with the Government of the United States of America, which shall notify all the signatory states of each deposit as well as the Secretary–General of the Organization when he has been appointed.

3.   The present Charter shall come into force upon the deposit of ratifications by the Republic of China, France, the Union of Soviet Socialist Republics, the United Kingdom of Great Britain and Northern Ireland, and the United States of America, and by a majority of the other signatory states. A protocol of the ratifications deposited shall thereupon be drawn up by the

4.   Amended text of Article 109 which came into force on 12 June 1968.

Government of the United States of America which shall communicate copies thereof to all the signatory states.

4. The states signatory to the present Charter which ratify it after it has come into force will become original Members of the United Nations on the date of the deposit of their respective ratifications.

Article 111

The present Charter, of which the Chinese, French, Russian, English, and Spanish texts are equally authentic, shall remain deposited in the archives of the Government of the United States of America. Duly certified copies thereof shall be transmitted by that Government to the Governments of the other signatory states.

1.4 STATUTE OF THE INTERNATIONAL COURT OF JUSTICE. Concluded at San Francisco, 26 June 1945. Entered into force, 24 October 1945. 1976 Y.B.U.N. 1052, 59 Stat. 1031, T.S. No. 993

Article 1

THE INTERNATIONAL COURT OF JUSTICE established by the Charter of the United Nations as the principal judicial organ of the United Nations shall be constituted and shall function in accordance with the provisions of the present Statute.

CHAPTER I. ORGANIZATION OF THE COURT

Article 2

The Court shall be composed of a body of independent judges, elected regardless of their nationality from among persons of high moral character, who possess the qualifications required in their respective countries for appointment to the highest judicial offices, or are jurisconsults of recognized competence in international law.

Article 3

1. The Court shall consist of fifteen members, no two of whom may be nationals of the same state.

2. A person who for the purposes of membership in the Court could be regarded as a national of more than one state shall be deemed to be a national of the one in which he ordinary exercises civil and political rights.

Article 4

1. The members of the Court shall be elected by the General Assembly and by the Security Council from a list of persons nominated by the national groups in the Permanent Court of Arbitration, in accordance with the following provisions.

2. In the case of Members of the United Nations not represented in the Permanent Court of Arbitration, candidates shall be nominated by national groups appointed for this purpose by their governments under the same conditions as those prescribed for members of the Permanent Court of Arbitration by Article 44 of the Convention of the Hague of 1907 for the pacific settlement of international disputes.

3. The conditions under which a state which is a party to the present Statute but is not a Member of the United Nations may participate in electing the members of the Court shall, in the absence of a special agreement, be laid down by the General Assembly upon recommendation of the Security Council.

Article 5

1. At least three months before the date of the election, the Secretary–General of the United Nations shall address a written request to the members of the Permanent Court of Arbitration belonging to the states which are parties to the present Statute, and to the members of the national groups appointed under Article 4, paragraph 2, inviting them to undertake, within a given time, by national groups, the nomination of persons in a position to accept the duties of a member of the Court.

2. No group may nominate more than four persons, not more than two of whom shall be of their own nationality. In no case may the number of

candidates nominated by a group be more than double the number of seats to be filled.

Article 6

Before making these nominations, each national group is recommended to consult its highest court of justice, its legal faculties and schools of law, and its national academies and national sections of international academies devoted to the study of law.

Article 7

1. The Secretary–General shall prepare a list in alphabetical order of all the persons thus nominated. Save as provided in Article 12, paragraph 2, these shall be the only persons eligible.

2. The Secretary–General shall submit this list to the General Assembly and to the Security Council.

Article 8

The General Assembly and the Security Council shall proceed independently of one another to elect the members of the Court.

Article 9

At every election, the electors shall bear in mind not only that the persons to be elected should individually possess the qualifications required, but also that in the body as a whole the representation of the main forms of civilization and of the principal legal systems of the world should be assured.

Article 10

1. Those candidates who obtain an absolute majority of votes in the General Assembly and in the Security Council shall be considered as elected.

2. Any vote of the Security Council, whether for the election of judges or for the appointment of members of the conference envisaged in Article 12, shall be taken without any distinction between permanent and non-permanent members of the Security Council.

3. In the event of more than one national of the same state obtaining an absolute majority of the votes both of the General Assembly and of the Security Council, the eldest of these only shall be considered as elected.

Article 11

If, after the first meeting held for the purpose of the election, one or more seats remain to be filled, a second and, if necessary, a third meeting shall take place.

Article 12

1. If, after the third meeting, one or more seats still remain unfilled, a joint conference consisting of six members, three appointed by the General Assembly and three by the Security Council, may be formed at any time at the request of either the General Assembly or the Security Council, for the purpose of choosing by the vote of an absolute majority one name for each seat still vacant, to submit to the General Assembly and the Security Council for their respective acceptance.

2. If the joint conference is unanimously agreed upon any person who fulfils the required conditions, he may be included in its list, even though he was not included in the list of nominations referred to in Article 7.

3. If the joint conference is satisfied that it will not be successful in procuring an election, those members of the Court who have already been elected shall, within a period to be fixed by the Security Council, proceed to fill the vacant seats by selection from among those candidates who have obtained votes either in the General Assembly or in the Security Council.

4. In the event of an equality of votes among the judges, the eldest judge shall have a casting vote.

Article 13

1. The members of the Court shall be elected for nine years and may be re-elected; provided, however, that of the judges elected at the first election, the terms of five judges shall expire at the end of three years and the terms of five more judges shall expire at the end of six years.

2. The judges whose terms are to expire at the end of the above-mentioned initial periods of three and six years shall be chosen by lot to be drawn by the Secretary–General immediately after the first election has been completed.

3. The members of the Court shall continue to discharge their duties until their places have been filled. Though replaced, they shall finish any cases which they may have begun.

4. In the case of the resignation of a member of the Court, the resignation shall be addressed to the President of the Court for transmission to the Secretary–General. This last notification makes the place vacant.

Article 14

Vacancies shall be filled by the same methods as that laid down for the first election, subject to the following provision: the Secretary–General shall, within one month of the occurrence of the vacancy, proceed to issue the invitations provided for in Article 5, and the date of the election shall be fixed by the Security Council.

Article 15

A member of the Court elected to replace a member whose term of office has not expired shall hold office for the remainder of his predecessor's term.

Article 16

1. No member of the Court may exercise any political or administrative function, or engage in any other occupation of a professional nature.

2. Any doubt on this point shall be settled by the decision of the Court.

Article 17

1. No member of the Court may act as agent, counsel, or advocate in any case.

2. No member may participate in the decision of any case in which he has previously taken part as agent, counsel, or advocate for one of the parties, or as a member of a national or international court, or of a commission of enquiry, or in any other capacity.

3. Any doubt on this point shall be settled by the decision of the Court.

Article 18

1. No member of the Court can be dismissed unless, in the unanimous opinion of the other members, he has ceased to fulfil the required conditions.

2. Formal notification thereof shall be made to the Secretary–General by the Registrar.

3. This notification makes the place vacant.

Article 19

The members of the Court, when engaged on the business of the Court, shall enjoy diplomatic privileges and immunities.

Article 20

Every member of the Court shall, before taking up his duties, make a solemn declaration in open court that he will exercise his powers impartially and conscientiously.

Article 21

1. The Court shall elect its President and Vice–President for three years; they may be re-elected.

2. The Court shall appoint its Registrar and may provide for the appointment of such other officers as may be necessary.

Article 22

1. The seat of the Court shall be established at The Hague. This, however, shall not prevent the Court from sitting and exercising its functions elsewhere whenever the Court considers it desirable.

2. The President and the Registrar shall reside at the seat of the Court.

Article 23

1. The Court shall remain permanently in session, except during the judicial vacations, the dates and duration which shall be fixed by the Court.

2. Members of the Court are entitled to periodic leave, the dates and duration of which shall be fixed by the Court, having in mind the distance between The Hague and the home of each judge.

3. Members of the Court shall be bound, unless they are on leave or prevented from attending by illness or other serious reasons duly explained to the President, to hold themselves permanently at the disposal of the Court.

Article 24

1. If, for some special reason, a member of the Court considers that he should not take part in the decision of a particular case, he shall so inform the President.

2. If the President considers that for some special reason one of the members of the Court should not sit in a particular case, he shall give him notice accordingly.

3. If in any such case the member of the Court and the President disagree, the matter shall be settled by the decision of the Court.

Article 25

1. The full Court shall sit except when it is expressly provided otherwise in the present Statute.

2. Subject to the condition that the number of judges available to constitute the Court is not thereby reduced below eleven, the Rules of the Court may provide for allowing one or more judges, according to circumstances and in rotation, to be dispensed from sitting.

3. A quorum of nine judges shall suffice to constitute the Court.

Article 26

1. The Court may from time to time form one or more chambers, composed of three or more judges as the Court may determine, for dealing with particular categories of cases; for example, labour cases and cases relating to transit and communications.

2. The Court may at any time form a chamber for dealing with a particular case. The number of judges to constitute such a chamber shall be determined by the Court with the approval of the parties.

3. Cases shall be heard and determined by the chambers provided for in this Article if the parties so request.

Article 27

A judgment given by any of the chambers provided for in Articles 26 and 29 shall be considered as rendered by the Court.

Article 28

The chambers provided for in Articles 26 and 29 may, with the consent of the parties, sit and exercise their functions elsewhere than at The Hague.

Article 29

With a view to the speedy dispatch of business, the Court shall form annually a chamber composed of five judges which, at the request of the parties, may hear and determine cases by summary procedure. In addition, two judges shall be selected for the purpose of replacing judges who find it impossible to sit.

Article 30

1. The Court shall frame rules for carrying out its functions. In particular, it shall lay down rules of procedure.

2. The Rules of the Court may provide for assessors to sit with the Court or with any of its chambers, without the right to vote.

Article 31

1. Judges of the nationality of each of the parties shall retain their right to sit in the case before the Court.

2. If the Court includes upon the Bench a judge of the nationality of one of the parties, any other party may choose a person to sit as judge. Such person shall be chosen preferably from among those persons who have been nominated as candidates as provided in Articles 4 and 5.

3. If the Court includes upon the Bench no judge of the nationality of the parties, each of these parties may proceed to choose a judge as provided in paragraph 2 of this Article.

4. The provisions of this article shall apply to the case of Articles 26 and 29. In such cases, the President shall request one or, if necessary, two of the members of the Court forming the chamber to give place to the members of the Court of the nationality of the parties concerned, and, failing such, or if they are unable to be present, to the judges specially chosen by the parties.

5. Should there be several parties in the same interest, they shall, for the purpose of the preceding provisions, be reckoned as one party only. Any doubt upon this point shall be settled by the decision of the Court.

6. Judges chosen as laid down in paragraphs 2, 3, and 4 of this Article shall fulfil the conditions required by Articles 2, 17 (paragraph 2), 20, and 24 of the present Statute. They shall take part in the decision on terms of complete equality with their colleagues.

Article 32

1. Each member of the Court shall receive an annual salary.

2. The President shall receive a special annual allowance.

3. The Vice-President shall receive a special allowance for every day on which he acts as President.

4. The judges chosen under Article 31, other than members of the Court, shall receive compensation for each day on which they exercise their functions.

5. These salaries, allowances, and compensation shall be fixed by the General Assembly. They may not be decreased during the term of office.

6. The salary of the Registrar shall be fixed by the General Assembly on the proposal of the Court.

7. Regulations made by the General Assembly shall fix the conditions under which retirement pensions may be given to members of the Court and to the Registrar, and the conditions under which members of the Court and the Registrar shall have their travelling expenses refunded.

8. The above salaries, allowances, and compensation shall be free of all taxation.

Article 33

The expenses of the Court shall be borne by the United Nations in such a manner as shall be decided by the General Assembly.

Chapter II. COMPETENCE OF THE COURT

Article 34

1. Only states may be parties in cases before the Court.

2. The Court, subject to and in conformity with its Rules, may request of public international organizations information relevant to cases before it, and shall receive such information presented by such organizations on their own initiative.

3.   Whenever the construction of the constituent instrument of a public international organization or of an international convention adopted thereunder is in question in a case before the Court, the Registrar shall so notify the public international organization concerned and shall communicate to it copies of all the written proceedings.

Article 35

1.   The Court shall be open to the states parties to the present Statute.

2.   The conditions under which the Court shall be open to other states shall, subject to the special provisions contained in treaties in force, be laid down by the Secretary Council, but in no case shall such conditions place the parties in a position of inequality before the Court.

3.   When a state which is not a Member of the United Nations is a party to a case, the Court shall fix the amount which that party is to contribute towards the expenses of the Court.   This provision shall not apply it such state is bearing a share of the expenses of the Court.

Article 36

1.   The jurisdiction of the Court comprises all cases which the parties refer to it and all matters specially provided for in the Charter of the United Nations or in treaties and conventions in force.

2.   The states parties to the present Statute may at any time declare that they recognize as compulsory *ipso facto* and without special agreement, in relation to any other state accepting the same obligation, the jurisdiction of the Court in all legal disputes concerning:

   a.   the interpretation of a treaty;

   b.   any question of international law;

   c.   the existence of any fact which, if established, would constitute a breach of an international obligation;

   d.   the nature or extent of the reparation to be made for the breach of an international obligation.

3.   The declarations referred to above may be made unconditionally or on condition of reciprocity on the part of several or certain states, or for a certain time.

4.   Such declarations shall be deposited with the Secretary–General of the United Nations, who shall transmit copies thereof to the parties to the Statute and to the Registrar of the Court.

5.   Declarations made under Article 36 of the Statute of the Permanent Court of International Justice and which are still in force shall be deemed, as between the parties to the present Statute, to be acceptances of the compulsory jurisdiction of the International Court of Justice for the period which they still have to run and in accordance with their terms.

6.   In the event of a dispute as to whether the Court has jurisdiction, the matter shall be settled by the decision of the Court.

Article 37

Wherever a treaty or convention in force provides for reference of a matter to a tribunal to have been instituted by the League of Nations, or to the Permanent Court of International Justice, the matter shall, as between the parties to the present Statute, be referred to the International Court of Justice.

Article 38

1. The Court, whose function is to decide in accordance with international law such disputes as are submitted to it, shall apply:

    a. international conventions, whether general or particular, establishing rules expressly recognized by the contesting states;

    b. international custom, as evidence of a general practice accepted as law;

    c. the general principles of law recognized by civilized nations;

    d. subject to the provisions of Article 59, judicial decisions and the teachings of the most highly qualified publicists of the various nations, as subsidiary means for the determination of rules of law.

2. This provision shall not prejudice the power of the Court to decide a case *ex aequo et bono,* if the parties agree thereto.

Chapter III. PROCEDURE

Article 39

1. The official languages of the Court shall be French and English. If the parties agree that the case shall be conducted in French, the judgment shall be delivered in French. If the parties agree that the case shall be conducted in English, the judgment shall be delivered in English.

2. In the absence of an agreement as to which language shall be employed, each party may, in the pleadings, use the language which it prefers; the decision of the Court shall be given in French and English. In this case the Court shall at the same time determine which of the two texts shall be considered as authoritative.

3. The Court shall, at the request of any party, authorize a language other than French or English to be used by that party.

Article 40

1. Cases are brought before the Court, as the case may be, either by the notification of the special agreement or by a written application addressed to the Registrar. In either case the subject of the dispute and the parties shall be indicated.

2. The Registrar shall forthwith communicate the application to all concerned.

3. He shall also notify the Members of the United Nations through the Secretary–General, and also any other states entitled to appear before the Court.

Article 41

1. The Court shall have the power to indicate, if it considers that circumstances so require, any provisional measures which ought to be taken to preserve the respective rights of either party.

2. Pending the final decision, notice of the measures suggested shall forthwith be given to the parties and to the Security Council.

Article 42

1. The parties shall be represented by agents.

2. They may have the assistance of counsel or advocates before the Court.

3. The agents, counsel, and advocates of parties before the Court shall enjoy the privileges and immunities necessary to the independent exercise of their duties.

Article 43

1. The procedure shall consist of two parts: written and oral.

2. The written proceedings shall consist of the communication to the Court and to the parties of memorials, counter-memorials and, if necessary, replies; also all papers and documents in support.

3. These communications shall be made through the Registrar, in the order and within the time fixed by the Court.

4. A certified copy of every document produced by one party shall be communicated to the other party.

5. The oral proceedings shall consist of the hearing by the Court of witnesses, experts, agents, counsel, and advocates.

Article 44

1. For the service of all notices upon persons other than the agents, counsel, and advocates, the Court shall apply direct to the government of the state upon whose territory the notice has to be served.

2. The same provision shall apply whenever steps are to be taken to procure evidence on the spot.

Article 45

The hearing shall be under the control of the President or, if he is unable to preside, of the Vice-President; if neither is able to preside, the senior judge present shall preside.

Article 46

The hearing in Court shall be public, unless the Court shall decide otherwise, or unless the parties demand that the public be not admitted.

Article 47

1. Minutes shall be made at each hearing and signed by the Registrar and the President.

2. These minutes alone shall be authentic.

Article 48

The Court shall make orders for the conduct of the case, shall decide the form and time in which each party must conclude its arguments, and make all arrangements connected with the taking of evidence.

Article 49

The Court may, even before the hearing begins, call upon the agents to produce any document or to supply any explanations. Formal note shall be taken of any refusal.

Article 50

The Court may, at any time, entrust any individual, body, bureau, commission, or other organization that it may select, with the task of carrying out an enquiry or giving an expert opinion.

Article 51

During the hearing any relevant questions are to be put to the witnesses and experts under the conditions laid down by the Court in the rules of procedure referred to in Article 30.

Article 52

After the Court has received the proofs and evidence within the time specified for the purpose, it may refuse to accept any further oral or written evidence that one party may desire to present unless the other side consents.

Article 53

1. Whenever one of the parties does not appear before the Court, or fails to defend its case, the other party may call upon the Court to decide in favour of its claim.

2. The Court must, before doing so, satisfy itself, not only that it has jurisdiction in accordance with Articles 36 and 37, but also that the claim is well founded in fact and law.

Article 54

1. When, subject to the control of the Court, the agents, counsel, and advocates have completed their presentation of the case, the President shall declare the hearing closed.

2. The Court shall withdraw to consider the judgment.

3. The deliberation of the Court shall take place in private and remain secret.

Article 55

1. All questions shall be decided by a majority of the judges present.

2. In the event of an equality of votes, the President or the judge who acts in his place shall have a casting vote.

Article 56

1. The judgment shall state the reasons on which it is based.

2. It shall contain the names of the judges who have taken part in the decision.

Article 57

If the judgment does not represent in whole or in part the unanimous opinion of the judges, any judge shall be entitled to deliver a separate opinion.

Article 58

The judgment shall be signed by the President and by the Registrar. It shall be read in open court, due notice having been given to the agents.

Article 59

The decision of the Court has no binding force except between the parties and in respect of that particular case.

Article 60

The judgment is final and without appeal. In the event of dispute as to the meaning or scope of the judgment, the Court shall construe it upon the request of any party.

Article 61

1. An application for revision of a judgment may be made only when it is based upon the discovery of some fact of such a nature as to be a decisive factor, which fact was, when the judgment was given, unknown to the Court and also to the party claiming revision, always provided that such ignorance was not due to negligence.

2. The proceedings for revision shall be opened by a judgment of the Court expressly recording the existence of the new fact, recognizing that it has such a character as to lay the case open to revision, and declaring the application admissible on this ground.

3. The Court may require previous compliance with the terms of the judgment before it admits proceedings in revision.

4. The application for revision must be made at latest within six months of the discovery of the new fact.

5. No application for revision may be made after the lapse of ten years from the date of the judgment.

Article 62

1. Should a state consider that it has an interest of a legal nature which may be affected by the decision in the case, it may submit a request to the Court to be permitted to intervene.

2. It shall be for the Court to decide upon this request.

Article 63

1. Whenever the construction of a convention to which states other than those concerned in the case are parties is in question, the Registrar shall notify all such states forthwith.

2. Every state so notified has the right to intervene in the proceedings; but if it uses this right, the construction given by the judgement will be equally binding upon it.

Article 64

Unless otherwise decided by the Court, each party shall bear its own costs.

CHAPTER IV. ADVISORY OPINIONS
Article 65

1. The Court may give an advisory opinion on any legal question at the request of whatever body may be authorized by or in accordance with the Charter of the United Nations to make such a request.

2. Questions upon which the advisory opinion of the Court is asked shall be laid before the Court by means of a written request containing an exact statement of the question upon which an opinion is required, and accompanied by all documents likely to throw light upon the question.

Article 66

1. The Registrar shall forthwith give notice of the request for an advisory opinion to all states entitled to appear before the Court.

2. The Registrar shall also, by means of a special and direct communication, notify any state entitled to appear before the Court or international organization considered by the Court, or, should it not be sitting, by the President, as likely to be able to furnish information on the question, that the Court will be prepared to receive, within a time limit to be fixed by the President, written statements, or to hear, at a public sitting to be held for the purpose, oral statements relating to the question.

3. Should any such state entitled to appear before the Court have failed to receive the special communication referred to in paragraph 2 of this Article, such state may express a desire to submit a written statement or to be heard; and the Court will decide.

4. States and organizations having presented written or oral statements or both shall be permitted to comment on the statements made by other states or organizations in the form, to the extent, and within the time limits which the Court, or, should it not be sitting, the President, shall decide in each particular case. Accordingly, the Registrar shall in due time communicate any such written statements to states and organizations having submitted similar statements.

Article 67

The Court shall deliver its advisory opinions in open court, notice having been given to the Secretary-General and to the representatives of Members of the United Nations, of other states and of international organizations immediately concerned.

Article 68

In the exercise of its advisory functions the Court shall further be guided by the provisions of the present Statute which apply in contentious cases to the extent to which it recognizes them to be applicable.

CHAPTER V. AMENDMENT
Article 69

Amendments to the present Statute shall be effected by the same procedure as is provided by the Charter of the United Nations for amendments to that Charter, subject however to any provisions which the General Assembly upon recommendation of the Security Council may adopt concerning the participation of states which are parties to the present Statute but are not Members of the United Nations.

Article 70

The Court shall have power to propose such amendments to the present Statute as it may deem necessary, through written communications to the Secretary–General, for consideration in conformity with the provisions of Article 69.

1.5 STATUTE OF THE INTERNATIONAL ATOMIC ENERGY AGENCY (IAEA) (AS AMENDED). Concluded at New York, 26 October 1956. Entered into force, 29 July 1957. 276 U.N.T.S. 3, T.I.A.S. 3873, 8 T.S. 1093; 471 U.N.T.S. 334, T.I.A.S. 5284, 14 T.S. 135; T.I.A.S. 7668, 24 T.S. 1637: *Arts. I, II, III, XI, XII*

Art. I. *Establishment of the agency*

The parties hereto establish an International Atomic Energy Agency (hereinafter referred to as "the Agency") upon the terms and conditions hereinafter set forth.

Art. II. *Objectives*

The agency shall seek to accelerate and enlarge the contribution of atomic energy to peace, health and prosperity throughout the world. It shall ensure, so far as it is able, that assistance provided by it or at its request or under its supervision or control is not used in such a way as to further any military purpose.

Art. III. *Functions*

(A) The agency is authorized:

1. To encourage and assist research on, and development and practical application, of atomic energy for peaceful uses throughout the world; and, if requested to do so, to act as an intermediary for the purposes of securing the performance of services or the supplying of materials, equipment, or facilities by one member of the agency for another; and to perform any operation or service useful in research on, or development or practical application of, atomic energy for peaceful purposes;

2. To make provision, in accordance with this statute, for materials, services, equipment, and facilities to meet the needs of research on, and development and practical application of, atomic energy for peaceful purposes, including the production of electric power, with due consideration for the needs of the under-developed areas of the world;

3. To foster the exchange of scientific and technical information on peaceful uses of atomic energy;

4. To encourage the exchange and training of scientists and experts in the field of peaceful uses of atomic energy;

5. To establish and administer safeguards designed to ensure that special fissionable and other materials, services, equipment, facilities and information made available by the agency or at its request or under its supervision or control are not used in such a way as to further any military purpose; and to apply safeguards, at the request of the parties, to any bilateral or multilateral arrangement, or, at the request of a state, to any of that state's activities in the field of atomic energy;

6. To establish or adopt, in consultation and, where appropriate, in collaboration with the competent organs of the United Nations and with the specialized agencies concerned, standards of safety for protection of health and minimization of danger to life and property (including such standards for labor conditions), and to provide for the application of these standards to its own operations as well as to the operations making use of materials, services, equipment, facilities and information made available

by the agency or at its request or under its control or supervision; and to provide for the application of these standards, at the request of the parties, to operations under any bilateral or multilateral arrangement, or, at the request of a state, to any of that state's activities in the field of atomic energy;

7. To acquire or establish any facilities, plant and equipment useful in carrying out its authorized functions, whenever the facilities, plant and equipment otherwise available to it in the area concerned are inadequate or available only on terms it deems unsatisfactory.

(B) In carrying out its functions, the agency shall:

1. Conduct its activities in accordance with the purposes and principles of the United Nations to promote peace and international cooperation, and in conformity with policies of the United Nations furthering the establishment of safeguarded world-wide disarmament and in conformity with any international agreements entered into pursuant to such policies;

2. Establish control over the use of special fissionable materials received by the agency, in order to ensure that these materials are used only for peaceful purposes;

3. Allocate its resources in such a manner as to secure efficient utilization and the greatest possible general benefit in all areas of the world, bearing in mind the special needs of the underdeveloped areas of the world;

4. Submit reports on its activities annually to the General Assembly of the United Nations and, when appropriate, to the Security Council: if in connection with the activities of the agency there should arise questions that are within the competence of the Security Council, the agency shall notify the Security Council, as the organ bearing the main responsibility for the maintenance of international peace and security, and may also take the measures open to it under this statute, including those provided in paragraph C of Article XII;

5. Submit reports to the Economic and Social Council and other organs of the United Nations on matters within the competence of these organs.

(C) In carrying out its functions, the agency shall not make assistance to members subject to any political, economic, military, or other conditions incompatible with the provisions of this statute.

(D) Subject to the provisions of this statute and to the terms of agreements concluded between a state or a group of states and the agency which shall be in accordance with the provisions of the statute, the activities of the agency shall be carried out with due observance of the sovereign rights of states.

* * *

Art. XI. *Agency projects*

(A) Any member or group of members of the agency desiring to set up any project for research on, or development or practical application of, atomic energy for peaceful purposes may request the assistance of the agency in securing special fissionable and other materials, services, equipment and facilities necessary for this purpose. Any such request shall be accompanied by an explanation of the purpose and extent of the project and shall be considered by the Board of Governors.

(B) Upon request, the agency may also assist any member or group of members to make arrangements to secure necessary financing from outside sources to carry out such projects. In extending this assistance, the agency will not be required to provide any guarantees or to assume any financial responsibilities for the project.

(C) The agency may arrange for the supplying of any materials, services, equipment, and facilities necessary for the project by one or more members or may itself undertake to provide any or all of these directly, taking into consideration the wishes of the member or members making the request.

(D) For the purpose of considering the request, the agency may send into the territory of the member or group of members making the request a person or persons qualified to examine the project. For this purpose the agency may, with the approval of the member or group of members making the request, use members of its own staff or employ suitably qualified nationals of any member.

(E) Before approving a project under this article, the Board of Governors shall give due consideration to:

     1. The usefulness of the project, including its scientific and technical feasibility;

     2. The adequacy of plans, funds, and technical personnel to assure the effective execution of the project;

     3. The adequacy of proposed health and safety standards for handling and storing materials and for operating facilities;

     4. The inability of the member or group of members making the request to secure the necessary finances, materials, facilities, equipment, and services;

     5. The equitable distribution of materials and other resources available to the agency;

     6. The special needs of the under-developed areas of the world; and

     7. Such other matters as may be relevant.

(F) Upon approving a project, the agency shall enter into an agreement with the member or group of members submitting the project, which agreement shall:

     1. Provide for allocation to the project of any required special fissionable or other materials;

     2. Provide for transfer of special fissionable materials from their then place of custody, whether the materials be in custody of the agency or of the member making them available for use in agency projects, to the member or group of members submitting the project, under conditions which ensure the safety of any shipment required and meet applicable health and safety standards;

3. Set forth the terms and conditions, including charges, on which any materials, services, equipment and facilities are to be provided by the agency itself, and, if any such materials, services, equipment and facilities are to be provided by a member, the terms and conditions as arranged for by the member or group of members submitting the project and the supplying member;

4. Include undertakings by the member or group of members submitting the project (*a*) that the assistance provided shall not be used in such a way as to further any military purpose; and (*b*) that the project shall be subject to the safeguards provided for in Article XII, the relevant safeguards being specified in the agreement;

5. Make appropriate provision regarding the rights and interests of the agency and the member or members concerned in any inventions or discoveries, or any patents therein, arising from the project;

6. Make appropriate provision regarding settlement of disputes;

7. Include such other provisions as may be appropriate.

(G) The provisions of this article shall also apply where appropriate to a request for materials, services, facilities, or equipment in connection with an existing project.

Art. XII. *Agency safeguards*

(A) With respect to any agency project or other arrangement where the agency is requested by the parties concerned to apply safeguards, the agency shall have the following rights and responsibilities to the extent relevant to the project or arrangement:

1. To examine the design of specialized equipment and facilities, including nuclear reactors, and to approve it only from the viewpoint of assuring that it will not further any military purpose, that it complies with applicable health and safety standards, and that it will permit effective application of the safeguards provided for in this article;

2. To require the observance of any health and safety measures prescribed by the agency;

3. To require the maintenance and production of operating records to assist in ensuring accountability for source and special fissionable materials used or produced in the project or arrangement;

4. To call for and receive progress reports;

5. To approve the means to be used for the chemical processing of irradiated materials solely to ensure that this chemical processing will not lend itself to diversion of materials for military purposes and will comply with applicable health and safety standards; to require that special fissionable materials recovered or produced as a by-product be used for peaceful purposes under continuing agency safeguards for research or in reactors, existing or under construction, specified by the member or members concerned; and to require deposit with the agency of any excess of any special fissionable materials recovered or produced as a by-product over what is needed for the above stated uses in order to prevent stockpiling of these materials, provided that thereafter at the request of the member or members concerned special fissionable materials so deposited

with the agency shall be returned promptly to the member or members concerned for use under the same provisions as stated above;

6. To send into the territory of the recipient state or states inspectors, designated by the agency after consultation with the state or states concerned, who shall have access at all times to all places and data and to any person who by reason of his occupation deals with materials, equipment, or facilities which are required by this statute to be safeguarded, as necessary to account for source and special fissionable materials supplied and fissionable products and to determine whether there is compliance with the undertaking against use in furtherance of any military purpose referred to in sub-Paragraph F–4 of Article XI, with the health and safety measures referred to in sub-Paragraph A–2 of this article, and with any other conditions prescribed in the agreement between the agency and the state or states concerned. Inspectors designated by the agency shall be accompanied by representatives of the authorities of the state concerned, if that state so requests, provided that the inspectors shall not thereby be delayed or otherwise impeded in the exercise of their functions;

7. In the event of non-compliance and failure by the recipient state or states to take requested corrective steps within a reasonable time, to suspend or terminate assistance and withdraw any materials and equipment made available by the agency or a member in furtherance of the project.

(B) The agency shall, as necessary, establish a staff of inspectors. The staff of inspectors shall have the responsibility of examining all operations conducted by the agency itself to determine whether the agency is complying with the health and safety measures prescribed by it for application to projects subject to its approval, supervision or control, and whether the agency is taking adequate measures to prevent the source and special fissionable materials in its custody or used or produced in its own operations from being used in furtherance of any military purpose. The agency shall take remedial action forthwith to correct any non-compliance or failure to take adequate measures.

(C) The staff of inspectors shall also have the responsibility of obtaining and verifying the accounting referred to in sub-Paragraph A–6 of this article and of determining whether there is compliance with the undertaking referred to in sub-Paragraph F–4 in Article XI, with the measures referred to in sub-Paragraph A–2 of this article, and with all other conditions of the project prescribed in the agreement between the agency and the state or states concerned. The inspectors shall report any non-compliance to the director general who shall thereupon transmit the report to the board of governors. The board shall call upon the recipient state or states to remedy forthwith any non-compliance which it finds to have occurred. The board shall report the non-compliance to all members and to the Security Council and General Assembly of the United Nations. In the event of failure of the recipient state or states to take fully corrective action within a reasonable time, the board may take one or both of the following measures: direct curtailment or suspension of assistance being provided by the agency or by a member, and call for the return of materials and equipment made available to the recipient member or group of members. The agency may also, in accordance with Article XIV, suspend any non-complying member from the exercise of the privileges and rights of membership.

1.6 TREATY ESTABLISHING THE EUROPEAN ECONOMIC COMMUNITY (WITHOUT ANNEXES AND PROTOCOLS).[1] Concluded at Rome, 25 March 1957. Entered into force, 1 January 1958. 298 U.N.T.S. 11: Arts. 1–6, 100

HIS MAJESTY THE KING OF THE BRITAINS, THE PRESIDENT OF THE FEDERAL REPUBLIC OF GERMANY, THE PRESIDENT OF THE FRENCH REPUBLIC, THE PRESIDENT OF THE ITALIAN REPUBLIC, HER ROYAL HIGHNESS THE GRAND DUCHESS OF LUXEMBOURG, HER MAJESTY THE QUEEN OF THE NETHERLANDS.

DETERMINED to establish the foundations of an ever closer union among the European peoples,

DECIDED to ensure the economic and social progress of their countries by common action in eliminating the barriers which divide Europe,

DIRECTING their efforts to the essential purpose of constantly improving the living and working conditions of their peoples,

RECOGNISING that the removal of existing obstacles calls for concerted action in order to guarantee a steady expansion, a balanced trade and fair competition,

ANXIOUS to strengthen the unity of their economies and to ensure their harmonious development by reducing the differences existing between the various regions and by mitigating the backwardness of the less favoured,

DESIROUS of contributing by means of a common commercial policy to the progressive abolition of restrictions on international trade,

INTENDING to confirm the solidarity which binds Europe and overseas countries, and desiring to ensure the development of their prosperity, in accordance with the principle of the Charter of the United Nations,

RESOLVED to strengthen the safeguards of peace and liberty by establishing this combination of resources, and calling upon the other peoples of Europe who share their ideal to join in their efforts,

HAVE decided to create a European Economic Community and to this end have designated as their plenipotentiaries * * *,

WHO, having exchanged their full powers, found in good and due form, have agreed, as follows:

PART ONE

PRINCIPLES

Article 1

By the present Treaty, the HIGH CONTRACTING PARTIES establish among themselves a EUROPEAN ECONOMIC COMMUNITY.

Article 2

It shall be the aim of the Community, by establishing a Common Market and progressively approximating the economic policies of Member States, to promote throughout the Community a harmonious development of economic activities, a continuous and balanced expansion, an increased stability, an

---

1. This treaty was amended by the Single European Act (Basic Document 1.10, *infra*).   *See also* The Treaty on European Union (Basic Document 1.12, *infra*).

accelerated raising of the standard of living and closer relations between its Member States.

Article 3

For the purposes set out in the preceding Article, the activities of the Community shall include, under the conditions and with the timing provided for in this Treaty:

(a) the elimination, as between Member States, of customs duties and of quantitative restrictions in regard to the importation and exportation of goods, as well as of all other measures with equivalent effect;

(b) the establishment of a common customs tariff and a common commercial policy towards third countries;

(c) the abolition, as between Member States, of the obstacles to the free movement of persons, services and capital;

(d) the inauguration of a common agricultural policy;

(e) the inauguration of a common transport policy;

(f) the establishment of a system ensuring that competition shall not be distorted in the Common Market;

(g) the application of procedures which shall make it possible to co-ordinate the economic policies of Member States and to remedy disequilibria in their balances of payments;

(h) the approximation of their respective municipal law to the extent necessary for the functioning of the Common Market;

(i) the creation of a European Social Fund in order to improve the possibilities of employment for workers and to contribute to the raising of their standard of living;

(j) the establishment of a European Investment Bank intended to facilitate the economic expansion of the Community through the creation of new resources; and

(k) the association of overseas countries and territories with the Community with a view to increasing trade and to pursuing jointly effort towards economic and social development.

Article 4

1. The achievement of the tasks entrusted to the Community shall be ensured by:

— an ASSEMBLY,

— a COUNCIL,

— a COMMISSION, and

— a COURT OF JUSTICE.

Each of these institutions shall act within the limits of the powers conferred upon it by this Treaty.

2. The Council and the Commission shall be assisted by an Economic and Social Committee acting in a consultative capacity.

Article 5

Member States shall take all general or particular measures which are appropriate for ensuring the carrying out of the obligations arising out of this Treaty or resulting from the acts of the institutions of the Community. They shall facilitate the achievement of the Community's aims.

They shall abstain from any measures likely to jeopardize the attainment of the objectives of this Treaty.

Article 6

1. Member States, acting in close collaboration with the institutions of the Community, shall co-ordinate their respective economic policies to the extent that is necessary to attain the objectives of this Treaty.

2. The institutions of the Community shall take care not to prejudice the internal and external financial stability of Member States.

* * *

Article 100

The Council, acting by means of a unanimous vote on a proposal of the Commission, shall issue directives for the approximation of such legislative and administrative provisions of the Member States as have a direct incidence on the establishment or functioning of the Common Market.

The Assembly and the Economic and Social Committee shall be consulted concerning any directives whose implementation in one or more of the Member States would involve amendment of legislative provisions.

1.7 VIENNA CONVENTION ON THE LAW OF TREATIES (WITH ANNEX). Concluded at Vienna, 23 May 1969. Entered into force, 27 January 1988. 1155 U.N.T.S. 331

The States Parties to the present Convention,

Considering the fundamental role of treaties in the history of international relations,

Recognizing the ever-increasing importance of treaties as a source of international law and as a means of developing peaceful co-operation among nations, whatever their constitutional and social systems,

Noting that the principles of free consent and of good faith and the *pacta sunt servanda* rule are universally recognized,

Affirming that disputes concerning treaties, like other international disputes, should be settled by peaceful means and in conformity with the principles of justice and international law,

Recalling the determination of the peoples of the United Nations to establish conditions under which justice and respect for the obligations arising from treaties can be maintained,

Having in mind the principles of international law embodied in the Charter of the United Nations, such as the principles of the equal rights and self-determination of peoples, of the sovereign equality and independence of all States, of noninterference in the domestic affairs of States, of the prohibition of the threat or use of force and of universal respect for, and observance of, human rights and fundamental freedoms for all,

Believing that the codification and progressive development of the law of treaties achieved in the present Convention will promote the purposes of the United Nations set forth in the Charter, namely, the maintenance of international peace and security, the development of friendly relations and the achievement of co-operation among nations,

Affirming that the rules of customary international law will continue to govern questions not regulated by the provisions of the present Convention,

Have agreed as follows:

PART I. INTRODUCTION

Article 1. SCOPE OF THE PRESENT CONVENTION

The present Convention applies to treaties between States

Article 2. USE OF TERMS

1. For the purposes of the present Convention:

(*a*) "Treaty" means an international agreement concluded between States in written form and governed by international law, whether embodied in a single instrument or in two or more related instruments and whatever its particular designation;

(*b*) "Ratification", "acceptance", "approval" and "accession" means in each case the international act so named whereby a State establishes on the international plane its consent to be bound by a treaty;

(*c*) "Full powers" means a document emanating from the competent authority of a State designating a person or persons to represent the

State for negotiating, adopting or authenticating the text of a treaty, for expressing the consent of the State to be bound by a treaty, or for accomplishing any other act with respect to a treaty;

(*d*) "Reservation" means a unilateral statement, however phrased or named, made by a State, when signing, ratifying, accepting, approving or acceding to a treaty, whereby it purports to exclude or to modify the legal effect of certain provisions of the treaty in their application to that State;

(*e*) "Negotiating State" means a State which took part in the drawing up and adoption of the text of the treaty;

(*f*) "Contracting State" means a State which has consented to be bound by the treaty, whether or not the treaty has entered into force;

(*g*) "Party" means a State which has consented to be bound by the treaty and for which the treaty is in force;

(*h*) "Third State" means a State not a party to the treaty;

(*i*) "International organization" means an intergovernmental organization.

2. The provisions of paragraph 1 regarding the use of terms in the present Convention are without prejudice to the use of those terms or to the meanings which may be given to them in the internal law of any State.

Article 3. INTERNATIONAL AGREEMENTS NOT WITHIN
THE SCOPE OF THE PRESENT CONVENTION

The fact that the present Convention does not apply to international agreements concluded between States and other subjects of international law or between such other subjects of international law, or to international agreements not in written form, shall not affect:

(*a*) The legal force of such agreements;

(*b*) The application to them of any of the rules set forth in the present Convention to which they would be subject under international law independently of the Convention;

(*c*) The application of the Convention to the relations of States as between themselves under international agreements to which other subjects of international law are also parties.

Article 4. NON-RETROACTIVITY OF THE PRESENT CONVENTION

Without prejudice to the application of any rules set forth in the present Convention to which treaties would be subject under international law independently of the Convention, the Convention applies only to treaties which are concluded by States after the entry into force of the present Convention with regard to such States.

Article 5. TREATIES CONSTITUTING INTERNATIONAL ORGANIZATIONS AND
TREATIES ADOPTED WITHIN AN INTERNATIONAL ORGANIZATION

The present Convention applies to any treaty which is the constituent instrument of an international organization and to any treaty adopted within an international organization without prejudice to any relevant rules of the organizations.

PART II.   CONCLUSION AND ENTRY INTO FORCE OF TREATIES

SECTION 1.   CONCLUSION OF TREATIES

Article 6.   CAPACITY OF STATES TO CONCLUDE TREATIES

Every State possesses capacity to conclude treaties.

Article 7.   FULL POWERS

1.   A person is considered as representing a State for the purpose of adopting or authenticating the text of a treaty or for the purpose of expressing the consent of the State to be bound by a treaty if:

(*a*) He produces appropriate full powers; or

(*b*) It appears from the practice of the States concerned or from other circumstances that their intention was to consider that person as representing the State for such purposes and to dispense with full powers.

2.   In virtue of their functions and without having to produce full powers, the following are considered as representing their State:

(*a*) Heads of State, Heads of Government and Ministers for Foreign Affairs, for the purpose of performing all acts relating to the conclusion of a treaty;

(*b*) Heads of diplomatic missions, for the purpose of adopting the text of a treaty between the accrediting State and the State to which they are accredited;

(*c*) Representatives accredited by States to an international conference or to an international organization or one of its organs, for the purpose of adopting the text of a treaty in that conference, organization or organ.

Article 8.   SUBSEQUENT CONFIRMATION OF AN
ACT PERFORMED WITHOUT AUTHORIZATION

An act relating to the conclusion of a treaty performed by a person who cannot be considered under article 7 as authorized to represent a State for that purpose is without legal effect unless afterwards confirmed by that State.

Article 9.   ADOPTION OF THE TEXT

1.   The adoption of the text of a treaty takes place by the consent of all the States participating in its drawing up except as provided in paragraph 2.

2.   The adoption of the text of a treaty at an international conference takes place by the vote of two thirds of the States present and voting, unless by the same majority they shall decide to apply a different rule.

Article 10.   AUTHENTICATION OF THE TEXT

The text of a treaty is established as authentic and definitive:

(*a*) By such procedure as may be provided for in the text or agreed upon by the States participating in its drawing up; or

(*b*) Failing such procedure, by the signature, signature ad referendum or initialling by the representatives of those States of the text of the treaty or of the Final Act of a conference incorporating the text.

Article 11. MEANS OF EXPRESSING CONSENT TO BE BOUND BY A TREATY

The consent of a State to be bound by a treaty may be expressed by signature, exchange of instruments constituting a treaty, ratification, acceptance, approval or accession, or by any other means if so agreed.

Article 12. CONSENT TO BE BOUND BY A TREATY EXPRESSED BY SIGNATURE

1. The consent of a State to be bound by a treaty is expressed by the signature of its representative when:

(*a*) The treaty provides that signature shall have that effect;

(*b*) It is otherwise established that the negotiating States were agreed that signature should have that effect; or

(*c*) The intention of the state to give that effect to the signature appears from the full powers of its representative or was expressed during the negotiation.

2. For the purposes of paragraph 1:

(*a*) The initialling of a text constitutes a signature of the treaty when it is established that the negotiating States so agreed;

(*b*) The signature *ad referendum* of a treaty by a representative, if confirmed by his State, constitutes a full signature of the treaty.

Article 13. CONSENT TO BE BOUND BY A TREATY EXPRESSED BY
AN EXCHANGE OF INSTRUMENTS CONSTITUTING A TREATY

The consent of States to be bound by a treaty constituted by instruments exchanged between them is expressed by that exchange when:

(*a*) The instruments provide that their exchange shall have that effect; or

(*b*) It is otherwise established that those States were agreed that the exchange of instruments shall have that effect.

Article 14. CONSENT TO BE BOUND BY A TREATY EXPRESSED
BY RATIFICATION, ACCEPTANCE OR APPROVAL

1. The consent of a State to be bound by a treaty is expressed by ratification when:

(*a*) The treaty provides for such consent to be expressed by means of ratification;

(*b*) It is otherwise established that the negotiating States were agreed that ratification should be required;

(*c*) The representative of the State has signed the treaty subject to ratification; or

(*d*) The intention of the State to sign the treaty subject to ratification appears from the full powers of its representative or was expressed during the negotiation.

2. The consent of a State to be bound by a treaty is expressed by acceptance or approval under conditions similar to those which apply to ratification.

Article 15.   Consent to be bound by a treaty expressed by accession

The consent of a State to be bound by a treaty is expressed by accession when:

(*a*) The treaty provides that such consent may be expressed by that State by means of accession;

(*b*) It is otherwise established that the negotiating States were agreed that such consent may be expressed by that State by means of accession; or

(*c*) All the parties have subsequently agreed that such consent may be expressed by that State by means of accession.

Article 16.   Exchange or deposit of instruments of
ratification, acceptance, approval or accession

Unless the treaty otherwise provides, instruments of ratification, acceptance, approval or accession establish the consent of a State to be bound by a treaty upon:

(*a*) Their exchange between the contracting States;

(*b*) Their deposit with the depositary; or

(*c*) Their notification to the contracting States or to the depositary, if so agreed.

Article 17.   Consent to be bound by part of a
treaty and choice of differing provisions

1. Without prejudice to articles 19 to 23, the consent of a State to be bound by part of a treaty is effective only if the treaty so permits or the other contracting States so agree.

2. The consent of a State to be bound by a treaty which permits a choice between differing provisions is effective only if it is made clear to which of the provisions the consent relates.

Article 18.   Obligation not to defeat the object and
purpose of a treaty prior to its entry into force

A State is obliged to refrain from acts which would defeat the object and purpose of a treaty when:

(*a*) It has signed the treaty or has exchanged instruments constituting the treaty subject to ratification, acceptance or approval, until it shall have made its intention clear not to become a party to the treaty; or

(*b*) It has expressed its consent to be bound by the treaty, pending the entry into force of the treaty and provided that such entry into force is not unduly delayed.

Section 2.   Reservations

Article 19.   Formulation of reservations

A State may, when signing, ratifying, accepting, approving or acceding to a treaty, formulate a reservation unless:

(*a*) The reservation is prohibited by the treaty;

(*b*) The treaty provides that only specified reservations, which do not include the reservation in question, may be made; or (*c*) In cases not falling under sub-paragraphs (*a*) and (*b*), the reservation is incompatible with the object and purpose of the treaty.

Article 20. ACCEPTANCE OF AND OBJECTION TO RESERVATIONS

1. A reservation expressly authorized by a treaty does not require any subsequent acceptance by the other contracting States unless the treaty so provides.

2. When it appears from the limited number of the negotiating States and the object and purpose of a treaty that the application of the treaty in its entirety between all the parties is an essential condition of the consent of each one to be bound by the treaty, a reservation requires acceptance by all the parties;

3. When a treaty is a constituent instrument of an international organization and unless it otherwise provides, a reservation requires the acceptance of the competent organ of that organization.

4. In cases not falling under the preceding paragraphs and unless the treaty otherwise provides:

(*a*) Acceptance by another contracting State of a reservation constitutes the reserving State a party to the treaty in relation to that other State if or when the treaty is in force for those States;

(*b*) An objection by another contracting State to a reservation does not preclude the entry into force of the treaty as between the objecting and reserving States unless a contrary intention is definitely expressed by the objecting State;

(*c*) An act expressing a State's consent to be bound by the treaty and containing a reservation is effective as soon as at least one other contracting State has accepted the reservation.

5. For the purposes of paragraphs 2 and 4 and unless the treaty otherwise provides, a reservation is considered to have been accepted by a State if it shall have raised no objection to the reservation by the end of a period of twelve months after it was notified of the reservation or by the date on which it expressed its consent to be bound by the treaty, whichever is later.

Article 21. LEGAL EFFECTS OF RESERVATIONS AND OF OBJECTIVES TO RESERVATIONS

1. A reservation established with regard to another party in accordance with articles 19, 20 and 23:

(*a*) Modifies for the reserving State in its relations with that other party the provisions of the treaty to which the reservation relates to the extent of the reservation; and

(*b*) Modifies those provisions to the same extent for that other party in its relations with the reserving State.

2. The reservation does not modify the provisions of the treaty for the other parties to the treaty *inter se.*

3. When a State objecting to a reservation has not opposed the entry into force of the treaty between itself and the reserving State, the provisions to which the reservation relates do not apply as between the two States to the extent of the reservation.

Article 22. WITHDRAWAL OF RESERVATIONS AND OF OBJECTIVES TO RESERVATIONS

1. Unless the treaty otherwise provides, a reservation may be withdrawn at any time and the consent of a State which has accepted the reservation is not required for its withdrawal.

2. Unless the treaty otherwise provides, an objection to a reservation may be withdrawn at any time.

3. Unless the treaty otherwise provides, or it is otherwise agreed:

(*a*) The withdrawal of a reservation becomes operative in relation to another contracting State only when notice of it has been received by that State;

(*b*) The withdrawal of an objection to a reservation becomes operative only when notice of it has been received by the State which formulated the reservation.

Article 23. PROCEDURE REGARDING RESERVATIONS

1. A reservation, an express acceptance of a reservation and an objection to a reservation must be formulated in writing and communicated to the contracting States and other States entitled to become parties to the treaty.

2. If formulated when signing the treaty subject to ratification, acceptance or approval, a reservation must be formally confirmed by the reserving State when expressing its consent to be bound by the treaty. In such a case the reservation shall be considered as having been made on the date of its confirmation.

3. An express acceptance of, or an objection to, a reservation made previously to confirmation of the reservation does not itself require confirmation.

4. The withdrawal of a reservation or of an objection to a reservation must be formulated in writing.

SECTION 3. ENTRY INTO FORCE PROVISIONAL APPLICATION OF TREATIES

Article 24. ENTRY INTO FORCE

1. A treaty enters into force in such manner and upon such date as it may provide or as the negotiating States may agree.

2. Failing any such provision or agreement, a treaty enters into force as soon as consent to be bound by the treaty has been established for all the negotiating States.

3. When the consent of a State to be bound by a treaty is established on a date after the treaty has come into force, the treaty enters into force for that State on that date, unless the treaty otherwise provides.

4. The provisions of a treaty regulating the authentication of its text, the establishment of the consent of States to be bound by the treaty, the manner or date of its entry into force, reservations, the functions of the depositary and other matters arising necessarily before the entry into force of the treaty apply from the time of the adoption of its text.

Article 25. PROVISIONAL APPLICATION

1. A treaty or a part of a treaty is applied provisionally pending its entry into force if:

(*a*) The treaty itself so provides; or

(*b*) The negotiating States have in some other manner so agreed.

2. Unless the treaty between provides or the negotiating States have otherwise agreed, the provisional application of a treaty or a part of a treaty with respect to a State shall be terminated if that State notifies the other States between which the treaty is being applied provisionally of its intention not to become a party to the treaty.

PART III.   OBSERVANCE, APPLICATION AND INTERPRETATION OF TREATIES

SECTION 1.   OBSERVANCE OF TREATIES

Article 26.   "PACTA SUNT SERVANDA"

Every treaty in force is binding upon the parties to it and must be performed by them in good faith.

Article 27.   INTERNAL LAW AND OBSERVANCE OF TREATIES

A party may not invoke the provisions of its internal law as justification for its failure to perform a treaty.   This rule is without prejudice to article 46.

SECTION 2.   APPLICATION OF TREATIES

Article 28.   NON-RETROACTIVITY OF TREATIES

Unless a different intention appears from the treaty or is otherwise established, its provisions do not bind a party in relation to any act or fact which took place or any situation which ceased to exist before the date of the entry into force of the treaty with respect to that party.

Article 29.   TERRITORIAL SCOPE OF TREATIES

Unless a different intention appears from the treaty or is otherwise established, a treaty is binding upon each party in respect of its entire territory.

Article 30.   APPLICATION OF SUCCESSIVE TREATIES
RELATING TO THE SAME SUBJECT-MATTER

1. Subject to Article 103 of the Charter of the United Nations, the rights and obligations of States parties to successive treaties relating to the same subject-matter shall be determined in accordance with the following paragraphs.

2. When a treaty specifies that it is subject to, or that it is not to be considered as incompatible with, an earlier or later treaty, the provisions of that other treaty prevail.

3. When all the parties to the earlier treaty are parties also to the later treaty but the earlier treaty is not terminated or suspended in operation under article 59, the earlier treaty applies only to the extent that its provisions are compatible with those of the later treaty.

4. When the parties to the later treaty do not include all the parties to the earlier one:

(*a*) As between States parties to both treaties the same rule applies as in paragraph 3;

(*b*) As between a State party to both treaties and a State party to only one of the treaties, the treaty to which both States are parties governs their mutual rights and obligations.

5. Paragraph 4 is without prejudice to article 41, or to any question of the termination or suspension of the operation of a treaty under article 60 or to any question of responsibility which may arise for a State from the conclusion or application of a treaty the provisions of which are incompatible with its obligations towards another State under another treaty.

SECTION 3. INTERPRETATION OF TREATIES

Article 31. GENERAL RULE OF INTERPRETATION

1. A treaty shall be interpreted in good faith in accordance with the ordinary meaning to be given to the terms of the treaty in their context and in the light of its object and purpose.

2. The context for the purpose of the interpretation of a treaty shall comprise, in addition to the text, including its preamble and annexes:

(*a*) Any agreement relating to the treaty which was made between all the parties in connexion with the conclusion of the treaty;

(*b*) Any instrument which was made by one or more parties in connexion with the conclusion of the treaty and accepted by the other parties as an instrument related to the treaty.

3. There shall be taken into account, together with the context:

(*a*) Any subsequent agreement between the parties regarding the interpretation of the treaty or the application of its provisions;

(*b*) Any subsequent practice in the application of the treaty which establishes the agreement of the parties regarding its interpretation;

(*c*) Any relevant rules of international law applicable in the relations between the parties.

4. A special meaning shall be given to a term if it is established that the parties so intended.

Article 32. SUPPLEMENTARY MEANS OF INTERPRETATION

Recourse may be had to supplementary means of interpretation, including the preparatory work of the treaty and the circumstances of its conclusion, in order to confirm the meaning resulting from the application of article 31, or to determine the meaning when the interpretation according to article 31:

(*a*) Leaves the meaning ambiguous or obscure; or

(*b*) Leads to a result which is manifestly absurd or unreasonable.

Article 33. INTERPRETATION OF TREATIES AUTHENTICATED
IN TWO OR MORE LANGUAGES

1. When a treaty has been authenticated in two or more languages, the text is equally authoritative in each language, unless the treaty provides or the parties agree that, in case of divergence, a particular text shall prevail.

2. A version of the treaty in a language other than one of those in which the text was authenticated shall be considered an authentic text only if the treaty so provides or the parties so agree.

3. The terms of the treaty are presumed to have the same meaning in each authentic text.

4. Except where a particular text prevails in accordance with paragraph 1, when a comparison of the authentic texts discloses a difference of meaning which the application of articles 31 and 32 does not remove, the meaning which best reconciles the texts, having regard to the object and purpose of the treaty, shall be adopted.

SECTION 4.   TREATIES AND THIRD STATES

Article 34.   GENERAL RULE REGARDING THIRD STATES

A treaty does not create either obligations or rights for a third State without its consent.

Article 35.   TREATIES PROVIDING FOR OBLIGATIONS FOR THIRD STATES

An obligation arises for a third State from a provision of a treaty if the parties to the treaty intend the provision to be the means of establishing the obligation and the third State expressly accepts that obligation in writing.

Article 36.   TREATIES PROVIDING FOR RIGHTS FOR THIRD STATES

1. A right arises for a third State from a provision of a treaty if the parties to the treaty intend the provision to accord that right either to the third State, or to a group of States to which it belongs, or to all States, and the third State assents thereto. Its assent shall be presumed so long as the contrary is not indicated, unless the treaty otherwise provides.

2. A State exercising a right in accordance with paragraph 1 shall comply with the conditions for its exercise provided for in the treaty or established in conformity with the treaty.

Article 37.   REVOCATION OR MODIFICATION OF
OBLIGATIONS OR RIGHTS OF THIRD STATES

1. When an obligation has arisen for a third State in conformity with article 35, the obligation may be revoked or modified only with the consent of the parties to the treaty and of the third State, unless it is established that they had otherwise agreed.

2. When a right has arisen for a third State in conformity with article 36, the right may not be revoked or modified by the parties if it is established that the right was intended not to be revocable or subject to modification without the consent of the third State.

Article 38.   RULES IN A TREATY BECOMING BINDING ON
THIRD STATES THROUGH INTERNATIONAL CUSTOM

Nothing in articles 34 to 37 precludes a rule set forth in a treaty from becoming binding upon a third State as a customary rule of international law, recognized as such.

PART IV.   AMENDMENT AND MODIFICATION OF TREATIES

Article 39.   GENERAL RULE REGARDING THE AMENDMENT OF TREATIES

A treaty may be amended by agreement between the parties. The rules laid down in Part II apply to such an agreement except in so far as the treaty may otherwise provide.

Article 40.   Amendment of multilateral treaties

1. Unless the treaty otherwise provides, the amendment of multilateral treaties shall be governed by the following paragraphs.

2. Any proposal to amend a multilateral treaty as between all the parties must be notified to all the contracting States, each one of which shall have the right to take part in:

(*a*) The decision as to the action to be taken in regard to such proposal;

(*b*) The negotiation and conclusion of any agreement for the amendment of the treaty.

3. Every State entitled to become a party to the treaty shall also be entitled to become a party to the treaty as amended.

4. The amending agreement does not bind any State already a party to the treaty which does not become a party to the amending agreement; article 30, paragraph 4(b), applies in relation to such State.

5. Any State which becomes a party to the treaty after the entry into force of the amending agreement shall, failing an expression of a different intention by that State:

(*a*) be considered as a party to the treaty as amended; and

(*b*) be considered as a party to the unamended treaty in relation to any party to the treaty not bound by the amending agreement.

Article 41.   Agreements to modify multilateral treaties
between certain of the parties only

1. Two or more of the parties to a multilateral treaty may conclude an agreement to modify the treaty as between themselves alone if:

(*a*) The possibility of such a modification is provided for by the treaty; or

(*b*) The modification in question is not prohibited by the treaty and:

(i) Does not affect the enjoyment by the other parties of their rights under the treaty or the performance of their obligations;

(ii) Does not relate to a provision, derogation from which is incompatible with the effective execution of the object and purpose of the treaty as a whole.

2. Unless in a case falling under paragraph 1(a) the treaty otherwise provides, the parties in question shall notify the other parties of their intention to conclude the agreement and of the modification to the treaty for which it provides.

PART V.   INVALIDITY, TERMINATION AND SUSPENSION OF THE OPERATION OF TREATIES

Section 1.   General provisions

Article 42.   Validity and continuance in force of treaties

1. The validity of a treaty or of the consent of a State to be bound by a treaty may be impeached only through the application of the present Convention.

2.   The termination of a treaty, its denunciation or the withdrawal of a party, may take place only as a result of the application of the provisions of the treaty or of the present Convention.   The same rule applies to suspension of the operation of a treaty.

Article 43.   OBLIGATIONS IMPOSED BY INTERNATIONAL
LAW INDEPENDENTLY OF A TREATY

The invalidity, termination or denunciation of a treaty, the withdrawal of a party from it, or the suspension of its operation, as a result of the application of the present Convention or of the provisions of the treaty, shall not in any way impair the duty of any State to fulfil any obligation embodied in the treaty to which it would be subject under international law independently of the treaty.

Article 44.   SEPARABILITY OF TREATY PROVISIONS

1.   A right of a party, provided for in a treaty or arising under article 56, to denounce, withdraw from or suspend the operation of the treaty may be exercised only with respect to the whole treaty unless the treaty otherwise provides or the parties otherwise agree.

2.   A ground for invalidating, terminating, withdrawing from or suspending the operation of a treaty recognized in the present Convention may be invoked only with respect to the whole treaty except as provided in the following paragraphs or in article 60.

3.   If the ground relates solely to particular clauses, it may be invoked only with respect to those clauses where:

(*a*) The said clauses are separable from the remainder of the treaty with regard to their application;

(*b*) It appears from the treaty or is otherwise established that acceptance of those clauses was not an essential basis of the consent of the other party or parties to be bound by the treaty as a whole;   and

(*c*) Continued performance of the remainder of the treaty would not be unjust.

4.   In cases falling under articles 49 and 50 the State entitled to invoke the fraud or corruption may do so with respect either to the whole treaty or, subject to paragraph 3, to the particular clauses alone.

5.   In cases falling under articles 51, 52 and 53, no separation of the provisions of the treaty is permitted.

Article 45.   LOSS OF A RIGHT TO INVOKE A GROUND FOR INVALIDATING, TERMINATING,
WITHDRAWING FROM OR SUSPENDING THE OPERATION OF A TREATY

A State may no longer invoke a ground for invalidating, terminating, withdrawing from or suspending the operation of a treaty under articles 46 to 50 or articles 60 and 62 if, after becoming aware of the facts:

(*a*) It shall have expressly agreed that the treaty is valid or remains in force or continues in operation, as the case may be;   or

(*b*) It must by reason of its conduct be considered as having acquiesced in the validity of the treaty or in its maintenance in force or in operation, as the case may be.

SECTION 2. INVALIDITY OF TREATIES

Article 46. PROVISIONS OF INTERNAL LAW REGARDING
COMPETENCE TO CONCLUDE TREATIES

1. A State may not invoke the fact that its consent to be bound by a treaty has been expressed in violation of a provision of its internal law regarding competence to conclude treaties as invalidating its consent unless that violation was manifest and concerned a rule of its internal law of fundamental importance.

2. A violation is manifest if it would be objectively evident to any State conducting itself in the matter in accordance with normal practice and in good faith.

Article 47. SPECIFIC RESTRICTIONS ON AUTHORITY
TO EXPRESS THE CONSENT OF A STATE

If the authority of a representative to express the consent of a State to be bound by a particular treaty has been made subject to a specific restriction, his omission to observe the restriction may not be invoked as invalidating the consent expressed by him unless the restriction was notified to the other negotiating States prior to his expressing such consent.

Article 48. ERROR

1. A State may invoke an error in a treaty as invalidating its consent to be bound by the treaty if the error relates to a fact or situation which was assumed by that State to exist at the time when the treaty was concluded and formed an essential basis of its consent to be bound by the treaty.

2. Paragraph 1 shall not apply if the State in question contributed by its own conduct to the error or if the circumstances were such as to put that State on notice of a possible error.

3. An error relating only to the wording of the text of a treaty does not affect its validity; article 79 then applies.

Article 49. FRAUD

If a State has been induced to conclude a treaty by the fraudulent conduct of another negotiating State, the State may invoke the fraud as invalidating its consent to be bound by the treaty.

Article 50. CORRUPTION OF A REPRESENTATIVE OF A STATE

If the expression of a State's consent to be bound by a treaty has been procured through the corruption of its representative directly or indirectly by another negotiating State, the State may invoke such corruption as invalidating its consent to be bound by the treaty

Article 51. COERCION OF A REPRESENTATIVE OF A STATE

The expression of a State's consent to be bound by a treaty which has been procured by the coercion of its representative through acts or threats directed against him shall be without any legal effect.

Article 52. COERCION OF A STATE BY THE THREAT OR USE OF FORCE

A treaty is void if its conclusion has been procured by the threat or use of force in violation of the principles of international law embodied in the Charter of the United Nations.

Article 53. TREATIES CONFLICTING WITH A PEREMPTORY NORM
OF GENERAL INTERNATIONAL LAW ("JUS COGENS")

A treaty is void if, at the time of its conclusion, it conflicts with a peremptory norm of general international law. For the purposes of the present Convention, a peremptory norm of general international law is a norm accepted and recognized by the international community of States as a whole as a norm from which no derogation is permitted and which can be modified only by a subsequent norm of general international law having the same character.

SECTION 3.   TERMINATION AND SUSPENSION OF THE OPERATION OF TREATIES

Article 54. TERMINATION OF OR WITHDRAWAL FROM A TREATY
UNDER ITS PROVISIONS OR BY CONSENT OF THE PARTIES

The termination of a treaty or the withdrawal of a party may take place:

(*a*) In conformity with the provisions of the treaty; or

(*b*) At any time by consent of all the parties after consultation with the other contracting States.

Article 55. REDUCTION OF THE PARTIES TO A MULTILATERAL TREATY
BELOW THE NUMBER NECESSARY FOR ITS ENTRY INTO FORCE

Unless the treaty otherwise provides a multilateral treaty does not terminate by reason only of the fact that the number of the parties falls below the number necessary for its entry into force.

Article 56. DENUNCIATION OF OR WITHDRAWAL FROM A TREATY CONTAINING
NO PROVISION REGARDING TERMINATION, DENUNCIATION OR WITHDRAWAL

1. A treaty which contains no provision regarding its termination and which does not provide for denunciation or withdrawal is not subject to denunciation or withdrawal unless:

(*a*) It is established that the parties intended to admit the possibility of denunciation or withdrawal; or

(*b*) A right of denunciation or withdrawal may be implied by the nature of the treaty.

2. A party shall give no less than twelve months' notice of its intention to denounce or withdraw from a treaty under paragraph 1.

Article 57. SUSPENSION OF THE OPERATION OF A TREATY UNDER
ITS PROVISIONS OR BY CONSENT OF THE PARTIES

The operation of a treaty in regard to all the parties or to a particular party may be suspended:

(*a*) In conformity with the provisions of the treaty; or

(*b*) At any time by consent of all the parties after consultation with the other contracting States.

Article 58. SUSPENSION OF THE OPERATION OF A MULTILATERAL TREATY
BY AGREEMENT BETWEEN CERTAIN OF THE PARTIES ONLY

1. Two or more parties to a multilateral treaty may conclude an agreement to suspend the operation of provisions of the treaty, temporarily and as between themselves alone, if:

(*a*) The possibility of such a suspension is provided for by the treaty; or

(*b*) The suspension in question is not prohibited by the treaty and:

(i) Does not affect the enjoyment by the other parties of their rights under the treaty or the performance of their obligations;

(ii) Is not incompatible with the object and purpose of the treaty.

2. Unless in a case falling under paragraph 1(*a*) the treaty otherwise provides, the parties in question shall notify the other parties of their intention to conclude the agreement and of those provisions of the treaty the operation of which they intend to suspend.

Article 59. Termination or suspension of the operation
of a treaty implied by conclusion of a later treaty

1. A treaty shall be considered as terminated if all the parties to it conclude a later treaty relating to the same subject-matter and:

(*a*) It appears from the later treaty or is otherwise established that the parties intended that the matter should be governed by that treaty; or

(*b*) The provisions of the later treaty are so far incompatible with those of the earlier one that the two treaties are not capable of being applied at the same time.

2. The earlier treaty shall be considered as only suspended in operation if it appears from the later treaty or is otherwise established that such was the intention of the parties.

Article 60. Termination or suspension of the operation
of a treaty as a consequence of its breach

1. A material breach of a bilateral treaty by one of the parties entitles the other to invoke the breach as a ground for terminating the treaty or suspending its operation in whole or in part.

2. A material breach of a multilateral treaty by one of the parties entitles:

(*a*) The other parties by unanimous agreement to suspend the operation of the treaty in whole or in part or to terminate it either:

(i) In the relations between themselves and the defaulting State, or

(ii) As between all the parties;

(*b*) A party specially affected by the breach to invoke it as a ground for suspending the operation of the treaty in whole or in part in the relations between itself and the defaulting State;

(*c*) Any party other than the defaulting State to invoke the breach as a ground for suspending the operation of the treaty in whole or in part with respect to itself if the treaty is of such a character that a material breach of its provisions by one party radically changes the position of every party with respect to the further performance of its obligations under the treaty.

3.   A material breach of a treaty, for the purposes of this article, consists in:

(*a*) A repudiation of the treaty not sanctioned by the present Convention; or

(*b*) The violation of a provision essential to the accomplishment of the object or purpose of the treaty.

4.   The foregoing paragraphs are without prejudice to any provision in the treaty applicable in the event of a breach.

5.   Paragraphs 1 to 3 do not apply to provisions relating to the protection of the human person contained in treaties of a humanitarian character, in particular to provisions prohibiting any form of reprisals against persons protected by such treaties.

Article 61.   SUPERVENING IMPOSSIBILITY OF PERFORMANCE

1.   A party may invoke the impossibility of performing a treaty as a ground for terminating or withdrawing from it if the impossibility results from the permanent disappearance or destruction of an object indispensable for the execution of the treaty. If the impossibility is temporary, it may be invoked only as a ground for suspending the operation of the treaty.

2.   Impossibility of performance may not be invoked by a party as a ground for terminating, withdrawing from or suspending the operation of a treaty if the impossibility is the result of a breach by that party either of an obligation under the treaty or of any other international obligation owed to any other party to the treaty.

Article 62.   FUNDAMENTAL CHANGE OF CIRCUMSTANCES

1.   A fundamental change of circumstances which has occurred with regard to those existing at the time of the conclusion of a treaty, and which was not foreseen by the parties, may not be invoked as a ground for terminating or withdrawing from the treaty unless:

(*a*) The existence of those circumstances constituted an essential basis of the consent of the parties to be bound by the treaty; and

(*b*) The effect of the change is radically to transform the extent of obligations still to be performed under the treaty.

2.   A fundamental change of circumstances may not be invoked as a ground for terminating or withdrawing from a treaty:

(*a*) If the treaty establishes a boundary; or

(*b*) If the fundamental change is the result of a breach by the party invoking it either of an obligation under the treaty or of any other international obligation owed to any other party to the treaty.

3.   If, under the foregoing paragraphs, a party may invoke a fundamental change of circumstances as a ground for terminating or withdrawing from a treaty it may also invoke the change as a ground for suspending the operation of the treaty.

Article 63.   SEVERANCE OF DIPLOMATIC OR CONSULAR RELATIONS

The severance of diplomatic or consular relations between parties to a treaty does not affect the legal relations established between them by the treaty except in so far as the existence of diplomatic or consular relations is indispensable for the application of the treaty.

Article 64.   Emergence of a new peremptory norm of
general international law ("JUS COGENS")

If a new peremptory norm of general international law emerges, any existing treaty which is in conflict with that norm becomes void and terminates.

Section 4.   Procedure

Article 65.   Procedure to be followed with respect to invalidity, termination,
withdrawal from or suspension of the operation of a treaty

1. A party which, under the provisions of the present Convention, invokes either a defect in its consent to be bound by a treaty or a ground for impeaching the validity of a treaty, terminating it, withdrawing from it or suspending its operation, must notify the other parties of its claim. The notification shall indicate the measure proposed to be taken with respect to the treaty and the reasons therefore.

2. If, after the expiry of a period which, except in cases of special urgency, shall not be less than three months after the receipt of the notification, no party has raised any objection, the party making the notification may carry out in the manner provided in article 67 the measure which it has proposed.

3. If, however, objection has been raised by any other party, the parties shall seek a solution through the means indicated in Article 33 of the Charter of the United Nations.

4. Nothing in the foregoing paragraphs shall affect the rights or obligations of the parties under any provisions in force binding the parties with regard to the settlement of disputes.

5. Without prejudice to article 45, the fact that a State has not previously made the notification prescribed in paragraph 1 shall not prevent it from making such notification in answer to another party claiming performance of the treaty or alleging its violation.

Article 66.   Procedures for judicial settlement, arbitration and conciliation

If, under paragraph 3 of article 65, no solution has been reached within a period of twelve months following the date on which the objection was raised, the following procedures shall be followed:

(*a*) Any one of the parties to a dispute concerning the application or the interpretation of articles 53 to 64 may, by a written application, submit it to the International Court of Justice for a decision unless the parties by common consent agree to submit the dispute to arbitration;

(*b*) Any one of the parties to a dispute concerning the application or the interpretation of any of the other articles in Part V of the present Convention may set in motion the procedure specified in the Annex to the Convention by submitting a request to that effect to the Secretary-General of the United Nations.

Article 67. INSTRUMENTS FOR DECLARING INVALID, TERMINATING, WITHDRAWING
FROM OR SUSPENDING THE OPERATION OF A TREATY

1. The notification provided for under article 65, paragraph 1 must be made in writing.

2. Any act declaring invalid, terminating, withdrawing from or suspending the operation of a treaty pursuant to the provisions of the treaty or of paragraphs 2 or 3 of article 65 shall be carried out through an instrument communicated to the other parties. If the instrument is not signed by the Head of State, Head of Government or Minister for Foreign Affair, the representative of the State communicating it may be called upon to produce full powers.

Article 68. REVOCATION OF NOTIFICATIONS AND INSTRUMENTS
PROVIDED FOR IN ARTICLES 65 AND 67

A notification or instrument provided for in articles 65 or 67 may be revoked at any time before it takes effect.

SECTION 5. CONSEQUENCES OF THE INVALIDITY, TERMINATION
OR SUSPENSION OF THE OPERATION OF A TREATY

Article 69. CONSEQUENCES OF THE INVALIDITY OF A TREATY

1. A treaty the invalidity of which is established under the present Convention is void. The provisions of a void treaty have no legal force.

2. If acts have nevertheless been performed in reliance on such a treaty:

(*a*) Each party may require any other party to establish as far as possible in their mutual relations the position that would have existed if the acts had not been performed;

(*b*) Acts performed in good faith before the invalidity was invoked are not rendered unlawful by reason only of the invalidity of the treaty.

3. In cases falling under articles 49, 50, 51 or 52, paragraph 2 does not apply with respect to the party to which the fraud, the act of corruption or the coercion is imputable.

4. In the case of the invalidity of a particular State's consent to be bound by a multilateral treaty, the foregoing rules apply in the relations between that State and the parties to the treaty.

Article 70. CONSEQUENCES OF THE TERMINATION OF A TREATY

1. Unless the treaty otherwise provides or the parties otherwise agree, the termination of a treaty under its provisions or in accordance with the present Convention:

(*a*) Releases the parties from any obligation further to perform the treaty;

(*b*) Does not affect any right, obligation or legal situation of the parties created through the execution of the treaty prior to its termination.

2. If a State denounces or withdraws from a multilateral treaty, paragraph 1 applies in the relations between that State and each of the other parties to the treaty from the date when such denunciation or withdrawal takes effect.

Article 71.   CONSEQUENCES OF THE INVALIDITY OF A TREATY WHICH CONFLICTS
WITH A PEREMPTORY NORM OF GENERAL INTERNATIONAL LAW

1.   In the case of a treaty which is void under article 53 the parties shall:

(*a*) Eliminate as far as possible the consequences of any act performed in reliance on any provision which conflicts with the peremptory norm of general international law; and

(*b*) Bring their mutual relations into conformity with the peremptory norm of general international law.

2.   In the case of a treaty which becomes void and terminates under article 64, the termination of the treaty:

(*a*) Releases the parties from any obligation further to perform the treaty;

(*b*) Does not affect any right, obligation or legal situation of the parties created through the execution of the treaty prior to its termination, provided that those rights, obligations or situations may thereafter be maintained only to the extent that their maintenance is not in itself in conflict with the new peremptory norm of general international law.

Article 72.   CONSEQUENCES OF THE SUSPENSION OF THE OPERATION OF A TREATY

1.   Unless the treaty otherwise provides or the parties otherwise agree, the suspension of the operation of a treaty under its provisions or in accordance with the present Convention:

(*a*) Release the parties between which the operation of the treaty is suspended from the obligation to perform the treaty in mutual relations during the period of the suspension;

(*b*) Does not otherwise affect the legal relations between the parties established by the treaty.

2.   During the period of the suspension the parties shall refrain from acts tending to obstruct the resumption of the operation of the treaty.

PART VI.   MISCELLANEOUS PROVISIONS

Article 73.   CASES OF STATE SUCCESSION, STATE RESPONSIBILITY
AND OUTBREAK OF HOSTILITIES

The provisions of the present Convention shall not prejudge any question that may arise in regard to a treaty from a succession of States or from the international responsibility of a State or from the outbreak of hostilities between States.

Article 74.   DIPLOMATIC AND CONSULAR RELATIONS AND THE CONCLUSION OF TREATIES

The severance or absence of diplomatic or consular relations between two or more States does not prevent the conclusion of treaties between those States.   The conclusion of a treaty does not in itself affect the situation in regard to diplomatic or consular relations.

Article 75.   CASE OF AN AGGRESSOR STATE

The provisions of the present Convention are without prejudice to any obligation in relation to a treaty which may arise for an aggressor State in consequence of measures taken in conformity with the Charter of the United Nations with reference to that State's aggression.

PART VII. DEPOSITARIES, NOTIFICATIONS, CORRECTIONS AND REGISTRATION

Article 76. DEPOSITARIES OF TREATIES

1. The designation of the depositary of a treaty may be made by the negotiating States, either in the treaty itself or in some other manner. The depositary may be one or more States, an international organization or the chief administrative officer of the organization.

2. The functions of the depositary of a treaty are international in character and the depositary is under an obligation to act impartially in their performance. In particular, the fact that a treaty has not entered into force between certain of the parties or that a difference has appeared between a State and a depositary with regard to the performance of the latter's functions shall not affect that obligation.

Article 77. FUNCTIONS OF DEPOSITARIES

1. The functions of a depositary, unless otherwise provided in the treaty or agreed by the contracting States, comprise in particular:

(*a*) Keeping custody of the original text of the treaty and of any full powers delivered to the depositary;

(*b*) Preparing certified copies of the original text and preparing any further text of the treaty in such additional languages as may be required by the treaty and transmitting them to the parties and to the States entitled to become parties to the treaty;

(*c*) Receiving any signatures to the treaty and receiving and keeping custody of any instruments, notifications and communications relating to it;

(*d*) Examining whether the signature or any instrument, notification or communication relating to the treaty is in due and proper form and, if need be, bringing the matter to the attention of the State in question;

(*e*) Informing the parties and the States entitled to become parties to the treaty of acts, notifications and communications relating to the treaty;

(*f*) Informing the States entitled to become parties to the treaty when the number of signatures or of instruments of ratification, acceptance, approval or accession required for the entry into force of the treaty has been received or deposited;

(*g*) Registering the treaty with the Secretariat of the United Nations;

(*h*) Performing the functions specified in other provisions of the present Convention.

2. In the event of any difference appearing between a State and the depositary as to the performance of the latter's functions, the depositary shall bring the question to the attention of the signatory States and the contracting

States or, where appropriate, of the competent organ of the international organization concerned.

Article 78. NOTIFICATIONS AND COMMUNICATIONS

Except as the treaty or the present Convention otherwise provides, any notification or communication to be made by any State under the present Convention shall:

(*a*) If there is no depositary, be transmitted direct to the States for which it is intended, or if there is a depositary, to the latter;

(*b*) Be considered as having been made by the State in question only upon its receipt by the State to which it was transmitted or, as the case may be, upon its receipt by the depositary;

(*c*) If transmitted to a depositary, be considered as received by the State for which it was intended only when the latter State has been informed by the depositary in accordance with article 77, paragraph 1(e).

Article 79. CORRECTION OF ERRORS IN TEXTS OR IN CERTIFIED COPIES OF TREATIES

1. Where, after the authentication of the text of a treaty, the signatory States and the contracting States are agreed that it contains an error, the error shall, unless they decide upon some other means of correction, be corrected:

(*a*) By having the appropriate correction made in the text and causing the correction to be initialled by duly authorized representatives;

(*b*) By executing or exchanging an instrument or instruments setting out the correction which it has been agreed to make; or

(*c*) By executing a corrected text of the whole treaty by the same procedure as in the case of the original text.

2. Where the treaty is one for which there is a depositary, the latter shall notify the signatory States and the contracting States of the error and of the proposal to correct it and shall specify an appropriate time-limit within which objection to the proposed correction may be raised. If, on the expiry of the time-limit:

(*a*) No objection has been raised, the depositary shall make and initial the correction in the text and shall execute a *process-verbal* of the rectification of the text and communicate a copy of it to the parties and to the States entitled to become parties to the treaty;

(*b*) An objection has been raised, the depositary shall communicate the objection to the signatory States and to the contracting States.

3. The rules in paragraphs 1 and 2 apply also where the text has been authenticated in two or more languages and it appears that there is a lack of concordance which the signatory States and the contracting States agree should be corrected.

4. The corrected text replaces the defective text *ab initio,* unless the signatory States and the contracting States otherwise decide.

5. The correction of the text of a treaty that has been registered shall be notified to the Secretariat of the United Nations.

6. Where an error is discovered in a certified copy of a treaty, the depositary shall execute a *process-verbal* specifying the rectification and communicate a copy of it to the signatory States and to the contracting States.

Article 80.   REGISTRATION AND PUBLICATION OF TREATIES

1. Treaties shall, after their entry into force, be transmitted to the Secretariat of the United Nations for registration or filing and recording, as the case may be, and for publication.

2. The designation of a depositary shall constitute authorization for it to perform the acts specified in the preceding paragraph.

PART VIII.   FINAL PROVISIONS

Article 81.   SIGNATURE

The present Convention shall be open for signature by all States Members of the United Nations or of any of the specialized agencies or of the International Atomic Energy Agency or parties to the Statute of the International Court of Justice, and by any other State invited by the General Assembly of the United Nations to become a party to the Convention, as follows: until 30 November 1969, at the Federal Ministry for Foreign Affairs of the Republic of Austria, and subsequently, until 30 April 1970, at United Nations Headquarters, New York.

Article 82.   RATIFICATION

The present Convention is subject to ratification. The instruments of ratification shall be deposited with the Secretary–General of the United Nations.

Article 83.   ACCESSION

The present Convention shall remain open for accession by any State belonging to any of the categories mentioned in article 81. The instruments of accession shall be deposited with the Secretary–General of the United Nations.

Article 84.   ENTRY INTO FORCE

1. The present Convention shall enter into force on the thirtieth day following the date of deposit of the thirty-fifth instrument of ratification or accession.

2. For each State ratifying or acceding to the Convention after the deposit of the thirty-fifth instrument of ratification or accession, the Convention shall enter into force on the thirtieth day after deposit by such State of its instrument of ratification or accession.

Article 85.   AUTHENTIC TEXTS

The original of the present Convention, of which the Chinese, English, French, Russian and Spanish texts are equally authentic, shall be deposited with the Secretary–General of the United Nations.

ANNEX

1. A list of conciliators consisting of qualified jurists shall be drawn up and maintained by the Secretary–General of the United Nations. To this end, every State which is a Member of the United Nations or a party to the present Convention shall be invited to nominate two conciliators, and the names of

the persons so nominated shall constitute the list. The term of a conciliator, including that of any conciliator nominated to fill a casual vacancy, shall be five years and may be renewed. A conciliator whose term expires shall continue to fulfil any function for which he shall have been chosen under the following paragraph.

2. When a request has been made to the Secretary–General under article 66, the Secretary–General shall bring the dispute before a conciliation commission constituted as follows:

The State or States constituting one of the parties to the dispute shall appoint:

(*a*) One conciliator of the nationality of that State or of one of those States, who may or may not be chosen from the list referred to in paragraph 1; and

(*b*) One conciliator not of the nationality of that State or of any of those States, who shall be chosen from the list.

The State or States constituting the other party to the dispute shall appoint two conciliators in the same way. The four conciliators chosen by the parties shall be appointed within sixty days following the date on which the Secretary–General receives the request.

The four conciliators shall, within sixty days following the date of the last of their own appointments, appoint a fifth conciliator chosen from the list, who shall be chairman.

If the appointment of the chairman or of any of the other conciliators has not been made within the period prescribed above for such appointment, it shall be made by the Secretary–General within sixty days following the expiry of that period. The appointment of the chairman may be made by the Secretary–General either from the list or from the membership of the International Law Commission. Any of the periods within which appointments must be made may be extended by agreement between the parties to the dispute.

Any vacancy shall be filled in the manner prescribed for the initial appointment.

3. The Conciliation Commission shall decide its own procedure. The Commission, with the consent of the parties to the dispute, may invite any party to the treaty to submit to it its views orally or in writing. Decisions and recommendations of the Commission shall be made by a majority vote of the five members.

4. The Commission may draw the attention of the parties to the dispute to any measures which might facilitate an amicable settlement.

5. The Commission shall hear the parties, examine the claims and objections, and make proposals to the parties with a view to reaching an amicable settlement of the dispute.

1.8 DECLARATION OF PRINCIPLES ON INTERNATIONAL LAW CONCERNING FRIENDLY RELATIONS AND CO-OPERATION AMONG STATES IN ACCORDANCE WITH THE CHARTER OF THE UNITED NATIONS. Adopted by the U.N. General Assembly, 24 October 1970. G.A.Res. 2625, U.N. GAOR, 25th Sess., Supp. No. 28, at 121, U.N.Doc. A/8028 (1971), 9 I.L.M. 1292 (1970)

THE GENERAL ASSEMBLY,

Reaffirming in the terms of the Charter that the maintenance of international peace and security and the development of friendly relations and co-operation between nations are among the fundamental purposes of the United Nations,

Recalling that the peoples of the United Nations are determined to practise tolerance and live together in peace with one another as good neighbours,

Bearing in mind the importance of maintaining and strengthening international peace and founded upon freedom, equality, justice and respect for fundamental human rights and of developing friendly relations among nations irrespective of their political, economic and social systems or the levels of their development,

Bearing in mind also the paramount importance of the Charter of the United Nations in the promotion of the rule of law among nations,

Considering that the faithful observance of the principles of international law concerning friendly relations and co-operation among States, and fulfilment in good faith of the obligation assumed by States, in accordance with the Charter, is of the greatest importance for the maintenance of international peace and security, and for the implementation of the other purposes of the United Nations,

Noting that the great political, economic and social changes and scientific progress which have taken place in the world since the adoption of the Charter of the United Nations give increased importance to these principles and to the need for their more effective application in the conduct of States wherever carried on,

Recalling the established principle that outer space, including the Moon and other celestial bodies, is not subject to national appropriation by claim of sovereignty by means of use or occupation or by any other means, and mindful of the fact that consideration is being given in the United Nations to the question of establishing other appropriate provisions similarly inspired,

Convinced that the strict observance by States of the obligation not to intervene in the affairs of any other State is an essential condition to ensure that nations live together in peace with one another since the practice of any form of intervention not only violates the spirit and letter of the Charter of the United Nations but also leads to the creation of situations which threaten international peace and security,

Recalling the duty of States to refrain in their international relations from military, political, economic or any other form of coercion aimed against the political independence or territorial integrity of any State,

Considering it essential that all States shall refrain in their international relations from the threat or use of force against the territorial integrity or political independence of any State, or in any other manner inconsistent with the purposes of the United Nations,

Considering it equally essential that all States shall settle their international disputes by peaceful means in accordance with the Charter,

Reaffirming, in accordance with the Charter, the basic importance of sovereign equality and stressing that the purposes of the United Nations can be implemented only if States enjoy sovereign equality and comply fully with the requirements of this principle in their international relations,

Convinced that the subjection of peoples to alien subjugation, domination and exploitation constitutes a major obstacle to the promotion of international peace and security,

Convinced that the principle of equal rights and self-determination of peoples constitutes a significant contribution to contemporary international law, and that its effective application is of paramount importance for the promotion of friendly relations among States, based on respect for the principle of sovereign equality,

Convinced in consequence that any attempt aimed at the partial or total disruption of the national unity and territorial integrity of a State or country or at its political independence is incompatible with the purposes and principles of the Charter,

Considering the provisions of the Charter as a whole and taking into account the role of relevant resolutions adopted by the competent organs of the United Nations relating to the content of the principles,

Considering that the progressive development and codification of the following principles:

(*a*) The principle that States shall refrain in their international relations from the threat or use of force against the territorial integrity or political independence of any State, or in any other manner inconsistent with the purposes of the United Nations,

(*b*) The principle that States shall settle their international disputes by peaceful means in such a manner that international peace and security and justice are not endangered,

(*c*) The duty not to intervene in matters within the domestic jurisdiction of any State, in accordance with the Charter,

(*d*) The duty of States to co-operate with one another in accordance with the Charter,

(*e*) The principle of equal rights and self-determination of peoples,

(*f*) The principle of sovereign equality of States,

(*g*) The principle that States shall fulfil in good faith the obligations assumed by them in accordance with the Charter, so as to secure their more effective application within the international community would promote the realization of the purposes of the United Nations,

Having considered the principles of international law relating to friendly relations and cooperation among States,

1. *Solemnly proclaims* the following principles:

The principle that States shall refrain in their international relations from the threat or use of force against the territorial integrity or political independence of any State, or in any other manner inconsistent with the purposes of the United Nations,

Every State has the duty to refrain in its international relations from the threat or use of force against the territorial integrity or political independence of any State, or in any other manner inconsistent with the purposes of the United Nations. Such a threat or use of force constitutes a violation of international law and the Charter of the United Nations and shall never be employed as a means of settling international issues.

A war of aggression constitutes a crime against the peace, for which there is responsibility under international law.

In accordance with the purposes and principles of the United Nations, States have the duty to refrain from propaganda for wars of aggression.

Every State has the duty to refrain from the threat or use of force to violate the existing international boundaries of another State or as a means of solving international disputes, including territorial disputes and problems concerning frontiers of States.

Every State likewise has the duty to refrain from the threat or use of force to violate international lines of demarcation, such as armistice lines, established by or pursuant to an international agreement to which it is a party or which it is otherwise bound to respect. Nothing in the foregoing shall be construed as prejudicing the positions of the parties concerned with regard to the status and effects of such lines under their special regimes or as affecting their temporary character.

States have a duty to refrain from acts of reprisal involving the use of force.

Every State has the duty to refrain from any forcible action which deprives peoples referred to in the elaboration of the principle of equal rights and self-determination of their right to self-determination and freedom and independence.

Every State has the duty to refrain from organizing or encouraging the organization of irregular forces or armed bands, including mercenaries, for incursion into the territory of another state.

Every State has the duty to refrain from organizing, instigating, assisting or participating in acts of civil strife or terrorist acts in another State or acquiescing in organized activities within its territory directed towards the commission of such acts, when the acts referred to in the present paragraph involve a threat or use of force.

The territory of a State shall not be the object of military occupation resulting from the use of force in contravention of the provisions of the Charter. The territory of a State shall not be the object of acquisition by another State resulting from the threat or use of force. No territorial acquisition resulting from the threat or use of force shall be recognized as legal. Nothing in the foregoing shall be construed as affecting:

(*a*) Provisions of the Charter or any international agreement prior to the Charter regime and valid under international law; or

(*b*) The powers of the Security Council under the Charter.

All States shall pursue in good faith negotiations for the early conclusion of a universal treaty on general and complete disarmament under effective international control and strive to adopt appropriate measures to reduce international tensions and strengthen confidence among States.

All States shall comply in good faith with their obligations under the generally recognized principles and rules of international law with respect to the maintenance of international peace and security, and shall endeavour to make the United Nations security system based upon the Charter more effective.

Nothing in the foregoing paragraphs shall be construed as enlarging or diminishing in any way the scope of the provisions of the Charter concerning cases in which the use of force is lawful.

The principle that States shall settle their international disputes by peaceful means in such a manner that international peace and security and justice are not endangered

Every State shall settle its international disputes with other States by peaceful means, in such a manner that international peace and security, and justice, are not endangered.

States shall accordingly seek early and just settlement of their international disputes by negotiation, inquiry, mediation, conciliation, arbitration, judicial settlement, resort to regional agencies or arrangements or other peaceful means of their choice. In seeking such a settlement, the parties shall agree upon such peaceful means as may be appropriate to the circumstances and nature of the dispute.

The parties to a dispute have the duty, in the event of failure to reach a solution by any one of the above peaceful means, to continue to seek a settlement of the dispute by other peaceful means agreed upon by them.

States parties to an international dispute, as well as other States, shall refrain from any action which may aggravate the situation so as to endanger the maintenance of international peace and security, and shall act in accordance with the purposes and principles of the United Nations.

International disputes shall be settled on the basis of the sovereign equality of States and in accordance with the principle of free choice of means. Recourse to, or acceptance of, a settlement procedure freely agreed to by States with regard to existing or future disputes to which they are parties shall not be regarded as incompatible with sovereign equality.

Nothing in the foregoing paragraphs prejudices or derogates from the applicable provisions of the Charter, in particular those relating to the pacific settlement of international disputes.

The principle concerning the duty not to intervene in matters within the domestic jurisdiction of any State, in accordance with the Charter

No State or group of States has the right to intervene, directly or indirectly, for any reason whatever, in the internal or external affairs of any other State. Consequently, armed intervention and all other forms of interference or attempted threats against the personality of the State or against its political, economic and cultural elements, are in violation of international law.

No State may use or encourage the use of economic, political or any other type of measures to coerce another State in order to obtain from it the subordination of the exercise of its sovereign rights and to secure from it advantages of any kind. Also, no State shall organize, assist, foment, finance, incite or tolerate subversive, terrorist or armed activities directed towards the violent overthrow of the regime of another State, or interfere in civil strife in another State.

The use of force to deprive peoples of their national identity constitutes a violation of their inalienable rights and of the principle of non-intervention.

Every State has an inalienable right to choose its political, economic, social and cultural systems, without interference in any form by another State.

Nothing in the foregoing paragraphs shall be construed as affecting the relevant provisions of the Charter relating to the maintenance of international peace and security.

The duty of States to co-operate with one another in accordance with the Charter

States have the duty to co-operate with one another, irrespective of the differences in their political, economic and social systems, in the various spheres of international relations, in order to maintain international peace and security and to promote international economic stability and progress, the general welfare of nations and international co-operation free from discrimination based on such differences.

To this end:

(a) States shall co-operate with other States in the maintenance of international peace and security;

(b) States shall co-operate in the promotion of universal respect for and observance of human rights and financial freedoms for all, and in the elimination of all forms of racial discrimination and all forms of religious intolerance;

(c) States shall conduct their international relations in the economic, social, cultural, technical and trade fields in accordance with the principles of sovereign equality and non-intervention;

(d) States Members of the United Nations have the duty to take joint and separate action in co-operation with the United Nations in accordance with the relevant provisions of the Charter.

States should co-operate in the economic, social and cultural fields as well as in the field of science and technology and for the promotion of international cultural and educational progress. States should co-operate in the promotion of economic growth throughout the world, especially that of the developing countries.

The principle of equal rights and self-determination of peoples

By virtue of the principle of equal rights and self-determination of peoples enshrined in the Charter, all peoples have the right freely to determine, without external interference, their political status and to pursue their economic, social and cultural development, and every State has the duty to respect this right in accordance with the provisions of the Charter.

Every State has the duty to promote, through joint and separate action, the realization of the principle of equal rights and self-determination of peoples, in accordance with the provisions of the Charter, and to render assistance to the United Nations in carrying out the responsibilities entrusted to it by the Charter regarding the implementation of the principle in order:

(*a*) To promote friendly relations and co-operation among States; and

(*b*) To bring a speedy end to colonialism, having due regard to the freely expressed will of the peoples concerned;

and bearing in mind that subjection of peoples to alien subjugation, domination and exploitation constitutes a violation of the principle, as well as a denial of fundamental human rights, and is contrary to the Charter of the United Nations.

Every State has the duty to promote through joint and separate action universal respect for and observance of human rights and fundamental freedoms in accordance with the Charter.

The establishment of a sovereign and independent State, the free association or integration with an independent State or the emergence into any other political status freely determined by a people constitute modes of implementing the right of self-determination by that peoples.

Every State has the duty to refrain from any forcible action which deprives peoples referred to above in the elaboration of the present principle of their right to self-determination and freedom and independence. In their actions against and resistance to such forcible action in pursuit of the exercise of their right to self-determination such peoples are entitled to seek and to receive support in accordance with the purposes and principles of the Charter of the United Nations.

The territory of a colony or other non-self-governing territory has, under the Charter of the United Nations, a status separate and distinct from the territory of the State administering it; and status separate and distinct from the territory of the State administering it; and such separate and distinct status under the Charter shall exist until the people of the colony or non-self-governing territory have exercised their right of self-determination in accordance with the Charter, and particularly its purposes and principles.

Nothing in the foregoing paragraphs shall be construed as authorizing or encouraging any action which would dismember or impair, totally or in part, the territorial integrity or political unity of sovereign and independent States conducting themselves in compliance with the principle of equal rights and self-determination of peoples as described above and thus possessed of a government representing the whole people belonging to the territory without distinction as to race, creed or colour.

Every State shall refrain from any action aimed at the partial or total disruption of the national unity and territorial integrity of any State or country.

The principle of sovereign equality of States

All States enjoy sovereign equality. They have equal right and duties and are equal members of the international community, notwithstanding differences of an economic, social, political or other nature.

In particular, sovereign equality includes the following elements:

(*a*) States are juridically equal;

(*b*) Each State enjoys the rights inherent in full sovereignty;

(*c*) Each State has the duty to respect the personality of other States;

(*d*) The territorial integrity and political independence of the State are inviolable;

(*e*) Each State has the right freely to choose and develop its political, social, economic and cultural systems;

(*f*) Each State has the duty to comply fully and in good faith with its international obligations and to live in peace with other States.

The principle that States shall fulfil in good faith the obligations assumed by them in accordance with the Charter

Every State has the duty to fulfil in good faith the obligations assumed by it in accordance with the Charter of the United Nations.

Every State has the duty to fulfil in good faith its obligations under the generally recognized principles and rules of international law.

Every State has the duty to fulfil in good faith its obligations under international agreements valid under the generally recognized principles and rules of international law.

Where obligations arising under international agreements are in conflict with the obligations of Members of the United Nations under the Charter of the United Nations, the obligations under the Charter shall prevail.

General part

2. *Declares* that:

In their interpretation and application the above principles are interrelated and each principle should be construed in the context of the other principles,

Nothing in this Declaration shall be construed as prejudicing in any manner the provisions of the Charter or the rights and duties of Member States under the Charter or the rights of peoples under the Charter taking into account the elaboration of these rights in this Declaration,

3. *Declares further* that:

The principles of the Charter which are embodied in this Declaration constitute basic principles of international law, and consequently appeals to all States to be guided by these principles in their international conduct and to develop their mutual relations on the basis of their strict observance.

1.9 INTERNATIONAL LAW COMMISSION DRAFT ARTICLES ON STATE RESPONSIBILITY. Adopted by the International Law Commission at its 1642nd mtg., 25 July 1980. Report of the International Law Commission on the Work of its Thirty–Second Session, 5 May–25 July 1980. U.N.Doc. A/35/10 (1981)

Chapter I. General Principles

Article I. *Responsibility of a State for its internationally wrongful acts*

Every internationally wrongful act of a State entails the international responsibility of that State.

Article 2. *Possibility that every State may be held to have committed an internationally wrongful act*

Every State is subject to the possibility of being held to have committed an internationally wrongful act entailing its international responsibility.

Article 3. *Elements of an internationally wrongful act of a State*

There is an internationally wrongful act of a State when:

(a) conduct consisting of an action or omission is attributable to the State under international law; and

(b) that conduct constitutes a breach of international obligation of the State.

Article 4. *Characterization of an act of a State as internationally wrongful*

An act of a State may only be characterized as internationally wrongful by international law. Such characterization cannot be affected by the characterization of the same act as lawful by internal law.

Chapter II. The "Act of the State" Under International Law

Article 5. *Attribution to the State of the conduct of its organs*

For the purposes of the present articles, conduct of any State organ having that status under the internal law of that State shall be considered as an act of the State concerned under international law, provided that organ was acting in that capacity in the case in question.

Article 6. *Irrelevance of the position of the organ in the organization of the State*

The conduct of an organ of the State shall be considered as an act of that State under international law whether that organ belongs to the constituent, legislative, executive, judicial or other power whether its functions are of an international or an internal character, and whether it holds a superior or a subordinate position in the organization of the State.

Article 7. *Attribution to the State of the conduct of other entities empowered to exercise elements of the government authority*

1. The conduct of an organ of a territorial governmental entity within a State shall also be considered as an act of that State under international law provided that organ was acting in that capacity in the case in question.

2. The conduct of an organ of an entity which is not part of the formal structure of the State or of a territorial governmental entity but which is empowered by the internal law of that State to exercise elements of the governmental authority shall also be considered as an act of the State under

international law provided that organ was acting in that capacity in the case in question.

Article 8. Attribution to the State of the conduct of persons acting in fact on behalf of the State

The conduct of a person or group of persons shall also be considered as an act of the State under international law if:

(a) it is established that such persons or group of persons was in fact acting on behalf of that State; or

(b) such person or group of persons was in fact exercising elements of the governmental authority in the absence of the official authorities and in circumstances which justified the exercise of those elements of authority.

Article 9. Attribution to the State of the conduct of organs placed at its disposal by another State or by an international organization

The conduct of an organ which has been placed at the disposal of a State by another State or by an international organization shall be considered as an act of the former State under international law, if that organ was acting in the exercise of elements of the governmental authority of the State at whose disposal it has been placed.

Article 10. Attribution to the State of conduct of organs acting outside their competence or contrary to instructions concerning their activity

The conduct of an organ of a State, of a territorial governmental entity or of an entity empowered to exercise elements of the governmental authority, such organ having acted in that capacity, shall be considered as an act of the State under international law even if, in the particular case, the organ exceeded its competence according to internal law or contravened instructions concerning its activity.

Article 11. Conduct of Persons not acting on behalf of the State

1. The conduct of person or a group of persons not acting on behalf of the State shall not be considered as an act of the State under international law.

2. Paragraph 1 is without prejudice to the attribution to the State of any other conduct which is related to that of the persons or groups of persons referred to in that paragraph and which is to be considered as an act of that State by virtue of articles 5 to 10.

Article 12. Conduct of organs of another State

1. The conduct of an organ of a State acting in that capacity which takes place in the territory of another State or in any other territory under its jurisdiction shall not be considered as an act of the latter State under international law.

2. Paragraph 1 is without prejudice to the attribution to a State of any other conduct which is related to that referred to in that paragraph and which is to be considered as an act of that State by virtue of articles 5 to 10.

Article 13.   Conduct of organs of an international organization

The conduct of an organ of an international organization acting in that capacity shall not be considered as an act of a State under international law by reason only of the fact that such conduct has taken place in the territory of that State or in any other territory under its jurisdiction.

Article 14.   Conduct of organs of an insurrectional movement

1.   The conduct of an organ of an insurrectional movement which is established in the territory of a State or in any other territory under its administration shall not be considered as an act of that State under international law.

2.   Paragraph 1 is without prejudice to the attribution to a State of any other conduct which is related to that of the organ of the insurrectional movement and which is to be considered as an act of that State by virtue of articles 5 to 10.

3.   Similarly paragraph 1 is without prejudice to the attribution of the conduct of the organ of the insurrectional movement to that movement in any case in which such attribution may be made under international law.

Article 15.   Attribution to the State of the act of an insurrectional movement which becomes the new government of a State or which results in the formation of a new State

1.   The act of an insurrectional movement which becomes the new government of a State shall be considered as an act of that State. However, such attribution shall be without prejudice to the attribution to that State of conduct which would have been previously considered as an act of the State by virtue of articles 5 to 10.

2.   The act of an insurrectional movement whose action results in the formation of a new State in part of the territory of a pre-existing State or in a territory under its administration shall be considered as an act of the new State.

Chapter III.   Breach of An International Obligation

Article 16.   Existence of a breach of an international obligation

There is a breach of an international obligation by a State when an act of that state is not in conformity with what is required of it by that obligation.

Article 17.   Irrelevance of the origin of the international obligation breached

1.   An act of a State which constitutes a breach of an international obligation is an internationally wrongful act regardless of the origin, whether customary, conventional, or other, of that obligation.

2.   The origin of the international obligation breached by a State does not affect the international responsibility arising from the internationally wrongful act of that State.

Article 18.   Requirement that the international obligation be in force for the State

1.   An act of the State which is not in conformity with what is required of it by an international obligation constitutes a breach of that obligation only

if the act was performed at the time when the obligation was in force for that State.

2. However, an act of the State which, at the time when it was performed was not in conformity with what was required of it by an international obligation in force for that State, ceases to be considered an internationally wrongful act if, subsequently, such an act has become compulsory by virtue of a peremptory norm of general international law.

3. If an act of the State which is not in conformity with what is required of it by an international obligation has a continuing character, there is a breach of that obligation only in respect of the period during which the act continues while the obligation is in force for that State.

4. If an act of the State which is not in conformity with what is required of it by an international obligation is composed of a series of actions or omissions in respect of separate cases, there is a breach of that obligation if such an act may be considered to be constituted by the actions or omissions occurring within the period during which the obligation is in force for that State.

5. If an act of the State which is not in conformity with what is required of it by an international obligation is a complex act constituted by actions or omissions by the same or different organs of the State in respect of the same case, there is a breach of that obligation if the complex act not in conformity with it begins with an action or omission occurring within the period during which the obligation is in force for that State, even if that act is completed after that period.

Article 19. *International crimes and international delicts*

1. An act of a State which constitutes a breach of an international obligation is an internationally wrongful act regardless of the subject-matter of the obligation breached.

2. An internationally wrongful act which results from the breach by a State of an international obligation so essential for the protection of fundamental interests of the international community that its breach is recognized as a crime by that community as a whole constitutes an international crime.

3. Subject to paragraph 2, and on the basis of the rules of international law in force, an international crime may result, *inter alia,* form:

(a) a serious breach of an international obligation of essential importance for the maintenance of international peace and security such, as that prohibiting aggression;

(b) a serious breach of an international obligation of essential importance for safeguarding the right of self-determination or peoples, such as that prohibiting the establishment or maintenance by force of colonial domination:

(c) a serious breach on a widespread scale of an international obligation of essential importance for safeguarding the human being such as those prohibiting slavery, genocide and *apartheid:*

(d) a serious breach of an international obligation of essential importance for the safeguarding and preservation of the human environment such as those prohibiting massive pollution of the atmosphere or of the seas.

4. Any internationally wrongful act which is not an international crime in accordance with paragraph 2 constitutes an international delict.

Article 20. *Breach of an international obligation requiring the adoption of a particular course of conduct*

There is a breach by a State of an international obligation requiring it to adopt a particular course of conduct when the conduct of that State is not in conformity with that required of it by that obligation.

Article 21. *Breach of an international obligation requiring the achievement of a specified result*

1. There is a breach by a State of an international obligation requiring it to achieve by means of its own choice a specified result if, by the conduct adopted, the State does not achieve the result required of it by that obligation.

2. When the conduct of the State has created a situation not in conformity with the result required of it by an international obligation but the obligation allows that this or an equivalent result may nevertheless be achieved by subsequent conduct of the State, there is a breach of the obligation only if the State also fails by its subsequent conduct to achieve the result required of it by that obligation.

Article 22. *Exhaustion of local remedies*

When the conduct of a State has created a situation not in conformity with the result required of it by an international obligation concerning the treatment to be accorded to aliens, whether natural or juridical persons, but the obligation allows that this or an equivalent result may nevertheless be achieved by subsequent conduct of the State, there is a breach of the obligation only if the aliens concerned have exhausted the effective local remedies available to them without obtaining the treatment called for by the obligation or, where that is not possible, an equivalent treatment.

Article 23. *Breach of an international obligation to prevent a given event*

When the result required of a State by an international obligation is the prevention by means of its own choice, of the occurrence of a given event, there is a breach of that obligation only if by the conduct adopted the State does not achieve that result.

Article 24. *Moment and duration of the breach of an international obligation by an act of the State not extending in time*

The breach of an international obligation by an act of the State not extending in time occurs at the moment when that act is performed. The time of commission of the breach does not extend beyond that moment, even if the effects of the act of the State continue subsequently.

Article 25. *Moment and duration of the breach of an international obligation by an act of the State extending in time*

1. The breach of an international obligation by an act of the State having a continuing character occurs at the moment when that act begins. Nevertheless the time of commission of the breach extends over the entire

period during which the act continues and remains not in conformity with the international obligation.

2.   The breach of an international obligation by an act of the State composed of a series of actions or omissions in respect of separate cases occurs at the moment when that action or omission of the series is accomplished which establishes the existence of the composite act.   Nevertheless, the time of commission of the breach extends over the entire period from the first of the actions or omissions constituting the composite act not in conformity with the international obligation and so long as such actions or omissions are repeated.

3.   The breach of an international obligation by a complex act of the State consisting of a succession of actions or omissions by the same or different organs of the State in respect of the same case occurs at the moment when the last constituent element of that complete act is accomplished. Nevertheless, the time of commission of the breach extends over the entire period between the action or omission which initiated the breach and that which completed it.

Article 26.   Moment and duration of the breach of an international obligation to prevent a given event

The breach of an international obligation requiring a State to prevent a given event occurs when the event begins.   Nevertheless the time of commission of the breach extends over the entire period during which the event continues.

Chapter IV.   Implication of a State in the Internationally Wrongful Act of Another State

Article 27.   Aid or assistance by a State to another State for the commission of an internationally wrongful act

Aid or assistance by a State to another State if it is established that it is rendered for the commission of an internationally wrongful act carried out by the latter, itself constitutes an internationally wrongful act even if taken alone such aid or assistance would not constitute the breach of an international obligation.

Article 28.   Responsibility of a State for an internationally wrongful act of another State

1.   An internationally wrongful act committed by a State in a field of activity in which that State is subject to the power of direction or control of another State entails the international responsibility of that other State.

2.   An internationally wrongful act committed by a State as the result of coercion exerted by another State to secure the commission of that act entails the international responsibility of that other State.

3.   Paragraphs 1 and 2 are without prejudice to the international responsibility, under the other articles of the present draft, of the State which has committed the internationally wrongful act.

Chapter V.   Circumstances Precluding Wrongfulness
Article 29.   Consent

1.   The consent validly given by a State to the commission by another State of a specified act not in conformity with an obligation of the latter State

towards the former State precludes the wrongfulness of the act in relation to that State to the extent that the act remains within the limits of that consent.

2. Paragraph 1 does not apply if the obligation arises out of a peremptory norm of general international law. For the purposes of the present draft articles, a peremptory norm of general international law is a norm accepted and recognized by the international community of States as a whole as a norm from which no derogation is permitted and which can be modified only by a subsequent norm of general international law having the same character.

Article 30. *Countermeasures in respect of an internationally wrongful act*

The wrongfulness of an act of a State not in conformity with an obligation of that State towards another State is precluded if the act constitutes a measure legitimate under international law against that other State in consequence of an internationally wrongful act of that other State.

Article 31. *Force Majeure and fortuitous event*

1. The wrongfulness of an act of a State not in conformity with an international obligation of that State is precluded if the act was due to an irresistible force or to an unforeseen external event beyond its control which made it materially impossible for the State to act in conformity with that obligation or to know that its conduct was not in conformity with that obligation.

2. Paragraph 1 shall not apply if the State in question has contributed to the occurrence of the situation of material impossibility.

Article 32. *Distress*

1. The wrongfulness of an act of a State not in conformity with an international obligation of that State is precluded if the author of the conduct which constitutes the act of that State had no other means in a situation of extreme distress of saving his life or that of persons entrusted to his care.

2. Paragraph 1 shall not apply if the State in question has contributed to the occurrence of the situation of extreme distress or if the conduct in question was likely to create a comparable or greater peril.

Article 33. *State of necessity*

1. A state of necessity may not be invoked by a State as a ground for precluding the wrongfulness of an act of that State not in conformity with an international obligation of the State unless:

(a) the act was the only means of safeguarding an essential interest of the State against a grave and imminent peril; and

(b) the act did not seriously impair an essential interest of the State towards which the obligation existed.

2. In any case, a state of necessity may not be invoked by a State as a ground for precluding wrongfulness:

(a) if the international obligation with which the act of the State is not in conformity arises out of a peremptory norm of general international law; or

(b) if the international obligation with which the act of the State is not in conformity is laid down by a treaty which explicitly or implicitly excludes the possibility of invoking the state of necessity with respect to that obligation; or

(c) if the State in question has contributed to the occurrence of the state of necessity.

Article 34. Self-defense

The wrongfulness of an act not in conformity with an international obligation of that State is precluded if the act constitutes a lawful measure of self-defence taken in conformity with the Charter of the United Nations.

Article 35. Reservation as to compensation for damage

Preclusion of the wrongfulness of an act of a State by virtue of the provisions of article 29, 31, 32 or 33 does not prejudge any question that may arise in regard to compensation for damage caused by that act.

1.10 **SINGLE EUROPEAN ACT. 169 O.J.E.C. 1 (1987) and Corr. 304 O.J.E.C.
46 (1987), 25 I.L.M. 503 (1987):** *Arts. 18 (amending Art. 100 of the
1957 Treaty Establishing the European Economic Community with
Art. 100A) and 25 (supplementing Part Three of the 1957 Treaty
Establishing the European Economic Community with a new Title
VII, including Arts. 130R–130T)* [1]

His Majesty the King of the Belgians,
Her Majesty the Queen of Denmark,
The President of the Federal Republic of Germany,
The President of the Hellenic Republic,
His Majesty the King of Spain,
The President of the French Republic,
The President of Ireland,
The President of the Italian Republic,
His Royal Highness the Grand Duke of Luxembourg,
Her Majesty the Queen of the Netherlands,
The President of the Portuguese Republic,
*Her Majesty the Queen of the United Kingdom of Great Britain and
Northern Ireland,*

Moved by the will to continue the work undertaken on the basis of the
Treaties establishing the European Communities and to transform relations
as a whole among their States into a European Union, in accordance with the
Solemn Declaration of Stuttgart of 19 June 1893.

Resolved to implement this European Union on the basis, firstly, of the
Communities operating in accordance with their own rules and, secondly, of
European Cooperation among the Signatory States in the sphere of foreign
policy and to invest this union with the necessary means of action,

Determined to work together to promote democracy on the basis of the
fundamental rights recognized in the constitutions and laws of the Member
States, in the Convention for the Protection of Human Rights and Fundamental Freedoms and the European Social Charter, notably freedom, equality and
social justice,

Convinced that the European idea, the results achieved in the fields of
economic integration and political cooperation, and the need for new developments correspond to the wishes of the democratic peoples of Europe, for
whom the European Parliament, elected by universal suffrage, is an indispensable means of expression,

Aware of the responsibility incumbent upon Europe to aim at speaking
ever increasingly with one voice and to act with consistency and solidarity in
order more effectively to protect its common interests and independence, in
particular to display the principles of democracy and compliance with the law
and with human rights to which they are attached, so that together they may
make their own contribution to the preservation of international peace and
security in accordance with the undertaking entered into by them within the
framework of the United Nations Charter,

1. *See also* Basic Documents 1.6, *supra,*
and 1.12, *infra.*

Determined to improve the economic and social situation by extending common policies and pursuing new objectives, and to ensure a smoother functioning of the Communities by enabling the institutions to exercise their powers under conditions most in keeping with Community interests,

Whereas at their Conference in Paris from 19 to 21 October 1972 the Heads of State or of Government approved the objective of the progressive realization of economic and monetary union;

Having regard to the Annex to the conclusions of the Presidency of the European Council in Bremen on 6 and 7 July 1978 and the Resolution of the European Council in Brussels on 5 December 1978 on the introduction of the European Monetary System (EMS) and related questions, and noting that in accordance with that Resolution, the Community and the Central Banks of the Member States have taken a number of measures intended to implement monetary cooperation,

Have decided to adopt this Act and to this end have designated ... as their plenipotentiaries ..., Who, having exchanged their full powers, found in good and due form, have agreed as follows:

* * *

Provisions relating to the foundations and the policy of the Community

Subsection I—Internal market

* * *

Article 13

The EEC Treaty shall be supplemented by the following provisions:

Article 100 A

1. By way of derogation from Article 100 and save where otherwise provided in this Treaty, the following provisions shall apply for the achievement of the objectives set out in Article 8A. The Council shall, acting by a qualified majority on a proposal from the Commission in cooperation with the European Parliament and the Economic and Social Committee, adopt the measures for the approximation of the provisions laid down by law, regulation or administrative action in Member States which have as their object the establishment and functioning of the internal market.

2. Paragraph 1 shall not apply to fiscal provisions, to those relating to the free movement of persons nor to those relating to the rights and interests of employed persons.

3. The Commission, in its proposals laid down in paragraph 1 concerning health, safety, environmental protection and consumer protection, will take as a base a high level of protection.

4. If, after the adoption of a harmonization measure by the Council acting by a qualified majority, a Member State deems it necessary to apply national provisions on grounds of major needs referred to in Article 36, or relating to protection of the environment or the working environment, it shall notify the Commission of these provisions.

The Commission shall confirm the provisions involved after having verified that they are not a means of arbitrary discrimination or a disguised restriction on trade between Member States.

By way of derogation from the procedure laid down in Articles 169 and 170, the Commission or any Member State may bring the matter directly before the Court of Justice if it considers that another Member State is making improper use of the powers provided for in this Article.

5. The harmonization measures referred to above shall, in appropriate cases, include a safeguard clause authorizing the Member States to take, for one or more of the non-economic reasons referred to in Article 36, provisional measures subject to a Community control procedure.'

* * *

Subsection VI—Environment

Article 25

A Title VII shall be added to Part Three of the EEC Treaty, reading as follows:

'*Title VII*

Environment

Article 130 R

1. Action by the Community relating to the environment shall have the following objectives:

(i) to preserve, protect and improve the quality of the environment;

(ii) to contribute towards protecting human health;

(iii) to ensure a prudent and rational utilization of natural resources.

2. Action by the Community relating to the environment shall be based on the principles that preventive action should be taken, that environmental damage should as a priority be rectified at source, and that the polluter should pay. Environmental protection requirements shall be a component of the Community's other policies.

3. In preparing its action relating to the environment, the Community shall take account of:

(i) available scientific and technical data;

(ii) environmental conditions in the various regions of the Community;

(iii) the potential benefits and costs of action or of lack of action;

(iv) the economic and social development of the Community as a whole and the balanced development of its regions.

4. The Community shall take action relating to the environment to the extent to which the objectives referred to in paragraph 1 can be attained better at Community level than at the level of the individual Member States. Without prejudice to certain measures of a Community nature, the Member States shall finance and implement the other measures.

5. Within their respective spheres of competence, the Community and the Member States shall cooperate with third countries and with the relevant international organizations. The arrangements for Community cooperation may be the subject of agreements between the Community and the third parties concerned, which shall be negotiated and concluded in accordance with Article 228.

The previous paragraph shall be without prejudice to Member States' competence to negotiate in international bodies and to conclude international agreements.

Article 130 S

The Council, acting unanimously on a proposal from the Commission and after consulting the European Parliament and the Economic and Social Committee, shall decide what action is to be taken by the Community.

The Council shall, under the conditions laid down in the preceding subparagraph, define those matters on which decisions are to be taken by a qualified majority.

Article 130 T

The protective measures adopted in common pursuant to Article 130 S shall not prevent any Member State from maintaining or introducing more stringent protective measures compatible with this Treaty.'

**1.11   INTERNATIONAL LAW COMMISSION DRAFT ARTICLES ON INTER-
NATIONAL LIABILITY FOR INJURIOUS CONSEQUENCES ARIS-
ING OUT OF ACTS NOT PROHIBITED BY INTERNATIONAL LAW.**
*Report of the International Law Commission on the Work of Its
Forty-first Session.*   U.N. GAOR, 44th Sess., Supp. No. 10, at 222,
U.N. Doc. A/44/10 (1989)

"CHAPTER I

GENERAL PROVISIONS

"Article 1

Scope of the present articles

The present articles shall apply with respect to activities carried out in
the territory of a State or in other places under its jurisdiction as recognized
by international law or, in the absence of such jurisdiction, under its control,
when the physical consequences of such activities cause, or create an appreciable risk of causing, transboundary harm throughout the process.

"Article 2

Use of terms

For the purposes of the present articles:

(a) 'Risk' means the risk occasioned by the use of things whose
physical properties, considered either intrinsically or in relation to the
place, environment or way in which they are used, make them likely to
cause transboundary harm throughout the process, notwithstanding any
precautions which might be taken in their regard.

'Appreciable risk' means the risk which may be identified through a
simple examination of the activity and the substances involved, in relation to
the place, environment or way in which they are used, and includes both the
low probability of very considerable (disastrous) transboundary harm and the
high probability of minor appreciable harm.

(b) 'Activities involving risk' means the activities referred to in the
preceding paragraph, in which harm is contingent, and 'activities with
harmful effects' means those causing appreciable transboundary harm
throughout the process.

(c) 'Transboundary harm' means the effect which arises as a physical
consequence of the activities referred to in article 1 and which, in the
territory or in places under the jurisdiction or control of another State, is
appreciably detrimental to persons or objects, to the use or enjoyment of
areas or to the environment, whether or not the States concerned have a
common border.   Under the régime of these articles, 'transboundary
harm' always refers to 'appreciable harm'.

(d) 'State of origin' means the State in whose territory or in places
under whose jurisdiction or control the activities referred to in article 1
take place.

(e) 'Affected State' means the State in whose territory or under
whose jurisdiction persons or objects, the use or enjoyment of areas, or
the environment, are or may be appreciably affected.

"Article 3
Assignment of obligations

The State of origin shall have the obligations established by the present articles, provided that it knew or had means of knowing that an activity referred to in article 1 was being, or was about to be, carried out in its territory or in other places under its jurisdiction or control.

Unless there is evidence to the contrary, it shall be presumed that the State of origin has the knowledge or the means of knowing referred to in the preceding paragraph.

"Article 4
Relationship between the present articles and other international agreements

Where States Parties to the present articles are also parties to another international agreement concerning activities referred to in article 1, in relations between such States the present articles shall apply, subject to that other international agreement.

"Article 5 [1]
Absence of effect upon other rules of international law

[The fact that the present articles do not specify circumstances in which the occurrence of transboundary harm arises from a wrongful act or omission of the State of origin shall be without prejudice to the operation of any other rule of international law.]

[The present articles are without prejudice to the operation of any other rule of international law establishing liability for transboundary harm resulting from a wrongful act.]

"CHAPTER II
PRINCIPLES
"Article 6
Freedom of action and the limits thereto

The sovereign freedom of States to carry out or permit human activities in their territory or in other places under their jurisdiction or control must be compatible with the protection of the rights emanating from the sovereignty of other States.

"Article 7
Co-operation

States shall co-operate in good faith among themselves, and request the assistance of any international organizations that might be able to help them, in trying to prevent any activities referred to in article 1 carried out in their territory or in other places under their jurisdiction or control from causing transboundary harm. If such harm occurs, the State of origin shall co-operate with the affected State in minimizing its effects. In the event of harm caused by an accident, the affected State shall, if possible, also co-operate with the State of origin with regard to any harmful effects which may have arisen in the territory of the State of origin or in other places under its jurisdiction or control.

---

1. The Special Rapporteur proposed two alternatives for article 5.

"Article 8

Prevention

States of origin shall take appropriate measures to prevent or, where necessary, minimize the risk of transboundary harm. To that end they shall, in so far as they are able, use the best practicable, available means with regard to activities referred to in article 1.

"Article 9

Reparation

To the extent compatible with the present articles, the State of origin shall make reparation for appreciable harm caused by an activity referred to in article 1. Such reparation shall be decided by negotiation between the State of origin and the affected State or States and shall be guided, in principle, by the criteria set forth in these articles, bearing in mind in particular that reparation should seek to restore the balance of interests affected by the harm."

"CHAPTER III

NOTIFICATION, INFORMATION AND WARNING
BY THE AFFECTED STATE

"Article 10

Assessment, notification and information

If a State has reason to believe that an activity referred to in article 1 is being, or is about to be, carried out in its territory or in other places under its jurisdiction or control, it shall:

(a) Review that activity to assess its potential transboundary effects and, if it finds that the activity may cause, or create the risk of causing, transboundary harm, determine the nature of the harm or risk to which it gives rise;

(b) Give the affected State or States timely notification of the conclusions of the aforesaid review;

(c) Accompany such notification by available technical data and information in order to enable the notified States to assess the potential effects of the activity in question;

(d) Inform them of the measures which it is attempting to take to comply with article 8 and, if it deems appropriate, those which might serve as a basis for a legal régime between the parties governing such activity.

"Article 11

Procedure for protecting national security or industrial secrets

If the State of origin invokes reasons of national security or the protection of industrial secrets in order not to reveal some information which it would otherwise have had to transmit to the affected State:

(a) It shall inform the affected State that it is withholding some information and shall indicate which of the two reasons mentioned above it is invoking for that purpose;

(b) If possible, it shall transmit to the affected State any information which does not affect the areas of reservation invoked, especially information on the type of risk or harm it considers foreseeable and the measures it proposes for establishing a régime to govern the activity in question.

"Article 12
Warning by the presumed affected State

If a State has serious reason to believe that it is, or may be, affected by an activity referred to in article 1 and that activity is being carried out in the territory or in other places under the jurisdiction or control of another State, it may request that State to apply the provisions of article 10. The request shall be accompanied by a technical, documented explanation setting forth the reasons for such belief.

"Article 13
Period for reply to notification. Obligation of the State of origin

Unless otherwise agreed, the notifying State shall allow the notified State or States a period of six months within which to study and evaluate the potential effects of the activity and to communicate their findings to it. During such period, the notifying State shall co-operate with the notified State or States by providing them, on request, with any additional data and information that is available and necessary for a better evaluation of the effects of the activity.

"Article 14
Reply to notification

The State which has been notified shall communicate its findings to the notifying State as early as possible, informing the notifying State of whether it accepts the measures proposed by that State and transmitting to that State any measures that it might itself propose in order to supplement or replace such proposed measures, together with a documented technical explanation setting forth the reasons for such findings.

"Article 15
Absence of reply to notification

If, within the period referred to in article 13, the notifying State receives no communication under article 14, it may consider that the preventive measures and, where appropriate, the legal régime which it proposed at the time of the notification are acceptable for the activity in question.

If it did not propose any measure for the establishment of a legal régime, the régime imposed by the present articles shall apply.

"Article 16
Obligation to negotiate
[Beginning identical in both formulations]

If the notifying State and the notified State or States disagree on:

(a) The nature of the activity or its effects; or

(b) The legal régime for such activity:

Alternative (A): They shall hold consultations without delay with a view to establishing the facts with certainty in the case of paragraph (a), and with a view to reaching agreement on the matter in question in the case of paragraph (b);

Alternative (B): They shall, unless otherwise agreed, establish fact-finding machinery, in accordance with the provisions laid down in the annex to the present articles, to determine the likely transboundary effects of the activity.

The report of that fact-finding machinery shall be of an advisory nature and shall not be binding on the States concerned.

Once the report has been completed, the States concerned shall hold consultations with a view to negotiating a suitable legal régime for the activity.

[End identical in both formulations]

Such consultations and negotiations shall be conducted on the basis of the principle of good faith and the principle that each State must show reasonable regard for the rights and legitimate interests of the other State or States.

"Article 17

Absence of reply to the notification under article 12

If the State notified under the provisions of article 12 does not give any reply within six months of receiving the warning, the presumed affected State may consider that the activity referred to in the notification has the characteristics attributed to it therein in which case the activity shall be subject to the régime laid down in the present articles."

1.12   TREATY ON EUROPEAN UNION.   Concluded at Maastricht, 7 February 1992.   Entered into force, 1 November 1993.   1 C.M.L.R. 573 (1992): *Arts: 100, 100a, 130r, 130s, 130t, 171, 189*[1]

* * *

(21) Article 100 shall be replaced by the following:

"Article 100

The Council shall, acting unanimously on a proposal from the Commission and after consulting the European Parliament and the Economic and Social Committee, issue directives for the approximation of such laws, regulations or administrative provisions of the Member States as directly affect the establishment or functioning of the common market."

(22) Article 100a(1) shall be replaced by the following:

"1.   By way of derogation from Article 100 and save where otherwise provided in this Treaty, the following provisions shall apply for the achievement of the objectives set out in Article 7a.   The Council shall, acting in accordance with the procedure referred to in Article 189b and after consulting the Economic and Social Committee, adopt the measures for the approximation of the provisions laid down by law, regulation or administrative action in Member States which have as their object the establishment and functioning of the internal market."

* * *

TITLE XVI
ENVIRONMENT
Article 130r

1.   Community policy on the environment shall contribute to pursuit of the following objectives:

— *preserving, protecting and improving the quality of the environment;*

— *protecting human health;*

— *prudent and rational utilization of natural resources;*

— *promoting measures at international level to deal with regional or worldwide environmental problems.*

2.   Community policy on the environment shall aim at a high level of protection taking into account the diversity of situations in the various regions of the Community.   It shall be based on the precautionary principle and on the principles that preventive action should be taken, that environmental damage should as a priority be rectified at source and that the polluter should pay. Environmental protection requirements must be integrated into the definition and implementation of other Community policies.

In this context, harmonization measures answering these requirements shall include, where appropriate, a safeguard clause allowing Member States to take provisional measures, for non-economic environmental reasons, subject to a Community inspection procedure.

1. *See also* Basic Documents 1.6 & 1.10, supra.

3. *In preparing its policy on the environment, the Community shall take account of:*

— *available scientific and technical data;*

— *environmental conditions in the various regions of the Community;*

— *the potential benefits and costs of action or lack of action;*

— *the economic and social development of the Community as a whole and the balanced development of its regions.*

4. *Within their respective spheres of competence, the Community and the Member States shall cooperate with third countries and with the competent international organizations. The arrangements for Community cooperation may be the subject of agreements between the Community and the third parties concerned, which shall be negotiated and concluded in accordance with Article 228.*

The previous subparagraph shall be without prejudice to Member States' competence to negotiate in international bodies and to conclude international agreements.

Article 130s

1. *The Council, acting in accordance with the procedure referred to in Article 189c and after consulting the Economic and Social Committee, shall decide what action is to be taken by the Community in order to achieve the objectives referred to in Article 130r.*

2. *By way of derogation from the decision-making procedure provided for in paragraph 1 and without prejudice to Article 100a, the Council, acting unanimously on a proposal from the Commission and after consulting the European Parliament and the Economic and Social Committee, shall adopt:*

— *provisions primarily of a fiscal nature;*

— *measures concerning town and country planning, land use with the exception of waste management and measures of a general nature, and management of water resources;*

— *measures significantly affecting a Member State's choice between different energy sources and the general structure of its energy supply.*

The Council may, under the conditions laid down in the preceding subparagraph, define those matters referred to in this paragraph on which decisions are to be taken by a qualified majority.

3. *In other areas, general action programmes setting out priority objectives to be attained shall be adopted by the Council, acting in accordance with the procedure referred to in Article 189b and after consulting the Economic and Social Committee.*

The Council, acting under the terms of paragraph 1 or paragraph 2 according to the case, shall adopt the measures necessary for the implementation of these programmes.

4. *Without prejudice to certain measures of a Community nature, the Member States shall finance and implement the environment policy.*

5. *Without prejudice to the principle that the polluter should pay, if a measure based on the provisions of paragraph 1 involves costs deemed dispro-*

portionate for the public authorities of a Member State, the Council shall, in the act adopting that measure, lay down appropriate provisions in the form of:

— temporary derogations, and/or

— financial support from the Cohesion Fund to be set up no later than 31 December 1993 pursuant to Article 130d.

Article 130t

The protective measures adopted pursuant to Article 130s shall not prevent any Member State from maintaining or introducing more stringent protective measures. Such measures must be compatible with this Treaty. They shall be notified to the Commission.

* * *

"Article 171

1. If the Court of Justice finds that a Member State has failed to fulfil an obligation under this Treaty, the State shall be required to take the necessary measures to comply with the judgment of the Court of Justice.

2. If the Commission considers that the Member State concerned has not taken such measures it shall, after giving that State the opportunity to submit its observations, issue a reasoned opinion specifying the points on which the Member State concerned has not complied with the judgment of the Court of Justice.

If the Member State concerned fails to take the necessary measures to comply with the Court's judgment within the time-limit laid down by the Commission, the latter may bring the case before the Court of Justice. In so doing it shall specify the amount of the lump sum or penalty payment to be paid by the Member State concerned which it considers appropriate in the circumstances.

If the Court of Justice finds that the Member State concerned has not complied with its judgment it may impose a lump sum or penalty payment on it.

This procedure shall be without prejudice to Article 170."

* * *

"Article 189

In order to carry out their task and in accordance with the provisions of this Treaty, the European Parliament acting jointly with the Council, the Council and the Commission shall make regulations and issue directives, take decisions, make recommendations or deliver opinions.

A regulation shall have general application. It shall be binding in its entirety and directly applicable in all Member States.

A directive shall be binding, as to the result to be achieved, upon each Member State to which it is addressed, but shall leave to the national authorities the choice of form and methods.

A decision shall be binding in its entirety upon those to whom it is addressed.

Recommendations and opinions shall have no binding force."

B. ENVIRONMENTAL

1.13   **RESOLUTION ON PERMANENT SOVEREIGNTY OVER NATURAL RE-SOURCES. Adopted by the U.N. General Assembly, 14 December 1962. G.A.Res. 1803, U.N.GAOR, 17th Sess., Supp. No. 17, at 15, U.N.Doc. A/5217 (1963), 16 U.N.Y.B. 503, 2 I.L.M. 223 (1963)**

The General Assembly,

Recalling its resolutions 523(VI) of 12 January 1952 and 626(VII) of 21 December 1952,

Bearing in mind its resolution 1314(XIII) of 12 December 1958, by which it established the Commission on Permanent Sovereignty over Natural Resources and instructed it to conduct a full survey of the status of permanent sovereignty over natural wealth and resources as a basic constituent of the right to self-determination, with recommendations, where necessary, for its strengthening, and decided further that, in the conduct of the full survey of the status of the permanent sovereignty of peoples and nations over their natural wealth and resources, due regard should be paid to the rights and duties of States under international law and to the importance of encouraging international co-operation in the economic development of developing countries,

Bearing in mind its resolution 1515(XV) of 15 December 1960, in which it recommended that the sovereign right of every State to dispose of its wealth and its natural resources should be respected,

Considering that any measure in this respect must be based on the recognition of the inalienable right of all States freely to dispose of their natural wealth and resources in accordance with their national interests, and on respect for the economic independence of States,

Considering that nothing in paragraph 4 below in any way prejudices the position of any Member State on any aspect of the question of the rights and obligations of successor States and Governments in respect of property acquired before the accession to complete sovereignty of countries formerly under colonial rule,

Noting that the subject of succession of States and Governments is being examined as a matter of priority by the International Law Commission,

Considering that it is desirable to promote international co-operation for the economic development of developing countries, and that economic and financial agreements between the developed and the developing countries must be based on the principles of equality and of the right of peoples and nations to self-determination,

Considering that the provision of economic and technical assistance, loans and increased foreign investment must not be subject to conditions which conflict with the interests of the recipient State,

Considering the benefits to be derived from exchanges of technical and scientific information likely to promote the development and use of such resources and wealth, and the important part which the United Nations and other international organizations are called upon to play in that connexion,

Attaching particular importance to the question of promoting the economic development of developing countries and securing their economic independence,

Noting that the creation and strengthening of the inalienable sovereignty of States over their natural wealth and resources reinforces their economic independence,

Desiring that there should be further consideration by the United Nations of the subject of permanent sovereignty over natural resources in the spirit of international co-operation in the field of economic development, particularly that of the developing countries,

I

Declares that:

1.   The right of peoples and nations to permanent sovereignty over their natural wealth and resources must be exercised in the interest of their national development and of the well-being of the people of the State concerned.

2.   The exploration, development and disposition of such resources, as well as the import of the foreign capital required for these purposes, should be in conformity with the rules and conditions which the peoples and nations freely consider to be necessary or desirable with regard to the authorization, restriction or prohibition of such activities.

3.   In cases where authorization is granted, the capital imported and the earnings on that capital shall be governed by the terms thereof, by the national legislation in force, and by international law.   The profits derived must be shared in the proportions freely agreed upon, in each case, between the investors and the recipient State, due care being taken to ensure that there is no impairment, for any reason, of that State's sovereignty over its natural wealth and resources.

4.   Nationalization, expropriation or requisitioning shall be based on grounds or reasons of public utility, security or the national interest which are recognized as overriding purely individual or private interests, both domestic and foreign.   In such cases the owner shall be paid appropriate compensation, in accordance with the rules in force in the State taking such measures in the exercise of its sovereignty and in accordance with international law.   In any case where the question of compensation gives rise to a controversy, the national jurisdiction of the State taking such measures shall be exhausted.   However, upon agreement by sovereign States and other parties concerned, settlement of the dispute should be made through arbitration or international adjudication.

5.   The free and beneficial exercise of the sovereignty of peoples and nations over their natural resources must be furthered by the mutual respect of States based on their sovereign equality.

6.   International co-operation for the economic development of developing countries, whether in the form of public or private capital investments, exchange of goods and services, technical assistance, or exchange of scientific information, shall be such as to further their independent national develop-

ment and shall be based upon respect for their sovereignty over their natural wealth and resources.

7.   Violation of the rights of peoples and nations to sovereignty over their natural wealth and resources is contrary to the spirit and principles of the Charter of the United Nations and hinders the development of international co-operation and the maintenance of peace.

8.   Foreign investment agreements freely entered into by or between sovereign States shall be observed in good faith: States and international organizations shall strictly and conscientiously respect the sovereignty of peoples and nations over their natural wealth and resources in accordance with the Charter and the principles set forth in the present resolution.

II

Welcomes the decision of the International Law Commission to speed up its work on the codification of the topic of responsibility of States for the consideration of the General Assembly;

III

Requests the Secretary–General to continue the study of the various aspects of permanent sovereignty over natural resources, taking into account the desire of Member States to ensure the protection of their sovereign rights while encouraging international co-operation in the field of economic development, and to report to the Economic and Social Council and to the General Assembly, if possible at its eighteenth session.

1.14 STOCKHOLM DECLARATION OF THE UNITED NATIONS CONFERENCE ON THE HUMAN ENVIRONMENT. Adopted by the U.N. Conference on the Human Environment at Stockholm, 16 June 1972. *Report of the UN Conference on the Human Environment, Stockholm, 5–16 June 1972,* U.N.Doc. A/CONF.48/14/Rev. 1 at 3 (1973), U.N.Doc. A/CONF.48/14 at 2–65, and Corr. 1 (1972), 11 I.L.M. 1416 (1972)

THE UNITED NATIONS CONFERENCE ON THE HUMAN ENVIRONMENT.

HAVING MET at Stockholm from 5 to 16 June 1972.

HAVING CONSIDERED the need for a common outlook and for common principles to inspire and guide the peoples of the world in the preservation and enhancement of the human environment.

I

PROCLAIMS THAT:

1. Man is both creature and moulder of his environment, which gives him physical sustenance and affords him the opportunity for intellectual, moral, social and spiritual growth. In the long and tortuous evolution of the human race on this planet a stage has been reached when, through the rapid acceleration of science and technology, man has acquired the power to transform his environment in countless ways and on an unprecedented scale. Both aspects of man's environment, the natural and the man-made, are essential to his well-being and to the enjoyment of basic human rights—even the right to life itself.

2. The protection and improvement of the human environment is a major issue which affects the well-being of peoples and economic development throughout the world; it is the urgent desire of the peoples of the whole world and the duty of all Governments.

3. Man has constantly to sum up experience and go on discovering, inventing, creating and advancing. In our time, man's capability to transform his surroundings, if used wisely, can bring to all peoples the benefits of development and the opportunity to enhance the quality of life. Wrongly or heedlessly applied, the same power can do incalculable harm to human beings and the human environment. We see around us growing evidence of man-made harm in many regions of the earth: dangerous levels of pollution in water, air, earth and living beings; major and undesirable disturbances to the ecological balance of the biosphere; destruction and depletion of irreplaceable resources; and gross deficiencies harmful to the physical, mental and social health of man, in the man-made environment, particularly in the living and working environment.

4. In the developing countries most of the environmental problems are caused by under-development. Millions continue to live far below the minimum levels required for a decent human existence, deprived of adequate food and clothing, shelter and education, health and sanitation. Therefore, the developing countries must direct their efforts to development, bearing in mind their priorities and the need to safeguard and improve the environment. For the same purpose, the industrialized countries should make efforts to reduce the gap between themselves and the developing countries. In the industrial-

ized countries, environmental problems are generally related to industrialization and technological development.

5. The natural growth of population continuously presents problems on the preservation of the environment, and adequate policies and measures should be adopted, as appropriate, to face these problems. Of all things in the world, people are the most precious. It is the people that propel social progress, create social wealth, develop science and technology and, through their hard work, continuously transform the human environment. Along with social progress and the advance of production, science and technology, the capability of man to improve the environment increases with each passing day.

6. A point has been reached in history when we must shape our actions throughout the world with a more prudent care for their environmental consequences. Through ignorance or indifference we can do massive and irreversible harm to the earthly environment on which our life and well-being depend. Conversely, through fuller knowledge and wiser action, we can achieve for ourselves and our posterity a better life in an environment more in keeping with human needs and hopes. There are broad vistas for the enhancement of environmental quality and the creation of a good life. What is needed is an enthusiastic but calm state of mind and intense but orderly work. For the purpose of attaining freedom in the world of nature, man must use knowledge to build, in collaboration with nature, a better environment. To defend and improve the human environment for present and future generations has become an imperative goal for mankind—a goal to be pursued together with, and in harmony with, the established and fundamental goals of peace and of world-wide economic and social development.

7. To achieve this environmental goal will demand the acceptance of responsibility by citizens and communities and by enterprises and institutions at every level, all sharing equitably in common efforts. Individuals in all walks of life as well as organizations in many fields, by their values and the sum of their actions, will shape the world environment of the future. Local and national governments will bear the greatest burden for large-scale environmental policy and action within their jurisdictions. International cooperation is also needed in order to raise resources to support the developing countries in carrying out their responsibilities in this field. A growing class of environmental problems, because they are regional or global in extent or because they affect the common international realm, will require extensive cooperation among nations and action by international organizations in the common interest. The Conference calls upon Governments and peoples to exert common efforts for the preservation and improvement of the human environment, for the benefit of all the people and for their posterity.

II
Principles

STATES THE COMMON CONVICTION THAT:

Principle 1

Man has the fundamental right to freedom, equality and adequate conditions of life, in an environment of a quality that permits a life of dignity and well-being, and he bears a solemn responsibility to protect and improve the environment for present and future generations. In this respect, policies promoting or perpetuating apartheid, racial segregation, discrimination, colonial and other forms of oppression and foreign domination stand condemned and must be eliminated.

Principle 2

The natural resources of the earth including the air, water, land, flora and fauna and especially representative samples of natural ecosystems must be safeguarded for the benefit of present and future generations through careful planning or management, as appropriate.

Principle 3

The capacity of the earth to produce vital renewable resources must be maintained and, wherever practicable, restored or improved.

Principle 4

Man has a special responsibility to safeguard and wisely manage the heritage of wildlife and its habitat which are now gravely imperilled by a combination of adverse factors. Nature conservation including wildlife must therefore receive importance in planning for economic development.

Principle 5

The non-renewable resources of the earth must be employed in such a way as to guard against the danger of their future exhaustion and to ensure that benefits from such employment are shared by all mankind.

Principle 6

The discharge of toxic substances or of other substances and the release of heat, in such quantities or concentrations as to exceed the capacity of the environment to render them harmless, must be halted in order to ensure that serious or irreversible damage is not inflicted upon ecosystems. The just struggle of the peoples of all countries against pollution should be supported.

Principle 7

States shall take all possible steps to prevent pollution of the seas by substances that are liable to create hazards to human health, to harm living resources and marine life, to damage amenities or to interfere with other legitimate uses of the sea.

Principle 8

Economic and social development is essential for ensuring a favourable living and working environment for man and for creating conditions on earth that are necessary for the improvement of the quality of life.

Principle 9

Environmental deficiencies generated by the conditions of underdevelopment and natural disasters pose grave problems and can best be remedied by accelerated development through the transfer of substantial quantities of financial and technological assistance as a supplement to the domestic effort of the developing countries and such timely assistance as may be required.

Principle 10

For the developing countries, stability of prices and adequate earnings for primary commodities and raw material are essential to environmental management since economic factors as well as ecological processes must be taken into account.

Principle 11

The environmental policies of all States should enhance and not adversely affect the present or future development potential of developing countries, nor should they hamper the attainment of better living conditions for all, and appropriate steps should be taken by States and international organizations with a view to reaching agreement on meeting the possible national and international economic consequences resulting from the application of environmental measures.

Principle 12

Resources should be made available to preserve and improve the environment, taking into account the circumstances and particular requirements of developing countries and any costs which may emanate from their incorporating environmental safeguards into their development planning and the need for making available to them, upon their request, additional international technical and financial assistance for this purpose.

Principle 13

In order to achieve a more rational management of resources and thus to improve the environment, State should adopt an integrated and co-ordinated approach to their development planning so as to ensure that development is compatible with the need to protect and improve the human environment for the benefit for their population.

Principle 14

Rational planning constitutes an essential tool for reconciling any conflict between the needs of development and the need to protect and improve the environment.

Principle 15

Planning must be applied to human settlements and urbanization with a view to avoiding adverse effects on the environment and obtaining maximum social, economic and environmental benefits for all. In this respect projects which are designed for colonialist and racist domination must be abandoned.

Principle 16

Demographic policies, which are without prejudice to basic human rights and which are deemed appropriate by Governments concerned, should be applied in those regions where the rate of population growth or excessive population concentrations are likely to have adverse effects on the environment or development, or where low population density may prevent improvement of the human environment and impede development.

Principle 17

Appropriate national institutions must be entrusted with the task of planning, managing or controlling the environmental resources of States with the view to enhancing environmental quality.

Principle 18

Science and technology, as part of their contribution to economic and social development, must be applied to the identification, avoidance and control of environmental risks and the solution of environmental problems and for the common good of mankind.

Principle 19

Education in environmental matters, for the younger generation as well as adults, giving due consideration to the underprivileged, is essential in order to broaden the basis for an enlightened opinion and responsible conduct by individuals, enterprises and communities in protecting and improving the environment in its full human dimension. It is also essential that mass media of communications avoid contributing to the deterioration of the environment, but, on the contrary, disseminate information of an educational nature, on the need to protect and improve the environment in order to enable man to develop in every respect.

Principle 20

Scientific research and development in the context of environmental problems, both national and multinational, must be promoted in all countries, especially the developing countries. In this connection, the free flow of up-to-date scientific information and transfer of experience must be supported and assisted, to facilitate the solution of environmental problems; environmental technologies should be made available to developing countries on terms which would encourage their wide dissemination without constituting an economic burden on the developing countries.

Principle 21

States have, in accordance with the Charter of the United Nations and the principles of international law, the sovereign right to exploit their own resources pursuant to their own environmental policies, and the responsibility to ensure that activities within their jurisdiction or control do not cause damage to the environment of other States or of areas beyond the limits of national jurisdiction.

Principle 22

States shall co-operate to develop further the international law regarding liability and compensation for the victims of pollution and other environmental damage caused by activities within the jurisdiction or control of such States to areas beyond their jurisdiction.

Principle 23

Without prejudice to such criteria as may be agreed upon by the international community, or to standards which will have to be determined nationally, it will be essential in all cases to consider the systems of values prevailing in each country, and the extent of the applicability of standards which are valid for the most advanced countries but which may be inappropriate and of unwarranted social cost for the developing countries.

Principle 24

International matters concerning the protection and improvement of the environment should be handled in a co-operative spirit by all countries, big or small, on an equal footing. Co-operation through multilateral or bilateral arrangements or other appropriate means is essential to effectively control, prevent, reduce and eliminate adverse environmental effects resulting from activities conducted in all spheres, in such a way that due account is taken of the sovereignty and interests of all States.

Principle 25

States shall ensure that international organizations play a co-ordinated, efficient and dynamic role for the protection and improvement of the environment.

Principle 26

Man and his environment must be spared the effects of nuclear weapons and all other means of mass destruction. States must strive to reach prompt agreement, in the relevant international organs, on the elimination and complete destruction of such weapons.

**1.15 RESOLUTION ON THE INSTITUTIONAL AND FINANCIAL ARRANGE-
MENT FOR INTERNATIONAL ENVIRONMENT COOPERATION
(ESTABLISHING THE UNITED NATIONS ENVIRONMENT PRO-
GRAM, UNEP).** Adopted by the U.N. General Assembly, 15 Decem-
ber 1972. G.A.Res. 2997, U.N. GAOR, 27th Sess., Supp. 30, at 42,
U.N.Doc. A/8370 (1973), 13 I.L.M. 234 (1974)

I

Governing Council of the United Nations Environment Programme

1. *Decides* to establish a Governing–Council of the United Nations
Environment Programme, composed of fifty-eight members elected by the
General Assembly for three-year terms on the following basis:

(*a*) Sixteen seats for African States;

(*b*) Thirteen seats for Asian States;

(*c*) Six seats for Eastern European States;

(*d*) Ten seats for Latin American States;

(*e*) Thirteen seats for Western European and other States;

2. *Decides* that the Governing Council shall have the following main
functions and responsibilities:

(*a*) To promote international co-operation in the field of the environment and to recommend, as appropriate, policies to this end;

(*b*) To provide general policy guidance for the direction and co-
ordination of environmental programmes within the United Nations
system;

(*c*) To receive and review the periodic reports of the Executive
Director, referred to in section II, paragraph 2, below, on the implementation of environmental programmes within the United Nations system;

(*d*) To keep under review the world environmental situation in order
to ensure that emerging environmental problems of wide international
significance receive appropriate and adequate consideration by Governments;

(*e*) To promote the contribution of the relevant international scientific and other professional communities to the acquisition, assessment and
exchange of environmental knowledge and information and, as appropriate, to the technical aspects of the formulation and implementation of
environmental programmes within the United Nations system;

(*f*) To maintain under continuing review the impact of national and
international environmental policies and measures on developing countries, as well as the problem of additional costs that may be incurred by
developing countries in the implementation of environmental programmes and projects, and to ensure that such programmes and projects
shall be compatible with the development plans and priorities of those
countries;

(*g*) To review and approve annually the programme of utilization of
resources of the Environment Fund referred to in section III below;

3. *Decides* that the Governing Council shall report annually to the
General Assembly through the Economic and Social Council, which will

transmit to the Assembly such comments on the report as it may deem necessary, particularly with regard to questions of co-ordination and to the relationship of environmental policies and programmes within the United Nations system to over-all economic and social policies and priorities;

II

Environment secretariat

1. *Decides* that a small secretariat shall be established in the United Nations to serve as a focal point for environmental action and co-ordination within the United Nations system in such a way as to ensure a high degree of effective management;

2. *Decides* that the environment secretariat shall be headed by the Executive Director of the United Nations Environment Programme, who shall be elected by the General Assembly on the nomination of the Secretary–General for a term of four years and who shall be entrusted, *inter alia*, with the following responsibilities:

(*a*) To provide substantive support to the Governing Council of the United Nations Environment Programme;

(*b*) To co-ordinate, under the guidance of the Governing Council, environmental programmes within the United Nations system to keep their implementation under review and to assess their effectiveness;

(*c*) To advise, as appropriate and under the guidance of the Governing Council, intergovernmental bodies of the United Nations system on the formulation and implementation of environmental programmes;

(*d*) To secure the effective co-operation of, and contribution from, the relevant scientific and other professional communities in all parts of the world;

(*e*) To provide, at the request of all parties concerned, advisory services for the promotion of international co-operation in the field of the environment;

(*f*) To submit to the Governing Council, on his own initiative or upon request, proposals embodying medium-range and long-range planning for United Nations programmes in the field of the environment;

(*g*) To bring to the attention of the Governing Council any matter which he deems to require consideration by it;

(*h*) To administer, under the authority and policy guidance of the Governing Council, the Environment Fund referred to in section III below;

(*i*) To report on environmental matters to the Governing Council;

(*j*) To perform such other functions as may be entrusted to him by the Governing Council;

3. *Decides* that the costs of servicing the Governing Council and providing the small secretariat referred to in paragraph 1 above shall be borne by the regular budget of the United Nations and that operational programme costs, programme support and administrative costs of the Environment Fund established under section III below shall be borne by the Fund;

III

Environment Fund

1. *Decides* that, in order to provide for additional financing for environmental programmes, a voluntary fund shall be established, with effect from 1 January 1973, in accordance with existing United Nations financial procedures;

2. *Decides* that, in order to enable the Governing Council of the United Nations Environment Programme to fulfil its policy-guidance role for the direction and co-ordination of environmental activities, the Environment Fund shall finance wholly or partly the costs of the new environmental initiatives undertaken within the United Nations system—which will include the initiatives envisaged in the Action Plan for the Human Environment adopted by the United Nations Conference on the Human Environment, with particular attention to integrated projects, and such other environmental activities as may be decided upon by the Governing Council—and that the Governing Council shall review these initiatives with a view to taking appropriate decisions as to their continued financing;

3. *Decides* that the Environment Fund shall be used for financing such programmes of general interest as regional and global monitoring, assessment and data-collecting systems, including, as appropriate, costs for national counterparts; the improvement of environmental quality management; environmental research; information exchange and dissemination; public education and training; assistance for national, regional and global environmental institutions; the promotion of environmental research and studies for the development of industrial and other technologies best suited to a policy of economic growth compatible with adequate environmental safeguards; and such other programmes as the Governing Council may decide upon, and that in the implementation of such programmes due account should be taken of the special needs of the developing countries;

4. *Decides* that, in order to ensure that the development priorities of developing countries shall not be adversely affected, adequate measures shall be taken to provide additional financial resources on terms compatible with the economic situation of the recipient developing country, and that, to this end, the Executive Director, in co-operation with competent organizations, shall keep this problem under continuing review;

5. *Decides* that the Environment Fund, in pursuance of the objectives stated in paragraphs 2 and 3 above, shall be directed to the need for effective co-ordination in the implementation of international environmental programmes of the organizations in the United Nations system and other international organizations;

6. *Decides* that, in the implementation of programmes to be financed by the Environment Fund, organizations outside the United Nations system, particularly those in the countries and regions concerned, shall also be utilized as appropriate, in accordance with the procedures established by the Governing Council, and that such organizations are invited to support the United Nations environmental programmes by complementary initiatives and contributions;

7. *Decides* that the Governing Council shall formulate such general procedures as are necessary to govern the operations of the Environment Fund.

IV
Environment Co-ordination Board

1. *Decides* that, in order to provide for the most efficient co-ordination of United Nations environmental programmes, an Environment Co-ordination Board, under the chairmanship of the Executive Director, shall be established under the auspices and within the framework of the Administrative Committee on Co-ordination;

2. *Further decides* that the Environment Co-ordination Board shall meet periodically for the purpose of ensuring co-operation and co-ordination among all bodies concerned in the implementation of environmental programmes and that it shall report annually to the Governing Council of the United Nations Environment Programme;

3. *Invites* the organizations of the United Nations system to adopt the measures that may be required to undertake concerted and co-ordinated programmes with regard to international environmental problems, taking into account existing procedures for prior consultation, particularly on programme and budgetary matters;

4. *Invites* the regional economic commissions and the United Nations Economic and Social Office at Beirut, in co-operation where necessary with other appropriate regional bodies, to intensify further their efforts directed towards contributing to the implementation of environmental programmes in view of the particular need for the rapid development of regional co-operation in this field;

5. *Also invites* other intergovernmental and those non-governmental organizations that have an interest in the field of the environment to lend their full support and collaboration to the United Nations with a view to achieving the largest possible degree of co-operation and co-ordination;

6. *Calls upon* Governments to ensure that appropriate national institutions shall be entrusted with the task of the co-ordination of environmental action, both national and international;

7. *Decides* to review as appropriate, at its thirty-first session, the above institutional arrangements, bearing in mind, *inter alia,* the responsibilities of the Economic and Social Council under the Charter of the United Nations.

**1.16 RESOLUTION ON CO–OPERATION IN THE FIELD OF THE ENVI-
RONMENT CONCERNING NATURAL RESOURCES SHARED BY
TWO OR MORE STATES. Adopted by the U.N. General Assembly,
13 December 1973. G.A.Res. 3129, U.N. GAOR, 28th Sess., Supp.
No. 30, at 48, U.N. Doc A/RES/3129 (1973), 13 I.L.M. 232 (1974)**

The General Assembly,

Reaffirming principles 21, 22 and 24 of the Declaration of the United
Nations Conference on the Human Environment, held at Stockholm from 5 to
16 June 1972,

Recalling its resolutions 2995 (XXVII), 2996 (XXVII) and 2997 (XXVII) of
15 December 1972 relating to co-operation between States in the field of the
environment, to international responsibility of States in regard to the environment and to the establishment of the Governing Council of the United
Nations Environment Programme, respectively,

Reaffirming the duty of the international community to adopt measures
to protect and improve the environment, and particularly the need for
continuous international collaboration to that end,

Convinced of the need to pursue, in the field of the environment, the
elaboration of international norms conducive to the achievement of those
purposes,

Taking note with satisfaction of the important Economic Declaration
adopted by the Fourth Conference of Heads of State or Government of Non–
Aligned Countries, held at Algiers from 5 to 9 September 1973,

Conscious of the importance and urgency of safeguarding the conservation and exploitation of the natural resources shared by two or more States,
by means of an effective system of co-operation, as indicated in the above-
mentioned Economic Declaration of Algiers,

1. *Considers* that it is necessary to ensure effective co-operation between
countries through the establishment of adequate international standards for
the conservation and harmonious exploitation of natural resources common to
two or more States in the context of the normal relations existing between
them;

2. *Considers further* that co-operation between countries sharing such
natural resources and interested in their exploitation must be developed on
the basis of a system of information and prior consultation within the
framework of the normal relations existing between them;

3. *Requests* the Governing Council of the United Nations Environment
Programme, in keeping with its function of promoting international co-
operation according to the mandate conferred upon it by the General Assembly, to take duly into account the preceding paragraphs and to report on
measures adopted for their implementation;

4. *Urges* Member States, within the framework of their mutual relations, to take fully into account the provisions of the present resolution.

1.17 RESOLUTION ON PERMANENT SOVEREIGNTY OVER NATURAL RE-SOURCES. Adopted by the U.N. General Assembly, 17 December 1973. G.A.Res. 3171, U.N.GAOR, 28th Sess., Supp. No. 30, at 52, U.N.Doc. A/9030 (1974), 13 I.L.M. 238 (1974)

The General Assembly,

Reiterating that the inalienable right of each State to the full exercise of national sovereignty over its natural resources has been repeatedly recognized by the international community in numerous resolutions of various organs of the United Nations,

Reiterating also that an intrinsic condition of the exercise of the sovereignty of every State is that it be exercised fully and effectively over all the natural resources of the State, whether found on land or in the sea,

Reaffirming the inviolable principle that every country has the right to adopt the economic and social system which it deems most favourable to its development,

Recalling its resolutions 1803 (XVII) of 14 December 1962, 2158 (XXI) of 25 November 1966, 2386 (XXIII) of 19 November 1968, 2625 (XXV) of 24 October 1970, 2692 (XXV) of 11 December 1970 and 3016 (XXVII) of 18 December 1972, and Security Council resolution 330 (1973) of 21 March 1973, which relate to permanent sovereignty over natural resources,

Recalling, in particular, the Declaration on Principles of International Law concerning Friendly Relations and Co-operation among States in accordance with the Charter of the United Nations, which proclaims that no State may use or encourage the use of economic, political or any other type of measures to coerce another State in order to obtain from it the subordination of the exercise of its sovereign rights and to secure from it advantages of any kind,

Considering that the full exercise by each State of sovereignty over its natural resources is an essential condition for achieving the objectives and targets of the Second United Nations Development Decade, and that this exercise requires that action by States aimed at achieving a better utilization and use of those resources must cover all stages, from exploration to marketing,

Taking note of section VII of the Economic Declaration adopted by the Fourth Conference of Heads of State or Government of Non–Aligned Countries, held at Algiers from 5 to 9 September 1973,

Taking note also of the report of the Secretary–General on permanent sovereignty over natural resources,

1. *Strongly reaffirms* the inalienable rights of States to permanent sovereignty over all their natural resources, on land within their international boundaries as well as those in the sea-bed and the subsoil thereof within their national jurisdiction and in the superjacent waters;

2. *Supports resolutely* the efforts of the developing countries and of the peoples of the territories under colonial and racial domination and foreign occupation in their struggle to regain effective control over their natural resources;

3. *Affirms* that the application of the principle of nationalization carried out by States, as an expression of their sovereignty in order to safeguard their natural resources, implies that each State is entitled to determine the amount of possible compensation and the mode of payment, and that any disputes which might arise should be settled in accordance with the national legislation of each State carrying out such measures;

4. *Deplores* acts of States which use force, armed aggression, economic coercion or any other illegal or improper means in resolving disputes concerning the exercise of the sovereign rights mentioned in paragraphs 1 to 3 above;

5. *Re-emphasizes* that actions, measures or legislative regulations by States aimed at coercing, directly or indirectly, other States or peoples engaged in the reorganization of their internal structure or in the exercise of their sovereign rights over their natural resources, both on land and in their coastal waters, are in violation of the Charter of the United Nations and of the Declaration contained in General Assembly resolution 2625 (XXV) and contradict the targets, objectives and policy measures of the International Development Strategy for the Second United Nations Development Decade, and that to persist therein could constitute a threat to international peace and security;

6. *Emphasizes* the duty of all States to refrain in their international relations from military, political, economic or any other form of coercion aimed against the territorial integrity of any State and the exercise of its national jurisdiction;

7. *Recognizes* that, as stressed in Economic and Social Council resolution 1737 (LIV) of 4 May 1973, one of the most effective ways in which the developing countries can protect their natural resources is to establish, promote or strengthen machinery for co-operation among them which has as its main purpose to concert pricing policies, to improve conditions of access to markets, to co-ordinate production policies and, thus, to guarantee the full exercise of sovereignty by developing countries over their natural resources;

8. *Requests* the Economic and Social Council, at its fifty-sixth session, to consider the report of the Secretary–General mentioned in the last preambular paragraph above and requests the Secretary–General to prepare a supplement to that report, in the light of the discussions that are to take place at the fifty-sixth session of the Council and of any other relevant developments, and to submit that supplementary report to the General Assembly at its twenty-ninth session.

1.18   CONVENTION ON THE PROTECTION OF THE ENVIRONMENT BE-TWEEN DENMARK, FINLAND, NORWAY AND SWEDEN (WITH PROTOCOL).   Concluded at Stockholm, 9 February 1974.   Entered into force, 5 October 1976.   1092 U.N.T.S. 279, 13 I.L.M. 591 (1974)

* * *

Article 1. For the purpose of this Convention, environmentally harmful activities shall mean the discharge from the soil or from buildings or installations of solid or liquid waste, gas or any other substance into watercourses, lakes or the sea and the use of land, the sea-bed, buildings or installations in any other way which entails, or may entail environmental nuisance by water pollution or any other effect on water conditions, sand drift, air pollution, noise, vibration, changes in temperature, ionizing radiation, light, etc.

The Convention shall not apply insofar as environmentally harmful activities are regulated by a special agreement between two or more of the Contracting States.

Article 2. In considering the permissibility of environmentally harmful activities, the nuisance which such activities entail or may entail in another Contracting State shall be equated with a nuisance in the State where the activities are carried out.

Article 3. Any person who is affected or may be affected by a nuisance caused by environmentally harmful activities in another Contracting State shall have the right to bring before the appropriate Court of Administrative Authority of that State the question of the permissibility of such activities, including the question of measures to prevent damage, and to appeal against the decision of the Court or the Administrative Authority to the same extent and on the same terms as a legal entity of the State in which the activities are being carried out.

The provisions of the first paragraph of this article shall be equally applicable in the case of proceedings concerning compensation for damage caused by environmentally harmful activities. The question of compensation shall not be judged by rules which are less favourable to the injured Party than the rules of compensation of the State in which the activities are being carried out.

Article 4. Each State shall appoint a special authority (supervisory authority) to be entrusted with the task of safeguarding general environmental interests insofar as regards nuisances arising out of environmentally harmful activities in another Contracting State.

For the purpose of safeguarding such interests, the supervisory authority shall have the right to institute proceedings before or be heard by the competent Court or Administrative Authority of another Contracting State regarding the permissibility of the environmentally harmful activities if an authority or other representative of general environmental interests in that State can institute proceedings or be heard in matters of this kind, as well as the right to appeal against the decision of the Court or the Administrative Authority in accordance with the procedures and rules of appeal applicable to such cases in the State concerned.

Article 5. If the Court or the Administrative Authority examining the permissibility of environmentally harmful activities (examining authority) finds that the activities entail or may entail nuisance of significance in another Contracting State, the examining authority shall, if proclamation or publication is required in cases of that nature, send as soon as possible a copy of the documents of the case to the supervisory authority of the other State, and afford it the opportunity of giving its opinion. Notification of the date and place of a meeting or inspection shall, where appropriate, be given well in advance to the supervisory authority which, moreover, shall be kept informed of any developments that may be of interest to it.

Article 6. Upon the request of the supervisory authority, the examining authority shall, in so far as compatible with the procedural rules of the State in which the activities are being carried out, require the applicant for a permit to carry out environmentally harmful activities to submit such additional particulars, drawings and technical specifications as the examining authority deems necessary for evaluating the effects in the other State.

Article 7. The supervisory authority, if it finds it necessary on account of public or private interests, shall publish communications from the examining authority in the local newspaper or in some other suitable manner. The supervisory authority shall also institute such investigations of the effects in its own State as it deems necessary.

Article 8. Each State shall defray the cost of the activities of its supervisory authority.

Article 9. If, in a particular case, the supervisory authority has informed the appropriate Court of Administrative authority of the State in which the activities are being carried out that in the case concerned the duties of the supervisory authority shall be discharged by another authority, the provisions of this Convention relating to supervisory activities shall, where appropriate, apply to that authority.

Article 10. If necessary for determining the damage caused in another State by environmentally harmful activities, the supervisory authority of that other State shall upon request of the examining authority of the State in which the activities are being carried out make arrangements for on-site inspection. The examining authority or an expert appointed by it may be present at such an inspection.

Where necessary, more detailed instructions concerning inspections such as referred to in the preceding paragraph shall be drawn up in consultation between the countries concerned.

Article 11. Where the permissibility of environmentally harmful activities which entail or may entail considerable nuisance in another Contracting State is being examined by the Government or by the appropriate Minister or Ministry of the State in which the activities are being carried out, consultations shall take place between the States concerned if the Government of the former State so requests.

Article 12. In cases such as those referred to in article 11, the Government of each State concerned may demand that an opinion be given by a Commission which, unless otherwise agreed, shall consist of a chairman from another Contracting State to be appointed jointly by the Parties and three members from each of the States concerned. Where such a Commission has been appointed, the case cannot be decided upon until the Commission has given its opinion.

Each State shall remunerate the members it has appointed. Fees or other remuneration of the Chairman as well as any other costs incidental to the activities of the Commission which are not manifestly the responsibility of one or the other State shall be equally shared by the States concerned.

Article 13. This Convention shall also apply to the continental shelf areas of the Contracting States.

Article 14. This Convention shall enter into force six months from the date on which all the Contracting States have notified the Swedish Ministry for Foreign Affairs that the constitutional measures necessary for the entry into force of the Convention have been implemented. The Swedish Ministry for Foreign Affairs shall notify the other Contracting States of the receipt of such communications.

Article 15. Actions or cases relevant to this Convention, which are pending before a Court or an Administrative Authority on the date when this Convention enters into force, shall be dealt with and judged according to provisions previously in force.

Article 16. Any Contracting State wishing to denounce this Convention shall give notice of its intention in writing to the Swedish Government, which shall forthwith inform the other Contracting States of the denunciation and of the date on which notice was received.

The denunciation shall take effect 12 months from the date on which the Swedish Government received such notification or on such later date as may be indicated in the notice of denunciation.

This Convention shall be deposited with the Swedish Ministry for Foreign Affairs, which shall send certified copies thereof to the Government of each Contracting State.

PROTOCOL

In connection with the signing today of the Nordic Environmental Protection Convention the duly authorized signatories agreed that the following comments on its application shall be appended to the Convention.

In the applications of article 1 discharge from the soil, or from buildings or installations of solid or liquid waste, gases or other substances into watercourses, lakes or the sea shall be regarded as environmentally harmful activities only if the discharge entails or may entail a nuisance to the surroundings.

The right established in article 3 for anyone who suffers injury as a result of environmentally harmful activities in a neighbouring State to institute proceedings for compensation before a court or administrative authority of that State shall, in principle, be regarded as including the right to demand the purchase of his real property.

Article 5 shall be regarded as applying also to application for permits where such applications are referred to certain authorities and organizations for their opinion but not in conjunction with proclamation or publication procedures.

The Contracting States shall require officials of the supervisory authority to observe professional secrecy as regards trade secrets, operational devices or business conditions of which they have become cognizant in dealing with cases concerning environmentally harmful activities in another State.

1.19 **FINAL ACT OF THE CONFERENCE ON SECURITY AND CO-OPERA-TION IN EUROPE.** Adopted by the Conference on Security and Co-operation in Europe at Helsinki, 1 August 1975. 14 I.L.M. 1292 (1975): *Co-operation in the Field of Economics, of Science and Technology and of the Environment*

* * *

Motivated by the political will, in the interest of peoples, to improve and intensify their relations and to contribute in Europe to peace, security, justice and co-operation as well as to rapprochement among themselves and with the other States of the world,

Determined, in consequence, to give full effect to the results of the Conference and to assure, among their States and throughout Europe, the benefits deriving from those results and thus to broaden, deepen and make continuing and lasting the process of detente.

The High Representatives of the participating States have solemnly adopted the following:

* * *

CO–OPERATION IN THE FIELD OF ECONOMICS, OF SCIENCE AND TECHNOLOGY AND OF THE ENVIRONMENT

The participating States,

Convinced that their efforts to develop co-operation in the fields of trade, industry, science and technology, the environment and other areas of economic activity contribute to the reinforcement of peace and security in Europe and in the world as a whole,

Recognizing that co-operation in these fields would promote economic and social progress and the improvement of the conditions of life,

Aware of the diversity of their economic and social systems,

Reaffirming their will to intensify such co-operation between one another, irrespective of their systems,

Recognizing that such co-operation, with due regard for the different levels of economic development, can be developed, on the basis of equality and mutual satisfaction of the partners, and of reciprocity permitting, as a whole, an equitable distribution of advantages and obligations of comparable scale, with respect for bilateral and multilateral agreements,

Taking into account the interests of the developing countries throughout the world, including those among the participating countries as long as they are developing from the economic point of view; reaffirming their will to co-operate for the achievement of the aims and objectives established by the appropriate bodies of the United Nations in the pertinent documents concerning development, it being understood that each participating State maintains the positions it has taken on them; giving special attention to the least developed countries,

Convinced that the growing world-wide, economic interdependence calls for increasing common and effective efforts towards the solution of major world economic problems such as food, energy, commodities, monetary and financial problems, and therefore emphasizes the need for promoting stable and equitable international economic relations, thus contributing to the continuous and diversified economic development of all countries,

Having taken into account the work already undertaken by relevant international organizations and wishing to take advantage of the possibilities offered by these organizations, in particular by the United Nations Economic Commission for Europe, for giving effect to the provisions of the final documents of the Conference,

Considering that the guidelines and concrete recommendations contained in the following texts are aimed at promoting further development of their mutual economic relations, and convinced that their co-operation in this field should take place in full respect for the principles guiding relations among participating States as set forth in the relevant document,

Have adopted the following:

* * *

5. Environment

The participating States,

Affirming that the protection and improvement of the environment, as well as the protection of nature and the rational utilization of its resources in the interests of present and future generations, is one of the tasks of major importance to the well-being of peoples and the economic development of all countries and the many environmental problems, particularly in Europe, can be solved effectively only through close international co-operation,

Acknowledging that each of the participating States, in accordance with the principles of international law, ought to ensure, in a spirit of co-operation, that activities carried out on its territory do not cause degradation of the environment in another State or in areas lying beyond the limits of national jurisdiction,

Considering that the success of any environmental policy presupposes that all population groups and social forces, aware of their responsibilities, help to protect and improve the environment, which necessitates continued and thorough educative action, particularly with regard to youth,

Affirming that experience has shown that economic development and technological progress must be compatible with the protection of the environment and the preservation of historical and cultural values; that damage to the environment is best avoided by preventive measures; and that the ecological balance must be preserved in the exploitation and management of natural resources,

Aims of co-operation

Agree to the following aims of co-operation, in particular:

— to study, with a view to their solution, those environmental problems which, by their nature, are of a multilateral, bilateral, regional or sub-regional dimension; as well as to encourage the development of an interdisciplinary approach to environmental problems;

— to increase the effectiveness of national and international measures for the protection of the environment, by the comparison and, if appropriate, the harmonization of methods of gathering and analyzing facts, by improving the knowledge of pollution phenomena and rational utilization of natural resources, by the exchange of information, by the harmonization of definitions and the adoption, as far as possible, of a common terminology in the field of the environment;

— to take the necessary measures to bring environmental policies closer together and, where appropriate and possible, to harmonize them;

— to encourage, where possible and appropriate, national and international efforts by their interested organizations, enterprises and firms in the development, production and improvement of equipment designed for monitoring, protecting and enhancing the environment.

Fields of co-operation

To attain these aims, the participating States will make use of every suitable opportunity to co-operate in the field of environment and, in particular, within the areas described below as examples:

Control of air pollution

Desulphurization of fossil fuels and exhaust gases; pollution control of heavy metals, particles, aerosols, nitrogen oxides, in particular those emitted by transport, power stations, and other industrial plants; systems and methods of observation and control of air pollution and its effects, including long-range transport of air pollutants;

Water pollution control and fresh water utilization

Prevention and control of water pollution, in particular of transboundary rivers and international lakes; techniques for the improvement of the quality of water and further development of ways and means for industrial and municipal sewage effluent purification; methods of assessment of fresh water resources and the improvement of their utilization, in particular by developing methods of production which are less polluting and lead to less consumption of fresh water;

Protection of the marine environment

Protection of the marine environment of participating States, and especially the Mediterranean Sea, from pollutants emanating from land-based sources and those from ships and other vessels, notably the harmful substances listed in Annexes I and II to the London Convention on the Prevention of Marine Pollution by the Dumping of Wastes and Other Matters; problems of maintaining marine ecological balances and food chains, in particular such problems as may arise from the exploration and exploitation of biological and mineral resources of the seas and the seabed;

Land utilization and soils

Problems associated with more effective use of lands, including land amelioration, reclamation and recultivation; control of soil pollution, water and air erosion, as well as other forms of soil degradation; maintaining and increasing the productivity of soils with due regard for the possible negative effects of the application of chemical fertilizers and pesticides;

Nature conservation and nature reserves

Protection of nature and nature reserves; conservation and maintenance of existing genetic resources, especially rare animal and plant species; conservation of natural ecological systems; establishment of nature reserves and other protected landscapes and areas, including their use for research, tourism, recreation and other purposes;

Improvement of environmental conditions in areas of human settlement

Environmental conditions associated with transport, housing, working areas, urban development and planning, water supply and sewage disposal systems; assessment of harmful effects of noise, and noise control methods; collection, treatment and utilization of wastes, including the recovery and recycling of materials; research on substitutes for non-biodegradable substances;

Fundamental research, monitoring, forecasting and assessment of environmental changes

Study of changes in climate, landscapes and ecological balances under the impact of both natural factors and human activities; forecasting of possible genetic changes in flora and fauna as a result of environmental pollution; harmonization of statistical data, development of scientific concepts and systems of monitoring networks, standardized methods of observation, measurement and assessment of changes in the biosphere; assessment of the effects of environmental pollution levels and degradation of the environment upon human health; study and development of criteria and standards for various environmental pollutants and regulation regarding production and use of various products;

Legal and administrative measures

Legal and administrative measures for the protection of the environment including procedures for establishing environmental impact assessments.

Forms and methods of co-operation

The participating States declare that problems relating to the protection and improvement of the environment will be solved on both a bilateral and multilateral, including regional and sub-regional, basis, making full use of existing patterns and forms of co-operation. They will develop co-operation in the field of the environment in particular by taking into consideration the Stockholm Declaration on the Human Environment, relevant resolutions of the United Nations General Assembly and the United Nations Economic Commission for Europe Prague symposium on environmental problems.

The participating States are resolved that co-operation in the field of the environment will be implemented in particular through:

— exchanges of scientific and technical information, documentation and research results, including information on the means of determining the possible effects on the environment of technical and economic activities;

— organization of conferences, symposia and meetings of experts;

— exchanges of scientists, specialists and trainees;

— joint preparation and implementation of programmes and projects for the study and solution of various problems of environmental protection;

— harmonization, where appropriate and necessary, of environmental protection standards and norms, in particular with the object of avoiding possible difficulties in trade which may arise from efforts to resolve ecological problems of production processes and which relate to the achievement of certain environmental qualities in manufactured products:

— consultations on various aspects of environmental protection, as agreed upon among countries concerned, especially in connection with problems which could have international consequences.

The participating States will further develop such co-operation by:

— promoting the progressive development, codification and implementation of international law as one means of preserving and enhancing the human environment, including principles and practices, as accepted by them, relating to pollution and other environmental damage caused by activities within the jurisdiction or control of their States affecting other countries and regions;

— supporting and promoting the implementation of relevant international Conventions to which they are parties, in particular those designed to prevent and combat marine and fresh water pollution, recommending States to ratify Conventions which have already been signed, as well as considering possibilities of accepting other appropriate Conventions to which they are not parties at present;

— advocating the inclusion, where appropriate and possible, of the various areas of co-operation into the programmes of work of the United Nations Economic Commission for Europe, supporting such co-operation within the framework of the Commission and of the United Nations Environment Programme, and taking into account the work of other competent international organizations of which they are members;

— making wider use in all types of co-operation, of information already available for national and international sources, including internationally agreed criteria, and utilizing the possibilities and capabilities of various competent international organizations.

The participating States agree on the following recommendations on specific measures:

— to develop through international co-operation an extensive programme for the monitoring and evaluation of the long-range transport of air pollutants, starting with sulphur dioxide and with possible extension to other pollutants, and to this end to take into account basic elements of a co-operation programme which were identified by the experts who met in Oslo in December 1974 at the invitation of the Norwegian Institute of Air Research;

— to advocate that within the framework of the United Nations Economic Commission for Europe a study be carried out of procedures and relevant experience relating to the activities of Governments in developing the capabilities of their countries to predict adequately environmental consequences of economic activities and technological development.

1.20 DRAFT PRINCIPLES OF CONDUCT IN THE FIELD OF THE ENVIRONMENT FOR GUIDANCE OF STATES IN THE CONSERVATION AND HARMONIOUS UTILIZATION OF NATURAL RESOURCES SHARED BY TWO OR MORE STATES. Adopted by the U.N. Environment Programme Governing Council, 19 May 1978. U.N.Doc. UNEP/IG12/2 (1978), 17 I.L.M. 1097 (1978)

Principle 1

It is necessary for States to co-operate in the field of the environment concerning the conservation and harmonious utilization of natural resources shared by two or more States. Accordingly, it is necessary that consistent with the concept of equitable utilization of shared natural resources, States co-operate with a view to controlling, preventing, reducing or eliminating adverse environmental effects which may result from the utilization of such resources. Such co-operation is to take place on an equal footing and taking into account the sovereignty, rights and interests of the States concerned.

Principle 2

In order to ensure effective international co-operation in the field of the environment concerning the conservation and harmonious utilization of natural resources shared by two or more States, States sharing such natural resources should endeavor to conclude bilateral or multilateral agreements between or among themselves in order to secure specific regulation of their conduct in this respect, applying as necessary the present principles in a legally binding manner or should endeavor to enter into other arrangements, as appropriate, for this purpose. In entering into such agreements or arrangements, States should consider the establishment of institutional structures, such as joint international commissions, for consultations on environmental problems relating to the protection and use of shared natural resources.

Principle 3

1. States have, in accordance with the Charter of the United Nations and the principles of international law, the sovereign right to exploit their own resources pursuant to their own environmental policies, and the responsibility to ensure that activities within their jurisdiction or control do not cause damage to the environment of other States or of areas beyond the limits of national jurisdiction.

2. The principles set forth in paragraph 1, as well as the other principles contained in this document, apply to shared natural resources.

3. Accordingly, it is necessary for each State to avoid to the maximum extent possible and to reduce to the minimum extent possible the adverse environmental effects beyond its jurisdiction of the utilization of a shared natural resource so as to protect the environment, in particular when such utilization might:

    (*a*) cause damage to the environment which could have repercussions on the utilization of the resource by another sharing State;

    (*b*) threaten the conservation of a shared renewable resource;

    (*c*) endanger the health of the population of another State.

Without prejudice to the generality of the above principle, it should be interpreted, taking into account, where appropriate, the practical capabilities of States sharing the natural resource.

Principle 4

States should make environmental assessments before engaging in any activity with respect to a shared natural resource which may create a risk of significantly [1] affecting the environment of another State or States sharing that resource.

Principle 5

States sharing a natural resource should, to the extent practicable, exchange information and engage in consultations on a regular basis on its environmental aspects.

Principle 6

1. It is necessary for every State sharing a natural resource with one or more other States:

  (*a*) to notify in advance the other State or States of the pertinent details of plans to initiate, or make a change in, the conservation or utilization of the resource which can reasonably be expected to affect significantly the environment in the territory of the other State or States; and

  (*b*) upon request of the other State or States, to enter into consultations concerning the above-mentioned plans; and

  (*c*) to provide, upon request to that effect by the other State or States, specific additional pertinent information concerning such plans; and

  (*d*) if there has been no advance notification as envisaged in subparagraph (a) above, to enter into consultations about such plans upon request of the other State or States.

2. In cases where the transmission of certain information is prevented by national legislation or international conventions, the State or States withholding such information shall nevertheless, on the basis, in particular, of the principle of good faith and in the spirit of good neighbourliness, co-operate with the other interested State or States with the aim of finding a satisfactory solution.

Principle 7

Exchange of information, notification, consultations and other forms of co-operation regarding shared natural resources are carried out on the basis of the principle of good faith and in the spirit of good neighbourliness and in such a way as to avoid any unreasonable delays either in the forms of co-operation or in carrying out development or conservation projects.

Principle 8

When it would be useful to clarify environmental problems relating to a shared natural resource, States should engage in joint scientific studies and

---

1. *See* "Definition" following Principle 15.

assessments, with a view to facilitating the finding of appropriate and satisfactory solutions to such problems on the basis of agreed data.

Principle 9

1. States have a duty urgently to inform other States which may be affected:

(*a*) Of any emergency situation arising from the utilization of a shared natural resource which might cause sudden harmful effects on their environment;

(*b*) Of any sudden grave natural events related to a shared natural resource which may affect the environment of such States.

2. States should also, when appropriate, inform the competent international organizations of any such situation or event.

3. States concerned should co-operate, in particular by means of agreed contingency plans, when appropriate, and mutual assistance, in order to avert grave situations, and to eliminate, reduce or correct, as far as possible, the effects of such situations or events.

Principle 10

States sharing a natural resource should, when appropriate, consider the possibility of jointly seeking the services of any competent international organization in clarifying the environmental problems relating to the conservation or utilization of such natural resource.

Principle 11

1. The relevant provisions of the Charter of the United Nations and of the Declaration of Principles of International Law concerning Friendly Relations and Co-operation among States in accordance with the Charter of the United Nations apply to the settlement of environmental disputes arising out of the conservation or utilization of shared natural resources.

2. In case negotiations or other non-binding means have failed to settle a dispute within a reasonable time, it is necessary for States to submit the dispute to an appropriate settlement procedure which is mutually agreed by them, preferably in advance. The procedure should be speedy, effective and binding.

3. It is necessary for the States parties to such a dispute to refrain from any action which may aggravate the situation with respect to the environment to the extent of creating an obstacle to the amicable settlement of the dispute.

Principle 12

1. States are responsible for the fulfillment of their international obligations in the field of the environment concerning the conservation and utilization of shared natural resources. They are subject to liability in accordance with applicable international law for environmental damage resulting from violations of these obligations caused to areas beyond their jurisdiction.

2. States should co-operate to develop further international law regarding liability and compensation for the victims of environmental damage

arising out of the utilization of a shared natural resource and caused to areas beyond their jurisdiction.

Principle 13

It is necessary for States, when considering, under their domestic environmental policy, the permissibility of domestic activities, to take into account the potential adverse environmental effects arising out of the utilization of shared natural resources, without discrimination as to whether the effects would occur within their jurisdiction or outside it.

Principle 14

States should endeavour, in accordance with their legal systems and, where appropriate, on a basis agreed by them, to provide persons in other States who have been or may be adversely affected by environmental damage resulting from the utilization of shared natural resources with equivalent access to and treatment in the same administrative and judicial proceedings, and make available to them the same remedies as are available to persons within their own jurisdictions who have been or may be similarly affected.

Principle 15

The present principles should be interpreted and applied in such a way as to enhance and not to affect adversely development and the interests of all countries, and in particular of the developing countries.

DEFINITION

In the present text, the expression "significantly affect" refers to any appreciable effects on a shared natural resource and excludes *"de minimis"* effects.

1.21　RESOLUTION ON HISTORICAL RESPONSIBILITY OF STATES FOR THE PRESERVATION OF NATURE FOR PRESENT AND FUTURE GENERATIONS. Adopted by the U.N. General Assembly, 30 October 1980. G.A.Res. 35/48, U.N. GAOR, 35th Sess, Supp. No. 48, at 15, U.N.Doc A/35/48 (1981)

The General Assembly,

Having considered the item entitled "Historical responsibility of States for the preservation of nature for present and future generations",

Conscious of the disastrous consequences which a war involving the use of nuclear weapons and other weapons of mass destruction would have on man and his environment,

Noting that the continuation of the arms race, including the testing of various types of weapons, especially nuclear weapons, and the accumulation of toxic chemicals are adversely affecting the human environment and damaging the vegetable and animal world,

Bearing in mind that the arms race is diverting material and intellectual resources from the solution of the urgent problems of preserving nature,

Attaching great importance to the development of planned, constructive international co-operation in solving the problems of preserving nature,

Recognizing that the prospects for solving problems so universal as the preservation of nature are closely linked to the strengthening and development of international detente and the creation of conditions which would banish war from the life of mankind,

Noting with satisfaction the drafting and signature in recent years of a number of international agreements designed to preserve the environment,

Determined to preserve nature as a prerequisite for the normal life of man,

1. *Proclaims* the historical responsibility of States for the preservation of nature for present and future generations;

2. *Draws the attention* of States to the fact that the continuing arms race has pernicious effects on the environment and reduces the prospects for the necessary international co-operation in preserving nature on our planet;

3. *Calls upon* States, in the interests of present and future generations, to demonstrate due concern and take the measures, including legislative measures, necessary for preserving nature, and also to promote international co-operation in this field;

4. *Requests* the Secretary–General, with the co-operation of the United Nations Environment Programme, to prepare a report on the pernicious effects of the arms race on nature and to seek the views of States on possible measures to be taken at the international level for the preservation of nature;

5. *Decides* to include in the provisional agenda of its thirty-sixth session an item entitled "Historical responsibility of States for the preservation of nature for present and future generations: report of the Secretary–General".

1.22 ILA RULES ON INTERNATIONAL LAW APPLICABLE TO TRANS-FRONTIER POLLUTION. Concluded at Montreal, 4 September 1982. 60 I.L.A. 158 (1983)

Article 1 (Applicability)

The following rules of international law concerning transfrontier pollution are applicable except as may be otherwise provided by convention, agreement or binding custom among the States concerned.

Article 2 (Definition)

(1) "Pollution" means any introduction by man, directly or indirectly, of substance or energy into the environment resulting in deleterious effects of such a nature as to endanger human health, harm living resources, ecosystems and material property and impair amenities or interfere with other legitimate uses of the environment.

(2) "Transfrontier pollution" means pollution of which the physical origin is wholly or in part situated within the territory of one State and which has deleterious effects in the territory of another State.

Article 3 (Prevention and Abatement)

(1) Without prejudice to the operation of the rules relating to the reasonable and equitable utilisation of shared natural resources States are in their legitimate activities under an obligation to prevent, abate and control transfrontier pollution to such an extent that no substantial injury is caused in the territory of another State.

(2) Furthermore States shall limit new and increased transfrontier pollution to the lowest level that may be reached by measures practicable and reasonable under the circumstances.

(3) States should endeavour to reduce existing transfrontier pollution, below the requirements of paragraph 1 of this Article, to the lowest level that may be reached by measures practicable and reasonable under the circumstances.

Article 4 (Highly Dangerous Substances)

Notwithstanding the provisions in Article 3 States shall refrain from causing transfrontier pollution by discharging into the environment substances generally considered as being highly dangerous to human health. If such substances are already being discharged, States shall eliminate the polluting discharge within a reasonable time.

Article 5 (Prior Notice)

(1) States planning to carry out activities which might entail a significant risk of transfrontier pollution shall give early notice to States likely to be affected. In particular they shall on their own initiative or upon request of the potentially affected States, communicate such pertinent information as will permit the recipient to make an assessment of the probable effects of the planned activities.

(2) In order to appraise whether a planned activity implies a significant risk of transfrontier pollution, States should make environmental assessment before carrying out such activities.

Article 6 (Consultations)

(1) Upon request of a potentially affected State, the State furnishing the information should enter into consultations on transfrontier pollution problems connected with the planned activities and pursue such consultations in good faith and over a reasonable period of time.

(2) States are under an obligation to enter into consultations whenever transfrontier pollution problems arise in connection with the equitable utilization of a shared natural resource as envisaged in Art. 5.

Article 7 (Emergency Situations)

When as a result of an emergency situation or of other circumstances activities already carried out in the territory of a State cause or might cause a sudden increase in the existing level of transfrontier pollution the State of origin is under a duty:

(a) to promptly warn the affected or potentially affected States;

(b) to provide them with such pertinent information as will enable them to minimize the transfrontier pollution damage;

(c) to inform them of the steps taken to abate the cause of the increased transfrontier pollution level.

1.23 WORLD CHARTER FOR NATURE. Adopted by the U.N. General Assembly, 28 October 1982. G.A. Res. 37/7 (Annex), U.N. GAOR, 37th Sess., Supp. No. 51, at 17, U.N. Doc. A/37/51, 22 I.L.M. 455 (1983)

The General Assembly,

Reaffirming the fundamental purposes of the United Nations, in particular the maintenance of international peace and security, the development of friendly relations among nations and the achievement of international cooperation in solving international problems of an economic, social, cultural, technical, intellectual or humanitarian character,

Aware that:

(*a*) Mankind is a part of nature and life depends on the uninterrupted functioning of natural systems which ensure the supply of energy and nutrients,

(*b*) Civilization is rooted in nature, which has shaped human culture and influenced all artistic and scientific achievement, and living in harmony with nature gives man the best opportunities for the development of his creativity, and for rest and recreation,

Convinced that:

(*a*) Every form of life is unique, warranting respect regardless of its worth to man, and, to accord other organisms such recognition, man must be guided by a moral code of action,

(*b*) Man can alter nature and exhaust natural resources by his action or its consequences and, therefore, must fully recognize the urgency of maintaining the stability and quality of nature and of conserving natural resources,

Persuaded that:

(*a*) Lasting benefits from nature depend upon the maintenance of essential ecological processes and life support systems, and upon the diversity of life forms, which are jeopardized through excessive exploitation and habitat destruction by man,

(*b*) The degradation of natural systems owing to excessive consumption and misuse of natural resources, as well as to failure to establish an appropriate economic order among peoples and among States, leads to the breakdown of the economic, social and political framework of civilization,

(*c*) Competition for scarce resources creates conflicts, whereas the conservation of nature and natural resources contributes to justice and the maintenance of peace and cannot be achieved until mankind learns to live in peace and to forsake war and armaments,

Reaffirming that man must acquire the knowledge to maintain and enhance his ability to use natural resources in a manner which ensures the preservation of the species and ecosystems for the benefit of present and future generations,

Firmly convinced of the need for appropriate measures, at the national and international, individual and collective, and private and public levels, to protect nature and promote international co-operation in this field,

Adopts, to these ends, the present World Charter for Nature, which proclaims the following principles of conservation by which all human conduct affecting nature is to be guided and judged.

I. General Principles

1. Nature shall be respected and its essential processes shall not be impaired.

2. The genetic viability on the earth shall not be compromised; the population levels of all life forms, wild and domesticated, must be at least sufficient for their survival, and to this end necessary habitats shall be safeguarded.

3. All areas of the earth, both land and sea, shall be subject to these principles of conservation; special protection shall be given to unique areas, to representative samples of all the different types of ecosystems and to the habitats of rare or endangered species.

4. Ecosystems and organisms, as well as the land, marine and atmospheric resources that are utilized by man, shall be managed to achieve and maintain optimum sustainable productivity, but not in such a way as to endanger the integrity of those other ecosystems or species with which they coexist.

5. Nature shall be secured against degradation caused by warfare or other hostile activities.

II. Functions

6. In the decision-making process it shall be recognized that man's needs can be met only by ensuring the proper functioning of natural systems and by respecting the principles set forth in the present Charter.

7. In the planning and implementation of social and economic development activities, due account shall be taken of the fact that the conservation of nature is an integral part of those activities.

8. In formulating long-term plans for economic development, population growth and the improvement of standards of living, due account shall be taken of the long-term capacity of natural systems to ensure the subsistence and settlement of the populations concerned, recognizing that this capacity may be enhanced through science and technology.

9. The allocation of areas of the earth to various uses shall be planned, and due account shall be taken of the physical constraints, the biological productivity and diversity and the natural beauty of the areas concerned.

10. Natural resources shall not be wasted, but used with a restraint appropriate to the principles set forth in the present Charter, in accordance with the following rules:

(*a*) Living resources shall not be utilized in excess of their natural capacity for regeneration;

(*b*) The productivity of soils shall be maintained or enhanced through measures which safeguard their long-term fertility and the process of organic decomposition, and prevent erosion and all other forms of degradation;

(*c*) Resources, including water, which are not consumed as they are used shall be reused or recycled;

(*d*) Non-renewable resources which are consumed as they are used shall be exploited with restraint, taking into account their abundance, the rational possibilities of converting them for consumption, and the compatibility of their exploitation with the functioning of natural systems.

11.   Activities which might have an impact on nature shall be controlled, and the best available technologies that minimize significant risks to nature or other adverse effects shall be used; in particular:

(*a*) Activities which are likely to cause irreversible damage to nature shall be avoided;

(*b*) Activities which are likely to pose a significant risk to nature shall be preceded by an exhaustive examination; their proponents shall demonstrate that expected benefits outweigh potential damage to nature, and where potential adverse effects are not fully understood, the activities should not proceed.

(*c*) Activities which may disturb nature shall be preceded by assessment of their consequences, and environmental impact studies of development projects shall be conducted sufficiently in advance, and if they are to be undertaken, such activities shall be planned and carried out so as to minimize potential adverse effects;

(*d*) Agriculture, grazing, forestry and fisheries practices shall be adapted to the natural characteristics and constraints of given areas;

(*e*) Areas degraded by human activities shall be rehabilitated for purposes in accord with their natural potential and compatible with the well-being of affected populations.

12.   Discharge of pollutants into natural systems shall be avoided and:

(*a*) Where this is not feasible, such pollutants shall be treated at the source, using the best practicable means available;

(*b*) Special precautions shall be taken to prevent discharge of radioactive or toxic wastes.

13.   Measures intended to prevent, control or limit natural disasters, infestations and diseases shall be specifically directed to the causes of these scourges and shall avoid adverse side-effects on nature.

III. Implementation

14.   The principles set forth in the present Charter shall be reflected in the law and practice of each State, as well as at the international level.

15.   Knowledge of nature shall be broadly disseminated by all possible means, particularly by ecological education as an integral part of general education.

16.   All planning shall include, among its essential elements, the formulation of strategies for the conservation of nature, the establishment of inventories of ecosystems and assessments of the effects on nature of proposed policies and activities; all of these elements shall be disclosed to the public by appropriate means in time to permit effective consultation and participation.

17. Funds, programmes and administrative structures necessary to achieve the objective of the conservation of nature shall be provided.

18. Constant efforts shall be made to increase knowledge of nature by scientific research and to disseminate such knowledge unimpeded by restrictions of any kind.

19. The status of natural processes, ecosystems and species shall be closely monitored to enable early detection of degradation or threat, ensure timely intervention and facilitate the evaluation of conservation policies and methods.

20. Military activities damaging to nature shall be avoided.

21. States and, to the extent they are able, other public authorities, international organizations, individuals, groups and corporations shall:

(*a*) Co-operate in the task of conserving nature through common activities and other relevant actions, including information exchange and consultations;

(*b*) Establish standards for products and manufacturing processes that may have adverse effects on nature, as well as agreed methodologies for assessing these effects;

(*c*) Implement the applicable international legal provisions for the conservation of nature and the protection of the environment;

(*d*) Ensure that activities within their jurisdictions or control do not cause damage to the natural systems located within other States or in the areas beyond the limits of national jurisdiction;

(*e*) Safeguard and conserve nature in areas beyond national jurisdiction.

22. Taking fully into account the sovereignty of States over their natural resources, each State shall give effect to the provisions of the present Charter through its competent organs and in co-operation with other States.

23. All persons, in accordance with their national legislation, shall have the opportunity to participate, individually or with others, in the formulation of decisions of direct concern to their environment, and shall have access to means of redress when their environment has suffered damage or degradation.

24. Each person has a duty to act in accordance with the provisions of the present Charter; acting individually, in association with others or through participation in the political process, each person shall strive to ensure that the objectives and requirements of the present Charter are met.

1.24 RESTATEMENT (THIRD) OF THE FOREIGN RELATIONS LAW OF THE UNITED STATES (1987): *§§ 601–604 (with comments)*

§ 601. State Obligations with Respect to Environment of Other States and the Common Environment

(1) A state is obligated to take such measures as may be necessary, to the extent practicable under the circumstances, to ensure that activities within its jurisdiction or control

(a) conform to generally accepted international rules and standards for the prevention, reduction, and control of injury to the environment of another state or of areas beyond the limits of national jurisdiction; and

(b) are conducted so as not to cause significant injury to the environment of another state or of areas beyond the limits of national jurisdiction.

(2) A state is responsible to all other states

(a) for any violation of its obligations under Subsection (1)(a), and

(b) for any significant injury, resulting from such violation, to the environment of areas beyond the limits of national jurisdiction.

(3) A state is responsible for any significant injury, resulting from a violation of its obligations under Subsection (1), to the environment of another state or to its property, or to persons or property within that state's territory or under its jurisdiction or control.

Comment:

a. Application of general principles of state responsibility. This Part applies to environmental questions the general principles of international law relating to the responsibility of states for injury to another state or its property or to persons within its territory or their property, or for injury to interests common to all states. A state is responsible under Subsections (2) and (3) for breach of any of its obligations under Subsection (1). It is responsible under Subsection (2) to all states, and any state may request that it abate a threat of pollution and make arrangements to prevent future violations. Under Subsection (3), it is responsible to an injured state for any significant injury and is required to make reparation for the injury. The conditions of responsibility and the remedies available may differ with the circumstances and with the interests affected. See Comment *d* and § 602; see also the general principles in § 711 and §§ 901–902.

b. "Generally accepted international rules and standards." This phrase is adopted from the law of the sea; see § 502, Comment *c*. The obligation under Subsection (1)(a) refers to both general rules of customary international law (see, *e.g.,* the *Trail Smelter* case, Reporters' Note 1) and those derived from international conventions, and from standards adopted by international organizations pursuant to such conventions, that deal with a specific subject, such as oil pollution or radioactive wastes. See Reporters' Notes 3–7 and § 603, Reporters' Notes 4 and 5; see also § 102, Comments *f* and *g,* and

§ 103, Comment *c*. A state is also obligated to comply with an environmental rule or standard that has been accepted by both it and an injured state, even if that rule or standard has not been generally accepted.

Where an international rule or standard has been violated, any state can object to the violation; where a state has been injured in consequence of such violation, it is entitled to damages or other appropriate relief from the responsible state; where there is a threat of injury, the threatened state, or any state acting on behalf of threatened common interests, is entitled to have the dangerous activity terminated. See § 602.

    c. "Activities within its jurisdiction" and "significant injury." An activity is considered to be within a state's jurisdiction under this section if the state may exercise jurisdiction to prescribe law with respect to that activity under §§ 402–403. The phrase "activities within its jurisdiction or control" includes activities in a state's territory, on the coastal waters that are under its jurisdiction, Part V, as well as activities on ships flying its flag or on installations on the high seas operating under its authority. See § 502(1)(b) and Comment *c* thereto, § 514, Comment *i* and § 521, Comment *c*. International law does not address internal pollution, but a state is responsible under this section if pollution within its jurisdiction causes significant injuries beyond its borders. "Significant injury" is not defined but references to "significant" impact on the environment are common in both international law and United States law. The word "significant" excludes minor incidents causing minimal damage. In special circumstances, the significance of injury to another state is balanced against the importance of the activity to the state causing the injury. See Reporters' Note 3.

    d. Conditions of responsibility. A state is responsible under Subsections (2) and (3) for both its own activities and those of individuals or private or public corporations under its jurisdiction. The state may be responsible, for instance, for not enacting necessary legislation, for not enforcing its laws against persons acting in its territory or against its vessels, or for not preventing or terminating an illegal activity, or for not punishing the person responsible for it. In the case of ships flying its flags, a state is responsible for injury due to the state's own defaults under Subsection (1) but is not responsible for injury due to fault of the operators of the ship. In both cases, a state is responsible only if it has not taken "such measures as may be necessary" to comply with applicable international standards and to avoid causing injury outside its territory, as required by Subsection (1). In general, the applicable international rules and standards do not hold a state responsible when it has taken the necessary and practicable measures; some international agreements provide also for responsibility regardless of fault in case of a discharge of highly dangerous (radioactive, toxic, etc.) substances, or an abnormally dangerous activity (*e.g.,* launching of space satellites). See also the principles applicable to weather modification, Comment *f.* In all cases, however, some defenses may be available to the state; *e.g.,* that it had acted pursuant to a binding decision of the Security Council of the United Nations, or that injury was due to the failure of the injured state to exercise reasonable care to avoid the threatened harm. Compare Restatement, Second, Torts §§ 519, 520, and 524. A state is not responsible for injury due to a natural disaster such as an eruption of a volcano, unless such disaster was triggered or aggravated by a human act, such as nuclear explosion in a volcano's vicinity. But a state is responsible if after a natural disaster has occurred it does not take necessary and practicable steps to prevent or reduce injury to other states.

Under Subsections (2)(b) and (3), responsibility of a state for a significant injury entails payment of appropriate damages if the complaining state proves the existence of a causal link between an activity within the jurisdiction of the responsible state and the injury to the complaining state. Determination of responsibility raises special difficulties in cases of long-range pollution where the link between multiple activities in some distant states and the pollution in the injured state might be difficult to prove. Where more than one state contributes to the pollution causing significant injury, the liability will be apportioned among the states, taking into account, where appropriate, the contribution to the injury of the injured state itself.

A state is responsible under this section for environmental harm proxi-mately caused by activity under its own jurisdiction, not for activity by another state. For instance, a state is not responsible under this section merely because it encourages activities in another state, such as plant eradi-cation programs, that inflict environmental injury in that state or in a third state. Similarly, if a group of states imposes economic sanctions on state A depriving it of oil supplies and requiring state A to use coal, which results in an increase in air pollution in state B, the boycotting states are not responsi-ble under principles of international environmental law for injury resulting to state B.

Although there has been no authoritative consideration of the issue, international environmental law has apparently not extended responsibility beyond the state directly responsible for the activities causing injury, under principles analogous to "product liability" which apply in some national legal systems. Thus, under this section, state A is responsible for a radioactive emission from a nuclear reactor operated in its territory that causes injury to state B, but there is no recognized responsibility to B by state C in which the defective reactor was manufactured or from which it was sold to state A. There may, however, be such responsibility pursuant to an international agreement between state A and state C, and in special circumstances under general principles of state responsibility. See, *e.g.*, §§ 207, 711, and 901. Also, there may be liability by the manufacturer or seller of the defective reactor, whether it is a state or a private person, under principles of national law applicable to the transaction. Compare, for example, Restatement, Sec-ond, Torts §§ 388–408.

Under this section, a state is obligated to take all necessary precautionary measures where an activity is contemplated that poses a substantial risk of a significant transfrontier environmental injury; if the activity has already taken place, the state is obligated to take all necessary measures to prevent or reduce pollution beyond its borders. Similarly, where a violation of interna-tional environmental rules and standards has already occurred, the violating state is obligated to take promptly all necessary preventive or remedial measures, even if no injury has yet taken place.

For the remedies for breach of obligations under this section, see § 602.

  e. Obligation to notify and consult. Under Subsection 1(a), a state has an obligation to warn another state promptly of any situation that may cause significant pollution damage in that state. A state has also an obligation to consult with another state if a proposed activity within its jurisdiction or control poses a substantial risk of significant injury to the environment of the other state, but it need not permit such consultations to delay the proposed activity unduly.

f. Weather modification. Weather modification programs are normally used either to prevent injuries to the environment (*e.g.,* by a storm) or to obtain some benefit (*e.g.,* by causing rain during a drought). A state's weather modification programs have sometimes caused injury to another state, *e.g.,* by bringing it excessive rain or by depriving it of rain, or, by changing the direction of a storm, causing injury to that state's ships at sea, to its shore, or to the marine environment. Under international law, a state engaged in weather modification activities is responsible for any significant injuries if causation can be proved, even if the injury was neither intended nor due to negligence, and even if the state took all necessary measures to prevent or reduce injury. Compare the rule as to abnormally dangerous activities, Comment *d.*

* * *

§ 602. Remedies for Violation of Environmental Obligations

(1) A state responsible to another state for violation of § 601 is subject to general interstate remedies (§ 902) to prevent, reduce, or terminate the activity threatening or causing the violation, and to pay reparation for injury caused.

(2) Where pollution originating in a state has caused significant injury to persons outside that state, or has created a significant risk of such injury, the state of origin is obligated to accord to the person injured or exposed to such risk access to the same judicial or administrative remedies as are available in similar circumstances to persons within the state.

Comment:

a. International law remedies. The remedies referred to in Subsection (1) usually begin with a protest against the violation, accompanied by a demand that the offending state terminate the violation, desist from further violations, and make reparation for past violations. If the matter is not resolved by diplomatic negotiations, the aggrieved state may resort to agreed third-party procedures, such as conciliation, mediation, arbitration, or adjudication. Some neighboring states have established international joint commissions to deal with transboundary problems, including pollution, but usually such commissions can only make recommendations. Strictly limited and reasonable measures of "self help" may be permitted in special circumstances. See § 905. Remedies under international law are to the injured state; whether that state is obligated to pay any reparation received over to any injured person in its territory is a matter of its domestic law. See § 902, Comments *i* and *l.*

Remedies under this section are available for injury to a state's environmental interests within its territory as well as to interests beyond its territory, such as injury to its fishing interests on the high seas; it may pursue remedies, not only for injury to state interests but also to those of its political subdivisions or of its inhabitants or nationals. A state may also pursue appropriate remedies for injury to the common interest in the global commons, such as the high seas.

Even where reparations for past injuries are not appropriate or feasible, a state may demand that violations be discontinued.

b. Local remedies. A state responsible for transfrontier pollution can fulfill its obligation to inhabitants of other states who suffered injuries by giving them access to its tribunals for adjudication of their claims. If such local remedies are available, the person who suffered injuries must exhaust these remedies before the state of which he is a national can bring an international claim on his behalf under Subsection (1). See § 703, Comment *d;* § 713, Comments *b* and *f;* § 902, Comment *k.* The two states, however, may agree at any time to settle the claim or include it in a lump-sum settlement. See § 902, Comment *i.*

Subsection (2) applies the principle of non-discrimination against foreign nationals (§ 711, Comment *f*). This principle requires that a state in which pollution originates avoid discrimination in the enforcement of applicable international rules and standards, as well as give to foreign victims the benefit of its own rules and standards for the protection of the environment, even if they are stricter than the international rules or standards. Subsection (2) applies the principle of nondiscrimination also to remedies. A state must provide the same procedures, and apply the same substantive law and the same measures of compensation, to persons outside its territory as are available to persons injured within its territory. Thus, a state applying the "polluter-pays" principle should apply it to all pollution originating within the state, whether it causes injury at home or abroad. If a state applies the principle of strict liability, a victim of transfrontier pollution will be entitled to the benefit of that principle. On the other hand, if the state makes liability conditional on fault or negligence, the foreign victim can be required to meet that condition even if in the place of injury fault or negligence is not a necessary element for liability. Similarly, if a state's law imposes an obligation to reduce pollution to the lowest level that is attainable by the application of the most advanced technology that is economically feasible, this requirement applies equally to pollution at home and abroad.

When environmental injury in one state results from private activity in another state, a remedy may sometimes be available in the courts of the victim state, or even of a third state, and if the victim has received satisfaction by such a remedy the interstate remedy would abate.

c. Availability of private remedies under state law. Under the law of many states, pollution damage is considered a local tort; suit for damages lies only in the state where the injury occurred, not in the state where the pollution originated. If personal jurisdiction over the person responsible for the pollution can be obtained in the state where the injury occurred, a suit for compensation or for an injunction would lie, but such suit might not be possible if the alleged polluter has no business or property in that state. Even if a suit there is brought under a long-arm statute and results in a default judgment, the judgment might not be enforceable in the polluter's home state. See § 421(2)(j) and § 481, Reporters' Note 4.

* * *

§ 603. State Responsibility for Marine Pollution

(1) A state is obligated

(a) to adopt laws and regulations to prevent, reduce, and control any significant pollution of the marine environment that are no less effective than generally accepted international rules and standards; and

(b) to ensure compliance with the laws and regulations adopted pursuant to clause (a) by ships flying its flag, and, in case of a violation, to impose adequate penalties on the owner or captain of the ship.

(2) A state is obligated to take, individually and jointly with other states, such measures as may be necessary, to the extent practicable under the circumstances, to prevent, reduce, and control pollution causing or threatening to cause significant injury to the marine environment.

Source Note:

This section is based on Articles 194, 207–12, 217, and 220 of the 1982 Convention on the Law of the Sea.

Comment:

a. State responsibility for marine pollution. This section applies the principles of § 601 to marine pollution. In fulfilling their obligations under this section, states must use "the best practicable means at their disposal and in accordance with their capabilities," and must "endeavour to harmonize their policies in this connection." LOS Convention, Article 194(1). In taking measures to prevent, reduce, or control pollution, states are obligated to implement any pertinent international rules and standards, and to refrain from unjustifiable interference with activities carried out by other states in exercise of their rights and in pursuance of their duties in conformity with international law. Articles 194(4) and 213–22.

The measures to be taken must "minimize to the fullest possible extent" the release of toxic, harmful, or noxious substances from land-based sources (such as rivers, estuaries, pipelines, and sewers), from or through the atmosphere, or by dumping of waste. Articles 194(3), 207, 210, and 212. In order to limit pollution from ships, all states must take measures for preventing accidents and dealing with emergencies, ensuring the safety of operations at sea, and preventing harmful discharges, whether intentional or unintentional. Navigational routing systems should also be designed to minimize the danger of accidents. Articles 194(3)(b) and 211(1). For the obligations of flag states, see Comment *b;* for the obligations of states engaged in sea-bed mining, see Comment *c.*

Under the principles of § 601(2) and (3), a state is responsible for injuries caused by pollution resulting from a violation of its obligations under this section to a coast or coastal waters of another state or to the marine areas beyond the limits of national jurisdiction, *i.e.,* areas of the sea not included in internal waters, the territorial sea, or the exclusive economic zone of a state, or in the archipelagic waters of an archipelagic state. See Article 86. State responsibility extends to injuries such as those caused by pollution, *e.g.,* by: toxic or noxious substances flowing down-river into the sea and moving into the coastal waters of a neighboring state; sewage drifting from the coastal waters of one state to the coast of another state; toxic or noxious substances dumped, or garbage or fuel discharged, by ships flying the flag of one state and landing on the coast of another state; or oil spills, mineral tailings, or other discharges from installations for exploration and exploitation of oil or polymetallic nodules that contaminate the high seas or are moved by currents to the waters or coast of another state.

b. Obligations of flag state. The flag state has the primary obligation to ensure that its ships respect generally accepted international anti-pollution rules and standards established through the competent international organization or general diplomatic conference, and that they comply with the state's laws and regulations implementing such rules and standards. A flag state is obligated to prohibit its ships from sailing unless they have complied with such international rules and standards, and have also met standards set by the state's own laws, especially those relating to design, construction, equipment, and manning of ships; to require its ships to carry on board certificates of compliance with the international rules; and to inspect its ships periodically to verify that their condition conforms to the certificates they carry. Other states must accept the certificates issued by the flag state as evidence of the condition of the ship, unless there are clear grounds for believing that the condition of the ship does not correspond substantially to the certificates. Article 217(1)–(3).

The flag state is obligated to provide for penalties for pollution by its vessels adequate in severity to discourage violations. Article 217(8). For further enforcement obligations of the flag state, see § 604, Comment *c.*

c. Obligations of sea-bed mining states. States are obligated to adopt laws, regulations, and other measures for preventing, reducing, and controlling pollution of the marine environment arising from or in connection with their exploration and exploitation of the sea-bed and subsoil, or from artificial islands, installations, and structures under their jurisdiction that are operating in the marine environment. Such laws, regulations, and measures must be no less effective than international rules, standards, and recommended practices and procedures. Articles 194(3)(c) and (d) and 208.

d. Protection of fragile ecosystems. States are obligated to take measures necessary to protect and preserve rare or fragile ecosystems, and the habitat of depleted, threatened, or endangered species and other forms of marine life. Where the area to be protected forms part of a state's exclusive economic zone, the competent international organization may authorize that state to implement special international rules and standards applicable to such zones. Articles 194(5) and 211(6).

A coastal state also has the right to adopt and enforce nondiscriminatory laws and regulations for the prevention, reduction, and control of marine pollution from vessels in ice-covered areas within the limits of its exclusive economic zone, where particularly severe climatic conditions and the presence of ice for most of the year create obstructions or exceptional hazards to navigation, and where pollution of the marine environment could cause major harm to, or irreversible disturbance of, the ecological balance. The coastal state is obligated to base such laws and regulations on the best available scientific evidence and to have due regard to navigation. Article 234.

e. Obligation to notify. When a state becomes aware that the marine environment has been injured or is in imminent danger of being injured, it is obligated immediately to notify other states likely to be affected by such injuries as well as the competent global or regional international organization. Article 198.

f. Joint action in emergencies. States in an area affected by a maritime pollution disaster are obligated to cooperate in eliminating the effects of pollution and in preventing or minimizing injury. To be able to deal better with such emergencies, neighboring states are obligated to develop and be ready to put into operation contingency plans for responding to pollution incidents affecting the marine environment in their vicinity. Article 199.

g. Pollution by aircraft. States are responsible under this section for pollution of the marine environment by aircraft of their registry, *e.g.,* by noxious emissions. States are obligated to adopt laws and regulations to prevent, reduce, and control such pollution, taking into account internationally agreed rules, standards, and recommended practices and procedures adopted by the International Civil Aviation Organization, but must not prejudice thereby the safety of air navigation. Article 212.

* * *

§ 604. Remedies for Marine Pollution

(1) A state responsible to another state for a violation of the principles of § 603 is subject to general interstate remedies (§ 902) to prevent, reduce, or terminate the activity threatening or causing pollution, and to pay reparation for injury caused.

(2) A state is obligated to ensure that a remedy is available, in accordance with its legal system, to provide prompt and adequate compensation or other relief for an injury to private interests caused by pollution of the marine environment resulting from a violation of § 603.

(3) In addition to remedies that may be available to it under Subsection (1):

    (a) a coastal state may detain, and institute proceedings against, a foreign ship:

        (i) navigating in its territorial sea, for a violation therein of antipollution laws that the coastal state adopted in accordance with applicable international rules and standards; or

        (ii) navigating in its territorial sea or its exclusive economic zone, for a violation in that zone of applicable international antipollution rules and standards that resulted in a discharge causing or threatening a major injury to the coastal state;

(b) a port state may institute proceedings against a foreign ship that has voluntarily come into that state's port,

(i) for a violation of the port state's antipollution laws adopted in accordance with applicable international rules and standards, if the violation had occurred in the port state's territorial sea or exclusive economic zone; or

(ii) for a discharge in violation of applicable international antipollution rules and standards that had occurred beyond the limits of national jurisdiction of any state; and

(c) a port state is obligated to investigate, as far as practicable, whether a foreign ship that has voluntarily come into that state's port was responsible for a discharge in violation of applicable international antipollution rules and standards,

(i) at the request of another state, where the discharge was alleged to have occurred in waters subject to that state's jurisdiction, or to have caused or threatened damage to that state; or

(ii) at the request of the flag state, irrespective of where the violation was alleged to have occurred.

Source Note:

This section is based on Articles 211, 217–18, 220, and 228 of the 1982 Convention on the Law of the Sea.

Comment:

a. Ordinary remedies between states. Subsection (1) states that ordinary international remedies are available for violations of obligations under § 603 as for violations of other obligations under international environmental law (§ 602), or of international obligations generally (§ 902). A state is responsible for a violation of international antipollution rules and standards, resulting from an act or omission by state officials or public vessels, or by ships, aircraft, platforms, or other structures at sea, or by natural or juridical persons, that are under the state's jurisdiction.

Interstate remedies may include claims for reparation for injury to the state or its political subdivisions, or injury to its nationals or inhabitants when they are not afforded reparation by domestic remedy in the offending state. See Subsection (2) and Comment *b.* The obligations of states in respect of the common environment are *erga omnes* and any state may pursue remedies for violations that inflict significant injury on that environment (for instance, to obtain termination of the wrongful conduct). See also Comment *c.*

b. Remedies for private injury. Under Subsection (2), when a natural or juridical person for whose acts a state is responsible under § 601 has caused injury to interests of a private person who is not the state's own national or resident, the state must provide to the injured person access to domestic remedies so that prompt and adequate compensation or preventive or injunctive relief may be obtained. See LOS Convention, Article 235. Where the injury results from a violation by a private ship or installation, the owner is presumably liable under domestic law, and the responsibility of the state is invoked only where adequate reparation is not obtained from the person responsible by domestic remedies. If complex patterns of ownership and agency make it difficult to determine who was legally liable under domestic law for the violation causing the injury, the state is responsible for ensuring that the injured person is compensated.

c. Enforcement by flag states. In addition to the remedies set forth in Comments *a* and *b,* if a ship has committed a violation of applicable international rules and standards, the flag state is obligated to investigate immediately and to institute appropriate proceedings, irrespective of the place of the violation or injury. See LOS Convention, Article 217. The state that is the victim of a violation by a ship (or, in case of pollution of the common environment, any state) may complain to the flag state and request that the guilty persons be punished and be enjoined from further pollution (see Articles 217(6) and 235); if dissatisfied with action taken by the flag state, it may invoke against the flag state the remedies available under international law. Subsection (1) and Comment *a.* In addition, if the flag state has repeatedly disregarded its obligations to enforce effectively the applicable international rules and standards in respect of violations committed by its ships, a port state where proceedings against a ship have been instituted under Subsection (3)(b) or (c) may continue such proceedings and impose penalties, regardless of a request of the flag state that the proceedings be transferred to it. See Comment *e;* LOS Convention, Article 228(1).

d. Enforcement by coastal states. The authority of the coastal state to bring proceedings against an offending foreign vessel (Subsection 3(a)) varies according to where the vessel is located and where the violation occurred. The coastal state has jurisdiction to prescribe, adjudicate, and enforce with respect to acts of pollution committed in its ports. The coastal state can also institute proceedings against a ship voluntarily in port, or against its crew, for a violation of its laws that occurred within its territorial sea or exclusive economic zone, provided that its laws were adopted in accordance with applicable international rules and standards. An offshore terminal is assimilated to a port for these purposes. LOS Convention, Article 220(1).

Where there are clear grounds for believing that a foreign ship, while passing through the territorial sea of the coastal state, violated laws and regulations of that state adopted in accordance with applicable international rules and standards, the coastal state may, subject to certain procedural safeguards (see Article 226), undertake physical inspection of the vessel in the territorial sea in order to ascertain the facts relating to the violation. Where evidence so warrants, the coastal state may institute proceedings against the ship, in accordance with its laws, and may detain the ship pending such proceedings. Article 220(2); see also Articles 19(2)(h), 21(1)(f), and 27.

When a violation of applicable international antipollution rules and standards is committed in the exclusive economic zone of the coastal state, and the ship is still in the zone or in the territorial sea of the coastal state, that state can take various steps, depending on the gravity of the violation. Where there are clear grounds for believing that a violation has occurred, the coastal state may require the ship to identify itself and its port of registry, indicate its last and its next port of call, and provide other relevant information needed to establish whether a violation has occurred. When there are clear grounds for believing that the violation resulted in "a substantial discharge causing or threatening significant pollution of the marine environment," and the ship either refuses to give information or the information supplied is manifestly at variance with the facts, the coastal state is entitled to proceed with a physical inspection. Only if there is "clear objective evidence" that the ship committed the violation and that the discharge is causing or threatens to cause "major damage to the coastline or related interests of the coastal state, or to any resources of its territorial sea or exclusive economic zone," is that state entitled to institute proceedings in accordance with its laws, and to detain the ship. Article 220(3)–(6).

To ensure that a ship is not unduly detained, appropriate procedures must be established, either through the competent international organization or by special agreement, for bonding or other appropriate financial security. If the ship makes the necessary arrangements, the coastal state is obligated to allow the vessel to proceed. Only monetary penalties may be imposed, unless the violation was committed in the territorial sea and the act of pollution was willful and serious, in which case the vessel may be confiscated and the person responsible may be tried and punished. Articles 220(7) and 230.

The principle of sovereign immunity protects warships, warplanes, and other government ships and aircraft on noncommercial service against coastal state proceedings, but the flag state is obligated to ensure that such ships or aircraft act in a manner consistent, as far as is reasonable and practicable, with applicable international rules and standards. Article 236.

e. Enforcement by port states. The jurisdiction of the port state with respect to a foreign ship voluntarily in its port or offshore terminal includes authority for the state to investigate and, where the evidence warrants, to institute proceedings with respect to any discharge from that ship that occurred on the high seas. The port state may also institute proceedings if an unlawful discharge outside its coastal waters caused or is likely to cause pollution within those waters. If the discharge occurred in the coastal waters of another state, the port state is obligated to institute proceedings, as far as practicable, when requested by that state. In addition, under Subsection (3)(c), the port state is obligated to conduct an investigation, as far as practicable, when so requested by the flag state, or by a state damaged or threatened by the discharge. LOS Convention, Article 218(1)–(4).

The records of the investigation carried out by a port state must be transmitted to the state that asked for the investigation if it so requests. The state in whose coastal waters the violation took place, but not the state where the injury occurred, is entitled to have the proceedings transferred to it. Once the records, the evidence, and the bonds (or other financial security) are transmitted to the requesting state, the proceedings in the port state must be suspended. Article 218(4).

The flag state is entitled to have penal proceedings against its ship in a foreign state suspended as soon as the flag state has itself instituted proceedings against the ship. However, the state that has instituted the proceedings need not suspend them (1) if the violation was committed in its territorial sea; (2) if the coastal state suffered major damage; or (3) if the flag state "has repeatedly disregarded its obligations to enforce effectively the applicable international rules and standards in respect of violations committed by its vessels." A proceeding that is suspended is to be terminated upon completion of proceedings in the flag state. Article 228(1). If the coastal state is dissatisfied with the action taken by the flag state after the case has been transferred, it may protest both to the flag state and to the competent international organization; and if the lack of enforcement recurs, the coastal state may refuse to suspend proceedings on a future occasion.

f. Liability for wrongful enforcement measures. If a state has taken measures against a foreign ship that were unlawful or exceeded those reasonably required in the light of available information, it is obligated to pay the flag state for any injury or loss attributable to such measures. It must provide for recourse in its courts for private actions in respect of such injury or loss. LOS Convention, Article 232.

1.25 EXPERTS GROUP ON ENVIRONMENTAL LAW OF THE WORLD COMMISSION ON ENVIRONMENT AND DEVELOPMENT, LEGAL PRINCIPLES FOR ENVIRONMENTAL PROTECTION AND SUSTAINABLE DEVELOPMENT. Adopted by the WCED Experts Group on Environmental Law, 4 August 1987. U.N.Doc. WCED/ 86/23/Add. 1 (1986)

USE OF TERMS

For the purposes of the present text:

(a) "use of a natural resource" means any human conduct, which, directly or indirectly, takes advantage of the benefits of a natural resource in the form of preservation, exploitation, consumption or otherwise of the natural resource, in so far as it does not result in an environmental interference as defined in Paragraph (f);

(b) "interference with the use of a natural resource" means any impairment, directly or indirectly, by man of the use of a natural resource in so far as it does not constitute an environmental interference as defined in Paragraph (f);

(c) "transboundary natural resource" means a natural resource which physically crosses the boundary between an area under the national jurisdiction of a State and an area under the national jurisdiction of another State or an area beyond the limits of national jurisdiction to the extent that its use in an area under the national jurisdiction of one State may affect its use in an area under the national jurisdiction of another State or in an area beyond the limits of national jurisdiction or vice versa;

(d) "transboundary interference with the use of a transboundary natural resource" means an interference with the use of a natural resource of which the physical origin is wholly or in part located outside the area under national jurisdiction of a State or outside the area beyond the limits of national jurisdiction in which the use takes place;

(e) "international natural resource" means a natural resource physically within an area beyond the limits of national jurisdiction to the extent that the origin and effects of any impairment of the use of the natural resource remain within the area beyond the limits of national jurisdiction;

(f) "environmental interference" means any impairment of human health, living resources, ecosystems, material property, amenities or other legitimate uses of a natural resource or the environment caused, directly or indirectly, by man through polluting substances, ionizing radiation, noise, explosions, vibration or other forms of energy, plants, animals, diseases, flooding, sand-drift or other similar means;

(g) "transboundary environmental interference" means an environmental interference of which the physical origin is wholly or in part located either outside the area under national jurisdiction of a State in which the effects caused by the interference occur, or outside the area beyond the limits of national jurisdiction in which the effects caused by the interference occur;

(h) "international environmental interference" means an environmental interference of which the physical origin and the effects are located within an area beyond the limits of national jurisdiction;

(i) "conservation" means the management of human use of a natural resource or the environment in such a manner that it may yield the greatest sustainable benefit to present generations while maintaining its potential to meet the needs and aspirations of future generations. It embraces preservation, maintenance, sustainable utilization, restoration and enhancement of a natural resource or the environment.

GENERAL PRINCIPLES CONCERNING NATURAL RESOURCES AND ENVIRONMENTAL INTERFERENCES

Article 1

Fundamental human right

All human beings have the fundamental right to an environment adequate for their health and well-being.

Article 2

Conservation for present and future generations

States shall ensure that the environment and natural resources are conserved and used for the benefit of present and future generations.

Article 3

Ecosystems, related ecological processes, biological diversity, and sustainability

States shall:

(a) maintain ecosystems and related ecological processes essential for the functioning of the biosphere in all its diversity, in particular those important for food production, health and other aspects of human survival and sustainable development;

(b) maintain maximum biological diversity by ensuring the survival and promoting the conservation in their natural habitat of all species of fauna and flora, in particular those which are rare, endemic or endangered;

(c) observe in the exploitation of living natural resources and ecosystems, the principle of optimum sustainable yield.

Article 4

Environmental standards and monitoring

States shall:

(a) establish specific environmental standards, in particular environmental quality standards, emission standards, technological standards and product standards aimed at preventing or abating interferences with natural resources or the environment;

(b) establish systems for the collection and dissemination of data and regular observation of natural resources and the environment in order to permit adequate planning of the use of natural resources and the environment, to permit early detection of interferences with natural resources or the environment and ensure timely intervention, and to facilitate the evaluation of conservation policies and methods.

Article 5
Assessment of planned activities

States planning to carry out or permit activities which may significantly affect a natural resource or the environment shall make or require an assessment of their effects before carrying out or permitting the planned activities.

Article 6
Timely information, access and due process

States shall inform all persons in a timely manner of activities which may significantly affect their use of a natural resource or their environment and shall grant the concerned persons access to and due process in administrative and judicial proceedings.

Article 7
Planning and implementation of development activities

1.   States shall ensure that the conservation of natural resources and the environment is treated as an integral part of the planning and implementation of development activities. Particular attention shall be paid to environmental problems arising in developing countries and to the need to incorporate environmental considerations in all development assistance programmes.

2.   States shall make available to other States, and especially to developing countries, upon their request and under agreed terms scientific and technical information and expertise, results of research programmes, training opportunities and specialized equipment and facilities which are needed by such other States to promote rational use of natural resources, and the environment or to prevent or abate interference with natural resources or the environment, in particular in cases of environmental emergencies.

Article 8
General obligation to co-operate

States shall co-operate in good faith with other States or through competent international organizations in the implementation of the provisions of the preceding articles.

PRINCIPLES SPECIFICALLY CONCERNING TRANSBOUNDARY NATURAL RESOURCES AND ENVIRONMENTAL INTERFERENCES

Article 9
Reasonable and equitable use of transboundary natural resources

States shall use transboundary natural resources in a reasonable and equitable manner.

Article 10
Prevention and abatement of a transboundary environmental interference

States shall, without prejudice to the principles laid down in Articles 11 and 12, prevent or abate any transboundary environmental interference or a significant risk thereof which causes substantial harm—i.e. harm which is not minor or insignificant.

Article 11
Liability for transboundary environmental interferences resulting from lawful activities

1.   If one or more activities create a significant risk of substantial harm as a result of a transboundary environmental interference, and if the overall technical and socio-economic cost or loss of benefits involved in preventing or reducing such risk far exceeds in the long run the advantage which such prevention or reduction would entail, the State which carried out or permitted the activities shall ensure that compensation is provided should substantial harm occur in an area under national jurisdiction of another State or in an area beyond the limits of national jurisdiction.

2.   A State shall ensure that compensation is provided for substantial harm caused by transboundary environmental interferences resulting from activities carried out or permitted by that State notwithstanding that the activities were not initially known to cause such interferences.

Article 12
Transboundary environmental interferences involving substantial harm far less than cost of prevention

1.   If a State is planning to carry out or permit an activity which will entail a transboundary environmental interference causing harm which is substantial but far less than the overall technical and socio-economic cost or loss of benefits involved in preventing or reducing such interference, such State shall enter into negotiations with the affected State on the equitable conditions, both technical and financial, under which the activity could be carried out.

2.   In the event of a failure to reach a solution on the basis of equitable principles within a period of 18 months after the beginning of the negotiations or within any other period of time agreed upon by the States concerned, the dispute shall at the request of any of the States concerned, and under the conditions set forth in Paragraphs 3 and 4 of Article 22, be submitted to conciliation or thereafter to arbitration or judicial settlement in order to reach a solution on the basis of equitable principles.

Article 13
Non-discrimination between domestic and transboundary environmental interferences

Without prejudice to the principles laid down in Articles 10, 11 and 12 when calling for a more stringent approach, States shall, when considering under their domestic policy or law the permissibility of an environmental interference or a significant risk thereof, take into account the detrimental effects which are or may be caused by the environmental interference without discrimination as to whether the effects would occur inside or outside the area under their national jurisdiction.

Article 14
General obligation to co-operate on transboundary environmental problems

1.   States shall co-operate in good faith with the other States concerned in maintaining or attaining for each of them a reasonable and equitable use of

a transboundary natural resource or in preventing or abating a transboundary environmental interference or significant risk thereof.

2.   The co-operation shall, as much as possible, be aimed at arriving at an optimal use of the transboundary natural resource or at maximizing the effectiveness of measures to prevent or abate a transboundary environmental interference.

Article 15
Exchange of information

States shall provide the other States concerned upon their request and in a timely manner with all relevant and reasonably available data concerning a transboundary natural resource, including the uses made of such a resource and transboundary interferences with them, or concerning a transboundary environmental interference.

Article 16
Prior notice of planned activities, environmental impact assessments

1.   States planning to carry out or permit activities which may entail a transboundary interference or a significant risk thereof with the reasonable and equitable use of a transboundary natural resource or which may entail a transboundary environmental interference or a significant risk thereof causing substantial harm in an area under national jurisdiction of another State or in an area beyond the limits of national jurisdiction shall give timely notice to the States concerned. In particular, they shall on their own initiative or upon request of the other States concerned provide such relevant information as will permit those other States to make an assessment of the probable effects of the planned activities.

2.   When a State has reasonable grounds for believing that planned activities may have the effects referred to in Paragraph 1, it shall make an assessment of those effects before carrying out or permitting the planned activities.

Article 17
Consultations

Consultations shall be held in good faith, upon request, at an early stage between, on the one hand, States whose reasonable and equitable use of a transboundary natural resource is or may be affected by a transboundary interference or whose environmental interests are or may be affected by a transboundary environmental interference and, on the other hand, States in whose area under national jurisdiction or under whose jurisdiction such a transboundary interference originates or may originate in connection with activities carried on or contemplated therein or thereunder.

Article 18
Co-operative arrangements for environmental assessment and protection

In order to maintain or attain a reasonable and equitable use of a transboundary natural resource or to prevent or abate transboundary environmental interferences or significant risks thereof the States concerned shall, inter alia:

(a) establish co-ordinated or unified systems for the collection and dissemination of data relating to the transboundary natural resource or for regular observation of transboundary environmental interferences;

(b) co-ordinate and, where appropriate, jointly undertake scientific or technical studies to that effect;

(c) establish by common agreement specific environmental standards, in particular environmental quality standards and emission standards;

(d) jointly establish or resort to an institutional mechanism or other appropriate arrangement.

Article 19
Emergency situations

1. In the case of an emergency situation or other change of circumstances suddenly giving rise to a transboundary interference or a significant risk thereof with the reasonable and equitable use of a transboundary natural resource or to a transboundary environmental interference or a significant risk thereof, causing substantial harm in an area under national jurisdiction of another State or in an area beyond the limits of national jurisdiction, the State in whose area under national jurisdiction or under whose jurisdiction the interference originates shall promptly warn the other States concerned, provide them with such pertinent information as will enable them to minimize the transboundary environmental interference, inform them of steps taken to abate the cause of the transboundary environmental interference, and co-operate with those States in order to prevent or minimize the harmful effects of such an emergency situation or other change of circumstances.

2. States shall develop contingency plans in order to prevent or minimize the harmful effects of an emergency situation or other change of circumstances referred to in Paragraph 1.

Article 20
Non-intergovernmental proceedings

States shall provide remedies for persons who have been or may be detrimentally affected by a transboundary interference with their use of a transboundary natural resource or by a transboundary environmental interference. In particular, States of origin shall grant those persons equal access as well as due process and equal treatment in the same administrative and judicial proceedings as are available to persons within their own jurisdiction who have been or may be similarly affected.

Article 21

1. A State is responsible under international law for a breach of an international obligation relating to the use of a natural resource or the prevention or abatement of an environmental interference.

2. In particular, it shall:

(a) cease the internationally wrongful act;

(b) as far as possible, re-establish the situation which would have existed if the internationally wrongful act had not taken place;

(c) provide compensation for the harm which results from the internationally wrongful act;

(d) where appropriate, give satisfaction for the internationally wrongful act.

PEACEFUL SETTLEMENT OF DISPUTES
Article 22

1. States, when they cannot avoid international disputes concerning the use of a natural resource or concerning an environmental interference in accordance with the preceding articles, shall settle such disputes by peaceful means in such a manner that international peace and security, and justice, are not endangered.

2. States shall accordingly seek a settlement of such disputes by negotiation, good offices, enquiry, mediation, conciliation, arbitration, judicial settlement, resort to appropriate bodies or arrangements, whether global or regional, or by any other peaceful means of their own choice.

3. In the event of a failure to reach a solution by another non-binding peaceful means within a period of 18 months after the dispute has arisen or within any other period of time agreed upon by the States concerned, the dispute shall be submitted to conciliation at the request of any of the States concerned, unless it is agreed to proceed with an already agreed peaceful means or to submit the dispute to another binding or non-binding means of peaceful settlement.

4. In the event that the conciliation envisaged in Paragraph 3, or any other non-binding means of peaceful settlement resorted to in lieu thereof, does not lead to a solution of the dispute, the dispute shall be submitted to arbitration or judicial settlement at the request of any of the States concerned, unless it is agreed to submit the dispute to another means of peaceful settlement.

1.26 DECLARATION OF THE HAGUE. Concluded at The Hague, 11 March 1989. U.N.Doc. A/44/340–E/1989/120 (Annex) (1989), 28 I.L.M. 1308 (1989)

The right to live is the right from which all other rights stem. Guaranteeing this right is the paramount duty of those in charge of all States throughout the world.

Today, the very conditions of life on our planet are threatened by the severe attacks to which the earth's atmosphere is subjected.

Authoritative scientific studies have shown the existence and scope of considerable dangers linked in particular to the warming of the atmosphere and to the deterioration of the ozone layer. The latter has already led to action, under the 1985 Vienna Convention for the Protection of the Ozone Layer and the 1987 Montreal Protocol, while the former is being addressed by the Intergovernmental Panel on Climatic Change established by UNEP and WMO, which has just begun its work. In addition the UN General Assembly adopted Resolution 43/53 on the Protection of the Global Climate in 1988, recognizing climate change as a common concern of mankind.

According to present scientific knowledge, the consequences of these phenomena may well jeopardize ecological systems as well as the most vital interests of mankind at large.

Because the problem is planet-wide in scope, solutions can only be devised on a global level. Because of the nature of the dangers involved, remedies to be sought involve not only the fundamental duty to preserve the ecosystem, but also the right to live in dignity in a viable global environment, and the consequent duty of the community of nations vis-à-vis present and future generations to do all that can be done to preserve the quality of the atmosphere.

Therefore we consider that, faced with a problem the solution to which has three salient features, namely that it is vital, urgent and global, we are in a situation that calls not only for implementation of existing principles but also for a new approach, through the development of new principles of international law including new and more effective decision-making and enforcement mechanisms.

What is needed here are regulatory, supportive and adjustment measures that take into account the participation and potential contribution of countries which have reached different levels of development. Most of the emissions that affect the atmosphere at present originate in the industrialized nations. And it is in these same nations that the room for change is greatest, and these nations are also those which have the greatest resources to deal with this problem effectively.

The international community and especially the industrialized nations have special obligations to assist developing countries which will be very negatively affected by changes in the atmosphere although the responsibility of many of them for the process may only be marginal today.

Financial institutions and development agencies, be they international or domestic, must coordinate their activities in order to promote sustainable development.

Without prejudice to the international obligations of each State, the signatories acknowledge and will promote the following principles:

(*a*) The principle of developing, within the framework of the United Nations, new institutional authority, either by strengthening existing institutions or by creating a new institution, which, in the context of the preservation of the earth's atmosphere, shall be responsible for combating any further global warming of the atmosphere and shall involve such decision-making procedures as may be effective even if, on occasion, unanimous agreement has not been achieved;

(*b*) The principle that this institutional authority undertake or commission the necessary studies, be granted appropriate information upon request, ensure the circulation and exchange of scientific and technological information—including facilitation of access to the technology needed—, develop instruments and define standards to enhance or guarantee the protection of the atmosphere and monitor compliance herewith;

(*c*) The principle of appropriate measures to promote the effective implementation of and compliance with the decisions of the new institutional authority, decisions which will be subject to control by the International Court of Justice;

(*d*) The principle that countries to which decisions taken to protect the atmosphere shall prove to be an abnormal or special burden, in view, inter alia, of the level of their development and actual responsibility for the deterioration of the atmosphere, shall receive fair and equitable assistance to compensate them for bearing such burden. To this end mechanisms will have to be developed;

(*e*) The negotiation of the necessary legal instruments to provide an effective and coherent foundation, institutionally and financially, for the aforementioned principles.

The Heads of State and Government or their representatives, who have expressed their endorsement of this Declaration by placing their signatures under it, stress their resolve to promote the principles thus defined by:

— furthering the development of their initiative within the United Nations and in close coordination and collaboration with existing agencies set up under the auspices of the United Nations;

— inviting all States of the world and the international organisations competent in this field to join in developing, taking into account studies by the IPCC, the framework conventions and other legal instruments necessary to establish institutional authority and to implement the other principles stated above to protect the atmosphere and to counter climate change, particularly global warming;

— urging all States of the world and the international organisations competent in this field to sign and ratify conventions relating to the protection of nature and the environment;

— calling upon all States of the world to endorse the present declaration.

The original of this Declaration, drawn up in French and English, will be transmitted to the Government of the Kingdom of the Netherlands, which will retain it in its archives. Each of the participating States will receive from the Government of the Kingdom of the Netherlands a true copy of this Declaration.

The Prime Minister of the Netherlands is requested to transmit the text of this Declaration, which is not eligible for registration under Article 102 of the Charter of the United Nations, to all members of the United Nations.

**1.27 THE LANGKAWI COMMONWEALTH HEADS OF GOVERNMENT DEC-
LARATION ON ENVIRONMENT. Adopted at Langkawi (Malaysia),
21 October 1989. 5 A.J.I.L. 589 (1990)**

We, the Heads of Government of the Commonwealth, representing a
quarter of the world's population and a broad cross-section of global interests,
are deeply concerned at the serious deterioration in the environment and the
threat this poses to the well-being of present and future generations. Any
delay in taking action to halt this progressive deterioration will result in
permanent and irreversible damage.

2. The current threat to the environment, which is a common concern of
all mankind, stems essentially from past neglect in managing the natural
environment and resources. The environment has been degraded by decades
of industrial and other forms of pollution, including unsafe disposal of toxic
wastes, the burning of fossil fuels, nuclear testing and non-sustainable practices in agriculture, fishery and forestry.

3. The main environment problems facing the world are the greenhouse
effect (which may lead to severe climatic changes that could induce floods,
droughts and rising sea levels), the depletion of the ozone layer, acid rain,
marine pollution, land degradation and the extinction of numerous animal
and plant species. Some developing countries also face distinct environmental problems arising from poverty and population pressure. In addition, some
islands and low-lying areas of other countries, are threatened by the prospect
of rising sea level.

4. Many environmental problems transcend national boundaries and
interests, necessitating a co-ordinated global effort. This is particularly true
in areas outside national jurisdiction, and where there is transboundary
pollution on land and in the oceans, atmosphere and outer space.

5. The need to protect the environment should be viewed in a balanced
perspective and due emphasis be accorded to promoting economic growth and
sustainable development, including eradication of poverty, meeting basic
needs, and enhancing the quality of life. The responsibility for ensuring a
better environment should be equitably shared and the ability of developing
countries to respond be taken into account.

6. To achieve sustainable development, economic growth is a compelling
necessity. Sustainable development implies the incorporation of environmental concerns into economic planning and policies. Environmental concerns
should not be used to introduce a new form of conditionality in aid and
development financing, nor as a pretext for creating unjustified barriers to
trade.

7. The success of global and national environmental programmes requires mutually reinforcing strategies and the participation and commitment
of all levels of society—government, individuals and organisations, industry
and the scientific community.

8. Recognising that our shared environment binds all countries to a
common future, we, the Heads of Government of the Commonwealth, resolved
to act collectively and individually, commit ourselves to the following programme of action:

— advance policies and programmes which help achieve sustainable development, including the development of new and better techniques in integrating the environmental dimension in economic decision-making;

— strengthen and support the development of international funding mechanisms and appropriate decision-making procedures to respond to environmental protection needs which will include assisting developing countries to obtain access to and transfer of needed environmental technologies and which should take account of proposals for an international environment fund/Planet Protection Fund;

— support the work of the UNEP/WMO Intergovernmental Panel on Climate Change (IPCC);

— call for the early conclusion of an international convention to protect and conserve the global climate and, in this context, applaud the efforts of member governments to advance the negotiation of a framework convention under UN auspices;

— support the findings and recommendations of the Commonwealth Expert Group's Report on Climate Change as a basis for achievable action to develop strategies for adapting to climate change and for reducing greenhouse gas emissions, as well as making an important contribution to the work of the IPCC;

— support measures to improve energy conservation and energy efficiency;

— promote the reduction and eventual phase-out of substances depleting the ozone layer;

— promote afforestation and agricultural practices in developed and developing countries to arrest the increase in atmospheric carbon dioxide and halt the deterioration of land and water resources;

— strengthen efforts by developing countries in sustainable forest management and their manufacture and export of higher value-added forest products and, in this regard, support the activities of the International Tropical Timber Organisation and the Food and Agriculture Organisation's Tropical Forestry Action Plan, as well as take note of the recommendations of the 13th Commonwealth Forestry Conference;

— support activities related to the conservation of biological diversity and genetic resources, including the conservation of significant areas of virgin forest and other protected natural habitats;

— support low-lying and island countries in their efforts to protect themselves and their vulnerable natural marine ecosystems from the effects of sea level rise;

— discourage and restrict non-sustainable fishing practices and seek to ban tangle net and pelagic drift net fishing;

— support efforts to prevent marine pollution including curbing ocean dumping of toxic wastes;

— strengthen international action to ensure the safe management and disposal of hazardous wastes and to reduce transboundary movements, particularly to prevent dumping in developing countries;

— participate in relevant international agreements relating to the environment and promote new and innovated instruments which will attract widespread support for protecting the global environment; and

— strengthen national, regional and international institutions responsible for environmental protection as well as the promotion of active programmes on environmental education to heighten public awareness and support.

9.   We, the Heads of Government of the Commonwealth, resolve to take immediate and positive actions on the basis of the above programme. In this regard, we pledge our full support for the convening of the 1992 UN Conference on Environment and Development.

10.   We call on the international community to join us in the endeavour.

1.28　AFRICAN, CARIBBEAN AND PACIFIC STATES—EUROPEAN ECONOMIC COMMUNITY CONVENTION (LOMÉ IV) (WITHOUT PROTOCOLS). Concluded at Lomé (Togo), 15 December 1989. Entered into force, 1 September 1991. 1990 E.C. 120, 29 I.L.M. 783 (1990): _Arts. 33–41 (Title I) and Annex VIII_

TITLE I

Environment

Article 33

In the framework of this Convention, the protection and the enhancement of the environment and natural resources, the halting of the deterioration of land and forests, the restoration of ecological balances, the preservation of natural resources and their rational exploitation are basic objectives that the ACP States concerned shall strive to achieve with Community support, with a view to bringing an immediate improvement in the living conditions of their populations and to safeguarding those of future generations.

Article 34

The ACP States and the Community recognize that the existence of some ACP States is under threat as a result of a rapid deterioration of the environment that hinders any development efforts, in particular those aimed at achieving the priority objectives of food self-sufficiency and food security.

For many ACP States, efforts to halt this deterioration of the environment and conserve natural resources are imperative and call for the preparation and implementation of coherent modes of development that have due regard for ecological balances.

Article 35

The dimension of the environmental problem and of the means to be deployed mean that operations will have to be carried out in the context of overall, long-term policies, drawn up and implemented by the ACP States at national, regional and international levels with international support.

To this end, the Parties agree to give priority in their activities to:

— a preventive approach aimed at avoiding harmful effects on the environment as a result of any programme or operation;

— a systematic approach that will ensure ecological viability at all stages, from identification to implementation;

— a trans-sectoral approach that takes into account not only the direct but also the indirect consequences of the operations undertaken.

Article 36

The protection of the environment and natural resources requires a comprehensive approach embracing the social and cultural dimensions.

In order to ensure that this specific dimension shall be taken into account, attention shall be given to incorporating suitable educational, training, information and research schemes in projects and programmes.

Article 37

Cooperation instruments appropriate to environmental needs shall be designed and implemented.

Where necessary, both qualitative and quantitative criteria may be used. Jointly approved check-lists shall be used to help estimate the environmental viability of proposed operations, whatever their scale. Environmental impact assessment will be carried out as appropriate in the case of large-scale projects and those posing a significant threat to the environment.

For the proper integration of environmental considerations, physical inventories, where possible translated into accounting terms, shall be drawn up.

The implementation of these instruments has to ensure that, should an adverse environmental impact be foreseen, the necessary corrective measures are formulated in the early stage of the preparation of the proposed project or programme so that it can go ahead in accordance with the planned timetable though improved in terms of environmental and natural resource protection.

Article 38

The Parties, desirous of bringing real protection and effective management to the environment and natural resources, consider that the areas of ACP–EEC cooperation covered in Part Two of this Convention shall be systematically examined and appraised in this light.

In this spirit the Community shall support efforts made by the ACP States at national, regional and international levels and also operations mounted by intergovernmental and nongovernmental organizations in furtherance of national and intergovernmental policies and priorities.

Article 39

1. The Contracting Parties undertake, for their part, to make every effort to ensure that international movements of hazardous waste and radioactive waste are generally controlled, and they emphasize the importance of efficient international cooperation in this area.

With this in view, the Community shall prohibit all direct or indirect export of such waste to the ACP States while at the same time the ACP States shall prohibit the direct or indirect import into their territory of such waste from the Community or from any other country, without prejudice to specific international undertakings to which the Contracting Parties have subscribed or may subscribe in the future in these two areas within the competent international fora.

These provisions do not prevent a Member State to which an ACP State has chosen to export waste for processing from returning the processed waste to the ACP State of origin.

The Contracting Parties shall expedite adoption of the necessary internal legislation and administrative regulations to implement this undertaking. At the request of one of the Parties, consultations may be held if delays are encountered. At the conclusion of such consultations each Party may take appropriate steps in the light of the situation.

2.   The Parties undertake to monitor strictly the implementation of the prohibition measures referred to in the second paragraph of paragraph 1. Should difficulties arise in this respect, consultations may be held subject to the same conditions as those provided for in the second paragraph of paragraph 1 and with the same effect.

3.   The term "hazardous waste" within the meaning of this Article shall cover categories of products listed in Annexes 1 and 2 to the Basle Convention on the Control of Transboundary Movements of Hazardous Wastes and their Disposal.

As regards radioactive waste, the applicable definitions and thresholds shall be those which will be laid down in the framework of the IAEA.   In the meantime, the said definitions and thresholds shall be those specified in the declaration in Annex VIII to this Convention.

* * *

Article 40

At the request of the ACP States, the Community shall provide available technical information on pesticides and other chemical products with a view to helping them develop or reinforce a suitable and safe use of these products. Where necessary and in accordance with the provisions for development finance cooperation, technical assistance can be given in order to ensure conditions of safety at all stages, from production to disposal of such products.

Article 41

The Parties recognize the value of exchanging views, using existing consultation mechanisms under this Convention, on major ecological hazards, whether on a planetary scale (such as the greenhouse effect, the deterioration of the ozone layer, tropical forests, etc.), or of a more specific scope resulting from the application of industrial technology.   Such consultations may be requested by either Party, insofar as these hazards may in practice affect the Contracting Parties, and will be aimed at assessing the scope for joint action to be undertaken within the terms of this Convention.   If necessary, the consultations will also provide for an exchange of views prior to discussions conducted on these subjects in the appropriate international fora.

* * *

ANNEX VIII
Joint declaration on Article 39 on movements of hazardous waste or radioactive waste

Keenly aware of the specific risks attaching to radioactive waste, the Contracting Parties will refrain from any practice of discharging such waste which would encroach upon the sovereignty of States or threaten the environment or public health in other countries.   They attach the greatest importance to developing international cooperation to protect the environment and public health against such risks.   They accordingly affirm their determination to play an active part in the work being done in the IAEA to produce an internationally approved code of good practice.

Until such time as a more precise definition is formulated in that framework, the term "radioactive waste" will be taken to mean any material for which no further use is envisaged and which contains or is contaminated by radionuclides of which the levels of radioactivity or the concentrations exceed the limits which the Community has set itself for protecting its own population in Article 4(a) and (b) of Directive 80/836 EURATOM, as last amended by Directive 84/467/EURATOM. As regards levels or radioactivity, these limits range from 5×10^3 becquerel for nuclides of very high radiotoxicity to 5×10^6 becquerel for those of low radiotoxicity. As regards concentrations, these limits are 100 $Bq.g^{-1}$ and 500 $Bq.g^{-1}$ for solid natural radioactive substances.

1.29 CONVENTION ON ENVIRONMENTAL IMPACT ASSESSMENT IN A TRANSBOUNDARY CONTEXT. Adopted at Espoo (Finland), 25 February 1991. Not in force as of 31 December 1992. 30 I.L.M. 800 (1991)

The Parties to this Convention,

Aware of the interrelationship between economic activities and their environmental consequences,

Affirming the need to ensure environmentally sound and sustainable development,

Determined to enhance international co-operation in assessing environmental impact, in particular in a transboundary context,

Mindful of the need and importance to develop anticipatory policies and of preventing, mitigating and monitoring significant adverse environmental impact in general and more specifically in a transboundary context,

Recalling the relevant provisions of the Charter of the United Nations, the Declaration of the Stockholm Conference on the Human Environment, the Final Act of the Conference on Security and Co-operation in Europe (CSCE) and the Concluding Documents of the Madrid and Vienna Meetings of Representatives of the Participating States of the CSCE,

Commending the ongoing activities of States to ensure that, through their national legal and administrative provisions and their national policies, environmental impact assessment is carried out,

Conscious of the need to give explicit consideration to environmental factors at an early stage in the decision-making process by applying environmental impact assessment, at all appropriate administrative levels, as a necessary tool to improve the quality of information presented to decision makers so that environmentally sound decisions can be made paying careful attention to minimizing significant adverse impact, particularly in a transboundary context,

Mindful of the efforts of international organizations to promote the use of environmental impact assessment both at the national and international levels, and taking into account work on environmental impact assessment carried out under the auspices of the United Nations Economic Commission for Europe, in particular results achieved by the Seminar on Environmental Impact Assessment (September 1987, Warsaw, Poland) as well as noting the Goals and Principles on environmental impact assessment adopted by the Governing Council of the United Nations Environment Programme, and the Ministerial Declaration on Sustainable Development (May 1990, Bergen, Norway),

Have agreed as follows:

Article 1

Definitions

For the purposes of this Convention;

(i) "Parties" means, unless the text otherwise indicates, the Contracting Parties to this Convention;

(ii) "Party of origin" means the Contracting Party or Parties to this Convention under whose jurisdiction a proposed activity is envisaged to take place;

(iii) "Affected Party" means the Contracting Party or Parties to this Convention likely to be affected by the transboundary impact of a proposed activity;

(iv) "Concerned Parties" means the Party of origin and the affected Party of an environmental impact assessment pursuant to this Convention;

(v) "Proposed activity" means any activity or any major change to an activity subject to a decision of a competent authority in accordance with an applicable national procedure;

(vi) "Environmental impact assessment" means a national procedure for evaluating the likely impact of a proposed activity on the environment;

(vii) "Impact" means any effect caused by a proposed activity on the environment including human health and safety, flora, fauna, soil, air, water, climate, landscape and historical monuments or other physical structures or the interaction among these factors; it also includes effects on cultural heritage or socio-economic conditions resulting from alterations to those factors;

(viii) "Transboundary impact" means any impact, not exclusively of a global nature, within an area under the jurisdiction of a Party caused by a proposed activity the physical origin of which is situated wholly or in part within the area under the jurisdiction of another Party;

* * *

(ix) "Competent authority" means the national authority or authorities designated by a Party as responsible for performing the tasks covered by this Convention and/or the authority or authorities entrusted by a Party with decision-making powers regarding a proposed activity;

(x) "The Public" means one or more natural or legal persons.

Article 2

General Provisions

1. The Parties shall, either individually or jointly, take all appropriate and effective measures to prevent, reduce and control significant adverse transboundary environmental impact from proposed activities.

2. Each Party shall take the necessary legal, administrative or other measures to implement the provisions of this Convention, including, with respect to proposed activities listed in Appendix I that are likely to cause significant adverse transboundary impact, the establishment of an environmental impact assessment procedure that permits public participation and preparation of the environmental impact assessment documentation described in Appendix II.

3. The Party of origin shall ensure that in accordance with the provisions of this Convention an environmental impact assessment is undertaken

prior to a decision to authorize or undertake a proposed activity listed in Appendix I that is likely to cause a significant adverse transboundary impact.

4. The Party of origin shall, consistent with the provisions of this Convention, ensure that affected Parties are notified of a proposed activity listed in Appendix I that is likely to cause a significant adverse transboundary impact.

5. Concerned Parties shall, at the initiative of any such Party, enter into discussions on whether one or more proposed activities not listed in Appendix I is or are likely to cause a significant adverse transboundary impact and thus should be treated as if it or they were so listed. Where those Parties so agree, the activity or activities shall be thus treated. General guidance for identifying criteria to determine significant adverse impact is set forth in Appendix III.

6. The Party of origin shall provide, in accordance with the provisions of this Convention, an opportunity to the public in the areas likely to be affected to participate in relevant environmental impact assessment procedures regarding proposed activities and shall ensure that the opportunity provided to the public of the affected Party is equivalent to that provided to the public of the Party of origin.

7. Environmental impact assessments as required by this Convention shall, as a minimum requirement, be undertaken at the project level of the proposed activity. To the extent appropriate, the Parties shall endeavour to apply the principles of environmental impact assessment to policies, plans and programmes.

8. The provisions of this Convention shall not affect the right of Parties to implement national laws, regulations, administrative provisions or accepted legal practices protecting information the supply of which would be prejudicial to industrial and commercial secrecy or national security.

9. The provisions of this Convention shall not affect the right of particular Parties to implement, by bilateral or multilateral agreement where appropriate, more stringent measures than those of this Convention.

10. The provisions of this Convention shall not prejudice any obligations of the Parties under international law with regard to activities having or likely to have a transboundary impact.

Article 3

Notification

1. For a proposed activity listed in Appendix I that is likely to cause a significant adverse transboundary impact, the Party of origin shall, for the purposes of ensuring adequate and effective consultations under Article 5, notify any Party which it considers may be an affected Party as early as possible and no later than when informing its own public about that proposed activity.

2. This notification shall contain, *inter alia:*

(a) Information on the proposed activity, including any available information on its possible transboundary impact;

(b) The nature of the possible decision; and

(c) An indication of a reasonable time within which a response under paragraph 3 of this Article is required, taking into account the nature of the proposed activity;

and may include the information set out in paragraph 5 of this Article.

3. The affected Party shall respond to the Party of origin within the time specified in the notification, acknowledging receipt of the notification, and shall indicate whether it intends to participate in the environmental impact assessment procedure.

4. If the affected Party indicates that it does not intend to participate in the environmental impact assessment procedure, or if it does not respond within the time specified in the notification, the provisions in paragraphs 5, 6, 7 and 8 of this Article and in Articles 4 to 7 will not apply. In such circumstances the right of a Party of origin to determine whether to carry out an environmental impact assessment on the basis of its national law and practice is not prejudiced.

5. Upon receipt of a response from the affected Party indicating its desire to participate in the environmental impact assessment procedure, the Party of origin shall, if it has not already done so, provide to the affected Party:

(a) Relevant information regarding the environmental impact assessment procedure, including an indication of the time schedule for transmittal of comments; and

(b) Relevant information on the proposed activity and its possible significant adverse transboundary impact.

6. An affected Party shall, at the request of the Party of origin, provide the latter with reasonably obtainable information relating to the potentially affected environment under the jurisdiction of the affected Party, where such information is necessary for the preparation of the environmental impact assessment documentation. The information shall be furnished promptly and, as appropriate, through a joint body where one exists.

7. When a Party considers that it would be affected by a significant adverse transboundary impact of a proposed activity listed in Appendix I, and when no notification has taken place in accordance with paragraph 1 of this Article, the concerned Parties shall, at the request of the affected Party, exchange sufficient information for the purposes of holding discussions on whether there is likely to be a significant adverse transboundary impact. If those Parties agree that there is likely to be a significant adverse transboundary impact, the provisions of this Convention shall apply accordingly. If those Parties cannot agree whether there is likely to be a significant adverse transboundary impact, any such Party may submit that question to an inquiry commission in accordance with the provisions of Appendix IV to advise on the likelihood of significant adverse transboundary impact, unless they agree on another method of settling this question.

8. The concerned Parties shall ensure that the public of the affected Party in the areas likely to be affected be informed of, and be provided with possibilities for making comments or objections on the proposed activity, and for the transmittal of these comments or objections to the competent authori-

ty of the Party of origin, either directly to this authority or, where appropriate, through the Party of origin.

Article 4

Preparation of the Environmental Impact Assessment Documentation

1. The environmental impact assessment documentation to be submitted to the competent authority of the Party of origin shall contain, at a minimum, the information described in Appendix II.

2. The Party of origin shall furnish the affected Party, as appropriate through a joint body where one exists, with the environmental impact assessment documentation. The concerned Parties shall arrange for distribution of the documentation to the authorities and the public of the affected Party in the areas likely to be affected and for the submission of comments to the competent authority of the Party of origin, either directly to this authority or, where appropriate, through the Party of origin within a reasonable time before the final decision is taken on the proposed activity.

Article 5

Consultations on the Basis of the Environmental Impact Assessment Documentation

The Party of origin shall, after completion of the environmental impact assessment documentation, without undue delay enter into consultations with the affected Party concerning, *inter alia,* the potential transboundary impact of the proposed activity and measures to reduce or eliminate its impact. Consultations may relate to:

(a) Possible alternatives to the proposed activity, including the no-action alternative and possible measures to mitigate significant adverse transboundary impact and to monitor the effects of such measures at the expense of the Party of origin;

(b) Other forms of possible mutual assistance in reducing any significant adverse transboundary impact of the proposed activity; and

(c) Any other appropriate matters relating to the proposed activity.

The Parties shall agree, at the commencement of such consultations, on a reasonable time-frame for the duration of the consultation period. Any such consultations may be conducted through an appropriate joint body, where one exists.

Article 6

Final Decision

1. The Parties shall ensure that, in the final decision on the proposed activity, due account is taken of the outcome of the environmental impact assessment, including the environmental impact assessment documentation, as well as the comments thereon received pursuant to Article 3, paragraph 8 and Article 4, paragraph 2, and the outcome of the consultations as referred to in Article 5.

2. The Party of origin shall provide to the affected Party the final decision on the proposed activity along with the reasons and considerations on which it was based.

3.   If additional information on the significant transboundary impact of a proposed activity, which was not available at the time a decision was made with respect to that activity and which could have materially affected the decision, becomes available to a concerned Party before work on that activity commences, that Party shall immediately inform the other concerned Party or Parties.   If one of the concerned Parties so requests, consultations shall be held as to whether the decision needs to be revised.

Article 7

Post–Project Analysis

1.   The concerned Parties, at the request of any such Party, shall determine whether, and if so to what extent, a post-project analysis shall be carried out, taking into account the likely significant adverse transboundary impact of the activity for which an environmental impact assessment has been undertaken pursuant to this Convention.   Any post-project analysis undertaken shall include, in particular, the surveillance of the activity and the determination of any adverse transboundary impact.   Such surveillance and determination may be undertaken with a view to achieving the objectives listed in Appendix V.

2.   When, as a result of post-project analysis, the Party of origin or the affected Party has reasonable grounds for concluding that there is a significant adverse transboundary impact or factors have been discovered which may result in such an impact, it shall immediately inform the other Party. The concerned Parties shall then consult on necessary measures to reduce or eliminate the impact.

Article 8

Bilateral and Multilateral Co-operation

The Parties may continue existing or enter into new bilateral or multilateral agreements or other arrangements in order to implement their obligations under this Convention.   Such agreements or other arrangements may be based on the elements listed in Appendix VI.

Article 9

Research Programmes

The Parties shall give special consideration to the setting up, or intensification of specific research programmes aimed at:

(a) Improving existing qualitative and quantitative methods for assessing the impacts of proposed activities;

(b) Achieving a better understanding of cause-effect relationships and their role in integrated environmental management;

(c) Analysing and monitoring the efficient implementation of decisions on proposed activities with the intention of minimizing or preventing impacts;

(d) Developing methods to stimulate creative approaches in the search for environmentally sound alternatives to proposed activities, production and consumption patterns;

(e) Developing methodologies for the application of the principles of environmental impact assessment at the macro-economic level.

The results of the programmes listed above shall be exchanged by the Parties.

Article 10

Status of the Appendices

The Appendices attached to this Convention form an integral part of the Convention.

Article 11

Meeting of Parties

1. The Parties shall meet, so far as possible, in connection with the annual sessions of the Senior Advisers to ECE Governments on Environmental and Water Problems. The first meeting of the Parties shall be convened not later than one year after the date of the entry into force of this Convention. Thereafter, meetings of the Parties shall be held at such other times as may be deemed necessary by a meeting of the Parties, or at the written request of any Party, provided that, within six months of the request being communicated to them by the secretariat, it is supported by at least one third of the Parties.

2. The Parties shall keep under continuous review the implementation of this Convention, and, with this purpose in mind, shall:

(a) Review the policies and methodological approaches to environmental impact assessment by the Parties with a view to further improving environmental impact assessment procedures in a transboundary context;

(b) Exchange information regarding experience gained in concluding and implementing bilateral and multilateral agreements or other arrangements regarding the use of environmental impact assessment in a transboundary context to which one or more of the Parties are party;

(c) Seek, where appropriate, the services of competent international bodies and scientific committees in methodological and technical aspects pertinent to the achievement of the purposes of this Convention;

(d) At their first meeting, consider and by consensus adopt rules of procedure for their meetings;

(e) Consider and, where necessary, adopt proposals for amendments to this Convention;

(f) Consider and undertake any additional action that may be required for the achievement of the purposes of this Convention.

Article 12

Right to vote

1. Each Party to this Convention shall have one vote.

2. Except as provided for in paragraph 1 of this Article, regional economic integration organizations, in matters within their competence, shall exercise their right to vote with a number of votes equal to the number of their member States which are Parties to this Convention. Such organizations shall not exercise their right to vote if their member States exercise theirs, and vice versa.

Article 13

Secretariat

The Executive Secretary of the Economic Commission for Europe shall carry out the following secretariat functions:

(a) The convening and preparing of meetings of the Parties;

(b) The transmission of reports and other information received in accordance with the provisions of this Convention to the Parties; and

(c) The performance of other functions as may be provided for in this Convention or as may be determined by the Parties.

Article 14

Amendments to the Convention

1. Any Party may propose amendments to this Convention.

2. Proposed amendments shall be submitted in writing to the secretariat, which shall communicate them to all Parties. The proposed amendments shall be discussed at the next meeting of the Parties, provided these proposals have been circulated by the secretariat to the Parties at least ninety days in advance.

3. The Parties shall make every effort to reach agreement on any proposed amendment to this Convention by consensus. If all efforts at consensus have been exhausted, and no agreement reached, the amendment shall as a last resort be adopted by a three-fourths majority vote of the Parties present and voting at the meeting.

4. Amendments to this Convention adopted in accordance with paragraph 3 of this Article shall be submitted by the Depositary to all Parties for ratification, approval or acceptance. They shall enter into force for Parties having ratified, approved or accepted them on the ninetieth day after the receipt by the Depositary of notification of their ratification, approval or acceptance by at least three-fourths of these Parties. Thereafter they shall enter into force for any other Party on the ninetieth day after that Party deposits its instrument of ratification, approval or acceptance of the amendments.

5. For the purpose of this Article, "Parties present and voting" means Parties present and casting an affirmative or negative vote.

6. The voting procedure set forth in paragraph 3 of this Article is not intended to constitute a precedent for future agreements negotiated within the Economic Commission for Europe.

Article 15

Settlement of Disputes

1. If a dispute arises between two or more Parties about the interpretation or application of this Convention, they shall seek a solution by negotiation or by any other method of dispute settlement acceptable to the parties to the dispute.

2. When signing, ratifying, accepting, approving or acceding to this Convention, or at any time thereafter, a Party may declare in writing to the Depositary that for a dispute not resolved in accordance with paragraph 1 of

this Article, it accepts one or both of the following means of dispute settlement as compulsory in relation to any Party accepting the same obligation:

(a) Submission of the dispute to the International Court of Justice;

(b) Arbitration in accordance with the procedure set out in Appendix VII.

3. If the parties to the dispute have accepted both means of dispute settlement referred to in paragraph 2 of this Article, the dispute may be submitted only to the International Court of Justice, unless the parties agree otherwise.

Article 16

Signature

This Convention shall be open for signature at Espoo (Finland) from 25 February to 1 March 1991 and thereafter at United Nations Headquarters in New York until 2 September 1991 by State members of the Economic Commission for Europe as well as States having consultative status with the Economic Commission for Europe pursuant to paragraph 8 of the Economic and Social Council resolution 36(IV) of 28 March 1947, and by regional economic integration organizations constituted by sovereign States members of the Economic Commission for Europe to which their member States have transferred competence in respect of matters governed by this Convention, including the competence to enter into treaties in respect of these matters.

Article 17

Ratification, Acceptance, Approval and Accession

1. This Convention shall be subject to ratification, acceptance or approval by signatory States and regional economic integration organizations.

2. This Convention shall be open for accession as from 3 September 1991 by the States and organizations referred to in Article 16.

3. The instruments of ratification, acceptance, approval or accession shall be deposited with the Secretary–General of the United Nations, who shall perform the functions of Depositary.

4. Any organization referred to in Article 16 which becomes a Party to this Convention without any of its member States being a Party shall be bound by all the obligations under this Convention. In the case of such organizations, one or more of whose member States is a Party to this Convention, the organization and its member States shall decide on their respective responsibilities for the performance of their obligations under this Convention. In such cases, the organization and the member States shall not be entitled to exercise rights under this Convention concurrently.

5. In their instruments of ratification, acceptance, approval or accession, the regional economic integration organizations referred to in Article 16 shall declare the extent of their competence with respect to the matters governed by this Convention. These organizations shall also inform the Depositary of any relevant modification to the extent of their competence.

Article 18

Entry into Force

1.   This Convention shall enter into force on the ninetieth day after the date of deposit of the sixteenth instrument of ratification, acceptance, approval or accession.

2.   For the purposes of paragraph 1 of this Article, any instrument deposited by a regional economic integration organization shall not be counted as additional to those deposited by States members of such an organization.

3.   For each State or organization referred to in Article 16 which ratifies, accepts or approves this Convention or accedes thereto after the deposit of the sixteenth instrument of ratification, acceptance, approval or accession, this Convention shall enter into force on the ninetieth day after the date of deposit by such State or organization of its instrument of ratification, acceptance, approval or accession.

Article 19

Withdrawal

At any time after four years from the date on which this Convention has come into force with respect to a Party, that Party may withdraw from this Convention by giving written notification to the Depositary.   Any such withdrawal shall take effect on the ninetieth day after the date of its receipt by the Depositary.   Any such withdrawal shall not affect the application of Articles 3 to 6 of this Convention to a proposed activity in respect of which a notification has been made pursuant to Article 3, paragraph 1, or a request has been made pursuant to Article 3, paragraph 7, before such withdrawal took effect.

Article 20

Authentic Texts

The original of this Convention, of which the English, French and Russian texts are equally authentic, shall be deposited with the Secretary-General of the United Nations.

1.30 RIO DECLARATION ON ENVIRONMENT AND DEVELOPMENT. Adopted by the U.N. Conference on Environment and Development (UNCED) at Rio de Janeiro, 13 June 1992. U.N.Doc. A/CONF.151/26 (vol. I) (1992), 31 I.L.M. 874 (1992)

The United Nations Conference on Environment and Development,

Having met at Rio de Janeiro from 3 to 14 June 1992,

Reaffirming the Declaration of the United Nations Conference on the Human Environment, adopted at Stockholm on 16 June 1972, and seeking to build upon it,

With the goal of establishing a new and equitable global partnership through the creation of new levels of cooperation among States, key sectors of societies and people,

Working towards international agreements which respect the interests of all and protect the integrity of the global environmental and developmental system,

Recognizing the integral and interdependent nature of the Earth, our home,

Proclaims that:

Principle 1

Human beings are at the centre of concerns for sustainable development. They are entitled to a healthy and productive life in harmony with nature.

Principle 2

States have, in accordance with the Charter of the United Nations and the principles of international law, the sovereign right to exploit their own resources pursuant to their own environmental and developmental policies, and the responsibility to ensure that activities within their jurisdiction or control do not cause damage to the environment of other States or of areas beyond the limits of national jurisdiction.

Principle 3

The right to development must be fulfilled so as to equitably meet developmental and environmental needs of present and future generations.

Principle 4

In order to achieve sustainable development, environmental protection shall constitute an integral part of the development process and cannot be considered in isolation from it.

Principle 5

All States and all people shall cooperate in the essential task of eradicating poverty as an indispensable requirement for sustainable development, in order to decrease the disparities in standards of living and better meet the needs of the majority of the people of the world.

Principle 6

The special situation and needs of developing countries, particularly the least developed and those most environmentally vulnerable, shall be given special priority. International actions in the field of environment and development should also address the interests and needs of all countries.

Principle 7

States shall cooperate in a spirit of global partnership to conserve, protect and restore the health and integrity of the Earth's ecosystem. In view of the different contributions to global environmental degradation, States have common but differentiated responsibilities. The developed countries acknowledge the responsibility that they bear in the international pursuit of sustainable development in view of the pressures their societies place on the global environment and of the technologies and financial resources they command.

Principle 8

To achieve sustainable development and a higher quality of life for all people, States should reduce and eliminate unsustainable patterns of production and consumption and promote appropriate demographic policies.

Principle 9

States should cooperate to strengthen endogenous capacity-building for sustainable development by improving scientific understanding through exchanges of scientific and technological knowledge, and by enhancing the development, adaptation, diffusion and transfer of technologies, including new and innovative technologies.

Principle 10

Environmental issues are best handled with the participation of all concerned citizens, at the relevant level. At the national level, each individual shall have appropriate access to information concerning the environment that is held by public authorities, including information on hazardous materials and activities in their communities, and the opportunity to participate in decision-making processes. States shall facilitate and encourage public awareness and participation by making information widely available. Effective access to judicial and administrative proceedings, including redress and remedy, shall be provided.

Principle 11

States shall enact effective environmental legislation. Environmental standards, management objectives and priorities should reflect the environmental and developmental context to which they apply. Standards applied by some countries may be inappropriate and of unwarranted economic and social cost to other countries, in particular developing countries.

Principle 12

States should cooperate to promote a supportive and open international economic system that would lead to economic growth and sustainable development in all countries, to better address the problems of environmental degradation. Trade policy measures for environmental purposes should not constitute a means of arbitrary or unjustifiable discrimination or a disguised restriction on international trade. Unilateral actions to deal with environmental challenges outside the jurisdiction of the importing country should be avoided. Environmental measures addressing transboundary or global environmental problems should, as far as possible, be based on an international consensus.

Principle 13

States shall develop national law regarding liability and compensation for the victims of pollution and other environmental damage. States shall also cooperate in an expeditious and more determined manner to develop further international law regarding liability and compensation for adverse effects of environmental damage caused by activities within their jurisdiction or control to areas beyond their jurisdiction.

Principle 14

States should effectively cooperate to discourage or prevent the relocation and transfer to other States of any activities and substances that cause severe environmental degradation or are found to be harmful to human health.

Principle 15

In order to protect the environment, the precautionary approach shall be widely applied by States according to their capabilities. Where there are threats of serious or irreversible damage, lack of full scientific certainty shall not be used as a reason for postponing cost-effective measures to prevent environmental degradation.

Principle 16

National authorities should endeavor to promote the internalization of environmental costs and the use of economic instruments, taking into account the approach that the polluter should, in principle, bear the cost of pollution, with due regard to the public interest and without distorting international trade and investment.

Principle 17

Environmental impact assessment, as a national instrument, shall be undertaken for proposed activities that are likely to have a significant adverse impact on the environment and are subject to a decision of a competent national authority.

Principle 18

States shall immediately notify other States of any natural disasters or other emergencies that are likely to produce sudden harmful effects on the environment of those States. Every effort shall be made by the international community to help States so afflicted.

Principle 19

States shall provide prior and timely notification and relevant information to potentially affected States on activities that may have a significant adverse transboundary environmental effect and shall consult with those States at an early stage and in good faith.

Principle 20

Women have a vital role in environmental management and development. Their full participation is therefore essential to achieve sustainable development.

Principle 21

The creativity, ideals and courage of the youth of the world should be mobilized to forge a global partnership in order to achieve sustainable development and ensure a better future for all.

Principle 22

Indigenous people and their communities and other local communities have a vital role in environmental management and development because of their knowledge and traditional practices. States should recognize and duly support their identity, culture and interests and enable their effective participation in the achievement of sustainable development.

Principle 23

The environment and natural resources of people under oppression, domination and occupation shall be protected.

Principle 24

Warfare is inherently destructive of sustainable development. States shall therefore respect international law providing protection for the environment in times of armed conflict and cooperate in its further development, as necessary.

Principle 25

Peace, development and environmental protection are interdependent and indivisible.

Principle 26

States shall resolve all their environmental disputes peacefully and by appropriate means in accordance with the Charter of the United Nations.

Principle 27

States and people shall cooperate in good faith and in a spirit of partnership in the fulfilment of the principles embodied in this Declaration and in the further development of international law in the field of sustainable development.

1.31 AGENDA 21. Adopted by the U.N. Conference on Environment and Development (UNCED) at Rio de Janeiro, 13 June 1992. U.N. Doc. A/CONF. 151/26 (vols. I, II, & III) (1992): *Table of Contents & Chs. 5, 15, 17, 20, 33*

Agenda 21 was adopted by the U.N. Conference on Environment and Development (UNCED) at Rio de Janeiro, 13 June 1992. The complete text is too lengthy for publication in this volume. The following table of contents provides a summary of its provisions. The full text may be found in the above-cited source.

* * *

Chapter 5
DEMOGRAPHIC DYNAMICS AND SUSTAINABILITY

5.1. This chapter contains the following programme areas:

(a) Developing and disseminating knowledge concerning the links between demographic trends and factors and sustainable development;

(b) Formulating integrated national policies for environment and development, taking into account demographic trends and factors;

(c) Implementing integrated, environment and development programmes at the local level, taking into account demographic trends and factors.

PROGRAMME AREAS

A. *Developing and disseminating knowledge concerning the links between demographic trends and factors and sustainable development*

Basis for action

5.2. Demographic trends and factors and sustainable development have a synergistic relationship.

5.3. The growth of world population and production combined with unsustainable consumption patterns places increasingly severe stress on the life-supporting capacities of our planet. These interactive processes affect the use of land, water, air, energy and other resources. Rapidly growing cities, unless well-managed, face major environmental problems. The increase in both the number and size of cities calls for greater attention to issues of local government and municipal management. The human dimensions are key elements to consider in this intricate set of relationships and they should be adequately taken into consideration in comprehensive policies for sustainable development. Such policies should address the linkages of demographic trends and factors, resource use, appropriate technology dissemination, and development. Population policy should also recognize the role played by human beings in environmental and development concerns. There is a need to increase awareness of this issue among decision makers at all levels and to provide both better information on which to base national and international policies and a framework against which to interpret this information.

5.4. There is a need to develop strategies to mitigate both the adverse impact on the environment of human activities and the adverse impact of environmental change on human populations. The world's population is expected to exceed 8 billion by the year 2020. Sixty per cent of the world's population already live in coastal areas, while 65 per cent of cities with populations above 2.5 million are located along the world coasts; several of them are already at or below the present sea level.

Objectives

5.5. The following objectives should be achieved as soon as practicable:

(a) To incorporate demographic trends and factors in the global analysis of environment and development issues;

(b) To develop a better understanding of the relationships among demographic dynamics, technology, cultural behaviour, natural resources and life support systems;

(c) To assess human vulnerability in ecologically sensitive areas and centres of population to determine the priorities for action at all levels, taking full account of community defined needs.

Activities

Research on the interaction between demographic trends and factors and sustainable development

5.6. Relevant international, regional and national institutions should consider undertaking the following activities:

(a) Identifying the interactions between demographic processes, natural resources and life support systems, bearing in mind regional and subregional variations deriving from, *inter alia*, different levels of development;

(b) Integrating demographic trends and factors into the ongoing study of environmental change, using the expertise of international, regional and national research networks and of local communities, first, to study the human dimensions of environmental change and, second, to identify vulnerable areas;

(c) Identifying priority areas for action and developing strategies and programmes to mitigate the adverse impact of environmental change on human populations, and vice versa.

Means of implementation

(a) *Financing and cost evaluation*

5.7. The Conference secretariat has estimated the average total annual cost (1993–2000) of implementing the activities of this programme to be about $10 million from the international community on grant or concessional terms. These are indicative and order-of-magnitude estimates only and have not been reviewed by Governments. Actual costs and financial terms, including any that are non-concessional, will depend upon, *inter alia,* the specific strategies and programmes Governments decide upon for implementation.

(b) *Strengthening research programmes that integrate population, environ- ment and development*

5.8. In order to integrate demographic analysis into a broader social science perspective on environment and development, interdisciplinary re- search should be increased. International institutions and networks of ex- perts should enhance their scientific capacity, taking full account of communi- ty experience and knowledge, and should disseminate the experience gained in multidisciplinary approaches and in linking theory to action.

5.9. Better modelling capabilities should be developed, identifying the range of possible outcomes of current human activities, especially the interre- lated impact of demographic trends and factors, per capita resource use and wealth distribution, as well as the major migration flows that may be expected with increasing climatic events and cumulative environmental change that may destroy people's local livelihoods.

(c) *Developing information and public awareness*

5.10. Socio-demographic information should be developed in a suitable format for interfacing with physical, biological and socio-economic data. Compatible spatial and temporal scales, cross-country and time-series infor- mation, as well as global behavioural indicators should be developed, learning from local communities' perceptions and attitudes.

5.11. Awareness should be increased at all levels concerning the need to optimize the sustainable use of resources through efficient resource manage- ment, taking into account the development needs of the populations of developing countries.

5.12. Awareness should be increased of the fundamental linkages be- tween improving the status of women and demographic dynamics, particularly through women's access to education, primary and reproductive health care programmes, economic independence and their effective, equitable partic- ipation in all levels of decision-making.

5.13. Results of research concerned with sustainable development issues should be disseminated through technical reports, scientific journals, the media, workshops, forums or other means so that the information can be used by decision makers at all levels and increase public awareness.

(d) *Developing and/or enhancing institutional capacity and collaboration*

5.14.   Collaboration and exchange of information should be increased between research institutions and international, regional and national agencies and all other sectors (including the private sector, local communities, non-governmental organizations and scientific institutions) from both the industrialized and developing countries, as appropriate.

5.15.   Efforts should be intensified to enhance the capacities of national and local governments, the private sector and non-governmental organizations in developing countries to meet the growing needs for improved management of rapidly growing urban areas.

B.   *Formulating integrated national policies for
environment and development, taking into account
demographic trends and factors*

Basis for action

5.16.   Existing plans for sustainable development have generally recognized demographic trends and factors as elements that have a critical influence on consumption patterns, production, lifestyles and long-term sustainability.   But in future, more attention will have to be given to these issues in general policy formulation and the design of development plans.   To do this, all countries will have to improve their own capacities to assess the environment and development implications of their demographic trends and factors. They will also need to formulate and implement policies and action programmes where appropriate.   Policies should be designed to address the consequences of population growth built into population momentum, while at the same time incorporating measures to bring about demographic transition. They should combine environmental concerns and population issues within a holistic view of development whose primary goals include the alleviation of poverty;   secure livelihoods;   good health;   quality of life;   improvement of the status and income of women and their access to schooling and professional training, as well as fulfilment of their personal aspirations;   and empowerment of individuals and communities.   Recognizing that large increases in the size and number of cities will occur in developing countries under any likely population scenario, greater attention should be given to preparing for the needs, in particular of women and children, for improved municipal management and local government.

Objective

5.17.   Full integration of population concerns into national planning, policy and decision-making processes should continue.   Population policies and programmes should be considered, with full recognition of women's rights.

Activities

5.18.   Governments and other relevant actors could, *inter alia,* undertake the following activities, with appropriate assistance from aid agencies, and report on their status of implementation to the International Conference on Population and Development to be held in 1994, especially to its committee on population and environment.

(a) *Assessing the implications of national demographic trends and factors*

5.19. The relationships between demographic trends and factors and environmental change and between environmental degradation and the components of demographic change should be analysed.

5.20. Research should be conducted on how environmental factors interact with socio-economic factors as a cause of migration.

5.21. Vulnerable population groups (such as rural landless workers, ethnic minorities, refugees, migrants, displaced people, women heads of household) whose changes in demographic structure may have specific impacts on sustainable development should be identified.

5.22. An assessment should be made of the implications of the age structure of the population on resource demand and dependency burdens, ranging from educational expenses for the young to health care and support for the elderly, and on household income generation.

5.23. An assessment should also be made of national population carrying capacity in the context of satisfaction of human needs and sustainable development, and special attention should be given to critical resources, such as water and land, and environmental factors, such as ecosystem health and biodiversity.

5.24. The impact of national demographic trends and factors on the traditional livelihoods of indigenous groups and local communities, including changes in traditional land use because of internal population pressures, should be studied.

(b) *Building and strengthening a national information base*

5.25. National databases on demographic trends and factors and environment should be built and/or strengthened, disaggregating data by ecological region (ecosystem approach), and population/environment profiles should be established by region.

5.26. Methodologies and instruments should be developed to identify areas where sustainability is, or may be, threatened by the environmental effects of demographic trends and factors, incorporating both current and projected demographic data linked to natural environmental processes.

5.27. Case-studies of local level responses by different groups to demographic dynamics should be developed, particularly in areas subject to environmental stress and in deteriorating urban centres.

5.28. Population data should be disaggregated by, *inter alia,* sex and age in order to take into account the implications of the gender division of labour for the use and management of natural resources.

(c) *Incorporating demographic features into policies and plans*

5.29. In formulating human settlements policies, account should be taken of resource needs, waste production and ecosystem health.

5.30. The direct and induced effects of demographic changes on environment and development programmes should, where appropriate, be integrated, and the impact on demographic features assessed.

5.31. National population policy goals and programmes that are consistent with national environment and development plans for sustainability and in keeping with the freedom, dignity and personally held values of individuals should be established and implemented.

5.32. Appropriate socio-economic policies for the young and the elderly, both in terms of family and state support systems, should be developed.

5.33. Policies and programmes should be developed for handling the various types of migrations that result from or induce environmental disruptions, with special attention to women and vulnerable groups.

5.34. Demographic concerns, including concerns for environmental migrants and displaced people, should be incorporated in the programmes for sustainable development of relevant international and regional institutions.

5.35. National reviews should be conducted and the integration of population policies in national development and environment strategies should be monitored nationally.

Means of implementation

(a) *Financing and cost evaluation*

5.36. The Conference secretariat has estimated the average total annual cost (1993–2000) of implementing the activities of this programme to be about $90 million from the international community on grant or concessional terms. These are indicative and order-of-magnitude estimates only and have not been reviewed by Governments. Actual costs and financial terms, including any that are non-concessional, will depend upon, *inter alia,* the specific strategies and programmes Governments decide upon for implementation.

(b) *Raising awareness of demographic and sustainable development interactions*

5.37. Understanding of the interactions between demographic trends and factors and sustainable development should be increased in all sectors of society. Stress should be placed on local and national action. Demographic and sustainable development education should be coordinated and integrated in both the formal and non-formal education sectors. Particular attention should be given to population literacy programmes, notably for women. Special emphasis should be placed on the linkage between these programmes, primary environmental care and the provision of primary health care and services.

(c) *Strengthening institutions*

5.38. The capacity of national, regional and local structures to deal with issues relating to demographic trends and factors and sustainable development should be enhanced. This would involve strengthening the relevant bodies responsible for population issues to enable them to elaborate policies consistent with the national prospects for sustainable development. Cooperation among government, national research institutions, non-governmental organizations and local communities in assessing problems and evaluating policies should also be enhanced.

5.39. The capacity of the relevant United Nations organs, organizations and bodies, international and regional intergovernmental bodies, non-governmental organizations and local communities should, as appropriate, be enhanced to help countries develop sustainable development policies on request and, as appropriate, provide assistance to environmental migrants and displaced people.

5.40. Inter-agency support for national sustainable development policies and programmes should be improved through better coordination of population and environment activities.

(d) *Promoting human resource development*

5.41. The international and regional scientific institutions should assist Governments, upon request, to include concerns regarding the population/environment interactions at the global, ecosystem and micro-levels in the training of demographers and population and environment specialists. Training should include research on linkages and ways to design integrated strategies.

C. *Implementing integrated environment and development programmes at the local level, taking into account demographic trends and factors*

Basis for action

5.42. Population programmes are more effective when implemented together with appropriate cross-sectoral policies. To attain sustainability at the local level, a new framework is needed that integrates demographic trends and factors with such factors as ecosystem health, technology and human settlements, and with socio-economic structures and access to resources. Population programmes should be consistent with socio-economic and environmental planning. Integrated sustainable development programmes should closely correlate action on demographic trends and factors with resource management activities and development goals that meet the needs of the people concerned.

Objective

5.43. Population programmes should be implemented along with natural resource management and development programmes at the local level that will ensure sustainable use of natural resources, improve the quality of life of the people and enhance environmental quality.

Activities

5.44. Governments and local communities, including community-based women's organizations and national non-governmental organizations, consistent with national plans, objectives, strategies and priorities, could, *inter alia*, undertake the activities set out below with the assistance and cooperation of international organizations, as appropriate. Governments could share their experience in the implementation of Agenda 21 at the International Conference on Population and Development, to be held in 1994, especially its committee on population and environment.

(a) *Developing a framework for action*

5.45. An effective consultative process should be established and implemented with concerned groups of society where the formulation and decision-making of all components of the programmes are based on a nationwide consultative process drawing on community meetings, regional workshops and national seminars, as appropriate. This process should ensure that views of women and men on needs, perspective and constraints are equally well reflected in the design of programmes, and that solutions are rooted in specific experience. The poor and underprivileged should be priority groups in this process.

5.46. Nationally determined policies for integrated and multifaceted programmes, with special attention to women, to the poorest people living in critical areas and to other vulnerable groups should be implemented, ensuring the involvement of groups with a special potential to act as agents for change and sustainable development. Special emphasis should be placed on those programmes that achieve multiple objectives, encouraging sustainable economic development, and mitigating adverse impacts of demographic trends and factors, and avoiding long-term environmental damage. Food security, access to secure tenure, basic shelter, and essential infrastructure, education, family welfare, women's reproductive health, family credit schemes, reforestation programmes, primary environmental care, women's employment should, as appropriate, be included among other factors.

5.47. An analytical framework should be developed to identify complementary elements of sustainable development policies as well as the national mechanisms to monitor and evaluate their effects on population dynamics.

5.48. Special attention should be given to the critical role of women in population/environment programmes and in achieving sustainable development. Projects should take advantage of opportunities to link social, economic and environmental gains for women and their families. Empowerment of women is essential and should be assured through education, training and policies to accord and improve women's rights and access to assets, human and civil rights, labour-saving measures, job opportunities and participation in decision-making. Population/environment programmes must enable women to mobilize themselves to alleviate their burden and improve their capacity to participate in and benefit from socio-economic development. Specific measures should be undertaken to close the gap between female and male illiteracy rates.

(b) *Supporting programmes that promote changes in demographic trends and factors towards sustainability*

5.49. Reproductive health programmes and services, should, as appropriate, be developed and enhanced to reduce maternal and infant mortality from all causes and enable women and men to fulfil their personal aspirations in terms of family size, in a way in keeping with their freedom and dignity and personally held values.

5.50. Governments should take active steps to implement, as a matter of urgency, in accordance with country-specific conditions and legal systems, measures to ensure that women and men have the same right to decide freely and responsibly on the number and spacing of their children, to have access to the information, education and means, as appropriate, to enable them to exercise this right in keeping with their freedom, dignity and personally held values taking into account ethical and cultural considerations.

5.51. Governments should take active steps to implement programmes to establish and strengthen preventive and curative health facilities that include women-centred, women-managed, safe and effective reproductive health care and affordable, accessible services, as appropriate, for the responsible planning of family size, in keeping with freedom, dignity and personally held values and taking into account ethical and cultural considerations. Programmes should focus on providing comprehensive health care, including pre-natal care, education and information on health and responsible parenthood and should provide the opportunity for all women to breast-feed fully, at least during the first four months post-partum. Programmes should fully support women's productive and reproductive roles and well being, with special attention to the need for providing equal and improved health care for all children and the need to reduce the risk of maternal and child mortality and sickness.

5.52. Consistent with national priorities, culturally based information and education programmes that transmit reproductive health messages to men and women that are easily understood should be developed.

(c) *Creating appropriate institutional conditions*

5.53. Constituencies and institutional conditions to facilitate the implementation of demographic activities should, as appropriate, be fostered. This requires support and commitment from political, indigenous, religious and traditional authorities, the private sector and the national scientific community. In developing these appropriate institutional conditions, countries should closely involve established national machinery for women.

5.54. Population assistance should be coordinated with bilateral and multilateral donors to ensure that population needs and requirements of all developing countries are addressed, fully respecting the overall coordinating responsibility and the choice and strategies of the recipient countries.

5.55. Coordination should be improved at local and international levels. Working practices should be enhanced in order to make optimum use of resources, draw on collective experience and improve the implementation of programmes. UNFPA and other relevant agencies should strengthen the coordination of international cooperation activities with recipient and donor countries in order to ensure that adequate funding is available to respond to growing needs.

5.56. Proposals should be developed for local, national and international population/environment programmes in line with specific needs for achieving sustainability. Where appropriate, institutional changes must be implemented so that old-age security does not entirely depend on input from family members.

Means of implementation

(a) *Financing and cost evaluation*

5.57. The Conference secretariat has estimated the average total annual cost (1993–2000) of implementing the activities of this programme to be about $7 billion, including about $3.5 billion from the international community on grant or concessional terms. These are indicative and order-of-magnitude estimates only and have not been reviewed by Governments. Actual costs and financial terms, including any that are non-concessional, will depend upon, *inter alia,* the specific strategies and programmes Governments decide upon for implementation.

(b) *Research*

5.58.   Research should be undertaken with a view to developing specific action programmes; it will be necessary to establish priorities between proposed areas of research.

5.59.   Socio-demographic research should be conducted on how populations respond to a changing environment.

5.60.   Understanding of socio-cultural and political factors that can positively influence acceptance of appropriate population policy instruments should be improved.

5.61.   Surveys of changes in needs for appropriate services relating to responsible planning of family size, reflecting variations among different socio-economic groups and variations in different geographical regions should be undertaken.

(c) *Human resource development and capacity-building*

5.62.   The areas of human resource development and capacity-building, with particular attention to the education and training of women, are areas of critical importance and are a very high priority in the implementation of population programmes.

5.63.   Workshops to help programme and projects managers to link population programmes to other development and environmental goals should be conducted.

5.64.   Educational materials, including guides/workbooks for planners and decision makers and other actors of population/environment/development programmes, should be developed.

5.65.   Cooperation should be developed between Governments, scientific institutions and non-governmental organizations within the region, and similar institutions outside the region.   Cooperation with local organizations should be fostered in order to raise awareness, engage in demonstration projects and report on the experience gained.

5.66.   The recommendations contained in this chapter should in no way prejudice discussions at the International Conference on Population and Development in 1994, which will be the appropriate forum for dealing with population and development issues, taking into account the recommendations of the International Conference on Population, held in Mexico City in 1984, and the Forward-looking Strategies for the Advancement of Women, adopted by the World Conference to Review and Appraise the Achievements of the United Decade for Women: Equality, Development and Peace, held in Nairobi in 1985.

* * *

Chapter 15

CONSERVATION OF BIOLOGICAL DIVERSITY

INTRODUCTION

15.1.   The objectives and activities in this chapter of Agenda 21 are intended to improve the conservation of biological diversity and the sustainable use of biological resources, as well as to support the Convention on Biological Diversity.

15.2. Our planet's essential goods and services depend on the variety and variability of genes, species, populations and ecosystems. Biological resources feed and clothe us and provide housing, medicines and spiritual nourishment. The natural ecosystems of forests, savannahs, pastures and rangelands, deserts, tundras, rivers, lakes and seas contain most of the Earth's biodiversity. Farmers' fields and gardens are also of great importance as repositories, while gene banks, botanical gardens, zoos and other germplasm repositories make a small but significant contribution. The current decline in biodiversity is largely the result of human activity and represents a serious threat to human development.

PROGRAMME AREA

Conservation of biological diversity

Basis for action

15.3. Despite mounting efforts over the past 20 years, the loss of the world's biological diversity, mainly from habitat destruction, over-harvesting, pollution and the inappropriate introduction of foreign plants and animals, has continued. Biological resources constitute a capital asset with great potential for yielding sustainable benefits. Urgent and decisive action is needed to conserve and maintain genes, species and ecosystems, with a view to the sustainable management and use of biological resources. Capacities for the assessment, study and systematic observation and evaluation of biodiversity need to be reinforced at national and international levels. Effective national action and international cooperation is required for the *in situ* protection of ecosystems, for the *ex situ* conservation of biological and genetic resources and for the enhancement of ecosystem functions. The participation and support of local communities are elements essential to the success of such an approach. Recent advances in biotechnology have pointed up the likely potential for agriculture, health and welfare and for the environmental purposes of the genetic material contained in plants, animals and microorganisms. At the same time, it is particularly important in this context to stress that States have the sovereign right to exploit their own biological resources pursuant to their environmental policies, as well as the responsibility to conserve their biodiversity and use their biological resources sustainably, and to ensure that activities within their jurisdiction or control do not cause damage to the biological diversity of other States or of areas beyond the limits of national jurisdiction.

Objectives

15.4. Governments at the appropriate level, with the cooperation of the relevant United Nations bodies and regional, intergovernmental and non-governmental organizations, the private sector and financial institutions, and taking into consideration indigenous people and their communities, as well as social and economic factors, should:

(a) Press for the early entry into force of the Convention on Biological Diversity, with the widest possible participation;

(b) Develop national strategies for the conservation of biological diversity and the sustainable use of biological resources;

(c) Integrate strategies for the conservation of biological diversity and the sustainable use of biological resources into national development strategies and/or plans;

(d) Take appropriate measures for the fair and equitable sharing of benefits derived from research and development and use of biological and genetic resources, including biotechnology, between the sources of those resources and those who use them;

(e) Carry out country studies, as appropriate, on the conservation of biological diversity and the sustainable use of biological resources, including analyses of relevant costs and benefits, with particular reference to socio-economic aspects;

(f) Produce regularly updated world reports on biodiversity based upon national assessments;

(g) Recognize and foster the traditional methods and the knowledge of indigenous people and their communities, emphasizing the particular role of women, relevant to the conservation of biological diversity and the sustainable use of biological resources, and ensure the opportunity for the participation of those groups in the economic and commercial benefits derived from the use of such traditional methods and knowledge;

(h) Implement mechanisms for the improvement, generation, development and sustainable use of biotechnology and its safe transfer, particularly to developing countries, taking account the potential contribution of biotechnology to the conservation of biological diversity and the sustainable use of biological resources;

(i) Promote broader international and regional cooperation in furthering scientific and economic understanding of the importance of biodiversity and its functions in ecosystems;

(j) Develop measures and arrangements to implement the rights of countries of origin of genetic resources or countries providing genetic resources, as defined in the Convention on Biological Diversity, particularly developing countries, to benefit from the biotechnological development and the commercial utilization of products derived from such resources.

Activities

(a) *Management-related activities*

15.5. Governments at the appropriate levels, consistent with national policies and practices, with the cooperation of the relevant United Nations bodies and, as appropriate, intergovernmental organizations and, with the support of indigenous people and their communities, non-governmental organizations and other groups, including the business and scientific communities, and consistent with the requirements of international law, should, as appropriate:

(a) Develop new or strengthen existing strategies, plans or programmes of action for the conservation of biological diversity and the sustainable use of biological resources, taking account of education and training needs;

(b) Integrate strategies for the conservation of biological diversity and the sustainable use of biological and genetic resources into relevant sectoral or cross-sectoral plans, programmes and policies, with particular reference to the special importance of terrestrial and aquatic biological and genetic resources for food and agriculture;

(c) Undertake country studies or use other methods to identify components of biological diversity important for its conservation and for the sustainable use of biological resources, ascribe values to biological and genetic resources, identify processes and activities with significant impacts upon biological diversity, evaluate the potential economic implications of the conservation of biological diversity and the sustainable use of biological and genetic resources, and suggest priority action;

(d) Take effective economic, social and other appropriate incentive measures to encourage the conservation of biological diversity and the sustainable use of biological resources, including the promotion of sustainable production systems, such as traditional methods of agriculture, agroforestry, forestry, range and wildlife management, which use, maintain or increase biodiversity;

(e) Subject to national legislation, take action to respect, record, protect and promote the wider application of the knowledge, innovations and practices of indigenous and local communities embodying traditional lifestyles for the conservation of biological diversity and the sustainable use of biological resources, with a view to the fair and equitable sharing of the benefits arising, and promote mechanisms to involve those communities, including women, in the conservation and management of ecosystems;

(f) Undertake long-term research into the importance of biodiversity for the functioning of ecosystems and the role of ecosystems in producing goods, environmental services and other values supporting sustainable development, with particular reference to the biology and reproductive capacities of key terrestrial and aquatic species, including native, cultivated and cultured species; new observation and inventory techniques; ecological conditions necessary for biodiversity conservation and continued evolution; and social behaviour and nutrition habits dependent on natural ecosystems, where women play key roles. The work should be undertaken with the widest possible participation, especially of indigenous people and their communities, including women;

(g) Take action where necessary for the conservation of biological diversity through the *in situ* conservation of ecosystems and natural habitats, as well as primitive cultivars and their wild relatives, and the maintenance and recovery of viable populations of species in their natural surroundings, and implement *ex situ* measures, preferably in the source country. *In situ* measures should include the reinforcement of terrestrial, marine and aquatic protected area systems and embrace, *inter alia*, vulnerable freshwater and other wetlands and coastal ecosystems, such as estuaries, coral reefs and mangroves;

(h) Promote the rehabilitation and restoration of damaged ecosystems and the recovery of threatened and endangered species;

(i) Develop policies to encourage the conservation of biodiversity and the sustainable use of biological and genetic resources on private lands;

(j) Promote environmentally sound and sustainable development in areas adjacent to protected areas with a view to furthering protection of these areas;

(k) Introduce appropriate environmental impact assessment procedures for proposed projects likely to have significant impacts upon biological diversity, providing for suitable information to be made widely available and for public participation, where appropriate, and encourage the assessment of the impacts of relevant policies and programmes on biological diversity;

(l) Promote, where appropriate, the establishment and strengthening of national inventory, regulation or management and control systems related to biological resources, at the appropriate level;

(m) Take measures to encourage a greater understanding and appreciation of the value of biological diversity, as manifested both in its component parts and in the ecosystem services provided.

(b) *Data and information*

15.6. Governments at the appropriate level, consistent with national policies and practices, with the cooperation of the relevant United Nations bodies and, as appropriate, intergovernmental organizations, and with the support of indigenous people and their communities, non-governmental organizations and other groups, including the business and scientific communities, and consistent with the requirements of international law, should, as appropriate:

(a) Regularly collate, evaluate and exchange information on the conservation of biological diversity and the sustainable use of biological resources;

(b) Develop methodologies with a view to undertaking systematic sampling and evaluation on a national basis of the components of biological diversity identified by means of country studies;

(c) Initiate or further develop methodologies and begin or continue work on surveys at the appropriate level on the status of ecosystems and establish baseline information on biological and genetic resources, including those in terrestrial, aquatic, coastal and marine ecosystems, as well as inventories undertaken with the participation of local and indigenous people and their communities;

(d) Identify and evaluate the potential economic and social implications and benefits of the conservation and sustainable use of terrestrial and aquatic species in each country, building upon the results of country studies;

(e) Undertake the updating, analysis and interpretation of data derived from the identification, sampling and evaluation activities described above;

(f) Collect, assess and make available relevant and reliable information in a timely manner and in a form suitable for decision-making at all levels, with the full support and participation of local and indigenous people and their communities.

(c) *International and regional cooperation and coordination*

15.7.   Governments at the appropriate level, with the cooperation of the relevant United Nations bodies and, as appropriate, intergovernmental organizations, and, with the support of indigenous people and their communities, non-governmental organizations and other groups, including the business and scientific communities, and consistent with the requirements of international law, should, as appropriate:

(a) Consider the establishment or strengthening of national or international capabilities and networks for the exchange of data and information of relevance to the conservation of biological diversity and the sustainable use of biological and genetic resources;

(b) Produce regularly updated world reports on biodiversity based upon national assessments in all countries;

(c) Promote technical and scientific cooperation in the field of conservation of biological diversity and the sustainable use of biological and genetic resources. Special attention should be given to the development and strengthening of national capabilities by means of human resource development and institution-building, including the transfer of technology and/or development of research and management facilities, such as herbaria, museums, gene banks, and laboratories, related to the conservation of biodiversity;

(d) Without prejudice to the relevant provisions of the Convention on Biological Diversity, facilitate for this chapter the transfer of technologies relevant to the conservation of biological diversity and the sustainable use of biological resources or technologies that make use of genetic resources and cause no significant damage to the environment, in conformity with chapter 34, and recognizing that technology includes biotechnology;

(e) Promote cooperation between the parties to relevant international conventions and action plans with the aim of strengthening and coordinating efforts to conserve biological diversity and the sustainable use of biological resources;

(f) Strengthen support for international and regional instruments, programmes and action plans concerned with the conservation of biological diversity and the sustainable use of biological resources;

(g) Promote improved international coordination of measures for the effective conservation and management of endangered/non-pest migratory species, including appropriate levels of support for the establishment and management of protected areas in transboundary locations;

(h) Promote national efforts with respect to surveys, data collection, sampling and evaluation, and the maintenance of gene banks.

Means of implementation

(a) *Financing and cost evaluation*

15.8.   The Conference secretariat has estimated the average total annual cost (1993–2000) of implementing the activities of this chapter to be about

$3.5 billion, including about $1.75 billion from the international community on grant or concessional terms. These are indicative and order-of-magnitude estimates only and have not been reviewed by Governments. Actual costs and financial terms, including any that are non-concessional, will depend upon, *inter alia,* the specific strategies and programmes Governments decide upon for implementation.

(b) *Scientific and technological means*

15.9. Specific aspects to be addressed include the need to develop:

(a) Efficient methodologies for baseline surveys and inventories, as well as for the systematic sampling and evaluation of biological resources;

(b) Methods and technologies for the conservation of biological diversity and the sustainable use of biological resources;

(c) Improved and diversified methods for *ex situ* conservation with a view to the long-term conservation of genetic resources of importance for research and development.

(c) *Human resource development*

15.10. There is a need, where appropriate, to:

(a) Increase the number and/or make more efficient use of trained personnel in scientific and technological fields relevant to the conservation of biological diversity and the sustainable use of biological resources;

(b) Maintain or establish programmes for scientific and technical education and training of managers and professionals, especially in developing countries, on measures for the identification, conservation of biological diversity and the sustainable use of biological resources;

(c) Promote and encourage understanding of the importance of the measures required for the conservation of biological diversity and the sustainable use of biological resources at all policy-making and decision-making levels in Governments, business enterprises and lending institutions, and promote and encourage the inclusion of these topics in educational programmes.

(d) *Capacity-building*

15.11. There is a need, where appropriate, to:

(a) Strengthen existing institutions and/or establish new ones responsible for the conservation of biological diversity and to consider the development of mechanisms such as national biodiversity institutes or centres;

(b) Continue to build capacity for the conservation of biological diversity and the sustainable use of biological resources in all relevant sectors;

(c) Build capacity, especially within Governments, business enterprises and bilateral and multilateral development agencies, for integrating biodiversity concerns, potential benefits and opportunity cost calculations into project design, implementation and evaluation processes, as well as for evaluating the impact on biological diversity of proposed development projects;

(d) Enhance the capacity of governmental and private institutions, at the appropriate level, responsible for protected area planning and management to undertake intersectoral coordination and planning with other governmental institutions, non-governmental organizations and, where appropriate, indigenous people and their communities.

* * *

Chapter 17
PROTECTION OF THE OCEANS, ALL KINDS OF SEAS, INCLUDING ENCLOSED AND SEMI-ENCLOSED SEAS, AND COASTAL AREAS AND THE PROTECTION, RATIONAL USE AND DEVELOPMENT OF THEIR LIVING RESOURCES

INTRODUCTION

17.1. The marine environment—including the oceans and all seas and adjacent coastal areas—forms an integrated whole that is an essential component of the global life-support system and a positive asset that presents opportunities for sustainable development. International law, as reflected in the provisions of the United Nations Convention on the Law of the Sea, referred to in this chapter of Agenda 21, sets forth rights and obligations of States and provides the international basis upon which to pursue the protection and sustainable development of the marine and coastal environment and its resources. This requires new approaches to marine and coastal area management and development at the national, subregional, regional and global levels, approaches that are integrated in content and are precautionary and anticipatory in ambit, as reflected in the following programme areas:

(a) Integrated management and sustainable development of coastal areas, including exclusive economic zones;

(b) Marine environmental protection;

(c) Sustainable use and conservation of marine living resources of the high seas;

(d) Sustainable use and conservation of marine living resources under national jurisdiction;

(e) Addressing critical uncertainties for the management of the marine environment and climate change;

(f) Strengthening international, including regional, cooperation and coordination;

(g) Sustainable development of small islands.

17.2. The implementation by developing countries of the activities set forth below shall be commensurate with their individual technological and financial capacities and priorities in allocating resources for development needs and ultimately depends on the technology transfer and financial resources required and made available to them.

PROGRAMME AREAS

A. *Integrated management and sustainable development of coastal and marine areas, including exclusive economic zones*

Basis for action

17.3. The coastal area contains diverse and productive habitats important for human settlements, development and local subsistence. More than half the world's population lives within 60 km of the shoreline, and this could rise to three quarters by the year 2020. Many of the world's poor are crowded in coastal areas. Coastal resources are vital for many local communities and indigenous people. The exclusive economic zone (EEZ) is also an important marine area where the States manage the development and conservation of natural resources for the benefit of their people. For small island States or countries, these are the areas most available for development activities.

17.4. Despite national, subregional, regional and global efforts, current approaches to the management of marine and coastal resources have not always proved capable of achieving sustainable development, and coastal resources and the coastal environment are being rapidly degraded and eroded in many parts of the world.

Objectives

17.5. Coastal States commit themselves to integrated management and sustainable development of coastal areas and the marine environment under their national jurisdiction. To this end, it is necessary to, *inter alia:*

(a) Provide for an integrated policy and decision-making process, including all involved sectors, to promote compatibility and a balance of uses;

(b) Identify existing and projected uses of coastal areas and their interactions;

(c) Concentrate on well-defined issues concerning coastal management;

(d) Apply preventive and precautionary approaches in project planning and implementation, including prior assessment and systematic observation of the impacts of major projects;

(e) Promote the development and application of methods, such as national resource and environmental accounting, that reflect changes in value resulting from uses of coastal and marine areas, including pollution, marine erosion, loss of resources and habitat destruction;

(f) Provide access, as far as possible, for concerned individuals, groups and organizations to relevant information and opportunities for consultation and participation in planning and decision-making at appropriate levels.

Activities

(a) *Management-related activities*

17.6. Each coastal State should consider establishing, or where necessary, strengthening, appropriate coordinating mechanisms (such as a high-level policy planning body) for integrated management and sustainable development of coastal and marine areas and their resources, at both the local and national levels. Such mechanisms should include consultation, as appropriate, with the academic and private sectors, non-governmental organizations, local communities, resource user groups, and indigenous people. Such national coordinating mechanisms could provide, *inter alia,* for:

(a) Preparation and implementation of land and water use and siting policies;

(b) Implementation of integrated coastal and marine management and sustainable development plans and programmes at appropriate levels;

(c) Preparation of coastal profiles identifying critical areas, including eroded zones, physical processes, development patterns, user conflicts and specific priorities for management;

(d) Prior environmental impact assessment, systematic observation and follow-up of major projects, including the systematic incorporation of results in decision-making;

(e) Contingency plans for human induced and natural disasters, including likely effects of potential climate change and sealevel rise, as well as contingency plans for degradation and pollution of anthropogenic origin, including spills of oil and other materials;

(f) Improvement of coastal human settlements, especially in housing, drinking water and treatment and disposal of sewage, solid wastes and industrial effluents;

(g) Periodic assessment of the impacts of external factors and phenomena to ensure that the objectives of integrated management and sustainable development of coastal areas and the marine environment are met;

(h) Conservation and restoration of altered critical habitats;

(i) Integration of sectoral programmes on sustainable development for settlements, agriculture, tourism, fishing, ports and industries affecting the coastal area;

(j) Infrastructure adaptation and alternative employment;

(k) Human resource development and training;

(l) Public education, awareness and information programmes;

(m) Promoting environmentally sound technology and sustainable practices;

(n) Development and simultaneous implementation of environmental quality criteria.

17.7. Coastal States, with the support of international organizations, upon request, should undertake measures to maintain biological diversity and productivity of marine species and habitats under national jurisdiction. *Inter alia,* these measures might include: surveys of marine biodiversity, inventories of endangered species and critical coastal and marine habitats; establishment and management of protected areas; and support of scientific research and dissemination of its results.

(b) *Data and information*

17.8. Coastal States, where necessary, should improve their capacity to collect, analyse, assess and use information for sustainable use of resources, including environmental impacts of activities affecting the coastal and marine areas. Information for management purposes should receive priority support in view of the intensity and magnitude of the changes occurring in the coastal and marine areas. To this end, it is necessary to, *inter alia:*

(a) Develop and maintain databases for assessment and management of coastal areas and all seas and their resources;

(b) Develop socio-economic and environmental indicators;

(c) Conduct regular environmental assessment of the state of the environment of coastal and marine areas;

(d) Prepare and maintain profiles of coastal area resources, activities, uses, habitats and protected areas based on the criteria of sustainable development;

(e) Exchange information and data.

17.9. Cooperation with developing countries, and, where applicable, subregional and regional mechanisms, should be strengthened to improve their capacities to achieve the above.

(c) *International and regional cooperation and coordination*

17.10. The role of international cooperation and coordination on a bilateral basis and, where applicable, within a subregional, interregional, regional or global framework, is to support and supplement national efforts of coastal States to promote integrated management and sustainable development of coastal and marine areas.

17.11. States should cooperate, as appropriate, in the preparation of national guidelines for integrated coastal zone management and development, drawing on existing experience. A global conference to exchange experience in the field could be held before 1994.

Means of implementation

(a) *Financing and cost evaluation*

17.12. The Conference secretariat has estimated the average total annual cost (1993–2000) of implementing the activities of this programme to be about $6 billion, including about $50 million from the international community on grant or concessional terms. These are indicative and order-of-magnitude estimates only and have not been reviewed by Governments. Actual costs and financial terms, including any that are non-concessional, will depend upon, *inter alia,* the specific strategies and programmes Governments decide upon for implementation.

(b) *Scientific and technological means*

17.13. States should cooperate in the development of necessary coastal systematic observation, research and information management systems. They should provide access to and transfer environmentally safe technologies and methodologies for sustainable development of coastal and marine areas to developing countries. They should also develop technologies and endogenous scientific and technological capacities.

17.14. International organizations, whether subregional, regional or global, as appropriate, should support coastal States, upon request, in these efforts, as indicated above, devoting special attention to developing countries.

(c) *Human resource development*

17.15.   Coastal States should promote and facilitate the organization of education and training in integrated coastal and marine management and sustainable development for scientists, technologists, managers (including community-based managers) and users, leaders, indigenous peoples, fisher-folk, women and youth, among others.   Management and development, as well as environmental protection concerns and local planning issues, should be incorporated in educational curricula and public awareness campaigns, with due regard to traditional ecological knowledge and socio-cultural values.

17.16.   International organizations, whether subregional, regional or global, as appropriate, should support coastal States, upon request, in the areas indicated above, devoting special attention to developing countries.

(d) *Capacity-building*

17.17.   Full cooperation should be extended, upon request, to coastal States in their capacity-building efforts and, where appropriate, capacity-building should be included in bilateral and multilateral development coopera-tion.   Coastal States may consider, *inter alia:*

(a) Ensuring capacity-building at the local level;

(b) Consulting on coastal and marine issues with local administra-tions, the business community, the academic sector, resource user groups and the general public;

(c) Coordinating sectoral programmes while building capacity;

(d) Identifying existing and potential capabilities, facilities and needs for human resource development and scientific and technological infra-structure;

(e) Developing scientific and technological means and research;

(f) Promoting and facilitating human resource development and edu-cation;

(g) Supporting "centres of excellence" in integrated coastal and marine resource management;

(h) Supporting pilot demonstration programmes and projects in inte-grated coastal and marine management.

B.   *Marine environmental protection*

Basis for action

17.18.   Degradation of the marine environment can result from a wide range of sources.   Land-based sources contribute 70 per cent of marine pollution, while maritime transport and dumping-at-sea activities contribute 10 per cent each.   The contaminants that pose the greatest threat to the marine environment are, in variable order of importance and depending on differing national or regional situations, sewage, nutrients, synthetic organic compounds, sediments, litter and plastics, metals, radionucleides, oil/hydrocar-bons and polycyclic aromatic hydrocarbons (PAHs).   Many of the polluting substances originating from land-based sources are of particular concern to the marine environment since they exhibit at the same time toxicity, persistence and bioaccumulation in the food chain. There is currently no global scheme to address marine pollution from land-based sources.

17.19. Degradation of the marine environment can also result from a wide range of activities on land. Human settlements, land use, construction of coastal infrastructure, agriculture, forestry, urban development, tourism and industry can affect the marine environment. Coastal erosion and siltation are of particular concern.

17.20. Marine pollution is also caused by shipping and sea-based activities. Approximately 600,000 tons of oil enter the oceans each year as a result of normal shipping operations, accidents and illegal discharges. With respect to offshore oil and gas activities, currently machinery space discharges are regulated internationally and six regional conventions to control platform discharges have been under consideration. The nature and extent of environmental impacts from offshore oil exploration and production activities generally account for a very small proportion of marine pollution.

17.21. A precautionary and anticipatory rather than a reactive approach is necessary to prevent the degradation of the marine environment. This requires, *inter alia,* the adoption of precautionary measures, environmental impact assessments, clean production techniques, recycling, waste audits and minimization, construction and/or improvement of sewage treatment facilities, quality management criteria for the proper handling of hazardous substances, and a comprehensive approach to damaging impacts from air, land and water. Any management framework must include the improvement of coastal human settlements and the integrated management and development of coastal areas.

Objectives

17.22. States, in accordance with the provisions of the United Nations Convention on the Law of the Sea on protection and preservation of the marine environment, commit themselves, in accordance with their policies, priorities and resources, to prevent, reduce and control degradation of the marine environment so as to maintain and improve its life-support and productive capacities. To this end, it is necessary to:

(a) Apply preventive, precautionary and anticipatory approaches so as to avoid degradation of the marine environment, as well as to reduce the risk of long-term or irreversible adverse effects upon it;

(b) Ensure prior assessment of activities that may have significant adverse impacts upon the marine environment;

(c) Integrate protection of the marine environment into relevant general environmental, social and economic development policies;

(d) Develop economic incentives, where appropriate, to apply clean technologies and other means consistent with the internalization of environmental costs, such as the polluter pays principle, so as to avoid degradation of the marine environment;

(e) Improve the living standards of coastal populations, particularly in developing countries, so as to contribute to reducing the degradation of the coastal and marine environment.

17.23. States agree that provision of additional financial resources, through appropriate international mechanisms, as well as access to cleaner technologies and relevant research, would be necessary to support action by developing countries to implement this commitment.

Activities

(a) *Management-related activities*

Prevention, reduction and control of degradation of the marine environment from land-based activities

17.24. In carrying out their commitment to deal with degradation of the marine environment from land-based activities, States should take action at the national level and, where appropriate, at the regional and subregional levels, in concert with action to implement programme area A, and should take account of the Montreal Guidelines for the Protection of the Marine Environment from Land–Based Sources.

17.25. To this end, States, with the support of the relevant international environmental, scientific, technical and financial organizations, should cooperate, *inter alia,* to:

(a) Consider updating, strengthening and extending the Montreal Guidelines, as appropriate;

(b) Assess the effectiveness of existing regional agreements and action plans, where appropriate, with a view to identifying means of strengthening action, where necessary, to prevent, reduce and control marine degradation caused by land-based activities;

(c) Initiate and promote the development of new regional agreements, where appropriate;

(d) Develop means of providing guidance on technologies to deal with the major types of pollution of the marine environment from land-based sources, according to the best scientific evidence;

(e) Develop policy guidance for relevant global funding mechanisms;

(f) Identify additional steps requiring international cooperation.

17.26. The UNEP Governing Council is invited to convene, as soon as practicable, an intergovernmental meeting on protection of the marine environment from land-based activities.

17.27. As concerns sewage, priority actions to be considered by States may include:

(a) Incorporating sewage concerns when formulating or reviewing coastal development plans, including human settlement plans;

(b) Building and maintaining sewage treatment facilities in accordance with national policies and capacities and international cooperation available;

(c) Locating coastal outfalls so as to maintain an acceptable level of environmental quality and to avoid exposing shell fisheries, water intakes and bathing areas to pathogens;

(d) Promoting environmentally sound co-treatments of domestic and compatible industrial effluents, with the introduction, where practicable, of controls on the entry of effluents that are not compatible with the system;

(e) Promoting primary treatment of municipal sewage discharged to rivers, estuaries and the sea, or other solutions appropriate to specific sites;

(f) Establishing and improving local, national, subregional and regional, as necessary, regulatory and monitoring programmes to control effluent discharge, using minimum sewage effluent guidelines and water quality criteria and giving due consideration to the characteristics of receiving bodies and the volume and type of pollutants.

17.28. As concerns other sources of pollution, priority actions to be considered by States may include:

(a) Establishing or improving, as necessary, regulatory and monitoring programmes to control effluent discharges and emissions, including the development and application of control and recycling technologies;

(b) Promoting risk and environmental impact assessments to help ensure an acceptable level of environmental quality;

(c) Promoting assessment and cooperation at the regional level, where appropriate, with respect to the input of point source pollutants from new installations;

(d) Eliminating the emission or discharge of organohalogen compounds that threaten to accumulate to dangerous levels in the marine environment;

(e) Reducing the emission or discharge of other synthetic organic compounds that threaten to accumulate to dangerous levels in the marine environment;

(f) Promoting controls over anthropogenic inputs of nitrogen and phosphorus that enter coastal waters where such problems as eutrophication threaten the marine environment or its resources;

(g) Cooperating with developing countries, through financial and technological support, to maximize the best practicable control and reduction of substances and wastes that are toxic, persistent or liable to bioaccumulate and to establish environmentally sound land-based waste disposal alternatives to sea dumping;

(h) Cooperating in the development and implementation of environmentally sound land-use techniques and practices to reduce run-off to water-courses and estuaries which would cause pollution or degradation of the marine environment;

(i) Promoting the use of environmentally less harmful pesticides and fertilizers and alternative methods for pest control, and considering the prohibition of those found to be environmentally unsound;

(j) Adopting new initiatives at national, subregional and regional levels for controlling the input of non-point source pollutants, which require broad changes in sewage and waste management, agricultural practices, mining, construction and transportation.

17.29. As concerns physical destruction of coastal and marine areas causing degradation of the marine environment, priority actions should include control and prevention of coastal erosion and siltation due to anthropogenic factors related to, *inter alia,* land-use and construction techniques and practices. Watershed management practices should be promoted so as to prevent, control and reduce degradation of the marine environment.

Prevention, reduction and control of degradation of the marine environment from sea-based activities

17.30.   States, acting individually, bilaterally, regionally or multilaterally and within the framework of IMO and other relevant international organizations, whether subregional, regional or global, as appropriate, should assess the need for additional measures to address degradation of the marine environment:

(a) From shipping, by:

(i) Supporting wider ratification and implementation of relevant shipping conventions and protocols;

(ii) Facilitating the processes in (i), providing support to individual States upon request to help them overcome the obstacles identified by them;

(iii) Cooperating in monitoring marine pollution from ships, especially from illegal discharges (e.g., aerial surveillance), and enforcing MARPOL discharge, provisions more rigorously;

(iv) Assessing the state of pollution caused by ships in particularly sensitive areas identified by IMO and taking action to implement applicable measures, where necessary, within such areas to ensure compliance with generally accepted international regulations;

(v) Taking action to ensure respect of areas designated by coastal States, within their exclusive economic zones, consistent with international law, in order to protect and preserve rare or fragile ecosystems, such as coral reefs and mangroves;

(vi) Considering the adoption of appropriate rules on ballast water discharge to prevent the spread of non-indigenous organisms;

(vii) Promoting navigational safety by adequate charting of coasts and ship-routing, as appropriate;

(viii) Assessing the need for stricter international regulations to further reduce the risk of accidents and pollution from cargo ships (including bulk carriers);

(ix) Encouraging IMO and IAEA to work together to complete consideration of a code on the carriage of irradiated nuclear fuel in flasks on board ships;

(x) Revising and updating the IMO Code of Safety for Nuclear Merchant Ships and considering how best to implement a revised code;

(xi) Supporting the ongoing activity within IMO regarding development of appropriate measures for reducing air pollution from ships;

(xii) Supporting the ongoing activity within IMO regarding the development of an international regime governing the transportation of hazardous and noxious substances carried by ships and further considering whether the compensation funds similar to the ones established under the Fund Convention would be appropriate in respect of pollution damage caused by substances other than oil;

(b) From dumping, by:

(i) Supporting wider ratification, implementation and participation in relevant Conventions on dumping at sea, including early conclusion of a future strategy for the London Dumping Convention;

(ii) Encouraging the London Dumping Convention parties to take appropriate steps to stop ocean dumping and incineration of hazardous substances;

(c) From offshore oil and gas platforms, by assessing existing regulatory measures to address discharges, emissions and safety and assessing the need for additional measures;

(d) From ports, by facilitating establishment of port reception facilities for the collection of oily and chemical residues and garbage from ships, especially in MARPOL special areas, and promoting the establishment of smaller scale facilities in marinas and fishing harbours.

17.31.   IMO and as appropriate, other competent United Nations organizations, when requested by the States concerned, should assess, where appropriate, the state of marine pollution in areas of congested shipping, such as heavily used international straits, with a view to ensuring compliance with generally accepted international regulations, particularly those related to illegal discharges from ships, in accordance with the provisions of Part III of the United Nations Convention on the Law of the Sea.

17.32.   States should take measures to reduce water pollution caused by organotin compounds used in anti-fouling paints.

17.33.   States should consider ratifying the Convention on Oil Pollution Preparedness, Response and Cooperation, which addresses, *inter alia,* the development of contingency plans on the national and international level, as appropriate, including provision of oil-spill response material and training of personnel, including its possible extension to chemical spill response.

17.34.   States should intensify international cooperation to strengthen or establish, where necessary, regional oil/chemical-spill response centres and/or, as appropriate, mechanisms in cooperation with relevant subregional, regional or global intergovernmental organizations and, where appropriate, industry-based organizations.

(b) *Data and information*

17.35.   States should, as appropriate, and in accordance with the means at their disposal and with due regard for their technical and scientific capacity and resources, make systematic observations on the state of the marine environment. To this end, States should, as appropriate, consider:

(a) Establishing systematic observation systems to measure marine environmental quality, including causes and effects of marine degradation, as a basis for management;

(b) Regularly exchanging information on marine degradation caused by land-based and sea-based activities and on actions to prevent, control and reduce such degradation;

(c) Supporting and expanding international programmes for systematic observations such as the mussel watch programme, building on existing facilities with special attention to developing countries;

(d) Establishing a clearing-house on marine pollution control information, including processes and technologies to address marine pollution control and to support their transfer to developing countries and other countries with demonstrated needs;

(e) Establishing a global profile and database providing information on the sources, types, amounts and effects of pollutants reaching the marine environment from land-based activities in coastal areas and sea-based sources;

(f) Allocating adequate funding for capacity-building and training programmes to ensure the full participation of developing countries, in particular, in any international scheme under the organs and organizations of the United Nations system for the collection, analysis and use of data and information.

Means of implementation

(a) *Financing and cost evaluation*

17.36.   The Conference secretariat has estimated the average total annual cost (1993–2000) of implementing the activities of this programme to be about $200 million from the international community on grant or concessional terms.   These are indicative and order-of-magnitude estimates only and have not been reviewed by Governments.   Actual costs and financial terms, including any that are non-concessional, will depend upon, *inter alia,* the specific strategies and programmes Governments decide upon for implementation.

(b) *Scientific and technological means*

17.37.   National, subregional and regional action programmes will, where appropriate, require technology transfer, in conformity with Chapter 34, and financial resources, particularly where developing countries are concerned, including:

(a) Assistance to industries in identifying and adopting clean production or cost-effective pollution control technologies;

(b) Planning development and application of low-cost and low-maintenance sewage installation and treatment technologies for developing countries;

(c) Equipment of laboratories to observe systematically human and other impacts on the marine environment;

(d) Identification of appropriate oil- and chemical-spill control materials, including low-cost locally available materials and techniques, suitable for pollution emergencies in developing countries;

(e) Study of the use of persistent organohalogens that are liable to accumulate in the marine environment to identify those that cannot be adequately controlled and to provide a basis for a decision on a time schedule for phasing them out as soon as practicable;

(f) Establishment of a clearing-house for information on marine pollution control, including processes and technologies to address marine pollution control, and support for their transfer to developing and other countries with demonstrated needs.

(c) *Human resource development*

17.38.   States individually or in cooperation with each other and with the support of international organizations, whether subregional, regional or global, as appropriate, should:

(a) Provide training for critical personnel required for the adequate protection of the marine environment as identified by training needs' surveys at the national, regional or subregional levels;

(b) Promote the introduction of marine environmental protection topics into the curriculum of marine studies programmes;

(c) Establish training courses for oil- and chemical-spill response personnel, in cooperation, where appropriate, with the oil and chemical industries;

(d) Conduct workshops on environmental aspects of port operations and development;

(e) Strengthen and provide secure financing for new and existing specialized international centres of professional maritime education;

(f) States should, through bilateral and multilateral cooperation, support and supplement the national efforts of developing countries as regards human resource development in relation to prevention and reduction of degradation of the marine environment.

(d) *Capacity-building*

17.39.   National planning and coordinating bodies should be given the capacity and authority to review all land-based activities and sources of pollution for their impacts on the marine environment and to propose appropriate control measures.

17.40.   Research facilities should be strengthened or, where appropriate, developed in developing countries for systematic observation of marine pollution, environmental impact assessment and development of control recommendations and should be managed and staffed by local experts.

17.41.   Special arrangements will be needed to provide adequate financial and technical resources to assist developing countries in preventing and solving problems associated with activities that threaten the marine environment.

17.42.   An international funding mechanism should be created for the application of appropriate sewage treatment technologies and building sewage treatment facilities, including grants or concessional loans from international agencies and appropriate regional funds, replenished at least in part on a revolving basis by user fees.

17.43.   In carrying out these programme activities, particular attention needs to be given to the problems of developing countries that would bear an unequal burden because of their lack of facilities, expertise or technical capacities.

C. *Sustainable use and conservation of marine living resources of the high seas*

Basis for action

17.44.   Over the last decade, fisheries on the high seas have considerably expanded and currently represent approximately 5 per cent of total world landings.   The provisions of the United Nations Convention on the Law of the Sea on the marine living resources of the high seas sets forth rights and obligations of States with respect to conservation and utilization of those resources.

17.45.   However, management of high seas fisheries, including the adoption, monitoring and enforcement of effective conservation measures, is inadequate in many areas and some resources are overutilized.   There are problems of unregulated fishing, overcapitalization, excessive fleet size, vessel reflagging to escape controls, insufficiently selective gear, unreliable databases and lack of sufficient cooperation between States.   Action by States whose nationals and vessels fish on the high seas, as well as cooperation at the bilateral, subregional, regional and global levels, is essential particularly for highly migratory species and straddling stocks.   Such action and cooperation should address inadequacies in fishing practices, as well as in biological knowledge, fisheries statistics and improvement of systems for handling data. Emphasis should also be on multi-species management and other approaches that take into account the relationships among species, especially in addressing depleted species, but also in identifying the potential of underutilized or unutilized populations.

Objectives

17.46.   States commit themselves to the conservation and sustainable use of marine living resources on the high seas.   To this end, it is necessary to:

(a) Develop and increase the potential of marine living resources to meet human nutritional needs, as well as social, economic and development goals;

(b) Maintain or restore populations of marine species at levels that can produce the maximum sustainable yield as qualified by relevant environmental and economic factors, taking into consideration relationships among species;

(c) Promote the development and use of selective fishing gear and practices that minimize waste in the catch of target species and minimize by-catch of non-target species;

* * *

Chapter 20
ENVIRONMENTALLY SOUND MANAGEMENT OF HAZARDOUS WASTES, INCLUDING PREVENTION OF ILLEGAL INTERNATIONAL TRAFFIC IN HAZARDOUS WASTES
INTRODUCTION

20.1.   Effective control of the generation, storage, treatment, recycling and reuse, transport, recovery and disposal of hazardous wastes is of paramount importance for proper health, environmental protection and natural resource management, and sustainable development. This will require the active cooperation and participation of the international community, Governments and industry. Industry, as referred to in this paper, shall include large industrial enterprises, including transnational corporations and domestic industry.

20.2. Prevention of the generation of hazardous wastes and the rehabilitation of contaminated sites are the key elements, and both require knowledge, experienced people, facilities, financial resources and technical and scientific capacities.

20.3. The activities outlined in the present chapter are very closely related to, and have implications for, many of the programme areas described in other chapters, so that an overall integrated approach to hazardous waste management is necessary.

20.4. There is international concern that part of the international movement of hazardous wastes is being carried out in contravention of existing national legislation and international instruments to the detriment of the environment and public health of all countries, particularly developing countries.

20.5. In section I of resolution 44/226 of 22 December 1989, the General Assembly requested each regional commission, within existing resources, to contribute to the prevention of the illegal traffic in toxic and dangerous products and wastes by monitoring and making regional assessments of that illegal traffic and its environmental and health implications. The Assembly also requested the regional commissions to interact among themselves and cooperate with the United Nations Environment Programme (UNEP), with a view to maintaining efficient and coordinated monitoring and assessment of the illegal traffic in toxic and dangerous products and wastes.

Overall objective

20.6. Within the framework of integrated life-cycle management, the overall objective is to prevent to the extent possible, and minimize, the generation of hazardous wastes, as well as to manage those wastes in such a way that they do not cause harm to health and the environment.

Overall targets

20.7. The overall targets are:

(a) Preventing or minimizing the generation of hazardous wastes as part of an overall integrated cleaner production approach; eliminating or reducing to a minimum transboundary movements of hazardous wastes, consistent with the environmentally sound and efficient management of those wastes; and ensuring that environmentally sound hazardous waste management options are pursued to the maximum extent possible within the country of origin (the self-sufficiency principle). The transboundary movements that take place should be on environmental and economic grounds and based upon agreements between the States concerned;

(b) Ratification of the Basel Convention on the Control of Transboundary Movements of Hazardous Wastes and their Disposal and the expeditious elaboration of related protocols, such as the protocol on liability and compensation, mechanisms and guidelines to facilitate the implementation of the Basel Convention;

(c) Ratification and full implementation by the countries concerned of the Bamako Convention on the Ban on the Import into Africa and the Control of Transboundary Movement of Hazardous Wastes within Africa and the expeditious elaboration of a protocol on liability and compensation;

(d) Elimination of the export of hazardous wastes to countries that, individually or through international agreements, prohibits the import of such wastes, such as, the contracting parties to the Bamako Convention, the fourth Lomé Convention or other relevant conventions, where such prohibition is provided for.

20.8. The following programme areas are included in this chapter:

(a) Promoting the prevention and minimization of hazardous waste;

(b) Promoting and strengthening institutional capacities in hazardous waste management;

(c) Promoting and strengthening international cooperation in the management of transboundary movements of hazardous wastes;

(d) Preventing illegal international traffic in hazardous wastes.

PROGRAMME AREAS

A. *Promoting the prevention and minimization of hazardous waste*

Basis for action

20.9. Human health and environmental quality are undergoing continuous degradation by the increasing amount of hazardous wastes being produced. There are increasing direct and indirect costs to society and to individual citizens in connection with the generation, handling and disposal of such wastes. It is therefore crucial to enhance knowledge and information on the economics of prevention and management of hazardous wastes, including the impact in relation to the employment and environmental benefits, in order to ensure that the necessary capital investment is made available in development programmes through economic incentives. One of the first priorities in hazardous waste management is minimization, as part of a broader approach to changing industrial processes and consumer patterns through pollution prevention and cleaner production strategies.

20.10. Among the most important factors in these strategies is the recovery of hazardous wastes and their transformation into useful material. Technology application, modification and development of new low-waste technologies are therefore currently a central focus of hazardous waste minimization.

Objectives

20.11. The objectives of this programme area are:

(a) To reduce the generation of hazardous wastes, to the extent feasible, as part of an integrated cleaner production approach;

(b) To optimize the use of materials by utilizing, where practicable and environmentally sound, the residues from production processes;

(c) To enhance knowledge and information on the economics of prevention and management of hazardous wastes.

20.12. To achieve those objectives, and thereby reduce the impact and cost of industrial development, countries that can afford to adopt the requisite technologies without detriment to their development should establish policies that include:

(a) Integration of cleaner production approaches and hazardous waste minimization in all planning, and the adoption of specific goals;

(b) Promotion of the use of regulatory and market mechanisms;

(c) Establishment of an intermediate goal for the stabilization of the quantity of hazardous waste generated;

(d) Establishment of long-term programmes and policies including targets where appropriate for reducing the amount of hazardous waste produced per unit of manufacture;

(e) Achievement of a qualitative improvement of waste streams, mainly through activities aimed at reducing their hazardous characteristics;

(f) Facilitation of the establishment of cost-effective policies and approaches to hazardous waste prevention and management, taking into consideration the state of development of each country.

Activities

(a) *Management-related activities*

20.13. The following activities should be undertaken:

(a) Governments should establish or modify standards or purchasing specifications to avoid discrimination against recycled materials, provided that those materials are environmentally sound;

(b) Governments, according to their possibilities and with the help of multilateral cooperation, should provide economic or regulatory incentives, where appropriate, to stimulate industrial innovation towards cleaner production methods, to encourage industry to invest in preventive and/or recycling technologies so as to ensure environmentally sound management of all hazardous wastes, including recyclable wastes, and to encourage waste minimization investments;

(c) Governments should intensify research and development activities on cost-effective alternatives for processes and substances that currently result in the generation of hazardous wastes that pose particular problems for environmentally sound disposal or treatment, the possibility of ultimate phase-out of those substances that present an unreasonable or otherwise unmanageable risk and are toxic, persistent and bio-accumulative to be considered as soon as practicable. Emphasis should be given to alternatives that could be economically accessible to developing countries;

(d) Governments, according to their capacities and available resources and with the cooperation of the United Nations and other relevant organizations and industries, as appropriate, should support the establishment of domestic facilities to handle hazardous wastes of domestic origin;

(e) Governments of developed countries should promote the transfer of environmentally sound technologies and know-how on clean technologies and low-waste production to developing countries in conformity with chapter 34, which will bring about changes to sustain innovation. Governments should cooperate with industry to develop guidelines and codes of conduct, where appropriate, leading to cleaner production through sectoral trade industry associations;

(f) Governments should encourage industry to treat, recycle, reuse and dispose of wastes at the source of generation, or as close as possible thereto, whenever hazardous waste generation is unavoidable and when it is both economically and environmentally efficient for industry to do so;

(g) Governments should encourage technology assessments, for example through the use of technology assessment centres;

(h) Governments should promote cleaner production through the establishment of centres providing training and information on environmentally sound technologies;

(i) Industry should establish environmental management systems, including environmental auditing of its production or distribution sites, in order to identify where the installation of cleaner production methods is needed;

(j) A relevant and competent United Nations organization should take the lead, in cooperation with other organizations, to develop guidelines for estimating the costs and benefits of various approaches to the adoption of cleaner production and waste minimization and environmentally sound management of hazardous wastes, including rehabilitation of contaminated sites, taking into account, where appropriate, the report of the 1991 Nairobi meeting of government-designated experts on an international strategy and an action programme, including technical guidelines for the environmentally sound management of hazardous wastes, in particular in the context of the work of the Basel Convention, being developed under the UNEP secretariat;

(k) Governments should establish regulations that lay down the ultimate responsibility of industries for environmentally sound disposal of the hazardous wastes their activities generate.

(b) *Data and information*

20.14. The following activities should be undertaken:

(a) Governments, assisted by international organizations, should establish mechanisms for assessing the value of existing information systems;

(b) Governments should establish nationwide and regional information collection and dissemination clearing-houses and networks that are easy for Government institutions and industry and other non-governmental organizations to access and use;

(c) International organizations, through the UNEP Cleaner Production programme and ICPIC, should extend and strengthen existing systems for collection of cleaner production information;

(d) All United Nations organs and organizations should promote the use and dissemination of information collected through the Cleaner Production network;

(e) OECD should, in cooperation with other organizations, undertake a comprehensive survey of, and disseminate information on, experiences of member countries in adopting economic regulatory schemes and incentive mechanisms for hazardous waste management and for the use of clean technologies that prevent such waste from being generated;

(f) Governments should encourage industries to be transparent in their operations and provide relevant information to the communities that might be affected by the generation, management and disposal of hazardous wastes.

(c) *International and regional cooperation and coordination*

20.15. International/regional cooperation should encourage the ratification by States of the Basel and Bamako Conventions and promote the implementation of those Conventions. Regional cooperation will be necessary for the development of similar conventions in regions other than Africa, if so required. In addition there is a need for effective coordination of international regional and national policies and instruments. Another activity proposed is cooperating in monitoring the effects of the management of hazardous wastes.

Means of implementation

(a) *Financing and cost evaluation*

20.16. The Conference secretariat has estimated the average total annual cost (1993–2000) of implementing the activities of this programme to be about $750 million from the international community on grant or concessional terms. These are indicative and order-of-magnitude estimates only and have not been reviewed by Governments. Actual costs and financial terms, including any that are non-concessional, will depend upon, *inter alia,* the specific strategies and programmes Governments decide upon for implementation.

(b) *Scientific and technological means*

20.17. The following activities related to technology development and research should be undertaken:

(a) Governments, according to their capacities and available resources and with the cooperation of the United Nations and other relevant organizations, and industries, as appropriate, should significantly increase financial support for cleaner technology research and development programmes, including the use of biotechnologies;

(b) States, with the cooperation of international organizations where appropriate, should encourage industry to promote and undertake research into the phase-out of the processes that pose the greatest environmental risk based on hazardous wastes generated;

(c) States should encourage industry to develop schemes to integrate the cleaner production approach into design of products and management practices;

(d) States should encourage industry to exercise environmentally responsible care through hazardous waste reduction and by ensuring the environmentally sound reuse, recycling and recovery of hazardous wastes, as well as their final disposal.

(c) *Human resource development*

20.18.   The following activities should be undertaken:

(a) Governments, international organizations and industry should encourage industrial training programmes, incorporating hazardous waste prevention and minimization techniques and launching demonstration projects at the local level to develop "success stories" in cleaner production;

(b) Industry should integrate cleaner production principles and case examples into training programmes and establish demonstration projects/networks by sector/country;

(c) All sectors of society should develop cleaner production awareness campaigns and promote dialogue and partnership with industry and other actors.

(d) *Capacity-building*

20.19.   The following activities should be undertaken:

(a) Governments of developing countries, in cooperation with industry and with the cooperation of appropriate international organizations, should develop inventories of hazardous waste production, in order to identify their needs with respect to technology transfer and implementation of measures for the sound management of hazardous wastes and their disposal;

(b) Governments should include in national planning and legislation an integrated approach to environmental protection, driven by prevention and source reduction criteria, taking into account the "polluter pays" principle, and adopt programmes for hazardous waste reduction, including targets and adequate environmental control;

(c) Governments should work with industry on sector-by-sector cleaner production and hazardous waste minimization campaigns, as well as on the reduction of such wastes and other emissions;

(d) Governments should take the lead in establishing and strengthening, as appropriate, national procedures for environmental impact assessment, taking into account the cradle-to-grave approach to the management of hazardous wastes, in order to identify options for minimizing the generation of hazardous wastes, through safer handling, storage, disposal and destruction;

(e) Governments, in collaboration with industry and appropriate international organizations, should develop procedures for monitoring the application of the cradle to grave approach, including environmental audits;

(f) Bilateral and multilateral development assistance agencies should substantially increase funding for cleaner technology transfer to developing countries, including small- and medium-sized enterprises.

B. *Promoting and strengthening institutional capacities in hazardous waste management*

Basis for action

20.20. Many countries lack the national capacity to handle and manage hazardous wastes. This is primarily due to inadequate infrastructure, deficiencies in regulatory frameworks, insufficient education and training programmes and lack of coordination between the different ministries and institutions involved in various aspects of waste management. In addition, there is a lack of knowledge about environmental contamination and pollution and the associated health risk from the exposure of populations, especially women and children, and ecosystems to hazardous wastes; assessment of risks; and the characteristics of wastes. Steps need to be taken immediately to identify populations at high risk and to take remedial measures, where necessary. One of the main priorities in ensuring environmentally sound management of hazardous wastes is to provide awareness, education and training programmes covering all levels of society. There is also a need to undertake research programmes to understand the nature of hazardous wastes, to identify their potential environmental effects and to develop technologies to safely handle those wastes. Finally, there is a need to strengthen the capacities of institutions that are responsible for the management of hazardous wastes.

Objectives

20.21. The objectives in this programme area are:

(a) To adopt appropriate coordinating, legislative and regulatory measures at the national level for the environmentally sound management of hazardous wastes, including the implementation of international and regional conventions;

(b) To establish public awareness and information programmes on hazardous waste issues and to ensure that basic education and training programmes are provided for industry and government workers in all countries;

(c) To establish comprehensive research programmes on hazardous wastes in countries;

(d) To strengthen service industries to enable them to handle hazardous wastes, and to build up international networking;

(e) To develop endogenous capacities in all developing countries to educate and train staff at all levels in environmentally sound hazardous waste handling and monitoring and in environmentally sound management;

(f) To promote human exposure assessment with respect to hazardous waste sites and identify the remedial measures required;

(g) To facilitate the assessment of impacts and risks of hazardous wastes on human health and the environment by establishing appropriate procedures, methodologies, criteria and/or effluent-related guidelines and standards;

(h) To improve knowledge regarding the effects of hazardous wastes on human health and the environment;

(i) To make information available to Governments and to the general public on the effects of hazardous wastes, including infectious wastes, on human health and the environment.

Activities

(a) *Management-related activities*

20.22.   The following activities should be undertaken:

(a) Governments should establish and maintain inventories, including computerized inventories, of hazardous wastes and their treatment/disposal sites, as well as of contaminated sites that require rehabilitation, and assess exposure and risk to human health and the environment; they should also identify the measures required to clean up the disposal sites. Industry should make the necessary information available;

(b) Governments, industry and international organizations should collaborate in developing guidelines and easy-to-implement methods for the characterization and classification of hazardous wastes;

(c) Governments should carry out exposure and health assessments of populations residing near uncontrolled hazardous waste sites and initiate remedial measures;

(d) International organizations should develop improved health-based criteria, taking into account national decision-making processes, and assist in the preparation of practical technical guidelines for the prevention, minimization and safe handling and disposal of hazardous wastes;

(e) Governments of developing countries should encourage interdisciplinary and intersectoral groups, in cooperation with international organizations and agencies, to implement training and research activities related to evaluation, prevention and control of hazardous waste health risks. Such groups should serve as models to develop similar regional programmes;

(f) Governments, according to their capacities and available resources and with the cooperation of the United Nations and other relevant organizations as appropriate, should encourage as far as possible the establishment of combined treatment/disposal facilities for hazardous wastes in small- and medium-sized industries;

(g) Governments should promote identification and clean-up of sites of hazardous wastes in collaboration with industry and international organizations. Technologies, expertise and financing should be available for this purpose, as far as possible and when appropriate with the application of the "polluter pays" principle;

(h) Governments should ascertain that their military establishments conform to their nationally applicable environmental norms in the treatment and disposal of hazardous wastes.

(b) *Data and information*

20.23.   The following activities should be undertaken:

(a) Governments, international and regional organizations and industry should facilitate and expand the dissemination of technical and scientific information dealing with the various health aspects of hazardous wastes, and promote its application;

(b) Governments should establish notification systems and registries of exposed populations and of adverse health effects and databases on risk assessments of hazardous wastes;

(c) Governments should endeavour to collect information on those who generate or dispose/recycle hazardous wastes and provide such information to the individuals and institutions concerned.

(c) *International and regional cooperation and coordination*

20.24. Governments, according to their capacities and available resources and with the cooperation of the United Nations and other relevant organizations, as appropriate, should:

(a) Promote and support the integration and operation, at the regional and local levels as appropriate, of institutional and interdisciplinary groups that collaborate, according to their capabilities, in activities oriented towards strengthening risk assessment, risk management and risk reduction with respect to hazardous wastes;

(b) Support capacity-building and technological development and research in developing countries in connection with human resource development, with particular support to be given to consolidating networks;

(c) Encourage self-sufficiency in hazardous waste disposal in the country of origin to the extent environmentally sound and feasible. The transboundary movements that take place should be on environmental and economic grounds and based upon agreements between all States concerned.

Means of implementation

(a) *Financing and cost evaluation*

20.25. The Conference secretariat has estimated the average total annual cost (1993–2000) of implementing the activities of this programme to be about $18.5 billion on a global basis with about $3.5 billion related to developing countries, including about $500 million from the international community on grant or concessional terms. These are indicative and order-of-magnitude estimates only and have not been reviewed by Governments. Actual costs and financial terms, including any that are non-concessional, will depend upon, *inter alia,* the specific strategies and programmes Governments decide upon for implementation.

(b) *Scientific and technological means*

20.26. The following activities should be undertaken:

(a) Governments, according to their capacities and available resources and with the cooperation of the United Nations and other relevant organizations and industry as appropriate, should increase support for hazardous waste research management in developing countries;

(b) Governments, in collaboration with international organizations, should conduct research on the health effects of hazardous wastes in developing countries, including the long-term effects on children and women;

(c) Governments should conduct research aimed at the needs of small- and medium-sized industries;

(d) Governments and international organizations in cooperation with industry should expand technological research on environmentally sound hazardous waste handling, storage, transport, treatment and disposal and on hazardous waste assessment, management and remediation;

(e) International organizations should identify relevant and improved technologies for handling, storage, treatment and disposal of hazardous wastes.

(c) *Human resource development*

20.27. Governments, according to their capacities and available resources and with the cooperation of the United Nations and other relevant organizations and industry as appropriate, should:

(a) Increase public awareness and information on hazardous waste issues and promote the development and dissemination of hazardous wastes information that the general public can understand;

(b) Increase participation in hazardous waste management programmes by the general public, particularly women, including participation at grass-roots levels;

(c) Develop training and education programmes for men and women in industry and Government aimed at specific real-life problems, for example, planning and implementing hazardous waste minimization programmes, conducting hazardous materials audits and establishing appropriate regulatory programmes;

(d) Promote the training of labour, industrial management and government regulatory staff in developing countries on technologies to minimize and manage hazardous wastes in an environmentally sound manner.

20.28. The following activities should also be undertaken:

(a) Governments, according to their capacities and available resources and with the cooperation of the United Nations, other organizations and non-governmental organizations, should collaborate in developing and disseminating educational materials concerning hazardous wastes and their effects on environment and human health, for use in schools, by women's groups and by the general public;

(b) Governments, according to their capacities and available resources and with the cooperation of the United Nations and other organizations, should establish or strengthen programmes for the environmentally sound management of hazardous wastes in accordance with, as appropriate, health and environmental standards, and extend surveillance systems for the purpose of identifying adverse effects on populations and the environment of exposure to hazardous wastes;

(c) International organizations should provide assistance to member States in assessing the health and environmental risks resulting from exposure to hazardous wastes, and in identifying their priorities for controlling the various categories or classes of wastes;

(d) Governments, according to their capacities and available resources and with the cooperation of the United Nations and other relevant organizations, should promote centres of excellence for training in hazardous waste management, building on appropriate national institutions and encouraging international cooperation, *inter alia,* through institutional links between developed and developing countries.

(d) *Capacity-building*

20.29. Wherever they operate, transnational corporations and other large-scale enterprises should be encouraged to introduce policies and make commitments to adopt standards of operation with reference to hazardous waste generation and disposal that are equivalent to or no less stringent than standards in the country of origin, and Governments are invited to make efforts to establish regulations requiring environmentally sound management of hazardous wastes.

20.30. International organizations should provide assistance to member States in assessing the health and environmental risks resulting from exposure to hazardous wastes and in identifying their priorities for controlling the various categories or classes of wastes.

20.31. Governments, according to their capacities and available resources and with the cooperation of the United Nations and other relevant organizations and industries, should:

(a) Support national institutions in dealing with hazardous wastes from the regulatory monitoring and enforcement perspectives, with such support including enabling of those institutions to implement international conventions;

(b) Develop industry-based institutions for dealing with hazardous wastes and service industries for handling hazardous wastes;

(c) Adopt technical guidelines for the environmentally sound management of hazardous wastes and support the implementation of regional and international conventions;

(d) Develop and expand international networking among professionals working in the area of hazardous wastes and maintain an information flow among countries;

(e) Assess the feasibility of establishing and operating national, subregional and regional hazardous wastes treatment centres. Such centres could be used for education and training, as well as for facilitation and promotion of the transfer of technologies for the environmentally sound management of hazardous wastes;

(f) Identify and strengthen relevant academic/research institutions or centres for excellence to enable them to carry out education and training activities in the environmentally sound management of hazardous wastes;

(g) Develop a programme for the establishment of national capacities and capabilities to educate and train staff at various levels in hazardous wastes management;

(h) Conduct environmental audits of existing industries to improve in-plant regimes for the management of hazardous wastes.

C. *Promoting and strengthening international cooperation in the management of transboundary movements of hazardous wastes*

Basis for action

20.32. In order to promote and strengthen international cooperation in the management, including control and monitoring, of transboundary movements of hazardous wastes, a precautionary approach should be applied. There is a need to harmonize the procedures and criteria used in various international and legal instruments. There is also a need to develop or harmonize existing criteria for identifying wastes dangerous to the environment and to build monitoring capacities.

Objectives

20.33. The objectives of this programme area are:

(a) To facilitate and strengthen international cooperation in the environmentally sound management of hazardous wastes, including control and monitoring of transboundary movements of such wastes, including wastes for recovery, by using internationally adopted criteria to identify and classify hazardous wastes and to harmonize relevant international legal instruments;

(b) To adopt a ban on or prohibit, as appropriate, the export of hazardous wastes to countries that do not have the capacity to deal with those wastes in an environmentally sound way or that have banned the import of such wastes;

(c) To promote the development of control procedures for the transboundary movement of hazardous wastes destined for recovery operations under the Basel Convention that encourage environmentally and economically sound recycling options.

Activities

(a) *Management-related activities*

Strengthening and harmonizing criteria and regulations

20.34. Governments, according to their capacities and available resources and with the cooperation of [the] United Nations and other relevant organizations, as appropriate, should:

(a) Incorporate the notification procedure called for in the Basel Convention and relevant regional conventions, as well as in their annexes, into national legislation;

(b) Formulate, where appropriate, regional agreements such as the Bamako Convention regulating the transboundary movement of hazardous wastes;

(c) Help promote the compatibility and complementarity of such regional agreements with international conventions and protocols;

(d) Strengthen national and regional capacities and capabilities to monitor and control the transboundary movement of hazardous wastes;

(e) Promote the development of clear criteria and guidelines, within the framework of the Basel Convention and regional conventions, as appropriate, for environmentally and economically sound operation in resource recovery, recycling reclamation, direct use or alternative uses and for determination of acceptable recovery practices, including recovery levels where feasible and appropriate, with a view to preventing abuses and false presentation in the above operations;

(f) Consider setting up, at national and regional levels, as appropriate, systems for monitoring and surveillance of the transboundary movements of hazardous wastes;

(g) Develop guidelines for the assessment of environmentally sound treatment of hazardous wastes;

(h) Develop guidelines for the identification of hazardous wastes at the national level, taking into account existing internationally—and, where appropriate, regionally—agreed criteria and prepare a list of hazard profiles for the hazardous wastes listed in national legislation;

(i) Develop and use appropriate methods for testing, characterizing and classifying hazardous wastes and adopt or adapt safety standards and principles for managing hazardous wastes in an environmentally sound way.

Implementing existing agreements

20.35. Governments are urged to ratify the Basel Convention and the Bamako Convention, as applicable, and to pursue the expeditious elaboration of related protocols, such as protocols on liability and compensation, and of mechanisms and guidelines to facilitate the implementation of the Conventions.

Means of implementation

(a) *Financing and cost evaluation*

20.36. Because this programme area covers a relatively new field of operation and because of the lack so far of adequate studies on costing of activities under this programme, no cost estimate is available at present. However, the costs for some of the activities related to capacity-building that are presented under this programme could be considered to have been covered under the costing of programme area B above.

20.37. The interim secretariat for the Basel Convention should undertake studies in order to arrive at a reasonable cost estimate for activities to be undertaken initially until the year 2000.

(b) *Capacity-building*

20.38. Governments, according to their capacities and available resources and with the cooperation of [the] United Nations and other relevant organizations, as appropriate, should:

(a) Elaborate or adopt policies for the environmentally sound management of hazardous wastes, taking into account existing international instruments;

(b) Make recommendations to the appropriate forums or establish or adapt norms, including the equitable implementation of the polluter pays principle, and regulatory measures to comply with obligations and principles of the Basel Convention, the Bamako Convention and other relevant existing or future agreements, including protocols, as appropriate, for setting appropriate rules and procedures in the field of liability and compensation for damage resulting from the transboundary movement and disposal of hazardous wastes;

(c) Implement policies for the implementation of a ban or prohibition, as appropriate, of exports of hazardous wastes to countries that do not have the capacity to deal with those wastes in an environmentally sound way or that have banned the import of such wastes;

(d) Study, in the context of the Basel Convention and relevant regional conventions, the feasibility of providing temporary financial assistance in the case of an emergency situation, in order to minimize damage from accidents arising from transboundary movements of hazardous wastes or during the disposal of those wastes.

D. *Preventing illegal international traffic in hazardous wastes*

Basis for action

20.39. The prevention of illegal traffic in hazardous wastes will benefit the environment and public health in all countries, particularly developing countries. It will also help to make the Basel Convention and regional international instruments, such as the Bamako Convention and the fourth Lomé Convention, more effective by promoting compliance with the controls established in those agreements. Article IX of the Basel Convention specifically addresses the issue of illegal shipments of hazardous wastes. Illegal traffic of hazardous wastes may cause serious threats to human health and the environment and impose a special and abnormal burden on the countries that receive such shipments.

20.40. Effective prevention requires action through effective monitoring and the enforcement and imposition of appropriate penalties.

Objectives

20.41. The objectives of this programme area are:

(a) To reinforce national capacities to detect and halt any illegal attempt to introduce hazardous wastes into the territory of any State in contravention of national legislation and relevant international legal instruments;

(b) To assist all countries, particularly developing countries, in obtaining all appropriate information concerning illegal traffic in hazardous wastes;

(c) To cooperate, within the framework of the Basel Convention, in assisting countries that suffer the consequences of illegal traffic.

Activities

(a) *Management-related activities*

20.42. Governments, according to their capacities and available resources and with the cooperation of the United Nations and other relevant organizations, as appropriate, should:

(a) Adopt, where necessary, and implement legislation to prevent the illegal import and export of hazardous wastes;

(b) Develop appropriate national enforcement programmes to monitor compliance with such legislation, detect and deter violations through appropriate penalties and give special attention to those who are known to have conducted illegal traffic in hazardous wastes and to hazardous wastes that are particularly susceptible to illegal traffic.

(b) *Data and information*

20.43. Governments should develop as appropriate, an information network and alert system to assist in detecting illegal traffic in hazardous wastes. Local communities and others could be involved in the operation of such a network and system.

20.44. Governments should cooperate in the exchange of information on illegal transboundary movements of hazardous wastes and should make such information available to appropriate United Nations bodies such as UNEP and the regional commissions.

(c) *International and regional cooperation*

20.45. The regional commissions, in cooperation with and relying upon expert support and advice from UNEP and other relevant bodies of the United Nations system, taking full account of the Basel Convention, shall continue to monitor and assess the illegal traffic in hazardous wastes, including its environmental, economic and health implications, on a continuing basis, drawing upon the results and experience gained in the joint UNEP/ESCAP preliminary assessment of illegal traffic.

20.46. Countries and international organizations, as appropriate, should cooperate to strengthen the institutional and regulatory capacities, in particular of developing countries, in order to prevent the illegal import and export of hazardous wastes.

* * *

SECTION IV. MEANS OF IMPLEMENTATION
Chapter 33
FINANCIAL RESOURCES AND MECHANISMS
INTRODUCTION

33.1. The General Assembly, in resolution 44/228 of 22 December 1989, *inter alia,* decided that the United Nations Conference on Environment and Development should:

Identify ways and means of providing new and additional financial resources, particularly to developing countries, for environmentally sound development programmes and projects in accordance with national development objectives, priorities and plans and to consider ways of effectively monitoring the provision of such new and additional financial resources, particularly to developing countries, so as to enable the international community to take further appropriate action on the basis of accurate and reliable data;

Identify ways and means of providing additional financial resources for measures directed towards solving major environmental problems of global concern and especially of supporting those countries, in particular developing countries, for which the implementation of such measures would entail a special or abnormal burden, owing, in particular, to their lack of financial resources, expertise or technical capacity;

Consider various funding mechanisms, including voluntary ones, and examine the possibility of a special international fund and other innovative approaches, with a view to ensuring, on a favourable basis, the most effective and expeditious transfer of environmentally sound technologies to developing countries;

Quantify the financial requirements for the successful implementation of Conference decisions and recommendations and identify possible sources, including innovative ones, of additional resources.

33.2.   This chapter deals with the financing of the implementation of Agenda 21, which reflects a global consensus integrating environmental considerations into an accelerated development process.   For each of the other chapters, the secretariat of the Conference has provided indicative estimates of the total costs of implementation for developing countries and the requirements for grant or other concessional financing needed from the international community.   These reflect the need for a substantially increased effort, both by countries themselves and by the international community.

BASIS FOR ACTION

33.3.   Economic growth, social development and poverty eradication are the first and overriding priorities in developing countries and are themselves essential to meeting national and global sustainability objectives.   In the light of the global benefits to be realized by the implementation of Agenda 21 as a whole, the provision to developing countries of effective means, *inter alia,* financial resources and technology, without which it will be difficult for them to fully implement their commitments, will serve the common interests of developed and developing countries and of humankind in general, including future generations.

33.4.   The cost of inaction could outweigh the financial costs of implementing Agenda 21.   Inaction will narrow the choices of future generations.

33.5.   For dealing with environmental issues, special efforts will be required.   Global and local environmental issues are interrelated.   The United Nations Framework Convention on Climate Change and the Convention on Biological Diversity address two of the most important global issues.

33.6.   Economic conditions, both domestic and international, that encourage free trade and access to markets will help make economic growth and environmental protection mutually supportive for all countries, particularly for developing countries and countries undergoing the process of transition to a market economy (see chapter 2 for a fuller discussion of these issues).

33.7. International cooperation for sustainable development should also be strengthened in order to support and complement the efforts of developing countries, particularly the least developed countries.

33.8. All countries should assess how to translate Agenda 21 into national policies and programmes through a process that will integrate environment and development considerations. National and local priorities should be established by means that include public participation and community involvement, promoting equal opportunity for men and women.

33.9. For an evolving partnership among all countries of the world, including, in particular, between developed and developing countries, sustainable development strategies and enhanced and predictable levels of funding in support of longer term objectives are required. For that purpose, developing countries should articulate their own priority actions and needs for support and developed countries should commit themselves to addressing these priorities. In this respect, consultative groups and round tables and other nationally based mechanisms can play a facilitative role.

33.10. The implementation of the huge sustainable development programmes of Agenda 21 will require the provision to developing countries of substantial new and additional financial resources. Grant or concessional financing should be provided according to sound and equitable criteria and indicators. The progressive implementation of Agenda 21 should be matched by the provision of such necessary financial resources. The initial phase will be accelerated by substantial early commitments of concessional funding.

OBJECTIVES

33.11. The objectives are as follows:

(a) To establish measures concerning financial resources and mechanisms for the implementation of Agenda 21;

(b) To provide new and additional financial resources that are both adequate and predictable;

(c) To seek full use and continuing qualitative improvement of funding mechanisms to be utilized for the implementation of Agenda 21.

ACTIVITIES

33.12. Fundamentally, the activities of this chapter are related to the implementation of all the other chapters of Agenda 21.

MEANS OF IMPLEMENTATION

33.13. In general, the financing for the implementation of Agenda 21 will come from a country's own public and private sectors. For developing countries, particularly the least developed countries, ODA is a main source of external funding, and substantial new and additional funding for sustainable development and implementation of Agenda 21 will be required. Developed countries reaffirm their commitments to reach the accepted United Nations target of 0.7 per cent of GNP for ODA and, to the extent that they have not yet achieved that target, agree to augment their aid programmes in order to reach that target as soon as possible and to ensure prompt and effective implementation of Agenda 21. Some countries have agreed to reach the target by the year 2000. It was decided that the Commission on Sustainable Development would regularly review and monitor progress towards this target. This review process should systematically combine the monitoring of the implementation of Agenda 21 with a review of the financial resources available. Those countries that have already reached the target are to be commended and encouraged to continue to contribute to the common effort to make available the substantial additional resources that have to be mobilized. Other developed countries, in line with their support for reform efforts in developing countries, agree to make their best efforts to increase their level of ODA. In this context, the importance of equitable burden-sharing among developed countries is recognized. Other countries, including those undergoing the process of transition to a market economy, may voluntarily augment the contributions of the developed countries.

33.14. Funding for Agenda 21 and other outcomes of the Conference should be provided in a way that maximizes the availability of new and additional resources and uses all available funding sources and mechanisms. These include, among others:

(a) The multilateral development banks and funds:

(i) *The International Development Association (IDA).* Among the various issues and options that IDA deputies will examine in connection with the forthcoming tenth replenishment of IDA, the statement made by the President of the World Bank at the United Nations Conference on Environment and Development should be given special consideration in order to help the poorest countries meet their sustainable development objectives as contained in Agenda 21;

(ii) *Regional and subregional development banks.* The regional and subregional development banks and funds should play an increased and more effective role in providing resources on concessional or other favourable terms needed to implement Agenda 21;

(iii) *The Global Environment Facility,* managed jointly by the World Bank, UNDP and UNEP, whose additional grant and concessional funding is designed to achieve global environmental benefits, should cover the agreed incremental costs of relevant activities under Agenda 21, in particular for developing countries. Therefore, it should be restructured so as to, *inter alia:*

Encourage universal participation;

Have sufficient flexibility to expand its scope and coverage to relevant programme areas of Agenda 21, with global environmental benefits, as agreed;

Ensure a governance that is transparent and democratic in nature, including in terms of decision-making and operations, by guaranteeing a balanced and equitable representation of the interests of developing countries and giving due weight to the funding efforts of donor countries;

Ensure new and additional financial resources on grant and concessional terms, in particular to developing countries;

Ensure predictability in the flow of funds by contributions from developed countries, taking into account the importance of equitable burden-sharing;

Ensure access to and disbursement of the funds under mutually agreed criteria without introducing new forms of conditionality;

(b) *The relevant specialized agencies, other United Nations bodies and other international organizations,* which have designated roles to play in supporting national Governments in implementing Agenda 21;

(c) *Multilateral institutions for capacity-building and technical cooperation.* Necessary financial resources should be provided to UNDP to use its network of field offices and its broad mandate and experience in the field of technical cooperation for facilitating capacity-building at the country level, making full use of the expertise of the specialized agencies and other United Nations bodies within their respective areas of competence, in particular UNEP and including the multilateral and regional development banks;

(d) *Bilateral assistance programmes.* These programmes will need to be strengthened in order to promote sustainable development;

(e) *Debt relief.* It is important to achieve durable solutions to the debt problems of low- and middle-income developing countries in order to provide them with the needed means for sustainable development. Measures to address the continuing debt problems of low- and middle-income countries should be kept under review. All creditors in the Paris Club should promptly implement the agreement of December 1991 to provide debt relief for the poorest heavily indebted countries pursuing structural adjustment; debt relief measures should be kept under review so as to address the continuing difficulties of those countries;

(f) *Private funding.* Voluntary contributions through non-governmental channels, which have been running at about 10 per cent of ODA, might be increased.

33.15. *Investment.* Mobilization of higher levels of foreign direct investment and technology transfers should be encouraged through national policies that promote investment and through joint ventures and other modalities.

33.16. *Innovative financing.* New ways of generating new public and private financial resources should be explored, in particular:

(a) Various forms of debt relief, apart from official or Paris Club debt, including greater use of debt swaps;

(b) The use of economic and fiscal incentives and mechanisms;

(c) The feasibility of tradeable permits;

(d) New schemes for fund-raising and voluntary contributions through private channels, including non-governmental organizations;

(e) The reallocation of resources at present committed to military purposes.

33.17. A supportive international and domestic economic climate conducive to sustained economic growth and development is important, particularly for developing countries, in order to achieve sustainability.

33.18. The secretariat of the Conference has estimated the average annual costs (1993–2000) of implementing in developing countries the activities in Agenda 21 to be over $600 billion, including about $125 billion on grant or concessional terms from the international community. These are indicative and order-of-magnitude estimates only, and have not been reviewed by Governments. Actual costs will depend upon, *inter alia,* the specific strategies and programmes Governments decide upon for implementation.

33.19. Developed countries and others in a position to do so should make initial financial commitments to give effect to the decisions of the Conference. They should report on such plans and commitments to the United Nations General Assembly at its forty-seventh session, in 1992.

33.20. Developing countries should also begin to draw up national plans for sustainable development to give effect to the decisions of the Conference.

33.21. Review and monitoring of the financing of Agenda 21 is essential. Questions related to the effective follow-up of the Conference are discussed in chapter 38 (International institutional arrangements). It will be important to review on a regular basis the adequacy of funding and mechanisms, including efforts to reach agreed objectives of the present chapter, including targets where applicable.

1.32 RESOLUTION ON INSTITUTIONAL ARRANGEMENT TO FOLLOW UP THE UNITED NATIONS CONFERENCE ON ENVIRONMENT AND DEVELOPMENT. Adopted by the U.N. General Assembly, 22 December 1992. U.N. Doc.A/47/191, 32 I.L.M. 238 (1993)

The General Assembly,

Welcoming the adoption by the United Nations Conference on Environment and Development of Agenda 21, in particular chapter 38, entitled "International institutional arrangements", which contains a set of important recommendations on institutional arrangements to follow up the Conference,

Stressing the overall objective of the integration of environment and development issues at the national, subregional, regional and international levels, including the United Nations system institutional arrangements, and the specific objectives recommended by the Conference in paragraph 38.8 of Agenda 21,

Taking note of the report of the Secretary–General, prepared with the assistance of the Secretary–General of the United Nations Conference on Environment and Development, on institutional arrangements to follow up the Conference, as well as the recommendations and proposals contained therein,

1. *Endorses* the recommendations on international institutional arrangements to follow up the United Nations Conference on Environment and Development as contained in chapter 38 of Agenda 21, particularly those on the establishment of a high-level Commission on Sustainable Development;

Commission on Sustainable Development

2. *Requests* the Economic and Social Council, at its organizational session for 1993, to set up a high-level Commission on Sustainable Development as a functional commission of the Council in accordance with Article 68 of the Charter of the United Nations in order to ensure the effective follow-up of the Conference, as well as to enhance international cooperation and rationalize the intergovernmental decision-making capacity for the integration of environment and development issues and to examine the progress of the implementation of Agenda 21 at the national, regional and international levels, fully guided by the principles of the Rio Declaration on Environment and Development and all other aspects of the Conference, in order to achieve sustainable development in all countries;

3. *Recommends* that the Commission shall have the following functions, as agreed in paragraphs 38.13, 33.13 and 33.21 of Agenda 21:

(a) To monitor progress in the implementation of Agenda 21 and activities related to the integration of environmental and developmental goals throughout the United Nations system through analysis and evaluation of reports from all relevant organs, organizations, programmes and institutions of the United Nations system dealing with various issues of environment and development, including those related to finance;

(b) To consider information provided by Governments, including, for example, in the form of periodic communications or national reports regarding the activities they undertake to implement Agenda 21, the problems they face, such as problems related to financial resources and technology transfer, and other environment and development issues they find relevant;

(c) To review the progress in the implementation of the commitments contained in Agenda 21, including those related to the provision of financial resources and transfer of technology;

(d) To review and monitor regularly progress towards the United Nations target of 0.7 per cent of the gross national product of developed countries for official development assistance. This review process should systematically combine the monitoring of the implementation of Agenda 21 with the review of financial resources available;

(e) To review on a regular basis the adequacy of funding and mechanisms, including efforts to reach agreed objectives of chapter 33 of Agenda 21, including targets where applicable;

(f) To receive and analyse relevant input from competent non-governmental organizations, including the scientific and the private sector, in the context of the overall implementation of Agenda 21;

(g) To enhance the dialogue, within the framework of the United Nations, with non-governmental organizations and the independent sector, as well as other entities outside the United Nations system;

(h) To consider, where appropriate, information regarding the progress made in the implementation of environmental conventions, which could be made available by the relevant Conferences of Parties;

(i) To provide appropriate recommendations to the General Assembly, through the Economic and Social Council, on the basis of an integrated consideration of the reports and issues related to the implementation of Agenda 21;

(j) To consider, at an appropriate time, the results of the review to be conducted expeditiously by the Secretary–General of all recommendations of the Conference for capacity-building programmes, information networks, task forces and other mechanisms to support the integration of environment and development at regional and subregional levels;

4. *Also recommends* that the Commission shall:

(a) Promote the incorporation of the principles of the Rio Declaration on Environment and Development in the implementation of Agenda 21;

(b) Promote the incorporation of the Non-legally Binding Authoritative Statement of Principles for a Global Consensus on the Management, Conservation and Sustainable Development of All Types of Forests in the implementation of Agenda 21, in particular in the context of the review of the implementation of chapter 11 thereof;

(c) Keep under review the implementation of Agenda 21, recognizing that it is a dynamic programme that could evolve over time, taking into account the agreement to review Agenda 21 in 1997, and make recommendations, as appropriate, on the need for new cooperative arrangements related to sustainable development to the Economic and Social Council and, through it, to the General Assembly;

5. *Decides* that the Commission, in the fulfilment of its functions, will also:

(a) Monitor progress in promoting, facilitating and financing, as appropriate, the access to and the transfer of environmentally sound technologies and corresponding know-how, in particular to developing countries, on favourable terms, including on concessional and preferential terms, as mutually agreed, taking into account the need to protect intellectual property rights as well as the special needs of developing countries for the implementation of Agenda 21;

(b) Consider issues related to the provision of financial resources from all available funding sources and mechanisms, as contained in paragraphs 33.13 to 33.16 of Agenda 21;

6. *Recommends* that the Commission consist of representatives of 53 States elected by the Economic and Social Council from among the Member States of the United Nations and its specialized agencies for three-year terms, with due regard to equitable geographical distribution. The regional allocation of seats could be the same as in the Commission on Science and Technology for Development, as decided in Economic and Social Council decision 1992/222 of 29 May 1992. Representation should be at a high level, including ministerial participation. Other Member States of the United Nations and its specialized agencies, as well as other observers of the United Nations, may participate in the Commission in the capacity of observer, in accordance with established practice;

7. *Also recommends* that the Commission should:

(a) Provide for representatives of various parts of the United Nations system and other intergovernmental organizations, including international financial institutions, the General Agreement on Tariffs and Trade, regional development banks, subregional financial institutions, relevant regional and subregional economic and technical cooperation organizations and regional economic integration organizations, to assist and advise the Commission in the performance of its functions within their respective areas of expertise and mandates, and participate actively in its deliberations; and provide for the European Economic Community, within its areas of competence, to participate—as will be appropriately defined in the rules of procedure of the Commission on Sustainable Development—fully, without the right to vote;

(b) Provide for non-governmental organizations, including those related to major groups as well as industry and the scientific and business communities, to participate effectively in its work and contribute within their areas of competence to its deliberations;

8. *Requests* the Secretary–General, in the light of paragraph 7 above, to submit, for the consideration of the the Economic and Social Council at its organizational session for 1993, his proposals on the rules of procedure of the Commission, including those related to participation of relevant intergovernmental and non-governmental organizations, as recommended by the United Nations Conference on Environment and Development, taking into account the following:

(a) The procedures, while ensuring the intergovernmental nature of the Commission, should allow its members to benefit from the expertise and competence of relevant intergovernmental and non-governmental organizations;

(b) The procedures should permit relevant intergovernmental organizations inside and outside the United Nations system, including multilateral financial institutions, to appoint special representatives to the Commission;

(c) The rules of procedure of the Economic and Social Council and the rules of procedure of its functional commissions;

(d) The rules of procedure of the United Nations Conference on Environment and Development;

(e) Decisions 1/1 and 2/1 of the Preparatory Committee for the United Nations Conference on Environment and Development;

(f) Paragraphs 38.11 and 38.44 of Agenda 21;

9. *Recommends* that the Commission on Sustainable Development shall meet once a year for a period of two to three weeks. The first substantive session of the Commission will be held in New York in 1993, without prejudice to the venue of its future sessions;

10. *Requests* the Committee on Conferences to consider the need for readjusting the calendar of meetings in order to take account of the interrelationship between the work of the Commission and the work of other relevant United Nations intergovernmental subsidiary organs, in order to ensure timely reporting to the Economic and Social Council;

11. *Recommends* that in 1993, as a transitional measure, the Commission hold a short organizational session in New York. At that session, the Commission will elect the Bureau of the Commission, consisting of a chairperson, three vice-chairpersons and a rapporteur, coming from each of the regional groups, decide on the agenda of its first substantive session and consider all other organizational issues as may be necessary. The agenda of the organizational session of the Commission shall be decided on by the Economic and Social Council at its organizational session of 1993;

12. *Also recommends* that the Commission, at its first substantive session, adopt a multi-year thematic programme of its work that will provide a framework to assess progress achieved in the implementation of Agenda 21 and ensure an integrated approach to all of its environment and development components as well as linkages between sectoral and cross-sectoral issues. This programme could be of clusters that would integrate in an effective manner related sectoral and cross-sectoral components of Agenda 21 in such a way as to allow the Commission to review the progress of the implementation of the entire Agenda 21 by 1997. This programme of work could be adjusted, as the need may arise, at the future sessions of the Commission;

13. *Requests* the Secretary–General to submit his proposals for such a programme of work during the organizational session of the Commission;

14. *Recommends* that in order to carry out its functions and implement its work programme effectively the Commission consider organizing its work on the following lines:

(a) Financial resources, mechanisms, transfer of technology, capacity-building and other cross-sectoral issues;

(b) Review of implementation of Agenda 21 at the international level, as well as at the regional and national levels, including the means of implementation, in accordance with paragraph 12 above and the functions of the Commission, taking into account, where appropriate, information regarding the progress in the implementation of relevant environmental conventions;

(c) A high-level meeting, with ministerial participation, to have an integrated overview of the implementation of Agenda 21, to consider emerging policy issues and to provide necessary political impetus to the implementation of decisions of the United Nations Conference on Environment and Development and commitments contained therein.

Review and consideration of implementation of Agenda 21 should be in an integrated manner;

15. *Requests* the Secretary–General to provide for each session of the Commission, in accordance with the programme of work mentioned in paragraph 12 above and in accordance with its organizational modalities, analytical reports containing information on relevant activities to implement Agenda 21, progress achieved and emerging issues to be addressed;

16. *Also requests* the Secretary–General to prepare, for the first substantive session of the Commission, reports containing information and proposals, as appropriate, on the following issues:

(a) Initial financial commitments, financial flows and arrangements to give effect to the decisions of the Conference from all available funding sources and mechanisms;

(b) Progress achieved in facilitating and promoting transfer of environmentally sound technologies, cooperation and capacity-building;

(c) Progress in the incorporation of recommendations of the United Nations Conference on Environment and Development in the activities of international organizations and measures undertaken by the Administrative Committee on Coordination to ensure that sustainable development principles are incorporated into programmes and processes within the United Nations system;

(d) Ways in which, upon request, the United Nations system and bilateral donors are assisting countries, particularly developing countries, in the preparation of national reports and national Agenda 21 action plans;

(e) Urgent and major emerging issues that may be addressed in the course of the high-level meeting;

17. *Decides* that organizational modalities for the Commission should be reviewed in the context of the overall review and appraisal of Agenda 21 during the special session of the General Assembly and adjusted, as may be required, to improve its effectiveness;

Relationship with other United Nations intergovernmental bodies

18. *Recommends* that the Commission, in discharging its functions, submit its consolidated recommendations to the Economic and Social Council and, through it, to the General Assembly, to be considered by the Council and the Assembly in accordance with their respective responsibilities as defined in the Charter of the United Nations and the relevant provisions of paragraphs 38.9 and 38.10 of Agenda 21;

19. *Also recommends* that the Commission actively interact with other intergovernmental United Nations bodies dealing with matters related to environment and development;

20. *Emphasizes* that the ongoing restructuring and revitalization of the United Nations in the economic, social and related fields should take into account the organizational modalities for the Commission on Sustainable Development, with a view to optimizing the work of the Commission and other intergovernmental United Nations bodies dealing with matters related to environment and development;

Coordination within the United Nations system

21. *Requests* all United Nations specialized agencies and related organizations of the United Nations system to strengthen and adjust their activities, programmes and medium-term plans, as appropriate, in line with Agenda 21, in particular regarding projects for promoting sustainable development, in accordance with paragraph 38.28 of Agenda 21, and make their reports on steps they have taken to give effect to this recommendation available to the Commission on Sustainable Development and the Economic and Social Council in 1993 or, at the latest, in 1994, in accordance with Article 64 of the Charter of the United Nations;

22. *Invites* all relevant governing bodies to ensure that the tasks assigned to them are carried out effectively, including the elaboration and publication on a regular basis of reports on the activities of the organs, programmes and organizations for which they are responsible, and that continuous reviews are undertaken of their policies, programmes, budgets and activities;

23. *Invites* the World Bank and other international, regional and subregional financial and development institutions, including the Global Environment Facility, to submit regularly to the Commission on Sustainable Development reports containing information on their experience, activities and plans to implement Agenda 21;

24. *Requests* the Secretary–General to submit to the Commission on Sustainable Development, at its substantive session of 1993, recommendations and proposals for improving coordination of programmes related to development data that exist within the United Nations system, taking into account provisions of paragraph 40.13 of Agenda 21, *inter alia,* regarding "Development Watch";

United Nations Environment Programme, United Nations Development Programme, United Nations Conference on Trade and Development and United Nations Sudano–Sahelian Office

25. *Requests* the Governing Councils of the United Nations Environment Programme, the United Nations Development Programme and the

Trade and Development Board to examine the relevant provisions of chapter 38 of Agenda 21 at their next sessions and submit reports on their specific plans to implement Agenda 21 to the General Assembly at its forty-eighth session, through the Commission on Sustainable Development and the Economic and Social Council;

26. *Takes note* of the work of the United Nations Centre on Urgent Environmental Assistance, established by the Governing Council of the United Nations Environment Programme on an experimental basis, and invites the Governing Council to report to the General Assembly at its forty-eighth session on the experience gained within the Centre;

Regional commissions

27. *Requests* United Nations regional commissions to examine the relevant provisions of chapter 38 of Agenda 21 at their next sessions and submit reports on their specific plans to implement Agenda 21;

28. *Requests* the Economic and Social Council to decide on the arrangements required so that the reports of regional commissions with the conclusions related to such a review be made available to the Commission on Sustainable Development in 1993, or at the latest in 1994;

High-level Advisory Board

29. *Endorses* the view of the Secretary–General that the High-level Advisory Board should consist of eminent persons broadly representative of all regions of the world, with recognized expertise on the broad spectrum of issues to be dealt with by the Commission on Sustainable Development, drawn from relevant scientific disciplines, industry, finance and other major non-governmental constituencies, as well as various disciplines related to environment and development, and that due account should also be given to gender balance;

30. *Decides* that the main task of this Board is to give broad consideration to issues related to implementation of Agenda 21, taking into account the thematic multi-year programme of work of the Commission on Sustainable Development, and provide expert advice in that regard to the Secretary–General and, through him to the Commission, the Economic and Social Council and the General Assembly;

31. *Takes note* of the views of the Secretary–General regarding the functions of the Board and of the Committee for Development Planning, and requests the Secretary–General to submit appropriate proposals to the Economic and Social Council at its organizational session for 1993, including the possibility of organizing expert rosters;

Secretariat support arrangements

32. *Takes note* of the decision of the Secretary–General to establish at the Under–Secretary–General level a new Department for Policy Coordination and Sustainable Development and in this context calls upon the Secretary–General to establish a clearly identifiable, highly qualified and competent secretariat support structure to provide support for the Commission on Sustainable Development, the Inter–Agency Committee on Sustainable Development and the High–Level Advisory Board, taking into account gender balance at all levels, the paramount importance of securing the highest

standards of efficiency, competence and integrity, and the importance of recruiting the staff on as wide a geographical basis as possible in accordance with Articles 8 and 101 of the Charter of the United Nations and the following criteria:

(a) It should draw on the expertise gained and the working methods and organizational structures developed during the preparatory process for the United Nations Conference on Environment and Development;

(b) It should work closely with United Nations and other expert bodies in the field of sustainable development and should cooperate closely and cooperatively with the economic and social entities of the Secretariat and the secretariats of relevant organs, organizations and bodies of the United Nations system, including the secretariats of international financial institutions, and it should provide for effective liaison with relevant non-governmental organizations, including those related to major groups, in particular non-governmental organizations from developing countries;

(c) The secretariat, which will be located in New York, should ensure easy access to all countries to its services; effective interaction with secretariats of other international organizations, financial institutions and relevant conventions whose secretariats have been established definitely or on an interim basis and should have a relevant office at Geneva to establish close links with activities related to follow-up of legal instruments, signed at or mandated by the United Nations Conference on Environment and Development, and to liaise with agencies in the fields of environment and development. The secretariat should also have a liaison office at Nairobi, on the basis of arrangements of the United Nations Conference on Environment and Development;

(d) It should be headed by a high-level official designated by the Secretary–General to work closely and directly with him and with assured access to him, as well as with the heads of relevant organizations of the United Nations system, including the multilateral financial and trade organizations, dealing with the implementation of Agenda 21;

(e) It should be funded from the United Nations regular budget and depend to the maximum extent possible upon existing budgetary resources;

(f) It should be supplemented or reinforced, as appropriate, by secondments from other relevant bodies and agencies of the United Nations system, especially the United Nations Environment Programme, the United Nations Development Programme and the World Bank, taking into account the need to ensure that the work programmes of those organizations are not negatively affected, and national Governments, as well as by appropriate specialists on limited-term contracts from outside the United Nations in such areas as may be required;

(g) It should take into account relevant resolutions and decisions of the General Assembly and the Economic and Social Council regarding women in the United Nations Secretariat;

(h) Sustainable development should be integrated and coordinated with other economic, social and environmental activities of the Secretariat. Organizational decisions should be consistent with consensus resolutions in the context of the restructuring and revitalization of the United Nations in the economic, social and related fields;

33. *Requests* the Secretary–General to make the necessary interim secretariat arrangements to ensure adequate preparations and support for the first session of the Commission on Sustainable Development and the work of the Inter–Agency Committee on Sustainable Development;

34. *Also requests* the Secretary–General to report to the General Assembly at its forty-eighth session on the implementation of the present resolution.

2. GLOBAL COMMONS: ANTARCTICA

2.1 ANTARCTIC TREATY.[1] Concluded at Washington, 1 December 1959. Entered into force, 23 June 1961. 402 U.N.T.S. 71, 12 U.S.T. 794, T.I.A.S. No. 4780, 19 I.L.M. 860 (1980)

The Governments of Argentina, Australia, Belgium, Chile, the French Republic, Japan, New Zealand, Norway, the Union of South Africa, the Union of Soviet Socialist Republics, the United Kingdom of Great Britain and Northern Ireland, and the United States of America,

Recognizing that it is in the interest of all mankind that Antarctica shall continue forever to be used exclusively for peaceful purposes and shall not become the scene or object of international discord;

Acknowledging the substantial contributions to scientific knowledge resulting from international cooperation in scientific investigation in Antarctica;

Convinced that the establishment of a firm foundation for the continuation and development of such cooperation on the basis of freedom of scientific investigation in Antarctica as applied during the International Geophysical Year accords with the interests of science and the progress of all mankind;

Convinced also that a treaty ensuring the use of Antarctica for peaceful purposes only and the continuance of international harmony in Antarctica will further the purposes and principles embodied in the Charter of the United Nations;

Have agreed as follows:

Article I

1. Antarctica shall be used for peaceful purposes only. There shall be prohibited, *inter alia,* any measures of a military nature, such as the establishment of military bases and fortifications, the carrying out of military maneuvers, as well as the testing of any type of weapons.

2. The present Treaty shall not prevent the use of military personnel or equipment for scientific research or for any other peaceful purpose.

Article II

Freedom of scientific investigation in Antarctica and cooperation toward that end, as applied during the International Geophysical Year, shall continue, subject to the provisions of the present Treaty.

Article III

1. In order to promote international cooperation in scientific investigation in Antarctica, as provided for in Article II of the present Treaty, the Contracting Parties agree that, to the greatest extent feasible and practicable:

(*a*) information regarding plans for scientific programs in Antarctica shall be exchanged to permit maximum economy and efficiency of operations;

---

1. *See also* Basic Document 2.9, *infra.*

(*b*) scientific personnel shall be exchanged in Antarctica between expeditions and stations;

(*c*) scientific observations and results from Antarctica shall be exchanged and made freely available.

2.   In implementing this Article, every encouragement shall be given to the establishment of cooperative working relations with those Specialized Agencies of the United Nations and other international organizations having a scientific or technical interest in Antarctica.

Article IV

1.   Nothing contained in the present Treaty shall be interpreted as:

(*a*) a renunciation by any Contracting Party of previously asserted rights of or claims to territorial sovereignty in Antarctica;

(*b*) a renunciation or diminution by any Contracting Party of any basis of claim to territorial sovereignty in Antarctica which it may have whether as a result of its activities or those of its nationals in Antarctica, or otherwise;

(*c*) prejudicing the position of any Contracting Party as regards its recognition or non-recognition of any other State's right of or claim or basis of claim to territorial sovereignty in Antarctica.

2.   No acts or activities taking place while the present Treaty is in force shall constitute a basis for asserting, supporting or denying a claim to territorial sovereignty in Antarctica or create any rights of sovereignty in Antarctica.   No new claim, or enlargement of an existing claim, to territorial sovereignty in Antarctica shall be asserted while the present Treaty is in force.

Article V

1.   Any nuclear explosions in Antarctica and the disposal there of radioactive waste material shall be prohibited.

2.   In the event of the conclusion of international agreements concerning the use of nuclear energy, including nuclear explosions and the disposal of radioactive waste material, to which all of the Contracting Parties whose representatives are entitled to participate in the meetings provided for under Article IX are parties, the rules established under such agreements shall apply in Antarctica.

Article VI

The provisions of the present Treaty shall apply to the area south of 60° South Latitude, including all ice shelves, but nothing in the present Treaty shall prejudice or in any way affect the rights, or the exercise of the rights, of any State under international law with regard to the high seas within that area.

Article VII

1.   In order to promote the objectives and ensure the observance of the provisions of the present Treaty, each Contracting Party whose representatives are entitled to participate in the meetings referred to in Article IX of the Treaty shall have the right to designate observers to carry out any inspection provided for by the present Article.   Observers shall be nationals of the

Contracting Parties which designate them. The names of observers shall be communicated to every other Contracting Party having the right to designate observers, and like notice shall be given of the termination of their appointment.

2. Each observer designated in accordance with the provisions of paragraph 1 of this Article shall have complete freedom of access at any time to any or all areas of Antarctica.

3. All areas of Antarctica, including all stations, installations and equipment within those areas, and all ships and aircraft at points of discharging or embarking cargoes or personnel in Antarctica, shall be open at all times to inspection by any observers designated in accordance with paragraph 1 of this Article.

4. Aerial observation may be carried out at any time over any or all areas of Antarctica by any of the Contracting Parties having the right to designate observers.

5. Each Contracting Party shall, at the time when the present Treaty enters into force for it, inform the other Contracting Parties, and thereafter shall give them notice in advance, of

(*a*) all expeditions to and within Antarctica, on the part of its ships or nationals, and all expeditions to Antarctica organized in or proceeding from its territory;

(*b*) all stations in Antarctica occupied by its nationals; and

(*c*) any military personnel or equipment intended to be introduced by it into Antarctica subject to the conditions prescribed in paragraph 2 of Article I of the present Treaty.

Article VIII

1. In order to facilitate the exercise of their functions under the present Treaty, and without prejudice to the respective positions of the Contracting Parties relating to jurisdiction over all other persons in Antarctica, observers designated under paragraph 1 of Article VII and scientific personnel exchanged under subparagraph 1(*b*) of Article III of the Treaty, and members of the staffs accompanying any such persons, shall be subject only to the jurisdiction of the Contracting Party of which they are nationals in respect of all acts or omissions occurring while they are in Antarctica for the purpose of exercising their functions.

2. Without prejudice to the provisions of paragraph 1 of this Article, and pending the adoption of measures in pursuance of subparagraph 1(*e*) of Article IX, the Contracting Parties concerned in any case of dispute with regard to the exercise of jurisdiction in Antarctica shall immediately consult together with a view to reaching a mutually acceptable solution.

Article IX

1. Representatives of the Contracting Parties named in the preamble to the present Treaty shall meet at the City of Canberra within two months after the date of entry into force of the Treaty, and thereafter at suitable intervals and places, for the purpose of exchanging information, consulting together on matters of common interest pertaining to Antarctica, and formulating and considering, and recommending to their Governments, measures in further-

ance of the principles and objectives of the Treaty, including measures regarding:

(*a*) use of Antarctica for peaceful purposes only;

(*b*) facilitation of scientific research in Antarctica;

(*c*) facilitation of international scientific cooperation in Antarctica;

(*d*) facilitation of the exercise of the rights of inspection provided for in Article VII of the Treaty;

(*e*) questions relating to the exercise of jurisdiction in Antarctica;

(*f*) preservation and conservation of living resources in Antarctica.

2. Each Contracting Party which has become a party to the present Treaty by accession under Article XIII shall be entitled to appoint representatives to participate in the meetings referred to in paragraph 1 of the present Article, during such time as that Contracting Party demonstrates its interest in Antarctica by conducting substantial scientific research activity there, such as the establishment of a scientific station or the despatch of a scientific expedition.

3. Reports from the observers referred to in Article VII of the present Treaty shall be transmitted to the representatives of the Contracting Parties participating in the meetings referred to in paragraph 1 of the present Article.

4. The measures referred to in paragraph 1 of this Article shall become effective when approved by all the Contracting Parties whose representatives were entitled to participate in the meetings held to consider those measures.

5. Any or all of the rights established in the present Treaty may be exercised as from the date of entry into force of the Treaty whether or not any measures facilitating the exercise of such rights have been proposed, considered or approved as provided in this Article.

Article X

Each of the Contracting Parties undertakes to exert appropriate efforts, consistent with the Charter of the United Nations, to the end that no one engages in any activity in Antarctica contrary to the principles or purposes of the present Treaty.

Article XI

1. If any dispute arises between two or more of the Contracting Parties concerning the interpretation or application of the present Treaty, those Contracting Parties shall consult among themselves with a view to having the dispute resolved by negotiation, inquiry, mediation, conciliation, arbitration, judicial settlement or other peaceful means of their own choice.

2. Any dispute of this character not so resolved shall, with the consent, in each case, of all parties to the dispute, be referred to the International Court of Justice for settlement; but failure to reach agreement on reference to the International Court shall not absolve parties to the dispute from the responsibility of continuing to seek to resolve it by any of the various peaceful means referred to in paragraph 1 of this Article.

Article XII

1. (*a*) The present Treaty may be modified or amended at any time by unanimous agreement of the Contracting Parties whose representatives are entitled to participate in the meetings provided for under Article IX. Any such modification or amendment shall enter into force when the depositary Government has received notice from all such Contracting Parties that they have ratified it.

(*b*) Such modification or amendment shall thereafter enter into force as to any other Contracting Party when notice of ratification by it has been received by the depositary Government. Any such Contracting Party from which no notice of ratification is received within a period of two years from the date of entry into force of the modification or amendment in accordance with the provisions of subparagraph 1 (*a*) of this Article shall be deemed to have withdrawn from the present Treaty on the date of the expiration of such period.

2. (*a*) If after the expiration of thirty years from the date of entry into force of the present Treaty, any of the Contracting Parties whose representatives are entitled to participate in the meetings provided for under Article IX so requests by a communication addressed to the depositary Government, a Conference of all the Contracting Parties shall be held as soon as practicable to review the operation of the Treaty.

(*b*) Any modification or amendment to the present Treaty which is approved at such a Conference by a majority of the Contracting Parties there represented, including a majority of those whose representatives are entitled to participate in the meetings provided for under Article IX, shall be communicated by the depositary Government to all the Contracting Parties immediately after the termination of the Conference and shall enter into force in accordance with the provisions of paragraph 1 of the present Article.

(*c*) If any such modification or amendment has not entered into force in accordance with the provisions of subparagraph 1 (*a*) of this Article within a period of two years after the date of its communication to all the Contracting Parties, any Contracting Party may at any time after the expiration of that period give notice to the depositary Government of its withdrawal from the present Treaty; and such withdrawal shall take effect two years after the receipt of the notice by the depositary Government.

Article XIII

1. The present Treaty shall be subject to ratification by the signatory States. It shall be open for accession by any State which is a Member of the United Nations, or by any other State which may be invited to accede to the Treaty with the consent of all the Contracting Parties whose representatives are entitled to participate in the meetings provided for under Article IX of the Treaty.

2. Ratification of or accession to the present Treaty shall be effected by each State in accordance with its constitutional processes.

3. Instruments of ratification and instruments of accession shall be deposited with the Government of the United States of America, hereby designated as the depositary Government.

4. The depositary Government shall inform all signatory and acceding States of the date of each deposit of an instrument of ratification or accession, and the date of entry into force of the Treaty and of any modification or amendment thereto.

5. Upon the deposit of instruments of ratification by all the signatory States, the present Treaty shall enter into force for those States and for States which have deposited instruments of accession. Thereafter the Treaty shall enter into force for any acceding State upon the deposit of its instrument of accession.

6. The present Treaty shall be registered by the depositary Government pursuant to Article 102 of the Charter of the United Nations.

Article XIV

The present Treaty, done in the English, French, Russian and Spanish languages, each version being equally authentic, shall be deposited in the archives of the Government of the United States of America, which shall transmit duly certified copies thereof to the Governments of the signatory and acceding States.

2.2   CERTAIN RECOMMENDATIONS OF THIRD ANTARCTIC TREATY CONSULTATIVE MEETING, ANNEX: AGREED MEASURES FOR THE CONSERVATION OF ANTARCTIC FAUNA AND FLORA. Concluded at Brussels, 13 June 1964.   17 U.S.T. 992, T.I.A.S. No. 6058

The Representatives, taking into consideration Article IX of the Antarctic Treaty, and recalling Recommendation I–VIII of the First Consultative Meeting and Recommendation II–II of the Second Consultative Meeting, recommend to their Governments that they approve as soon as possible and implement without delay the annexed "Agreed Measures for the Conservation of Antarctic Fauna and Flora".

Preamble

The Governments participating in the Third Consultative Meeting under Article IX of the Antarctic Treaty,

Desiring to implement the principles and purposes of the Antarctic Treaty;

Recognising the scientific importance of the study of Antarctic fauna and flora, their adaptation to their rigorous environment, and their interrelationship with that environment;

Considering the unique nature of these fauna and flora, their circumpolar range, and particularly their defencelessness and susceptibility to extermination;

Desiring by further international collaboration within the framework of the Antarctic Treaty to promote and achieve the objectives of protection, scientific study, and rational use of these fauna and flora; and

Having particular regard to the conservation principles developed by the Scientific Committee on Antarctic Research (SCAR) of the International Council of Scientific Unions;

Hereby consider the Treaty Area as a Special Conservation Area and have agreed on the following measures:

Article I

1.   These Agreed Measures shall apply to the same area to which the Antarctic Treaty is applicable (hereinafter referred to as the Treaty Area) namely the area south of 60° South Latitude, including all ice shelves.

However, nothing in these Agreed Measures shall prejudice or in any way affect the rights, or the exercise of the rights, of any State under international law with regard to the high seas within the Treaty Area, or restrict the implementation of the provisions of the Antarctic Treaty with respect to inspection.

2.   The Annexes to these Agreed Measures shall form an integral part thereof, and all references to the Agreed Measures shall be considered to include the Annexes.

Article II

For the purposes of these Agreed Measures:

a) "Native mammal" means any member, at any stage of its life cycle, of any species belonging to the Class Mammalia indigenous to the

Antarctic or occurring there through natural agencies of dispersal, excepting whales;

b) "native bird" means any member, at any stage of its life cycle (including eggs), of any species of the Class Aves indigenous to the Antarctic or occurring there through natural agencies of dispersal;

c) "native plant" means any kind of vegetation at any stage of its life cycle (including seeds), indigenous to the Antarctic or occurring there through natural agencies of dispersal;

d) "appropriate authority" means any person authorised by a Participating Government to issue permits under these Agreed Measures;

e) "permit" means a formal permission in writing issued by an appropriate authority;

f) "participating government" means any Government for which these Agreed Measures have become effective in accordance with Article XIII of these Agreed Measures.

Article III

Each Participating Government shall take appropriate action to carry out these Agreed Measures.

Article IV

The Participating Governments shall prepare and circulate to members of expeditions and stations information to ensure understanding and observance of the provisions of these Agreed Measures, setting forth in particular prohibited activities, and providing lists of specially protected species and specially protected areas.

Article V

The provisions of these Agreed Measures shall not apply in cases of extreme emergency involving possible loss of human life or involving the safety of ships or aircraft.

Article VI

1. Each Participating Government shall prohibit within the Treaty Area the killing, wounding, capturing or molesting of any native mammal or native bird, or any attempt at any such act, except in accordance with a permit.

2. Such permits shall be drawn in terms as specific as possible and issued only for the following purposes:

a) to provide indispensable food for men or dogs in the Treaty Area in limited quantities, and in conformity with the purposes and principles of these Agreed Measures;

b) to provide specimens for scientific study or scientific information;

c) to provide specimens for museums, zoological gardens, or other educational or cultural institutions or uses.

3. Permits for Specially Protected Areas shall be issued only in accordance with the provisions of Article VIII.

4. Participating Governments shall limit the issue of such permits so as to ensure as far as possible that:

a) no more native mammals or birds are killed or taken in any year than can normally be replaced by natural reproduction in the following breeding season;

b) the variety of species and the balance of the natural ecological systems existing within the Treaty Area are maintained.

5. The species of native mammals and birds listed in Annex A of these Measures shall be designated "Specially Protected Species", and shall be accorded special protection by Participating Governments.

6. A Participating Government shall not authorise an appropriate authority to issue a permit with respect to a Specially Protected Species except in accordance with paragraph 7 of this Article.

7. A permit may be issued under this Article with respect to a Specially Protected Species, provided that:

a) it is issued for a compelling scientific purpose, and;

b) the actions permitted thereunder will not jeopardise the existing natural ecological system or the survival of that species.

Article VII

1. Each Participating Government shall take appropriate measures to minimize harmful interference within the Treaty Area with the normal living conditions of any native mammal or bird, or any attempt at such harmful interference, except as permitted under Article VI.

2. The following acts and activities shall be considered as harmful interference:

a) allowing dogs to run free;

b) flying helicopters or other aircraft in a manner which would unnecessarily disturb bird and seal concentrations, or landing close to such concentrations (e.g. within 200 metres);

c) driving vehicles unnecessarily close to concentrations of birds and seals (e.g. within 200 metres);

d) use of explosives close to concentrations of birds and seals;

e) discharge of firearms close to bird and seal concentrations (e.g. within 300 metres);

f) any disturbance of bird and seal colonies during the breeding period by persistent attention from persons on foot.

However, the above activities, with the exception of those mentioned in a) and e) may be permitted to the minimum extent necessary for the establishment, supply and operation of stations.

3. Each Participating Government shall take all reasonable steps towards the alleviation of pollution of the waters adjacent to the coast and ice shelves.

Article VIII

1. The areas of outstanding scientific interest listed in Annex B shall be designated "Specially Protected Areas" and shall be accorded special protec-

tion by the Participating Governments in order to preserve their unique natural ecological system.

2. In addition to the prohibitions and measures of protection dealt with in other Articles of these Agreed Measures, the Participating Governments shall in Specially Protected Areas further prohibit:

 a) the collection of any native plant, except in accordance with a permit;

 b) the driving of any vehicle.

3. A permit issued under Article VI shall not have effect within a Specially Protected Area except in accordance with paragraph 4 of the present Article.

4. A permit shall have effect within a Specially Protected Area provided that:

 a) it was issued for a compelling scientific purpose which cannot be served elsewhere; and

 b) the actions permitted thereunder will not jeopardise the natural ecological system existing in that Area.

Article IX

1. Each Participating Government shall prohibit the bringing into the Treaty Area of any species of animal or plant not indigenous to that Area, except in accordance with a permit.

2. Permits under paragraph 1 of this Article shall be drawn in terms as specific as possible and shall be issued to allow the importation only of the animals and plants listed in Annex C. When any such animal or plant might cause harmful interference with the natural system if left unsupervised within the Treaty Area, such permits shall require that it be kept under controlled conditions and, after it has served its purpose, it shall be removed from the Treaty Area or destroyed.

3. Nothing in paragraphs 1 and 2 of this Article shall apply to the importation of food into the Treaty Area so long as animals and plants used for this purpose are kept under controlled conditions.

4. Each Participating Government undertakes to ensure that all reasonable precautions shall be taken to prevent the accidental introduction of parasites and diseases into the Treaty Area. In particular, the precautions listed in Annex D shall be taken.

Article X

Each Participating Government undertakes to exert appropriate efforts, consistent with the Charter of the United Nations, to the end that no one engages in any activity in the Treaty Area contrary to the principles or purposes of these Agreed Measures.

Article XI

Each Participating Government whose expeditions use ships sailing under flags of nationalities other than its own shall, as far as feasible, arrange with the owners of such ships that the crews of these ships observe these Agreed Measures.

Article XII

1.   The Participating Governments may make such arrangements as may be necessary for the discussion of such matters as:

a) the collection and exchange of records (including records of permits) and statistics concerning the numbers of each species of native mammal and bird killed or captured annually in the Treaty Area;

b) the obtaining and exchange of information as to the status of native mammals and birds in the Treaty Area, and the extent to which any species needs protection;

c) the number of native mammals or birds which should be permitted to be harvested for food, scientific study, or other uses in the various regions;

d) the establishment of a common form in which this information shall be submitted by Participating Governments in accordance with paragraph 2 of this Article.

2.   Each Participating Government shall inform the other Governments in writing before the end of November of each year of the steps taken and information collected in the preceding period of July 1st to June 30th relating to the implementation of these Agreed Measures.   Governments exchanging information under paragraph 5 of Article VII of the Antarctic Treaty may at the same time transmit the information relating to the implementation of these Agreed Measures.

Article XIII

1.   After the receipt by the Government designated in Recommendation I–XIV (5) of notification of approval by all Governments whose representatives are entitled to participate in meetings provided for under Article IX of the Antarctic Treaty, these Agreed Measures shall become effective for those Governments.

2.   Thereafter any other Contracting Party to the Antarctic Treaty may, in consonance with the purposes of Recommendation III–VII, accept these Agreed Measures by notifying the designated Government of its intention to apply the Agreed Measures and to be bound by them.   The Agreed Measures shall become effective with regard to such Governments on the date of receipt of such notification.

3.   The designated Government shall inform the Governments referred to in paragraph 1 of this Article of each notification of approval, the effective date of these Agreed Measures and of each notification of acceptance.   The designated Government shall also inform any Government which has accepted these Agreed Measures of each subsequent notification of acceptance.

Article XIV

1.   These Agreed Measures may be amended at any time by unanimous agreement of the Governments whose Representatives are entitled to participate in meetings under Article IX of the Antarctic Treaty.

2.   The Annexes, in particular, may be amended as necessary through diplomatic channels.

3. An amendment proposed through diplomatic channels shall be submitted in writing to the designated Government which shall communicate it to the Governments referred to in paragraph 1. of the present Article for approval; at the same time, it shall be communicated to the other Participating Governments.

4. Any amendment shall become effective on the date on which notifications of approval have been received by the designated Government from all of the Governments referred to in paragraph 1. of this article.

5. The designated Government shall notify those same Governments of the date of receipt of each approval communicated to it and the date on which the amendment will become effective for them.

6. Such amendment shall become effective on that same date for all other Participating Governments, except those which before the expiry of two months after that date notify the designated Government that they do not accept it.

ANNEXES TO THESE AGREED MEASURES
Annex A

Specially protected species

. . . .

. . . .

Annex B

Specially protected areas

. . . .

. . . .

Annex C

Importation of animals and plants

The following animals and plants may be imported into the Treaty Area in accordance with permits issued under Article IX (2) of these Agreed Measures:

    a) sledge dogs;

    b) domestic animals and plants;

    c) laboratory animals and plants.

Annex D

Precautions to prevent accidental introduction of parasites and diseases into the Treaty Area

The following precautions shall be taken:

1. <u>Dogs:</u> All dogs imported into the Treaty Area shall be inoculated against the following diseases:
   a) distemper;
   b) contagious canine hepatitis;
   c) rabies
   d) leptospirosis (*L. canicola* and *L. icterohaemorrhagicae*).

Each dog shall be inoculated at least two months before the time of its arrival in the Treaty Area.

2. <u>Poultry</u>:   Notwithstanding the provisions of Article IX (3) of these Agreed Measures, no living poultry shall be brought into the Treaty Area after July 1st 1966.

2.3 CONVENTION FOR THE CONSERVATION OF ANTARCTIC SEALS (WITH ANNEX). Concluded at London, 11 February 1972. Entered into force, 11 March 1978. 11 ILM 251 (1972). 29 U.S.T. 441, T.I.A.S. No. 8826, 11 I.L.M. 251 (1972)

The Contracting Parties,

Recalling the Agreed Measures for the Conservation of Antarctic Fauna and Flora, adopted under the Antarctic Treaty signed at Washington on 1 December 1959;

Recognizing the general concern about the vulnerability of Antarctic seals to commercial exploitation and the consequent need for effective conservation measures;

Recognizing that the stocks of Antarctic seals are an important living resource in the marine environment which requires an international agreement for its effective conservation;

Recognizing that this resource should not be depleted by over-exploitation, and hence that any harvesting should be regulated so as not to exceed the levels of the optimum sustainable yield;

Recognizing that in order to improve scientific knowledge and so place exploitation on a rational basis, every effort should be made both to encourage biological and other research on Antarctic seal populations and to gain information from such research and from the statistics of future sealing operations, so that further suitable regulations may be formulated;

Noting that the Scientific Committee on Antarctic Research of the International Council of Scientific Unions (SCAR) is willing to carry out the tasks requested of it in this Convention;

Desiring to promote and achieve the objectives of protection, scientific study and rational use of Antarctic seals, and to maintain a satisfactory balance within the ecological system,

Have agreed as follows:

Article 1

Scope

1. This Convention applies to the seas south of 60° South Latitude, in respect of which the Contracting Parties affirm the provisions of Article IV of the Antarctic Treaty.

2. This Convention may be applicable to any or all of the following species:

Southern elephant seal *Mirounga leonina,*

Leopard seal *Hydrurga leptonyx,*

Weddell seal *Leptonychotes weddelli,*

Crabeater seal *Lobodon carcinophagus,*

Ross seal *Ommatophoca rossi,*

Southern fur seals *Arctocephalus* sp.

3. The Annex to this Convention forms an integral part thereof.

Article 2

Implementation

1.   The Contracting Parties agree that the species of seals enumerated in Article 1 shall not be killed or captured within the Convention area by their nationals or vessels under their respective flags except in accordance with the provisions of this Convention.

2.   Each Contracting Party shall adopt for its nationals and for vessels under its flag such laws, regulations and other measures, including a permit system as appropriate, as may be necessary to implement this Convention.

Article 3

Annexed Measures

1.   This Convention includes an Annex specifying measures which the Contracting Parties hereby adopt.   Contracting Parties may from time to time in the future adopt other measures with respect to the conservation, scientific study and rational and humane use of seal resources, prescribing *inter alia:*

(a) permissible catch;

(b) protected and unprotected species;

(c) open and closed seasons;

(d) open and closed areas, including the designation of reserves;

(e) the designation of special areas where there shall be no disturbance of seals;

(f) limits relating to sex, size, or age for each species;

(g) restrictions relating to time of day and duration, limitations of effort and methods of sealing;

(h) types and specifications of gear and apparatus and appliances which may be used;

(i) catch returns and other statistical and biological records;

(j) procedures for facilitating the review and assessment of scientific information;

(k) other regulatory measures including an effective system of inspection.

2.   The measures adopted under paragraph 1 of this Article shall be based upon the best scientific and technical evidence available.

3.   The Annex may from time to time be amended in accordance with the procedures provided for in Article 9.

Article 4

Special Permits

1.   Notwithstanding the provisions of this Convention, any Contracting Party may issue permits to kill or capture seals in limited quantities and in conformity with the objectives and principles of this Convention for the following purposes:

(a) to provide indispensable food for men or dogs;

(b) to provide for scientific research; or

(c) to provide specimens for museums, educational or cultural institutions.

2. Each Contracting Party shall, as soon as possible, inform the other Contracting Parties and SCAR of the purpose and content of all permits issued under paragraph 1 of this Article and subsequently of the numbers of seals killed or captured under these permits.

Article 5

Exchange of Information and Scientific Advice

1. Each Contracting Party shall provide to the other Contracting Parties and to SCAR the information specified in the Annex within the period indicated therein.

2. Each Contracting Party shall also provide to the other Contracting Parties and to SCAR before 31 October each year information on any steps it has taken in accordance with Article 2 of this Convention during the preceding period 1 July to 30 June.

3. Contracting Parties which have no information to report under the two preceding paragraphs shall indicate this formally before 31 October each year.

4. SCAR is invited:

(a) to assess information received pursuant to this Article; encourage exchange of scientific data and information among the Contracting Parties; recommend programmes for scientific research; recommend statistical and biological data to be collected by sealing expeditions within the Convention area; and suggest amendments to the Annex; and

(b) to report on the basis of the statistical, biological and other evidence available when the harvest of any species of seal in the Convention area is having a significantly harmful effect on the total stocks of such species or on the ecological system in any particular locality.

5. SCAR is invited to notify the Depositary which shall report to the Contracting Parties when SCAR estimates in any sealing season that the permissible catch limits for any species are likely to be exceeded and, in that case, to provide an estimate of the date upon which the permissible catch limits will be reached. Each Contracting Party shall then take appropriate measures to prevent its nationals and vessels under its flag from killing or capturing seals of that species after the estimated date until the Contracting Parties decide otherwise.

6. SCAR may if necessary seek the technical assistance of the Food and Agriculture Organization of the United Nations in making its assessments.

7. Notwithstanding the provisions of paragraph 1 of Article 1 the Contracting Parties shall, in accordance with their internal law, report to each other and to SCAR, for consideration statistics relating to the Antarctic seals listed in paragraph 2 of Article 1 which have been killed or captured by their nationals and vessels under their respective flags in the area of floating sea ice north of 60° South Latitude.

Article 6

Consultations Between Contracting Parties

1. At any time after commercial sealing has begun a Contracting Party may propose through the Depositary that a meeting of Contracting Parties be convened with a view to:

(a) establishing by a two-third majority of the Contracting Parties, including the concurring votes of all States signatory to this Convention present at the meeting, an effective system of control, including inspection, over the implementation of the provisions of this Convention;

(b) establishing a commission to perform such functions under this Convention as the Contracting Parties may deem necessary; or

(c) considering other proposals, including:

(i) the provision of independent scientific advice;

(ii) the establishment, by a two-thirds majority, of a scientific advisory committee which may be assigned some or all of the functions requested of SCAR under this Convention, if commercial sealing reaches significant proportions;

(iii) the carrying out of scientific programmes with the participation of the Contracting Parties; and

(iv) the provision of further regulatory measures, including moratoria.

2. If one-third of the Contracting Parties indicate agreement the Depositary shall convene such a meeting, as soon as possible.

3. A meeting shall be held at the request of any Contracting Party, if SCAR reports that the harvest of any species of Antarctic seal in the area to which this Convention applies is having a significantly harmful effect on the total stocks or the ecological system in any particular locality.

Article 7

Review of Operations

The Contracting Parties shall meet within five years after the entry into force of this Convention and at least every five years thereafter to review the operation of the Convention.

Article 8

Amendments to the Convention

1. This Convention may be amended at any time. The text of any amendment proposed by a Contracting Party shall be submitted to the Depositary, which shall transmit it to all the Contracting Parties.

2. If one third of the Contracting Parties request a meeting to discuss the proposed amendment the Depositary shall call such a meeting.

3. An amendment shall enter into force when the Depositary has received instruments of ratification or acceptance thereof from all the Contracting Parties.

Article 9

Amendments to the Annex

1. Any Contracting Party may propose amendments to the Annex to this Convention. The text of any such proposed amendment shall be submitted to the Depositary which shall transmit it to all Contracting Parties.

2. Each such proposed amendment shall become effective for all Contracting Parties six months after the date appearing on the notification from the Depositary to the Contracting Parties, if within 120 days of the notification date, no objection has been received and two-thirds of the Contracting Parties have notified the Depositary in writing of their approval.

3. If an objection is received from any Contracting Party within 120 days of the notification date, the matter shall be considered by the Contracting Parties at their next meeting. If unanimity on the matter is not reached at the meeting, the Contracting Parties shall notify the Depositary within 120 days from the date of closure of the meeting of their approval or rejection of the original amendment or of any new amendment proposed by the meeting. If, by the end of this period, two-thirds of the Contracting Parties have approved such amendment, it shall become effective six months from the date of the closure of the meeting for those Contracting Parties which have by then notified their approval.

4. Any Contracting Party which has objected to a proposed amendment may at any time withdraw that objection, and the proposed amendment shall become effective with respect to such Party immediately if the amendment is already in effect, or at such time as it becomes effective under the terms of this Article.

5. The Depositary shall notify each Contracting Party immediately upon receipt of each approval or objection, of each withdrawal of objection, and of the entry into force of any amendment.

6. Any State which becomes a party to this Convention after an amendment to the Annex has entered into force shall be bound by the Annex as so amended. Any State which becomes a Party to this Convention during the period when a proposed amendment is pending may approve or object to such an amendment within the time limits applicable to other Contracting Parties.

Article 10

Signature

This Convention shall be open for signature at London from 1 June to 31 December 1972 by States participating in the Conference on the Conservation of Antarctic Seals held at London from 3 to 11 February 1972.

Article 11

Ratification

This Convention is subject to ratification or acceptance. Instruments of ratification or acceptance shall be deposited with the Government of the United Kingdom of Great Britain and Northern Ireland, hereby designated as the Depositary.

Article 12

Accession

The Convention shall be open for accession by any State which may be invited to accede to this Convention with the consent of all the Contracting Parties.

Article 13

Entry into Force

1. This Convention shall enter into force on the thirtieth day following the date of deposit of the seventh instrument of ratification or acceptance.

2. Thereafter this Convention shall enter into force for each ratifying, accepting or acceding State on the thirtieth day after deposit by such State of its instrument of ratification, acceptance or accession.

Article 14

Withdrawal

Any Contracting Party may withdraw from this Convention on 30 June of any year by giving notice on or before 1 January of the same year to the Depositary which upon receipt of such a notice shall at once communicate it to the other Contracting Parties. Any other Contracting Party may, in like manner, within one month of the receipt of a copy of such a notice from the Depositary, give notice of withdrawal, so that the Convention shall cease to be in force on 30 June of the same year with respect to the Contracting Party giving such notice.

Article 15

Notification by the Depositary

The Depositary shall notify all signatory and acceding States of the following:

(a) signatures of this Convention, the deposit of instruments of ratification, acceptance or accession and notices of withdrawal;

(b) the date of entry into force of this Convention and of any amendments to it or its Annex.

Article 16

Certified Copies and Registration

1. This Convention, done in the English, French, Russian and Spanish languages, each version being equally authentic, shall be deposited in the archives of the Government of the United Kingdom of Great Britain and Northern Ireland, which shall transmit duly certified copies thereof to all signatory and acceding States.

2. This Convention shall be registered by the Depositary pursuant to Article 102 of the Charter of the United Nations.

ANNEX

1. *Permissible Catch*

The Contracting Parties shall in any one year, which shall run from 1 July to 30 June inclusive, restrict the total number of seals of each species killed or captured to the numbers specified below. These numbers are subject to review in the light of scientific assessments.

(a) in the case of Crabeater seals *Lobodon carcinophague* 175,000

(b) in the case of Leopard seals *Hydrurga leptonyx* 12,000

(c) in the case of Weddell seals *Leptonychotes weddelli,* 5,000

2. *Protected Species*

(a) It is forbidden to kill or capture Ross seals *Ommatophoca rossi,* Southern elephant seals *Mirounga leonina,* or fur seals of the genus *Arctocephalus.*

(b) In order to protect the adult breeding stock during the period when it is most concentrated and vulnerable, it is forbidden to kill or capture any Weddell seal *Leptonychotes weddelli* one year old or older between 1 September and 31 January inclusive.

3. *Closed Season and Sealing Season*

The period between 1 March and 31 August inclusive is a Closed Season, during which the killing or capturing of seals is forbidden. The period 1 September to the last day in February constitutes a Sealing Season.

4. *Sealing Zones*

Each of the sealing zones listed in this paragraph shall be closed in numerical sequence to all sealing operations for the seal species listed in paragraph 1 of this Annex for the period 1 September to the last day of February inclusive. Such closures shall begin with the same zone as is closed under paragraph 2 of Annex B to Annex 1 of the Report of the Fifth Antarctic Treaty Consultative Meeting at the moment the Convention enters into force. Upon the expiration of each closed period, the affected zone shall reopen.

Zone 1— between 60° and 120° West Longitude

Zone 2— between 0° and 60° West Longitude, together with that part of the Weddell Sea lying westward of 60° West Longitude

Zone 3— between 0° and 70° East Longitude

Zone 4— between 70° and 130° East Longitude

Zone 5— between 130° East Longitude and 170° West Longitude

Zone 6— between 120° and 170° West Longitude.

5. *Seal Reserves*

It is forbidden to kill or capture seals in the following reserves, which are seal breeding areas or the site of long-term scientific research:

(a) The area around the South Orkmov Islands between 60° 20′ and 60° 56′ South Latitude and 44° 05′ and 46° 25′ West Longitude.

(b) The area of the southwestern Ross Sea south of 76° South Latitude and west of 170° East Longitude.

(c) The area of Edisto Inlet south and west of a line drawn between Cape Hallet at 72° 19′ South Latitude, 170° 18′ East Longitude, and Helm Point, at 72° 11′ South Latitude, 72° 11′ South Latitude, 170° 00′ East Longitude.

6. *Exchange of Information*

(a) Contracting Parties shall provide before 31 October each year to other Contracting Parties and to SCAR a summary of statistical information on all seals killed or captured by their respective flags in the Convention areas, in respect of the preceding period 1 July to 30 June. This information shall include by zones and months:

(i) The gross and nett [sic] tonnage, brake horse-power, number of crew, and number of days' operation of vessels under the flag of the Contracting Party:

(ii) The number of adult individuals and pups of each species taken. When specifically requested, this information shall be provided in respect of each ship, together with its daily position at noon each operating day and the catch on that day.

(b) When an industry has started, reports of the number of seals of each species killed or captured in each zone shall be made to SCAR in the form and at the intervals (not shorter than once a week) requested by that body.

(c) Contracting Parties shall provide to SCAR biological information concerning in particular

(i) Sex

(ii) Reproductive condition

(iii) Age

SCAR may request additional information or material with the approval of the Contracting Parties.

(d) Contracting Parties shall provide to other Contracting Parties and to SCAR at least 30 days in advance of departure from their home ports, information on proposed sealing expenditures.

7. *Sealing Methods*

(a) SCAR is invited to report on methods of sealing and to make recommendations with a view to ensuring that the killing or capturing of seals is quick, painless and efficient. Contracting Parties, as appropriate, shall adopt rules for their nationals and vessels under their respective flags engaged in the killing and capturing of seals, giving due consideration to the views of SCAR.

(b) In the light of the available scientific and technical data, Contracting Parties agree to take appropriate steps to ensure that their nationals and vessels under their respective flags refrain from killing, or capturing seals in the water, except in limited quantities to provide for scientific research in conformity with the objectives and principles of this Convention. Such research shall include studies as to the effectiveness of methods of sealing from the viewpoint of the management and humane and rational utilization of the Antarctic seal resources for conservation purposes. The undertaking and the results of any such scientific research programme shall be communicated to SCAR and the Depositary which shall transmit them to the Contracting Parties.

2.4 CONVENTION ON THE CONSERVATION OF ANTARCTIC MARINE LIVING RESOURCES (CCAMLR) (WITHOUT ANNEX). Concluded at Canberra, 20 May 1980. Entered into force, 7 April 1982. L252 O.J.E.C. 27 (1981), T.I.A.S. No. 10240, 19 I.L.M. 841 (1980)

THE CONTRACTING PARTIES,

RECOGNIZING the importance of safeguarding the environment and protecting the integrity of the ecosystem of the seas surrounding Antarctica;

NOTING the concentration of marine living resources found in Antarctic waters and the increased interest in the possibilities offered by the utilization of these resources as a source of protein;

CONSCIOUS of the urgency of ensuring the conservation of Antarctic marine living resources;

CONSIDERING that it is essential to increase knowledge of the Antarctic marine ecosystem and its components so as to be able to base decisions on harvesting on sound scientific information;

BELIEVING that the conservation of Antarctic marine living resources calls for international cooperation with due regard for the provisions of the Antarctic Treaty and with the active involvement of all States engaged in research or harvesting activities in Antarctic waters;

RECOGNIZING the prime responsibilities of the Antarctic Treaty Consultative Parties for the protection and preservation of the Antarctic environment and, in particular, their responsibilities under Article IX, paragraph 1(f) of the Antarctic Treaty in respect of the preservation and conservation of living resources in Antarctica;

RECALLING the action already taken by the Antarctic Treaty Consultative Parties including, in particular, the agreed measures for the conservation of Antarctic fauna and flora, as well as the provisions of the Convention for the conservation of Antarctic seals;

BEARING in mind the concern regarding the conservation of Antarctic marine living resources expressed by the consultative parties at the ninth consultative meeting of the Antarctic Treaty and the importance of the provisions of recommendations IX–2 which led to the establishment of the present convention;

BELIEVING that it is in the interest of all mankind to preserve the waters surrounding the Antarctic continent for peaceful purposes only and to prevent their becoming the scene or object of international discord;

RECOGNIZING, in the light of the foregoing, that it is desirable to establish suitable machinery for recommending, promoting, deciding upon and coordinating the measures and scientific studies needed to ensure the conservation of Antarctic marine living organisms,

HAVE AGREED AS FOLLOWS:

Article I

1. This Convention applies to the Antarctic marine living resources of the area south of 60° South latitude and to the Antarctic marine living resources of the area between that latitude and the Antarctic Convergence which form part of the Antarctic marine ecosystem.

2. Antarctic marine living resources means the populations of fin fish, molluscs, crustaceans and all other species of living organisms, including birds, found south of the Antarctic Convergence.

3. The Antarctic marine ecosystem means the complex of relationships of Antarctic marine living resources with each other and with their physical environment.

4. The Antarctic Convergence shall be deemed to be a line joining the following points along parallels of latitude and meridians of longitude:

50°S, 0°; 50°S, 30°E; 45°S, 30°E; 45°S, 80°E; 55°S, 80°E; 55°S, 150°E; 60°S, 150°E; 60°S, 50°W; 50°S, 50°W; 50°S, 0°.

Article II

1. The objective of this Convention is the Conservation of Antarctic marine living resources.

2. For the purposes of this Convention, the term "conservation" includes rational use.

3. Any harvesting and associated activities in the area to which this Convention applies shall be conducted in accordance with the provisions of this Convention and with the following principles of conservation:

(a) prevention of decrease in the size of any harvested population to levels below those which ensure its stable recruitment. For this purpose its size should not be allowed to fall below a level close to that which ensures the greatest net annual increment;

(b) maintenance of the ecological relationships between harvested, dependent and related populations of Antarctic marine living resources and the restoration of depleted populations to the levels defined in subparagraph (a) above;

and

(c) prevention of changes or minimization of the risk of changes in the marine ecosystem which are not potentially reversible over two or three decades, taking into account the state of available knowledge of the direct and indirect impact of harvesting, the effect of the introduction of alien species, the effects of associated activities on the marine ecosystem and of the effects of environmental changes, with the aim of making possible the sustained conservation of Antarctic marine living resources.

Article III

The Contracting Parties, whether or not they are Parties to the Antarctic Treaty, agree that they will not engage in any activities in the Antarctic Treaty area contrary to the principles and purposes of that Treaty and that, in their relations with each other, they are bound by the obligations contained in Articles I and V of the Antarctic Treaty.

Article IV

1. With respect to the Antarctic Treaty area, all Contracting Parties, whether or not they are Parties to the Antarctic Treaty, are bound by Articles IV and VI of the Antarctic Treaty in their relations with each other.

2. Nothing in this Convention and no acts or activities taking place while the present Convention is in force shall:

(*a*) constitute a basis for asserting, supporting or denying a claim to territorial sovereignty in the Antarctic Treaty area or create any rights of sovereignty in the Antarctic Treaty area;

(*b*) be interpreted as a renunciation or diminution by any Contracting Party of, or as prejudicing, any right or claim or basis of claim to exercise coastal state jurisdiction under international law within the area to which this Convention applies;

(*c*) be interpreted as prejudicing the position of any Contracting Party as regards its recognition or non-recognition of any such right, claim or basis of claim;

(*d*) affect the provision of Article IV, paragraph 2, of the Antarctic Treaty that no new claim, or enlargement of an existing claim, to territorial sovereignty in Antarctica shall be asserted while the Antarctic Treaty is in force.

Article V

1. The Contracting Parties which are not Parties to the Antarctic Treaty acknowledge the special obligations and responsibilities of the Antarctic Treaty Consultative Parties for the protection and preservation of the environment of the Antarctic Treaty area.

2. The Contracting Parties which are not Parties to the Antarctic Treaty agree that, in their activities in the Antarctic Treaty area, they will observe as and when appropriate the Agreed Measures for the Conservation of Antarctic Fauna and Flora and such other measures as have been recommended by the Antarctic Treaty Consultative Parties in fulfilment of their responsibility for the protection of the Antarctic environment from all forms of harmful human interference.

3. For the purposes of this Convention, "Antarctic Treaty Consultative Parties" means the Contracting Parties to the Antarctic Treaty whose Representatives participate in meetings under Article IX of the Antarctic Treaty.

Article VI

Nothing in this Convention shall derogate from the rights and obligations of Contracting Parties under the International Convention for the Regulation of Whaling and the Convention for the Conservation of Antarctic Seals.

Article VII

1. The Contracting Parties hereby establish and agree to maintain the Commission for the Conservation of Antarctic Marine Living Resources (hereinafter referred to as "the Commission").

2. Membership in the Commission shall be as follows:

(*a*) each Contracting Party which participated in the meeting at which this Convention was adopted shall be a Member of the Commission;

(*b*) each State Party which has acceded to this Convention pursuant to Article XXIX shall be entitled to be a Member of the Commission during such time as that acceding party is engaged in research or harvesting activities in relation to the marine living resources to which this Convention applies;

(c) each regional economic integration organization which has acceded to this Convention pursuant to Article XXIX shall be entitled to be a Member of the Commission during such time as its States members are so entitled;

(d) a Contracting Party seeking to participate in the work of the Commission pursuant to sub-paragraphs (b) and (c) above shall notify the Depositary of the basis upon which it seeks to become a Member of the Commission and of its willingness to accept conservation measures in force. The Depositary shall communicate to each Member of the Commission such notification and accompanying information. Within two months of receipt of such communication from the Depositary, any Member of the Commission may request that a special meeting of the Commission be held to consider the matter. Upon receipt of such request, the Depositary shall call such a meeting. If there is no request for a meeting, the Contracting Party submitting the notification shall be deemed to have satisfied the requirements for Commission Membership.

3. Each Member of the Commission shall be represented by one representative who may be accompanied by alternate representatives and advisers.

Article VIII

The Commission shall have legal personality and shall enjoy in the territory of each of the States Parties such legal capacity as may be necessary to perform its function and achieve the purposes of this Convention. The privileges and immunities to be enjoyed by the Commission and its staff in the territory of a State Party shall be determined by agreement between the Commission and the State Party concerned.

Article IX

1. The function of the Commission shall be to give effect to the objective and principles set out in Article II of this Convention. To this end, it shall:

(a) facilitate research into and comprehensive studies of Antarctic marine living resources and of the Antarctic marine ecosystem;

(b) compile data on the status of and changes in population of Antarctic marine living resources and on factors affecting the distribution, abundance and productivity of harvested species and dependent or related species or populations;

(c) ensure the acquisition of catch and effort statistics on harvested populations;

(d) analyse, disseminate and publish the information referred to in subparagraphs (b) and (c) above and the reports of the Scientific Committee;

(e) identify conservation needs and analyse the effectiveness of conservation measures;

(f) formulate, adopt and revise conservation measures on the basis of the best scientific evidence available, subject to the provisions of paragraph 5 of this Article;

(*g*) implement the system of observation and inspection established under Article XXIV of this Convention;

(*h*) carry out such other activities as are necessary to fulfil the objective of this Convention.

2. The conservation measures referred to in paragraph 1(f) above include the following:

(*a*) the designation of the quantity of any species which may be harvested in the area to which this Convention applies;

(*b*) the designation of regions and sub-regions based on the distribution of populations of Antarctic marine living resources;

(*c*) the designation of the quantity which may be harvested from the populations of regions and sub-regions;

(*d*) the designation of protected species;

(*e*) the designation of the size, age and, as appropriate, sex of species which may be harvested;

(*f*) the designation of open and closed seasons for harvesting;

(*g*) the designation of the opening and closing of areas, regions or sub-regions for purposes of scientific study or conservation, including special areas for protection and scientific study;

(*h*) regulation of the effort employed and methods of harvesting, including fishing gear, with a view, inter alia, to avoiding undue concentration of harvesting in any region or sub-region;

(*i*) the taking of such other conservation measures as the Commission considers necessary for the fulfilment of the objective of this Convention, including measures concerning the effects of harvesting and associated activities on components of the marine ecosystem other than the harvested populations.

3. The Commission shall publish and maintain a record of all conservation measures in force.

4. In exercising its functions under paragraph 1 above, the Commission shall take full account of the recommendations and advice of the Scientific Committee.

5. The Commission shall take full account of any relevant measures or regulations established or recommended by the Consultative Meetings pursuant to Article IX of the Antarctic Treaty or by existing fisheries commissions responsible for species which may enter the area to which this Convention applies, in order that there shall be no inconsistency between the rights and obligations of a Contracting Party under such regulations or measures and conservation measures which may be adopted by the Commission.

6. Conservation measures adopted by the Commission in accordance with this Convention shall be implemented by Members of the Commission in the following manner:

(*a*) the Commission shall notify conservation measures to all Members of the Commission;

(*b*) conservation measures shall become binding upon all Members of the Commission 180 days after such notification, except as provided in subparagraphs (c) and (d) below;

(*c*) if a Member of the Commission, within ninety days following the notification specified in sub-paragraph (a), notifies the Commission that it is unable to accept the conservation measure, in whole or in part, the measure shall not, to the extent stated, be binding upon that Member of the Commission;

(*d*) in the event that any Member of the Commission invokes the procedure set forth in sub-paragraph (c) above, the Commission shall meet at the request of any Member of the Commission to review the conservation measure. At the time of such meeting and within thirty days following the meeting, any Member of the Commission shall have the right to declare that it is no longer able to accept the conservation measure, in which case the Member shall no longer be bound by such measure.

Article X

1. The Commission shall draw the attention of any State which is not a Party to this Convention to any activity undertaken by its nationals or vessels which, in the opinion of the Commission, affects the implementation of the objective of this Convention.

2. The Commission shall draw the attention of all Contracting Parties to any activity which, in the opinion of the Commission, affects the implementation by a Contracting Party of the objective of this Convention or the compliance by that Contracting Party with its obligations under this Convention.

Article XI

The Commission shall seek to cooperate with Contracting Parties which may exercise jurisdiction in marine areas adjacent to the area to which this Convention applies in respect of the conservation of any stock or stocks of associated species which occur both within those areas and the area to which this Convention applies, with a view to harmonizing the conservation measures adopted in respect of such stocks.

Article XII

1. Decisions of the Commission on matters of substance shall be taken by consensus. The question of whether a matter is one of substance shall be treated as a matter of substance.

2. Decisions on matters other than those referred to in paragraph 1 above shall be taken by a simple majority of the Members of the Commission present and voting.

3. In Commission consideration of any item requiring a decision, it shall be made clear whether a regional economic integration organization will participate in the taking of the decision and, if so, whether any of its member States will also participate. The number of Contracting Parties so participating shall not exceed the number of member States of the regional economic integration organization which are Members of the Commission.

4.   In the taking of decisions pursuant to this Article, a regional economic integration organization shall have only one vote.

Article XIII

1.   The headquarters of the Commission shall be established at Hobart, Tasmania, Australia.

2.   The Commission shall hold a regular annual meeting. Other meetings shall also be held at the request of one-third of its members and as otherwise provided in this Convention. The first meeting of the Commission shall be held within three months of the entry into force of this Convention, provided that among the Contracting Parties there are at least two States conducting harvesting activities within the area to which this Convention applies. The first meeting shall, in any event, be held within one year of the entry into force of this Convention. The Depositary shall consult with the signatory States regarding the first Commission meeting, taking into account that a broad representation of such States is necessary for the effective operation of the Commission.

3.   The Depositary shall convene the first meeting of the Commission at the headquarters of the Commission. Thereafter, meetings of the Commission shall be held at its headquarters, unless it decides otherwise.

4.   The Commission shall elect from among its members a Chairman and Vice–Chairman, each of whom shall serve for a term of two years and shall be eligible for re-election for one additional term. The first Chairman shall, however, be elected for an initial term of three years. The Chairman and Vice–Chairman shall not be representatives of the same Contracting Party.

5.   The Commission shall adopt and amend as necessary the rules of procedure for the conduct of its meetings, except with respect to the matters dealt with in Article XII of this Convention.

6.   The Commission may establish such subsidiary bodies as are necessary for the performance of its functions.

Article XIV

1.   The Contracting Parties hereby establish the Scientific Committee for the Conservation of Antarctic Marine Living Resources (hereinafter referred to as "the Scientific Committee") which shall be a consultative body to the Commission. The Scientific Committee shall normally meet at the headquarters of the Commission unless the Scientific Committee decides otherwise.

2.   Each Member of the Commission shall be a member of the Scientific Committee and shall appoint a representative with suitable scientific qualifications who may be accompanied by other experts and advisers.

3.   The Scientific Committee may seek the advice of other scientists and experts as may be required on an ad hoc basis.

Article XV

1.   The Scientific Committee shall provide a forum for consultation and cooperation concerning the collection, study and exchange of information with respect to the marine living resources to which this Convention applies. It shall encourage and promote cooperation in the field of scientific research in

order to extend knowledge of the marine living resources of the Antarctic marine ecosystem.

2. The Scientific Committee shall conduct such activities as the Commission may direct in pursuance of the objective of this Convention and shall:

(*a*) establish criteria and methods to be used for determinations concerning the conservation measures referred to in Article IX of this Convention;

(*b*) regularly assess the status and trends of the populations of Antarctic marine living resources;

(*c*) analyse data concerning the direct and indirect effects of harvesting on the populations of Antarctic marine living resources;

(*d*) assess the effects of proposed changes in the methods or levels of harvesting and proposed conservation measures;

(*e*) transmit assessments, analyses, reports and recommendations to the Commission as requested or on its own initiative regarding measures and research to implement the objective of this Convention;

(*f*) formulate proposals for the conduct of international and national programs of research into Antarctic marine living resources.

3. In carrying out its functions, the Scientific Committee shall have regard to the work of other relevant technical and scientific organizations and to the scientific activities conducted within the framework of the Antarctic Treaty.

Article XVI

1. The first meeting of the Scientific Committee shall be held within three months of the first meeting of the Commission. The Scientific Committee shall meet thereafter as often as may be necessary to fulfil its functions.

2. The Scientific Committee shall adopt and amend as necessary its rules of procedure. The rules and any amendments thereto shall be approved by the Commission. The rules shall include procedures for the presentation of minority reports.

3. The Scientific Committee may establish, with the approval of the Commission, such subsidiary bodies as are necessary for the performance of its functions.

Article XVII

1. The Commission shall appoint an Executive Secretary to serve the Commission and Scientific Committee according to such procedures and on such terms and conditions as the Commission may determine. His term of office shall be for four years and he shall be eligible for reappointment.

2. The Commission shall authorize such staff establishment for the Secretariat as may be necessary and the Executive Secretary shall appoint, direct and supervise such staff according to such rules and procedures and on such terms and conditions as the Commission may determine.

3. The Executive Secretary and Secretariat shall perform the functions entrusted to them by the Commission.

Article XVIII

The official languages of the Commission and of the Scientific Committee shall be English, French, Russian and Spanish.

Article XIX

1. At each annual meeting, the Commission shall adopt by consensus its budget and the budget of the Scientific Committee.

2. A draft budget for the Commission and the Scientific Committee and any subsidiary bodies shall be prepared by the Executive Secretary and submitted to the Members of the Commission at least sixty days before the annual meeting of the Commission.

3. Each Member of the Commission shall contribute to the budget. Until the expiration of five years after the entry into force of this Convention, the contribution of each Member of the Commission shall be equal. Thereafter the contribution shall be determined in accordance with two criteria: the amount harvested and an equal sharing among all Members of the Commission. The Commission shall determine by consensus the proportion in which these two criteria shall apply.

4. The financial activities of the Commission and Scientific Committee shall be conducted in accordance with financial regulations adopted by the Commission and shall be subject to an annual audit by external auditors selected by the Commission.

5. Each Member of the Commission shall meet its own expenses arising from attendance at meetings of the Commission and of the Scientific Committee.

6. A Member of the Commission that fails to pay its contributions for two consecutive years shall not, during the period of its default, have the right to participate in the taking of decisions in the Commission.

Article XX

1. The Members of the Commission shall, to the greatest extent possible, provide annually to the Commission and to the Scientific Committee such statistical, biological and other data and information as the Commission and Scientific Committee may require in the exercise of their functions.

2. The Members of the Commission shall provide, in the manner and at such intervals as may be prescribed, information about their harvesting activities, including fishing areas and vessels, so as to enable reliable catch and effort statistics to be compiled.

3. The Members of the Commission shall provide to the Commission at such intervals as may be prescribed information on steps taken to implement the conservation measures adopted by the Commission.

4. The Members of the Commission agree that in any of their harvesting activities, advantage shall be taken of opportunities to collect data needed to assess the impact of harvesting.

Article XXI

1. Each Contracting Party shall take appropriate measures within its competence to ensure compliance with the provisions of this Convention and

with conservation measures adopted by the Commission to which the Party is bound in accordance with Article IX of this Convention.

2.   Each Contracting Party shall transmit to the Commission information on measures taken pursuant to paragraph 1 above, including the imposition of sanctions for any violation.

Article XXII

1.   Each Contracting Party undertakes to exert appropriate efforts, consistent with the Charter of the United Nations, to the end that no one engages in any activity contrary to the objective of this Convention.

2.   Each Contracting Party shall notify the Commission of any such activity which comes to its attention.

Article XXIII

1.   The Commission and the Scientific Committee shall co-operate with the Antarctic Treaty Consultative Parties on matters falling within the competence of the latter.

2.   The Commission and the Scientific Committee shall co-operate, as appropriate, with the Food and Agriculture Organization of the United Nations and with other Specialised Agencies.

3.   The Commission and the Scientific Committee shall seek to develop co-operative working relationships, as appropriate, with inter-governmental and non-governmental organizations which could contribute to their work, including the Scientific Committee on Antarctic Research, the Scientific Committee on Oceanic Research and the International Whaling Commission.

4.   The Commission may enter into agreements with the organizations referred to in this Article and with other organizations as may be appropriate. The Commission and the Scientific Committee may invite such organizations to send observers to their meetings and to meetings of their subsidiary bodies.

Article XXIV

1.   In order to promote the objective and ensure observance of the provisions of this Convention, the Contracting Parties agree that a system of observation and inspection shall be established.

2.   The system of observation and inspection shall be elaborated by the Commission on the basis of the following principles:

(a) Contracting Parties shall cooperate with each other to ensure the effective implementation of the system of observation and inspection, taking account of the existing international practice. This system shall include, inter alia, procedures for boarding and inspection by observers and inspectors designated by the Members of the Commission and procedures for flag state prosecution and sanctions on the basis of evidence resulting from such boarding and inspections. A report of such prosecutions and sanctions imposed shall be included in the information referred to in Article XXI of this Convention;

(b) in order to verify compliance with measures adopted under this Convention, observation and inspection shall be carried out on board vessels engaged in scientific research or harvesting of marine living resources in the area to which this Convention applies, through observers and inspectors designated by the Members of the Commission and operating under terms and conditions to be established by the Commission;

(c) designated observers and inspectors shall remain subject to the jurisdiction of the Contracting Party of which they are nationals. They shall report to the Member of the Commission by which they have been designated which in turn shall report to the Commission.

3. Pending the establishment of the system of observation and inspection, the Members of the Commission shall seek to establish interim arrangements to designate observers and inspectors and such designated observers and inspectors shall be entitled to carry out inspections in accordance with the principles set out in paragraph 2 above.

Article XXV

1. If any dispute arises between two or more of the Contracting Parties concerning the interpretation or application of this Convention, those Contracting Parties shall consult among themselves with a view to having the dispute resolved by negotiation, inquiry, mediation, conciliation, arbitration, judicial settlement or other peaceful means of their own choice.

2. Any dispute of this character not so resolved shall, with the consent in each case of all Parties to the dispute, be referred for settlement to the International Court of Justice or to arbitration; but failure to reach agreement on reference to the International Court or to arbitration shall not absolve Parties to the dispute from the responsibility of continuing to seek to resolve it by any of the various peaceful means referred to in paragraph 1 above.

3. In cases where the dispute is referred to arbitration, the arbitral tribunal shall be constituted as provided in the Annex to this Convention.

Article XXVI

1. This Convention shall be open for signature at Canberra from 1 August to 31 December 1980 by the States participating in the Conference on the Conservation of Antarctic Marine Living Resources held at Canberra from 7 to 20 May 1980.

2. The States which so sign will be the original signatory States of the Convention.

Article XXVII

1. This Convention is subject to ratification, acceptance or approval by signatory States.

2. Instruments of ratification, acceptance or approval shall be deposited with the Government of Australia, hereby designated as the Depositary.

Article XXVIII

1. This Convention shall enter into force on the thirtieth day following the date of deposit of the eighth instrument of ratification, acceptance or approval by States referred to in paragraph 1 of Article XXVI of this Convention.

2. With respect to each State or regional economic integration organization which subsequent to the date of entry into force of this Convention

deposits an instrument of ratification, acceptance, approval or accession, the Convention shall enter into force on the thirtieth day following such deposit.

Article XXIX

1.   This Convention shall be open for accession by any State interested in research or harvesting activities in relation to the marine living resources to which this Convention applies.

2.   This Convention shall be open for accession by regional economic integration organizations constituted by sovereign States which include among their members one or more States Members of the Commission and to which the States members of the organization have transferred, in whole or in part, competences with regard to the matters covered by this Convention. The accession of such regional economic integration organizations shall be the subject of consultations among Members of the Commission.

Article XXX

1.   This Convention may be amended at any time.

2.   If one-third of the Members of the Commission request a meeting to discuss a proposed amendment the Depositary shall call such a meeting.

3.   An amendment shall enter into force when the Depositary has received instruments of ratification, acceptance or approval thereof from all the Members of the Commission.

4.   Such amendment shall thereafter enter into force as to any other Contracting Party when notice of ratification, acceptance or approval by it has been received by the Depositary. Any such Contracting Party from which no such notice has been received within a period of one year from the date of entry into force of the amendment in accordance with paragraph 3 above shall be deemed to have withdrawn from this Convention.

Article XXXI

1.   Any Contracting Party may withdraw from this Convention on 30 June of any year, by giving written notice not later than 1 January of the same year to the Depositary, which, upon receipt of such a notice, shall communicate it forthwith to the other Contracting Parties.

2.   Any other Contracting Party may, within sixty days of the receipt of a copy of such a notice from the Depositary, give written notice of withdrawal to the Depositary in which case the Convention shall cease to be in force on 30 June of the same year with respect to the Contracting Party giving such notice.

3.   Withdrawal from this Convention by any Member of the Commission shall not affect its financial obligations under this Convention.

Article XXXII

The Depositary shall notify all Contracting Parties of the following:

(a) signatures of this Convention and the deposit of instruments of ratification, acceptance, approval or accession;

(b) the date of entry into force of this Convention and of any amendment thereto.

Article XXXIII

1.   This Convention, of which the English, French, Russian and Spanish texts are equally authentic, shall be deposited with the Government of Australia which shall transmit duly certified copies thereof to all signatory and acceding Parties.

2.   This Convention shall be registered by the Depositary pursuant to Article 102 of the Charter of the United Nations.

2.5   RESOLUTION ON THE QUESTION OF ANTARCTICA.   Adopted by the UN General Assembly, 15 December 1983.   G.A.Res. 38/77, U.N. GAOR, 38th Sess., Supp. No. 47, at 69, U.N.Doc. A/38/69 (1983)

The General Assembly,

Having considered the item entitled "Question of Antarctica",

Conscious of the increasing international awareness of and interest in Antarctica,

Bearing in mind the Antarctic Treaty and the significance of the system it has developed,

Taking into account the debate on this item at its thirty-eighth session,

Convinced of the advantages of a better knowledge of Antarctica,

Affirming the conviction that, in the interest of all mankind, Antarctica should continue forever to be used exclusively for peaceful purposes and that it should not become the scene or object of international discord,

Recalling the relevant paragraphs of the Economic Declaration adopted by the Seventh Conference of Heads of State or Government of the Non–Aligned Countries, held at New Delhi from 7 to 12 March 1983,

1.   *Requests* the Secretary–General to prepare a comprehensive, factual and objective study on all aspects of Antarctica, taking fully into account the Antarctica Treaty system and other relevant factors;

2.   *Also requests* the Secretary–General to seek the views of all Member States in the preparation of the study;

3.   *Requests* those States conducting scientific research in Antarctica, other interested States, the relevant specialized agencies, organs, organizations and bodies of the United Nations system and relevant international organizations having scientific or technical information on Antarctica to lend the Secretary–General whatever assistance he may request for the purpose of carrying out the study;

4.   *Requests* the Secretary–General to report to the General Assembly at its thirty-ninth session;

5.   *Decides* to include in the provisional agenda of its thirty-ninth session the item entitled "Question of Antarctica".

2.6 RESOLUTION ON THE QUESTION OF ANTARCTICA. Adopted by the UN General Assembly, 17 December 1984. G.A. Res. 39/152, U.N. GAOR, 39th Sess., Supp. No. 51, at 94, U.N. Doc. A/39/51 (1984)

The General Assembly,

Recalling its resolution 38/77 of 15 December 1983,

Having considered the item entitled "Question of Antarctica",

Taking note of the study on the question of Antarctica,

Conscious of the increasing international awareness of and interest in Antarctica,

Bearing in mind the Antarctic Treaty and the significance of the system it has developed,

Taking into account the debate on this item at its thirty-ninth session,

Convinced of the advantages of a better knowledge of Antarctica,

Affirming the conviction that, in the interest of all mankind, Antarctica should continue forever to be used exclusively for peaceful purposes and that it should not become the scene or object of international discord,

Recalling the relevant paragraphs of the Economic Declaration adopted at the Seventh Conference of Heads of State or Government of Non–Aligned Countries, held at New Delhi from 7 to 12 March 1983,

1. *Expresses its appreciation* to the Secretary–General for the study on the question of Antarctica;

2. *Decides* to include in the provisional agenda of its fortieth session the item entitled "Question of Antarctica".

**2.7 CONVENTION ON THE REGULATION OF ANTARCTIC MINERAL RE-
SOURCE ACTIVITIES (CRAMRA) (WITHOUT ANNEX FOR ARBI-
TRAL TRIBUNAL). Concluded at Wellington, 2 June 1988. Not in
force as of 31 December 1992. Doc AMR/SCM/88/78, 27 I.L.M. 859
(1988)**

CHAPTER I: GENERAL PROVISIONS
Article 1
Definitions

For the purposes of this Convention:

1. "Antarctic Treaty" means the Antarctic Treaty done at Washington
on 1 December 1959.

2. "Antarctic Treaty Consultative Parties" means the Contracting Parties to the Antarctic Treaty entitled to appoint representatives to participate
in the meetings referred to in Article IX of that Treaty.

3. "Antarctic Treaty area" means the area to which the provisions of
the Antarctic Treaty apply in accordance with Article VI of that Treaty.

4. "Convention for the Conservation of Antarctic Seals" means the
Convention done at London on 1 June 1972.

5. "Convention on the Conservation of Antarctic Marine Living Resources" means the Convention done at Canberra on 20 May 1980.

6. "Mineral resources" means all non-living natural non-renewable resources, including fossil fuels, metallic and non-metallic minerals.

7. "Antarctic mineral resource activities" means prospecting, exploration or development, but does not include scientific research activities within
the meaning of Article III of the Antarctic Treaty.

8. "Prospecting" means activities, including logistic support, aimed at
identifying areas of mineral resource potential for possible exploration and
development, including geological, geochemical and geophysical investigations
and field observations, the use of remote sensing techniques and collection of
surface, seafloor and sub-ice samples. Such activities do not include dredging
and excavations, except for the purpose of obtaining small-scale samples, or
drilling, except shallow drilling into rock and sediment to depths not exceeding 25 metres, or such other depth as the Commission may determine for
particular circumstances.

9. "Exploration" means activities, including logistic support, aimed at
identifying and evaluating specific mineral resource occurrences or deposits,
including exploratory drilling, dredging and other surface or subsurface excavations required to determine the nature and size of mineral resource deposits
and the feasibility of their development, but excluding pilot projects or
commercial production.

10. "Development" means activities, including logistic support, which
take place following exploration and are aimed at or associated with exploitation of specific mineral resource deposits, including pilot projects, processing,
storage and transport activities.

11. "Operator" means:

(*a*) a Party; or

(*b*) an agency or instrumentality of a Party; or

(*c*) a juridical person established under the law of a Party or;

(*d*) a joint venture consisting exclusively of any combination of any of the foregoing,

which is undertaking Antarctic mineral resource activities and for which there is a Sponsoring State.

12. "Sponsoring State" means the Party with which an Operator has a substantial and genuine link, through being:

(*a*) in the case of a Party, that Party;

(*b*) in the case of an agency or instrumentality of a Party, that Party;

(*c*) in the case of a juridical person other than an agency or instrumentality of a Party, the Party:

(i) under whose law that juridical person is established and to whose law it is subject, without prejudice to any other law which might be applicable, and

(ii) in whose territory the management of that juridical person is located, and

(iii) to whose effective control that juridical person is subject;

(*d*) in the case of a joint venture not constituting a juridical person:

(i) where the managing member of the joint venture is a Party or an agency or instrumentality of a Party, that Party; or

(ii) in any other cases, where in relation to a Party the managing member of the joint venture satisfies the requirements of subparagraph (c) above, that Party.

13. "Managing member of the joint venture" means that member which the participating members in the joint venture have by agreement designated as having responsibility for central management of the joint venture, including the functions of organising and supervising the activities to be undertaken, and controlling the financial resources involved.

14. "Effective control" means the ability of the Sponsoring State to ensure the availability of substantial resources of the Operator for purposes connected with the implementation of this Convention, through the location of such resources in the territory of the Sponsoring State or otherwise.

15. "Damage to the Antarctic environment or dependent or associated ecosystems" means any impact on the living or non-living components of that environment or those ecosystems, including harm to atmospheric, marine or terrestrial life, beyond that which is negligible or which has been assessed and judged to be acceptable pursuant to this Convention.

16. "Commission" means the Antarctic Mineral Resources Commission established pursuant to Article 18.

17. "Regulatory Committee" means an Antarctic Mineral Resources Regulatory Committee established pursuant to Article 39.

18. "Advisory Committee" means the Scientific, Technical and Environmental Advisory Committee established pursuant to Article 13.

19. "Special Meeting of Parties" means the Meeting referred to in Article 28.

20. "Arbitral Tribunal" means an Arbitral Tribunal constituted as provided for in the Annex, which forms an integral part of this Convention.

Article 2
Objectives and General Principles

1. This Convention is an integral part of the Antarctic Treaty system, comprising the Antarctic Treaty, the measures in effect under that Treaty, and its associated separate legal instruments, the prime purpose of which is to ensure that Antarctica shall continue forever to be used exclusively for peaceful purposes and shall not become the scene or object of international discord. The Parties provide through this Convention, the principles it establishes, the rules it prescribes, the institutions it creates and the decisions adopted pursuant to it, a means for:

(a) assessing the possible impact on the environment of Antarctic mineral resource activities;

(b) determining whether Antarctic mineral resource activities are acceptable;

(c) governing the conduct of such Antarctic mineral resource activities as may be found acceptable; and

(d) ensuring that any Antarctic mineral resource activities are undertaken in strict conformity with this Convention.

2. In implementing this Convention, the Parties shall ensure that Antarctic mineral resource activities, should they occur, take place in a manner consistent with all the components of the Antarctic Treaty system and the obligations flowing therefrom.

3. In relation to Antarctic mineral resource activities, should they occur, the Parties acknowledge the special responsibility of the Antarctic Treaty Consultative Parties for the protection of the environment and the need to:

(a) protect the Antarctic environment and dependent and associated ecosystems;

(b) respect Antarctica's significance for, and influence on, the global environment;

(c) respect other legitimate uses of Antarctica;

(d) respect Antarctica's scientific value and aesthetic and wilderness qualities;

(e) ensure the safety of operations in Antarctica;

(f) promote opportunities for fair and effective participation of all Parties; and

(g) take into account the interests of the international community as a whole.

Article 3
Prohibition of Antarctic Mineral Resource
Activities Outside This Convention

No Antarctic mineral resource activities shall be conducted except in accordance with this Convention and measures in effect pursuant to it and, in the case of exploration or development, with a Management Scheme approved pursuant to Article 48 or 54.

Article 4
Principles Concerning Judgments on Antarctic
Mineral Resource Activities

1.   Decisions about Antarctic mineral resource activities shall be based upon information adequate to enable informed judgments to be made about their possible impacts and no such activities shall take place unless this information is available for decisions relevant to those activities.

2.   No Antarctic mineral resource activity shall take place until it is judged, based upon assessment of its possible impacts on the Antarctic environment and on dependent and on associated ecosystems, that the activity in question would not cause:

(*a*) significant adverse effects on air and water quality;

(*b*) significant changes in atmospheric, terrestrial or marine environments;

(*c*) significant change in the distribution, abundance or productivity of populations of species of fauna or flora;

(*d*) further jeopardy to endangered or threatened species or populations of such species; or

(*e*) degradation of, or substantial risk to, areas of special biological, scientific, historic, aesthetic or wilderness significance.

3.   No Antarctic mineral resource activity shall take place until it is judged, based upon assessment of its possible impacts, that the activity in question would not cause significant adverse effects on global or regional climate or weather patterns.

4.   No Antarctic mineral resource activity shall take place until it is judged that:

(*a*) technology and procedures are available to provide for safe operations and compliance with paragraphs 2 and 3 above;

(*b*) there exists the capacity to monitor key environmental parameters and ecosystem components so as to identify any adverse effects of such activity and to provide for the modification of operating procedures as may be necessary in the light of the results of monitoring or increased knowledge of the Antarctic environment or dependent or associated ecosystems; and

(*c*) there exists the capacity to respond effectively to accidents, particularly those with potential environmental effects.

5.   The judgments referred to in paragraphs 2, 3 and 4 above shall take into account the cumulative impacts of possible Antarctic mineral resource

activities both by themselves and in combination with other such activities and other uses of Antarctica.

Article 5
Area of Application

1. This Convention shall, subject to paragraphs 2, 3 and 4 below, apply to the Antarctic Treaty area.

2. Without prejudice to the responsibilities of the Antarctic Treaty Consultative Parties under the Antarctic Treaty and measures pursuant to it, the Parties agree that this Convention shall regulate Antarctic mineral resource activities which take place on the continent of Antarctica and all Antarctic islands, including all ice shelves, south of 60° south latitude and in the seabed and subsoil of adjacent offshore areas up to the deep seabed.

3. For the purposes of this Convention "deep seabed" means the seabed and subsoil beyond the geographic extent of the continental shelf as the term continental shelf is defined in accordance with international law.

4. Nothing in this Article shall be construed as limiting the application of other Articles of this Convention in so far as they relate to possible impacts outside the area referred to in paragraphs 1 and 2 above, including impacts on dependent or on associated ecosystems.

Article 6
Cooperation and International Participation

In the implementation of this Convention cooperation within its framework shall be promoted and encouragement given to international participation in Antarctic mineral resource activities by interested Parties which are Antarctic Treaty Consultative Parties and by other interested Parties, in particular, developing countries in either category. Such participation may be realised through the Parties themselves and their Operators.

Article 7
Compliance with This Convention

1. Each Party shall take appropriate measures within its competence to ensure compliance with this Convention and any measures in effect pursuant to it.

2. If a Party is prevented by the exercise of jurisdiction by another Party from ensuring compliance in accordance with paragraph 1 above, it shall not, to the extent that it is so prevented, bear responsibility for that failure to ensure compliance.

3. If any jurisdictional dispute related to compliance with this Convention or any measure in effect pursuant to it arises between two or more Parties, the Parties concerned shall immediately consult together with a view to reaching a mutually acceptable solution.

4. Each Party shall notify the Executive Secretary, for circulation to all other Parties, of the measures taken pursuant to paragraph 1 above.

5. Each Party shall exert appropriate efforts, consistent with the Charter of the United Nations, to the end that no one engages in any Antarctic mineral resource activities contrary to the objectives and principles of this Convention.

6. Each Party may, whenever it deems it necessary, draw the attention of the Commission to any activity which in its opinion affects the implementation of the objectives and principles of this Convention.

7. The Commission shall draw the attention of all Parties to any activity which, in the opinion of the Commission, affects the implementation of the objectives and principles of this Convention or the compliance by any Party with its obligations under this Convention and any measures in effect pursuant to it.

8. The Commission shall draw the attention of any State which is not a Party to this Convention to any activity undertaken by that State, its agencies or instrumentalities, natural or juridical persons, ships, aircraft or other means of transportation which, in the opinion of the Commission, affects the implementation of the objectives and principles of this Convention. The Commission shall inform all Parties accordingly.

9. Nothing in this Article shall affect the operation of Article 12(7) of this Convention or Article VIII of the Antarctic Treaty.

Article 8
Response Action and Liability

1. An Operator undertaking any Antarctic mineral resource activity shall take necessary and timely response action, including prevention, containment, clean up and removal measures, if the activity results in or threatens to result in damage to the Antarctic environment or dependent or associated ecosystems. The Operator, through its Sponsoring State, shall notify the Executive Secretary, for circulation to the relevant institutions of this Convention and to all Parties, of action taken pursuant to this paragraph.

2. An Operator shall be strictly liable for:

(*a*) damage to the Antarctic environment or dependent or associated ecosystems arising from its Antarctic mineral resource activities, including payment in the event that there has been no restoration to the *status quo ante;*

(*b*) loss of or impairment to an established use, as referred to in Article 15, or loss of or impairment to an established use of dependent or associated ecosystems, arising directly out of damage described in subparagraph (a) above;

(*c*) loss of or damage to property of a third party or loss of life or personal injury of a third party arising directly out of damage described in subparagraph (a) above; and

(*d*) reimbursement of reasonable costs by whomsoever incurred relating to necessary response action, including prevention, containment, clean up and removal measures, and action taken to restore the *status quo ante* where Antarctic mineral resource activities undertaken by that Operator result in or threaten to result in damage to the Antarctic environment or dependent or associated ecosystems.

3. (*a*) Damage of the kind referred to in paragraph 2 above which would not have occurred or continued if the Sponsoring State had carried out its obligations under this Convention with respect to its Operator shall, in accordance with international law, entail liability of that Sponsoring State.

Such liability shall be limited to that portion of liability not satisfied by the Operator or otherwise.

(*b*) Nothing in subparagraph (a) above shall affect the application of the rules of international law applicable in the event that damage not referred to in that subparagraph would not have occurred or continued if the Sponsoring State had carried out its obligations under this Convention with respect to its Operator.

4.   An Operator shall not be liable pursuant to paragraph 2 above if it proves that the damage has been caused directly by, and to the extent that it has been caused directly by:

(*a*) an event constituting in the circumstances of Antarctica a natural disaster of an exceptional character which could not reasonably have been foreseen; or

(*b*) armed conflict, should it occur notwithstanding the Antarctic Treaty, or an act of terrorism directed against the activities of the Operator, against which no reasonable precautionary measures could have been effective.

5.   Liability of an Operator for any loss of life, personal injury or loss of or damage to property other than that governed by this Article shall be regulated by applicable law and procedures.

6.   If an Operator proves that damage has been caused totally or in part by an intentional or grossly negligent act or omission of the party seeking redress, that Operator may be relieved totally or in part from its obligation to pay compensation in respect of the damage suffered by such party.

7.   (*a*) Further rules and procedures in respect of the provisions on liability set out in this Article shall be elaborated through a separate Protocol which shall be adopted by consensus by the members of the Commission and shall enter into force according to the procedure provided for in Article 62 for the entry into force of this Convention.

(*b*) Such rules and procedures shall be designed to enhance the protection of the Antarctic environment and dependent and associated ecosystems.

(*c*) Such rules and procedures:

(i) may contain provisions for appropriate limits on liability, where such limits can be justified:

(ii) without prejudice to Article 57, shall prescribe means and mechanisms such as a claims tribunal or other fora by which claims against Operators pursuant to this Article may be assessed and adjudicated:

(iii) shall ensure that a means is provided to assist with immediate response action, and to satisfy liability under paragraph 2 above in the event, *inter alia,* that an Operator liable is financially incapable of meeting its obligation in full that it exceeds any relevant limits of liability, that there is a defence to liability or that the loss or damage is of undetermined origin.

Unless it is determined during the elaboration of the Protocol that there are other effective means of meeting these objectives, the Protocol shall establish a Fund or Funds and make provision in respect of such Fund or Funds, *inter alia,* for the following:

— financing by Operators or on industry wide bases;

— ensuring the permanent liquidity and mandatory supplementation thereof in the event of insufficiency;

— reimbursement of costs of response action, by whomsoever incurred.

8. Nothing in paragraphs 4, 6 and 7 above or in the Protocol adopted pursuant to paragraph 7 shall affect in any way the provisions of paragraph 1 above.

9. No application for an exploration or development permit shall be made until the Protocol provided for in paragraph 7 above is in force for the Party lodging such application.

10. Each Party, pending the entry into force for it of the Protocol provided for in paragraph 7 above, shall ensure, consistently with Article 7 and in accordance with its legal system, that recourse is available in its national courts for adjudicating liability claims pursuant to paragraphs 2, 4 and 6 above against Operators which are engaged in prospecting. Such recourse shall include the adjudication of claims against any Operator it has sponsored. Each Party shall also ensure, in accordance with its legal system, that the Commission has the right to appear as a party in its national courts to pursue relevant liability claims under paragraph 2(a) above.

11. Nothing in this Article or in the Protocol provided for in paragraph 7 above shall be construed so as to:

(*a*) preclude the application of existing rules on liability, and the development in accordance with international law of further such rules, which may have application to either States or Operators; or

(*b*) affect the right of an Operator incurring liability pursuant to this Article to seek redress from another party which caused or contributed to the damage in question.

12. When compensation has been paid other than under this Convention liability under this Convention shall be offset by the amount of such payment.

Article 9

Protection of Legal Positions under the Antarctic Treaty

Nothing in this Convention and no acts or activities taking place while this Convention is in force shall:

(*a*) constitute a basis for asserting, supporting or denying a claim to territorial sovereignty in the Antarctic Treaty area or create any rights of sovereignty in the Antarctic Treaty area;

(*b*) be interpreted as a renunciation or diminution by any Party of, or as prejudicing, any right or claim or basis of claim to territorial sovereignty in Antarctica or to exercise coastal state jurisdiction under international law;

(c) be interpreted as prejudicing the position of any Party as regards its recognition or non-recognition of any such right, claim or basis of claim; or

(d) affect the provision of Article IV(2) of the Antarctic Treaty that no new claim, or enlargement of an existing claim, to territorial sovereignty in Antarctica shall be asserted while the Antarctic Treaty is in force.

Article 10
Consistency with the Other Components of the Antarctic Treaty System

1. Each Party shall ensure that Antarctic mineral resource activities take place in a manner consistent with the components of the Antarctic Treaty system, including the Antarctic Treaty, the Convention for the Conservation of Antarctic Seals and the Convention on the Conservation of Antarctic Marine Living Resources and the measures in effect pursuant to those instruments.

2. The Commission shall consult and cooperate with the Antarctic Treaty Consultative Parties, the Contracting Parties to the Convention for the Conservation of Antarctic Seals, and the Commission for the Conservation of Antarctic Marine Living Resources with a view to ensuring the achievement of the objectives and principles of this Convention and avoiding any interference with the achievement of the objectives and principles of the Antarctic Treaty, the Convention for the Conservation of Antarctic Seals or the Convention on the Conservation of Antarctic Marine Living Resources, or inconsistency between the measures in effect pursuant to those instruments and measures in effect pursuant to this Convention.

Article 11
Inspection under the Antarctic Treaty

All stations, installations and equipment, in the Antarctic Treaty area, relating to Antarctic mineral resource activities, as well as ships and aircraft supporting such activities at points of discharging or embarking cargoes or personnel at such stations and installations, shall be open at all times to inspection by observers designated under Article VII of the Antarctic Treaty for the purposes of that Treaty.

Article 12
Inspection under This Convention

1. In order to promote the objectives and principles and to ensure the observance of this Convention and measures in effect pursuant to it, all stations, installations and equipment relating to Antarctic mineral resource activities in the area in which these activities are regulated by this Convention, as well as ships and aircraft supporting such activities at points of discharging or embarking cargoes or personnel anywhere in that area shall be open at all times to inspection by:

(a) observers designated by any member of the Commission who shall be nationals of that member; and

(b) observers designated by the Commission or relevant Regulatory Committees.

2. Aerial inspection may be carried out at any time over the area in which Antarctic mineral resource activities are regulated by this Convention.

3. The Commission shall maintain an up-to-date list of observers designated pursuant to paragraph 1(a) and (b) above.

4. Reports from the observers shall be transmitted to the Commission and to any Regulatory Committee having competence in the area where the inspection has been carried out.

5. Observers shall avoid interference with the safe and normal operations of stations, installations and equipment visited and shall respect measures adopted by the Commission to protect confidentiality of data and information.

6. Inspections undertaken pursuant to paragraph 1(a) and (b) above shall be compatible and reinforce each other and shall not impose an undue burden on the operation of stations, installations and equipment visited.

7. In order to facilitate the exercise of their functions under this Convention, and without prejudice to the respective positions of the Parties relating to jurisdiction over all other persons in the area in which Antarctic mineral resource activities are regulated by this Convention, observers designated under this Article shall be subject only to the jurisdiction of the Party of which they are nationals in respect of all acts or omissions occurring while they are in that area for the purpose of exercising their functions.

8. No exploration or development shall take place in an area identified pursuant to Article 41 until effective provision has been made for inspection in that area.

Article 13
Protected Areas

1. Antarctic mineral resource activities shall be prohibited in any area designated as a Specially Protected Area or a Site of Special Scientific Interest under Article IX(1) of the Antarctic Treaty. Such activities shall also be prohibited in any other area designated as a protected area in accordance with Article IX(1) of the Antarctic Treaty, except to the extent that the relevant measure provides otherwise pending any designation becoming effective in accordance with Article IX(4) of the Antarctic Treaty, no Antarctic mineral resource activities shall take place in any such area which would prejudice the purpose for which it was designated.

2. The Commission shall also prohibit or restrict Antarctic mineral resource activities in any area which, for historic, ecological, environmental, scientific or other reasons, it has designated as a protected area.

3. In exercising its powers under paragraph 2 above or under Article 41 the Commission shall consider whether to restrict or prohibit Antarctic mineral resource activities in any area, in addition to those referred to in paragraph 1 above, protected or set aside pursuant to provisions of other components of the Antarctic Treaty system, to ensure the purposes which they are designated.

4. In relation to any area in which Antarctic mineral resource activities are prohibited or restricted in accordance with paragraph 1, 2 or 3 above, the Commission shall consider whether, for the purposes of Article 4(2)(e), it

would be prudent, additionally, to prohibit or restrict Antarctic mineral resource activities in adjacent areas for the purpose of creating a buffer zone.

5. The Commission shall give effect to Article 10(2) in acting pursuant to paragraphs 2, 3 and 4 above.

6. The Commission shall, where appropriate, bring any decisions it takes pursuant to this Article to the attention of the Antarctic Treaty Consultative Parties, the Contracting Parties to the Convention for the Conservation of Antarctic Seals, the Commission for the Conservation of Antarctic Marine Living Resources and the Scientific Committee on Antarctic Research.

Article 14

Non–Discrimination

In the implementation of this Convention there shall be no discrimination against any Party or its Operators.

Article 15

Respect for Other Uses of Antarctica

1. Decisions about Antarctic mineral resource activities shall take into account the need to respect other established uses of Antarctica, including:

(a) the operation of stations and their associated installations, support facilities and equipment in Antarctica;

(b) scientific investigation in Antarctic and cooperation therein;

(c) the conservation, including national use, of Antarctic marine living resources;

(d) tourism;

(e) the preservation of historic monuments; and

(f) navigation and aviation, that are consistent with the Antarctic Treaty system.

2. Antarctic mineral resource activities shall be conducted so as to respect any uses of Antarctica as referred to in paragraph 1 above.

Article 16

Availability and Confidentiality of Data and Information

Data and information obtained from Antarctic mineral resource activities shall, to the greatest extent practicable and feasible, be made freely available, provided that:

(a) as regards data and information of commercial value deriving from prospecting, they may be retained by the Operator in accordance with Article 37;

(b) as regards data and information deriving from exploration or development, the Commission shall adopt measures relating, as appropriate, to their release and to ensure the confidentiality of data and information of commercial value.

Article 17
Notifications and Provisional Exercise of
Functions of the Executive Secretary

1. Where in this Convention there is a reference to the provision of information, a notification or a report to any institution provided for in this Convention and that institution has not been established, the information, notification or report shall be provided to the Executive Secretary who shall circulate it as required.

2. Where in this Convention a function is assigned to the Executive Secretary and no Executive Secretary has been appointed under Article 33, that function shall be performed by the Depositary.

CHAPTER II: INSTITUTIONS
Article 18
Commission

1. There is hereby established the Antarctic Mineral Resources Commission.

2. Membership of the Commission shall be as follows:

(*a*) each Party which was an Antarctic Treaty Consultative Party on the date when this Convention was opened for signature; and

(*b*) each other Party during such time as it is actively engaged in substantial scientific, technical or environmental research in the area to which this Convention applies directly relevant to decisions about Antarctic mineral resource activities, particularly the assessments and judgments called for in Article 4; and

(*c*) each other Party sponsoring Antarctic mineral resource exploration or development during such time as the relevant Management Scheme is in force.

3. A Party seeking to participate in the work of the Commission pursuant to subparagraph (b) or (c) above shall notify the Depositary of the basis upon which it seeks to become a member of the Commission. In the case of a Party which is not an Antarctic Treaty Consultative Party, such notification shall include a declaration of intent to abide by recommendations pursuant to Article IX(1) of the Antarctic Treaty. The Depositary shall communicate to each member of the Commission such notification and accompanying information.

4. The Commission shall consider the notification at its next meeting. In the event that a Party referred to in paragraph 2(b) above submitting a notification pursuant to paragraph 3 above is an Antarctic Treaty Consultative Party, it shall be deemed to have satisfied the requirements for Commission membership unless more than one-third of the members of the Commission object at the meeting at which such notification is considered. Any other Party submitting a notification shall be deemed to have satisfied the requirements for Commission membership if no member of the Commission objects at the meeting at which such notification is considered.

5. Each member of the Commission shall be represented by one representative who may be accompanied by alternate representatives and advisers.

6.   Observer status in the Commission shall be open to any Party and to any Contracting Party to the Antarctic Treaty which is not a Party to this Convention.

Article 19
Commission Meetings

1.   (*a*) The first meeting of the Commission, held for the purpose of taking organizational, financial and other decisions necessary for the effective functioning of this Convention and its institutions, shall be convened within six months of the entry into force of this Convention.

(*b*) After the Commission has held the meeting or meetings necessary to take the decisions referred to in subparagraph (a) above, the Commission shall not hold further meetings except in accordance with paragraph 2 or 3 below.

2.   Meetings of the Commission shall be held within two months of:

(*a*) receipt of a notification pursuant to Article 39;

(*b*) a request by at least six members of the Commission; or

(*c*) a request by a member of a Regulatory Committee in accordance with Article 49(1).

3.   The Commission may establish a regular schedule of meetings if it determines that it is necessary for the effective functioning of this Convention.

4.   Unless the Commission decides otherwise, its meetings shall be convened by the Executive Secretary

5.   Each member of the Commission shall be represented by one representative who may be accompanied by alternate representatives and advisers.

6.   Observer status in the Commission shall be open to any Party and to any Contracting Party to the Antarctic Treaty which is not a Party to this Convention.

Article 20
Commission Procedure

1.   The Commission shall elect from among its members a Chairman and two Vice–Chairmen, each of whom shall be a representative of a different Party.

2.   (*a*) Until such time as the Commission has established a regular schedule of meetings in accordance with Article 19(3), the Chairman and Vice–Chairmen shall be elected to serve for a period of two years, provided that if no meeting is held during that period they shall continue to serve until the conclusion of the first meeting held thereafter.

(*b*) When a regular schedule of meetings has been established, the Chairman and Vice–Chairmen shall be elected to serve for a period of two years.

3.   The Commission shall adopt its rules of procedure. Such rules may include provisions concerning the number of terms of office which the Chairman and Vice–Chairmen may serve and for the rotation of such offices.

4.   The Commission may establish such subsidiary bodies as are necessary for the performance of its functions.

5.   The Commission may decide to establish a permanent headquarters which shall be in New Zealand.

6.   The Commission shall have legal personality and shall enjoy in the territory of each Party such legal capacity as may be necessary to perform its functions and achieve the objectives of this Convention.

7.   The privileges and immunities to be enjoyed by the Commission, the Secretariat and representatives attending meetings in the territory of a Party shall be determined by agreement between the Commission and the Party concerned.

Article 21
Functions of the Commission

1.   The functions of the Commission shall be:

(*a*) to facilitate and promote the collection and exchange of scientific, technical and other information and research projects necessary to predict, detect and assess the possible environmental impact of Antarctic mineral resource activities, including the monitoring of key environmental parameters and ecosystem components;

(*b*) to designate areas in which Antarctic mineral resource activities shall be prohibited or restricted in accordance with Article 13, and to perform the related functions assigned to it in that Article;

(*c*) to adopt measures for the protection of the Antarctic environment and dependent and associated ecosystems and for the promotion of safe and effective exploration and development techniques and, as it may deem appropriate, to make available a handbook of such measures;

(*d*) to determine, in accordance with Article 41, whether or not to identify an area for possible exploration and development, and to perform the related functions assigned to it in Article 42;

(*e*) to adopt measures relating to prospecting applicable to all relevant Operators:

(i) to determine for particular circumstances maximum drilling depths in accordance with Article 1(8);

(ii) to restrict or prohibit prospecting consistently with Articles 13, 37 and 38;

(*f*) to ensure the effective application of Articles 12(4), 37(7) and (8), 38(2) and 39(2), which require the submission to the Commission of information, notifications and reports;

(*g*) to give advance public notice of matters upon which it is requesting the advice of the Advisory Committee;

(*h*) to adopt measures relating to the availability and confidentiality of data and information, including measures pursuant to Article 16;

(*i*) to elaborate the principle of non-discrimination set forth in Article 14;

(*j*) to adopt measures with respect to maximum block sizes;

(*k*) to perform the functions assigned to it in Article 29;

(*l*) to review action by Regulatory Committees in accordance with Article 49;

(*m*) to adopt measures in accordance with Articles 6 and 41(1)(d) related to the promotion of cooperation and to participation in Antarctic mineral resource activities;

(*n*) to adopt general measures pursuant to Article 51(6);

(*o*) to take decisions on budgetary matters and adopt financial regulations in accordance with Article 35;

(*p*) to adopt measures regarding fees payable in connection with notifications submitted pursuant to Articles 37 and 39 and applications lodged pursuant to Articles 44 and 53, the purpose of which fees shall be to cover the administrative costs of handling such notifications and applications;

(*q*) to adopt measures regarding levies payable by Operators engaged in exploration and development, the principal purpose of which levies shall be to cover the costs of the institutions of this Convention;

(*r*) to determine in accordance with Article 35(7) the disposition of revenues, if any, accruing to the Commission which are surplus to the requirements for financing the budget pursuant to Article 35;

(*s*) to perform the functions assigned to it in Article 7(7) and (8);

(*t*) to perform the functions relating to inspection assigned to it in Article 12;

(*u*) to consider monitoring reports received pursuant to Article 52;

(*v*) to perform the functions relating to dispute settlement assigned to it in Article 59;

(*w*) to perform the functions relating to consultation and cooperation assigned to it in Article 10(2) and 34;

(*x*) to keep under review the conduct of Antarctic mineral resource activities with a view to safeguarding the protection of the Antarctic environment in the interest of all mankind; and

(*y*) to perform such other functions as are provided for elsewhere in this Convention.

2. In performing its functions the Commission shall seek and take full account of the views of the Advisory Committee provided in accordance with Article 26.

3. Each measure adopted by the Commission shall specify the date on which it comes into effect.

4. The Commission shall, subject to Article 16 and measures in effect pursuant to it and paragraph 1(h) above, ensure that a publicly available record of its meetings and decisions and of information, notifications and reports submitted to it is maintained.

Article 22

Decision Making in the Commission

1. The Commission shall take decisions on matters of substance by a three-quarters majority of the members present and voting. When a question arises as to whether a matter is one of substance or not, that matter shall be treated as one of substance unless otherwise decided by a three-quarters majority of the members present and voting.

2. Notwithstanding paragraph 1 above, consensus shall be required for the following:

(*a*) the adoption of the budget and decisions on budgetary and related matters pursuant to Article 22(1)(p), (q) and (r) and Article 35(1), (2), (3), (4) and (5);

(*b*) decisions taken pursuant to Article 21(1)(i);

(*c*) decisions taken pursuant to Article 41(2).

3. Decisions on matters of procedure shall be taken by a simple majority of the members present and voting.

4. Nothing in this Article shall be interpreted as preventing the Commission, in taking decisions on matters of substance, from endeavouring to reach a consensus.

5. For the purposes of this Article, consensus means the absence of a formal objection. If, with respect to any decision covered by paragraph 2(c) above, the Chairman of the Commission determines that there would be such an objection he shall consult the members of the Commission. If, as a result of these consultations, the Chairman determines that an objection would remain, he shall convene those members most directly interested for the purpose of seeking to reconcile the differences and producing a generally acceptable proposal.

Article 23

Advisory Committee

1. There is hereby established the Scientific, Technical and Environmental Advisory Committee.

2. Membership of the Advisory Committee shall be open to all Parties.

3. Each member of the advisory Committee shall be represented by one representative with suitable scientific, technical or environmental competence who may be accompanied by alternate representatives and by experts and advisers.

4. Observer status in the Advisory Committee shall be open to any Contracting Party to the Antarctic Treaty or to the Convention on the Conservation of Antarctic Marine Living Resources which is not a Party to this Convention.

Article 24

Advisory Committee Meetings

1. Unless the Commission decides otherwise, the Advisory Committee shall be convened for its first meeting within six months of the first meeting

of the Commission. It shall meet thereafter as necessary to fulfill its functions on the basis of a schedule established by the Commission.

2. Meetings of the Advisory Committee, in addition to those scheduled pursuant to paragraph 1 above, shall be convened at the request of at least six members of the Commission or pursuant to Article 40(1).

3. Unless the Commission decides otherwise, the meetings of the Advisory Committee shall be convened by the Executive Secretary.

Article 25

Advisory Committee Procedure

1. The Advisory Committee shall elect from among its members a Chairman and two Vice–Chairmen, each of whom shall be a representative of a different Party.

2. (*a*) Until such time as the Commission has established a schedule of meetings in accordance with Article 24(1), the Chairman and Vice–Chairmen shall be elected to serve for a period of two years, provided that if no meeting is held during that period they shall continue to serve until the conclusion of the first meeting held thereafter.

(*b*) When a schedule of meetings has been established, the Chairman and Vice–Chairmen shall be elected to serve for a period of two years.

3. The Advisory Committee shall give advance public notice of its meetings and of matters to be considered at each meeting so as to permit the receipt and consideration of views on such matters from international organizations having an interest in them. For this purpose the Advisory Committee may, subject to review by the Commission, establish procedures for the transmission of relevant information to these organizations.

4. The Advisory Committee shall, by a two-thirds majority of the members present and voting, adopt its rules of procedure. Such rules may include provisions concerning the number of terms of office which the Chairman and Vice–Chairmen may serve and for the rotation of such offices. The rules of procedure and any amendments thereto shall be subject to approval by the Commission.

5. The Advisory Committee may establish such subcommittees, subject to budgetary approval, as may be necessary for the performance of its functions.

Article 26

Functions of the Advisory Committee

1. The Advisory Committee shall advise the Commission and Regulatory Committees, as required by this Convention, or as requested by them, on the scientific, technical and environmental aspects of Antarctic mineral resources activities. It shall provide a forum for consultation and cooperation concerning the collection, exchange and evaluation of information related to the scientific, technical and environmental aspects of Antarctic mineral resource activities.

2. It shall provide advice to:

(*a*) the Commission relating to its functions under Articles 21(1)(a) to (f), (u) and 35(7)(a) (in matters relating to scientific research) as well as on the implementation of Article 4; and

(*b*) Regulatory Committees with respect to:

(i) the implementation of Article 4;

(ii) scientific, technical and environmental aspects of Articles 43(3) and (5), 45, 47, 51, 52 and 54;

(iii) data to be collected and reported in accordance with Articles 47 and 52; and

(iv) the scientific, technical and environmental implications of reports and reported data provided in accordance with Articles 47 and 53.

3. It shall provide advice to the Commission and to Regulatory Committees on:

(*a*) criteria in respect of the judgments required under Article 4(2) and (3) for the purposes of Article 4(1);

(*b*) types of data and information required to carry out its functions, and how they should be collected reported and archived;

(*c*) scientific research which would contribute to the base of data and information required in subparagraph (b) above;

(*d*) effective procedures and systems for data and information analysis, evaluation, presentation and dissemination to facilitate the judgments referred to in Article 4; and

(*e*) possibilities for scientific, technical and environmental cooperation amongst interested Parties which are developing countries and other Parties.

4. The Advisory Committee, in providing advice on decisions to be taken in accordance with Articles 41, 43, 45 and 54 shall, in each case, undertake a comprehensive environmental and technical assessment of the proposed actions. Such assessments shall be based on all information, and any amplifications thereof, available to the Advisory Committee, including the information provided pursuant to Articles 39(2)(e), 44(2)(b)(iii) and 53(2)(b). The assessments of the Advisory Committee shall, in each case, address the nature and scope of the decisions to be taken and shall include consideration, as appropriate, of, *inter alia:*

(*a*) the adequacy of existing information to enable informed judgments to be made;

(*b*) the nature, extent, duration and intensity of likely direct environmental impacts resulting from the proposed activity;

(*c*) possible indirect impacts;

(*d*) means and alternatives by which such direct or indirect impacts might be reduced, including environmental consequences of the alternative of not proceeding;

(*e*) cumulative impacts of the proposed activity in the light of existing or planned activities;

(*f*) capacity to respond effectively to accidents with potential environmental effects;

(*g*) the environmental significance of unavoidable impacts; and

(*h*) the probabilities of accidents and their environmental consequences.

5. In preparing its advice the Advisory Committee may seek information and advice from other scientists and experts or scientific organizations as may be required on an *ad hoc* basis.

6. The Advisory Committee shall, with a view to promoting international participation in Antarctic mineral resource activities as provided for in Article 6, provide advice concerning the availability to interested developing country Parties and other Parties, of the information referred to in paragraph 3 above, of training programmes related to scientific, technical and environmental matters bearing on Antarctic mineral resource activities, and of opportunities for cooperation among Parties in these programmes.

Article 27

Reporting by the Advisory Committee

The Advisory Committee shall present a report on each of its meetings to the Commission and to any relevant Regulatory Committee. The report shall cover all matters considered at the meeting and shall reflect the conclusions reached and all the views expressed by members of the Advisory Committee. The report shall be circulated by the Executive Secretary to all Parties, and to observers attending the meeting, and shall thereupon be made publicly available.

Article 28

Special Meeting of Parties

1. A Special Meeting of Parties shall, as required, be convened in accordance with Article 40(2) and shall have the functions, in relation to the identification of an area for possible exploration and development, specified in Article 40(3).

2. Membership of a Special Meeting of Parties shall be open to all Parties, each of which shall be represented by one representative who may be accompanied by alternate representative who may be accompanied by alternate representatives and advisers.

3. Observer status at a Special Meeting of Parties shall be open to any Contracting Party to the Antarctic Treaty which is not a Party to this Convention.

4. Each Special Meeting of Parties shall elect from among its members a Chairman and Vice–Chairman, each of whom shall serve for the duration of that meeting. The Chairman and Vice–Chairman shall not be representatives of the same Party.

5. The Special Meeting of Parties shall, by a two-thirds majority of the members present and voting, adopt its rules of procedure. Until such time as this has been done the Special Meeting of Parties shall apply provisional rules of procedure drawn up by the Commission.

6. Unless the Commission decides otherwise, a Special Meeting of Parties shall be convened by the Executive Secretary and shall be held at the same venue as the meeting of the Commission convened to consider the identification of an area for possible exploration and development.

Article 29
Regulatory Committees

1. An Antarctic Mineral Resources Regulatory Committee shall be established for each area identified by the Commission pursuant to Article 41.

2. Subject to paragraph 6 below, each Regulatory Committee shall consist of 10 members. Membership shall be determined by the Commission in accordance with this Article and, taking into account Article 9, shall include:

(*a*) the member, if any, or if there are more than one, those members of the Commission identified by reference to Article 9(b) which assert rights or claims in the identified area;

(*b*) the two members of the Commission also identified by reference to Article 9(b) which assert a basis of claim in Antarctica;

(*c*) other members of the Commission determined in accordance with this Article so that the Regulatory Committee shall, subject to paragraph 6 below, consist, in total, of 10 members;

(i) four members identified by reference to Article 9(b) which assert rights or claims, including the member or members, if any, referred to in subparagraph (a) above; and

(ii) six members which do not assert rights or claims as described in Article 9(b), including the two members referred to in subparagraph (b) above.

3. Upon the identification of an area in accordance with Article 41(2), the Chairman of the Commission shall, as soon as possible and in any event within 90 days, make a recommendation to the Commission concerning the membership of the Regulatory Committee. To this end the Chairman shall consult, as appropriate, with the Chairman of the Advisory Committee and all members of the Commission. Such recommendation shall comply with the requirements of paragraphs 2 and 4 of this Article and shall ensure:

(*a*) the inclusion of members of the Commission which, whether through prospecting, scientific research or otherwise, have contributed substantial scientific, technical or environmental information relevant to the identification of the area by the Commission pursuant to Article 41;

(*b*) adequate and equitable representation of developing country members of the Commission, having regard to the overall balance between developed and developing country members of the Commission, including at least three developing country members of the Commission;

(*c*) that account is taken of the value of a rotation of membership of Regulatory Committees as a further means of ensuring equitable representation of members of the Commission.

4. (*a*) When there are one or more members of the Regulatory Committee referred to in paragraph 2(a) above, the Chairman of the Commission shall

make the recommendation in respect of paragraph 2(c)(i) above upon the nomination, if any, of such member or members which shall take into account paragraph 3 above, in particular subparagraph (b) of that paragraph.

(*b*) in making the recommendation in respect of paragraph 2(c)(ii) above, the Chairman of the Commission shall give full weight to the views (which shall take into account paragraph 3 above) which may be presented on behalf of those members of the Commission which do not assert rights of or claims to territorial sovereignty in Antarctica and, with reference to the requirements of paragraph 3(b) above, to the views which may be presented on behalf of the developing countries among them.

5.   The recommendation of the Chairman of the Commission shall be deemed to have been approved by the Commission if it does not decide otherwise at the same meeting as the recommendation is submitted.   In taking any decision in accordance with this Article the Commission shall ensure that the requirements of paragraphs 2 and 3 above are complied with and that the nomination, if any, referred to in paragraph 4(a) above is given effect.

6.   (*a*) If a member of the Commission which has sponsored prospecting in the identified area and submitted the notification pursuant to Article 39 upon which the Commission based its identification of the area pursuant to Article 41, is not a member of the Regulatory Committee by virtue of paragraphs 2 and 3 above, that member of the Commission shall be a member of the Regulatory Committee until such time as an application for an exploration permit is lodged pursuant to Article 44.

(*b*) If a Party lodging an application for an exploration permit pursuant to Article 44 is not a member of the Regulatory Committee by virtue of paragraphs 2 and 3 above, that Party shall be a member of the Regulatory Committee for its consideration of that application.   Should such application result in approval of a Management Scheme pursuant to Article 48, the Party in question shall remain a member of the Regulatory Committee during such time as that Management Scheme is in force with the right to take part in decisions on matters affecting that Management Scheme.

7.   Nothing in this Article shall be interpreted as affecting Article IV of the Antarctic Treaty.

Article 30
Regulatory Committee Procedure

1.   The first meeting of each Regulatory Committee shall be convened by the Executive Secretary in accordance with Article 43(1).   Each Regulatory Committee shall meet thereafter when and where necessary to fulfill its functions.

2.   Each member of a Regulatory Committee shall be represented by one representative who may be accompanied by alternate representatives and advisers.

3.   Each Regulatory Committee shall elect from among its members a Chairman and Vice–Chairman.   The Chairman and Vice–Chairman shall not be representatives of the same Party.

4. Any Party may attend meetings of a Regulatory Committee as an observer.

5. Each Regulatory Committee shall adopt its rules of procedure. Such rules may include provisions concerning the period and number of terms of office which the Chairman and Vice–Chairman may serve and for the rotation of such offices.

Article 31
Functions of Regulatory Committees

1. The Functions of each Regulatory Committee shall be:

(*a*) to undertake the preparatory work provided for in Article 43;

(*b*) to consider application for exploration and development permits in accordance with Articles 45, 46 and 54;

(*c*) to approve Management Schemes and issue exploration and development permits in accordance with Articles 47, 48 and 54;

(*d*) to monitor exploration and development activities in accordance with Article 52;

(*e*) to perform the functions assigned to it in Article 51;

(*f*) to perform the functions relating to inspection assigned to it in Article 12;

(*g*) to perform the functions relating to dispute settlement assigned to it in Article 47(r); and

(*h*) to perform such other functions as are provided for elsewhere in this Convention.

2. In performing its functions each Regulatory Committee shall seek and take full account of the views of the Advisory Committee provided in accordance with Article 26.

3. Each Regulatory Committee shall, subject to Article 16 and measures in effect pursuant to it and Article 21(1)(h), ensure that a publicly available record of its decisions, and of Management Scheme in force, is maintained.

Article 32
Decision Making in Regulatory Committees

1. Decisions by a Regulatory Committee pursuant to Articles 48 and 54(5) shall be taken by a two-thirds majority of the members present and voting, which majority shall include a simple majority of those members present and voting referred to in Article 29(2)(*c*)(i) and also a simple majority of those members present and voting referred to in Article 29(2)(*c*)(ii).

2. Decisions by a Regulatory Committee pursuant to Article 43(3) and (5) shall be taken by a two-thirds majority of the members present and voting, which majority shall include at least half of those members present and voting referred to in Article 29(2)(c)(i) and also at least half of those members present and voting referred to in Article 29(2)(c)(ii).

3. Decisions on all other matters of substance shall be taken by a two-thirds majority of the members present and voting. When a question arises as to whether a matter is one of substance or not, that matter shall be treated

as one of substance unless otherwise decided by a two-thirds majority of the members present and voting.

4.   Decisions on matters of procedure shall be taken by a simple majority of the members present and voting.

5.   Nothing in this Article shall be interpreted as preventing a Regulatory Committee, in taking decisions on matters of substance, from endeavoring to reach a consensus.

Article 33

Secretariat

1.   The Commission may establish a Secretariat to serve the Commission, Regulatory Committees, the Advisory Committee, the Special Meeting of Parties and any subsidiary bodies established.

2.   The Commission may appoint an Executive Secretary, who shall be the head of the Secretariat, according to such procedures and on such terms and conditions as the Commission may determine.   The Executive Secretary shall serve for a four year term and may be reappointed.

3.   The Commission may, with due regard to the need for efficiency and economy, authorize such staff establishment for the Secretariat as may be necessary.   The Executive Secretary shall appoint, direct and supervise the staff according to such rules and procedures and on such terms and conditions as the Commission may determine.

4.   The Secretariat shall perform the functions specified in this Convention and, subject to the approved budget, the tasks entrusted to it by the Commission, Regulatory Committees, the Advisory Committee and the Special Meeting of Parties.

Article 34

Cooperation with International Organizations

1.   The Commission and, as appropriate, the Advisory Committee shall cooperate with the Antarctic Treaty Consultative Parties, the Contracting Parties to the Convention for the Conservation of Antarctic Seals, the Commission for the Conservation of Antarctic Marine Living Resources, and the Scientific Committee on Antarctic Research.

2.   The Commission shall cooperate with the United Nations, its relevant Specialized Agencies, and, as appropriate, any international organization which may have competence in respect of mineral resources in areas adjacent to those covered by this Convention.

3.   The Commission shall also, as appropriate, cooperate with the International Union for the Conservation of Nature and Natural Resources, and with other relevant international organizations, including non-governmental organizations, having a scientific, technical or environmental interest in Antarctica.

4.   The Commission may, as appropriate, accord observer status in the Commission and in the Advisory Committee to such relevant international organizations, including non-governmental organizations, as might assist in the work of the institution in question.   Observer status at a Special Meeting

of Parties shall be open to such organizations as have been accorded observer status in the Commission or the Advisory Committee.

5. The Commission may enter into agreements with the organizations referred to in this Article.

Article 35
Financial Provisions

1. The Commission shall adopt a budget, on an annual or other appropriate basis, for:

(*a*) its activities and the activities of Regulatory Committees, the Advisory Committee, the Special Meeting of Parties, any subsidiary bodies established and the Secretariat; and

(*b*) the progressive reimbursement of any contributions paid under paragraphs 5 and 6 below whenever revenues under paragraph 4 below exceed expenditure.

2. The first draft budget shall be submitted by the Depositary at least 90 days before the first meeting of the Commission. At that meeting the Commission shall adopt its first budget and decide upon arrangements for the preparation of subsequent budgets.

3. The Commission shall adopt financial regulations.

4. Subject to paragraph 5 below, the budget shall be financed, *inter alia*, by:

(*a*) fees prescribed pursuant, to Articles 21(1)(p) and 43(2)(b);

(*b*) levies on Operators, subject to any measures adopted by the Commission in accordance with Article 21(1)(q), pursuant to Article 47(k)(i); and

(*c*) such other financial payments by Operators pursuant to Article 47(k)(ii) as may be required to be paid to the institutions of this Convention.

5. If the budget is not fully financed by revenues in accordance with paragraph 4 above, and subject to reimbursement in accordance with paragraph 1(b) above, the budget shall, to the extent of any shortfall and subject to paragraph 6 below, be financed by contributions from the members of the Commission. To this end, the Commission shall adopt as soon as possible a method of equitable sharing of contributions to the budget. The budget shall, in the meantime, to the extent of any shortfall, be financed by equal contributions from each member of the Commission.

6. In adopting the method of contributions referred to in paragraph 5 above the Commission shall consider the extent to which members of and observers at institutions of this Convention may be called upon to contribute to the cost of those institutions.

7. The Commission, in determining the disposition of revenues accruing to it, which are surplus to the requirements for financing the budget pursuant to this Article, shall:

(*a*) promote scientific research in Antarctica, particularly that related to the Antarctic environment and Antarctic resources, and a wide spread of participation in such research by all Parties, in particular developing country Parties;

(*b*) ensure that the interests of the members of Regulatory Committees having the most direct interest in the matter in relation to the areas in question are respected in any disposition of that surplus.

8.   The finances of the Commission, Regulatory Committees, the Advisory Committee, the Special Meeting of Parties, any subsidiary bodies established and the Secretariat shall accord with the financial regulations adopted by the Commission and shall be subject to an annual audit by external auditors selected by the Commission.

9.   Each member of the Commission, Regulatory Committees, the Advisory Committee, the Special Meeting of Parties and any subsidiary bodies established, as well as any observer at a meeting of any of the institutions of this Convention, shall meet its own expenses arising from attendance at meetings.

10.   A member of the Commission that fails to pay its contribution for two consecutive years shall not, during the period of its continuing subsequent default, have the right to participate in the taking of decisions in any of the institutions of this Convention.   If it continues to be in default for a further two consecutive years, Commission shall decide what further action should be taken, which may include loss by that member of the right to participate in meetings of the institutions of this Convention.   Such member shall resume the full enjoyment of its rights upon payment of the outstanding contributions.

11.   Nothing in this Article shall be construed as prejudicing the position of any member of a Regulatory Committee on the outcome of consideration by the Regulatory Committee of terms and conditions in a Management Scheme pursuant to Article 47(k)(ii).

Article 36
Official and Working Languages

The official and working languages of the Commission, Regulatory Committees, the Advisory Committee, the Special Meeting of Parties and any meeting convened under Article 64 shall be English, French, Russian and Spanish.

CHAPTER III: PROSPECTING
Article 37
Prospecting

1.   Prospecting shall not confer upon any Operator any right to Antarctic mineral resources.

2.   Prospecting shall at all times be conducted in compliance with this Convention and with measures in effect pursuant to this Convention, but shall not require authorization by the institutions of this Convention.

3.   (*a*) The Sponsoring State shall ensure that its Operators undertaking prospecting maintain the necessary financial and technical means to comply with Article 8(1), and, to the extent that any such Operator fails to take

response action as required in Article 8(1), shall ensure that this is undertaken.

(*b*) The Sponsoring State shall also ensure that its Operators undertaking prospecting maintain financial capacity, commensurate with the nature and level of the activity undertaken and the risks involved, to comply with Article 8(2).

4. In cases where more than one Operator is engaged in prospecting in the same general area, the Sponsoring State or States shall ensure that those cooperators conduct their activities with due regard to each others' rights.

5. Where an Operator wishes to conduct prospecting in an area identified under Article 41 in which another Operator has been authorized to undertake exploration or development, the Sponsoring State shall ensure that such prospecting is carried out subject to the rights of any authorized Operator and any requirements to protect its rights specified by the relevant Regulatory Committee.

6. Each Operator shall ensure upon cessation of prospecting the removal of all installations and equipment and site rehabilitation. On the request of the Sponsoring State, the Commission may waive the obligation to remove installations and equipment.

7. The Sponsoring State shall notify the Commission at least nine months in advance of the commencement of planned prospecting. The notification shall be accompanied by such fees as may be established by the Commission in accordance with Article 21(1)(p) and shall:

(*a*) identify, by reference to coordinates of latitude and longitude or identifiable geographic features, the general area in which the prospecting is to take place;

(*b*) broadly identify the mineral resource or resources which are to be the subject of the prospecting;

(*c*) describe the prospecting, including the methods to be used, and the general programme of work to be undertaken and its expected duration;

(*d*) provide an assessment of the possible environmental and other impacts of the prospecting, taking into account possible cumulative impacts as referred to in Article 4(5);

(*e*) describe the measures, including monitoring programmes, to be adopted to avoid harmful environmental consequences or undue interference with other established uses of Antarctica, and outline the measures to be put into effect in the event of any accident and contingency plans for evacuation in an emergency;

(*f*) provide details on the Operator and certify that it:

(i) has a substantial and genuine link with the Sponsoring State as defined in Article 1(12); and

(ii) is financially and technically qualified to carry out the proposed prospecting in accordance with this Convention; and

(*g*) provide such further information as may be required by measures adopted by the Commission.

8.   The Sponsoring State shall subsequently provide to the Commission:

(*a*) notification of any changes to the information referred to in paragraph 7 above;

(*b*) notification of the cessation of prospecting, including removal of any installations and equipment as well as site rehabilitation; and

(*c*) a general annual report on the prospecting undertaken by the Operator.

9.   Notifications and reports submitted pursuant to this Article shall be circulated by the Executive Secretary without delay to all Parties and observers attending Commission meetings.

10.   Paragraphs 7, 8 and 9 above shall not be interpreted as requiring the disclosure of data and information of commercial value.

11.   The Sponsoring State shall ensure that basic data and information of commercial value generated by prospecting are maintained in archives and may at any time release part of or all such data and information, on conditions which it shall establish, for scientific or environmental purposes.

12.   The Sponsoring State shall ensure that basic data and information, other than interpretative data, generated by prospecting are made readily available when such data and information are not, or are no longer, of commercial value and, in any event, no later than 10 years after the year the data and information were collected, unless it certifies to the Commission that the data and information continue to have commercial value. It shall review at regular intervals whether such data and information may be released and shall report the results of such reviews to the Commission.

13.   The Commission may adopt measures consistent with this Article relating to the release of data and information of commercial value including requirements for certifications, the frequency of reviews and maximum time limits for extensions of the protection of such data and information.

Article 38
Consideration of Prospecting by the Commission

1.   If a member of the Commission considers that a notification submitted in accordance with Article 37(7) or (8), or ongoing prospecting, causes concern as to consistency with this Convention or measures in effect pursuant thereto, that member may request the Sponsoring State to provide a clarification. If that member considers that an adequate response is not forthcoming from the Sponsoring State within a reasonable time, the member may request that the Commission be convened in accordance with Article 19(2)(b) to consider the question and take appropriate action.

2.   If measures applicable to all relevant Operators are adopted by the Commission following a request made in accordance with paragraph 1 above, Sponsoring States that have submitted notifications in accordance with Article 37(7) or (8), and Sponsoring States whose Operators are conducting prospecting, shall ensure that the plans and activities of their Operators are modified to the extent necessary to conform with those measures within such time limit as the Commission may prescribe, and shall notify the Commission accordingly.

CHAPTER IV: EXPLORATION
Article 39
Requests for Identification of an Area for Possible Exploration and Development

1. Any Party may submit to the Executive Secretary a notification requesting that the Commission identify an area for possible exploration and development of a particular mineral resource or resources.

2. Any such notification shall be accompanied by such fees as may be established by the Commission in accordance with Article 21(1)(p) and shall contain:

(*a*) a precise delineation, including coordinates, of the area proposed for identification;

(*b*) specification of the resource or resources for which the area would be identified and any relevant data and information, excluding data and information of commercial value, concerning that resource or those resources, including a geological description of the proposed area;

(*c*) a detailed description of the physical and environmental characteristics of the proposed area;

(*d*) a description of the likely scale of exploration and development for the resource or resources involved in the proposed area and of the methods which could be employed in such exploration and development;

(*e*) a detailed assessment of the environmental and other impacts of possible exploration and development for the resource or resources involved, taking into account Articles 15 and 26(4); and

(*f*) such other information as may be required pursuant to measures adopted by the Commission.

3. A notification under paragraph 1 above shall be referred promptly by the Executive Secretary to all Parties and shall be circulated to observers attending the meeting of the Commission to be convened pursuant to Article 19(2)(a).

Article 40
Action by the Advisory Committee and Special Meeting of Parties

1. The Advisory Committee shall meet as soon as possible after the meeting of the Commission convened pursuant to Article 19(2)(a) has commenced. The Advisory Committee shall provide advice to the Commission on the notification submitted pursuant to Article 39(1). The Commission may prescribe a time limit for the provision of such advice.

2. A Special Meeting of Parties shall meet as soon as possible after circulation of the report of the Advisory Committee and in any event not later than two months after that report has been circulated.

3. The Special Meeting of Parties shall consider whether identification of an area by the Commission in accordance with the request contained in the notification would be consistent with this Convention, and shall report thereon to the Commission as soon as possible and in any event not later than 21 days from the commencement of the meeting.

4.   The report of the Special Meeting of Parties to the Commission shall reflect the conclusions reached and all the views expressed by Parties participating in the meeting.

Article 41
Action by the Commission

1.   The Commission shall, as soon as possible after receipt of the report of the Special Meeting of Parties, consider whether or not it will identify an area as requested. Taking full account of the views and giving special weight to the conclusions of the Special Meeting of Parties, and taking full account of the views and the conclusions of the Advisory Committee, the Commission shall determine whether such identification would be consistent with this Convention. For this purpose:

(*a*) the Commission shall ensure that an area to be identified shall be such that, taking into account all factors relevant to such identification, including the physical, geological, environmental and other characteristics of such area, it forms a coherent unit for the purposes of resource management. The Commission shall thus consider whether an area to be identified should include all or part of that which was requested in the notification and, subject to the necessary assessments having been made, adjacent areas not covered by that notification;

(*b*) the Commission shall consider whether there are, within an area requested or to be identified, any areas in which exploration and development are or should be prohibited or restricted in accordance with Article 13;

(*c*) the Commission shall specify the mineral resource or resources for which the area would be identified;

(*d*) the Commission shall give effect to Article 6, by elaborating opportunities for joint ventures or different forms of participation, up to a defined level, including procedures for offering such participation, in possible exploration and development, within the area, by interested Parties which are Antarctic Treaty Consultative Parties and by other interested Parties, in particular, developing countries in either category;

(*e*) the Commission shall prescribe any additional associated conditions necessary to ensure that an area to be identified is consistent with other provisions of this Convention and may prescribe general guidelines relating to the operational requirements for exploration and development in an area to be identified including measures establishing maximum block sizes and advice concerning related support activities; and

(*f*) the Commission shall give effect to the requirement in Article 59 to establish additional procedures for the settlement of disputes.

2.   After it has completed its consideration in accordance with paragraph 1 above, the Commission shall identify an area for possible exploration and development if there is a consensus of Commission members that such identification is consistent with this Convention.

Article 42
Revision in the Scope of an Identified Area

1.   If, after an area has been identified in accordance with Article 41, a Party requests identification of an area, all or part of which is contained

within the boundaries of the area already identified but in respect of a mineral resource or resources different from any resource in respect of which the area has already been identified, the request shall be dealt with in accordance with Articles 39, 40 and 41. Should the Commission identify an area in respect of such different mineral resource or resources, it shall have regard, in addition to the requirements of Article 41(1)(a), to the desirability of specifying the boundaries of the area in such a way that it can be assigned to the Regulatory Committee with competence for the area already identified.

2. In the light of increased knowledge bearing on the effective management of the area, and after seeking the views of the Advisory Committee and the relevant Regulatory Committee, the Commission may amend the boundaries of any area it has identified. In making any such amendment the Commission shall ensure that authorized exploration and development in the area are not adversely affected. Unless there are compelling reasons for doing so, the Commission shall not amend the boundaries of an area it has identified in such a way as to involve a change in the composition of the relevant Regulatory Committee.

Article 43
Preparatory Work by Regulatory Committees

1. As soon as possible after the identification of an area pursuant to Article 41, the relevant Regulatory Committee established in accordance with Article 29 shall be convened.

2. The Regulatory Committee shall:

(*a*) subject to any measures adopted by the Commission pursuant to Article 21(1)(j) relating to maximum block sizes, divide its area of competence into blocks in respect of which applications for exploration and development may be submitted and make provision for a limit in appropriate circumstances on the number of blocks to be accorded to any Party;

(*b*) subject to any measures adopted by the Commission pursuant to Article 21(1)(p), establish fees to be paid with any application for an exploration or development permit lodged pursuant to Article 44 or 53;

(*c*) establish periods within which applications for exploration and development may be lodged, all applications received within each such period being considered as simultaneous;

(*d*) establish procedures for the handling of applications; and

(*e*) determine a method of resolving competing applications which are not resolved in accordance with Article 45(4)(a), which method shall, provided that all other requirements of this Convention are satisfied and consistently with measures adopted pursuant to Article 41(1)(d), include priority for the application with the broadest participation among interested Parties which are Antarctic Treaty Consultative Parties and other interested Parties, in particular, developing countries in either category.

3. The Regulatory Committee shall adopt guidelines which are consistent with, and which taken together with, the provisions of this Convention and measures of general applicability adopted by the Commission, as well as associated conditions and general guidelines adopted by the Commission when

identifying the area, shall, by addressing the relevant items in Article 47, identify the general requirements for exploration and development in its area of competence.

4.   Upon adoption of guidelines under paragraph 3 above the Executive Secretary shall, without delay, inform all members of the Commission of the decisions taken by the Regulatory Committee pursuant to paragraphs 2 and 3 above and shall make them publicly available together with relevant measures, associated conditions and general guidelines adopted by the Commission.

5.   The Regulatory Committee may from time to time revise guidelines adopted under paragraph 3 above, taking into account any views of the Commission.

6.   In performing its functions under paragraphs 3 and 5 above, the Regulatory Committee shall seek and take full account of the views of the Advisory Committee provided in accordance with Article 26.

Article 44
Application for an Exploration Permit

1.   Following completion of the work undertaken pursuant to Article 43, any Party, on behalf of an Operator for which it is the Sponsoring State, may lodge with the Regulatory Committee an application for an exploration permit within the periods established by the Regulatory Committee pursuant to Article 43(2)(c).

2.   An application shall be accompanied by the fees established by the Regulatory Committee in accordance with Article 43(2)(b) and shall contain:

(*a*) a detailed description of the Operator, including its managerial structure, financial composition and resources and technical expertise, and, in the case of an Operator being a joint venture, the inclusion of a detailed description of the degree to which Parties are involved in the Operator through, *inter alia,* juridical persons with which Parties have substantial and genuine links, so that each component of the joint venture can be easily attributed to a Party or Parties for the purposes of identifying the level of Antarctic mineral resource activities thereof, which description of substantial and genuine links shall include a description of equity sharing;

(*b*) a detailed description of the proposed exploration activities and a description in as much detail as possible of proposed development activities, including:

(i) an identification of the mineral resource or resources and the block to which the application applies;

(ii) a detailed explanation of how the proposed activities conform with the general requirements referred to in Article 43(3);

(iii) a detailed assessment of the environmental and other impacts of the proposed activities, taking into account Articles 15 and 26(4); and

(iv) a description of the capacity to respond effectively to accidents, especially those with potential environmental effects;

(*c*) a certification by the Sponsoring State of the capacity of the Operator to comply with the general requirements referred to in Article 43(3);

(*d*) a certification by the Sponsoring State of the technical competence and financial capacity of the Operator and that the Operator has a substantial and genuine link with it as defined in Article 1(12);

(*e*) a description of the manner in which the application complies with any measures adopted by the Commission pursuant to Article 41(1)(d), and

(*f*) such further information as may be required by the Regulatory Committee or in measures adopted by the Commission.

Article 45
Examination of Applications

1. The Regulatory Committee shall meet as soon as possible after an application has been lodged pursuant to Article 44, for the purpose of elaborating a Management Scheme. In performing this function it shall:

(*a*) determine whether the application contains sufficient or adequate information pursuant to Article 44(2). To this end, it may at any time seek further information from the Sponsoring State consistent with Article 44(2);

(*b*) consider the exploration and development activities, proposed in the application, and such elaborations, revisions or adaptations as necessary:

(i) to ensure their consistency with this Convention as well as measures in effect pursuant thereto and the general requirements referred to in Article 43(3); and

(ii) to prescribe the specific terms and conditions of a Management Scheme in accordance with Article 47.

2. At any time during the process of consideration described above, the Regulatory Committee may decline the application if it considers that the activities proposed therein cannot be elaborated, revised or adapted to ensure consistency with this Convention as well as measures in effect pursuant thereto and the general requirements referred to in Article 43(3).

3. In performing its functions under this Article, the Regulatory Committee shall seek and take full account of the views of the Advisory Committee. To that end the Regulatory Committee shall refer to the Advisory Committee all parts of the application which are necessary for it to provide advice pursuant to Article 26, together with any other relevant information.

4. If two or more applications meeting the requirements of Article 44(2) are lodged in respect of the same block:

(*a*) the competing applicants shall be invited by the Regulatory Committee to resolve the competition amongst themselves, by means of their own choice within a prescribed period;

(*b*) if the competition is not resolved pursuant to subparagraph (a) above it shall be resolved by the Regulatory Committee in accordance with the method determined by it pursuant to Article 43(2)(e).

Article 46
Management Scheme

In performing its functions under Article 45, including the preparation of a Management Scheme, and under Article 54, the Regulatory Committee shall have recourse to the Sponsoring State and the member or members, if any, referred to in Article 29(2)(a) and, as may be required, one or two additional members of the Regulatory Committee.

Article 47
Scope of the Management Scheme

The Management Scheme shall prescribe the specific terms and conditions for exploration and development of the mineral resource or resources concerned within the relevant block. Such terms and conditions shall be consistent with the general requirements referred to in Article 43(3), and shall cover, *inter alia:*

(*a*) duration of exploration and development permits;

(*b*) measures and procedures for the protection of the Antarctic environment and dependent and associated ecosystems, including methods, activities and undertakings by the Operator to minimize environmental risks and damage;

(*c*) provision for necessary and timely response action, including prevention, containment and clean up and removal measures, for restoration to the *status quo ante,* and for contingency plans, resources and equipment to enable such action to be taken;

(*d*) procedures for the implementation of different stages of exploration and development;

(*e*) performance requirements;

(*f*) technical and safety specifications, including standards and procedures to ensure safe operations;

(*g*) monitoring and inspection;

(*h*) liability;

(*i*) procedures for the development of mineral deposits which extend outside the area covered by a permit;

(*j*) resource conservation requirements;

(*k*) financial obligations of the Operator including:

(i) levies in accordance with measures adopted pursuant to Article 21(1)(q);

(ii) payments in the nature of and similar to taxes, royalties or payments in kind;

(*l*) financial guarantees and insurance;

(*m*) assignment and relinquishment;

(*n*) suspension and modification of the Management Scheme, or cancellation of the Management Scheme, exploration or development permit, and the imposition of monetary penalties, in accordance with Article 51;

(*o*) procedures for agreed modifications;

(*p*) enforcement of the Management Scheme;

(*q*) applicable law to the extent necessary;

(*r*) effective additional procedures for the settlement of disputes;

(*s*) provisions to avoid and to resolve conflict with other legitimate uses of Antarctica;

(*t*) data and information collection, reporting and notification requirements;

(*u*) confidentiality; and

(*v*) removal of installations and equipment, as well as site rehabilitation.

Article 48
Approval of the Management Scheme

A Management Scheme prepared in accordance with Articles 45, 46 and 47 shall be subject to approval pursuant to Article 32. Such approval shall constitute authorization for the issue without delay of an exploration permit by the Regulatory Committee. The exploration permit shall accord exclusive rights to the Operator to explore and, subject to Articles 53 and 54, to develop the mineral resource or resources which are the subject of the Management Scheme exclusively in accordance with the terms and conditions of the Management Scheme.

Article 49
Review

1. Any member of the Commission, or any member of a Regulatory Committee, may within one month of a decision by that Regulatory Committee to approve a Management Scheme or issue a development permit, request that the Commission be convened in accordance with Article 19(2)(b) or (c), as the case may be, to review the decision of the Regulatory Committee for consistency with the decision taken by the Commission to identify the area pursuant to Article 41 and any measures in effect relevant to that decision.

2. The Commission shall complete its consideration within three months of a request made pursuant to paragraph 1 above. In performing its functions the Commission shall not assume the functions of the Regulatory Committee, nor shall it substitute its discretion for that of the Regulatory Committee.

3. Should the Commission determine that a decision to approve a Management Scheme or issue a development permit is inconsistent with the decision taken by the Commission to identify the area pursuant to Article 41 and any measures in effect relevant to that decision, it may request that Regulatory Committee to reconsider its decision.

Article 50
Rights of Authorized Operators

1. No Management Scheme shall be suspended or modified and no Management Scheme, exploration or development permit shall be cancelled

without the consent of the Sponsoring State except pursuant to Article 51, or Article 54 or the Management Scheme itself.

2.   Each Operator authorized to conduct activities pursuant to a Management Scheme shall exercise its rights with due regard to the rights of other Operators undertaking exploration or development in the same identified area.

Article 51

Suspension, Modification or Cancellation of the Management Scheme and Monetary Penalties

1.   If a Regulatory Committee determines that exploration or development authorised pursuant to a Management Scheme has resulted or is about to result in impacts on the Antarctic environment or dependent or associated ecosystems beyond those judged acceptable pursuant to this Convention, it shall suspend the relevant activities and as soon as possible modify the Management Scheme so as to avoid such impacts. If such impacts cannot be avoided by the modification of the Management Scheme, the Regulatory Committee shall suspend it, or cancel it and the exploration or development permit.

2.   In performing its functions under paragraph 1 above a Regulatory Committee shall, unless emergency action is required, seek and take into account the views of the Advisory Committee.

3.   If a Regulatory Committee determines that an Operator has failed to comply with this Convention or with measures in effect pursuant to it or a Management Scheme applicable to that Operator, the Regulatory Committee may do all or any of the following:

   (a) modify the Management Scheme;

   (b) suspend the Management Scheme;

   (c) cancel the Management Scheme and the exploration or development permit; and

   (d) impose a monetary penalty.

4.   Sanctions determined pursuant to paragraph 3(a) to (d) above shall be proportionate to the seriousness of the failure to comply.

5.   A Regulatory Committee shall cancel a Management Scheme and the exploration or development permit if an Operator ceases to have a substantial and genuine link with the Sponsoring State as defined in Article 1(12).

6.   The Commission shall adopt general measures, which may include mitigation, relating to action by Regulatory Committees pursuant to paragraphs 1 and 3 above and, as appropriate, to the consequences of such action. No application pursuant to Article 44 may be lodged until such measures have come into effect.

Article 52

Monitoring in Relation to Management Schemes

1.   Each Regulatory Committee shall monitor the compliance of Operators with Management Schemes within its area of competence.

2. Each Regulatory Committee, taking into account the advice of the Advisory Committee, shall monitor and assess the effects on the Antarctic environment and on dependent and on associated ecosystems of Antarctic mineral resource activities within its area of competence, particularly by reference to key environmental parameters and ecosystem components.

3. Each Regulatory Committee shall, as appropriate, inform the Commission and the Advisory Committee in a timely fashion of monitoring under this Article.

CHAPTER V: DEVELOPMENT
Article 53
Application for a Development Permit

1. At any time during the period in which an approved Management Scheme and exploration permit are in force for an Operator, the Sponsoring State may, on behalf of that Operator, lodge with the Regulatory Committee an application for a development permit.

2. An application shall be accompanied by the fees established by the Regulatory Committee in accordance with Article 43(2)(b) and shall contain:

(*a*) an updated description of the planned development identifying any modifications proposed to the approved Management Scheme and any additional measures to be taken, consequent upon such modifications, to ensure consistency with this Convention, including any measures in effect pursuant thereto and the general requirements referred to in Article 43(3);

(*b*) a detailed assessment of the environmental and other impacts of the planned development, taking into account Articles 15 and 26(4);

(*c*) a recertification by the Sponsoring State of the technical competence and financial capacity of the Operator and that the Operator has a substantial and genuine link with it as defined in Article 1(12);

(*d*) a recertification by the Sponsoring State of the capacity of the Operator to comply with the general requirements referred to in Article 43(3);

(*e*) updated information in relation to all other matters specified in Article 44(2); and

(*f*) such further information as may be required by the Regulatory Committee or in measures adopted by the Commission.

Article 54
Examination of Applications and Issue of Development Permits

1. The Regulatory Committee shall meet as soon as possible after an application has been lodged pursuant to Article 53.

2. The Regulatory Committee shall determine whether the application contains sufficient or adequate information pursuant to Article 53(2). In performing this function it may at any time seek further information from the Sponsoring State consistent with Article 53(2).

3. The Regulatory Committee shall consider whether:

(*a*) the application reveals modifications to the planned development previously envisaged;

(*b*) the planned development would cause previously unforeseen impacts on the Antarctic environment or dependent or associated ecosystems, either as a result of any modifications referred to in subparagraph (a) above or in the light of increased knowledge.

4. The Regulatory Committee shall consider any modifications to the Management Scheme necessary in the light of paragraph 3 above to ensure that the development activities proposed would be undertaken consistently with this Convention as well as measures in effect pursuant thereto and the general requirements referred to in Article 43(3). However, the financial obligations specified in the approved Management Scheme may not be revised without the consent of the Sponsoring State, unless provided for in the Management Scheme itself.

5. If the Regulatory Committee in accordance with Article 32 approves modifications under paragraph 4 above, or if it does not consider that such modifications are necessary, the Regulatory Committee shall issue without delay a development permit.

6. In performing its functions under this Article, the Regulatory Committee shall seek and take full account of the views of the Advisory Committee. To that end the Regulatory Committee shall refer to the Advisory Committee all parts of the application which are necessary for it to provide advice pursuant to Article 26, together with any other relevant information.

CHAPTER VI: DISPUTES SETTLEMENT
Article 55
Disputes Between Two or More Parties

Articles 56, 57 and 58 apply to disputes between two or more Parties.

Article 56
Choice of Procedure

1. Each Party, when signing, ratifying, accepting, approving or acceding to this Convention, or at any time thereafter, may choose, by written declaration, one or both of the following means for the settlement of disputes concerning the interpretation or application of this Convention:

(*a*) the International Court of Justice;

(*b*) the Arbitral Tribunal.

2. A declaration made under paragraph 1 above shall not affect the operation of Article 57(1), (3), (4) and (5).

3. A Party that has not made a declaration under paragraph 1 above or in respect of which a declaration is no longer in force shall be deemed to have accepted the competence of the Arbitral Tribunal.

4. If the parties to a dispute have accepted the same means for the settlement of a dispute, the dispute may be submitted only to that procedure, unless the parties otherwise agree.

5. If the parties to a dispute have not accepted the same means for the settlement of a dispute, or if they have both accepted both means, the dispute

may be submitted only to the Arbitral Tribunal, unless the parties otherwise agree.

6. A declaration made under paragraph 1 above shall remain in force until it expires in accordance with its terms or until 3 months after written notice of revocation has been deposited with the Depositary.

7. A new declaration, a notice of revocation or the expiry of a declaration shall not in any way affect proceedings pending before the International Court of Justice or the Arbitral Tribunal, unless the parties to the dispute otherwise agree.

8. Declarations and notices referred to in this Article shall be deposited with the Depositary who shall transmit copies thereof to all Parties.

Article 57
Procedure for Dispute Settlement

1. If a dispute arises concerning the interpretation or application of this Convention, the parties to the dispute shall, at the request of any one of them, consult among themselves as soon as possible with a view to having the dispute resolved by negotiation, enquiry, mediation, conciliation, arbitration, judicial settlement or other peaceful means of their choice.

2. If the parties to a dispute concerning the interpretation or application of this Convention have not agreed on a means for resolving it within 12 months of the request for consultation pursuant to paragraph 1 above, the dispute shall be referred, at the request of any party to the dispute, for settlement in accordance with the procedure determined by the operation of Article 56(4) and (5).

3. If a dispute concerning the interpretation or application of this Convention relates to a measure in effect pursuant to this Convention or a Management Scheme and the parties to such a dispute:

(a) have not agreed on a means for resolving the dispute within 6 months of the request for consultation pursuant to paragraph 1 above, the dispute shall be referred, at the request of any party to the dispute, for discussion in the institution which adopted the instrument in question;

(b) have not agreed on a means for resolving the dispute within 12 months of the request for consultation pursuant to paragraph 1 above, the dispute shall be referred for settlement, at the request of any party to the dispute, to the Arbitral Tribunal.

4. The Arbitral Tribunal shall not be competent to decide or otherwise rule upon any matter within the scope of Article 9. In addition, nothing in this Convention shall be interpreted as conferring competence or jurisdiction on the International Court of Justice or any other tribunal established for the purpose of settling disputes between Parties to decide or otherwise rule upon any matter within the scope of Article 9.

5. The Arbitral Tribunal shall not be competent with regard to the exercise by an institution of its discretionary powers in accordance with this Convention; in no case shall the Arbitral Tribunal substitute its discretion for that of an institution. In addition, nothing in this Convention shall be interpreted as conferring competence or jurisdiction on the International

Court of Justice or any other tribunal established for the purpose of settling disputes between Parties with regard to the exercise by an institution of its discretionary powers or to substitute its discretion for that of an institution.

Article 58
Exclusion of Categories of Disputes

1.   Any Party, when signing, ratifying, accepting, approving or acceding to this Convention, or at any time thereafter, may, by written declaration, exclude the operation of Article 57(2) or (3) without its consent with respect to a category or categories of disputes specified in the declaration.   Such declaration may not cover disputes concerning the interpretation or application of:

(a) any provision of this Convention or of any measure in effect pursuant to it relating to the protection of the Antarctic environment or dependent or associated ecosystems;

(b) Article 7(1);

(c) Article 8;

(d) Article 12;

(e) Article 14;

(f) Article 15; or

(g) Article 37.

2.   Nothing in paragraph 1 above or in any declaration made under it shall affect the operation of Article 57(1), (4) and (5).

3.   A declaration made under paragraph 1 above shall remain in force until it expires in accordance with its terms or until 3 months after written notice of revocation has been deposited with the Depositary.

4.   A new declaration, a notice of revocation or the expiry of a declaration shall not in any way affect proceedings pending before the International Court of Justice or the Arbitral Tribunal, unless the parties to the dispute otherwise agree.

5.   Declarations and notices referred to in this Article shall be deposited with the Depositary who shall transmit copies thereof to all Parties.

6.   A Party which, by declaration made under paragraph 1 above, has excluded specific category or categories of disputes from the operation of Article 57(2) or (3) without its consent shall not be entitled to submit any dispute falling within that category or those categories for settlement pursuant to Article 57(2) or (3), as the case may be, without the consent of the other party or parties to the dispute.

Article 59
Additional Dispute Settlement Procedures

1.   The Commission, in conjunction with its responsibilities pursuant to Article 41(1), shall establish additional procedures for third-party settlement, by the Arbitral Tribunal or through other similar procedures, of disputes which may arise if it is alleged that a violation of this Convention has occurred by virtue of:

(a) a decision to decline a Management Scheme;

(*b*) a decision to decline the issue of a development permit; or

(*c*) a decision to suspend, modify or cancel a Management Scheme or to impose monetary penalties.

2. Such procedures shall:

(*a*) permit, as appropriate, Parties and Operators under their sponsorship, but not both in respect of any particular dispute, to initiate proceedings against a Regulatory Committee;

(*b*) require disputes to which they relate to be referred in the first instance to the relevant Regulatory Committee for consideration;

(*c*) incorporate the rules in Article 57(4) and (5).

CHAPTER VII: FINAL CLAUSES
Article 60
Signature

This Convention shall be open for signature at Wellington from 25 November 1988 to 25 November 1989 by States which participated in the final session of the Fourth Special Antarctic Treaty Consultative Meeting.

Article 61
Ratification, Acceptance, Approval or Accession

1. This Convention is subject to ratification, acceptance or approval by Signatory States.

2. After 25 November 1989 this Convention shall be open for accession by any State which is a Contracting Party to the Antarctic Treaty.

3. Instruments of ratification, acceptance, approval or accession shall be deposited with the Government of New Zealand, hereby designated as the Depositary.

Article 62
Entry Into Force

1. This Convention shall enter into force on the thirtieth day following the date of deposit of instruments of ratification, acceptance, approval or accession by 16 Antarctic Treaty Consultative Parties which participated as such in the final session of the Fourth Special Antarctic Treaty Consultative Meeting, provided that number includes all the States necessary in order to establish all of the institutions of the Convention in respect of every area of Antarctica, including 5 developing countries and 11 developed countries.

2. For each State which, subsequent to the date of entry into force of this Convention, deposits an instrument of ratification, acceptance, approval or accession, the Convention shall enter into force on the thirtieth by following such deposit.

Article 63
Reservations, Declarations and Statements

1. Reservations to this Convention shall not be permitted. This does not preclude a State, when signing, ratifying, accepting, approving or acceding to this Convention, from making declarations or statements, however phrased or named, with a view, *inter alia,* to the harmonization of its laws and

regulations with this Convention, provided that such declarations or statements do not purport to exclude or to modify the legal effect of this Convention in its application to that State.

2.   The provisions of this Article are without prejudice to the right to make written declarations in accordance with Article 58.

Article 64
Amendment

1.   This Convention shall not be subject to amendment until after the expiry of 10 years from the date of its entry into force.   Thereafter, any Party may, by written communication addressed to the Depositary, propose a specific amendment to this Convention and request the convening of a meeting to consider such proposed amendment.

2.   The Depositary shall circulate such communication to all Parties.   If within 12 months of the date of circulation of the communication at least one-third of the Parties reply favorably to the request, the Depositary shall convene the meeting.

3.   The adoption of an amendment considered at such a meeting shall require the affirmative votes of two-thirds of the Parties present and voting including the concurrent votes of the members of the Commission attending the meeting.

4.   The adoption of any amendment relating to the Special Meeting of Parties or to the Advisory Committee shall require the affirmative votes of three-quarters of the Parties present and voting, including the concurrent votes of the members of the Commission attending the meeting.

5.   An amendment shall enter into force for those Parties having deposited instruments of ratification, acceptance or approval thereof 30 days after the Depositary has received such instruments of ratification, acceptance or approval from all the members of the Commission.

6.   Such amendment shall thereafter enter into force for any other Party 30 days after the Depositary has received its instrument of ratification, acceptance or approval thereof.

7.   An amendment that has entered into force pursuant to this Article shall be without prejudice to the provisions of any Management Scheme approved before the date on which the amendment entered into force.

Article 65
Withdrawal

1.   Any Party may withdraw from this Convention by giving to the Depositary notice in writing of its intention to withdraw.   Withdrawal shall take effect two years after the date of receipt of such notice by the Depositary.

2.   Any Party which ceases to be a Contracting Party to the Antarctic Treaty shall be deemed to have withdrawn from this Convention on the date that it ceases to be a Contracting Party to the Antarctic Treaty.

3.   Where an amendment has entered into force pursuant to Article 64(5), any Party from which no instrument of ratification, acceptance or approval of the amendment has been received by the Depositary within a period of two years from the date of the entry into force of the amendment

shall be deemed to have withdrawn from this Convention on the date of the expiration of a further two year period.

4.   Subject to paragraph 5 and 6 below, the rights and obligations of any Operator pursuant to this Convention shall cease at the time its Sponsoring State withdraws or is deemed to have withdrawn from this Convention.

5.   Such Sponsoring State shall ensure that the obligations of its Operators have been discharged no later than the date on which its withdrawal takes effect.

6.   Withdrawal from this Convention by any Party shall not affect its financial or other obligations under this Convention pending on the date withdrawal takes effect.   Any dispute settlement procedure in which that Party is involved and which has been commenced prior to that date shall continue to its conclusion unless agreed otherwise by the parties to the dispute.

Article 66
Notifications by the Depositary

The Depositary shall notify all Contracting Parties to the Antarctic Treaty of the following:

(*a*) signatures of this Convention and the deposit of instruments of ratification, acceptance, approval or accession;

(*b*) the deposit of instruments of ratification, acceptance or approval of any amendment adopted pursuant to Article 64;

(*c*) the date of entry into force of this Convention and of any amendment thereto;

(*d*) the deposit of declarations and notices pursuant to Articles 56 and 58;

(*e*) notifications pursuant to Article 18; and

(*f*) the withdrawal of a Party pursuant to Article 65.

Article 67
Authentic Texts, Certified Copies and Registration
with the United Nations

1.   This Convention of which the Chinese, English, French, Russian and Spanish texts are equally authentic shall be deposited with the Government of New Zealand which shall transmit duly certified copies thereof to all Signatory and Acceding States.

2.   The Depositary shall also transmit duly certified copies to all Signatory and Acceding States of the text of this Convention in any additional language of a Signatory or Acceding State which submits such text to the Depositary.

3.   This Convention shall be registered by the Depositary pursuant to Article 102 of the Charter of the United Nations.

2.8 RESOLUTION ON THE QUESTION OF ANTARCTICA. Adopted by the UN General Assembly, 15 December 1989. G.A. Res. 44/124, U.N. GAOR, 44th Sess., Supp. No. 49, at 91, U.N. Doc. A/44/49 (1989)

A

The General Assembly,

Recalling its resolution 43/83 B of 7 December 1988,

Having considered the item entitled "Question of Antarctica",

Noting with regret that the racist *apartheid* régime of South Africa, which has been suspended from participation in the General Assembly of the United Nations, has continued to participate in the meetings of the Antarctic Treaty Consultative Parties,

Recalling the resolution adopted by the Council of Ministers of the Organization of African Unity at its fiftieth ordinary session, held at Addis Ababa from 17 to 22 July 1989,

Recalling also the final document on Antarctica adopted by the Ninth Conference of Heads of State or Government of Non–Aligned Countries, held at Belgrade from 4 to 7 September 1989,

Recalling further that the Antarctic Treaty is, by its terms, intended to further the purposes and principles embodied in the Charter of the United Nations,

Noting that the policy of *apartheid* practised by the racist minority régime of South Africa, which has been universally condemned, constitutes a threat to regional and international peace and security,

1. *Views with concern* the continuing participation of the *apartheid* régime of South Africa in the meetings of the Antarctic Treaty Consultative Parties;

2. *Appeals once again* to the Antarctic Treaty Consultative Parties to take urgent measures to exclude the racist *apartheid* régime of South Africa from participation in the meetings of the Consultative Parties at the earliest possible date;

3. *Invites* the States parties to the Antarctic Treaty to inform the Secretary–General of the actions taken regarding the provisions of the present resolution;

4. *Requests* the Secretary–General to submit a report in this regard to the General Assembly at its forty-fifth session;

5. *Decides* to include in the provisional agenda of its forty-fifth session the item entitled "Question of Antarctica".

B

The General Assembly,

Having considered the item entitled "Question of Antarctica",

Recalling its resolutions 38/77 of 15 December 1983, 39/152 of 17 December 1984, 40/156 A and B of 16 December 1985, 41/88 A and B of 4 December 1986, 42/46 A and B of 30 November 1987 and 43/83 A and B of 7 December 1988,

Recalling also the relevant paragraphs of the Political Declaration adopted by the Eighth Conference of Heads of State or Government of Non–Aligned Countries, held at Harare from 1 to 6 September 1986, and the resolution on Antarctica adopted by the Council of Ministers of the Organization of African Unity at its forty-second ordinary session, held at Addis Ababa from 10 to 17 July 1985, as well as the relevant paragraphs of the decision of the Council of Ministers of the League of Arab States meeting at Tunis on 17 and 18 September 1986 and resolution 25/5–P(IS) adopted by the Fifth Islamic Summit Conference of the Organization of the Islamic Conference, held at Kuwait from 26 to 29 January 1987, the final document on Antarctica adopted by the Ninth Conference of Heads of State or Government of Non–Aligned Countries, held at Belgrade from 4 to 7 September 1989 and the communiqué issued by Commonwealth Heads of Government at Kuala Lumpur on 24 October 1989,

Taking into account the debates on this item held since its thirty-eighth session,

Welcoming the increasing awareness of and interest in Antarctica shown by the international community,

Convinced of the advantages to the whole of mankind of a better knowledge of Antarctica,

Affirming its conviction that, in the interest of all mankind, Antarctica should continue forever to be used exclusively for peaceful purposes and that it should not become the scene or object of international discord,

Reaffirming the principle that the international community is entitled to information covering all aspects of Antarctica and that the United Nations should be made the repository for all such information in accordance with General Assembly resolutions 41/88 A, 42/46 B and 43/83 A,

Conscious of the particular significance of Antarctica to the international community in terms, *inter alia,* of international peace and security, environment, its effects on global climatic conditions, economy and scientific research,

Conscious also of the interrelationship between Antarctica and the physical, chemical and biological processes that regulate the total Earth system,

Reaffirming that the management and use of Antarctica should be conducted in accordance with the purposes and principles of the Charter of the United Nations and in the interest of maintaining international peace and security and of promoting international co-operation for the benefit of mankind as a whole,

Affirming the necessity of ensuring, in the interest of all mankind, comprehensive environmental protection and conservation of the Antarctic environment and its dependent and associated ecosystems through negotiations with the full participation of all members of the international community,

Conscious of the environmental degradation that prospecting and mining in and around Antarctica would pose to the Antarctic and global environment and ecosystems,

Convinced of the need to prevent or minimize any impact of human activity resulting from the large number of scientific stations and expeditions in Antarctica on the environment and its dependent and associated ecosystems,

Taking into account all aspects pertaining to all areas covered by the Antarctic Treaty system,

Taking note with appreciation of the reports of the Secretary–General on the question of Antarctica,

1. *Expresses its regret* that, despite the numerous resolutions in which it has called upon the Antarctic Treaty Consultative Parties to invite the Secretary–General or his representative to their meetings, including their consultative meetings, the Secretary–General was not invited to the Preparatory Meeting of the XVth Antarctic Treaty Consultative Meeting or to the XVth Consultative Meeting, held in Paris from 9 to 13 May and from 9 to 20 October 1989, respectively;

2. *Reiterates its call* upon the Antarctic Treaty Consultative Parties to invite the Secretary–General or his representative to all meetings of the Treaty parties, including their consultative meetings;

3. *Requests* the Secretary–General to submit a report on his evaluations thereon to the General Assembly at its forty-fifth session;

4. *Expresses the conviction* that, in view of the significant impact that Antarctica exerts on the global environment and ecosystems, any régime to be established for the protection and conservation of the Antarctic environment and its dependent and associated ecosystems, in order to be for the benefit of mankind as a whole and in order to gain the universal acceptability necessary to ensure full compliance and enforcement, must be negotiated with the full participation of all members of the international community;

5. *Urges* all members of the international community to support all efforts to ban prospecting and mining in and around Antarctica and to ensure that all activities are carried out exclusively for the purpose of peaceful scientific investigation and that all such activities ensure the maintenance of international peace and security in Antarctica and the protection of its environment and are for the benefit of all mankind;

6. *Expresses its conviction* that the establishment, through negotiations with the full participation of all members of the international community, of Antarctica as a nature reserve or a world park would ensure the protection and conservation of its environment and its dependent and associated ecosystems for the benefit of all mankind;

7. *Also expresses its conviction,* in view of the large number of scientific stations and expeditions, that international scientific research should be enhanced through the establishment of international stations devoted to scientific investigations of global significance, regulated by stringent environmental safeguards, so as to avoid or minimize any adverse impact of human activities on the Antarctic environment and its dependent and associated ecosystems;

8. *Urges* all States Members of the United Nations to co-operate with the Secretary–General and to continue consultations on all aspects relating to Antarctica;

9. *Decides* to include in the provisional agenda of its forty-fifth session the item entitled "Question of Antarctica".

2.9 PROTOCOL ON ENVIRONMENTAL PROTECTION TO THE ANTARCTIC TREATY (WITH ANNEXES I & III ONLY).[1] Concluded at Madrid, 4 October 1991. Not in force as of 31 December 1992. XI ATSCM/2, 30 I.L.M. 1461 (1991)

PREAMBLE

The States Parties to this Protocol to the Antarctic Treaty, hereinafter referred to as the Parties,

Convinced of the need to enhance the protection of the Antarctic environment and dependent and associated ecosystems;

Convinced of the need to strengthen the Antarctic Treaty system so as to ensure that Antarctica shall continue forever to be used exclusively for peaceful purposes and shall not become the scene or object of international discord;

Bearing in mind the special legal and political status of Antarctica and the special responsibility of the Antarctic Treaty Consultative Parties to ensure that all activities in Antarctica are consistent with the purposes and principles of the Antarctic Treaty;

Recalling the designation of Antarctica as a Special Conservation Area and other measures adopted under the Antarctic Treaty system to protect the Antarctic environment and dependent and associated ecosystems;

Acknowledging further the unique opportunities Antarctica offers for scientific monitoring of and research on processes of global as well as regional importance;

Reaffirming the conservation principles of the Convention on the Conservation of Antarctic Marine Living Resources;[2]

Convinced that the development of a comprehensive regime for the protection of the Antarctic environment and dependent and associated ecosystems is in the interest of mankind as a whole;

Desiring to supplement the Antarctic Treaty to this end;

Have agreed as follows:

ARTICLE 1
DEFINITIONS

For the purposes of this Protocol:

(a) "The Antarctic Treaty" means the Antarctic Treaty done at Washington on 1 December 1959;

(b) "Antarctic Treaty area" means the area to which the provisions of the Antarctic Treaty apply in accordance with Article VI of that Treaty;

(c) "Antarctic Treaty Consultative Meetings" means the meetings referred to in Article IX of the Antarctic Treaty;

(d) "Antarctic Treaty Consultative Parties" means the Contracting Parties to the Antarctic Treaty entitled to appoint representatives to participate in the meetings referred to in Article IX of that Treaty;

---

1. *See also* Basic Document 2.1, *supra.*   **2.** *See* Basic Document 2.4, *supra.*

(e) "Antarctic Treaty system" means the Antarctic Treaty, the measures in effect under that Treaty, its associated separate international instruments in force and the measures in effect under those instruments;

(f) "Arbitral Tribunal" means the Arbitral Tribunal established in accordance with the Schedule to this Protocol, which forms an integral part thereof;

(g) "Committee" means the Committee for Environmental Protection established in accordance with Article 11.

ARTICLE 2
OBJECTIVE AND DESIGNATION

The Parties commit themselves to the comprehensive protection of the Antarctic environment and dependent and associated ecosystems and hereby designate Antarctica as a natural reserve, devoted to peace and science.

ARTICLE 3
ENVIRONMENTAL PRINCIPLES

1. The protection of the Antarctic environment and dependent and associated ecosystems and the intrinsic value of Antarctica, including its wilderness and aesthetic values and its value as an area for the conduct of scientific research, in particular research essential to understanding the global environment, shall be fundamental considerations in the planning and conduct of all activities in the Antarctic Treaty area.

2. To this end:

(a) activities in the Antarctic Treaty area shall be planned and conducted so as to limit adverse impacts on the Antarctic environment and dependent and associated ecosystems;

(b) activities in the Antarctic Treaty area shall be planned and conducted so as to avoid:

(i) adverse effects on climate or weather patterns;

(ii) significant adverse effects on air or water quality;

(iii) significant changes in the atmospheric, terrestrial (including aquatic), glacial or marine environments;

(iv) detrimental changes in the distribution, abundance or productivity of species or populations of species of fauna and flora;

(v) further jeopardy to endangered or threatened species or populations of such species; or

(vi) degradation of, or substantial risk to, areas of biological, scientific, historic, aesthetic or wilderness significance;

(c) activities in the Antarctic Treaty area shall be planned and conducted on the basis of information sufficient to allow prior assessments of, and informed judgments about, their possible impacts on the Antarctic environment and dependent and associated ecosystems and on the value of Antarctica for the conduct of scientific research; such judgments shall take full account of:

(i) the scope of the activity, including its area, duration and intensity;

(ii) the cumulative impacts of the activity, both by itself and in combination with other activities in the Antarctic Treaty area;

(iii) whether the activity will detrimentally affect any other activity in the Antarctic Treaty area;

(iv) whether technology and procedures are available to provide for environmentally safe operations;

(v) whether there exists the capacity to monitor key environmental parameters and ecosystem components so as to identify and provide early warning of any adverse effects of the activity and to provide for such modification of operating procedures as may be necessary in the light of the results of monitoring or increased knowledge of the Antarctic environment and dependent and associated ecosystems; and

(vi) whether there exists the capacity to respond promptly and effectively to accidents, particularly those with potential environmental effects;

(d) regular and effective monitoring shall take place to allow assessment of the impacts of ongoing activities, including the verification of predicted impacts;

(e) regular and effective monitoring shall take place to facilitate early detection of the possible unforeseen effects of activities carried on both within and outside the Antarctic Treaty area on the Antarctic environment and dependent and associated ecosystems.

3. Activities shall be planned and conducted in the Antarctic Treaty area so as to accord priority to scientific research and to preserve the value of Antarctica as an area for the conduct of such research, including research essential to understanding the global environment.

4. Activities undertaken in the Antarctic Treaty area pursuant to scientific research programmes, tourism and all other governmental and nongovernmental activities in the Antarctic Treaty area for which advance notice is required in accordance with Article VII(5) of the Antarctic Treaty, including associated logistic support activities, shall:

(a) take place in a manner consistent with the principles in this Article; and

(b) be modified, suspended or cancelled if they result in or threaten to result in impacts upon the Antarctic environment or dependent or associated ecosystems inconsistent with those principles.

ARTICLE 4

RELATIONSHIP WITH THE OTHER COMPONENTS OF THE ANTARCTIC TREATY SYSTEM

1. This Protocol shall supplement the Antarctic Treaty and shall neither modify nor amend that Treaty.

2. Nothing in this Protocol shall derogate from the rights and obligations of the Parties to this Protocol under the other international instruments in force within the Antarctic Treaty system.

ARTICLE 5
CONSISTENCY WITH THE OTHER COMPONENTS OF THE ANTARCTIC TREATY SYSTEM

The Parties shall consult and co-operate with the Contracting Parties to the other international instruments in force within the Antarctic Treaty system and their respective institutions with a view to ensuring the achievement of the objectives and principles of this Protocol and avoiding any interference with the achievement of the objectives and principles of those instruments or any inconsistency between the implementation of those instruments and of this Protocol.

ARTICLE 6
CO–OPERATION

1.   The Parties shall co-operate in the planning and conduct of activities in the Antarctic Treaty area. To this end, each Party shall endeavour to:

(a) promote co-operative programmes of scientific, technical and educational value, concerning the protection of the Antarctic environment and dependent and associated ecosystems;

(b) provide appropriate assistance to other Parties in the preparation of environmental impact assessments;

(c) provide to other Parties upon request information relevant to any potential environmental risk and assistance to minimize the effects of accidents which may damage the Antarctic environment or dependent and associated ecosystems;

(d) consult with other Parties with regard to the choice of sites for prospective stations and other facilities so as to avoid the cumulative impacts caused by their excessive concentration in any location;

(e) where appropriate, undertake joint expeditions and share the use of stations and other facilities; and

(f) carry out such steps as may be agreed upon at Antarctic Treaty Consultative Meetings.

2.   Each Party undertakes, to the extent possible, to share information that may be helpful to other Parties in planning and conducting their activities in the Antarctic Treaty area, with a view to the protection of the Antarctic environment and dependent and associated ecosystems.

3.   The Parties shall co-operate with those Parties which may exercise jurisdiction in areas adjacent to the Antarctic Treaty area with a view to ensuring that activities in the Antarctic Treaty area do not have adverse environmental impacts on those areas.

ARTICLE 7
PROHIBITION OF MINERAL RESOURCE ACTIVITIES

Any activity relating to mineral resources, other than scientific research, shall be prohibited.

ARTICLE 8
ENVIRONMENTAL IMPACT ASSESSMENT

1.   Proposed activities referred to in paragraph 2 below shall be subject to the procedures set out in Annex I for prior assessment of the impacts of

those activities on the Antarctic environment or on dependent or associated ecosystems according to whether those activities are identified as having:

(a) less than a minor or transitory impact;

(b) a minor or transitory impact; or

(c) more than a minor or transitory impact.

2. Each Party shall ensure that the assessment procedures set out in Annex I are applied in the planning processes leading to decisions about any activities undertaken in the Antarctic Treaty area pursuant to scientific research programmes, tourism and all other governmental and non-governmental activities in the Antarctic Treaty area for which advance notice is required under Article VII(5) of the Antarctic Treaty, including associated logistic support activities.

3. The assessment procedures set out in Annex I shall apply to any change in an activity whether the change arises from an increase or decrease in the intensity of an existing activity, from the addition of an activity, the decommissioning of a facility, or otherwise.

4. Where activities are planned jointly by more than one Party, the Parties involved shall nominate one of their number to coordinate the implementation of the environmental impact assessment procedures set out in Annex I.

ARTICLE 9
ANNEXES

1. The Annexes to this Protocol shall form an integral part thereof.

2. Annexes, additional to Annexes I–IV, may be adopted and become effective in accordance with Article IX of the Antarctic Treaty.

3. Amendments and modifications to Annexes may be adopted and become effective in accordance with Article IX of the Antarctic Treaty, provided that any Annex may itself make provision for amendments and modifications to become effective on an accelerated basis.

4. Annexes and any amendments and modifications thereto which have become effective in accordance with paragraphs 2 and 3 above shall, unless an Annex itself provides otherwise in respect of the entry into effect of any amendment or modification thereto, become effective for a Contracting Party to the Antarctic Treaty which is not an Antarctic Treaty Consultative Party, or which was not an Antarctic Treaty Consultative Party at the time of the adoption, when notice of approval of that Contracting Party has been received by the Depositary.

5. Annexes shall, except to the extent that an Annex provides otherwise, be subject to the procedures for dispute settlement set out in Articles 18 to 20.

ARTICLE 10
ANTARCTIC TREATY CONSULTATIVE MEETINGS

1. Antarctic Treaty Consultative Meetings shall, drawing upon the best scientific and technical advice available:

(a) define, in accordance with the provisions of this Protocol, the general policy for the comprehensive protection of the Antarctic environment and dependent and associated ecosystems; and

(b) adopt measures under Article IX of the Antarctic Treaty for the implementation of this Protocol.

2. Antarctic Treaty Consultative Meetings shall review the work of the Committee and shall draw fully upon its advice and recommendations in carrying out the tasks referred to in paragraph 1 above, as well as upon the advice of the Scientific Committee on Antarctic Research.

ARTICLE 11
COMMITTEE FOR ENVIRONMENTAL PROTECTION

1. There is hereby established the Committee for Environmental Protection.

2. Each Party shall be entitled to be a member of the Committee and to appoint a representative who may be accompanied by experts and advisers.

3. Observer status in the Committee shall be open to any Contracting Party to the Antarctic Treaty which is not a Party to this Protocol.

4. The Committee shall invite the President of the Scientific Committee on Antarctic Research and the Chairman of the Scientific Committee for the Conservation of Antarctic Marine Living Resources to participate as observers at its sessions. The Committee may also, with the approval of the Antarctic Treaty Consultative Meeting, invite such other relevant scientific, environmental and technical organisations which can contribute to its work to participate as observers at its sessions.

5. The Committee shall present a report on each of its sessions to the Antarctic Treaty Consultative Meeting. The report shall cover all matters considered at the session and shall reflect the views expressed. The report shall be circulated to the Parties and to observers attending the session, and shall thereupon be made publicly available.

6. The Committee shall adopt its rules of procedure which shall be subject to approval by the Antarctic Treaty Consultative Meeting.

ARTICLE 12
FUNCTIONS OF THE COMMITTEE

1. The functions of the Committee shall be to provide advice and formulate recommendations to the Parties in connection with the implementation of this Protocol, including the operation of its Annexes, for consideration at Antarctic Treaty Consultative Meetings, and to perform such other functions as may be referred to it by the Antarctic Treaty Consultative Meetings. In particular, it shall provide advice on:

(a) the effectiveness of measures taken pursuant to this Protocol;

(b) the need to update, strengthen or otherwise improve such measures;

(c) the need for additional measures, including the need for additional Annexes, where appropriate;

(d) the application and implementation of the environmental impact assessment procedures set out in Article 8 and Annex I;

(e) means of minimising or mitigating environmental impacts of activities in the Antarctic Treaty area;

(f) procedures for situations requiring urgent action, including response action in environmental emergencies;

(g) the operation and further elaboration of the Antarctic Protected Area system;

(h) inspection procedures, including formats for inspection reports and checklists for the conduct of inspections;

(i) the collection, archiving, exchange and evaluation of information related to environmental protection;

(j) the state of the Antarctic environment; and

(k) the need for scientific research, including environmental monitoring, related to the implementation of this Protocol.

2. In carrying out its functions, the Committee shall, as appropriate, consult with the Scientific Committee on Antarctic Research, the Scientific Committee for the Conservation of Antarctic Marine Living Resources and other relevant scientific, environmental and technical organizations.

ARTICLE 13
COMPLIANCE WITH THIS PROTOCOL

1. Each Party shall take appropriate measures within its competence, including the adoption of laws and regulations, administrative actions and enforcement measures, to ensure compliance with this Protocol.

2. Each Party shall exert appropriate efforts, consistent with the Charter of the United Nations, to the end that no one engages in any activity contrary to this Protocol.

3. Each Party shall notify all other Parties of the measures it takes pursuant to paragraphs 1 and 2 above.

4. Each Party shall draw the attention of all other Parties to any activity which in its opinion affects the implementation of the objectives and principles of this Protocol.

5. The Antarctic Treaty Consultative Meetings shall draw the attention of any State which is not a Party to this Protocol to any activity undertaken by that State, its agencies, instrumentalities, natural or juridical persons, ships, aircraft or other means of transport which affects the implementation of the objectives and principles of this Protocol.

ARTICLE 14
INSPECTION

1. In order to promote the protection of the Antarctic environment and dependent and associated ecosystems, and to ensure compliance with this Protocol, the Antarctic Treaty Consultative Parties shall arrange, individually or collectively, for inspections by observers to be made in accordance with Article VII of the Antarctic Treaty.

2.   Observers are:

(a) observers designated by any Antarctic Treaty Consultative Party who shall be nationals of that Party; and

(b) any observers designated at Antarctic Treaty Consultative Meetings to carry out inspections under procedures to be established by an Antarctic Treaty Consultative Meeting.

3.   Parties shall co-operate fully with observers undertaking inspections, and shall ensure that during inspections, observers are given access to all parts of stations, installations, equipment, ships and aircraft open to inspection under Article VII(3) of the Antarctic Treaty, as well as to all records maintained thereon which are called for pursuant to this Protocol.

4.   Reports of inspections shall be sent to the Parties whose stations, installations, equipment, ships or aircraft are covered by the reports. After those Parties have been given the opportunity to comment, the reports and any comments thereon shall be circulated to all the Parties and to the Committee, considered at the next Antarctic Treaty Consultative Meeting, and thereafter made publicly available.

ARTICLE 15
EMERGENCY RESPONSE ACTION

1.   In order to respond to environmental emergencies in the Antarctic Treaty area, each Party agrees to:

(a) provide for prompt and effective response action to such emergencies which might arise in the performance of scientific research programmes, tourism and all other governmental and nongovernmental activities in the Antarctic Treaty area for which advance notice is required under Article VII(5) of the Antarctic Treaty, including associated logistic support activities; and

(b) establish contingency plans for response to incidents with potential adverse effects on the Antarctic environment or dependent and associated ecosystems.

2.   To this end, the Parties shall:

(a) co-operate in the formulation and implementation of such contingency plans; and

(b) establish procedures for immediate notification of, and co-operative response to, environmental emergencies.

3.   In the implementation of this Article, the Parties shall draw upon the advice of the appropriate international organisations.

ARTICLE 16
LIABILITY

Consistent with the objectives of this Protocol for the comprehensive protection of the Antarctic environment and dependent and associated ecosystems, the Parties undertake to elaborate rules and procedures relating to liability for damage arising from activities taking place in the Antarctic Treaty area and covered by this Protocol. Those rules and procedures shall be included in one or more Annexes to be adopted in accordance with Article 9(2).

ARTICLE 17
ANNUAL REPORT BY PARTIES

1. Each Party shall report annually on the steps taken to implement this Protocol. Such reports shall include notifications made in accordance with Article 13(3), contingency plans established in accordance with Article 15 and any other notifications and information called for pursuant to this Protocol for which there is no other provision concerning the circulation and exchange of information.

2. Reports made in accordance with paragraph 1 above shall be circulated to all Parties and to the Committee, considered at the next Antarctic Treaty Consultative Meeting, and made publicly available.

ARTICLE 18
DISPUTE SETTLEMENT

If a dispute arises concerning the interpretation or application of this Protocol, the parties to the dispute shall, at the request of any one of them, consult among themselves as soon as possible with a view to having the dispute resolved by negotiation, inquiry, mediation, conciliation, arbitration, judicial settlement or other peaceful means to which the parties to the dispute agree.

ARTICLE 19
CHOICE OF DISPUTE SETTLEMENT PROCEDURE

1. Each Party, when signing, ratifying, accepting, approving or acceding to this Protocol, or at any time thereafter, may choose, by written declaration, one or both of the following means for the settlement of disputes concerning the interpretation or application of Articles 7, 8 and 15 and, except to the extent that an Annex provides otherwise, the provisions of any Annex and, insofar as it relates to these Articles and provisions, Article 13:

(a) the International Court of Justice;

(b) the Arbitral Tribunal.

2. A declaration made under paragraph 1 above shall not affect the operation of Article 18 and Article 20(2).

3. A Party which has not made a declaration under paragraph 1 above or in respect of which a declaration is no longer in force shall be deemed to have accepted the competence of the Arbitral Tribunal.

4. If the parties to a dispute have accepted the same means for the settlement of a dispute, the dispute may be submitted only to that procedure, unless the parties otherwise agree.

5. If the parties to a dispute have not accepted the same means for the settlement of a dispute, or if they have both accepted both means, the dispute may be submitted only to the Arbitral Tribunal, unless the parties otherwise agree.

6. A declaration made under paragraph 1 above shall remain in force until it expires in accordance with its terms or until three months after written notice of revocation has been deposited with the Depositary.

7. A new declaration, a notice of revocation or the expiry of a declaration shall not in any way affect proceedings pending before the International Court of Justice or the Arbitral Tribunal, unless the parties to the dispute otherwise agree.

8. Declarations and notices referred to in this Article shall be deposited with the Depositary who shall transmit copies thereof to all Parties.

ARTICLE 20
DISPUTE SETTLEMENT PROCEDURE

1. If the parties to a dispute concerning the interpretation or application of Articles 7, 8 or 15 or, except to the extent that an Annex provides otherwise, the provisions of any Annex or, insofar as it relates to these Articles and provisions, Article 13, have not agreed on a means for resolving it within 12 months of the request for consultation pursuant to Article 18, the dispute shall be referred, at the request of any party to the dispute, for settlement in accordance with the procedure determined by Article 19(4) and (5).

2. The Arbitral Tribunal shall not be competent to decide or rule upon any matter within the scope of Article IV of the Antarctic Treaty. In addition, nothing in this Protocol shall be interpreted as conferring competence or jurisdiction on the International Court of Justice or any other tribunal established for the purpose of settling disputes between Parties to decide or otherwise rule upon any matter within the scope of Article IV of the Antarctic Treaty.

ARTICLE 21
SIGNATURE

This Protocol shall be open for signature at Madrid on the 4th of October 1991 and thereafter at Washington until the 3rd of October 1992 by any State which is a Contracting Party to the Antarctic Treaty.

ARTICLE 22
RATIFICATION, ACCEPTANCE, APPROVAL OR ACCESSION

1. This Protocol is subject to ratification, acceptance or approval by signatory States.

2. After the 3rd of October 1992 this Protocol shall be open for accession by any State which is a Contracting Party to the Antarctic Treaty.

3. Instruments of ratification, acceptance, approval or accession shall be deposited with the Government of the United States of America, hereby designated as the Depositary.

4. After the date on which this Protocol has entered into force, the Antarctic Treaty Consultative Parties shall not act upon a notification regarding the entitlement of a Contracting Party to the Antarctic Treaty to appoint representatives to participate in Antarctic Treaty Consultative Meetings in accordance with Article IX(2) of the Antarctic Treaty unless that Contracting Party has first ratified, accepted, approved or acceded to this Protocol.

ARTICLE 23
ENTRY INTO FORCE

1. This Protocol shall enter into force on the thirtieth day following the date of deposit of instruments of ratification, acceptance, approval or acces-

sion by all States which are Antarctic Treaty Consultative Parties at the date on which this Protocol is adopted.

2. For each Contracting Party to the Antarctic Treaty which, subsequent to the date of entry into force of this Protocol, deposits an instrument of ratification, acceptance, approval or accession, this Protocol shall enter into force on the thirtieth day following such deposit.

ARTICLE 24
RESERVATIONS

Reservations to this Protocol shall not be permitted.

ARTICLE 25
MODIFICATION OR AMENDMENT

1. Without prejudice to the provisions of Article 9, this Protocol may be modified or amended at any time in accordance with the procedures set forth in Article XII(1)(a) and (b) of the Antarctic Treaty.

2. If, after the expiration of 50 years from the date of entry into force of this Protocol, any of the Antarctic Treaty Consultative Parties so requests by a communication addressed to the Depositary, a conference shall be held as soon as practicable to review the operation of this Protocol.

3. A modification or amendment proposed at any Review Conference called pursuant to paragraph 2 above shall be adopted by a majority of the Parties, including ¾ of the States which are Antarctic Treaty Consultative Parties at the time of adoption of this Protocol.

4. A modification or amendment adopted pursuant to paragraph 3 above shall enter into force upon ratification, acceptance, approval or accession by ¾ of the Antarctic Treaty Consultative Parties, including ratification, acceptance, approval or accession by all States which are Antarctic Treaty Consultative Parties at the time of adoption of this Protocol.

5. (a) With respect to Article 7, the prohibition on Antarctic mineral resource activities contained therein shall continue unless there is in force a binding legal regime on Antarctic mineral resource activities that includes an agreed means for determining whether, and, if so, under which conditions, any such activities would be acceptable. This regime shall fully safeguard the interests of all States referred to in Article IV of the Antarctic Treaty and apply the principles thereof. Therefore, if a modification or amendment to Article 7 is proposed at a Review Conference referred to in paragraph 2 above, it shall include such a binding legal regime.

(b) If any such modification or amendment has not entered into force within 3 years of the date of its adoption, any Party may at any time thereafter notify the Depositary of its withdrawal from this Protocol, and such withdrawal shall take effect 2 years after receipt of the notification by the Depositary.

ARTICLE 26
NOTIFICATIONS BY THE DEPOSITARY

The Depositary shall notify all Contracting Parties to the Antarctic Treaty of the following:

(a) signatures of this Protocol and the deposit of instruments of ratification, acceptance, approval or accession;

(b) the date of entry into force of this Protocol and any additional Annex thereto;

(c) the date of entry into force of any amendment or modification to this Protocol;

(d) the deposit of declarations and notices pursuant to Article 19; and

(e) any notification received pursuant to Article 25(5)(b)

ARTICLE 27

AUTHENTIC TEXTS AND REGISTRATION WITH THE UNITED NATIONS

1. This Protocol, done in the English, French, Russian and Spanish languages, each version being equally authentic, shall be deposited in the archives of the Government of the United States of America, which shall transmit duly certified copies thereof to all Contracting Parties to the Antarctic Treaty.

2. This Protocol shall be registered by the Depositary pursuant to Article 102 of the Charter of the United Nations.

* * *

Annex I to the Protocol on Environmental Protection to the Antarctic Treaty

ENVIRONMENTAL IMPACT ASSESSMENT

Article 1

Preliminary Stage

1. The environmental impacts of proposed activities referred to in Article 8 of the Protocol shall, before their commencement, be considered in accordance with appropriate national procedures.

2. If an activity is determined as having less than a minor or transitory impact, the activity may proceed forthwith.

Article 2

Initial Environmental Evaluation

1. Unless it has been determined that an activity will have less than a minor or transitory impact, or unless a Comprehensive Environmental Evaluation is being prepared in accordance with Article 3, an Initial Environmental Evaluation shall be prepared. It shall contain sufficient detail to assess whether a proposed activity may have more than a minor or transitory impact and shall include:

(a) a description of the proposed activity, including its purpose, location, duration, and intensity; and

(b) consideration of alternatives to the proposed activity and any impacts that the activity may have, including consideration of cumulative impacts in the light of existing and known planned activities.

2. If an Initial Environmental Evaluation indicates that a proposed activity is likely to have no more than a minor or transitory impact, the activity may proceed, provided that appropriate procedures, which may include monitoring, are put in place to assess and verify the impact of the activity.

Article 3

Comprehensive Environmental Evaluation

1. If an Initial Environmental Evaluation indicates or if it is otherwise determined that a proposed activity is likely to have more than a minor or transitory impact, a Comprehensive Environmental Evaluation shall be prepared.

2. A Comprehensive Environmental Evaluation shall include:

(a) a description of the proposed activity including its purpose, location, duration and intensity, and possible alternatives to the activity, including the alternatives of not proceeding, and the consequences of those alternatives;

(b) a description of the initial environmental reference state with which predicted changes are to be compared and a prediction of the future environmental reference state in the absence of the proposed activity;

(c) a description of the methods and data used to forecast the impacts of the proposed activity;

(d) estimation of the nature, extent, duration, and intensity of the likely direct impacts of the proposed activity;

(e) consideration of possible indirect or second order impacts of the proposed activity;

(f) consideration of cumulative impacts of the proposed activity in the light of existing activities and other known planned activities;

(g) identification of measures, including monitoring programmes, that could be taken to minimise or mitigate impacts of the proposed activity and to detect unforeseen impacts and that could provide early warning of any adverse effects of the activity as well as to deal promptly and effectively with accidents;

(h) identification of unavoidable impacts of the proposed activity;

(i) consideration of the effects of the proposed activity on the conduct of scientific research and on other existing uses and values;

(j) an identification of gaps in knowledge and uncertainties encountered in compiling the information required under this paragraph;

(k) a non-technical summary of the information provided under this paragraph; and

(*l*) the name and address of the person or organization which prepared the Comprehensive Environmental Evaluation and the address to which comments thereon should be directed.

3. The draft Comprehensive Environmental Evaluation shall be made publicly available and shall be circulated to all Parties, which shall also make

it publicly available, for comment. A period of 90 days shall be allowed for the receipt of comments.

4. The draft Comprehensive Environmental Evaluation shall be forwarded to the Committee at the same time as it is circulated to the Parties, and at least 120 days before the next Antarctic Treaty Consultative Meeting, for consideration as appropriate.

5. No final decision shall be taken to proceed with the proposed activity in the Antarctic Treaty area unless there has been an opportunity for consideration of the draft Comprehensive Environmental Evaluation by the Antarctic Treaty Consultative Meeting on the advice of the Committee, provided that no decision to proceed with a proposed activity shall be delayed through the operation of this paragraph for longer than 15 months from the date of circulation of the draft Comprehensive Environmental Evaluation.

6. A final Comprehensive Environmental Evaluation shall address and shall include or summarise comments received on the draft Comprehensive Environmental Evaluation. The final Comprehensive Environmental Evaluation, notice of any decisions relating thereto, and any evaluation of the significance of the predicted impacts in relation to the advantages of the proposed activity, shall be circulated to all Parties, which shall also make them publicly available, at least 60 days before the commencement of the proposed activity in the Antarctic Treaty area.

Article 4

Decisions to Be Based on Comprehensive Environmental Evaluations

Any decision on whether a proposed activity, to which Article 3 applies, should proceed, and, if so, whether in its original or in a modified form, shall be based on the Comprehensive Environmental Evaluation as well as other relevant considerations.

Article 5

Monitoring

1. Procedures shall be put in place, including appropriate monitoring of key environmental indicators, to assess and verify the impact of any activity that proceeds following the completion of a Comprehensive Environmental Evaluation.

2. The procedures referred to in paragraph 1 above and in Article 2(2) shall be designed to provide a regular and verifiable record of the impacts of the activity in order, *inter alia*, to:

(a) enable assessments to be made of the extent to which such impacts are consistent with the Protocol; and

(b) provide information useful for minimising or mitigating impacts, and, where appropriate, information on the need for suspension, cancellation or modification of the activity.

Article 6

Circulation of Information

1. The following information shall be circulated to the Parties, forwarded to the Committee and made publicly available:

(a) a description of the procedures referred to in Article 1;

(b) an annual list of any Initial Environmental Evaluations prepared in accordance with Article 2 and any decisions taken in consequence thereof;

(c) significant information obtained, and any action taken in consequence thereof, from procedures put in place in accordance with Articles 2(2) and 5; and

(d) information referred to in Article 3(6).

2. Any Initial Environmental Evaluation prepared in accordance with Article 2 shall be made available on request.

Article 7

Cases of Emergency

1. This Annex shall not apply in cases of emergency relating to the safety of human life or of ships, aircraft, or equipment and facilities of high value, or the protection of the environment, which require an activity to be undertaken without completion of the procedures set out in this Annex.

2. Notice of activities undertaken in cases of emergency, which would otherwise have required preparation of a Comprehensive Environmental Evaluation, shall be circulated immediately to all Parties and to the Committee and a full explanation of the activities carried out shall be provided within 90 days of those activities.

Article 8

Amendment or Modification

1. This Annex may be amended or modified by a measure adopted in accordance with Article IX(1) of the Antarctic Treaty. Unless the measure specifies otherwise, the amendment or modification shall be deemed to have been approved, and shall become effective, one year after the close of the Antarctic Treaty Consultative Meeting at which it was adopted, unless one or more of the Antarctic Treaty Consultative Parties notifies the Depositary, within that period, that it wishes an extension of that period or that it is unable to approve the measure.

2. Any amendment or modification of this Annex which becomes effective in accordance with paragraph 1 above shall thereafter become effective as to any other Party when notice of approval by it has been received by the Depositary.

* * *

Annex III to the Protocol on Environmental Protection to the Antarctic Treaty

WASTE DISPOSAL AND WASTE MANAGEMENT

Article 1

General Obligations

1. This Annex shall apply to activities undertaken in the Antarctic Treaty area pursuant to scientific research programmes, tourism and all other governmental and non-governmental activities in the Antarctic Treaty area

for which advance notice is required under Article VII (5) of the Antarctic Treaty, including associated logistic support activities.

2.   The amount of wastes produced or disposed of in the Antarctic Treaty area shall be reduced as far as practicable so as to minimise impact on the Antarctic environment and to minimise interference with the natural values of Antarctica, with scientific research and with other uses of Antarctica which are consistent with the Antarctic Treaty.

3.   Waste storage, disposal and removal from the Antarctic Treaty area, as well as recycling and source reduction, shall be essential considerations in the planning and conduct of activities in the Antarctic Treaty area.

4.   Wastes removed from the Antarctic Treaty area shall, to the maximum extent practicable, be returned to the country from which the activities generating the waste were organized or to any other country in which arrangements have been made for the disposal of such wastes in accordance with relevant international agreements.

5.   Past and present waste disposal sites on land and abandoned work sites of Antarctic activities shall be cleaned up by the generator of such wastes and the user of such sites.   This obligation shall not be interpreted as requiring:

(a) the removal of any structure designated as a historic site or monument; or

(b) the removal of any structure or waste material in circumstances where the removal by any practical option would result in greater adverse environmental impact than leaving the structure or waste material in its existing location.

Article 2

Waste Disposal by Removal From the Antarctic Treaty Area

1.   The following wastes, if generated after entry into force of this Annex, shall be removed from the Antarctic Treaty area by the generator of such wastes:

(a) radio-active materials;

(b) electrical batteries;

(c) fuel, both liquid and solid;

(d) wastes containing harmful levels of heavy metals or acutely toxic or harmful persistent compounds;

(e) poly-vinyl chloride (PVC), polyurethane foam, polystyrene foam, rubber and lubricating oils, treated timbers and other products which contain additives that could produce harmful emissions if incinerated;

(f) all other plastic wastes, except low density polyethylene containers (such as bags for storing wastes), provided that such containers shall be incinerated in accordance with Article 3(1);

(g) fuel drums; and

(h) other solid, non-combustible wastes;

provided that the obligation to remove drums and solid non-combustible wastes contained in subparagraphs (g) and (h) above shall not apply in circumstances where the removal of such wastes by any practical option would result in greater adverse environmental impact than leaving them in their existing locations.

2.   Liquid wastes which are not covered by paragraph 1 above and sewage and domestic liquid wastes, shall, to the maximum extent practicable, be removed from the Antarctic Treaty area by the generator of such wastes.

3.   The following wastes shall be removed from the Antarctic Treaty area by the generator of such wastes, unless incinerated, autoclaved or otherwise treated to be made sterile:

(a) residues of carcasses of imported animals;

(b) laboratory culture of micro-organisms and plant pathogens; and

(c) introduced avian products.

Article 3

Waste Disposal by Incineration

1.   Subject to paragraph 2 below, combustible wastes, other than those referred to in Article 2(1), which are not removed from the Antarctic Treaty area shall be burnt in incinerators which to the maximum extent practicable reduce harmful emissions.   Any emissions standards and equipment guidelines which may be recommended by, inter alia, the Committee and the Scientific Committee on Antarctic Research shall be taken into account.   The solid residue of such incineration shall be removed from the Antarctic Treaty area.

2.   All open burning of wastes shall be phased out as soon as practicable, but no later than the end of the 1998/1999 season.   Pending the completion of such phase-out, when it is necessary to dispose of wastes by open burning, allowance shall be made for the wind direction and speed and the type of wastes to be burnt to limit particulate deposition and to avoid such deposition over areas of special biological, scientific, historic, aesthetic or wilderness significance including, in particular, areas accorded protection under the Antarctic Treaty.

Article 4

Other Waste Disposal on Land

1.   Wastes not removed or disposed of in accordance with Articles 2 and 3 shall not be disposed of onto ice-free areas or into fresh water systems.

2.   Sewage, domestic liquid wastes and other liquid wastes not removed from the Antarctic Treaty area in accordance with Article 2, shall, to the maximum extent practicable, not be disposed of onto sea ice, ice shelves or the grounded ice-sheet, provided that such wastes which are generated by stations located inland on ice shelves or on the grounded ice-sheet may be disposed of in deep ice pits where such disposal is the only practicable option.   Such pits shall not be located on known ice-flow lines which terminate at ice-free areas or in areas of high ablation.

3.   Wastes generated at field camps shall, to the maximum extent practicable, be removed by the generator of such wastes to supporting stations or ships for disposal in accordance with this Annex.

Article 5

Disposal of Waste in the Sea

1. Sewage and domestic liquid wastes may be discharged directly into the sea, taking into account the assimilative capacity of the receiving marine environment and provided that:

(a) such discharge is located, wherever practicable, where conditions exist for initial dilution and rapid dispersal; and

(b) large quantities of such wastes (generated in a station where the average weekly occupancy over the austral summer is approximately 30 individuals or more) shall be treated at least by maceration.

2. The by-product of sewage treatment by the Rotary Biological Contactor process or similar processes may be disposed of into the sea provided that such disposal does not adversely affect the local environment, and provided also that any such disposal at sea shall be in accordance with Annex IV to the Protocol.

Article 6

Storage of Waste

All wastes to be removed from the Antarctic Treaty area, or otherwise disposed of, shall be stored in such a way as to prevent their dispersal into the environment.

Article 7

Prohibited Products

No polychlorinated biphenyls (PCBs), non-sterile soil, polystyrene beads, chips or similar forms of packaging, or pesticides (other than those required for scientific, medical or hygiene purposes) shall be introduced onto land or ice shelves or into water in the Antarctic Treaty area.

Article 8

Waste Management Planning

1. Each Party which itself conducts activities in the Antarctic Treaty area shall, in respect of those activities, establish a waste disposal classification system as a basis for recording wastes and to facilitate studies aimed at evaluating the environmental impacts of scientific activity and associated logistic support. To that end, wastes produced shall be classified as:

(a) sewage and domestic liquid wastes (Group 1);

(b) other liquid wastes and chemicals, including fuels and lubricants (Group 2);

(c) solids to be combusted (Group 3);

(d) other solid wastes (Group 4); and

(e) radioactive material (Group 5).

2. In order to reduce further the impact of waste on the Antarctic environment, each such Party shall prepare and annually review and update its waste management plans (including waste reduction, storage and disposal), specifying for each fixed site, for field camps generally, and for each ship

(other than small boats that are part of the operations of fixed sites or of ships and taking into account existing management plans for ships):

(a) programmes for cleaning up existing waste disposal sites and abandoned work sites;

(b) current and planned waste management arrangements, including final disposal;

(c) current and planned arrangements for analysing the environmental effects of waste and waste management; and

(d) other efforts to minimise any environmental effects of wastes and waste management.

3. Each such Party shall, as far as is practicable, also prepare an inventory of locations of past activities (such as traverses, fuel depots, field bases, crashed aircraft) before the information is lost, so that such locations can be taken into account in planning future scientific programmes (such as snow chemistry, pollutants in lichens or ice core drilling).

Article 9

Circulation and Review of Waste Management Plans

1. The waste management plans prepared in accordance with Article 8, reports on their implementation, and the inventories referred to in Article 8(3), shall be included in the annual exchanges of information in accordance with Articles III and VII of the Antarctic Treaty and related Recommendations under Article IX of the Antarctic Treaty.

2. Each Party shall send copies of its waste management plans, and reports on their implementation and review, to the Committee.

3. The Committee may review waste management plans and reports thereon and may offer comments, including suggestions for minimising impacts and modifications and improvement to the plans, for the consideration of the Parties.

4. The Parties may exchange information and provide advice on, inter alia, available low waste technologies, reconversion of existing installations, special requirements for effluents, and appropriate disposal and discharge methods.

Article 10

Management Practices

Each Party shall:

(a) designate a waste management official to develop and monitor waste management plans; in the field, this responsibility shall be delegated to an appropriate person at each site;

(b) ensure that members of its expeditions receive training designed to limit the impact of its operations on the Antarctic environment and to inform them of requirements of this Annex; and

(c) discourage the use of poly-vinyl chloride (PVC) products and ensure that its expeditions to the Antarctic Treaty area are advised of any PVC products they may introduce into that area in order that these products may be removed subsequently in accordance with this Annex.

Article 11

Review

This Annex shall be subject to regular review in order to ensure that it is updated to reflect improvement in waste disposal technology and procedures and to ensure thereby maximum protection of the Antarctic environment.

Article 12

Cases of Emergency

1. This Annex shall not apply in cases of emergency relating to the safety of human life or of ships, aircraft or equipment and facilities of high value or the protection of the environment.

2. Notice of activities undertaken in cases of emergency shall be circulated immediately to all Parties and to the Committee.

Article 13

Amendment or Modification

1. This Annex may be amended or modified by a measure adopted in accordance with Article IX(1) of the Antarctic Treaty. Unless the measure specifies otherwise, the amendment or modification shall be deemed to have been approved, and shall become effective, one year after the close of the Antarctic Treaty Consultative Meeting at which it was adopted, unless one or more of the Antarctic Treaty Consultative Parties notifies the Depositary, within that time period, that it wishes an extension of that period or that it is unable to approve the amendment.

2. Any amendment or modification of this Annex which becomes effective in accordance with paragraph 1 above shall thereafter become effective as to any other Party when notice of approval by it has been received by the Depositary.

3. ATMOSPHERE/SPACE

3.1 CONVENTION ON THIRD PARTY LIABILITY IN THE FIELD OF NUCLEAR ENERGY (AS AMENDED THROUGH 1964).[1] Concluded at Paris, 29 July 1960. Entered into force, 1 April 1968. 956 U.N.T.S. 251

THE GOVERNMENTS of the Federal Republic of Germany, the Republic of Austria, the Kingdom of Belgium, the Kingdom of Denmark, Spain, the French Republic, the Kingdom of Greece, the Italian Republic, the Grand Duchy of Luxembourg, the Kingdom of Norway, the Kingdom of the Netherlands, the Portuguese Republic, the United Kingdom of Great Britain and Northern Ireland, the Kingdom of Sweden, the Swiss Confederation and the Turkish Republic;

Considering that the OECD Nuclear Energy Agency, established within the framework of the Organisation for Economic Co-operation and Development (hereinafter referred to as the "Organisation"), is charged with encouraging the elaboration and harmonization of legislation relating to nuclear energy in participating countries, in particular with regard to third party liability and insurance against atomic risks;

DESIROUS of ensuring adequate and equitable compensation for persons who suffer damage caused by nuclear incidents whilst taking the necessary steps to ensure that the development of the production and uses of nuclear energy for peaceful purposes is not thereby hindered;

Convinced of the need for unifying the basic rules applying in the various countries to the liability incurred for such damage, whilst leaving these countries free to take, on a national basis, any additional measures which they deem appropriate;

Article 1

(*a*) For the purposes of this Convention:

(i) "A nuclear incident" means any occurrence or succession of occurrences having the same origin which causes damage, provided that such occurrence or succession of occurrences, or any of the damage caused, arises out of or results either from the radioactive properties, or a combination of radioactive properties with toxic, explosive, or other hazardous properties of nuclear fuel or radioactive products or waste or with any of them, or from ionizing radiations emitted by any other source of radiation inside a nuclear installation.

(ii) "Nuclear installation" means reactors other than those comprised in any means of transport; factories for the manufacture or processing of nuclear substances; factories for the separation of isotopes of nuclear fuel; factories for the reprocessing of irradiated nuclear fuel; facilities for the storage of nuclear substances other than storage incidental to the carriage of such substances; and such other installations in

---

1. *See also* Basic Documents 3.2 and 3.3, *infra.*

which there are nuclear fuel or radioactive products or waste as the Steering Committee for Nuclear Energy of the Organisation (hereinafter referred to as the "Steering Committee") shall from time to time determine; any Contracting Party may determine that two or more nuclear installations of one operator which are located on the same site shall, together with any other premises on that site where radioactive material is held, be treated as a single nuclear installation.

(iii) "Nuclear fuel" means fissionable material in the form of uranium metal, alloy, or chemical compound (including natural uranium), plutonium metal, alloy, or chemical compound, and such other fissionable material as the Steering Committee shall from time to time determine.

(iv) "Radioactive products or waste" means any radioactive material produced in or made radioactive by exposure to the radiation incidental to the process of producing or utilizing nuclear fuel, but does not include (1) nuclear fuel, or (2) radioisotopes outside a nuclear installation which have reached the final stage of fabrication so as to be usable for any industrial, commercial, agricultural, medical, scientific or educational purpose.

(v) "Nuclear substances" means nuclear fuel (other than natural uranium and other than depleted uranium) and radioactive products or waste.

(vi) "Operator" in relation to a nuclear installation means the person designated or recognized by the competent public authority as the operator of that installation.

(b) The Steering Committee may, if in its view the small extent of the risks involved so warrants, exclude any nuclear installation, nuclear fuel, or nuclear substances from the application of this Convention.

Article 2

This Convention does not apply to nuclear incidents occurring in the territory of non-Contracting States or to damage suffered in such territory, unless otherwise provided by the legislation of the Contracting Party in whose territory the nuclear installation of the operator liable is situated, and except in regard to rights referred to in article 6(e).

Article 3

(a) The operator of a nuclear installation shall be liable, in accordance with this Convention, for:

(i) damage to or loss of life of any person; and

(ii) damage to or loss of any property other than

1. the nuclear installation itself and any other nuclear installation, including a nuclear installation under construction, on the site where that installation is located; and

2. any property on that same site which is used or to be used in connection with any such installation, upon proof that such damage or loss (hereinafter referred to as "damage") was caused by a nuclear incident in such installation or involving nuclear substances coming from such installation, except as otherwise provided for in Article 4.

(*b*) Where the damage or loss is caused jointly by a nuclear incident and by an incident other than a nuclear incident, that part of the damage or loss which is caused by such other incident shall, to the extent that it is not reasonably separable from the damage or loss caused by the nuclear incident, be considered to be damage caused by the nuclear incident. Where the damage or loss is caused jointly by a nuclear incident and by an emission of ionizing radiation not covered by this Convention, nothing in this Convention shall limit or otherwise affect the liability of any person in connection with that emission of ionizing radiation.

Article 4

In the case of carriage of nuclear substances, including storage incidental thereto, without prejudice to article 2:

(*a*) The operator of a nuclear installation shall be liable, in accordance with this Convention, for damage upon proof that it was caused by a nuclear incident outside that installation and involving nuclear substances in the course of carriage therefrom, only if the incident occurs:

(i) before liability with regard to nuclear incidents involving the nuclear substances has been assumed, pursuant to the express terms of a contract in writing, by the operator of another nuclear installation;

(ii) in the absence of such express terms, before the operator of another nuclear installation has taken charge of the nuclear substances; or

(iii) where the nuclear substances are intended to be used in a reactor comprised in a means of transport, before the person duly authorized to operate that reactor has taken charge of the nuclear substances; but

(iv) where the nuclear substances have been sent to a person within the territory of a non-Contracting State, before they have been unloaded from the means of transport by which they have arrived in the territory of that non-Contracting State.

(*b*) The operator of a nuclear installation shall be liable, in accordance with this Convention, for damage upon proof that it was caused by a nuclear incident outside that installation and involving nuclear substances in the course of carriage thereto, only if the incident occurs:

(i) after liability with regard to nuclear incidents involving the nuclear substances has been assumed by him, pursuant to the express terms of a contract in writing, from the operator of another nuclear installation;

(ii) in the absence of such express terms, after he has taken charge of the nuclear substances; or

(iii) after he has taken charge of the nuclear substances from a person operating a reactor comprised in a means of transport; but

(iv) where the nuclear substances have, with the written consent of the operator, been sent from a person within the territory of a non-Contracting State, after they have been loaded on the means of transport by which they are to be carried from the territory of that State.

(*c*) The operator liable in accordance with this Convention shall provide the carrier with a certificate issued by or on behalf of the insurer or other financial guarantor furnishing the security required pursuant to Article 10. However, a Contracting Party may exclude this obligation in relation to carriage which takes place wholly within its own territory. The certificate shall state the name and address of that operator and the amount, type and duration of the security, and these statements may not be disputed by the person by whom or on whose behalf the certificate was issued. The certificate shall also indicate the nuclear substances and the carriage in respect of which the security applies and shall include a statement by the competent public authority that the person named is an operator within the meaning of this Convention.

(*d*) A Contracting Party may provide by legislation that, under such terms as may be contained therein and upon fulfilment of the requirements of article 10(*a*), a carrier may, at his request and with the consent of an operator of a nuclear installation situated in its territory, by decision of the competent public authority, be liable in accordance with this Convention in place of that operator. In such case for all the purposes of this Convention the carrier shall be considered, in respect of nuclear incidents occurring in the course of carriage of nuclear substances, as an operator of a nuclear installation on the territory of the Contracting Party whose legislation so provides.

Article 5

(*a*) If the nuclear fuel or radioactive products or waste involved in a nuclear incident have been in more than one nuclear installation and are in a nuclear installation at the time damage is caused, no operator of any nuclear installation in which they have previously been shall be liable for the damage.

(*b*) Where, however, damage is caused by a nuclear incident occurring in a nuclear installation and involving only nuclear substances stored therein incidentally to their carriage, the operator of the nuclear installation shall not be liable where another operator or person is liable pursuant to article 4.

(*c*) If the nuclear fuel or radioactive products or waste involved in a nuclear incident have been in more than one nuclear installation and are not in a nuclear installation at the time damage is caused, no operator other than the operator of the last nuclear installation in which they were before the damage was caused or an operator who has subsequently taken them in charge, or has assumed liability therefor pursuant to the express terms of a contract in writing shall be liable for the damage.

(*d*) If damage gives rise to liability of more than one operator in accordance with this Convention, the liability of these operators shall be joint and several: provided that where such liability arises as a result of damage caused by a nuclear incident involving nuclear substances in the course of carriage in one and the same means of transport, or, in the case of storage incidental to the carriage, in one and the same nuclear installation, the maximum total amount for which such operators shall be liable shall be the highest amount established with respect to any of them pursuant to article 7 and provided that in no case shall any one operator be required, in respect of a nuclear incident, to pay more than the amount established with respect to him pursuant to article 7.

Article 6

(*a*) The right to compensation for damage caused by a nuclear incident may be exercised only against an operator liable for the damage in accordance with this Convention, or, if a direct right of action against the insurer or other financial guarantor furnishing the security required pursuant to article 10 is given by national law, against the insurer or other financial guarantor.

(*b*) Except as otherwise provided in this article, no other person shall be liable for damage caused by a nuclear incident, but this provision shall not affect the application of any international agreement in the field of transport in force or open for signature, ratification or accession at the date of this Convention.

(*c*)(i) Nothing in this Convention shall affect the liability:

    1. of any individual for damage caused by a nuclear incident for which the operator, by virtue of article 3(*a*)(ii)(1) and (2) or Article 9, is not liable under this Convention and which results from an act or omission of that individual done with intent to cause damage;

    2. of a person duly authorized to operate a reactor comprised in a means of transport for damage caused by a nuclear incident when an operator is not liable for such damage pursuant to article 4(*a*)(iii) or (*b*)(iii).

(ii) The operator shall incur no liability outside this Convention for damage caused by a nuclear incident.

(*d*) Any person who has paid compensation in respect of damage caused by a nuclear incident under any international agreement referred to in paragraph (*b*) of this article or under any legislation of a non-Contracting State shall, up to the amount which he has paid, acquire by subrogation the rights under this Convention of the person suffering damage whom he has so compensated.

(*e*) Any person who has his principal place of business in the territory of a Contracting Party or who is the servant of such a person and who has paid compensation in respect of damage caused by a nuclear incident occurring in the territory of a non-Contracting State or in respect of damage suffered in such territory shall, up to the amount which he has paid, acquire the rights which the person so compensated would have had against the operator but for the provisions of article 2.

(*f*) The operator shall have a right of recourse only:

    (i) if the damage caused by a nuclear incident results from an act or omission done with intent to cause damage, against the individual acting or omitting to act with such intent;

    (ii) if and to the extent that it is so provided expressly by contract.

(*g*) If the operator has a right of recourse to any extent pursuant to paragraph (*f*) of this article against any person, that person shall not, to that extent, have a right against the operator under paragraphs (d) or (e) of this article.

(h) Where provisions of national or public health insurance, social security, workmen's compensation or occupational disease compensation systems include compensation for damage caused by a nuclear incident, rights of beneficiaries of such systems and rights of recourse by virtue of such systems shall be determined by the law of the Contracting Party or by the regulations of the inter-Governmental organization which has established such systems.

Article 7

(a) The aggregate of compensation required to be paid in respect of damage caused by a nuclear incident shall not exceed the maximum liability established in accordance with this article.

(b) The maximum liability of the operator in respect of damage caused by a nuclear incident shall be 15,000,000 Special Drawing Rights as defined by the International Monetary Fund and used by it for its own operations and transactions (hereinafter referred to as "Special Drawing Rights"). However,

(i) any Contracting Party, taking into account the possibilities for the operator of obtaining the insurance or other financial security required pursuant to Article 10, may establish by legislation a greater or lesser amount;

(ii) any Contracting Party, having regard to the nature of the nuclear installation or the nuclear substances involved and to the likely consequences of an incident originating therefrom, may establish a lower amount;

provided that in no event shall any amounts so established be less than 5,000,000 Special Drawing Rights. The sums mentioned above may be converted into national currency in round figures.

(c) Compensation for damage caused to the means of transport on which the nuclear substances involved were at the time of the nuclear incident shall not have the effect of reducing the liability of the operator in respect of other damage to an amount less than either 5,000,000 Special Drawing Rights, or any higher amount established by the legislation of a Contracting Party.

(d) The amount of liability of operators of nuclear installations in the territory of a Contracting Party established in accordance with paragraph (b) of this article as well as the provisions of any legislation of a Contracting Party pursuant to paragraph (c) of this article shall apply to the liability of such operators wherever the nuclear incident occurs.

(e) A Contracting Party may subject the transit of nuclear substances through its territory to the condition that the maximum amount of liability of the foreign operator concerned be increased, if it considers that such amount does not adequately cover the risks of a nuclear incident in the course of the transit: provided that the maximum amount thus increased shall not exceed the maximum amount of liability of operators of nuclear installations situated in its territory.

(f) The provisions of paragraph (e) of this article shall not apply:

(i) to carriage by sea where, under international law, there is a right of entry in cases of urgent distress into the ports of such Contracting Party or a right of innocent passage through its territory; or

(ii) to carriage by air where, by agreement or under international law there is a right to fly over or land on the territory of such Contracting Party.

(*g*) Any interest and costs awarded by a court in actions for compensation under this Convention shall not be considered to be compensation for the purposes of this Convention and shall be payable by the operator in addition to any sum for which he is liable in accordance with this article.

Article 8

(*a*) The right of compensation under this Convention shall be extinguished if an action is not brought within ten years from the date of the nuclear incident. National legislation may, however, establish a period longer than ten years if measures have been taken by the Contracting Party in whose territory the nuclear installation of the operator liable is situated to cover the liability of that operator in respect of any actions for compensation begun after the expiry of the period of ten years and during such longer period: provided that such extension of the extinction period shall in no case affect the right of compensation under this Convention of any person who has brought an action in respect of loss of life or personal injury against the operator before the expiry of the period of ten years.

(*b*) In the case of damage caused by a nuclear incident involving nuclear fuel or radioactive products or waste which, at the time of the incident have been stolen, lost, jettisoned or abandoned and have not yet been recovered, the period established pursuant to paragraph (*a*) of this article shall be computed from the date of that nuclear incident, but the period shall in no case exceed twenty years from the date of the theft, loss, jettison or abandonment.

(*c*) National legislation may establish a period of not less than two years for the extinction of the right or as a period of limitation either from the date at which the person suffering damage has knowledge or from the date at which he ought reasonably to have known of both the damage and the operator liable: provided that the period established pursuant to paragraphs (*a*) and (*b*) of this article shall not be exceeded.

(*d*) Where the provisions of article 13(*c*)(ii) are applicable, the right of compensation shall not, however, be extinguished if, within the time provided for in paragraphs (*a*), (*b*) and (*c*) of this Article.

(i) prior to the determination by the Tribunal referred to in article 17, an action has been brought before any of the courts from which the Tribunal can choose; if the Tribunal determines that the competent court is a court other than that before which such action has already been brought, it may fix a date by which such action has to be brought before the competent court so determined; or

(ii) a request has been made to a Contracting Party concerned to initiate a determination by the Tribunal of the competent court pursuant to article 13(*c*)(ii) and an action is brought subsequent to such determination within such time as may be fixed by the Tribunal.

(*e*) Unless national law provides to the contrary, any person suffering damage caused by a nuclear incident who has brought an action for compensation within the period provided for in this article may amend his claim in respect of any aggravation of the damage after the expiry of such period provided that final judgment has not been entered by the competent court.

Article 9

The operator shall not be liable for damage caused by a nuclear incident directly due to an act of armed conflict, hostilities, civil war, insurrection or, except in so far as the legislation of the Contracting Party in whose territory his nuclear installation is situated may provide to the contrary, a grave natural disaster of an exceptional character.

Article 10

(*a*) To cover the liability under this Convention, the operator shall be required to have and maintain insurance or other financial security of the amount established pursuant to article 7 and of such type and terms as the competent public authority shall specify.

(*b*) No insurer or other financial guarantor shall suspend or cancel the insurance or other financial security provided for in paragraph (*a*) of this article without giving notice in writing of at least two months to the competent public authority or in so far as such insurance or other financial security relates to the carriage of nuclear substances, during the period of the carriage in question.

(*c*) The sums provided as insurance, reinsurance, or other financial security may be drawn upon only for compensation for damage caused by a nuclear incident.

Article 11

The nature, form and extent of the compensation, within the limits of this Convention, as well as the equitable distribution thereof, shall be governed by national law.

Article 12

Compensation payable under this Convention, insurance and reinsurance premiums, sums provided as insurance, reinsurance, or other financial security required pursuant to article 10, and interest and costs referred to in article 7(*g*), shall be freely transferable between the monetary areas of the Contracting Parties.

Article 13

(*a*) Except as otherwise provided in this article, jurisdiction over actions under articles 3, 4, 6(*a*) and 6(*e*) shall lie only with the courts of the Contracting Party in whose territory the nuclear incident occurred.

(*b*) Where a nuclear incident occurs outside the territory of the Contracting Parties, or where the place of the nuclear incident cannot be determined with certainty, jurisdiction over such actions shall lie with the courts of the Contracting Party in whose territory the nuclear installation of the operator liable is situated.

(*c*) Where jurisdiction would lie with the courts of more than one Contracting Party by virtue of paragraphs (*a*) or (*b*) of this article, jurisdiction shall lie,

(i) if the nuclear incident occurred partly outside the territory of any Contracting Party and partly in the territory of a single Contracting Party, with the courts of that Contracting Party; and

(ii) in any other case, with the courts of the Contracting Party determined, at the request of a Contracting Party concerned, by the Tribunal referred to in article 17 as being the most closely related to the case in question.

(*d*) Judgments entered by the competent court under this article after trial, or by default, shall, when they have become enforceable under the law applied by that court, become enforceable in the territory of any of the other Contracting Parties as soon as the formalities required by the Contracting Party concerned have been complied with. The merits of the case shall not be the subject of further proceedings. The foregoing provisions shall not apply to interim judgements.

(*e*) If an action is brought against a Contracting Party under this Convention, such Contracting Party may not, except in respect of measures of execution, invoke any jurisdictional immunities before the court competent in accordance with this article.

Article 14

(*a*) This Convention shall be applied without any discrimination based upon nationality, domicile, or residence.

(*b*) "National law" and "national legislation" mean the national law or the national legislation of the court having jurisdiction under this Convention over claims arising out of a nuclear incident, and that law or legislation shall apply to all matters both substantive and procedural not specifically governed by this Convention.

(*c*) That law and legislation shall be applied without any discrimination based upon nationality, domicile, or residence.

Article 15

(*a*) Any Contracting Party may take such measures as it deems necessary to provide for an increase in the amount of compensation specified in this Convention.

(*b*) In so far as compensation for damage involves public funds and is in excess of the 5,000,000 Special Drawing Rights referred to in Article 7, any such measure in whatever form may be applied under conditions which may derogate from the provisions of this Convention.

Article 16

Decisions taken by the Steering Committee under article 1(*a*)(ii), 1(*a*)(iii) and 1(*b*) shall be adopted by mutual agreement of the members representing the Contracting Parties.

Article 17

Any dispute arising between two or more Contracting Parties concerning the interpretation or application of this Convention shall be examined by the

Steering Committee and in the absence of friendly settlement shall, upon the request of a Contracting Party concerned, be submitted to the Tribunal established by the Convention of 20th December, 1957, on the Establishment of a Security Control in the Field of Nuclear Energy.

Article 18

(a) Reservations to one or more of the provisions of this Convention may be made at any time prior to ratification of or accession to this Convention or prior to the time of notification under article 23 in respect of any territory or territories mentioned in the notification, and shall be admissible only if the terms of these reservations have been expressly accepted by the signatories.

(b) Such acceptance shall not be required from a signatory which has not itself ratified this Convention within a period of twelve months after the date of notification to it of such reservation by the Secretary–General of the Organisation in accordance with article 24.

(c) Any reservation admitted in accordance with this article may be withdrawn at any time by notification addressed to the Secretary–General of the Organisation.

Article 19

(a) This Convention shall be ratified. Instruments of ratification shall be deposited with the Secretary–General of the Organisation.

(b) This Convention shall come into force upon the deposit of instruments of ratification by not less than five of the signatories. For each Signatory ratifying thereafter, this Convention shall come into force upon the deposit of its instrument of ratification.

Article 20

Amendments to this Convention shall be adopted by mutual agreement of all the Contracting Parties. They shall come into force when ratified or confirmed by two-thirds of the Contracting Parties. For each Contracting Party ratifying or confirming thereafter, they shall come into force at the date of such ratification or confirmation.

Article 21

(a) The Government of any Member or Associate country of the Organisation which is not a signatory to this Convention may accede thereto by notification addressed to the Secretary–General of the Organisation.

(b) The Government of any other country which is not a signatory to this Convention may accede thereto by notification addressed to the Secretary–General of the Organisation and with the unanimous assent of the Contracting Parties. Such accession shall take effect from the date of such assent.

Article 22

(a) This Convention shall remain in effect for a period of ten years as from the date of its coming into force. Any Contracting Party may, by giving twelve months' notice to the Secretary–General of the Organisation, terminate the application of this Convention to itself at the end of the period of ten years.

(b) This Convention shall, after the period of ten years, remain in force for a period of five years for such Contracting Parties as have not terminated its application in accordance with paragraph *(a)* of this article, and thereafter for successive periods of five years for such Contracting Parties as have not terminated its application at the end of one of such periods of five years by giving twelve months' notice to that effect to the Secretary–General of the Organisation.

(c) A conference shall be convened by the Secretary–General of the Organisation in order to consider revisions to this Convention after a period of five years as from the date of its coming into force or, at any other time, at the request of a Contracting Party, within six months from the date of such request.

Article 23

(a) This Convention shall apply to the metropolitan territories of the Contracting Parties.

(b) Any signatory or Contracting Party may, at the time of signature or ratification of or accession to this Convention or at any later time, notify the Secretary–General of the Organisation that this Convention shall apply to those of its territories, including the territories for whose international relations it is responsible, to which this Convention is not applicable in accordance with paragraph *(a)* of this article and which are mentioned in the notification. Any such notification may in respect of any territory or territories mentioned therein be withdrawn by giving twelve months' notice to that effect to the Secretary–General of the Organisation.

(c) Any territories of a Contracting Party, including the territories for whose international relations it is responsible, to which this Convention does not apply shall be regarded for the purposes of this Convention as being a territory of a non-Contracting State.

Article 24

The Secretary–General of the Organisation shall give notice to all Signatories and acceding Governments of the receipt of any instrument of ratification, accession, withdrawal, notification under article 23, and decisions of the Steering Committee under article 1*(a)* (ii), 1*(a)* (iii) and 1*(b)*. He shall also notify them of the date on which this Convention comes into force, the text of any amendment thereto and of the date on which such amendment comes into force, and any reservation made in accordance with article 18.

3.2 CONVENTION SUPPLEMENTARY TO THE 1960 CONVENTION ON THIRD PARTY LIABILITY IN THE FIELD OF NUCLEAR ENERGY (WITH ANNEX AND AS AMENDED THROUGH 1964).[1] Concluded at Brussels, 31 January 1963. Entered into force, 4 December 1974. 2 I.L.M. 685 (1963)

* * *

Article 1

The system instituted by this Convention is supplementary to that of the Paris Convention, shall be subject to the provisions of the Paris Convention, and shall be applied in accordance with the following Articles.

Article 2

(a) The system of this Convention shall apply to damage caused by nuclear incidents, other than those occurring entirely in the territory of a State which is not a Party to this Convention:

(i) for which an operator of a nuclear installation, used for peaceful purposes, situated in the territory of a Contracting Party to this Convention (hereinafter referred to as a "Contracting Party"), and which appears on the list established and kept up to date in accordance with the terms of Article 13, is liable under the Paris Convention, and

(ii) suffered

(1) in the territory of a Contracting Party; or

(2) on or over the high seas on board a ship or aircraft registered in the territory of a Contracting Party; or

(3) on or over the high seas by a national of a Contracting Party, provided that, in the case of damage to a ship or an aircraft, the ship or aircraft is registered in the territory of a Contracting Party;

provided that the courts of a Contracting Party have jurisdiction pursuant to the Paris Convention.

(b) Any Signatory or acceding Government may, at the time of signature of or accession to this Convention or on the deposit of its instrument of ratification, declare that, for the purposes of the application of paragraph (a)(ii)(3) of this Article, individuals or certain categories thereof, considered under its law as having their habitual residence in its territory, are assimilated to its own nationals.

(c) In this Article, the expression "a national of a Contracting Party" shall include a Contracting Party or any of its constituent sub-divisions, or a partnership, or any public or private body whether corporate or not established in the territory of a Contracting Party.

Article 3

(a) Under the conditions established by this Convention, the Contracting Parties undertake that compensation in respect of the damage referred to in Article 2 shall be provided up to the amount of 300 million Special Drawing Rights per incident.

(b) Such compensation shall be provided:

---

1. *See also* Basic Documents 3.1 and 3.3, *supra.*

(i) up to an amount of at least 5 million Special Drawing Rights, out of funds provided by insurance or other financial security, such amount to be established by the legislation of the Contracting Party in whose territory the nuclear installation of the operator liable is situated;

(ii) between this amount and 175 million Special Drawing Rights, out of public funds to be made available by the Contracting Party in whose territory the nuclear installation of the operator liable is situated;

(iii) between 175 million and 300 million Special Drawing Rights, out of public funds to be made available by the Contracting Parties according to the formula for contributions specified in Article 12.

(c) For this purpose, each Contracting Party shall either:

(i) establish the maximum liability of the operator, pursuant to Article 7 of the Paris Convention, at 300 million Special Drawing Rights, and provide that such liability shall be covered by all the funds referred to in paragraph (b) of this Article; or

(ii) establish the maximum liability of the operator at an amount at least equal to that established pursuant to paragraph (b)(i) of this Article and provide that, in excess of such amount and up to 300 million Special Drawing Rights, the public funds referred to in paragraph (b)(ii) and (iii) of this Article shall be made available by some means other than as cover for the liability of the operator, provided that the rules of substance and procedure laid down in this Convention are not thereby affected.

(d) The obligation of the operator to pay compensation, interest or costs out of public funds made available pursuant to paragraphs (b)(ii) and (iii), and (f) of this Article shall only be enforceable against the operator as and when such funds are in fact made available.

(e) The Contracting Parties, in carrying out this Convention, undertake not to make use of the right provided for in Article 15(b) of the Paris Convention to apply special conditions:

(i) in respect of compensation for damage provided out of the funds referred to in paragraph (b)(i) of this Article;

(ii) other than those laid down in this Convention in respect of compensation for damage provided out of the public funds referred to in paragraph (b)(ii) and (iii) of this Article.

(f) The interest and costs referred to in Article 7(g) of the Paris Convention are payable in addition to the amounts referred to in paragraph (b) of this Article and shall be borne in so far as they are awarded in respect of compensation payable out of the funds referred to in:

(i) paragraph (b)(i) of this Article, by the operator liable;

(ii) paragraph (b)(ii) of this Article, by the Contracting Party in whose territory the nuclear installation of that operator is situated;

(iii) paragraph (b)(iii) of this Article, by the Contracting Parties together.

(g) For the purposes of this Convention, "Special Drawing Right" means the Special Drawing Right as it is defined by the International Monetary Fund. The amounts mentioned in this Convention shall be converted into the national currency of a Contracting Party in accordance with the value of that currency at the date of the incident, unless another date is fixed for a given incident by agreement between the Contracting Parties. The equivalent in Special Drawings Rights of the national currency of a Contracting Party shall be calculated in accordance with the method of valuation applied at the date in question by the International Monetary Fund for its own operations and transactions.

Article 4

(a) If a nuclear incident causes damage which gives rise to liability of more than one operator, the aggregate liability provided for in Article 5(d) of the Paris Convention shall not, to the extent that public funds have to be made available pursuant to Article 3(b)(ii) and (iii), exceed 300 million Special Drawing Rights.

(b) The total amount of the public funds made available pursuant to Article 3 (b)(ii) and (iii) shall not, in such event, exceed the difference between 300 million Special Drawing Rights and the sum of the amounts established with respect to such operators pursuant to Article 3(b)(i) or, in the case of an operator whose nuclear installation is situated in the territory of a State which is not a Party to this Convention, the amount established pursuant to Article 7 of the Paris Convention. If more than one Contracting Party is required to make available public funds pursuant to Article 3(b)(ii), such funds shall be made available by them in proportion to the number of nuclear installations situated in their respective territories, which are involved in the nuclear incident and of which the operators are liable.

Article 5

(a) Where the operator liable has a right of recourse pursuant to Article 6(f) of the Paris Convention, the Contracting Party in whose territory the nuclear installation of that operator is situated shall take such legislative measures as are necessary to enable both that Contracting Party and the other Contracting Parties to benefit from this recourse to the extent that public funds have been made available pursuant to Article 3(b)(ii) and (iii), and (f).

(b) Such legislation may provide for the recovery of public funds made available pursuant to Article 3(b)(ii) and (iii), and (f) from such operator if the damage results from fault on his part.

Article 6

In calculating the public funds to be made available pursuant to this Convention, account shall be taken only of those rights to compensation exercised within ten years from the date of the nuclear incident. In the case of damage caused by a nuclear incident involving nuclear fuel or radioactive products or waste which, at the time of the incident have been stolen, lost, jettisoned, or abandoned and have not yet been recovered such period shall not in any case exceed twenty years from the date of the theft, loss, jettison or abandonment. It shall also be extended in the cases and under the conditions laid down in Article 8(d) of the Paris Convention. Amendments made to claims after the expiry of this period, under the conditions laid down in Article 8(e) of the Paris Convention, shall also be taken into account.

Article 7

Where a Contracting Party makes use of the right provided for in Article 8(c) of the Paris Convention, the period which it establishes shall be a period of prescription of three years either from the date at which the person suffering damage has knowledge or from the date at which he ought reasonably to have known of both the damage and the operator liable.

Article 8

Any person who is entitled to benefit from the provisions of this Convention shall have the right to full compensation in accordance with national law for damage suffered, provided that, where the amount of damage exceeds or is likely to exceed:

(i) 300 million Special Drawing Rights; or

(ii) if there is aggregate liability under Article 5(d) of the Paris Convention and a higher sum results therefrom, such higher sum;

any Contracting Party may establish equitable criteria for apportionment. Such criteria shall be applied whatever the origin of the funds and, subject to the provisions of Article 2, without discrimination based on the nationality, domicile or residence of the person suffering the damage.

Article 9

(a) The system of disbursements by which the public funds required under Article 3(b)(ii) and (iii), and (f) are to be made available shall be that of the Contracting Party whose courts have jurisdiction.

(b) Each Contracting Party shall ensure that persons suffering damage may enforce their rights to compensation without having to bring separate proceedings according to the origin of the funds provided for such compensation.

(c) No Contracting Party shall be required to make available the public funds referred to in Article 3(b)(ii) and (iii) so long as any of the funds referred to in Article 3(b)(i) remain available.

Article 10

(a) The Contracting Party whose courts have jurisdiction shall be required to inform the other Contracting Parties of a nuclear incident and its circumstances as soon as it appears that the damage caused by such incident exceeds, or is likely to exceed, 175 million Special Drawing Rights. The Contracting Parties shall without delay make all the necessary arrangements to settle the procedure for their relations in this connection.

(b) Only the Contracting Party whose courts have jurisdiction shall be entitled to request the other Contracting Parties to make available the public funds required under Article 3(b)(iii) and (f) and shall have exclusive competence to disburse such funds.

(c) Such Contracting Party shall, when the occasion arises, exercise the right of recourse provided for in Article 5 on behalf of the other Contracting Parties who have made available public funds pursuant to Article 3(b)(iii) and (f).

(d) Settlements effected in respect of the payment of compensation out of the public funds referred to in Article 8(b)(ii) and (iii) in accordance with the conditions established by national legislation shall be recognized by the other Contracting Parties, and judgements entered by the competent courts in respect of such compensation shall become enforceable in the territory of the other Contracting Parties in accordance with the provisions of Article 13(d) of the Paris Convention.

Article 11

(a) If the courts having jurisdiction are those of a Contracting Party other than the Contracting Party in whose territory the nuclear installation of the operator liable is situated, the public funds required under Article 3(b)(ii) and (f) shall be made available by the first-named Contracting Party. The Contracting Party in whose territory the nuclear installation of the operator liable is situated shall reimburse to the other Contracting Party the sums paid. These two Contracting Parties shall agree on the procedure for reimbursement.

(b) In adopting all legislative, regulatory or administrative provisions, after the nuclear incident has occurred, concerning the nature, form and extent of the compensation, the procedure for making available the public funds required under Article 3(b)(ii) and, if necessary, the criteria for the apportionment of such funds, the Contracting Party whose courts have jurisdiction shall consult the Contracting Party in whose territory the nuclear installation of the operator liable is situated. It shall further take all measures necessary to enable the latter to intervene in proceedings and to participate in any settlement concerning compensation.

Article 12

(a) The formula for contributions according to which the Contracting Parties shall make available the public funds referred to in Article 3(b)(iii) shall be determined as follows:

(i) as to 50%, on the basis of the ratio between the gross national product at current prices of each Contracting Party and the total of the gross national products at current prices of all Contracting Parties as shown by the official statistics published by the Organisation for Economic Co-operation and Development for the year preceding the year in which the nuclear incident occurs;

(ii) as to 50%, on the basis of the ratio between the thermal power of the reactors situated in the territory of each Contracting Party and the total thermal power of the reactors situated in the territories of all the Contracting Parties. This calculation shall be made on the basis of the thermal power of the reactors shown at the date of the nuclear incident in the list referred to in Article 2(a)(i): provided that a reactor shall only be taken into consideration for the purposes of this calculation as from the date when it first reaches criticality.

(b) For the purposes of this Convention, "thermal power" means

(i) before the issue of a final operating licence, the planned thermal power;

(ii) after the issue of such licence, the thermal power authorized by the competent national authorities.

Article 13

(a) Each Contracting Party shall ensure that all nuclear installations used for peaceful purposes situated in its territory, and falling within the definition in Article 1 of the Paris Convention, appear in the list referred to in Article 2(a)(i).

(b) For this purpose, each Signatory or acceding Government shall, on the deposit of its instrument of ratification or accession, communicate to the Belgian Government full particulars of such installations.

(c) Such particulars shall indicate:

(i) in the case of all installations not yet completed, the expected date on which the risk of a nuclear incident will exist;

(ii) and further, in the case of reactors, the expected date on which they will first reach criticality, and also their thermal power.

(d) Each Contracting Party shall also communicate to the Belgian Government the exact date of the existence of the risk of a nuclear incident and, in the case of reactors, the date on which they first reached criticality.

(e) Each Contracting Party shall also communicate to the Belgian Government all modifications to be made to the list. Where such modifications include the addition of a nuclear installation, the communication must be made at least three months before the expected date on which the risk of a nuclear incident will exist.

(f) If a Contracting Party is of the opinion that the particulars, or any modification to be made to the list, communicated by another Contracting Party do not comply with the provisions of Article 2(a)(i) and of this Article, it may raise objections thereto only by addressing them to the Belgian Government within three months from the date on which it has received notice pursuant to paragraph (h) of this Article.

(g) If a Contracting Party is of the opinion that a communication required in accordance with this Article has not been made within the time prescribed in this Article, it may raise objections only by addressing them to the Belgian Government within three months from the date on which it knew of the facts which, in its opinion, ought to have been communicated.

(h) The Belgian Government shall give notice as soon as possible to each Contracting Party of the communications and objections which it has received pursuant to this Article.

(i) The list referred to in Article 2(a)(i) shall consist of all the particulars and modifications referred to in paragraphs (b), (c), (d) and (e) of this Article, it being understood that objections submitted pursuant to paragraphs (f) and (g) of this Article shall have effect retrospective to the date on which they were raised, if they are sustained.

(j) The Belgian Government shall supply any Contracting Party on demand with an up-to-date statement of the nuclear installations covered by this Convention and the details supplied in respect of them pursuant to this Article.

Article 14

(a) Except insofar as this Convention otherwise provides, each Contracting Party may exercise the powers vested in it by virtue of the Paris Convention, and any provisions made thereunder may be invoked against the other Contracting Parties in order that the public funds referred to in Article 3(b)(ii) and (iii) be made available.

(b) Any such provisions made by a Contracting Party pursuant to Articles 2 and 9 of the Paris Convention as a result of which the public funds referred to in Article 3(b)(ii) and (iii) are required to be made available may not be invoked against any other Contracting Party unless it has consented thereto.

(c) Nothing in this Convention shall prevent a Contracting Party from making provisions outside the scope of the Paris Convention and of this Convention, provided that such provisions shall not involve any further obligation on the part of the other Contracting Parties insofar as their public funds are concerned.

Article 15

(a) Any Contracting Party may conclude an agreement with a State which is not a Party to this Convention concerning compensation out of public funds for damage caused by a nuclear incident.

(b) To the extent that the conditions for payment of compensation under any such agreement are not more favourable than those which result from the measures adopted by the Contracting Party concerned for the application of the Paris Convention and of this Convention, the amount of damage caused by a nuclear incident covered by this Convention and for which compensation is payable by virtue of such an agreement may be taken into consideration, where the proviso to Article 8 applies, in calculating the total amount of damage caused by that incident.

(c) The provisions of paragraphs (a) and (b) of this Article shall in no case affect the obligations under Article 3(b)(ii) and (iii) of those Contracting Parties which have not given their consent to such agreement.

(d) Any Contracting Party intending to conclude such an agreement shall notify the other Contracting Parties of its intention. Agreements concluded shall be notified to the Belgian Government.

Article 16

(a) The Contracting Parties shall consult each other upon all problems of common interest raised by the application of this Convention and of the Paris Convention, especially Articles 20 and 22(c) of the latter Convention.

(b) They shall consult each other on the desirability of revising this Convention after a period of five years from the date of its coming into force, and at any other time upon the request of a Contracting Party.

Article 17

Any dispute arising between two or more Contracting Parties concerning the interpretation or application of this Convention shall, upon the request of a Contracting Party concerned, be submitted to the European Nuclear Energy

Tribunal established by the Convention of 20th December 1957 on the Establishment of a Security Control in the Field of Nuclear Energy.

Article 18

(a) Reservations to one or more of the provisions of this Convention may be made at any time prior to ratification of this Convention if the terms of these reservations have been expressly accepted by all Signatories or, at the time of accession or of the application of the provisions of Articles 21 and 24, if the terms of these reservations have been expressly accepted by all Signatories and acceding Governments.

(b) Such acceptance shall not be required from a Signatory which has not itself ratified this Convention within a period of twelve months after the date of notification to it of such reservation by the Belgian Government in accordance with Article 25.

(c) Any reservation accepted in accordance with the provisions of paragraph (a) of this Article may be withdrawn at any time by notification addressed to the Belgian Government.

Article 19

No State may become or continue to be a Contracting Party to this Convention unless it is a Contracting Party to the Paris Convention.

Article 20

(a) The Annex to this Convention shall form an integral part thereof.

(b) This Convention shall be ratified. Instruments of ratification shall be deposited with the Belgian Government.

(c) This Convention shall come into force three months after the deposit of the sixth instrument of ratification.

(d) For each Signatory ratifying this Convention after the deposit of the sixth instrument of ratification, it shall come into force three months after the date of the deposit of its instrument of ratification.

Article 21

Amendments to this Convention shall be adopted by agreement among all the Contracting Parties. They shall come into force on the date when all Contracting Parties have ratified or confirmed them.

Article 22

(a) After the coming into force of this Convention, any Contracting Party to the Paris Convention which has not signed this Convention may request accession to this Convention by notification addressed to the Belgian Government.

(b) Such accession shall require the unanimous assent of the Contracting Parties.

(c) Once such assent has been given, the Contracting Party to the Paris Convention requesting accession shall deposit its instrument of accession with the Belgian Government.

(d) The accession shall take effect three months from the date of deposit of the instrument of accession.

Article 23

(a) This Convention shall remain in force until the expiry of the Paris Convention.

(b) Any Contracting Party may, by giving twelve months' notice to the Belgian Government, terminate the application of this Convention to itself after the end of the period of ten years specified in Article 22(a) of the Paris Convention. Within six months after receipt of such notice, any other Contracting Party may, by notice to the Belgian Government, terminate the application of this Convention to itself as from the date when it ceases to have effect in respect of the Contracting Party which first gave notice.

(c) The expiry of this Convention or the withdrawal of a Contracting Party shall not terminate the obligations assumed by each Contracting Party under this Convention to pay compensation for damage caused by nuclear incidents occurring before the date of such expiry or withdrawal.

(d) The Contracting Parties shall, in good time, consult each other on what measures should be taken after the expiry of this Convention or the withdrawal of one or more of the Contracting Parties, to provide compensation comparable to that accorded by this Convention for damage caused by nuclear incidents occurring after the date of such expiry or withdrawal and for which the operator of a nuclear installation in operation before such date within the territories of the Contracting Parties is liable.

Article 24

(a) This Convention shall apply to the metropolitan territories of the Contracting Parties.

(b) Any Contracting Party desiring the application of this Convention to one or more of the territories in respect of which, pursuant to Article 23 of the Paris Convention, it has given notification of application of that Convention, shall address a request to the Belgian Government.

(c) The application of this Convention to any such territory shall require the unanimous assent of the Contracting Parties.

(d) Once such assent has been given, the Contracting Party concerned shall address to the Belgian Government a notification which shall take effect as from the date of its receipt.

(e) Such notification may, as regards any territory mentioned therein, be withdrawn by the Contracting Party which has made it by giving twelve months' notice to that effect to the Belgian Government.

(f) If the Paris Convention ceases to apply to any such territory, this Convention shall also cease to apply thereto.

Article 25

The Belgian Government shall notify all Signatories and acceding Governments of the receipt of any instrument of ratification, accession or withdrawal, and shall also notify them of the date on which this Convention comes into force, the text of any amendment thereto and the date on which such amendment comes into force, any reservations made in accordance with Article 18, and all notifications which it has received.

ANNEX

THE GOVERNMENTS OF THE CONTRACTING PARTIES declare that compensation for damage caused by a nuclear incident not covered by the Supplementary Convention solely by reason of the fact that the relevant nuclear installation, on account of its utilization, is not on the list referred to in Article 2 of the Supplementary Convention, (including the case where such installation is considered by one or more but not all of the Governments to be outside the Paris Convention):

— shall be provided without discrimination among the nationals of the Contracting Parties to the Supplementary Convention; and

— shall not be limited to less than 300 million Special Drawing Rights.

In addition, if they have not already done so, they shall endeavor to make the rules for compensation of persons suffering damage caused by such incidents as similar as possible to those established in respect of nuclear incidents occurring in connection with nuclear installations covered by the Supplementary Convention.

3.3 **VIENNA CONVENTION ON CIVIL LIABILITY FOR NUCLEAR DAMAGE (WITHOUT OPTIONAL PROTOCOL).**[1] **Concluded at Vienna, 21 May 1963. Entered into force, 12 November 1977. 1063 U.N.T.S. 265, 7 I.L.M. 727 (1968)**

* * *

Article I. 1. For the purposes of this Convention:

(a) "Person" means any individual, partnership, any private or public body, whether corporate or not, any international organization enjoying legal personality under the law of the Installation State, and any State or any of its constituent sub-divisions.

(b) "National of a Contracting Party" includes a Contracting Party or any of its constituent sub-divisions, a partnership, or any private or public body, whether corporate or not, established within the territory of a Contracting Party.

(c) "Operator", in relation to a nuclear installation, means the person designated or recognized by the Installation State as the operator of that installation.

(d) "Installation State", in relation to a nuclear installation, means the Contracting Party within whose territory that installation is situated or, if it is not situated within the territory of any State, the Contracting Party by which or under the authority of which the nuclear installation is operated.

(e) "Law of the competent court" means the law of the court having jurisdiction under this Convention, including any rules of such law relating to conflict of laws.

(f) "Nuclear fuel" means any material which is capable of producing energy by a self-sustaining chain process of nuclear fission.

(g) "Radioactive products or waste" means any radioactive material produced in, or any material made radioactive by exposure to the radiation incidental to, the production or utilization of nuclear fuel, but does not include radioisotopes which have reached the final stage of fabrication so as to be usable for any scientific, medical, agricultural, commercial or industrial purpose.

(h) "Nuclear material" means:

(i) nuclear fuel, other than natural uranium and depleted uranium, capable of producing energy by a self-sustaining chain process of nuclear fission outside a nuclear reactor, either alone or in combination with some other material; and

(ii) radioactive products or waste.

(i) "Nuclear reactor" means any structure containing nuclear fuel in such an arrangement that a self-sustaining chain process of nuclear fission can occur therein without an additional source of neutrons.

(j) "Nuclear installation" means:

---

1. *See also* Basic Documents 3.1 and 3.2, *supra.*

    (i) any nuclear reactor other than one with which a means of sea or air transport is equipped for use as a source of power, whether for propulsion thereof or for any other purpose;

    (ii) any factory using nuclear fuel for the production of nuclear material, or any factory for the processing of nuclear material, including any factory for the re-processing of irradiated nuclear fuel; and

    (iii) any facility where nuclear material is stored, other than storage incidental to the carriage of such material;

provided that the Installation State may determine that several nuclear installations of one operator which are located at the same site shall be considered as a single nuclear installation.

    (k) "Nuclear damage" means:

    (i) loss of life, any personal injury or any loss of, or damage to, property which arises out of or results from the radioactive properties or a combination of radioactive properties with toxic, explosive or other hazardous properties of nuclear fuel or radioactive products or waste in, or of nuclear material coming from, originating in, or sent to, a nuclear installation;

    (ii) any other loss or damage so arising or resulting if and to the extent that the law of the competent court so provides; and

    (iii) if the law of the Installation State so provides, loss of life, any personal injury or any loss of, or damage to, property which arises out of or results from other ionizing radiation emitted by any other source of radiation inside a nuclear installation.

    (l) "Nuclear incident" means any occurrence or series of occurrences having the same origin which causes nuclear damage.

    2. An Installation State may, if the small extent of the risks involved so warrants, exclude any small quantities of nuclear material from the application of this Convention, provided that:

    (a) maximum limits for the exclusion of such quantities have been established by the Board of Governors of the International Atomic Energy Agency; and

    (b) any exclusion by an Installation State is within such established limits.

The maximum limits shall be reviewed periodically by the Board of Governors.

    Article II. 1. The operator of a nuclear installation shall be liable for nuclear damage upon proof that such damage has been caused by a nuclear incident:

    (a) in his nuclear installation; or

    (b) involving nuclear material coming from or originating in his nuclear installation, and occurring:

(i) before liability with regard to nuclear incidents involving the nuclear material has been assumed, pursuant to the express terms of a contract in writing, by the operator of another nuclear installation;

(ii) in the absence of such express terms, before the operator of another nuclear installation has taken charge of the nuclear material; or

(iii) where the nuclear material is intended to be used in a nuclear reactor with which a means of transport is equipped for use as a source of power, whether for propulsion thereof or for any other purpose, before the person duly authorized to operate such reactor has taken charge of the nuclear material; but

(iv) where the nuclear material has been sent to a person within the territory of a non-Contracting State, before it has been unloaded from the means of transport by which it has arrived in the territory of that non-Contracting State;

(c) involving nuclear material sent to his nuclear installation, and occurring:

(i) after liability with regard to nuclear incidents involving the nuclear material has been assumed by him, pursuant to the express terms of a contract in writing, from the operator of another nuclear installation;

(ii) in the absence of such express terms, after he has taken charge of the nuclear material; or

(iii) after he has taken charge of the nuclear material from a person operating a nuclear reactor with which a means of transport is equipped for use as a source of power, whether for propulsion thereof or for any other purpose; but

(iv) where the nuclear material has, with the written consent of the operator, been sent from a person within the territory of a non-Contracting State, only after it has been loaded on the means of transport by which it is to be carried from the territory of that State;

provided that, if nuclear damage is caused by a nuclear incident occurring in a nuclear installation and involving nuclear material stored therein incidentally to the carriage of such material, the provisions of sub-paragraph *(a)* of this paragraph shall not apply where another operator or person is solely liable pursuant to the provisions of sub-paragraph *(b)* or *(c)* of this paragraph.

2.   The Installation State may provide by legislation that, in accordance with such terms as may be specified therein, a carrier of nuclear material or a person handling radioactive waste may, at his request and with the consent of the operator concerned, be designated or recognized as operator in the place of that operator in respect of such nuclear material or radioactive waste respectively. In this case such carrier or such person shall be considered, for all the purposes of this Convention, as an operator of a nuclear installation situated within the territory of that State.

3.   *(a)* Where nuclear damage engages the liability of more than one operator, the operators involved shall, in so far as the damage attributable to each operator is not reasonably separable, be jointly and severally liable.

(b) Where a nuclear incident occurs in the course of carriage of nuclear material, either in one and the same means of transport, or, in the case of storage incidental to the carriage, in one and the same nuclear installation, and causes nuclear damage which engages the liability of more than one operator, the total liability shall not exceed the highest amount applicable with respect to any one of them pursuant to article V.

(c) In neither of the cases referred to in sub-paragraphs *(a)* and *(b)* of this paragraph shall the liability of any one operator exceed the amount applicable with respect to him pursuant to article V.

4. Subject to the provisions of paragraph 3 of this article, where several nuclear installations of one and the same operator are involved in one nuclear incident, such operator shall be liable in respect of each nuclear installation involved up to the amount applicable with respect to him pursuant to article V.

5. Except as otherwise provided in this Convention, no person other than the operator shall be liable for nuclear damage. This, however, shall not affect the application of any international convention in the field of transport in force or open for signature, ratification or accession at the date on which this Convention is opened for signature.

6. No person shall be liable for any loss or damage which is not nuclear damage pursuant to sub-paragraph *(k)* of paragraph 1 of article I but which could have been included as such pursuant to sub-paragraph *(k)* (ii) of that paragraph.

7. Direct action shall lie against the person furnishing financial security pursuant to article VII, if the law of the competent court so provides.

Article III. The operator liable in accordance with this Convention shall provide the carrier with a certificate issued by or on behalf of the insurer or other financial guarantor furnishing the financial security required pursuant to article VII. The certificate shall state the name and address of that operator and the amount, type and duration of the security, and these statements may not be disputed by the person by whom or on whose behalf the certificate was issued. The certificate shall also indicate the nuclear material in respect of which the security applies and shall include a statement by the competent public authority of the Installation State that the person named is an operator within the meaning of this Convention.

Article IV. 1. The liability of the operator for nuclear damage under this Convention shall be absolute.

2. If the operator proves that the nuclear damage resulted wholly or partly either from the gross negligence of the person suffering the damage or from an act or omission of such person done with intent to cause damage, the competent court may, if its law so provides, relieve the operator wholly or partly from his obligation to pay compensation in respect of the damage suffered by such person.

3. *(a)* No liability under this Convention shall attach to an operator for nuclear damage caused by a nuclear incident directly due to an act of armed conflict, hostilities, civil war or insurrection.

(b) Except in so far as the law of the Installation State may provide to the contrary, the operator shall not be liable for nuclear damage caused by a nuclear incident directly due to a grave natural disaster of an exceptional character.

4. Whenever both nuclear damage and damage other than nuclear damage have been caused by a nuclear incident or jointly by a nuclear incident and one or more other occurrences, such other damage shall, to the extent that it is not reasonably separable from the nuclear damage, be deemed, for the purposes of this Convention, to be nuclear damage caused by that nuclear incident. Where, however, damage is caused jointly by a nuclear incident covered by this Convention and by an emission of ionizing radiation not covered by it, nothing in this Convention shall limit or otherwise affect the liability, either as regards any person suffering nuclear damage or by way of recourse or contribution, of any person who may be held liable in connection with that emission of ionizing radiation.

5. The operator shall not be liable under this Convention for nuclear damage:

(a) to the nuclear installation itself or to any property on the site of that installation which is used or to be used in connection with that installation; or

(b) to the means of transport upon which the nuclear material involved was at the time of the nuclear incident.

6. Any Installation State may provide by legislation that sub-paragraph *(b)* of paragraph 5 of this article shall not apply, provided that in no case shall the liability of the operator in respect of nuclear damage, other than nuclear damage to the means of transport, be reduced to less than US $5 million for any one nuclear incident.

7. Nothing in this Convention shall affect:

(a) the liability of any individual for nuclear damage for which the operator, by virtue of paragraph 3 or 5 of this article, is not liable under this Convention and which that individual caused by an act or omission done with intent to cause damage; or

(b) the liability outside this Convention of the operator for nuclear damage for which, by virtue of sub-paragraph *(b)* of paragraph 5 of this article, he is not liable under this Convention.

Article V. 1. The liability of the operator may be limited by the Installation State to not less than US $5 million for any one nuclear incident.

2. Any limits of liability which may be established pursuant to this article shall not include any interest or costs awarded by a court in actions for compensation of nuclear damage.

3. The United States dollar referred to in this Convention is a unit of account equivalent to the value of the United States dollar in terms of gold on 29 April 1963, that is to say US $35 per one troy ounce of fine gold.

4. The sum mentioned in paragraph 6 of article IV and in paragraph 1 of this article may be converted into national currency in round figures.

Article VI. 1. Rights of compensation under this Convention shall be extinguished if an action is not brought within ten years from the date of the nuclear incident. If, however, under the law of the Installation State the liability of the operator is covered by insurance or other financial security or by State funds for a period longer than ten years, the law of the competent court may provide that rights of compensation against the operator shall only be extinguished after a period which may be longer than ten years, but shall not be longer than the period for which his liability is so covered under the law of the Installation State. Such extension of the extinction period shall in no case affect rights of compensation under this Convention of any person who has brought an action for loss of life or personal injury against the operator before the expiry of the aforesaid period of ten years.

2. Where nuclear damage is caused by a nuclear incident involving nuclear material which at the time of the nuclear incident was stolen, lost, jettisoned or abandoned, the period established pursuant to paragraph 1 of this article shall be computed from the date of that nuclear incident, but the period shall in no case exceed a period of twenty years from the date of the theft, loss, jettison or abandonment.

3. The law of the competent court may establish a period of extinction or prescription of not less than three years from the date on which the person suffering nuclear damage had knowledge or should have had knowledge of the damage and of the operator liable for the damage, provided that the period established pursuant to paragraphs 1 and 2 of this article shall not be exceeded.

4. Unless the law of the competent court otherwise provides, any person who claims to have suffered nuclear damage and who has brought an action for compensation within the period applicable pursuant to this article may amend his claim to take into account any aggravation of the damage, even after the expiry of that period, provided that final judgment has not been entered.

5. Where jurisdiction is to be determined pursuant to sub-paragraph *(b)* of paragraph 3 of article XI and a request has been made within the period applicable pursuant to this article to any one of the Contracting Parties empowered so to determine, but the time remaining after such determination is less than six months, the period within which an action may be brought shall be six months, reckoned from the date of such determination.

Article VII. 1. The operator shall be required to maintain insurance or other financial security covering his liability for nuclear damage in such amount, of such type and in such terms as the Installation State shall specify. The Installation State shall ensure the payment of claims for compensation for nuclear damage which have been established against the operator by providing the necessary funds to the extent that the yield of insurance or other financial security is inadequate to satisfy such claims, but not in excess of the limit, if any, established pursuant to article V.

2. Nothing in paragraph 1 of this article shall require a Contracting Party or any of its constituent sub-divisions, such as States or Republics, to maintain insurance or other financial security to cover their liability as operators.

3.   The funds provided by insurance, by other financial security or by the Installation State pursuant to paragraph 1 of this article shall be exclusively available for compensation due under this Convention.

4.   No insurer or other financial guarantor shall suspend or cancel the insurance or other financial security provided pursuant to paragraph 1 of this article without giving notice in writing of at least two months to the competent public authority or, in so far as such insurance or other financial security relates to the carriage of nuclear material, during the period of the carriage in question.

Article VIII.   Subject to the provisions of this Convention, the nature, form and extent of the compensation, as well as the equitable distribution thereof, shall be governed by the law of the competent court.

Article IX.   1.   Where provisions of national or public health insurance, social insurance, social security, workmen's compensation or occupational disease compensation systems include compensation for nuclear damage, rights of beneficiaries of such systems to obtain compensation under this Convention and rights of recourse by virtue of such systems against the operator liable shall be determined, subject to the provisions of this Convention, by the law of the Contracting Party in which such systems have been established, or by the regulations of the intergovernmental organization which has established such systems.

2.   *(a)* If a person who is a national of a Contracting Party, other than the operator, has paid compensation for nuclear damage under an international convention or under the law of a non-Contracting State, such person shall, up to the amount which he has paid, acquire by subrogation the rights under this Convention of the person so compensated.   No rights shall be so acquired by any person to the extent that the operator has a right of recourse against such person under this Convention.

(b) Nothing in this Convention shall preclude an operator who has paid compensation for nuclear damage out of funds other than those provided pursuant to paragraph 1 of article VII from recovering from the person providing financial security pursuant to that paragraph or from the Installation State, up to the amount he has paid, the sum which the person so compensated would have obtained under this Convention.

Article X.   The operator shall have a right of recourse only:

(a) if this is expressly provided for by a contract in writing; or

(b) if the nuclear incident results from an act or omission done with intent to cause damage, against the individual who has acted or omitted to act with such intent.

Article XI.   1.   Except as otherwise provided in this article, jurisdiction over actions under article II shall lie only with the courts of the Contracting Party within whose territory the nuclear incident occurred.

2.   Where the nuclear incident occurred outside the territory of any Contracting Party, or where the place of the nuclear incident cannot be determined with certainty, jurisdiction over such actions shall lie with the courts of the Installation State of the operator liable.

3. Where under paragraph 1 or 2 of this article, jurisdiction would lie with the courts of more than one Contracting Party, jurisdiction shall lie:

(*a*) if the nuclear incident occurred partly outside the territory of any Contracting Party, and partly within the territory of a single Contracting Party, with the courts of the latter; and

(*b*) in any other case, with the courts of that Contracting Party which is determined by agreement between the Contracting Parties whose courts would be competent under paragraph 1 or 2 of this article.

Article XII. 1. A final judgment entered by a court having jurisdiction under article XI shall be recognized within the territory of any other Contracting Party, except:

(*a*) where the judgment was obtained by fraud;

(*b*) where the party against whom the judgment was pronounced was not given a fair opportunity to present his case; or

(*c*) where the judgment is contrary to the public policy of the Contracting Party within the territory of which recognition is sought, or is not in accord with fundamental standards of justice.

2. A final judgment which is recognized shall, upon being presented for enforcement in accordance with the formalities required by the law of the Contracting Party where enforcement is sought, be enforceable as if it were a judgment of a court of that Contracting Party.

3. The merits of a claim on which the judgment has been given shall not be subject to further proceedings.

Article XIII. This Convention and the national law applicable thereunder shall be applied without any discrimination based upon nationality, domicile or residence.

Article XIV. Except in respect of measures of execution, jurisdictional immunities under rules of national or international law shall not be invoked in actions under this Convention before the courts competent pursuant to article XI.

Article XV. The Contracting Parties shall take appropriate measures to ensure that compensation for nuclear damage, interest and costs awarded by a court in connection therewith, insurance and reinsurance premiums and funds provided by insurance, reinsurance or other financial security, or funds provided by the Installation State, pursuant to this Convention, shall be freely transferable into the currency of the Contracting Party within whose territory the damage is suffered, and of the Contracting Party within whose territory the claimant is habitually resident, and, as regards insurance or reinsurance premiums and payments, into the currencies specified in the insurance or reinsurance contract.

Article XVI. No person shall be entitled to recover compensation under this Convention to the extent that he has recovered compensation in respect of the same nuclear damage under another international convention on civil liability in the field of nuclear energy.

Article XVII. This Convention shall not, as between the parties to them, affect the application of any international agreements or international conventions on civil liability in the field of nuclear energy in force, or open for signature, ratification or accession at the date on which this Convention is opened for signature.

Article XVIII. This Convention shall not be construed as affecting the rights, if any, of a Contracting Party under the general rules of public international law in respect of nuclear damage.

Article XIX. 1. Any Contracting Party entering into an agreement pursuant to sub-paragraph *(b)* of paragraph 3 of article XI shall furnish without delay to the Director General of the International Atomic Energy Agency for information and dissemination to the other Contracting Parties a copy of such agreement.

2. The Contracting Parties shall furnish to the Director General for information and dissemination to the other Contracting Parties copies of their respective laws and regulations relating to matters covered by this Convention.

Article XX. Notwithstanding the termination of the application of this Convention to any Contracting Party, either by termination pursuant to article XXV or by denunciation pursuant to article XXVI, the provisions of this Convention shall continue to apply to any nuclear damage caused by a nuclear incident occurring before such termination.

Article XXI. This Convention shall be open for signature by the States represented at the International Conference on Civil Liability for Nuclear Damage held in Vienna from 29 April to 19 May 1963.

Article XXII. This Convention shall be ratified, and the instruments of ratification shall be deposited with the Director General of the International Atomic Energy Agency.

Article XXIII. This Convention shall come into force three months after the deposit of the fifth instrument of ratification, and, in respect of each State ratifying it thereafter, three months after the deposit of the instrument of ratification by that State.

Article XXIV. 1. All States Members of the United Nations, or of any of the specialized agencies or of the International Atomic Energy Agency not represented at the International Conference on Civil Liability for Nuclear Damage, held in Vienna from 29 April to 19 May 1963, may accede to this Convention.

2. The instruments of accession shall be deposited with the Director General of the International Atomic Energy Agency.

3. This Convention shall come into force in respect of the acceding State three months after the date of deposit of the instrument of accession of that State but not before the date of the entry into force of this Convention pursuant to article XXIII.

Article XXV. 1. This Convention shall remain in force for a period of ten years from the date of its entry into force. Any Contracting Party may, by giving before the end of that period at least twelve months' notice to that effect to the Director General of the International Atomic Energy Agency, terminate the application of this Convention to itself at the end of that period of ten years.

2. This Convention shall, after that period of ten years, remain in force for a further period of five years for such Contracting Parties as have not terminated its application pursuant to paragraph 1 of this article, and thereafter for successive periods of five years each for those Contracting Parties which have not terminated its application at the end of one of such periods, by giving, before the end of one of such periods, at least twelve months' notice to that effect to the Director General of the International Atomic Energy Agency.

Article XXVI. 1. A conference shall be convened by the Director General of the International Atomic Energy Agency at any time after the expiry of a period of five years from the date of the entry into force of this Convention in order to consider the revision thereof, if one-third of the Contracting Parties express a desire to that effect.

2. Any Contracting Party may denounce this Convention by notification to the Director General of the International Atomic Energy Agency within a period of twelve months following the first revision conference held pursuant to paragraph 1 of this article.

3. Denunciation shall take effect one year after the date on which notification to that effect has been received by the Director General of the International Atomic Energy Agency.

Article XXVII. The Director General of the International Atomic Energy Agency shall notify the States invited to the International Conference on Civil Liability for Nuclear Damage held in Vienna from 29 April to 19 May 1963 and the States which have acceded to this Convention of the following:

(a) signatures and instruments of ratification and accession received pursuant to articles XXI, XXII and XXIV;

(b) the date on which this Convention will come into force pursuant to article XXIII;

(c) notifications of termination and denunciation received pursuant to articles XXV and XXVI;

(d) requests for the convening of a revision conference pursuant to article XXVI.

Article XXVIII. This Convention shall be registered by the Director General of the International Atomic Energy Agency in accordance with Article 102 of the Charter of the United Nations.

Article XXIX. The original of this Convention, of which the English, French, Russian and Spanish texts are equally authentic, shall be deposited with the Director General of the International Atomic Energy Agency, who shall issue certified copies.

3.4 TREATY ON PRINCIPLES GOVERNING THE ACTIVITIES OF STATES IN THE EXPLORATION AND USE OF OUTER SPACE, INCLUDING THE MOON AND OTHER CELESTIAL BODIES.[1] Concluded at London, Moscow, and Washington, 27 January 1967. Entered into force, 10 October 1967. 610 U.N.T.S. 205, 6 I.L.M. 386 (1967)

Article I

The exploration and use of outer space, including the moon and other celestial bodies, shall be carried out for the benefit and in the interests of all countries, irrespective of their degree of economic or scientific development, and shall be the province of all mankind.

Outer space, including the moon and other celestial bodies, shall be free for exploration and use by all States without discrimination of any kind, on a basis of equality and in accordance with international law, and there shall be free access to all areas of celestial bodies.

There shall be freedom of scientific investigation in outer space, including the moon and other celestial bodies, and States shall facilitate and encourage international co-operation in such investigation.

Article II

Outer space, including the moon and other celestial bodies, is not subject to national appropriation by claim of sovereignty, by means of use or occupation, or by any other means.

Article III

States Parties to the Treaty shall carry on activities in the exploration and use of outer space, including the moon and other celestial bodies, in accordance with international law, including the Charter of the United Nations, in the interest of maintaining international peace and security and promoting international co-operation and understanding.

Article IV

States Parties to the Treaty undertake not to place in orbit around the earth any objects carrying nuclear weapons or any other kinds of weapons of mass destruction, instal such weapons on celestial bodies, or station such weapons in outer space in any other manner.

The moon and other celestial bodies shall be used by all States Parties to the Treaty exclusively for peaceful purposes. The establishment of military bases, installations and fortifications, the testing of any type of weapons and the conduct of military manoeuvres on celestial bodies shall be forbidden. The use of military personnel for scientific research or for any other peaceful purposes shall not be prohibited. The use of any equipment or facility necessary for peaceful exploration of the moon and other celestial bodies shall also not be prohibited.

Article V

States Parties to the Treaty shall regard astronauts as envoys of mankind in outer space and shall render to them all possible assistance in the event of accident, distress, or emergency landing on the territory of another State

---

1. Also known as "the Outer Space Treaty."

Party or on the high seas. When astronauts make such a landing, they shall be safely and promptly returned to the State of registry of their space vehicle.

In carrying on activities in outer space and on celestial bodies, the astronauts of one State Party shall render all possible assistance to the astronauts of other States Parties.

States Parties to the Treaty shall immediately inform the other States Parties to the Treaty or the Secretary–General of the United Nations of any phenomena they discover in outer space, including the moon and other celestial bodies, which could constitute a danger to the life or health of astronauts.

Article VI

States Parties to the Treaty shall bear international responsibility for national activities in outer space, including the moon and other celestial bodies, whether such activities are carried on by governmental agencies or by non-governmental entities, and for assuring that national activities are carried out in conformity with the provisions set forth in the present Treaty. The activities of non-governmental entities in outer space, including the moon and other celestial bodies, shall require authorization and continuing supervision by the appropriate State Party to the Treaty. When activities are carried on in outer space, including the moon and other celestial bodies, by an international organization, responsibility for compliance with this Treaty shall be borne both by the international organization and by the States Parties to the Treaty participating in such organization.

Article VII

Each State Party to the Treaty that launches or procures the launching of an object into outer space, including the moon and other celestial bodies, and each State Party from whose territory or facility an object is launched, is internationally liable for damage to another State Party to the Treaty or to its natural or juridical persons by such object or its component parts on the Earth, in air space or in outer space, including the moon and other celestial bodies.

Article VIII

A State Party to the Treaty on whose registry an object launched into outer space is carried shall retain jurisdiction and control over such object, and over any personnel thereof, while in outer space or on a celestial body. Ownership of objects launched into outer space, including objects landed or constructed on a celestial body, and of their component parts, is not affected by their presence in outer space or on a celestial body or by their return to the Earth. Such objects or component parts found beyond the limits of the State Party to the Treaty on whose registry they are carried shall be returned to that State Party, which shall, upon request, furnish identifying data prior to their return.

Article IX

In the exploration and use of outer space, including the moon and other celestial bodies, States Parties to the Treaty shall be guided by the principle of co-operation and mutual assistance and shall conduct all their activities in outer space, including the moon and other celestial bodies, with due regard to the corresponding interests of all other States Parties to the Treaty. States Parties to the Treaty shall pursue studies of outer space, including the moon and other celestial bodies, and conduct exploration of them so as to avoid their harmful contamination and also adverse changes in the environment of the Earth resulting from the introduction of extraterrestrial matter and, where necessary, shall adopt appropriate measures for this purpose. If a State Party to the Treaty has reason to believe that an activity or experiment planned by it or its nationals in outer space, including the moon and other celestial bodies, would cause potentially harmful interference with activities of other States Parties in the peaceful exploration and use of outer space, including the moon and other celestial bodies, it shall undertake appropriate international consultations before proceeding with any such activity or experiment. A State Party to the Treaty which has reason to believe that an activity or experiment planned by another State Party in outer space, including the moon and other celestial bodies, would cause potentially harmful interference with activities in the peaceful exploration and use of outer space, including the moon and other celestial bodies, may request consultation concerning the activity or experiment.

Article X

In order to promote international co-operation in the exploration and use of outer space, including the moon and other celestial bodies, in conformity with the purposes of this Treaty, the States Parties to the Treaty shall consider on a basis of equality any requests by other States Parties to the Treaty to be afforded an opportunity to observe the flight of space objects launched by those States.

The nature of such an opportunity for observation and the conditions under which it could be afforded shall be determined by agreement between the States concerned.

Article XI

In order to promote international co-operation in the peaceful exploration and use of outer space, States Parties to the Treaty conducting activities in outer space, including the moon and other celestial bodies, agree to inform the Secretary–General of the United Nations as well as the public and the international scientific community, to the greatest extent feasible and practicable, of the nature, conduct, locations and results of such activities. On receiving the said information, the Secretary–General of the United Nations should be prepared to disseminate it immediately and effectively.

Article XII

All stations, installations, equipment and space vehicles on the moon and other celestial bodies shall be open to representatives of other States Parties to the Treaty on a basis of reciprocity. Such representatives shall give reasonable advance notice of a projected visit, in order that appropriate consultations may be held and that maximum precautions may be taken to assure safety and to avoid interference with normal operations in the facility to be visited.

Article XIII

The provisions of this Treaty shall apply to the activities of States Parties to the Treaty in the exploration and use of outer space, including the moon and other celestial bodies, whether such activities are carried on by a single State Party to the Treaty or jointly with other States, including cases where they are carried on within the framework of international inter-governmental organizations.

Any practical questions arising in connexion with activities carried on by international inter-governmental organizations in the exploration and use of outer space, including the moon and other celestial bodies, shall be resolved by the States Parties to the Treaty either with the appropriate international organization or with one or more States members of that international organization, which are Parties to this Treaty.

Article XIV

1. This Treaty shall be open to all States for signature. Any State which does not sign this Treaty before its entry into force in accordance with paragraph 3 of this Article may accede to it at any time.

2. This Treaty shall be subject to ratification by signatory States. Instruments of ratification and instruments of accession shall be deposited with the Governments of the United Kingdom of Great Britain and Northern Ireland, the Union of Soviet Socialist Republics and the United States of America, which are hereby designated the Depositary Governments.

3. This Treaty shall enter into force upon the deposit of instruments of ratification by five Governments including the Governments designated as Depositary Governments under this Treaty.

4. For States whose instruments of ratification or accession are deposited subsequent to the entry into force of this Treaty, it shall enter into force on the date of the deposit of their instruments of ratification or accession.

5. The Depositary Governments shall promptly inform all signatory and acceding States of the date of each signature, the date of deposit of each instrument of ratification of and accession to this Treaty, the date of its entry into force and other notices.

6. This Treaty shall be registered by the Depositary Governments pursuant to Article 102 of the Charter of the United Nations.

Article XV

Any State Party to the Treaty may propose amendments to this Treaty. Amendments shall enter into force for each State Party to the Treaty accepting the amendments upon their acceptance by a majority of the States Parties to the Treaty and thereafter for each remaining State Party to the Treaty on the date of acceptance by it.

Article XVI

Any State Party to the Treaty may give notice of its withdrawal from the Treaty one year after its entry into force by written notification to the Depositary Governments. Such withdrawal shall take effect one year from the date of receipt of this notification.

Article XVII

This Treaty, of which the English, Russian, French, Spanish and Chinese texts are equally authentic, shall be deposited in the archives of the Depositary Governments. Duly certified copies of this Treaty shall be transmitted by the Depositary Governments to the Governments of the signatory and acceding States.

3.5 COUNCIL OF EUROPE COMMITTEE OF MINISTERS RESOLUTION ON AIR POLLUTION IN FRONTIER AREAS. Adopted 26 March 1971. C/E Res. 71(5), 19 E.Y.B. 263

The Committee of Ministers,

Having regard to the Declaration of Principles on Air Pollution Control (Resolution (68) 4) and specially to Title II, Chapter 7 concerning pollution in frontier areas;

Considering that it is in the common interest to prevent so far as possible the occurrence of problems caused by transfrontier air pollution;

Considering that the comments of the inhabitants of regions beyond the frontier should be examined in the same spirit as those made by the inhabitants of the country where the pollution plant is situated or planned,

Recommends that governments of member States of the Council of Europe ensure for the inhabitants of regions beyond their frontiers the same protection against air pollution in frontier areas as is provided for their own inhabitants.

To this end they should in particular ensure that the competent authorities should inform each other in good time about any project for installations liable to pollute the atmosphere beyond the frontier.

The competent authorities beyond the frontier should be able to make their comments on such projects. These comments should be given the same consideration and treatment as if they had been made by the inhabitants of the country where the plant is situated or proposed.

3.6 CONVENTION ON INTERNATIONAL LIABILITY FOR DAMAGE CAUSED BY SPACE OBJECTS. Concluded at Washington, London, and Moscow, 29 March 1972. Entered into force, 1 September 1972. 961 U.N.T.S. 187, 24 U.S.T. 2389, T.I.A.S. No. 7762

Article I. For the purposes of this Convention:

(*a*) The term "damage" means loss of life, personal injury or other impairment of health; or loss of or damage to property of States or of persons, natural or juridical, or property of international intergovernmental organisations;

(*b*) The term "launching" includes attempted launching;

(*c*) The term "launching State" means:

(i) a state which launches or procures the launching of a space object;

(ii) a State from whose territory or facility a space object is launched;

(*d*) The term "space object" includes component parts of a space object as well as its launch vehicle and parts thereof.

Article II. A launching State shall be absolutely liable to pay compensation for damage caused by its space object on the surface of the earth or to aircraft in flight.

Article III. In the event of damage being caused elsewhere than on the surface of the earth to a space object of one launching State or to persons or property on board such a space object by a space object of another launching State, the latter shall be liable only if the damage is due to its fault or the fault of persons for whom it is responsible.

Article IV. 1. In the event of damage being caused elsewhere than on the surface of the earth to a space object of one launching State or to persons or property on board such a space object by a space object of another launching State, and of damage thereby being caused to a third State or to its natural or juridical persons, the first two States shall be jointly and severally liable to the third State, to the extent indicated by the following:

(*a*) If the damage has been caused to the third State on the surface of the earth or to aircraft in flight, their liability to the third State shall be absolute;

(*b*) If the damage has been caused to a space object of the third State or to persons or property on board that space object elsewhere than on the surface of the earth, their liability to the third State shall be based on the fault of either of the first two States or on the fault of persons for whom either is responsible.

2. In all cases of joint and several liability referred to in paragraph 1 of this Article, the burden of compensation for the damage shall be apportioned between the first two States in accordance with the extent to which they were at fault; if the extent of the fault of each of these States cannot be established, the burden of compensation shall be apportioned equally between them. Such apportionment shall be without prejudice to the right of the third State to seek the entire compensation due under this Convention from any or all of the launching States which are jointly and severally liable.

Article V. 1. Whenever two or more States jointly launch a space object, they shall be jointly and severally liable for any damage caused.

2. A launching State which has paid compensation for damage shall have the right to present a claim for indemnification to other participants in the joint launching. The participants in a joint launching may conclude agreements regarding the apportioning among themselves of the financial obligation in respect of which they are jointly and severally liable. Such agreements shall be without prejudice to the right of a State sustaining damage to seek the entire compensation due under this Convention from any or all of the launching States which are jointly and severally liable.

3. A State from whose territory or facility a space object is launched shall be regarded as a participant in a joint launching.

Article VI. 1. Subject to the provisions of paragraph 2 of this Article, exoneration from absolute liability shall be granted to the extent that a launching State establishes that the damage has resulted either wholly or partially from gross negligence or from an act or omission done with intent to cause damage on the part of a claimant State or of natural or juridical persons it represents.

2. No exoneration whatever shall be granted in cases where the damage has resulted from activities conducted by a launching State which are not in conformity with international law including, in particular, the Charter of the United Nations and the Treaty on Principles Governing the Activities of States in the Exploration and Use of Outer Space, including the Moon and Other Celestial Bodies.

Article VII. The provisions of this Convention shall not apply to damage caused by a space object of a launching State to:

(a) nationals of that launching State;

(b) foreign nationals during such time as they are participating in the operation of that space object from the time of its launching or at any stage thereafter until its descent, or during such time as they are in the immediate vicinity of a planned launching or recovery area as the result of an invitation by that launching State.

Article VIII. 1. A State which suffers damage, or whose natural or juridical persons suffer damage, may present to a launching State a claim for compensation for such damage.

2. If the State of nationality has not presented a claim, another State may, in respect of damage sustained in its territory by any natural or juridical person, present a claim to a launching State.

3. If neither the State of nationality nor the State in whose territory the damage was sustained has presented a claim or notified its intention of presenting a claim, another State may, in respect of damage sustained by its permanent residents, present a claim to a launching State.

Article IX. A claim for compensation for damage shall be presented to a launching State through diplomatic channels. If a State does not maintain diplomatic relations with the launching State concerned, it may request another State to present its claim to that launching State or otherwise represent its interests under this Convention. It may also present its claim through the Secretary–General of the United Nations, provided the claimant State and the launching State are both Members of the United Nations.

Article X. 1. A claim for compensation for damage may be presented to a launching State not later than one year following the date of the occurrence of the damage or the identification of the launching State which is liable.

2. If, however, a State does not know of the occurrence of the damage or has not been able to identify the launching State which is liable, it may present a claim within one year following the date on which it learned of the aforementioned facts; however, this period shall in no event exceed one year following the date on which the State could reasonably be expected to have learned of the facts through the exercise of due diligence.

3. The time-limits specified in paragraphs 1 and 2 of this Article shall apply even if the full extent of the damage may not be known. In this event, however, the claimant State shall be entitled to revise the claim and submit additional documentation after the expiration of such time-limits until one year after the full extent of the damage is known.

Article XI. 1. Presentation of a claim to a launching State for compensation for damage under this Convention shall not require the prior exhaustion of any local remedies which may be available to a claimant State or to natural or juridical persons it represents.

2. Nothing in this Convention shall prevent a State, or natural or juridical persons it might represent, from pursuing a claim in the courts or administrative tribunals or agencies of a launching State. A State shall not, however, be entitled to present a claim under this Convention in respect of the same damage for which a claim is being pursued in the courts or administrative tribunals or agencies of a launching State or under another international agreement which is binding on the States concerned.

Article XII. The compensation which the launching State shall be liable to pay for damage under this Convention shall be determined in accordance with international law and the principles of justice and equity, in order to provide such reparation in respect of the damage as will restore the person, natural or juridical, State or international organisation on whose behalf the claim is presented to the condition which would have existed if the damage had not occurred.

Article XIII. Unless the claimant State and the State from which compensation is due under this Convention agree on another form of compensation, the compensation shall be paid in the currency of the claimant State or, if that State so requests, in the currency of the State from which compensation is due.

Article XIV. If no settlement of a claim is arrived at through diplomatic negotiations as provided for in Article IX, within one year from the date on which the claimant State notifies the launching State that it has submitted the documentation of its claim, the parties concerned shall establish a Claims Commission at the request of either party.

Article XV. 1. The Claims Commission shall be composed of three members: one appointed by the claimant State, one appointed by the launching State and the third member, the Chairman, to be chosen by both parties jointly. Each party shall make its appointment within two months of the request for the establishment of the Claims Commission.

2. If no agreement is reached on the choice of the Chairman within four months of the request for the establishment of the Commission, either party may request the Secretary–General of the United Nations to appoint the Chairman within a further period of two months.

Article XVI. 1. If one of the parties does not make its appointment within the stipulated period, the Chairman shall, at the request of the other party, constitute a single-member Claims Commission.

2. Any vacancy which may arise in the Commission for whatever reason shall be filled by the same procedure adopted for the original appointment.

3. The Commission shall determine its own procedure.

4. The Commission shall determine the place or places where it shall sit and all other administrative matters.

5. Except in the case of decisions and awards by a single-member Commission, all decisions and awards of the Commission shall be by majority vote.

Article XVII. No increase in the membership of the Claims Commission shall take place by reason of two or more claimant States or launching States being joined in any one proceeding before the Commission. The claimant States so joined shall collectively appoint one member of the Commission in the same manner and subject to the same conditions as would be the case for a single claimant State. When two or more launching States are so joined, they shall collectively appoint one member of the Commission in the same way. If the claimant States or the launching States do not make the appointment within the stipulated period, the Chairman shall constitute a single-member Commission.

Article XVIII. The Claims Commission shall decide the merits of the claim for compensation and determine the amount of compensation payable, if any.

Article XIX. 1. The Claims Commission shall act in accordance with the provisions of Article XII.

2. The decision of the Commission shall be final and binding if the parties have so agreed; otherwise the Commission shall render a final and recommendatory award, which the parties shall consider in good faith. The Commission shall state the reasons for its decision or award.

3. The Commission shall give its decision or award as promptly as possible and no later than one year from the date of its establishment, unless an extension of this period is found necessary by the Commission.

4. The Commission shall make its decision or award public. It shall deliver a certified copy of its decision or award to each of the parties and to the Secretary–General of the United Nations.

Article XX. The expenses in regard to the Claims Commission shall be borne equally by the parties, unless otherwise decided by the Commission.

Article XXI. If the damage caused by a space object presents a large-scale danger to human life or seriously interferes with the living conditions of the population or the functioning of vital centres, the States Parties, and in particular the launching State, shall examine the possibility of rendering appropriate and rapid assistance to the State which has suffered the damage, when it so requests. However, nothing in this Article shall affect the rights or obligations of the States Parties under this Convention.

Article XXII. 1. In this Convention, with the exception of Articles XXIV to XXVII, references to States shall be deemed to apply to any international intergovernmental organisation which conducts space activities if the organisation declares its acceptance of the rights and obligations provided for in this Convention and if a majority of the States members of the organisation are States Parties to this Convention and to the Treaty on Principles Governing the Activities of States in the Exploration and Use of Outer Space, including the Moon and Other Celestial Bodies.

2. States members of any such organisation which are States Parties to this Convention shall take all appropriate steps to ensure that the organisation makes a declaration in accordance with the preceding paragraph.

3. If an international intergovernmental organisation is liable for damage by virtue of the provisions of this Convention, that organisation and those of its members which are States Parties to this Convention shall be jointly and severally liable; provided, however, that:

(*a*) any claim for compensation in respect of such damage shall be first presented to the organisation;

(*b*) only where the organisation has not paid, within a period of six months, any sum agreed or determined to be due as compensation for such damage, may the claimant State invoke the liability of the members which are States Parties to this Convention for the payment of that sum.

4. Any claim, pursuant to the provisions of this Convention, for compensation in respect of damage caused to an organisation which has made a declaration in accordance with paragraph 1 of this Article shall be presented by a State member of the organisation which is a State Party to this Convention.

Article XXIII. 1. The provisions of this Convention shall not affect other international agreements in force in so far as relations between the States Parties to such agreements are concerned.

2. No provision of this Convention shall prevent States from concluding international agreements reaffirming, supplementing or extending its provisions.

Article XXIV. 1. This Convention shall be open to all States for signature. Any State which does not sign this Convention before its entry into force in accordance with paragraph 3 of this Article may accede to it at any time.

2. This Convention shall be subject to ratification by signatory States. Instruments of ratification and instruments of accession shall be deposited with the Governments of the United Kingdom of Great Britain and Northern Ireland, the Union of Soviet Socialist Republics and the United States of America, which are hereby designated the Depositary Governments.

3. This Convention shall enter into force on the deposit of the fifth instrument of ratification.

4. For States whose instruments of ratification or accession are deposited subsequent to the entry into force of this Convention, it shall enter into force on the date of the deposit of their instruments of ratification or accession.

5. The Depositary Governments shall promptly inform all signatory and acceding States of the date of each signature, the date of deposit of each instrument of ratification of and accession to this Convention, the date of its entry into force and other notices.

6. This Convention shall be registered by the Depositary Governments pursuant to Article 102 of the Charter of the United Nations.

Article XXV. Any State Party to this Convention may propose amendments to this Convention. Amendments shall enter into force for each State Party to the Convention accepting the amendments upon their acceptance by a majority of the States Parties to the Convention and thereafter for each remaining State Party on the date of acceptance by it.

Article XXVI. Ten years after the entry into force of this Convention, the question of the review of this Convention shall be included in the provisional agenda of the United Nations General Assembly in order to consider, in the light of past application of the Convention, whether it requires revision. However, at any time after the Convention has been in force for five years, and at the request of one third of the States Parties to the Convention, and with the concurrence of the majority of the States Parties, a conference of the States Parties shall be convened to review this Convention.

Article XXVII. Any State Party to this Convention may give notice of its withdrawal from the Convention one year after its entry into force by written notification to the Depositary Governments. Such withdrawal shall take effect one year from the date of receipt of this notification.

Article XXVIII. This Convention, of which the English, Russian, French, Spanish and Chinese texts are equally authentic, shall be deposited in the archives of the Depositary Governments. Duly certified copies of this Convention shall be transmitted by the Depositary Governments to the Governments of the signatory and acceding States.

3.7 OECD COUNCIL RECOMMENDATION ON PRINCIPLES CONCERNING TRANSFRONTIER POLLUTION (WITH ANNEX). Adopted 14 November 1974. 1974 O.E.C.D. C224, O.E.C.D. 142, 14 I.L.M. 242 (1975)

The Council,

Having regard to Article 5(b) of the Convention on the Organization for Economic Co-operation and Development of 14th December, 1960;

Considering that the protection and improvement of the environment are common objectives of Member countries;

Considering that the common interests of countries concerned by transfrontier pollution should induce them to co-operate more closely in a spirit of international solidarity and to initiate concerted action for preventing and controlling transfrontier pollution;

Having regard to the Recommendations of the United Nations Conference on the Human Environment held in Stockholm in June 1972 and in particular those Principles of the Declaration on the Human Environment which are relevant to transfrontier pollution;

On the proposal of the Environment Committee;

I. RECOMMENDS that, without prejudice to future developments in international law and international co-operation in relation to transfrontier pollution, Member countries should be guided in their environmental policy by the principles concerning transfrontier pollution contained in this Recommendation and its Annex, which is an integral part of this Recommendation.

II. INSTRUCTS the Environment Committee to prepare without delay, taking account of the work undertaken by other international organizations, a programme of work designed to elaborate further these principles and to facilitate their practical implementation.

III. RECOMMENDS Member countries to co-operate in developing international law applicable to transfrontier pollution.

IV. INSTRUCTS the Environment Committee, within the framework of its mandate, to examine or investigate further, as the case may be, the issues related to the Principles of the Stockholm Declaration regarding responsibility and liability, taking into account the work undertaken by other international organizations, to submit a first report to the Council on its work by 1st March, 1976 and to seek to formulate as soon as possible Draft Recommendations.

V. INSTRUCTS the Environment Committee to investigate further the issues concerning equal right of hearing, to formulate as soon as possible Draft Recommendations and to report to the Council on its work by 1st July, 1975.

Annex
Some Principles Concerning Transfrontier Pollution

Title A—Introduction

This Annex sets forth some principles designed to facilitate the development of harmonized environmental policies with a view to solving transfrontier pollution problems. Their implementation should be based on a fair balance of rights and obligations among countries concerned by transfrontier pollution.

These principles should subsequently be supplemented and developed in the light of work undertaken by the OECD or other appropriate international organizations.

For the purpose of these principles, pollution means the introduction by man, directly or indirectly, of substances or energy into the environment resulting in deleterious effects of such a nature as to endanger human health, harm living resources and ecosystems, and impair or interfere with amenities and other legitimate uses of the environment.

Unless otherwise specified, these principles deal with pollution originating in one country and having effects within other countries.

Title B—International Solidarity

1. Countries should define a concerted long-term policy for the protection and improvement of the environment in zones liable to be affected by transfrontier pollution.

Without prejudice to their rights and obligations under international law and in accordance with their responsibility under Principle 21 of the Stockholm Declaration, countries should seek, as far as possible, an equitable balance of their rights and obligations as regards the zones concerned by transfrontier pollution.

In implementing this concerted policy, countries should among other things:

(a) take account of:

— levels of existing pollution and the present quality of the environment concerned;

— the nature and quantities of pollutants;

— the assimilative capacity of the environment, as established by mutual agreement by the countries concerned, taking into account the particular characteristics and use of the affected zone;

— activities at the source of pollution and activities and uses sensitive to such pollution;

— the situation, prospective use and development of the zones concerned from a socio-economic stand-point;

(b) define:

— environmental quality objectives and corresponding protective measures:

(c) promote:

— guidelines for a land-use planning policy consistent with the requirements both of environmental protection and socio-economic development;

(d) draw up and maintain up to date:

(i) list of particularly dangerous substances regarding which efforts should be made to eliminate polluting discharges, if necessary by stages, and

(ii) lists of substances regarding which polluting discharges should be subject to very strict control.

2. Pending the definition of such concerted long-term policies countries should, individually and jointly, take all appropriate measures to prevent and control transfrontier pollution, and harmonize as far as possible their relevant policies.

3. Countries should endeavour to prevent any increase in transfrontier pollution, including that stemming from new or additional substances and activities, and to reduce, and as far as possible eliminate any transfrontier pollution existing between them within time limits to be specified.

Title C—Principle of non-discrimination

4. Countries should initially base their action on the principle of nondiscrimination, whereby:

(*a*) polluters causing transfrontier pollution should be subject to legal or statutory provisions no less severe than those which would apply for any equivalent pollution occurring within their country, under comparable conditions and in comparable zones, taking into account, when appropriate, the special nature and environmental needs of the zone affected;

(*b*) in particular, without prejudice to quality objectives or standards applying to transfrontier pollution mutually agreed upon by the countries concerned, the levels of transfrontier pollution entering into the zones liable to be affected by such pollution should not exceed those considered acceptable under comparable conditions and in comparable zones inside the country in which it originates, taking into account, when appropriate, the special state of the environment in the affected country;

(*c*) any country whenever it applies the Polluter–Pays Principle should apply it to all polluters within this country without making any difference according to whether pollution affects this country or another country;

(*d*) persons affected by transfrontier pollution should be granted no less favourable treatment than persons affected by a similar pollution in the country from which such transfrontier pollution originates.

Title D—Principle of equal right of hearing

5. Countries should make every effort to introduce, where not already in existence, a system affording equal right of hearing, according to which:

(*a*) whenever a project, a new activity or a course of conduct may create a significant risk of transfrontier pollution and is investigated by public authorities, those who may be affected by such pollution should have the same rights of standing in judicial or administrative proceedings in the country where it originates as those of that country;

(*b*) whenever transfrontier pollution gives rise to damage in a country, those who are affected by such pollution should have the same rights of standing in judicial or administrative proceedings in the country where such pollution originates as those of that country, and they should be extended procedural rights equivalent to the rights extended to those of that country.

Title E—Principle of information and consultation

6. Prior to the initiation in a country of works or undertakings which might create a significant risk of transfrontier pollution, this country should provide early information to other countries which are or may be affected. It should provide these countries with relevant information and data, the transmission of which is not prohibited by legislative provisions or prescriptions or applicable international conventions, and should invite their comments.

7. Countries should enter into consultation on an existing or foreseeable transfrontier pollution problem at the request of a country which is or may be directly affected and should diligently pursue such consultations on this particular problem over a reasonable period of time.

8. Countries should refrain from carrying out projects or activities which might create a significant risk of transfrontier pollution without first informing the countries which are or may be affected and, except in cases of extreme urgency, providing a reasonable amount of time in the light of circumstances for diligent consultation. Such consultations held in the best spirit of co-operation and good neighbourliness should not enable a country to unreasonably delay or to impede the activities or projects on which consultations are taking place.

Title F—Warning systems and incidents

9. Countries should promptly warn other potentially affected countries of any situation which may cause any sudden increase in the level of pollution in areas outside the country of origin of pollution, and take all appropriate steps to reduce the effects of any such sudden increase.

10. Countries should assist each other, wherever necessary, in order to prevent incidents which may result in transfrontier pollution, and to minimise, and if possible eliminate, the effects of such incidents, and should develop contingency plans to this end.

Title G—Exchange of scientific information, monitoring measures and research

11. Countries concerned should exchange all relevant scientific information and data on transfrontier pollution, when not prohibited by legislative provisions or prescriptions or by applicable international conventions. They should develop and adopt pollution measurement methods providing results which are compatible.

12. They should, when appropriate, co-operate in scientific and technical research programmes inter alio for identifying the origin and pathways of transfrontier pollution, any damage caused and the best methods of pollution prevention and control, and should share all information and data thus obtained.

They should, where necessary, consider setting up jointly, in zones affected by transfrontier pollution, a permanent monitoring system or network for assessing the levels of pollution and the effectiveness of measures taken by them to reduce pollution.

Title H—Institutions

13. Countries concerned by a particular problem of transfrontier pollution should consider the advantages of co-operation, by setting up international commissions or other bodies, or by strengthening existing institutions, in order to deal more effectively with particular aspects of such problems.

Such institutions could be authorised to collect any data needed for a proper evaluation of the problem and its causes, and make to the countries concerned practical proposals for concerted efforts to combat transfrontier pollution. With the consent of the States concerned, they could also carry out any necessary additional investigations into the origin and degree of pollution, review the effectiveness of any pollution prevention and control measures which have been taken, and publish reports of their findings.

Title I—Disputes

14. Should negotiations and other means of diplomatically settling disputes concerning transfrontier pollution fail, countries should have the opportunity to submit such a dispute to a procedure of legal settlement which is prompt, effective and binding.

Title J—International agreements

15. Countries should endeavour to conclude, where necessary, bilateral or multilateral agreements for the abatement of transfrontier pollution in accordance with the above principles, to bring promptly into force any agreements which may already have been signed.

16. When negotiating new bilateral or multilateral agreements countries should, while taking into account the principles set out above, strive for the application of efficient pollution prevention and control measures in accordance with the Polluter–Pays Principle.

Such agreements could, inter alia, include provisions for practical procedures promoting the prompt and equitable compensation of persons affected by transfrontier pollution, and could also contain procedures facilitating the provision of information and consultation.

3.8 OECD COUNCIL RECOMMENDATION FOR THE IMPLEMENTATION OF A REGIME OF EQUAL RIGHT OF ACCESS AND NON-DISCRIMINATION IN RELATION TO TRANSFRONTIER POLLUTION (WITH ANNEX). Adopted 17 May 1977. 1977 O.E.C.D. C(77)28, O.E.C.D. 150, 16 I.L.M. 977 (1977)

The Council,

Having regard to Article 5(b) of the Convention on the Organisation for Economic Co-operation and Development of 14th December, 1960;

Having regard to the Declaration on the Human Environment adopted in Stockholm in June 1972 and in particular Principles 21, 22, 23 and 24 of that Declaration;

Having regard to the Recommendations of the Council of 14th November, 1974, on Principles concerning Transfrontier Pollution and of 11th May, 1976, on Equal Right of Access in relation to Transfrontier Pollution (C(74)224 and C(76)55(Final) and without prejudice to such Recommendations;

Having regard to the Report by the Secretary–General of 18th March, 1977 on the Implementation of a Regime of Equal Right of Access and Non-discrimination in relation to Transfrontier Pollution;

Considering that the protection and improvement of the environment are common objectives of Member countries;

Conscious that pollution originating in the area within the national jurisdiction of a State may have effects on the environment outside this jurisdiction;

Considering that the implementation of a regime of equal right of access and non-discrimination among Member countries should lead to improved protection of the environment without prejudice to other channels available for the solution of transfrontier problems;

On the proposal of the Environment Committee;

RECOMMENDS that Member Countries, in regard to each other, take into account the principles concerning transfrontier pollution set forth in the Annex to this Recommendation, which is an integral part of it, in their domestic legislation, possibly on the basis of reciprocity, notably regarding individual rights, and in bilateral or multilateral international agreements.

ANNEX

Introduction

This Annex sets out a number of principles intended to promote the implementation between Member countries of a regime of equal right of access and non-discrimination in matters of transfrontier pollution, while maintaining a fair balance of rights and obligations between Countries concerned by such pollution.

These principles do not prejudice any more favourable measures for the protection of the environment and of persons whose property, rights or interests are or could be affected by pollution the origin of which is situated within the area under the jurisdiction of a Member country.

For the purposes of this Recommendation:

a) "Pollution" means any introduction by man, directly or indirectly, of substance or energy into the environment resulting in deleterious effects of such a nature as to endanger human health, harm living resources and eco-systems, impair amenities or interfere with other legitimate uses of the environment;

b) "Domestic pollution" means any intentional or unintentional pollution, the physical origin of which is situated wholly within the area under the national jurisdiction of one Country and which has effects within that area only.

c) "Transfrontier pollution" means any intentional or unintentional pollution whose physical origin is subject to, and situated wholly or in part within the area under, the national jurisdiction of one Country and which has effects in the area under the national jurisdiction of another Country;

d) "Country" means any Member country which participates in this Recommendation;

e) "Country of origin" means any Country within which, and subject to the jurisdiction of which, transfrontier pollution originates or could originate in connection with activities carried on or contemplated in that Country;

f) "Exposed Country" means any Country affected by transfrontier pollution or exposed to a significant risk of transfrontier pollution;

g) "Countries concerned" means any Country of origin of transfrontier pollution and any Country exposed to such pollution;

h) "Regions concerned by transfrontier pollution" means any region of origin of transfrontier pollution in the Country of origin and any regions of the Country of origin and of any exposed Country where such pollution produces or might produce its effects;

i) "Persons" means any natural or legal person, either private or public;

j) "Regime of environmental protection" means any set of statutory and administrative measures related to the protection of the environment, including those concerning the property, rights or interests of persons.

Title A. PRINCIPLES TO FACILITATE THE SOLUTION AT INTER-STATE LEVEL OF TRANSFRONTIER POLLUTION PROBLEMS

1. When preparing and giving effect to their policies affecting the environment, Countries should, consistent with their obligations and rights as regards the protection of the environment, take fully into consideration the effects of such policies on the environment of exposed Countries so as to protect such environment against transfrontier pollution.

2. With a view to improved protection of the environment, Countries should attempt by common agreement to:

a) make their environmental policies mutually compatible, particularly those bearing on regions concerned by transfrontier pollution;

b) bring closer together quality objectives and environmental standards adopted by Countries, apply them systematically to cases of transfrontier pollution and, where necessary, improve those already in force;

c) work out additional rules of conduct of States to be applied in matters of transfrontier pollution.

3. a) Pending the implementation of the objectives laid down in paragraph 2, and without prejudice to more favourable measures taken in accordance with paragraphs 1 and 2 above, each Country should ensure that its regime of environmental protection does not discriminate between pollution originating from it which affects or is likely to affect the area under its national jurisdiction and pollution originating from it which affects or is likely to affect an exposed Country.

b) Thus, transfrontier pollution problems should be treated by the Country of origin in an equivalent way to similar domestic pollution problems occurring under comparable conditions in the Country of origin.

c) In the event of difficulties arising between Countries concerned because the situations resulting from transfrontier pollution and domestic pollution are manifestly not comparable, for example as a result of uncoordinated land use policies in regions concerned by transfrontier pollution, those countries should strive to arrive at a mutually agreed arrangement which ensures to the largest extent possible the application of the principle referred to in sub-paragraph (a) of this paragraph.

Title B. LEGAL PROTECTION OF PERSONS

4. a) Countries of origin should ensure that any person who has suffered transfrontier pollution damage or is exposed to a significant risk of transfrontier pollution, shall at least receive equivalent treatment to that afforded in the Country of origin in cases of domestic pollution and in comparable circumstances, to persons of equivalent condition or status.

b) From a procedural standpoint, this treatment includes the right to take part in, or have resort to, all administrative and judicial procedures existing within the Country of origin, in order to prevent domestic pollution, to have it abated and/or to obtain compensation for the damage caused.

5. Where in spite of the existence of a liability ceiling instituted by an international agreement, there exists in a Country a system of additional compensation financed or administered by the public authorities, then such Country should not be required in the absence of reciprocal arrangements to grant entitlement to such additional compensation to victims of transfrontier pollution, but it should in advance inform the exposed Countries of the particular situation.

6. a) Where the domestic law of Countries permits private non profit legal persons that are resident within their own territories, such as environmental defence associations, to commence proceedings to safeguard environmental interests which it is their aim to protect, those Countries should grant the same right for comparable matters to similar legal persons resident in exposed Countries, provided that the latter satisfy the conditions laid down for the former in the Country of origin.

b) When some of the conditions concerning matters of form laid down in the Country of origin cannot reasonably be imposed on legal persons resident in an exposed Country, these latter should be entitled to commence proceedings in the Country of origin if they satisfy comparable conditions.

7. When the law of a Country of origin permits a public authority to participate in administrative or judicial proceedings in order to safeguard general environmental interests, the Country of origin should consider, if its legal system allows it, providing, by means of international agreement if it deems it necessary, competent public authorities of exposed Countries with access to such proceedings.

Title C. EXCHANGE OF INFORMATION AND CONSULTATION

8. a) The Country of origin, on its own initiative or at the request of an exposed Country, should communicate to the latter appropriate information concerning it in matters of transfrontier pollution or significant risk of such pollution (and enter into consultations with it)

b) In order to enable a Country of origin to implement adequately the principles set out in Title A of this Recommendation, each exposed Country should, on its own initiative or at the request of the Country of origin, supply appropriate information of mutual concern.

c) Each Country should designate one or more authorities entitled to receive directly information communicated under subparagraphs (a) and (b) of this paragraph.

9. a) Countries of origin should take any appropriate measures to provide persons exposed to a significant risk of transfrontier pollution with sufficient information to enable them to exercise in a timely manner the rights referred to in this Recommendation. As far as possible, such information should be equivalent to that provided in the Country of origin in cases of comparable domestic pollution.

b) Exposed Countries should designate one or more authorities which will have the duty to receive and the responsibility to disseminate such information within limits of time compatible with the exercise of existing procedures in the Country of origin.

10. Countries should encourage and facilitate regular contacts between representatives designated by them at regional and/or local levels in order to examine such transfrontier pollution matters as may arise.

3.9 CONVENTION ON LONG–RANGE TRANSBOUNDARY AIR POLLUTION (LRTAP) (WITHOUT PROTOCOLS).[1] But see Basic Document 3.19, infra. Concluded at Geneva, 13 November 1979. Entered into force, 16 March 1983. 1302 U.N.T.S. 217, 18 I.L.M. 1442 (1979), T.I.A.S. No. 10541

The Parties to the present Convention,

Determined to promote relations and co-operation in the field of environmental protection,

Aware of the significance of the activities of the United Nations Economic Commission for Europe in strengthening such relations and co-operation, particularly in the field of air pollution including long-range transport of air pollutants,

Recognizing the contribution of the Economic Commission for Europe to the multilateral implementation of the pertinent provisions of the Final Act of the Conference on Security and Co-operation in Europe,

Cognizant of the references in the chapter on environment of the Final Act of the Conference on Security and Co-operation in Europe calling for co-operation to control air pollution and its effects, including long-range transport of air pollutants, and to the development through international co-operation of an extensive programme for the monitoring and evaluation of long-range transport of air pollutants, starting with sulphur dioxide and with possible extension to other pollutants,

Considering the pertinent provisions of the Declaration of the United Nations Conference on the Human Environment, and in particular principle 21, which expresses the common conviction that States have, in accordance with the Charter of the United Nations and the principles of international law, the sovereign right to exploit their own resources pursuant to their own environmental policies, and the responsibility to ensure that activities within their jurisdiction or control do not cause damage to the environment of other States or of areas beyond the limits of natural jurisdiction,

Recognizing the existence of possible adverse effects, in the short and long term, of air pollution including transboundary air pollution,

Concerned that a rise in the level of emissions of air pollutants within the region as forecast may increase such adverse effects,

Recognizing the need to study the implications of the long-range transport of air pollutants and the need to seek solutions for the problems identified,

Affirming their willingness to reinforce active international co-operation to develop appropriate national policies and by means of exchange of information, consultation, research and monitoring, to co-ordinate national action for combating air pollution including long-range transboundary air pollution,

Have agreed as follows:

DEFINITIONS
Article 1

For the purposes of the present Convention:

1. *But see* Basic Document 3.19, *infra.*

(a) *"air pollution"* means the introduction by man, directly or indirectly, of substances or energy into the air resulting in deleterious effects of such a nature as to endanger human health, harm living resources and ecosystems and material property and impair or interfere with amenities and other legitimate uses of the environment, and "air pollutants" shall be construed accordingly;

(b) *"long-range transboundary air pollution"* means air pollution whose physical origin is situated wholly or in part within the area under the national jurisdiction of one State and which has adverse effects in the area under the jurisdiction of another State at such a distance that it is not generally possible to distinguish the contribution of individual emission sources or groups of sources.

FUNDAMENTAL PRINCIPLES

Article 2

The Contracting Parties, taking due account of the facts and problems involved, are determined to protect man and his environment against air pollution and shall endeavour to limit and, as far as possible, gradually reduce and prevent air pollution including long-range transboundary air pollution.

Article 3

The Contracting Parties, within the framework of the present Convention, shall by means of exchanges of information, consultation, research and monitoring, develop without undue delay policies and strategies which shall serve as a means of combating the discharge of air pollutants, taking into account efforts already made at national and international levels.

Article 4

The Contracting Parties shall exchange information on and review their policies, scientific activities and technical measures aimed at combating, as far as possible, the discharge of air pollutants which may have adverse effects, thereby contributing to the reduction of air pollution including long-range transboundary air pollution.

Article 5

Consultations shall be held, upon request, at an early stage between, on the one hand, Contracting Parties which are actually affected by or exposed to a significant risk of long-range transboundary air pollution and, on the other hand, Contracting Parties within which and subject to whose jurisdiction a significant contribution to long-range transboundary air pollution originates, or could originate, in connexion with activities carried on or contemplated therein.

AIR QUALITY MANAGEMENT

Article 6

Taking into account articles 2 to 5, the ongoing research, exchange of information and monitoring and the results thereof, the cost and effectiveness of local and other remedies and, in order to combat air pollution, in particular that originating from new or rebuilt installations, each Contracting Party undertakes to develop the best policies and strategies including air quality management systems and, as part of them, control measures compatible with balanced development, in particular by using the best available technology which is economically feasible and low- and non-waste technology.

RESEARCH AND DEVELOPMENT

Article 7

The Contracting Parties, as appropriate to their needs, shall initiate and co-operate in the conduct of research into and/or development of:

(a) existing and proposed technologies for reducing emissions of sulphur compounds and other major air pollutants, including technical and economic feasibility, and environmental consequences;

(b) instrumentation and other techniques for monitoring and measuring emission rates and ambient concentrations of air pollutants;

(c) improved models for a better understanding of the transmission of long-range transboundary air pollutants;

(d) the effects of sulphur compounds and other major air pollutants on human health and the environment, including agriculture, forestry, materials, aquatic and other natural ecosystems and visibility, with a view to establishing a scientific basis for dose/effect relationships designed to protect the environment;

(e) the economic, social and environmental assessment of alternative measures for attaining environmental objectives including the reduction of long-range transboundary air pollution;

(f) education and training programmes related to the environmental aspects of pollution by sulphur compounds and other major air pollutants.

EXCHANGE OF INFORMATION

Article 8

The Contracting Parties, within the framework of the Executive Body referred to in article 10 and bilaterally, shall, in their common interests, exchange available information on:

(a) data on emissions at periods of time to be agreed upon, of agreed air pollutants, starting with sulphur dioxide, coming from grid-units of agreed size; or on the fluxes of agreed air pollutants, starting with sulphur dioxide, across national borders, at distances and at periods of time to be agreed upon;

(b) major changes in national policies and in general industrial development, and their potential impact, which would be likely to cause significant changes in long-range transboundary air pollution;

(c) control technologies for reducing air pollution relevant to long-range transboundary air pollution;

(d) the projected cost of the emission control of sulphur compounds and other major air pollutants on a national scale;

(e) meteorological and physico-chemical data relating to the processes during transmission;

(f) physico-chemical and biological data relating to the effects of long-range transboundary air pollution and the extent of the damage which these data indicate can be attributed to long-range transboundary air pollution;

(g) national, subregional and regional policies and strategies for the control of sulphur compounds and other major air pollutants.

IMPLEMENTATION AND FURTHER DEVELOPMENT OF THE CO–OPERATIVE PROGRAMME FOR THE MONITORING AND EVALUATION OF THE LONG–RANGE TRANSMISSION OF AIR POLLUTANTS IN EUROPE

Article 9

The Contracting Parties stress the need for the implementation of the existing "Co-operative programme for the monitoring and evaluation of the long-range transmission of air pollutants in Europe" (hereinafter referred to as EMEP) and, with regard to the further development of this programme, agree to emphasize:

(a) the desirability of Contracting Parties joining in and fully implementing EMEP which, as a first step, is based on the monitoring of sulphur dioxide and related substances;

(b) the need to use comparable or standardized procedures for monitoring whenever possible;

(c) the desirability of basing the monitoring programme on the framework of both national and international programmes. The establishment of monitoring stations and the collection of data shall be carried out under the national jurisdiction of the country in which the monitoring stations are located;

(d) the desirability of establishing a framework for a co-operative environmental monitoring programme, based on and taking into account present and future national, subregional, regional and other international programmes;

(e) the need to exchange data on emissions at periods of time to be agreed upon, of agreed air pollutants, starting with sulphur dioxide, coming from grid-units of agreed size; or on the fluxes of agreed air pollutants, starting with sulphur dioxide, across national borders, at distances and at periods of time to be agreed upon. The method, including the model, used to determine the fluxes, as well as the method, including the model, used to determine the transmission of air pollutants based on the emissions per grid-unit, shall be made available and periodically reviewed, in order to improve the methods and the models;

(f) their willingness to continue the exchange and periodic updating of national data on total emissions of agreed air pollutants, starting with sulphur dioxide;

(g) the need to provide meteorological and physico-chemical data relating to processes during transmission;

(h) the need to monitor chemical components in other media such as water, soil and vegetation, as well as a similar monitoring programme to record effects on health and environment;

(i) the desirability of extending the national EMEP networks to make them operational for control and surveillance purposes.

EXECUTIVE BODY
Article 10

1.   The representatives of the Contracting Parties shall, within the framework of the Senior Advisers to ECE Governments on Environmental Problems, constitute the Executive Body of the present Convention, and shall meet at least annually in that capacity.

2.   The Executive Body shall:

(a) review the implementation of the present Convention;

(b) establish, as appropriate, working groups to consider matters related to the implementation and development of the present Convention and to this end to prepare appropriate studies and other documentation and to submit recommendations to be considered by the Executive Body;

(c) fulfil such other functions as may be appropriate under the provisions of the present Convention.

3.   The Executive Body shall utilize the Steering Body for the EMEP to play an integral part in the operation of the present Convention, in particular with regard to data collection and scientific co-operation.

4.   The Executive Body, in discharging its functions, shall, when it deems appropriate, also make use of information from other relevant international organizations.

SECRETARIAT
Article 11

The Executive Secretary of the Economic Commission for Europe shall carry out, for the Executive Body, the following secretariat functions:

(a) to convene and prepare the meetings of the Executive Body;

(b) to transmit to the Contracting Parties reports and other information received in accordance with the provisions of the present Convention;

(c) to discharge the functions assigned by the Executive Body.

AMENDMENTS TO THE CONVENTION
Article 12

1.   Any Contracting Party may propose amendments to the present Convention.

2.   The text of proposed amendments shall be submitted in writing to the Executive Secretary of the Economic Commission for Europe, who shall communicate them to all Contracting Parties. The Executive Body shall discuss proposed amendments at its next annual meeting provided that such proposals have been circulated by the Executive Secretary of the Economic Commission for Europe to the Contracting Parties at least ninety days in advance.

3.   An amendment to the present Convention shall be adopted by consensus of the representatives of the Contracting Parties, and shall enter into

force for the Contracting Parties which have accepted it on the ninetieth day after the date on which two-thirds of the Contracting Parties have deposited their instruments of acceptance with the depositary. Thereafter, the amendment shall enter into force for any other Contracting Party on the ninetieth day after the date on which that Contracting Party deposits its instrument of acceptance of the amendment.

SETTLEMENT OF DISPUTES
Article 13

If a dispute arises between two or more Contracting Parties to the present Convention as to the interpretation or application of the Convention, they shall seek a solution by negotiation or by any other method of dispute settlement acceptable to the parties to the dispute.

SIGNATURE
Article 14

1. The present Convention shall be open for signature at the United Nations Office at Geneva from 13 to 16 November 1979 on the occasion of the High-level Meeting within the framework of the Economic Commission for Europe on the Protection of the Environment, by the member States of the Economic Commission for Europe as well as States having consultative status with the Economic Commission for Europe, pursuant to paragraph 8 of Economic and Social Council resolution 36 (IV) of 28 March 1947, and by regional economic integration organizations, constituted by sovereign States members of the Economic Commission for Europe, which have competence in respect of the negotiation, conclusion and application of international agreements in matters covered by the present Convention.

2. In matters within their competence, such regional economic integration organizations shall, on their own behalf, exercise the rights and fulfil the responsibilities which the present Convention attributes to their member States. In such cases, the member States of these organizations shall not be entitled to exercise such rights individually.

RATIFICATION, ACCEPTANCE, APPROVAL AND ACCESSION
Article 15

1. The present Convention shall be subject to ratification, acceptance or approval.

2. The present Convention shall be open for accession as from 17 November 1979 by the States and organizations referred to in article 14, paragraph 1.

3. The instruments of ratification, acceptance, approval or accession shall be deposited with the Secretary–General of the United Nations, who will perform the functions of the depositary.

ENTRY INTO FORCE
Article 16

1. The present Convention shall enter into force on the ninetieth day after the date of deposit of the twenty-fourth instrument of ratification, acceptance, approval or accession.

2. For each Contracting Party which ratifies, accepts or approves the present Convention or accedes thereto after the deposit of the twenty-fourth instrument of ratification, acceptance, approval or accession, the Convention shall enter into force on the ninetieth day after the date of deposit by such Contracting Party of its instrument of ratification, acceptance, approval or accession.

WITHDRAWAL
Article 17

At any time after five years from the date on which the present Convention has come into force with respect to a Contracting Party, that Contracting Party may withdraw from the Convention by giving written notification to the depositary. Any such withdrawal shall take effect on the ninetieth day after the date of its receipt by the depositary.

AUTHENTIC TEXTS
Article 18

The original of the present Convention, of which the English, French and Russian texts are equally authentic, shall be deposited with the Secretary-General of the United Nations.

3.10 AGREEMENT GOVERNING THE ACTIVITIES OF STATES ON THE MOON AND OTHER CELESTIAL BODIES.[1] Concluded at New York, 5 December 1979. Entered into force, 11 July 1984. G.A.Res. 34/68, U.N. GAOR, 34th Sess., Supp. No. 46, at 77, U.N. Doc. A/RES/ 34/68 (1979), 18 I.L.M. 1434 (1979)

Article 1

1. The provisions of this Agreement relating to the moon shall also apply to other celestial bodies within the solar system, other than the earth, except in so far as specific legal norms enter into force with respect to any of these celestial bodies.

2. For the purposes of this Agreement reference to the moon shall include orbits around or other trajectories to or around it.

3. This Agreement does not apply to extraterrestrial materials which reach the surface of the earth by natural means.

Article 2

All activities on the moon, including its exploration and use, shall be carried out in accordance with international law, in particular the Charter of the United Nations, and taking into account the Declaration on Principles of International Law concerning Friendly Relations and Co-operation among States in accordance with the Charter of the United Nations, adopted by the General Assembly on 24 October 1970, in the interests of maintaining international peace and security and promoting international co-operation and mutual understanding, and with due regard to the corresponding interests of all other States Parties.

Article 3

1. The moon shall be used by all States Parties exclusively for peaceful purposes.

2. Any threat or use of force or any other hostile act or threat of hostile act on the moon is prohibited. It is likewise prohibited to use the moon in order to commit any such act or to engage in any such threat in relation to the earth, the moon, spacecraft, the personnel of spacecraft or man-made space objects.

3. States Parties shall not place in orbit around or other trajectory to or around the moon objects carrying nuclear weapons or any other kinds of weapons of mass destruction or place or use such weapons on or in the moon.

4. The establishment of military bases, installations and fortifications, the testing of any type of weapons and the conduct of military manoeuvres on the moon shall be forbidden. The use of military personnel for scientific research or for any other peaceful purposes shall not be prohibited. The use of any equipment or facility necessary for peaceful exploration and use of the moon shall also not be prohibited.

Article 4

1. The exploration and use of the moon shall be the province of all mankind and shall be carried out for the benefit and in the interests of all countries, irrespective of their degree of economic or scientific development.

---

1. Also known as "the Moon Treaty."

Due regard shall be paid to the interests of present and future generations as well as to the need to promote higher standards of living and conditions of economic and social progress and development in accordance with the Charter of the United Nations.

2. States Parties shall be guided by the principle of co-operation and mutual assistance in all their activities concerning the exploration and use of the moon. International co-operation in pursuance of this Agreement should be as wide as possible and may take place on a multilateral basis, on a bilateral basis or through international intergovernmental organizations.

Article 5

1. States Parties shall inform the Secretary–General of the United Nations as well as the public and the international scientific community, to the greatest extent feasible and practicable, of their activities concerned with the exploration and use of the moon. Information on the time, purposes, locations, orbital parameters and duration shall be given in respect of each mission to the moon as soon as possible after launching, while information on the results of each mission, including scientific results, shall be furnished upon completion of the mission. In the case of a mission lasting more than thirty days, information on conduct of the mission, including any scientific results, shall be given periodically at thirty-day intervals. For missions lasting more than six months, only significant additions to such information need be reported thereafter.

2. If a State Party becomes aware that another State Party plans to operate simultaneously in the same area of or in the same orbit around or trajectory to or around the moon, it shall promptly inform the other State of the timing of and plans for its own operations.

3. In carrying out activities under this Agreement, States Parties shall promptly inform the Secretary–General, as well as the public and the international scientific community, of any phenomena they discover in outer space, including the moon, which could endanger human life or health, as well as of any indication of organic life.

Article 6

1. There shall be freedom of scientific investigation on the moon by all States Parties without discrimination of any kind, on the basis of equality and in accordance with international law.

2. In carrying out scientific investigations and in furtherance of the provisions of this Agreement, the States Parties shall have the right to collect on and remove from the moon samples of its mineral and other substances. Such samples shall remain at the disposal of those States Parties which caused them to be collected and may be used by them for scientific purposes. States Parties shall have regard to the desirability of making a portion of such samples available to other interested States Parties and the international scientific community for scientific investigation. States Parties may in the course of scientific investigations also use mineral and other substances of the moon in quantities appropriate for the support of their missions.

3. States Parties agree on the desirability of exchanging scientific and other personnel on expeditions to or installations on the moon to the greatest extent feasible and practicable.

Article 7

1. In exploring and using the moon, States Parties shall take measures to prevent the disruption of the existing balance of its environment whether by introducing adverse changes in that environment, by its harmful contamination through the introduction of extra-environmental matter or otherwise. States Parties shall also take measures to avoid harmfully affecting the environment of the earth through the introduction of extraterrestrial matter or otherwise.

2. States Parties shall inform the Secretary–General of the United Nations of the measures being adopted by them in accordance with paragraph 1 of this article and shall also, to the maximum extent feasible, notify him in advance of all placements by them of radio-active materials on the moon and of the purposes of such placements.

3. States Parties shall report to other States Parties and to the Secretary–General concerning areas of the moon having special scientific interest in order that, without prejudice to the rights of other States Parties, consideration may be given to the designation of such areas as international scientific preserves for which special protective arrangements are to be agreed upon in consultation with the competent bodies of the United Nations.

Article 8

1. States Parties may pursue their activities in the exploration and use of the moon anywhere on or below its surface, subject to the provisions of this Agreement.

2. For these purposes States Parties may, in particular:

(a) Land their space objects on the moon and launch them from the moon;

(b) Place their personnel, space vehicles, equipment, facilities, stations and installations anywhere on or below the surface of the moon.

Personnel, space vehicles, equipment, facilities, stations and installations may move or be moved freely over or below the surface of the moon.

3. Activities of States Parties in accordance with paragraphs 1 and 2 of this article shall not interfere with the activities of other States Parties on the moon. Where such interference may occur, the States Parties concerned shall undertake consultations in accordance with article 15, paragraphs 2 and 3 of this Agreement.

Article 9

1. States Parties may establish manned and unmanned stations on the moon. A State Party establishing a station shall use only that area which is required for the needs of the station and shall immediately inform the Secretary–General of the United Nations of the location and purposes of that station. Subsequently, at annual intervals that State shall likewise inform the Secretary–General whether the station continues in use and whether its purposes have changed.

2. Stations shall be installed in such a manner that they do not impede the free access to all areas of the moon by personnel, vehicles and equipment of other States Parties conducting activities on the moon in accordance with

the provisions of this Agreement or of article I of the Treaty on Principles Governing the Activities of States in the Exploration and Use of Outer Space, including the Moon and Other Celestial Bodies.

Article 10

1.   States Parties shall adopt all practicable measures to safeguard the life and health of persons on the moon.   For this purpose they shall regard any person on the moon as an astronaut within the meaning of article V of the Treaty on Principles Governing the Activities of States in the Exploration and Use of Outer Space, including the Moon and Other Celestial Bodies and as part of the personnel of a spacecraft within the meaning of the Agreement on the Rescue of Astronauts, the Return of Astronauts and the Return of Objects Launched into Outer Space.

2.   States Parties shall offer shelter in their stations, installations, vehicles and other facilities to persons in distress on the moon.

Article 11

1.   The moon and its natural resources are the common heritage of mankind, which finds its expression in the provisions of this Agreement and in particular in paragraph 5 of this article.

2.   The moon is not subject to national appropriation by any claim of sovereignty, by means of use or occupation, or by any other means.

3.   Neither the surface nor the subsurface of the moon, nor any part thereof or natural resources in place, shall become property of any State, international intergovernmental or non-governmental organization, national organization or non-governmental entity or of any natural person.   The placement of personnel, space vehicles, equipment, facilities, stations and installations on or below the surface of the moon, including structures connected with its surface or subsurface, shall not create a right of ownership over the surface or the subsurface of the moon or any areas thereof.   The foregoing provisions are without prejudice to the international régime referred to in paragraph 5 of this article.

4.   States Parties have the right to exploration and use of the moon without discrimination of any kind, on a basis of equality and in accordance with international law and the terms of this Agreement.

5.   States Parties to this Agreement hereby undertake to establish an international régime, including appropriate procedures, to govern the exploitation of the natural resources of the moon as such exploitation is about to become feasible.   This provision shall be implemented in accordance with article 18 of this Agreement.

6.   In order to facilitate the establishment of the international régime referred to in paragraph 5 of this article, States Parties shall inform the Secretary–General of the United Nations as well as the public and the international scientific community, to the greatest extent feasible and practicable, of any natural resources they may discover on the moon.

7.   The main purposes of the international régime to be established shall include:

(a) The orderly and safe development of the natural resources of the moon;

(b) The rational management of those resources;

(c) The expansion of opportunities in the use of those resources;

(d) An equitable sharing by all States Parties in the benefits derived from those resources, whereby the interests and needs of the developing countries, as well as the efforts of those countries which have contributed either directly or indirectly to the exploration of the moon, shall be given special consideration.

8. All the activities with respect to the natural resources of the moon shall be carried out in a manner compatible with the purposes specified in paragraph 7 of this article and the provisions of article 6, paragraph 2, of this Agreement.

Article 12

1. States Parties shall retain jurisdiction and control over their personnel, vehicles, equipment, facilities, stations and installations on the moon. The ownership of space vehicles, equipment, facilities, stations and installations shall not be affected by their presence on the moon.

2. Vehicles, installations and equipment or their component parts found in places other than their intended location shall be dealt with in accordance with article 5 of the Agreement on Rescue of Astronauts, the Return of Astronauts and the Return of Objects Launched into Outer Space.

3. In the event of an emergency involving a threat to human life, States Parties may use the equipment, vehicles, installations, facilities or supplies of other States Parties on the moon. Prompt notification of such use shall be made to the Secretary–General of the United Nations or the State Party concerned.

Article 13

A State Party which learns of the crash landing, forced landing or other unintended landing on the moon of a space object, or its component parts, that were not launched by it, shall promptly inform the launching State Party and the Secretary–General of the United Nations.

Article 14

1. States Parties to this Agreement shall bear international responsibility for national activities on the moon, whether such activities are carried on by governmental agencies or by non-governmental entities, and for assuring that national activities are carried out in conformity with the provisions set forth in this Agreement. States Parties shall ensure that non-governmental entities under their jurisdiction shall engage in activities on the moon only under the authority and continuing supervision of the appropriate State Party.

2. States Parties recognize that detailed arrangements concerning liability for damage caused on the moon, in addition to the provisions of the Treaty on Principles Governing the Activities of States in the Exploration and Use of Outer Space, including the Moon and Other Celestial Bodies and the Convention on International Liability for Damage Caused by Space Objects, may become necessary as a result of more extensive activities on the moon. Any such arrangements shall be elaborated in accordance with the procedure provided for in article 18 of this Agreement.

Article 15

1.   Each State Party may assure itself that the activities of other States Parties in the exploration and use of the moon are compatible with the provisions of this Agreement.   To this end, all space vehicles, equipment, facilities, stations and installations on the moon shall be open to other States Parties.   Such States Parties shall give reasonable advance notice of a projected visit, in order that appropriate consultations may be held and that maximum precautions may be taken to assure safety and to avoid interference with normal operations in the facility to be visited.   In pursuance of this article, any State Party may act on its own behalf or with the full or partial assistance of any other State Party or through appropriate international procedures within the framework of the United Nations and in accordance with the Charter.

2.   A State Party which has reason to believe that another State Party is not fulfilling the obligations incumbent upon it pursuant to this Agreement or that another State Party is interfering with the rights which the former State has under this Agreement may request consultations with that State Party. A State Party receiving such a request shall enter into such consultations without delay.   Any other State Party which requests to do so shall be entitled to take part in the consultations.   Each State Party participating in such consultations shall seek a mutually acceptable resolution of any controversy and shall bear in mind the rights and interests of all States Parties. The Secretary–General of the United Nations shall be informed of the results of the consultations and shall transmit the information received to all States Parties concerned.

3.   If the consultations do not lead to a mutually acceptable settlement which has due regard for the rights and interests of all States Parties, the parties concerned shall take all measures to settle the dispute by other peaceful means of their choice appropriate to the circumstances and the nature of the dispute.   If difficulties arise in connexion with the opening of consultations or if consultations do not lead to a mutually acceptable settlement, any State Party may seek the assistance of the Secretary–General, without seeking the consent of any other State Party concerned, in order to resolve the controversy.   A State Party which does not maintain diplomatic relations with another State Party concerned shall participate in such consultations, at its choice, either itself or through another State Party or the Secretary–General as intermediary.

Article 16

With the exception of articles 17 to 21, references in this Agreement to States shall be deemed to apply to any international intergovernmental organization which conducts space activities if the organization declares its acceptance of the rights and obligations provided for in this Agreement and if a majority of the States members of the organization are States Parties to this Agreement and to the Treaty on Principles Governing the Activities of States in the Exploration and Use of Outer Space, including the Moon and Other Celestial Bodies.   States members of any such organization which are States Parties to this Agreement shall take all appropriate steps to ensure that the organization makes a declaration in accordance with the foregoing.

Article 17

Any State Party to this Agreement may propose amendments to the Agreement. Amendments shall enter into force for each State Party to the Agreement accepting the amendments upon their acceptance by a majority of the States Parties to the Agreement and thereafter for each remaining State Party to the Agreement on the date of acceptance by it.

Article 18

Ten years after the entry into force of this Agreement, the question of the review of the Agreement shall be included in the provisional agenda of the General Assembly of the United Nations in order to consider, in the light of past application of the Agreement, whether it requires revision. However, at any time after the Agreement has been in force for five years, the Secretary–General of the United Nations, as depository, shall, at the request of one third of the States Parties to the Agreement and with the concurrence of the majority of the States Parties, convene a conference of the States Parties to review this Agreement. A review conference shall also consider the question of the implementation of the provisions of article 11, paragraph 5, on the basis of the principle referred to in paragraph 1 of that article and taking into account in particular any relevant technological developments.

Article 19

1. This Agreement shall be open for signature by all States at United Nations Headquarters in New York.

2. This Agreement shall be subject to ratification by signatory States. Any State which does not sign this Agreement before its entry into force in accordance with paragraph 3 of this article may accede to it at any time. Instruments of ratification or accession shall be deposited with the Secretary–General of the United Nations.

3. This Agreement shall enter into force on the thirtieth day following the date of deposit of the fifth instrument of ratification.

4. For each State depositing its instrument of ratification or accession after the entry into force of this Agreement, it shall enter into force on the thirtieth day following the date of deposit of any such instrument.

5. The Secretary–General shall promptly inform all signatory and acceding States of the date of each signature, the date of deposit of each instrument of ratification or accession to this Agreement, the date of its entry into force and other notices.

Article 20

Any State Party to this Agreement may give notice of its withdrawal from the Agreement one year after its entry into force by written notification to the Secretary–General of the United Nations. Such withdrawal shall take effect one year from the date of receipt of this notification.

3.11 EUROPEAN COMMUNITIES COUNCIL DIRECTIVE NO. 80/779 ON AIR QUALITY LIMIT VALUES (WITHOUT ANNEXES BUT AS AMENDED). Adopted at Brussels, 15 July 1980. L229 O.J.E.C. 30 (1980)

THE COUNCIL OF THE EUROPEAN COMMUNITIES,

Having regard to the Treaty establishing the European Economic Community, and in particular Articles 100 and 235 thereof,

Having regard to the proposal from the Commission,

Having regard to the opinion of the European Parliament,

Having regard to the opinion of the Economic and Social Committee,

Whereas the European Communities' programmes of action on the environment of 1973 and 1977 provide that priority is to be given to measures against sulphur dioxide and suspended particulates because of their toxicity and the current state of knowledge of their effects on human health and the environment;

Whereas, since any discrepancy between the provisions already applicable or being prepared in the various Member States with regard to sulphur dioxide and suspended particulates could give rise to unequal conditions of competition and could consequently directly affect the functioning of the common market, the legislative provisions in this area should be harmonized as prescribed in Article 100 of the Treaty;

Whereas one of the basic tasks of the European Economic Community is to promote throughout the Community a harmonious development of economic activities and a continued and balanced expansion; whereas such an achievement is inconceivable without measures to combat pollution, improve the quality of life and protect the environment; whereas, since the Treaty has not provided the necessary powers in this field, Article 235 of the Treaty must be invoked;

Whereas, in order to protect human health in particular, it is necessary to set for these two pollutants limit values which must not be exceeded in the territory of the Member States during specified periods; whereas these values should be based on the findings reached in the framework of the WHO, particularly with regard to the dose/effect relationships established for sulphur dioxide and suspended particulates taken together;

Whereas, despite the measures taken, it may not be possible to comply with these limit values in certain zones; whereas the Member States must therefore be allowed temporary derogations on condition that they forward to the Commission plans for the progressive improvement of the quality of the air in those zones;

Whereas guide values should also be set to serve as long-term precautions for health and the environment and as reference points for the establishment of specific schemes within zones determined by the Member States;

Whereas the measures taken pursuant to this Directive must be economically feasible and compatible with balanced development;

Whereas it is necessary to establish suitable monitoring of air quality and particularly of observance of the limit values; whereas the Member States should therefore be obliged to establish measuring stations to supply the data necessary for the application of the Directive;

Whereas since different sampling and analysis methods are applied in the Member States, it is necessary to permit, under certain conditions, the use of sampling and measurement methods other than the reference methods laid down in the Directive;

Whereas, since some Member States use particular methods of sampling and analysis which cannot easily be correlated with the reference methods, it is necessary that the Directive specify different limit values which are to be respected where such methods are used; whereas the Member States concerned should also carry out parallel measurements at a series of representative stations using the reference methods in addition to their own methods of measurement; whereas the Commission must make further proposals in the light of these parallel measurements and of the need to avoid discriminatory provisions;

Whereas the subsequent development of reference methods of sampling and analysis referred to in this Directive may be desirable in the light of technical and scientific progress in this area; whereas in order to facilitate implementation of the work necessary to this end, a procedure should be set up to establish close cooperation between the Member States and the Commission within a Committee on Adaptation to Scientific and Technical Progress,

HAS ADOPTED THIS DIRECTIVE:

Article 1

The purpose of this Directive is to fix limit values (Annex I) and guide values (Annex II) for sulphur dioxide and suspended particulates in the atmosphere and the conditions for their application in order to improve:

— the protection of human health,

— the protection of the environment.

Article 2

1. 'Limit values' means:

— the concentrations of sulphur dioxide and suspended particulates considered simultaneously in accordance with Table A in Annex I, and

— the concentrations of suspended particulates considered separately in accordance with Table B in Annex I,

which, in order to protect human health in particular, must not be exceeded throughout the territory of the Member States during specified periods and under the conditions laid down in the following Articles.

2. 'Guide values' means the concentrations of sulphur dioxide and suspended particulates over specified periods which are given in Annex II and are intended to serve as:

— long-term precautions for health and the environment,

— reference points for the establishment of specific schemes within zones determined by the Member States.

Article 3

1. Member States shall take appropriate measures to ensure that as from 1 April 1983 the concentrations of sulphur dioxide and suspended particulates in the atmosphere are not greater than the limit values given in Annex I, without prejudice to the following provisions.

2. Where a Member State considers that there is a likelihood that, despite the measures taken, the concentrations of sulphur dioxide and suspended particulates in the atmosphere might, after 1 April 1983, exceed in certain zones the limit values given in Annex I, it shall inform the Commission thereof before 1 October 1982.

It shall at the same time forward to the Commission plans for the progressive improvement of the quality of the air in those zones. These plans, drawn up on the basis of relevant information on the nature, origin and evolution of the pollution, shall describe in particular the measures taken or to be taken and the procedures implemented or to be implemented by the Member State concerned. These measures and procedures must bring the concentrations of sulphur dioxide and suspended particulates in the atmosphere within these zones to values below or equal to the limit values given in Annex I as soon as possible and by 1 April 1993 at the latest.

Article 4

1. In the zones in which the Member State concerned considers it necessary to limit or prevent a foreseeable increase in pollution by sulphur dioxide and suspended particulates in the wake of development, in particular urban or industrial development, the Member State shall, taking the guide values in Annex II as a reference point, fix values which must be lower than the limit values in Annex I.

2. In zones on its territory which the Member State concerned considers should be afforded special environmental protection, the Member State shall fix values which are generally lower than the guide values in Annex II.

3. Member States shall inform the Commission of the values, deadlines and timetables they have laid down for the zones referred to in paragraphs 1 and 2, and of any appropriate measures they have taken.

Article 5

In addition to the provisions referred to in Article 3(1) and Article 4(1), Member States shall, with the object of taking further precautions for the protection of health and the environment, endeavour to move towards the guide values in Annex II wherever the measured concentrations are higher than these values.

Article 6

Member States shall establish measuring stations designed to supply the data necessary for the application of this Directive, in particular in zones where the limit values referred to in Article 3(1) are likely to be approached or exceeded and in the zones referred to in Article 3(2); the stations must be located at sites where pollution is thought to be greatest and where the measured concentrations are representative of local conditions.

Article 7

1.   Following the entry into force of this Directive, Member States shall inform the Commission, not later than six months after the end (31 March) of the annual reference period, of instances in which the limit values laid down in Annex I have been exceeded and of the concentrations recorded.

2.   They shall also notify the Commission, not later than one year after the end of the annual reference period, of the reasons for such instances and of the measures they have taken to avoid their recurrence.

3.   In addition, Member States shall forward information to the Commission, at its request, on the concentrations of sulphur dioxide and suspended particulates in any zones they have designated pursuant to Article 4(1) and (2).

Article 8

The Commission shall each year publish a summary report on the application of this Directive.

Article 9

Application of the measures taken pursuant to this Directive must not bring about a significant deterioration in the quality of the air where the level of pollution by sulphur dioxide and suspended particulates at the time of implementation of this Directive is low in relation to the limit values set out in Annex I.

Article 10

1.   For the purposes of applying this Directive, the Member States shall use either the reference methods of sampling and analysis referred to in Annex III or any other method of sampling and analysis in respect of which they demonstrate to the Commission at regular intervals:

— either that it ensures satisfactory correlation of results with those obtained using the reference method;

— or that measurements taken in parallel with the reference method at a series of representative stations chosen in accordance with the requirements laid down in Article 6 show that there is a reasonably stable relationship between the results obtained using that method and those obtained using the reference method.

2.   Without prejudice to the provisions of this Directive, a Member State may also use, pending the decision of the Council on the proposals from the Commission referred to in paragraph 4, the sampling and analysis methods laid down in Annex IV and the values associated with these methods also laid down in Annex IV in substitution for the limit values set out in Annex I.

3.   A Member State which decides to avail itself of the provisions of paragraph 2 must however take measurements in parallel at a series of representative measuring stations, chosen in accordance with the requirements of Article 6, in order to verify the corresponding stringency of the limit values set out in Annex IV and Annex I.   The results of these parallel measurements, including in particular instances in which the limit values laid down in Annex I have been exceeded and the concentrations recorded, shall be

forwarded to the Commission at regular intervals, and at least twice a year, for incorporation in the annual report provided for in Article 8.

4. The Commission shall, after five years, but within six years of the expiry of the limit of 24 months specified in Article 15(1), submit a report to the Council on the results of the parallel measurements carried out under paragraph 3 and shall, having regard in particular to these results and to the need to avoid discriminatory provisions, make proposals relating to paragraph 2 and Annex IV. In the report provided for in Article 8 the Commission will indicate whether it has noted instances in which the limit values fixed in Annex I have been exceeded to a significant extent on repeated occasions.

5. The Commission shall, in selected locations in the Member States and in cooperation with the latter, carry out studies on the sampling and analysis of sulphur dioxide, and of black smoke and suspended particulates. These studies shall be designed in particular to promote the harmonization of methods of sampling and analysis of these pollutants.

Article 11

1. Where Member States fix in border regions values for concentrations of sulphur dioxide and suspended particulates in the atmosphere in accordance with Article 4(1) and (2), they shall hold prior consultations. The Commission may attend such consultations.

2. Where the limit values given in Annex I or the values referred to in Article 4(1) and (2), inasmuch as the latter values have been the subject of consultations in accordance with paragraph 1, are or might be exceeded following significant pollution which originates or may have originated in another Member State, the Member States concerned shall hold consultations with a view to remedying the situation. The Commission may attend such consultations.

Article 12

The procedure laid down in Articles 13 and 14 for the adaptation on this Directive to technical progress shall cover the subsequent development of the reference methods of sampling and analysis referred to in Annex III. This adaptation must not result in any direct or indirect modification of effective concentration values given in Annexes I and II.

Article 13

1. For the purpose of Article 12 a Committee on the adaptation of this Directive to scientific and technical progress, hereinafter called 'the Committee', shall be set up; it shall consist of representatives of the Member States, with a Commission representative as chairman.

2. The Committee shall adopt its own rules of procedure.

Article 14

1. Where the procedure laid down in this Article is invoked, the Committee shall be convened by the chairman, either on his own initiative or at the request of the representative of a Member State.

2. The Commission representative shall submit a draft of the measures to be taken to the Committee. The Committee shall give its opinion on the draft within a time limit set by the chairman having regard to the urgency of

the matter. Decisions shall be taken by a majority of 41 votes, the votes of the Member States being weighted as provided in Article 148(2) of the Treaty. The chairman shall not vote.

3. The Commission shall adopt the proposed measures if they are consistent with the opinion of the Committee.

Where the proposed measures are not consistent with the opinion of the Committee, or if no opinion is delivered, the Commission shall without delay submit to the Council a proposal on the measures to be taken. The Council shall decide by a qualified majority.

If within three months of the proposal being submitted to it the Council has not acted, the proposed measures shall be adopted by the Commission.

Article 15

1. Member States shall bring into force the laws, regulations and administrative provisions necessary to comply with this Directive within 24 months of its notification and shall forthwith inform the Commission thereof.

2. Member States shall communicate to the Commission the texts of the provisions of national law which they adopt in the field covered by this Directive.

Article 16

This Directive is addressed to the Member States.

AMENDMENT TO DIRECTIVE NO. 80/779/EEC (89/427/EEC, 14 July 1989)

THE COUNCIL OF THE EUROPEAN COMMUNITIES,

Having regard to the Treaty establishing the European Economic Community, and in particular Article 130s thereof,

Having regard to the proposal from the Commission,

Having regard to the opinion of the European Parliament,

Having regard to the opinion of the Economic and Social Committee,

Whereas the European Communities' 1973, 1977, 1983 and 1987 action programmes on the environment put the accent on harmonization of the action taken to protect the environment and on the need to reduce the concentrations of the principal pollutants in the air to levels considered acceptable for protecting sensitive ecosystems;

Whereas Council Directive 80/779/EEC, as last amended by the 1985 Act of Accession, offers a choice between two methods of sampling and analysis and two sets of associated limit values;

Whereas Article 10(4) of the abovementioned Directive requires the submission between July 1987 and July 1988, of proposals on this parallel application of two different sets of measurement methods and limit values;

Whereas these proposals must take account of the results of the parallel measurements referred to in Article 10(3) and of the need to avoid discriminatory provisions;

Whereas the results of the parallel measurements have shown that the limit values set out in Annex I and Annex IV to this Directive do not correspond as regards their stringency;

Whereas some Member States apply the limit values in Annex I and others those in Annex IV;

Whereas this has led to the use of different methods of sampling which are difficult to compare;

Whereas it is essential to harmonize the measurement methods and whereas, therefore, reference methods or technical specifications for the analysis and sampling of sulphur dioxide and suspended particulates in the air must be defined and finalized;

Whereas the Member States have taken measures to observe the limit values in the exempted zones as soon as possible and by 1 April 1993 at the latest;

Whereas these measures are based on one or other of the two measurement methods and associated values laid down by Directive 80/779/EEC;

Whereas the dual approach for measuring suspended particulates in the air causes discrimination between Member States;

Whereas a two-stage review is needed to draft proposals to avoid this dual approach without calling into question completion of the measures already taken by the Member States to observe the limit values;

Whereas these amendments must be taken into account in the obligations imposed by Article 3 of the said Directive on Member States applying Annex IV thereof,

HAS ADOPTED THIS DIRECTIVE:

Article 1

Directive 80/779/EEC is hereby amended as follows:

1.   Article 10(1), (3) and (4) is replaced by the following:

'1.   For the purposes of applying this Directive, Member States shall use either the reference methods of sampling and analysis referred to in Annex III for sulphur dioxide and for suspended particulates measured by the black smoke method or in Annex IV for suspended particulates measured by the gravimetric method, or any other method of sampling and analysis in respect of which they demonstrate to the Commission at regular intervals:

— either that it ensures satisfactory correlation of results with those obtained using the reference method,

— or that measurements taken in parallel with the reference method at a series of representative stations chosen in accordance with the requirements laid down in Article 6 show that there is a reasonably stable relationship between the results obtained using that method and those obtained using the reference method.'

'3.   By way of derogation from Article 3, Member States which decide to avail themselves of the provisions of paragraph 2 shall:

— inform the Commission, before 1 January 1991, of any zones where they consider that there is a likelihood that the concentrations of sulphur dioxide and suspended particulates in the air might exceed the limit values set out in Annex IV after 1 January 1991,

— forward to the Commission, as from 1 April 1991, plans for the progressive improvement of air quality in those zones. These plans, drawn up on the basis of relevant information on the nature, origin and development of the pollution, shall describe in particular the measures taken or to be taken and the procedures implemented or to be implemented by the Member States concerned. These measures and procedures must bring the concentrations of sulphur dioxide and suspended particulates in the air in these zones to values below or equal to the limit values set out in Annex IV as soon as possible and by 1 April 1993 at the latest.'

'4. To overcome the disadvantages of the dual approach currently laid down in Annexes I and IV, which are not completely equivalent, by 31 December 1992 the Commission shall submit to the Council a proposal for a general review of this Directive. The proposal shall take account of the experience acquired from the studies referred to in paragraph 5 and of the results of subsequent measurements taken using technical specifications or reference methods for determining suspended particulates and sulphur dioxide. These technical specifications or reference methods must be finalized by the Commission, in agreement with the Member States, by 31 December 1990.

This proposal shall cover any other aspects in need of review in the light of scientific knowledge and of the experience acquired over the period of application of this Directive. It shall take account of, *inter alia,* aspects connected with the design of the networks for measuring air pollution and with the installation of measuring equipment as well as the quality and comparability of the measurements taken.'

2. Annex IV shall be amended in accordance with the Annex to this Directive.

Article 2

1. Member States shall bring into force the laws, regulations and administrative provisions necessary to comply with this Directive within 18 months of its notification. They shall forthwith inform the Commission thereof.

2. Member States shall see to it that they communicate to the Commission the texts of the provisions of national law which they adopt in the field covered by this Directive.

Article 3

This Directive is addressed to the Member States.

3.12 MEMORANDUM OF INTENT BETWEEN CANADA AND THE UNITED STATES CONCERNING TRANSBOUNDARY AIR POLLUTION (WITHOUT ANNEX). Concluded at Washington, 5 August 1980. 32 U.S.T. 2521, T.I.A.S. No. 9856, 20 I.L.M. 690 (1981)

The Government of the United States of America and the Government of Canada,

Share a concern about actual and potential damage resulting from transboundary air pollution, (which is the short and long range transport of air pollutants between their countries), including the already serious problem of acid rain;

Recognize this is an important and urgent bilateral problem as it involves the flow of air pollutants in both directions across the international boundary, especially the long range transport of air pollutants;

Share also a common determination to combat transboundary air pollution in keeping with their existing international rights, obligations, commitments and cooperative practices, including those set forth in the 1909 Boundary Waters Treaty, the 1972 Stockholm Declaration on the Human Environment, the 1978 Great Lakes Water Quality Agreement, and the 1979 ECE Convention on Long Range Transboundary Air Pollution;

Undertook in July 1979 to develop a bilateral cooperative agreement on air quality which would deal effectively with transboundary air pollution;

Are resolved as a matter of priority both to improve scientific understanding of the long range transport of air pollutants and its effects and to develop and implement policies, practices and technologies to combat its impact;

Are resolved to protect the environment in harmony with measures to meet energy needs and other national objectives;

Note scientific findings which indicate that continued pollutant loadings will result in extensive acidification in geologically sensitive areas during the coming years, and that increased pollutant loadings will accelerate this process;

Are concerned that environmental stress could be increased if action is not taken to reduce transboundary air pollution;

Are convinced that the best means to protect the environment from the effects of transboundary air pollution is through the achievement of necessary reductions in pollutant loadings;

Are convinced also that this common problem requires cooperative action by both countries;

Intend to increase bilateral cooperative action to deal effectively with transboundary air pollution, including acid rain.

In particular, the Government of the United States of America and the Government of Canada intend:

1. to develop a bilateral agreement which will reflect and further the development of effective domestic control programs and other measures to combat transboundary air pollution;

2. to facilitate the conclusion of such an agreement as soon as possible; and,

3. pending conclusion of such an agreement, to take interim actions available under current authority to combat transboundary air pollution.

The specific undertakings of both Governments at this time are outlined below.

INTERIM ACTIONS

1. *Transboundary Air Pollution Agreement*

Further to their Joint Statement of July 26, 1979, and subsequent bilateral discussions, both Governments shall take all necessary steps forthwith:

(a) to establish a United States/Canada Coordinating Committee which will undertake preparatory discussions immediately and commence formal negotiations no later than June 1, 1981, of a cooperative agreement on transboundary air pollution; and

(b) to provide the necessary resources for the Committee to carry out its work, including the working group structure as set forth in the Annex. Members will be appointed to the work groups by each Government as soon as possible.

2. *Control Measures*

To combat transboundary air pollution both Governments shall:

(a) develop domestic air pollution control policies and strategies, and as necessary and appropriate, seek legislative or other support to give effect to them;

(b) promote vigorous enforcement of existing laws and regulations as they require limitation of emissions from new, substantially modified and existing facilities in a way which is responsive to the problems of transboundary air pollution; and

(c) share information and consult on actions being taken pursuant to (a) and (b) above.

3. *Notification and Consultation*

Both Governments shall continue and expand their long-standing practice of advance notification and consultation on proposed actions involving a significant risk or potential risk of causing or increasing transboundary air pollution, including:

(a) proposed major industrial development or other actions which may cause significant increases in transboundary air pollution; and

(b) proposed changes of policy, regulations or practices which may significantly affect transboundary air pollution.

4. *Scientific Information, Research and Development*

In order to improve understanding of their common problem and to increase their capability for controlling transboundary air pollution both Governments shall:

(a) exchange information generated in research programs being undertaken in both countries on the atmospheric aspects of the transport of air pollutants and on their effects on aquatic and terrestrial ecosystems and on human health and property;

(b) maintain and further develop a coordinated program for monitoring and evaluation of the impacts of transboundary air pollution, including the maintenance of a United States/Canada sampling network and exchange of data on current and projected emissions of major air pollutants; and

(c) continue to exchange information on research to develop improved technologies for reducing emissions of major air pollutants of concern.

The Memorandum of Intent will become effective on signature and will remain in effect until revised by mutual agreement.

3.13 MEXICO–UNITED STATES AGREEMENT TO CO-OPERATE IN THE SOLUTION OF ENVIRONMENTAL PROBLEMS IN THE BORDER AREA (WITHOUT ANNEXES). Concluded at La Paz (Mexico), 14 August 1983. Entered into force, 16 February 1984. 22 I.L.M. 1025 (1983)

Whereas, the Governments of Mexico and the United States share many environmental problems related to large and expanding urban populations, substantial industrial activity, and a common border between the two countries; and both countries possess many areas of natural and man-made scenic and recreational value; and

Whereas, the Subsecretariat for Environmental Improvement of Mexico (SMA) and the Environmental Protection Agency (EPA) of the United States share a concern for protecting and improving the human and natural environments of their respective nations, and a common interest in the cause of global as well as common border environmental protection and improvement; and

Whereas, the Governments of Mexico and the U.S. have pledged increased cooperation through the Consultative Mechanism set up by the two Presidents to include environmental cooperation;

It is Hereby AGREED that:

1. The SMA and EPA will initiate a cooperative effort to resolve environmental problems of mutual concern in border areas as well as any environmental protection matter through exchanges of information and personnel, and the establishment of parallel projects which the two parties consider appropriate to adopt.

2. The SMA and EPA will accomplish parallel activities, while allowing for the possibility that, at any given time, through special agreement, joint actions tending to resolve specific problems, may be conducted.

3. SMA and EPA senior officials will meet annually, unless they mutually agree otherwise, to discuss overall policies, programs and problems which are of common concern. The annual meeting will be held, alternately in each country, at a mutually agreeable time and site.

4. Experts designated by SMA and EPA will meet periodically or as necessary to review technical issues and plan parallel projects, including pollution abatement and control, regulations, quality assurance, research, and monitoring, that are of common interest or concern to both Mexico and the United States. An annual meeting of designated experts will be held at a site mutually agreed to by both parties and may coincide with the U.S./Mexico Border Health Association annual meetings or with other meetings. The SMA and EPA experts may make policy recommendations for consideration by the respective heads of SMA and EPA.

5. The meetings of the SMA and EPA representatives will not be limited to consideration of border problems alone but may include discussions of all areas of environmental protection and enhancement. It is understood that the Water Treaty of 1944 between the two Governments entrusted the solution of border sanitation problems to the International Boundary and Water Commission.

6. Each Party will name one person to act as coordinator to facilitate exchanges of information and other cooperation under this Memorandum of Understanding. The coordinators will establish procedures and details for the meetings of the senior officials as well as experts, including the time, place and agenda.

7. The coordinators may invite representatives of federal, state and local government agencies, international organizations, members of private organizations or other private citizens to participate in meetings, conferences, and other parallel activities as deemed appropriate.

8. Parallel activities may be conducted when approved by appropriate authorities of the respective governments and may include but will not be limited to the following:

— Development of pollution abatement and control programs directed toward specific pollution problems affecting either or both countries along the border.

— Development of an early warning system to alert the two Governments to potential environmental problems.

— Review and consultation regarding national environmental policies and strategies of Mexico and the United States.

— Development of data gathering, processing and mechanisms for the exchanges of information of common interest.

9. The coordinators will be responsible for the general management of programs, workshops, projects and activities undertaken pursuant to this Memorandum of Understanding. This includes definition of each program, workshop or project as to scope, priority, and completion schedules. The coordinators may delegate work on a special problem area to a special subcommittee which shall examine the problem in detail and make recommendations to the Governments through the SMA and EPA, respectively.

10. Unless otherwise agreed, each Party will bear the cost of its participation, including personnel costs, in activities undertaken pursuant to this Memorandum of Understanding.

11. Work under this Memorandum of Understanding is subject to the availability of funds and other resources to each Party, and to the laws and regulations of Mexico and the United States.

12. Results of work accomplished under this Memorandum of Understanding will be fully available to both parties and either Party may release information in its possession to the public on 10 days notice to the other Party.

13. This Memorandum of Understanding will enter into force when signed by both Parties and approved by the two Governments through an exchange of notes. The Memorandum of Understanding will remain in force indefinitely until either Party notifies the other of its intent to terminate the agreement, with 90 days notification.

3.14 EUROPEAN COMMUNITIES COUNCIL DIRECTIVE NO. 85/203/EEC ON AIR QUALITY STANDARDS FOR NITROGEN DIOXIDE. Adopted at Brussels, 7 March 1985. L87 O.J.E.C. (1985)

THE COUNCIL OF THE EUROPEAN COMMUNITIES,

Having regard to the Treaty establishing the European Economic Community, and in particular Articles 100 and 235 thereof,

Having regard to the proposal from the Commission,

Having regard to the opinion of the European Parliament,

Having regard to the opinion of the Economic and Social Committee,

Whereas the programmes of action of the European Communities on the environment of 1973, 1977 and 1982 provide that priority is to be given to measures against nitrogen dioxide because of its noxiousness and having regard to the current state of knowledge of its effects on human health and the environment;

Whereas insufficient technical and scientific information is available to enable the Council to lay down specific standards for the environment generally and whereas the adoption of limit values for the protection of human health will contribute to the protection of the environment as well;

Whereas any discrepancy between the provisions already applicable or being drawn up in the various Member States with regard to nitrogen dioxide in the air could give rise to unequal conditions of competition and could in consequence directly affect the functioning of the common market; whereas, therefore, the approximation of laws prescribed in Article 100 of the Treaty should be carried out in this area;

Whereas one of the basic tasks of the Community is to promote throughout the Community a harmonious development of economic activities and a continued and balanced expansion, which is inconceivable without an attack on pollution and nuisance or an improvement in the quality of life and the protection of the environment; whereas, since the Treaty has not provided the necessary powers, recourse must be had to Article 235 of the Treaty;

Whereas, in order to protect in particular human health and the environment, it is necessary to set for nitrogen dioxide a limit value which must not be exceeded in the territory of the Member States during specified periods and whereas this value should be based on the results of work carried out for the World Health Organization, particularly with regard to the dose/effect relationships established for this pollutant;

Whereas, despite the measures taken, it may not be possible to comply with the limit value in certain zones; whereas the Member States may be allowed temporary derogations on condition that they forward to the Commission plans for the gradual improvement of the quality of the air in these zones;

Whereas it is expected that the Council will shortly establish a further legal act enabling Member States to impose significantly lower limit values for exhaust gases from motor vehicles;

Whereas the measures taken pursuant to this Directive must be economically feasible and compatible with balanced development;

Whereas nitrogen dioxide is also a precursor in the formation of photo-chemical oxidants which can be harmful to man and the environment and whereas preventive action can help reduce their formation;

Whereas it is necessary to establish measuring stations to monitor compliance with the limit value for nitrogen dioxide and whereas it is desirable that these stations also measure nitric oxide which is an intermediary step in the formation of nitrogen dioxide;

Whereas, in view of the existence of different methods of analysis in the Member States, it is necessary to permit, under certain conditions, the use of methods of analysis other than the reference method laid down in the Directive;

Whereas, in addition to the limit value, there is a need to provide for guide values to improve the protection of human health and contribute to the long-term protection of the environment;

Whereas subsequent changes in the reference method of analysis referred to in this Directive may be desirable in the light of technical and scientific progress in this area; whereas, in order to facilitate the implementation of the work necessary to this end, a procedure should be set up to establish close cooperation between Member States and the Commission within a Committee on Adaptation to Scientific and Technical Progress,

HAS ADOPTED THIS DIRECTIVE:

Article 1

1.   The purpose of this Directive is to:

— fix a limit value (Annex I) for nitrogen dioxide in the atmosphere specifically to help protect human beings against the effects of nitrogen dioxide in the environment,

— lay down guide values (Annex II) for nitrogen dioxide in the atmosphere in order to improve the protection of human health and contribute to the long-term protection of the environment.

2.   This Directive shall not apply to exposure at work or inside buildings.

Article 2

For the purposes of this Directive:

— 'limit value' means the concentration of nitrogen dioxide as defined in the table in Annex I which must not be exceeded throughout the territory of the Member States during specified periods and under the conditions laid down in the following Articles,

— 'guide values' means the concentrations of nitrogen dioxide as given in Annex II considered over specified periods and intended, in particular, to serve as reference points for the establishment of specific schemes within zones determined by the Member States.

Article 3

1.   Member States shall take the necessary measures to ensure that as from 1 July 1987 the concentrations of nitrogen dioxide in the atmosphere measured in accordance with Annex III are not greater than the limit value given in Annex I.

2. However, when in particular circumstances the nitrogen dioxide concentrations in the atmosphere in certain zones are likely, despite the measures taken, to exceed the limit value in Annex I after 1 July 1987, the Member State concerned shall inform the Commission thereof before 1 July 1987.

It shall forward plans for the gradual improvement of the quality of the air in these zones to the Commission as soon as possible. These plans, drawn up on the basis of relevant information on the nature, origin and development of this pollution, shall describe, in particular, the measures taken or to be taken and the procedures implemented or to be implemented by the Member State concerned. These measures and procedures must aim at reducing the nitrogen dioxide concentrations in the atmosphere within these zones to values not exceeding the limit value given in Annex I as rapidly as possible and by 1 January 1994 at the latest.

Article 4

1. In the zones in which the Member State concerned considers it necessary to limit or prevent a foreseeable increase in pollution by nitrogen dioxide in the wake of urban or industrial development in particular, it may fix values lower than the limit value in Annex I.

2. In zones which the Member State concerned considers should be afforded special environmental protection, it may fix values which are generally lower than the guide values in Annex II.

Article 5

Member States may, at any time, fix values more stringent than those laid down in this Directive.

Article 6

Member States shall establish measuring stations to supply the data necessary for the application of this Directive in accordance with the specifications in Annex III, in particular in zones where the limit value is exceeded or likely to be exceeded and in the zones referred to in Article 4.

Such stations may also measure concentrations of nitric oxide.

Article 7

1. From 1 July 1987 Member States shall inform the Commission, not later than six months after the end (31 December) of the annual reference period, of instances in which the limit value laid down in Annex I has been exceeded and of the concentrations recorded.

2. Member States shall also notify the Commission, not later than one year after the end of the annual reference period, of the reasons for such instances and of the measures they have taken to deal with them.

3. In addition, Member States shall inform the Commission, at its request, of:

— the concentrations they have measured,

— the limit values, deadlines and timetables they have laid down,

— any appropriate measures they have taken,

concerning the zones referred to in Article 4(1) and (2).

This information must also be made available to the public.

Article 8

The Commission shall publish periodically a summary report on the application of this Directive.

Article 9

The application of the measures taken pursuant to this Directive must not lead to a significant deterioration in the quality of the air in zones, outside urban areas, where the level of pollution by nitrogen dioxide at the time of implementation of this Directive is low in relation to the limit value laid down in Annex I.

Article 10

In applying this Directive, Member States shall use:

— either the reference method of analysis referred to in Annex IV,

— or any other method of analysis which the Commission has been shown is equivalent to the reference method.

Article 11

1. Where a Member State intends to fix, in a region near the border with one or more other Member States, values for concentrations of nitrogen dioxide in the atmosphere in accordance with Article 4(1) and (2), it shall hold prior consultations with the Member States concerned. The Commission shall be informed and may attend such consultations.

2. Where the limit value given in Annex I or the values referred to in Article 4(1) and (2)—provided that the latter values have been the subject of consultations in accordance with paragraph 1—are or are likely to be exceeded following significant pollution which originates or may originate in another Member State, the Member States concerned shall hold consultations with a view to remedying the situation. The Commission shall be informed and may attend such consultations.

Article 12

The amendments necessary to adapt the specifications in Annex IV to technical progress shall be adopted in accordance with the procedure described in Article 14. These amendments shall not be such as to alter, directly or indirectly, the limit value laid down in Annex I.

Article 13

1. For the purposes of Article 12, a Committee on the Adaptation of this Directive to Scientific and Technical Progress, hereinafter called 'the Committee', shall be set up, composed of representatives of the Member States with a Commission representative as Chairman.

2. The Committee shall adopt its own rules of procedure.

Article 14

1. Where the procedure laid down in this Article is to be followed, matters shall be referred to the Committee by its Chairman, either on his own initiative or at the request of the representative of a Member State.

2. The Commission representative shall submit a draft of the measures to be taken to the Committee. The Committee shall give its opinion on the draft within a time limit set by the Chairman having regard to the urgency of the matter. Decisions shall be taken by a majority of 54 votes, the votes of the Member States being weighted as provided in Article 148(2) of the Treaty. The Chairman shall not vote.

3. The Commission shall adopt the proposed measures if they are consistent with the opinion of the Committee.

Where the proposed measures are not consistent with the opinion of the Committee, or if no opinion is delivered, the Commission shall without delay submit to the Council a proposal on the measures to be taken. The Council shall decide by a qualified majority.

If, within three months of the proposal being submitted to it, the Council has not acted, the proposed measures shall be adopted by the Commission.

Article 15

1. Member States shall bring into force the laws, regulations and administrative provisions necessary to comply with this Directive by 1 January 1987 at the latest and shall forthwith inform the Commission thereof.

2. Member States shall communicate to the Commission the texts of the provisions of national law which they adopt in the field covered by this Directive.

Article 16

This Directive is addressed to the Member States.

3.15 VIENNA CONVENTION FOR THE PROTECTION OF THE OZONE LAYER (WITH ANNEXES I & II).[1] Concluded at Vienna, 22 March 1985. Entered into force, 22 September 1988. UNEP Doc. IG.53/5, 26 I.L.M. 1529 (1987)

ARTICLE 1

DEFINITIONS

For the purposes of this Convention:

1. 'The ozone layer' means the layer of atmospheric ozone above the planetary boundary layer.

2. 'Adverse effects' means changes in the physical environment or biota, including changes in climate, which have significant deleterious effects on human health or on the composition, resilience and productivity of natural and managed ecosystems, or on materials useful to mankind.

3. 'Alternative technologies or equipment' means technologies or equipment the use of which makes it possible to reduce or effectively eliminate emissions of substances which have or are likely to have adverse effects on the ozone layer.

4. 'Alternative substances' means substances which reduce, eliminate or avoid adverse effects on the ozone layer.

5. 'Parties' means, unless the text otherwise indicates, Parties to this Convention.

6. 'Regional economic integration organization' means an organization constituted by sovereign States of a given region which has competence in respect of matters governed by this Convention or its protocols and has been duly authorized, in accordance with its internal procedures, to sign, ratify, accept, approve or accede to the instruments concerned.

7. 'Protocols' means protocols to this Convention.

ARTICLE 2

GENERAL OBLIGATIONS

1. The Parties shall take appropriate measures in accordance with the provisions of this Convention and of those protocols in force to which they are party to protect human health and the environment against adverse effects resulting or likely to result from human activities which modify or are likely to modify the ozone layer.

2. To this end the Parties shall, in accordance with the means at their disposal and their capabilities:

(a) Co-operate by means of systematic observations, research and information exchange in order to better understand and assess the effects of human activities on the ozone layer and the effects on human health and the environment from modification of the ozone layer;

(b) Adopt appropriate legislative or administrative measures and co-operate in harmonizing appropriate policies to control, limit, reduce or prevent human activities under their jurisdiction or control should it be

---

1. *See also* Basic Documents 3.17, 3.20, 3.21 and 3.23, *infra*.

found that these activities have or are likely to have adverse effects resulting from modification or likely modification of the ozone layer;

(c) Co-operate in the formulation of agreed measures, procedures and standards for the implementation of this Convention, with a view to the adoption of protocols and annexes;

(d) Co-operate with competent international bodies to implement effectively this Convention and protocols to which they are party.

3. The provisions of this Convention shall in no way affect the right of Parties to adopt, in accordance with international law, domestic measures additional to those referred to in paragraphs 1 and 2 above, nor shall they affect additional domestic measures already taken by a Party, provided that these measures are not incompatible with their obligations under this Convention.

4. The application of this article shall be based on relevant scientific and technical considerations.

ARTICLE 3

RESEARCH AND SYSTEMATIC OBSERVATIONS

1. The Parties undertake, as appropriate, to initiate and co-operate in, directly or through competent international bodies, the conduct of research and scientific assessments on:

(a) The physical and chemical processes that may affect the ozone layer;

(b) The human health and other biological effects deriving from any modifications of the ozone layer, particularly those resulting from changes in ultra-violet solar radiation having biological effects (UV–B);

(c) Climatic effects deriving from any modifications of the ozone layer;

(d) Effects deriving from any modifications of the ozone layer and any consequent change in UV–B radiation on natural and synthetic materials useful to mankind;

(e) Substances, practices, processes and activities that may affect the ozone layer, and their cumulative effects;

(f) Alternative substances and technologies;

(g) Related socio-economic matters;

and as further elaborated in annexes I and II.

2. The Parties undertake to promote or establish, as appropriate, directly or through competent international bodies and taking fully into account national legislation and relevant ongoing activities at both the national and international levels, joint or complementary programmes for systematic observation of the state of the ozone layer and other relevant parameters, as elaborated in annex I.

3. The Parties undertake to co-operate, directly or through competent international bodies, in ensuring the collection, validation and transmission of research and observational data through appropriate world data centres in a regular and timely fashion.

ARTICLE 4

CO-OPERATION IN THE LEGAL, SCIENTIFIC AND TECHNICAL FIELDS

1.   The Parties shall facilitate and encourage the exchange of scientific, technical, socio-economic, commercial and legal information relevant to this Convention as further elaborated in annex II.   Such information shall be supplied to bodies agreed upon by the Parties.   Any such body receiving information regarded as confidential by the supplying Party shall ensure that such information is not disclosed and shall aggregate it to protect its confidentiality before it is made available to all Parties.

2.   The Parties shall co-operate, consistent with their national laws, regulations and practices and taking into account in particular the needs of the developing countries, in promoting, directly or through competent international bodies, the development and transfer of technology and knowledge. Such co-operation shall be carried out particularly through:

(a) Facilitation of the acquisition of alternative technologies by other Parties;

(b) Provision of information on alternative technologies and equipment, and supply of special manuals or guides to them;

(c) The supply of necessary equipment and facilities for research and systematic observations;

(d) Appropriate training of scientific and technical personnel.

ARTICLE 5

TRANSMISSION OF INFORMATION

The Parties shall transmit, through the secretariat, to the Conference of the Parties established under article 6 information on the measures adopted by them in implementation of this Convention and of protocols to which they are party in such form and at such intervals as the meetings of the parties to the relevant instruments may determine.

ARTICLE 6

CONFERENCE OF THE PARTIES

1.   A Conference of the Parties is hereby established.   The first meeting of the Conference of the Parties shall be convened by the secretariat designated on an interim basis under article 7 not later than one year after entry into force of this Convention.   Thereafter, ordinary meetings of the Conference of the Parties shall be held at regular intervals to be determined by the Conference at its first meeting.

2.   Extraordinary meetings of the Conference of the Parties shall be held at such other times as may be deemed necessary by the Conference, or at the written request of any Party, provided that, within six months of the request being communicated to them by the secretariat, it is supported by at least one third of the Parties.

3.   The Conference of the Parties shall by consensus agree upon and adopt rules of procedure and financial rules for itself and for any subsidiary bodies it may establish, as well as financial provisions governing the functioning of the secretariat.

4. The Conference of the Parties shall keep under continuous review the implementation of this Convention, and, in addition, shall:

(a) Establish the form and the intervals for transmitting the information to be submitted in accordance with article 5 and consider such information as well as reports submitted by any subsidiary body;

(b) Review the scientific information on the ozone layer, on its possible modification and on possible effects of any such modification;

(c) Promote, in accordance with article 2, the harmonization of appropriate policies, strategies and measures for minimizing the release of substances causing or likely to cause modification of the ozone layer, and make recommendations on any other measures relating to this Convention;

(d) Adopt, in accordance with articles 3 and 4, programmes for research, systematic observations, scientific and technological co-operation, the exchange of information and the transfer of technology and knowledge;

(e) Consider and adopt, as required, in accordance with articles 9 and 10, amendments to this Convention and its annexes;

(f) Consider amendments to any protocol, as well as to any annexes thereto, and, if so decided, recommend their adoption to the parties to the protocol concerned;

(g) Consider and adopt, as required, in accordance with article 10, additional annexes to this Convention;

(h) Consider and adopt, as required, protocols in accordance with article 8;

(i) Establish such subsidiary bodies as are deemed necessary for the implementation of this Convention;

(j) Seek, where appropriate, the services of competent international bodies and scientific committees, in particular the World Meteorological Organization and the World Health Organization, as well as the Coordinating Committee on the Ozone Layer, in scientific research, systematic observations and other activities pertinent to the objectives of this Convention, and make use as appropriate of information from these bodies and committees;

(k) Consider and undertake any additional action that may be required for the achievement of the purposes of this Convention.

5. The United Nations, its specialized agencies and the International Atomic Energy Agency, as well as any State not party to this Convention, may be represented at meetings of the Conference of the Parties by observers. Any body or agency, whether national or international, governmental or non-governmental, qualified in fields relating to the protection of the ozone layer which has informed the secretariat of its wish to be represented at a meeting of the Conference of the Parties as an observer may be admitted unless at least one-third of the Parties present object. The admission and participation of observers shall be subject to the rules of procedure adopted by the Conference of the Parties.

ARTICLE 7

SECRETARIAT

1.   The functions of the secretariat shall be:

(a) To arrange for and service meetings provided for in articles 6, 8, 9 and 10;

(b) To prepare and transmit reports based upon information received in accordance with articles 4 and 5, as well as upon information derived from meetings of subsidiary bodies established under article 6;

(c) To perform the functions assigned to it by any protocol;

(d) To prepare reports on its activities carried out in implementation of its functions under this Convention and present them to the Conference of the Parties;

(e) To ensure the necessary co-ordination with other relevant international bodies, and in particular to enter into such administrative and contractual arrangements as may be required for the effective discharge of its functions;

(f) To perform such other functions as may be determined by the Conference of the Parties.

2.   The secretariat functions will be carried out on an interim basis by the United Nations Environment Programme until the completion of the first ordinary meeting of the Conference of the Parties held pursuant to article 6. At its first ordinary meeting, the Conference of the Parties shall designate the secretariat from amongst those existing competent international organizations which have signified their willingness to carry out the secretariat functions under this Convention.

ARTICLE 8

ADOPTION OF PROTOCOLS

1.   The Conference of the Parties may at a meeting adopt protocols pursuant to article 2.

2.   The text of any proposed protocol shall be communicated to the Parties by the secretariat at least six months before such a meeting.

ARTICLE 9

AMENDMENT OF THE CONVENTION OR PROTOCOLS

1.   Any Party may propose amendments to this Convention or to any protocol. Such amendments shall take due account, *inter alia,* of relevant scientific and technical considerations.

2.   Amendments to this Convention shall be adopted at a meeting of the Conference of the Parties. Amendments to any protocol shall be adopted at a meeting of the Parties to the protocol in question. The text of any proposed amendment to this Convention or to any protocol, except as may otherwise be provided in such protocol, shall be communicated to the Parties by the secretariat at least six months before the meeting at which it is proposed for adoption. The secretariat shall also communicate proposed amendments to the signatories to this Convention for information.

3. The Parties shall make every effort to reach agreement on any proposed amendment to this Convention by consensus. If all efforts at consensus have been exhausted, and no agreement reached, the amendment shall as a last resort be adopted by a three-fourths majority vote of the Parties present and voting at the meeting, and shall be submitted by the Depositary to all Parties for ratification, approval or acceptance.

4. The procedure mentioned in paragraph 3 above shall apply to amendments to any protocol, except that a two-thirds majority of the parties to that protocol present and voting at the meeting shall suffice for their adoption.

5. Ratification, approval or acceptance of amendments shall be notified to the Depositary in writing. Amendments adopted in accordance with paragraph 3 or 4 above shall enter into force between parties having accepted them on the ninetieth day after the receipt by the Depositary of notification of their ratification, approval or acceptance by at least three-fourths of the Parties to this Convention or by at least two-thirds of the parties to the protocol concerned, except as may otherwise be provided in such protocol. Thereafter the amendments shall enter into force for any other Party on the ninetieth day after that Party deposits its instrument of ratification, approval or acceptance of the amendments.

6. For the purposes of this article, "Parties present and voting" means Parties present and casting an affirmative or negative vote.

ARTICLE 10

ADOPTION AND AMENDMENT OF ANNEXES

1. The annexes to this Convention or to any protocol shall form an integral part of this Convention or of such protocol, as the case may be, and, unless expressly provided otherwise, a reference to this Convention or its protocols constitutes at the same time a reference to any annexes thereto. Such annexes shall be restricted to scientific, technical and administrative matters.

2. Except as may be otherwise provided in any protocol with respect to its annexes, the following procedure shall apply to the proposal, adoption and entry into force of additional annexes to this Convention or of annexes to a protocol:

(a) Annexes to this Convention shall be proposed and adopted according to the procedure laid down in article 9, paragraphs 2 and 3, while annexes to any protocol shall be proposed and adopted according to the procedure laid down in article 9, paragraphs 2 and 4;

(b) Any party that is unable to approve an additional annex to this Convention or an annex to any protocol to which it is party shall so notify the Depositary, in writing, within six months from the date of the communication of the adoption by the Depositary. The Depositary shall without delay notify all Parties of any such notification received. A Party may at any time substitute an acceptance for a previous declaration of objection and the annexes shall thereupon enter into force for that Party;

(c) On the expiry of six months from the date of the circulation of the communication by the Depositary, the annex shall become effective for all Parties to this Convention or to any protocol concerned which have not submitted a notification in accordance with the provision of subparagraph (b) above.

3. The proposal, adoption and entry into force of amendments to annexes to this Convention or to any protocol shall be subject to the same procedure as for the proposal, adoption and entry into force of annexes to the Convention or annexes to a protocol. Annexes and amendments thereto shall take due account, *inter alia,* of relevant scientific and technical considerations.

4. If an additional annex or an amendment to an annex involves an amendment to this Convention or to any protocol, the additional annex or amended annex shall not enter into force until such time as the amendment to this Convention or to the protocol concerned enters into force.

ARTICLE 11
SETTLEMENT OF DISPUTES

1. In the event of a dispute between Parties concerning the interpretation or application of this Convention, the parties concerned shall seek solution by negotiation.

2. If the parties concerned cannot reach agreement by negotiation, they may jointly seek the good offices of, or request mediation by, a third party.

3. When ratifying, accepting, approving or acceding to this Convention, or at any time thereafter, a State or regional economic integration organization may declare in writing to the Depositary that for a dispute not resolved in accordance with paragraph 1 or paragraph 2 above, it accepts one or both of the following means of dispute settlement as compulsory:

(a) Arbitration in accordance with procedures to be adopted by the Conference of the Parties at its first ordinary meeting;

(b) Submission of the dispute to the International Court of Justice.

4. If the parties have not, in accordance with paragraph 3 above, accepted the same or any procedure, the dispute shall be submitted to conciliation in accordance with paragraph 5 below unless the parties otherwise agree.

5. A conciliation commission shall be created upon the request of one of the parties to the dispute. The commission shall be composed of an equal number of members appointed by each party concerned and a chairman chosen jointly by the members appointed by each party. The commission shall render a final and recommendatory award, which the parties shall consider in good faith.

6. The provisions of this article shall apply with respect to any protocol except as otherwise provided in the protocol concerned.

ARTICLE 12
SIGNATURE

This Convention shall be open for signature by States and by regional economic integration organizations at the Federal Ministry for Foreign Affairs of the Republic of Austria in Vienna from 22 March 1985 to 21 September 1985, and at United Nations Headquarters in New York from 22 September 1985 to 21 March 1986.

ARTICLE 13

RATIFICATION, ACCEPTANCE OR APPROVAL

1. This Convention and any protocol shall be subject to ratification, acceptance or approval by States and by regional economic integration organizations. Instruments of ratification, acceptance or approval shall be deposited with the Depositary.

2. Any organization referred to in paragraph 1 above which becomes a Party to this Convention or any protocol without any of its member States being a Party shall be bound by all the obligations under the Convention or the protocol, as the case may be. In the case of such organizations, one or more of whose member States is a Party to the Convention or relevant protocol, the organization and its member States shall decide on their respective responsibilities for the performance of their obligation under the Convention or protocol, as the case may be. In such cases, the organization and the member States shall not be entitled to exercise rights under the Convention or relevant protocol concurrently.

3. In their instruments of ratification, acceptance or approval, the organizations referred to in paragraph 1 above shall declare the extent of their competence with respect to the matters governed by the Convention or the relevant protocol. These organizations shall also inform the Depositary of any substantial modification in the extent of their competence.

ARTICLE 14

ACCESSION

1. This Convention and any protocol shall be open for accession by States and by regional economic integration organizations from the date on which the Convention or the protocol concerned is closed for signature. The instruments of accession shall be deposited with the Depositary.

2. In their instruments of accession, the organizations referred to in paragraph 1 above shall declare the extent of their competence with respect to the matters governed by the Convention or the relevant protocol. These organizations shall also inform the Depositary of any substantial modification in the extent of their competence.

3. The provisions of article 13, paragraph 2, shall apply to regional economic integration organizations which accede to this Convention or any protocol.

ARTICLE 15

RIGHT TO VOTE

1. Each Party to this Convention or to any protocol shall have one vote.

2. Except as provided for in paragraph 1 above, regional economic integration organizations, in matters within their competence, shall exercise their right to vote with a number of votes equal to the number of their member States which are Parties to the Convention or the relevant protocol. Such organizations shall not exercise their right to vote if their member States exercise theirs, and vice versa.

ARTICLE 16

RELATIONSHIP BETWEEN THE CONVENTION AND ITS PROTOCOLS

1. A State or a regional economic integration organization may not become a party to a protocol unless it is, or becomes at the same time, a Party to the Convention.

2. Decisions concerning any protocol shall be taken only by the parties to the protocol concerned.

ARTICLE 17

ENTRY INTO FORCE

1. This Convention shall enter into force on the ninetieth day after the date of deposit of the twentieth instrument of ratification, acceptance, approval or accession.

2. Any protocol, except as otherwise provided in such protocol, shall enter into force on the ninetieth day after the date of deposit of the eleventh instrument of ratification, acceptance or approval of such protocol or accession thereto.

3. For each Party which ratifies, accepts or approves this Convention or accedes thereto after the deposit of the twentieth instrument of ratification, acceptance, approval or accession, it shall enter into force on the ninetieth day after the date of deposit by such Party of its instrument of ratification, acceptance, approval or accession.

4. Any protocol, except as otherwise provided in such protocol, shall enter into force for a party that ratifies, accepts or approves that protocol or accedes thereto after its entry into force pursuant to paragraph 2 above, on the ninetieth day after the date on which that party deposits its instrument of ratification, acceptance, approval or accession, or on the date on which the Convention enters into force for that Party, whichever shall be the later.

5. For the purposes of paragraphs 1 and 2 above, any instrument deposited by a regional economic integration organization shall not be counted as additional to those deposited by member States of such organization.

ARTICLE 18

RESERVATIONS

No reservations may be made to this Convention.

ARTICLE 19

WITHDRAWAL

1. At any time after four years from the date on which this Convention has entered into force for a Party, that Party may withdraw from the Convention by giving written notification to the Depositary.

2. Except as may be provided in any protocol, at any time after four years from the date on which such protocol has entered into force for a party, that party may withdraw from the protocol by giving written notification to the Depositary.

3. Any such withdrawal shall take effect upon expiry of one year after the date of its receipt by the Depositary, or on such later date as may be specified in the notification of the withdrawal.

4. Any Party which withdraws from this Convention shall be considered as also having withdrawn from any protocol to which it is party.

ARTICLE 20
DEPOSITARY

1. The Secretary–General of the United Nations shall assume the functions of Depositary of this Convention and any protocols.

2. The Depositary shall inform the Parties, in particular, of:

(a) The signature of this Convention and of any protocol, and the deposit of instruments of ratification, acceptance, approval or accession in accordance with articles 13 and 14;

(b) The date on which the Convention and any protocol will come into force in accordance with article 17;

(c) Notifications of withdrawal made in accordance with article 19;

(d) Amendments adopted with respect to the Convention and any protocol, their acceptance by the parties and their date of entry into force in accordance with article 9;

(e) All communications relating to the adoption and approval of annexes and to the amendment of annexes in accordance with article 10;

(f) Notifications by regional economic integration organizations of the extent of their competence with respect to matters governed by this Convention and any protocols, and of any modifications thereof;

(g) Declarations made in accordance with article 11, paragraph 3.

ARTICLE 21
AUTHENTIC TEXTS

The original of this Convention, of which the Arabic, Chinese, English, French, Russian and Spanish texts are equally authentic, shall be deposited with the Secretary–General of the United Nations.

ANNEX I
RESEARCH AND SYSTEMATIC OBSERVATIONS

1. The Parties to the Convention recognize that the major scientific issues are:

(a) Modification of the ozone layer which would result in a change in the amount of solar ultra-violet radiation having biological effects (UV–B) that reaches the Earth's surface and the potential consequences for human health, for organisms, ecosystems and materials useful to mankind;

(b) Modification of the vertical distribution of ozone, which could change the temperature structure of the atmosphere and the potential consequences for weather and climate.

2. The Parties to the Convention, in accordance with article 3, shall cooperate in conducting research and systematic observations and in formulating recommendations for future research and observation in such areas as:

(a) *Research into the physics and chemistry of the atmosphere*

(i) Comprehensive theoretical models: further development of models which consider the interaction between radiative, dynamic and chemical processes; studies of the simultaneous effects of various man-made and naturally occurring species upon atmospheric ozone; interpretation of satellite and non-satellite measurement data sets; evaluation of trends in atmospheric and geophysical parameters, and the development of methods for attributing changes in these parameters to specific causes;

(ii) Laboratory studies of: rate coefficients, absorption cross-sections and mechanisms of tropospheric and stratospheric chemical and photochemical processes; spectroscopic data to support field measurements in all relevant spectral regions;

(iii) Field measurements: the concentration and fluxes of key source gases of both natural and anthropogenic origin; atmospheric dynamics studies; simultaneous measurements of photochemically-related species down to the planetary boundary layer, using *in situ* and remote sensing instruments; intercomparison of different sensors, including co-ordinated correlative measurements for satellite instrumentation; three-dimensional fields of key atmospheric trace constituents, solar spectral flux and meteorological parameters;

(iv) Instrument development, including satellite and non-satellite sensors for atmospheric trace constituents, solar flux and meteorological parameters;

(b) *Research into health, biological and photodegradation effects*

(i) The relationship between human exposure to visible and ultra-violet solar radiation and (a) the development of both non-melanoma and melanoma skin cancer and (b) the effects on the immunological system;

(ii) Effects of UV–B radiation, including the wavelength dependence, upon (a) agricultural crops, forests and other terrestial ecosystems and (b) the aquatic food web and fisheries, as well as possible inhibition of oxygen production by marine phytoplankton;

(iii) The mechanisms by which UV–B radiation acts on biological materials, species and ecosystems, including: the relationship between dose, dose rate, and response; photorepair, adaptation, and protection;

(iv) Studies of biological action spectra and the spectral response using polychromatic radiation in order to include possible interactions of the various wavelength regions;

(v) The influence of UV–B radiation on: the sensitivities and activities of biological species important to the biospheric balance; primary processes such as photosynthesis and biosynthesis;

(vi) The influence of UV–B radiation on the photodegradation of pollutants, agricultural chemicals and other materials;

(c) *Research on effects on climate*

(i) Theoretical and observational studies of the radiative effects of ozone and other trace species and the impact on climate parameters, such as land and ocean surface temperatures, precipitation patterns, the exchange between the troposphere and stratosphere;

(ii) The investigation of the effects of such climate impacts on various aspects of human activity;

(d) *Systematic observations on:*

(i) The status of the ozone layer (i.e. the spatial and temporal variability of the total column content and vertical distribution) by making the Global Ozone Observing System, based on the integration of satellite and ground-based systems, fully operational;

(ii) The tropospheric and stratospheric concentrations of source gases for the HO_x, NO_x, $C1O_x$ and carbon families;

(iii) The temperature from the ground to the mesosphere, utilizing both ground-based and satellite systems;

(iv) Wavelength-resolved solar flux reaching, and thermal radiation leaving, the Earth's atmosphere, utilizing satellite measurements;

(v) Wavelength-resolved solar flux reaching the Earth's surface in the ultra-violet range having biological effects (UV–B);

(vi) Aerosol properties and distribution from the ground to the mesosphere, utilizing ground-based, airborne and satellite systems;

(vii) Climatically important variables by the maintenance of programmes of high-quality meteorological surface measurements;

(viii) Trace species, temperatures, solar flux and aerosols utilizing improved methods for analysing global data.

3. The Parties to the Convention shall co-operate, taking into account the particular needs of the developing countries, in promoting the appropriate scientific and technical training required to participate in the research and systematic observations outlined in this annex. Particular emphasis should be given to the intercalibration of observational instrumentation and methods with a view to generating comparable or standardized scientific data sets.

4. The following chemical substances of natural and anthropogenic origin, not listed in order of priority, are thought to have the potential to modify the chemical and physical properties of the ozone layer.

(a) Carbon substances

(i) *Carbon monoxide (CO)*

Carbon monoxide has significant natural and anthropogenic sources, and is thought to play a major direct role in tropospheric photochemistry, and an indirect role in stratospheric photochemistry.

(ii) *Carbon dioxide (CO_2)*

Carbon dioxide has significant natural and anthropogenic sources, and affects stratospheric ozone by influencing the thermal structure of the atmosphere.

(iii) *Methane (CH_4)*

Methane has both natural and anthropogenic sources, and affects both tropospheric and stratospheric ozone.

(iv) *Non-methane hydrocarbon species*

Non-methane hydrocarbon species, which consist of a large number of chemical substances, have both natural and anthropogenic sources, and play a direct role in tropospheric photochemistry and an indirect role in stratospheric photochemistry.

(b) Nitrogen substances

(i) *Nitrous oxide (N_2O)*

The dominant sources of N_2O are natural, but anthropogenic contributions are becoming increasingly important. Nitrous oxide is the primary source of stratospheric NO_x, which play a vital role in controlling the abundance of stratospheric ozone.

(ii) *Nitrogen oxides (NO_x)*

Ground-level sources of NO_x play a major direct role only in tropospheric photochemical processes and an indirect role in stratospheric photochemistry, whereas injection of NO_x close to the tropopause may lead directly to a change in upper tropospheric and stratospheric ozone.

(c) Chlorine substances

(i) *Fully halogenated alkanes, e.g. CCl_4, $CFCl_3$ (CFC–11), CF_2Cl_2 (CFC–12), $C_2F_3Cl_3$ (CFC–113), $C_2F_4Cl_2$ (CFC–114)*

Fully halogenated alkanes are anthropogenic and act as a source of $C1O_x$, which plays a vital role in ozone photochemistry, especially in the 30–50 km altitude region.

(ii) *Partially halogenated alkanes, e.g. CH_3Cl, CHF_2Cl (CFC–22), CH_3CCl_3, $CHFCl_2$ (CFC–21)*

The sources of CH_3Cl are natural, whereas the other partially halogenated alkanes mentioned above are anthropogenic in origin. These gases also act as a source of stratospheric $C1O_x$.

(d) Bromine substances

Fully halogenated alkanes, e.g. CF_3Br

These gases are anthropogenic and act as a source of BrO_x, which behaves in a manner similar to ClO_x.

(e) Hydrogen substances

(i) *Hydrogen (H_2)*

Hydrogen, the source of which is natural and anthropogenic, plays a minor role in stratospheric photochemistry.

(ii) *Water (H_2O)*

Water, the source of which is natural, plays a vital role in both tropospheric and stratospheric photochemistry. Local sources of water vapour in the stratosphere include the oxidation of methane and, to a lesser extent, of hydrogen.

ANNEX II

INFORMATION EXCHANGE

1. The Parties to the Convention recognize that the collection and sharing of information is an important means of implementing the objectives of this Convention and of assuring that any actions that may be taken are appropriate and equitable. Therefore, Parties shall exchange scientific, technical, socio-economic, business, commercial and legal information.

2. The Parties to the Convention, in deciding what information is to be collected and exchanged, should take into account the usefulness of the information and the costs of obtaining it. The Parties further recognize that co-operation under this annex has to be consistent with national laws, regulations and practices regarding patents, trade secrets, and protection of confidential and proprietary information.

3. *Scientific information*

This includes information on:

(a) Planned and ongoing research, both governmental and private, to facilitate the co-ordination of research programmes so as to make the most effective use of available national and international resources;

(b) The emission data needed for research;

(c) Scientific results published in peer-reviewed literature on the understanding of the physics and chemistry of the Earth's atmosphere and of its susceptibility to change, in particular on the state of the ozone layer and effects on human health, environment and climate which would result from changes on all time-scales in either the total column content or the vertical distribution of ozone;

(d) The assessment of research results and the recommendations for future research.

4. *Technical information*

This includes information on:

(a) The availability and cost of chemical substitutes and of alternative technologies to reduce the emissions of ozone-modifying substances and related planned and ongoing research;

(b) The limitations and any risks involved in using chemical or other substitutes and alternative technologies.

5. *Socio-economic and commercial information on the substances referred to in annex I*

This includes information on:

(a) Production and production capacity;

(b) Use and use patterns;

(c) Imports/exports;

(d) The costs, risks and benefits of human activities which may indirectly modify the ozone layer and of the impacts of regulatory actions taken or being considered to control these activities.

6. *Legal information*

This includes information on:

(a) National laws, administrative measures and legal research relevant to the protection of the ozone layer;

(b) International agreements, including bilateral agreements, relevant to the protection of the ozone layer;

(c) Methods and terms of licensing and availability of patents relevant to the protection of the ozone layer.

**3.16 IAEA CONVENTION ON EARLY NOTIFICATION OF A NUCLEAR AC-
CIDENT. Concluded at Vienna and New York, 26 September 1986.
Entered into force, 27 October 1986. IAEA INFCIRC 335, IAEA
Leg. Ser. No. 14, 25 I.L.M. 1369 (1986)**

Article 1
General provisions

1.   The States Parties shall cooperate between themselves and with the
International Atomic Energy Agency (hereinafter referred to as the "Agency") in accordance with the provisions of this Convention to facilitate prompt
assistance in the event of a nuclear accident or radiological emergency to
minimize its consequences and to protect life, property and the environment
from the effects of radioactive releases.

2.   To facilitate such cooperation States Parties may agree on bilateral or
multilateral arrangements or, where appropriate, a combination of these, for
preventing or minimizing injury and damage which may result in the event of
a nuclear accident or radiological emergency.

3.   The States Parties request the Agency, acting within the framework
of its Statute, to use its best endeavours in accordance with the provisions of
this Convention to promote, facilitate and support the cooperation between
States Parties provided for in this Convention.

Article 2
Provision of assistance

1.   If a State Party needs assistance in the event of a nuclear accident or
radiological emergency, whether or not such accident or emergency originates
within its territory, jurisdiction or control, it may call for such assistance from
any other State Party, directly or through the Agency, and from the Agency,
or, where appropriate, from other international intergovernmental organizations (hereinafter referred to as "international organizations").

2.   A State Party requesting assistance shall specify the scope and type of
assistance required and, where practicable, provide the assisting party with
such information as may be necessary for that party to determine the extent
to which it is able to meet the request. In the event that it is not practicable
for the requesting State Party to specify the scope and type of assistance
required, the requesting State Party and the assisting party shall, in consultation, decide upon the scope and type of assistance required.

3.   Each State Party to which a request for such assistance is directed
shall promptly decide and notify the requesting State Party, directly or
through the Agency, whether it is in a position to render the assistance
requested, and the scope and terms of the assistance that might be rendered.

4.   States Parties shall, within the limits of their capabilities, identify
and notify the Agency of experts, equipment and materials which could be
made available for the provision of assistance to other States Parties in the
event of a nuclear accident or radiological emergency as well as the terms,
especially financial, under which such assistance could be provided.

5.   Any State Party may request assistance relating to medical treatment
or temporary relocation into the territory of another State Party of people
involved in a nuclear accident or radiological emergency.

6. The Agency shall respond, in accordance with its Statute and as provided for in this Convention, to a requesting State Party's or a Member State's request for assistance in the event of a nuclear accident or radiological emergency by:

(a) making available appropriate resources allocated for this purpose;

(b) transmitting promptly the request to other States and international organizations which, according to the Agency's information, may possess the necessary resources; and

(c) if so requested by the requesting State, co-ordinating the assistance at the international level which may thus become available.

Article 3

Direction and control of assistance

Unless otherwise agreed:

(a) the overall direction, control, co-ordination and supervision of the assistance shall be the responsibility within its territory of the requesting State. The assisting party should, where the assistance involves personnel, designate in consultation with the requesting State, the person who should be in charge of and retain immediate operational supervision over the personnel and the equipment provided by it. The designated person should exercise such supervision in cooperation with the appropriate authorities of the requesting State;

(b) the requesting State shall provide, to the extent of its capabilities, local facilities and services for the proper and effective administration of the assistance. It shall also ensure the protection of personnel, equipment and materials brought into its territory by or on behalf of the assisting party for such purpose;

(c) ownership of equipment and materials provided by either party during the periods of assistance shall be unaffected, and their return shall be ensured;

(d) a State Party providing assistance in response to a request under paragraph 5 of article 2 shall co-ordinate that assistance within its territory.

Article 4

Competent authorities and points of contact

1. Each State Party shall make known to the Agency and to other States Parties, directly or through the Agency, its competent authorities and point of contact authorized to make and receive requests for and to accept offers of assistance. Such points of contact and a focal point within the Agency shall be available continuously.

2. Each State Party shall promptly inform the Agency of any changes that may occur in the information referred to in paragraph 1.

3. The Agency shall regularly and expeditiously provide to States Parties, Member States and relevant international organizations the information referred to in paragraphs 1 and 2.

Article 5

Functions of the Agency

The States Parties request the Agency, in accordance with paragraph 3 of article 1 and without prejudice to other provisions of this Convention, to:

(a) collect and disseminate to States Parties and Member States information concerning:

(i) experts, equipment and materials which could be made available in the event of nuclear accidents or radiological emergencies;

(ii) methodologies, techniques and available results of research relating to response to nuclear accidents or radiological emergencies;

(b) assist a State Party or a Member State when requested in any of the following or other appropriate matters:

(i) preparing both emergency plans in the case of nuclear accidents and radiological emergencies and the appropriate legislation;

(ii) developing appropriate training programs for personnel to deal with nuclear accidents and radiological emergencies;

(iii) transmitting requests for assistance and relevant information in the event of a nuclear accident or radiological emergency;

(iv) developing appropriate radiation monitoring programmes, procedures and standards;

(v) conducting investigations into the feasibility of establishing appropriate radiation monitoring systems;

(c) make available to a State Party or a Member State requesting assistance in the event of a nuclear accident or radiological emergency appropriate resources allocated for the purpose of conducting an initial assessment of the accident or emergency;

(d) offer its good offices to the States Parties and Member States in the event of a nuclear accident or radiological emergency;

(e) establish and maintain liaison with relevant international organizations for the purposes of obtaining and exchanging relevant information and data, and make a list of such organizations available to States Parties, Member States and the aforementioned organizations.

Article 6

Confidentiality and public statements

1. The requesting State and the assisting party shall protect the confidentiality of any confidential information that becomes available to either of them in connection with the assistance in the event of a nuclear accident or radiological emergency. Such information shall be used exclusively for the purpose of the assistance agreed upon.

2. The assisting party shall make every effort to coordinate with the requesting State before releasing information to the public on the assistance provided in connection with a nuclear accident or radiological emergency.

Article 7
Reimbursement of costs

1.   An assisting party may offer assistance without costs to the requesting State. When considering whether to offer assistance on such a basis, the assisting party shall take into account:

(a) the nature of the nuclear accident or radiological emergency;

(b) the place of origin of the nuclear accident or radiological emergency;

(c) the needs of developing countries;

(d) the particular needs of countries without nuclear facilities; and

(e) any other relevant factors.

2.   When assistance is provided wholly or partly on a reimbursement basis, the requesting State shall reimburse the assisting party for the costs incurred for the services rendered by persons or organizations acting on its behalf, and for all expenses in connection with the assistance to the extent that such expenses are not directly defrayed by the requesting State. Unless otherwise agreed, reimbursement shall be provided promptly after the assisting party has presented its request for reimbursement to the requesting State, and in respect of costs other than local costs, shall be freely transferrable.

3.   Notwithstanding paragraph 2, the assisting party may at any time waive, or agree to the postponement of, the reimbursement in whole or in part. In considering such waiver or postponement, assisting parties shall give due consideration to the needs of developing countries.

Article 8
Privileges, immunities and facilities

1.   The requesting State shall afford to personnel of the assisting party and personnel acting on its behalf the necessary privileges, immunities and facilities for the performance of their assistance functions.

2.   The requesting State shall afford the following privileges and immunities to personnel of the assisting party or personnel acting on its behalf who have been duly notified to and accepted by the requesting State:

(a) immunity from arrest, detention and legal process, including criminal, civil and administrative jurisdiction, of the requesting State, in respect of acts or omissions in the performance of their duties; and

(b) exemption from taxation, duties or other charges, except those which are normally incorporated in the price of goods or paid for services rendered, in respect of the performance of their assistance functions.

3.   The requesting State shall:

(a) afford the assisting party exemption from taxation, duties or other charges on the equipment and property brought into the territory of the requesting State by the assisting party for the purpose of the assistance; and

(b) provide immunity from seizure, attachment or requisition of such equipment and property.

4. The requesting State shall ensure the return of such equipment and property. If requested by the assisting party, the requesting State shall arrange, to the extent it is able to do so, for the necessary decontamination of recoverable equipment involved in the assistance before its return.

5. The requesting State shall facilitate the entry into, stay in and departure from its national territory of personnel notified pursuant to paragraph 2 and of equipment and property involved in the assistance.

6. Nothing in this article shall require the requesting State to provide its nationals or permanent residents with the privileges and immunities provided for in the foregoing paragraphs.

7. Without prejudice to the privileges and immunities, all beneficiaries enjoying such privileges and immunities under this article have a duty to respect the laws and regulations of the requesting State. They shall also have the duty not to interfere in the domestic affairs of the requesting State.

8. Nothing in this article shall prejudice rights and obligations with respect to privileges and immunities afforded pursuant to other international agreements or the rules of customary international law.

9. When signing, ratifying, accepting, approving or acceding to this Convention, a State may declare that it does not consider itself bound in whole or in part by paragraphs 2 and 3.

10. A State Party which has made a declaration in accordance with paragraph 9 may at any time withdraw it by notification to the depositary.

Article 9

Transit of personnel, equipment and property

Each State Party shall, at the request of the requesting State or the assisting party, seek to facilitate the transit through its territory of duly notified personnel, equipment and property involved in the assistance to and from the requesting State.

Article 10

Claims and compensation

1. The States Parties shall closely cooperate in order to facilitate the settlement of legal proceedings and claims under this article.

2. Unless otherwise agreed, a requesting State shall in respect of death or of injury to persons, damage to or loss of property, or damage to the environment caused within its territory or other area under its jurisdiction or control in the course of providing the assistance requested:

    (a) not bring any legal proceedings against the assisting party or persons or other legal entities acting on its behalf;

    (b) assume responsibility for dealing with legal proceedings and claims brought by third parties against the assisting party or against persons or other legal entities acting on its behalf;

    (c) hold the assisting party or persons or other legal entities acting on its behalf harmless in respect of legal proceedings and claims referred to in sub-paragraph (b); and

(d) compensate the assisting party or persons or other legal entities acting on its behalf for:

(i) death of or injury to personnel of the assisting party or persons acting on its behalf;

(ii) loss of or damage to non-consumable equipment or materials related to the assistance;

except in cases of wilful misconduct by the individuals who caused the death, injury, loss or damage.

3.   This article shall not prevent compensation or indemnity available under any applicable international agreement or national law of any State.

4.   Nothing in this article shall require the requesting State to apply paragraph 2 in whole or in part to its nationals or permanent residents.

5.   When signing, ratifying, accepting, approving or acceding to this Convention, a State may declare:

(a) that it does not consider itself bound in whole or in part by paragraph 2;

(b) that it will not apply paragraph 2 in whole or in part in cases of gross negligence by the individuals who caused the death, injury, loss or damage.

6.   A State Party which has made a declaration in accordance with paragraph 5 may at any time withdraw it by notification to the depositary.

Article 11
Termination of assistance

The requesting State or the assisting party may at any time, after appropriate consultations and by notification in writing, request the termination of assistance received or provided under this Convention. Once such a request has been made, the parties involved shall consult with each other to make arrangements for the proper conclusion of the assistance.

Article 12
Relationship to other international agreements

This Convention shall not affect the reciprocal rights and obligations of States Parties under existing international agreements which relate to the matters covered by this Convention, or under future international agreements concluded in accordance with the object and purpose of this Convention.

Article 13
Settlement of disputes

1.   In the event of a dispute between States Parties, or between a State Party and the Agency, concerning the interpretation or application of this Convention, the parties to the dispute shall consult with a view to the settlement of the dispute by negotiation or by any other peaceful means of settling disputes acceptable to them.

2.   If a dispute of this character between States Parties cannot be settled within one year from the request for consultation pursuant to paragraph 1, it shall, at the request of any party to such dispute, be submitted to arbitration or referred to the International Court of Justice for decision. Where a

dispute is submitted to arbitration, if, within six months from the date of the request, the parties to the dispute are unable to agree on the organization of the arbitration, a party may request the President of the International Court of Justice or the Secretary–General of the United Nations to appoint one or more arbitrators. In cases of conflicting requests by the parties to the dispute, the request to the Secretary–General of the United Nations shall have priority.

3. When signing, ratifying, accepting, approving or acceding to this Convention, a State may declare that it does not consider itself bound by either or both of the dispute settlement procedures provided for in paragraph 2. The other States Parties shall not be bound by a dispute settlement procedure provided for in paragraph 2 with respect to a State Party for which such a declaration is in force.

4. A State Party which has made a declaration in accordance with paragraph 3 may at any time withdraw it by notification to the depositary.

Article 14
Entry into force

1. This Convention shall be open for signature by all States and Namibia, represented by the United Nations Council for Namibia, at the Headquarters of the International Atomic Energy Agency in Vienna and at the Headquarters of the United Nations in New York, from 26 September 1986 and 6 October 1986 respectively, until its entry into force or for twelve months, whichever period is longer.

2. A State and Namibia, represented by the United Nations Council for Namibia, may express its consent to be bound by this Convention either by signature, or by deposit of an instrument of ratification, acceptance or approval following signature made subject to ratification, acceptance or approval, or by deposit of an instrument of accession. The instruments of ratification, acceptance, approval or accession shall be deposited with the depositary.

3. This Convention shall enter into force thirty days after consent to be bound has been expressed by three States.

4. For each State expressing consent to be bound by this Convention after its entry into force, this Convention shall enter into force for that State thirty days after the date of expression of consent.

5. (a) This Convention shall be open for accession, as provided for in this article, by international organizations and regional integration organizations constituted by sovereign States, which have competence in respect of the negotiation, conclusion and application of international agreements in matters covered by this Convention.

(b) In matters within their competence such organizations shall, on their own behalf, exercise the rights and fulfil the obligations which this Convention attributes to States Parties.

(c) When depositing its instrument of accession, such an organization shall communicate to the depositary a declaration indicating the extent of its competence in respect of matters covered by this Convention.

(d) Such an organization shall not hold any vote additional to those of its Member States.

Article 15
Provisional application

A State may, upon signature or at any later date before this Convention enters into force for it, declare that it will apply this Convention provisionally.

Article 16
Amendments

1. A State Party may propose amendments to this Convention. The proposed amendment shall be submitted to the depositary who shall circulate it immediately to all other States Parties.

2. If a majority of the States Parties request the depositary to convene a conference to consider the proposed amendments, the depositary shall invite all States Parties to attend such a conference to begin not sooner than thirty days after the invitations are issued. Any amendment adopted at the conference by a two-thirds majority of all States Parties shall be laid down in a protocol which is open to signature in Vienna and New York by all States Parties.

3. The protocol shall enter into force thirty days after consent to be bound has been expressed by three States. For each State expressing consent to be bound by the protocol after its entry into force, the protocol shall enter into force for that State thirty days after the date of expression of consent.

Article 17
Denunciation

1. A State Party may denounce this Convention by written notification to the depositary.

2. Denunciation shall take effect one year following the date on which the notification is received by the depositary.

Article 18
Depositary

1. The Director General of the Agency shall be the depositary of this Convention.

2. The Director General of the Agency shall promptly notify States Parties and all other States of:

(a) each signature of this Convention or any protocol of amendment;

(b) each deposit of an instrument of ratification, acceptance, approval or accession concerning this Convention or any protocol of amendment;

(c) any declaration or withdrawal thereof in accordance with articles 8, 10 and 13;

(d) any declaration of provisional application of this Convention in accordance with article 15;

(e) the entry into force of this Convention and of any amendment thereto; and

(f) any denunciation made under article 17.

Article 19
Authentic texts and certified copies

The original of this Convention, of which the Arabic, Chinese, English, French, Russian and Spanish texts are equally authentic, shall be deposited with the Director General of the International Atomic Energy Agency who shall send certified copies to States Parties and all other States.

3.17 IAEA CONVENTION ON ASSISTANCE IN THE CASE OF A NUCLEAR ACCIDENT OR RADIOLOGICAL EMERGENCY. Concluded at Vienna and New York, 26 September 1986. Entered into force, 26 September 1987. IAEA INFCIRC 336, 25 I.L.M. 1377 (1986)

Article 1
Scope of application

1. This Convention shall apply in the event of any accident involving facilities or activities of a State Party or of persons or legal entities under its jurisdiction or control, referred to in paragraph 2 below, from which a release of radioactive material occurs or is likely to occur and which has resulted or may result in an international transboundary release that could be of radiological safety significance for another State.

2. The facilities and activities referred to in paragraph 1 are the following:

(a) any nuclear reactor wherever located;

(b) any nuclear fuel cycle facility;

(c) any radioactive waste management facility;

(d) the transport and storage of nuclear fuels or radioactive wastes;

(e) the manufacture, use, storage, disposal and transport of radioisotopes for agricultural, industrial, medical and related scientific and research purposes; and

(f) the use of radioisotopes for power generation in space objects.

Article 2
Notification and information

In the event of an accident specified in article 1 (hereinafter referred to as a "nuclear accident"), the State Party referred to in that article shall:

(a) forthwith notify, directly or through the International Atomic Energy Agency (hereinafter referred to as the "Agency"), those States which are or may be physically affected as specified in article 1 and the Agency of the nuclear accident, its nature, the time of its occurrence and its exact location where appropriate; and

(b) promptly provide the States referred to in sub-paragraph (a), directly or through the Agency, and the Agency with such available information relevant to minimizing the radiological consequences in those States, as specified in article 5.

Article 3
Other Nuclear Accidents

With a view to minimizing the radiological consequences, States Parties may notify in the event of nuclear accidents other than those specified in article 1.

Article 4
Functions of the Agency

The Agency shall:

(a) forthwith inform States Parties, Member States, other States which are or may be physically affected as specified in article 1 and relevant international intergovernmental organizations (hereinafter referred to as "international organizations") of a notification received pursuant to sub-paragraph (a) of article 2; and

(b) promptly provide any State Party, Member State or relevant international organization, upon request, with the information received pursuant to sub-paragraph (b) of article 2.

Article 5

Information to be provided

1. The information to be provided pursuant to sub-paragraph (b) of article 2 shall comprise the following data as then available to the notifying State Party:

(a) the time, exact location where appropriate, and the nature of the nuclear accident;

(b) the facility or activity involved;

(c) the assumed or established cause and the foreseeable development of the nuclear accident relevant to the transboundary release of the radioactive materials;

(d) the general characteristics of the radioactive release, including, as far as is practicable and appropriate, the nature, probable physical and chemical form and the quantity, composition and effective height of the radioactive release;

(e) information on current and forecast meteorological and hydrological conditions, necessary for forecasting the transboundary release of the radioactive materials;

(f) the results of environmental monitoring relevant to the transboundary release of the radioactive materials;

(g) the off-site protective measures taken or planned;

(h) the predicted behaviour over time of the radioactive release.

2. Such information shall be supplemented at appropriate intervals by further relevant information on the development of the emergency situation, including its foreseeable or actual termination.

3. Information received pursuant to sub-paragraph (b) of article 2 may be used without restriction, except when such information is provided in confidence by the notifying State Party.

Article 6

Consultations

A State Party providing information pursuant to sub-paragraph (b) of article 2 shall, as far as is reasonably practicable, respond promptly to a request for further information or consultations sought by an affected State Party with a view to minimizing the radiological consequences in that State.

Article 7
Competent authorities and points of contact

1. Each State Party shall make known to the Agency and to other States Parties, directly or through the Agency, its competent authorities and point of contact responsible for issuing and receiving the notification and information referred to in article 2. Such points of contact and a focal point within the Agency shall be available continuously.

2. Each State Party shall promptly inform the Agency of any changes that may occur in the information referred to in paragraph 1.

3. The Agency shall maintain an up-to-date list of such national authorities and points of contact as well as points of contact of relevant international organizations and shall provide it to States Parties and Member States and to relevant international organizations.

Article 8
Assistance to States Parties

The Agency shall, in accordance with its Statute and upon a request of a State Party which does not have nuclear activities itself and borders on a State having an active nuclear programme but not Party, conduct investigations into the feasibility and establishment of an appropriate radiation monitoring system in order to facilitate the achievement of the objectives of this Convention.

Article 9
Bilateral and multilateral arrangements

In furtherance of their mutual interests, States Parties may consider, where deemed appropriate, the conclusion of bilateral or multilateral arrangements relating to the subject matter of this Convention.

Article 10
Relationship to other international agreements

This Convention shall not affect the reciprocal rights and obligations of States Parties under existing international agreements which relate to the matters covered by this Convention, or under future international agreements concluded in accordance with the object and purpose of this Convention.

Article 11
Settlement of disputes

1. In the event of a dispute between States Parties, or between a State Party and the Agency, concerning the interpretation or application of this Convention, the parties to the dispute shall consult with a view to the settlement of the dispute by negotiation or by any other peaceful means of settling disputes acceptable to them.

2. If a dispute of this character between States Parties cannot be settled within one year from the request for consultation pursuant to paragraph 1, it shall, at the request of any party to such dispute, be submitted to arbitration or referred to the International Court of Justice for decision. Where a dispute is submitted to arbitration, if, within six months from the date of the request, the parties to the dispute are unable to agree on the organization of the arbitration, a party may request the President of the International Court

of Justice or the Secretary–General of the United Nations to appoint one or more arbitrators. In cases of conflicting requests by the parties to the dispute, the request to the Secretary–General of the United Nations shall have priority.

3. When signing, ratifying, accepting, approving or acceding to this Convention, a State may declare that it does not consider itself bound by either or both of the dispute settlement procedures provided for in paragraph 2. The other States Parties shall not be bound by a dispute settlement procedure provided for in paragraph 2 with respect to a State Party for which such a declaration is in force.

4. A State Party which has made a declaration in accordance with paragraph 3 may at any time withdraw it by notification to the depositary.

Article 12

Entry into force

1. This Convention shall be open for signature by all States and Namibia, represented by the United Nations Council for Namibia, at the headquarters of the International Atomic Energy Agency in Vienna and at the headquarters of the United Nations in New York, from 26 September 1986 and 6 October 1986 respectively, until its entry into force or for twelve months, whichever period is longer.

2. A State and Namibia, represented by the United Nations Council for Namibia, may express its consent to be bound by this Convention either by signature, or by deposit of an instrument of ratification, acceptance or approval following signature made subject to ratification, acceptance or approval, or by deposit of an instrument of accession. The instruments of ratification, acceptance, approval or accession shall be deposited with the depositary.

3. This Convention shall enter into force thirty days after consent to be bound has been expressed by three States.

4. For each State expressing consent to be bound by this Convention after its entry into force, this Convention shall enter into force for that State thirty days after the date of expression of consent.

5. (a) This Convention shall be open for accession, as provided for in this article, by international organizations and regional integration organizations constituted by sovereign States, which have competence in respect of the negotiation, conclusion and application of international agreements in matters covered by this Convention.

(b) In matters within their competence such organizations shall, on their own behalf, exercise the rights and fulfil the obligations which this Convention attributes to States Parties.

(c) When depositing its instrument of accession, such an organization shall communicate to the depositary a declaration indicating the extent of its competence in respect of matters covered by this Convention.

(d) Such an organization shall not hold any vote additional to those of its Member States.

Article 13
Provisional application

A State may, upon signature or at any later date before this Convention enters into force for it, declare that it will apply this Convention provisionally.

Article 14
Amendments

1. A State Party may propose amendments to this Convention. The proposed amendment shall be submitted to the depositary who shall circulate it immediately to all other States Parties.

2. If a majority of the States Parties request the depositary to convene a conference to consider the proposed amendments, the depositary shall invite all States Parties to attend such a conference to begin not sooner than thirty days after the invitations are issued. Any amendment adopted at the conference by a two-thirds majority of all States Parties shall be laid down in a protocol which is open to signature in Vienna and New York by all States Parties.

3. The protocol shall enter into force thirty days after consent to be bound has been expressed by three States. For each State expressing consent to be bound by the protocol after its entry into force, the protocol shall enter into force for that State thirty days after the date of expression of consent.

Article 15
Denunciation

1. A State Party may denounce this Convention by written notification to the depositary.

2. Denunciation shall take effect one year following the date on which the notification is received by the depositary.

Article 16
Depositary

1. The Director General of the Agency shall be the depositary of this Convention.

2. The Director General of the Agency shall promptly notify States Parties and all other States of:

(a) each signature of this Convention or any protocol of amendment;

(b) each deposit of an instrument of ratification, acceptance, approval or accession concerning this Convention or any protocol of amendment;

(c) any declaration or withdrawal thereof in accordance with article 11;

(d) any declaration of provisional application of this Convention in accordance with article 13;

(e) the entry into force of this Convention and of any amendment thereto; and

(f) any denunciation made under article 15.

Article 17
Authentic texts and certified copies

The original of this Convention, of which the Arabic, Chinese, English, French, Russian and Spanish texts are equally authentic, shall be deposited with the Director General of the International Atomic Energy Agency who shall send certified copies to States Parties and all other States.

3.18 MONTREAL PROTOCOL ON SUBSTANCES THAT DEPLETE THE OZONE LAYER (WITH ANNEX A AND AS ADJUSTED).[1] Concluded at Montreal, 16 September 1987. Entered into force, 1 January 1989. 26 I.L.M. 1550 (1987)

ARTICLE 1. DEFINITIONS

For the purposes of this Protocol:

1. "Convention" means the Vienna Convention for the Protection of the Ozone Layer, adopted on 22 March 1985.

2. "Parties" means, unless the text otherwise indicates, Parties to this Protocol.

3. "Secretariat" means the secretariat of the Convention.

4. "Controlled substance" means a substance listed in Annex A to this Protocol, whether existing alone or in a mixture. It excludes, however, any such substance or mixture which is in a manufactured product other than a container used for the transportation or storage of the substance listed.

5. "Production" means the amount of controlled substances produced minus the amount destroyed by technologies to be approved by the Parties.

6. "Consumption" means production plus imports minus exports of controlled substances.

7. "Calculated levels" of production, imports, exports and consumption means levels determined in accordance with Article 3.

8. "Industrial rationalization" means the transfer of all or a portion of the calculated level of production of one Party to another, for the purpose of achieving economic efficiencies or responding to anticipated shortfalls in supply as a result of plant closures.

ARTICLE 2. CONTROL MEASURES

5. Any Party whose calculated level of production in 1986 of the controlled substances in Group I of Annex A was less than twenty-five kilotonnes may, for the purposes of industrial rationalization, transfer to or receive from any other Party, production in excess of the limits set out in paragraphs 1, 3 and 4 provided that the total combined calculated levels of production of the Parties concerned does not exceed the production limits set out in this Article. Any transfer of such production shall be notified to the secretariat, no later than the time of the transfer.

6. Any Party not operating under Article 5, that has facilities for the production of controlled substances under construction, or contracted for, prior to 16 September 1987, and provided for in national legislation prior to 1 January 1987, may add the production from such facilities to its 1986 production of such substances for the purposes of determining its calculated level of production for 1986, provided that such facilities are completed by 31 December 1990 and that such production does not raise that Party's annual calculated level of consumption of the controlled substances above 0.5 kilograms per capita.

1. *See also* Basic Documents 3.15, *supra,*
3.20, 3.21, and 3.23 *infra.*

7. Any transfer of production pursuant to paragraph 5 or any addition of production pursuant to paragraph 6 shall be notified to the secretariat, no later than the time of the transfer or addition.

8. (a) Any Parties which are Member States of a regional economic integration organization as defined in Article 1(6) of the Convention may agree that they shall jointly fulfil their obligations respecting consumption under this Article provided that their total combined calculated level of consumption does not exceed the levels required by this Article.

(b) The Parties to any such agreement shall inform the secretariat of the terms of the agreement before the date of the reduction in consumption with which the agreement is concerned.

(c) Such agreement will become operative only if all Member States of the regional economic integration organization and the organization concerned are Parties to the Protocol and have notified the secretariat of their manner of implementation.

9. (a) Based on the assessments made pursuant to Article 6, the Parties may decide whether:

(i) adjustments to the ozone depleting potentials specified in Annex A should be made and, if so, what the adjustments should be; and

(ii) further adjustments and reductions of production or consumption of the controlled substances from 1986 levels should be undertaken and, if so, what the scope, amount and timing of any such adjustments and reductions should be.

(b) Proposals for such adjustments shall be communicated to the Parties by the secretariat at least six months before the meeting of the Parties at which they are proposed for adoption.

(c) In taking such decisions, the Parties shall make every effort to reach agreement by consensus. If all efforts at consensus have been exhausted, and no agreement reached, such decisions shall, as a last resort, be adopted by a two-thirds majority vote of the Parties present and voting representing at least fifty per cent of the total consumption of the controlled substances of the Parties.

(d) The decisions, which shall be binding on all Parties, shall forthwith be communicated to the Parties by the Depositary. Unless otherwise provided in the decisions, they shall enter into force on the expiry of six months from the date of the circulation of the communication by the Depositary.

10. (a) Based on the assessments made pursuant to Article 6 of this Protocol and in accordance with the procedure set out in Article 9 of the Convention, the Parties may decide:

(i) whether any substances, and if so which, should be added to or removed from any annex to this Protocol; and

(ii) the mechanism, scope and timing of the control measures that should apply to those substances;

(b) Any such decision shall become effective, provided that it has been accepted by a two-thirds majority vote of the Parties present and voting.

11. Notwithstanding the provisions contained in this Article, Parties may take more stringent measures than those required by this Article.

Article 2A. CFCS

1. Each Party shall ensure that for the twelve-month period commencing on the first day of the seventh month following the date of the entry into force of this Protocol, and in each twelve-month period thereafter, its calculated level of consumption of the controlled substances in Group I of Annex A does not exceed its calculated level of consumption in 1986. By the end of the same period, each Party producing one or more of these substances shall ensure that its calculated level of production of the substances does not exceed its calculated level of production in 1986, except that such level may have increased by no more than ten per cent based on the 1986 level. Such increase shall be permitted only so as to satisfy the basic domestic needs of the Parties operating under Article 5 and for the purposes of industrial rationalization between Parties.

2. Each Party shall ensure that for the period from 1 July 1991 to 31 December 1992 its calculated levels of consumption and production of the controlled substances in Group I of Annex A do not exceed 150 per cent of its calculated levels of production and consumption of those substances in 1986; with effect from 1 January 1993, the twelve-month control period for these controlled substances shall run from 1 January to 31 December each year.

3. Each Party shall ensure that for the twelve-month period commencing on 1 January 1995, and in each twelve-month period thereafter, its calculated level of consumption of the controlled substances in Group I of Annex A does not exceed, annually, fifty per cent of its calculated level of consumption in 1986. Each Party producing one or more of these substances shall, for the same periods, ensure that its calculated level of production of the substances does not exceed, annually, fifty per cent of its calculated level of production in 1986. However, in order to satisfy the basic domestic needs of the Parties operating under paragraph 1 of Article 5, its calculated level of production may exceed that limit by up to ten per cent of its calculated level of production in 1986.

4. Each Party shall ensure that for the twelve-month period commencing on 1 January 1997, and in each twelve-month period thereafter, its calculated level of consumption of the controlled substances in Group I of Annex A does not exceed, annually, fifteen per cent of its calculated level of consumption in 1986. Each Party producing one or more of these substances shall, for the same periods, ensure that its calculated level of production of the substances does not exceed, annually, fifteen per cent of its calculated level of production in 1986. However, in order to satisfy the basic domestic needs of the Parties operating under paragraph 1 of Article 5, its calculated level of production may exceed that limit by up to 10 per cent of its calculated level of production in 1986.

5. Each Party shall ensure that for the twelve-month period commencing on 1 January 2000, and in each twelve-month period thereafter, its

calculated level of consumption of the controlled substances in Group I of Annex A does not exceed zero. Each Party producing one or more of these substances shall, for the same periods, ensure that its calculated level of production of the substances does not exceed zero. However, in order to satisfy the basic domestic needs of the Parties operating under paragraph 1 of Article 5, its calculated level of production may exceed that limit by up to fifteen percent of its calculated level of production in 1986.

6. In 1992, the Parties will review the situation with the objective of accelerating the reduction schedule.

Article 2B.   Halons

1. Each Party shall ensure that for the twelve-month period commencing on 1 January 1992, and in each twelve-month period thereafter, its calculated level of consumption of the controlled substances in Group II of Annex A does not exceed, annually, its calculated level of consumption in 1986. Each Party producing one or more of these substances shall, for the same periods, ensure that its calculated level of production of the substances does not exceed, annually, its calculated level of production in 1986. However, in order to satisfy the basic domestic needs of the Parties operating under paragraph 1 of Article 5, its calculated level of production may exceed that limit by up to ten per cent of its calculated level of production in 1986.

2. Each Party shall ensure that for the twelve-month period commencing on 1 January 1995, and in each twelve-month period thereafter, its calculated level of consumption of the controlled substances in Group II of Annex A does not exceed, annually, fifty per cent of its calculated level of consumption in 1986. Each Party producing one or more of these substances shall, for the same periods, ensure that its calculated level of production of the substances does not exceed, annually, fifty per cent of its calculated level of production in 1986. However, in order to satisfy the basic domestic needs of the Parties operating under paragraph 1 of Article 5, its calculated level of production may exceed that limit by up to ten per cent of its calculated level of production in 1986. This paragraph will apply save to the extent that the Parties decide to permit the level of production or consumption that is necessary to satisfy essential uses for which no adequate alternatives are available.

3. Each Party shall ensure that for the twelve-month period commencing on 1 January 2000, and in each twelve-month period thereafter, its calculated level of consumption of the controlled substances in Group II of Annex A does not exceed zero. Each Party producing one or more of these substances shall, for the same periods, ensure that its calculated level of production of the substances does not exceed zero. However, in order to satisfy the basic domestic needs of the Parties operating under paragraph 1 of Article 5, its calculated level of production may exceed that limit by up to fifteen per cent of its calculated level of production in 1986. This paragraph will apply save to the extent that the Parties decide to permit the level of production or consumption that is necessary to satisfy essential uses for which no adequate alternatives are available.

4. By 1 January 1993, the Parties shall adopt a decision identifying essential uses, if any, for the purposes of paragraphs 2 and 3 of this Article. Such decision shall be reviewed by the Parties at their subsequent meetings.

ARTICLE 3. CALCULATION OF CONTROL LEVELS

For the purposes of Articles 2 and 5, each Party shall, for each Group of substances in Annex A, determine its calculated levels of:

(a) production by:

(i) multiplying its annual production of each controlled substance by the ozone depleting potential specified in respect of it in Annex A; and

(ii) adding together, for each such Group, the resulting figures;

(b) imports and exports, respectively, by following, *mutatis mutandis,* the procedure set out in subparagraph (a); and

(c) consumption by adding together its calculated levels of production and imports and subtracting its calculated level of exports as determined in accordance with subparagraphs (a) and (b). However, beginning on 1 January 1993, any export of controlled substances to non-Parties shall not be subtracted in calculating the consumption level of the exporting Party.

ARTICLE 4. CONTROL OF TRADE WITH NON–PARTIES

1. Within one year of the entry into force of this Protocol, each Party shall ban the import of controlled substances from any State not party to this Protocol.

2. Beginning on 1 January 1993, no Party operating under paragraph 1 of Article 5 may export any controlled substance to any State not party to this Protocol.

3. Within three years of the date of the entry into force of this Protocol, the Parties shall, following the procedures in Article 10 of the Convention, elaborate in an annex a list of products containing controlled substances. Parties that have not objected to the annex in accordance with those procedures shall ban, within one year of the annex having become effective, the import of those products from any State not party to this Protocol.

4. Within five years of the entry into force of this Protocol, the Parties shall determine the feasibility of banning or restricting, from States not party to this Protocol, the import of products produced with, but not containing, controlled substances. If determined feasible, the Parties shall, following the procedures in Article 10 of the Convention, elaborate in an annex a list of such products. Parties that have not objected to it in accordance with those procedures shall ban or restrict, within one year of the annex having become effective, the import of those products from any State not party to this Protocol.

5. Each Party shall discourage the export, to any State not party to this Protocol, of technology for producing and for utilizing controlled substances.

6. Each Party shall refrain from providing new subsidies, aid, credits, guarantees or insurance programmes for the export to States not party to this Protocol of products, equipment, plants or technology that would facilitate the production of controlled substances.

7. Paragraphs 5 and 6 shall not apply to products, equipment, plants or technology that improve the containment, recovery, recycling or destruction of

controlled substances, promote the development of alternative substances, or otherwise contribute to the reduction of emissions of controlled substances.

8. Notwithstanding the provisions of this Article, imports referred to in paragraphs 1, 3 and 4 may be permitted from any State not party to this Protocol if that State is determined, by a meeting of the Parties, to be in full compliance with Article 2 and this Article, and has submitted data to that effect as specified in Article 7.

ARTICLE 5.   SPECIAL SITUATION OF DEVELOPING COUNTRIES

1. Any Party that is a developing country and whose annual calculated level of consumption of the controlled substances is less than 0.3 kilograms per capita on the date of the entry into force of the Protocol for it, or any time thereafter within ten years of the date of entry into force of the Protocol shall, in order to meet its basic domestic needs, be entitled to delay its compliance with the control measures set out in paragraphs 1 to 4 of Article 2 by ten years after that specified in those paragraphs. However, such Party shall not exceed an annual calculated level of consumption of 0.3 kilograms per capita. Any such Party shall be entitled to use either the average of its annual calculated level of consumption for the period 1995 to 1997 inclusive or a calculated level of consumption of 0.3 kilograms per capita, whichever is the lower, as the basis for its compliance with the control measures.

2. The Parties undertake to facilitate access to environmentally safe alternative substances and technology for Parties that are developing countries and assist them to make expeditious use of such alternatives.

3. The Parties undertake to facilitate bilaterally or multilaterally the provision of subsidies, aid, credits, guarantees or insurance programmes to Parties that are developing countries for the use of alternative technology and for substitute products.

ARTICLE 6.   ASSESSMENT AND REVIEW OF CONTROL MEASURES

Beginning in 1990, and at least every four years thereafter, the Parties shall assess the control measures provided for in Article 2 on the basis of available scientific, environmental, technical and economic information. At least one year before each assessment, the Parties shall convene appropriate panels of experts qualified in the fields mentioned and determine the composition and terms of reference of any such panels. Within one year of being convened, the panels will report their conclusions, through the secretariat, to the Parties.

ARTICLE 7.   REPORTING OF DATA

1. Each Party shall provide to the secretariat, within three months of becoming a Party, statistical data on its production, imports and exports of each of the controlled substances for the year 1986, or the best possible estimates of such data where actual data are not available.

2. Each Party shall provide statistical data to the secretariat on its annual production (with separate data on amounts destroyed by technologies to be approved by the Parties), imports, and exports to Parties and non-Parties, respectively, of such substances for the year during which it becomes a Party and for each year thereafter. It shall forward the data no later than nine months after the end of the year to which the data relate.

ARTICLE 8. NON–COMPLIANCE

The Parties, at their first meeting, shall consider and approve procedures and institutional mechanisms for determining non-compliance with the provisions of this Protocol and for treatment of Parties found to be in non-compliance.

ARTICLE 9. RESEARCH, DEVELOPMENT, PUBLIC AWARENESS AND EXCHANGE OF INFORMATION

1. The Parties shall co-operate, consistent with their national laws, regulations and practices and taking into account in particular the needs of developing countries, in promoting, directly or through competent international bodies, research, development and exchange of information on:

(a) best technologies for improving the containment, recovery, recycling or destruction of controlled substances or otherwise reducing their emissions;

(b) possible alternatives to controlled substances, to products containing such substances, and to products manufactured with them; and

(c) costs and benefits of relevant control strategies.

2. The Parties, individually, jointly or through competent international bodies, shall co-operate in promoting public awareness of the environmental effects of the emissions of controlled substances and other substances that deplete the ozone layer.

3. Within two years of the entry into force of this Protocol and every two years thereafter, each Party shall submit to the secretariat a summary of the activities it has conducted pursuant to this Article.

ARTICLE 10. TECHNICAL ASSISTANCE

1. The Parties shall, in the context of the provisions of Article 4 of the Convention, and taking into account in particular the needs of developing countries, co-operate in promoting technical assistance to facilitate participation in and implementation of this Protocol.

2. Any Party or Signatory to this Protocol may submit a request to the secretariat for technical assistance for the purposes of implementing or participating in the Protocol.

3. The Parties, at their first meeting, shall begin deliberations on the means of fulfilling the obligations set out in Article 9, and paragraphs 1 and 2 of this Article, including the preparation of workplans. Such workplans shall pay special attention to the needs and circumstances of the developing countries. States and regional economic integration organizations not party to the Protocol should be encouraged to participate in activities specified in such workplans.

ARTICLE 11. MEETINGS OF THE PARTIES

1. The Parties shall hold meetings at regular intervals. The secretariat shall convene the first meeting of the Parties not later than one year after the date of the entry into force of this Protocol and in conjunction with a meeting of the Conference of the Parties to the Convention, if a meeting of the latter is scheduled within that period.

2. Subsequent ordinary meetings of the Parties shall be held, unless the Parties otherwise decide, in conjunction with meetings of the Conference of the Parties to the Convention. Extraordinary meetings of the Parties shall be held at such other times as may be deemed necessary by a meeting of the Parties, or at the written request of any Party, provided that, within six months of such a request being communicated to them by the secretariat, it is supported by at least one third of the Parties.

3. The Parties, at their first meeting, shall:

(a) adopt by consensus rules of procedure for their meetings;

(b) adopt by consensus the financial rules referred to in paragraph 2 of Article 13;

(c) establish the panels and determine the terms of reference referred to in Article 6;

(d) consider and approve the procedures and institutional mechanisms specified in Article 8; and

(e) begin preparation of workplans pursuant to paragraph 3 of Article 10.

4. The functions of the meetings of the Parties shall be to:

(a) review the implementation of this Protocol;

(b) decide on any adjustments or reductions referred to in paragraph 9 of Article 2;

(c) decide on any addition to, insertion in or removal from any annex of substances and on related control measures in accordance with paragraph 10 of Article 2;

(d) establish, where necessary, guidelines or procedures for reporting of information as provided for in Article 7 and paragraph 3 of Article 9;

(e) review requests for technical assistance submitted pursuant to paragraph 2 of Article 10;

(f) review reports prepared by the secretariat pursuant to subparagraph (c) of Article 12;

(g) assess, in accordance with Article 6, the control measures provided for in Article 2;

(h) consider and adopt, as required, proposals for amendment of this Protocol or any annex and for any new annex;

(i) consider and adopt the budget for implementing this Protocol; and

(j) consider and undertake any additional action that may be required for the achievement of the purposes of this Protocol.

5. The United Nations, its specialized agencies and the International Atomic Energy Agency, as well as any State not party to this Protocol, may be represented at meetings of the Parties as observers. Any body or agency, whether national or international, governmental or non-governmental, qualified in fields relating to the protection of the ozone layer which has informed the secretariat of its wish to be represented at a meeting of the Parties as an observer may be admitted unless at least one third of the Parties present

object. The admission and participation of observers shall be subject to the rules of procedure adopted by the Parties.

ARTICLE 12. SECRETARIAT

For the purposes of this Protocol, the secretariat shall:

(a) arrange for and service meetings of the Parties as provided for in Article 11;

(b) receive and make available, upon request by a Party, data provided pursuant to Article 7;

(c) prepare and distribute regularly to the Parties reports based on information received pursuant to Articles 7 and 9;

(d) notify the Parties of any request for technical assistance received pursuant to Article 10 so as to facilitate the provision of such assistance;

(e) encourage non-Parties to attend the meetings of the Parties as observers and to act in accordance with the provisions of this Protocol;

(f) provide, as appropriate, the information and requests referred to in subparagraphs (c) and (d) to such non-party observers; and

(g) perform such other functions for the achievement of the purposes of this Protocol as may be assigned to it by the Parties.

ARTICLE 13. FINANCIAL PROVISIONS

1. The funds required for the operation of this Protocol, including those for the functioning of the secretariat related to this Protocol, shall be charged exclusively against contributions from the Parties.

2. The Parties, at their first meeting, shall adopt by consensus financial rules for the operation of this Protocol.

ARTICLE 14. RELATIONSHIP OF THIS PROTOCOL TO THE CONVENTION

Except as otherwise provided in this Protocol, the provisions of the Convention relating to its protocols shall apply to this Protocol.

ARTICLE 15. SIGNATURE

This Protocol shall be open for signature by States and by regional economic integration organizations in Montreal on 16 September 1987, in Ottawa from 17 September 1987 to 16 January 1988, and at United Nations Headquarters in New York from 17 January 1988 to 15 September 1988.

ARTICLE 16. ENTRY INTO FORCE

1. This Protocol shall enter into force on 1 January 1989, provided that at least eleven instruments of ratification, acceptance, approval of the Protocol or accession thereto have been deposited by States or regional economic integration organizations representing at least two-thirds of 1986 estimated global consumption of the controlled substances, and the provisions of paragraph 1 of Article 17 of the Convention have been fulfilled. In the event that these conditions have not been fulfilled by that date, the Protocol shall enter into force on the ninetieth day following the date on which the conditions have been fulfilled.

2.   For the purposes of paragraph 1, any such instrument deposited by a regional economic integration organization shall not be counted as additional to those deposited by member States of such organization.

3.   After the entry into force of this Protocol, any State or regional economic integration organization shall become a Party to it on the ninetieth day following the date of deposit of its instrument of ratification, acceptance, approval or accession.

ARTICLE 17.   PARTIES JOINING AFTER ENTRY INTO FORCE

Subject to Article 5, any State or regional economic integration organization which becomes a Party to this Protocol after the date of its entry into force, shall fulfil forthwith the sum of the obligations under Article 2, as well as under Article 4, that apply at that date to the States and regional economic integration organizations that became Parties on the date the Protocol entered into force.

ARTICLE 18.   RESERVATIONS

No reservations may be made to this Protocol.

ARTICLE 19.   WITHDRAWAL

For the purposes of this Protocol, the provisions of Article 19 of the Convention relating to withdrawal shall apply, except with respect to Parties referred to in paragraph 1 of Article 5.   Any such Party may withdraw from this Protocol by giving written notification to the Depositary at any time after four years of assuming the obligations specified in paragraphs 1 to 4 of Article 2.   Any such withdrawal shall take effect upon expiry of one year after the date of its receipt by the Depositary, or on such later date as may be specified in the notification of the withdrawal.

ARTICLE 20.   AUTHENTIC TEXTS

The original of this Protocol, of which the Arabic, Chinese, English, French, Russian and Spanish texts are equally authentic, shall be deposited with the Secretary–General of the United Nations.

ANNEX A
CONTROLLED SUBSTANCES

Group	Substance	Ozone Depleting Potential
Group I		
	$CFCl_3$ (CFC–11)	1.0
	CF_2Cl_2 (CFC–12)	1.0
	$C_2F_3Cl_3$ (CFC–113)	0.8
	$C_2F_4Cl_2$ (CFC–114)	1.0
	C_2F_5Cl (CFC–115)	0.6
Group II		
	CF_2BrCl (halon–1211)	3.0
	CF_3Br (halon–1301)	10.0
	$C_2F_4Br_2$ (halon–2402)	(to be determined)

3.19 PROTOCOL TO THE 1979 CONVENTION ON LONG–RANGE TRANS-BOUNDARY AIR POLLUTION CONCERNING THE CONTROL OF EMISSIONS OF NITROGEN OXIDES OR THEIR TRANSBOUN-DARY FLUXES.[1] Concluded at Sofia, 31 October 1988. Entered into force, 14 February 1991. EB.AIR/21, 28 I.L.M. 212 (1989)

Article 1

Definitions

For the purposes of the present Protocol,

1. "Convention" means the Convention on Long-range Transboundary Air Pollution, adopted in Geneva on 13 November 1979;

2. "EMEP" means the Co-operative Programme for Monitoring and Evaluation of the Long-range Transmission of Air Pollutants in Europe;

3. "Executive Body" means the Executive Body for the Convention constituted under article 10, paragraph 1 of the Convention;

4. "Geographical scope of EMEP" means the area defined in article 1, paragraph 4 of the Protocol to the 1979 Convention on Long-range Trans-boundary Air Pollution on Long-term Financing of the Co-operative Pro-gramme for Monitoring and Evaluation of the Long-range Transmission of Air Pollutants in Europe (EMEP), adopted in Geneva on 28 September 1984;

5. "Parties" means, unless the context otherwise requires, the Parties to the present Protocol;

6. "Commission" means the United Nations Economic Commission for Europe;

7. "Critical load" means a quantitative estimate of the exposure to one or more pollutants below which significant harmful effects on specified sensitive elements of the environment do not occur according to present knowledge;

8. "Major existing stationary source" means any existing stationary source the thermal input of which is at least 100 MW;

9. "Major new stationary source" means any new stationary source the thermal input of which is at least 50 MW;

10. "Major source category" means any category of sources which emit or may emit air pollutants in the form of nitrogen oxides, including the categories described in the Technical Annex, and which contribute at least 10 per cent of the total national emissions of nitrogen oxides on an annual basis as measured or calculated in the first calendar year after the date of entry into force of the present Protocol, and every fourth year thereafter;

11. "New stationary source" means any stationary source the construc-tion or substantial modification of which is commenced after the expiration of two years from the date of entry into force of this Protocol;

12. "New mobile source" means a motor vehicle or other mobile source which is manufactured after the expiration of two years from the date of entry into force of the present Protocol.

---

1. *See* Basic Document 3.9, *supra.*

Article 2

Basic obligations

1. The Parties shall, as soon as possible and as a first step, take effective measures to control and/or reduce their national annual emissions of nitrogen oxides or their transboundary fluxes so that these, at the latest by 31 December 1994, do not exceed their national annual emissions of nitrogen oxides or transboundary fluxes of such emissions for the calendar year 1987 or any previous year to be specified upon signature of, or accession to, the Protocol, provided that in addition, with respect to any Party specifying such a previous year, its national average annual transboundary fluxes or national average annual emissions of nitrogen oxides for the period from 1 January 1987 to 1 January 1996 do not exceed its transboundary fluxes or national emissions for the calendar year 1987.

2. Furthermore, the Parties shall in particular, and no later than two years after the date of entry into force of the present Protocol:

(a) Apply national emissions standards to major new stationary sources and/or source categories, and to substantially modified stationary sources in major source categories, based on the best available technologies which are economically feasible, taking into consideration the Technical Annex;

(b) Apply national emission standards to new mobile sources in all major source categories based on the best available technologies which are economically feasible, taking into consideration the Technical Annex and the relevant decisions taken within the framework of the Inland Transport Committee of the Commission; and

(c) Introduce pollution control measures for major existing stationary sources, taking into consideration the Technical Annex and the characteristics of the plant, its age and its rate of utilization and the need to avoid undue operational disruption.

3. (a) The Parties shall, as a second step, commence negotiations, no later than six months after the date of entry into force of the present Protocol, on further steps to reduce national annual emissions of nitrogen oxides or transboundary fluxes of such emissions, taking into account the best available scientific and technological developments, internationally accepted critical loads and other elements resulting from the work programme undertaken under article 6.

(b) To this end, the Parties shall co-operate in order to establish:

(i) Critical loads;

(ii) Reductions in national annual emissions of nitrogen oxides or transboundary fluxes of such emissions as required to achieve agreed objectives based on critical loads; and

(iii) Measures and a time-table commencing no later than 1 January 1996 for achieving such reductions.

4. Parties may take more stringent measures than those required by the present article.

Article 3

Exchange of technology

1.   The Parties shall, consistent with their national laws, regulations and practices, facilitate the exchange of technology to reduce emissions of nitrogen oxides, particularly through the promotion of:

(a) Commercial exchange of available technology;

(b) Direct industrial contacts and co-operation, including joint ventures;

(c) Exchange of information and experience; and

(d) Provision of technical assistance.

2.   In promoting the activities specified in subparagraphs (a) to (d) above, the Parties shall create favourable conditions by facilitating contacts and co-operation among appropriate organizations and individuals in the private and public sectors that are capable of providing technology, design and engineering services, equipment or finance.

3.   The Parties shall, no later than six months after the date of entry into force of the present Protocol, commence consideration of procedures to create more favourable conditions for the exchange of technology to reduce emissions of nitrogen oxides.

Article 4

Unleaded fuel

The Parties shall, as soon as possible and no later than two years after the date of entry into force of the present Protocol, make unleaded fuel sufficiently available, in particular cases as a minimum along main international transit routes, to facilitate the circulation of vehicles equipped with catalytic converters.

Article 5

Review process

1.   The Parties shall regularly review the present Protocol, taking into account the best available scientific substantiation and technological development.

2.   The first review shall take place no later than one year after the date of entry into force of the present Protocol.

Article 6

Work to be undertaken

The Parties shall give high priority to research and monitoring related to the development and application of an approach based on critical loads to determine, on a scientific basis, necessary reductions in emissions of nitrogen oxides.   The Parties shall, in particular, through national research programmes, in the work plan of the Executive Body and through other co-operative programmes within the framework of the Convention, seek to:

(a) Identify and quantify effects of emissions of nitrogen oxides on humans, plant and animal life, waters, soils and materials, taking into account the impact on these of nitrogen oxides from sources other than atmospheric deposition;

(b) Determine the geographical distribution of sensitive areas;

(c) Develop measurements and model calculations including harmonized methodologies for the calculation of emissions, to quantify the long-range transport of nitrogen oxides and related pollutants;

(d) Improve estimates of the performance and costs of technologies for control of emissions of nitrogen oxides and record the development of improved and new technologies; and

(e) Develop, in the context of an approach based on critical loads, methods to integrate scientific, technical and economic data in order to determine appropriate control strategies.

Article 7

National programmes, policies and strategies

The Parties shall develop without undue delay national programmes, policies and strategies to implement the obligations under the present Protocol that shall serve as a means of controlling and reducing emissions of nitrogen oxides or their transboundary fluxes.

Article 8

Information exchange and annual reporting

1. The Parties shall exchange information by notifying the Executive Body of the national programmes, policies and strategies that they develop in accordance with article 7 and by reporting to it annually on progress achieved under, and any changes to, those programmes, policies and strategies, and in particular on:

(a) The levels of national annual emissions of nitrogen oxides and the basis upon which they have been calculated;

(b) Progress in applying national emission standards required under article 2, subparagraphs 2(a) and 2(b), and the national emission standards applied or to be applied, and the sources and/or source categories concerned;

(c) Progress in introducing the pollution control measures required under article 2, subparagraph 2(c), the sources concerned and the measures introduced or to be introduced;

(d) Progress in making unleaded fuel available;

(e) Measures taken to facilitate the exchange of technology; and

(f) Progress in establishing critical loads.

2. Such information shall, as far as possible, be submitted in accordance with a uniform reporting framework.

Article 9

Calculations

EMEP shall, utilizing appropriate models and in good time before the annual meetings of the Executive Body, provide to the Executive Body calculations of nitrogen budgets and also of transboundary fluxes and deposition of nitrogen oxides within the geographical scope of EMEP. In areas outside the geographical scope of EMEP, models appropriate to the particular circumstances of Parties to the Convention therein shall be used.

Article 10

Technical Annex

The Technical Annex to the present Protocol is recommendatory in character. It shall form an integral part of the Protocol.

Article 11

Amendments to the Protocol

1. Any Party may propose amendments to the present Protocol.

2. Proposed amendments shall be submitted in writing to the Executive Secretary of the Commission who shall communicate them to all Parties. The Executive Body shall discuss the proposed amendments at its next annual meeting provided that these proposals have been circulated by the Executive Secretary to the Parties at least ninety days in advance.

3. Amendments to the Protocol, other than amendments to its Technical Annex, shall be adopted by consensus of the Parties present at a meeting of the Executive Body, and shall enter into force for the Parties which have accepted them on the ninetieth day after the date on which two-thirds of the Parties have deposited their instruments of acceptance thereof. Amendments shall enter into force for any Party which has accepted them after two-thirds of the Parties have deposited their instruments of acceptance of the amendment, on the ninetieth day after the date on which that Party deposited its instrument of acceptance of the amendments.

4. Amendments to the Technical Annex shall be adopted by consensus of the Parties present at a meeting of the Executive Body and shall become effective thirty days after the date on which they have been communicated in accordance with paragraph 5 below.

5. Amendments under paragraphs 3 and 4 above shall, as soon as possible after their adoption, be communicated by the Executive Secretary to all Parties.

Article 12

Settlement of disputes

If a dispute arises between two or more Parties as to the interpretation or application of the present Protocol, they shall seek a solution by negotiation or by any other method of dispute settlement acceptable to the parties to the dispute.

Article 13

Signature

1. The present Protocol shall be open for signature at Sofia from 1 November 1988 until 4 November 1988 inclusive, then at the Headquarters of the United Nations in New York until 5 May 1989, by the member States of the Commission as well as States having consultative status with the Commission, pursuant to paragraph 8 of Economic and Social Council resolution 36 (IV) of 28 March 1947, and by regional economic integration organizations, constituted by sovereign States members of the Commission, which have competence in respect of the negotiation, conclusion and application of international agreements in matters covered by the Protocol, provided that the States and organizations concerned are Parties to the Convention.

2.   In matters within their competence, such regional economic integration organizations shall, on their own behalf, exercise the rights and fulfil the responsibilities which the present Protocol attributes to their member States. In such cases, the member States of these organizations shall not be entitled to exercise such rights individually.

Article 14
Ratification, acceptance, approval and accession

1.   The present Protocol shall be subject to ratification, acceptance or approval by Signatories.

2.   The present Protocol shall be open for accession as from 6 May 1989 by the States and organizations referred to in article 13, paragraph 1.

3.   A State or organization which accedes to the present Protocol after 31 December 1993 may implement articles 2 and 4 no later than 31 December 1995.

4.   The instruments of ratification, acceptance, approval or accession shall be deposited with the Secretary–General of the United Nations, who will perform the functions of depositary.

Article 15
Entry into force

1.   The present Protocol shall enter into force on the ninetieth day following the date on which the sixteenth instrument of ratification, acceptance, approval or accession has been deposited.

2.   For each State and organization referred to in article 13, paragraph 1, which ratifies, accepts or approves the present Protocol or accedes thereto after the deposit of the sixteenth instrument of ratification, acceptance, approval, or accession, the Protocol shall enter into force on the ninetieth day following the date of deposit by such Party of its instrument of ratification, acceptance, approval, or accession.

Article 16
Withdrawal

At any time after five years from the date on which the present Protocol has come into force with respect to a Party, that Party may withdraw from it by giving written notification to the depositary. Any such withdrawal shall take effect on the ninetieth day following the date of its receipt by the depositary, or on such later date as may be specified in the notification of the withdrawal.

Article 17
Authentic texts

The original of the present Protocol, of which the English, French and Russian texts are equally authentic, shall be deposited with the Secretary–General of the United Nations.

3.20 HELSINKI DECLARATION ON THE PROTECTION OF THE OZONE LAYER.[1] Adopted at the First Meetings of the Parties to the 1985 Vienna Convention and the 1987 Montreal Protocol at Helsinki, 2 May 1989. 28 I.L.M. 1335 (1989)

The Governments and the European Communities represented at the First Meetings of the Parties to the Vienna Convention and the Montreal Protocol

Aware of the wide agreement among scientists that depletion of the ozone layer will threaten present and future generations unless more stringent control measures are adopted

Mindful that some ozone depleting substances are powerful greenhouse gases leading to global warming

Aware also of the extensive and rapid technological development of environmentally acceptable substitutes for the substances that deplete the ozone layer and the urgent need to facilitate the transfer of technologies of such substitutes especially to developing countries

ENCOURAGE all states that have not done so to join the Vienna Convention for the Protection of the Ozone Layer and its Montreal Protocol

AGREE to phase out the production and the consumption of CFC's controlled by the Montreal Protocol as soon as possible but not later than the year 2000 and for that purpose to tighten the timetable agreed upon in the Montreal Protocol taking due account of the special situation of developing countries

AGREE to both phase out halons and control and reduce other ozone-depleting substances which contribute significantly to ozone depletion as soon as feasible

AGREE to commit themselves, in proportion to their means and resources, to accelerate the development of environmentally acceptable substituting chemicals, products and technologies

AGREE to facilitate the access of developing countries to relevant scientific information, research results and training and to seek to develop appropriate funding mechanisms to facilitate the transfer of technology and replacement of equipment at minimum cost to developing countries.

1. *See also* Basic Documents 3.15 and 3.17 *supra,* 3.21 and 3.23 *infra.*

3.21 LONDON AMENDMENTS TO THE MONTREAL PROTOCOL ON SUB-STANCES THAT DEPLETE THE OZONE LAYER WITH ANNEXES (1990).[1] Adopted at London by Decisions II/2 at the Second Meeting of Parties to the Montreal Protocol, 29 June 1990. Not in force as of 31 December 1992. UNEP/Oz.L.Pro.2/3 (Annex II)

A. Preambular paragraphs

1. The 6th preambular paragraph of the Protocol shall be replaced by the following:

Determined to protect the ozone layer by taking precautionary measures to control equitably total global emissions of substances that deplete it, with the ultimate objective of their elimination on the basis of developments in scientific knowledge, taking into account technical and economic considerations and bearing in mind the developmental needs of developing countries.

2. The 7th preambular paragraph of the Protocol shall be replaced by the following:

Acknowledging that special provision is required to meet the needs of developing countries, including the provision of additional financial resources and access to relevant technologies, bearing in mind that the magnitude of funds necessary is predictable, and the funds can be expected to make a substantial difference in the world's ability to address the scientifically established problem of ozone depletion and its harmful effects.

3. The 9th preambular paragraph of the Protocol shall be replaced by the following:

Considering the importance of promoting international co-operation in the research, development and transfer of alternative technologies relating to the control and reduction of emissions of substances that deplete the ozone layer, bearing in mind in particular the needs of developing countries.

B. Article 1: Definitions

1. Paragraph 4 of Article 1 of the Protocol shall be replaced by the following paragraph:

4. "Controlled substance" means a substance in Annex A or in Annex B to this Protocol, whether existing alone or in a mixture. It includes the isomers of any such substance, except as specified in the relevant Annex, but excludes any controlled substance or mixture which is in a manufactured product other than a container used for the transportation or storage of that substance.

2. Paragraph 5 of Article 1 of the Protocol shall be replaced by the following paragraph:

5. "Production" means the amount of controlled substances produced, minus the amount destroyed by technologies to be approved by the Parties and minus the amount entirely used as feedstock in the manufac-

1. *See also* Basic Documents 3.15, 3.17, 3.20, *supra,* and 3.23, *infra.*

ture of other chemicals. The amount recycled and reused is not to be considered as "production".

3.   The following paragraph shall be added to Article 1 of the Protocol:

9.   "Transitional substance" means a substance in Annex C to this Protocol, whether existing alone or in a mixture. It includes the isomers of any such substance, except as may be specified in Annex C, but excludes any transitional substance or mixture which is in a manufactured product other than a container used for the transportation or storage of that substance.

C.   Article 2, paragraph 5

Paragraph 5 of Article 2 of the Protocol shall be replaced by the following paragraph:

5.   Any Party may, for any one or more control periods, transfer to another Party any portion of its calculated level of production set out in Articles 2A to 2E, provided that the total combined calculated levels of production of the Parties concerned for any group of controlled substances do not exceed the production limits set out in those Articles for that group. Such transfer of production shall be notified to the Secretariat by each of the Parties concerned, stating the terms of such transfer and the period for which it is to apply.

D.   Article 2, paragraph 6

The following words shall be inserted in paragraph 6 of Article 2 before the words "controlled substances" the first time they occur:

Annex A or Annex B

E.   Article 2, paragraph 8(a)

The following words shall be added after the words "this Article" wherever they appear in paragraph 8(a) of Article 2 of the Protocol:

and Articles 2A to 2E

F.   Article 2, paragraph 9(a)(i)

The following words shall be added after "Annex A" in paragraph 9(a)(i) of Article 2 of the Protocol:

and/or Annex B

G.   Article 2, paragraph 9(a)(ii)

The following words shall be deleted from paragraph 9(a)(ii) of Article 2 of the Protocol:

form 1986 levels

H.   Article 2, paragraph 9(c)

The following words shall be deleted from paragraph 9(c) of Article 2 of the Protocol:

representing at least fifty per cent of the total consumption of the controlled substances of the Parties

and replaced by:

representing a majority of the Parties operating under paragraph 1 of Article 5 present and voting and a majority of the Parties not so operating present and voting

I. Article 2, paragraph 10(b)

Paragraph 10(b) of Article 2 of the Protocol shall be deleted, and paragraph 10(a) of Article 2 shall become paragraph 10.

J. Article 2, paragraph 11

The following words shall be added after the words "this Article" wherever they occur in paragraph 11 of Article 2 of the Protocol:

and Articles 2A to 2E

K. Article 2C: Other fully halogenated CFCs

The following paragraphs shall be added to the Protocol as Article 2C:

Article 2C: Other fully halogenated CFCs

1. Each Party shall ensure that for the twelve-month period commencing on 1 January 1993, and in each twelve-month period thereafter, its calculated level of consumption of the controlled substances in Group I of Annex B does not exceed, annually, eighty per cent of its calculated level of consumption in 1989. Each Party producing one or more of these substances shall, for the same periods, ensure that its calculated level of production of the substances does not exceed, annually, eighty per cent of its calculated level of production in 1989. However, in order to satisfy the basic domestic needs of the Parties operating under paragraph 1 of Article 5, its calculated level of production may exceed that limit by up to ten per cent of its calculated level of production in 1989.

2. Each Party shall ensure that for the twelve-month period commencing on 1 January 1997, and in each twelve-month period thereafter, its calculated level of consumption of the controlled substances in Group I of Annex B does not exceed, annually, fifteen per cent of its calculated level of consumption in 1989. Each Party producing one or more of these substances shall, for the same periods, ensure that its calculated level of production of the substances does not exceed, annually, fifteen per cent of its calculated level of production in 1989. However, in order to satisfy the basic domestic needs of the Parties operating under paragraph 1 of Article 5, its calculated level of production may exceed that limit by up to ten per cent of its calculated level of production in 1989.

3. Each Party shall ensure that for the twelve-month period commencing on 1 January 2000, and in each twelve-month period thereafter, its calculated level of consumption of the controlled substances in Group I of Annex B does not exceed zero. Each Party producing one or more of these substances shall, for the same periods, ensure that its calculated level of production of the substances does not exceed zero. However, in order to satisfy the basic domestic needs of the Parties operating under paragraph 1 of Article 5, its calculated level of production may exceed that limit by up to fifteen per cent of its calculated level of production in 1989.

L. Article 2D: Carbon tetrachloride

The following paragraphs shall be added to the Protocol as Article 2D:

Article 2D: Carbon tetrachloride

1. Each Party shall ensure that for the twelve-month period commencing on 1 January 1995, and in each twelve-month period thereafter, its calculated level of consumption of the controlled substance in Group II of Annex B does not exceed, annually, fifteen per cent of its calculated level of consumption in 1989. Each Party producing the substance shall, for the same periods, ensure that its calculated level of production of the substance does not exceed, annually, fifteen per cent of its calculated level of production in 1989. However, in order to satisfy the basic domestic needs of the Parties operating under paragraph 1 of Article 5, its calculated level of production may exceed that limit by up to ten per cent of its calculated level of production in 1989.

2. Each Party shall ensure that for the twelve-month period commencing on 1 January 2000, and in each twelve-month period thereafter, its calculated level of consumption of the controlled substance in Group II of Annex B does not exceed zero. Each Party producing the substance shall, for the same periods, ensure that its calculated level of production of the substance does not exceed zero. However, in order to satisfy the basic domestic needs of the Parties operating under paragraph 1 of Article 5, its calculated level of production may exceed that limit by up to fifteen per cent of its calculated level of production in 1989.

M. Article 2E: 1.1.1–trichloroethane (methyl chloroform)

The following paragraphs shall be added to the Protocol as Article 2E:

Article 2E: 1.1.1–trichloroethane (methyl chloroform)

1. Each Party shall ensure that for the twelve-month period commencing on 1 January 1993, and in each twelve month period thereafter, its calculated level of consumption of the controlled substance in Group III of Annex B does not exceed, annually, its calculated level of consumption in 1989. Each Party producing the substance shall, for the same periods, ensure that its calculated level of production of the substance does not exceed, annually, its calculated level of production in 1989. However, in order to satisfy the basic domestic needs of the Parties operating under paragraph 1 of Article 5, its calculated level of production may exceed that limit by up to ten per cent of its calculated level of production in 1989.

2. Each Party shall ensure that for the twelve-month period commencing on 1 January 1995, and in each twelve-month period thereafter, its calculated level of consumption of the controlled substance in Group III of Annex B does not exceed, annually, seventy per cent of its calculated level of consumption in 1989. Each Party producing the substance shall, for the same periods, ensure that its calculated level of production of the substance does not exceed, annually, seventy per cent of its calculated level of consumption in 1989. However, in order to satisfy the basic domestic needs of the Parties operating under paragraph 1 of Article 5, its calculated level of production may exceed that limit by up to ten per cent of its calculated level of production in 1989.

3. Each Party shall ensure that for the twelve-month period commencing on 1 January 2000, and in each twelve-month period thereafter, its calculated level of consumption of the controlled substance in Group III of

Annex B does not exceed, annually, thirty per cent of its calculated level of consumption in 1989. Each Party producing the substance shall, for the same periods, ensure that its calculated level of production of the substance does not exceed, annually, thirty per cent of its calculated level of production in 1989. However, in order to satisfy the basic domestic needs of Parties operating under paragraph 1 of Article 5, its calculated level of production may exceed that limit by up to ten per cent of its calculated level of production in 1989.

4. Each Party shall ensure that for the twelve-month period commencing on 1 January 2005, and in each twelve-month period thereafter, its calculated level of consumption of the controlled substance in Group III of Annex B does not exceed zero. Each Party producing the substance shall, for the same periods, ensure that its calculated level of production of the substance does not exceed zero. However, in order to satisfy the basic domestic needs of the Parties operating under paragraph 1 of Article 5, its calculated level of production may exceed that limit by up to fifteen per cent of its calculated level of production in 1989.

5. The parties shall review, in 1992, the feasibility of a more rapid schedule of reductions than that set out in this Article.

N. Article 3: Calculation of control levels

1. The following shall be added after "Articles 2" in Article 3 of the Protocol:

2A to 2E.

2. The following words shall be added after "Annex A" each time it appears in Article 3 of the Protocol:

or Annex B

O. Article 4: Control of trade with non-Parties

1. Paragraphs 1 to 5 of Article 4 shall be replaced by the following paragraphs:

1. As of 1 January 1990, each Party shall ban the import of the controlled substances in Annex A from any State not party to this Protocol.

1 *bis*. Within one year of the date of the entry into force of this paragraph, each Party shall ban the import of the controlled substances in Annex B from any State not party to this Protocol.

2. As of 1 January 1993, each Party shall ban the export of any controlled substances in Annex A to any State not party to this Protocol.

2 *bis*. Commencing one year after the date of entry into force of this paragraph, each Party shall ban the export of any controlled substances in Annex B to any State not party to this Protocol.

3. By 1 January 1992, the Parties shall, following the procedures in Article 10 of the Convention, elaborate in an annex a list of products containing controlled substances in Annex A. Parties that have not objected to the annex in accordance with those procedures shall ban, within one year of the annex having become effective, the import of those products from any State not party to this Protocol.

3 *bis.* Within three years of the date of the entry into force of this paragraph, the Parties shall, following the procedures in Article 10 of the Convention, elaborate in an annex a list of products containing controlled substances in Annex B. Parties that have not objected to the annex in accordance with those procedures shall ban, within one year of the annex having become effective, the import of those products from any State not party to this Protocol.

4. By 1 January 1994, the Parties shall determine the feasibility of banning or restricting, from States not party to this Protocol, the import of products produced with, but not containing, controlled substances in Annex A. If determined feasible, the Parties shall, following the procedures in Article 10 of the Convention, elaborate in an annex a list of such products. Parties that have not objected to the annex in accordance with those procedures shall ban, within one year of the annex having become effective, the import of those products from any State not party to this Protocol.

4 *bis.* Within five years of the date of the entry into force of this paragraph, the Parties shall determine the feasibility of banning or restricting, from States not party to this Protocol, the import of products produced with, but not containing, controlled substances in Annex B. If determined feasible, the Parties shall, following the procedures in Article 10 of the Convention, elaborate in an annex a list of such products. Parties that have not objected to the annex in accordance with those procedures shall ban or restrict, within one year of the annex having become effective, the import of those products from any State not party to this Protocol.

5. Each Party undertakes to the fullest practicable extent to discourage the export to any State not party to this Protocol of technology for producing and for utilizing controlled substances.

2. Paragraph 8 of Article 4 of the Protocol shall be replaced by the following paragraph:

8. Notwithstanding the provisions of this Article, imports referred to in paragraphs 1, 1 *bis,* 3, 3 *bis,* 4 and 4 *bis,* and exports referred to in paragraphs 2 and 2 *bis,* may be permitted from, or to, any State not party to this Protocol, if that State is determined by a meeting of the Parties to be in full compliance with Article 2, Articles 2A to 2E, and this Article and have submitted data to that effect as specified in Article 7.

3. The following paragraph shall be added to Article 4 of the Protocol as paragraph 9:

9. For the purposes of this Article, the term "State not party to this Protocol" shall include, with respect to a particular controlled substance, a State or regional economic integration organization that has not agreed to be bound by the control measures in effect for that substance.

P. Article 5: Special situation of developing countries

Article 5 of the Protocol shall be replaced by the following:

1. Any Party that is a developing country and whose annual calculated level of consumption of the controlled substances in Annex A is less

than 0.3 kilograms per capita on the date of the entry into force of the Protocol for it, or any time thereafter until 1 January 1999, shall in order to meet its basic domestic needs, be entitled to delay for ten years its compliance with the control measures set out in Articles 2A to 2E.

2. However, any Party operating under paragraph 1 of this Article shall exceed neither an annual calculated level of consumption of the controlled substances in Annex A of 0.3 kilograms per capita nor an annual calculated level of consumption of the controlled substances of Annex B of 0.2 kilograms per capita.

3. When implementing the control measures set out in Articles 2A to 2E, any Party operating under paragraph 1 of this Article shall be entitled to use:

(*a*) For controlled substances under Annex A, either the average of its annual calculated level of consumption for the period 1995 to 1997 inclusive or a calculated level of consumption of 0.3 kilograms per capita, whichever is the lower, as the basis for determining its compliance with the control measures;

(*b*) For controlled substances under Annex B, the average of its annual calculated level of consumption for the period 1998 to 2000 inclusive or a calculated level of consumption of 0.2 kilograms per capita, whichever is the lower, as the basis for determining its compliance with the control measures.

4. If a Party operating under paragraph 1 of this Article, at any time before the control measures obligations in Articles 2A to 2E become applicable to it, finds itself unable to obtain an adequate supply of controlled substances, it may notify this to the Secretariat. The Secretariat shall forthwith transmit a copy of such notification to the Parties, which shall consider the matter at their next Meeting, and decide upon appropriate action to be taken.

5. Developing the capacity to fulfil the obligations of the Parties operating under paragraph 1 of this Article to comply with the control measures set out in Articles 2A to 2E and their implementation by those same Parties will depend upon the effective implementation of the financial co-operation as provided by Article 10 and transfer of technology as provided by Article 10A.

6. Any Party operating under paragraph 1 of this Article may, at any time, notify the Secretariat in writing that, having taken all practicable steps it is unable to implement any or all of the obligations laid down in Articles 2A to 2E due to the inadequate implementation of Articles 10 and 10A. The Secretariat shall forthwith transmit a copy of the notification to the Parties, which shall consider the matter at their next Meeting, giving due recognition to paragraph 5 of this Article and shall decide upon appropriate action to be taken.

7. During the period between notification and the Meeting of the Parties at which the appropriate action referred to in paragraph 6 above is to be decided, or for a further period if the Meeting of the Parties so decides, the non-compliance procedures referred to in Article 8 shall not be invoked against the notifying Party.

8. A Meeting of the Parties shall review, not later than 1995, the situation of the Parties operating under paragraph 1 of this Article, including the effective implementation of financial co-operation and transfer of technology to them, and adopt such revisions that may be deemed necessary regarding the schedule of control measures applicable to those Parties.

9. Decisions of the Parties referred to in paragraphs 4, 6 and 7 of this Article shall be taken according to the same procedure applied to decision-making under Article 10.

Q. Article 6: Assessment and review of control measures

The following words shall be added after "Article 2" in Article 6 of the Protocol:

Articles 2A to 2E, and the situation regarding production, imports and exports of the transitional substances in Group I of Annex C.

R. Article 7: Reporting of data

1. Article 7 of the Protocol shall be replaced by the following:

1. Each Party shall provide to the Secretariat, within three months of becoming a Party, statistical data on its production, imports and exports of each of the controlled substances in Annex A for the year 1986, or the best possible estimates of such data where actual data are not available.

2. Each Party shall provide to the Secretariat statistical data on its production, imports and exports of each of the controlled substances in Annex B and each of the transitional substances in Group I of Annex C, for the year 1989, or the best possible estimates of such data where actual data are not available, not later than three months after the date when the provisions set out in the Protocol with regard to the substances in Annex B enter into force for that Party.

3. Each Party shall provide statistical data to the Secretariat on its annual production (as defined in paragraph 5 of Article 1), and, separately.

—amounts used for feedstocks,

—amounts destroyed by technologies approved by the Parties,

—imports and exports to Parties and non-Parties respectively,

of each of the controlled substances listed in Annexes A and B as well as of the transitional substances in Group I of Annex C, for the year during which provisions concerning the substances in Annex B entered into force for that Party and for each year thereafter. Data shall be forwarded not later than nine months after the end of the year to which the data relate.

4. For Parties operating under the provisions of paragraph 8(a) of Article 2, the requirements in paragraphs 1, 2 and 3 of this Article in respect of statistical data on imports and exports shall be satisfied if the regional economic integration organization concerned provides data on imports and exports between the organization and States that are not members of that organization.

S.　Article 9:　Research, development, public awareness and exchange of information

Paragraph 1(a) of Article 9 of the Protocol shall be replaced by the following:

(*a*) Best technologies for improving the containment, recovery, recycling, or destruction of controlled and transitional substances or otherwise reducing their emissions;

T.　Article 10:　Financial mechanism

Article 10 of the Protocol shall be replaced by the following:

Article 10:　Financial mechanism

1.　The Parties shall establish a mechanism for the purposes of providing financial and technical co-operation, including the transfer of technologies, to Parties operating under paragraph 1 of Article 5 of this Protocol to enable their compliance with the control measures set out in Articles 2A to 2E of the Protocol.　The mechanism, contributions to which shall be additional to other financial transfers to Parties operating under that paragraph, shall meet all agreed incremental costs of such Parties in order to enable their compliance with the control measures of the Protocol.　An indicative list of the categories of incremental costs shall be decided by the meeting of the Parties.

2.　The mechanism established under paragraph 1 shall include a Multilateral Fund.　It may also include other means of multilateral, regional and bilateral co-operation.

3.　The Multilateral Fund shall:

(*a*) Meet, on a grant or concessional basis as appropriate, and according to criteria to be decided upon by the Parties, the agreed incremental costs:

(*b*) Finance clearing-house functions to:

(i) Assist Parties operating under paragraph 1 of Article 5, through country specific studies and other technical co-operation, to identify their needs for co-operation;

(ii) Facilitate technical co-operation to meet these identified needs;

(iii) Distribute, as provided for in Article 9, information and relevant materials, and hold workshops, training sessions, and other related activities, for the benefit of Parties that are developing countries;　and

(iv) Facilitate and monitor other multilateral, regional and bilateral co-operation available to Parties that are developing countries;

(*c*) Finance the secretarial services of the Multilateral Fund and related support costs.

4.　The Multilateral Fund shall operate under the authority of the Parties who shall decide on its overall policies.

5. The Parties shall establish an Executive Committee to develop and monitor the implementation of specific operational policies, guidelines and administrative arrangements, including the disbursement of resources, for the purpose of achieving the objectives of the Multilateral Fund. The Executive Committee shall discharge its tasks and responsibilities, specified in its terms of reference as agreed by the Parties, with the co-operation and assistance of the International Bank for Reconstruction and Development (World Bank), the United Nations Environment Programme, the United Nations Development Programme or other appropriate agencies depending on their respective areas of expertise. The members of the Executive Committee, which shall be selected on the basis of a balanced representation of the Parties operating under paragraph 1 of Article 5 and of the Parties not so operating, shall be endorsed by the Parties.

6. The Multilateral Fund shall be financed by contributions from Parties not operating under paragraph 1 of Article 5 in convertible currency or, in certain circumstances, in kind and/or in national currency, on the basis of the United Nations scale of assessments. Contributions by other Parties shall be encouraged. Bilateral and, in particular cases agreed by a decision of the Parties, regional co-operation may, up to a percentage and consistent with any criteria to be specified by decision of the Parties, be considered as a contribution to the Multilateral Fund, provided that such co-operation, as a minimum:

   (*a*) Strictly relates to compliance with the provisions of this Protocol;

   (*b*) Provides additional resources; and

   (*c*) Meets agreed incremental costs.

7. The Parties shall decide upon the programme budget of the Multilateral Fund for each fiscal period and upon the percentage of contributions of the individual Parties thereto.

8. Resources under the Multilateral Fund shall be disbursed with the concurrence of the beneficiary Party.

9. Decisions by the Parties under this Article shall be taken by consensus whenever possible. If all efforts at consensus have been exhausted and no agreement reached, decisions shall be adopted by a two-thirds majority vote of the Parties present and voting, representing a majority of the Parties operating under paragraph 1 of Article 5 present and voting and a majority of the Parties not so operating present and voting.

10. The financial mechanism set out in this Article is without prejudice to any future arrangements that may be developed with respect to other environmental issues.

U. Article 10A: Transfer of technology

The following Article shall be added to the Protocol as Article 10A:

Article 10A: Transfer of technology

Each Party shall take every practicable step, consistent with the programmes supported by the financial mechanism, to ensure:

(*a*) That the best available, environmentally safe substitutes and related technologies are expeditiously transferred to Parties operating under paragraph 1 of Article 5; and

(*b*) That the transfers referred to in subparagraph (a) occur under fair and most favourable conditions.

V. Article 11: Meetings of the Parties

Paragraph 4(g) of Article 11 of the Protocol shall be replaced by the following:

(*g*) Assess, in accordance with Article 6, the control measures and the situation regarding transitional substances;

W. Article 17: Parties joining after entry into force

The following words shall be added after "as well as under" in Article 17:

Articles 2A to 2E, and

X. Article 19: Withdrawal

Article 19 of the Protocol shall be replaced by the following paragraph:

Any Party may withdraw from this Protocol by giving written notification to the Depositary at any time after four years of assuming the obligations specified in paragraph 1 of Article 2A. Any such withdrawal shall take effect upon expiry of one year after the date of its receipt by the Depositary, or on such later date as may be specified in the notification of the withdrawal.

Annexes

The following annexes shall be added to the Protocol:

Annex B
Controlled substances

Group	Substance	Ozone-depleting potential
Group I		
CF_3Cl	(CFC–13)	1.0
C_2FCl_5	(CFC–111)	1.0
$C_2F_2Cl_4$	(CFC–112)	1.0
C_3FCl_7	(CFC–211)	1.0
$C_3F_2Cl_6$	(CFC–212)	1.0
$C_3F_3Cl_5$	(CFC–213)	1.0
$C_3F_4Cl_4$	(CFC–214)	1.0
$C_3F_5Cl_3$	(CFC–215)	1.0
$C_3F_6Cl_2$	(CFC–216)	1.0
C_3F_7Cl	(CFC–217)	1.0
Group II		
CCl_4	carbon tetrachloride	1.1
Group III		
$C_2H_3Cl_3$ *	1,1,1–trichloroethane (methyl chloroform)	0.1

* This formula does not refer to 1,1,2–trichloroethane.

Annex C
Transitional substances

Group	Substance
Group I	
$CHFCl_2$	(HCFC–21)
CHF_2Cl	(HCFC–22)
CHF_2Cl	(HCFC–31)
C_2HFCl_4	(HCFC–121)
$C_2HF_2Cl_3$	(HCFC–122)
$C_2HF_3Cl_2$	(HCFC–123)
C_2HF_4Cl	(HCFC–124)
$C_2H_2FCl_3$	(HCFC–131)
$C_2H_2F_2Cl_2$	(HCFC–132)
$C_2H_2F_3Cl$	(HCFC–133)
$C_2H_3FCl_2$	(HCFC–141)
$C_2H_3F_2Cl$	(HCFC–142)
C_2H_4FCl	(HCFC–151)
C_3HFCl_6	(HCFC–221)
$C_3HF_2Cl_5$	(HCFC–222)
$C_3HF_3Cl_4$	(HCFC–223)
$C_3HF_4Cl_3$	(HCFC–224)
$C_3HF_5Cl_2$	(HCFC–225)
C_3HP_6Cl	(HCFC–226)
$C_3H_2FCl_5$	(HCFC–231)
$C_3H_2F_2Cl_4$	(HCFC–232)
$C_3H_2F_3Cl_3$	(HCFC–233)
$C_3H_2F_4Cl_2$	(HCFC–234)
$C_3H_2F_5Cl$	(HCFC–235)
$C_3H_3FCl_4$	(HCFC–241)
$C_3H_3F_2Cl_3$	(HCFC–242)
$C_3H_3F_3Cl_2$	(HCFC–243)
$C_3H_3F_4Cl$	(HCFC–244)
$C_3H_4FCl_3$	(HCFC–251)
$C_3H_4F_2Cl_2$	(HCFC–252)
$C_3H_4F_3Cl$	(HCFC–253)
$C_3H_5FCl_2$	(HCFC–261)
$C_3H_5F_2Cl$	(HCFC–262)
C_3H_6FCl	(HCFC–271)

Article 2
Entry into force

1.   This Amendment shall enter into force on 1 January 1992, provided that at least twenty instruments of ratification, acceptance or approval of the Amendment have been deposited by States or regional economic integration organizations that are Parties to the Montreal Protocol on Substances that Deplete the Ozone Layer.   In the event that this condition has not been fulfilled by that date, the Amendment shall enter into force on the ninetieth day following the date on which it has been fulfilled.

2.   For the purposes of paragraph 1, any such instrument deposited by a regional economic integration organization shall not be counted as additional to those deposited by member States of such organization.

3.   After the entry into force of this Amendment as provided under paragraph 1, it shall enter into force for any other Party to the Protocol on the ninetieth day following the date of deposit of its instrument of ratification, acceptance or approval.

Annex III
Non-compliance procedure

1. If one or more Parties have reservations regarding another Party's implementation of its obligations under the Protocol, those concerns may be addressed in writing to the Secretariat. Such a submission shall be supported by corroborating information.

2. The Party whose implementation is at issue is to be given the submission and a reasonable opportunity to reply. Such reply and information in support thereof is to be submitted to the Secretariat and to the Parties involved. The Secretariat shall then transmit the submission, the reply and the information provided by the Parties, to the Implementation Committee referred to in paragraph 3, which shall consider the matter as soon as practicable.

3. An Implementation Committee is hereby established. It shall consist of five Parties elected by the Meeting of the Parties for two years, based on equitable geographical distribution. Outgoing Parties may also be re-elected for one immediate consecutive term. At the first election, two Parties shall be elected for a one-year term.

4. The Committee shall meet as necessary to perform its functions.

5. The functions of the Committee shall be to receive, consider and report on:

(a) Any submission made by one or more Parties in accordance with paragraphs 1 and 2;

(b) Any information or observations forwarded by the Secretariat in connection with the preparation of the report referred to in Article 12(c) of the Protocol.

6. The Committee shall consider the submissions, information and observations referred to in paragraph 5 with a view to securing an amicable resolution of the matter on the basis of respect for the provisions of the Protocol.

7. The Committee shall report to the Meeting of the Parties. After receiving a report by the Committee the Parties may, taking into consideration the circumstances of the case, decide upon and call for steps to bring about full compliance with the Protocol, including measures to assist the Party's compliance with the Protocol, and to further the Protocol's objectives.

8. The Parties involved in a matter referred to in paragraph 5 shall inform, through the Secretariat, the Meeting of the Parties of the results of proceedings taken under Article 11 of the Convention regarding possible non-compliance, about implementation of those results and about implementation of any decision of the Parties pursuant to paragraph 7.

9. The Meeting of the Parties may, pending completion of proceedings initiated under Article 11 of the Convention, issue an interim call and/or recommendations.

3.22 UNITED NATIONS FRAMEWORK CONVENTION ON CLIMATE CHANGE (WITHOUT ANNEXES I & II). Concluded at Rio de Janeiro, 29 May 1992. Entered into force 21 March 1994. 31 I.L.M. 849 (1992)

The Parties to this Convention,

Acknowledging that change in the Earth's climate and its adverse effects are a common concern of humankind,

Concerned that human activities have been substantially increasing the atmospheric concentrations of greenhouse gases, that these increases enhance the natural greenhouse effect, and that this will result on average in an additional warming of the Earth's surface and atmosphere and may adversely affect natural ecosystems and humankind,

Noting that the largest share of historical and current global emissions of greenhouse gases has originated in developed countries, that per capita emissions in developing countries are still relatively low and that the share of global emissions originating in developing countries will grow to meet their social and development needs,

Aware of the role and importance in terrestrial and marine ecosystems of sinks and reservoirs of greenhouse gases,

Noting that there are many uncertainties in predictions of climate change, particularly with regard to the timing, magnitude and regional patterns thereof,

Acknowledging that the global nature of climate change calls for the widest possible cooperation by all countries and their participation in an effective and appropriate international response, in accordance with their common but differentiated responsibilities and respective capabilities and their social and economic conditions,

Recalling the pertinent provisions of the Declaration of the United Nations Conference on the Human Environment, adopted at Stockholm on 16 June 1972,

Recalling also that States have, in accordance with the Charter of the United Nations and the principles of international law, the sovereign right to exploit their own resources pursuant to their own environmental and developmental policies, and the responsibility to ensure that activities within their jurisdiction or control do not cause damage to the environment of other States or of areas beyond the limits of national jurisdiction,

Reaffirming the principle of sovereignty of States in international cooperation to address climate change,

Recognizing that States should enact effective environmental legislation, that environmental standards, management objectives and priorities should reflect the environmental and developmental context to which they apply, and that standards applied by some countries may be inappropriate and of unwarranted economic and social cost to other countries, in particular developing countries,

Recalling the provisions of General Assembly resolution 44/228 of 22 December 1989 on the United Nations Conference on Environment and Development, and resolutions 43/53 of 6 December 1988, 44/207 of 22 December 1989, 45/212 of 21 December 1990 and 46/169 of 19 December 1991 on protection of global climate for present and future generations of mankind,

Recalling also the provisions of General Assembly resolution 44/206 of 22 December 1989 on the possible adverse effects of sealevel rise on islands and coastal areas, particularly low-lying coastal areas and the pertinent provisions of General Assembly resolution 44/172 of 19 December 1989 on the implementation of the Plan of Action to Combat Desertification,

Recalling further the Vienna Convention for the Protection of the Ozone Layer, 1985, and the Montreal Protocol on Substances that Deplete the Ozone Layer, 1987, as adjusted and amended on 29 June 1990,

Noting the Ministerial Declaration of the Second World Climate Conference adopted on 7 November 1990,

Conscious of the valuable analytical work being conducted by many States on climate change and of the important contributions of the World Meteorological Organization, the United Nations Environment Programme and other organs, organizations and bodies of the United Nations system, as well as other international and intergovernmental bodies, to the exchange of results of scientific research and the coordination of research,

Recognizing that steps required to understand and address climate change will be environmentally, socially and economically most effective if they are based on relevant scientific, technical and economic considerations and continually re-evaluated in the light of new findings in these areas,

Recognizing that various actions to address climate change can be justified economically in their own right and can also help in solving other environmental problems,

Recognizing also the need for developed countries to take immediate action in a flexible manner on the basis of clear priorities, as a first step towards comprehensive response strategies at the global, national and, where agreed, regional levels that take into account all greenhouse gases, with due consideration of their relative contributions to the enhancement of the greenhouse effect,

Recognizing further that low-lying and other small island countries, countries with low-lying coastal, arid and semi-arid areas or areas liable to floods, drought and desertification, and developing countries with fragile mountainous ecosystems are particularly vulnerable to the adverse effects of climate change,

Recognizing the special difficulties of those countries, especially developing countries, whose economies are particularly dependent on fossil fuel production, use and exportation, as a consequence of action taken on limiting greenhouse gas emissions,

Affirming that responses to climate change should be coordinated with social and economic development in an integrated manner with a view to avoiding adverse impacts on the latter, taking into full account the legitimate priority needs of developing countries for the achievement of sustained economic growth and the eradication of poverty,

Recognizing that all countries, especially developing countries, need access to resources required to achieve sustainable social and economic development and that, in order for developing countries to progress towards that goal, their energy consumption will need to grow taking into account the possibilities for achieving greater energy efficiency and for controlling greenhouse gas emissions in general, including through the application of new technologies on terms which make such an application economically and socially beneficial,

Determined to protect the climate system for present and future generations,

Have agreed as follows:

ARTICLE 1
DEFINITIONS

For the purposes of this Convention:

1. "Adverse effects of climate change" means changes in the physical environment or biota resulting from climate change which have significant deleterious effects on the composition, resilience or productivity of natural and managed ecosystems or on the operation of socio-economic systems or on human health and welfare.

2. "Climate change" means a change of climate which is attributed directly or indirectly to human activity that alters the composition of the global atmosphere and which is in addition to natural climate variability observed over comparable time periods.

3. "Climate system" means the totality of the atmosphere, hydrosphere, biosphere and geosphere and their interactions.

4. "Emissions" means the release of greenhouse gases and/or their precursors into the atmosphere over a specified area and period of time.

5. "Greenhouse gases" means those gaseous constituents of the atmosphere, both natural and anthropogenic, that absorb and re-emit infrared radiation.

6. "Regional economic integration organization" means an organization constituted by sovereign States of a given region which has competence in respect of matters governed by this Convention or its protocols and has been duly authorized, in accordance with its internal procedures, to sign, ratify, accept, approve or accede to the instruments concerned.

7. "Reservoir" means a component or components of the climate system where a greenhouse gas or a precursor of a greenhouse gas is stored.

8. "Sink" means any process, activity or mechanism which removes a greenhouse gas, an aerosol or a precursor of a greenhouse gas from the atmosphere.

9. "Source" means any process or activity which releases a greenhouse gas, an aerosol or a precursor of a greenhouse gas into the atmosphere.

ARTICLE 2
OBJECTIVE

The ultimate objective of this Convention and any related legal instruments that the Conference of the Parties may adopt is to achieve, in accordance with the relevant provisions of the Convention, stabilization of greenhouse gas concentrations in the atmosphere at a level that would prevent dangerous anthropogenic interference with the climate system. Such a level should be achieved within a time-frame sufficient to allow ecosystems to adapt naturally to climate change, to ensure that food production is not threatened and to enable economic development to proceed in a sustainable manner.

ARTICLE 3

PRINCIPLES

In their actions to achieve the objective of the Convention and to implement its provisions, the Parties shall be guided, *inter alia,* by the following:

1. The Parties should protect the climate system for the benefit of present and future generations of humankind, on the basis of equity and in accordance with their common but differentiated responsibilities and respective capabilities. Accordingly, the developed country Parties should take the lead in combating climate change and the adverse effects thereof.

2. The specific needs and special circumstances of developing country Parties, especially those that are particularly vulnerable to the adverse effects of climate change, and of those Parties, especially developing country Parties, that would have to bear a disproportionate or abnormal burden under the Convention, should be given full consideration.

3. The Parties should take precautionary measures to anticipate, prevent or minimize the causes of climate change and mitigate its adverse effects. Where there are threats of serious or irreversible damage, lack of full scientific certainty should not be used as a reason for postponing such measures, taking into account that policies and measures to deal with climate change should be cost-effective so as to ensure global benefits at the lowest possible cost. To achieve this, such policies and measures should take into account different socio-economic contexts, be comprehensive, cover all relevant sources, sinks and reservoirs of greenhouse gases and adaptation, and comprise all economic sectors. Efforts to address climate change may be carried out cooperatively by interested Parties.

4. The Parties have a right to, and should, promote sustainable development. Policies and measures to protect the climate system against human-induced change should be appropriate for the specific conditions of each Party and should be integrated with national development programmes, taking into account that economic development is essential for adopting measures to address climate change.

5. The Parties should cooperate to promote a supportive and open international economic system that would lead to sustainable economic growth and development in all Parties, particularly developing country Parties, thus enabling them better to address the problems of climate change. Measures taken to combat climate change, including unilateral ones, should not constitute a means of arbitrary or unjustifiable discrimination or a disguised restriction on international trade.

ARTICLE 4
COMMITMENTS

1. All Parties, taking into account their common but differentiated responsibilities and their specific national and regional development priorities, objectives and circumstances, shall:

(a) Develop, periodically update, publish and make available to the Conference of the Parties, in accordance with Article 12, national inventories of anthropogenic emissions by sources and removals by sinks of all greenhouse gases not controlled by the Montreal Protocol, using comparable methodologies to be agreed upon by the Conference of the Parties;

(b) Formulate, implement, publish and regularly update national and, where appropriate, regional programmes containing measures to mitigate climate change by addressing anthropogenic emissions by sources and removals by sinks of all greenhouse gases not controlled by the Montreal Protocol, and measures to facilitate adequate adaptation to climate change;

(c) Promote and cooperate in the development, application and diffusion, including transfer, of technologies, practices and processes that control, reduce or prevent anthropogenic emissions of greenhouse gases not controlled by the Montreal Protocol in all relevant sectors, including the energy, transport, industry, agriculture, forestry and waste management sectors;

(d) Promote sustainable management, and promote and cooperate in the conservation and enhancement, as appropriate, of sinks and reservoirs of all greenhouse gases not controlled by the Montreal Protocol, including biomass, forests and oceans as well as other terrestrial, coastal and marine ecosystems;

(e) Cooperate in preparing for adaptation to the impacts of climate change; develop and elaborate appropriate and integrated plans for coastal zone management, water resources and agriculture, and for the protection and rehabilitation of areas, particularly in Africa, affected by drought and desertification, as well as floods;

(f) Take climate change considerations into account, to the extent feasible, in their relevant social, economic and environmental policies and actions, and employ appropriate methods, for example impact assessments, formulated and determined nationally, with a view to minimizing adverse effects on the economy, on public health and on the quality of the environment, of projects or measures undertaken by them to mitigate or adapt to climate change;

(g) Promote and cooperate in scientific, technological, technical, socio-economic and other research, systematic observation and development of data archives related to the climate system and intended to further the understanding and to reduce or eliminate the remaining uncertainties regarding the causes, effects, magnitude and timing of climate change and the economic and social consequences of various response strategies;

(h) Promote and cooperate in the full, open and prompt exchange of relevant scientific, technological, technical, socio-economic and legal information related to the climate system and climate change, and to the economic and social consequences of various response strategies;

(i) Promote and cooperate in education, training and public awareness related to climate change and encourage the widest participation in this process, including that of non-governmental organizations; and

(j) Communicate to the Conference of the Parties information related to implementation, in accordance with Article 12.

2.   The developed country Parties and other Parties included in annex I commit themselves specifically as provided for in the following:

(a) Each of these Parties shall adopt national policies and take corresponding measures on the mitigation of climate change, by limiting its anthropogenic emissions of greenhouse gases and protecting and enhancing its greenhouse gas sinks and reservoirs. These policies and measures will demonstrate that developed countries are taking the lead in modifying longer-term trends in anthropogenic emissions consistent with the objective of the Convention, recognizing that the return by the end of the present decade to earlier levels of anthropogenic emissions of carbon dioxide and other greenhouse gases not controlled by the Montreal Protocol would contribute to such modification, and taking into account the differences in these Parties' starting points and approaches, economic structures and resource bases, the need to maintain strong and sustainable economic growth, available technologies and other individual circumstances, as well as the need for equitable and appropriate contributions by each of these Parties to the global effort regarding that objective. These Parties may implement such policies and measures jointly with other Parties and may assist other Parties in contributing to the achievement of the objective of the Convention and, in particular, that of this subparagraph;

(b) In order to promote progress to this end, each of these Parties shall communicate, within six months of the entry into force of the Convention for it and periodically thereafter, and in accordance with Article 12, detailed information on its policies and measures referred to in subparagraph (a) above, as well as on its resulting projected anthropogenic emissions by sources and removals by sinks of greenhouse gases not controlled by the Montreal Protocol for the period referred to in subparagraph (a), with the aim of returning individually or jointly to their 1990 levels these anthropogenic emissions of carbon dioxide and other greenhouse gases not controlled by the Montreal Protocol. This information will be reviewed by the Conference of the Parties, at its first session and periodically thereafter, in accordance with Article 7;

(c) Calculations of emissions by sources and removals by sinks of greenhouse gases for the purposes of subparagraph (b) above should take into account the best available scientific knowledge, including the effective capacity of sinks and the respective contributions of such gases to climate change. The Conference of the Parties shall consider and agree on methodologies for these calculations at its first session and review them regularly thereafter;

(d) The Conference of the Parties shall, at its first session, review the adequacy of subparagraphs (a) and (b) above. .Such review shall be carried out in the light of the best available scientific information and assessment on climate change and its impacts, as well as relevant technical, social and economic information. Based on this review, the Conference of the Parties shall take appropriate action, which may include the adoption of amendments to the commitments in subparagraphs (a) and (b) above. The Conference of the Parties, at its first session, shall also take decisions regarding criteria for joint implementation as indicated in subparagraph (a) above. A second review of subparagraphs (a) and (b) shall take place not later than 31 December 1998, and thereafter at regular intervals determined by the Conference of the Parties, until the objective of the Convention is met;

(e) Each of these Parties shall:

(i) coordinate as appropriate with other such Parties, relevant economic and administrative instruments developed to achieve the objective of the Convention; and

(ii) identify and periodically review its own policies and practices which encourage activities that lead to greater levels of anthropogenic emissions of greenhouse gases not controlled by the Montreal Protocol than would otherwise occur;

(f) The Conference of the Parties shall review, not later than 31 December 1998, available information with a view to taking decisions regarding such amendments to the lists in annexes I and II as may be appropriate, with the approval of the Party concerned;

(g) Any Party not included in annex I may, in its instrument of ratification, acceptance, approval or accession, or at any time thereafter, notify the Depositary that it intends to be bound by subparagraphs (a) and (b) above. The Depositary shall inform the other signatories and Parties of any such notification.

3. The developed country Parties and other developed Parties included in annex II shall provide new and additional financial resources to meet the agreed full costs incurred by developing country Parties in complying with their obligations under Article 12, paragraph 1. They shall also provide such financial resources, including for the transfer of technology, needed by the developing country Parties to meet the agreed full incremental costs of implementing measures that are covered by paragraph 1 of this Article and that are agreed between a developing country Party and the international entity or entities referred to in Article 11, in accordance with that Article. The implementation of these commitments shall take into account the need for adequacy and predictability in the flow of funds and the importance of appropriate burden sharing among the developed country Parties.

4. The developed country Parties and other developed Parties included in annex II shall also assist the developing country Parties that are particularly vulnerable to the adverse effects of climate change in meeting costs of adaptation to those adverse effects.

5. The developed country Parties and other developed Parties included in annex II shall take all practicable steps to promote, facilitate and finance,

as appropriate, the transfer of, or access to, environmentally sound technologies and know-how to other Parties, particularly developing country Parties, to enable them to implement the provisions of the Convention. In this process, the developed country Parties shall support the development and enhancement of endogenous capacities and technologies of developing country Parties. Other Parties and organizations in a position to do so may also assist in facilitating the transfer of such technologies.

6. In the implementation of their commitments under paragraph 2 above, a certain degree of flexibility shall be allowed by the Conference of the Parties to the Parties included in annex I undergoing the process of transition to a market economy, in order to enhance the ability of these Parties to address climate change, including with regard to the historical level of anthropogenic emissions of greenhouse gases not controlled by the Montreal Protocol chosen as a reference.

7. The extent to which developing country Parties will effectively implement their commitments under the Convention will depend on the effective implementation by developed country Parties of their commitments under the Convention related to financial resources and transfer of technology and will take fully into account that economic and social development and poverty eradication are the first and overriding priorities of the developing country Parties.

8. In the implementation of the commitments in this Article, the Parties shall give full consideration to what actions are necessary under the Convention, including actions related to funding, insurance and the transfer of technology, to meet the specific needs and concerns of developing country Parties arising from the adverse effects of climate change and/or the impact of the implementation of response measures, especially on:

(a) Small island countries;

(b) Countries with low-lying coastal areas;

(c) Countries with arid and semi-arid areas, forested areas and areas liable to forest decay;

(d) Countries with areas prone to natural disasters;

(e) Countries with areas liable to drought and desertification;

(f) Countries with areas of high urban atmospheric pollution;

(g) Countries with areas with fragile ecosystems, including mountainous ecosystems;

(h) Countries whose economies are highly dependent on income generated from the production, processing and export, and/or on consumption of fossil fuels and associated energy-intensive products; and

(i) Land-locked and transit countries.

Further, the Conference of the Parties may take actions, as appropriate, with respect to this paragraph.

9. The Parties shall take full account of the specific needs and special situations of the least developed countries in their actions with regard to funding and transfer of technology.

10.   The Parties shall, in accordance with Article 10, take into consideration in the implementation of the commitments of the Convention the situation of Parties, particularly developing country Parties, with economies that are vulnerable to the adverse effects of the implementation of measures to respond to climate change.   This applies notably to Parties with economies that are highly dependent on income generated from the production, processing and export, and/or consumption of fossil fuels and associated energy-intensive products and/or the use of fossil fuels for which such Parties have serious difficulties in switching to alternatives.

ARTICLE 5
RESEARCH AND SYSTEMATIC OBSERVATION

In carrying out their commitments under Article 4, paragraph 1(g), the Parties shall:

(a) Support and further develop, as appropriate, international and intergovernmental programmes and networks or organizations aimed at defining, conducting, assessing and financing research, data collection and systematic observation, taking into account the need to minimize duplication of effort;

(b) Support international and intergovernmental efforts to strengthen systematic observation and national scientific and technical research capacities and capabilities, particularly in developing countries, and to promote access to, and the exchange of, data and analyses thereof obtained from areas beyond national jurisdiction; and

(c) Take into account the particular concerns and needs of developing countries and cooperate in improving their endogenous capacities and capabilities to participate in the efforts referred to in subparagraphs (a) and (b) above.

ARTICLE 6
EDUCATION, TRAINING AND PUBLIC AWARENESS

In carrying out their commitments under Article 4, paragraph 1(i), the Parties shall:

(a) Promote and facilitate at the national and, as appropriate, subregional and regional levels, and in accordance with national laws and regulations, and within their respective capacities:

(i) the development and implementation of educational and public awareness programmes on climate change and its effects;

(ii) public access to information on climate change and its effects;

(iii) public participation in addressing climate change and its effects and developing adequate responses; and

(iv) training of scientific, technical and managerial personnel.

(b) Cooperate in and promote, at the international level, and, where appropriate, using existing bodies:

(i) the development and exchange of educational and public awareness material on climate change and its effects; and

(ii) the development and implementation of education and training programmes, including the strengthening of national institutions and the exchange or secondment of personnel to train experts in this field, in particular for developing countries.

ARTICLE 7
CONFERENCE OF THE PARTIES

1.   A Conference of the Parties is hereby established.

2.   The Conference of the Parties, as the supreme body of this Convention, shall keep under regular review the implementation of the Convention and any related legal instruments that the Conference of the Parties may adopt, and shall make, within its mandate, the decisions necessary to promote the effective implementation of the Convention.   To this end, it shall:

(a) Periodically examine the obligations of the Parties and the institutional arrangements under the Convention, in the light of the objective of the Convention, the experience gained in its implementation and the evolution of scientific and technological knowledge;

(b) Promote and facilitate the exchange of information on measures adopted by the Parties to address climate change and its effects, taking into account the differing circumstances, responsibilities and capabilities of the Parties and their respective commitments under the Convention;

(c) Facilitate, at the request of two or more Parties, the coordination of measures adopted by them to address climate change and its effects, taking into account the differing circumstances, responsibilities and capabilities of the Parties and their respective commitments under the Convention;

(d) Promote and guide, in accordance with the objective and provisions of the Convention, the development and periodic refinement of comparable methodologies, to be agreed on by the Conference of the Parties, *inter alia,* for preparing inventories of greenhouse gas emissions by sources and removals by sinks, and for evaluating the effectiveness of measures to limit the emissions and enhance the removals of these gases;

(e) Assess, on the basis of all information made available to it in accordance with the provisions of the Convention, the implementation of the Convention by the Parties, the overall effects of the measures taken pursuant to the Convention, in particular environmental, economic and social effects as well as their cumulative impacts and the extent to which progress towards the objective of the Convention is being achieved;

(f) Consider and adopt regular reports on the implementation of the Convention and ensure their publication;

(g) Make recommendations on any matters necessary for the implementation of the Convention;

(h) Seek to mobilize financial resources in accordance with Article 4, paragraphs 3, 4 and 5, and Article 11;

(i) Establish such subsidiary bodies as are deemed necessary for the implementation of the Convention;

(j) Review reports submitted by its subsidiary bodies and provide guidance to them;

(k) Agree upon and adopt, by consensus, rules of procedure and financial rules for itself and for any subsidiary bodies;

(*l*) Seek and utilize, where appropriate, the services and cooperation of, and information provided by, competent international organizations and intergovernmental and non-governmental bodies; and

(m) Exercise such other functions as are required for the achievement of the objective of the Convention as well as all other functions assigned to it under the Convention.

3.   The Conference of the Parties shall, at its first session, adopt its own rules of procedure as well as those of the subsidiary bodies established by the Convention, which shall include decision-making procedures for matters not already covered by decision-making procedures stipulated in the Convention. Such procedures may include specified majorities required for the adoption of particular decisions.

4.   The first session of the Conference of the Parties shall be convened by the interim secretariat referred to in Article 21 and shall take place not later than one year after the date of entry into force of the Convention. Thereafter, ordinary sessions of the Conference of the Parties shall be held every year unless otherwise decided by the Conference of the Parties.

5.   Extraordinary sessions of the Conference of the Parties shall be held at such other times as may be deemed necessary by the Conference, or at the written request of any Party, provided that, within six months of the request being communicated to the Parties by the secretariat, it is supported by at least one-third of the Parties.

6.   The United Nations, its specialized agencies and the International Atomic Energy Agency, as well as any State member thereof or observers thereto not Party to the Convention, may be represented at sessions of the Conference of the Parties as observers. Any body or agency, whether national or international, governmental or non-governmental, which is qualified in matters covered by the Convention, and which has informed the secretariat of its wish to be represented at a session of the Conference of the Parties as an observer, may be so admitted unless at least one-third of the Parties present object. The admission and participation of observers shall be subject to the rules of procedure adopted by the Conference of the Parties.

ARTICLE 8
SECRETARIAT

1.   A secretariat is hereby established.

2.   The functions of the secretariat shall be:

(a) To make arrangements for sessions of the Conference of the Parties and its subsidiary bodies established under the Convention and to provide them with services as required;

(b) To compile and transmit reports submitted to it;

(c) To facilitate assistance to the Parties, particularly developing country Parties, on request, in the compilation and communication of information required in accordance with the provisions of the Convention;

(d) To prepare reports on its activities and present them to the Conference of the Parties;

(e) To ensure the necessary coordination with the secretariats of other relevant international bodies;

(f) To enter, under the overall guidance of the Conference of the Parties, into such administrative and contractual arrangements as may be required for the effective discharge of its functions; and

(g) To perform the other secretariat functions specified in the Convention and in any of its protocols and such other functions as may be determined by the Conference of the Parties.

3. The Conference of the Parties, at its first session, shall designate a permanent secretariat and make arrangements for its functioning.

ARTICLE 9
SUBSIDIARY BODY FOR SCIENTIFIC AND TECHNOLOGICAL ADVICE

1. A subsidiary body for scientific and technological advice is hereby established to provide the Conference of the Parties and, as appropriate, its other subsidiary bodies with timely information and advice on scientific and technological matters relating to the Convention. This body shall be open to participation by all Parties and shall be multidisciplinary. It shall comprise government representatives competent in the relevant field of expertise. It shall report regularly to the Conference of the Parties on all aspects of its work.

2. Under the guidance of the Conference of the Parties, and drawing upon existing competent international bodies, this body shall:

(a) Provide assessments of the state of scientific knowledge relating to climate change and its effects;

(b) Prepare scientific assessments on the effects of measures taken in the implementation of the Convention;

(c) Identify innovative, efficient and state-of-the-art technologies and know-how and advise on the ways and means of promoting development and/or transferring such technologies;

(d) Provide advice on scientific programmes, international cooperation in research and development related to climate change, as well as on ways and means of supporting endogenous capacity-building in developing countries; and

(e) Respond to scientific, technological and methodological questions that the Conference of the Parties and its subsidiary bodies may put to the body.

3. The functions and terms of reference of this body may be further elaborated by the Conference of the Parties.

ARTICLE 10
SUBSIDIARY BODY FOR IMPLEMENTATION

1. A subsidiary body for implementation is hereby established to assist the Conference of the Parties in the assessment and review of the effective implementation of the Convention. This body shall be open to participation by all Parties and comprise government representatives who are experts on matters related to climate change. It shall report regularly to the Conference of the Parties on all aspects of its work.

2. Under the guidance of the Conference of the Parties, this body shall:

(a) Consider the information communicated in accordance with Article 12, paragraph 1, to assess the overall aggregated effect of the steps taken by the Parties in the light of the latest scientific assessments concerning climate change;

(b) Consider the information communicated in accordance with Article 12, paragraph 2, in order to assist the Conference of the Parties in carrying out the reviews required by Article 4, paragraph 2(d); and

(c) Assist the Conference of the Parties, as appropriate, in the preparation and implementation of its decisions.

ARTICLE 11
FINANCIAL MECHANISM

1. A mechanism for the provision of financial resources on a grant or concessional basis, including for the transfer of technology, is hereby defined. It shall function under the guidance of and be accountable to the Conference of the Parties, which shall decide on its policies, programme priorities and eligibility criteria related to this Convention. Its operation shall be entrusted to one or more existing international entities.

2. The financial mechanism shall have an equitable and balanced representation of all Parties within a transparent system of governance.

3. The Conference of the Parties and the entity or entities entrusted with the operation of the financial mechanism shall agree upon arrangements to give effect to the above paragraphs, which shall include the following:

(a) Modalities to ensure that the funded projects to address climate change are in conformity with the policies, programme priorities and eligibility criteria established by the Conference of the Parties;

(b) Modalities by which a particular funding decision may be reconsidered in light of these policies, programme priorities and eligibility criteria;

(c) Provision by the entity or entities of regular reports to the Conference of the Parties on its funding operations, which is consistent with the requirement for accountability set out in paragraph 1 above; and

(d) Determination in a predictable and identifiable manner of the amount of funding necessary and available for the implementation of this Convention and the conditions under which that amount shall be periodically reviewed.

4. The Conference of the Parties shall make arrangements to implement the above-mentioned provisions at its first session, reviewing and taking into account the interim arrangements referred to in Article 21, paragraph 3, and shall decide whether these interim arrangements shall be maintained. Within four years thereafter, the Conference of the Parties shall review the financial mechanism and take appropriate measures.

5. The developed country Parties may also provide and developing country Parties avail themselves of, financial resources related to the implementation of the Convention through bilateral, regional and other multilateral channels.

ARTICLE 12
COMMUNICATION OF INFORMATION
RELATED TO IMPLEMENTATION

1. In accordance with Article 4, paragraph 1, each Party shall communicate to the Conference of the Parties, through the secretariat, the following elements of information:

(a) A national inventory of anthropogenic emissions by sources and removals by sinks of all greenhouse gases not controlled by the Montreal Protocol, to the extent its capacities permit, using comparable methodologies to be promoted and agreed upon by the Conference of the Parties;

(b) A general description of steps taken or envisaged by the Party to implement the Convention; and

(c) Any other information that the Party considers relevant to the achievement of the objective of the Convention and suitable for inclusion in its communication, including, if feasible, material relevant for calculations of global emission trends.

2. Each developed country Party and each other Party included in annex I shall incorporate in its communication the following elements of information:

(a) A detailed description of the policies and measures that it has adopted to implement its commitment under Article 4, paragraphs 2(a) and 2(b); and

(b) A specific estimate of the effects that the policies and measures referred to in subparagraph (a) immediately above will have on anthropogenic emissions by its sources and removals by its sinks of greenhouse gases during the period referred to in Article 4, paragraph 2(a).

3. In addition, each developed country Party and each other developed Party included in annex II shall incorporate details of measures taken in accordance with Article 4, paragraphs 3, 4 and 5.

4. Developing country Parties may, on a voluntary basis, propose projects for financing, including specific technologies, materials, equipment, techniques or practices that would be needed to implement such projects, along with, if possible, an estimate of all incremental costs, of the reductions of emissions and increments of removals of greenhouse gases, as well as an estimate of the consequent benefits.

5.   Each developed country Party and each other Party included in annex I shall make its initial communication within six months of the entry into force of the Convention for that Party. Each Party not so listed shall make its initial communication within three years of the entry into force of the Convention for that Party, or of the availability of financial resources in accordance with Article 4, paragraph 3. Parties that are least developed countries may make their initial communication at their discretion. The frequency of subsequent communications by all Parties shall be determined by the Conference of the Parties, taking into account the differentiated timetable set by this paragraph.

6.   Information communicated by Parties under this Article shall be transmitted by the secretariat as soon as possible to the Conference of the Parties and to any subsidiary bodies concerned. If necessary, the procedures for the communication of information may be further considered by the Conference of the Parties.

7.   From its first session, the Conference of the Parties shall arrange for the provision to developing country Parties of technical and financial support, on request, in compiling and communicating information under this Article, as well as in identifying the technical and financial needs associated with proposed projects and response measures under Article 4. Such support may be provided by other Parties, by competent international organizations and by the secretariat, as appropriate.

8.   Any group of Parties may, subject to guidelines adopted by the Conference of the Parties, and to prior notification to the Conference of the Parties, make a joint communication in fulfilment of their obligations under this Article, provided that such a communication includes information on the fulfilment by each of these Parties of its individual obligations under the Convention.

9.   Information received by the secretariat that is designated by a Party as confidential, in accordance with criteria to be established by the Conference of the Parties, shall be aggregated by the secretariat to protect its confidentiality before being made available to any of the bodies involved in the communication and review of information.

10.   Subject to paragraph 9 above, and without prejudice to the ability of any Party to make public its communication at any time, the secretariat shall make communications by Parties under this Article publicly available at the time they are submitted to the Conference of the Parties.

ARTICLE 13
RESOLUTION OF QUESTIONS REGARDING IMPLEMENTATION

The Conference of the Parties shall, at its first session, consider the establishment of a multilateral consultative process, available to Parties on their request, for the resolution of questions regarding the implementation of the Convention.

ARTICLE 14
SETTLEMENT OF DISPUTES

1.   In the event of a dispute between any two or more Parties concerning the interpretation or application of the Convention, the Parties concerned

shall seek a settlement of the dispute through negotiation or any other peaceful means of their own choice.

2. When ratifying, accepting, approving or acceding to the Convention, or at any time thereafter, a Party which is not a regional economic integration organization may declare in a written instrument submitted to the Depositary that, in respect of any dispute concerning the interpretation or application of the Convention, it recognizes as compulsory *ipso facto* and without special agreement, in relation to any Party accepting the same obligation:

(a) Submission of the dispute to the International Court of Justice, and/or

(b) Arbitration in accordance with procedures to be adopted by the Conference of the Parties as soon as practicable, in an annex on arbitration.

A Party which is a regional economic integration organization may make a declaration with like effect in relation to arbitration in accordance with the procedures referred to in subparagraph (b) above.

3. A declaration made under paragraph 2 above shall remain in force until it expires in accordance with its terms or until three months after written notice of its revocation has been deposited with the Depositary.

4. A new declaration, a notice of revocation or the expiry of a declaration shall not in any way affect proceedings pending before the International Court of Justice or the arbitral tribunal, unless the parties to the dispute otherwise agree.

5. Subject to the operation of paragraph 2 above, if after twelve months following notification by one Party to another that a dispute exists between them, the Parties concerned have not been able to settle their dispute through the means mentioned in paragraph 1 above, the dispute shall be submitted, at the request of any of the parties to the dispute, to conciliation.

6. A conciliation commission shall be created upon the request of one of the parties to the dispute. The commission shall be composed of an equal number of members appointed by each party concerned and a chairman chosen jointly by the members appointed by each party. The commission shall render a recommendatory award, which the parties shall consider in good faith.

7. Additional procedures relating to conciliation shall be adopted by the Conference of the Parties, as soon as practicable, in an annex on conciliation.

8. The provisions of this Article shall apply to any related legal instrument which the Conference of the Parties may adopt, unless the instrument provides otherwise.

ARTICLE 15
AMENDMENTS TO THE CONVENTION

1. Any Party may propose amendments to the Convention.

2. Amendments to the Convention shall be adopted at an ordinary session of the Conference of the Parties. The text of any proposed amendment to the Convention shall be communicated to the Parties by the secretariat at least six months before the meeting at which it is proposed for adoption.

The secretariat shall also communicate proposed amendments to the signatories to the Convention and, for information, to the Depositary.

3.   The Parties shall make every effort to reach agreement on any proposed amendment to the Convention by consensus.   If all efforts at consensus have been exhausted, and no agreement reached, the amendment shall as a last resort be adopted by a three-fourths majority vote of the Parties present and voting at the meeting.   The adopted amendment shall be communicated by the secretariat to the Depositary, who shall circulate it to all Parties for their acceptance.

4.   Instruments of acceptance in respect of an amendment shall be deposited with the Depositary.   An amendment adopted in accordance with paragraph 3 above shall enter into force for those Parties having accepted it on the ninetieth day after the date of receipt by the Depositary of an instrument of acceptance by at least three-fourths of the Parties to the Convention.

5.   The amendment shall enter into force for any other Party on the ninetieth day after the date on which that Party deposits with the Depositary its instrument of acceptance of the said amendment.

6.   For the purposes of this Article, "Parties present and voting" means Parties present and casting an affirmative or negative vote.

ARTICLE 16
ADOPTION AND AMENDMENT OF ANNEXES
TO THE CONVENTION

1.   Annexes to the Convention shall form an integral part thereof and, unless otherwise expressly provided, a reference to the Convention constitutes at the same time a reference to any annexes thereto.   Without prejudice to the provisions of Article 14, paragraphs 2(b) and 7, such annexes shall be restricted to lists, forms and any other material of a descriptive nature that is of a scientific, technical, procedural or administrative character.

2.   Annexes to the Convention shall be proposed and adopted in accordance with the procedure set forth in Article 15, paragraphs 2, 3, and 4.

3.   An annex that has been adopted in accordance with paragraph 2 above shall enter into force for all Parties to the Convention six months after the date of the communication by the Depositary to such Parties of the adoption of the annex, except for those Parties that have notified the Depositary, in writing, within that period of their non-acceptance of the annex.   The annex shall enter into force for Parties which withdraw their notification of non-acceptance on the ninetieth day after the date on which withdrawal of such notification has been received by the Depositary.

4.   The proposal, adoption and entry into force of amendments to annexes to the Convention shall be subject to the same procedure as that for the proposal, adoption and entry into force of annexes to the Convention in accordance with paragraphs 2 and 3 above.

5.   If the adoption of an annex or an amendment to an annex involves an amendment to the Convention, that annex or amendment to an annex shall not enter into force until such time as the amendment to the Convention enters into force.

ARTICLE 17
PROTOCOLS

1.   The Conference of the Parties may, at any ordinary session, adopt protocols to the Convention.

2.   The text of any proposed protocol shall be communicated to the Parties by the secretariat at least six months before such a session.

3.   The requirements for the entry into force of any protocol shall be established by that instrument.

4.   Only Parties to the Convention may be Parties to a protocol.

5.   Decisions under any protocol shall be taken only by the Parties to the protocol concerned.

ARTICLE 18
RIGHT TO VOTE

1.   Each Party to the Convention shall have one vote, except as provided for in paragraph 2 below.

2.   Regional economic integration organizations, in matters within their competence, shall exercise their right to vote with a number of votes equal to the number of their member States that are Parties to the Convention. Such an organization shall not exercise its right to vote if any of its member States exercises its right, and vice versa.

ARTICLE 19
DEPOSITARY

The Secretary–General of the United Nations shall be the Depositary of the Convention and of protocols adopted in accordance with Article 17.

ARTICLE 20
SIGNATURE

This Convention shall be open for signature by States Members of the United Nations or of any of its specialized agencies or that are Parties to the Statute of the International Court of Justice and by regional economic integration organizations at Rio de Janeiro, during the United Nations Conference on Environment and Development, and thereafter at United Nations Headquarters in New York from 20 June 1992 to 19 June 1993.

ARTICLE 21
INTERIM ARRANGEMENTS

1.   The secretariat functions referred to in Article 8 will be carried out on an interim basis by the secretariat established by the General Assembly of the United Nations in its resolution 45/212 of 21 December 1990, until the completion of the first session of the Conference of the Parties.

2.   The head of the interim secretariat referred to in paragraph 1 above will cooperate closely with the Intergovernmental Panel on Climate Change to ensure that the Panel can respond to the need for objective scientific and technical advice. Other relevant scientific bodies could also be consulted.

3.   The Global Environment Facility of the United Nations Development Programme, the United Nations Environment Programme and the Interna-

tional Bank for Reconstruction and Development shall be the international entity entrusted with the operation of the financial mechanism referred to in Article 11 on an interim basis. In this connection, the Global Environment Facility should be appropriately restructured and its membership made universal to enable it to fulfil the requirements of Article 11.

ARTICLE 22
RATIFICATION, ACCEPTANCE, APPROVAL OR ACCESSION

1. The Convention shall be subject to ratification, acceptance, approval or accession by States and by regional economic integration organizations. It shall be open for accession from the day after the date on which the Convention is closed for signature. Instruments of ratification, acceptance, approval or accession shall be deposited with the Depositary.

2. Any regional economic integration organization which becomes a Party to the Convention without any of its member States being a Party shall be bound by all the obligations under the Convention. In the case of such organizations, one or more of whose member States is a Party to the Convention, the organization and its member States shall decide on their respective responsibilities for the performance of their obligations under the Convention. In such cases, the organization and the member States shall not be entitled to exercise rights under the Convention concurrently.

3. In their instruments of ratification, acceptance, approval or accession, regional economic integration organizations shall declare the extent of their competence with respect to the matters governed by the Convention. These organizations shall also inform the Depositary, who shall in turn inform the Parties, of any substantial modification in the extent of their competence.

ARTICLE 23
ENTRY INTO FORCE

1. The Convention shall enter into force on the ninetieth day after the date of deposit of the fiftieth instrument of ratification, acceptance, approval or accession.

2. For each State or regional economic integration organization that ratifies, accepts or approves the Convention or accedes thereto after the deposit of the fiftieth instrument of ratification, acceptance, approval or accession, the Convention shall enter into force on the ninetieth day after the date of deposit by such State or regional economic integration organization of its instrument of ratification, acceptance, approval or accession.

3. For the purposes of paragraphs 1 and 2 above, any instrument deposited by a regional economic integration organization shall not be counted as additional to those deposited by States members of the organization.

ARTICLE 24
RESERVATIONS

No reservations may be made to the Convention.

ARTICLE 25
WITHDRAWAL

1. At any time after three years from the date on which the Convention has entered into force for a Party, that Party may withdraw from the Convention by giving written notification to the Depositary.

2. Any such withdrawal shall take effect upon expiry of one year from the date of receipt by the Depositary of the notification of withdrawal, or on such later date as may be specified in the notification of withdrawal.

3. Any Party that withdraws from the Convention shall be considered as also having withdrawn from any protocol to which it is a Party.

ARTICLE 26
AUTHENTIC TEXTS

The original of this Convention, of which the Arabic, Chinese, English, French, Russian and Spanish texts are equally authentic, shall be deposited with the Secretary–General of the United Nations.

**3.23 MONTREAL PROTOCOL PARTIES: ADJUSTMENTS AND AMEND-
MENTS TO THE MONTREAL PROTOCOL ON SUBSTANCES THAT
DEPLETE THE OZONE LAYER (WITH ANNEXES).[1] Adopted at
Copenhagen, 23–25 November 1992. 32 I.L.M. 874 (1993)**

* * *

The Secretary–General of the United Nations, acting in his capacity as depositary, communicates the following:

I

At the Fourth Meeting of the Parties to the above-mentioned Protocol, held in Copenhagen from 23 to 25 November 1992, the Parties adopted Adjustments to the Protocol (Decisions IV/2 and IV/3), pursuant to article 2(9)(c) of the Protocol.

The text of the said Adjustments is transmitted herewith in the six languages of their conclusion, as Annexes I and II to this notification.

The Adjustments will enter into force on the expiry of six months from the date of the present notification issued pursuant to article 2(9)(d) of the Protocol.

II

Also, at their Fourth Meeting, the Parties further adopted, pursuant to article 9(4) of the 1985 Vienna Convention for the Protection of the Ozone Layer, an Amendment to the Protocol (Decision IV/4).

The text of the above-mentioned Amendment, in the six official languages of its conclusion, is attached as Annex III to this notification.

In accordance with its Article 3, paragraph 1, "the Amendment shall enter into force on 1 January 1994, provided that at least twenty instruments of ratification, acceptance or approval have been deposited by States or regional economic integration organizations that are parties to the Montreal Protocol on Substances that Deplete the Ozone Layer. In the event that this condition has not been fulfilled by that date, the Amendment shall enter into force on the ninetieth day following the date on which it has been fulfilled."

After its entry into force, the Amendment, in accordance with its Article 3, paragraph 3, shall enter into force for any other Party to the Protocol on the ninetieth day following the date of deposit of the instrument of ratification, acceptance or approval.

22 March 1993

Annex I

ADJUSTMENTS TO ARTICLES 2A AND 2B OF THE
MONTREAL PROTOCOL ON SUBSTANCES
THAT DEPLETE THE OZONE LAYER

The Fourth Meeting of the Parties to the Montreal Protocol on Substances that Deplete the Ozone Layer decides, on the basis of the assessments made pursuant to Article 6 of the Protocol, to adopt adjustments and reductions of production and consumption of the controlled substances in Annex A to the Protocol as follows:

---

1. *See also* Basic Documents 3.15, 3.17,
3.20 and 3.21 *supra.*

A. *Article 2A: CFCs*

Paragraphs 3 to 6 of Article 2A of the Protocol shall be replaced by the following paragraphs, which shall be numbered paragraphs 3 and 4 of Article 2A:

3. Each Party shall ensure that for the twelve-month period commencing on 1 January 1994, and in each twelve-month period thereafter, its calculated level of consumption of the controlled substances in Group I of Annex A does not exceed, annually, twenty-five per cent of its calculated level of consumption in 1986. Each Party producing one or more of these substances shall, for the same periods, ensure that its calculated level of production of the substances does not exceed, annually, twenty-five per cent of its calculated level of production in 1986. However, in order to satisfy the basic domestic needs of the Parties operating under paragraph 1 of Article 5, its calculated level of production may exceed that limit by up to ten per cent of its calculated level of production in 1986.

4. Each Party shall ensure that for the twelve-month period commencing on 1 January 1996, and in each twelve-month period thereafter, its calculated level of consumption of the controlled substances in Group I of Annex A does not exceed zero. Each Party producing one or more of these substances shall, for the same periods, ensure that its calculated level of production of the substances does not exceed zero. However, in order to satisfy the basic domestic needs of the Parties operating under paragraph 1 of Article 5, its calculated level of production may exceed that limit by up to fifteen per cent of its calculated level of production in 1986. This paragraph will apply save to the extent that the Parties decide to permit the level of production or consumption that is necessary to satisfy uses agreed by them to be essential.

B. *Article 2B: Halons*

Paragraphs 2 to 4 of Article 2B of the Protocol shall be replaced by the following paragraph, which shall be numbered paragraph 2 of Article 2B:

2. Each Party shall ensure that for the twelve-month period commencing on 1 January 1994, and in each twelve-month period thereafter, its calculated level of consumption of the controlled substances in Group II of Annex A does not exceed zero. Each Party producing one or more of these substances shall, for the same periods, ensure that its calculated level of production of the substances does not exceed zero. However, in order to satisfy the basic domestic needs of the Parties operating under paragraph 1 of Article 5, its calculated level of production may exceed that limit by up to fifteen per cent of its calculated level of production in 1986. This paragraph will apply save to the extent that the Parties decide to permit the level of production or consumption that is necessary to satisfy uses agreed by them to be essential.

Annex II

ADJUSTMENTS TO ARTICLES 2C, 2D AND 2E OF THE MONTREAL PROTOCOL ON SUBSTANCES THAT DEPLETE THE OZONE LAYER

The Fourth Meeting of the Parties to the Montreal Protocol on Substances that Deplete the Ozone Layer decides, on the basis of the assessments made pursuant to Article 6 of the Protocol, to adopt adjustments and reductions of production and consumption of the controlled substances in Annex B to the Protocol as follows:

A. *Article 2C: Other Fully Halogenated CFCs*

Article 2C of the Protocol shall be replaced by the following Article:

Article 2C: Other Fully Halogenated CFCs

1. Each Party shall ensure that for the twelve-month period commencing on 1 January 1993, its calculated level of consumption of the controlled substances in Group I of Annex B does not exceed, annually, eighty per cent of its calculated level of consumption in 1989. Each Party producing one or more of these substances shall, for the same period, ensure that its calculated level of production of the substances does not exceed, annually, eighty per cent of its calculated level of production in 1989. However, in order to satisfy the basic domestic needs of the Parties operating under paragraph 1 of Article 5, its calculated level of production may exceed that limit by up to ten per cent of its calculated level of production in 1989.

2. Each Party shall ensure that for the twelve-month period commencing on 1 January 1994, and in each twelve-month period thereafter, its calculated level of consumption of the controlled substances in Group I of Annex B does not exceed, annually, twenty-five per cent of its calculated level of consumption in 1989. Each Party producing one or more of these substances shall, for the same periods, ensure that its calculated level of production of the substances does not exceed, annually, twenty-five per cent of its calculated level of production in 1989. However, in order to satisfy the basic domestic needs of the Parties operating under paragraph 1 of Article 5, its calculated level of production may exceed that limit by up to ten per cent of its calculated level of production in 1989.

3. Each Party shall ensure that for the twelve-month period commencing on 1 January 1996, and in each twelve-month period thereafter, its calculated level of consumption of the controlled substances in Group I of Annex B does not exceed zero. Each Party producing one or more of these substances shall, for the same periods, ensure that its calculated level of production of the substances does not exceed zero. However, in order to satisfy the basic domestic needs of the Parties operating under paragraph 1 of Article 5, its calculated level of production may exceed that limit by up to fifteen per cent of its calculated level of production in 1989. This paragraph will apply save to the extent that the Parties decide to permit the level of production or consumption that is necessary to satisfy uses agreed by them to be essential.

B. *Article 2D: Carbon Tetrachloride*

Article 2D of the Protocol shall be replaced by the following Article:

Article 2D: Carbon Tetrachloride

1. Each Party shall ensure that for the twelve-month period commencing on 1 January 1995, its calculated level of consumption of the controlled substances in Group II of Annex B does not exceed, annually, fifteen per cent of its calculated level of consumption in 1989. Each Party producing the substance shall, for the same period, ensure that its calculated level of

production of the substance does not exceed, annually, fifteen per cent of its calculated level of production in 1989. However, in order to satisfy the basic domestic needs of the Parties operating under paragraph 1 of Article 5, its calculated level of production may exceed that limit by up to ten per cent of its calculated level of production in 1989.

2. Each Party shall ensure that for the twelve-month period commencing on 1 January 1996, and in each twelve-month period thereafter, its calculated level of consumption of the controlled substance in Group II of Annex B does not exceed zero. Each Party producing the substance shall, for the same periods, ensure that its calculated level of production of the substance does not exceed zero. However, in order to satisfy the basic domestic needs of the Parties operating under paragraph 1 of Article 5, its calculated level of production may exceed that limit by up to fifteen per cent of its calculated level of production in 1989. This paragraph will apply save to the extent that the Parties decide to permit the level of production or consumption that is necessary to satisfy uses agreed by them to be essential.

C. *Article 2E: 1,1,1–Trichloroethane (Methyl Chloroform)*

Article 2E of the Protocol shall be replaced by the following Article:

Article 2E: 1,1,1–Trichloroethane (Methyl Chloroform)

1. Each Party shall ensure that for the twelve-month period commencing on 1 January 1993, its calculated level of consumption of the controlled substance in Group III of Annex B does not exceed, annually, its calculated level of consumption in 1989. Each Party producing the substance shall, for the same period, ensure that its calculated level of production of the substance does not exceed, annually, its calculated level of production in 1989. However, in order to satisfy the basic domestic needs of the Parties operating under paragraph 1 of Article 5, its calculated level of production may exceed that limit by up to ten per cent of its calculated level of production in 1989.

2. Each Party shall ensure that for the twelve-month period commencing on 1 January 1994, and in each twelve-month period thereafter, its calculated level of consumption of the controlled substance in Group III of Annex B does not exceed, annually, fifty per cent of its calculated level of consumption in 1989. Each Party producing the substance shall, for the same periods, ensure that its calculated level of production of the substance does not exceed, annually, fifty per cent of its calculated level of production in 1989. However, in order to satisfy the basic domestic needs of the Parties operating under paragraph 1 of Article 5, its calculated level of production may exceed that limit by up to ten per cent of its calculated level of production in 1989.

3. Each Party shall ensure that for the twelve-month period commencing on 1 January 1996, and in each twelve-month period thereafter, its calculated level of consumption of the controlled substance in Group III of Annex B does not exceed zero. Each Party producing the substance shall, for the same periods, ensure that its calculated level of production of the substance does not exceed zero. However, in order to satisfy the basic domestic needs of the Parties operating under paragraph 1 of Article 5, its calculated level of production may exceed that limit by up to fifteen per cent of its calculated level of production for 1989. This paragraph will apply save

to the extent that the Parties decide to permit the level of production or consumption that is necessary to satisfy uses agreed by them to be essential.

Annex III

AMENDMENT TO THE MONTREAL PROTOCOL ON SUBSTANCES THAT DEPLETE THE OZONE LAYER

ARTICLE 1: AMENDMENT

A. *Article 1, paragraph 4*

In paragraph 4 of Article 1 of the Protocol, for the words:

or in Annex B

there shall be substituted:

Annex B, Annex C or Annex E

B. *Article 1, paragraph 9*

Paragraph 9 of Article 1 of the Protocol shall be deleted.

C. *Article 2, paragraph 5*

In paragraph 5 of Article 2 of the Protocol, after the words:

Articles 2A to 2E

there shall be added:

and Article 2H

D. *Article 2, paragraph 5 bis*

The following paragraph shall be inserted after paragraph 5 of Article 2 of the Protocol:

5 *bis.* Any Party not operating under paragraph 1 of Article 5 may, for one or more control periods, transfer to another such Party any portion of its calculated level of consumption set out in Article 2F, provided that the calculated level of consumption of controlled substances in Group I of Annex A of the Party transferring the portion of its calculated level of consumption did not exceed 0.25 kilograms per capita in 1989 and that the total combined calculated levels of consumption of the Parties concerned do not exceed the consumption limits set out in Article 2F. Such transfer of consumption shall be notified to the Secretariat by each of the Parties concerned, stating the terms of such transfer and the period for which it is to apply.

E. *Article 2, paragraphs 8(a) and 11*

In paragraphs 8(a) and 11 of Article 2 of the Protocol, for the words:

Articles 2A to 2E

there shall be substituted each time they occur:

Articles 2A to 2H

F. *Article 2, paragraph 9(a)(i)*

In paragraph 9(a)(i) of Article 2 of the Protocol, for the words:

and/or Annex B

there shall be substituted:

Annex B, Annex C and/or Annex E

G. *Article 2F: Hydrochlorofluorocarbons*

The following Article shall be inserted after Article 2E of the Protocol:

Article 2F: Hydrochlorofluorocarbons

1. Each Party shall ensure that for the twelve-month period commencing on 1 January 1996, and in each twelve-month period thereafter, its calculated level of consumption of the controlled substances in Group I of Annex C does not exceed, annually, the sum of:

(a) Three point one per cent of its calculated level of consumption in 1989 of the controlled substances in Group I of Annex A; and

(b) Its calculated level of consumption in 1989 of the controlled substances in Group I of Annex C.

2. Each Party shall ensure that for the twelve-month period commencing on 1 January 2004, and in each twelve-month period thereafter, its calculated level of consumption of the controlled substances in Group I of Annex C does not exceed, annually, sixty-five per cent of the sum referred to in paragraph 1 of this Article.

3. Each Party shall ensure that for the twelve-month period commencing on 1 January 2010, and in each twelve-month period thereafter, its calculated level of consumption of the controlled substances in Group I of Annex C does not exceed, annually, thirty-five per cent of the sum referred to in paragraph 1 of this Article.

4. Each Party shall ensure that for the twelve-month period commencing on 1 January 2015, and in each twelve-month period thereafter, its calculated level of consumption of the controlled substances in Group I of Annex C does not exceed, annually, ten per cent of the sum referred to in paragraph 1 of this Article.

5. Each Party shall ensure that for the twelve-month period commencing on 1 January 2020, and in each twelve-month period thereafter, its calculated level of consumption of the controlled substances in Group I of Annex C does not exceed, annually, zero point five per cent of the sum referred to in paragraph 1 of this Article.

6. Each Party shall ensure that for the twelve-month period commencing on 1 January 2030, and in each twelve-month period thereafter, its calculated level of consumption of the controlled substances in Group I of Annex C does not exceed zero.

7. As of 1 January 1996, each Party shall endeavour to ensure that:

(a) The use of controlled substances in Group I of Annex C is limited to those applications where other more environmentally suitable alternative substances or technologies are not available;

(b) The use of controlled substances in Group I of Annex C is not outside the areas of application currently met by controlled substances in Annexes A, B and C, except in rare cases for the protection of human life or human health; and

(c) Controlled substances in Group I of Annex C are selected for use in a manner that minimizes ozone depletion, in addition to meeting other environmental, safety and economic considerations.

H. *Article 2G: Hydrobromofluorocarbons*

The following Article shall be inserted after Article 2F of the Protocol:

Article 2G: Hydrobromofluorocarbons

Each Party shall ensure that for the twelve-month period commencing on 1 January 1996, and in each twelve-month period thereafter, its calculated level of consumption of the controlled substances in Group II of Annex C does not exceed zero. Each Party producing the substances shall, for the same periods, ensure that its calculated level of production of the substances does not exceed zero. This paragraph will apply save to the extent that the Parties decide to permit the level of production or consumption that is necessary to satisfy uses agreed by them to be essential.

I. *Article 2H: Methyl Bromide*

The following Article shall be inserted after Article 2G of the Protocol:

Article 2H: Methyl Bromide

Each Party shall ensure that for the twelve-month period commencing on 1 January 1995, and in each twelve-month period thereafter, its calculated level of consumption of the controlled substance in Annex E does not exceed, annually, its calculated level of consumption in 1991. Each Party producing the substance shall, for the same periods, ensure that its calculated level of production of the substance does not exceed, annually, its calculated level of production in 1991. However, in order to satisfy the basic domestic needs of the Parties operating under paragraph 1 of Article 5, its calculated level of production may exceed that limit by up to ten per cent of its calculated level of production in 1991. The calculated levels of consumption and production under this Article shall not include the amounts used by the Party for quarantine and pre-shipment applications.

J. *Article 3*

In Article 3 of the Protocol, for the words:

2A to 2E

there shall be substituted:

2A to 2H

and for the words

or Annex B

there shall be substituted each time they occur:

Annex B, Annex C or Annex E

K. *Article 4, paragraph 1 ter*

The following paragraph shall be inserted after paragraph 1 *bis* of Article 4 of the Protocol:

1 ter. Within one year of the date of entry into force of this paragraph, each Party shall ban the import of any controlled substances in Group II of Annex C from any State not party to this Protocol.

L. *Article 4, paragraph 2 ter*

The following paragraph shall be inserted after paragraph 2 *bis* of Article 4 of the Protocol:

2 ter. Commencing one year after the date of entry into force of this paragraph, each Party shall ban the export of any controlled substances in Group II of Annex C to any State not party to this Protocol.

M. *Article 4, paragraph 3 ter*

The following paragraph shall be inserted after paragraph 3 *bis* of Article 4 of the Protocol:

3 ter. Within three years of the date of entry into force of this paragraph, the Parties shall, following the procedures in Article 10 of the Convention, elaborate in an annex a list of products containing controlled substances in Group II of Annex C. Parties that have not objected to the annex in accordance with those procedures shall ban, within one year of the annex having become effective, the import of those products from any State not party to this Protocol.

N. *Article 4, paragraph 4 ter*

The following paragraph shall be inserted after paragraph 4 *bis* of Article 4 of the Protocol:

4 ter. Within five years of the date of entry into force of this paragraph, the Parties shall determine feasibility of banning or restricting, from States not party to this Protocol, the import of products produced with, but not containing, controlled substances in Group II of Annex C. If determined feasible, the Parties shall, following the procedures in Article 10 of the Convention, elaborate in an annex a list of such products. Parties that have not objected to the annex in accordance with those procedures shall ban or restrict, within one year of the annex having become effective, the import of those products from any State not party to this Protocol.

O. *Article 4, paragraphs 5, 6 and 7*

In paragraphs 5, 6 and 7 of Article 4 of the Protocol, for the words:

controlled substances

there shall be substituted:

controlled substances in Annexes A and B and Group II of Annex C

P. *Article 4, paragraph 8*

In paragraph 8 of Article 4 of the Protocol, for the words:

referred to in paragraphs 1, 1 *bis,* 3, 3 *bis,* 4 and 4 *bis* and exports referred to in paragraphs 2 and 2 *bis*

there shall be substituted:

and exports referred to in paragraphs 1 to 4 *ter* of this Article

and after the words:

Articles 2A to 2E

there shall be added:

Article 2G

Q. *Article 4, paragraph 10*

The following paragraph shall be inserted after paragraph 9 of Article 4 of the Protocol:

10. By 1 January 1996, the Parties shall consider whether to amend this Protocol in order to extend the measures in this Article to trade in controlled substances in Group I of Annex C and in Annex E with States not party to the Protocol.

R. *Article 5, paragraph 1*

The following words shall be added at the end of paragraph 1 of Article 5 of the Protocol:

provided that any further amendments to the adjustments or Amendments adopted at the Second Meeting of the Parties in London, 29 June 1990, shall apply to the Parties operating under this paragraph after the review provided for in paragraph 8 of this Article has taken place and shall be based on the conclusions of that review.

S. *Article 5, paragraph 1 bis*

The following paragraph shall be added after paragraph 1 of Article 5 of the Protocol:

1 *bis*. The Parties shall, taking into account the review referred to in paragraph 8 of this Article, the assessments made pursuant to Article 6 and any other relevant information, decide by 1 January 1996, through the procedure set forth in paragraph 9 of Article 2:

(a) With respect to paragraphs 1 to 6 of Article 2F, what base year, initial levels, control schedules and phase-out date for consumption of the controlled substances in Group I of Annex C will apply to Parties operating under paragraph 1 of this Article;

(b) With respect to Article 2G, what phase-out date for production and consumption of the controlled substances in Group II of Annex C will apply to Parties operating under paragraph 1 of this Article; and

(c) With respect to Article 2H, what base year, initial levels and control schedules for consumption and production of the controlled substance in Annex E will apply to Parties operating under paragraph 1 of this Article.

T. *Article 5 paragraph 4*

In paragraph 4 of Article 5 of the Protocol, for the words:

Articles 2A to 2E

there shall be substituted:

Articles 2A to 2H

U. *Article 5, paragraph 5*

In paragraph 5 of Article 5 of the Protocol, after the words:

set out in Articles 2A to 2E

there shall be added:

and any control measures in Articles 2F to 2H that are decided pursuant to paragraph 1 *bis* of this Article,

V. *Article 5, paragraph 6*

In paragraph 6 of Article 5 of the Protocol, after the words:

obligations laid down in Articles 2A to 2E

there shall be added:

or any or all obligations in Articles 2F to 2H that are decided pursuant to paragraph 1 *bis* of this Article,

W. *Article 6*

The following words shall be deleted from Article 6 of the Protocol:

Articles 2A to 2E, and the situation regarding production, imports and exports of the transitional substances in Group I of Annex C

and replaced by

Articles 2A to 2H

X. *Article 7, paragraphs 2 and 3*

Paragraphs 2 and 3 of Article 7 of the Protocol shall be replaced by the following:

2. Each Party shall provide to the Secretariat statistical data on its production, imports and exports of each of the controlled substances

—in Annexes B and C, for the year 1989,

—in Annex E, for the year 1991,

or the best possible estimates of such data where actual data are not available, not later than three months after the date when the provisions set out in the Protocol with regard to the substances in Annexes B, C and E respectively enter into force for that Party.

3. Each Party shall provide to the Secretariat statistical data on its annual production (as defined in paragraph 5 of Article 1) of each of the controlled substances listed in Annexes A, B, C and E and, separately, for each substance,

— Amounts used for feedstocks,

— Amounts destroyed by technologies approved by the Parties, and

— Imports from and exports to Parties and non-Parties respectively,

for the year during which provisions concerning the substances in Annexes A B, C and E respectively entered into force for that Party and for each year thereafter. Data shall be forwarded not later than nine months after the end of the year to which the data relate.

Y. *Article 7, paragraph 3 bis*

The following paragraph shall be inserted after paragraph 3 of Article 7 of the Protocol:

3 *bis*. Each Party shall provide to the Secretariat separate statistical data of its annual imports and exports of each of the controlled substances listed in Group II of Annex A and Group I of Annex C that have been recycled.

Z. *Article 7, paragraph 4*

In paragraph 4 of Article 7 of the Protocol, for the words:

in paragraphs 1, 2 and 3

there shall be substituted:

in paragraphs 1, 2, 3 and 3 *bis*

AA. *Article 9, paragraph 1(a)*

The following words shall be deleted from paragraph 1(a) of Article 9 of the Protocol:

and transitional

BB. *Article 10, paragraph 1*

In paragraph 1 of Article 10 of the Protocol, after the words:

Articles 2A to 2E

there shall be added:

and any control measures in Articles 2F to 2H that are decided pursuant to paragraph 1 *bis* of Article 5.

CC. *Article 11, paragraph 4(g)*

The following words shall be deleted from paragraph 4(g) of Article 11 of the Protocol:

and the situation regarding transitional substances

DD. *Article 17*

In Article 17 of the Protocol, for the words:

Articles 2A to 2E

there shall be substituted:

Articles 2A to 2H

EE. *Annexes*

1. *Annex C*

The following annex shall replace Annex C of the Protocol:

Annex C
Controlled substances

Group	Substance	Number of Isomers	Ozone Depleting Potential *
Group I			
$CHFCl_2$	(HCFC–21) **	1	0.04
CHF_2Cl	(HCFC–22) **	1	0.055
CH_2FCl	(HCFC–31)	1	0.02
C_2HFCl_4	(HCFC–121)	2	0.01–0.04
$C_2HF_2Cl_3$	(HCFC–122)	3	0.02–0.08
$C_2HF_3Cl_2$	(HCFC–123)	3	0.02–0.06
$CHCl_2CF_3$	(HCFC–123) **	—	0.02
C_2HF_4Cl	(HCFC–124)	2	0.02–0.04
$CHFClCF_3$	(HCFC–124) **	—	0.022
$C_2H_2FCl_3$	(HCFC–131)	3	0.007–0.05
$C_2H_2F_2Cl_2$	(HCFC–132)	4	0.008–0.05
$C_2H_2F_3Cl$	(HCFC–133)	3	0.02–0.06

Group	Substance	Number of Isomers	Ozone Depleting Potential *
$C_2H_3FCl_2$	(HCFC–141)	3	0.005–0.07
CH_3CFCl_2	(HCFC–141b) **	—	0.11
$C_2H_3F_2Cl$	(HCFC–142)	3	0.008–0.07
CH_3CF_2Cl	(HCFC–142b) **	—	0.065
C_2H_4FCl	(HCFC–151)	2	0.003–0.005
C_3HFCl_6	(HCFC–221)	5	0.015–0.07
$C_3HF_2Cl_5$	(HCFC–222)	9	0.01–0.09
$C_3HF_3Cl_4$	(HCFC–223)	12	0.01–0.08
$C_3HF_4Cl_3$	(HCFC–224)	12	0.01–0.09
$C_3HF_5Cl_2$	(HCFC–225)	9	0.02–0.07
$CF_3CF_2CHCl_2$	(HCFC–225ca) **	—	0.025
CF_2ClCF_2CHClF	(HCFC–225cb) **	—	0.033
C_3HF_6Cl	(HCFC–226)	5	0.02–0.10
$C_3H_2FCl_5$	(HCFC–231)	9	0.05–0.09
$C_3H_2F_2Cl_4$	(HCFC–232)	16	0.008–0.10
$C_3H_2F_3Cl_3$	(HCFC–233)	18	0.007–0.23
$C_3H_2F_4Cl_2$	(HCFC–234)	16	0.01–0.28
$C_3H_2F_5Cl$	(HCFC–235)	9	0.03–0.52
$C_3H_3FCl_4$	(HCFC–241)	12	0.004–0.09
$C_3H_3F_2Cl_3$	(HCFC–242)	18	0.005–0.13

* Where a range of ODPs is indicated, the highest value in that range shall be used for the purposes of the Protocol. The ODPs listed as a single value have been determined from calculations based on laboratory measurements. Those listed as a range are based on estimates and are less certain. The range pertains to an isomeric group. The upper value is the estimate of the ODP of the isomer with the highest ODP, and the lower value is the estimate of the ODP of the isomer with the lowest ODP.

** Identifies the most commercially viable substances with ODP values listed against them to be used for the purposes of the Protocol.

4. HYDROSPHERE

4.1 TREATY BETWEEN CANADA AND THE UNITED STATES OF AMERICA RELATING TO BOUNDARY WATERS AND QUESTIONS ARISING ALONG THE BOUNDARY BETWEEN THE UNITED STATES AND CANADA.[1] Concluded at Washington, 11 January 1909. Entered into force, 5 May 1910. 36 Stat. 2448, T.S. No. 548

The United States of America and His Majesty the King of the United Kingdom of Great Britain and Ireland and of the British Dominions beyond the Seas, Emperor of India, being equally desirous to prevent disputes regarding the use of boundary waters and to settle all questions which are now pending between the United States and the Dominion of Canada involving the rights, obligations, or interests of either in relation to the other or to the inhabitants of the other, along their common frontier, and to make provision for the adjustment and settlement of all such questions as may hereafter arise, have resolved to conclude a treaty in furtherance of these ends, and for that purpose have appointed as their respective plenipotentiaries:

The President of the United States of America, Elihu Root, Secretary of State of the United States; and

His Britannic Majesty, the Right Honorable James Bryce, O.M., His Ambassador Extraordinary and Plenipotentiary at Washington;

Who, after having communicated to one another their full powers, found in good and due form, have agreed upon the following articles:

PRELIMINARY ARTICLE

For the purposes of this treaty boundary waters are defined as the waters from main shore to main shore of the lakes and rivers and connecting waterways, or the portions thereof, along which the international boundary between the United States and the Dominion of Canada passes, including all bays, arms, and inlets thereof, but not including tributary waters which in their natural channels would flow into such lakes, rivers, and waterways, or waters flowing from such lakes, rivers, and waterways, or the waters of rivers flowing across the boundary.

ARTICLE I

The High Contracting Parties agree that the navigation of all navigable boundary waters shall forever continue free and open for the purposes of commerce to the inhabitants and to the ships, vessels, and boats of both countries equally, subject, however, to any laws and regulations of either country, within its own territory, not inconsistent with such privilege of free navigation and applying equally and without discrimination to the inhabitants, ships, vessels, and boats of both countries.

It is further agreed that so long as this treaty shall remain in force, this same right of navigation shall extend to the waters of Lake Michigan and to

---

1. Article 5 terminated by treaty of 27 February 1950.

all canals connecting boundary waters, and now existing or which may hereafter be constructed on either side of the line. Either of the High Contracting Parties may adopt rules and regulations governing the use of such canals within its own territory and may charge tolls for the use thereof, but all such rules and regulations and all tolls charged shall apply alike to the subjects or citizens of the High Contracting Parties and the ships, vessels, and boats of both of the High Contracting Parties, and they shall be placed on terms of equality in the use thereof.

ARTICLE II

Each of the High Contracting Parties reserves to itself or to the several State Governments on the one side and the Dominion or Provincial Governments on the other as the case may be, subject to any treaty provisions now existing with respect thereto, the exclusive jurisdiction and control over the use and diversion, whether temporary or permanent, of all waters on its own side of the line which in their natural channels would flow across the boundary or into boundary waters; but it is agreed that any interference with or diversion from their natural channel of such waters on either side of the boundary, resulting in any injury on the other side of the boundary, shall give rise to the same rights and entitle the injured parties to the same legal remedies as if such injury took place in the country where such diversion or interference occurs; but this provision shall not apply to cases already existing or to cases expressly covered by special agreement between the parties hereto.

It is understood, however, that neither of the High Contracting Parties intends by the foregoing provision to surrender any right, which it may have, to object to any interference with or diversions of waters on the other side of the boundary the effect of which would be productive of material injury to the navigation interests on its own side of the boundary.

ARTICLE III

It is agreed that, in addition to the uses, obstructions, and diversions heretofore permitted or hereafter provided for by special agreement between the Parties hereto, no further or other uses or obstructions or diversions, whether temporary or permanent, of boundary waters on either side of the line, affecting the natural level or flow of boundary waters on the other side of the line, shall be made except by authority of the United States or the Dominion of Canada within their respective jurisdictions and with the approval, as hereinafter provided, of a joint commission, to be known as the International Joint Commission.

The foregoing provisions are not intended to limit or interfere with the existing rights of the Government of the United States on the one side and the Government of the Dominion of Canada on the other, to undertake and carry on governmental works in boundary waters for the deepening of channels, the construction of breakwaters, the improvement of harbors, and other governmental works for the benefit of commerce and navigation, provided that such works are wholly on its own side of the line and do not materially affect the level or flow of the boundary waters on the other, nor are such provisions intended to interfere with the ordinary use of such waters for domestic and sanitary purposes.

ARTICLE IV

The High Contracting Parties agree that, except in cases provided for by special agreement between them, they will not permit the construction or maintenance on their respective sides of the boundary of any remedial or protective works or any dams or other obstructions in waters flowing from boundary waters or in waters at a lower level than the boundary in rivers flowing across the boundary, the effect of which is to raise the natural level of waters on the other side of the boundary unless the construction or maintenance thereof is approved by the aforesaid International Joint Commission.

It is further agreed that the waters herein defined as boundary waters and waters flowing across the boundary shall not be polluted on either side to the injury of health or property on the other.

ARTICLE V

The High Contracting Parties agree that it is expedient to limit the diversion of waters from the Niagara River so that the level of Lake Erie and the flow of the stream shall not be appreciably affected. It is the desire of both Parties to accomplish this object with the least possible injury to investments which have already been made in the construction of power plants on the United States side of the river under grants of authority from the State of New York, and on the Canadian side of the river under licenses authorized by the Dominion of Canada and the Province of Ontario.

So long as this treaty shall remain in force, no diversion of the waters of the Niagara River above the Falls from the natural course and stream thereof shall be permitted except for the purposes and to the extent hereinafter provided.

The United States may authorize and permit the diversion within the State of New York of the waters of said river above the Falls of Niagara, for power purposes, not exceeding in the aggregate a daily diversion at the rate of twenty thousand cubic feet of water per second.

The United Kingdom, by the Dominion of Canada, or the Province of Ontario, may authorize and permit the diversion within the Province of Ontario of the waters of said river above the Falls of Niagara, for power purposes, not exceeding in the aggregate a daily diversion at the rate of thirty-six thousand cubic feet of water per second.

The prohibitions of this article shall not apply to the diversion of water for sanitary or domestic purposes, or for the service of canals for the purposes of navigation.

ARTICLE VI

The High Contracting Parties agree that the St. Mary and Milk Rivers and their tributaries (in the State of Montana and the Provinces of Alberta and Saskatchewan) are to be treated as one stream for the purposes of irrigation and power, and the waters thereof shall be apportioned equally between the two countries, but in making such equal apportionment more than half may be taken from one river and less than half from the other by either country so as to afford a more beneficial use to each. It is further agreed that in the division of such waters during the irrigation season, between the 1st of April and 31st of October, inclusive, annually, the United

States is entitled to a prior appropriation of 500 cubic feet per second of the waters of the Milk River, or so much of such amount as constitutes three-fourths of its natural flow, and that Canada is entitled to a prior appropriation of 500 cubic feet per second of the flow of the St. Mary River, or so much of such amount as constitutes three-fourths of its natural flow.

The channel of the Milk River in Canada may be used at the convenience of the United States for the conveyance, while passing through Canadian territory, of waters diverted from the St. Mary River. The provisions of Article II of this treaty shall apply to any injury resulting to property in Canada from the conveyance of such waters through the Milk River.

The measurement and apportionment of the water to be used by each country shall from time to time be made jointly by the properly constituted reclamation officers of the United States and the properly constituted irrigation officers of His Majesty under the direction of the International Joint Commission.

ARTICLE VII

The High Contracting Parties agree to establish and maintain an International Joint Commission of the United States and Canada composed of six commissioners, three on the part of the United States appointed by the President thereof, and three on the part of the United Kingdom appointed by His Majesty on the recommendation of the Governor in Council of the Dominion of Canada.

ARTICLE VIII

This International Joint Commission shall have jurisdiction over and shall pass upon all cases involving the use or obstruction or diversion of the waters with respect to which under Articles III and IV of this treaty the approval of this Commission is required, and in passing upon such cases the Commission shall be governed by the following rules or principles which are adopted by the High Contracting Parties for this purpose:

The High Contracting Parties shall have, each on its own side of the boundary, equal and similar rights in the use of the waters hereinbefore defined as boundary waters.

The following order of precedence shall be observed among the various uses enumerated hereinafter for these waters, and no use shall be permitted which tends materially to conflict with or restrain any other use which is given preference over it in this order of precedence:

(1) Uses for domestic and sanitary purposes;

(2) Uses for navigation, including the service of canals for the purposes of navigation;

(3) Uses for power and for irrigation purposes.

The foregoing provisions shall not apply to or disturb any existing uses of boundary waters on either side of the boundary.

The requirement for an equal division may in the discretion of the Commission be suspended in cases of temporary diversions along boundary waters at points where such equal division can not be made advantageously on account of local conditions, and where such diversion does not diminish elsewhere the amount available for use on the other side.

The Commission in its discretion may make its approval in any case conditional upon the construction of remedial or protective works to compensate so far as possible for the particular use or diversion proposed, and in such cases may require that suitable and adequate provision, approved by the Commission, be made for the protection and indemnity against injury of any interests on either side of the boundary.

In cases involving the elevation of the natural level of waters on either side of the line as a result of the construction or maintenance on the other side of remedial or protective works or dams or other obstructions in boundary waters or in waters flowing therefrom or in waters below the boundary in rivers flowing across the boundary, the Commission shall require, as a condition of its approval thereof, that suitable and adequate provision, approved by it, be made for the protection and indemnity of all interests on the other side of the line which may be injured thereby.

The majority of the Commissioners shall have power to render a decision. In case the Commission is evenly divided upon any question or matter presented to it for decision, separate reports shall be made by the Commissioners on each side to their own Government. The High Contracting Parties shall thereupon endeavor to agree upon an adjustment of the question or matter of difference, and if an agreement is reached between them, it shall be reduced to writing in the form of a protocol, and shall be communicated to the Commissioners, who shall take such further proceedings as may be necessary to carry out such agreement.

ARTICLE IX

The High Contracting Parties further agree that any other questions or matters of difference arising between them involving the rights, obligations, or interests of either in relation to the other or to the inhabitants of the other along the common frontier between the United States and the Dominion of Canada, shall be referred from time to time to the International Joint Commission for examination and report, whenever either the Government of the United States or the Government of the Dominion of Canada shall request that such questions or matters of difference be so referred.

The International Joint Commission is authorized in each case so referred to examine into and report upon the facts and circumstances of the particular questions and matters referred, together with such conclusions and recommendations as may be appropriate, subject, however, to any restrictions or exceptions which may be imposed with respect thereto by the terms of the reference.

Such reports of the Commission shall not be regarded as decisions of the questions or matters so submitted either on the facts or the law, and shall in no way have the character of an arbitral award.

The Commission shall make a joint report to both Governments in all cases in which all or a majority of the Commissioners agree, and in case of disagreement the minority may make a joint report to both Governments, or separate reports to their respective Governments.

In case the Commission is evenly divided upon any question or matter referred to it for report, separate reports shall be made by the Commissioners on each side to their own Government.

ARTICLE X

Any questions or matters of difference arising between the High Contracting Parties involving the rights, obligations, or interests of the United States or of the Dominion of Canada either in relation to each other or to their respective inhabitants, may be referred for decision to the International Joint Commission by the consent of the two Parties, it being understood that on the part of the United States any such action will be by and with the advice and consent of the Senate, and on the part of His Majesty's Government with the consent of the Governor General in Council. In each case so referred, the said Commission is authorized to examine into and report upon the facts and circumstances of the particular questions and matters referred, together with such conclusions and recommendations as may be appropriate, subject, however, to any restrictions or exceptions which may be imposed with respect thereto by the terms of the reference.

A majority of the said Commission shall have power to render a decision or finding upon any of the questions or matters so referred.

If the said Commission is equally divided or otherwise unable to render a decision or finding as to any questions or matters so referred, it shall be the duty of the Commissioners to make a joint report to both Governments, or separate reports to their respective Governments, showing the different conclusions arrived at with regard to the matters or questions so referred, which questions or matters shall thereupon be referred for decision by the High Contracting Parties to an umpire chosen in accordance with the procedure prescribed in the fourth, fifth, and sixth paragraphs of Article XLV of The Hague Convention for the pacific settlement of international disputes, dated October 18, 1907. Such umpire shall have power to render a final decision with respect to those matters and questions so referred on which the Commission failed to agree.

ARTICLE XI

A duplicate original of all decisions rendered and joint reports made by the Commission shall be transmitted to and filed with the Secretary of State of the United States and the Governor General of the Dominion of Canada, and to them shall be addressed all communications of the Commission.

ARTICLE XII

The International Joint Commission shall meet and organize at Washington promptly after the members thereof are appointed, and when organized the Commission may fix such times and places for its meetings as may be necessary, subject at all times to special call or direction by the two Governments. Each Commissioner, upon the first joint meeting of the Commission after his appointment, shall, before proceeding with the work of the Commission, make and subscribe a solemn declaration in writing that he will faithfully and impartially perform the duties imposed upon him under this treaty, and such declaration shall be entered on the records of the proceedings of the Commission.

The United States and Canadian sections of the Commission may each appoint a secretary, and these shall act as joint secretaries of the Commission at its joint sessions, and the Commission may employ engineers and clerical assistants from time to time as it may deem advisable. The salaries and personal expenses of the Commission and of the secretaries shall be paid by their respective Governments, and all reasonable and necessary joint expenses of the Commission, incurred by it, shall be paid in equal moieties by the High Contracting Parties.

The Commission shall have power to administer oaths to witnesses, and to take evidence on oath whenever deemed necessary in any proceeding, or inquiry, or matter within its jurisdiction under this treaty, and all parties interested therein shall be given convenient opportunity to be heard, and the High Contracting Parties agree to adopt such legislation as may be appropriate and necessary to give the Commission the powers above mentioned on each side of the boundary, and to provide for the issue of subpoenas and for compelling the attendance of witnesses in proceedings before the Commission. The Commission may adopt such rules of procedure as shall be in accordance with justice and equity, and may make such examination in person and through agents or employees as may be deemed advisable.

ARTICLE XIII

In all cases where special agreements between the High Contracting Parties hereto are referred to in the foregoing articles, such agreements are understood and intended to include not only direct agreements between the High Contracting Parties, but also any mutual arrangement between the United States and the Dominion of Canada expressed by concurrent or reciprocal legislation on the part of Congress and the Parliament of the Dominion.

ARTICLE XIV

The present treaty shall be ratified by the President of the United States of America, by and with the advice and consent of the Senate thereof, and by His Britannic Majesty. The ratifications shall be exchanged at Washington as soon as possible and the treaty shall take effect on the date of the exchange of its ratifications. It shall remain in force for five years, dating from the day of exchange of ratifications, and thereafter until terminated by twelve months' written notice given by either High Contracting Party to the other.

4.2 INTERNATIONAL CONVENTION FOR THE PREVENTION OF POLLU-TION OF THE SEA BY OIL (OILPOL) (WITHOUT ANNEXES BUT AS AMENDED TO 1971).[1] Concluded at London, 12 May 1954. Entered into force, 26 July 1958. 327 U.N.T.S. 3, 12 U.S.T. 2989, T.I.A.S. No. 4900; 600 U.N.T.S. 332, 17 U.S.T. 1523, T.I.A.S. No. 6109; 28 U.S.T. 1205, T.I.A.S. No. 8505

Article I

(1) For the purposes of the present Convention, the following expressions shall (unless the context otherwise requires) have the meanings hereby respectively assigned to them that is to say:

'The Bureau' has the meaning assigned to it by Article XXI;

'Discharge' in relation to oil or to oily mixture means any discharge or escape howsoever caused;

'Heavy diesel oil' means diesel oil, other than those distillates of which more than 50 per cent by volume distils at a temperature not exceeding 340°C. when tested by A.S.T.M. Standard Method D.86/59;

'Instantaneous rate of discharge of oil content' means the rate of discharge of oil in litres per hour at any instant divided by the speed of the ship in knots at the same instant;

'Mile' means a nautical mile of 6,080 feet or 1,852 metres;

'Nearest land.' The term 'from the nearest land' means from the baseline from which the territorial sea of the territory in question is established in accordance with the Geneva Convention on the Territorial Sea and the Contiguous Zone, 1958, except that, for the purposes of this Convention 'from the nearest land' off the north-eastern coast of Australia shall mean from a line drawn from a point on the coast of Australia in latitude 11° south, longitude 142° 08' east to a point in latitude 10° 35' south, longitude 141° 55' east—

thence to a point latitude 10° 00' south, longitude 142° 00' east

thence to a point latitude 9° 10' south, longitude 143° 52' east

thence to a point latitude 9° 00' south, longitude 144° 30' east

thence to a point latitude 13° 00' south, longitude 144° 00' east

thence to a point latitude 15° 00' south, longitude 146° 00' east

thence to a point latitude 18° 00' south, longitude 147° 00' east

thence to a point latitude 21° 00' south, longitude 153° 00' east

thence to a point on the coast of Australia in latitude 24° 42' south, longitude 153° 15' east.

'Oil' means crude oil, fuel oil, heavy diesel oil and lubricating oil, and 'oily' shall be construed accordingly;

'Oily mixture' means a mixture with any oil content;

'Organization' means the Inter–Governmental Maritime Consultative Organization;

1. The Convention was superseded by the Protocol of 1978 Relating to the International Convention for the Prevention of Pollution from Ships (Basic Document 4.23 *infra*) as between the States Parties thereto.

'Ship' means any sea-going vessel of any type whatsoever, including floating craft, whether self-propelled or towed by another vessel, making a sea voyage; and 'tanker' means a ship in which the greater part of the cargo space is constructed or adapted for the carriage of liquid cargoes in bulk and which is not, for the time being, carrying a cargo other than oil in that part of its cargo space.

(2) For the purposes of the present Convention, the territories of a Contracting Government mean the territory of the country of which it is the Government and any other territory for the international relations of which it is responsible and to which the Convention shall have been extended under Article XVIII.

Article II

(1) The present Convention shall apply to ships registered in any of the territories of a Contracting Government and to unregistered ships having the nationality of a Contracting Party, except:

(a) tankers of under 150 tons gross tonnage and other ships of under 500 tons gross tonnage, provided that each Contracting Government will take the necessary steps, so far as is reasonable and practicable, to apply the requirements of the Convention to such ships also, having regard to their size, service and the type of fuel used for their propulsion;

(b) ships for the time being engaged in the whaling industry when actually employed on whaling operations;

(c) ships for the time being navigating the Great Lakes of North America and their connecting and tributary waters as far east as the lower exit of St. Lambert Lock at Montreal in the Province of Quebec, Canada;

(d) naval ships and ships for the time being used as naval auxiliaries.

(2) Each Contracting Government undertakes to adopt appropriate measures ensuring that requirements equivalent to those of the present Convention are, so far as is reasonable and practicable, applied to the ships referred to in subparagraph (d) of paragraph (1) of this Article.

Article III

Subject to the provisions of Articles IV and V:

(a) the discharge from a ship to which the present Convention applies, other than a tanker, of oil or oily mixture shall be prohibited except when the following conditions are all satisfied:

(i) the ship is proceeding en route;

(ii) the instantaneous rate of discharge of oil content does not exceed 60 litres per mile;

(iii) the oil content of the discharge is less than 100 parts per 1,000,000 parts of the mixture;

(iv) the discharge is made as far as practicable from the nearest land;

(*b*) the discharge from a tanker to which the present Convention applies of oil or oily mixture shall be prohibited except when the following conditions are all satisfied:

(i) the tanker is proceeding en route;

(ii) the instantaneous rate of discharge of oil content does not exceed 60 litres per mile;

(iii) the total quantity of oil discharged on a ballast voyage does not exceed 1/15,000 of the total cargo-carrying capacity;

(iv) the tanker is more than 50 miles from the nearest land;

(*c*) the provisions of sub-paragraph (*b*) of this Article shall not apply to:

(i) the discharge of ballast from a cargo tank which, since the cargo was last carried therein, has been so cleaned that any effluent therefrom, if it were discharged from a stationary tanker into clean calm water on a clear day, would produce no visible traces of oil on the surface of the water; or

(ii) the discharge of oil or oily mixture from machinery space bilges, which shall be governed by the provisions of sub-paragraph (*a*) of this Article.

Article IV

Article III shall not apply to:

(*a*) the discharge of oil or of oily mixture from a ship for the purpose of securing the safety of a ship, preventing damage to a ship or cargo, or saving life at sea;

(*b*) the escape of oil or of oily mixture resulting from damage to a ship or unavoidable leakage, if all reasonable precautions have been taken after the occurrence of the damage or discovery of the leakage for the purpose of preventing or minimizing the escape.

Article V

Article III shall not apply to the discharge of oily mixture from the bilges of a ship during the period of twelve months following the date on which the present Convention comes into force for the relevant territory in accordance with paragraph (1) of Article II.

Article VI

(1) Any contravention of Articles III and IX shall be an offence punishable under the law of the relevant territory in respect of the ship in accordance with paragraph (1) of Article II.

(2) The penalties which may be imposed under the law of any of the territories of a Contracting Government in respect of the unlawful discharge from a ship of oil or oily mixture outside the territorial sea of that territory shall be adequate in severity to discourage any such unlawful discharge and shall not be less than the penalties which may be imposed under the law of that territory in respect of the same infringements within the territorial sea.

(3) Each Contracting Government shall report to the Organization the penalties actually imposed for each infringement.

Article VI bis

(1) Every tanker to which the present Convention applies and for which the building contract is placed on or after the date of coming into force of this Article shall be constructed in accordance with the provisions of Annex C.[2] In addition, every tanker to which the present Convention applies and for which the building contract is placed, or in the absence of a building contract the keel of which is laid or which is at a similar stage of construction, before the date of coming into force of this Article shall be required, within two years after that date, to comply with the provisions of Annex C, where such a tanker falls into either of the following categories:

(*a*) a tanker, the delivery of which is after 1 January 1977; or

(*b*) a tanker to which both the following conditions apply:

(i) delivery is not later than 1 January 1977; and

(ii) the building contract is placed after 1 January 1972, or in cases where no building contract has previously been placed the keel is laid, or the tanker is at a similar stage of construction, after 30 June 1972.

(2) A tanker required under paragraph (1) of this Article to be constructed in accordance with Annex C and so constructed shall carry on board a certificate issued or authorized by the responsible Contracting Government attesting such compliance. A tanker which under paragraph (1) of this Article is not required to be constructed in accordance with Annex C shall carry on board a certificate to that effect issued or authorized by the responsible Contracting Government, or if the tanker does comply with Annex C although not required to do so, it may carry on board a certificate issued or authorized by the responsible Contracting Government attesting such compliance. A Contracting Government shall not permit such tankers under its flag to trade unless the appropriate certificate has been issued.

(3) Certificates issued under the authority of a Contracting Government shall be accepted by the other Contracting Governments for all purposes covered by the present Convention. They shall be regarded by the other Contracting Governments as having the same force as certificates issued by them.

(4) If a Contracting Government has clear grounds for believing that a tanker required under paragraph (1) of this Article to be constructed in accordance with Annex C entering ports in its territory or using off-shore terminals under its control does not in fact comply with Annex C, such Contracting Government may request consultation with the Government with which the tanker is registered. If, after such consultation or otherwise, the Contracting Government is satisfied that the tanker does not comply with Annex C, such Contracting Government may for this reason deny such a tanker access to ports in its territorial waters or to off-shore terminals under its control until such time as the Contracting Government is satisfied that the tanker does comply.

---

2. As of 31 December 1982 (date of entry into force of the 1971 Amendments) Annex C became Annex B and Annex B became Annex A.

Article VII

(1) As from a date twelve months after the present Convention comes into force for the relevant territory in respect of a ship in accordance with paragraph (1) of Article II, such a ship shall be required to be so fitted as to prevent, as far as reasonable and practicable, the escape of oil into bilges, unless effective means are provided to ensure that the oil in the bilges is not discharged in contravention of this Convention.

(2) Carrying water ballast in oil fuel tanks shall be avoided if possible.

Article VIII

(1) Each Contracting Government shall take all appropriate steps to promote the provision of facilities as follows:

(a) according to the needs of ships using them, ports shall be provided with facilities adequate for the reception, without causing undue delay to ships, of such residues and oily mixtures as would remain for disposal from ships other than tankers if the bulk of the water had been separated from the mixture;

(b) oil loading terminals shall be provided with facilities, adequate for the reception of such residues and oily mixtures as would similarly remain for disposal by tankers;

(c) ship repair ports shall be provided with facilities adequate for the reception of such residues and oily mixtures as would similarly remain for disposal by all ships entering for repairs.

(2) Each Contracting Government shall determine which are the ports and oil loading terminals in its territories suitable for the purposes of sub-paragraphs (a), (b) and (c) of paragraph (1) of this Article.

(3) As regards paragraph (1) of this Article, each Contracting Government shall report to the Organization, for transmission to the Contracting Government concerned, all cases where the facilities are alleged to be inadequate.

Article IX

(1) Of the ships to which the present Convention applies, every ship which uses oil fuel and every tanker shall be provided with an oil record book, whether as part of the ship's official log book or otherwise, in the form specified in the Annex to this Convention.

(2) The oil record book shall be completed on each occasion, on a tank-to-tank basis, whenever any of the following operations take place in the ship:

(a) *for tankers:*

    (i) loading of oil cargo;

    (ii) transfer of oil cargo during voyage;

    (iii) discharge of oil cargo;

    (iv) ballasting of cargo tanks;

    (v) cleaning of cargo tanks;

    (vi) discharge of dirty ballast;

    (vii) discharge of water from slop-tanks;

(viii) disposal of residues;

(ix) discharge overboard of bilge water containing oil which has accumulated in machinery spaces whilst in port, and the routine discharge at sea of bilge water containing oil unless the latter has been entered in the appropriate log book;

(*b*) *for ships other than tankers:*

(i) ballasting or cleaning of bunker fuel tanks;

(ii) discharge of dirty ballast or cleaning water from tanks referred to under (i) of this sub-paragraph;

(iii) disposal of residues;

(iv) discharge overboard of bilge water containing oil which has accumulated in machinery spaces whilst in port, and the routine discharge at sea of bilge water containing oil unless the latter has been entered in the appropriate log book.

In the event of such discharge or escape of oil or oily mixture as is referred to in Article IV, a statement shall be made in the oil record book of the circumstances of, and the reason for, the discharge or escape.

(3) Each operation described in paragraph (2) of this Article shall be fully recorded without delay in the oil record book so that all the entries in the book appropriate to that operation are completed. Each page of the book shall be signed by the officer or officers in charge of the operations concerned and, when the ship is manned, by the master of the ship. The written entries in the oil record book shall be in an official language of the relevant territory in respect of the ship in accordance with paragraph (1) of Article II, or in English or French.

(4) Oil record books shall be kept in such a place as to be readily available for inspection at all reasonable times, and, except in the case of unmanned ships under tow, shall be kept on board the ship. They shall be preserved for a period of two years after the last entry has been made.

(5) The competent authorities of any of the territories of a Contracting Government may inspect on board any ship to which the present Convention applies, while within a port in that territory, the oil record book required to be carried in the ship in compliance with the provisions of this Article, and may make a true copy of any entry in that book and may require the master of the ship to certify that the copy is a true copy of such entry. Any copy so made which purports to have been certified by the master of the ship as a true copy of an entry in the ship's oil record book shall be made admissible in any judicial proceedings as evidence of the facts stated in the entry. Any action by the competent authorities under this paragraph shall be taken as expeditiously as possible and the ship shall not be delayed.

Article X

(1) Any Contracting Government may furnish to the Government of the relevant territory in respect of the ship in accordance with paragraph (1) of Article II particulars in writing of evidence that any provision of the present Convention has been contravened in respect of that ship, wheresoever the alleged contravention may have taken place. If it is practicable to do so, the

competent authorities of the former Government shall notify the master of the ship of the alleged contravention.

(2) Upon receiving such particulars, the Government so informed shall investigate the matter, and may request the other Government to furnish further or better particulars of the alleged contravention. If the Government so informed is satisfied that sufficient evidence is available in the form required by its law to enable proceedings against the owner or master of the ship to be taken in respect of the alleged contravention, it shall cause such proceedings to be taken as soon as possible. That Government shall promptly inform the Government whose official has reported the alleged contravention, as well as the Organization, of the action taken as a consequence of the information communicated.

Article XI

Nothing in the present Convention shall be construed as derogating from the powers of any Contracting Government to take measures within its jurisdiction in respect of any matter to which the Convention relates or as extending the jurisdiction of any Contracting Government.

Article XII

Each Contracting Government shall send to the Bureau and to the appropriate organ of the United Nations:

(a) the text of laws, decrees, orders and regulations in force in its territories which give effect to the present Convention;

(b) all official reports or summaries of official reports in so far as they show the results of the application of the provisions of the Convention, provided always that such reports or summaries are not, in the opinion of that Government, of a confidential nature.

Article XIII

Any dispute between Contracting Governments relating to the interpretation or application of the present Convention which cannot be settled by negotiation shall be referred at the request of either party to the International Court of Justice for decision unless the parties in dispute agree to submit it to arbitration.

Article XIV

(1) The present Convention shall remain open for signature for three months from this day's date and shall thereafter remain open for acceptance.

(2) Subject to Article XV, the Governments of States Members of the United Nations or of any of the Specialized Agencies or parties to the Statute of the International Court of Justice may become parties to the present Convention by:

(a) signature without reservation as to acceptance;

(b) signature subject to acceptance followed by acceptance; or

(c) acceptance.

(3) Acceptance shall be effected by the deposit of an instrument of acceptance with the Bureau, which shall inform all Governments that have

already signed or accepted the present Convention of each signature and deposit of an acceptance and of the date of such signature or deposit.

Article XV

(1) The present Convention shall come into force twelve months after the date on which not less than ten Governments have become parties to the Convention, including five Governments of countries each with not less than 500,000 gross tons of tanker tonnage.

(2)(*a*) For each Government which signs the Convention without reservation as to acceptance or accepts the Convention before the date on which the Convention comes into force in accordance with paragraph (1) of this Article it shall come into force on that date. For each Government which accepts the Convention on or after that date, it shall come into force three months after the date of the deposit of that Government's acceptance.

(*b*) The Bureau shall, as soon as possible, inform all Governments which have signed or accepted the Convention of the date on which it will come into force.

Article XVI

(1)(*a*) The present Convention may be amended by unanimous agreement between the Contracting Governments.

(*b*) Upon request of any Contracting Government a proposed amendment shall be communicated by the Organization to all Contracting Governments for consideration and acceptance under this paragraph.

(2)(*a*) An amendment to the present Convention may be proposed to the Organization at any time by any Contracting Government, and such proposal if adopted by a two-thirds majority of the Assembly of the Organization upon recommendation adopted by a two-thirds majority of the Maritime Safety Committee of the Organization shall be communicated by the Organization to all Contracting Governments for their acceptance.

(*b*) Any such recommendation by the Maritime Safety Committee shall be communicated by the Organization to all Contracting Governments for their consideration at least six months before it is considered by the Assembly.

(3)(*a*) A conference of Governments to consider amendments to the present Convention proposed by any Contracting Government shall at any time be convened by the Organization upon the request of one-third of the Contracting Governments.

(*b*) Every amendment adopted by such conference by a two-thirds majority of the Contracting Governments shall be communicated by the Organization to all Contracting Governments for their acceptance.

(4) Any amendment communicated to Contracting Governments for their acceptance under paragraph (2) or (3) of this Article shall come into force for all Contracting Governments, except those which before it comes into force make a declaration that they do not accept the amendment, twelve months after the date on which the amendment is accepted by two-thirds of the Contracting Governments.

(5) The Assembly, by a two-thirds majority vote, including two-thirds of the Governments represented on the Maritime Safety Committee, and subject to the concurrence of two-thirds of the Contracting Governments to the present Convention, or a conference convened under paragraph (3) of this Article by a two-thirds majority vote, may determine at the time of its adoption that the amendment is of such an important nature that any Contracting Government which makes a declaration under paragraph (4) of this Article and which does not accept the amendment within a period of twelve months after the amendment comes into force, shall, upon the expiry of this period, cease to be a party to the present Convention.

(6) The Organization shall inform all Contracting Governments of any amendments which come into force under this Article, together with the date on which such amendments shall come into force.

(7) Any acceptance or declaration under this Article shall be made by a notification in writing to the Organization which shall notify all Contracting Governments of the receipt of the acceptance or declaration.

Article XVII

(1) The present Convention may be denounced by any Contracting Government at any time after the expiration of a period of five years from the date on which the Convention comes into force for that Government.

(2) Denunciation shall be effected by a notification in writing addressed to the Bureau, which shall notify all the Contracting Governments of any denunciation received and of the date of its receipt.

(3) A denunciation shall take effect twelve months, or such longer period as may be specified in the notification, after its receipt by the Bureau.

Article XVIII

(1)(*a*) The United Nations in cases where they are the administering authority for a territory or any Contracting Government responsible for the international relations of a territory shall as soon as possible consult with such territory in an endeavour to extend the present Convention to that territory and may at any time by notification in writing given to the Bureau declare that the Convention shall extend to such territory.

(*b*) The present Convention shall from the date of the receipt of the notification or from such other date as may be specified in the notification extend to the territory named therein.

(2)(*a*) The United Nations in cases where they are the administering authority for a territory or any Contracting Government which has made a declaration under paragraph (1) of this Article, at any time after the expiry of a period of five years from the date on which the present Convention has been so extended to any territory, may by a notification in writing given to the Bureau after consultation with such territory declare that the Convention shall cease to extend to any such territory named in the notification.

(*b*) The present Convention shall cease to extend to any territory mentioned in such notification one year, or such longer period as may be specified therein, after the date of receipt of the notification by the Bureau.

(3) The Bureau shall inform all the Contracting Governments of the extension of the present Convention to any territory under paragraph (1) of this Article, and of the termination of any such extension under the provisions of paragraph (2) stating in each case the date from which the Convention has been or will cease to be so extended.

Article XIX

(1) In case of war or other hostilities, a Contracting Government which considers that it is affected, whether as a belligerent or as a neutral, may suspend the operation of the whole or any part of the present Convention in respect of all or any of its territories. The suspending Government shall immediately give notice of any such suspension to the Bureau.

(2) The suspending Government may at any time terminate such suspension and shall in any event terminate it as soon as it ceases to be justified under paragraph (1) of this Article. Notice of such termination shall be given immediately to the Bureau by the Government concerned.

(3) The Bureau shall notify all Contracting Governments of any suspension or termination of suspension under this Article.

Article XX

As soon as the present Convention comes into force it shall be registered by the Bureau with the Secretary–General of the United Nations.

Article XXI

The duties of the Bureau shall be carried out by the Government of the United Kingdom of Great Britain and Northern Ireland unless and until the Inter–Governmental Maritime Consultative Organization comes into being and takes over the duties assigned to it under the Convention signed at Geneva on the 6th day of March, 1948, and thereafter the duties of the Bureau shall be carried out by the said Organization.

4.3   CONVENTION ON THE HIGH SEAS.[1]   Concluded at Geneva, 29 April 1958.   Entered into force, 30 September 1962.   450 U.N.T.S. 82, 13 U.S.T. 2312, T.I.A.S. No. 5200

Article 1

The term "high seas" means all parts of the sea that are not included in the territorial sea or in the internal waters of a State.

Article 2

The high seas being open to all nations, no State may validly purport to subject any part of them to its sovereignty. Freedom of the high seas is exercised under the conditions laid down by these articles and by the other rules of international law. It comprises, *inter alia,* both for coastal and non-coastal States:

(1) Freedom of navigation;

(2) Freedom of fishing;

(3) Freedom to lay submarine cables and pipelines;

(4) Freedom to fly over the high seas.

These freedoms, and others which are recognized by the general principles of international law, shall be exercised by all States with reasonable regard to the interests of other States in their exercise of the freedom of the high seas.

Article 3

1. In order to enjoy the freedom of the seas on equal terms with coastal States, States having no sea-coast should have free access to the sea. To this end States situated between the sea and a State having no sea-coast shall by common agreement with the latter, and in conformity with existing international conventions, accord:

    (*a*) To the State having no sea-coast, on a basis of reciprocity, free transit through their territory; and

    (*b*) To ships flying the flag of that State treatment equal to that accorded to their own ships, or to the ships of any other States, as regards access to seaports and the use of such ports.

2. States situated between the sea and a State having no sea-coast shall settle, by mutual agreement with the latter, and taking into account the rights of the coastal State or State of transit and the special conditions of the State having no sea-coast, all matters relating to freedom of transit and equal treatment in ports, in case such States are not already parties to existing international conventions.

Article 4

Every State, whether coastal or not, has the right to sail ships under its flag on the high seas.

---

1. *See also* Optional Protocol to the 1958 Law of the Sea Conventions Concerning the Compulsory Settlement of Disputes (which provides for reference to the International Court of Justice of disputes arising out of this agreement), concluded 29 April 1958 and entered into force 30 September 1962 (450 UNTS 169).

Article 5

1. Each State shall fix the conditions for the grant of its nationality to ships, for the registration of ships in its territory, and for the right to fly its flag. Ships have the nationality of the State whose flag they are entitled to fly. There must exist a genuine link between the State and the ship; in particular, the State must effectively exercise its jurisdiction and control in administrative, technical and social matters over ships flying its flag.

2. Each State shall issue to ships to which it has granted the right to fly its flag documents to that effect.

Article 6

1. Ships shall sail under the flag of one State only and, save in exceptional cases expressly provided for in international treaties or in these articles, shall be subject to its exclusive jurisdiction on the high seas. A ship may not change its flag during a voyage or while in a port of call, save in the case of a real transfer of ownership or change of registry.

2. A ship which sails under the flags of two or more States, using them according to convenience, may not claim any of the nationalities in question with respect to any other State, and may be assimilated to a ship without nationality.

Article 7

The provisions of the preceding articles do not prejudice the question of ships employed on the official service of an inter-governmental organization flying the flag of the organization.

Article 8

1. Warships on the high seas have complete immunity from the jurisdiction of any State other than the flag State.

2. For the purposes of these articles, the term "warship" means a ship belonging to the naval forces of a State and bearing the external marks distinguishing warships of its nationality, under the command of an officer duly commissioned by the government and whose name appears in the Navy List, and manned by a crew who are under regular naval discipline.

Article 9

Ships owned or operated by a State and used only on government non-commercial service shall, on the high seas, have complete immunity from the jurisdiction of any State other than the flag State.

Article 10

1. Every State shall take such measures for ships under its flag as are necessary to ensure safety at sea with regard *inter alia* to:

    (*a*) The use of signals, the maintenance of communications and the prevention of collisions;

    (*b*) The manning of ships and labour conditions for crews taking into account the applicable international labour instruments;

    (*c*) The construction, equipment and seaworthiness of ships.

2. In taking such measures each State is required to conform to generally accepted international standards and to take any steps which may be necessary to ensure their observance.

Article 11

1. In the event of a collision or of any other incident of navigation concerning a ship on the high seas, involving the penal or disciplinary responsibility of the master or of any other person in the service of the ship, no penal or disciplinary proceedings may be instituted against such persons except before the judicial or administrative authorities either of the flag State or of the State of which such person is a national.

2. In disciplinary matters, the State which has issued a master's certificate or a certificate of competence or license shall alone be competent, after due legal process, to pronounce the withdrawal of such certificates, even if the holder is not a national of the State which issued them.

3. No arrest or detention of the ship, even as a measure of investigation, shall be ordered by any authorities other than those of the flag State.

Article 12

1. Every State shall require the master of a ship sailing under its flag, in so far as he can do so without serious danger to the ship, the crew or the passengers,

(*a*) To render assistance to any person found at sea in danger of being lost;

(*b*) To proceed with all possible speed to the rescue of persons in distress if informed of their need of assistance, in so far as such action may reasonably be expected of him;

(*c*) After a collision, to render assistance to the other ship, her crew and her passengers and, where possible, to inform the other ship of the name of his own ship, her port of registry and the nearest port at which she will call.

2. Every coastal State shall promote the establishment and maintenance of an adequate and effective search and rescue service regarding safety on and over the sea and—where circumstances so require—by way of mutual regional arrangements co-operate with neighbouring States for this purpose.

Article 13

Every State shall adopt effective measures to prevent and punish the transport of slaves in ships authorized to fly its flag, and to prevent the unlawful use of its flag for that purpose. Any slave taking refuge on board any ship, whatever its flag, shall *ipso facto* be free.

Article 14

All States shall co-operate to the fullest possible extent in the repression of piracy on the high seas or in any other place outside the jurisdiction of any State.

Article 15

Piracy consists of any of the following acts:

(1) Any illegal acts of violence, detention or any act of depredation, committed for private ends by the crew or the passengers of a private ship or a private aircraft, and directed:

    (*a*) On the high seas, against another ship or aircraft, or against persons or property on board such ship or aircraft;

    (*b*) Against a ship, aircraft, persons or property in a place outside the jurisdiction of any State;

(2) Any act of voluntary participation in the operation of a ship or of an aircraft with knowledge of facts making it a pirate ship or aircraft;

(3) Any act of inciting or of intentionally facilitating an act described in sub-paragraph 1 or sub-paragraph 2 of this article.

Article 16

The acts of piracy, as defined in article 15, committed by a warship, government ship or government aircraft whose crew has mutinied and taken control of the ship or aircraft are assimilated to acts committed by a private ship.

Article 17

A ship or aircraft is considered a pirate ship or aircraft if it is intended by the persons in dominant control to be used for the purpose of committing one of the acts referred to in article 15. The same applies if the ship or aircraft has been used to commit any such act, so long as it remains under the control of the persons guilty of that act.

Article 18

A ship or aircraft may retain its nationality although it has become a pirate ship or aircraft. The retention or loss of nationality is determined by the law of the State from which such nationality was derived.

Article 19

On the high seas, or in any other place outside the jurisdiction of any State, every State may seize a pirate ship or aircraft, or a ship taken by piracy and under the control of pirates, and arrest the persons and seize the property on board. The courts of the State which carried out the seizure may decide upon the penalties to be imposed, and may also determine the action to be taken with regard to the ships, aircraft or property, subject to the rights of third parties acting in good faith.

Article 20

Where the seizure of a ship or aircraft on suspicion of piracy has been effected without adequate grounds, the State making the seizure shall be liable to the State the nationality of which is possessed by the ship or aircraft, for any loss or damage caused by the seizure.

Article 21

A seizure on account of piracy may only be carried out by warships or military aircraft, or other ships or aircraft on government service authorized to that effect.

Article 22

1.   Except where acts of interference derive from powers conferred by treaty, a warship which encounters a foreign merchant ship on the high seas is not justified in boarding her unless there is reasonable ground for suspecting:

   (*a*) That the ship is engaged in piracy; or

   (*b*) That the ship is engaged in the slave trade; or

   (*c*) That though flying a foreign flag or refusing to show its flag, the ship is, in reality, of the same nationality as the warship.

2.   In the cases provided for in sub-paragraphs (*a*), (*b*) and (*c*) above, the warship may proceed to verify the ship's right to fly its flag. To this end, it may send a boat under the command of an officer to the suspected ship. If suspicion remains after the documents have been checked, it may proceed to a further examination on board the ship, which must be carried out with all possible consideration.

3.   If the suspicions prove to be unfounded, and provided that the ship boarded has not committed any act justifying them, it shall be compensated for any loss or damage that may have been sustained.

Article 23

1.   The hot pursuit of a foreign ship may be undertaken when the competent authorities of the coastal State have good reason to believe that the ship has violated the laws and regulations of that State. Such pursuit must be commenced when the foreign ship or one of its boats is within the internal waters or the territorial sea or the contiguous zone of the pursuing State, and may only be continued outside the territorial sea or the contiguous zone if the pursuit has not been interrupted. It is not necessary that, at the time when the foreign ship within the territorial sea or the contiguous zone receives the order to stop, the ship giving the order should likewise be within the territorial sea or the contiguous zone. If the foreign ship is within a contiguous zone, as defined in article 24 of the Convention on the Territorial Sea and the Contiguous Zone, the pursuit may only be undertaken if there has been a violation of the rights for the protection of which the zone was established.

2.   The right of hot pursuit ceases as soon as the ship pursued enters the territorial sea of its own country or of a third State.

3.   Hot pursuit is not deemed to have begun unless the pursuing ship has satisfied itself by such practicable means as may be available that the ship pursued or one of its boats or other craft working as a team and using the ship pursued as a mother ship are within the limits of the territorial sea, or as the case may be within the contiguous zone. The pursuit may only be commenced after a visual or auditory signal to stop has been given at a distance which enables it to be seen or heard by the foreign ship.

4.   The right of hot pursuit may be exercised only by warships or military aircraft, or other ships or aircraft on government service specially authorized to that effect.

5. Where hot pursuit is effected by an aircraft:

(*a*) The provisions of paragraph 1 to 3 of this article shall apply *mutatis mutandis;*

(*b*) The aircraft giving the order to stop must itself actively pursue the ship until a ship or aircraft of the coastal State, summoned by the aircraft, arrives to take over the pursuit, unless the aircraft is itself able to arrest the ship. It does not suffice to justify an arrest on the high seas that the ship was merely sighted by the aircraft as an offender or suspected offender, if it was not both ordered to stop and pursued by the aircraft itself or other aircraft or ship which continue the pursuit without interruption.

6. The release of a ship arrested within the jurisdiction of a State and escorted to a port of that State for the purposes of an enquiry before the competent authorities may not be claimed solely on the ground that the ship, in the course of its voyage, was escorted across a portion of the high seas, if the circumstances rendered this necessary.

7. Where a ship has been stopped or arrested on the high seas in circumstances which do not justify the exercise of the right of hot pursuit, it shall be compensated for any loss or damage that may have been thereby sustained.

Article 24

Every State shall draw up regulations to prevent pollution of the seas by the discharge of oil from ships or pipelines or resulting from the exploitation and exploration of the seabed and its subsoil, taking account of existing treaty provisions on the subject.

Article 25

1. Every State shall take measures to prevent pollution of the seas from the dumping of radio-active waste, taking into account any standards and regulations which may be formulated by the competent international organizations.

2. All States shall co-operate with the competent international organizations in taking measures for the prevention of pollution of the seas or air space above, resulting from any activities with radio-active materials or other harmful agents.

Article 26

1. All States shall be entitled to lay submarine cables and pipelines on the bed of the high seas.

2. Subject to its right to take reasonable measures for the exploration of the continental shelf and the exploitation of its natural resources, the coastal State may not impede the laying or maintenance of such cables or pipelines.

3. When laying such cables or pipelines the State in question shall pay due regard to cables or pipelines already in position on the seabed. In particular, possibilities of repairing existing cables or pipelines shall not be prejudiced.

Article 27

Every State shall take the necessary legislative measures to provide that the breaking or injury by a ship flying its flag or by a person subject to its jurisdiction of a submarine cable beneath the high seas done wilfully or through culpable negligence, in such a manner as to be liable to interrupt or obstruct telegraphic or telephonic communications, and similarly the breaking or injury of a submarine pipeline or high-voltage power cable shall be a punishable offence. This provision shall not apply to any break or injury caused by persons who acted merely with the legitimate object of saving their lives or their ships, after having taken all necessary precautions to avoid such break or injury.

Article 28

Every State shall take the necessary legislative measures to provide that, if persons subject to its jurisdiction who are the owners of a cable or pipeline beneath the high seas, in laying or repairing that cable or pipeline, cause a break in or injury to another cable or pipeline, they shall bear the cost of the repairs.

Article 29

Every State shall take the necessary legislative measures to ensure that the owners of ships who can prove that they have sacrificed an anchor, a net or any other fishing gear, in order to avoid injuring a submarine cable or pipeline, shall be indemnified by the owner of the cable or pipeline, provided that the owner of the ship has taken all reasonable precautionary measures beforehand.

Article 30

The provisions of this Convention shall not affect conventions or other international agreements already in force, as between States Parties to them.

Article 31

This Convention shall, until 31 October 1958, be open for signature by all States Members of the United Nations or of any of the specialized agencies, and by any other State invited by the General Assembly of the United Nations to become a Party to the Convention.

Article 32

This Convention is subject to ratification. The instruments of ratification shall be deposited with the Secretary–General of the United Nations.

Article 33

This Convention shall be open for accession by any States belonging to any of the categories mentioned in article 31. The instruments of accession shall be deposited with the Secretary–General of the United Nations.

Article 34

1. This Convention shall come into force on the thirtieth day following the date of deposit of the twenty-second instrument of ratification or accession with the Secretary–General of the United Nations.

2. For each State ratifying or acceding to the Convention after the deposit of the twenty-second instrument of ratification or accession, the Convention shall enter into force on the thirtieth day after deposit by such State of its instrument of ratification or accession.

Article 35

1. After the expiration of a period of five years from the date on which this Convention shall enter into force, a request for the revision of this Convention may be made at any time by any Contracting Party by means of a notification in writing addressed to the Secretary–General of the United Nations.

2. The General Assembly of the United Nations shall decide upon the steps, if any, to be taken in respect of such request.

Article 36

The Secretary–General of the United Nations shall inform all States Members of the United Nations and the other States referred to in article 31:

(*a*) Of signatures to this Convention and of the deposit of instruments of ratification or accession, in accordance with articles 31, 32 and 33;

(*b*) Of the date on which this Convention will come into force, in accordance with article 34;

(*c*) Of requests for revision in accordance with article 35.

Article 37

The original of this Convention, of which the Chinese, English, French, Russian and Spanish texts are equally authentic, shall be deposited with the Secretary–General of the United Nations, who shall send certified copies thereof to all States referred to in article 31.

4.4 CONVENTION ON THE CONTINENTAL SHELF.[1] Concluded at Geneva, 29 April 1958. Entered into force, 10 June 1964. 499 U.N.T.S. 311, 15 U.S.T. 471, T.I.A.S. No. 5578

Article 1

For the purpose of these articles, the term "continental shelf" is used as referring (a) to the seabed and subsoil of the submarine areas adjacent to the coast but outside the area of the territorial sea, to a depth of 200 metres or, beyond that limit, to where the depth of the superjacent waters admits of the exploitation of the natural resources of the said areas; (b) to the seabed and subsoil of similar submarine areas adjacent to the coasts of islands.

Article 2

1. The coastal State exercises over the continental shelf sovereign rights for the purpose of exploring it and exploiting its natural resources.

2. The rights referred to in paragraph 1 of this article are exclusive in the sense that if the coastal State does not explore the continental shelf or exploit its natural resources, no one may undertake these activities, or make a claim to the continental shelf, without the express consent of the coastal State.

3. The rights of the coastal State over the continental shelf do not depend on occupation, effective or notional, or on any express proclamation.

4. The natural resources referred to in these articles consist of the mineral and other non-living resources of the seabed and subsoil together with living organisms belonging to sedentary species, that is to say, organisms which, at the harvestable stage, either are immobile on or under the seabed or are unable to move except in constant physical contact with the seabed or the subsoil.

Article 3

The rights of the coastal State over the continental shelf do not affect the legal status of the superjacent waters as high seas, or that of the airspace above those waters.

Article 4

Subject to its right to take reasonable measures for the exploration of the continental shelf and the exploitation of its natural resources, the coastal State may not impede the laying or maintenance of submarine cables or pipe lines on the continental shelf.

Article 5

1. The exploration of the continental shelf and the exploitation of its natural resources must not result in any unjustifiable interference with navigation, fishing or the conservation of the living resources of the sea, nor result in any interference with fundamental oceanographic or other scientific research carried out with the intention of open publication.

---

1. *See also* Optional Protocol to the 1958 Law of the Sea Conventions Concerning the Compulsory Settlement of Disputes (which provides for reference to the International Court of Justice of disputes arising out of this agreement), concluded 29 April 1958 and entered into force 30 September 1962 (450 UNTS 169).

2. Subject to the provisions of paragraphs 1 and 6 of this article, the coastal State is entitled to construct and maintain or operate on the continental shelf installations and other devices necessary for its exploration and the exploitation of its natural resources, and to establish safety zones around such installations and devices and to take in those zones measures necessary for their protection.

3. The safety zones referred to in paragraph 2 of this article may extend to a distance of 500 metres around the installations and other devices which have been erected, measured from each point of their outer edge. Ships of all nationalities must respect these safety zones.

4. Such installations and devices, though under the jurisdiction of the coastal State, do not possess the status of islands. They have no territorial sea of their own, and their presence does not affect the delimitation of the territorial sea of the coastal State.

5. Due notice must be given of the construction of any such installations, and permanent means for giving warning of their presence must be maintained. Any installations which are abandoned or disused must be entirely removed.

6. Neither the installations or devices, nor the safety zones around them, may be established where interference may be caused to the use of recognized sea lanes essential to international navigation.

7. The coastal State is obliged to undertake, in the safety zones, all appropriate measures for the protection of the living resources of the sea from harmful agents.

8. The consent of the coastal State shall be obtained in respect of any research concerning the continental shelf and undertaken there. Nevertheless the coastal State shall not normally withhold its consent if the request is submitted by a qualified institution with a view to purely scientific research into the physical or biological characteristics of the continental shelf, subject to the proviso that the coastal State shall have the right, if it so desires, to participate or to be represented in the research, and that in any event the results shall be published.

Article 6

1. Where the same continental shelf is adjacent to the territories of two or more States whose coasts are opposite each other, the boundary of the continental shelf appertaining to such States shall be determined by agreement between them. In the absence of agreement, and unless another boundary line is justified by special circumstances, the boundary is the median line, every point of which is equidistant from the nearest points of the baselines from which the breadth of the territorial sea of each State is measured.

2. Where the same continental shelf is adjacent to the territories of two adjacent States, the boundary of the continental shelf shall be determined by agreement between them. In the absence of agreement, and unless another boundary line is justified by special circumstances, the boundary shall be determined by application of the principle of equidistance from the nearest points of the baselines from which the breadth of the territorial sea of each State is measured.

3. In delimiting the boundaries of the continental shelf, any lines which are drawn in accordance with the principles set out in paragraphs 1 and 2 of this article should be defined with reference to charts and geographical features as they exist at a particular date, and reference should be made to fixed permanent identifiable points on the land.

Article 7

The provisions of these articles shall not prejudice the right of the coastal State to exploit the subsoil by means of tunnelling irrespective of the depth of water above the subsoil.

Article 8

This Convention shall, until 31 October 1958, be open for signature by all States Members of the United Nations or of any of the specialized agencies, and by any other State invited by the General Assembly of the United Nations to become a Party to the Convention.

Article 9

This Convention is subject to ratification. The instruments of ratification shall be deposited with the Secretary–General of the United Nations.

Article 10

This Convention shall be open for accession by any States belonging to any of the categories mentioned in article 8. The instruments of accession shall be deposited with the Secretary–General of the United Nations.

Article 11

1. This Convention shall come into force on the thirtieth day following the date of deposit of the twenty-second instrument of ratification or accession with the Secretary–General of the United Nations.

2. For each State ratifying or acceding to the Convention after the deposit of the twenty-second instrument of ratification or accession, the Convention shall enter into force on the thirtieth day after deposit by such State of its instrument of ratification or accession.

Article 12

1. At the time of signature, ratification or accession, any State may make reservations to articles of the Convention other than to articles 1 to 3 inclusive.

2. Any Contracting State making a reservation in accordance with the preceding paragraph may at any time withdraw the reservation by a communication to that effect addressed to the Secretary–General of the United Nations.

Article 13

1. After the expiration of a period of five years from the date on which this Convention shall enter into force, a request for the revision of this Convention may be made at any time by any Contracting Party by means of a notification in writing addressed to the Secretary–General of the United Nations.

2. The General Assembly of the United Nations shall decide upon the steps, if any, to be taken in respect of such request.

Article 14

The Secretary–General of the United Nations shall inform all States Members of the United Nations and the other States referred to in article 8:

(*a*) Of signatures to this Convention and of the deposit of instruments of ratification or accession, in accordance with articles 8, 9 and 10;

(*b*) Of the date on which this Convention will come into force, in accordance with article 11;

(*c*) Of requests for revision in accordance with article 13;

(*d*) Of reservations to this Convention, in accordance with article 12.

Article 15

The original of this Convention, of which the Chinese, English, French, Russian and Spanish texts are equally authentic, shall be deposited with the Secretary–General of the United Nations, who shall send certified copies thereof to all States referred to in article 8.

4.5 CONVENTION ON THE TERRITORIAL SEA AND CONTIGUOUS ZONE.[1] Concluded at Geneva, 29 April 1958. Entered into force, 10 September 1964. 516 U.N.T.S. 205, 15 U.S.T. 1606, T.I.A.S. No. 5639

PART I

TERRITORIAL SEA

SECTION I. GENERAL

Article 1

1. The sovereignty of a State extends, beyond its land territory and its internal waters, to a belt of sea adjacent to its coast, described as the territorial sea.

2. This sovereignty is exercised subject to the provisions of these articles and to other rules of international law.

Article 2

The sovereignty of a coastal State extends to the air space over the territorial sea as well as to its bed and subsoil.

SECTION II. LIMITS OF THE TERRITORIAL SEA

Article 3

Except where otherwise provided in these articles, the normal baseline for measuring the breadth of the territorial sea is the low-water line along the coast as marked on large-scale charts officially recognized by the coastal State.

Article 4

1. In localities where the coast line is deeply indented and cut into, or if there is a fringe of islands along the coast in its immediate vicinity, the method of straight baselines joining appropriate points may be employed in drawing the baseline from which the breadth of the territorial sea is measured.

2. The drawing of such baselines must not depart to any appreciable extent from the general direction of the coast, and the sea areas lying within the lines must be sufficiently closely linked to the land domain to be subject to the régime of internal waters.

3. Baselines shall not be drawn to and from low-tide elevations, unless lighthouses or similar installations which are permanently above sea level have been built on them.

4. Where the method of straight baselines is applicable under the provisions of paragraph 1, account may be taken, in determining particular baselines, of economic interests peculiar to the region concerned, the reality and the importance of which are clearly evidenced by a long usage.

5. The system of straight baselines may not be applied by a State in such a manner as to cut off from the high seas the territorial sea of another State.

---

1. *See also* Optional Protocol to the 1958 Law of the Sea Conventions Concerning the Compulsory Settlement of Disputes (which provides for reference to the International Court of Justice of disputes arising out of this agreement), concluded 29 April 1958 and entered into force 30 September 1962 (450 UNTS 169).

6. The coastal State must clearly indicate straight baselines on charts, to which due publicity must be given.

Article 5

1. Waters on the landward side of the baseline of the territorial sea form part of the internal waters of the State.

2. Where the establishment of a straight baseline in accordance with article 4 has the effect of enclosing as internal waters areas which previously had been considered as part of the territorial sea or of the high seas, a right of innocent passage, as provided in articles 14 to 23, shall exist in those waters.

Article 6

The outer limit of the territorial sea is the line every point of which is at a distance from the nearest point of the baseline equal to the breadth of the territorial sea.

Article 7

1. This article relates only to bays the coasts of which belong to a single State.

2. For the purposes of these articles, a bay is a well-marked indentation whose penetration is in such proportion to the width of its mouth as to contain landlocked waters and constitute more than a mere curvature of the coast. An indentation shall not, however, be regarded as a bay unless its area is as large as, or larger than, that of the semi-circle whose diameter is a line drawn across the mouth of that indentation.

3. For the purpose of measurement, the area of an indentation is that lying between the low-water mark around the shore of the indentation and a line joining the low-water marks of its natural entrance points. Where, because of the presence of islands, an indentation has more than one mouth, the semi-circle shall be drawn on a line as long as the sum total of the lengths of the lines across the different mouths. Islands within an indentation shall be included as if they were part of the water areas of the indentation.

4. If the distance between the low-water marks of the natural entrance points of a bay does not exceed twenty-four miles, a closing line may be drawn between these two low-water marks, and the waters enclosed thereby shall be considered as internal waters.

5. Where the distance between the low-water marks of the natural entrance points of a bay exceeds twenty-four miles, a straight baseline of twenty-four miles shall be drawn within the bay in such a manner as to enclose the maximum area of water that is possible with a line of that length.

6. The foregoing provisions shall not apply to so-called "historic" bays, or in any case where the straight baseline system provided for in article 4 is applied.

Article 8

For the purpose of delimiting the territorial sea, the outermost permanent harbour works which form an integral part of the harbour system shall be regarded as forming part of the coast.

Article 9

Roadsteads which are normally used for the loading, unloading and anchoring of ships, and which would otherwise be situated wholly or partly outside the outer limit of the territorial sea, are included in the territorial sea. The coastal State must clearly demarcate such roadsteads and indicate them on charts together with their boundaries, to which due publicity must be given.

Article 10

1. An island is a naturally-formed area of land, surrounded by water, which is above water at high-tide.

2. The territorial sea of an island is measured in accordance with the provisions of these articles.

Article 11

1. A low-tide elevation is a naturally-formed area of land which is surrounded by and above water at low-tide but submerged at high-tide. Where a low-tide elevation is situated wholly or partly at a distance not exceeding the breadth of the territorial sea from the mainland or an island, the low-water line on that elevation may be used as the baseline for measuring the breadth of the territorial sea.

2. Where a low-tide elevation is wholly situated at a distance exceeding the breadth of the territorial sea from the mainland or an island, it has no territorial sea of its own.

Article 12

1. Where the coasts of two States are opposite or adjacent to each other, neither of the two States is entitled, failing agreement between them to the contrary, to extend its territorial sea beyond the median line every point of which is equidistant from the nearest points on the baselines from which the breadth of the territorial seas of each of the two States is measured. The provisions of this paragraph shall not apply, however, where it is necessary by reason of historic title or other special circumstances to delimit the territorial seas of the two States in a way which is at variance with this provision.

2. The line of delimitation between the territorial seas of two States lying opposite to each other or adjacent to each other shall be marked on large-scale charts officially recognized by the coastal States.

Article 13

If a river flows directly into the sea, the baseline shall be a straight line across the mouth of the river between points on the low-tide line of its banks.

SECTION III. RIGHT OF INNOCENT PASSAGE

SUB-SECTION A. RULES APPLICABLE TO ALL SHIPS

Article 14

1. Subject to the provisions of these articles, ships of all States, whether coastal or not, shall enjoy the right of innocent passage through the territorial sea.

2. Passage means navigation through the territorial sea for the purpose either of traversing that sea without entering internal waters, or of proceeding to internal waters, or of making for the high seas from internal waters.

3. Passage includes stopping and anchoring, but only in so far as the same are incidental to ordinary navigation or are rendered necessary by *force majeure* or by distress.

4. Passage is innocent so long as it is not prejudicial to the peace, good order or security of the coastal State. Such passage shall take place in conformity with these articles and with other rules of international law.

5. Passage of foreign fishing vessels shall not be considered innocent if they do not observe such laws and regulations as the coastal State may make and publish in order to prevent these vessels from fishing in the territorial sea.

6. Submarines are required to navigate on the surface and to show their flag.

Article 15

1. The coastal State must not hamper innocent passage through the territorial sea.

2. The coastal State is required to give appropriate publicity to any dangers to navigation, of which it has knowledge, within its territorial sea.

Article 16

1. The coastal State may take the necessary steps in its territorial sea to prevent passage which is not innocent.

2. In the case of ships proceeding to internal waters, the coastal State shall also have the right to take the necessary steps to prevent any breach of the conditions to which admission of those ships to those waters is subject.

3. Subject to the provisions of paragraph 4, the coastal State may, without discrimination amongst foreign ships, suspend temporarily in specified areas of its territorial sea the innocent passage of foreign ships if such suspension is essential for the protection of its security. Such suspension shall take effect only after having been duly published.

4. There shall be no suspension of the innocent passage of foreign ships through straits which are used for international navigation between one part of the high seas and another part of the high seas or the territorial sea of a foreign State.

Article 17

Foreign ships exercising the right of innocent passage shall comply with the laws and regulations enacted by the coastal State in conformity with these articles and other rules of international law and, in particular, with such laws and regulations relating to transport and navigation.

SUB-SECTION B. RULES APPLICABLE TO MERCHANT SHIPS

Article 18

1. No charge may be levied upon foreign ships by reason only of their passage through the territorial sea.

2. Charges may be levied upon a foreign ship passing through the territorial sea as payment only for specific services rendered to the ship. These charges shall be levied without discrimination.

Article 19

1. The criminal jurisdiction of the coastal State should not be exercised on board a foreign ship passing through the territorial sea to arrest any person or to conduct any investigation in connexion with any crime committed on board the ship during its passage, save only in the following cases:

(a) If the consequences of the crime extend to the coastal State; or

(b) If the crime is of a kind to disturb the peace of the country or the good order of the territorial sea; or

(c) If the assistance of the local authorities has been requested by the captain of the ship or by the consul of the country whose flag the ship flies; or

(d) If it is necessary for the suppression of illicit traffic in narcotic drugs.

2. The above provisions do not affect the right of the coastal State to take any steps authorized by its laws for the purpose of an arrest or investigation on board a foreign ship passing through the territorial sea after leaving internal waters.

3. In the cases provided for in paragraphs 1 and 2 of this article, the coastal State shall, if the captain so requests, advise the consular authority of the flag State before taking any steps, and shall facilitate contact between such authority and the ship's crew. In cases of emergency this notification may be communicated while the measures are being taken.

4. In considering whether or how an arrest should be made, the local authorities shall pay due regard to the interests of navigation.

5. The coastal State may not take any steps on board a foreign ship passing through the territorial sea to arrest any person or to conduct any investigation in connexion with any crime committed before the ship entered the territorial sea, if the ship, proceeding from a foreign port, is only passing through the territorial sea without entering internal waters.

Article 20

1. The coastal State should not stop or divert a foreign ship passing through the territorial sea for the purpose of exercising civil jurisdiction in relation to a person on board the ship.

2. The coastal State may not levy execution against or arrest the ship for the purpose of any civil proceedings, save only in respect of obligations or liabilities assumed or incurred by the ship itself in the course or for the purpose of its voyage through the waters of the coastal State.

3. The provisions of the previous paragraph are without prejudice to the right of the coastal State, in accordance with its laws, to levy execution against or to arrest, for the purpose of any civil proceedings, a foreign ship lying in the territorial sea, or passing through the territorial sea after leaving internal waters.

SUB-SECTION C. RULES APPLICABLE TO GOVERNMENT SHIPS OTHER THAN WARSHIPS

Article 21

The rules contained in sub-sections A and B shall also apply to government ships operated for commercial purposes.

Article 22

1. The rules contained in sub-section A and in article 18 shall apply to government ships operated for non-commercial purposes.

2. With such exceptions as are contained in the provisions referred to in the preceding paragraph, nothing in these articles affects the immunities which such ships enjoy under these articles or other rules of international law.

SUB-SECTION D. RULE APPLICABLE TO WARSHIPS

Article 23

If any warship does not comply with the regulations of the coastal State concerning passage through the territorial sea and disregards any request for compliance which is made to it, the coastal State may require the warship to leave the territorial sea.

PART II

CONTIGUOUS ZONE

Article 24

1. In a zone of the high seas contiguous to its territorial sea, the coastal State may exercise the control necessary to:

(a) Prevent infringement of its customs, fiscal, immigration or sanitary regulations within its territory or territorial sea;

(b) Punish infringement of the above regulations committed within its territory or territorial sea.

2. The contiguous zone may not extend beyond twelve miles from the baseline from which the breadth of the territorial sea is measured.

3. Where the coasts of two States are opposite or adjacent to each other, neither of the two States is entitled, failing agreement between them to the contrary, to extend its contiguous zone beyond the median line every point of which is equidistant from the nearest points on the baselines from which the breadth of the territorial seas of the two States is measured.

PART III

FINAL ARTICLES

Article 25

The provisions of this Convention shall not affect conventions or other international agreements already in force, as between States Parties to them.

Article 26

This Convention shall, until 31 October 1958, be open for signature by all States Members of the United Nations or of any of the specialized agencies, and by any other State invited by the General Assembly of the United Nations to become a Party to the Convention.

Article 27

This Convention is subject to ratification. The instruments of ratification shall be deposited with the Secretary–General of the United Nations.

Article 28

This Convention shall be open for accession by any States belonging to any of the categories mentioned in article 26. The instruments of accession shall be deposited with the Secretary–General of the United Nations.

Article 29

1. This Convention shall come into force on the thirtieth day following the date of deposit of the twenty-second instrument of ratification or accession with the Secretary–General of the United Nations.

2. For each State ratifying or acceding to the Convention after the deposit of the twenty-second instrument of ratification or accession, the Convention shall enter into force on the thirtieth day after deposit by such State of its instrument of ratification or accession.

Article 30

1. After the expiration of a period of five years from the date on which this Convention shall enter into force, a request for the revision of this Convention may be made at any time by any Contracting Party by means of a notification in writing addressed to the Secretary–General of the United Nations.

2. The General Assembly of the United Nations shall decide upon the steps, if any, to be taken in respect of such request.

Article 31

The Secretary–General of the United Nations shall inform all States Members of the United Nations and the other States referred to in article 26:

(*a*) Of signatures to this Convention and of the deposit of instruments of ratification or accession, in accordance with articles 26, 27 and 28;

(*b*) Of the date on which this Convention will come into force, in accordance with article 29;

(*c*) Of requests for revision in accordance with article 30.

Article 32

The original of this Convention, of which the Chinese, English, French, Russian and Spanish texts are equally authentic, shall be deposited with the Secretary–General of the United Nations, who shall send certified copies thereof to all States referred to in article 26.

4.6 CONVENTION ON THE LIABILITY OF OPERATORS OF NUCLEAR SHIPS. Concluded at Brussels, 25 May 1962. Entered into force, 15 July 1975. IAEA Leg.Ser. No. 4 at 34, 57 A.J.I.L. 268 (1963)

The contracting Parties,

Having recognized the desirability of determining by agreement certain uniform rules concerning the liability of operators of nuclear ships,

Have decided to conclude a Convention for this purpose, and thereto agreed as follows:

Article I

For the purpose of this Convention:

1. "Nuclear ship" means any ship equipped with a nuclear power plant.

2. "Licensing State" means the Contracting State which operates or which has authorized the operation of a nuclear ship under its flag.

3. "Person" means any individual or partnership, or any public or private body whether corporate or not, including a State or any of its constituent subdivisions.

4. "Operator" means the person authorized by the licensing State to operate a nuclear ship, or where a Contracting State operates a nuclear ship, that State.

5. "Nuclear fuel" means any material which is capable of producing energy by a self-sustaining process of nuclear fission and which is used or intended for use in a nuclear ship.

6. "Radioactive products or waste" means any material, including nuclear fuel, made radioactive by neutron irradiation incidental to the utilization of nuclear fuel in a nuclear ship.

7. "Nuclear damage" means loss of life or personal injury and loss or damage to property which arises out of or results from the radioactive properties or a combination of radioactive properties with toxic, explosive or other hazardous properties of nuclear fuel or of radioactive products or waste; any other loss, damage or expense so arising or resulting shall be included only if and to the extent that the applicable national law so provides.

8. "Nuclear incident" means any occurence or series of occurences having the same origin which causes nuclear damage.

9. "Nuclear power plant" means any power plant in which a nuclear reactor is, or is to be used as, the source of power, whether for propulsion of the ship or for any other purpose.

10. "Nuclear reactor" means any installation containing nuclear fuel in such an arrangement that a self-sustained chain process of nuclear fission can occur therein without an additional source of neutrons.

11. "Warship" means any ship belonging to the naval forces of a State and bearing the external marks distinguishing warships of its nationality, under the command of an officer duly commissioned by the Government of such State and whose name appears in the Navy List, and manned by a crew who are under regular naval discipline.

12. "Applicable national law" means the national law of the court having jurisdiction under the Convention including any rules of such national law relating to conflict of laws.

Article II

1. The operator of a nuclear ship shall be absolutely liable for any nuclear damage upon proof that such damage has been caused by a nuclear incident involving the nuclear fuel of, or radioactive products or waste produced in such ship.

2. Except as otherwise provided in this Convention no person other than the operator shall be liable for such nuclear damage.

3. Nuclear damage suffered by the nuclear ship itself, its equipment, fuel or stores shall not be covered by the operator's liability as defined in this Convention.

4. The operator shall not be liable with respect to nuclear incidents occuring before the nuclear fuel has been taken in charge by him or after the nuclear fuel or radioactive products or waste have been taken in charge by another person duly authorized by law and liable for any nuclear damage that may be caused by them.

5. If the operator proves that the nuclear damage resulted wholly or partially from an act or omission done with intent to cause damage by the individual who suffered the damage, the competent courts may exonerate the operator wholly or partially from his liability to such individual.

6. Notwithstanding the provisions of paragraph 1 of this Article, the operator shall have a right of recourse:

a) If the nuclear incident results from a personal act or omission done with intent to cause damage, in which event recourse shall lie against the individual who has acted, or omitted to act, with such intent;

b) If the nuclear incident occurred as a consequence of any wreck-raising operation, against the person or persons who carried out such operation without the authority of the operator or of the State having licensed the sunken ship or of the State in whose waters the wreck is situated;

c) If recourse is expressly provided for by contract.

Article III

1. The liability of the operator as regards one nuclear ship shall be limited to 1500 million francs in respect of any one nuclear incident, notwithstanding that the nuclear incident may have resulted from any fault of privity of that operator; such limit shall include neither any interest nor costs awarded by a court in actions for compensation under this Convention.

2. The operator shall be required to maintain insurance, or other financial security covering his liability for nuclear damage, in such amount, of such type and in such terms as the licensing State shall specify. The licensing State shall ensure the payment of claims for compensation for nuclear damage established against the operator by providing the necessary funds up to the limit laid down in paragraph 1 of this Article to the extent

that the yield of the insurance or the financial security is inadequate to satisfy such claims.

3. However, nothing in paragraph 2 of this Article shall require any Contracting State or any of its constituent subdivisions, such as States, Republics or Cantons, to maintain insurance or other financial security to cover their liability as operators of nuclear ships.

4. The franc mentioned in paragraph 1 of this Article is a unit of account constituted by sixty-five and one half milligrams of gold of millesimal fineness nine hundred. The amount awarded may be converted into each national currency in round figures. Conversion into national currencies other than gold shall be effected on the basis of their gold at the date of payment.

Article IV

Whenever both nuclear damage and damage other than nuclear damage have been caused by a nuclear incident or jointly by a nuclear incident and one or more other occurrences and the nuclear damage and such other damage are not reasonably separable, the entire damage shall, for the purposes of this Convention, be deemed to be nuclear damage exclusively caused by the nuclear incident. However, where damage is caused jointly by a nuclear incident covered by this Convention and by an emission of ionizing radiation or by an emission of ionizing radiation in combination with the toxic, explosive or other hazardous properties of the source of radiation not covered by it, nothing in this Convention shall limit or otherwise affect the liability, either as regards the victims or by way of recourse or contribution, of any person who may be held liable in connection with the emission of ionizing radiation or by the toxic explosive or other hazardous properties of the source of radiation not covered by this Convention.

Article V

1. Rights of compensation under this Convention shall be extinguished if an action is not brought within ten years from the date of the nuclear incident. If, however, under the law of the licensing State the liability of the operator is covered by insurance or other financial security or State indemnification for a period longer than ten years, the applicable national law may provide that rights of compensation against the operator shall only be extinguished after a period which may be longer than ten years but shall not be longer than the period for which his liability is so covered under the law of the licensing State. However, such extension of the extinction period shall in no case affect the right of compensation under this Convention of any person who has brought an action for loss of life or personal injury against the operator before the expiry of the aforesaid period of ten years.

2. Where nuclear damage is caused by nuclear fuel, radioactive products or waste which were stolen, lost, jettisoned, or abandoned, the period established under paragraph 1 of this Article shall be computed from the date of the nuclear incident causing the nuclear damage, but the period shall in no case exceed a period of twenty years from the date of the theft, loss, jettison or abandonment.

3. The applicable national law may establish a period of extinction or prescription of not less than three years from the date on which the person who claims to have suffered nuclear damage had knowledge or ought reason-

ably to have had knowledge of the damage and of the person responsible for the damage, provided that the period established under paragraphs 1 and 2 of this Article shall not be exceeded.

4. Any person who claims to have suffered nuclear damage and who has brought an action for compensation within the period applicable under this Article may amend his claim to take into account any aggravation of the damage, even after the expiry of that period, provided that final judgment has not been entered.

Article VI

Where provisions of national health insurance, social security, workmen's compensation or occupational disease compensation systems include compensation for nuclear damage, rights of beneficiaries under such systems and rights of subrogation, or of recourse against the operator, by virtue of such systems, shall be determined by the law of the Contracting State having established such systems. However, if the law of such Contracting State allows claims of beneficiaries of such systems and such rights of subrogation and recourse to be brought against the operator in conformity with the terms of this Convention, this shall not result in the liability of the operator exceeding the amount specified in paragraph 1 of Article III.

Article VII

1. Where nuclear damage engages the liability of more than one operator and the damage attributable to each operator is not reasonably separable, the operators involved shall be jointly and severally liable for such damage. However, the liability of any one operator shall not exceed the limit laid down in Article III.

2. In the case of a nuclear incident where the nuclear damage arises out of or results from nuclear fuel or radioactive products or waste of more than one nuclear ship of the same operator, that operator shall be liable in respect of each ship up to the limit laid down in Article III.

3. In case of joint and several liability, and subject to the provisions of paragraph 1 of this Article:

a) Each operator shall have a right of contribution against the others in proportion to the fault attaching to each of them;

b) Where circumstances are such that the degree of fault cannot be apportioned, the total liability shall be borne in equal parts.

Article VIII

No liability under this Convention shall attach to an operator in respect to nuclear damage caused by a nuclear incident directly due to an act of war, hostilities, civil war or insurrection.

Article IX

The sums provided by insurance, by other financial security or by State indemnification in conformity with paragraph 2 of this Article III shall be exclusively available for compensation due under this Convention.

Article X

1. Any action for compensation shall be brought, at the option of the claimant, either before the courts of the licensing State or before the courts of

the Contracting State or States in whose territory nuclear damage has been sustained.

2. If the licensing State has been or might be called upon to ensure the payment of claims for compensation in accordance with paragraph 2 of Article III of this Convention, it may intervene as party in any proceedings brought against the operator.

3. Any immunity from legal processes pursuant to rules of national or international law shall be waived with respect to duties or obligations arising under, or for the purpose of, this Convention. Nothing in this Convention shall make warships or other State-owned or State-operated ships on non-commercial service liable to arrest, attachment or seizure or confer jurisdiction in respect of warships on the courts of any foreign State.

Article XI

1. When, having regard to the likelihood of any claims arising out of a nuclear incident exceeding the amount specified in Article III of this Convention, a court of the licensing State, at the request of the operator, a claimant or the licensing State, so certifies, the operator or the licensing State shall make that amount available in that court to pay any such claims; that amount shall be regarded as constituting the limitation fund in respect of that incident.

2. The amount may be made available for the purposes of the preceding paragraph by payment into court or by the provision of security or guarantees sufficient to satisfy the court that the money will be available when required to meet any established claim.

3. After the fund has been constituted in accordance with paragraph 1 of this Article the court of the licensing State shall be exclusively competent to determine all matters relating to the apportionment and distribution of the fund.

4. a) A final judgment entered by a court having jurisdiction under Article X shall be recognized in the territory of any other Contracting State, except:

i) where the judgment was obtained by fraud; or

ii) the operator was not given a fair opportunity to present his case;

b) A final judgment which is recognized shall, upon being presented for enforcement in accordance with the formalities required by the law of the Contracting State where enforcement is sought, be enforceable as if it were a judgment of a court of that State;

c) The merits of a claim on which the judgment has been given shall not be subject to further proceedings.

5. a) If a person who is a national of a Contracting State, other than the operator, has paid compensation for nuclear damage under an International Convention or under the law of a non-Contracting State, such person shall, up to the amount which he has paid, acquire by subrogation the rights which the person so compensated would have enjoyed under this Convention. However, no rights shall be so acquired by any person if and to the extent that the

operator has a right of recourse or contribution against such person under this Convention;

    b) If a limitation fund has been set up and

        i) the operator has paid, prior to its being set up, compensation for nuclear damage; or

        ii) the operator has paid, after it has been set up, compensation for nuclear damage under an International Convention or the law of a non-Contracting State,

he shall be entitled to recover from the fund, up to the amount which he has paid, the amount which the person so compensated would have obtained in the distribution of the fund;

    c) If no limitation fund is set up, nothing in this Convention shall preclude an operator, who has paid compensation for nuclear damage out of funds other than those provided pursuant to paragraph 2 of Article III, from recovering from the person providing financial security under paragraph 2 of Article III or from the licensing State, up to the amount he has paid, the sum which the person so compensated would have obtained under this Convention;

    d) In this paragraph the expression "a national of a Contracting State" shall include a Contracting State or any of its constituent subdivisions or a partnership or any public or private body whether corporate or not established in a Contracting State.

6. Where no fund has been constituted under the provisions of this Article, the licensing State shall adopt such measures as are necessary to ensure that adequate sums provided by it or by insurance or other financial security in accordance with paragraph 2 of Article III, shall be available for the satisfaction of any claim established by a judgment of a court of any other Contracting State which would be recognized under paragraph 4 of this Article; the sums shall be made available, at the option of the claimant, either in the licensing State or in the Contracting State in which the damage was sustained or in the Contracting State in which the claimant is habitually resident.

7. After the limitation fund has been constituted in accordance with paragraph 1 of this Article or, where no such fund has been constituted, if the sums provided by the licensing State, or by insurance, or other financial security are available in accordance with paragraph 6 of this Article to meet a claim for compensation, the claimant shall not be entitled to exercise any right against any other asset of the operator in respect of his claim for nuclear damage, and any bail or security (other than security for costs) given by or on behalf of that operator in any Contracting State shall be released.

Article XII

1. The Contracting States undertake to adopt such measures as are necessary to ensure implementation of the provisions of this Convention, including any appropriate measures for the prompt and equitable distribution of the sums available for compensation for nuclear damage.

2. The Contracting States undertake to adopt such measures as are necessary to ensure that insurance and reinsurance premiums and sums

provided by insurance, reinsurance or other financial security, or provided by them in accordance with paragraph 2 of Article III, shall be freely transferable into the currency of the Contracting State in which the damage was sustained, of the Contracting State in which the claimant is habitually resident or, as regards insurance and reinsurance premiums and payments, in the currencies specified in the insurance or reinsurance contract.

3. This Convention shall be applied without discrimination based upon nationality, domicile or residence.

Article XIII

This Convention applies to nuclear damage caused by a nuclear incident occurring in any part of the world and involving the nuclear fuel of, or radioactive products or waste produced in, a nuclear ship flying the flag of a Contracting State.

Article XIV

This Convention shall supersede any International Conventions in force or open for signature, ratification or accession at the date on which this Convention is opened for signature, but only to the extent that such Conventions would be in conflict with it; however, nothing in this Article shall affect the obligations of Contracting States to non-Contracting States arising under such International Conventions.

Article XV

1. Each Contracting State undertakes to take all measures necessary to prevent a nuclear ship flying its flag from being operated without a licence or authority granted by it.

2. In the event of nuclear damage involving the nuclear fuel of, or radioactive products or waste produced in a nuclear ship flying the flag of a Contracting State, the operation of which was not at the time of the nuclear incident licensed or authorized by such Contracting State, the owner of the nuclear ship at the time of the nuclear incident shall be deemed to be the operator of the nuclear ship for all the purposes of this Convention, except that his liability shall not be limited in amount.

3. In such an event, the Contracting State whose flag the nuclear ship flies shall be deemed to be the licensing State for all the purposes of this Convention and shall, in particular, be liable for compensation for victims in accordance with the obligations imposed on a licensing State by Article III and up to the limit laid down therein.

4. Each Contracting State undertakes not to grant a licence or authority to operate a nuclear ship flying the flag of another State. However, nothing in this paragraph shall prevent a Contracting State from implementing the requirements of its national law concerning the operation of a nuclear ship within its internal waters and territorial sea.

Article XVI

This Convention shall apply to a nuclear ship from the date of her launching. Between her launching and the time she is authorized to fly a flag, the nuclear ship shall be deemed to be operated by the owner and to be flying the flag of the State in which she was built.

Article XVII

Nothing in this Convention shall affect any right which a Contracting State may have under international law to deny access to its waters and harbours to nuclear ships licensed by another Contracting State, even when it has formally complied with all the provisions of this Convention.

Article XVIII

An action for compensation for nuclear damage shall be brought against the operator; it may also be brought against the insurer or any person other than the licensing State who has provided financial security to the operator pursuant to paragraph 2 of Article III, if the right to bring an action against the insurer or such other person is provided under the applicable national law.

Article XIX

Notwithstanding the termination of this Convention or the termination of its application to any Contracting State pursuant to Article XXVII, the provisions of the Convention shall continue to apply with respect to any nuclear damage caused by a nuclear incident involving the nuclear fuel of, or radioactive products or waste produced in, a nuclear ship licensed or otherwise authorized for operation by any Contracting State prior to the date of such termination, provided the nuclear incident occurred prior to the date of such termination or, in the event of a nuclear incident occurring subsequent to the date of such termination, prior to the expiry of a period of twenty-five years after the date of such licensing or other authorization to operate such ship.

Article XX

Without prejudice to Article X, any dispute between two or more Contracting Parties concerning the interpretation or application of this Convention which cannot be settled through negociation, shall, at the request of one of them, be submitted to arbitration. If within six months from the date of the request for arbitration the Parties are unable to agree on the organization of the arbitration, any one of those Parties may refer the dispute to the International Court of Justice by request in conformity with the Statute of the Court.

Article XXI

1. Each Contracting Party may at the time of signature or ratification of this Convention or accession thereto, declare that it does not consider itself bound by Article XX of the Convention. The other Contracting Parties shall not be bound by this Article with respect to any Contracting Party having made such a reservation.

2. Any Contracting Party having made a reservation in accordance with paragraph 1 may at any time withdraw this reservation by notification to the Belgian Government.

Article XXII

This Convention shall be open for signature by the States represented at the eleventh session (1961–1962) of the Diplomatic Conference on Maritime Law.

Article XXIII

This Convention shall be ratified and the instruments of ratification shall be deposited with the Belgian Government.

Article XXIV

1. This Convention shall come into force three months after the deposit of an instrument of ratification by at least one licencing State and one other State.

2. This Convention shall come into force, in respect of each signatory State which ratifies it after its entry into force as provided in paragraph 1 of this Article, three months after the date of deposit of the instrument of ratification of that State.

Article XXV

1. States Members of the United Nations Members of the specialized agencies and of the International Atomic Energy Agency not represented at the eleventh session of the Diplomatic Conference on Maritime Law, may accede to this Convention.

2. The instruments of accession shall be deposited with the Belgian Government.

3. The Convention shall come into force in respect of the acceding State three months after the date of deposit of the instrument of accession of that State, but not before the date of entry into force of the Convention as established by Article XXIV.

Article XXVI

1. A conference for the purpose of revising this Convention shall be convened by the Belgian Government and the International Atomic Energy Agency after the Convention has been in force five years.

2. Such a conference shall also be convened by the Belgian Government and the International Atomic Energy Agency before the expiry of this term or thereafter, if one third of the Contracting States express a desire to that effect.

Article XXVII

1. Any Contracting State may denounce this Convention by notification to the Belgian Government at any time after the first revision Conference held in accordance with the provisions of Article XXVI 1.

2. This denunciation shall take effect one year after the date on which the notification has been received by the Belgian Government.

Article XXVIII

The Belgian Government shall notify the States represented at the eleventh session of the Diplomatic Conference on Maritime Law, and the States acceding to this Convention, of the following:

1. Signatures, ratifications and accessions received in accordance with Article XXII, XXIII and XXV.

2. The date on which the Convention will come into force in accordance with Article XXIV.

3. Denunciations received in accordance with Article XXVII.

**4.7 HELSINKI RULES ON THE USES OF THE WATERS OF INTERNA-
TIONAL RIVERS (WITHOUT COMMENTS AND ANNEX). Adopted
by the International Law Association at Helsinki, 20 August 1966.
52 I.L.A. 484 (1967)**

CHAPTER 1
GENERAL
Article I

The general rules of international law as set forth in these chapters are
applicable to the use of the waters of an international drainage basin except
as may be provided otherwise by convention, agreement or binding custom
among the basin States.

Article II

An international drainage basin is a geographical area extending over two
or more States determined by the watershed limits of the system of waters,
including surface and underground waters, flowing into a common terminus.

Article III

A "basin State" is a state the territory of which includes a portion of an
international drainage basin.

CHAPTER 2
EQUITABLE UTILIZATION OF THE WATERS OF
AN INTERNATIONAL DRAINAGE BASIN
Article IV

Each basin State is entitled, within its territory, to a reasonable and
equitable share in the beneficial uses of the waters of an international
drainage basin.

Article V

(1) What is a reasonable and equitable share within the meaning of
Article IV is to be determined in the light of all the relevant factors in each
particular case.

(2) Relevant factors which are to be considered include, but are not
limited to:

(a) the geography of the basin, including in particular the extent of
the drainage area in the territory of each basin State;

(b) the hydrology of the basin, including in particular the contribution of water by each basin State;

(c) the climate affecting the basin;

(d) the past utilization of the waters of the basin, including in
particular existing utilization;

(e) the economic and social needs of each basin State;

(f) the population dependent on the waters of the basin in each basin
State;

(g) the comparative costs of alternative means of satisfying the
economic and social needs of each basin State;

(h) the availability of other resources;

(i) the avoidance of unnecessary waste in the utilization of waters of the basin;

(j) the practicability of compensation to one or more of the co-basin States as a means of adjusting conflicts among uses; and

(k) the degree to which the needs of a basin State may be satisfied, without causing substantial injury to a co-basin State.

(3) The weight to be given to each factor is to be determined by its importance in comparison with that of other relevant factors. In determining what is a reasonable and equitable share, all relevant factors are to be considered together and a conclusion reached on the basis of the whole.

Article VI

A use or category of uses is not entitled to any inherent preference over any other use or category of uses.

Article VII

A basin State may not be denied the present reasonable use of the waters of an international drainage basin to reserve for a co-basin State a future use of such waters.

Article VIII

1. An existing reasonable use may continue in operation unless the factors justifying its continuance are outweighed by other factors leading to the conclusion that it be modified or terminated so as to accommodate a competing incompatible use.

2. (a) A use that is in fact operational is deemed to have been an existing use from the time of the initiation of construction directly related to the use or, where such construction is not required, the undertaking of comparable acts of actual implementation.

(b) Such a use continues to be an existing use until such time as it is discontinued with the intention that it be abandoned.

3. A use will not be deemed an existing use if at the time of becoming operational it is incompatible with an already existing reasonable use.

CHAPTER 3
POLLUTION
Article IX

As used in this Chapter, the term "water pollution" refers to any detrimental change resulting from human conduct in the natural composition, content, or quality of the waters of an international drainage basin.

Article X

1. Consistent with the principle of equitable utilization of the waters of an international drainage basin, a State

(a) must prevent any new form of water pollution or any increase in the degree of existing water pollution in an international drainage basin which would cause substantial injury in the territory of a co-basin State, and

(b) should take all reasonable measures to abate existing water pollution in an international drainage basin to such an extent that no substantial damage is caused in the territory of a co-basin State.

2. The rule stated in paragraph 1 of this Article applies to water pollution originating

(a) within a territory of the State, or

(b) outside the territory of the State, if it is caused by the State's conduct.

Article XI

1. In the case of a violation of the rule stated in paragraph 1(a) of Article X of this Chapter, the State responsible shall be required to cease the wrongful conduct and compensate the injured co-basin State for the injury that has been caused to it.

2. In a case falling under the rule stated in paragraph 1(b) of Article X, if a State fails to take reasonable measures, it shall be required promptly to enter into negotiations with the injured State with a view toward reaching a settlement equitable under the circumstances.

CHAPTER 4
NAVIGATION
Article XII

1. This Chapter refers to those rivers and lakes portions of which are both navigable and separate or traverse the territories of two or more States.

2. Rivers or lakes are "navigable" if in their natural or canalized state they are currently used for commercial navigation or are capable by reason of their natural condition of being so used.

3. In this Chapter the term "riparian State" refers to a State through or along which the navigable portion of a river flows or a lake lies.

Article XIII

Subject to any limitations or qualifications referred to in these Chapters, each riparian State is entitled to enjoy rights of free navigation on the entire course of a river or lake.

Article XIV

"Free navigation", as the term is used in this Chapter, includes the following freedoms for vessels of a riparian State on a basis of equality:

(a) freedom of movement on the entire navigable course of the river or lake;

(b) freedom to enter ports and to make use of plants and docks; and

(c) freedom to transport goods and passengers, either directly or through trans-shipment, between the territory of one riparian State and the territory of another riparian State and between the territory of a riparian State and the open sea.

Article XV

A riparian State may exercise rights of police, including but not limited to the protection of public safety and health, over that portion of the river or lake subject to its jurisdiction, provided the exercise of such rights does not unreasonably interfere with the enjoyment of the rights of free navigation defined in Articles XIII and XIV.

Article XVI

Each riparian State may restrict or prohibit the loading by vessels of a foreign State of goods and passengers in its territory for discharge in such territory.

Article XVII

A riparian State may grant rights of navigation to non-riparian State on rivers or lakes within its territory.

Article XVIII

Each riparian State is, to the extent of the means available or made available to it, required to maintain in good order that portion of the navigable course of a river or lake within its jurisdiction.

Article XIX

The rules stated in this Chapter are not applicable to the navigation of vessels of war or of vessels performing police or administrative functions, or, in general, exercising any other form of public authority.

Article XX

In time of war, other armed conflict, or public emergency constituting a threat to the life of the State, a riparian State may take measures derogating from its obligations under this Chapter to the extent strictly required by the exigencies of the situation, provided that such measures are not inconsistent with its other obligations under international law. The riparian State shall in any case facilitate navigation for humanitarian purposes.

CHAPTER 5
TIMBER FLOATING
Article XXI

The floating of timber on a watercourse which flows through or between the territories of two or more States is governed by the following Articles except in cases in which floating is governed by rules of navigation according to applicable law or custom binding upon the riparians.

ARTICLE XXII

The States riparian to an international watercourse utilized for navigation may determine by common consent whether and under what conditions timber floating may be permitted upon the watercourse.

Article XXIII

1. It is recommended that each State riparian to an international watercourse not used for navigation should, with due regard to other uses of the watercourse, authorise the co-riparian States to use the watercourse and its banks within the territory of each riparian State for the floating of timber.

2. This authorization should extend to all necessary work along the banks by the floating crew and to the installation of such facilities as may be required for the timber floating.

Article XXIV

If a riparian State requires permanent installation for floating inside a territory of a co-riparian State or if it is necessary to regulate the flow of the watercourse, all questions connected with these installations and measures should be determined by agreement between the States concerned.

Article XXV

Co-riparian States of a watercourse which is, or is to be used for floating timber should negotiate in order to come to an agreement governing the administrative regime of floating, and if necessary to establish a joint agency or commission in order to facilitate the regulation of floating in all aspects.

CHAPTER 6
PROCEDURES FOR THE PREVENTION
AND SETTLEMENT OF DISPUTES
Article XXVI

This Chapter relates to procedures for the prevention and settlement of international disputes as to the legal rights or other interests of basin States and of other States in the waters of an international drainage basin.

Article XXVII

1. Consistently with the Charter of the United Nations, States are under an obligation to settle international disputes as to their legal rights or other interests by peaceful means in such a manner that international peace and security, and justice are not endangered.

2. It is recommended that States resort progressively to the means of prevention and settlement of disputes stipulated in Articles XXIX to XXXIV of this Chapter.

Article XXVIII

1. States are under a primary obligation to resort to means of prevention and settlement of disputes stipulated in the applicable treaties binding upon them.

2. States are limited to the means of prevention and settlement of disputes stipulated in treaties binding upon them only to the extent provided by the applicable treaties.

Article XXIX

1. With a view to preventing disputes from arising between basin States as to their legal rights or other interest, it is recommended that each basin State furnish relevant and reasonably available information to the other basin States concerning the waters of a drainage basin within its territory and its use of, and activities with respect to such waters.

2. A State, regardless of its location in a drainage basin, should in particular furnish to any other basin State, the interests of which may be substantially affected, notice of any proposed construction or installation which would alter the regime of the basin in a way which might give rise to a dispute as defined in Article XXVI. The notice should include such essential facts as will permit the recipient to make an assessment of the probable effect of the proposed alteration.

3. A State providing the notice referred to in paragraph 2 of this Article should afford to the recipient a reasonable period of time to make an assessment of the probable effect of the proposed construction or installation and to submit its views thereon to the State furnishing the notice.

4. If a State has failed to give the notice referred to in paragraph 2 of this Article, the alteration by the State in the regime of the drainage basin shall not be given the weight normally accorded to temporal priority in use in the event of a determination of what is a reasonable and equitable share of the waters of the basin.

Article XXX

In case of a dispute between States as to their legal rights or other interests, as defined in Article XXVI, they should seek a solution by negotiation.

Article XXXI

1. If a question or dispute arises which relates to the present or future utilization of the waters of an international drainage basin, it is recommended that the basin States refer the question or dispute to a joint agency and that they request the agency to survey the international drainage basin and to formulate plans or recommendations for the fullest and most efficient use thereof in the interests of all such States.

2. It is recommended that the joint agency be instructed to submit reports on all matters within its competence to the appropriate authorities of the member States concerned.

3. It is recommended that the member States of the joint agency in appropriate cases invite non-basin States which by treaty enjoy a right in the use of the waters and an international drainage basin to associate themselves with the work of the joint agency or that they be permitted to appear before the agency.

Article XXXII

If a question or a dispute is one which is considered by the States concerned to be incapable of resolution in the manner set forth in Article XXXI, it is recommended that they seek the good offices, or jointly request the mediation of a third State, of a qualified international organisation or of a qualified person.

Article XXXIII

1. If the States concerned have not been able to resolve their dispute through negotiation or have been unable to agree on the measures described in Article XXXI and XXXII, it is recommended that they form a commission of inquiry or an ad hoc conciliation commission, which shall endeavour to find a solution, likely to be accepted by the States concerned, of any dispute as to their legal rights.

2. It is recommended that the conciliation commission be constituted in the manner set forth in the Annex.

Article XXXIV

It is recommended that the States concerned agree to submit their legal disputes to an *ad hoc* arbitral tribunal, to a permanent arbitral tribunal or to the International Court of Justice if:

(a) A commission has not been formed as provided in Article XXXIII, or

(b) The commission has not been able to find a solution to be recommended, or

(c) A solution recommended has not been accepted by the States concerned, and

(d) An agreement has not been otherwise arrived at.

Article XXXV

It is recommended that in the event of arbitration the States concerned have recourse to the Model Rules on Arbitral Procedure prepared by the International Law Commission of the United Nations at its tenth session in 1958.

Article XXXVI

Recourse to arbitration implies the undertaking by the States concerned to consider the award to be given as final and to submit in good faith to its execution.

Article XXXVII

The means of settlement referred to in the preceding Articles of this Chapter are without prejudice to the utilization of means of settlement recommended to, or required of, members of regional arrangements or agencies and of other international organizations.

4.8 INTERNATIONAL CONVENTION ON CIVIL LIABILITY FOR OIL POL-LUTION DAMAGE (WITHOUT ANNEX AND PROTOCOLS).[1] Concluded at Brussels, 29 November 1969. Entered into force, 19 June 1975. 973 U.N.T.S. 3, 9 I.L.M. 45 (1970)

Article I

For the purposes of this Convention:

1. "Ship" means any sea-going vessel and any seaborne craft of any type whatsoever, actually carrying oil in bulk as cargo.

2. "Person" means any individual or partnership or any public or private body, whether corporate or not, including a State or any of its constituent subdivisions.

3. "Owner" means the person or persons registered as the owner of the ship or, in the absence of registration, the person or persons owning the ship. However in the case of a ship owned by a State and operated by a company which in that State is registered as the ship's operator, "owner" shall mean such company.

4. "State of the ship's registry" means in relation to registered ships the State of registration of the ship, and in relation to unregistered ships the State whose flag the ship is flying.

5. "Oil" means any persistent oil such as crude oil, fuel oil, heavy diesel oil, lubricating oil and whale oil, whether carried on board a ship as cargo or in the bunkers of such a ship.

6. "Pollution damage" means loss or damage caused outside the ship carrying oil by contamination resulting from the escape or discharge of oil from the ship, wherever such escape or discharge may occur, and includes the costs of preventive measures and further loss or damage caused by preventive measures.

7. "Preventive measures" means any reasonable measures taken by any person after an incident has occurred to prevent or minimize pollution damage.

8. "Incident" means any occurrence, or series of occurrences having the same origin, which causes pollution damage.

9. "Organization" means the Inter–Governmental Maritime Consultative Organization.

Article II

This Convention shall apply exclusively to pollution damage caused on the territory including the territorial sea of a Contracting State and to preventive measures taken to prevent or minimize such damage.

Article III

1. Except as provided in paragraphs 2 and 3 of this Article, the owner of a ship at the time of an incident, or where the incident consists of a series of occurrences at the time of the first such occurrence, shall be liable for any pollution damage caused by oil which has escaped or been discharged from the ship as a result of the incident.

---

1. *But see* Basic Document 4.18 and 4.28, *infra.*

2. No liability for pollution damage shall attach to the owner if he proves that the damage:

(a) resulted from an act of war, hostilities, civil war, insurrection or a natural phenomenon of an exceptional, inevitable and irresistible character, or

(b) was wholly caused by an act or omission done with intent to cause damage by a third party, or

(c) was wholly caused by the negligence or other wrongful act of any Government or other authority responsible for the maintenance of lights or other navigational aids in the exercise of that function.

3. If the owner proves that the pollution damage resulted wholly or partially either from an act or omission done with intent to cause damage by the person who suffered the damage or from the negligence of that person, the owner may be exonerated wholly or partially from his liability to such person.

4. No claim for compensation for pollution damage shall be made against the owner otherwise than in accordance with this Convention. No claim for pollution damage under this Convention or otherwise may be made against the servants or agents of the owner.

5. Nothing in this Convention shall prejudice any right of recourse of the owner against third parties.

Article IV

When oil has escaped or has been discharged from two or more ships, and pollution damage results therefrom, the owners of all the ships concerned, unless exonerated under Article III, shall be jointly and severally liable for all such damage which is not reasonably separable.

Article V

1. The owner of a ship shall be entitled to limit his liability under this Convention in respect of any one incident to an aggregate amount of 133 units of account for each ton of the ship's tonnage. However, this aggregate amount shall not in any event exceed 14 million units of account.

2. If the incident occurred as a result of the actual fault or privity of the owner, he shall not be entitled to avail himself of the limitation provided in paragraph 1 of this Article.

3. For the purpose of availing himself of the benefit of limitation provided for in paragraph 1 of this Article the owner shall constitute a fund for the total sum representing the limit of his liability with the Court or other competent authority of any one of the Contracting States in which action is brought under Article IX. The fund can be constituted either by depositing the sum or by producing a bank guarantee or other guarantee, acceptable under the legislation of the Contracting State where the fund is constituted, and considered to be adequate by the Court or another competent authority.

4. The fund shall be distributed among the claimants in proportion to the amounts of their established claims.

5. If before the fund is distributed the owner or any of his servants or agents or any person providing him insurance or other financial security has as a result of the incident in question, paid compensation for pollution

damage, such person shall, up to the amount he has paid, acquire by subrogation the rights which the person so compensated would have enjoyed under this Convention.

6. The right of subrogation provided for in paragraph 5 of this Article may also be exercised by a person other than those mentioned therein in respect of any amount of compensation for pollution damage which he may have paid but only to the extent that such subrogation is permitted under the applicable national law.

7. Where the owner or any other person establishes that he may be compelled to pay at a later date in whole or in part any such amount of compensation, with regard to which such person would have enjoyed a right of subrogation under paragraph 5 or 6 of this Article, had the compensation been paid before the fund was distributed, the Court or other competent authority of the State where the fund has been constituted may order that a sufficient sum shall be provisionally set aside to enable such person at such later date to enforce his claim against the fund.

8. Claims in respect of expenses reasonably incurred or sacrifices reasonably made by the owner voluntarily to prevent or minimize pollution damage shall rank equally with other claims against the fund.

9(a) The "unit of account" referred to in paragraph 1 of this Article is the Special Drawing Right as defined by the International Monetary Fund. The amounts mentioned in paragraph 1 shall be converted into the national currency of the State in which the fund is being constituted on the basis of the value of that currency by reference to the Special Drawing Right on the date of the constitution of the fund. The value of the national currency, in terms of the Special Drawing Right, of a Contracting State which is a member of the International Monetary Fund, shall be calculated in accordance with the method of valuation applied by the International Monetary Fund in effect at the date in question for its operations and transactions. The value of the national currency, in terms of the Special Drawing Right, of a Contracting State which is not a member of the International Monetary Fund, shall be calculated in a manner determined by that State.

9(b) Nevertheless, a Contracting State which is not a member of the International Monetary Fund and whose law does not permit the application of the provisions of paragraph 9(a) of this Article may, at the time of ratification, acceptance, approval of or accession to the present Convention, or at any time thereafter, declare that the limits of liability provided for in paragraph 1 to be applied in its territory shall, in respect of any one incident, be an aggregate of 2,000 monetary units for each ton of the ship's tonnage provided that this aggregate amount shall not in any event exceed 210 million monetary units. The monetary unit referred to in this paragraph corresponds to sixty-five and a half milligrammes of gold of millesimal fineness nine hundred. The conversion of these amounts into the national currency shall be made according to the law of the State concerned.

9(c) The calculation mentioned in the last sentence of paragraph 9(a) and the conversion mentioned in paragraph 9(b) shall be made in such a manner as to express in the national currency of the Contracting State as far as possible the same real value for the amounts in paragraph 1 as is expressed there in units of account. Contracting States shall communicate to the depositary the manner of calculation pursuant to paragraph 9(a), or the result of the conversion in paragraph 9(b) as the case may be, when depositing an instrument referred to in Article IV and whenever there is a change in either.

10. For the purpose of this Article the ship's tonnage shall be the net tonnage of the ship with the addition of the amount deducted from the gross tonnage on account of engine room space for the purpose of ascertaining the net tonnage. In the case of a ship which cannot be measured in accordance with the normal rules of tonnage measurement, the ship's tonnage shall be deemed to be 40 per cent of the weight in tons (of 2240 lbs) of oil which the ship is capable of carrying.

11. The insurer or other person providing financial security shall be entitled to constitute a fund in accordance with this Article on the same conditions and having the same effect as if it were constituted by the owner. Such a fund may be constituted even in the event of the actual fault or privity of the owner but its constitution shall in that case not prejudice the rights of any claimant against the owner.

Article VI

1. Where the owner, after an incident, has constituted a fund in accordance with Article V, and is entitled to limit his liability,

(a) no person having a claim for pollution damage arising out of that incident shall be entitled to exercise any right against any other assets of the owner in respect of such claim;

(b) the Court or other competent authority of any Contracting State shall order the release of any ship or other property belonging to the owner which has been arrested in respect of a claim for pollution damage arising out of that incident, and shall similarly release any bail or other security furnished to avoid such arrest.

2. The foregoing shall, however, only apply if the claimant has access to the Court administering the fund and the fund is actually available in respect or his claim.

Article VII

1. The owner of a ship registered in a Contracting State and carrying more than 2,000 tons of oil in bulk as cargo shall be required to maintain insurance or other financial security, such as the guarantee of a bank or a certificate delivered by an international compensation fund, in the sums fixed by applying the limits of liability prescribed in Article V, paragraph 1 to cover his liability for pollution damage under this Convention.

2. A certificate attesting that insurance or other financial security is in force in accordance with the provisions of this Convention shall be issued to each ship. It shall be issued or certified by the appropriate authority of the State of the ship's registry after determining that the requirements of paragraph 1 of this Article have been complied with. This certificate shall be in the form of the annexed model and shall contain the following particulars:

(a) name of ship and port of registration;

(b) name and principal place of business of owner;

(c) type of security;

(d) name and principal place of business of insurer or other person giving security and, where appropriate, place of business where the insurance or security is established;

(e) period of validity of certificate which shall not be longer than the period of validity of the insurance or other security.

3. The certificate shall be in the official language or languages of the issuing State. If the language used is neither English nor French, the text shall include a translation into one of these languages.

4. The certificate shall be carried on board the ship and a copy shall be deposited with the authorities who keep the record of the ship's registry.

5. An insurance or other financial security shall not satisfy the requirements of this Article if it can cease, for reasons other than the expiry of the period of validity of the insurance or security specified in the certificate under paragraph 2 of this Article, before three months have elapsed from the date on which notice of its termination is given to the authorities referred to in paragraph 4 of this Article, unless the certificate has been surrendered to these authorities or a new certificate has been issued within the said period. The foregoing provisions shall similarly apply to any modification which results in the insurance or security no longer satisfying the requirements of this Article.

6. The State of registry shall, subject to the provisions of this Article, determine the conditions of issue and validity of the certificate.

7. Certificates issued or certified under the authority of a Contracting State shall be accepted by other Contracting States for the purposes of this Convention and shall be regarded by other Contracting States as having the same force as certificates issued or certified by them. A Contracting State may at any time request consultation with the State of a ship's registry should it believe that the insurer or guarantor named in the certificate is not financially capable of meeting the obligations imposed by this Convention.

8. Any claim for compensation for pollution damage may be brought directly against the insurer or other person providing financial security for the owner's liability for pollution damage. In such case the defendant may, irrespective of the actual fault or privity of the owner, avail himself of the limits of liability prescribed in Article V, paragraph 1. He may further avail himself of the defences (other than the bankruptcy or winding up of the owner) which the owner himself would have been entitled to invoke. Furthermore, the defendant may avail himself of the defence that the pollution damage resulted from the wilful misconduct of the owner himself, but the defendant shall not avail himself of any other defence which he might have been entitled to invoke in proceedings brought by the owner against him. The defendant shall in any event have the right to require the owner to be joined in the proceedings.

9. Any sums provided by insurance or by other financial security maintained in accordance with paragraph 1 of this Article shall be available exclusively for the satisfaction of claims under this Convention.

10. A Contracting State shall not permit a ship under its flag to which this Article applies to trade unless a certificate has been issued under paragraph 2 or 12 of this Article.

11.   Subject to the provisions of this Article, each Contracting State shall ensure, under its national legislation, that insurance or other security to the extent specified in paragraph 1 of this Article is in force in respect of any ship, wherever registered, entering or leaving a port in its territory, or arriving at or leaving an off-shore terminal in its territorial sea, if the ship actually carries more than 2,000 tons of oil in bulk as cargo.

12.   If insurance or other financial security is not maintained in respect of a ship owned by a Contracting State, the provisions of this Article relating thereto shall not be applicable to such ship, but the ship shall carry a certificate issued by the appropriate authorities of the State of the ship's registry stating that the ship is owned by that State and that the ship's liability is covered within the limits prescribed by Article V, paragraph 1. Such a certificate shall follow as closely as practicable the model prescribed by paragraph 2 of this Article.

Article VIII

Rights of compensation under this Convention shall be extinguished unless an action is brought thereunder within three years from the date when the damage occurred. However, in no case shall an action be brought after six years from the date of the incident which caused the damage. Where this incident consists of a series of occurrences, the six-years period shall run from the date of the first such occurrence.

Article IX

1.   Where an incident has caused pollution damage in the territory including the territorial sea of one or more Contracting States, or preventive measures have been taken to prevent or minimize pollution damage in such territory including the territorial sea, actions for compensation may only be brought in the Courts of any such Contracting State or States. Reasonable notice of any such action shall be given to the defendant.

2.   Each Contracting State shall ensure that its Courts possess the necessary jurisdiction to entertain such actions for compensation.

3.   After the fund has been constituted in accordance with Article V the Courts of the State in which the fund is constituted shall be exclusively competent to determine all matters relating to the apportionment and distribution of the fund.

Article X

1.   Any judgment given by a Court with jurisdiction in accordance with Article IX which is enforceable in the State of origin where it is no longer subject to ordinary forms of review, shall be recognized in any Contracting State, except:

(a) where the judgment was obtained by fraud; or

(b) where the defendant was not given reasonable notice and a fair opportunity to present his case.

2.   A judgment recognized under paragraph 1 of this Article shall be enforceable in each Contracting State as soon as the formalities required in that State have been complied with. The formalities shall not permit the merits of the case to be re-opened.

Article XI

1. The provisions of this Convention shall not apply to warships or other ships owned or operated by a State and used, for the time being, only on government non-commercial service.

2. With respect to ships owned by a Contracting State and used for commercial purposes, each State shall be subject to suit in the jurisdictions set forth in Article IX and shall waive all defences based on its status as a sovereign State.

Article XII

This Convention shall supersede any International Conventions in force or open for signature, ratification or accession at the date on which the Convention is opened for signature, but only to the extent that such Conventions would be in conflict with it; however, nothing in this Article shall affect the obligations of Contracting States to non-Contracting States arising under such International Conventions.

Article XIII

1. The present Convention shall remain open for signature until 31 December 1970 and shall thereafter remain open for accession.

2. States Members of the United Nations or any of the Specialized Agencies or of the International Atomic Energy Agency or Parties to the Statute of the International Court of Justice may become Parties to this Convention by:

(a) signature without reservation as to ratification, acceptance or approval;

(b) signature subject to ratification, acceptance or approval followed by ratification, acceptance or approval; or

(c) accession.

Article XIV

1. Ratification, acceptance, approval or accession shall be effected by the deposit of a formal instrument to that effect with the Secretary–General of the Organization.

2. Any instrument of ratification, acceptance, approval or accession deposited after the entry into force of an amendment to the present Convention with respect to all existing Contracting States, or after the completion of all measures required for the entry into force of the amendment with respect to those Contracting States shall be deemed to apply to the Convention as modified by the amendment.

Article XV

1. The present Convention shall enter into force on the ninetieth day following the date on which Governments of eight States including five States each with not less than 1,000,000 gross tons of tanker tonnage have either signed it without reservation as to ratification, acceptance or approval or have deposited instruments of ratification, acceptance, approval or accession with the Secretary–General of the Organization.

2. For each State which subsequently ratifies, accepts, approves or accedes to it the present Convention shall come into force on the ninetieth day after deposit by such State of the appropriate instrument.

Article XVI

1. The present Convention may be denounced by any Contracting State at any time after the date on which the Convention comes into force for that State.

2. Denunciation shall be effected by the deposit of an instrument with the Secretary–General of the Organization.

3. A denunciation shall take effect one year, or such longer period as may be specified in the instrument of denunciation, after its deposit with the Secretary–General of the Organization.

Article XVII

1. The United Nations, where it is the administering authority for a territory, or any Contracting State responsible for the international relations of a territory, shall as soon as possible consult with the appropriate authorities of such territory or take such other measures as may be appropriate, in order to extend the present Convention to that territory and may at any time by notification in writing to the Secretary–General of the Organization declare that the present Convention shall extend to such territory.

2. The present Convention shall, from the date of receipt of the notification or from such other date as may be specified in the notification, extend to the territory named therein.

3. The United Nations, or any Contracting State which has made a declaration under paragraph 1 of this Article may at any time after the date on which the Convention has been so extended to any territory declare by notification in writing to the Secretary–General of the Organization that the present Convention shall cease to extend to any such territory named in the notification.

4. The present Convention shall cease to extend to any territory mentioned in such notification one year, or such longer period as may be specified therein, after the date of receipt of the notification by the Secretary–General of the Organization.

Article XVIII

1. A Conference for the purpose of revising or amending the present Convention may be convened by the Organization.

2. The Organization shall convene a Conference of the Contracting States for revising or amending the present Convention at the request of not less than one-third of the Contracting States.

Article XIX

1. The present Convention shall be deposited with the Secretary–General of the Organization.

2.   The Secretary–General of the Organization shall:

(a) inform all States which have signed or acceded to the Convention of:

(i) each new signature or deposit of instrument together with the date thereof;

(ii) the deposit of any instrument of denunciation of this Convention together with the date of the deposit;

(iii) the extension of the present Convention to any territory under paragraph 1 of Article XVII and of the termination of any such extension under the provisions of paragraph 4 of that Article stating in each case the date on which the present Convention has been or will cease to be so extended;

(b) transmit certified true copies of the present Convention to all Signatory States and to all States which accede to the present Convention.

Article XX

As soon as the present Convention comes into force, the text shall be transmitted by the Secretary–General of the Organization to the Secretariat of the United Nations for registration and publication in accordance with Article 102 of the Charter of the United Nations.

Article XXI

The present Convention is established in a single copy in the English and French languages, both texts being equally authentic. Official translations in the Russian and Spanish languages shall be prepared and deposited with the signed original.

4.9 INTERNATIONAL CONVENTION RELATING TO INTERVENTION ON THE HIGH SEAS IN CASES OF OIL POLLUTION CASUALTIES (WITHOUT ANNEX AND PROTOCOL). Concluded at Brussels, 29 November 1969. Entered into force, 6 May 1975. 970 U.N.T.S. 211, 26 U.S.T. 765, T.I.A.S. No. 8068, 9 I.L.M. 25 (1986)

Article I. 1. Parties to the present Convention may take such measures on the high seas as may be necessary to prevent, mitigate or eliminate grave and imminent danger to their coastline or related interests from pollution or threat of pollution of the sea by oil, following upon a maritime casualty or acts related to such a casualty, which may reasonably be expected to result in major harmful consequences.

2. However, no measures shall be taken under the present Convention against any warship or other ship owned or operated by a State and used, for the time being, only on government non-commercial service.

Article II. For the purposes of the present Convention:

1. "Maritime casualty" means a collision of ships, stranding or other incident of navigation, or other occurrence on board a ship or external to it resulting in material damage or imminent threat of material damage to a ship or cargo.

2. "Ship" means:

(*a*) any sea-going vessel of any type whatsoever, and

(*b*) any floating craft, with the exception of an installation or device engaged in the exploration and exploitation of the resources of the sea-bed and the ocean floor and the subsoil thereof.

3. "Oil" means crude oil, fuel oil, diesel oil and lubricating oil.

4. "Related interests" means the interests of a coastal State directly affected or threatened by the maritime casualty, such as:

(*a*) maritime coastal, port or estuarine activities, including fisheries activities, constituting an essential means of livelihood of the persons concerned;

(*b*) tourist attractions of the area concerned;

(*c*) the health of the coastal population and the well-being of the area concerned, including conservation of living marine resources and of wildlife.

5. "Organization" means the Inter–Governmental Maritime Consultative Organization.

Article III. When a coastal State is exercising the right to take measures in accordance with Article I, the following provisions shall apply:

(*a*) before taking any measures, a coastal State shall proceed to consultations with other States affected by the maritime casualty, particularly with the flag State or States;

(*b*) the coastal State shall notify without delay the proposed measures to any persons physical or corporate known to the coastal State, or made known to it during the consultations, to have interests which can reasonably be expected to be affected by those measures. The coastal State shall take into account any views they may submit;

(*c*) before any measure is taken, the coastal State may proceed to a consultation with independent experts, whose names shall be chosen from a list maintained by the Organization;

(*d*) in cases of extreme urgency requiring measures to be taken immediately, the coastal State may take measures rendered necessary by the urgency of the situation, without prior notification or consultation or without continuing consultations already begun;

(*e*) a coastal State shall, before taking such measures and during their course, use its best endeavours to avoid any risk to human life, and to afford persons in distress any assistance of which they may stand in need, and in appropriate cases to facilitate the repatriation of ships' crews, and to raise no obstacle thereto;

(*f*) measures which have been taken in application of Article I shall be notified without delay to the States and to the known physical or corporate persons concerned, as well as to the Secretary–General of the Organization.

Article IV. 1. Under the supervision of the Organization, there shall be set up and maintained the list of experts contemplated by Article III of the present Convention, and the Organization shall make necessary and appropriate regulations in connexion therewith, including the determination of the required qualifications.

2. Nominations to the list may be made by Member States of the Organization and by Parties to this Convention. The experts shall be paid on the basis of services rendered by the States utilizing those services.

Article V. 1. Measures taken by the coastal State in accordance with Article I shall be proportionate to the damage actual or threatened to it.

2. Such measures shall not go beyond what is reasonably necessary to achieve the end mentioned in Article I and shall cease as soon as that end has been achieved; they shall not unnecessarily interfere with the rights and interests of the flag State, third States and of any persons, physical or corporate, concerned.

3. In considering whether the measures are proportionate to the damage, account shall be taken of:

(*a*) the extent and probability of imminent damage if those measures are not taken; and

(*b*) the likelihood of those measures being effective; and

(*c*) the extent of the damage which may be caused by such measures.

Article VI. Any Party which has taken measures in contravention of the provisions of the present Convention causing damage to others, shall be obliged to pay compensation to the extent of the damage caused by measures which exceed those reasonably necessary to achieve the end mentioned in Article I.

Article VII. Except as specifically provided, nothing in the present Convention shall prejudice any otherwise applicable right, duty, privilege or immunity or deprive any of the Parties or any interested physical or corporate person of any remedy otherwise applicable.

Article VIII. 1. Any controversy between the Parties as to whether measures taken under Article I were in contravention of the provisions of the present Convention, to whether compensation is obliged to be paid under Article VI, and to the amount of such compensation shall, if settlement by negotiation between the Parties involved or between the Party which took the measures and the physical or corporate claimants has not been possible, and if the Parties do not otherwise agree, be submitted upon request of any of the Parties concerned to conciliation or, if conciliation does not succeed, to arbitration, as set out in the Annex to the present Convention.

2. The Party which took the measures shall not be entitled to refuse a request for conciliation or arbitration under provisions of the preceding paragraph solely on the grounds that any remedies under municipal law in its own courts have not been exhausted.

Article IX. 1. The present Convention shall remain open for signature until 31 December 1970 and shall thereafter remain open for accession.

2. States Members of the United Nations or any of the Specialized Agencies or of the International Atomic Energy Agency or Parties to the Statute of the International Court of Justice may become Parties to this Convention by:

    (*a*) signature without reservation as to ratification, acceptance or approval;

    (*b*) signature subject to ratification, acceptance or approval followed by ratification, acceptance or approval; or

    (*c*) accession.

Article X. 1. Ratification, acceptance, approval or accession shall be effected by the deposit of a formal instrument to that effect with the Secretary–General of the Organization.

2. Any instrument of ratification, acceptance, approval or accession deposited after the entry into force of an amendment to the present Convention with respect to all existing Parties or after the completion of all measures required for the entry into force of the amendment with respect to those Parties shall be deemed to apply to the Convention as modified by the amendment.

Article XI. 1. The present Convention shall enter into force on the ninetieth day following the date on which Governments of fifteen States have either signed it without reservation as to ratification, acceptance or approval or have deposited instruments of ratification, acceptance, approval or accession with the Secretary–General of the Organization.

2. For each State which subsequently ratifies, accepts, approves or accedes to it the present Convention shall come into force on the ninetieth day after deposit by such State of the appropriate instrument.

Article XII. 1. The present Convention may be denounced by any Party at any time after the date on which the Convention comes into force for that State.

2. Denunciation shall be effected by the deposit of an instrument with the Secretary–General of the Organization.

3. A denunciation shall take effect one year, or such longer period as may be specified in the instrument of denunciation, after its deposit with the Secretary–General of the Organization.

Article XIII. 1. The United Nations where it is the administering authority for a territory, or any State Party to the present Convention responsible for the international relations of a territory, shall as soon as possible consult with the appropriate authorities of such territories or take such other measures as may be appropriate, in order to extend the present Convention to that territory and may at any time by notification in writing to the Secretary–General of the Organization declare that the present Convention shall extend to such territory.

2. The present Convention shall, from the date of receipt of the notification or from such other date as may be specified in the notification, extend to the territory named therein.

3. The United Nations, or any Party which has made a declaration under paragraph 1 of this Article may at any time after the date on which the Convention has been so extended to any territory declare by notification in writing to the Secretary–General of the Organization that the present Convention shall cease to extend to any such territory named in the notification.

4. The present Convention shall cease to extend to any territory mentioned in such notification one year, or such longer period as may be specified therein, after the date of receipt of the notification by the Secretary–General of the Organization.

Article XIV. 1. A Conference for the purpose of revising or amending the present Convention may be convened by the Organization.

2. The Organization shall convene a Conference of the States Parties to the present Convention for revising or amending the present Convention at the request of not less than one-third of the Parties.

Article XV. 1. The present Convention shall be deposited with the Secretary–General of the Organization.

2. The Secretary–General of the Organization shall:

(*a*) inform all States which have signed or acceded to the Convention of:

(i) each new signature or deposit of instrument together with the date thereof;

(ii) the deposit of any instrument of denunciation of this Convention together with the date of the deposit;

(iii) the extension of the present Convention to any territory under paragraph 1 of Article XIII and of the termination of any such extension under the provisions of paragraph 4 of that Article stating in each case the date on which the present Convention has been or will cease to be so extended;

(*b*) transmit certified true copies of the present Convention to all Signatory States and to all States which accede to the present Convention.

Article XVI. As soon as the present Convention comes into force, the text shall be transmitted by the Secretary–General of the Organization to the Secretariat of the United Nations for registration and publication in accordance with Article 102 of the Charter of the United Nations.

Article XVII. The present Convention is established in a single copy in the English and French languages, both texts being equally authentic. Official translations in the Russian and Spanish languages shall be prepared and deposited with the signed original.

4.10 DECLARATION OF PRINCIPLES GOVERNING THE SEA–BED AND THE OCEAN FLOOR, AND THE SUBSOIL THEREOF, BEYOND THE LIMITS OF NATIONAL JURISDICTION. Adopted by the U.N. General Assembly, 17 December 1970. U.N. Doc. A/RES/2749(XXV), 10 I.L.M. 220 (1971)

THE GENERAL ASSEMBLY,

Recalling its resolutions 2340 (XXII) of 18 December 1967, 2467 (XXIII) of 21 December 1968 and 2574 (XXIV) of 15 December 1969, concerning the area to which the title of the item refers.

Affirming that there is an area of the sea-bed and the ocean floor, and the subsoil thereof, beyond the limits of national jurisdiction, the precise limits of which are yet to be determined.

Recognizing that the existing legal régime of the high seas does not provide substantive rules for regulating the exploration of the aforesaid area and the exploitation of its resources.

Convinced that the area shall be reserved exclusively for peaceful purposes and that the exploration of the area and the exploitation of its resources shall be carried out for the benefit of mankind as a whole.

Believing it essential that an international régime applying to the area and its resources and including appropriate international machinery should be established as soon as possible.

Bearing in mind that the development and use of the area and its resources shall be undertaken in such a manner as to foster healthy development of the world economy and balanced growth of international trade, and to minimize any adverse economic effects caused by fluctuation of prices of raw materials resulting from such activities.

Solemnly declares that:

1. The sea-bed and ocean floor, and the subsoil thereof, beyond the limits of national jurisdiction (hereinafter referred to as the area), as well as the resources of the area, are the common heritage of mankind.

2. The area shall not be subject to appropriation by any means by States or persons, natural or juridical, and no State shall claim or exercise sovereignty or sovereign rights over any part thereof.

3. No State or person, natural or juridical, shall claim, exercise or acquire rights with respect to the area or its resources incompatible with the international régime to be established and the principles of this Declaration.

4. All activities regarding the exploration and exploitation of the resources of the area and other related activities shall be governed by the international régime to be established.

5. The area shall be open to use exclusively for peaceful purposes by all States whether coastal or land-locked, without discrimination, in accordance with international régime to be established.

6. States shall act in the area in accordance with the applicable principles and rules of international law including the Charter of the United Nations and the Declaration on Principles of International Law concerning Friendly Relations and Co-operation among States in accordance with the

Charter of the United Nations, adopted by the General Assembly on 24 October 1970, in the interests of maintaining international peace and security and promoting international co-operation and mutual understanding.

7. The exploration of the area and the exploitation of its resources shall be carried out for the benefit of mankind as a whole, irrespective of the geographical location of States, whether land-locked or coastal, and taking into particular consideration the interests and needs of the developing countries.

8. The area shall be reserved exclusively for peaceful purposes, without prejudice to any measures which have been or may be agreed upon in the context of international negotiations undertaken in the field of disarmament and which may be applicable to a broader area. One or more international agreements shall be concluded as soon as possible in order to implement effectively this principle and to constitute a step towards the exclusion of the sea-bed, the ocean floor and the subsoil thereof from the arms race.

9. On the basis of the principles of this Declaration, an international régime applying to the area and its resources and including appropriate international machinery to give effect to its provisions shall be established by an international treaty of a universal character, generally agreed upon. The régime shall, *inter alia,* provide for the orderly and safe development and rational management of the area and its resources and for expanding opportunities in the use thereof and ensure the equitable sharing by States in the benefits derived therefrom, taking into particular consideration the interests and needs of the developing countries, whether land-locked or coastal.

10. States shall promote international co-operation in scientific research exclusively for peaceful purposes:

(a) By participation in international programmes and by encouraging co-operation in scientific research by personnel of different countries;

(b) Through effective publication of research programmes and dissemination of the results of research through international channels;

(c) By co-operation in measures to strengthen research capabilities of developing countries, including the participation of their nationals in research programmes. No such activity shall form the legal basis for any claims with respect to any part of the area or its resources.

11. With respect to activities in the area and acting in conformity with the international régime to be established, States shall take appropriate measures for and shall co-operate in the adoption and implementation of international rules, standards and procedures for, *inter alia:*

(a) Prevention of pollution and contamination, and other hazards to the marine environment, including the coastline, and of interference with the ecological balance of the marine environment;

(b) Protection and conservation of the natural resources of the area and prevention of damage to the flora and fauna of the marine environment.

12. In their activities in the area, including those relating to its resources, States shall pay due regard to the rights and legitimate interests of coastal States in the region of such activities, as well as of all other States

which may be affected by such activities. Consultations shall be maintained with the coastal States concerned with respect to activities relating to the exploration of the area and the exploitation of its resources with a view to avoiding infringement of such rights and interests.

13. Nothing herein shall affect:

(a) The legal status of the waters superjacent to the area or that of the air space above those waters;

(b) The rights of coastal States with respect to measures to prevent, mitigate or eliminate grave and imminent danger to their coastline or related interests from pollution or threat thereof resulting from, or from other hazardous occurrences caused by, any activities in the area, subject to the international régime to be established.

14. Every State shall have the responsibility to ensure that activities in the area, including those relating to its resources, whether undertaken by governmental agencies, or nongovernmental entities or persons under its jurisdiction, or acting on its behalf, shall be carried out in conformity with the international régime to be established. The same responsibility applies to international organizations and their members for activities undertaken by such organizations or on their behalf. Damage caused by such activities shall entail liability.

15. The parties to any dispute relating to activities in the area and its resources shall resolve such dispute by the measures mentioned in Article 33 of the Charter of the United Nations and such procedures for settling disputes as may be agreed upon in the international régime to be established.

4.11 CONVENTION RELATING TO CIVIL LIABILITY IN THE FIELD OF MARITIME CARRIAGE OF NUCLEAR MATERIAL (WITHOUT FINAL ACT). Concluded at Brussels, 17 December 1971. Entered into force, 15 July 1975. 974 U.N.T.S. 255

The High Contracting Parties,

Considering that the Paris Convention of 29 July 1960 on Third Party Liability in the Field of Nuclear Energy and its Additional Protocol of 28 January 1964 (hereinafter referred to as "the Paris Convention") and the Vienna Convention of 21 May 1963 on Civil Liability for Nuclear Damage (hereinafter referred to as "the Vienna Convention") provide that, in the case of damage caused by a nuclear incident occurring in the course of maritime carriage of nuclear material covered by such Conventions, the operator of a nuclear installation is the person liable for such damage,

Considering that similar provisions exist in the national law in force in certain States,

Considering that the application of any preceding international Convention in the field of maritime transport is however maintained,

Desirous of ensuring that the operator of a nuclear installation will be exclusively liable for damage caused by a nuclear incident occurring in the course of maritime carriage of nuclear material,

Have agreed as follows:

Article 1. Any person who by virtue of an international convention or national law applicable in the field of maritime transport might be held liable for damage caused by a nuclear incident shall be exonerated from such liability:

(*a*) if the operator of a nuclear installation is liable for such damage under either the Paris or the Vienna Convention, or

(*b*) if the operator of a nuclear installation is liable for such damage by virtue of a national law governing the liability for such damage, provided that such law is in all respects as favourable to persons who may suffer damage as either the Paris or the Vienna Convention.

Article 2. 1. The exoneration provided for in Article I shall also apply in respect of damage caused by a nuclear incident:

(*a*) to the nuclear installation itself or to any property on the site of that installation which is used or to be used in connexion with that installation, or

(*b*) to the means of transport upon which the nuclear material involved was at the time of the nuclear incident,

for which the operator of the nuclear installation is not liable because his liability for such damage has been excluded pursuant to the provisions of either the Paris or the Vienna Convention, or, in cases referred to in Article 1(*b*), by equivalent provisions of the national law referred to therein.

2. The provisions of paragraph 1 shall not, however, affect the liability of any individual who has caused the damage by an act or omission done with intent to cause damage.

Article 3. No provision of the present Convention shall affect the liability of the operator of a nuclear ship in respect of damage caused by a nuclear incident involving the nuclear fuel of or radioactive products or waste produced in such ship.

Article 4. The present Convention shall supersede any international Conventions in the field of maritime transport which, at the date on which the present Convention is opened for signature, are in force or open for signature, ratification or accession but only to the extent that such Conventions would be in conflict with it; however, nothing in this Article shall affect the obligations of the Contracting Parties to the present Convention to non-Contracting States arising under such international Conventions.

Article 5. 1. The present Convention shall be opened for signature in Brussels and shall remain open for signature in London at the Headquarters of the Inter–Governmental Maritime Consultative Organization (hereinafter referred to as "the Organization") until 31 December 1972 and shall thereafter remain open for accession.

2. States Members of the United Nations or any of the Specialized Agencies or of the International Atomic Energy Agency or Parties to the Statute of the International Court of Justice may become Parties to the present Convention by:

(*a*) signature without reservation as to ratification, acceptance or approval;

(*b*) signature subject to ratification, acceptance or approval followed by ratification, acceptance or approval; or

(*c*) accession.

3. Ratification, acceptance, approval or accession shall be effected by the deposit of a formal instrument to that effect with the Secretary–General of the Organization.

Article 6. 1. The present Convention shall enter into force on the ninetieth day following the date on which five States have either signed it without reservation as to ratification, acceptance or approval or have deposited instruments of ratification, acceptance, approval or accession with the Secretary–General of the Organization.

2. For any State which subsequently signs the present Convention without reservation as to ratification, acceptance or approval, or deposits its instrument of ratification, acceptance, approval or accession, the Convention shall come into force on the ninetieth day after the date of such signature or deposit.

Article 7. 1. The present Convention may be denounced by any Contracting Party to it at any time after the date on which the Convention comes into force for that State.

2. Denunciation shall be effected by a notification in writing delivered to the Secretary–General of the Organization.

3. A denunciation shall take effect one year, or such longer period as may be specified in the notification, after its receipt by the Secretary–General of the Organization.

4. Notwithstanding a denunciation by a Contracting Party pursuant to this Article the provisions of the present Convention shall continue to apply to any damage caused by a nuclear incident occurring before the denunciation takes effect.

Article 8. 1. The United Nations where it is the administering authority for a territory, or any Contracting Party to the present Convention responsible for the international relations of a territory, may at any time by notification in writing to the Secretary–General of the Organization declare that the present Convention shall extend to such territory.

2. The present Convention shall, from the date of receipt of the notification or from such other date as may be specified in the notification, extend to the territory named therein.

3. The United Nations, or any Contracting Party which had made a declaration under paragraph 1 of this Article may at any time after the date on which the Convention has been so extended to any territory declare by notification in writing to the Secretary–General of the Organization that the present Convention shall cease to extend to any such territory named in the notification.

4. The present Convention shall cease to extend to any territory mentioned in such notification one year, or such longer period as may be specified therein, after the date of receipt of the notification by the Secretary–General of the Organization.

Article 9. 1. A Conference for the purpose of revising or amending the present Convention may be convened by the Organization.

2. The Organization shall convene a Conference of the Contracting Parties to the present Convention for revising or amending it at the request of not less than one-third of the Contracting Parties.

Article 10. A Contracting Party may make reservations corresponding to those which it has validly made to the Paris or Vienna Convention. A reservation may be made at the time of signature, ratification, acceptance, approval or accession.

Article 11. 1. The present Convention shall be deposited with the Secretary–General of the Organization.

2. The Secretary–General of the Organization shall:

(*a*) inform all States which have signed or acceded to the present Convention of:

    (i) each new signature and each deposit of an instrument together with the date thereof;

    (ii) any reservation made in conformity with the present Convention;

    (iii) the date of entry into force of the present Convention;

    (iv) any denunciation of the present Convention and the date on which it takes effect;

    (v) the extension of the present Convention to any territory under paragraph 1 of Article 8 and of the termination of any such extension under the provisions of paragraph 4 of that Article stating in each case the date on which the present Convention has been or will cease to be so extended;

(*b*) transmit certified true copies of the present Convention to all Signatory States and to all States which have acceded to the present Convention.

3. As soon as the present Convention comes into force, a certified true copy thereof shall be transmitted by the Secretary–General of the Organization to the Secretariat of the United Nations for registration and publication in accordance with Article 102 of the Charter of the United Nations.

Article 12. The present Convention is established in a single original in the English and French languages, both texts being equally authentic. Official translations in the Russian and Spanish languages shall be prepared by the Secretariat of the Organization and deposited with the signed original.

4.12 INTERNATIONAL CONVENTION ON THE ESTABLISHMENT OF AN INTERNATIONAL FUND FOR COMPENSATION FOR OIL POLLUTION DAMAGE (WITHOUT ANNEX AND PROTOCOLS).[1] Concluded at Brussels, 18 December 1971. Entered into force, 16 October 1978. 1971 U.N.J.Y.B. 103

* * *

GENERAL PROVISIONS

Article 1. For the purposes of this Convention:

1. "Liability Convention" means the International Convention on Civil Liability for Oil Pollution Damage, adopted at Brussels on 29 November 1969.

2. "Ship", "Person", "Owner", "Oil", "Pollution Damage", "Preventive Measures", "Incident" and "Organization", have the same meaning as in Article I of the Liability Convention, provided however that, for the purposes of these terms, "oil" shall be confined to persistent hydrocarbon mineral oils.

3. "Contributing Oil" means crude oil and fuel oil as defined in subparagraphs (*a*) and (*b*) below:

(*a*) "Crude Oil" means any liquid hydrocarbon mixture occurring naturally in the earth whether or not treated to render it suitable for transportation. It also includes crude oils from which certain distillate fractions have been removed (sometimes referred to as "topped crudes") or to which certain distillate fractions have been added (sometimes referred to as "spiked" or "reconstituted" crudes).

(*b*) "Fuel Oil" means heavy distillates or residues from crude oil or blends of such materials intended for use as a fuel for the production of heat or power of a quality equivalent to the "American Society for Testing and Materials' Specification for Number Four Fuel Oil (Designation D 396–69)", or heavier.

4. "Franc" means the unit referred to in Article V, paragraph 9, of the Liability Convention.

5. "Ship's tonnage" has the same meaning as in Article V, paragraph 10, of the Liability Convention.

6. "Ton", in relation to oil, means a metric ton.

7. "Guarantor" means any person providing insurance or other financial security to cover an owner's liability in pursuance of Article VII, paragraph 1, of the Liability Convention.

8. "Terminal installation" means any site for the storage of oil in bulk which is capable of receiving oil from waterborne transportation, including any facility situated off-shore and linked to such site.

9. Where an incident consists of a series of occurrences, it shall be treated as having occurred on the date of the first such occurrence.

Article 2. 1. An International Fund for compensation for pollution damage, to be named "the International Oil Pollution Compensation Fund" and hereinafter referred to as "the Fund", is hereby established with the following aims:

---

1. *But see* Basic Document 4.19 and 4.29, *infra.*

(*a*) To provide compensation for pollution damage to the extent that the protection afforded by the Liability Convention is inadequate;

(*b*) To give relief to shipowners in respect of the additional financial burden imposed on them by the Liability Convention, such relief being subject to conditions designed to ensure compliance with safety at sea and other conventions;

(*c*) To give effect to the related purposes set out in this Convention.

2. The Fund shall in each Contracting State be recognized as a legal person capable under the laws of that State of assuming rights and obligations and of being a party in legal proceedings before the courts of that State. Each Contracting State shall recognize the Director of the Fund (hereinafter referred to as "the Director") as the legal representative of the Fund.

Article 3. This Convention shall apply:

1. With regard to compensation according to Article 4, exclusively to pollution damage caused on the territory including the territorial sea of a Contracting State, and to preventive measures taken to prevent or minimize such damage;

2. With regard to indemnification of shipowners and their guarantors according to Article 5, exclusively in respect of pollution damage caused on the territory, including the territorial sea, of a State party to the Liability Convention by a ship registered in or flying the flag of a Contracting State and in respect of preventive measures taken to prevent or minimize such damage.

COMPENSATION AND INDEMNIFICATION

Article 4. 1. For the purpose of fulfilling its function under Article 2, paragraph 1(*a*), the Fund shall pay compensation to any person suffering pollution damage if such person has been unable to obtain full and adequate compensation for the damage under the terms of the Liability Convention,

(*a*) Because no liability for the damage arises under the Liability Convention;

(*b*) Because the owner liable for the damage under the Liability Convention is financially incapable of meeting his obligations in full and any financial security that may be provided under Article VII of that Convention does not cover or is insufficient to satisfy the claims for compensation for the damage; an owner being treated as financially incapable of meeting his obligations and a financial security being treated as insufficient if the person suffering the damage has been unable to obtain full satisfaction of the amount of compensation due under the Liability Convention after having taken all reasonable steps to pursue the legal remedies available to him;

(*c*) Because the damage exceeds the owner's liability under the Liability Convention as limited pursuant to Article V, paragraph 1, of that Convention or under the terms of any other international Convention in force or open for signature, ratification or accession at the date of this Convention.

Expenses reasonably incurred or sacrifices reasonably made by the owner voluntarily to prevent or minimize pollution damage shall be treated as pollution damage for the purposes of this Article.

2. The Fund shall incur no obligation under the preceding paragraph if:

(*a*) It proves that the pollution damage resulted from an act of war, hostilities, civil war or insurrection or was caused by oil which has escaped or been discharged from a warship or other ship owned or operated by a State and used, at the time of the incident, only on Government non-commercial service; or

(*b*) The claimant cannot prove that the damage resulted from an incident involving one or more ships.

3. If the Fund proves that the pollution damage resulted wholly or partially either from an act or omission done with intent to cause damage by the person who suffered the damage or from the negligence of that person, the Fund may be exonerated wholly or partially from its obligation to pay compensation to such person provided, however, that there shall be no such exoneration with regard to such preventive measures which are compensated under paragraph 1. The Fund shall in any event be exonerated to the extent that the shipowner may have been exonerated under Article III, paragraph 3, of the Liability Convention.

4. (*a*) Except as otherwise provided in subparagraph (*b*) of this paragraph, the aggregate amount of compensation payable by the Fund under this Article shall in respect of any one incident be limited, so that the total sum of that amount and the amount of compensation actually paid under the Liability Convention for pollution damage caused in the territory of the Contracting States, including any sums in respect of which the Fund is under an obligation to indemnify the owner pursuant to Article 5, paragraph 1, of this Convention, shall not exceed 450 million francs.

(*b*) The aggregate amount of compensation payable by the Fund under this Article for pollution damage resulting from a natural phenomenon of an exceptional, inevitable and irresistible character shall not exceed 450 million francs.

5. Where the amount of established claims against the Fund exceeds the aggregate amount of compensation payable under paragraph 4, the amount available shall be distributed in such a manner that the proportion between any established claim and the amount of compensation actually recovered by the claimant under the Liability Convention and this Convention shall be the same for all claimants.

6. The Assembly of the Fund (hereinafter referred to as "the Assembly") may, having regard to the experience of incidents which have occurred and in particular the amount of damage resulting therefrom and to changes in the monetary values, decide that the amount of 450 million francs referred to in paragraph 4, sub-paragraphs (*a*) and (*b*), shall be changed; provided, however, that this amount shall in no case exceed 900 million francs or be lower than 450 million francs. The changed amount shall apply to incidents which occur after the date of the decision effecting the change.

7. The Fund shall, at the request of a Contracting State, use its good offices as necessary to assist that State to secure promptly such personnel,

material and services as are necessary to enable the State to take measures to prevent or mitigate pollution damage arising from an incident in respect of which the Fund may be called upon to pay compensation under this Convention.

8. The Fund may, on conditions to be laid down in the Internal Regulations, provide credit facilities with a view to the taking of preventive measures against pollution damage arising from a particular incident in respect of which the Fund may be called upon to pay compensation under this Convention.

Article 5. 1. For the purpose of fulfilling its function under Article 2, paragraph 1(*b*), the Fund shall indemnify the owner and his guarantor for that portion of the aggregate amount of liability under the Liability Convention which:

(*a*) Is in excess of an amount equivalent to 1,500 francs for each ton of the ship's tonnage or of an amount of 125 million francs, whichever is the less, and

(*b*) Is not in excess of an amount equivalent to 2,000 francs for each ton of the said tonnage or an amount of 210 million francs, whichever is the less,

provided, however, that the Fund shall incur no obligation under this paragraph where the pollution damage resulted from the wilful misconduct of the owner himself.

2. The Assembly may decide that the Fund shall, on conditions to be laid down in the Internal Regulations, assume the obligations of a guarantor in respect of ships referred to in Article 3, paragraph 2, with regard to the portion of liability referred to in paragraph 1 of this Article. However, the Fund shall assume such obligations only if the owner so requests and if he maintains adequate insurance or other financial security covering the owner's liability under the Liability Convention up to an amount equivalent to 1,500 francs for each ton of the ship's tonnage or an amount of 125 million francs, whichever is the less. If the Fund assumes such obligations, the owner shall in each Contracting State be considered to have complied with Article VII of the Liability Convention in respect of the portion of his liability mentioned above.

3. The Fund may be exonerated wholly or partially from its obligations under paragraph 1 towards the owner and his guarantor if the Fund proves that as a result of the actual fault or privity of the owner:

(*a*) The ship from which the oil causing the pollution damage escaped did not comply with the requirements laid down in:

(i) The International Convention for the Prevention of Pollution of the Sea by Oil, 1954, as amended in 1962; or

(ii) The International Convention for the Safety of Life at Sea, 1960; or

(iii) The International Convention on Load Lines, 1966; or

(iv) The International Regulations for Preventing Collisions at Sea, 1960; or

(v) Any amendments to the above-mentioned Conventions which have been determined as being of an important nature in accordance with Article XVI(5) of the Convention mentioned under (i), Article IX(*e*) of the Convention mentioned under (ii) or Article 29(3)(*d*) or (4)(*d*) of the Convention mentioned under (iii), provided, however, that such amendments had been in force for at least twelve months at the time of the incident; and

(*b*) The incident or damage was caused wholly or partially by such non-compliance.

The provisions of this paragraph shall apply irrespective of whether the Contracting State in which the ship was registered or whose flag it was flying is a Party to the relevant Instrument.

4. Upon the entry into force of a new Convention designed to replace, in whole or in part, any of the Instruments specified in paragraph 3, the Assembly may decide at least six months in advance a date on which the new Convention will replace such Instrument or part thereof for the purpose of paragraph 3.   However, any State Party to this Convention may declare to the Director before that date that it does not accept such replacement;   in which case the decision of the Assembly shall have no effect in respect of a ship registered in, or flying the flag of, that State at the time of the incident. Such a declaration may be withdrawn at any later date and shall in any event cease to have effect when the State in question becomes a party to such new Convention.

5. A ship complying with the requirements in an amendment to an Instrument specified in paragraph 3 or with requirements in a new Convention, where the amendment or Convention is designed to replace in whole or in part such Instrument, shall be considered as complying with the requirements in the said Instrument for the purposes of paragraph 3.

6. Where the Fund, acting as a guarantor by virtue of paragraph 2, has paid compensation for pollution damage in accordance with the Liability Convention, it shall have a right of recovery from the owner if and to the extent that the Fund would have been exonerated pursuant to paragraph 3 from its obligations under paragraph 1 to indemnify the owner.

7. Expenses reasonably incurred and sacrifices reasonably made by the owner voluntarily to prevent or minimize pollution damage shall be treated as included in the owner's liability for the purposes of this Article.

Article 6.   1. Rights to compensation under Article 4 or indemnification under Article 5 shall be extinguished unless an action is brought thereunder or a notification has been made pursuant to Article 7, paragraph 6, within three years from the date when the damage occurred.   However, in no case shall an action be brought after six years from the date of the incident which caused the damage.

2. Notwithstanding paragraph 1, the right of the owner or his guarantor to seek indemnification from the Fund pursuant to Article 5, paragraph 1, shall in no case be extinguished before the expiry of a period of six months as from the date on which the owner or his guarantor acquired knowledge of the bringing of an action against him under the Liability Convention.

Article 7. 1. Subject to the subsequent provisions of this Article, any action against the Fund for compensation under Article 4 or indemnification under Article 5 of this Convention shall be brought only before a court competent under Article IX of the Liability Convention in respect of actions against the owner who is or who would, but for the provisions of Article III, paragraph 2, of that Convention, have been liable for pollution damage caused by the relevant incident.

2. Each Contracting State shall ensure that its courts possess the necessary jurisdiction to entertain such actions against the Fund as are referred to in paragraph 1.

3. Where an action for compensation for pollution damage has been brought before a court competent under Article IX of the Liability Convention against the owner of a ship or his guarantor, such court shall have exclusive jurisdictional competence over any action against the Fund for compensation or indemnification under the provisions of Article 4 or 5 of this Convention in respect of the same damage. However, where an action for compensation for pollution damage under the Liability Convention has been brought before a court in a State Party to the Liability Convention but not to this Convention, any action against the Fund under Article 4 or under Article 5, paragraph 1, of this Convention shall at the option of the claimant be brought either before a court of the State where the Fund has its headquarters or before any court of a State Party to this Convention competent under Article IX of the Liability Convention.

4. Each Contracting State shall ensure that the Fund shall have the right to intervene as a party to any legal proceedings instituted in accordance with Article IX of the Liability Convention before a competent court of that State against the owner of a ship or his guarantor.

5. Except as otherwise provided in paragraph 6, the Fund shall not be bound by any judgment or decision in proceedings to which it has not been a party or by any settlement to which it is not a party.

6. Without prejudice to the provisions of paragraph 4, where an action under the Liability Convention for compensation for pollution damage has been brought against an owner or his guarantor before a competent court in a Contracting State, each party to the proceedings shall be entitled under the national law of that State to notify the Fund of the proceedings. Where such notification has been made in accordance with the formalities required by the law of the court seized and in such time and in such a manner that the Fund has in fact been in a position effectively to intervene as a party to the proceedings, any judgment rendered by the court in such proceedings shall, after it has become final and enforceable in the State where the judgment was given, become binding upon the Fund in the sense that the facts and findings in that judgment may not be disputed by the Fund even if the Fund has not actually intervened in the proceedings.

Article 8. Subject to any decision concerning the distribution referred to in Article 4, paragraph 5, any judgment given against the Fund by a court having jurisdiction in accordance with Article 7, paragraphs 1 and 3, shall, when it has become enforceable in the State of origin and is in that State no longer subject to ordinary forms of review, be recognized and enforceable in each Contracting State on the same conditions as are prescribed in Article X of the Liability Convention.

Article 9. 1. Subject to the provisions of Article 5, the Fund shall, in respect of any amount of compensation for pollution damage paid by the Fund in accordance with Article 4, paragraph 1, of this Convention, acquire by subrogation the rights that the person so compensated may enjoy under the Liability Convention against the owner or his guarantor.

2. Nothing in this Convention shall prejudice any right of recourse or subrogation of the Fund against persons other than those referred to in the preceding paragraph. In any event the right of the Fund to subrogation against such person shall not be less favourable than that of an insurer of the person to whom compensation or indemnification has been paid.

3. Without prejudice to any other rights of subrogation or recourse against the Fund which may exist, a Contracting State or agency thereof which has paid compensation for pollution damage in accordance with provisions of national law shall acquire by subrogation the rights which the person so compensated would have enjoyed under this Convention.

CONTRIBUTIONS

Article 10. 1. Contributions to the Fund shall be made in respect of each Contracting State by any person who, in the calendar year referred to in Article 11, paragraph 1, as regards initial contributions and in Article 12, paragraphs 2(*a*) or (*b*), as regards annual contributions, has received in total quantities exceeding 150,000 tons:

(*a*) In the ports or terminal installations in the territory of that State contributing oil carried by sea to such ports or terminal installations; and

(*b*) In any installations situated in the territory of that Contracting State contributing oil which has been carried by sea and discharged in a port or terminal installation of a non-Contracting State, provided that contributing oil shall only be taken into account by virtue of this sub-paragraph on first receipt in a Contracting State after its discharge in that non-Contracting State.

2. (*a*) For the purposes of paragraph 1, where the quantity of contributing oil received in the territory of a Contracting State by any person in a calendar year when aggregated with the quantity of contributing oil received in the same Contracting State in that year by any associated person or persons exceeds 150,000 tons, such person shall pay contributions in respect of the actual quantity received by him notwithstanding that that quantity did not exceed 150,000 tons.

(*b*) "Associated person" means any subsidiary or commonly controlled entity. The question whether a person comes within this definition shall be determined by the national law of the State concerned.

Article 11. 1. In respect of each Contracting State initial contributions shall be made of an amount which shall for each person referred to in Article 10 be calculated on the basis of a fixed sum for each ton of contributing oil received by him during the calendar year preceding that in which this Convention entered into force for that State.

2. The sum referred to in paragraph 1 shall be determined by the Assembly within two months after the entry into force of this Convention. In performing this function the Assembly shall, to the extent possible, fix the sum in such a way that the total amount of initial contributions would, if contributions were to be made in respect of 90 per cent of the quantities of contributing oil carried by sea in the world, equal 75 million francs.

3. The initial contributions shall in respect of each Contracting State be paid within three months following the date at which the Convention entered into force for that State.

Article 12. 1. With a view to assessing for each person referred to in Article 10 the amount of annual contributions due, if any, and taking account of the necessity to maintain sufficient liquid funds, the Assembly shall for each calendar year make an estimate in the form of a budget of:

(i) Expenditure

(*a*) Costs and expenses of the administration of the Fund in the relevant year and any deficit from operations in preceding years;

(*b*) Payments to be made by the Fund in the relevant year for the satisfaction of claims against the Fund due under Article 4 or 5, including repayment on loans previously taken by the Fund for the satisfaction of such claims, to the extent that the aggregate amount of such claims in respect of any one incident does not exceed 15 million francs;

(*c*) Payments to be made by the Fund in the relevant year for the satisfaction of claims against the Fund due under Article 4 or 5, including repayments on loans previously taken by the Fund for the satisfaction of such claims, to the extent that the aggregate amount of such claims in respect of any one incident is in excess of 15 million francs;

(ii) Income

(*a*) Surplus funds from operations in preceding years, including any interest;

(*b*) Initial contributions to be paid in the course of the year;

(*c*) Annual contributions, if required to balance the budget;

(*d*) Any other income.

2. For each person referred to in Article 10 the amount of his annual contribution shall be determined by the Assembly and shall be calculated in respect of each Contracting State:

(*a*) In so far as the contribution is for the satisfaction of payments referred to in paragraph 1(i)(*a*) and (*b*) on the basis of a fixed sum for each ton of contributing oil received in the relevant State by such persons during the preceding calendar year; and

(*b*) In so far as the contribution is for the satisfaction of payments referred to in paragraph 1(i)(*c*) of this Article on the basis of a fixed sum for each ton of contributing oil received by such person during the calendar year preceding that in which the incident in question occurred, provided that State was a party to this Convention at the date of the incident.

3. The sums referred to in paragraph 2 above shall be arrived at by dividing the relevant total amount of contributions required by the total amount of contributing oil received in all Contracting States in the relevant year.

4. The Assembly shall decide the portion of the annual contribution which shall be immediately paid in cash and decide on the date of payment. The remaining part of each annual contribution shall be paid upon notification by the Director.

5. The Director may, in cases and in accordance with conditions to be laid down in the Internal Regulations of the Fund, require a contributor to provide financial security for the sums due from him.

6. Any demand for payments made under paragraph 4 shall be called rateably from all individual contributors.

Article 13. 1. The amount of any contribution due under Article 12 and which is in arrears shall bear interest at a rate which shall be determined by the Assembly for each calendar year provided that different rates may be fixed for different circumstances.

2. Each Contracting State shall ensure that any obligation to contribute to the Fund arising under this Convention in respect of oil received within the territory of that State is fulfilled and shall take any appropriate measures under its law, including the imposing of such sanctions as it may deem necessary, with a view to the effective execution of any such obligation; provided, however, that such measures shall only be directed against those persons who are under an obligation to contribute to the Fund.

3. Where a person who is liable in accordance with the provisions of Articles 10 and 11 to make contributions to the Fund does not fulfil his obligations in respect of any such contribution or any part thereof and is in arrears for a period exceeding three months, the Director shall take all appropriate action against such person on behalf of the Fund with a view to the recovery of the amount due. However, where the defaulting contributor is manifestly insolvent or the circumstances otherwise so warrant, the Assembly may, upon recommendation of the Director, decide that no action shall be taken or continued against the contributor.

Article 14. 1. Each Contracting State may at the time when it deposits its instrument of ratification or accession or at any time thereafter declare that it assumes itself obligations that are incumbent under this Convention on any person who is liable to contribute to the Fund in accordance with Article 10, paragraph 1, in respect of oil received within the territory of that State. Such declaration shall be made in writing and shall specify which obligations are assumed.

2. Where a declaration under paragraph 1 is made prior to the entry into force of this Convention in accordance with Article 40, it shall be deposited with the Secretary–General of the Organization who shall after the entry into force of the Convention communicate the declaration to the Director.

3. A declaration under paragraph 1 which is made after the entry into force of this Convention shall be deposited with the Director.

4. A declaration made in accordance with this Article may be withdrawn by the relevant State giving notice thereof in writing to the Director. Such notification shall take effect three months after the Director's receipt thereof.

5. Any State which is bound by a declaration made under this Article shall, in any proceedings brought against it before a competent court in respect of any obligation specified in the declaration, waive any immunity that it would otherwise be entitled to invoke.

Article 15. 1. Each Contracting State shall ensure that any person who receives contributing oil within its territory in such quantities that he is liable to contribute to the Fund appears on a list to be established and kept up to date by the Director in accordance with the subsequent provisions of this Article.

2. For the purposes set out in paragraph 1, each Contracting State shall communicate, at a time and in the manner to be prescribed in the Internal Regulations, to the Director the name and address of any person who in respect of that State is liable to contribute to the Fund pursuant to Article 10, as well as data on the relevant quantities of contributing oil received by any such person during the preceding calendar year.

3. For the purposes of ascertaining who are, at any given time, the persons liable to contribute to the Fund in accordance with Article 10, paragraph 1, and of establishing, where applicable, the quantities of oil to be taken into account for any such person when determining the amount of his contribution, the list shall be *prima facie* evidence of the facts stated therein.

ORGANIZATION AND ADMINISTRATION

Article 16. The Fund shall have an Assembly, a Secretariat headed by a Director and, in accordance with the provisions of Article 21, an Executive Committee.

ASSEMBLY

Article 17. The Assembly shall consist of all Contracting States to this Convention.

Article 18. The functions of the Assembly shall, subject to the provisions of Article 26, be:

1. To elect at each regular session its Chairman and two Vice–Chairmen who shall hold office until the next regular session;

2. To determine its own rules of procedure, subject to the provisions of this Convention;

3. To adopt Internal Regulations necessary for the proper functioning of the Fund;

4. To appoint the Director and make provisions for the appointment of such other personnel as may be necessary and determine the terms and conditions of service of the Director and other personnel;

5. To adopt the annual budget and fix the annual contributions;

6. To appoint auditors and approve the accounts of the Fund;

7. To approve settlements of claims against the Fund, to take decisions in respect of the distribution among claimants of the available amount of compensation in accordance with Article 4, paragraph 5, and to determine the terms and conditions according to which provisional payments in respect of claims shall be made with a view to ensuring that victims of pollution damage are compensated as promptly as possible;

8. To elect the members of the Assembly to be represented on the Executive Committee, as provided in Articles 21, 22 and 23;

9. To establish any temporary or permanent subsidiary body it may consider to be necessary;

10. To determine which non-Contracting States and which intergovernmental and international non-governmental organizations shall be admitted to take part, without voting rights, in meetings of the Assembly, the Executive Committee, and subsidiary bodies;

11. To give instructions concerning the administration of the Fund to the Director, the Executive Committee and subsidiary bodies;

12. To review and approve the reports and activities of the Executive Committee;

13. To supervise the proper execution of the Convention and of its own decisions;

14. To perform such other functions as are allocated to it under the Convention or are otherwise necessary for the proper operation of the Fund.

Article 19. 1. Regular sessions of the Assembly shall take place once every calendar year upon convocation by the Director; provided, however, that if the Assembly allocates to the Executive Committee the functions specified in Article 18, paragraph 5, regular sessions of the Assembly shall be held once every two years.

2. Extraordinary sessions of the Assembly shall be convened by the Director at the request of the Executive Committee or of at least one third of the members of the Assembly and may be convened on the Director's own initiative after consultation with the Chairman of the Assembly. The Director shall give members at least thirty days' notice of such sessions.

Article 20. A majority of the members of the Assembly shall constitute a quorum for its meetings.

EXECUTIVE COMMITTEE

Article 21. The Executive Committee shall be established at the first regular session of the Assembly after the date on which the number of Contracting States reaches fifteen.

Article 22. 1. The Executive Committee shall consist of one third of the members of the Assembly but of not less than seven or more than fifteen members. Where the number of members of the Assembly is not divisible by three, the one third referred to shall be calculated on the next higher number which is divisible by three.

2. When electing the members of the Executive Committee the Assembly shall:

(*a*) Secure an equitable geographical distribution of the seats on the Committee on the basis of an adequate representation of Contracting States particularly exposed to the risks of oil pollution and of Contracting States having large tanker fleets; and

(*b*) Elect one half of the members of the Committee, or in case the total number of members to be elected is uneven, such number of the members as is equivalent to one half of the total number less one, among those Contracting States in the territory of which the largest quantities of oil to be taken into account under Article 10 were received during the preceding calendar year, provided that the number of States eligible under this sub-paragraph shall be limited as shown in the table below:

Total number of Members on the Committee	Number of States eligible under sub-paragraph (b)	Number of States to be elected under sub-paragraph (b)
7	5	3
8	6	4
9	6	4
10	8	5
11	8	5
12	9	6
13	9	6
14	11	7
15	11	7

3. A member of the Assembly which was eligible but was not elected under sub-paragraph (*b*) shall not be eligible to be elected for any remaining seat on the Executive Committee.

Article 23. 1. Members of the Executive Committee shall hold office until the end of the next regular session of the Assembly.

2. Except to the extent that may be necessary for complying with the requirements of Article 22, no State Member of the Assembly may serve on the Executive Committee for more than two consecutive terms.

Article 24. The Executive Committee shall meet at least once every calendar year at thirty days' notice upon convocation by the Director, either on his own initiative or at the request of its Chairman or of at least one third of its members. It shall meet at such places as may be convenient.

Article 25. At least two thirds of the members of the Executive Committee shall constitute a quorum for its meetings.

Article 26. 1. The functions of the Executive Committee shall be:

(*a*) To elect its Chairman and adopt its own rules of procedure, except as otherwise provided in this Convention;

(*b*) To assume and exercise in place of the Assembly the following functions:

(i) Making provision for the appointment of such personnel, other than the Director, as may be necessary and determining the terms and conditions of service of such personnel;

(ii) Approving settlements of claims against the Fund and taking all other steps envisaged in relation to such claims in Article 18, paragraph 7;

(iii) Giving instructions to the Director concerning the administration of the Fund and supervising the proper execution by him of the Convention, of the decisions of the Assembly and of the Committee's own decisions; and

(c) To perform such other functions as are allocated to it by the Assembly.

2. The Executive Committee shall each year prepare and publish a report of the activities of the Fund during the previous calendar year.

Article 27. Members of the Assembly who are not members of the Executive Committee shall have the right to attend its meetings as observers.

SECRETARIAT

Article 28. 1. The Secretariat shall comprise the Director and such staff as the administration of the Fund may require.

2. The Director shall be the legal representative of the Fund.

Article 29. 1. The Director shall be the chief administrative officer of the Fund and shall, subject to the instructions given to him by the Assembly and by the Executive Committee, perform those functions which are assigned to him by this Convention, the Internal Regulations, the Assembly and the Executive Committee.

2. The Director shall in particular:

(a) Appoint the personnel required for the administration of the Fund;

(b) Take all appropriate measures with a view to the proper administration of the Fund's assets;

(c) Collect the contributions due under this Convention while observing in particular the provisions of Article 13, paragraph 3;

(d) To the extent necessary to deal with claims against the Fund and carry out the other functions of the Fund, employ the services of legal, financial and other experts;

(e) Take all appropriate measures for dealing with claims against the Fund within the limits and on conditions to be laid down in the Internal Regulations, including the final settlement of claims without the prior approval of the Assembly or the Executive Committee where these Regulations so provide;

(f) Prepare and submit to the Assembly or to the Executive Committee, as the case may be, the financial statements and budget estimates for each calendar year;

(g) Assist the Executive Committee in the preparation of the report referred to in Article 26, paragraph 2;

(h) Prepare, collect and circulate the papers, documents, agenda, minutes and information that may be required for the work of the Assembly, the Executive Committee and subsidiary bodies.

Article 30. In the performance of their duties the Director and the staff and experts appointed by him shall not seek or receive instructions from any Government or from any authority external to the Fund. They shall refrain from any action which might reflect on their position as international officials. Each Contracting State on its part undertakes to respect the exclusively international character of the responsibilities of the Director and the staff and experts appointed by him, and not to seek to influence them in the discharge of their duties.

FINANCES

Article 31. 1. Each Contracting State shall bear the salary, travel and other expenses of its own delegation to the Assembly and of its representatives on the Executive Committee and on subsidiary bodies.

2. Any other expenses incurred in the operation of the Fund shall be borne by the Fund.

VOTING

Article 32. The following provisions shall apply to voting in the Assembly and the Executive Committee:

(*a*) Each member shall have one vote;

(*b*) Except as otherwise provided in Article 33, decisions of the Assembly and the Executive Committee shall be by a majority vote of the members present and voting;

(*c*) Decisions where a three-fourths or a two-thirds majority is required shall be by a three-fourths or two-thirds majority vote, as the case may be, of those present;

(*d*) For the purpose of this Article the phrase "members present" means "members present at the meeting at the time of the vote", and the phrase "members present and voting" means "members present and casting an affirmative or negative vote". Members who abstain from voting shall be considered as not voting.

Article 33. 1. The following decisions of the Assembly shall require a three-fourths majority:

(*a*) An increase in accordance with Article 4, paragraph 6, in the maximum amount of compensation payable by the Fund;

(*b*) A determination, under Article 5, paragraph 4, relating to the replacement of the Instruments referred to in that paragraph;

(*c*) The allocation to the Executive Committee of the functions specified in Article 18, paragraph 5.

2. The following decisions of the Assembly shall require a two-thirds majority:

(*a*) A decision under Article 13, paragraph 3, not to take or continue action against a contributor;

(*b*) The appointment of the Director under Article 18, paragraph 4;

(*c*) The establishment of subsidiary bodies, under Article 18, paragraph 9.

Article 34. 1. The Fund, its assets, income, including contributions, and other property shall enjoy in all Contracting States exemption from all direct taxation.

2. When the Fund makes substantial purchases of movable or immovable property, or has important work carried out which is necessary for the exercise of its official activities and the cost of which includes indirect taxes or sales taxes, the Governments of Member States shall take, whenever possible, appropriate measures for the remission or refund of the amount of such duties and taxes.

3. No exemption shall be accorded in the case of duties, taxes or dues which merely constitute payment for public utility services.

4. The Fund shall enjoy exemption from all customs duties, taxes and other related taxes on articles imported or exported by it or on its behalf for its official use. Articles thus imported shall not be transferred either for consideration or gratis on the territory of the country into which they have been imported except on conditions agreed by the government of that country.

5. Persons contributing to the Fund and victims and owners of ships receiving compensation from the Fund shall be subject to the fiscal legislation of the State where they are taxable, no special exemption or other benefit being conferred on them in this respect.

6. Information relating to individual contributors supplied for the purpose of this Convention shall not be divulged outside the Fund except in so far as it may be strictly necessary to enable the Fund to carry out its functions including the bringing and defending of legal proceedings.

7. Independently of existing or future regulations concerning currency or transfers, Contracting States shall authorize the transfer and payment of any contribution to the Fund and of any compensation paid by the Fund without any restriction.

Transitional Provisions

Article 35. 1. The Fund shall incur no obligation whatsoever under Article 4 or 5 in respect of incidents occurring within a period of one hundred and twenty days after the entry into force of this Convention.

2. Claims for compensation under Article 4 and claims for indemnification under Article 5, arising from incidents occurring later than one hundred and twenty days but not later than two hundred and forty days after the entry into force of this Convention may not be brought against the Fund prior to the elapse of the two hundred and fortieth day after the entry into force of this Convention.

Article 36. The Secretary–General of the Organization shall convene the first session of the Assembly. This session shall take place as soon as possible after entry into force of this Convention and, in any case, not more than thirty days after such entry into force.

Final Clauses

Article 37. 1. This Convention shall be open for signature by the States which have signed or which accede to the Liability Convention, and by any State represented at the Conference on the Establishment of an International

Fund for Compensation for Oil Pollution Damage, 1971. The Convention shall remain open for signature until 31 December 1972.

2. Subject to paragraph 4, this Convention shall be ratified, accepted or approved by the States which have signed it.

3. Subject to paragraph 4, this Convention is open for accession by States which did not sign it.

4. This Convention may be ratified, accepted, approved or acceded to, only by States which have ratified, accepted, approved or acceded to the Liability Convention.

Article 38. 1. Ratification, acceptance, approval or accession shall be effected by the deposit of a formal instrument to that effect with the Secretary–General of the Organization.

2. Any instrument of ratification, acceptance, approval or accession deposited after the entry into force of an amendment to this Convention with respect to all existing Contracting States or after the completion of all measures required for the entry into force of the amendment with respect to those Parties shall be deemed to apply to the Convention as modified by the amendment.

Article 39. Before this Convention comes into force a State shall, when depositing an instrument referred to in Article 38, paragraph 1, and annually thereafter at a date to be determined by the Secretary–General of the Organization, communicate to him the name and address of any person who in respect of that State would be liable to contribute to the Fund pursuant to Article 10 as well as data on the relevant quantities of contributing oil received by any such person in the territory of that State during the preceding calendar year.

Article 40. 1. This Convention shall enter into force on the ninetieth day following the date on which the following requirements are fulfilled:

(*a*) At least eight States have deposited instruments of ratification, acceptance, approval or accession with the Secretary–General of the Organization, and

(*b*) The Secretary–General of the Organization has received information in accordance with Article 39 that those persons in such States who would be liable to contribute pursuant to Article 10 have received during the preceding calendar year a total quantity of at least 750 million tons of contributing oil.

2. However, this Convention shall not enter into force before the Liability Convention has entered into force.

3. For each State which subsequently ratifies, accepts, approves or accedes to it, this Convention shall enter into force on the ninetieth day after deposit by such State of the appropriate instrument.

Article 41. 1. This Convention may be denounced by any Contracting State at any time after the date on which the Convention comes into force for that State.

2. Denunciation shall be effected by the deposit of an instrument with the Secretary–General of the Organization.

3. A denunciation shall take effect one year, or such longer period as may be specified in the instrument of denunciation, after its deposit with the Secretary–General of the Organization.

4. Denunciation of the Liability Convention shall be deemed to be a denunciation of this Convention. Such denunciation shall take effect on the same date as the denunciation of the Liability Convention takes effect according to paragraph 3 of Article XVI of that Convention.

5. Notwithstanding a denunciation by a Contracting State pursuant to this Article, any provisions of this Convention relating to the obligations to make contributions under Article 10 with respect to an incident referred to in Article 12, paragraph 2(b), and occurring before the denunciation takes effect shall continue to apply.

Article 42. 1. Any Contracting State may, within ninety days after the deposit of an instrument of denunciation the result of which it considers will significantly increase the level of contributions for remaining Contracting States, request the Director to convene an extraordinary session of the Assembly. The Director shall convene the Assembly to meet not later than sixty days after receipt of the request.

2. The Director may convene, on his own initiative, an extraordinary session of the Assembly to meet within sixty days after the deposit of any instrument of denunciation, if he considers that such denunciation will result in a significant increase in the level of contributions for the remaining Contracting States.

3. If the Assembly at an extraordinary session convened in accordance with paragraph 1 or 2 decides that the denunciation will result in a significant increase in the level of contributions for the remaining Contracting States, any such State may, not later than one hundred and twenty days before the date on which that denunciation takes effect, denounce this Convention with effect from the same date.

Article 43. 1. This Convention shall cease to be in force on the date when the number of Contracting States falls below three.

2. Contracting States which are bound by this Convention on the date before the day it ceases to be in force shall enable the Fund to exercise its functions as described under Article 44 and shall, for that purpose only, remain bound by this Convention.

Article 44. 1. If this Convention ceases to be in force, the Fund shall nevertheless

(a) Meet its obligations in respect of any incident occurring before the Convention ceased to be in force;

(b) Be entitled to exercise its rights to contributions to the extent that these contributions are necessary to meet the obligations under subparagraph (a), including expenses for the administration of the Fund necessary for this purpose.

2. The Assembly shall take all appropriate measures to complete the winding up of the Fund, including the distribution in an equitable manner of any remaining assets among those persons who have contributed to the Fund.

3. For the purposes of this Article the Fund shall remain a legal person.

Article 45. 1. A Conference for the purpose of revising or amending this Convention may be convened by the Organization.

2. The Organization shall convene a Conference of the Contracting States for the purpose of revising or amending this Convention at the request of not less than one-third of all Contracting States.

Article 46. 1. This Convention shall be deposited with the Secretary–General of the Organization.

2. The Secretary–General of the Organization shall:

(*a*) Inform all States which have signed or acceded to this Convention of:

(i) Each new signature or deposit of instrument and the date thereof;

(ii) The date of entry into force of the Convention;

(iii) Any denunciation of the Convention and the date on which it takes effect;

(*b*) Transmit certified true copies of this Convention to all Signatory States and to all States which accede to the Convention.

Article 47. As soon as this Convention enters into force, a certified true copy thereof shall be transmitted by the Secretary–General of the Organization to the Secretariat of the United Nations for registration and publication in accordance with Article 102 of the Charter of the United Nations.

Article 48. This Convention is established in a single original in the English and French languages, both texts being equally authentic. Official translations in the Russian and Spanish languages shall be prepared by the Secretariat of the Organization and deposited with the signed original.

4.13   ILA DRAFT ARTICLES ON MARINE POLLUTION OF CONTINENTAL ORIGIN (WITHOUT COMMENTS). Adopted 26 August 1972. 55 I.L.A. XVII 97 (1972)

Article I

As used in this chapter "Continental sea-water pollution" means any detrimental change in the natural composition, content or quality of sea water resulting from human conduct taking place within the limits of the national jurisdiction of a State.

This conduct shall include, *inter alia,* the discharge or introduction of substances directly into the sea from pipelines, extended outlets, or ships, or indirectly through rivers or other watercourses whether natural or artificial, or through atmospheric fall-out.

Article II

Taking into account all relevant factors referred to in Article III, a State

(a) shall prevent any new form of continental sea-water pollution or any increase in the degree of existing continental sea-water pollution which would cause substantial injury in the territory of another State or to any of its rights under international law or to the marine environment, and

(b) shall take all reasonable measures to abate existing continental sea-water pollution to such an extent that no substantial injury of the kind referred to in paragraph (a) is caused.

Article III

(a) States should establish, as soon as possible, international standards for the control of sea-water pollution, having regard to all relevant factors, including the following:—

— the geography and hydrography of the area (inland waters, territorial sea, contiguous zone and continental shelf);

— climatological conditions;

— quality and composition of affected sea waters;

— the conservation of the maritime environment (flora and fauna);

— the resources of the sea-bed and the subsoil and their economic value for present and potential users;

— the recreational facilities of the coastal area;

— the past, present and future utilization of the coastal area and sea water;

— the economic and social needs of the (coastal) States involved;

— the existence of alternative means for waste disposal;

— the adaptation of detrimental changes to beneficial human uses;

— the avoidance of unnecessary waste-disposal;

(b) Until such standards are established, the existence of substantial injury from pollution shall be determined by taking into consideration all relevant factors, including those referred to in paragraph (a).

(c) The weight to be given to each factor is to be determined by its importance in comparison with that of other relevant factors.

Article IV

When it is contended that the conduct of a State is not in accordance with its obligations under these Articles, that State shall promptly enter into negotiations with the complainant with a view to reaching a solution that is equitable under the circumstances.

Article V

In the case of violation of the rules in Article II, the State responsible shall cease the wrongful conduct and shall compensate the injured State for the injury that has been caused to it.

Article VI

In case of a dispute, Articles XXXI to XXXVII of the Helsinki Rules are, so far as may be, applicable.

4.14 CONVENTION ON THE PREVENTION OF MARINE POLLUTION BY DUMPING OF WASTES AND OTHER MATTER (WITH ANNEXES AND AS AMENDED TO 1989 BUT WITHOUT ADDENDUM). Concluded at Washington, 29 December 1972. Entered into force, 30 August 1975. 1046 U.N.T.S. 120, 26 U.S.T. 2403, T.I.A.S. No. 8165, 11 I.L.M. 1294 (1973)

The Contracting Parties to this Convention,

Recognizing that the marine environment and the living organisms which it supports are of vital importance to humanity, and all people have an interest in assuring that it is so managed that its quality and resources are not impaired;

Recognizing that the capacity of the sea to assimilate wastes and render them harmless, and its ability to regenerate natural resources is not unlimited;

Recognizing that States have, in accordance with the Charter of the United Nations and the principles of international law, the sovereign right to exploit their own resources pursuant to their own environmental policies, and the responsibility to ensure that activities within their jurisdiction or control do not cause damage to the environment of other States or of areas beyond the limits of national jurisdiction;

Recognizing resolution 2749 (XXV) of the General Assembly of the United Nations on the principles governing the sea-bed and the ocean floor and the subsoil thereof, beyond the limits of national jurisdiction;

Noting that marine pollution originates in many sources, such as dumping and discharges through the atmosphere, rivers, estuaries, outfalls and pipelines, and that it is important that States use the best practicable means to prevent such pollution and develop products and processes which will reduce the amount of harmful wastes to be disposed of;

Being convinced that international action to control the pollution of the sea by dumping can and must be taken without delay but that this action should not preclude discussion of measures to control other sources of marine pollution as soon as possible; and

Wishing to improve protection of the marine environment by encouraging States with a common interest in particular geographical areas to enter into appropriate agreements supplementary to this Convention;

Have agreed as follows:

Article I. Contracting Parties shall individually and collectively promote the effective control of all sources of pollution of the marine environment, and pledge themselves especially to take all practicable steps to prevent the pollution of the sea by the dumping of waste and other matter that is liable to create hazards to human health, to harm living resources and marine life, to damage amenities or to interfere with other legitimate uses of the sea.

Article II. Contracting Parties shall, as provided for in the following Articles, take effective measures individually, according to their scientific, technical and economic capabilities, and collectively, to prevent marine pollution caused by dumping and shall harmonize their policies in this regard.

Article III. For the purposes of this Convention:

1. (*a*) "Dumping" means:

(i) any deliberate disposal at sea of wastes or other matter from vessels, aircraft, platforms or other man-made structures at sea;

(ii) any deliberate disposal at sea of vessels, aircraft, platforms or other man-made structures at sea.

(*b*) "Dumping" does not include:

(i) the disposal at sea of wastes or other matter incidental to, or derived from the normal operations of vessels, aircraft, platforms or other man-made structures at sea and their equipment, other than wastes or other matter transported by or to vessels, aircraft, platforms or other man-made structures at sea, operating for the purpose of disposal of such matter or derived from the treatment of such wastes or other matter on such vessels, aircraft, platforms or structures;

(ii) placement of matter for a purpose other than the mere disposal thereof, provided that such placement is not contrary to the aims of this Convention.

(*c*) The disposal of wastes or other matter directly arising from, or related to the exploration, exploitation and associated off-shore processing of sea-bed mineral resources will not be covered by the provisions of this Convention.

2. "Vessels and aircraft" means waterborne or airborne craft of any type whatsoever. This expression includes air-cushioned craft and floating craft, whether self-propelled or not.

3. "Sea" means all marine waters other than the internal waters of States.

4. "Wastes or other matter" means material and substance of any kind, form or description.

5. "Special permit" means permission granted specifically on application in advance and in accordance with Annex II and Annex III.

6. "General permit" means permission granted in advance and in accordance with Annex III.

7. The "Organisation" means the Organisation designated by the Contracting Parties in accordance with Article XIV(2).

Article IV. 1. In accordance with the provisions of this Convention, Contracting Parties shall prohibit the dumping of any wastes or other matter in whatever form or condition except as otherwise specified below:

(*a*) the dumping of wastes or other matter listed in Annex I is prohibited;

(*b*) the dumping of wastes or other matter listed in Annex II requires a prior special permit;

(*c*) the dumping of all other wastes or matter requires a prior general permit.

2. Any permit shall be issued only after careful consideration of all the factors set forth in Annex III, including prior studies of the characteristics of the dumping site, as set forth in Sections B and C of that Annex.

3. No provision of this Convention is to be interpreted as preventing a Contracting Party from prohibiting, insofar as that Party is concerned, the dumping of wastes or other matter not mentioned in Annex I. That Party shall notify such measures to the Organisation.

Article V. 1. The provisions of Article IV shall not apply when it is necessary to secure the safety of human life or of vessels, aircraft, platforms or other man-made structures at sea in cases of *force majeure* caused by stress of weather, or in any case which constitutes a danger to human life or a real threat to vessels, aircraft, platforms or other man-made structures at sea, if dumping appears to be the only way of averting the threat and if there is every probability that the damage consequent upon such dumping will be less than would otherwise occur. Such dumping shall be so conducted as to minimise the likelihood of damage to human or marine life and shall be reported forthwith to the Organisation.

2. A Contracting Party may issue a special permit as an exception to Article IV(1)(*a*), in emergencies, posing unacceptable risk relating to human health and admitting no other feasible solution. Before doing so the Party shall consult any other country or countries that are likely to be affected and the Organisation which, after consulting other Parties, and international organisations as appropriate, shall, in accordance with Article XIV promptly recommend to the Party the most appropriate procedures to adopt. The Party shall follow these recommendations to the maximum extent feasible consistent with the time within which action must be taken and with the general obligation to avoid damage to the marine environment and shall inform the Organisation of the action it takes. The Parties pledge themselves to assist one another in such situations.

3. Any Contracting Party may waive its rights under paragraph (2) at the time of, or subsequent to ratification of, or accession to this Convention.

Article VI. 1. Each Contracting Party shall designate an appropriate authority or authorities to:

(*a*) issue special permits which shall be required prior to, and for, the dumping of matter listed in Annex II and in the circumstances provided for in Article V(2);

(*b*) issue general permits which shall be required prior to, and for, the dumping of all other matter;

(*c*) keep records of the nature and quantities of all matter permitted to be dumped and the location, time and method of dumping;

(*d*) monitor individually, or in collaboration with other Parties and competent international organisations, the condition of the seas for the purposes of this Convention.

2. The appropriate authority or authorities of a Contracting Party shall issue prior special or general permits in accordance with paragraph (1) in respect of matter intended for dumping:

(*a*) loaded in its territory;

(*b*) loaded by a vessel or aircraft registered in its territory or flying its flag, when the loading occurs in the territory of a State not party to this Convention.

3. In issuing permits under sub-paragraphs (1)(*a*) and (*b*) above, the appropriate authority or authorities shall comply with Annex III, together with such additional criteria, measures and requirements as they may consider relevant.

4. Each Contracting Party, directly or through a Secretariat established under a regional agreement, shall report to the Organisation, and where appropriate to other Parties, the information specified in sub-paragraphs (*c*) and (*d*) of paragraph (1) above, and the criteria, measures and requirements it adopts in accordance with paragraph (3) above. The procedure to be followed and the nature of such reports shall be agreed by the Parties in consultation.

Article VII. 1. Each Contracting Party shall apply the measures required to implement the present Convention to all:

(*a*) vessels and aircraft registered in its territory or flying its flag;

(*b*) vessels and aircraft loading in its territory or territorial seas matter which is to be dumped;

(*c*) vessels and aircraft and fixed or floating platforms under its jurisdiction believed to be engaged in dumping.

2. Each Party shall take in its territory appropriate measures to prevent and punish conduct in contravention of the provisions of this Convention.

3. The Parties agree to co-operate in the development of procedures for the effective application of this Convention particularly on the high seas, including procedures for the reporting of vessels and aircraft observed dumping in contravention of the Convention.

4. This Convention shall not apply to those vessels and aircraft entitled to sovereign immunity under international law. However, each Party shall ensure by the adoption of appropriate measures that such vessels and aircraft owned or operated by it act in a manner consistent with the object and purpose of this Convention, and shall inform the Organisation accordingly.

5. Nothing in this convention shall affect the right of each Party to adopt other measures, in accordance with the principles of international law, to prevent dumping at sea.

Article VIII. In order to further the objectives of this Convention, the Contracting Parties with common interests to protect in the marine environment in a given geographical area shall endeavour, taking into account characteristic regional features, to enter into regional agreements consistent with this Convention for the prevention of pollution, especially by dumping. The Contracting Parties to the present Convention shall endeavour to act consistently with the objectives and provisions of such regional agreements, which shall be notified to them by the Organisation. Contracting Parties shall seek to co-operate with the Parties to regional agreements in order to develop harmonized procedures to be followed by Contracting Parties to the different conventions concerned. Special attention shall be given to co-operation in the field of monitoring and scientific research.

Article IX. The Contracting Parties shall promote, through collaboration within the Organisation and other international bodies, support for those Parties which request it for:

(*a*) the training of scientific and technical personnel;

(*b*) the supply of necessary equipment and facilities for research and monitoring;

(*c*) the disposal and treatment of waste and other measures to prevent or mitigate pollution caused by dumping;

preferably within the countries concerned, so furthering the aims and purposes of this Convention.

Article X. In accordance with the principles of international law regarding State responsibility for damage to the environment of other States or to any other area of the environment, caused by dumping of wastes and other matter of all kinds, the Contracting Parties undertake to develop procedures for the assessment of liability and the settlement of disputes regarding dumping.

Article XI. The Contracting Parties shall at their first consultative meeting consider procedures for the settlement of disputes concerning the interpretation and application of this Convention.

Article XII. The Contracting Parties pledge themselves to promote, within the competent specialised agencies and other international bodies, measures to protect the marine environment against pollution caused by:

(*a*) hydrocarbons, including oil, and their wastes;

(*b*) other noxious or hazardous matter transported by vessels for purposes other than dumping;

(*c*) wastes generated in the course of operation of vessels, aircraft, platforms and other man-made structures at sea;

(*d*) radio-active pollutants from all sources, including vessels;

(*e*) agents of chemical and biological warfare;

(*f*) wastes or other matter directly arising from, or related to the exploration, exploitation and associated off-shore processing of sea-bed mineral resources.

The Parties will also promote, within the appropriate international organisation, the codification of signals to be used by vessels engaged in dumping.

Article XIII. Nothing in this Convention shall prejudice the codification and development of the law of the sea by the United Nations Conference on the Law of the Sea convened pursuant to Resolution 2750 C(XXV) of the General Assembly of the United Nations nor the present or future claims and legal views of any State concerning the law of the sea and the nature and extent of coastal and flag State jurisdiction. The Contracting Parties agree to consult at a meeting to be convened by the Organisation after the Law of the Sea Conference, and in any case not later than 1976, with a view to defining the nature and extent of the right and the responsibility of a coastal State to apply the Convention in a zone adjacent to its coast.

Article XIV. 1. The Government of the United Kingdom of Great Britain and Northern Ireland as a depositary shall call a meeting of the Contracting Parties not later than three months after the entry into force of this Convention to decide on organisational matters.

2. The Contracting Parties shall designate a competent Organisation existing at the time of that meeting to be responsible for Secretariat duties in relation to this Convention. Any Party to this Convention not being a member of this Organisation shall make an appropriate contribution to the expenses incurred by the Organisation in performing these duties.

3. The Secretariat duties of the Organisation shall include:

(*a*) the convening of consultative meetings of the Contracting Parties not less frequently than once every two years and of special meetings of the Parties at any time on the request of two thirds of the Parties;

(*b*) preparing and assisting, in consultation with the Contracting Parties and appropriate International Organisations, in the development and implementation of procedures referred to in sub-paragraph (4)(*e*) of this Article;

(*c*) considering enquiries by, and information from the Contracting Parties, consulting with them and with the appropriate International Organisations, and providing recommendations to the Parties on questions related to, but not specifically covered by the Convention;

(*d*) conveying to the Parties concerned all notifications received by the Organisation in accordance with Articles IV(3), V(1) and (2), VI(4), XV, XX and XXI.

Prior to the designation of the Organisation these functions shall, as necessary, be performed by the depositary, who for this purpose shall be the Government of the United Kingdom of Great Britain and Northern Ireland.

4. Consultative or special meetings of the Contracting Parties shall keep under continuing review the implementation of this Convention and may, *inter alia:*

(*a*) review and adopt amendments to this Convention and its Annexes in accordance with Article XV;

(*b*) invite the appropriate scientific body or bodies to collaborate with and to advise the Parties or the Organisation on any scientific or technical aspect relevant to this Convention, including particularly the content of the Annexes;

(*c*) receive and consider reports made pursuant to Article VI(4);

(*d*) promote co-operation with and between regional organisations concerned with the prevention of marine pollution;

(*e*) develop or adopt, in consultation with appropriate International Organisations, procedures referred to in Article V(2), including basic criteria for determining exceptional and emergency situations, and procedures for consultative advice and the safe disposal of matter in such circumstances, including the designation of appropriate dumping areas, and recommend accordingly;

(*f*) consider any additional action that may be required.

5. The Contracting Parties at their first consultative meeting shall establish rules of procedure as necessary.

Article XV. 1. (*a*) At meetings of the Contracting Parties called in accordance with Article XIV amendments to this Convention may be adopted by a two-thirds majority of those present. An amendment shall enter into force for the Parties which have accepted it on the sixtieth day after two thirds of the Parties shall have deposited an instrument of acceptance of the amendment with the Organisation. Thereafter the amendment shall enter into force for any other Party 30 days after that Party deposits its instrument of acceptance of the amendment.

(*b*) The Organisation shall inform all Contracting Parties of any request made for a special meeting under Article XIV and of any amendments adopted at meetings of the Parties and of the date on which each such amendment enters into force for each Party.

2. Amendments to the Annexes will be based on scientific or technical considerations. Amendments to the Annexes approved by a two-thirds majority of those present at a meeting called in accordance with Article XIV shall enter into force for each Contracting Party immediately on notification of its acceptance to the Organisation and 100 days after approval by the meeting for all other Parties except for those which before the end of the 100 days make a declaration that they are not able to accept the amendment at that time. Parties should endeavour to signify their acceptance of an amendment to the Organisation as soon as possible after approval at a meeting. A Party may at any time substitute an acceptance for a previous declaration of objection and the amendment previously objected to shall thereupon enter into force for that Party.

3. An acceptance or declaration of objection under this Article shall be made by the deposit of an instrument with the Organisation. The Organisation shall notify all Contracting Parties of the receipt of such instruments.

4. Prior to the designation of the Organisation, the Secretarial functions herein attributed to it shall be performed temporarily by the Government of the United Kingdom of Great Britain and Northern Ireland, as one of the depositaries of this Convention.

Article XVI. This Convention shall be open for signature by any State at London, Mexico City, Moscow and Washington from 29 December 1972 until 31 December 1973.

Article XVII. This Convention shall be subject to ratification. The instruments of ratification shall be deposited with the Governments of Mexico, the Union of Soviet Socialist Republics, the United Kingdom of Great Britain and Northern Ireland, and the United States of America.

Article XVIII. After 31 December 1973, this Convention shall be open for accession by any State. The instruments of accession shall be deposited with the Governments of Mexico, the Union of Soviet Socialist Republics, the United Kingdom of Great Britain and Northern Ireland, and the United States of America.

Article XIX. 1. This Convention shall enter into force on the thirtieth day following the date of deposit of the fifteenth instrument of ratification or accession.

2. For each Contracting Party ratifying or acceding to the Convention after the deposit of the fifteenth instrument of ratification or accession, the Convention shall enter into force on the thirtieth day after deposit by such Party of its instrument of ratification or accession.

Article XX. The depositaries shall inform Contracting Parties:

(*a*) of signatures to this Convention and of the deposit of instruments of ratification, accession or withdrawal, in accordance with Articles XVI, XVII, XVIII and XXI, and

(*b*) of the date on which this Convention will enter into force, in accordance with Article XIX.

Article XXI. Any Contracting Party may withdraw from this Convention by giving six months' notice in writing to a depositary, which shall promptly inform all Parties of such notice.

Article XXII. The original of this Convention of which the English, French, Russian and Spanish texts are equally authentic, shall be deposited with the Governments of Mexico, the Union of Soviet Socialist Republics, the United Kingdom of Great Britain and Northern Ireland and the United States of America who shall send certified copies thereof to all States.

ANNEX I

1. Organohalogen compounds.

2. Mercury and mercury compounds.

3. Cadmium and cadmium compounds.

4. Persistent plastics and other persistent synthetic materials, for example, netting and ropes, which may float or may remain in suspension in the sea in such a manner as to interfere materially with fishing, navigation or other legitimate uses of the sea.

5. Crude oil and its wastes, refined petroleum products, petroleum distillate residues, and any mixtures containing any of these, taken on board for the purpose of dumping.

6. High-level radio-active wastes or other high-level radio-active matter, defined on public health, biological or other grounds, by the competent international body in this field, at present the International Atomic Energy Agency, as unsuitable for dumping at sea.

7. Materials in whatever form (e.g. solids, liquids, semi-liquids, gases or in a living state) produced for biological and chemical warfare.

8. The preceding paragraphs of this Annex do not apply to substances which are rapidly rendered harmless by physical, chemical or biological processes in the sea provided they do not:

(i) make edible marine organisms unpalatable, or

(ii) endanger human health or that of domestic animals.

The consultative procedure provided for under Article XIV should be followed by a Party if there is doubt about the harmlessness of the substances.

9. This Annex does not apply to wastes or other materials (e.g. sewage sludges and dredged spoils) containing the matter referred to in paragraphs

1–5 above as trace contaminants. Such wastes shall be subject to the provisions of Annexes II and III as appropriate.

10. Paragraphs 1 and 5 of this annex do not apply to the disposal of wastes or other matter referred to in these paragraphs by means of incineration at sea. Incineration of such wastes or other matter at sea requires a prior special permit. In the issue of special permits for incineration, the Contracting Parties shall apply the regulations for the control of incineration of wastes and other matter at sea set forth in the addendum to this annex (which shall constitute an integral part of this annex) and take full account of the technical guidelines on the control of incineration of wastes and other matter at sea adopted by the Contracting Parties in consultation.

ANNEX II

The following substances and materials requiring special care are listed for the purposes of Article VI(1)(a).

A. Wastes containing significant amounts of the matters listed below:

arsenic)
lead)
copper) and their compounds
zinc)

organosilicon compounds
cyanides
fluorides
pesticides and their by-products not covered in Annex I.

B. In the issue of permits for the dumping of large quantities of acids and alkalis, consideration shall be given to the possible presence in such wastes of the substances listed in paragraph A and to the following additional substances:

beryllium)
chromium)
nickel) and their compounds
vanadium)

C. Containers, scrap metal and other bulky wastes liable to sink to the sea bottom which may present a serious obstacle to fishing or navigation.

D. Radio-active wastes or other radio-active matter not included in Annex I. In the issue of permits for the dumping of this matter, the Contracting Parties should take full account of the recommendations of the competent international body in this field, at present the International Atomic Energy Agency.

E. In the issue of special permits for the incineration of substances and materials listed in this annex, the Contracting Parties shall apply the regulations for the control of incineration of wastes and other matter at sea set forth in the addendum to annex I and take full account of the technical guidelines on the control of incineration of wastes and other matter at sea adopted by the Contracting Parties in consultation, to the extent specified in these regulations and guidelines.

F. Substances which, though of a non-toxic nature, may become harmful due to the quantities in which they are dumped, or which are liable to seriously reduce amenities.

ANNEX III

Provisions to be considered in establishing criteria governing the issue of permits for the dumping of matter at sea, taking into account Article IV(2), include:

A. CHARACTERISTICS AND COMPOSITION OF THE MATTER

1. Total amount and average composition of matter dumped (e.g. per year).

2. Form, e.g. solid, sludge, liquid, or gaseous.

3. Properties: physical (e.g. solubility and density), chemical and biochemical (e.g. oxygen demand, nutrients) and biological (e.g. presence of viruses, bacteria, yeasts, parasites).

4. Toxicity.

5. Persistence: physical, chemical and biological.

6. Accumulation and biotransformation in biological materials or sediments.

7. Susceptibility to physical, chemical and biochemical changes and interaction in the aquatic environment with other dissolved organic and inorganic materials.

8. Probability of production of taints or other changes reducing marketability of resources (fish, shellfish, etc.).

B. CHARACTERISTICS OF DUMPING SITE AND METHOD OF DEPOSIT

1. Location (e.g. co-ordinates of the dumping area, depth and distance from the coast), location in relation to other areas (e.g. amenity areas, spawning, nursery and fishing areas and exploitable resources).

2. Rate of disposal per specific period (e.g. quantity per day, per week, per month).

3. Methods of packaging and containment, if any.

4. Initial dilution achieved by proposed method of release.

5. Dispersal characteristics (e.g. effects of currents, tides and wind on horizontal transport and vertical mixing).

6. Water characteristics (e.g. temperature, pH, salinity, stratification, oxygen indices of pollution—dissolved oxygen (DO), chemical oxygen demand (COD), biochemical oxygen demand (BOD)—nitrogen present in organic and mineral form including ammonia, suspended matter, other nutrients and productivity).

7. Bottom characteristics (e.g. topography, geochemical and geological characteristics and biological productivity).

8. Existence and effects of other dumpings which have been made in the dumping area (e.g. heavy metal background reading and organic carbon content).

9. In issuing a permit for dumping, Contracting Parties should consider whether an adequate scientific basis exists for assessing the consequences of such dumping, as outlined in this Annex, taking into account seasonal variations.

C. General considerations and conditions

1. Possible effects on amenities (e.g. presence of floating or stranded material, turbidity, objectionable odour, discolouration and foaming).

2. Possible effects on marine life, fish and shellfish culture, fish stocks and fisheries, seaweed harvesting and culture.

3. Possible effects on other uses of the sea (e.g. impairment of water quality for industrial use, underwater corrosion of structures, interference with ship operations from floating materials, interference with fishing or navigation through deposit of waste or solid objects on the sea floor and protection of areas of special importance for scientific or conservation purposes).

4. The practical availability of alternative land-based methods of treatment, disposal or elimination, or of treatment to render the matter less harmful for dumping at sea.

**4.15 INTERNATIONAL CONVENTION FOR THE PREVENTION OF POLLU-
TION FROM SHIPS (MARPOL) (WITH ANNEXES I, II, & V AND AS
AMENDED BUT WITHOUT APPENDICES).[1] Concluded at London,
2 November 1973. IMCO Doc. MP/CONF/WP.35 (1973), 12 I.L.M.
1319 (1973)**

ARTICLE 1

General Obligations under the Convention

(1) The Parties to the Convention undertake to give effect to the provisions of the present Convention and those Annexes thereto by which they are bound, in order to prevent the pollution of the marine environment by the discharge of harmful substances or effluents containing such substances in contravention of the Convention.

(2) Unless expressly provided otherwise, a reference to the present Convention constitutes at the same time a reference to its Protocols and to the Annexes.

ARTICLE 2

Definitions

For the purposes of the present Convention, unless expressly provided otherwise:

(1) "Regulations" means the Regulations contained in the Annexes to the present Convention.

(2) "Harmful substance" means any substance which, if introduced into the sea, is liable to create hazards to human health, to harm living resources and marine life, to damage amenities or to interfere with other legitimate uses of the sea, and includes any substance subject to control by the present Convention.

(3)(a) "Discharge", in relation to harmful substances or effluents containing such substances, means any release howsoever caused from a ship and includes any escape, disposal, spilling, leaking, pumping, emitting or emptying;

(b) "Discharge" does not include:

(i) dumping within the meaning of the Convention on the Prevention of Marine Pollution by Dumping of Wastes and Other Matter, done at London on 13 November 1972; or

(ii) release of harmful substances directly arising from the exploration, exploitation and associated off-shore processing of sea-bed mineral resources; or

(iii) release of harmful substances for purposes of legitimate scientific research into pollution abatement or control.

(4) "Ship" means a vessel of any type whatsoever operating in the marine environment and includes hydrofoil boats, air-cushion vehicles, submersibles, floating craft and fixed or floating platforms.

(5) "Administration" means the Government of the State under whose authority the ship is operating. With respect to a ship entitled to fly a flag of

---

1. *See also* Basic Document 4.23 *infra*.

any State, the Administration is the Government of that State. With respect to fixed or floating platforms engaged in exploration and exploitation of the sea-bed and subsoil thereof adjacent to the coast over which the coastal State exercises sovereign rights for the purposes of exploration and exploitation of their natural resources, the Administration is the Government of the coastal State concerned.

(6) "Incident" means an event involving the actual or probable discharge into the sea of a harmful substance, or effluents containing such a substance.

(7) "Organization" means the Inter–Governmental Maritime Consultative Organization.

ARTICLE 3

Application

(1) The present Convention shall apply to:

    (a) ships entitled to fly the flag of a Party to the Convention; and

    (b) ships not entitled to fly the flag of a Party but which operate under the authority of a Party.

(2) Nothing in the present Article shall be construed as derogating from or extending the sovereign rights of the Parties under international law over the sea-bed and subsoil thereof adjacent to their coasts for the purposes of exploration and exploitation of their natural resources.

(3) The present Convention shall not apply to any warship, naval auxiliary or other ship owned or operated by a State and used, for the time being, only on government non-commercial service. However, each Party shall ensure by the adoption of appropriate measures not impairing the operations or operational capabilities of such ships owned or operated by it, that such ships act in a manner consistent, so far as is reasonable and practicable, with the present Convention.

ARTICLE 4

Violation

(1) Any violation of the requirements of the present Convention shall be prohibited and sanctions shall be established therefor under the law of the Administration of the ship concerned wherever the violation occurs. If the Administration is informed of such a violation and is satisfied that sufficient evidence is available to enable proceedings to be brought in respect of the alleged violation, it shall cause such proceedings to be taken as soon as possible, in accordance with its law.

(2) Any violation of the requirements of the present Convention within the jurisdiction of any Party to the Convention shall be prohibited and sanctions shall be established therefor under the law of that Party. Whenever such a violation occurs, that Party shall either:

    (a) cause proceedings to be taken in accordance with its law; or

    (b) furnish to the Administration of the ship such information and evidence as may be in its possession that a violation has occurred.

(3) Where information or evidence with respect to any violation of the present Convention by a ship is furnished to the Administration of that ship,

the Administration shall promptly inform the Party which has furnished the information or evidence, and the Organization, of the action taken.

(4) The penalties specified under the law of a Party pursuant to the present Article shall be adequate in severity to discourage violations of the present Convention and shall be equally severe irrespective of where the violations occur.

ARTICLE 5

Certificates and Special Rules on Inspection of Ships

(1) Subject to the provisions of paragraph (2) of the present Article a certificate issued under the authority of a Party to the Convention in accordance with the provisions of the Regulations shall be accepted by the other Parties and regarded for all purposes covered by the present Convention as having the same validity as a certificate issued by them.

(2) A ship required to hold a certificate in accordance with the provisions of the Regulations is subject, while in the ports or off-shore terminals under the jurisdiction of a Party, to inspection by officers duly authorized by that Party. Any such inspection shall be limited to verifying that there is on board a valid certificate, unless there are clear grounds for believing that the condition of the ship or its equipment does not correspond substantially with the particulars of that certificate. In that case, or if the ship does not carry a valid certificate, the Party carrying out the inspection shall take such steps as will ensure that the ship shall not sail until it can proceed to sea without presenting an unreasonable threat of harm to the marine environment. That Party may, however, grant such a ship permission to leave the port or off-shore terminal for the purpose of proceeding to the nearest appropriate repair yard available.

(3) If a Party denies a foreign ship entry to the ports or off-shore terminals under its jurisdiction or takes any action against such a ship for the reason that the ship does not comply with the provisions of the present Convention, the Party shall immediately inform the consul or diplomatic representative of the Party whose flag the ship is entitled to fly, or if this is not possible, the Administration of the ship concerned. Before denying entry or taking such action the Party may request consultation with the Administration of the ship concerned. Information shall also be given to the Administration when a ship does not carry a valid certificate in accordance with the provisions of the Regulations.

(4) With respect to the ships of non-Parties to the Convention, Parties shall apply the requirements of the present Convention as may be necessary to ensure that no more favorable treatment is given to such ships.

ARTICLE 6

Detection of Violations and Enforcement of the Convention

(1) Parties to the Convention shall co-operate in the detection of violations and the enforcement of the provisions of the present Convention, using all appropriate and practicable measures of detection and environmental monitoring, adequate procedures for reporting and accumulation of evidence.

(2) A ship to which the present Convention applies may, in any port or off-shore terminal of a Party, be subject to inspection by officers appointed or

authorized by that Party for the purpose of verifying whether the ship has discharged any harmful substances in violation of the provisions of the Regulations. If an inspection indicates a violation of the Convention, a report shall be forwarded to the Administration for any appropriate action.

(3) Any Party shall furnish to the Administration evidence, if any, that the ship has discharged harmful substances or effluents containing such substances in violation of the provisions of the Regulations. If it is practicable to do so, the competent authority of the former Party shall notify the Master of the ship of the alleged violation.

(4) Upon receiving such evidence, the Administration so informed shall investigate the matter, and may request the other party to furnish further or better evidence of the alleged contravention. If the Administration is satisfied that sufficient evidence is available to enable proceedings to be brought in respect of the alleged violation, it shall cause such proceedings to be taken in accordance with its law as soon as possible. The Administration shall promptly inform the Party which has reported the alleged violation, as well as the Organization, of the action taken.

(5) A Party may also inspect a ship to which the present Convention applies when it enters the ports or off-shore terminals under its jurisdiction, if a request for an investigation is received from any Party together with sufficient evidence that the ship has discharged harmful substances or effluents containing such substances in any place. The report of such investigation shall be sent to the Party requesting it and to the Administration so that the appropriate action may be taken under the present Convention.

ARTICLE 7
Undue Delay to Ships

(1) All possible efforts shall be made to avoid a ship being unduly detained or delayed under Articles 4, 5 or 6 of the present Convention.

(2) When a ship is unduly detained or delayed under Articles 4, 5 or 6 of the present Convention, it shall be entitled to compensation for any loss or damage suffered.

ARTICLE 8
Reports on Incidents Involving Harmful Substances

(1) A report of an incident shall be made without delay to the fullest extent possible in accordance with the provisions of Protocol I to the present Convention.

(2) Each Party to the Convention shall:

(a) make all arrangements necessary for an appropriate officer or agency to receive and process all reports on incidents; and

(b) notify the Organization with complete details of such arrangements for circulation to other Parties and Member States of the Organization.

(3) Whenever a Party receives a report under the provisions of the present Article, that Party shall relay the report without delay to:

(a) the Administration of the ship involved; and

(b) any other State which may be affected.

(4) Each Party to the Convention undertakes to issue instructions to its maritime inspection vessels and aircraft and to other appropriate services, to report to its authorities any incident referred to in Protocol I to the present Convention. That Party shall, if it considers it appropriate, report accordingly to the Organization and to any other party concerned.

ARTICLE 9

Other Treaties and Interpretation

(1) Upon its entry into force, the present Convention supersedes the International Convention for the Prevention of Pollution of the Sea by Oil, 1954, as amended, as between Parties to that Convention.

(2) Nothing in the present Convention shall prejudice the codification and development of the law of the sea by the United Nations Conference on the Law of the Sea convened pursuant to Resolution 2750 C(XXV) of the General Assembly of the United Nations nor the present or future claims and legal views of any State concerning the law of the sea and the nature and extent of coastal and flag State jurisdiction.

(3) The term "jurisdiction" in the present Convention shall be construed in the light of international law in force at the time of application or interpretation of the present Convention.

ARTICLE 10

Settlement of Disputes

Any dispute between two or more Parties to the Convention concerning the interpretation or application of the present Convention shall, if settlement by negotiation between the Parties involved has not been possible, and if these Parties do not otherwise agree, be submitted upon request of any of them to arbitration as set out in Protocol II to the present Convention.

ARTICLE 11

Communication of Information

(1) The Parties to the Convention undertake to communicate to the Organization:

(a) the text of laws, orders, decrees and regulations and other instruments which have been promulgated on the various matters within the scope of the present Convention;

(b) a list of non-governmental agencies which are authorized to act on their behalf in matters relating to the design, construction and equipment of ships carrying harmful substances in accordance with the provisions of the Regulations;

(c) a sufficient number of specimens of their certificates issued under the provisions of the Regulations;

(d) a list of reception facilities including their location, capacity and available facilities and other characteristics;

(e) official reports or summaries of official reports in so far as they show the results of the application of the present Convention; and

(f) an annual statistical report, in a form standardized by the Organization, of penalties actually imposed for infringement of the present Convention.

(2) The Organization shall notify Parties of the receipt of any communications under the present Article and circulate to all Parties any information communicated to it under sub-paragraphs (1)(b) to (f) of the present Article.

ARTICLE 12
Casualties to Ships

(1) Each Administration undertakes to conduct an investigation of any casualty occurring to any of its ships subject to the provisions of the Regulations if such casualty has produced a major deleterious effect upon the marine environment.

(2) Each Party to the Convention undertakes to supply the Organization with information concerning the findings of such investigation, when it judges that such information may assist in determining what changes in the present Convention might be desirable.

ARTICLE 13
Signature, Ratification, Acceptance, Approval and Accession

(1) The present Convention shall remain open for signature at the Headquarters of the Organization from 15 January 1974 until 31 December 1974 and shall thereafter remain open for accession. States may become Parties to the present Convention by:

(a) signature without reservation as to ratification, acceptance or approval; or

(b) signature subject to ratification, acceptance or approval, followed by ratification, acceptance or approval; or

(c) accession.

(2) Ratification, acceptance, approval or accession shall be effected by the deposit of an instrument to that effect with the Secretary–General of the Organization.

(3) The Secretary–General of the Organization shall inform all States which have signed the present Convention or acceded to it of any signature or of the deposit of any new instrument of ratification, acceptance, approval or accession and the date of its deposit.

ARTICLE 14
Optional Annexes

(1) A State may at the time of signing, ratifying, accepting, approving or acceding to the present Convention declare that it does not accept any one or all of Annexes III, IV and V (hereinafter referred to as "Optional Annexes") of the present Convention. Subject to the above, Parties to the Convention shall be bound by any Annex in its entirety.

(2) A State which has declared that it is not bound by an Optional Annex may at any time accept such Annex by depositing with the Organization an instrument of the kind referred to in Article 13(2).

(3) A State which makes a declaration under paragraph (1) of the present Article in respect of an Optional Annex and which has not subsequently accepted that Annex in accordance with paragraph (2) of the present Article shall not be under any obligation nor entitled to claim any privileges under the present Convention in respect of matters related to such Annex and all references to Parties in the present Convention shall not include that State in so far as matters related to such Annex are concerned.

(4) The Organization shall inform the States which have signed or acceded to the present Convention of any declaration under the present Article as well as the receipt of any instrument deposited in accordance with the provisions of paragraph (2) of the present Article.

ARTICLE 15
Entry into Force

(1) The present Convention shall enter into force twelve months after the date on which not less than 15 States, the combined merchant fleets of which constitute not less than fifty per cent of the gross tonnage of the world's merchant shipping, have become parties to it in accordance with Article 13.

(2) An Optional Annex shall enter into force twelve months after the date on which the conditions stipulated in paragraph (1) of the present Article have been satisfied in relation to that Annex.

(3) The Organization shall inform the States which have signed the present Convention or acceded to it of the date on which it enters into force and of the date on which an Optional Annex enters into force in accordance with paragraph (2) of the present Article.

(4) For States which have deposited an instrument of ratification, acceptance, approval or accession in respect of the present Convention or any Optional Annex after the requirements for entry into force thereof have been met but prior to the date of entry into force, the ratification, acceptance, approval or accession shall take effect on the date of entry into force of the Convention or such Annex or three months after the date of deposit of the instrument whichever is the later date.

(5) For States which have deposited an instrument of ratification, acceptance, approval or accession after the date on which the Convention or an Optional Annex entered into force, the Convention or the Optional Annex shall become effective three months after the date of deposit of the instrument.

(6) After the date on which all the conditions required under Article 16 to bring an amendment to the present Convention or an Optional Annex into force have been fulfilled, any instrument of ratification, acceptance, approval or accession deposited shall apply to the Convention or Annex as amended.

ARTICLE 16
Amendments

(1) The present Convention may be amended by any of the procedures specified in the following paragraphs.

(2) Amendments after consideration by the Organization:

(a) any amendment proposed by a Party to the Convention shall be submitted to the Organization and circulated by its Secretary–General to all Members of the Organization and all Parties at least six months prior to its consideration;

(b) any amendment proposed and circulated as above shall be submitted to an appropriate body by the Organization for consideration;

(c) Parties to the Convention, whether or not Members of the Organization, shall be entitled to participate in the proceedings of the appropriate body;

(d) amendments shall be adopted by a two-thirds majority of only the Parties to the Convention present and voting;

(e) if adopted in accordance with sub-paragraph (d) above, amendments shall be communicated by the Secretary–General of the Organization to all the Parties to the Convention for acceptance;

(f) an amendment shall be deemed to have been accepted in the following circumstances:

(i) an amendment to an Article of the Convention shall be deemed to have been accepted on the date on which it is accepted by two-thirds of the Parties, the combined merchant fleets of which constitute not less than fifty per cent of the gross tonnage of the world's merchant fleet;

(ii) an amendment to an Annex to the Convention shall be deemed to have been accepted in accordance with the procedure specified in sub-paragraph (f)(iii) unless the appropriate body, at the time of its adoption, determines that the amendment shall be deemed to have been accepted on the date on which it is accepted by two-thirds of the Parties, the combined merchant fleets of which constitute not less than fifty per cent of the gross tonnage of the world's merchant fleet. Nevertheless, at any time before the entry into force of an amendment to an Annex to the Convention, a Party may notify the Secretary–General of the Organization that its express approval will be necessary before the amendment enters into force for it. The latter shall bring such notification and the date of its receipt to the notice of Parties;

(iii) an amendment to an Appendix to an Annex to the Convention shall be deemed to have been accepted at the end of a period to be determined by the appropriate body at the time of its adoption, which period shall be not less than ten months, unless within that period an objection is communicated to the Organization by not less than one-third of the Parties or by the Parties the combined merchant fleets of which constitute not less than fifty per cent of the gross tonnage of the world's merchant fleet whichever condition is fulfilled;

(iv) an amendment to Protocol I to the Convention shall be subject to the same procedures as for the amendments to the Annexes to the Convention, as provided for in sub-paragraphs (f)(ii) or (f)(iii) above;

(v) an amendment to Protocol II to the Convention shall be subject to the same procedures as for the amendments to an Article of the Convention, as provided for in sub-paragraph (f)(i) above;

(g) the amendment shall enter into force under the following conditions:

(i) in the case of an amendment to an Article of the Convention, to Protocol II, or to Protocol I or to an Annex to the Convention not under the procedure specified in sub-paragraph (f)(iii), the amendment accepted in conformity with the foregoing provisions shall enter into force six months after the date of its acceptance with respect to the Parties which have declared that they have accepted it;

(ii) in the case of an amendment to Protocol I, to an Appendix to an Annex or to an Annex to the Convention under the procedure specified in sub-paragraph (f)(iii), the amendment deemed to have been accepted in accordance with the foregoing conditions shall enter into force six months after its acceptance for all the Parties with the exception of those which, before that date, have made a declaration that they do not accept it or a declaration under subparagraph (f)(ii), that their express approval is necessary.

(3) Amendment by a Conference:

(a) Upon the request of a Party, concurred in by at least one-third of the Parties, the Organization shall convene a Conference of Parties to the Convention to consider amendments to the present Convention.

(b) Every amendment adopted by such a Conference by a two-thirds majority of those present and voting of the Parties shall be communicated by the Secretary–General of the Organization to all Contracting Parties for their acceptance.

(c) Unless the Conference decides otherwise, the amendment shall be deemed to have been accepted and to have entered into force in accordance with the procedures specified for that purpose in paragraph (2)(f) and (g) above.

(4)(a) In the case of an amendment to an Optional Annex, a reference in the present Article to a "Party to the Convention" shall be deemed to mean a reference to a Party bound by that Annex.

(b) Any Party which has declined to accept an amendment to an Annex shall be treated as a non-Party only for the purpose of application of that amendment.

(5) The adoption and entry into force of a new Annex shall be subject to the same procedures as for the adoption and entry into force of an amendment to an Article of the Convention.

(6) Unless expressly provided otherwise, any amendment to the present Convention made under this Article, which relates to the structure of a ship, shall apply only to ships for which the building contract is placed, or in the absence of a building contract, the keel of which is laid, on or after the date on which the amendment comes into force.

(7) Any amendment to a Protocol or to an Annex shall relate to the substance of that Protocol or Annex and shall be consistent with the Articles of the present Convention.

(8) The Secretary–General of the Organization shall inform all Parties of any amendments which enter into force under the present Article, together with the date on which each such amendment enters into force.

(9) Any declaration of acceptance or of objection to an amendment under the present article shall be notified in writing to the Secretary–General of the Organization. The latter shall bring such notification and the date of its receipt to the notice of the Parties to the Convention.

ARTICLE 17
Promotion of Technical Co-operation

The Parties to the Convention shall promote, in consultation with the Organization and other international bodies, with assistance and co-ordination by the Executive Director of the United Nations Environment Programme, support for those Parties which request technical assistance for:

(a) the training of scientific and technical personnel;

(b) the supply of necessary equipment and facilities for reception and monitoring;

(c) the facilitation of other measures and arrangements to prevent or mitigate pollution of the marine environment by ships; and

(d) the encouragement of research;

preferably within the countries concerned, so furthering the aims and purposes of the present Convention.

ARTICLE 18
Denunciation

(1) The present Convention or any Optional Annex may be denounced by any Parties to the Convention at any time after the expiry of five years from the date on which the Convention or such Annex enters into force for that Party.

(2) Denunciation shall be effected by notification in writing to the Secretary–General of the Organization who shall inform all the other Parties of any such notification received and of the date of its receipt as well as the date on which such denunciation takes effect.

(3) A denunciation shall take effect twelve months after receipt of the notification of denunciation by the Secretary–General of the Organization or after the expiry of any other longer period which may be indicated in the notification.

ARTICLE 19
Deposit and Registration

(1) The present Convention shall be deposited with the Secretary–General of the Organization who shall transmit certified true copies thereof to all States which have signed the present Convention or acceded to it.

(2) As soon as the present Convention enters into force, the text shall be transmitted by the Secretary–General of the Organization to the Secretary–

General of the United Nations for registration and publication, in accordance with Article 102 of the Charter of the United Nations.

ARTICLE 20

Languages

The present Convention is established in a single copy in the English, French, Russian and Spanish languages, each text being equally authentic. Official translations in the Arabic, German, Italian and Japanese languages shall be prepared and deposited with the signed original.

ANNEX I [2]
OF MARPOL 73/78
INCLUDING PROPOSED AMENDMENTS
REGULATIONS FOR THE PREVENTION OF POLLUTION BY OIL
CHAPTER I—GENERAL
Regulation 1
Definitions

For the purposes of this Annex:

(1) "Oil" means petroleum in any form including crude oil, fuel oil, sludge, oil refuse and refined products (other than petrochemicals which are subject to the provisions of Annex II of the present Convention) and, without limiting the generality of the foregoing, includes the substances listed in Appendix I to this Annex.

(2) "Oily mixture" means a mixture with any oil content.

(3) "Oil fuel" means any oil used as fuel in connexion with the propulsion and auxiliary machinery of the ship in which such oil is carried.

(4) "Oil tanker" means a ship constructed or adapted primarily to carry oil in bulk in its cargo spaces and includes combination carriers and any "chemical tanker" as defined in Annex II of the present Convention when it is carrying a cargo or part cargo of oil in bulk.

(5) "Combination carrier" means a ship designed to carry either oil or solid cargoes in bulk.

(6) "New ship" means a ship:

(a) for which the building contract is placed after 31 December 1975; or

(b) in the absence of a building contract, the keel of which is laid or which is at a similar stage of construction after 30 June 1976; or

(c) the delivery of which is after 31 December 1979; or

(d) which has undergone a major conversion:

(i) for which the contract is placed after 31 December 1975; or

(ii) in the absence of a contract, the construction work of which is begun after 30 June 1976; or

(iii) which is completed after 31 December 1979.

(7) "Existing ship" means a ship which is not a new ship.

2. *See* Basic Document 4.23, *infra,* for amendments to Annex I.

(8)(a) "Major conversion" means a conversion of an existing ship:

(i) which substantially alters the dimensions or carrying capacity of the ship; or

(ii) which changes the type of the ship; or

(iii) the intent of which in the opinion of the Administration is substantially to prolong its life; or

(iv) which otherwise so alters the ship that, if it were a new ship, it would become subject to relevant provisions of the present Convention not applicable to it as an existing ship.

(b) Notwithstanding the provisions of sub-paragraph (a) of this paragraph, conversion of an existing oil tanker of 20,000 tons deadweight and above to meet the requirements of Regulation 13 of this Annex shall not be deemed to constitute a major conversion for the purposes of this Annex.

(9) "Nearest land". The term "from the nearest land" means from the baseline from which the territorial sea of the territory in question is established in accordance with international law, except that, for the purposes of the present Convention "from the nearest land" off the north eastern coast of Australia shall mean from a line drawn from a point on the coast of Australia in

latitude 11°00′ South, longitude 142°08′ East to a point in latitude 10°35′ South,

longitude 141°55′ East, thence to a point latitude 10°00′ South,

longitude 142°00′ East, thence to a point latitude 9°10′ South,

longitude 143°52′ East, thence to a point latitude 9°00′ South,

longitude 144°30′ East, thence to a point latitude 13°00′ South,

longitude 144°00′ East, thence to a point latitude 15°00′ South,

longitude 146°00′ East, thence to a point latitude 18°00′ South,

longitude 147°00′ East, thence to a point latitude 21°00′ South,

longitude 153°00′ East, thence to a point on the coast of Australia in latitude 24°42′ South, longitude 153°15′ East.

(10) "Special area" means a sea area where for recognized technical reasons in relation to its oceanographical and ecological condition and to the particular character of its traffic the adoption of special mandatory methods for the prevention of sea pollution by oil is required. Special areas shall include those listed in Regulation 10 of this Annex.

(11) "Instantaneous rate of discharge of oil content" means the rate of discharge of oil in litres per hour at any instant divided by the speed of the ship in knots at the same instant.

(12) "Tank" means an enclosed space which is formed by the permanent structure of a ship and which is designed for the carriage of liquid in bulk.

(13) "Wing tank" means any tank adjacent to the side shell plating.

(14) "Centre tank" means any tank inboard of a longitudinal bulkhead.

(15) "Slop tank" means a tank specifically designated for the collection of tank drainings, tank washings and other oily mixtures.

(16) "Clean ballast" means the ballast in a tank which since oil was last carried therein, has been so cleaned that effluent therefrom if it were discharged from a ship which is stationary into clean calm water on a clear day would not produce visible traces of oil on the surface of the water or on adjoining shorelines or cause a sludge or emulsion to be deposited beneath the surface of the water or upon adjoining shorelines. If the ballast is discharged through an oil discharge monitoring and control system approved by the Administration, evidence based on such a system to the effect that the oil content of the effluent did not exceed 15 parts per million shall be determinative that the ballast was clean, notwithstanding the presence of visible traces.

(17) "Segregated ballast" means the ballast water introduced into a tank which is completely separated from the cargo oil and oil fuel system and which is permanently allocated to the carriage of ballast or to the carriage of ballast or cargoes other than oil or noxious substances as variously defined in the Annexes of the present Convention.

(18) "Length" (L) means 96 per cent of the total length on a waterline at 85 per cent of the least moulded depth measured from the top of the keel, or the length from the foreside of the stem to the axis of the rudder stock on that waterline, if that be greater. In ships designed with a rake of keel the waterline on which this length is measured shall be parallel to the designed waterline. The length (L) shall be measured in metres.

(19) "Forward and after perpendiculars" shall be taken at the forward and after ends of the length (L). The forward perpendicular shall coincide with the foreside of the stem on the waterline on which the length is measured.

(20) "Amidships" is at the middle of the length (L).

(21) "Breadth" (B) means the maximum breadth of the ship, measured amidships to the moulded line of the frame in a ship with a metal shell and to the outer surface of the hull in a ship with a shell of any other material. The breadth (B) shall be measured in metres.

(22) "Deadweight" (DW) means the difference in metric tons between the displacement of a ship in water of a specific gravity of 1.025 at the load waterline corresponding to the assigned summer freeboard and the lightweight of the ship.

(23) "Lightweight" means the displacement of a ship in metric tons without cargo, fuel, lubricating oil, ballast water, fresh water and feed water in tanks, consumable stores, and passengers and crew and their effects.

(24) "Permeability" of a space means the ratio of the volume within that space which is assumed to be occupied by water to the total volume of that space.

(25) "Volumes" and "areas" in a ship shall be calculated in all cases to moulded lines.

(26) Notwithstanding the provisions of paragraph (6) of this Regulation, for the purposes of Regulations 13, 13B, 13E and 18(4) of this Annex, "new oil tanker" means an oil tanker:

(a) for which the building contract is placed after 1 June 1979; or

(b) in the absence of a building contract, the keel of which is laid or which is at a similar stage of construction after 1 January 1980; or

(c) the delivery of which is after 1 June 1982; or

(d) which has undergone a major conversion:

(i) for which the contract is placed after 1 June 1979; or

(ii) in the absence of a contract, the construction work of which is begun after 1 January 1980; or

(iii) which is completed after 1 June 1982;

except that, for oil tankers of 70,000 tons deadweight and above, the definition in paragraph (6) of this Regulation shall apply for the purposes of Regulation 13(1) of this Annex.

(27) Notwithstanding the provisions of paragraph (7) of this Regulation, for the purposes of Regulations 13, 13A, 13B, 13C, 13D, 18(5) and 18(6)(c) of this Annex, "existing oil tanker" means an oil tanker which is not a new oil tanker as defined in paragraph (26) of this Regulation.

(28) "Crude oil" means any liquid hydrocarbon mixture occurring naturally in the earth whether or not treated to render it suitable for transportation and includes:

(a) crude oil from which certain distillate fractions may have been removed; and

(b) crude oil to which certain distillate fractions may have been added.

(29) "Crude oil tanker" means an oil tanker engaged in the trade of carrying crude oil.

(30) "Product carrier" means an oil tanker engaged in the trade of carrying oil other than crude oil.

Regulation 2
Application

(1) Unless expressly provided otherwise, the provisions of this Annex shall apply to all ships.

(2) In ships other than oil tankers fitted with cargo spaces which are constructed and utilized to carry oil in bulk of an aggregate capacity of 200 cubic metres or more, the requirements of Regulations 9, 10, 14, 15(1), (2) and (3), 18, 20 and 24(4) of this Annex for oil tankers shall also apply to the construction and operation of those spaces, except that where such aggregate capacity is less than 1,000 cubic metres the requirements of Regulation 15(4) of this Annex may apply in lieu of Regulation 15(1), (2) and (3).

(3) Where a cargo subject to the provisions of Annex II of the present Convention is carried in a cargo space of an oil tanker, the appropriate requirements of Annex II of the present Convention shall also apply.

(4)(a) Any hydrofoil, air-cushion vehicle and other new type of vessel (near-surface craft, submarine craft, etc.) whose constructional features are such as to render the application of any of the provisions of Chapters II and

III of this Annex relating to construction and equipment unreasonable or impracticable may be exempted by the Administration from such provisions, provided that the construction and equipment of that ship provides equivalent protection against pollution by oil, having regard to the service for which it is intended.

(b) Particulars of any such exemption granted by the Administration shall be indicated in the Certificate referred to in Regulation 5 of this Annex.

(c) The Administration which allows any such exemption shall, as soon as possible, but not more than ninety days thereafter, communicate to the Organization particulars of same and the reasons, therefor, which the Organization shall circulate to the Parties to the Convention for their information and appropriate action, if any.

Regulation 3
Equivalents

(1) The Administration may allow any fitting, material, appliance or apparatus to be fitted in a ship as an alternative to that required by this Annex if such fitting, material, appliance or apparatus is at least as effective as that required by this Annex. This authority of the Administration shall not extend to substitution of operational methods to effect the control of discharge of oil as equivalent to those design and construction features which are prescribed by Regulations in this Annex.

(2) The Administration which allows a fitting, material, appliance or apparatus, as an alternative to that required by this Annex shall communicate to the Organization for circulation to the Parties to the Convention particulars thereof, for their information and appropriate action, if any.

Regulation 4
Surveys and Inspections

(1) Every oil tanker of 150 tons gross tonnage and above, and every other ship of 400 tons gross tonnage and above shall be subject to the surveys specified below:

(a) An initial survey before the ship is put in service or before the Certificate required under Regulation 5 of this Annex is issued for the first time, which shall include a complete survey of its structure, equipment, systems, fittings, arrangements and material in so far as the ship is covered by this Annex. This survey shall be such as to ensure that the structure, equipment, systems, fittings, arrangements and material fully comply with the applicable requirements of this Annex.

(b) Periodical surveys at intervals specified by the Administration, but not exceeding five years, which shall be such as to ensure that the structure, equipment, systems, fittings, arrangements and material fully comply with the requirements of this Annex.

(c) A minimum of one intermediate survey during the period of validity of the Certificate which shall be such as to ensure that the equipment and associated pump and piping systems, including oil discharge monitoring and control systems, crude oil washing systems, oily-water separating equipment and oil filtering systems, fully comply with the applicable requirements of this Annex and are in good working order. In cases where only one such intermediate survey is carried out in any one Certificate validity period, it shall be held not before six months prior to, nor later than six months after the half-way date of the Certificate's period of validity. Such intermediate surveys shall be endorsed on the Certificate issued under Regulation 5 of this Annex.

(2) The Administration shall establish appropriate measures for ships which are not subject to the provisions of paragraph (1) of this Regulation in order to ensure that the applicable provisions of this Annex are complied with.

(3)(a) Surveys of ships as regards the enforcement of the provisions of this Annex shall be carried out by officers of the Administration. The Administration may, however, entrust the surveys either to surveyors nominated for the purpose or to organizations recognized by it.

(b) The Administration shall institute arrangements for unscheduled inspections to be carried out during the period of validity of the Certificate. Such inspections shall ensure that the ship and its equipment remain in all respects satisfactory for the service for which the ship is intended. These inspections may be carried out by their own inspection services, or by nominated surveyors or by recognized organizations, or by other Parties upon request of the Administration. Where the Administration, under the provisions of paragraph (1) of this Regulation, establishes mandatory annual surveys, the above unscheduled inspections shall not be obligatory.

(c) An Administration nominating surveyors or recognizing organizations to conduct surveys and inspections as set forth in sub-paragraphs (a) and (b) of this paragraph, shall as a minimum empower any nominated surveyor or recognized organization to:

(i) require repairs to a ship; and

(ii) carry out surveys and inspections if requested by the appropriate authorities of a Port State.

The Administration shall notify the Organization of the specific responsibilities and conditions of the authority delegated to the nominated surveyors or recognized organizations, for circulation to Parties to the present Protocol for the information of their officers.

(d) When a nominated surveyor or recognized organization determines that the condition of the ship or its equipment does not correspond substantially with the particulars of the Certificate or is such that the ship is not fit to proceed to sea without presenting an unreasonable threat of harm to the marine environment, such surveyor or organization shall immediately ensure that corrective action is taken and shall in due course notify the Administration. If such corrective action is not taken the Certificate should be withdrawn and the Administration shall be notified immediately; and if the ship is in a port of another Party, the appropriate authorities of the Port State shall also be notified immediately. When an officer of the Administration, a nominated surveyor or recognized organization has notified the appropriate authorities of the Port State, the Government of the Port State concerned shall give such officer, surveyor or organization any necessary assistance to carry out their obligations under this Regulation. When applicable, the Government of the Port State concerned shall take such steps as will ensure that the ship shall not sail until it can proceed to sea or leave the port for the purpose of proceeding to the nearest appropriate repair yard available without presenting an unreasonable threat of harm to the marine environment.

(e) In every case, the Administration concerned shall fully guarantee the completeness and efficiency of the survey and inspection and shall undertake to ensure the necessary arrangements to satisfy this obligation.

(4)(a) The condition of the ship and its equipment shall be maintained to conform with the provisions of the present Convention to ensure that the ship in all respects will remain fit to proceed to sea without presenting an unreasonable threat of harm to the marine environment.

(b) After any survey of the ship under paragraph (1) of this Regulation has been completed, no change shall be made in the structure, equipment, systems, fittings, arrangements or material covered by the survey, without the sanction of the Administration, except the direct replacement of such equipment and fittings.

(c) Whenever an accident occurs to a ship or a defect is discovered which substantially affects the integrity of the ship or the efficiency or completeness of its equipment covered by this Annex the master or owner of the ship shall report at the earliest opportunity to the Administration, the recognized organization or the nominated surveyor responsible for issuing the relevant Certificate, who shall cause investigations to be initiated to determine whether a survey as required by paragraph (1) of this Regulation is necessary. If the ship is in a port of another Party, the master or owner shall also report immediately to the appropriate authorities of the Port State and the nominated surveyor or recognized organization shall ascertain that such report has been made.

Regulation 5
Issue of Certificate

(1) An International Oil Pollution Prevention Certificate shall be issued, after survey in accordance with the provisions of Regulation 4 of this Annex, to any oil tanker of 150 tons gross tonnage and above and any other ships of 400 tons gross tonnage and above which are engaged in voyages to ports or off-shore terminals under the jurisdiction of other Parties to the Convention. In the case of existing ships this requirement shall apply twelve months after the date of entry into force of the present Convention.

(2) Such Certificate shall be issued either by the Administration or by any persons or organization duly authorized by it. In every case the Administration assumes full responsibility for the Certificate.

Regulation 6
Issue of a Certificate by another Government

(1) The Government of a Party to the Convention may, at the request of the Administration, cause a ship to be surveyed and, if satisfied that the provisions of this Annex are complied with, shall issue or authorize the issue

of an International Oil Pollution Prevention Certificate to the ship in accordance with this Annex.

(2) A copy of the Certificate and a copy of the survey report shall be transmitted as soon as possible to the requesting Administration.

(3) A Certificate so issued shall contain a statement to the effect that it has been issued at the request of the Administration and it shall have the same force and receive the same recognition as the Certificate issued under Regulation 5 of this Annex.

(4) No International Oil Pollution Prevention Certificate shall be issued to a ship which is entitled to fly the flag of a State which is not a Party.

Regulation 7
Form of Certificate

The International Oil Pollution Prevention Certificate shall be drawn up in an official language of the issuing country in the form corresponding to the model given in Appendix II to this Annex. If the language used is neither English nor French, the text shall include a translation into one of these languages.

Regulation 8
Duration of Certificate

(1) An International Oil Pollution Prevention Certificate shall be issued for a period specified by the Administration, which shall not exceed five years from the date of issue, provided that in the case of an oil tanker operating with dedicated clean ballast tanks for a limited period specified in Regulation 13(9) of this Annex, the period of validity of the Certificate shall not exceed such specified period.

(2) A Certificate shall cease to be valid if significant alterations have taken place in the construction, equipment, systems, fittings, arrangements or material required without the sanction of the Administration, except the direct replacement of such equipment or fittings, or if intermediate surveys as specified by the Administration under Regulation 4(1)(c) of this Annex are not carried out.

(3) A Certificate issued to a ship shall also cease to be valid upon transfer of the ship to the flag of another State. A new Certificate shall only be issued when the Government issuing the new Certificate is fully satisfied that the ship is in full compliance with the requirements of Regulation 4(4)(a) and (b) of this Annex. In the case of a transfer between Parties, if requested within three months after the transfer has taken place, the Government of the Party whose flag the ship was formerly entitled to fly shall transmit as soon as possible to the Administration a copy of the Certificate carried by the ship before the transfer and, if available, a copy of the relevant survey report.

CHAPTER II—REQUIREMENTS FOR CONTROL OF OPERATIONAL POLLUTION
Regulation 9
Control of Discharge of Oil

(1) Subject to the provisions of Regulations 10 and 11 of this Annex and paragraph (2) of this Regulation, any discharge into the sea of oil or oily

mixtures from ships to which this Annex applies shall be prohibited except when all the following conditions are satisfied:

(a) for an oil tanker, except as provided for in sub-paragraph (b) of this paragraph:

(i) the tanker is not within a special area;

(ii) the tanker is more than 50 nautical miles from the nearest land;

(iii) the tanker is proceeding en route;

(iv) the instantaneous rate of discharge of oil content does not exceed 60 litres per nautical mile;

(v) the total quantity of oil discharged into the sea does not exceed for existing tankers 1/15,000 of the total quantity of the particular cargo of which the residue formed a part, and for new tankers 1/30,000 of the total quantity of the particular cargo of which the residue formed a part; and

(vi) the tanker has in operation an oil discharge monitoring and control system and a slop tank arrangement as required by Regulation 15 of this Annex.

(b) from a ship of 400 tons gross tonnage and above other than an oil tanker and from machinery space bilges excluding cargo pump room bilges of an oil tanker unless mixed with oil cargo residue:

(i) the ship is not within a special area;

(ii) the ship is more than 12 nautical miles from the nearest land;

(iii) the ship is proceeding en route;

(iv) the oil content of the effluent is less than 100 parts per million; and

(v) the ship has in operation an oil discharge monitoring and control system, oily-water separating equipment, oil filtering equipment or other installation as required by Regulation 16 of this Annex.

(2) In the case of a ship of less than 400 tons gross tonnage other than an oil tanker whilst outside the special area, the Administration shall ensure that it is equipped as far as practicable and reasonable with installations to ensure the storage of oil residues on board and their discharge to reception facilities or into the sea in compliance with the requirements of paragraph (1)(b) of this Regulation.

(3) Whenever visible traces of oil are observed on or below the surface of the water in the immediate vicinity of a ship or its wake, Governments of Parties to the Convention should, to the extent they are reasonably able to do so, promptly investigate the facts bearing on the issue of whether there has been a violation of the provisions of this Regulation or Regulation 10 of this Annex. The investigation should include, in particular, the wind and sea conditions, the track and speed of the ship, other possible sources of the visible traces in the vicinity, and any relevant oil discharge records.

(4) The provisions of paragraph (1) of this Regulation shall not apply to the discharge of clean or segregated ballast or unprocessed oily mixtures which without dilution have an oil content not exceeding 15 parts per million and which do not originate from cargo pump-room bilges and are not mixed with oil cargo residues. The provisions of sub-paragraph (1)(b) of this Regulation shall not apply to the discharge of the processed oily mixture, provided that all of the following conditions are satisfied:

(a) the oily mixture does not originate from cargo pump-room bilges;

(b) the oily mixture is not mixed with oil cargo residues;

(c) the oil content of the effluent without dilution does not exceed 15 parts per million; and

(d) the ship has in operation oil filtering equipment complying with Regulation 16(7) of this Annex.

(5) No discharge into the sea shall contain chemicals or other substances in quantities or concentrations which are hazardous to the marine environment or chemicals or other substances introduced for the purpose of circumventing the conditions of discharge specified in this Regulation.

(6) The oil residues which cannot be discharged into the sea in compliance with paragraphs (1), (2) and (4) of this Regulation shall be retained on board or discharged to reception facilities.

Regulation 10

*Methods for the Prevention of Oil Pollution from
Ships while operating in Special Areas*

(1) For the purposes of this Annex the special areas are the Mediterranean Sea area, the Baltic Sea area, the Black Sea area, the Red Sea area and the "Gulfs area" which are defined as follows:

(a) The Mediterranean Sea area means the Mediterranean Sea proper including the gulfs and seas therein with the boundary between the Mediterranean and the Black Sea constituted by the 41°N parallel and bounded to the west by the Straits of Gibraltar at the meridian of 5°36'W.

(b) The Baltic Sea area means the Baltic Sea proper with the Gulf of Bothnia, the Gulf of Finland and the entrance to the Baltic Sea bounded by the parallel of the Skaw in the Skagerrak at 57°44.8'N.

(c) The Black Sea area means the Black Sea proper with the boundary between the Mediterranean and the Black Sea constituted by the parallel 41°N.

(d) The Red Sea area means the Red Sea proper including the Gulfs of Suez and Aqaba bounded at the south by the rhumb line between Ras si Ane (12°8.5'N, 43°19.6'E) and Husn Murad (12°40.4'N, 43°30.2'E).

(e) The Gulfs area means the sea area located north west of the rhumb line between Ras al Hadd (22°30'N, 59°48'E) and Ras Al Fasteh (25°04'N, 61°25'E).

(2) Subject to the provisions of Regulation 11 of this Annex:

(a) Any discharge into the sea of oil or oily mixture from any oil tanker and any ship of 400 tons gross tonnage and above other than an oil tanker shall be prohibited while in a special area;

(b) any discharge into the sea of oil or oily mixture from a ship of less than 400 tons gross tonnage, other than an oil tanker, shall be prohibited while in a special area, except when the oil content of the effluent without dilution does not exceed 15 parts per million or alternatively when all of the following conditions are satisfied:

(i) the ship is proceeding en route;

(ii) the oil content of the effluent is less than 100 parts per million; and

(iii) the discharge is made as far as practicable from the land, but in no case less than 12 nautical miles from the nearest land.

(3)(a) The provisions of paragraph (2) of this Regulation shall not apply to the discharge of clean or segregated ballast.

(b) The provisions of sub-paragraph (2)(a) of this Regulation shall not apply to the discharge of processed bilge water from machinery spaces, provided that all of the following conditions are satisfied:

(i) the bilge water does not originate from cargo pump room bilges;

(ii) the bilge water is not mixed with oil cargo residues;

(iii) the ship is proceeding en route;

(iv) the oil content of the effluent without dilution does not exceed 15 parts per million;

(v) the ship has in operation oil filtering equipment complying with Regulation 16(7) of this Annex; and

(vi) the filtering system is equipped with a stopping device which will ensure that the discharge is automatically stopped when the oil content of the effluent exceeds 15 parts per million.

(4)(a) No discharge into the sea shall contain chemicals or other substances in quantities or concentrations which are hazardous to the marine environment or chemicals or other substances introduced for the purpose of circumventing the conditions of discharge specified in this Regulation.

(b) The oil residues which cannot be discharged into the sea in compliance with paragraph (2) or (3) of this Regulation shall be retained on board or discharged to reception facilities.

(5) Nothing in this Regulation shall prohibit a ship on a voyage only part of which is in a special area from discharging outside the special area in accordance with Regulation 9 of this Annex.

(6) Whenever visible traces of oil are observed on or below the surface of the water in the immediate vicinity of a ship or its wake, the Governments of Parties to the Convention should, to the extent they are reasonably able to do so, promptly investigate the facts bearing on the issue of whether there has been a violation of the provisions of this Regulation or Regulation 9 of this Annex. The investigation should include, in particular, the wind and sea

conditions, the track and speed of the ship, other possible sources of the visible traces in the vicinity, and any relevant oil discharge records.

(7) Reception facilities within special areas:

(a) Mediterranean Sea, Black Sea and Baltic Sea areas:

(i) The Government of each Party to the Convention, the coast-line of which borders on any given special area undertakes to ensure that not later than 1 January 1977 all oil loading terminals and repair ports within the special area are provided with facilities adequate for the reception and treatment of all the dirty ballast and tank washing water from oil tankers. In addition all ports within the special area shall be provided with adequate reception facilities for other residues and oily mixtures from all ships. Such facilities shall have adequate capacity to meet the needs of the ships using them without causing undue delay.

(ii) The Government of each Party having under its jurisdiction entrances to seawater courses with low depth contour which might require a reduction of draught by the discharge of ballast undertakes to ensure the provision of the facilities referred to in sub-paragraph (a)(i) of this paragraph but with the proviso that ships required to discharge slops or dirty ballast could be subject to some delay.

(iii) During the period between the entry into force of the present Convention (if earlier than 1 January 1977) and 1 January 1977 ships while navigating in the special areas shall comply with the requirements of Regulation 9 of this Annex. However, the Governments of Parties the coastlines of which border any of the special areas under this sub-paragraph may establish a date earlier than 1 January 1977, but after the date of entry into force of the present Convention, from which the requirements of this Regulation in respect of the special areas in question shall take effect:

(1) if all the reception facilities required have been provided by the date so established; and

(2) provided that the Parties concerned notify the Organization of the date so established at least six months in advance, for circulation to other Parties.

(iv) After 1 January 1977, or the date established in accordance with sub-paragraph (a)(iii) of this paragraph if earlier, each Party shall notify the Organization for transmission to the Contracting Governments concerned of all cases where the facilities are alleged to be inadequate.

(b) Red Sea area and Gulfs area:

(i) The Government of each Party the coastline of which borders on the special areas undertakes to ensure that as soon as possible all oil loading terminals and repair ports within these special areas are provided with facilities adequate for the reception and treatment of all the dirty ballast and tank washing water from tankers. In addition all ports within the special area shall be provided with adequate reception facilities for other residues and oily mixtures from all ships. Such facilities shall have adequate capacity to meet the needs of the ships using them without causing undue delay.

(ii) The Government of each Party having under its jurisdiction entrances to seawater courses with low depth contour which might require a reduction of draught by the discharge of ballast shall undertake to ensure the provision of the facilities referred to in sub-paragraph (b)(i) of this paragraph but with the proviso that ships required to discharge slops or dirty ballast could be subject to some delay.

(iii) Each Party concerned shall notify the Organization of the measures taken pursuant to provisions of sub-paragraph (b)(i) and (ii) of this paragraph. Upon receipt of sufficient notifications the Organization shall establish a date from which the requirements of this Regulation in respect of the area in question shall take effect. The Organization shall notify all Parties of the date so established no less than twelve months in advance of that date.

(iv) During the period between the entry into force of the present Convention and the date so established, ships while navigating in the special area shall comply with the requirements of Regulation 9 of this Annex.

(v) After such date oil tankers loading in ports in these special areas where such facilities are not yet available shall also fully comply with the requirements of this Regulation. However, oil tankers entering these special areas for the purpose of loading shall make every effort to enter the area with only clean ballast on board.

(vi) After the date on which the requirements for the special area in question take effect, each Party shall notify the Organization for transmission to the Parties concerned of all cases where the facilities are alleged to be inadequate.

(vii) At least the reception facilities as prescribed in Regulation 12 of this Annex shall be provided by 1 January 1977 or one year after the date of entry into force of the present Convention, whichever occurs later.

Regulation 11

Exceptions

Regulations 9 and 10 of this Annex shall not apply to:

(a) the discharge into the sea of oil or oily mixture necessary for the purpose of securing the safety of a ship or saving life at sea; or

(b) the discharge into the sea of oil or oily mixture resulting from damage to a ship or its equipment:

(i) provided that all reasonable precautions have been taken after the occurrence of the damage or discovery of the discharge for the purpose of preventing or minimizing the discharge; and

(ii) except if the owner or the Master acted either with intent to cause damage, or recklessly and with knowledge that damage would probably result; or

(c) the discharge into the sea of substances containing oil, approved by the Administration, when being used for the purpose of combating specific pollution incidents in order to minimize the damage from pollution. Any such discharge shall be subject to the approval of any Government in whose jurisdiction it is contemplated the discharge will occur.

Regulation 12
Reception Facilities

(1) Subject to the provisions of Regulation 10 of this Annex, the Government of each Party undertakes to ensure the provision at oil loading terminals, repair ports, and in other ports in which ships have oily residues to discharge, of facilities for the reception of such residues and oily mixtures as remain from oil tankers and other ships adequate to meet the needs of the ships using them without causing undue delay to ships.

(2) Reception facilities in accordance with paragraph (1) of this Regulation shall be provided in:

(a) all ports and terminals in which crude oil is loaded into oil tankers where such tankers have immediately prior to arrival completed a ballast voyage of not more than 72 hours or not more than 1,200 nautical miles;

(b) all ports and terminals in which oil other than crude oil in bulk is loaded at an average quantity of more than 1,000 metric tons per day;

(c) all ports having ship repair yards or tank cleaning facilities;

(d) all ports and terminals which handle ships provided with the sludge tank(s) required by Regulation 17 of this Annex;

(e) all ports in respect of oily bilge waters and other residues, which cannot be discharged in accordance with Regulation 9 of this Annex; and

(f) all loading ports for bulk cargoes in respect of oil residues from combination carriers which cannot be discharged in accordance with Regulation 9 of this Annex.

(3) The capacity for the reception facilities shall be as follows:

(a) Crude oil loading terminals shall have sufficient reception facilities to receive oil and oily mixtures which cannot be discharged in accordance with the provisions of Regulation 9(1)(a) of this Annex from all oil tankers on voyages as described in paragraph (2)(a) of this Regulation.

(b) Loading ports and terminals referred to in paragraph (2)(b) of this Regulation shall have sufficient reception facilities to receive oil and oily mixtures which cannot be discharged in accordance with the provisions of Regulation 9(1)(a) of this Annex from oil tankers which load oil other than crude oil in bulk.

(c) All ports having ship repair yards or tank cleaning facilities shall have sufficient reception facilities to receive all residues and oily mixtures which remain on board for disposal from ships prior to entering such yards or facilities.

(d) All facilities provided in ports and terminals under paragraph (2)(d) of this Regulation shall be sufficient to receive all residues retained according to Regulation 17 of this Annex from all ships that may reasonably be expected to call at such ports and terminals.

(e) All facilities provided in ports and terminals under this Regulation shall be sufficient to receive only bilge waters and other residues which cannot be discharged in accordance with Regulation 9 of this Annex.

(f) The facilities provided in loading ports for bulk cargoes shall take into account the special problems of combination carriers as appropriate.

(4) The reception facilities prescribed in paragraphs (2) and (3) of this Regulation shall be made available no later than one year from the date of entry into force of the present Convention or by 1 January 1977, whichever occurs later.

(5) Each Party shall notify the Organization for transmission to the Parties concerned of all cases where the facilities provided under this Regulation are alleged to be inadequate.

Regulation 13

Segregated Ballast Tanks, Dedicated Clean Ballast Tanks and Crude Oil Washing

Subject to the provisions of Regulations 13C and 13D of this Annex, oil tankers shall comply with the requirements of this Regulation.

New oil tankers of 20,000 tons deadweight and above

(1) Every new crude oil tanker of 20,000 tons deadweight and above and every new product carrier of 30,000 tons deadweight and above shall be provided with segregated ballast tanks and shall comply with paragraphs (2), (3) and (4), or paragraph (5) as appropriate, of this Regulation.

(2) The capacity of the segregated ballast tanks shall be so determined that the ship may operate safely on ballast voyages without recourse to the use of cargo tanks for water ballast except as provided for in paragraph (3) or (4) of this Regulation. In all cases, however, the capacity of segregated ballast tanks shall be at least such that, in any ballast condition at any part of the voyage, including the conditions consisting of lightweight plus segregated ballast only, the ship's draughts and trim can meet each of the following requirements:

(a) the moulded draught amidships (dm) in metres (without taking into account any ship's deformation) shall not be less than:

$$dm = 2.0 + 0.02L;$$

(b) the draughts at the forward and after perpendiculars shall correspond to those determined by the draught amidships (dm) as specified in subparagraph (a) of this paragraph, in association with the trim by the stern of not greater than 0.015L; and

(c) in any case the draught at the after perpendicular shall not be less than that which is necessary to obtain full immersion of the propeller(s).

(3) In no case shall ballast water be carried in cargo tanks, except:

(a) on those rare voyages when weather conditions are so severe that, in the opinion of the master, it is necessary to carry additional ballast water in cargo tanks for the safety of the ship;

(b) in exceptional cases where the particular character of the operation of an oil tanker renders it necessary to carry ballast water in excess of the quantity required under paragraph (2) of this Regulation, provided that such operation of the oil tanker falls under the category of exceptional cases as established by the Organization.

Such additional ballast water shall be processed and discharged in compliance with Regulation 9 of this Annex and in accordance with the requirements of Regulation 15 of this Annex and an entry shall be made in the Oil Record Book referred to in Regulation 20 of this Annex.

(4) In the case of new crude oil tankers, the additional ballast permitted in paragraph (3) of this Regulation shall be carried in cargo tanks only if such tanks have been crude oil washed in accordance with Regulation 13B of this Annex before departure from an oil unloading port or terminal.

(5) Notwithstanding the provisions of paragraph (2) of this Regulation, the segregated ballast conditions for oil tankers less than 150 metres in length shall be to the satisfaction of the Administration.

(6) Every new crude oil tanker of 20,000 tons deadweight and above shall be fitted with a cargo tank cleaning system using crude oil washing. The Administration shall undertake to ensure that the system fully complies with the requirements of Regulation 13B of this Annex within one year after the tanker was first engaged in the trade of carrying crude oil or by the end of the third voyage carrying crude oil suitable for crude oil washing, whichever occurs later. Unless such oil tanker carries crude oil which is not suitable for crude oil washing, the oil tanker shall operate the system in accordance with the requirements of that Regulation.

Existing crude oil tankers of 40,000 tons deadweight and above

(7) Subject to the provisions of paragraphs (8) and (9) of this Regulation every existing crude oil tanker of 40,000 tons deadweight and above shall be provided with segregated ballast tanks and shall comply with the requirements of paragraphs (2) and (3) of this Regulation from the date of entry into force of the present Convention.

(8) Existing crude oil tankers referred to in paragraph (7) of this Regulation may, in lieu of being provided with segregated ballast tanks, operate with a cargo tank cleaning procedure using crude oil washing in accordance with Regulation 13B of this Annex unless the crude oil tanker is intended to carry crude oil which is not suitable for crude oil washing.

(9) Existing crude oil tankers referred to in paragraph (7) or (8) of this Regulation may, in lieu of being provided with segregated ballast tanks or operating with a cargo tank cleaning procedure using crude oil washing, operate with dedicated clean ballast tanks in accordance with the provisions of Regulation 13A of this Annex for the following period:

(a) for crude oil tankers of 70,000 tons deadweight and above, until two years after the date of entry into force of the present Convention; and

(b) for crude oil tankers of 40,000 tons deadweight and above but below 70,000 tons deadweight, until four years after the date of entry into force of the present Convention.

Existing product carriers of 40,000 tons deadweight and above

(10) From the date of entry into force of the present Convention, every existing product carrier of 40,000 tons deadweight and above shall be provided with segregated ballast tanks and shall comply with the requirements of paragraphs (2) and (3) of this Regulation, or, alternatively, operate with dedicated clean ballast tanks in accordance with the provisions of Regulation 13A of this Annex.

An oil tanker qualified as a segregated ballast oil tanker

(11) Any oil tanker which is not required to be provided with segregated ballast tanks in accordance with paragraph (1), (7) or (10) of this Regulation may, however, be qualified as a segregated ballast tanker, provided that it complies with the requirements of paragraphs (2) and (3), or paragraph (5) as appropriate, of this Regulation.

Regulation 13A

Requirements for Oil Tankers with Dedicated Clean Ballast Tanks

(1) An oil tanker operating with dedicated clean ballast tanks in accordance with the provisions of Regulation 13(9) or (10) of this Annex, shall have adequate tank capacity, dedicated solely to the carriage of clean ballast as defined in Regulation 1(16) of this Annex, to meet the requirements of Regulation 13(2) and (3) of this Annex.

(2) The arrangements and operational procedures for dedicated clean ballast tanks shall comply with the requirements established by the Administration. Such requirements shall contain at least all the provisions of the Specifications for Oil Tankers with Dedicated Clean Ballast Tanks adopted by the International Conference on Tanker Safety and Pollution Prevention, 1978, in Resolution 14 and as may be revised by the Organization.

(3) An oil tanker operating with dedicated clean ballast tanks shall be equipped with an oil content meter, approved by the Administration on the basis of specifications recommended by the Organization, to enable supervision of the oil content in ballast water being discharged. The oil content meter shall be installed no later than at the first scheduled shipyard visit of the tanker following the entry into force of the present Convention. Until such time as the oil content meter is installed, it shall immediately before discharge of ballast be established by examination of the ballast water from dedicated tanks that no contamination with oil has taken place.

(4) Every oil tanker operating with dedicated clean ballast tanks shall be provided with a Dedicated Clean Ballast Tank Operation Manual detailing the system and specifying operational procedures. Such a Manual shall be to the satisfaction of the Administration and shall contain all the information set out in the Specifications referred to in paragraph (2) of this Regulation. If an alteration affecting the dedicated clean ballast tank system is made, the Operation Manual shall be revised accordingly.

Regulation 13B
Requirements for Crude Oil Washing

(1) Every crude oil washing system required to be provided in accordance with Regulation 13(6) and (8) of this Annex shall comply with the requirements of this Regulation.

(2) The crude oil washing installation and associated equipment and arrangements shall comply with the requirements established by the Administration. Such requirements shall contain at least all the provisions of the Specifications for the Design, Operation and Control of Crude Oil Washing Systems adopted by the International Conference on Tanker Safety and Pollution Prevention, 1978, in Resolution 15 and as may be revised by the Organization.

(3) An inert gas system shall be provided in every cargo tank and slop tank in accordance with the appropriate Regulations of Chapter II–2 of the International Convention for the Safety of Life at Sea, 1974, as modified and added to by the Protocol of 1978 Relating to the International Convention for the Safety of Life at Sea, 1974 and as may be further amended.

(4) With respect to the ballasting of cargo tanks, sufficient cargo tanks shall be crude oil washed prior to each ballast voyage in order that, taking into account the tanker's trading pattern and expected weather conditions, ballast water is put only into cargo tanks which have been crude oil washed.

(5) Every oil tanker operating with crude oil washing systems shall be provided with an Operations and Equipment Manual detailing the system and equipment and specifying operational procedures. Such a Manual shall be to the satisfaction of the Administration and shall contain all the information set out in the Specifications referred to in paragraph (2) of this Regulation. If an alteration affecting the crude oil washing system is made, the Operations and Equipment Manual shall be revised accordingly.

Regulation 13C
Existing Tankers Engaged in Specific Trades

(1) Subject to the provisions of paragraph (2) of this Regulation, Regulation 13(7) to (10) of this Annex shall not apply to an existing oil tanker solely engaged in specific trades between:

    (a) ports or terminals within a State Party to the present Convention; or

    (b) ports or terminals of States Parties to the present Convention, where:

        (i) the voyage is entirely within a Special Area as defined in Regulation 10(1) of this Annex; or

        (ii) the voyage is entirely within other limits designated by the Organization.

(2) The provisions of paragraph (1) of this Regulation shall only apply when the ports or terminals where cargo is loaded on such voyages are provided with reception facilities adequate for the reception and treatment of all the ballast and tank washing water from oil tankers using them and all the following conditions are complied with:

(a) subject to the exceptions provided for in Regulation 11 of this Annex, all ballast water, including clean ballast water, and tank washing residues are retained on board and transferred to the reception facilities and the appropriate entry in the Oil Record Book referred to in Regulation 20 of this Annex is endorsed by the competent Port State Authority;

(b) agreement has been reached between the Administration and the Governments of the Port States referred to in sub-paragraph (1)(a) or (b) of this Regulation concerning the use of an existing oil tanker for a specific trade;

(c) the adequacy of the reception facilities in accordance with the relevant provisions of this Annex at the ports or terminals referred to above, for the purpose of this Regulation, is approved by the Governments of the States Parties to the present Convention within which such ports or terminals are situated; and

(d) the International Oil Pollution Prevention Certificate is endorsed to the effect that the oil tanker is solely engaged in such specific trade.

Regulation 13D

Existing Oil Tankers Having Special Ballast Arrangements

(1) Where an existing oil tanker is so constructed or operates in such a manner that it complies at all times with the draught and trim requirements set out in Regulation 13(2) of this Annex without recourse to the use of ballast water, it shall be deemed to comply with the segregated ballast tank requirements referred to in Regulation 13(7) of this Annex, provided that all of the following conditions are complied with:

(a) operational procedures and ballast arrangements are approved by the Administration;

(b) agreement is reached between the Administration and the Governments of the Port States Parties to the present Convention concerned when the draught and trim requirements are achieved through an operational procedure; and

(c) the International Oil Pollution Prevention Certificate is endorsed to the effect that the oil tanker is operating with special ballast arrangements.

(2) In no case shall ballast water be carried in oil tanks except on those rare voyages when weather conditions are so severe that, in the opinion of the master, it is necessary to carry additional ballast water in cargo tanks for the safety of the ship. Such additional ballast water shall be processed and discharged in compliance with Regulation 9 of this Annex and in accordance with the requirements of Regulation 15 of this Annex, and entry shall be made in the Oil Record Book referred to in Regulation 20 of this Annex.

(3) An Administration which has endorsed a Certificate in accordance with subparagraph (1)(c) of this Regulation shall communicate to the Organization the particulars thereof for circulation to the Parties to the present Convention.

Regulation 13E
Protective Location of Segregated Ballast Spaces

(1) In every new crude oil tanker of 20,000 tons deadweight and above and every new product carrier of 30,000 tons deadweight and above, the segregated ballast tanks required to provide the capacity to comply with the requirements of Regulation 13 of this Annex which are located within the cargo tank length, shall be arranged in accordance with the requirements of paragraphs (2), (3) and (4) of this Regulation to provide a measure of protection against oil outflow in the event of grounding or collision.

(2) Segregated ballast tanks and spaces other than oil tanks within the cargo tank length (L_t) shall be so arranged as to comply with the following requirement:

$$\Sigma\, PA_c + \Sigma\, PA_s \geq J[L_t\,(B + 2D)\,]$$

where: PA_c　=　the side shell area in square metres for each segregated ballast tank or space other than an oil tank based on projected moulded dimensions.

　　　　PA_s　=　the bottom shell area in square metres for each such tank or space based on projected moulded dimensions.

　　　　L_t　=　length in metres between the forward and after extremities of the cargo tanks.

　　　　B　=　maximum breadth of the ship in metres as defined in Regulation l(21) of this Annex.

　　　　D　=　moulded depth in metres measured vertically from the top of the keel to the top of the freeboard deck beam at side amidships. In ships having rounded gunwales, the moulded depth shall be measured to the point of intersection of the moulded lines of the deck and side shell plating, the lines extending as though the gunwale were of angular design.

　　　　J　=　0.45 for oil tankers of 20,000 tons deadweight, 0.30 for oil tankers of 200,000 tons deadweight and above, subject to the provisions of paragraph (3) of this Regulation.

　　　　　　For intermediate values of deadweight the value of "J" shall be determined by linear interpolation.

Whenever symbols given in this paragraph appear in this Regulation, they have the meaning as defined in this paragraph.

(3) For tankers of 200,000 tons deadweight and above the value of "J" may be reduced as follows:

$$J\ reduced = \left[J - \left(a - \frac{O_c + O_s}{40_A} \right) \right]\ or\ 0.2\ whichever\ is\ greater$$

where: a　=　0.25 for oil tankers of 200,000 tons deadweight

　　　　a　=　0.40 for oil tankers of 300,000 tons deadweight

　　　　a　=　0.50 for oil tankers of 420,000 tons deadweight and above,

　　　　For intermediate values of deadweight the value of "a" shall be determined by linear interpolation.

　　　　O_c　=　as defined in Regulation 23(1)(a) of this Annex,

　　　　O_s　=　as defined in Regulation 23(1)(b) of this Annex,

　　　　O_A　=　the allowable oil outflow as required by Regulation 24(2) of this Annex,

(4) In the determination of "PA_c" and "PA_s" for segregated ballast tanks and spaces other than oil tanks the following shall apply:

(a) the minimum width of each wing tank or space either of which extends for the full depth of the ship's side or from the deck to the top of the double bottom shall be not less than 2 metres. The width shall be measured inboard from the ship's side at right angles to the centre line. Where a lesser width is provided the wing tank or space shall not be taken into account when calculating the protecting area "PA_c"; and

(b) the minimum vertical depth of each double bottom tank or space shall be B/15 or 2 metres, whichever is the lesser. Where a lesser depth is provided the bottom tank or space shall not be taken into account when calculating the protecting area "PA_s".

The minimum width and depth of wing tanks and double bottom tanks shall be measured clear of the bilge area and, in the case of minimum width, shall be measured clear of any rounded gunwale area.

Regulation 14

Segregation of Oil and Water Ballast and
Carriage of Oil in Forepeak Tanks

(1) Except as provided in paragraph (2) of this Regulation, in new ships of 4,000 tons gross tonnage and above other than oil tankers, and in new oil tankers of 150 tons gross tonnage and above, no ballast water shall be carried in any oil fuel tank.

(2) Where abnormal conditions or the need to carry large quantities of oil fuel render it necessary to carry ballast water which is not a clean ballast in any oil fuel tank, such ballast water shall be discharged to reception facilities or into the sea in compliance with Regulation 9 using the equipment specified in Regulation 16(2) of this Annex, and an entry shall be made in the Oil Record Book to this effect.

(3) All other ships shall comply with the requirements of paragraph (1) of this Regulation as far as reasonable and practicable.

(4) In a ship of 400 tons gross tonnage and above, for which the building contract is placed after 1 January 1982 or, in the absence of a building contract, the keel of which is laid or which is at a similar stage of construction after 1 July 1982, oil shall not be carried in a forepeak tank or a tank forward of the collision bulkhead.

(5) All ships other than those subject to paragraph (4) of this Regulation shall comply with the provisions of that paragraph, as far as is reasonable and practicable.

Regulation 15

Retention of Oil on Board

(1) Subject to the provisions of paragraphs (5) and (6) of this Regulation, oil tankers of 150 tons gross tonnage and above shall be provided with arrangements in accordance with the requirements of paragraphs (2) and (3) of this Regulation, provided that in the case of existing tankers the require-

ments for oil discharge monitoring and control systems and slop tank arrangements shall apply three years after the date of entry into force of the present Convention.

(2)(a) Adequate means shall be provided for cleaning the cargo tanks and transferring the dirty ballast residue and tank washings from the cargo tanks into a slop tank approved by the Administration. In existing oil tankers, any cargo tank may be designated as a slop tank.

(b) In this system arrangements shall be provided to transfer the oily waste into a slop tank or combination of slop tanks in such a way that any effluent discharged into the sea will be such as to comply with the provisions of Regulation 9 of this Annex.

(c) The arrangements of the slop tank or combination of slop tanks shall have a capacity necessary to retain the slop generated by tank washings, oil residues and dirty ballast residues. The total capacity of the slop tank or tanks shall not be less than 3 per cent of the oil carrying capacity of the ships, except that the Administration may accept:

(i) 2 per cent for such oil tankers where the tank washing arrangements are such that once the slop tank or tanks are charged with washing water, this water is sufficient for tank washing and, where applicable, for providing the driving fluid for eductors, without the introduction of additional water into the system;

(ii) 2 per cent where segregated ballast tanks or dedicated clean ballast tanks are provided in accordance with Regulation 13 of this Annex, or where a cargo tank cleaning system using crude oil washing is fitted in accordance with Regulation 13B of this Annex. This capacity may be further reduced to 1.5 per cent for such oil tankers where the tank washing arrangements are such that once the slop tank or tanks are charged with washing water, this water is sufficient for tank washing and, where applicable, for providing the driving fluid for eductors, without the introduction of additional water into the system;

(iii) 1 per cent for combination carriers where oil cargo is only carried in tanks with smooth walls. This capacity may be further reduced to 0.8 per cent where the tank washing arrangements are such that once the slop tank or tanks are charged with washing water, this water is sufficient for tank washing and, where applicable, for providing the driving fluid for eductors, without the introduction of additional water into the system.

New oil tankers of 70,000 tons deadweight and above shall be provided with at least two slop tanks.

(d) Slop tanks shall be so designed particularly in respect of the position of inlets, outlets, baffles or weirs where fitted, so as to avoid excessive turbulence and entrainment of oil or emulsion with the water.

(3)(a) An oil discharge monitoring and control system approved by the Administration shall be fitted. In considering the design of the oil content meter to be incorporated in the system, the Administration shall have regard to the specification recommended by the Organization. The system shall be fitted with a recording device to provide a continuous record of the discharge in litres per nautical mile and total quantity discharged, or the oil content and rate of discharge. This record shall be identifiable as to time and date and shall be kept for at least three years. The oil discharge monitor and control system shall come into operation when there is any discharge of effluent into the sea and shall be such as will ensure that any discharge of oily mixture is automatically stopped when the instantaneous rate of discharge of oil exceeds that permitted by Regulation 9(1)(a) of this Annex. Any failure of this monitoring and control system shall stop the discharge and be noted in the Oil Record Book. A manually operated alternative method shall be provided and may be used in the event of such failure, but the defective unit shall be made operable before the oil tanker commences its next ballast voyage unless it is proceeding to a repair port. The oil discharge monitoring and control system shall be designed and installed in compliance with the Guidelines and Specifications for Oil Discharge Monitoring and Control Systems for Oil Tankers developed by the Organization. Administrations may accept such specific arrangements as detailed in the Guidelines and Specifications.

(b) Effective oil/water interface detectors approved by the Administration shall be provided for a rapid and accurate determination of the oil/water interface in slop tanks and shall be available for use in other tanks where the separation of oil and water is effected and from which it is intended to discharge effluent direct to the sea.

(c) Instructions as to the operation of the system shall be in accordance with an operational manual approved by the Administration. They shall cover manual as well as automatic operations and shall be intended to ensure that at no time shall oil be discharged except in compliance with the conditions specified in Regulation 9 of this Annex.

(4) The requirements of paragraphs (1), (2) and (3) of this Regulation shall not apply to oil tankers of less than 150 tons gross tonnage, for which the control of discharge of oil under Regulation 9 of this Annex shall be effected by the retention of oil on board with subsequent discharge of all contaminated washings to reception facilities. The total quantity of oil and water used for washing and returned to a storage tank shall be recorded in the Oil Record Book. This total quantity shall be discharged to reception facilities unless adequate arrangements are made to ensure that any effluent which is allowed to be discharged into the sea is effectively monitored to ensure that the provisions of Regulation 9 of this Annex are complied with.

(5)(a) The Administration may waive the requirements of paragraphs (1), (2) and (3) of this Regulation for any oil tanker which engages exclusively on voyages both of 72 hours or less in duration and within 50 miles from the nearest land, provided that the oil tanker is engaged exclusively in trades between ports or terminals within a State Party to the present Convention. Any such waiver shall be subject to the requirement that the oil tanker shall retain on board all oily mixtures for subsequent discharge to reception facilities and to the determination by the Administration that facilities available to receive such oily mixtures are adequate.

(b) The Administration may waive the requirements of paragraph (3) of this Regulation for oil tankers other than those referred to in subparagraph (a) of this paragraph in cases where:

(i) the tanker is an existing oil tanker of 40,000 tons deadweight or above, as referred to in Regulation 13C(1) of this Annex, engaged in specific trades, and the conditions specified in Regulation 13C(2) are complied with; or

(ii) the tanker is engaged exclusively in one or more of the following categories of voyages:

(1) voyages within special areas; or

(2) voyages within 50 miles from the nearest land outside special areas where the tanker is engaged in:

(aa) trades between ports or terminals of a State Party to the present Convention; or

(bb) restricted voyages as determined by the Administration, and of 72 hours or less in duration;

provided that all of the following conditions are complied with:

(3) all oily mixtures are retained on board for subsequent discharge to reception facilities;

(4) for voyages specified in sub-paragraph (b)(ii)(2) of this paragraph, the Administration has determined that adequate reception facilities are available to receive such oily mixtures in those oil loading ports or terminals the tanker calls at;

(5) the International Oil Pollution Prevention Certificate, when required, is endorsed to the effect that the ship is exclusively engaged in one or more of the categories of voyages specified in sub-paragraphs (b)(ii)(1) and (b)(ii)(2)(bb) of this paragraph; and

(6) the quantity, time and port of the discharge are recorded in the Oil Record Book.

(6) Where in the view of the Organization equipment required by Regulation 9(1)(a)(vi) of this Annex and specified in sub-paragraph (3)(a) of this Regulation is not obtainable for the monitoring of discharge of light refined products (white oils), the Administration may waive compliance with such requirement, provided that discharge shall be permitted only in compliance with procedures established by the Organization which shall satisfy the conditions of Regulation 9(1)(a) of this Annex except the obligation to have an oil discharge monitoring and control system in operation. The Organization shall review the availability of equipment at intervals not exceeding twelve months.

(7) The requirements of paragraphs (1), (2) and (3) of this Regulation shall not apply to oil tankers carrying asphalt or other products subject to the provisions of this Annex, which through their physical properties inhibit effective product/water separation and monitoring, for which the control of discharge under Regulation 9 of this Annex shall be effected by the retention of residues on board with discharge of all contaminated washings to reception facilities.

Regulation 16

*Oil Discharge Monitoring and Control System and Oily–
Water Separating and Oil Filtering Equipment*

(1) Any ship of 400 tons gross tonnage and above but less than 10,000 tons gross tonnage shall be fitted with oily-water separating equipment (100 ppm equipment) complying with paragraph (6) of this Regulation. Any such ship which carries large quantities of oil fuel shall comply with paragraph (2) of this Regulation or paragraph (1) of Regulation 14.

(2) Any ship of 10,000 tons gross tonnage and above shall be fitted either:

(a) with oily-water separating equipment (100 ppm equipment) complying with paragraph (6) of this Regulation and with an oil discharge monitoring and control system complying with paragraph (5) of this Regulation; or

(b) with oil filtering equipment (15 ppm equipment) complying with paragraph (7) of this Regulation.

(3)(a) The Administration may waive the requirements of paragraphs (1) and (2) of this Regulation for any ship engaged exclusively on:

(i) voyages within special areas; or

(ii) voyages within 12 miles of the nearest land outside special areas, provided the ship is in:

(1) trade between ports or terminals within a State Party to the present Convention; or

(2) restricted voyages as determined by the Administration;

provided that all of the following conditions are complied with:

(iii) the ship is fitted with a holding tank having a volume adequate, to the satisfaction of the Administration, for the total retention on board of the oily bilge water;

(iv) all oily bilge water is retained on board for subsequent discharge to reception facilities;

(v) the Administration has determined that adequate reception facilities are available to receive such oily bilge water in a sufficient number of ports or terminals the ship calls at;

(vi) the International Oil Pollution Prevention Certificate, when required, is endorsed to the effect that the ship is exclusively engaged on the voyages specified in sub-paragraph (a)(i) or (a)(ii)(2) of this paragraph; and

(vii) the quantity, time, and port of the discharge are recorded in the Oil Record Book.

(b) The Administration shall ensure that ships of less than 400 tons gross tonnage are equipped, as far as practicable, to retain on board oil or oily mixtures or discharge them in accordance with the requirements of Regulation 9(1)(b) of this Annex.

(4) For existing ships the requirements of paragraphs (1), (2) and (3) of this Regulation shall apply three years after the date of entry into force of the present Convention.

(5) An oil discharge monitoring and control system shall be of a design approved by the Administration. In considering the design of the oil content meter to be incorporated into the system, the Administration shall have regard to the specification recommended by the Organization. The system shall be fitted with a recording device to provide a continuous record of the oil content in parts per million. This record shall be identifiable as to time and date and shall be kept for at least three years. The system shall come into operation when there is any discharge of effluent into the sea and shall be such as will ensure that any discharge of oily mixture is automatically stopped when the oil content of effluent exceeds that permitted by Regulation 9(1)(b) of this Annex. Any failure of the system shall stop the discharge and be noted in the Oil Record Book. The defective unit shall be made operable before the ship commences its next voyage unless it is proceeding to a repair port. Existing ships shall comply with all of the provisions specified above except that the stopping of the discharge may be performed manually.

(6) Oily-water separating equipment referred to in paragraphs (1) and (2)(a) of this Regulation shall be of a design approved by the Administration and shall be such as will ensure that any oily mixture discharged into the sea after passing through the system has an oil content of less than 100 parts per million. In considering the design of such equipment, the Administration shall have regard to the specification recommended by the Organization.

(7) Oil filtering equipment referred to in paragraph (2)(b) of this Regulation shall be of a design approved by the Administration and shall be such as will ensure that any oily mixture discharged into the sea after passing through the system or systems has an oil content not exceeding 15 parts per million. It shall be provided with alarm arrangements to indicate when this level cannot be maintained. In considering the design of such equipment, the Administration shall have regard to the specification recommended by the Organization. In the case of ships less than 10,000 tons gross tonnage, other than those carrying large quantities of oil fuel or those discharging bilge water under Regulation 10(3)(b), which are provided with oil filtering equipment in lieu of oily-water separating equipment, the requirements for the alarm arrangements shall be complied with as far as reasonable and practicable.

Regulation 17
Tanks for Oil Residues (Sludge)

(1) Every ship of 400 tons gross tonnage and above shall be provided with a tank or tanks of adequate capacity, having regard to the type of machinery and length of voyage, to receive the oily residue (sludges) which cannot be dealt with otherwise in accordance with the requirements of this Annex, such as those resulting from the purification of fuel and lubricating oils and oil leakages in the machinery spaces.

(2) In new ships, such tanks shall be designed and constructed so as to facilitate their cleaning and the discharge of residues to reception facilities. Existing ships shall comply with this requirement as far as is reasonable and practicable.

Regulation 18

Pumping, Piping and Discharge Arrangements of Oil Tankers

(1) In every oil tanker, a discharge manifold for connexion to reception facilities for the discharge of dirty ballast water or oil contaminated water shall be located on the open deck on both sides of the ship.

(2) In every oil tanker, pipelines for the discharge to the sea of ballast water or oil-contaminated water from cargo tank areas which may be permitted under Regulation 9 or Regulation 10 of this Annex shall be led to the open deck or to the ship's side above the waterline in the deepest ballast condition. Different piping arrangements to permit operation in the manner permitted in sub-paragraphs (6)(a) to (e) of this Regulation may be accepted.

(3) In new oil tankers means shall be provided for stopping the discharge into the sea of ballast water or oil-contaminated water from cargo tank areas, other than those discharges below the waterline permitted under paragraph (6) of this Regulation, from a position on the upper deck or above located so that the manifold in use referred to in paragraph (1) of this Regulation and the discharge to the sea from the pipelines referred to in paragraph (2) of this Regulation may be visually observed. Means for stopping the discharge need not be provided at the observation position if a positive communication system such as a telephone or radio system is provided between the observation position and the discharge control position.

(4) Every new oil tanker required to be provided with segregated ballast tanks or fitted with a crude oil washing system shall comply with the following requirements:

(a) it shall be equipped with oil piping so designed and installed that oil retention in the lines is minimized; and

(b) means shall be provided to drain all cargo pumps and all oil lines at the completion of cargo discharge, where necessary by connexion to a stripping device. The line and pump drainings shall be capable of being discharged both ashore and to a cargo tank or a slop tank. For discharge ashore a special small diameter line shall be provided and shall be connected outboard of the ship's manifold valves.

(5) Every existing crude oil tanker required to be provided with segregated ballast tanks, or to be fitted with a crude oil washing system, or to operate with dedicated clean ballast tanks, shall comply with the provisions of paragraph (4)(b) of this Regulation.

(6) On every oil tanker the discharge of ballast water or oil contaminated water from cargo tank areas shall take place above the waterline, except as follows:

(a) Segregated ballast and clean ballast may be discharged below the waterline:

(i) in ports or at offshore terminals, or

(ii) at sea by gravity,

provided that the surface of the ballast water has been examined immediately before the discharge to ensure that no contamination with oil has taken place.

(b) Existing oil tankers which, without modification, are not capable of discharging segregated ballast above the waterline may discharge segregated ballast below the waterline at sea, provided that the surface of the ballast water has been examined immediately before the discharge to ensure that no contamination with oil has taken place.

(c) Existing oil tankers operating with dedicated clean ballast tanks, which without modification are not capable of discharging ballast water from dedicated clean ballast tanks above the waterline, may discharge this ballast below the waterline provided that the discharge of the ballast water is supervised in accordance with Regulation 13A(3) of this Annex.

(d) On every oil tanker at sea, dirty ballast water or oil contaminated water from tanks in the cargo area, other than slop tanks, may be discharged by gravity below the waterline, provided that sufficient time has elapsed in order to allow oil/water separation to have taken place and the ballast water has been examined immediately before the discharge with an oil/water interface detector referred to in Regulation 15(3)(b) of this Annex, in order to ensure that the height of the interface is such that the discharge does not involve any increased risk of harm to the marine environment.

(e) On existing oil tankers at sea, dirty ballast water or oil contaminated water from cargo tank areas may be discharged below the waterline, subsequent to or in lieu of the discharge by the method referred to in sub-paragraph (d) of this paragraph, provided that:

(i) a part of the flow of such water is led through permanent piping to a readily accessible location on the upper deck or above where it may be visually observed during the discharge operation; and

(ii) such part flow arrangements comply with the requirements established by the Administration, which shall contain at least all the provisions of the Specifications for the Design, Installation and Operation of a Part Flow System for Control of Overboard Discharges adopted by the Organization.

Regulation 19

Standard Discharge Connection

To enable pipes of reception facilities to be connected with the ship's discharge pipeline for residues from machinery bilges, both lines shall be fitted with a standard discharge connection in accordance with the following table:

STANDARD DIMENSIONS OF FLANGES FOR DISCHARGE CONNECTIONS

Description	Dimension
Outside diameter	215 mm
Inner diameter	According to pipe outside diameter
Bolt circle diameter	183 mm
Slots in flange	6 holes 22 mm in diameter equidistantly placed on a bolt circle of the above diameter, slotted to the flange periphery. The slot width to be 22 mm

Flange thickness	20 mm
Bolts and nuts: quantity, diameter	6, each of 20 mm in diameter and of suitable length

The flange is designed to accept pipes up to a maximum internal diameter of 125 mm and shall be of steel or other equivalent material having a flat face. This flange, together with a gasket of oilproof material, shall be suitable for a service pressure of 6 kg cm²

Regulation 20

Oil Record Book

(1) Every oil tanker of 150 tons gross tonnage and above and every ship of 400 tons gross tonnage and above other than an oil tanker shall be provided with an Oil Record Book Part I (Machinery Space Operations). Every oil tanker of 150 tons gross tonnage and above shall also be provided with an Oil Record Book Part II (Cargo Ballast Operations). The Oil Record Book(s), whether as a part of the ship's official log book or otherwise, shall be in the Form(s) specified in Appendix III to this Annex.

(2) The Oil Record Book shall be completed on each occasion, on a tank to tank basis if appropriate, whenever any of the following operations take place in the ship:

(a) for machinery space operations (all ships):

(i) ballasting or cleaning of oil fuel tanks;

(ii) discharge of dirty ballast or cleaning water from tanks referred to under (i) of the sub-paragraph;

(iii) disposal of oily residues (sludge);

(iv) discharge overboard or disposal otherwise of bilge water which has accumulated in machinery spaces.

(b) for cargo/ballast operations (oil tankers):

(i) loading of oil cargo;

(ii) internal transfer of oil cargo during voyage;

(iii) unloading of oil cargo;

(iv) ballasting of cargo tanks and dedicated clean ballast tanks;

(v) cleaning of cargo tanks including crude oil washing;

(vi) discharge of ballast except from segregated ballast tanks;

(vii) discharge of water from slop tanks;

(viii) closing of all applicable valves or similar devices after slop tank discharge operations;

(ix) closing of valves necessary for isolation of dedicated clean ballast tanks from cargo and stripping lines after slop tank discharge operations;

(x) disposal of residues.

(3) In the event of such discharge of oil or oily mixture as is referred to in Regulation 11 of this Annex or in the event of accidental or other exceptional discharge of oil not excepted by that Regulation, a statement shall be made in

the Oil Record Book of the circumstances of, and the reasons for, the discharge.

(4) Each operation described in paragraph (2) of this Regulation shall be fully recorded without delay in the Oil Record Book so that all the entries in the book appropriate to that operation are completed. Each completed operation shall be signed by the officer or officers in charge of the operations concerned and each completed page shall be signed by the master of the ship. The entries in the Oil Record Book shall be in an official language of the State whose flag the ship is entitled to fly, and, for ships holding an International Oil Pollution Prevention Certificate, in English or French. The entries in an official national language of the State whose flag the ship is entitled to fly shall prevail in case of a dispute or discrepancy.

(5) The Oil Record Book shall be kept in such a place as to be readily available for inspection at all reasonable times and, except in the case of unmanned ships under tow, shall be kept on board the ship. It shall be preserved for a period of three years after the last entry has been made.

(6) The competent authority of the Government of a Party to the Convention may inspect the Oil Record Book on board any ship to which this Annex applies while the ship is in its port or offshore terminals and may make a copy of any entry in that book and may require the Master of the ship to certify that the copy is a true copy of such entry. Any copy so made which has been certified by the Master of the ship as a true copy of an entry in the ship's Oil Record Book shall be made admissible in any judicial proceedings as evidence of the facts stated in the entry. The inspection of an Oil Record Book and the taking of a certified copy by the competent authority under this paragraph shall be performed as expeditiously as possible without causing the ship to be unduly delayed.

(7) For oil tankers of less than 150 tons gross tonnage operating in accordance with Regulation 15(4) of this Annex an appropriate Oil Record Book should be developed by the Administration.

Regulation 21
Special Requirements for Drilling Rigs and other Platforms

Fixed and floating drilling rigs when engaged in the exploration, exploitation and associated offshore processing of sea-bed mineral resources and other platforms shall comply with the requirements of this Annex applicable to ships of 400 tons gross tonnage and above other than oil tankers, except that:

(a) they shall be equipped as far as practicable with the installations required in Regulations 16 and 17 of this Annex:

(b) they shall keep a record of all operations involving oil or oily mixture discharges, in a form approved by the Administration; and

(c) in any special area and subject to the provisions of Regulation 11 of this Annex, the discharge into the sea of oil or oily mixture shall be prohibited except when the oil content of the discharge without dilution does not exceed 15 parts per million.

(d) Outside special areas and more than 12 nautical miles from the nearest land and subject to the provisions of Regulation 11 of this Annex, the discharge from such drilling rigs and platforms when stationary into the sea of oil or oily mixtures shall be prohibited except when the oil content of the discharges without dilution does not exceed 100 parts per million unless there are appropriate national regulations which are more stringent, in which case the appropriate national regulations shall apply.

CHAPTER III—REQUIREMENTS FOR MINIMIZING OIL POLLUTION FROM OIL TANKERS DUE TO SIDE AND BOTTOM DAMAGES

Regulation 22

Damage Assumptions

(1) For the purpose of calculating hypothetical oil outflow from oil tankers, three dimensions of the extent of damage of a parallelepiped on the side and bottom of the ship are assumed as follows. In the case of bottom damages two conditions are set forth to be applied individually to the stated portions of the oil tanker.

(a) *Side damage*

    (i) Longitudinal extent (l_c): $\frac{1}{3}L^{\frac{2}{3}}$ or 14.5 metres, whichever is less

    (ii) Transverse extent (t_c): (inboard from the ship's side at right angles to the centreline at the level corresponding to the assigned summer free-board) $\frac{B}{5}$ or 11.5 metres, whichever is less

    (iii) Vertical extent (v_c):   from the base line upwards without limit

(b) *Bottom damage*

	For 0.3L from the forward perpendicular of the ship	Any other part of the ship
(i) Longitudinal extent (l_s):	$\frac{L}{10}$	$\frac{L}{10}$ or 5 metres. whichever is less
(ii) Transverse extent (t_s):	$\frac{B}{6}$ or 10 metres, whichever is less but not less than 5 metres	5 metres
(iii) Vertical extent from the base line (v_s):	$\frac{B}{15}$ or 6 metres, whichever is less	

(2) Wherever the symbols given in this Regulation appear in this Chapter, they have the meaning as defined in this Regulation.

Regulation 23

Hypothetical Outflow of Oil

(1) The hypothetical outflow of oil in the case of side damage (O_c) and bottom damage (O_s) shall be calculated by the following formulae with respect

to compartments breached by damage to all conceivable locations along the length of the ship to the extent as defined in Regulation 22 of this Annex.

(a) for side damages:

$$O_c = \Sigma W_i + \Sigma K_i C_i \qquad\qquad\text{(I)}$$

(b) for bottom damages:

$$O_s = \tfrac{1}{3}(\Sigma Z_i W_i + \Sigma Z_i C_i) \qquad\qquad\text{(II)}$$

where: W_i = volume of a wing tank in cubic metres assumed to be breached by the damage as specified in Regulation 22 of this Annex: W_i for a segregated ballast tank may be taken equal to zero.

C_i = volume of a centre tank in cubic metres assumed to be breached by the damage as specified in Regulation 22 of this Annex: C_i for a segregated ballast tank may be taken equal to zero.

K_i = $1 - \dfrac{b_i}{t_c}$ when b_i is equal to or greater than t_c, K_i shall be taken equal to zero.

Z_i = $1 - \dfrac{h_i}{v_s}$ when h_i is equal to or greater than v_s, Z_i shall be taken equal to zero.

b_i = width of wing tank in metres under consideration measured inboard from the ship's side at right angles to the centreline at the level corresponding to the assigned summer freeboard.

h_i = minimum depth of the double bottom in metres under consideration: where no double bottom is fitted h_i shall be taken equal to zero.

Whenever symbols given in this paragraph appear in this Chapter, they have the meaning as defined in this Regulation.

(2) If a void space or segregated ballast tank of a length less than l_c as defined in Regulation 22 of this Annex is located between wing oil tanks. O_c in formula (I) may be calculated on the basis of volume W_i being the actual volume of one such tank (where they are of equal capacity) or the smaller of the two tanks (if they differ in capacity) adjacent to such space, multiplied by S_i as defined below and taking for all other wing tanks involved in such a collision the value of the actual full volume.

$$S_i = 1 \; \frac{l_i}{l_c}$$

where l_i = length in metres of void space or segregated ballast tank under consideration.

(3) (a) Credit shall only be given in respect of double bottom tanks which are either empty or carrying clean water when cargo is carried in the tanks above.

(b) Where the double bottom does not extend for the full length and width of the tank involved, the double bottom is considered non-existent and the volume of the tanks above the area of the bottom damage shall be included in formula (II) even if the tank is not considered breached because of the installation of such a partial double bottom.

(c) Suction wells may be neglected in the determination of the value h_i provided such wells are not excessive in area and extend below the tank for a minimum distance and in no case more than half the height of the double bottom. If the depth of such a well exceeds half the height of the double bottom, h_i shall be taken equal to the double bottom height minus the well height.

Piping serving such wells if installed within the double bottom shall be fitted with valves or other closing arrangements located at the point of connexion to the tank served to prevent oil outflow in the event of damage to the piping. Such piping shall be installed as high from the bottom shell as possible. These valves shall be kept closed at sea at any time when the tank contains oil cargo, except that they may be opened only for cargo transfer needed for the purpose of trimming of the ship.

(4) In the case where bottom damage simultaneously involves four centre tanks, the value of O_s may be calculated according to the formula

$$O_s = \frac{1}{4}\Sigma Z_i W_i + \Sigma Z_i C_i) \qquad \text{(III)}$$

(5) An Administration may credit as reducing oil outflow in case of bottom damage, an installed cargo transfer system having an emergency high suction in each cargo oil tank, capable of transferring from a breached tank or tanks to segregated ballast tanks or to available cargo tankage if it can be assured that such tanks will have sufficient ullage. Credit for such a system would be governed by ability to transfer in two hours of operation oil equal to one half of the largest of the breached tanks involved and by availability of equivalent receiving capacity in ballast or cargo tanks. The credit shall be confined to permitting calculcation of O_s according to formula (III). The pipes for such suctions shall be installed at least at a height not less than the vertical extent of the bottom damage v_s. The Administration shall supply the Organization with the information concerning the arrangements accepted by it, for circulation to other Parties to the Convention.

Regulation 24
Limitation of Size and Arrangement of Cargo Tanks

(1) Every new oil tanker shall comply with the provisions of this Regulation. Every existing oil tanker shall be required, within two years after the date of entry into force of the present Convention, to comply with the provisions of this Regulation if such a tanker falls into either of the following categories:

(a) a tanker, the delivery of which is after 1 January 1977; or
(b) a tanker to which both the following conditions apply:
  (i) delivery is not later than 1 January 1977; and
  (ii) the building contract is placed after 1 January 1974, or in cases where no building contract has previously been placed, the keel is laid or the tanker is at a similar stage of construction after 30 June 1974.

(2) Cargo tanks of oil tankers shall be of such size and arrangements that the hypothetical outflow O_c or O_s calculated in accordance with the provisions of Regulation 23 of this Annex anywhere in the length of the ship does not

exceed 30,000 cubic metres or 400 $\sqrt[3]{DW}$, whichever is the greater, but subject to a maximum of 40,000 cubic metres.

(3) The volume of any one wing cargo oil tank of an oil tanker shall not exceed seventy-five per cent of the limits of the hypothetical oil outflow referred to in paragraph (2) of this Regulation. The volume of any one centre cargo oil tank shall not exceed 50,000 cubic metres. However, in segregated ballast oil tankers as defined in Regulation 13 of this Annex, the permitted volume of a wing cargo oil tank situated between two segregated ballast tanks, each exceeding l_c in length, may be increased to the maximum limit of hypothetical oil outflow provided that the width of the wing tanks exceeds 1_c.

(4) The length of each cargo tank shall not exceed 10 metres or one of the following values, whichever is the greater:

(a) where no longitudinal bulkhead is provided:

0.1L

(b) where a longitudinal bulkhead is provided at the centreline only:

0.15L

(c) Where two or more longitudinal bulkheads are provided:

(i) for wing tanks:

0.2L

(ii) for centre tanks:

(1) if $\dfrac{b_i}{B}$ is equal to or greater than $\frac{1}{5}$:

0.2L

(2) if $\dfrac{b_i}{B}$ is less than $\frac{1}{5}$:

—where no centreline longitudinal bulkhead is provided:

$(0.5 \dfrac{b_i}{B} + 0.1)L$

—where a centreline longitudinal bulkhead is provided:

$(0.25 \dfrac{b_i}{B} + 0.15)L$

(5) In order not to exceed the volume limits established by paragraphs (2), (3) and (4) of this Regulation and irrespective of the accepted type of cargo transfer system installed, when such system interconnects two or more cargo tanks, valves or other similar closing devices shall be provided for separating the tanks from each other. These valves or devices shall be closed when the tanker is at sea.

(6) Lines of piping which run through cargo tanks in a position less than t_c from the ship's side or less than v_c from the ship's bottom shall be fitted with valves or similar closing devices at the point at which they open into any cargo tank. These valves shall be kept closed at sea at any time when the tanks contain cargo oil, except that they may be opened only for cargo transfer needed for the purpose of trimming of the ship.

Regulation 25
Subdivision and Stability

(1) Every new oil tanker shall comply with the subdivision and damage stability criteria as specified in paragraph (3) of this Regulation, after the

assumed side or bottom damage as specified in paragraph (2) of this Regulation, for any operating draught reflecting actual partial or full load conditions consistent with trim and strength of the ship as well as specific gravities of the cargo. Such damage shall be applied to all conceivable locations along the length of the ship as follows:

(a) in tankers of more than 225 metres in length, anywhere in the ship's length;

(b) in tankers of more than 150 metres, but not exceeding 225 metres in length, anywhere in the ship's length except involving either after or forward bulkhead bounding the machinery space located aft. The machinery space shall be treated as a single floodable compartment;

(c) in tankers not exceeding 150 metres in length, anywhere in the ship's length between adjacent transverse bulkheads with the exception of the machinery space. For tankers of 100 metres or less in length where all requirements of paragraph (3) of this Regulation cannot be fulfilled without materially impairing the operational qualities of the ship. Administrations may allow relaxations from these requirements.

Ballast conditions where the tanker is not carrying oil in cargo tanks excluding any oil residue, shall not be considered.

(2) The following provisions regarding the extent and the character of the assumed damage shall apply:

(a) Side damage

(i) Longitudinal extent — $\frac{1}{8}(L^i)$ or 14.5 metres. whichever is less

(ii) Transverse extent — $\frac{B}{5}$ or 11.5 metres, whichever is less

(Inboard from the ship's side at right angles to the centreline at the level of the summer load line)

(iii) Vertical extent — From the moulded line of the bottom shell plating at centreline, upwards without limit

(b) Bottom damage	For 0.3L from the forward perpendicular of the ship	Any other part of the ship
(i) Longitudinal extent	$\frac{1}{8}(L^{\frac{2}{1}})$ or 14.5 metres. whichever is less	$\frac{1}{8}(L^{\frac{2}{1}})$ or 5 metres. whichever is less
Transverse extent	$\frac{B}{6}$ or 10 metres. whichever is less	$\frac{B}{6}$ or 5 metres. whichever is less
(iii) Vertical extent	$\frac{B}{15}$ or 6 metres. whichever is less, measured from the moulded line of the	$\frac{B}{15}$ or 6 metres. whichever is less, measured from the moulded line of the

bottom shell plating bottom shell plating
at centreline at centreline

(c) If any damage of a lesser extent than the maximum extent of damage specified in sub-paragraphs (a) and (b) of this paragraph would result in a more severe condition, such damage shall be considered.

(d) Where the damage involving transverse bulkheads is envisaged as specified in sub-paragraphs (1)(a) and (b) of this Regulation, transverse watertight bulkheads shall be spaced at least at a distance equal to the longitudinal extent of assumed damage specified in sub-paragraph (a) of this paragraph in order to be considered effective. Where transverse bulkheads are spaced at a lesser distance, one or more of these bulkheads within such extent of damage shall be assumed as non-existent for the purpose of determining flooded compartments.

(e) Where the damage between adjacent transverse watertight bulkheads is envisaged as specified in sub-paragraph (1)(c) of this Regulation, no main transverse bulkhead or a transverse bulkhead bounding side tanks or double bottom tanks shall be assumed damaged, unless:

(i) the spacing of the adjacent bulkheads is less than the longitudinal extent of assumed damage specified in sub-paragraph (a) of this paragraph: or

(ii) there is a step or a recess in a transverse bulkhead of more than 3.05 metres in length, located within the extent of penetration of assumed damage. The step formed by the after peak bulkhead and after peak tank top shall not be regarded as a step for the purpose of this Regulation.

(f) If pipes, ducts or tunnels are situated within the assumed extent of damage, arrangements shall be made so that progressive flooding cannot thereby extend to compartments other than those assumed to be floodable for each case of damage.

(3) Oil tankers shall be regarded as complying with the damage stability criteria if the following requirements are met:

(a) The final waterline, taking into account sinkage, heel and trim, shall be below the lower edge of any opening through which progressive flooding may take place. Such openings shall include air pipes and those which are closed by means of weathertight doors or hatch covers and may exclude those openings closed by means of watertight manhole covers and flush scuttles, small watertight cargo tank hatch covers which maintain the high integrity of the deck, remotely operated watertight sliding doors, and side scuttles of the non-opening type.

(b) In the final stage of flooding, the angle of heel due to unsymmetrical flooding shall not exceed 25 degrees, provided that this angle may be increased up to 30 degrees if no deck edge immersion occurs.

(c) The stability in the final stage of flooding shall be investigated and may be regarded as sufficient if the righting lever curve has at least a range of 20 degrees beyond the position of equilibrium in association with a maximum residual righting lever of at least 0.1 metre within the 20 degrees range; the area under the curve within this range shall not be less than 0.0175 metre radians. Unprotected openings shall not be immersed within this range unless the space concerned is assumed to be flooded. Within this range, the immersion of any of the openings listed in sub-paragraph (a) of this paragraph and other openings capable of being closed weathertight may be permitted.

(d) The Administration shall be satisfied that the stability is sufficient during intermediate stages of flooding.

(e) Equalization arrangements requiring mechanical aids such as valves or cross-levelling pipes, if fitted, shall not be considered for the purpose of reducing an angle of heel or attaining the minimum range of residual stability to meet the requirements of sub-paragraphs (a), (b) and (c) of this paragraph and sufficient residual stability shall be maintained during all stages where equalization is used. Spaces which are linked by ducts of a large cross-sectional area may be considered to be common.

(4) The requirements of paragraph (1) of this Regulation shall be confirmed by calculations which take into consideration the design characteristics of the ship, the arrangements, configuration and contents of the damaged compartments; and the distribution, specific gravities and the free surface effect of liquids. The calculations shall be based on the following:

(a) Account shall be taken of any empty or partially filled tank, the specific gravity of cargoes carried, as well as any outflow of liquids from damaged compartments.

(b) The permeabilities assumed for spaces flooded as a result of damage shall be as follows:

Spaces	Permeabilities
Appropriated to stores	0.60
Occupied by accommodation	0.95
Occupied by machinery	0.85
Voids	0.95
Intended for consumable liquids	0 to 0.95
Intended for other liquids	0 to 0.95

(c) The buoyancy of any superstructure directly above the side damage shall be disregarded. The unflooded parts of superstructures beyond the extent of damage, however, may be taken into consideration provided that they are separated from the damaged space by watertight bulkheads and the requirements of sub-paragraph (3)(a) of this Regulation in respect of these intact spaces are complied with. Hinged watertight doors may be acceptable in watertight bulkheads in the superstructure.

(d) The free surface effect shall be calculated at an angle of heel of 5 degrees for each individual compartment. The Administration may require or allow the free surface corrections to be calculated at an angle of heel greater than 5 degrees for partially filled tanks.

(c) In calculating the effect of free surfaces of consumable liquids it shall be assumed that, for each type of liquid at least one transverse pair or a single centreline tank has a free surface and the tank or combination of tanks to be taken into account shall be those where the effect of free surfaces is the greatest.

(5) The Master of every new oil tanker and the person in charge of a new nonself-propelled oil tanker to which this Annex applies shall be supplied in an approved form with:

(a) information relative to loading and distribution of cargo necessary to ensure compliance with the provisions of this Regulation; and

(b) data on the ability of the ship to comply with damage stability criteria as determined by this Regulation, including the effect of relaxations that may have been allowed under sub-paragraph (1)(c) of this Regulation.

Appendix I
LIST OF OILS

Asphalt solutions
Blending Stocks
Roofers Flux
Straight Run Residue

Oils
Clarified
Crude Oil
Mixtures containing crude oil
Diesel Oil
Fuel Oil No. 4
Fuel Oil No. 5
Fuel Oil No. 6
Residual Fuel Oil
Road Oil
Transformer Oil
Aromatic Oil (excluding vegetable oil)
Lubricating Oils and Blending Stocks
Mineral Oil
Motor Oil
Penetrating Oil
Spindle Oil
Turbine Oil

Distillates
Straight Run
Flashed Feed Stocks

Gas Oil
Cracked

Gasoline Blending Stocks
Alkylates—fuel
Reformates
Polymer—fuel

Gasolines
Casinghead (natural)
Automotive
Aviation
Straight Run
Fuel Oil No. 1 (Kerosene)
Fuel Oil No. 1–D
Fuel Oil No. 2
Fuel Oil No. 2–D

Jet Fuels
JP–1 (Kerosene)
JP–3
JP–4
JP–5 (Kerosene, Heavy)
Turbo Fuel
Kerosene
Mineral Spirit

Naphtha
Solvent
Petroleum
Heartcut Distillate Oil

ANNEX II

REGULATIONS FOR THE CONTROL OF POLLUTION BY NOXIOUS LIQUID SUBSTANCES IN BULK

Regulation 1

Definitions

For the purposes of this Annex:

(1) "Chemical tanker" means a ship constructed or adapted primarily to carry a cargo of noxious liquid substances in bulk and includes an "oil tanker" as defined in Annex I of the present Convention when carrying a cargo or part cargo of noxious liquid substances in bulk.

(2) "Clean ballast" means ballast carried in a tank which, since it was last used to carry a cargo containing a substance in Category A, B, C or D has been thoroughly cleaned and the residues resulting therefrom have been discharged and the tank emptied in accordance with the appropriate requirements of this Annex.

(3) "Segregated ballast" means ballast water introduced into a tank permanently allocated to the carriage of ballast or to the carriage of ballast or cargoes other than oil or noxious liquid substances as variously defined in the Annexes of the present Convention, and which is completely separated from the cargo and oil fuel system.

(4) "Nearest land" is as defined in Regulation 1(9) of Annex I of the present Convention.

(5) "Liquid substances" are those having a vapour pressure not exceeding 2.8 kp/cm^2 at a temperature of 37.8°C.

(6) "Noxious liquid substance" means any substance designated in Appendix II to this Annex or provisionally assessed under the provisions of Regulation 3(4) as falling into Category A, B, C or D.

(7) "Special area" means a sea area where for recognized technical reasons in relation to its oceanographic and ecological condition and to its peculiar transportation traffic the adoption of special mandatory methods for the prevention of sea pollution by noxious liquid substances is required.

Special areas shall be:

    (a) The Baltic Sea Area, and

    (b) The Black Sea Area.

(8) "Baltic Sea Area" is as defined in Regulation 10(1)(b) of Annex I of the present Convention.

(9) "Black Sea Area" is as defined in Regulation 10(1)(c) of Annex I of the present Convention.

(10) "International Bulk Chemical Code" means the International Code for the Construction and Equipment of Ships Carrying Dangerous Chemicals in Bulk adopted by the Marine Environment Protection Committee of the Organization by resolution MEPC 19(22), as may be amended by the Organization, provided that such amendments are adopted and brought into force in accordance with the provisions of Article 16 of the present Convention concerning amendment procedures applicable to an Appendix to an Annex.

(11) "Bulk Chemical Code" means the Code for the Construction and Equipment of Ships Carrying Dangerous Chemicals in Bulk adopted by the Marine Environment Protection Committee of the Organization by resolution MEPC 20(22), as may be amended by the Organization, provided that such amendments are adopted and brought into force in accordance with the provisions of Article 16 of the present Convention concerning amendment procedures applicable to an Appendix to an Annex.

(12) "Ship constructed" means a ship the keel of which is laid or which is at a similar stage of construction. A ship converted to a chemical tanker, irrespective of the date of construction, shall be treated as a chemical tanker constructed on the date on which such conversion commenced. This conver-

sion provision shall not apply to the modification of a ship which complies with all of the following conditions:

(a) the ship is constructed before 1 July 1986; and

(b) the ship is certified under the Bulk Chemical Code to carry only those products identified by the Code as substances with pollution hazards only.

(13) "Similar stage of construction" means the stage at which:

(a) construction identifiable with a specific ship begins; and

(b) assembly of that ship has commenced comprising at least 50 tons or one per cent of the estimated mass of all structural material, whichever is less.

Regulation 2

Application

(1) Unless expressly provided otherwise the provisions of this Annex shall apply to all ships carrying noxious liquid substances in bulk.

(2) Where a cargo subject to the provisions of Annex I of the present Convention is carried in a cargo space of a chemical tanker, the appropriate requirements of Annex I of the present Convention shall also apply.

(3) Regulation 13 of this Annex shall apply only to ships carrying substances which are categorized for discharge control purposes in Category A, B or C.

(4) For ships constructed before 1 July 1986, the provisions of Regulation 5 of this Annex in respect of the requirement to discharge below the waterline and maximum concentration in the wake astern of the ship shall apply as from 1 January 1988.

(5) The Administration may allow any fitting, material, appliance or apparatus to be fitted in a ship as an alternative to that required by this Annex if such fitting, material, appliance or apparatus is at least as effective as that required by this Annex. This authority of the Administration shall not extend to the substitution of operational methods to effect the control of discharge of noxious liquid substances as equivalent to those design and construction features which are prescribed by Regulations in this Annex.

(6) The Administration which allows a fitting, material, appliance or apparatus as alternative to that required by this Annex, under paragraph (5) of this Regulation, shall communicate to the Organization for circulation to the Parties to the Convention, particulars thereof, for their information and appropriate action, if any.

Regulation 3

Categorization and Listing of Noxious Liquid Substances

(1) For the purpose of the Regulations of this Annex, noxious liquid substances shall be divided into four categories as follows:

(a) Category A—Noxious liquid substances which if discharged into the sea from tank cleaning or deballasting operations would present a major hazard to either marine resources or human health or cause serious harm to amenities or other legitimate uses of the sea and therefore justify the application of stringent anti-pollution measures.

(b) Category B—Noxious liquid substances which if discharged into the sea from tank cleaning or deballasting operations would present a hazard to either marine resources or human health or cause harm to amenities or other legitimate uses of the sea and therefore justify the application of special anti-pollution measures.

(c) Category C—Noxious liquid substances which if discharged into the sea from tank cleaning or deballasting operations would present a minor hazard to either marine resources or human health or cause minor harm to amenities or other legitimate uses of the sea and therefore require special operational conditions.

(d) Category D—Noxious liquid substances which if discharged into the sea from tank cleaning or deballasting operations would present a recognizable hazard to either marine resources or human health or cause minimal harm to amenities or other legitimate uses of the sea and therefore require some attention in operational conditions.

(2) Guidelines for use in the categorization of noxious liquid substances are given in Appendix I to this Annex.

(3) The list of noxious substances carried in bulk and presently categorized which are subject to the provisions of this Annex is set out in Appendix II to this Annex.

(4) Where it is proposed to carry a liquid substance in bulk which has not been categorized under paragraph (1) of this Regulation or evaluated as referred to in Regulation 4(1) of this Annex, the Governments of Parties to the Convention involved in the proposed operation shall establish and agree on a provisional assessment for the proposed operation on the basis of the guidelines referred to in paragraph (2) of this Regulation. Until full agreement between the Governments involved has been reached, the substance shall be carried under the most severe conditions proposed. As soon as possible, but not later than ninety days after its first carriage, the Administration concerned shall notify the Organization and provide details of the substance and the provisional assessment for prompt circulation to all Parties for their information and consideration. The Government of each Party shall have a period of ninety days in which to forward its comments to the Organization, with a view to the assessment of the substance.

Regulation 4
Other Liquid Substances

(1) The substances listed in Appendix III to this Annex have been evaluated and found to fall outside the Categories A, B, C and D, as defined in Regulation 3(1) of this Annex because they are presently considered to present no harm to human health, marine resources, amenities or other legitimate uses of the sea, when discharged into the sea from tank cleaning or deballasting operations.

(2) The discharge of bilge or ballast water or other residues or mixtures containing only substances listed in Appendix III to this Annex shall not be subject to any requirement of this Annex.

(3) The discharge into the sea of clean ballast or segregated ballast shall not be subject to any requirement of this Annex.

Regulation 5

Discharge of Noxious Liquid Substances

Categories A, B and C Substances outside Special Areas and Category D Substances in all Areas

Subject to the provisions of Regulation 6 of this Annex,

(1) The discharge into the sea of substances in Category A as defined in Regulation 3(1)(a) of this Annex or of those provisionally assessed as such, or ballast water, tank washings, or other residues or mixtures containing such substances shall be prohibited. If tanks containing such substances or mixtures are to be washed, the resulting residues shall be discharged to a reception facility until the concentration of the substance in the effluent to such facility is at or below the residual concentration prescribed for that substance in column III of Appendix II to this Annex and until the tank is empty. Any water subsequently added to the tank may be discharged into the sea when all the following conditions are satisfied:

(a) the ship is proceeding en route at a speed of at least 7 knots in the case of self-propelled ships or at least 4 knots in the case of ships which are not self-propelled;

(b) the discharge is made below the waterline, taking into account the location of the seawater intakes; and

(c) the discharge is made at a distance of not less than 12 nautical miles from the nearest land and in a depth of water of not less than 25 metres.

(2) The discharge into the sea of substances in Category B as defined in Regulation 3(1)(b) of this Annex or of those provisionally assessed as such, or ballast water, tank washings, or other residues or mixtures containing such substances shall be prohibited except when all the following conditions are satisfied:

(a) the ship is proceeding en route at a speed of at least 7 knots in the case of self-propelled ships or at least 4 knots in the case of ships which are not self-propelled;

(b) the procedures and arrangements for discharge are approved by the Administration. Such procedures and arrangements shall be based upon standards developed by the Organization and shall ensure that the concentration and rate of discharge of the effluent is such that the concentration of the substance in the wake astern of the ship does not exceed 1 part per million;

(c) the maximum quantity of cargo discharged from each tank and its associated piping system does not exceed the maximum quantity approved in accordance with the procedures referred to in sub-paragraph (b) of this paragraph, which shall in no case exceed the greater of 1 cubic metre or 1/3,000 of the tank capacity in cubic metres;

(d) the discharge is made below the waterline, taking into account the location of the seawater intakes; and

(e) the discharge is made at a distance of not less than 12 nautical miles from the nearest land and in a depth of water of not less than 25 metres.

(3) The discharge into the sea of substances in Category C as defined in Regulation 3(1)(c) of this Annex or of those provisionally assessed as such, or ballast water, tank washings, or other residues or mixtures containing such substances shall be prohibited except when all the following conditions are satisfied:

(a) the ship is proceeding en route at a speed of at least 7 knots in the case of self-propelled ships or at least 4 knots in the case of ships which are not self-propelled;

(b) the procedures and arrangements for discharge are approved by the Administration. Such procedures and arrangements shall be based upon standards developed by the Organization and shall ensure that the concentration and rate of discharge of the effluent is such that the concentration of the substance in the wake astern of the ship does not exceed 10 parts per million;

(c) the maximum quantity of cargo discharged from each tank and its associated piping system does not exceed the maximum quantity approved in accordance with the procedures referred to in sub-paragraph (b) of this paragraph, which shall in no case exceed the greater of 3 cubic metres or 1/1,000 of the tank capacity in cubic metres;

(d) the discharge is made below the waterline, taking into account the location of the seawater intakes; and

(e) the discharge is made at a distance of not less than 12 nautical miles from the nearest land and in a depth of water of not less than 25 metres.

(4) The discharge into the sea of substances in Category D as defined in Regulation 3(1)(d) of this Annex, or of those provisionally assessed as such, or ballast water, tank washings, or other residues or mixtures containing such substances shall be prohibited except when all the following conditions are satisfied:

(a) the ship is proceeding en route at a speed of at least 7 knots in the case of self-propelled ships or at least 4 knots in the case of ships which are not self-propelled;

(b) such mixtures are of a concentration not greater than one part of the substance in ten parts of water; and

(c) the discharge is made at a distance of not less than 12 nautical miles from the nearest land.

(5) Ventilation procedures approved by the Administration may be used to remove cargo residues from a tank. Such procedures shall be based upon standards developed by the Organization. Any water subsequently introduced into the tank shall be regarded as clean and shall not be subject to paragraph (1), (2), (3) or (4) of this Regulation.

(6) The discharge into the sea of substances which have not been categorized, provisionally assessed, or evaluated as referred to in Regulation 4(1) of

this Annex, or of ballast water, tank washings, or other residues or mixtures containing such substances shall be prohibited.

Categories A, B and C Substances within Special Areas

Subject to the provisions of Regulation 6 of this Annex,

(7) The discharge into the sea of substances in Category A as defined in Regulation 3(1)(a) of this Annex or of those provisionally assessed as such, or ballast water, tank washings, or other residues or mixtures containing such substances shall be prohibited. If tanks containing such substances or mixtures are to be washed the resulting residues shall be discharged to a reception facility which the States bordering the special area shall provide in accordance with Regulation 7 of this Annex, until the concentration of the substance in the effluent to such facility is at or below the residual concentration prescribed for that substance in column IV of Appendix II to this Annex and until the tank is empty. Any water subsequently added to the tank may be discharged into the sea when all the following conditions are satisfied:

(a) the ship is proceeding en route at a speed of at least 7 knots in the case of self-propelled ships or at least 4 knots in the case of ships which are not self-propelled;

(b) the discharge is made below the waterline, taking into account the location of the seawater intakes; and

(c) the discharge is made at a distance of not less than 12 nautical miles from the nearest land and in a depth of water of not less than 25 metres.

(8) The discharge into the sea of substances in Category B as defined in Regulation 3(1)(b) of this Annex or of those provisionally assessed as such, or ballast water, tank washings, or other residues or mixtures containing such substances shall be prohibited except when all the following conditions are satisfied:

(a) the tank has been prewashed in accordance with the procedure approved by the Administration and based on standards developed by the Organization and the resulting tank washings have been discharged to a reception facility;

(b) the ship is proceeding en route at a speed of at least 7 knots in the case of self-propelled ships or at least 4 knots in the case of ships which are not self-propelled;

(c) the procedures and arrangements for discharge and washings are approved by the Administration. Such procedures and arrangements shall be based upon standards developed by the Organization and shall ensure that the concentration and rate of discharge of the effluent is such that the concentration of the substance in the wake astern of the ship does not exceed 1 part per million;

(d) the discharge is made below the waterline, taking into account the location of the seawater intakes; and

(e) the discharge is made at a distance of not less than 12 nautical miles from the nearest land and in a depth of water of not less than 25 metres.

(9) The discharge into the sea of substances in Category C as defined in Regulation 3(1)(c) of this Annex or of those provisionally assessed as such, or ballast water, tank washings, or other residues or mixtures containing such substances shall be prohibited except when all the following conditions are satisfied:

(a) the ship is proceeding en route at a speed of at least 7 knots in the case of self-propelled ships or at least 4 knots in the case of ships which are not self-propelled;

(b) the procedures and arrangements for discharge are approved by the Administration. Such procedures and arrangements shall be based upon standards developed by the Organization and shall ensure that the concentration and rate of discharge of the effluent is such that the concentration of the substance in the wake astern of the ship does not exceed 1 part per million;

(c) the maximum quantity of cargo discharged from each tank and its associated piping system does not exceed the maximum quantity approved in accordance with the procedures referred to in sub-paragraph (b) of this paragraph which shall in no case exceed the greater of 1 cubic metre or 1/3,000 of the tank capacity in cubic metres;

(d) the discharge is made below the waterline, taking into account the location of the seawater intakes; and

(e) the discharge is made at a distance of not less than 12 nautical miles from the nearest land and in a depth of water of not less than 25 metres.

(10) Ventilation procedures approved by the Administration may be used to remove cargo residues from a tank. Such procedures shall be based upon standards developed by the Organization. Any water subsequently introduced into the tank shall be regarded as clean and shall not be subject to paragraph (7), (8) or (9) of this Regulation.

(11) The discharge into the sea of substances which have not been categorized, provisionally assessed or evaluated as referred to in Regulation 4(1) of this Annex, or of ballast water, tank washings, or other residues or mixtures containing such substances shall be prohibited.

(12) Nothing in this Regulation shall prohibit a ship from retaining on board the residues from a Category B or C cargo and discharging such residues into the sea outside a special area in accordance with paragraph (2) or (3) of this Regulation, respectively.

(13)(a) The Governments of Parties to the Convention, the coastlines of which border on any given special area, shall collectively agree and establish a date by which time the requirement of Regulation 7(1) of this Annex will be fulfilled and from which the requirements of paragraphs (7), (8), (9) and (10) of this Regulation in respect of that area shall take effect and notify the Organization of the date so established at least six months in advance of that date. The Organization shall then promptly notify all Parties of that date.

(b) If the date of entry into force of the present Convention is earlier than the date established in accordance with sub-paragraph (a) of this paragraph, the requirements of paragraphs (1), (2) and (3) of this Regulation shall apply during the interim period.

Regulation 5A

Pumping, Piping and Unloading Arrangements

(1) Every ship constructed on or after 1 July 1986 shall be provided with pumping and piping arrangements to ensure, through testing under favourable pumping conditions, that each tank designated for the carriage of a Category B substance does not retain a quantity of residue in excess of 0.1 cubic metres in the tank's associated piping and in the immediate vicinity of that tank's suction point.

(2)(a) Subject to the provisions of sub-paragraph (b) of this paragraph, every ship constructed before 1 July 1986 shall be provided with pumping and piping arrangements to ensure, through testing under favourable pumping conditions, that each tank designated for the carriage of a Category B substance does not retain a quantity of residue in excess of 0.3 cubic metres in the tank's associated piping and in the immediate vicinity of that tank's suction point.

(b) Until 2 October 1994 ships referred to in sub-paragraph (a) of this paragraph if not in compliance with the requirements of that sub-paragraph shall, as a minimum, be provided with pumping and piping arrangements to ensure, through testing under favourable pumping conditions and surface residue assessment, that each tank designated for the carriage of a Category B substance does not retain a quantity of residue in excess of 1 cubic metre or 1/3,000 of the tank capacity in cubic metres, whichever is greater, in that tank and the associated piping.

(3) Every ship constructed on or after 1 July 1986 shall be provided with pumping and piping arrangements to ensure, through testing under favourable pumping conditions, that each tank designated for the carriage of a Category C substance does not retain a quantity of residue in excess of 0.3 cubic metres in the tank's associated piping and in the immediate vicinity of that tank's suction point.

(4)(a) Subject to the provisions of sub-paragraph (b) of this paragraph, every ship constructed before 1 July 1986 shall be provided with pumping and piping arrangements to ensure, through testing under favourable pumping conditions, that each tank designated for the carriage of a Category C substance does not retain a quantity of residue in excess of 0.9 cubic metres in the tank's associated piping and in the immediate vicinity of that tank's suction point.

(b) Until 2 October 1994 the ships referred to in sub-paragraph (a) of this paragraph if not in compliance with the requirements of that sub-paragraph shall, as a minimum, be provided with pumping and piping arrangements to ensure, through testing under favourable pumping conditions and surface residue assessment, that each tank designated for the carriage of a Category C substance does not retain a quantity of residue in excess of 3 cubic metres or 1/1,000 of the tank capacity in cubic metres, whichever is greater, in that tank and the associated piping.

(5) Pumping conditions referred to in paragraphs (1), (2), (3) and (4) of this Regulation shall be approved by the Administration and based on

standards developed by the Organization. Pumping efficiency tests referred to in paragraphs (1), (2), (3) and (4) of this Regulation shall use water as the test medium and shall be approved by the Administration and based on standards developed by the Organization. The residues on cargo tank surfaces, referred to in paragraphs (2)(b) and (4)(b) of this Regulation shall be determined based on standards developed by the Organization.

(6)(a) Subject to the provision of sub-paragraph (b) of this paragraph, the provisions of paragraphs (2) and (4) of this Regulation need not apply to a ship constructed before 1 July 1986 which is engaged in restricted voyages as determined by the Administration between:

(i) ports or terminals within a State Party to the present Convention; or

(ii) ports or terminals of States Parties to the present Convention.

(b) The provisions of sub-paragraph (a) of this paragraph shall only apply to a ship constructed before 1 July 1986 if:

(i) each time a tank containing Category B or C substances or mixtures is to be washed or ballasted, the tank is washed in accordance with a pre-wash procedure approved by the Administration and based on Standards developed by the Organization and the tank washings are discharged to a reception facility;

(ii) subsequent washings or ballast water are discharged to a reception facility or at sea in accordance with other provisions of this Annex;

(iii) the adequacy of the reception facilities at the ports or terminals referred to above, for the purpose of this paragraph, is approved by the Governments of the States Parties to the present Convention within which such ports or terminals are situated;

(iv) in the case of ships engaged in voyages to ports or terminals under the jurisdiction of other States Parties to the present Convention, the Administration communicates to the Organization, for circulation to the Parties to the Convention, particulars of the exemption, for their information and appropriate action, if any; and

(v) the Certificate required under this Annex is endorsed to the effect that the ship is solely engaged in such restricted voyages.

(7) For a ship whose constructional and operational features are such that ballasting of cargo tanks is not required and cargo tank washing is only required for repair or dry-docking, the Administration may allow exemption from the provisions of paragraphs (1), (2), (3) and (4) of this Regulation, provided that all the following conditions are complied with:

(a) the design, construction and equipment of the ship are approved by the Administration, having regard to the service for which it is intended;

(b) any effluent from tank washings which may be carried out before a repair or dry-docking is discharged to a reception facility, the adequacy of which is ascertained by the Administration;

(c) the Certificate required under this Annex indicates:

(i) that each cargo tank is certified for the carriage of only one named substance; and

(ii) the particulars of the exemption;

(d) the ship carries a suitable operational manual approved by the Administration; and

(e) in the case of ships engaged in voyages to ports or terminals under the jurisdiction of other States Parties to the present Convention, the Administration communicates to the Organization, for circulation to the Parties to the Convention, particulars of the exemption, for their information and appropriate action, if any.

Regulation 6

Exceptions

Regulation 5 of this Annex shall not apply to:

(a) the discharge into the sea of noxious liquid substances or mixtures containing such substances necessary for the purpose of securing the safety of a ship or saving life at sea; or

(b) the discharge into the sea of noxious liquid substances or mixtures containing such substances resulting from damage to a ship or its equipment:

(i) provided that all reasonable precautions have been taken after the occurrence of the damage or discovery of the discharge for the purpose of preventing or minimizing the discharge; and

(ii) except if the owner or the Master acted either with intent to cause damage, or recklessly and with knowledge that damage would probably result; or

(c) the discharge into the sea of noxious liquid substances or mixtures containing such substances, approved by the Administration, when being used for the purpose of combating specific pollution incidents in order to minimize the damage from pollution. Any such discharge shall be subject to the approval of any Government in whose jurisdiction it is contemplated the discharge will occur.

Regulation 7

Reception Facilities and Cargo Unloading Terminal Arrangements

(1) The Government of each Party to the Convention undertakes to ensure the provision of reception facilities according to the needs of ships using its ports, terminals or repair ports as follows:

(a) cargo loading and unloading ports and terminals shall have facilities adequate for reception without undue delay to ships of such residues and mixtures containing noxious liquid substances as would remain for disposal from ships carrying them as a consequence of the application of this Annex; and

(b) ship repair ports undertaking repairs to chemical tankers shall have facilities adequate for the reception of residues and mixtures containing noxious liquid substances.

(2) The Government of each Party shall determine the types of facilities provided for the purpose of paragraph (1) of this Regulation at each cargo loading and unloading port, terminal and ship repair port in its territories and notify the Organization thereof.

(3) The Government of each Party to the Convention shall undertake to ensure that cargo unloading terminals shall provide arrangements to facilitate stripping of cargo tanks of ships unloading noxious liquid substances at these terminals. Cargo hoses and piping systems of the terminal, containing noxious liquid substances received from ships unloading these substances at the terminal, shall not be drained back to the ship.

(4) Each Party shall notify the Organization, for transmission to the Parties concerned, of any case where facilities required under paragraph (1) or arrangements required under paragraph (3) of this Regulation are alleged to be inadequate.

Regulation 8
Measures of Control

(1)(a) The Government of each Party to the Convention shall appoint or authorize surveyors for the purpose of implementing this Regulation. The surveyors shall execute control in accordance with control procedures developed by the Organization.

(b) The Master of a ship carrying noxious liquid substances in bulk shall ensure that the provisions of Regulation 5 and this Regulation have been complied with and that the Cargo Record Book is completed in accordance with Regulation 9 of this Annex whenever operations as referred to in that Regulation take place.

(c) An exemption referred to in paragraph (2)(b), (5)(b), (6)(c) or (7)(c) of this Regulation may only be granted by the Government of the receiving Party to a ship engaged in voyages to ports or terminals under the jurisdiction of other States Parties to the present Convention. When such an exemption has been granted, the appropriate entry made in the Cargo Record Book shall be endorsed by the surveyor referred to in sub-paragraph (a) of this paragraph.

Category A substances in all areas

(2) With respect to Category A substances the following provisions shall apply in all areas:

(a) A tank which has been unloaded shall, subject to the provisions of sub-paragraph (b) of this paragraph, be washed in accordance with the requirements of paragraph (3) or (4) of this Regulation before the ship leaves the port of unloading.

(b) At the request of the ship's master, the Government of the receiving Party may exempt the ship from the requirements referred to in sub-paragraph (a) of this paragraph, where it is satisfied that:

(i) the tank unloaded is to be reloaded with the same substance or another substance compatible with the previous one and that the tank will not be washed or ballasted prior to loading; or

(ii) the tank unloaded is neither washed nor ballasted at sea and the provisions of paragraph (3) or (4) of this Regulation are complied with at another port provided that it has been confirmed in writing that a reception facility at that port is available and is adequate for such a purpose; or

(iii) the cargo residues will be removed by a ventilation procedure approved by the Administration and based on standards developed by the Organization.

(3) If the tank is to be washed in accordance with sub-paragraph (2)(a) of this Regulation, the effluent from the tank washing operation shall be discharged to a reception facility at least until the concentration of the substance in the discharge, as indicated by analyses of samples of the effluent taken by the surveyor, has fallen to the residual concentration specified for that substance in Appendix II to this Annex. When the required residual concentration has been achieved, remaining tank washings shall continue to be discharged to the reception facility until the tank is empty. Appropriate entries of these operations shall be made in the Cargo Record Book and endorsed by the surveyor referred to under paragraph (1)(a) of this Regulation.

(4) Where the Government of the receiving party is satisfied that it is impracticable to measure the concentration of the substance in the effluent without causing undue delay to the ship, that Party may accept an alternative procedure as being equivalent to paragraph (3) of this Regulation provided that:

(a) The tank is prewashed in accordance with a procedure approved by the Administration and based on standards developed by the Organization; and

(b) The surveyor referred to under paragraph (1)(a) certifies in the Cargo Record Book that:

(i) the tank, its pump and piping systems have been emptied; and

(ii) the prewash has been carried out in accordance with the prewash procedure approved by the Administration for that tank and that substance; and

(iii) the tank washings resulting from such prewash have been discharged to a reception facility and the tank is empty.

Category B and C substances outside Special Areas

(5) With respect to Category B and C substances, the following provisions shall apply outside Special Areas:

(a) A tank which has been unloaded shall, subject to the provisions of sub-paragraph (b) of this paragraph, be prewashed before the ship leaves the port of unloading, whenever:

(i) the substance unloaded is identified in the standards developed by the Organization as resulting in a residue quantity exceeding the maximum quantity which may be discharged into the sea under Regulation 5(2) or (3) of this Annex in case of Category B or C substances respectively; or

(ii) the unloading is not carried out in accordance with the pumping conditions for the tank approved by the Administration and based on standards developed by the Organization as referred to under Regulation 5A(5) of this Annex, unless alternative measures are taken to the satisfaction of the surveyor referred to in paragraph (1)(a) of this Regulation, to remove the cargo residues from the ship to quantities specified in Regulation 5A of this Annex as applicable.

The prewash procedure used shall be approved by the Administration and based on standards developed by the Organization and the resulting tank washings shall be discharged to a reception facility at the port of unloading.

(b) At the request of the ship's Master, the Government of the receiving party may exempt the ship from the requirements of sub-paragraph (a) of this paragraph, where it is satisfied that:

(i) the tank unloaded is to be reloaded with the same substance or another substance compatible with the previous one and that the tank will not be washed nor ballasted prior to loading; or

(ii) the tank unloaded is neither washed nor ballasted at sea and the tank is prewashed in accordance with a procedure approved by the Administration and based on standards developed by the Organization and resulting tank washings are discharged to a reception facility at another port, provided that it has been confirmed in writing that a reception facility at that port is available and adequate for such a purpose; or

(iii) the cargo residues will be removed by a ventilation procedure approved by the Administration and based on standards developed by the Organization.

Category B substances within Special Areas

(6) With respect to Category B substances, the following provisions shall apply within Special Areas:

(a) A tank which has been unloaded shall, subject to the provisions of sub-paragraphs (b) and (c), be prewashed before the ship leaves the port of unloading. The prewash procedure used shall be approved by the Administration and based on standards developed by the Organization and the resulting tank washings shall be discharged to a reception facility at the port of unloading.

(b) The requirements of sub-paragraph (a) of this paragraph do not apply when all the following conditions are satisfied:

(i) the Category B substance unloaded is identified in the standards developed by the Organization as resulting in a residue quantity not exceeding the maximum quantity which may be discharged into the sea outside Special Areas under Regulation 5(2) of this Annex, and the residues are retained on board for subsequent discharge into the sea outside the Special Area in compliance with Regulation 5(2) of this Annex; and

(ii) the unloading is carried out in accordance with the pumping conditions for the tank approved by the Administration and based on standards developed by the Organization as referred to under Regulation 5A(5) of this Annex, or failing to comply with the approved pumping conditions, alternative measures are taken to the satisfaction of the surveyor referred to in paragraph (1)(a) of this Regulation, to remove the cargo residues from the ship to quantities specified in Regulation 5A of this Annex as applicable.

(c) At the request of the ship's master, the Government of the receiving party may exempt the ship from the requirements of sub-paragraph (a) of this paragraph, where it is satisfied:

(i) that the tank unloaded is to be reloaded with the same substance or another substance compatible with the previous one and that the tank will not be washed or ballasted prior to loading; or

(ii) that the tank unloaded is neither washed nor ballasted at sea and the tank is prewashed in accordance with a procedure approved by the Administration and based on standards developed by the Organization and resulting tank washings are discharged to a reception facility at another port, provided that it has been confirmed in writing that a reception facility at that port is available and adequate for such a purpose; or

(iii) that the cargo residues will be removed by a ventilation procedure approved by the Administration and based on standards developed by the Organization.

Category C substances within Special Areas

(7) With respect to Category C substances, the following provisions shall apply within Special Areas:

(a) A tank which has been unloaded shall, subject to the provisions of sub-paragraphs (b) and (c) of this paragraph, be prewashed before the ship leaves the port of unloading, whenever:

(i) the Category C substance unloaded is identified in the standards developed by the Organization as resulting in a residue quantity exceeding the maximum quantity which may be discharged into the sea under Regulation 5(9) of this Annex; or

(ii) the unloading is not carried out in accordance with the pumping conditions for the tank approved by the Administration and based on standards developed by the Organization as referred to under Regulation 5A(5) of this Annex, unless alternative measures are taken to the satisfaction of the surveyor referred to in paragraph (1)(a) of this Regulation, to remove the cargo residues from the ship to quantities specified in Regulation 5A of this Annex as applicable.

The prewash procedure used shall be approved by the Administration and based on standards developed by the Organization and the resulting tank washings shall be discharged to a reception facility at the port of unloading.

(b) The requirements of sub-paragraph (a) of this paragraph do not apply when all the following conditions are satisfied:

(i) the Category C substance unloaded is identified in the standards developed by the Organization as resulting in a residue quantity not exceeding the maximum quantity which may be discharged into the sea outside Special Areas under Regulation 5(3) of this Annex, and the residues are retained on board for subsequent discharge into the sea outside the Special Area in compliance with Regulation 5(3) of this Annex; and

(ii) the unloading is carried out in accordance with the pumping conditions for the tank approved by the Administration and based on standards developed by the Organization as referred to under Regulation 5A(5) of this Annex, or failing to comply with the approved pumping conditions, alternative measures are taken to the satisfaction of the surveyor referred to in paragraph (1)(a) of this Regulation, to remove the cargo residues from the ship to quantities specified in Regulation 5A of this Annex as applicable.

(c) At the request of the ship's master, the Government of the receiving party may exempt the ship from the requirements of subparagraph (a) of this paragraph, where it is satisfied:

(i) that the tank unloaded is to be reloaded with the same substance or another substance compatible with the previous one and that the tank will not be washed or ballasted prior to loading; or

(ii) that the tank unloaded is neither washed nor ballasted at sea and the tank is prewashed in accordance with a procedure approved by the Administration and based on standards developed by the Organization and resulting tank washings are discharged to a reception facility at another port, provided that it has been confirmed in writing that a reception facility at that port is available and adequate for such a purpose; or

(iii) that the cargo residues will be removed by a ventilation procedure approved by the Administration and based on standards developed by the Organization.

Category D substances in all areas

(8) With respect to Category D substances, a tank which has been unloaded shall either be washed and the resulting tank washings shall be discharged to a reception facility, or the remaining residues in the tank shall be diluted and discharged into the sea in accordance with Regulation 5(4) of this Annex.

Discharge from a slop tank

(9) Any residues retained on board in a slop tank, including those from cargo pump room bilges, which contain a Category A substance, or within a special area either a Category A or a Category B substance, shall be discharged to a reception facility in accordance with the provisions of Regulation 5(1), (7) or (8) of this Annex, whichever is applicable.

Regulation 9
Cargo Record Book

(1) Every ship to which this Annex applies shall be provided with a Cargo Record Book, whether as part of the ship's official log book or otherwise, in the form specified in Appendix IV to this Annex.

(2) The Cargo Record Book shall be completed, on a tank-to-tank basis, whenever any of the following operations with respect to a noxious liquid substance take place in the ship:

        (i) loading of cargo;

        (ii) internal transfer of cargo;

        (iii) unloading of cargo;

        (iv) cleaning of cargo tanks;

        (v) ballasting of cargo tanks;

        (vi) discharge of ballast from cargo tanks;

        (vii) disposal of residues to reception facilities;

        (viii) discharge into the sea or removal by ventilation of residues in accordance with Regulation 5 of this Annex.

(3) In the event of any discharge of the kind referred to in Article 8 of the present Convention and Regulation 6 of this Annex of any noxious liquid substance or mixture containing such substance, whether intentional or accidental, an entry shall be made in the Cargo Record Book stating the circumstances of, and the reason for, the discharge.

(4) When a surveyor appointed or authorized by the Government of the Party to the Convention to supervise any operations under this Annex has inspected a ship, then that surveyor shall make an appropriate entry in the Cargo Record Book.

(5) Each operation referred to in paragraphs (2) and (3) of this Regulation shall be fully recorded without delay in the Cargo Record Book so that all the entries in the Book appropriate to that operation are completed. Each entry shall be signed by the officer or officers in charge of the operation concerned and each page shall be signed by the Master of the ship. The entries in the Cargo Record Book shall be in an official language of the State whose flag the ship is entitled to fly, and, for ships holding an International Pollution Prevention Certificate for the Carriage of Noxious Liquid Substances in Bulk or a Certificate referred to in Regulation 12A of this Annex in English or French. The entries in an official national language of the State whose flag the ship is entitled to fly shall prevail in case of a dispute or discrepancy.

(6) The Cargo Record Book shall be kept in such a place as to be readily available for inspection and, except in the case of unmanned ships under tow, shall be kept on board the ship. It shall be retained for a period of three years after the last entry has been made.

(7) The competent authority of the Government of a Party may inspect the Cargo Record Book on board any ship to which this Annex applies while the ship is in its port, and may make a copy of any entry in that book and may require the Master of the ship to certify that the copy is a true copy of such entry. Any copy so made which has been certified by the Master of the ship as a true copy of an entry in the ship's Cargo Record Book shall be made admissible in any judicial proceedings as evidence of the facts stated in the entry. The inspection of a Cargo Record Book and the taking of a certified

copy by the competent authority under this paragraph shall be performed as expeditiously as possible without causing the ship to be unduly delayed.

Regulation 10

Surveys

(1) Ships carrying noxious liquid substances in bulk shall be subject to the surveys specified below:

(a) An initial survey before the ship is put in service or before the Certificate required under Regulation 11 of this Annex is issued for the first time, and which shall include a complete survey of its structure, equipment, systems, fittings, arrangements and material in so far as the ship is covered by this Annex. This survey shall be such as to ensure that the structure, equipment, systems, fittings, arrangements and material fully comply with the applicable requirements of this Annex.

(b) Periodical surveys at intervals specified by the Administration, but not exceeding five years, and which shall be such as to ensure that the structure, equipment, systems, fittings, arrangements and material fully comply with the requirements of this Annex.

(c) A minimum of one intermediate survey during the period of validity of the Certificate and which shall be such as to ensure that the equipment and associated pump and piping systems fully comply with the applicable requirements of this Annex and are in good working order. In cases where only one such intermediate survey is carried out in any one Certificate validity period, it shall be held not before six months prior to, nor later than six months after the half-way date of the Certificate's period of validity. Such intermediate surveys shall be endorsed on the Certificate issued under Regulation 11 of this Annex.

(d) An annual survey within 3 months before or after the day and the month of the date of issue of the Certificate and which shall include a general examination to ensure that the structure, fittings, arrangements and materials remain in all respects satisfactory for the service for which the ship is intended. Such annual surveys shall be endorsed on the Certificate issued under Regulation 11 of this Annex.

(2)(a) Surveys of ships as regards the enforcement of the provisions of this Annex shall be carried out by officers of the Administration. The Administration may, however, entrust the surveys either to surveyors nominated for the purpose or to organizations recognized by it.

(b) An Administration nominating surveyors or recognizing organizations to conduct surveys and inspections as set forth in sub-paragraph (a) of this paragraph, shall as a minimum empower any nominated surveyor or recognized organization to:

(i) require repairs to a ship; and

(ii) carry out surveys and inspections if requested by the appropriate authorities of a port State.

The Administration shall notify the Organization of the specific responsibilities and conditions of the authority delegated to the nominated surveyors or recognized organizations, for circulation to

Parties to the present Convention for the information of their officers.

(c) When a nominated surveyor or recognized organization determines that the condition of the ship or its equipment does not correspond substantially with the particulars of the Certificate, or is such that the ship is not fit to proceed to sea without presenting an unreasonable threat of harm to the marine environment, such surveyor or organization shall immediately ensure that corrective action is taken and shall in due course notify the Administration. If such corrective action is not taken the Certificate should be withdrawn and the Administration shall be notified immediately; and if the ship is in a port of another Party, the appropriate authorities of the port State shall also be notified immediately. When an officer of the Administration, a nominated surveyor or recognized organization has notified the appropriate authorities of the port State, the Government of the port State concerned shall give such officer, surveyor, or organization any necessary assistance to carry out their obligations under this Regulation. When applicable, the Government of the port State concerned shall take such steps as will ensure that the ship shall not sail until it can proceed to sea or leave the port for the purpose of proceeding to the nearest appropriate repair yard available without presenting an unreasonable threat of harm to the marine environment.

(d) In every case, the Administration concerned shall fully guarantee the completeness and efficiency of the survey and inspection and shall undertake to ensure the necessary arrangements to satisfy this obligation.

(3)(a) The condition of the ship and its equipment shall be maintained to conform with the provisions of the present Convention to ensure that the ship in all respects will remain fit to proceed to sea without presenting an unreasonable threat of harm to the marine environment.

(b) After any survey of the ship under paragraph (1) of this Regulation has been completed, no change shall be made in the structure, equipment, systems, fittings, arrangements or material covered by the survey, without the sanction of the Administration, except the direct replacement of such equipment and fittings.

(c) Whenever an accident occurs to a ship or a defect is discovered which substantially affects the integrity of the ship or the efficiency or completeness of its equipment covered by this Annex, the master or owner of the ship shall report at the earliest opportunity to the Administration, the recognized organization or the nominated surveyor responsible for issuing the relevant Certificate, who shall cause investigations to be initiated to determine whether a survey as required by paragraph (1) of this Regulation is necessary. If the ship is in a port of another Party, the master or owner shall also report immediately to the appropriate authorities of the port State and the nominated surveyor or recognized organization shall ascertain that such report has been made.

Regulation 11
Issue of Certificate

(1) An International Pollution Prevention Certificate for the Carriage of Noxious Liquid Substances in Bulk shall be issued, after survey in accordance

with the provisions of Regulation 10 of this Annex, to any ship carrying noxious liquid substances in bulk and which is engaged in voyages to ports or terminals under the jurisdiction of other Parties to the Convention.

(2) Such Certificate shall be issued either by the Administration or by any person or organization duly authorized by it. In every case, the Administration assumes full responsibility for the Certificate.

(3)(a) The Government of a Party to the Convention may, at the request of the Administration, cause a ship to be surveyed and, if satisfied that the provisions of this Annex are complied with, shall issue or authorize the issue of an International Pollution Prevention Certificate for the Carriage of Noxious Liquid Substances in Bulk to the ship in accordance with this Annex.

(b) A copy of the Certificate and a copy of the survey report shall be transmitted as soon as possible to the requesting Administration.

(c) A Certificate so issued shall contain a statement to the effect that it has been issued at the request of the Administration and it shall have the same force and receive the same recognition as the Certificate issued under paragraph (1) of this Regulation.

(d) No International Pollution Prevention Certificate for the Carriage of Noxious Liquid Substances in Bulk shall be issued to a ship which is entitled to fly the flag of a State which is not a Party.

(4) The International Pollution Prevention Certificate for the Carriage of Noxious Liquid Substances in Bulk shall be drawn up in an official language of the issuing country in the form corresponding to the model given in Appendix V to this Annex. If the language used is neither English nor French, the text shall include a translation into one of these languages.

Regulation 12
Duration of Certificate

(1) An International Pollution Prevention Certificate for the Carriage of Noxious Liquid Substances in Bulk shall be issued for a period specified by the Administration, which shall not exceed five years from the date of issue.

(2) A Certificate shall cease to be valid if significant alterations have taken place in the construction, equipment, systems, fittings, arrangements or material required without the sanction of the Administration, except the direct replacement of such equipment or fittings, or if intermediate or annual surveys as specified by the Administration under Regulation 10(1)(c) or (d) of this Annex are not carried out.

(3) A Certificate issued to a ship shall also cease to be valid upon transfer of the ship to the flag of another State. A new Certificate shall be issued only when the Government issuing the new Certificate is fully satisfied that the ship is in full compliance with the requirements of Regulation 10(3)(a) and (b) of this Annex. In the case of a transfer between Parties, if requested within three months after the transfer has taken place, the Government of the Party whose flag the ship was formerly entitled to fly shall transmit as soon as possible to the Administration a copy of the Certificate carried by the ship before the transfer and, if available, a copy of the relevant survey report.

Regulation 12A

Survey and Certification of Chemical Tankers

Notwithstanding the provisions of Regulations 10, 11 and 12 of this Annex, chemical tankers which have been surveyed and certified by States Parties to the present Convention in accordance with the provisions of the International Bulk Chemical Code or the Bulk Chemical Code, as applicable, shall be deemed to have complied with the provisions of the said Regulations, and the Certificate issued under that Code shall have the same force and receive the same recognition as the Certificate issued under Regulation 11 of this Annex.

Regulation 13

Requirements for Minimizing Accidental Pollution

(1) The design, construction, equipment and operation of ships carrying noxious liquid substances of Category A, B or C in bulk, shall be such as to minimize the uncontrolled discharge into the sea of such substances.

(2) Chemical tankers constructed on or after 1 July 1986 shall comply with the requirements of the International Bulk Chemical Code.

(3) Chemical tankers constructed before 1 July 1986 shall comply with the following requirements:

(a) The following chemical tankers shall comply with the requirements of the Bulk Chemical Code as applicable to ships referred to in 1.7.2 of that Code:

(i) ships for which the building contract is placed on or after 2 November 1973 and which are engaged on voyages to ports or terminals under the jurisdiction of other States Parties to the Convention; and

(ii) ships constructed on or after 1 July 1983 which are engaged solely on voyages between ports or terminals within the State the flag of which the ship is entitled to fly;

(b) The following chemical tankers shall comply with the requirements of the Bulk Chemical Code as applicable to ships referred to in 1.7.3 of that Code:

(i) ships for which the building contract is placed before 2 November 1973 and which are engaged on voyages to ports or terminals under the jurisdiction of other States Parties to the Convention; and

(ii) ships constructed before 1 July 1983 which are engaged on voyages between ports or terminals within the State the flag of which the ship is entitled to fly, except that for ships of less than 1,600 tons gross tonnage compliance with the Code in respect of construction and equipment shall take effect not later than 1 July 1994.

(4) In respect of ships other than chemical tankers carrying noxious liquid substances of Category A, B or C in bulk, the Administration shall establish appropriate measures based on the Guidelines developed by the Organization in order to ensure that the provisions of paragraph (1) of this Regulation are complied with.

Regulation 14
Carriage and Discharge of Oil-like Substances

Notwithstanding the provisions of other Regulations of this Annex, noxious liquid substances designated in Appendix II of this Annex as falling under Category C or D and identified by the Organization as oil-like substances under the criteria developed by the Organization, may be carried on an oil tanker as defined in Annex I of the Convention and discharged in accordance with the provisions of Annex I of the present Convention, provided that all of the following conditions are complied with:

(a) the ship complies with the provisions of Annex I of the present Convention as applicable to product carriers as defined in that Annex;

(b) the ship carries an International Oil Pollution Prevention Certificate and its Supplement B and the Certificate is endorsed to indicate that the ship may carry oil-like substances in conformity with this Regulation and the endorsement includes a list of oil-like substances the ship is allowed to carry;

(c) in the case of Category C substances the ship complies with the ship type 3 damage stability requirements of:

(i) the International Bulk Chemical Code in the case of a ship constructed on or after 1 July 1986; or

(ii) the Bulk Chemical Code, as applicable under Regulation 13 of this Annex, in the case of a ship constructed before 1 July 1986; and

(d) the oil content meter in the oil discharge monitoring and control system of the ship is approved by the Administration for use in monitoring the oil-like substances to be carried.

ANNEX V
REGULATIONS FOR THE PREVENTION OF POLLUTION BY GARBAGE FROM SHIPS
Regulation 1
Definitions

For the purposes of this Annex:

(1) "Garbage" means all kinds of victual, domestic and operational waste excluding fresh fish and parts thereof, generated during the normal operation of the ship and liable to be disposed of continuously or periodically except those substances which are defined or listed in other Annexes to the present Convention.

(2) "Nearest land". The term "from the nearest land" means from the baseline from which the territorial sea of the territory in question is established in accordance with international law except that, for the purposes of the present Convention "from the nearest land" off the north eastern coast of Australia shall mean from a line drawn from a point on the coast of Australia in latitude 11° South, longitude 142°08' East to a point in latitude 10°35' South,

longitude 141°55' East, thence to a point latitude 10°00' South,

longitude 142°00' East, thence to a point latitude 9°10' South, longitude 143°52′ East, thence to a point latitude 9°00′ South,

longitude 144°30′ East, thence to a point latitude 13°00′ South,

longitude 144°00′ East, thence to a point latitude 15°00′ South,

longitude 146°00′ East, thence to a point latitude 18°00′ South,

longitude 147°00′ East, thence to a point latitude 21°00′ South,

longitude 153°00′ East, thence to a point on the coast of Australia in latitude 24°42′ South, longitude 153°15′ East.

(3) "Special area" means a sea area where for recognized technical reasons in relation to its oceanographical and ecological condition and to the particular character of its traffic the adoption of special mandatory methods for the prevention of sea pollution by garbage is required. Special areas shall include those listed in Regulation 5 of this Annex.

Regulation 2
Application

The provisions of this Annex shall apply to all ships.

Regulation 3
Disposal of Garbage Outside Special Areas

(1) Subject to the provisions of Regulations 4, 5 and 6 of this Annex:

(a) the disposal into the sea of all plastics, including but not limited to synthetic ropes, synthetic fishing nets and plastic garbage bags is prohibited;

(b) the disposal into the sea of the following garbage shall be made as far as practicable from the nearest land but in any case is prohibited if the distance from the nearest land is less than:

(i) 25 nautical miles for dunnage, lining and packing materials which will float;

(ii) 12 nautical miles for food wastes and all other garbage including paper products, rags, glass, metal, bottles, crockery and similar refuse;

(c) disposal into the sea of garbage specified in sub-paragraph (b)(ii) of this Regulation may be permitted when it is passed through a comminuter or grinder and made as far as practicable from the nearest land but in any case is prohibited if the distance from the nearest land is less than 3 nautical miles. Such comminuted or ground garbage shall be capable of passing through a screen with openings no greater than 25 millimetres.

(2) When the garbage is mixed with other discharges having different disposal or discharge requirements the more severe requirements shall apply.

Regulation 4
Disposals from Drilling Rigs

(1) Fixed or floating platforms engaged in the exploration, exploitation and associated offshore processing of sea-bed mineral resources, and all other ships when alongside such platforms or within 500 metres of such platforms, are forbidden to dispose of any materials regulated by this Annex, except as permitted by paragraph (2) of this Regulation.

(2) The disposal into the sea of food wastes when passed through a comminuter or grinder from such fixed or floating drilling rigs located more than 12 nautical miles from land and all other ships when positioned as above. Such comminuted or ground food wastes shall be capable of passing through a screen with openings no greater than 25 millimetres.

Regulation 5

Disposal of Garbage within Special Areas

(1) For the purpose of this Annex the special areas are the Mediterranean Sea area, the Baltic Sea area, the Black Sea area, the Red Sea area and the "Gulfs area" which are defined as follows:

(a) The Mediterranean Sea area means the Mediterranean Sea proper including the gulfs and seas therein with the boundary between the Mediterranean and the Black Sea constituted by the 41°N parallel and bounded to the west by the Straits of Gibraltar at the meridian of 5°36'W.

(b) The Baltic Sea area means the Baltic Sea proper with the Gulf of Bothnia and the Gulf of Finland and the entrance to the Baltic Sea bounded by the parallel of the Skaw in the Skagerrak at 57°44.8'N.

(c) The Black Sea area means the Black Sea proper with the boundary between the Mediterranean and the Black Sea constituted by the parallel 41°N.

(d) The Red Sea area means the Red Sea proper including the Gulfs of Suez and Aqaba bounded at the south by the rhumb line between Ras si Ane (12°8.5'N, 43°19.6'E) and Husn Murad (12°40.4'N, 43°30.2'E).

(e) The "Gulfs area" means the sea area located north west of the rhumb line between Ras al Hadd (22°30'N, 59°48'E) and Ras al Fasteh (25°04'N, 61°25'E).

(2) Subject to the provisions of Regulation 6 of this Annex:

(a) disposal into the sea of the following is prohibited:

(i) all plastics, including but not limited to synthetic ropes, synthetic fishing nets and plastic garbage bags;

(ii) all other garbage, including paper products, rags, glass, metal, bottles, crockery, dunnage, lining and packing materials;

(b) disposal into the sea of food wastes shall be made as far as practicable from land, but in any case not less than 12 nautical miles from the nearest land.

(3) When the garbage is mixed with other discharges having different disposal or discharge requirements the more severe requirements shall apply.

(4) Reception facilities within special areas.

(a) The Government of each party to the Convention, the coast line of which borders a special area undertakes to ensure that as soon as possible in all ports within a special area, adequate reception facilities are provided in accordance with Regulation 7 of this Annex, taking into account the special needs of ships operating in these areas.

(b) The Government of each party concerned shall notify the Organization of the measures taken pursuant to sub-paragraph (a) of this

Regulation. Upon receipt of sufficient notifications the Organization shall establish a date from which the requirements of this Regulation in respect of the area in question shall take effect. The Organization shall notify all parties of the date so established no less than twelve months in advance of that date.

(c) After date so established, ships calling also at ports in these special areas where such facilities are not yet available, shall fully comply with the requirements of this Regulation.

Regulation 6

Exception

Regulations 3, 4 and 5 of this Annex shall not apply to:

(a) the disposal of garbage from a ship necessary for the purpose of securing the safety of a ship, the health of its personnel, or saving life at sea;

(b) the escape of garbage resulting from damage to a ship or its equipment provided all reasonable precautions have been taken before and after the occurrence of the damage, for the purpose of preventing or minimizing the escape;

(c) the accidental loss of synthetic fishing nets or synthetic material incidental to the repair of such nets, provided that all reasonable precautions have been taken to prevent such loss.

Regulation 7

Reception Facilities

(1) The Government of each party to the Convention undertakes to ensure the provisions of facilities at ports and terminals for the reception of garbage, without causing undue delay to ships, and according to the needs of the ships using them.

(2) The Government of each party shall notify the Organization for transmission to the parties concerned of all cases where the facilities provided under this Regulation are alleged to be inadequate.

4.16 CONVENTION ON THE PROTECTION OF THE MARINE ENVIRON-MENT OF THE BALTIC SEA AREA (WITHOUT ANNEXES). Concluded at Helsinki, 22 March 1974. Entered into force, 3 May 1980. 13 I.L.M. 546 (1974)

THE STATES PARTIES TO THIS CONVENTION,

CONSCIOUS of the indispensable economic, social and cultural values of the marine environment of the Baltic Sea Area and its living resources for the peoples of the Contracting Parties;

BEARING in mind the exceptional hydrographic and ecological characteristics of the Baltic Sea Area and the sensitivity of its living resources to changes in the environment;

NOTING the rapid development of human activities at the Baltic Sea Area, the considerable population living within its catchment area and the highly urbanized and industrialized state of the Contracting Parties as well as their intensive agriculture and forestry;

NOTING with deep concern the increasing pollution of the Baltic Sea Area, originating from many sources such as discharges through rivers, estuaries, outfalls and pipelines, dumping and normal operations of vessels as well as through airborne pollutants;

CONSCIOUS of the responsibility of the Contracting Parties to protect and enhance the values of the marine environment of the Baltic Sea Area for the benefit of their peoples;

RECOGNIZING that the protection and enhancement of the marine environment of the Baltic Sea Area are tasks that cannot effectively be accomplished by national efforts only but that also close regional co-operation and other appropriate international measures aiming at fulfilling these tasks are urgently needed;

NOTING that the relevant recent international conventions even after having entered into force for the respective Contracting Parties do not cover all special requirements to protect and enhance the marine environment of the Baltic Sea Area;

NOTING the importance of scientific and technological co-operation in the protection and enhancement of the marine environment of the Baltic Sea Area, particularly between the Contracting Parties;

DESIRING to develop further regional co-operation in the Baltic Sea Area, the possibilities and requirements of which were confirmed by the signing of the Convention on Fishing and Conservation of the Living Resources in the Baltic Sea and the Belts, Gdansk 1973;

CONSCIOUS of the importance of regional intergovernmental co-operation in the protection of the marine environment of the Baltic Sea Area as an integral part of the peaceful co-operation and mutual understanding between all European States;

HAVE AGREED as follows:

Article 1
Convention area

For the purposes of the present Convention "the Baltic Sea Area" shall be the Baltic Sea proper with the Gulf of Bothnia, the Gulf of Finland and the entrance to the Baltic Sea bounded by the parallel of the Skaw in the Skagerrak at 57°44'8"N. It does not include internal waters of the Contracting Parties.

Article 2
Definitions

For the purposes of the present Convention:

1. "Pollution" means introduction by man, directly or indirectly, of substances or energy into the marine environment, including estuaries, resulting in such deleterious effects as hazard to human health, harm to living resources and marine life, hindrance to legitimate uses of the sea including fishing, impairment of the quality for use of sea water, and reduction of amenities;

2. "Land-based pollution" means pollution of the sea caused by discharges from land reaching the sea waterborne, airborne or directly from the coast, including outfalls from pipelines;

3. a) "Dumping" means:

(i) any deliberate disposal at sea of wastes or other matter from vessels, aircraft, platforms or other man-made structures at sea;

(ii) any deliberate disposal at sea of vessels, aircraft, platforms or other man-made structures at sea;

b) "Dumping" does not include:

(i) the disposal at sea of wastes or other matter incidental to, or derived from the normal operations of vessels, aircraft, platforms or other man-made structures at sea and their equipment, other than wastes or other matter transported by or to vessels, aircraft, platforms or other man-made structures at sea, operating for the purpose of disposal of such matter or derived from the treatment of such wastes or other matter on such vessels, aircraft, platforms or structures;

(ii) placement of matter for a purpose other than the mere disposal thereof, provided that such placement is not contrary to the aims of the present Convention;

4. "Vessels and aircraft" means waterborne or airborne craft of any type whatsoever. This expression includes hydrofoil boats, air-cushion vehicles, submersibles, floating craft whether self-propelled or not, and fixed or floating platforms;

5. "Oil" means petroleum in any form including crude oil, fuel oil, sludge, oil refuse and refined products;

6. "Harmful substance" means any hazardous, noxious, or other substance, which, if introduced into the sea, is liable to cause pollution;

7. "Incident" means an event involving the actual or probable discharge into the sea of a harmful substance, or effluents containing such a substance.

Article 3
Fundamental principles and obligations

1. The Contracting Parties shall individually or jointly take all appropriate legislative, administrative or other relevant measures in order to prevent

and abate pollution and to protect and enhance the marine environment of the Baltic Sea Area.

2.   The Contracting Parties shall use their best endeavours to ensure that the implementation of the present Convention shall not cause an increase in the pollution of sea areas outside the Baltic Sea Area.

Article 4

Application

1.   The present Convention shall apply to the protection of the marine environment of the Baltic Sea Area which comprises the water-body and the sea-bed including their living resources and other forms of marine life.

2.   Without prejudice to the sovereign rights in regard to their territorial sea, each Contracting Party shall implement the provisions of the present Convention within its territorial sea through its national authorities.

3.   While the provisions of the present Convention do not apply to internal waters, which are under the sovereignty of each Contracting Party, the Contracting Parties undertake, without prejudice to their sovereign rights, to ensure that the purposes of the present Convention will be obtained in these waters.

4.   The present Convention shall not apply to any warship, naval auxiliary, military aircraft or other ship and aircraft owned or operated by a State and used, for the time being, only on government non-commercial service.

However, each Contracting Party shall ensure, by the adoption of appropriate measures not impairing the operations or operational capabilities of such ships and aircraft owned or operated by it, that such ships and aircraft act in a manner consistent, so far as is reasonable and practicable, with the present Convention.

Article 5

Hazardous substances

The Contracting Parties undertake to counteract the introduction, whether airborne, waterborne or otherwise, into the Baltic Sea Area of hazardous substances as specified in Annex I of the present Convention.

Article 6

Principles and obligations concerning land-based pollution

1.   The Contracting Parties shall take all appropriate measures to control and minimize land-based pollution of the marine environment of the Baltic Sea Area.

2.   In particular, the Contracting Parties shall take all appropriate measures to control and strictly limit pollution by noxious substances and materials in accordance with Annex II of the present Convention. To this end they shall, inter alia, as appropriate co-operate in the development and adoption of specific programmes, guidelines, standards or regulations concerning discharges, environmental quality, and products containing such substances and materials and their use.

3.   The substances and materials listed in Annex II of the present Convention shall not be introduced into the marine environment of the Baltic

Sea Area in significant quantities without a prior special permit, which may be periodically reviewed, by the appropriate national authority.

4. The appropriate national authority will inform the Commission referred to in Article 12 of the present Convention of the quantity, quality and way of discharge if it considers that significant quantities of substances and materials listed in Annex II of the present Convention were discharged.

5. The Contracting Parties shall endeavor to establish and adopt common criteria for issuing permits for discharges.

6. To control and minimize pollution of the Baltic Sea Area by harmful substances the Contracting Parties shall, in addition to the provisions of Article 5 of the present Convention, aim at attaining the goals and applying the criteria enumerated in Annex III of the present Convention.

7. If the discharge from a watercourse, flowing through the territories of two or more Contracting Parties or forming a boundary between them, is liable to cause pollution of the marine environment of the Baltic Sea Area, the Contracting Parties concerned shall in common take appropriate measures in order to prevent and abate such pollution.

8. The Contracting Parties shall endeavour to use best practicable means in order to minimize the airborne pollution of the Baltic Sea Area by noxious substances.

Article 7
Prevention of pollution from ships

1. In order to protect the Baltic Sea Area from pollution by deliberate, negligent or accidental release of oil, harmful substances other than oil, and by the discharge of sewage and garbage from ships, the Contracting Parties shall take measures as set out in Annex IV of the present Convention.

2. The Contracting Parties shall develop and apply uniform requirements for the capacity and location of facilities for the reception of residues of oil, harmful substances other than oil, including sewage and garbage, taking into account inter alia the special needs of passenger ships and combination carriers.

Article 8
Pleasure craft

The Contracting Parties shall, in addition to implementing those provisions of the present Convention which can appropriately be applied to pleasure craft, take special measures in order to abate harmful effects on the marine environment of the Baltic Sea Area of pleasure craft activities. The measures shall inter alia deal with adequate reception facilities for wastes from pleasure craft.

Article 9
Prevention of dumping

1. The Contracting Parties shall, subject to Paragraphs 2 and 4 of this Article, prohibit dumping in the Baltic Sea Area.

2. Dumping of dredged spoils shall be subject to a prior special permit by the appropriate national authority in accordance with the provisions of Annex V of the present Convention.

3. Each Contracting Party undertakes to ensure compliance with the provisions of this Article by vessels and aircraft:

a) registered in its territory or flying its flag;

b) loading, within its territory or territorial sea, matter which is to be dumped; or

c) believed to be engaged in dumping within its territorial sea.

4. The provisions of this Article shall not apply when the safety of human life or of a vessel or aircraft at sea is threatened by the complete destruction or total loss of the vessel or aircraft, or in any case which constitutes a danger to human life, if dumping appears to be the only way of averting the threat and if there is every probability that the damage consequent upon such dumping will be less than would otherwise occur. Such dumping shall be so conducted as to minimize the likelihood of damage to human or marine life.

5. Dumping made under the provisions of Paragraph 4 of this Article shall be reported and dealt with in accordance with Annex VI of the present Convention and shall also be reported forthwith to the Commission referred to in Article 12 of the present Convention in accordance with the provisions of Regulation 4 of Annex V of the present Convention.

6. In case of dumping suspected to be in contravention of the provisions of this Article the Contracting Parties shall co-operate in investigating the matter in accordance with Regulation 2 of Annex IV of the present Convention.

Article 10

Exploration and exploitation of the sea-bed and its subsoil

Each Contracting Party shall take all appropriate measures in order to prevent pollution of the marine environment of the Baltic Sea Area resulting from exploration or exploitation of its part of the sea-bed and its subsoil or from any associated activities thereon. It shall also ensure that adequate equipment is at hand to start an immediate abatement of pollution in that area.

Article 11

Co-operation in combatting marine pollution

The Contracting Parties shall take measures and co-operate as set out in Annex VI of the present Convention in order to eliminate or minimize pollution of the Baltic Sea Area by oil or other harmful substances.

Article 12

Institutional and organizational framework

1. The Baltic Marine Environment Protection Commission, hereinafter referred to as "the Commission", is hereby established for the purposes of the present Convention.

2. The chairmanship of the Commission shall be given to each Contracting Party in turn in alphabetical order of the names of the States in the English language.

The Chairman shall serve for a period of two years, and cannot during the period of his chairmanship serve as representative of his country.

Should the chairmanship fall vacant, the Contracting Party chairing the Commission shall nominate a successor to remain in office until the term of chairmanship of that Contracting Party expires.

3. Meetings of the Commission shall be held at least once a year upon convocation by the Chairman. Upon the request of a Contracting Party, provided it is endorsed by another Contracting Party, the Chairman shall, as soon as possible, summon an extraordinary meeting at such time and place as the Chairman determines, however, not later than ninety days from the date of the submission of the request.

4. The first meeting of the Commission shall be called by the Depositary Government and shall take place within a period of ninety days from the date following the entry into force of the present Convention.

5. Each Contracting Party shall have one vote in the Commission. Unless otherwise provided under the present Convention, the Commission shall take its decisions unanimously.

Article 13

The duties of the Commission

The duties of the Commission shall be:

a) To keep the implementation of the present Convention under continuous observation;

b) To make recommendations on measures relating to the purposes of the present Convention;

c) To keep under review the contents of the present Convention including its Annexes and to recommend to the Contracting Parties such amendments to the present Convention including its Annexes as may be required including changes in the lists of substances and materials as well as the adoption of new Annexes;

d) To define pollution control criteria, objectives for the reduction of pollution, and objectives concerning measures, particularly according to Annex III of the present Convention;

e) To promote in close co-operation with appropriate governmental bodies, taking into consideration Sub–Paragraph f) of this Article, additional measures to protect the marine environment of the Baltic Sea Area and for this purpose:

(i) to receive, process, summarize and disseminate from available sources relevant scientific, technological and statistical information; and

(ii) to promote scientific and technological research;

f) To seek, when appropriate, the services of competent regional and other international organizations to collaborate in scientific and technological research as well as other relevant activities pertinent to the objectives of the present Convention;

g) To assume such other functions as may be appropriate under the terms of the present Convention.

Article 14
Administrative provisions for the Commission

1.   The working language of the Commission shall be English.

2.   The Commission shall adopt its Rules of Procedure.

3.   The office of the Commission, hereafter referred to as the "Secretariat", shall be in Helsinki.

4.   The Commission shall appoint an Executive Secretary and make provisions for the appointment of such other personnel as may be necessary, and determine the duties, terms and conditions of the Executive Secretary.

5.   The Executive Secretary shall be the chief administrative official of the Commission and shall perform the functions that are necessary for the administration of the present Convention, the work of the Commission and other tasks entrusted to the Executive Secretary by the Commission and its Rules of Procedure.

Article 15
Financial provisions for the Commission

1.   The Commission shall adopt its Financial Rules.

2.   The Commission shall adopt an annual or biennial budget of proposed expenditures and budget estimates for the fiscal period following thereafter.

3.   The total amount of the budget, including any supplementary budget adopted by the Commission, shall be contributed by the Contracting Parties in equal parts, unless the Commission unanimously decides otherwise.

4.   Each Contracting Party shall pay the expenses related to the participation in the Commission of its representatives, experts and advisers.

Article 16
Scientific and technological co-operation

1.   The Contracting Parties undertake directly, or when appropriate through competent regional or other international organizations, to co-operate in the fields of science, technology and other research, and to exchange data as well as other scientific information for the purposes of the present Convention.

2.   Without prejudice to Paragraphs 1, 2 and 3 of Article 4 of the present Convention the Contracting Parties undertake directly, or when appropriate through competent regional or other international organizations, to promote studies, undertake, support or contribute to programmes aimed at developing ways and means for the assessment of the nature and extent of pollution, pathways, exposures, risks and remedies in the Baltic Sea Area, and particularly to develop alternative methods of treatment, disposal and elimination of such matter and substances that are likely to cause pollution of the marine environment of the Baltic Sea Area.

3.   The Contracting Parties undertake directly, or when appropriate through competent regional or other international organizations, and, on the basis of the information and data acquired pursuant to Paragraphs 1 and 2 of

this Article, to co-operate in developing inter-comparable observation methods, in performing baseline studies and in establishing complementary or joint programmes for monitoring.

4. The organization and scope of work connected with the implementation of tasks referred to in the preceding Paragraphs should primarily be outlined by the Commission.

Article 17

Responsibility for damage

The Contracting Parties undertake, as soon as possible, jointly to develop and accept rules concerning responsibility for damage resulting from acts or omissions in contravention of the present Convention, including, inter alia, limits of responsibility, criteria and procedures for the determination of liability and available remedies.

Article 18

Settlement of disputes

1. In case of a dispute between Contracting Parties as to the interpretation or application of the present Convention, they should seek a solution by negotiation. If the Parties concerned cannot reach agreement they should seek the good offices of or jointly request the mediation by a third Contracting Party, a qualified international organization or a qualified person.

2. If the Parties concerned have not been able to resolve their dispute through negotiation or have been unable to agree on measures as described above, such disputes shall be, upon common agreement, submitted to an ad-hoc arbitration tribunal, to a permanent arbitration tribunal, or to the International Court of Justice.

Article 19

Safeguard of certain freedoms

Nothing in the present Convention shall be construed as infringing upon the freedom of navigation, fishing, marine scientific research and other legitimate uses of the high seas, as well as upon the right of innocent passage through the territorial sea.

Article 20

Status of Annexes

The Annexes attached to the present Convention form an integral part of the Convention.

Article 21

Relation to other Conventions

The provisions of the present Convention shall be without prejudice to the rights and obligations of the Contracting Parties under treaties concluded previously as well as under treaties which may be concluded in the future, furthering and developing the general principles of the Law of the Sea that the present Convention is based upon and in particular provisions concerning the prevention of pollution of the marine environment.

Article 22

Revision of the Convention

A conference for the purpose of a general revision of the present Convention may be convened with the consent of the Contracting Parties or at the request of the Commission.

Article 23

Amendments to the Articles of the Convention

1. Each Contracting Party may propose amendments to the Articles of the present Convention. Any such proposed amendment shall be submitted to the Depositary Government and communicated by it to all Contracting Parties, which shall inform the Depositary Government of either their acceptance or rejection of the amendment as soon as possible after the receipt of the communication.

The amendment shall enter into force ninety days after the Depositary Government has received notifications of acceptance of that amendment from all Contracting Parties.

2. With the consent of the Contracting Parties or at the request of the Commission a conference may be convened for the purpose of amending the present Convention.

Article 24

Amendments to the Annexes and the adoption of Annexes

1. Any amendment to the Annexes proposed by a Contracting Party shall be communicated to the other Contracting Parties by the Depositary Government and considered in the Commission. If adopted by the Commission, the amendment shall be communicated to the Contracting Parties and recommended for acceptance.

2. Such amendment shall be deemed to have been accepted at the end of a period determined by the Commission unless within that period any one of the Contracting Parties has objected to the amendment. The accepted amendment shall enter into force on a date determined by the Commission.

The period determined by the Commission shall be prolonged for an additional period of six months and the date of entry into force of the amendment postponed accordingly, if, in exceptional cases, any Contracting Party before the expiring of the period determined by the Commission informs the Depositary Government, that, although it intends to accept the proposal, the constitutional requirements for such an acceptance are not yet fulfilled in its State.

3. An Annex to the present Convention may be adopted in accordance with the provisions of this Article.

4. The Depositary Government shall inform all Contracting Parties of any amendments or the adoption of a new Annex which enter into force under this Article and of the date on which such amendment or new Annex enters into force.

5. Any objection under this Article shall be made by notification in writing to the Depositary Government which shall notify all Contracting

Parties and the Executive Secretary of any such notification and the date of its receipt.

Article 25

Reservations

1. The provisions of the present Convention shall not be subject to reservations.

2. The provision of Paragraph 1 of this Article does not prevent a Contracting Party from suspending for a period not exceeding one year the application of an Annex of the present Convention or part thereof or an amendment thereto after the Annex in question or the amendment thereto has entered into force.

3. If after the entry into force of the present Convention a Contracting Party invokes the provisions of Paragraph 2 of this Article it shall inform the other Contracting Parties, at the time of the adoption by the Commission of an amendment to an Annex or a new Annex, of those provisions which will be suspended in accordance with Paragraph 2 of this Article.

Article 26

Signature, ratification, approval, and accession

1. The present Convention shall be open for signature in Helsinki on 22 March 1974 by the Baltic Sea States participating in the Diplomatic Conference on the Protection of the Marine Environment of the Baltic Sea Area, held in Helsinki from 18 to 22 March 1974. The present Convention shall be open for accession to any other State interested in fulfilling the aims and purposes of the present Convention, provided that this State is invited by all the Contracting Parties.

2. The present Convention shall be subject to ratification or approval by the States which have signed it.

3. The instruments of ratification, approval, or accession shall be deposited with the Government of Finland, which will perform the duties of the Depositary Government.

Article 27

Entry into force

The present Convention shall enter into force two months after the deposit of the seventh instrument of ratification or approval.

Article 28

Withdrawal

1. At any time after the expiry of five years from the date of entry into force of the present Convention any Contracting Party may, by giving written notification to the Depositary Government, withdraw from the present Convention. The withdrawal shall take effect for such Contracting Party on the thirty-first day of December of the year which follows the year in which the Depositary Government was notified of the withdrawal.

2. In case of notification of withdrawal by a Contracting Party the Depositary Government shall convene a meeting of the Contracting Parties for the purpose of considering the effect of the withdrawal.

Article 29

Language

The present Convention has been drawn up in a single copy in the English language. Official translations into the Danish, Finnish, German, Polish, Russian, and Swedish languages shall be prepared and deposited with the signed original.

4.17 CONVENTION FOR THE PREVENTION OF MARINE POLLUTION FROM LAND–BASED SOURCES (WITHOUT ANNEXES BUT AS AMENDED). Concluded at Paris, 4 June 1974. Entered into force, 6 May 1978. 13 I.L.M. 352 (1974)

THE CONTRACTING PARTIES:

RECOGNIZING that the marine environment and the living resources which it supports are of vital importance to all nations;

MINDFUL that the ecological equilibrium and the legitimate uses of the sea are increasingly threatened by pollution;

CONSIDERING the recommendations of the United Nations Conference on the Human Environment, held in Stockholm in June 1972;

RECOGNIZING that concerted action at national, regional and global levels is essential to prevent and combat marine pollution;

CONVINCED that international action to control the pollution of the sea from land-based sources can and should be taken without delay, as part of progressive and coherent measures to protect the marine environment from pollution, whatever its origin, including current efforts to combat the pollution of international waterways;

CONSIDERING that the common interests of States concerned with the same marine area should induce them to cooperate at regional or sub-regional levels;

RECALLING the Convention for the Prevention of Marine Pollution by Dumping from Ships and Air-craft concluded in Oslo on 15 February 1972;

Have agreed as follows:

ARTICLE I

1. The Contracting Parties pledge themselves to take all possible steps to prevent pollution of the sea, by which is meant the introduction by man, directly or indirectly, of substances or energy into the marine environment (including estuaries) resulting in such deleterious effects as hazards to human health, harm to living resources and to marine eco-systems, damage to amenities or interference with other legitimate uses of the sea.

2. The Contracting Parties shall adopt individually and jointly measures to combat marine pollution from land-based sources in accordance with the provisions of the present convention and shall harmonize their policies in this regard.

ARTICLE 2

The present Convention shall apply to the maritime area within the following limits:

a) those parts of the Atlantic and Arctic Oceans and the dependent seas which lie North of 36° north latitude and between 42° west longitude and 51° east longitude, but excluding:

i) the Baltic Sea and Belts lying to the south and east of lines drawn from Hasenore Head to Gniben Point, from Korshage to Spodsbierg and from Gilbierg Head to Kulien, and

ii) the Mediterranean Sea and its dependent seas as far as the point of intersection of the parallel of 36° north latitude and the meridian of 5°36′ west longitude;

b) that part of the Atlantic Ocean north of 59° north latitude and between 44° west longitude and 42° west longitude.

ARTICLE 3

For the purpose of the present Convention:

a) *"Maritime area"*—means the high seas, the territorial seas of Contracting Parties and waters on the landward side of the base lines from which the breadth of the territorial sea is measured, extending, in the case of watercourses up to the freshwater limit unless otherwise decided under Article 16 of the present Convention;

b) *"Freshwater limit"*—means the place in the watercourse where, at low tide and in a period of low freshwater flow, there is an appreciable increase in salinity due to the presence of sea-water;

c) *"Pollution from land-based sources"*—means the pollution of the maritime area:

i) through watercourses,

ii) from the coast, including introduction through underwater or other pipelines,

iii) from man-made structures placed under the jurisdiction of a Contracting Party within the limits of the area to which the present Convention applies.

iv) by emissions into the atmosphere from land or from man-made structures as defined in subparagraph iii, above.

ARTICLE 4

1.   The Contracting Parties undertake:

a) to eliminate, if necessary by stages, pollution of the maritime area from land-based sources of substances listed in Part I of Annex A to the present Convention;

b) to limit strictly pollution of the maritime area from land-based sources of the substances listed in Part II of Annex A to the present Convention.

2.   In order to carry out the undertakings in paragraph 1 of this Article, the Contracting Parties, jointly or individually as appropriate, shall implement programmes and measures:

a) for the elimination, as a matter of urgency, of pollution of the maritime area from land-based sources by substances listed in Part I of Annex A to the present Convention;

b) for the reduction or, as appropriate, elimination of pollution of the maritime area from land-based sources by substances listed in Part II of Annex A to the present Convention. These substances shall be discharged only after approval has been granted by the appropriate Authorities within each contracting State. Such approval shall be periodically reviewed.

3. The programmes and measures adopted under paragraph 2 above shall include, as appropriate, specific regulations or standards governing the quality of the environment, discharges into the maritime area, such discharges into watercourses and emissions into the atmosphere as affect the maritime area, and the composition and use of substances and products and shall take into account the latest technical developments.

The programmes shall contain time-limits for their completion.

4. Furthermore, the Contracting Parties may, jointly or individually as appropriate, implement programmes or measures to forestall, reduce or eliminate pollution of the maritime area from land-based sources by a substance not then listed in Annex A to the present Convention, if scientific evidence has established that a serious hazard may be created in the maritime area by that substance and if urgent action is necessary.

ARTICLE 5

1. The Contracting Parties undertake to adopt measures to forestall and, as appropriate, eliminate pollution of the maritime area from land-based sources by radio-active substances referred to in Part III of Annex A of the present Convention.

2. Without prejudice to their obligations under other Treaties and Conventions, in implementing this undertaking the Contracting Parties shall:

a) take full account of the recommendations of the appropriate international Organizations and Agencies;

b) take account of the monitoring procedures recommended by these international Organisations and Agencies;

c) coordinate their monitoring and study of radio-active substances in accordance with Article 10 and 11 of the present Convention.

ARTICLE 6

1. With a view to preserving and enhancing the quality of the marine environment, the Contracting Parties, without prejudice to the provisions of Article 4, shall endeavour:

a) to reduce existing pollution from land-based sources;

b) to forestall any new pollution from land-based sources, including that which derives from new substances.

2. In implementing this undertaking, the Contracting Parties shall take account of:

a) the nature and quantities of the pollutants under consideration;

b) the level of existing pollution;

c) the quality and absorptive capacity of the receiving waters of the maritime area;

d) the need for an integrated planning policy, consistent with the requirement of environmental protection.

ARTICLE 7

The Contracting Parties agree to apply the measures they adopt in such a way as to avoid increasing pollution:

— in the seas outside the area to which the present Convention applies;

— in the maritime area covered by the present Convention, originating otherwise than from land-based sources.

ARTICLE 8

No provision of the present Convention may be interpreted as preventing the Contracting Parties from taking more stringent measures to combat marine pollution from land-based sources.

ARTICLE 9

1. When pollution from land-based sources originating from the territory of a Contracting Party by substances not listed in Part 1 of Annex A of the present Convention is likely to prejudice the interests of one or more of the other Parties to the Convention, the Contracting Parties concerned undertake to enter into consultation, at the request of any one of them, with a view to negotiating a co-operation agreement.

2. At the request of any Contracting Party concerned, the Commission referred to in Article 15 of the present Convention shall consider the question and may make recommendations with a view to reaching a satisfactory solution.

3. The special agreements specified in Paragraph 1 of this Article may, among other things, define the areas to which they shall apply, the quality objectives to be achieved, and the methods for achieving these objectives including methods for the application of appropriate standards, and the scientific and technical information to be collected.

4. The Contracting Parties signatory to these agreements shall, through the medium of the Commission, inform the other Contracting Parties of their purport and of the progress made in putting them into effect.

ARTICLE 10

The Contracting Parties agree to establish complementary or joint programmes of scientific and technical research, including research into the best methods of eliminating or replacing noxious substances so as to reduce marine pollution from land-based sources, and to transmit to each other the information so obtained. In doing so they will have regard to the work carried out, in these fields, by the appropriate international Organizations and Agencies.

ARTICLE 11

The Contracting Parties agree to set up progressively, and to operate within the area covered by the present Convention, a permanent monitoring system allowing of:

— the earliest possible assessment of the existing level of marine pollution;

— the assessment of the effectiveness of measures for the reduction of marine pollution from land-based sources taken under the terms of the present Convention.

For this purpose the Contracting Parties shall lay down the ways and means of pursuing individually or jointly systematic and ad hoc monitoring programmes. These programmes shall take into account the deployment of research vessels and other facilities in the monitoring area.

The programmes will take into account similar programmes pursued in accordance with Conventions already in force and by the appropriate international Organisations and Agencies.

ARTICLE 12

1. Each Contracting Party undertakes to ensure compliance with the provisions of this Convention and to take in its territory appropriate measures to prevent and punish conduct in contravention of the provisions of the present Convention.

2. The Contracting Parties shall inform the Commission of the legislative and administrative measures they have taken to implement the provisions of the above paragraph.

ARTICLE 13

The Contracting Parties undertake to assist one another as appropriate to prevent incidents which may result in pollution from land-based sources, to minimize and eliminate the consequences of such incidents, and to exchange information to that end.

ARTICLE 14

1. The provisions of the present Convention may not be invoked against a Contracting Party to the extent that the latter is prevented, as a result of pollution having its origin in the territory of a non-Contracting State, from ensuring their full application.

2. However, the said Contracting Party shall endeavour to co-operate with the non-Contracting State so as to make possible the full application of the present Convention.

ARTICLE 15

A Commission made of representatives of each of the Contracting Parties is hereby established. The Commission shall meet at regular intervals and at any time, when due to special circumstances it is so decided in accordance with the rules of procedure.

ARTICLE 16

It shall be the duty of the Commission:

a) to exercise overall supervision over the implementation of the present Convention;

b) to review generally the condition of the seas within the area to which the present Convention applies, the effectiveness of the control measures being adopted and the need for any additional or different measures;

c) to examine the feasibility of and, as appropriate to fix, if necessary, in accordance with Article 3(a), on the proposal of the Contracting Party or Parties bordering on the same watercourse and following a standard procedure, the limit to which the maritime area shall extend in this watercourse;

d) to draw up, in accordance with Article 4 of the present Convention, programmes and measures for the elimination or reduction of pollution from land-based sources;

e) to make recommendations in accordance with the provisions of Article 9;

f) to receive and review information and distribute it to the Contracting Parties in accordance with the provisions of Article 11, 12, and 17 of the present Convention;

g) to make, in accordance with Article 13, recommendations regarding any amendment to the lists of substances included in Annex A of the present Convention;

h) to discharge such other functions, as may be appropriate, under the terms of the present Convention.

ARTICLE 17

The Contracting Parties, in accordance with a standard procedure, shall transmit to the Commission:

a) the results of monitoring pursuant to Article (11).

b) the most detailed information available on the substances listed in the Annexes to the present Convention and liable to find their way into the maritime area.

The Contracting Parties shall endeavour to improve progressively techniques for gathering such information which can contribute to the revision of the pollution reduction programmes adopted in accordance with Article 4.

ARTICLE 18

1. The Commission shall draw up its own Rules of Procedure which shall be adopted by unanimous vote.

2. The Commission shall draw up its own Financial Regulations which shall be adopted by unanimous vote.

3. The Commission shall adopt, by unanimous vote, programmes and measures for the reduction or elimination of pollution from land-based sources as provided for in Article 4, and for scientific research and monitoring as provided for in Articles 10 and 11 and the decisions under Article 16c.

Such programmes and measures shall commence for, and be applied by, all Contracting Parties two hundred days after adoption, unless the Commission specifies another date.

Should unanimity not be attainable, the Commission may nonetheless adopt a programme or measures by a three quarters majority vote of its members. Such programmes or measures shall commence for those Contracting Parties which voted for them two hundred days after their adoption, unless the Commission specifies another date, and for any other Contracting Party after it has explicitly accepted the programme or measures which it may do at any time.

The Commission may adopt, in accordance with Article 16g, recommendations for amendments to Annex A to the present Convention by a three quarters majority vote of its members and shall submit them for the approval of the Governments of the Contracting Parties. Any Government of a Contracting Party that is unable to approve an amendment shall notify the Depositary Government in writing within a period of two hundred days after the adoption of the Recommendation of amendment in the Commission.

Should no such notification be received, the amendment shall enter into force for all Contracting Parties two hundred and thirty days after the vote in the Commission. The Depositary Government shall notify the Contracting Parties as soon as possible of the receipt of any notification.

ARTICLE 19

Within its competences, the European Economic Community is entitled to a number of votes equal to the number of its member States which are Contracting Parties to the present Convention.

The European Economic Community shall not exercise its right to vote in cases where its member States exercise theirs and conversely.

ARTICLE 20

The depositary Government shall convene the first meeting of the Commission as soon as possible after the coming into force of the present Convention.

ARTICLE 21

Any dispute between Contracting Parties relating to the interpretation or application of the present Convention, which cannot be settled otherwise by the parties concerned, for instance by means of inquiry or conciliation within the Commission, shall, at the request of any of those Parties be submitted to arbitration under the conditions laid down in Annex B to the Convention.

ARTICLE 22

The present Convention shall be open at Paris, from 4th June 1974 to 30th June 1975, for signature by the States invited to the Diplomatic Conference on the Convention for the prevention of Marine Pollution from Land–Based Sources held at Paris and by the European Economic Community.

ARTICLE 23

The present Convention shall be subject to ratification, acceptance or approval. The instruments of ratification, acceptance or approval shall be deposited with the Government of the French Republic.

ARTICLE 24

1. After 30th June 1975, the present Convention shall be open for accession by States referred to in Article 22 and by the European Economic Community.

2. The present Convention shall also be open for accession from the same date by any other Contracting Party to the Convention for the prevention of Marine Pollution by Dumping from Ships and Aircraft opened for signature at Oslo on 15th February 1972.

3. From the date of its entry into force, the present Convention shall be open for accession by any State not referred to in Article 22 located upstream on watercourses crossing the territory of one or more Contracting Parties to the present Convention and reaching the maritime area defined in Article 2.

4. The Contracting Parties may, by unanimous vote, invite other States to accede to the present Convention. In that case the maritime area defined

in Article 2 may, if necessary, be amended in accordance with Article 27 of the present Convention.

5.   The instruments of accession shall be deposited with the Government of the French Republic.

ARTICLE 25

1.   The present Convention shall come into force on the thirtieth day following the date of deposit of the seventh instrument of ratification, approval, acceptance or accession.

2.   For each Party ratifying, accepting or approving the present Convention or acceding to it after the deposit of the seventh instrument of ratification, approval, acceptance or accession, the present Convention shall enter into force on the thirtieth day after deposit by that Party of its instrument of ratification, acceptance, approval or accession.

ARTICLE 26

At any time after the expiry of two years from the date of coming into force of the present Convention in relation to any Contracting Party such Party may withdraw from the Convention by notice in writing to the depositary Government. Such notice shall take effect one year after the date on which it is received.

ARTICLE 27

1.   The depositary Government shall, at the request of the Commission on a decision taken by a two-thirds majority of its members, call a Conference for the purpose of revising or amending the present Convention.

2.   Upon accession by a State as provided for in Paragraphs 2, 3, and 4 of Article 24, the maritime area defined in Article 2 may be amended upon a proposal by the Commission adopted by a unanimous vote. Such amendments shall enter into force after unanimous approval by the Contracting Parties.

ARTICLE 28

The depositary Government shall inform the Contracting Parties and those referred to in Article 22:

(a) of signatures to the present Convention, of the deposit of instruments or ratification, acceptance, approval or accession, and of notices of withdrawal in accordance with Articles 22, 23, 24 and 26;

(b) of the date on which the present Convention comes into force in accordance with Article 25;

(c) of the receipt of notifications of approval or of objection to the present Convention and its annexes, and of the entry into force of amendments thereto, in accordance with Articles 18 and 27 of the present Convention.

ARTICLE 29

The original of the present Convention of which the French and English texts shall be equally authentic, shall be deposited with the Government of the French Republic which shall send certified copies thereof to the Contracting Parties and the States referred to in Article 22 and shall deposit a certified copy with the Secretary General of the United Nations for registration and publication in accordance with Article 102 of the United Nations Charter.

4.18 PROTOCOL TO THE 1969 INTERNATIONAL CONVENTION ON CIVIL LIABILITY FOR OIL POLLUTION DAMAGE.[1] Concluded at London, 19 November 1976. Entered into force, 8 April 1981. 16 I.L.M. 617 (1977)

* * *

THE PARTIES TO THE PRESENT PROTOCOL,

BEING PARTIES to the International Convention on Civil Liability for Oil Pollution Damage, done at Brussels on 29 November 1969;

HAVE AGREED AS FOLLOWS:

Article I

For the purpose of the present Protocol:

1. "Convention" means the International Convention on Civil Liability for Oil Pollution Damage, 1969.

2. "Organization" has the same meaning as in the Convention.

3. "Secretary–General" means the Secretary–General of the Organization.

Article II

Article V of the Convention is amended as follows:

(1) Paragraph 1 is replaced by the following text:

"The owner of a ship shall be entitled to limit his liability under this Convention in respect of any one incident to an aggregate amount of 133 units of account for each ton of the ship's tonnage. However, this aggregate amount shall not in any event exceed 14 million units of account."

(2) Paragraph 9 is replaced by the following text:

"9(a) The "unit of account" referred to in paragraph 1 of this Article is the Special Drawing Right as defined by the International Monetary Fund. The amounts mentioned in paragraph 1 shall be converted into the national currency of the State in which the fund is being constituted on the basis of the value of that currency by reference to the Special Drawing Right on the date of the constitution of the fund. The value of the national currency, in terms of the Special Drawing Right, of a Contracting State which is a member of the International Monetary Fund, shall be calculated in accordance with the method of valuation applied by the International Monetary Fund in effect at the date in question for its operations and transactions. The value of the national currency, in terms of the Special Drawing Right, of a Contracting State which is not a member of the International Monetary Fund, shall be calculated in a manner determined by that State.

9(b) Nevertheless, a Contracting State which is not a member of the International Monetary Fund and whose law does not permit the application of the provisions of paragraph 9(a) of this Article may, at the time of ratification, acceptance, approval of or accession to the present Convention, or at any time thereafter, declare that the limits of liability provided

---

1. *See* Basic Document 4.8, *supra,* and 4.28, *infra.*

for in paragraph 1 to be applied in its territory shall, in respect of any one incident, be an aggregate of 2,000 monetary units for each ton of the ship's tonnage provided that this aggregate amount shall not in any event exceed 210 million monetary units. The monetary unit referred to in this paragraph corresponds to sixty-five and a half milligrammes of gold of millesimal fineness nine hundred. The conversion of these amounts into the national currency shall be made according to the law of the State concerned.

9(c) The calculation mentioned in the last sentence of paragraph 9(a) and the conversion mentioned in paragraph 9(b) shall be made in such a manner as to express in the national currency of the Contracting State as far as possible the same real value for the amounts in paragraph 1 as is expressed there in units of account. Contracting States shall communicate to the depositary the manner of calculation pursuant to paragraph 9(a), or the result of the conversion in paragraph 9(b) as the case may be, when depositing an instrument referred to in Article IV and whenever there is a change in either."

Article III

1. The present Protocol shall be open for signature by any State which has signed the Convention or acceded thereto and by any State invited to attend the Conference to Revise the Unit of Account Provisions of the Convention on Civil Liability for Oil Pollution Damage, 1969, held in London from 17 to 19 November 1976. The Protocol shall be open for signature from 1 February 1977 to 31 December 1977 at the Headquarters of the Organization.

2. Subject to paragraph 4 of this Article, the present Protocol shall be subject to ratification, acceptance or approval by the States which have signed it.

3. Subject to paragraph 4 of this Article, this Protocol shall be open for accession by States which did not sign it.

4. The present Protocol may be ratified, accepted, approved or acceded to by States Parties to the Convention.

Article IV

1. Ratification, acceptance, approval or accession shall be effected by the deposit of a formal instrument to that effect with the Secretary–General.

2. Any instrument of ratification, acceptance, approval or accession deposited after the entry into force of an amendment to the present Protocol with respect to all existing Parties or after the completion of all measures required for the entry into force of the amendment with respect to all existing Parties, shall be deemed to apply to the Protocol as modified by the amendment.

Article V

1. The present Protocol shall enter into force for the States which have ratified, accepted, approved or acceded to it on the ninetieth day following the date on which eight States including five States each with not less than 1,000,000 gross tons of tanker tonnage have deposited instruments of ratification, acceptance, approval or accession with the Secretary–General.

2. For each State which subsequently ratifies, accepts, approves or accedes to it, the present Protocol shall enter into force on the ninetieth day after the deposit by such State of the appropriate instrument.

Article VI

1. The present Protocol may be denounced by any Party at any time after the date on which the Protocol enters into force for that Party.

2. Denunciation shall be effected by the deposit of an instrument to that effect with the Secretary–General.

3. Denunciation shall take effect one year, or such longer period as may be specified in the instrument of denunciation, after its deposit with the Secretary–General.

Article VII

1. A Conference for the purpose of revising or amending the present Protocol may be convened by the Organization.

2. The Organization shall convene a Conference of Parties to the present Protocol for the purpose of revising or amending it at the request of not less than one-third of the Parties.

Article VIII

1. The present Protocol shall be deposited with the Secretary–General.

2. The Secretary–General shall:

(a) inform all States which have signed the present Protocol or acceded thereto of:

(i) each new signature or deposit of an instrument together with the date thereof;

(ii) the date of entry into force of the present Protocol;

(iii) the deposit of any instrument of denunciation of the present Protocol together with the date on which the denunciation takes effect;

(iv) any amendments to the present Protocol;

(b) transmit certified true copies of the present Protocol to all States which have signed the present Protocol or acceded thereto.

Article IX

As soon as the present Protocol enters into force, a certified true copy thereof shall be transmitted by the Secretary–General to the Secretariat of the United Nations for registration and publication in accordance with Article 102 of the Charter of the United Nations.

Article X

The present Protocol is established in a single original in the English and French languages, both texts being equally authentic. Official translations in the Russian and Spanish languages shall be prepared and deposited with the signed original.

4.19 PROTOCOL TO THE 1971 INTERNATIONAL CONVENTION ON THE ESTABLISHMENT OF AN INTERNATIONAL FUND FOR COMPENSATION FOR OIL POLLUTION DAMAGE.[1] Concluded at London, 19 November 1976. Entered into force, 8 April 1981. 16 I.L.M. 621 (1977)

Article I

For the purpose of the present Protocol:

1. "Convention" means the International Convention on the Establishment of an International Fund for Compensation for Oil Pollution Damage, 1971.

2. "Liability Convention" has the same meaning as in the Convention.

3. "Organization" has the same meaning as in the Convention.

4. "Secretary–General" means the Secretary–General of the Organization.

Article II

Article 1, paragraph 4 of the Convention is replaced by the following text:

" 'Unit of Account' or 'Monetary Unit' means the unit of account or monetary unit as the case may be, referred to in Article V of the Liability Convention, as amended by the Protocol thereto adopted on 19 November 1976."

Article III

The amounts referred to in the Convention shall wherever they appear be amended as follows:

(a) Article 4:

(i) "450 million francs" is replaced by "30 million units of account or 450 million monetary units";

(ii) "900 million francs" is replaced by "60 million units of account or 900 million monetary units".

(b) In Article 5:

(i) "1,500 francs" is replaced by "100 units of account or 1,500 monetary units";

(ii) "125 million francs" is replaced by "8,333,000 units of account or 125 million monetary units";

(iii) "2,000 francs" is replaced by "133 units of account or 2,000 monetary units";

(iv) "210 million francs" is replaced by "14 million units of account or 210 million monetary units".

(c) In Article 11, "75 million francs" is replaced by "5 million units of account or 75 million monetary units".

(d) In Article 12, "15 million francs" is replaced by "1 million units of account or 15 million monetary units".

---

1. *See* Basic Document 4.12, *supra,* and 4.29, *infra.*

Article IV

1. The present Protocol shall be open for signature by any State which has signed the Convention or acceded thereto and by any State invited to attend the Conference to Revise the Unit of Account Provisions in the International Convention on the Establishment of an International Fund for Compensation for Oil Pollution Damage, 1971, held in London from 17 to 19 November 1976. The Protocol shall be open for signature from 1 February 1977 to 31 December 1977 at the Headquarters of the Organization.

2. Subject to paragraph 4 of this Article, the present Protocol shall be subject to ratification, acceptance or approval by the States which have signed it.

3. Subject to paragraph 4 of this Article, this Protocol shall be open for accession by States which did not sign it.

4. The present Protocol may be ratified, accepted, approved or acceded to by States Parties to the Convention.

Article V

1. Ratification, acceptance, approval or accession shall be effected by the deposit of a formal instrument to that effect with the Secretary–General.

2. Any instrument of ratification, acceptance, approval or accession deposited after the entry into force of an amendment to the present Protocol with respect to all existing Parties or after the completion of all measures required for the entry into force of the amendment with respect to all existing Parties shall be deemed to apply to the Protocol as modified by the amendment.

Article VI

1. The present Protocol shall enter into force for the States which have ratified, accepted, approved or acceded to it on the ninetieth day following the date on which the following requirements are fulfilled:

(a) at least eight States have deposited instruments of ratification, acceptance, approval or accession with the Secretary–General, and

(b) the Secretary–General has received information in accordance with Article 39 of the Convention that those persons in such States who would be liable to contribute pursuant to Article 10 of the Convention have received during the preceding calendar year a total quantity of at least 750 million tons of contributing oil.

2. However, the present Protocol shall not enter into force before the Convention has entered into force.

3. For each State which subsequently ratifies, accepts, approves or accedes to it, the present Protocol shall enter into force on the ninetieth day after deposit by such State of the appropriate instrument.

Article VII

1. The present Protocol may be denounced by any Party at any time after the date on which the Protocol enters into force for that Party.

2. Denunciation shall be effected by the deposit of an instrument with the Secretary–General.

3. Denunciation shall take effect one year, or such longer period as may be specified in the instrument of denunciation, after its deposit with the Secretary–General.

Article VIII

1. A conference for the purpose of revising or amending the present Protocol may be convened by the Organization.

2. The Organization shall convene a Conference of Parties to the present Protocol for the purpose of revising or amending it at the request of not less than one-third of the Parties.

Article IX

1. The present Protocol shall be deposited with the Secretary–General.

2. The Secretary–General shall:

(a) inform all States which have signed the present Protocol or acceded thereto of:

(i) each new signature or deposit of an instrument together with the date thereof;

(ii) the date of entry into force of the present Protocol;

(iii) the deposit of any instrument of denunciation of the present Protocol together with the date on which the denunciation takes effect;

(iv) any amendments to the present Protocol;

(b) transmit certified true copies of the present Protocol to all States which have signed the present Protocol or acceded thereto.

Article X

As soon as this Protocol enters into force, a certified true copy thereof shall be transmitted by the Secretary–General to the Secretariat of the United Nations for registration and publication in accordance with Article 102 of the Charter of the United Nations.

Article XI

The present Protocol is established in a single original in the English and French languages, both texts being equally authentic. Official translations in the Russian and Spanish languages shall be prepared by the Secretariat of the Organization and deposited with the signed original.

4.20 CONVENTION FOR THE PROTECTION OF THE MEDITERRANEAN SEA AGAINST POLLUTION (WITHOUT PROTOCOLS AND ANNEX). Concluded at Barcelona, 16 February 1976. Entered into force, 12 February 1978. 15 I.L.M. 290 (1976)

THE CONTRACTING PARTIES,

Conscious of the economic, social, health and cultural value of the marine environment of the Mediterranean Sea Area,

Fully aware of their responsibility to preserve this common heritage for the benefit and enjoyment of present and future generations,

Recognizing the threat posed by pollution to the marine environment, its ecological equilibrium, resources and legitimate uses,

Mindful of the special hydrographic and ecological characteristics of the Mediterranean Sea Area and its particular vulnerability to pollution,

Noting that existing international conventions on the subject do not cover, in spite of the progress achieved, all aspects and sources of marine pollution and do not entirely meet the special requirements of the Mediterranean Sea Area,

Realizing fully the need for close co-operation among the States and international organizations concerned in a co-ordinated and comprehensive regional approach for the protection and enhancement of the marine environment in the Mediterranean Sea Area,

HAVE AGREED AS FOLLOWS:

Article 1

Geographical coverage

1. For the purposes of this Convention, the Mediterranean Sea Area shall mean the maritime waters of the Mediterranean Sea proper, including its gulfs and seas bounded to the west by the meridian passing through Cape Spartel lighthouse, at the entrance of the Straits of Gibraltar, and to the East by the southern limits of the Straits of the Dardanelles between Mehmetcik and Kumkale lighthouses.

2. Except as may be otherwise provided in any protocol to this Convention the Mediterranean Sea Area shall not include internal waters of the Contracting Parties.

Article 2

Definitions

For the purposes of this Convention:

a) "pollution" means the introduction by man, directly or indirectly, of substances or energy into the marine environment resulting in such deleterious effects as harm to living resources, hazards to human health, hindrance to marine activities including fishing, impairment of quality for use of sea water and reduction of amenities.

b) "organization" means the body designated as responsible for carrying out secretariat functions pursuant to article 13 of this Convention.

Article 3
General provisions

1. The Contracting Parties may enter into bilateral or multilateral agreements, including regional or sub-regional agreements, for the protection of the marine environment of the Mediterranean Sea against pollution, provided that such agreements are consistent with this Convention and conform to international law. Copies of such agreements between Contracting Parties to this Convention shall be communicated to the Organization.

2. Nothing in this Convention shall prejudice the codification and development of the Law of the Sea by the United Nations Conference on the Law of the Sea convened pursuant to Resolution 2750 C (XXV) of the General Assembly of the United Nations, nor the present or future claims and legal views of any State concerning the law of the sea and nature and extent of coastal and flag State jurisdiction.

Article 4
General undertakings

1. The Contracting Parties shall individually or jointly take all appropriate measures in accordance with the provisions of this Convention and those protocols in force to which they are party, to prevent, abate and combat pollution of the Mediterranean Sea Area and to protect and enhance the marine environment in that Area.

2. The Contracting Parties shall co-operate in the formulation and adoption of protocols, in addition to the protocols opened for signature at the same time as this Convention, prescribing agreed measures, procedures and standards for the implementation of this Convention.

3. The Contracting Parties further pledge themselves to promote, within the international bodies considered to be competent by the Contracting Parties, measures concerning the protection of the marine environment in the Mediterranean Sea Area from all types and sources of pollution.

Article 5
Pollution caused by dumping from ships and aircraft

The Contracting Parties shall take all appropriate measures to prevent and abate pollution of the Mediterranean Sea Area caused by dumping from ships and aircraft.

Article 6
Pollution from ships

The Contracting Parties shall take all measures in conformity with international law to prevent, abate and combat pollution of the Mediterranean Sea Area caused by discharges from ships and to ensure the effective implementation in that Area of the rules which are generally recognized at the international level relating to the control of this type of pollution.

Article 7
Pollution resulting from exploration and exploitation of the continental shelf and the seabed and its subsoil

The Contracting Parties shall take all appropriate measures to prevent, abate and combat pollution of the Mediterranean Sea Area resulting from exploration and exploitation of the continental shelf and the seabed and its subsoil.

Article 8

Pollution from land-based sources

The Contracting Parties shall take all appropriate measures to prevent, abate and combat pollution of the Mediterranean Sea Area caused by discharges from rivers, coastal establishments or outfalls, or emanating from any other land-based sources within their territories.

Article 9

Co-operation in dealing with pollution emergencies

1. The Contracting Parties shall co-operate in taking the necessary measures for dealing with pollution emergencies in the Mediterranean Sea Area, whatever the causes of such emergencies, and reducing or eliminating damage resulting therefrom.

2. Any Contracting Party which becomes aware of any pollution emergency in the Mediterranean Sea Area shall without delay notify, the Organization and, either through the Organization or directly, any Contracting Party likely to be affected by such emergency.

Article 10

Monitoring

1. The Contracting Parties shall endeavor to establish, in close co-operation with the international bodies which they consider competent, complementary or joint programmes including, as appropriate, programmes at the bilateral or multilateral levels, for pollution monitoring in the Mediterranean Sea Area and shall endeavor to establish a pollution monitoring system for that Area.

2. For this purpose, the Contracting Parties shall designate the competent authorities responsible for pollution monitoring within areas under their national jurisdiction and participate as far as practicable in international arrangements for pollution monitoring in areas beyond national jurisdiction.

3. The Contracting Parties undertake to co-operate in the formulation, adoption and implementation of such annexes to this Convention as may be required to prescribe common procedures and standards for pollution monitoring.

Article 11

Scientific and technological co-operation

1. The Contracting Parties undertake as far as possible to co-operate directly, or when appropriate through competent regional or other international organizations, in the fields of science and technology, and to exchange data as well as other scientific information for the purpose of this Convention.

2. The Contracting Parties undertake as far as possible to develop and co-ordinate their national research programmes relating to all types of marine pollution in the Mediterranean Sea Area and to co-operate in the establishment and implementation of regional and other international research programmes for the purposes of this Convention.

3. The Contracting Parties undertake to co-operate in the provision of technical and other possible assistance in fields relating to marine pollution, with priority to be given to the special needs of developing countries in the Mediterranean region.

Article 12

Liability and compensation

The Contracting Parties undertake to co-operate as soon as possible in the formulation and adoption of appropriate procedures for the determination of liability and compensation for damage resulting from the pollution of the marine environment deriving from violations of the provisions of this Convention and applicable protocols.

Article 13

Institutional arrangements

The Contracting Parties designate the United Nations Environment Programme as responsible for carrying out the following secretariat functions:

(i) To convene and prepare the meetings of Contracting Parties and conferences provided for in articles 14, 15, and 16;

(ii) To transmit to the Contracting Parties notifications, reports and other information received in accordance with articles 3, 9, and 20;

(iii) To consider inquiries by, and information from, the Contracting Parties, and to consult with them on questions relating to this Convention and the protocols and annexes thereto;

(iv) To perform the functions assigned to it by the protocols to this Convention;

(v) To perform such other functions as may be assigned to it by the Contracting Parties;

(vi) To ensure the necessary co-ordination with other international bodies which the Contracting Parties consider competent, and in particular to enter into such administrative arrangements as may be required for the effective discharge of the secretariat functions.

Article 14

Meetings of the Contracting Parties

1. The Contracting Parties shall hold ordinary meetings once every two years, and extraordinary meetings at any other time deemed necessary, upon the request of the Organization or at the request of any Contracting Party, provided that such requests are supported by at least two Contracting Parties.

2. It shall be the function of the meetings of the Contracting Parties to keep under review the implementation of this Convention and the protocols and, in particular:

(i) To review generally the inventories carried out by Contracting Parties and competent international organizations on the state of marine pollution and its effects in the Mediterranean Sea Area;

(ii) To consider reports submitted by the Contracting Parties under article 20;

(iii) To adopt, review and amend as required the annexes to this Convention and to the protocols, in accordance with the procedure established in article 17;

(iv) To make recommendations regarding the adoption of any additional protocols or any amendments to this Convention or the protocols in accordance with the provisions of articles 15 and 16;

(v) To establish working groups as required to consider any matters related to this Convention and the protocols and annexes;

(vi) To consider and undertake any additional action that may be required for the achievement of the purposes of this Convention and the protocols.

Article 15

Adoption of additional protocols

1. The Contracting Parties, at a diplomatic conference, may adopt additional protocols to this Convention pursuant to paragraph 2 of article 4.

2. A diplomatic conference for the purpose of adopting additional protocols shall be convened by the Organization at the request of two thirds of the Contracting Parties.

3. Pending the entry into force of this Convention the Organization may, after consulting with the signatories to this Convention, convene a diplomatic conference for the purpose of adopting additional protocols.

Article 16

Amendment of the Convention or protocols

1. Any Contracting Party to this Convention may propose amendments to the Convention. Amendments shall be adopted by a diplomatic conference which shall be convened by the Organization at the request of two thirds of the Contracting Parties.

2. Any Contracting Party to this Convention may propose amendments to any protocol. Such amendments shall be adopted by a diplomatic conference which shall be convened by the Organization at the request of two thirds of the Contracting Parties to the protocol concerned.

3. Amendments to this Convention shall be adopted by a three-fourths majority vote of the Contracting Parties to the Convention which are represented at the diplomatic conference, and shall be submitted by the Depositary for acceptance by all Contracting Parties to the Convention. Amendments to any protocol shall be adopted by a three-fourths majority vote of the Contracting Parties to such protocol which are represented at the diplomatic conference, and shall be submitted by the Depositary for acceptance by all Contracting Parties to such protocol.

4. Acceptance of amendments shall be notified to the Depositary in writing. Amendments adopted in accordance with paragraph 3 of this article shall enter into force between Contracting Parties having accepted such amendments on the thirtieth day follow the receipt by the Depositary of notification of their acceptance by at least three fourths of the Contracting Parties to this Convention or to the protocol concerned, as the case may be.

5. After the entry into force of an amendment to this Convention or to a protocol, any new Contracting Party to this Convention or such protocol shall become a Contracting Party to the instrument as amended.

Article 17
Annexes and amendments to annexes

1. Annexes to this Convention or to any protocol shall form an integral part of the Convention or such protocol, as the case may be.

2. Except as may be otherwise provided in any protocol, the following procedure shall apply to the adoption and entry into force of any amendments to annexes to this Convention or to any protocol, with the exception of amendments to the annex on arbitration:

(i) Any Contracting Party may propose amendments to the annexes to this Convention or to protocols at the meetings referred to in article 14:

(ii) Such amendments shall be adopted by a three-fourths majority vote of the Contracting Parties to the instrument in question;

(iii) The Depositary shall without delay communicate the amendments so adopted to all Contracting Parties;

(iv) Any Contracting Party that is unable to approve an amendment to the annexes to this Convention or to any protocol shall so notify in writing the Depositary within a period determined by the Contracting Parties concerned when adopting the amendment;

(v) The Depositary shall without delay notify all Contracting Parties of any notification received pursuant to the preceding sub-paragraph;

(vi) On expiry of the period referred to in sub-paragraph (iv) above, the amendment to the annex shall become effective for all Contracting Parties to this Convention or to the protocol concerned which have not submitted a notification in accordance with the provisions of that sub-paragraph.

3. The adoption and entry into force of a new annex to this Convention or to any protocol shall be subject to the same procedure as for the adoption and entry into force, provided that, if any amendment to the Convention or the protocol concerned is involved the new annex shall not enter into force until such time as the amendment to the Convention or the protocol concerned enters into force.

4. Amendments to the annex on arbitration shall be considered to be amendments to this Convention and shall be proposed and adopted in accordance with the procedures set out in article 16 above.

Article 18
Rules of procedure and financial rules

1. The Contracting Parties shall adopt rules of procedure for their meetings and conferences envisaged in articles 14, 15, and 16 above.

2. The Contracting Parties shall adopt financial rules, prepared in consultation with the Organization, to determine, in particular, their financial participation.

Article 19

Special exercise of voting right

Within the areas of their competence, the European Economic Community and any regional economic grouping referred to in article 24 of this Convention shall exercise their right to vote with a number of votes equal to the number of their member States which are Contracting Parties to this Convention and to one or more protocols; the European Economic Community and any grouping as referred to above shall not exercise their right to vote in cases where the member States concerned exercise theirs, and conversely.

Article 20

Reports

The Contracting Parties shall transmit to the Organization reports on the measures adopted in implementation of this Convention and of protocols to which they are Parties, in such form and at such intervals as the meetings of Contracting Parties may determine.

Article 21

Compliance control

The Contracting Parties undertake to co-operate in the development of procedures enabling them to control the application of this Convention and the protocols.

Article 22

Settlement of disputes

1. In case of a dispute between Contracting Parties as to the interpretation or application of this Convention or the protocols, they shall seek a settlement of the dispute through negotiation or any other peaceful means of their own choice.

2. If the parties concerned cannot settle their dispute through the means mentioned in the preceding paragraph, the dispute shall upon common agreement be submitted to arbitration under the conditions laid down in Annex A to this Convention.

3. Nevertheless, the Contracting Parties may at any time declare that they recognize as compulsory *ipso-facto* and without special agreement, in relation to any other Party accepting the same obligation, the application of the arbitration procedure in conformity with the provisions of Annex A. Such declaration shall be notified in writing to the Depositary, who shall communicate it to the other Parties.

Article 23

Relationship between the Convention and protocols

1. No one may become a Contracting Party to this Convention unless it becomes at the same time a Contracting Party to at least one of the protocols. No one may become a Contracting Party to a protocol unless it is, or becomes at the same time a Contracting Party to this Convention.

2. Any protocol to this Convention shall be binding only on the Contracting Parties to the protocol in question.

3. Decisions concerning any protocol pursuant to articles 14, 16 and 17 of this Convention shall be taken only by the Parties to the protocol concerned.

Article 24

Signature

This Convention, the Protocol for the Prevention of Pollution of the Mediterranean Sea by Dumping from Ships and Aircraft and the Protocol Concerning Co-operation in Combating Pollution of the Mediterranean Sea by Oil and Other Harmful Substances in Cases of Emergency shall be open for signature in Barcelona on 16 February 1976 and in Madrid from 17 February 1976 to 16 February 1977 by any State invited as a participant in the Conference of Plenipotentiaries of the Coastal States of the Mediterranean Region on the Protection of the Mediterranean Sea, held in Barcelona from 2 to 16 February 1976, and by any State entitled to sign any protocol in accordance with the provisions of such protocol. They shall also be open until the same date for signature by the European Economic Community and by any similar regional economic grouping at least one member of which is a coastal State of the Mediterranean Sea Area and which exercise competences in fields covered by this Convention, as well as by any protocol affecting them.

Article 25

Ratification, acceptance or approval

This Convention and any protocol thereto shall be subject to ratification, acceptance, or approval. Instruments of ratification, acceptance or approval shall be deposited with the Government of Spain, which will assume the functions of Depositary.

Article 26

Accession

1. As from 17 February 1977, the present Convention, the Protocol for the Prevention of Pollution of the Mediterranean Sea by Dumping from Ships and Aircraft, and the Protocol Concerning Co-operation in Combating Pollution of the Mediterranean Sea by Oil and Other Harmful Substances in Cases of Emergency shall be open for accession by the States, by the European Economic Community and by any grouping as referred to in article 24.

2. After the entry into force of the Convention and of any protocol, any State not referred to in article 24 may accede to this Convention and to any protocol, subject to prior approval by three-fourths of the Contracting Parties to the protocol concerned.

3. Instruments of accession shall be deposited with the Depositary.

Article 27

Entry into force

1. This Convention shall enter into force on the same date as the protocol first entering into force.

2. The Convention shall also enter into force with regard to the States, the European Economic Community and any regional economic grouping referred to in article 24 if they have complied with the formal requirements

for becoming Contracting Parties to any other protocol not yet entered into force.

3. Any protocol to this Convention, except as otherwise provided in such protocol, shall enter into force on the thirtieth day following the date of deposit of at least six instruments of ratification, acceptance, or approval of, or accession to, such protocol by the Parties referred to in article 24.

4. Thereafter, this Convention and any protocol shall enter into force with respect to any State, the European Economic Community and any regional economic grouping referred to in article 24 on the thirtieth day following the date of deposit of the instruments of ratification, acceptance, approval or accession.

Article 28
Withdrawal

1. At any time after three years from the date of entry into force of this Convention, any Contracting Party may withdraw from this Convention by giving written notification of withdrawal.

2. Except as may be otherwise provided in any protocol to this Convention, any Contracting Party may, at any time after three years from the date of entry into force of such protocol, withdraw from such protocol by giving written notification of withdrawal.

3. Withdrawal shall take effect 90 days after the date on which notification of withdrawal is received by the Depositary.

4. Any Contracting Party which withdraws from this Convention shall be considered as also having withdrawn from any protocol to which it was a Party.

5. Any Contracting Party which, upon its withdrawal from a protocol, is no longer a Party to any protocol to this Convention, shall be considered as also having withdrawn from this Convention.

Article 29
Responsibilities of the Depository

1. The Depositary shall inform the Contracting Parties, any other Party referred in article 24, and the Organizations:

(i) Of the signature of this Convention and of any protocol thereto, and of the deposit of instruments of ratification, acceptance, approval or accession in accordance with articles 24, 25 and 26;

(ii) Of the date on which the Convention and any protocol will come into force in accordance with the provisions of article 27;

(iii) Of notifications of withdrawal made in accordance with article 28;

(iv) Of the amendments adopted with respect to the Convention and to any protocol, their acceptance by the Contracting Parties and the date of entry into force of those amendments in accordance with the provisions of article 16;

(v) Of the adoption of new annexes and of the amendment of any annex in accordance with article 17;

(vi) Of declarations recognizing as compulsory the application of the arbitration procedure mentioned in paragraph 3 of article 22.

2. The original of this Convention and of any protocol thereto shall be deposited with the Depositary, the Government of Spain, which shall send certified copies thereof to the Contracting Parties, to the Organization, and to the Secretary–General of the United Nations for registration and publication in accordance with Article 102 of the United Nations Charter.

4.21 CONVENTION FOR THE PROTECTION OF THE RHINE RIVER AGAINST POLLUTION BY CHEMICAL POLLUTION (WITHOUT ANNEXES). Concluded at Bonn, 3 December 1976. Entered into force, 2 January 1979. 1124 U.N.T.S. 375, 6 I.L.M. 242 (1967)

The Government of the Federal Republic of Germany, the Government of the French Republic, the Government of the Grand Duchy of Luxembourg, the Government of the Kingdom of the Netherlands, the Government of the Swiss Confederation and the European Economic Community,

Referring to the Agreement of 29 April 1963 and the Additional Agreement of 3 December 1976 on the International Commission for the Protection of the Rhine against Pollution,

Considering that chemical pollution of the waters of the Rhine is a threat to its flora and fauna and also has undesirable effects on sea water,

Conscious of the dangers for certain uses of the waters of the Rhine that may result from such pollution,

Desiring to improve the quality of the waters of the Rhine with these uses in mind,

Considering that the Rhine is also used for other purposes, in particular for shipping and for receiving effluents,

Convinced that international action to protect the waters of the Rhine against chemical pollution must be evaluated in conjunction with other efforts to protect these waters, in particular efforts aimed at the conclusion of agreements to counter pollution by chlorides and thermal pollution, and that such action forms part of the continuing and interrelated measures to protect both fresh water and sea water against pollution,

Considering the action taken by the European Economic Community to protect the waters, in particular under the Council's directive of 4 May 1976 concerning pollution resulting from specific dangerous substances discharged into the water environment of the Community,

Referring to the results of the ministerial conferences held on 25 and 26 October 1972 in The Hague, 4 and 5 December 1973 in Bonn and 1 April 1976 in Paris, on protection of the Rhine against pollution,

Have agreed as follows:

Article 1. (1) In order to improve the quality of the waters of the Rhine, the Contracting Parties, in accordance with the following provisions, shall take appropriate action:

(*a*) To eliminate pollution of the surface waters of the Rhine basin by the dangerous substances included in the families and groupings of substances specified in annex I (hereinafter referred to as "substances listed in annex I"); they shall aim gradually to eliminate discharges of these substances, taking into account the findings of research carried out by specialists on each of these substances, as well as the technical means available;

(*b*) To reduce pollution of the waters of the Rhine by those dangerous substances included in the families and groups of substances listed in annex II (hereinafter referred to as "substances listed in annex II").

(2) When taking the action referred to in paragraph 1, reasonable consideration shall be given to the fact that the waters of the Rhine are used for the following purposes:

(a) Supplying drinking water for human consumption,

(b) Consumption by domestic and wild animals,

(c) Conserving and developing the natural flora and fauna, and maintaining the self-purifying capacity of the waters,

(d) Fishing,

(e) Recreation, taking hygienic and aesthetic requirements into consideration,

(f) Direct or indirect supply of fresh water to agricultural land,

(g) Production of water for industrial uses, and the need to preserve an acceptable quality of sea water.

(3) The provisions of this Agreement are only the first step towards achieving the aim referred to in paragraph 1 of this article.

(4) Annex A of this Agreement provides a description of what the Contracting Parties understand by the term "Rhine" for purposes of implementing the Agreement.

Article 2. (1) The Governments Parties to this Agreement shall, in accordance with the provisions of annex III, paragraph 1, draw up a national list of those discharges into the surface waters of the Rhine basin that may contain substances covered in annex I to which emission standards may be applicable.

(2) The Governments shall, in accordance with the provisions of annex III, paragraph 2, inform the International Commission for the Protection of the Rhine against Pollution (hereinafter referred to as "the International Commission"), of the items on this list, which shall be updated regularly and at least once every three years.

(3) The proposals made by the International Commission, referred to in article 6, paragraph 3, may, if necessary, contain a list of various substances listed in annex II.

Article 3. (1) Every discharge into the surface waters of the Rhine basin that may contain one of the substances listed in annex I shall require prior approval by the competent authority of the Government concerned.

(2) In the case of discharges of those substances into the surface waters of the Rhine basin and when required for the implementation of this Agreement, in the case of discharges of those substances into drains, the approval shall specify emission standards which shall not exceed the limits set in article 5.

(3) So far as current discharges of those substances are concerned, the approval shall set a deadline for compliance with its terms. This deadline shall not exceed the limits set in article 5, paragraph 3.

(4) Approval shall be given only for a limited period. It may be renewed in the light of any changes made in the limits referred to in article 5.

Article 4. (1) The emission standards specified in the approval granted under article 3 shall determine:

(a) The permissible maximum concentration of a substance in discharges; in cases of dilution, the limits referred to in article 5, paragraph 2, subparagraph (a), shall be divided by the dilution factor;

(b) The permissible maximum quantity of a substance in discharges over one or more fixed periods of time; if necessary, this maximum may also be expressed as a unit of weight of the pollutant per unit of the characteristic component of the polluting action (for instance, per unit of weight of raw material or per unit of product).

(2) If the discharger declares that he cannot comply with the prescribed emission standards, or if the competent authority of the Government concerned confirms this, permission shall be refused.

(3) If the emission standards are not being adhered to, the competent authority of the Government concerned shall take all appropriate steps to ensure that the terms of the approval are complied with and, where necessary, that the discharge is forbidden.

Article 5. (1) The International Commission shall propose the limits referred to in article 3, paragraph 2, and, where necessary, their applicability to discharges into drains. These limits shall be set in accordance with the procedure laid down in article 14. Once adopted, they shall be included in annex IV.

(2) These limits shall be determined:

(a) By the permissible maximum concentration of a substance in the discharges; and

(b) Where appropriate, by the permissible maximum quantity of such a substance, expressed as a unit of weight of the pollutant per unit of the component characteristic of the polluting action (for instance, per unit of weight of raw material or per unit of product).

Where appropriate, the limits applicable to industrial effluents shall be determined by sector and by product type.

The limits applicable to the substances listed in annex I shall be determined primarily on the basis of:

— Toxicity,

— Persistence,

— Bio-accumulation,

taking into consideration the best technical facilities available.

(3) The International Commission shall propose to the Parties to the Agreement the deadlines referred to in article 3, paragraph 3, taking into account the distinctive characteristics of the industrial sectors concerned and, where appropriate, of product types. These deadlines shall be established in accordance with the procedure laid down in article 14.

(4) The International Commission shall use the findings obtained at the international measurement points in order to establish to what extent the

content of substances listed in annex I in the waters of the Rhine has changed after implementation of the foregoing provisions.

(5) The International Commission, if this is required from the point of view of the quality of the waters of the Rhine, may propose other measures aimed at reducing the pollution of the waters of the Rhine, particularly with regard to toxicity, persistence and bio-accumulation of the substance concerned. These proposals shall be adopted in accordance with the procedure laid down in article 14.

Article 6. (1) Every discharge of one of the substances listed in annex II which could detrimentally affect the quality of the waters of the Rhine shall be regulated by the national authorities with a view to introducing rigorous restrictions.

(2) The Governments Parties to this Agreement shall endeavour, within a period of two years from the entry into force of this Agreement, to establish national programmes reducing pollution of the waters of the Rhine by the substances listed in annex II; for their implementation they shall apply in particular the measures indicated in paragraphs 1, 4, 6 and 7 of this article.

(3) Before establishing these national programmes, the Contracting Parties shall confer in the International Commission in order to co-ordinate them. To this end, the International Commission shall regularly compare the draft national programmes in order to ensure their compatibility in terms of aims and means, and shall make proposals, in particular for the achievement of common aims relating to reducing the pollution of the waters of the Rhine. These proposals shall be adopted in accordance with the procedure laid down in article 14 of this Agreement. Comparison of national draft programmes shall not be allowed to cause delays in the implementation, at the national or regional level, of measures intended to reduce the pollution of the waters of the Rhine.

(4) For each discharge that may contain one of the substances listed in annex II, prior authorization shall be required from the competent authority of the Government concerned which establishes the emission standards. The standards shall be determined in terms of the quality goals indicated in paragraph 5.

(5) The programmes referred to in paragraph 2 of this article shall prescribe quality goals for the waters of the Rhine.

(6) The programmes may also include specific provisions concerning the composition and use of substances or groups of substances and of products, and shall take account of the latest economically viable technical developments.

(7) The programmes shall set deadlines for their implementation.

(8) The International Commission shall be provided with a summary of the programmes and the results of their implementation.

Article 7. (1) The Contracting Parties shall take all necessary statutory and administrative action in order to guarantee that storage of the substances listed in annexes I and II is organized so as to avoid any danger of polluting the waters of the Rhine.

(2) The International Commission shall, as necessary, propose to the Contracting Parties appropriate measures for protecting groundwater in order to prevent pollution of the waters of the Rhine by the substances covered in annexes I and II.

Article 8. (1) The Contracting Parties shall ensure that discharges are regulated in accordance with this Agreement.

(2) They shall inform the International Commission annually of their experiences.

Article 9. Implementation of the measures adopted under this Agreement shall in no case lead to a direct or indirect increase in the pollution of the waters of the Rhine.

Article 10. (1) In order to monitor the proportion of substances covered in annexes I and II in the waters of the Rhine, each Government concerned shall be responsible for the installation and operation of measuring instruments and systems, at the agreed measurement stations on the Rhine, which shall serve to determine the concentration of these substances.

(2) Each Government concerned shall inform the International Commission regularly, and at least once annually, of the results of this monitoring process.

(3) The International Commission shall prepare an annual report which summarizes the results of the monitoring process and makes it possible to keep track of the changes in the quality of the waters of the Rhine.

Article 11. When a Government Party to this Agreement discovers in the waters of the Rhine a sudden and large increase of substances listed in annexes I and II, or becomes aware of an accident which may result in a serious threat to the quality of those waters, it shall immediately inform the International Commission and those Contracting Parties which may be affected, using a procedure to be established by the International Commission.

Article 12. (1) The Contracting Parties shall regularly inform the International Commission of the experience they have acquired through implementation of this Agreement.

(2) The International Commission shall draw up, as necessary, recommendations for progressive improvement in the implementation of this Agreement.

Article 13. The International Commission shall draw up recommendations for achieving comparability of results through the use of appropriate methods of measurement and analysis.

Article 14. (1) Annexes I to IV, which form an integral part of this Agreement, may be amended and supplemented in order to bring them into line with scientific and technical developments or to make the efforts to counter chemical pollution of the waters of the Rhine more effective.

(2) To this end, the International Commission shall recommend such amendments or additions as it deems useful.

(3) The amended or supplemented texts shall enter into force after their unanimous adoption by the Contracting Parties.

Article 15. Any dispute between the Contracting Parties, relating to the interpretation or implementation of this Agreement, which cannot be settled by negotiation shall, unless the Parties to the dispute decide otherwise, be submitted, at the request of either of them, to arbitration in accordance with the provisions of annex B which forms an integral part of this Agreement.

Article 16. In implementing this Agreement the European Economic Community and its member States shall take action with regard to those areas which fall within their respective jurisdictions.

Article 17. (1) Each signatory Party shall notify the Government of the Swiss Confederation of the completion of the procedures incumbent on such Party for the entry into force of this Agreement.

(2) Subject to notification by all Parties of the completion of the procedures required for the entry into force of the Additional Agreement to the Agreement on the International Commission for the Protection of the Rhine against Pollution, the present Agreement shall enter into force on the first day of the second month following receipt of the last notification specified in the previous paragraph.

Article 18. Upon the expiry of a period of three years after its entry into force, this Agreement may be denounced at any time by any of the Contracting Parties by means of a declaration addressed to the Government of the Swiss Confederation. The denunciation shall enter into force, for the denouncing Party, six months after receipt of the declaration by the Government of the Swiss Confederation.

Article 19. The Government of the Swiss Confederation shall inform the Contracting Parties of the date of receipt of each notification or declaration received in pursuance of articles 14, 17 and 18.

Article 20. (1) If the Agreement on the International Commission for the Protection of the Rhine against Pollution of 29 April 1963 is denounced by one of the Parties to that Agreement, the Contracting Parties shall immediately consult each other concerning the measures required to ensure the continuing discharge of the functions incumbent upon the International Commission under this Agreement.

(2) If no agreement has been reached within six months after the start of these consultations, each of the Contracting Parties may at any time denounce this Agreement in accordance with article 18, without waiting for the expiry of the three-year period.

Article 21. This Agreement, prepared in a single original in the German, French and Dutch languages, all three texts being equally authentic, shall be deposited in the archives of the Government of the Swiss Confederation, which shall transmit an authenticated copy thereof to each of the Contracting Parties.

* * *

4.22 CONVENTION FOR THE PROTECTION OF THE RHINE RIVER AGAINST POLLUTION BY CHLORIDES (WITHOUT ANNEXES). Concluded at Bonn, 3 December 1976. Entered into force, 5 July 1985. 16 I.L.M. 265 (1977)

The Government of the Federal Republic of Germany,
The Government of the French Republic,
The Government of the Grand Duchy of Luxembourg,
The Government of the Kingdom of the Netherlands,
and the Government of the Swiss Confederation,

Referring to the Agreement of April 29, 1963 concerning the International Commission for the Protection of the Rhine against Pollution,

Considering the present amount of chloride ions in the Rhine,

Aware of the damage that could result therefrom,

Referring to the findings and results of the Conference of Ministers on the Pollution of the Rhine, which took place at The Hague on October 25–26, 1972, during the course of which the desire was expressed to improve progressively the quality of the waters of the Rhine so that at the German–Netherlands border the chloride ion content will not be greater than 200 mg/l, Have agreed on the following:

Article 1

1. The Contracting Parties will strengthen their cooperation for the purpose of fighting against the pollution of the Rhine by chloride ions on the basis, during an initial stage, of the provisions of this Convention.

2. Annex A to the Convention specifies what the Contracting Parties understand by the term "Rhine" for the purposes of the application of the aforementioned Convention.

Article 2

1. The discharge of chloride ions into the Rhine will be reduced by at least 60 kg/s of chloride ions (annual average). This objective will be achieved gradually and in French territory.

2. In order to achieve the objective indicated in the preceding paragraph, the French Government will, under the conditions set forth in Annex I of this Convention, install an injection system in the subsoil of Alsace in order to reduce over a period of ten years the discharges from the Alsace Potassium Mines by an initial quantity of 20 kg/s of chloride ions. The installation shall be constructed as soon as possible, no later than 18 months after the entry into force of the Convention. The French Government will report regularly to the International Commission for the Protection of the Rhine against Pollution (hereinafter designated "the International Commission").

3. The Contracting Parties are agreed that the French Government will, after consideration of the results obtained during the initial stage described in paragraph 2, take all steps necessary to achieve before January 1, 1980 the objective set forth in paragraph 1, by injection into the Alsatian sub-soil or by other means, subject to an agreement on the technical terms and conditions of the project and on the financing of the costs relating thereto.

4.   The French Government will present an over-all plan on the technical terms and conditions and the costs of the measures to be taken pursuant to paragraph 3.

Article 3

1.   The Contracting Parties will take in their own territory, the necessary measures to prevent an increase in the amounts of chloride ions discharged into the Rhine basin.   The national concentration figures are shown in Annex II.

2.   An increase in the amounts of chloride ions from isolated discharges shall be admissible only to the extent that the Contracting Parties concerned will offset such concentration in their respective territories or if a general method of offsetting it is found within the framework of the International Commission.   This provision shall not hinder the application of Article 6.

3.   A Contracting Party may, in exceptional cases and for imperative reasons, after having requested the opinion of the International Commission, authorize an increase in concentration without immediately offsetting it.

4.   The Contracting Parties will control all discharges of chloride ions greater than 1 kg/s in the basin of the Rhine in their territory.

5.   Each Contracting Party will send an annual report to the International Commission which shall indicate as precisely as possible the increase in the chloride-ion concentration in the waters of the Rhine.   This report shall be based on all significant data from pertinent national programs and shall distinguish discharges greater than 1 Kg/s from other discharges.   Should such a distinction be impossible to make, it must be reported to the International Commission.

6.   The Annex mentioned previously in paragraph 1 as well as the maximum concentration of 1 kg/s of chloride ions shall be reviewed each year by the International Commission as the situation develops.   If necessary, the International Commission shall propose changes in the Annex to the Governments.

Article 4

1.   The French Government, on its own initiative or at the request of another Contracting Party, may have the process of injection or resorption of chloride ions halted when there is evidence of serious danger to the environment and particularly to the water table.

2.   The French Government, or any other requesting Party, will immediately inform the International Commission of the situation and will provide data on the extent and nature of the danger.

3.   The French Government will immediately take the steps rendered necessary by the situation and will report them to the International Commission.   When the situation is no longer considered dangerous, the chloride-ion injection or resorption process is to be resumed without delay.

4.   The Contracting Parties will, at the request of one of them, consult among themselves within the International Commission if the need for additional measures should arise.

Article 5

If the process of injection or resorption of chloride ions causes damage for which compensation cannot be guaranteed fully or in part by the constructors of the works or by third parties, the Contracting Parties will consult among themselves at the request of one among them regarding a possible contribution that may be paid to the French Government.

Article 6

The International Commission shall present to the Contracting Parties within four years of the entry into force of the Convention proposals concerning the means to achieve progressively a new chloride-ion concentration limitation over the entire course of the Rhine.

Article 7

1. The expenses resulting from injection as provided in Article 2 paragraph 2 and from the preparatory works will be assumed by the French Party.

2. The Contracting Parties mentioned below will contribute to the total cost of 132 million French francs by means of a lump sum payment, prorated as follows:

Federal Republic of Germany	30%
Kingdom of the Netherlands	34%
Swiss Confederation	6%

The payments shall be made no later than three months after the entry into force of this Convention.

3. The Contracting Parties will deliberate, following the presentation of the over-all plan provided for in Article 2(4) and at the request of the French Government, on the financing of the measures to be carried out in application of Article 2(3) on the basis of the prorating given in paragraph 2 above. The costs of preliminary research, particularly relating to studies and exploration, and, in addition, the unforeseen expenses not covered by the financing of the first stage shall likewise be included in the financing plan.

Article 8

The payments specified in Article 7(2) shall be made in French francs to account No. 440–09/line 1 in the Central Accounting Agency of the French Treasury.

Article 9

When, following the entry into force of this Convention, the International Commission ascertains that at one of the measuring points the load and concentration of chloride ions shows a continuing tendency to increase, it shall request each Contracting Party in whose territory the cause of this increase is located to take the necessary steps to halt it.

Article 10

1. If any difficulties should result from the application of Article 9, and a period of six months has gone by since such difficulties were noted by the International Commission, the latter, in order to present a report to the Governments, may call upon the services of an independent expert at the request of a Contracting Party.

2. The expenses relating to the inquiry, including the expert's fee shall be divided among the Contracting Parties mentioned below, as follows:

Federal Republic of Germany	two sevenths (²⁄₇)
French Republic	two sevenths (²⁄₇)
Kingdom of the Netherlands	two sevenths (²⁄₇)
Swiss Confederation	one seventh (¹⁄₇)

The International Commission may, in certain cases, establish a different method for dividing the expenses.

Article 11

When a Contracting Party notes a sudden and sizeable increase in chloride ions in the waters of the Rhine or has knowledge of an accident that may seriously endanger the quality of those waters, it will report it without delay to the International Commission and to the Contracting Parties likely to be affected, according to a procedure to be established by the International Commission.

Article 12

1. Each Contracting Party concerned will be responsible at the appropriate measuring stations, for the installation and operation of the measuring equipment and systems serving to check the concentration of chloride ions in the waters of the Rhine.

2. The chloride-ion concentrations shall be determined on the basis of the measurements carried out according to the recommendations of the International Commission.

3. The Contracting Parties will report to the International Commission regularly and at least every six months the results of the checks carried out pursuant to paragraph 1 above.

Any dispute between the Contracting Parties regarding the interpretation or application of the present Convention that cannot be settled by negotiation shall, except when the Parties to the dispute decide otherwise, be subject, at the request of one of them, to arbitration in accordance with the provisions of Annex B. The latter, as well as Annexes A, I, and II shall form an integral part of this Convention.

Article 14

Each Signatory Party will notify the Government of the Swiss Confederation of the execution of the procedures required for the entry into force of this Convention. It shall enter into force on the first day of the second month following receipt of the last notification.

Article 15

At the end of three years following its entry into force, this Convention may be denounced at any time by any of the Contracting Parties by means of a statement addressed to the Government of the Swiss Confederation. The denunciation shall take effect, for the denouncing Party, six months following receipt of the statement by the Government of the Swiss Confederation. This shall not have the effect of compromising the continued execution of tasks for which international financing has been obtained.

Article 16

The Government of the Swiss Confederation will inform the Contracting Parties of the date of receipt of any notification or statement received pursuant to Articles 14 and 15.

Article 17

1. If the April 29, 1963 Agreement concerning the International Commission for the Protection of the Rhine Against Pollution is denounced by one of the Parties to the aforementioned Agreement, the Contracting Parties will consult without delay on the measures necessary to ensure the continued execution of the tasks that, according to this Convention, are the responsibility of the International Commission.

2. If an agreement is not reached in the six months following the opening of discussions, each of the Contracting Parties may denounce this Convention at anytime in accordance with Article 15, without waiting for the three-year period to elapse.

Article 18

This Convention, drawn up in a single copy in German, French and Dutch, the three texts being equally authentic shall be deposited in the Archives of the Government of the Swiss Confederation, which shall transmit a certified copy to each of the Contracting Parties.

4.23 PROTOCOL OF 1978 RELATING TO THE INTERNATIONAL CONVEN-TION FOR THE PREVENTION OF POLLUTION FROM SHIPS, 1973 (MARPOL)[1] (WITH ANNEXES BUT WITHOUT APPENDICES THERETO). Concluded at London, 17 February 1978. Entered into force, 2 October 1983. 1341 U.N.T.S. 3, 17 I.L.M. 546 (1978)

THE PARTIES TO THE PRESENT PROTOCOL,

RECOGNIZING the significant contribution which can be made by the International Convention for the Prevention of Pollution from Ships, 1973, to the protection of the marine environment from pollution from ships,

RECOGNIZING ALSO the need to improve further the prevention and control of marine pollution from ships, particularly oil tankers,

RECOGNIZING FURTHER the need for implementing the Regulations for the Prevention of Pollution by Oil contained in Annex I of that Convention as early and as widely as possible,

ACKNOWLEDGING HOWEVER the need to defer the application of Annex II of that Convention until certain technical problems have been satisfactorily resolved,

CONSIDERING that these objectives may best be achieved by the conclusion of a Protocol Relating to the International Convention for the Prevention of Pollution from Ships, 1973,

HAVE AGREED as follows:

ARTICLE I
General Obligations

1. The Parties to the present Protocol undertake to give effect to the provisions of:

(a) the present Protocol and the Annex hereto which shall constitute an integral part of the present Protocol; and

(b) the International Convention for the Prevention of Pollution from Ships, 1973 (hereinafter referred to as "the Convention"), subject to the modifications and additions set out in the present Protocol.

2. The provisions of the Convention and the present Protocol shall be read and interpreted together as one single instrument.

3. Every reference to the Protocol constitutes at the same time a reference to the Annex hereto.

ARTICLE II
Implementation of Annex II of the Convention

1. Notwithstanding the provisions of Article 14(1) of the Convention, the Parties to the present Protocol agree that they shall not be bound by the provisions of Annex II of the Convention for a period of three years from the date of entry into force of the present Protocol or for such longer period as may be decided by a two-thirds majority of the Parties to the present Protocol in the Marine Environment Protection Committee (hereinafter referred to as "the Committee") of the Inter–Governmental Maritime Consultative Organization (hereinafter referred to as "the Organization").

---

1. *See* Basic Document 4.15, *supra.*

2. During the period specified in paragraph 1 of this Article, the Parties to the present Protocol shall not be under any obligations nor entitled to claim any privileges under the Convention in respect of matters relating to Annex II of the Convention and all reference to Parties in the Convention shall not include the Parties to the present Protocol in so far as matters relating to that Annex are concerned.

ARTICLE III

Communication of Information

The text of Article 11(1)(b) of the Convention is replaced by the following:

"a list of nominated surveyors or recognized organizations which are authorized to act on their behalf in the administration of matters relating to the design, construction, equipment and operation of ships carrying harmful substances in accordance with the provisions of the Regulations for circulation to the Parties for information of their officers. The Administration shall therefore notify the Organization of the specific responsibilities and conditions of the authority delegated to nominated surveyors or recognized organizations."

ARTICLE IV

Signature, Ratification, Acceptance, Approval and Accession

1. The present Protocol shall be open for signature at the Headquarters of the Organization from 1 June 1978 to 31 May 1979 and shall thereafter remain open for accession. States may become Parties to the present Protocol by:

(a) signature without reservation as to ratification, acceptance or approval; or

(b) signature, subject to ratification, acceptance or approval, followed by ratification, acceptance or approval; or

(c) accession.

2. Ratification, acceptance, approval or accession shall be effected by the deposit of an instrument to that effect with the Secretary–General of the Organization.

ARTICLE V

Entry into Force

1. The present Protocol shall enter into force twelve months after the date on which not less than fifteen States, the combined merchant fleets of which constitute not less than fifty per cent of the gross tonnage of the world's merchant shipping, have become Parties to it in accordance with Article IV of the present Protocol.

2. Any instrument of ratification, acceptance, approval or accession deposited after the date on which the present Protocol enters into force shall take effect three months after the date of deposit.

3. After the date on which an amendment to the present Protocol is deemed to have been accepted in accordance with Article 16 of the Convention, any instrument of ratification, acceptance, approval or accession deposited shall apply to the present Protocol as amended.

ARTICLE VI

Amendments

The procedures set out in Article 16 of the Convention in respect of amendments to the Articles, an Annex and an Appendix to an Annex of the Convention shall apply respectively to amendments to the Articles, the Annex and an Appendix to the Annex of the present Protocol.

ARTICLE VII

Denunciation

1.   The present Protocol may be denounced by any Party to the present Protocol at any time after the expiry of five years from the date on which the Protocol enters into force for that Party.

2.   Denunciation shall be effected by the deposit of an instrument of denunciation with the Secretary–General of the Organization.

3.   A denunciation shall take effect twelve months after receipt of the notification by the Secretary–General of the Organization or after the expiry of any other longer period which may be indicated in the notification.

ARTICLE VIII

Depositary

1.   The present Protocol shall be deposited with the Secretary–General of the Organization (hereinafter referred to as "the Depositary").

2.   The Depositary shall:

(a) inform all States which have signed the present Protocol or acceded thereto of:

(i) each new signature or deposit of an instrument of ratification, acceptance, approval or accession, together with the date thereof;

(ii) the date of entry into force of the present protocol;

(iii) the deposit of any instrument of denunciation of the present Protocol together with the date on which it was received and the date on which the denunciation takes effect;

(iv) any decision made in accordance with Article II(1) of the present Protocol;

(b) transmit certified true copies of the present Protocol to all States which have signed the present Protocol or acceded thereto.

3.   As soon as the present Protocol enters into force, a certified true copy thereof shall be transmitted by the Depositary to the Secretariat of the United Nations for registration and publication in accordance with Article 102 of the Charter of the United Nations.

ARTICLE IX

Languages

The present Protocol is established in a single original in the English, French, Russian and Spanish languages, each text being equally authentic.

Official translations in the Arabic, German, Italian and Japanese languages shall be prepared and deposited with the signed original.

* * *

ANNEX I
REGULATIONS FOR THE PREVENTION OF POLLUTION BY OIL
Regulation 1
Definitions

Paragraphs (1) to (7), (9) to (22) and (24) to (25)—*No change*

The existing text of paragraph (8) is replaced by the following:

(8)(a) "Major conversion" means a conversion of an existing ship:

(i) which substantially alters the dimensions or carrying capacity of the ship; or

(ii) which changes the type of the ship; or

(iii) the intent of which in the opinion of the Administration is substantially to prolong its life; or

(iv) which otherwise so alters the ship that if it were a new ship, it would become subject to relevant provisions of the present Protocol not applicable to it as an existing ship.

(b) Notwithstanding the provisions of sub-paragraph (a) of this paragraph, conversion of an existing oil tanker of 20,000 tons deadweight and above to meet the requirements of Regulation 13 of this Annex shall not be deemed to constitute a major conversion for the purposes of this Annex.

The existing text of paragraph (23) is replaced by the following:

(23) 'Lightweight' means the displacement of a ship in metric tons without cargo, fuel, lubricating oil, ballast water, fresh water and feed water in tanks, consumable stores, and passengers and crew and their effects.

The following paragraphs are added to the existing text:

(26) Notwithstanding the provisions of paragraph (6) of this Regulation, for the purposes of Regulations 13, 13B, 13E and 18(5) of this Annex, "new oil tanker" means an oil tanker:

(a) for which the building contract is placed after 1 June 1979; or

(b) in the absence of a building contract, the keel of which is laid, or which is at a similar stage of construction after 1 January 1980; or

(c) the delivery of which is after 1 June 1982; or

(d) which has undergone a major conversion:

(i) for which the contract is placed after 1 June 1979; or

(ii) in the absence of a contract, the construction work of which is begun after 1 January 1980; or

(iii) which is completed after 1 June 1982,

except that for oil tankers of 70,000 tons deadweight and above the definition in paragraph (6) of this Regulation shall apply for the purposes of Regulation 13(1) of this Annex.

(27) Notwithstanding the provisions of paragraph (7) of this Regulation, for the purposes of Regulations 13, 13A, 13B, 13C, 13D and 18(6) of this Annex, "existing oil tanker" means an oil tanker which is not a new oil tanker as defined in paragraph (26) of this Regulation.

(28) "Crude oil" means any oil occurring naturally in the earth whether or not treated to render it suitable for transportation and includes:

(a) crude oil from which certain distillate fractions may have been removed; and

(b) crude oil to which certain distillate fractions may have been added.

(29) "Crude oil tanker" means an oil tanker engaged in the trade of carrying crude oil.

(30) "Product carrier" means an oil tanker engaged in the trade of carrying oil other than crude oil.

Regulations 2 and 3—*No change*
Regulation 4
Surveys and Inspections

The existing text of Regulation 4 is replaced by the following:

(1) Every oil tanker of 150 tons gross tonnage and above, and every other ship of 400 tons gross tonnage and above shall be subject to the surveys specified below:

(a) An initial survey before the ship is put in service or before the Certificate required under Regulation 5 of this Annex is issued for the first time, which shall include a complete survey of its structure, equipment, systems, fittings, arrangements and material in so far as the ship is covered by this Annex. This survey shall be such as to ensure that the structure, equipment, systems, fittings, arrangements and material fully comply with the applicable requirements of this Annex.

(b) Periodical surveys at intervals specified by the Administration, but not exceeding five years, which shall be such as to ensure that the structure, equipment, systems, fittings, arrangements and material fully comply with the requirements of this Annex.

(c) A minimum of one intermediate survey during the period of validity of the Certificate which shall be such as to ensure that the equipment and associated pump and piping systems, including oil discharge monitoring and control systems, crude oil washing systems, oily-water separating equipment and oil filtering systems, fully comply with the applicable requirements of this Annex and are in good working order. In cases where only one such intermediate survey is carried out in any one certificate validity period, it shall be held not before six months prior to, nor later than six months after the half-way date of the certificate's period of validity. Such intermediate surveys shall be endorsed on the Certificate issued under Regulation 5 of this Annex.

(2) The Administration shall establish appropriate measures for ships which are not subject to the provisions of paragraph (1) of this Regulation in order to ensure that the applicable provisions of this Annex are complied with.

(3)(a) Surveys of ships as regards the enforcement of the provisions of this Annex shall be carried out by officers of the Administration. The Administration may, however, entrust the surveys either to surveyors nominated for the purpose or to organizations recognized by it.

(b) The Administration shall institute arrangements for unscheduled inspections to be carried out during the period of validity of the Certificate. Such inspections shall ensure that the ship and its equipment remain in all respects satisfactory for the service for which the ship is intended. These inspections may be carried out by their own inspection services, or by nominated surveyors or by recognized organizations, or by other Parties upon request of the Administration. Where the Administration, under the provisions of paragraph (1) of this Regulation, establishes mandatory annual surveys, the above unscheduled inspections shall not be obligatory.

(c) An Administration nominating surveyors or recognizing organizations to conduct surveys and inspections as set forth in sub-paragraphs (a) and (b) of this paragraph, shall as a minimum empower any nominated surveyor or recognized organization to:

(i) require repairs to a ship; and

(ii) carry out surveys and inspections if requested by the appropriate authorities of a Port State.

The Administration shall notify the Organization of the specific responsibilities and conditions of the authority delegated to the nominated surveyors or recognized organizations, for circulation to Parties to the present Protocol for the information of their officers.

(d) When a nominated surveyor or recognized organization determines that the condition of the ship or its equipment does not correspond substantially with the particulars of the Certificate or is such that the ship is not fit to proceed to sea without presenting an unreasonable threat of harm to the marine environment, such surveyor or organization shall immediately ensure that corrective action is taken and shall in due course notify the Administration. If such corrective action is not taken the Certificate should be withdrawn and the Administration shall be notified immediately; and if the ship is in the port of another Party, the appropriate authorities of the Port State shall also be notified immediately. When an officer of the Administration, a nominated surveyor or recognized organization has notified the appropriate authorities of the Port State, the Government of the Port State concerned shall give such officer, surveyor or organization any necessary assistance to carry out their obligations under this Regulation. When applicable the Government of the Port State concerned shall take such steps as will ensure that the ship shall not sail until it can proceed to sea or leave the port for the purpose of proceeding to the nearest appropriate repair yard available without presenting an unreasonable threat of harm to the marine environment.

(e) In every case, the Administration concerned shall fully guarantee the completeness and efficiency of the survey and inspection and shall undertake to ensure the necessary arrangements to satisfy this obligation.

(4)(a) The condition of the ship and its equipment shall be maintained to conform with the provisions of the present Protocol to ensure that the ship in all respects will remain fit to proceed to sea without presenting an unreasonable threat of harm to the marine environment.

(b) After any survey of the ship under paragraph (1) of this Regulation has been completed, no change shall be made in the structure, equipment, systems, fittings, arrangements or material covered by the survey, without the sanction of the Administration, except the direct replacement of such equipment and fittings.

(c) Whenever an accident occurs to a ship or a defect is discovered which substantially affects the integrity of the ship or the efficiency or completeness of its equipment covered by this Annex the master or owner of the ship shall report at the earliest opportunity to the Administration, the recognized organization or the nominated surveyor responsible for issuing the relevant Certificate, who shall cause investigations to be initiated to determine whether a survey as required by paragraph (1) of this Regulation is necessary. If the ship is in the port of another Party, the master or owner shall also report immediately to the appropriate authorities of the Port State and the nominated surveyor or recognized organization shall ascertain that such report has been made.

Regulations 5, 6 and 7

In the existing text of these Regulations, delete all references to "(1973)" in relation to the International Oil Pollution Prevention Certificate.

Regulation 8

Duration of Certificate

The existing text of Regulation 8 is replaced by the following:

(1) An International Oil Pollution Prevention Certificate shall be issued for a period specified by the Administration, which shall not exceed five years from the date of issue, provided that in the case of an oil tanker operating with dedicated clean ballast tanks for a limited period specified in Regulation 13(9) of this Annex, the period of validity of the Certificate shall not exceed the expiry date of such specified period.

(2) A Certificate shall cease to be valid if significant alterations have taken place in the construction, equipment, systems, fittings, arrangements or material required without the sanction of the Administration, except the direct replacement of such equipment or fittings, or if intermediate surveys as specified by the Administration under Regulation 4(1)(c) of this Annex are not carried out.

(3) A Certificate issued to a ship shall also cease to be valid upon transfer of the ship to the flag of another State. A new Certificate shall only be issued when the Government issuing the new Certificate is fully satisfied that the ship is in full compliance with the requirements of Regulation 4(4)(a) and (b) of this Annex. In the case of a transfer between Parties, if requested within

three months after the transfer has taken place, the Government of the Party whose flag the ship was formerly entitled to fly shall transmit as soon as possible to the Administration a copy of the Certificate carried by the ship before the transfer and, if available, a copy of the relevant survey report.

Regulations 9–12—No change

The existing text of Regulation 13 is replaced by the following Regulations:

Regulation 13

Segregated Ballast Tanks, Dedicated Clean Ballast
Tanks and Crude Oil Washing

Subject to the provisions of Regulations 13C and 13D of this Annex, oil tankers shall comply with the requirements of this Regulation.

New oil tankers of 20,000 tons deadweight and above

(1) Every new crude oil tanker of 20,000 tons deadweight and above and every new product carrier of 30,000 tons deadweight and above shall be provided with segregated ballast tanks and shall comply with paragraphs (2), (3) and (4), or paragraph (5) as appropriate, of this Regulation.

(2) The capacity of the segregated ballast tanks shall be so determined that the ship may operate safely on ballast voyages without recourse to the use of cargo tanks for water ballast except as provided for in paragraph (3) or (4) of this Regulation. In all cases, however, the capacity of segregated ballast tanks shall be at least such that in any ballast condition at any part of the voyage, including the conditions consisting of lightweight plus segregated ballast only, the ship's draughts and trim can meet each of the following requirements:

(a) the moulded draught amidships (dm) in metres (without taking into account any ship's deformation) shall not be less than:

$$dm = 2.0 + 0.02L;$$

(b) the draughts at the forward and after perpendiculars shall correspond to those determined by the draught amidships (dm) as specified in sub-paragraph (a) of this paragraph, in association with the trim by the stern of not greater than 0.015L; and

(c) in any case the draught at the after perpendicular shall not be less than that which is necessary to obtain full immersion of the propeller(s).

(3) In no case shall ballast water be carried in cargo tanks except on those rare voyages when weather conditions are so severe that, in the opinion of the master, it is necessary to carry additional ballast water in cargo tanks for the safety of the ship. Such additional ballast water shall be processed and discharged in compliance with Regulation 9 of this Annex and in accordance with the requirements of Regulation 15 of this Annex and an entry shall be made in the Oil Record Book referred to in Regulation 20 of this Annex.

(4) In the case of new crude oil tankers, the additional ballast permitted in paragraph (3) of this Regulation shall be carried in cargo tanks only if such tanks have been crude oil washed in accordance with Regulation 13B of this Annex before departure from an oil unloading port or terminal.

(5) Notwithstanding the provisions of paragraph (2) of this Regulation, the segregated ballast conditions for oil tankers less than 150 metres in length shall be to the satisfaction of the Administration.

(6) Every new crude oil tanker of 20,000 tons deadweight and above shall be fitted with a cargo tank cleaning system using crude oil washing. The Administration shall undertake to ensure that the system fully complies with the requirements of Regulation 13B of this Annex within one year after the tanker was first engaged in the trade of carrying crude oil or by the end of the third voyage carrying crude oil suitable for crude oil washing, whichever occurs later. Unless such oil tanker carries crude oil which is not suitable for crude oil washing, the oil tanker shall operate the system in accordance with the requirements of that Regulation.

Existing crude oil tankers of 40,000 tons deadweight and above

(7) Subject to the provisions of paragraphs (8) and (9) of this Regulation every existing crude oil tanker of 40,000 tons deadweight and above shall be provided with segregated ballast tanks and shall comply with the requirements of paragraphs (2) and (3) of this Regulation from the date of entry into force of the present Protocol.

(8) Existing crude oil tankers referred to in paragraph (7) of this Regulation may, in lieu of being provided with segregated ballast tanks, operate with a cargo tank cleaning procedure using crude oil washing in accordance with Regulation 13B of this Annex unless the crude oil tanker is intended to carry crude oil which is not suitable for crude oil washing.

(9) Existing crude oil tankers referred to in paragraph (7) or (8) of this Regulation may, in lieu of being provided with segregated ballast tanks or operating with a cargo tank cleaning procedure using crude oil washing, operate with dedicated clean ballast tanks in accordance with the provisions of Regulation 13A of this Annex for the following period:

    (a) for crude oil tankers of 70,000 tons deadweight and above, until two years after the date of entry into force of the present Protocol; and

    (b) for crude oil tankers of 40,000 tons deadweight and above but below 70,000 tons deadweight, until four years after the date of entry into force of the present Protocol.

Existing product carriers of 40,000 tons deadweight and above

(10) From the date of entry into force of the present Protocol, every existing product carrier of 40,000 tons deadweight and above shall be provided with segregated ballast tanks and shall comply with the requirements of paragraphs (2) and (3) of this Regulation or, alternatively, operate with dedicated clean ballast tanks in accordance with the provisions of Regulation 13A of this Annex.

An oil tanker qualified as a segregated ballast oil tanker

(11) Any oil tanker which is not required to be provided with segregated ballast tanks in accordance with paragraph (1), (7) or (10) of this Regulation may, however, be qualified as a segregated ballast tanker, provided that it complies with the requirements of paragraphs (2) and (3), or paragraph (5) as appropriate, of this Regulation.

Regulation 13A
Requirements for Oil Tankers with Dedicated Clean Ballast Tanks

(1) An oil tanker operating with dedicated clean ballast tanks in accordance with the provisions of Regulation 13(9) or (10) of this Annex, shall have adequate tank capacity, dedicated solely to the carriage of clean ballast, as defined in Regulation 1(16) of this Annex, to meet the requirements of Regulation 13(2) and (3) of this Annex.

(2) The arrangements and operational procedures for dedicated clean ballast tanks shall comply with the requirements established by the Administration. Such requirements shall contain at least all the provisions of the Specifications for Oil Tankers with Dedicated Clean Ballast Tanks adopted by the International Conference on Tanker Safety and Pollution Prevention, 1978, in Resolution 14 and as may be revised by the Organization.

(3) An oil tanker operating with dedicated clean ballast tanks shall be equipped with an oil content meter, approved by the Administration on the basis of specifications recommended by the Organization, to enable supervision of the oil content in ballast water being discharged. The oil content meter shall be installed no later than at the first scheduled shipyard visit of the tanker following the entry into force of the present Protocol. Until such time as the oil content meter is installed, it shall immediately before discharge of ballast be established by examination of the ballast water from dedicated tanks that no contamination with oil has taken place.

(4) Every oil tanker operating with dedicated clean ballast tanks shall be provided with:

(a) a Dedicated Clean Ballast Tank Operation Manual detailing the system and specifying operational procedures. Such a Manual shall be to the satisfaction of the Administration and shall contain all the information set out in the Specifications referred to in paragraph (2) of this Regulation. If an alteration affecting the dedicated clean ballast tank system is made, the Operation Manual shall be revised accordingly; and

(b) a Supplement to the Oil Record Book referred to in Regulation 20 of this Annex as set out in Supplement 1 to Appendix III of this Annex. The Supplement shall be permanently attached to the Oil Record Book.

Regulation 13B
Requirements for Crude Oil Washing

(1) Every crude oil washing system required to be provided in accordance with Regulation 13(6) and (8) of this Annex shall comply with the requirements of this Regulation.

(2) The crude oil washing installation and associated equipment and arrangements shall comply with the requirements established by the Administration. Such requirements shall contain at least all the provisions of the Specifications for the Design, Operation and Control of Crude Oil Washing Systems adopted by the International Conference on Tanker Safety and Pollution Prevention, 1978, in Resolution 15 and as may be revised by the Organization.

(3) An inert gas system shall be provided in every cargo tank and slop tank in accordance with the appropriate Regulations of Chapter II-2 of the

International Convention for the Safety of Life at Sea, 1974 as modified and added to by the Protocol of 1978 Relating to the International Convention for the Safety of Life at Sea, 1974.

(4) With respect to the ballasting of cargo tanks, sufficient cargo tanks shall be crude oil washed prior to each ballast voyage in order that, taking into account the tanker's trading pattern and expected weather conditions, ballast water is put only into cargo tanks which have been crude oil washed.

(5) Every oil tanker operating with crude oil washing systems shall be provided with:

(a) an Operations and Equipment Manual detailing the system and equipment and specifying operational procedures. Such a Manual shall be to the satisfaction of the Administration and shall contain all the information set out in the Specifications referred to in paragraph (2) of this Regulation. If an alteration affecting the crude oil washing system is made, the Operations and Equipment Manual shall be revised accordingly; and

(b) a Supplement to the Oil Record Book referred to in Regulation 20 of this Annex as set out in Supplement 2 to Appendix III of this Annex. The Supplement shall be permanently attached to the Oil Record Book.

Regulation 13C

Existing Tankers Engaged in Specific Trades

(1) Subject to the provisions of paragraphs (2) and (3) of this Regulation, Regulation 13(7) to (10) of this Annex shall not apply to an existing oil tanker solely engaged in specific trades between:

(a) ports or terminals within a State Party to the present Protocol; or

(b) ports or terminals of States Parties to the present Protocol, where

(i) the voyage is entirely within a Special Area as defined in Regulation 10(1) of this Annex; or

(ii) the voyage is entirely within other limits designated by the Organization.

(2) The provisions of paragraph (1) of this Regulation shall only apply when the ports or terminals where cargo is loaded on such voyages are provided with reception facilities adequate for the reception and treatment of all the ballast and tank washing water from oil tankers using them and all the following conditions are complied with:

(a) subject to the exceptions as provided for in Regulation 11 of this Annex, all ballast water including clean ballast water and tank washing residues are retained on board and transferred to the reception facilities and the entry in the appropriate Sections of the Supplement to the Oil Record Book referred to in paragraph (3) of this Regulation is endorsed by the competent Port State authority;

(b) agreement has been reached between the Administration and the Governments of the Port States referred to in sub-paragraph (1)(a) or (b) of this Regulation concerning the use of an existing oil tanker for a specific trade;

(c) the adequacy of the reception facilities in accordance with the relevant provisions of this Annex at the ports or terminals referred to above, for the purpose of this Regulation, is approved by the Governments of the Parties to the present Protocol, within which such ports or terminals are situated; and

(d) the International Oil Pollution Prevention Certificate is endorsed to the effect that the oil tanker is solely engaged in such specific trade.

(3) Every oil tanker engaged in a specific trade shall be provided with a Supplement to the Oil Record Book referred to in Regulation 20 of this Annex as set out in Supplement 3 to Appendix III of this Annex. The Supplement shall be permanently attached to the Oil Record Book.

Regulation 13D
Existing Oil Tankers Having Special Ballast Arrangements

(1) Where an existing oil tanker is so constructed or operates in such a manner that at all times it complies with the minimum draught and trim requirements set out in Regulation 13(2) of this Annex without recourse to the use of ballast water, it shall be deemed to comply with the segregated ballast tank requirements referred to in Regulation 13(7) of this Annex, provided that all of the following conditions are complied with:

(a) operational procedures and ballast arrangements are approved by the Administration;

(b) agreement is reached between the Administration and the Governments of the Port States Parties to the present Protocol concerned when the draught and trim requirements are achieved through an operational procedure; and

(c) the International Oil Pollution Prevention Certificate is endorsed to the effect that the oil tanker is operating with special ballast arrangements.

(2) In no case shall ballast water be carried in oil tanks except on those rare voyages when weather conditions are so severe that, in the opinion of the master, it is necessary to carry additional ballast water in cargo tanks for the safety of the ship. Such additional ballast water shall be processed and discharged in compliance with Regulation 9 of this Annex and in accordance with the requirements of Regulation 15 of this Annex, and an entry shall be made in the Oil Record Book referred to in Regulation 20 of this Annex.

(3) An Administration which has endorsed a certificate in accordance with sub-paragraph (1)(c) of this Regulation shall communicate to the Organization the particulars thereof for circulation to the Parties to the present Protocol.

Regulation 13E
Protective Location of Segregated Ballast Spaces

(1) In every new crude oil tanker of 20,000 tons deadweight and above and every new product carrier of 30,000 tons deadweight and above, the segregated ballast tanks required to provide the capacity to comply with the

requirements of Regulation 13 of this Annex which are located within the cargo tank length, shall be arranged in accordance with the requirements of paragraphs (2), (3) and (4) of this Regulation to provide a measure of protection against oil outflow in the event of grounding or collision.

(2) Segregated ballast tanks and spaces other than oil tanks within the cargo tank length (L_t) shall be so arranged as to comply with the following requirement:

$$\Sigma PA_c + \Sigma PA_s \geq J[L_t\,(B + 2D)\,]$$

where: PA_c = the side shell area in square metres for each segregated ballast tank or space other than an oil tank based on projected moulded dimensions,

       PA_s = the bottom shell area in square metres for each such tank or space based on projected moulded dimensions,

       L_t = length in metres between the forward and after extremities of the cargo tanks,

       B = maximum breadth of the ship in metres as defined in Regulation 1(21) of this Chapter,

       D = moulded depth in metres measured vertically from the top of the keel to the top of the freeboard deck beam at side amidships. In ships having rounded gunwales, the moulded depth shall be measured to the point of intersection of the moulded lines of the deck and side shell plating, the lines extending as though the gunwale were of angular design,

       J = 0.45 for oil tankers of 20,000 tons deadweight,

              0.30 for oil tankers of 200,000 tons deadweight and above, subject to the provisions of paragraph (3) of this Regulation.

              For intermediate values of deadweight the value of "J" shall be determined by linear interpolation.

Whenever symbols given in this paragraph appear in this Regulation, they have the meaning as defined in this paragraph.

(3) For tankers of 200,000 tons deadweight and above the value of "J" may be reduced as follows:

$$J \text{ reduced} = \left[J - \left(a - \frac{0_c + 0_s}{4\,0_A} \right) \right] \text{ or } 0.2 \text{ whichever is greater}$$

where: a = 0.25 for oil tankers of 200,000 tons deadweight

       a = 0.40 for oil tankers of 300,000 tons deadweight

       a = 0.50 for oil tankers of 420,000 tons deadweight and above,

       For intermediate values of deadweight the value of "a" shall be determined by linear interpolation.

       0_c = as defined in Regulation 23(1)(a) of this Annex,

       0_s = as defined in Regulation 23(1)(b) of this Annex,

       0_A = the allowable oil outflow as required by Regulation 24(2) of this Annex.

(4) In the determination of "PA$_c$" and "PA$_s$" for segregated ballast tanks and spaces other than oil tanks the following shall apply:

(a) the minimum width of each wing tank or space either of which extends for the full depth of the ship's side or from the deck to the top of the double bottom shall be not less than 2 metres. The width shall be measured inboard from the ship's side at right angles to the centre line. Where a lesser width is provided the wing tank or space shall not be taken into account when calculating the protecting area "PA$_c$"; and

(b) the minimum vertical depth of each double bottom tank or space shall be B/15 or 2 metres, whichever is the lesser. Where a lesser depth is provided the bottom tank or space shall not be taken into account when calculating the protecting area "PA$_s$".

The minimum width and depth of wing tanks and double bottom tanks shall be measured clear of the bilge area and in the case of minimum width, shall be measured clear of any rounded gunwale area.

Regulation 13F

Prevention of Oil Pollution in the Event of Collision or Stranding

(1) This regulation shall apply to oil tankers of 600 tons deadweight and above:

(a) for which the building contract is placed on or after 6 July 1993, or

(b) in the absence of a building contract, the keels of which are laid or which are at a similar stage of construction on or after 6 January 1994, or

(c) the delivery of which is on or after 6 July 1996, or

(d) which have undergone a major conversion:

(i) for which the contract is placed after 6 July 1993; or

(ii) in the absence of a contract, the construction work of which is begun after 6 January 1994; or

(iii) which is completed after 6 July 1996.

(2) Every oil tanker of 5,000 tons deadweight and above shall:

(a) in lieu of regulation 13E, as applicable, comply with the requirements of paragraph (3) unless it is subject to the provisions of paragraphs (4) and (5); and

(b) comply, if applicable, with the requirements of paragraph (6).

(3) The entire cargo tank length shall be protected by ballast tanks or spaces other than cargo and fuel oil tanks as follows:

(a) *Wing tanks or spaces*

Wing tanks or spaces shall extend either for the full depth of the ship's side or from the top of the double bottom to the uppermost deck, disregarding a rounded gunwale where fitted. They shall be arranged such that the cargo tanks are located inboard of the moulded line of the side shell plating, nowhere less than the distance *w* which, as shown in figure 1, is measured at any cross-section at right angles to the side shell, as specified below:

Figure 1 – *Cargo tank boundary lines for the purpose of paragraph (3)*

$$w = 0.5 + \frac{DW}{20,000} \text{ (m) or}$$

w = 2.0 m, whichever is the lesser.

The minimum value of w = 1.0 m.

(b) *Double bottom tanks or spaces*

At any cross-section the depth of each double bottom tank or space shall be such that the distance h between the bottom of the cargo tanks and the moulded line of the bottom shell plating measured at right angles to the bottom shell plating as shown in figure 1 is not less than specified below:

h = B/15 (m) or

h = 2.0 m, whichever is the lesser.

The minimum value of h = 1.0 m.

(c) *Turn of the bilge area or at locations without a clearly defined turn of the bilge*

When the distance h and w are different, the distance w shall have preference at levels exceeding 1.5h above the baseline as shown in figure 1.

(d) *The aggregate capacity of ballast tanks*

On crude oil tankers of 20,000 tons deadweight and above and product carriers of 30,000 tons deadweight and above, the aggregate capacity of wing tanks, double bottom tanks, forepeak tanks and afterpeak tanks shall not be less than the capacity of segregated ballast tanks necessary to meet the requirements of regulation 13. Wing tanks or spaces and double bottom tanks used to meet the requirements of regulation 13 shall be located as uniformly as practicable along the cargo tank length. Additional segregated ballast capacity provided for reducing longitudinal hull girder bending stress, trim, etc., may be located anywhere within the ship.

(e) *Suction wells in cargo tanks*

Suction wells in cargo tanks may protrude into the double bottom below the boundary line defined by the distance h provided that such wells are as small as practicable and the distance between the well bottom and bottom shell plating is not less than $0.5h$.

(f) *Ballast and cargo piping*

Ballast piping and other piping such as sounding and vent piping to ballast tanks shall not pass through cargo tanks. Cargo piping and similar piping to cargo tanks shall not pass through ballast tanks. Exemptions to this requirement may be granted for short lengths of piping, provided that they are completely welded or equivalent.

(4)(a) Double bottom tanks or spaces as required by paragraph (3)(b) may be dispensed with, provided that the design of the tanker is such that the cargo and vapour pressure exerted on the bottom shell plating forming a single boundary between the cargo and the sea does not exceed the external hydrostatic water pressure, as expressed by the following formula:

$$\Gamma \times h_e \times \rho_c \times g + 100\Delta\rho \leq d_n \times \rho_s \times g$$

where:

h_e = height of cargo in contact with the bottom shell plating in metres

ρ_c = maximum cargo density in t/m^3

d_n = minimum operating draught under any expected loading condition in metres

ρ_s = density of seawater in t/m^3

$\Delta\rho$ = maximum set pressure of pressure/vacuum valve provided for the cargo tank in bars

f = safety factor = 1.1

g = standard acceleration of gravity ($9.81 \ m/s^2$).

(b) Any horizontal partition necessary to fulfill the above requirements shall be located at a height of not less than B/6 or 6 m, whichever is the lesser, but not more than 0.6D, above the baseline where D is the moulded depth amidships.

(c) The location of wing tanks or spaces shall be as defined in paragraph (e)(a) except that, below a level $1.5h$ above the baseline where h is as defined in paragraph (3)(b), the cargo tank boundary line may be vertical down to the bottom plating, as shown in figure 2.

Figure 2 − *Cargo tank boundary lines for the purpose of paragraph (4)*

(5) Other methods of design and construction of oil tankers may also be accepted as alternatives to the requirements prescribed in paragraph (3), provided that such methods ensure at least the same level of protection against oil pollution in the event of collision or stranding and are approved in principle by the Marine Environment Protection Committee based on guidelines developed by the Organization.

(6) For all tankers of 20,000 tons deadweight and above the damage assumptions prescribed in regulation 25(2)(b) shall be supplemented by the following assumed bottom raking damage:

(a) longitudinal extent:

(i) ships of 75,000 tons deadweight and above: $0.6L$ measured from the forward perpendicular;

(ii) ships of less than 75,000 tons deadweight: $0.4L$ measured from the forward perpendicular;

(b) transverse extent: $\beta/3$ anywhere in the bottom;

(c) vertical extent; breach of the outer hull.

(7) Oil tankers of less than 5,000 tons deadweight shall:

(a) at least be fitted with double bottom tanks or spaces having such a depth that the distance h specified in paragraph (3)(b) complies with the following:

$$h = \beta/15 \text{ (m)}$$

with a minimum value of $h = 07.6$ m;

in the turn of the bilge area and at locations without a clearly defined turn of the bilge, the cargo tank boundary line shall run parallel to the line of the midship flat bottom as shown in figure 3; and

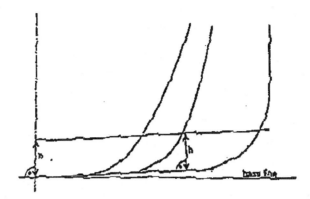

Figure 3 – Cargo tank boundary lines for the purpose of paragraph (7)

(b) be provided with cargo tanks so arranged that the capacity of each cargo tank does not exceed 700 m^3 unless wing tanks or spaces are arranged in accordance with paragraph (3)(a) complying with the following:

$$w = 0.4 - \frac{2.4 \text{ DW}}{20,000} \text{ (m)}$$

with a minimum value of w = 0.76 m.

(8) Oil shall not be carried in any space extending forward of a collision bulkhead located in accordance with regulation 11–1/11 of the International Convention for the Safety of Life at Sea, 1974, as amended. An oil tanker that is not required to have a collision bulkhead in accordance with that regulation shall not carry oil in any space extending forward of the transverse plane perpendicular to the centreline that is located as if it were a collision bulkhead located in accordance with that regulation.

(9) In approving the design and construction of oil tankers to be built in accordance with the provisions of this regulation, Administrations shall have due regard to the general safety aspects including the need for the maintenance and inspections of wing and double bottom tanks or spaces.

Regulation 13G

Prevention of Oil Pollution in the Event of Collision or Stranding
Measures for Existing Tankers

(1) This regulation shall:

(a) apply to crude oil tankers of 20,000 tons deadweight and above and to product carriers of 30,000 tons deadweight and above, which are contracted, the keels of which are laid, or which are delivered before the dates specified in regulation 13F(1) of this annex; and

(b) not apply to oil tankers complying with regulation 13F of this annex, which are contacted, the keels of which are laid, or are delivered before the dates specified in regulation 13F(1) of this annex; and

(c) not apply to oil tankers covered by subparagraph (a) above which comply with regulation 13F(3)(a) and (b) or 13F(4) or 13F(5) of this annex, except that the requirement for minimum distances between the cargo tank boundaries and the ship side and bottom plating need not be met in all respects. In that event, the side protection distances shall not be less than those specified in the International Bulk Chemical Code for type 2 cargo tank location and the bottom protection shall comply with regulation 13E(4)(b) of this annex.

(2) The requirements of this regulation shall take effect as from 6 July 1995.

(3)(a) An oil tanker to which this regulation applies shall be subject to an enhanced programme of inspections during periodical, intermediate and annual surveys, the scope and frequency of which shall at least comply with the guidelines developed by the Organization.

(b) An oil tanker over five years of age to which this regulation applies shall have on board, available to the competent authority of any Government of a State Party to the present Convention, a complete file of the survey reports, including the results of all scantling measurements required, as well as the statement of structural work carried out.

(c) This file shall be accompanied by a condition evaluation report, containing conclusions on the structural condition of the ship and its residual scantlings, endorsed to indicate that it has been accepted by or on behalf of the flag Administration. This file and condition evaluation report shall be prepared in a standard format as contained in the guidelines developed by the Organization.

(4) An oil tanker not meeting the requirements of a new oil tanker as defined in regulation 1(26) of this annex shall comply with the requirements of regulation 13F of this annex not later than 25 years after its date of delivery, unless wing tanks or double bottom spaces, not used for the carriage of oil and meeting the width and height requirements of regulation 13E(4), cover at least 30% of L, for the full depth of the ship on each side or at least 30% of the projected bottom shell area EPAs within the length L_1, where L, and the projected bottom shell area EPAs area as defined in regulation 13E(2), in which case compliance with regulation 13F is required not later than 30 years after its date of delivery.

(5) An oil tanker meeting the requirements of a new oil tanker as defined in regulation 1(26) of this annex shall comply with the requirements of regulation 13F of this annex not later than 30 years after its date of delivery.

(6) Any new ballast and load conditions resulting form the application of paragraph (4) of this regulation shall be subject to approval of the Administration which shall have regard, in particular, to longitudinal and local strength, intact stability and, if applicable, damage stability.

(7) Other structural or operational arrangements such as hydrostatically balanced loading may be accepted as alternatives to the requirements prescribed in paragraph (4), provided that such alternatives ensure at least the same level of protection against oil pollution in the event of collision or stranding and are approved by the Administration based on guidelines developed by the Organization.

Regulation 14—*No change*
Regulation 15

In the existing text of this Regulation, delete reference to "(1973)" in relation to the International Oil Pollution Prevention Certificate.

Regulations 16 and 17—*No change*
Regulation 18

Pumping, Piping and Discharge Arrangements of Oil Tankers

Paragraphs (1) to (4)—*No change*

The following paragraphs are added to the existing text:

(5) Every new oil tanker required to be provided with segregated ballast tanks, or fitted with a crude oil washing system shall comply with the following requirements:

(a) it shall be equipped with oil piping so designed and installed such that oil retention in the lines is minimized; and

(b) means shall be provided to drain all cargo pumps and all oil lines at the completion of cargo discharge, where necessary by connexion to a stripping device. The line and pump drainings shall be capable of being discharged both ashore and to a cargo tank or a slop tank. For discharge ashore a special small diameter line shall be provided for that purpose and connected outboard of the ship's manifold valves.

(6) Every existing crude oil carrier required to be provided with segregated ballast tanks, or fitted with a crude oil washing system or operated with dedicated clean ballast tanks, shall comply with the provisions of paragraph (5)(b) of this Regulation.

Regulation 19—*No change*
Regulation 20

In the existing text of this Regulation, delete reference to "(1973)" in relation to the International Oil Pollution Prevention Certificate.

Regulations 21 to 25—*No change*
Appendix I—LIST OF OILS

No change

4.24 KUWAIT REGIONAL CONVENTION FOR CO-OPERATION ON THE PROTECTION OF THE MARINE ENVIRONMENT FROM POLLUTION (WITHOUT 1978 PROTOCOL). Concluded at Kuwait, 24 April 1978. Entered into force, 30 June 1979. 1140 U.N.T.S. 133, 17 I.L.M. 511 (1978)

* * *

The Government of the State of Bahrain, the Imperial Government of Iran, the Government of the Republic of Iraq, the Government of the State of Kuwait, the Government of the Sultanate of Oman, the Government of the State of Qatar, the Government of the Kingdom of Saudi Arabia, the Government of the United Arab Emirates,

Realizing that pollution of the marine environment in the Region shared by Bahrain, Iran, Iraq, Kuwait, Oman, Qatar, Saudi Arabia and the United Arab Emirates, by oil and other harmful or noxious materials arising from human activities on land or at sea, especially through indiscriminate and uncontrolled discharge of these substances, presents a growing threat to marine life, fisheries, human health, recreational uses of beaches and other amenities,

Mindful of the special hydrographic and ecological characteristics of the marine environment of the Region and its particular vulnerability to pollution,

Conscious of the need to ensure that the processes of urban and rural development and resultant land use should be carried out in such a manner as to preserve, as far as possible, marine resources and coastal amenities, and that such development should not lead to deterioration of the marine environment,

Convinced of the need to ensure that the processes of industrial development should not, in any way, cause damage to the marine environment of the Region, jeopardize its living resources or create hazards to human health,

Recognizing the need to develop an integrated management approach to the use of the marine environment and the coastal areas which will allow the achievement of environmental and development goals in a harmonious manner,

Recognizing also the need for a carefully planned research, monitoring and assessment programme in view of the scarcity of scientific information on marine pollution in the Region,

Considering that the States sharing the Region have a special responsibility to protect its marine environment,

Aware of the importance of co-operation and co-ordination of action on a regional basis with the aim of protecting the marine environment of the Region for the benefit of all concerned, including future generations,

Bearing in mind the existing international conventions relevant to the present Convention,

Have agreed as follows:

Article I. DEFINITIONS

For the purpose of the present Convention:

(*a*) "Marine pollution" means the introduction by man, directly or indirectly, of substances or energy into the marine environment resulting or likely to result in such deleterious effects as harm to living resources, hazards to human health, hindrance to marine activities including fishing, impairment of quality for use of sea water and reduction of amenities;

(*b*) "National Authority" means the authority designated by each Contracting State as responsible for the co-ordination of national efforts for implementing the Convention and its protocols;

(*c*) "Organization" means the organization established by the Contracting States in accordance with article XVI;

(*d*) "Secretariat" means the organ of the Organization established in accordance with article XVI;

(*e*) "Action Plan" means the Action Plan for the Development and Protection of the Marine Environment and the Coastal Areas of Bahrain, Iran, Iraq, Kuwait, Oman, Qatar, Saudi Arabia and the United Arab Emirates adopted at the Kuwait Regional Conference of Plenipotentiaries on the Protection and Development of the Marine Environment and the Coastal Areas, convened from 15 to 23 April 1978.

Article II. GEOGRAPHICAL COVERAGE

(*a*) The present Convention shall apply to the sea area in the Region bounded in the south by the following rhumb lines: from Ras Dharbat Ali in (16°39′ N, 53°3′30″ E) then to a position in (16°00′ N, 53°25′ E) then to a position in (17°00′ N, 56°30′ E) then to a position in (20°30′ N, 60°00′ E) then to Ras AlFasteh in (25°04′ N, 61°25′ E) (hereinafter referred to as the "Sea Area");

. (*b*) The Sea Area shall not include internal waters of the Contracting States unless it is otherwise stated in the present Convention or in any of its protocols.

Article III. GENERAL OBLIGATIONS

(*a*) The Contracting States shall, individually and/or jointly, take all appropriate measures in accordance with the present Convention and those protocols in force to which they are party to prevent, abate and combat pollution of the marine environment in the Sea Area;

(*b*) In addition to the Protocol Concerning Regional Co-operation in Combating Pollution by Oil and Other Harmful Substances in Cases of Emergency opened for signature at the same time as the present Convention, the Contracting States shall co-operate in the formulation and adoption of other protocols prescribing agreed measures, procedures and standards for the implementation of the Convention;

(*c*) The Contracting States shall establish national standards, laws and regulations as required for the effective discharge of the obligation prescribed in paragraph (*a*) of this article, and shall endeavour to harmonise their national policies in this regard and for this purpose appoint the National Authority;

(*d*) The Contracting States shall co-operate with the competent international, regional and sub-regional organizations to establish and adopt regional standards, recommended practices and procedures to prevent, abate and combat pollution from all sources in conformity with the objectives of the present Convention, and to assist each other in fulfilling their obligations under the present Convention;

(e) The Contracting States shall use their best endeavour to ensure that the implementation of the present Convention shall not cause transformation of one type of pollution to another which could be more detrimental to the environment.

Article IV. Pollution from ships

The Contracting States shall take all appropriate measures in conformity with the present Convention and the applicable rules of international law to prevent, abate and combat pollution in the Sea Area caused by intentional or accidental discharges from ships, and shall ensure effective compliance in the Sea Area with applicable international rules relating to the control of this type of pollution, including load-on-top, segregated ballast and crude oil washing procedures for tankers.

Article V. Pollution caused by dumping from ships and aircraft

The Contracting States shall take all appropriate measures to prevent, abate and combat pollution in the Sea Area caused by dumping of wastes and other matter from ships and aircraft, and shall ensure effective compliance in the Sea Area with applicable international rules relating to the control of this type of pollution as provided for in relevant international conventions.

Article VI. Pollution from land-based sources

The Contracting States shall take all appropriate measures to prevent, abate and combat pollution caused by discharges from land reaching the Sea Area whether water-borne, air-borne, or directly from the coast including outfalls and pipelines.

Article VII. Pollution resulting from exploration and exploitation of the bed of the territorial sea and its sub-soil and the continental shelf

The Contracting States shall take all appropriate measures to prevent, abate and combat pollution in the Sea Area resulting from exploration and exploitation of the bed of the territorial sea and its sub-soil and the continental shelf, including the prevention of accidents and the combating of pollution emergencies resulting in damage to the marine environment.

Article VIII. Pollution from other human activities

The Contracting States shall take all appropriate measures to prevent, abate and combat pollution of the Sea Area resulting from land reclamation and associated suction dredging and coastal dredging.

Article IX. Co-operation in dealing with pollution emergencies

(a) The Contracting States shall, individually and/or jointly, take all necessary measures, including those to ensure that adequate equipment and qualified personnel are readily available, to deal with pollution emergencies in the Sea Area, whatever the cause of such emergencies, and to reduce or eliminate damage resulting therefrom;

(b) Any Contracting State which becomes aware of any pollution emergency in the Sea Area shall, without delay, notify the Organization referred to under article XVI and, through the secretariat, any Contracting State likely to be affected by such emergency.

Article X. SCIENTIFIC AND TECHNOLOGICAL CO-OPERATION

(*a*) The Contracting States shall co-operate directly, or, where appropriate, through competent international and regional organizations, in the field of scientific research, monitoring and assessment concerning pollution in the Sea Area, and shall exchange data as well as other scientific information for the purpose of the present Convention and any of its protocols;

(*b*) The Contracting States shall co-operate further to develop and co-ordinate national research and monitoring programmes relating to all types of pollution in the Sea Area and to establish in co-operation with competent regional or international organizations, a regional network of such programmes to ensure compatible results. For this purpose, each Contracting State shall designate the National Authority responsible for pollution research and monitoring within the areas under its national jurisdiction. The Contracting States shall participate in international arrangements for pollution research and monitoring in areas beyond their national jurisdiction.

Article XI. ENVIRONMENTAL ASSESSMENT

(*a*) Each Contracting State shall endeavour to include an assessment of the potential environmental effects in any planning activity entailing projects within its territory, particularly in the coastal areas, which may cause significant risks of pollution in the Sea Area;

(*b*) The Contracting States may, in consultation with the secretariat, develop procedures for dissemination of information of the assessment of the activities referred to in paragraph (*a*) above;

(*c*) The Contracting States undertake to develop, individually or jointly, technical and other guidelines in accordance with standard scientific practice to assist the planning of their development projects in such a way as to minimize their harmful impact on the marine environment. In this regard international standards may be used where appropriate.

Article XII. TECHNICAL AND OTHER ASSISTANCE

The Contracting States shall co-operate directly or through competent regional or international organizations in the development of programmes of technical and other assistance in fields relating to marine pollution in co-ordination with the Organization referred to in article XVI.

Article XIII. LIABILITY AND COMPENSATION

The Contracting States undertake to co-operate in the formulation and adoption of appropriate rules and procedures for the determination of:

(*a*) Civil liability and compensation for damage resulting from pollution of the marine environment, bearing in mind applicable international rules and procedures relating to those matters; and

(*b*) Liability and compensation for damage resulting from violation of obligations under the present Convention and its protocols.

Article XIV. Sovereign immunity

Warships or other ships owned or operated by a State, and used only on Government non-commercial service, shall be exempted from the application of the provisions of the present Convention. Each Contracting State shall, as far as possible, ensure that its warships or other ships owned or operated by that State, and used only on Government non-commercial service, shall comply with the present Convention in the prevention of pollution to the marine environment.

Article XV. Disclaimer

Nothing in the present Convention shall prejudice or affect the rights or claims of any Contracting State in regard to the nature or extent of its maritime jurisdiction which may be established in conformity with international law.

Article XVI. Regional Organization for the Protection of the Marine Environment

(*a*) The Contracting States hereby establish a Regional Organization for the Protection of the Marine Environment, the permanent headquarters of which shall be located in Kuwait;

(*b*) The Organization shall consist of the following organs:

(i) A Council which shall be comprised of the Contracting States and shall perform the functions set forth in paragraph (*d*) of article XVII;

(ii) A Secretariat which shall perform the functions set forth in paragraph (*a*) of article XVIII; and

(iii) A Judicial Commission for the Settlement of Disputes whose composition, terms of reference and rules of procedure shall be established at the first meeting of the Council.

Article XVII. Council

(*a*) The meetings of the Council shall be convened in accordance with paragraph (*a*) of article XVIII and paragraph (*b*) of article XXX. The Council shall hold ordinary meetings once a year. Extraordinary meetings of the Council shall be held upon the request of at least one Contracting State endorsed by at least one other Contracting State, or upon the request of the Executive Secretary endorsed by at least two Contracting States. Meetings of the Council shall be convened at the headquarters of the Organization or at any other place agreed upon by consultation amongst the Contracting States. Three fourths of the Contracting States shall constitute a quorum;

(*b*) The Chairmanship of the Council shall be given to each Contracting State in turn in alphabetical order of the names of the States in the English language. The Chairman shall serve for a period of one year and cannot during the period of chairmanship serve as a representative of his State. Should the chairmanship fall vacant, the Contracting State chairing the Council shall designate a successor to remain in office until the term of chairmanship of that Contracting State expires;

(*c*) The voting procedure in the Council shall be as follows:

(i) Each Contracting State shall have one vote;

(ii) Decisions on substantive matters shall be taken by a unanimous vote of the Contracting States present and voting;

(iii) Decisions on procedural matters shall be taken by three-fourths majority vote of the Contracting States present and voting.

(*d*) The functions of the Council shall be:

(i) To keep under review the implementation of the Convention and its protocols, and the Action Plan referred to in paragraph (*e*) of article I;

(ii) To review and evaluate the state of marine pollution and its effects on the Sea Area on the basis of reports provided by the Contracting States and the competent international or regional organizations;

(iii) To adopt, review and amend as required in accordance with procedures established in article XXI, the annexes to the Convention and to its protocols;

(iv) To receive and to consider reports submitted by the Contracting States under articles IX and XXIII;

(v) To consider reports prepared by the Secretariat on questions relating to the Convention and to matters relevant to the administration of the Organization;

(vi) To make recommendations regarding the adoption of any additional protocols or any amendments to the Convention or to its protocols in accordance with articles XIX and XX;

(vii) To establish subsidiary bodies and *ad hoc* working groups as required to consider any matters related to the Convention and its protocols and annexes to the Convention and its protocols;

(viii) To appoint an Executive Secretary and to make provision for the appointment by the Executive Secretary of such other personnel as may be necessary;

(ix) To review periodically the functions of the Secretariat;

(x) To consider and to undertake any additional action that may be required for the achievement of the purposes of the Convention and its protocols.

Article XVIII. Secretariat

(*a*) The Secretariat shall be comprised of an Executive Secretary and the personnel necessary to perform the following functions:

(i) To convene and to prepare the meetings of the Council and its subsidiary bodies and *ad hoc* working groups as referred to in article XVII, and conferences as referred to in articles XIX and XX;

(ii) To transmit to the Contracting States notifications, reports and other information received in accordance with articles IX and XXIII;

(iii) To consider enquiries by, and information from, the Contracting States and to consult with them on questions relating to the Convention and its protocols and annexes thereto;

(iv) To prepare reports on matters relating to the Convention and to the administration of the Organization;

(v) To establish, maintain and disseminate an up-to-date collection of national laws of all States concerned relevant to the protection of the marine environment;

(vi) To arrange, upon request, for the provision of technical assistance and advice for the drafting of appropriate national legislation for the effective implementation of the Convention and its protocols;

(vii) To arrange for training programmes in areas related to the implementation of the Convention and its protocols;

(viii) To carry out its assignments under the protocols to the Convention;

(ix) To perform such other functions as may be assigned to it by the Council for the implementation of the Convention and its protocols.

(*b*) The Executive Secretary shall be the chief administrative official of the Organization and shall perform the functions that are necessary for the administration of the present Convention, the work of the Secretariat and other tasks entrusted to the Executive Secretary by the Council and as provided for in its rules of procedure and financial rules.

Article XIX. ADOPTION OF ADDITIONAL PROTOCOLS

Any Contracting State may propose additional protocols to the present Convention pursuant to paragraph (*b*) of article III at a diplomatic conference of the Contracting States to be convened by the Secretariat at the request of at least three Contracting States. Additional protocols shall be adopted by a unanimous vote of the Contracting States present and voting.

Article XX. AMENDMENTS TO THE CONVENTION AND ITS PROTOCOLS

(*a*) Any Contracting State to the present Convention or to any of its protocols may propose amendments to the Convention or to the protocol concerned at a diplomatic conference to be convened by the Secretariat at the request of at least three Contracting States. Amendments to the Convention and its protocols shall be adopted by a unanimous vote of the Contracting States present and voting;

(*b*) Amendments to the Convention or any protocol adopted by a diplomatic conference shall be submitted by the Depositary for acceptance by all Contracting States. Acceptance of amendments to the Convention or to any protocol shall be notified to the Depositary in writing. Amendments adopted in accordance with this article shall enter into force for all Contracting States, except those which have notified the Depositary of a different intention, on the thirtieth day following the receipt by the Depositary of notification of their acceptance by at least three-fourths of the Contracting States to the Convention or any protocol concerned as the case may be;

(*c*) After the entry into force of an amendment to the Convention or to a protocol, any new Contracting State to the Convention or such protocol shall become a Contracting State to the instrument as amended.

Article XXI. ANNEXES AND AMENDMENTS TO ANNEXES

(*a*) Annexes to the Convention or to any protocol shall form an integral part of the Convention or such protocol;

(*b*) Except as may be otherwise provided in any protocol, the following procedure shall apply to the adoption and entry into force of any amendments to annexes to the Convention or to any protocol:

(i) Any Contracting State to the Convention or to a protocol may propose amendments to the annexes to the instrument in question at the meetings of the Council referred to in article XVII;

(ii) Such amendments shall be adopted at such meetings by a unanimous vote;

(iii) The Depositary referred to in article XXX shall communicate amendments so adopted to all Contracting States without delay;

(iv) Any Contracting State which has a different intention with respect to an amendment to the annexes to the Convention or to any protocol shall notify the Depositary in writing within a period determined by the Contracting States concerned when adopting the amendment;

(v) The Depositary shall notify all Contracting States without delay of any notification received pursuant to the preceding sub-paragraph;

(vi) On the expiry of the period referred to in sub-paragraph (iv) above, the amendment to the annex shall become effective for all Contracting States to the Convention or to the protocol concerned which have not submitted a notification in accordance with the provisions of that sub-paragraph;

(*c*) The adoption and entry into force of a new annex to the Convention or to any protocol shall be subject to the same procedure as for the adoption and entry into force of an amendment to an annex in accordance with the provisions of this article, provided that, if any amendment to the Convention or the protocol concerned is involved, the new annex shall not enter into force until such time as the amendment to the Convention or the protocol concerned enters into force.

Article XXII. RULES OF PROCEDURE AND FINANCIAL RULES

(*a*) The Council shall, at its first meeting, adopt its own rules;

(*b*) The Council shall adopt financial rules to determine, in particular, the financial participation of the Contracting States.

Article XXIII. REPORTS

Each Contracting State shall submit to the Secretariat reports on measures adopted in implementation of the provisions of the Convention and its protocols in such form and at such intervals as may be determined by the Council.

Article XXIV. COMPLIANCE CONTROL

The Contracting States shall co-operate in the development of procedures for the effective application of the Convention and its protocols, including detection of violations, using all appropriate and practicable measures of detection and environmental monitoring, including adequate procedures for reporting and accumulation of evidence.

Article XXV. SETTLEMENT OF DISPUTES

(*a*) In case of a dispute as to the interpretation or application of this Convention or its protocols, the Contracting States concerned shall seek a settlement of the dispute through negotiation or any other peaceful means of their own choice.

(*b*) If the Contracting States concerned cannot settle the dispute through the means mentioned in paragraph (*a*) of this article, the dispute shall be submitted to the Judicial Commission for the Settlement of Disputes referred to in paragraph (*b*)(iii) of article XVI.

Article XXVI. SIGNATURE

The present Convention together with the Protocol Concerning Regional Co-operation in Combating Pollution by Oil and other Harmful Substances in Cases of Emergency shall be open for signature in Kuwait from 24 April to 23 July 1978 by any State invited as a participant in the Kuwait Regional Conference of Plenipotentiaries on the Protection and Development of the Marine Environment and the Coastal Areas, convened from 15 to 23 April 1978 for the purpose of adopting the Convention and the Protocol.

Article XXVII. RATIFICATION, ACCEPTANCE, APPROVAL OR ACCESSION

(*a*) The present Convention together with the Protocol concerning Regional Co-operation in Combating Pollution by Oil and other Harmful Substances in Cases of Emergency and any other protocol thereto shall be subject to ratification, acceptance, or approval by the States referred to in article XXVI.

(*b*) As from 24 July 1978, this Convention together with the Protocol Concerning Regional Co-operation in Combating Pollution by Oil and other Harmful Substances in Cases of Emergency shall be open for accession by the States referred to in article XXVI;

(*c*) Any State which has ratified, accepted, approved or acceded to the present Convention shall be considered as having ratified, accepted, approved or acceded to the Protocol Concerning Regional Co-operation in Combating Pollution by Oil and other Harmful Substances in Cases of Emergency;

(*d*) Instruments of ratification, acceptance, approval or accession shall be deposited with the Government of Kuwait which will assume the functions of Depositary.

Article XXVIII. ENTRY INTO FORCE

(*a*) The present Convention together with the Protocol Concerning Regional Co-operation in Combating Pollution by Oil and other Harmful Substances in Cases of Emergency shall enter into force on the ninetieth day following the date of deposit of at least five instruments of ratification, acceptance or approval of, or accession to, the Convention;

(*b*) Any other protocol to this Convention, except as otherwise provided in such protocol, shall enter into force on the ninetieth day following the date of deposit of at least five instruments of ratification, acceptance or approval of, or accession to, such protocol;

(*c*) After the date of deposit of five instruments of ratification, acceptance or approval of, or accession to, this Convention or any other protocol, this Convention or any such protocol shall enter into force with respect to any State on the ninetieth day following the date of deposit by that State of the instrument of ratification, acceptance, approval or accession.

Article XXIX. Withdrawal

(*a*) At any time after five years from the date of entry into force of this Convention, any Contracting State may withdraw from this Convention by giving written notification of withdrawal to the Depositary;

(*b*) Except as may be otherwise provided in any other protocol to the Convention, any Contracting State may, at any time after five years from the date of entry into force of such protocol, withdraw from such protocol by giving written notification of withdrawal to the Depositary;

(*c*) Withdrawal shall take effect ninety days after the date on which notification of withdrawal is received by the Depositary;

(*d*) Any Contracting State which withdraws from the Convention shall be considered as also having withdrawn from any protocol to which it was a party;

(*e*) Any Contracting State which withdraws from the Protocol concerning Regional Co-operation in Combating Pollution by Oil and other Harmful Substances in Cases of Emergency shall be considered as also having withdrawn from the Convention.

Article XXX. Responsibilities of the Depositary

(*a*) The Depositary shall inform the Contracting States and the Secretariat of the following:

(i) Signature of this Convention and of any protocol thereto, and of the deposit of the instruments of ratification, acceptance, approval or accession in accordance with article XXVII;

(ii) Date on which Convention and any protocol will enter into force in accordance with the provisions of article XXVIII;

(iii) Notification of a different intention made in accordance with articles XX and XXI;

(iv) Notification of withdrawal made in accordance with article XXIX;

(v) Amendments adopted with respect to the Convention and to any protocol, their acceptance by the Contracting State and the date of entry into force of those amendments in accordance with the provisions of article XX;

(vi) Adoption of new annexes and of the amendment of any annex in accordance with article XXI;

(*b*) The Depositary shall call the first meeting of the Council within six months of the date on which the Convention enters into force.

The original of this Convention, of any protocol thereto, of any annex to the Convention or to a protocol, or of any amendment to the Convention, to a protocol or to an annex of the Convention or of a protocol shall be deposited with the Depositary, the Government of Kuwait who shall send copies thereof to all States concerned and shall register all such instruments and all subsequent actions in respect of them with the Secretariat of the United Nations in accordance with Article 102 of the Charter of the United Nations.

4.25 PROTOCOL FOR THE PROTECTION OF THE MEDITERRANEAN SEA AGAINST POLLUTION FROM LAND–BASED SOURCES (WITHOUT ANNEXES). Concluded at Athens, 17 May 1980. Entered into force, 17 June 1983. 19 I.L.M. 869 (1980)

The Contracting Parties to the present Protocol,

Being Parties to the Convention for the Protection of the Mediterranean Sea against Pollution, adopted at Barcelona on 16 February 1976,

Desirous of implementing article 4, paragraph 2, and articles 8 and 15 of the said Convention,

Noting the rapid increase of human activities in the Mediterranean Sea Area, particularly in the fields of industrialization and urbanization, as well as the seasonal increase in the coastal population due to tourism,

Recognizing the danger posed to the marine environment and to human health by pollution from land-based sources and the serious problems resulting therefrom in many coastal waters and river estuaries of the Mediterranean Sea, primarily due to the release of untreated, insufficiently treated or inadequately disposed domestic or industrial discharges,

Recognizing the differences in levels of development between the coastal States, and taking account of the economic and social imperatives of the developing countries,

Determined to take in close co-operation the necessary measures to protect the Mediterranean Sea against pollution from land-based sources,

Have agreed as follows:

Article 1

The Contracting Parties to this Protocol (hereinafter referred to as "the Parties") shall take all appropriate measures to prevent, abate, combat and control pollution of the Mediterranean Sea Area caused by discharges from rivers, coastal establishments or outfalls, or emanating from any other land-based sources within their territories.

Article 2

For the purposes of this Protocol:

(a) "The Convention" means the Convention for the Protection of the Mediterranean Sea against Pollution, adopted at Barcelona on 16 February 1976;

(b) "Organization" means the body referred to in article 13 of the Convention;

(c) "Freshwater limit" means the place in watercourses where, at low tides and in a period of low freshwater flow, there is an appreciable increase in salinity due to the presence of sea water.

Article 3

The area to which this Protocol applies (hereinafter referred to as the "Protocol Area") shall be:

(a) the Mediterranean Sea Area as defined in article 1 of the Convention;

(b) waters on the landward side of the baselines from which the breadth of the territorial sea is measured and extending, in the case of watercourses, up to the freshwater limit;

(c) saltwater marshes communicating with the sea.

Article 4

1. This Protocol shall apply:

(a) to polluting discharges reaching the Protocol Area from land-based sources within the territories of the Parties, in particular:

— directly, from outfalls discharging into the sea or through coastal disposal;

— indirectly, through rivers, canals or other watercourses, including underground watercourses, or through run-off;

(b) to pollution from land-based sources transported by the atmosphere, under conditions to be defined in an additional annex to this Protocol and accepted by the Parties in conformity with the provisions of article 17 of the Convention.

2. This Protocol shall also apply to polluting discharges from fixed man-made off-shore structures which are under the jurisdiction of a Party and which serve purposes other than exploration and exploitation of mineral resources of the continental shelf and the sea-bed and its sub-soil.

Article 5

1. The Parties undertake to eliminate pollution of the Protocol Area from land-based sources by substances listed in annex I to this Protocol.

2. To this end they shall elaborate and implement, jointly or individually, as appropriate, the necessary programmes and measures.

3. These programmes and measures shall include, in particular, common emission standards and standards for use.

4. The standards and the time-tables for the implementation of the programmes and measures aimed at eliminating pollution from land-based sources shall be fixed by the Parties and periodically reviewed, if necessary every two years, for each of the substances listed in annex I, in accordance with the provisions of article 15 of this Protocol.

Article 6

1. The Parties shall strictly limit pollution from land-based sources in the Protocol Area by substances or sources listed in annex II to this Protocol.

2. To this end they shall elaborate and implement, jointly or individually, as appropriate, suitable programmes and measures.

3. Discharges shall be strictly subject to the issue, by the competent national authorities, of an authorization taking due account of the provisions of annex III to this Protocol.

Article 7

1. The Parties shall progressively formulate and adopt, in co-operation with the competent international organizations, common guidelines and, as appropriate, standards or criteria dealing in particular with:

(a) the length, depth and position of pipelines for coastal outfalls, taking into account, in particular, the methods used for pretreatment of effluents;

(b) special requirements for effluents necessitating separate treatment;

(c) the quality of sea water used for specific purposes that is necessary for the protection of human health, living resources and ecosystems;

(d) the control and progressive replacement of products, installations and industrial and other processes causing significant pollution of the marine environment;

(e) specific requirements concerning the quantities of the substances listed in annexes I and II discharged, their concentration in effluents and methods of discharging them.

2. Without prejudice to the provisions of article 5 of this Protocol, such common guidelines, standards or criteria shall take into account local ecological, geographical and physical characteristics, the economic capacity of the Parties and their need for development, the level of existing pollution and the real absorptive capacity of the marine environment.

3. The programmes and measures referred to in articles 5 and 6 shall be adopted by taking into account, for their progressive implementation, the capacity to adapt and reconvert existing installations, the economic capacity of the Parties and their need for development.

Article 8

Within the framework of the provisions of, and the monitoring programmes provided for in, article 10 of the Convention, and if necessary in cooperation with the competent international organizations, the Parties shall carry out at the earliest possible date monitoring activities in order:

(a) systematically to assess, as far as possible, the levels of pollution along their coasts, in particular with regard to the substances or sources listed in annexes I and II, and periodically to provide information in this respect;

(b) to evaluate the effects of measures taken under this Protocol to reduce pollution of the marine environment.

Article 9

In conformity with article 11 of the Convention, the Parties shall co-operate as far as possible in scientific and technological fields related to pollution from land-based sources, particularly research on inputs, pathways and effects of pollutants and on the development of new methods for their treatment, reduction or elimination. To this end the Parties shall, in particular, endeavour to:

(a) exchange scientific and technical information;

(b) co-ordinate their research programmes.

Article 10

1. The Parties shall, directly or with the assistance of competent regional or other international organizations or bilaterally, co-operate with a view to

formulating and, as far as possible, implementing programmes of assistance to developing countries, particularly in the fields of science, education and technology, with a view to preventing pollution from land-based sources and its harmful effects in the marine environment.

2. Technical assistance would include, in particular, the training of scientific and technical personnel, as well as the acquisition, utilization and production by those countries of appropriate equipment on advantageous terms to be agreed upon among the Parties concerned.

Article 11

1. If discharges from a watercourse which flows through the territories of two or more Parties or forms a boundary between them are likely to cause pollution of the marine environment of the Protocol Area, the Parties in question, respecting the provisions of this Protocol in so far as each of them is concerned, are called upon to co-operate with a view to ensuring its full application.

2. A Party shall not be responsible for any pollution originating on the territory of a non-contracting State. However, the said Party shall endeavour to co-operate with the said State so as to make possible full application of the Protocol.

Article 12

1. Taking into account article 22, paragraph 1, of the Convention, when land-based pollution originating from the territory of one Party is likely to prejudice directly the interests of one or more of the other Parties, the Parties concerned shall, at the request of one or more of them, undertake to enter into consultation with a view to seeking a satisfactory solution.

2. At the request of any Party concerned, the matter shall be placed on the agenda of the next meeting of the Parties held in accordance with article 14 of this Protocol; the meeting may make recommendations with a view to reaching a satisfactory solution.

Article 13

1. The Parties shall inform one another through the Organization of measures taken, of results achieved and, if the case arises, of difficulties encountered in the application of this Protocol. Procedures for the collection and submission of such information shall be determined at the meetings of the Parties.

2. Such information shall include, *inter alia:*

(a) statistical data on the authorizations granted in accordance with article 6 of this Protocol;

(b) data resulting from monitoring as provided for in article 8 of this Protocol;

(c) quantities of pollutants discharged from their territories;

(d) measures taken in accordance with articles 5 and 6 of this Protocol.

Article 14

1. Ordinary meetings of the Parties shall take place in conjunction with ordinary meetings of the Contracting Parties to the Convention held pursuant to article 14 of the Convention. The Parties may also hold extraordinary meetings in accordance with article 14 of the Convention.

2. The functions of the meetings of the Parties to this Protocol shall be, *inter alia:*

(a) to keep under review the implementation of this Protocol and to consider the efficacy of the measures adopted and the advisability of any other measures, in particular in the form of annexes;

(b) to revise and amend any annex to this Protocol, as appropriate;

(c) to formulate and adopt programmes and measures in accordance with articles 5, 6 and 15 of this Protocol;

(d) to adopt, in accordance with article 7 of this Protocol, common guidelines, standards or criteria, in any form decided upon by the Parties;

(e) to make recommendations in accordance with article 12, paragraph 2, of this Protocol;

(f) to consider the information submitted by the Parties under article 13 of this Protocol;

(g) to discharge such other functions as may be appropriate for the application of this Protocol.

Article 15

1. The meeting of the Parties shall adopt, by a two-thirds majority, the programmes and measures for the abatement or the elimination of pollution from land-based sources which are provided for in articles 5 and 6 of this Protocol.

2. The Parties which are not able to accept a programme or measures shall inform the meeting of the Parties of the action they intend to take as regards the programme or measures concerned, it being understood that these Parties may, at any time, give their consent to the programme or measures that have been adopted.

Article 16

1. The provisions of the Convention relating to any Protocol shall apply with respect to this Protocol.

2. The rules of procedure and the financial rules adopted pursuant to article 18 of the Convention shall apply with respect to this Protocol, unless the Parties to this Protocol agree otherwise.

3. This Protocol shall be open for signature, at Athens from 17 May 1980 to 16 June 1980, and at Madrid from 17 June 1980 to 16 May 1981, by any State invited to the Conference of Plenipotentiaries of the Coastal States of the Mediterranean Region for the Protection of the Mediterranean Sea against Pollution from Land–Based Sources held at Athens from 12 May to 17 May 1980. It shall also be open until the same dates for signature by the European Economic Community and by any similar regional economic group-

ing of which at least one member is a coastal State of the Mediterranean Sea Area and which exercises competence in fields covered by this Protocol.

4. This Protocol shall be subject to ratification, acceptance or approval. Instruments of ratification, acceptance or approval shall be deposited with the Government of Spain, which will assume the functions of Depositary.

5. As from 17 May 1981, this Protocol shall be open for accession by the States referred to in paragraph 3 above, by the European Economic Community and by any grouping referred to in that paragraph.

6. This Protocol shall enter into force on the thirtieth day following the deposit of at least six instruments of ratification, acceptance or approval of, or accession to, the Protocol by the Parties referred to in paragraph 3 of this article.

4.26   UNITED NATIONS CONVENTION ON THE LAW OF THE SEA (WITH ANNEX V).[1] Concluded at Montego Bay, 10 December 1982. Enters into force, 16 November 1994. U.N. Doc. A/CONF.62/122, 21 I.L.M. 1261 (1982)

The States Parties to this Convention,

Prompted by the desire to settle, in a spirit of mutual understanding and co-operation, all issues relating to the law of the sea and aware of the historic significance of this Convention as an important contribution to the maintenance of peace, justice and progress for all peoples of the world,

Noting that developments since the United Nations Conferences on the Law of the Sea held at Geneva in 1958 and 1960 have accentuated the need for a new and generally acceptable Convention on the law of the sea,

Conscious that the problems of ocean space are closely interrelated and need to be considered as a whole,

Recognizing the desirability of establishing through this Convention, with due regard for the sovereignty of all States, a legal order for the seas and oceans which will facilitate international communication, and will promote the peaceful uses of the seas and oceans, the equitable and efficient utilization of their resources, the conservation of their living resources, and the study, protection and preservation of the marine environment,

Bearing in mind that the achievement of these goals will contribute to the realization of a just and equitable international economic order which takes into account the interests and needs of mankind as a whole and, in particular, the special interests and needs of developing countries, whether coastal or land-locked,

Desiring by this Convention to develop the principles embodied in resolution 2749 (XXV) of 17 December 1970 in which the General Assembly of the United Nations solemnly declared *inter alia* that the area of the sea-bed and ocean floor and the subsoil thereof, beyond the limits of national jurisdiction, as well as its resources, are the common heritage of mankind, the exploration and exploitation of which shall be carried out for the benefit of mankind as a whole, irrespective of the geographical location of States,

Believing that the codification and progressive development of the law of the sea achieved in this Convention will contribute to the strengthening of peace, security, co-operation and friendly relations among all nations in conformity with the principles of justice and equal rights and will promote the economic and social advancement of all peoples of the world, in accordance with the Purposes and Principles of the United Nations as set forth in the Charter,

Affirming that matters not regulated by this Convention continue to be governed by the rules and principles of general international law,

Have agreed as follows:

---

1. The Convention will supersede the 1958 Geneva law of the sea conventions (Basic Documents 4.3, 4.4, 4.5, *supra,* and 6.3, *infra*) upon entry into force for the parties.

PART I

INTRODUCTION

Article 1

Use of terms and scope

1. For the purposes of this Convention:

(1) "Area" means the sea-bed and ocean floor and subsoil thereof, beyond the limits of national jurisdiction;

(2) "Authority" means the International Sea–Bed Authority;

(3) "activities in the Area" means all activities of exploration for, and exploitation of, the resources of the Area;

(4) "pollution of the marine environment" means the introduction by man, directly or indirectly, of substances or energy into the marine environment, including estuaries, which results or is likely to result in such deleterious effects as harm to living resources and marine life, hazards to human health, hindrance to marine activities, including fishing and other legitimate uses of the sea, impairment of quality for use of sea water and reduction of amenities;

(5)(a) "dumping" means:

(i) any deliberate disposal of wastes or other matter from vessels, aircraft, platforms or other man-made structures at sea;

(ii) any deliberate disposal of vessels, aircraft, platforms or other man-made structures at sea;

(b) "dumping" does not include:

(i) the disposal of wastes or other matter incidental to, or derived from the normal operations of vessels, aircraft, platforms or other man-made structures at sea and their equipment, other than wastes or other matter transported by or to vessels, aircraft, platforms or other man-made structures at sea, operating for the purpose of disposal of such matter or derived from the treatment of such wastes or other matter on such vessels, aircraft, platforms or structures;

(ii) placement of matter for a purpose other than the mere disposal thereof, provided that such placement is not contrary to the aims of this Convention.

2. (1) "States Parties" means States which have consented to be bound by this Convention and for which this Convention is in force.

(2) This Convention applies *mutatis mutandis* to the entities referred to in article 305, paragraph 1(b), (c), (d), (e) and (f), which become Parties to this Convention in accordance with the conditions relevant to each, and to that extent "States Parties" refers to those entities.

PART II
TERRITORIAL SEA AND CONTIGUOUS ZONE
SECTION 1. GENERAL PROVISIONS
Article 2
Legal status of the territorial sea, of the air space over
the territorial sea and of its bed and subsoil

1. The sovereignty of a coastal State extends, beyond its land territory and internal waters and, in the case of an archipelagic State, its archipelagic waters, to an adjacent belt of sea, described as the territorial sea.

2. This sovereignty extends to the air space over the territorial sea as well as to its bed and subsoil.

3. The sovereignty over the territorial sea is exercised subject to this Convention and to other rules of international law.

SECTION 2. LIMITS OF THE TERRITORIAL SEA
Article 3
Breadth of the territorial sea

Every State has the right to establish the breadth of its territorial sea up to a limit not exceeding 12 nautical miles, measured from baselines determined in accordance with this Convention.

Article 4
Outer limit of the territorial sea

The outer limit of the territorial sea is the line every point of which is at a distance from the nearest point of the baseline equal to the breadth of the territorial sea.

Article 5
Normal baseline

Except where otherwise provided in this Convention, the normal baseline for measuring the breadth of the territorial sea is the low-water line along the coast as marked on large-scale charts officially recognized by the coastal State.

Article 6
Reefs

In the case of islands situated on atolls or of islands having fringing reefs, the baseline for measuring the breadth of the territorial sea is the seaward low-water line of the reef, as shown by the appropriate symbol on charts officially recognized by the coastal State.

Article 7
Straight baselines

1. [*See* Basic Document 4.5, Art. 4(1).]

2. Where because of the presence of a delta and other natural conditions the coastline is highly unstable, the appropriate points may be selected along the furthest seaward extent of the low-water line and, notwithstanding subsequent regression of the low-water line, the straight baselines shall remain effective until changed by the coastal State in accordance with this Convention.

3. [*See* Basic Document 4.5, Art. 4(2).]

4. Straight baselines shall not be drawn to and from low-tide elevations, unless lighthouses or similar installations which are permanently above sea level have been built on them or except in instances where the drawing of baselines to and from such elevations has received general international recognition.

5. [*See* Basic Document 4.5, Art. 4(4).]

6. The system of straight baselines may not be applied by a State in such a manner as to cut off the territorial sea of another State from the high seas or an exclusive economic zone.

Article 8

Internal waters

1. Except as provided in Part IV, waters on the landward side of the baseline of the territorial sea form part of the internal waters of the State.

2. Where the establishment of a straight baseline in accordance with the method set forth in article 7 has the effect of enclosing as internal waters areas which had not previously been considered as such, a right of innocent passage as provided in this Convention shall exist in those waters.

Article 9

Mouths of rivers

[*See* Basic Document 4.5, Art. 13.]

Article 10

Bays

1. [*See* Basic Document 4.5, Art. 7(1).]

2. [*See* Basic Document 4.5, Art. 7(2).]

3. [*See* Basic Document 4.5, Art. 7(3).]

4. [*See* Basic Document 4.5, Art. 7(4).]

5. [*See* Basic Document 4.5, Art. 7(5).]

6. The foregoing provisions do not apply to so-called "historic" bays, or in any case where the system of straight baselines provided for in article 7 is applied.

Article 11

Ports

For the purpose of delimiting the territorial sea, the outermost permanent harbour works which form an integral part of the harbour system are regarded as forming part of the coast. Off-shore installations and artificial islands shall not be considered as permanent harbour works.

Article 12

Roadsteads

Roadsteads which are normally used for the loading, unloading and anchoring of ships, and which would otherwise be situated wholly or partly outside the outer limit of the territorial sea, are included in the territorial sea.

Article 13

Low-tide elevations

[*See* Basic Document 4.5, Art. 11.]

Article 14

Combination of methods for determining baselines

The coastal State may determine baselines in turn by any of the methods provided for in the foregoing articles to suit different conditions.

Article 15

Delimitation of the territorial sea between States with opposite or adjacent coasts

[*See* Basic Document 4.5, Art. 12(1).]

Article 16

Charts and lists of geographical co-ordinates

1.   The baselines for measuring the breadth of the territorial sea determined in accordance with articles 7, 9 and 10, or the limits derived therefrom, and the lines of delimitation drawn in accordance with articles 12 and 15 shall be shown on charts of a scale or scales adequate for ascertaining their position. Alternatively, a list of geographical co-ordinates of points, specifying the geodetic datum, may be substituted.

2.   The coastal State shall give due publicity to such charts or lists of geographical co-ordinates and shall deposit a copy of each such chart or list with the Secretary–General of the United Nations.

SECTION 3.   INNOCENT PASSAGE IN THE TERRITORIAL SEA
SUBSECTION A.   RULES APPLICABLE TO ALL SHIPS

Article 17

Right of innocent passage

[*See* Basic Document 4.5, Art. 14(1).]

Article 18

Meaning of passage

1.   Passage means navigation through the territorial sea for the purpose of:

(a) traversing that sea without entering internal waters or calling at a roadstead or port facility outside internal waters; or

(b) proceeding to or from internal waters or a call at such roadstead or port facility.

2.   Passage shall be continuous and expeditious. However, passage includes stopping and anchoring, but only in so far as the same are incidental to ordinary navigation or are rendered necessary by *force majeure* or distress or for the purpose of rendering assistance to persons, ships or aircraft in danger or distress.

Article 19

Meaning of innocent passage

1.   [*See* Basic Document 4.5, Art. 14(4).]

2. Passage of a foreign ship shall be considered to be prejudicial to the peace, good order or security of the coastal State if in the territorial sea it engages in any of the following activities:

(a) any threat or use of force against the sovereignty, territorial integrity or political independence of the coastal State, or in any other manner in violation of the principles of international law embodied in the Charter of the United Nations;

(b) any exercise or practice with weapons of any kind;

(c) any act aimed at collecting information to the prejudice of the defence or security of the coastal State;

(d) any act of propaganda aimed at affecting the defence or security of the coastal State;

(e) the launching, landing or taking on board of any aircraft;

(f) the launching, landing or taking on board of any military device;

(g) the loading or unloading of any commodity, currency or person contrary to the customs, fiscal, immigration or sanitary laws and regulations of the coastal State;

(h) any act of wilful and serious pollution contrary to this Convention;

(i) any fishing activities;

(j) the carrying out of research or survey activities;

(k) any act aimed at interfering with any systems of communication or any other facilities or installations of the coastal State;

(*l*) any other activity not having a direct bearing on passage.

Article 20
Submarines and other underwater vehicles

In the territorial sea, submarines and other underwater vehicles are required to navigate on the surface and to show their flag.

Article 21
Laws and regulations of the coastal State relating to innocent passage

1. The coastal State may adopt laws and regulations, in conformity with the provisions of this Convention and other rules of international law, relating to innocent passage through the territorial sea, in respect of all or any of the following:

(a) the safety of navigation and the regulation of maritime traffic;

(b) the protection of navigational aids and facilities and other facilities or installations;

(c) the protection of cables and pipelines;

(d) the conservation of the living resources of the sea;

(e) the prevention of infringement of the fisheries laws and regulations of the coastal State;

(f) the preservation of the environment of the coastal State and the prevention, reduction and control of pollution thereof;

(g) marine scientific research and hydrographic surveys;

(h) the prevention of infringement of the customs, fiscal, immigration or sanitary laws and regulations of the coastal State.

2. Such laws and regulations shall not apply to the design, construction, manning or equipment of foreign ships unless they are giving effect to generally accepted international rules or standards.

3. The coastal State shall give due publicity to all such laws and regulations.

4. Foreign ships exercising the right of innocent passage through the territorial sea shall comply with all such laws and regulations and all generally accepted international regulations relating to the prevention of collisions at sea.

Article 22
Sea lanes and traffic separation schemes in the territorial sea

1. The coastal State may, where necessary, having regard to the safety of navigation, require foreign ships exercising the right of innocent passage through its territorial sea to use such sea lanes and traffic separation schemes as it may designate or prescribe for the regulation of the passage of ships.

2. In particular, tankers, nuclear-powered ships and ships carrying nuclear or other inherently dangerous or noxious substances or materials may be required to confine their passage to such sea lanes.

3. In the designation of sea lanes and the prescription of traffic separation schemes under this article, the coastal State shall take into account:

(a) the recommendations of the competent international organization;

(b) any channels customarily used for international navigation;

(c) the special characteristics of particular ships and channels; and

(d) the density of traffic.

4. The coastal State shall clearly indicate such sea lanes and traffic separation schemes on charts to which due publicity shall be given.

Article 23
*Foreign nuclear-powered ships and ships carrying nuclear
or other inherently dangerous or noxious substances*

Foreign nuclear-powered ships and ships carrying nuclear or other inherently dangerous or noxious substances shall, when exercising the right of innocent passage through the territorial sea, carry documents and observe special precautionary measures established for such ships by international agreements.

Article 24
Duties of the coastal State

1. The coastal State shall not hamper the innocent passage of foreign ships through the territorial sea except in accordance with this Convention. In particular, in the application of this Convention or of any laws or regulations adopted in conformity with this Convention, the coastal State shall not:

(a) impose requirements on foreign ships which have the practical effect of denying or impairing the right of innocent passage; or

(b) discriminate in form or in fact against the ships of any State or against ships carrying cargoes to, from or on behalf of any State.

2. [*See* Basic Document 4.5, Art. 15(2).]

Article 25

Rights of protection of the coastal State

1. [*See* Basic Document 4.5, Art. 16(1).]

2. In the case of ships proceeding to internal waters or a call at a port facility outside internal waters, the coastal State also has the right to take the necessary steps to prevent any breach of the conditions to which admission of those ships to internal waters or such a call is subject.

3. The coastal State may, without discrimination in form or in fact among foreign ships, suspend temporarily in specified areas of its territorial sea the innocent passage of foreign ships if such suspension is essential for the protection of its security, including weapons exercises. Such suspension shall take effect only after having been duly published.

Article 26

Charges which may be levied upon foreign ships

[*See* Basic Document 4.5, Art. 18.]

SUBSECTION B. RULES APPLICABLE TO MERCHANT SHIPS AND GOVERNMENT SHIPS OPERATED FOR COMMERCIAL PURPOSES

Article 27

Criminal jurisdiction on board a foreign ship

1. The criminal jurisdiction of the coastal State should not be exercised on board a foreign ship passing through the territorial sea to arrest any person or to conduct any investigation in connection with any crime committed on board the ship during its passage, save only in the following cases:

(a) if the consequences of the crime extend to the coastal State;

(b) if the crime is of a kind to disturb the peace of the country or the good order of the territorial sea;

(c) if the assistance of the local authorities has been requested by the master of the ship or by a diplomatic agent or consular officer of the flag State; or

(d) if such measures are necessary for the suppression of illicit traffic in narcotic drugs or psychotropic substances.

2. [*See* Basic Document 4.5, Art. 19(2).]

3. [*See* Basic Document 4.5, Art. 19(3).]

4. [*See* Basic Document 4.5, Art. 19(4).]

5. Except as provided in Part XII or with respect to violations of laws and regulations adopted in accordance with Part V, the coastal State may not take any steps on board a foreign ship passing through the territorial sea to arrest any person or to conduct any investigation in connection with any

crime committed before the ship entered the territorial sea, if the ship, proceeding from a foreign port, is only passing through the territorial sea without entering internal waters.

Article 28
Civil jurisdiction in relation to foreign ships

[*See* Basic Document 4.5, Art. 20.]

SUBSECTION C. RULES APPLICABLE TO WARSHIPS AND OTHER GOVERNMENT SHIPS OPERATED FOR NON–COMMERCIAL PURPOSES

Article 29
Definition of warships

For the purposes of this Convention, "warship" means a ship belonging to the armed forces of a State bearing the external marks distinguishing such ships of its nationality, under the command of an officer duly commissioned by the government of the State and whose name appears in the appropriate service list or its equivalent, and manned by a crew which is under regular armed forces discipline.

Article 30
Non-compliance by warships with the laws and regulations of the coastal State

If any warship does not comply with the laws and regulations of the coastal State concerning passage through the territorial sea and disregards any request for compliance therewith which is made to it, the coastal State may require it to leave the territorial sea immediately.

Article 31
Responsibility of the flag State for damage caused by a warship or other government ship operated for non-commercial purposes

The flag State shall bear international responsibility for any loss or damage to the coastal State resulting from the non-compliance by a warship or other government ship operated for non-commercial purposes with the laws and regulations of the coastal State concerning passage through the territorial sea or with the provisions of this Convention or other rules of international law.

Article 32
Immunities of warships and other government ships operated for non-commercial purposes

With such exceptions as are contained in subsection A and in articles 30 and 31, nothing in this Convention affects the immunities of warships and other government ships operated for non-commercial purposes.

SECTION 4. CONTIGUOUS ZONE

Article 33
Contiguous zone

1.   [*See* Basic Document 4.5, Art. 24(1).]

2.   The contiguous zone may not extend beyond 24 nautical miles from the baselines from which the breadth of the territorial sea is measured.

PART III
STRAITS USED FOR INTERNATIONAL NAVIGATION
SECTION 1. GENERAL PROVISIONS
Article 34
Legal status of waters forming straits used for international navigation

1. The régime of passage through straits used for international naviga-tion established in this Part shall not in other respects affect the legal status of the waters forming such straits or the exercise by the States bordering the straits of their sovereignty or jurisdiction over such waters and their air space, bed and subsoil.

2. The sovereignty or jurisdiction of the States bordering the straits is exercised subject to this Part and to other rules of international law.

Article 35
Scope of this Part

Nothing in this Part affects:

(a) any areas of internal waters within a strait, except where the establishment of a straight baseline in accordance with the method set forth in article 7 has the effect of enclosing as internal waters areas which had not previously been considered as such;

(b) the legal status of the waters beyond the territorial seas of States bordering straits as exclusive economic zones or high seas; or

(c) the legal régime in straits in which passage is regulated in whole or in part by long-standing international conventions in force specifically relating to such straits.

Article 36
High seas routes or routes through exclusive economic zones through straits used for international navigation

This Part does not apply to a strait used for international navigation if there exists through the strait a route through the high seas or through an exclusive economic zone of similar convenience with respect to navigational and hydrographical characteristics; in such routes, the other relevant Parts of this Convention, including the provisions regarding the freedoms of naviga-tion and overflight, apply.

SECTION 2. TRANSIT PASSAGE
Article 37
Scope of this section

This section applies to straits which are used for international navigation between one part of the high seas or an exclusive economic zone and another part of the high seas or an exclusive economic zone.

Article 38
Right of transit passage

1. In straits referred to in article 37, all ships and aircraft enjoy the right of transit passage, which shall not be impeded; except that, if the strait is formed by an island of a State bordering the strait and its mainland, transit passage shall not apply if there exists seaward of the island a route through

the high seas or through an exclusive economic zone of similar convenience with respect to navigational and hydrographical characteristics.

2. Transit passage means the exercise in accordance with this Part of the freedom of navigation and overflight solely for the purpose of continuous and expeditious transit of the strait between one part of the high seas or an exclusive economic zone and another part of the high seas or an exclusive economic zone. However, the requirement of continuous and expeditious transit does not preclude passage through the strait for the purpose of entering, leaving or returning from a State bordering the strait, subject to the conditions of entry to that State.

3. Any activity which is not an exercise of the right of transit passage through a strait remains subject to the other applicable provisions of this Convention.

Article 39
Duties of ships and aircraft during transit passage

1. Ships and aircraft, while exercising the right of transit passage, shall:

(a) proceed without delay through or over the strait;

(b) refrain from any threat or use of force against the sovereignty, territorial integrity or political independence of States bordering the strait, or in any other manner in violation of the principles of international law embodied in the Charter of the United Nations;

(c) refrain from any activities other than those incident to their normal modes of continuous and expeditious transit unless rendered necessary by *force majeure* or by distress;

(d) comply with other relevant provisions of this Part.

* * *

Article 40
Research and survey activities

During transit passage, foreign ships, including marine scientific research and hydrographic survey ships, may not carry out any research or survey activities without the prior authorization of the States bordering straits.

Article 41
Sea lanes and traffic separation schemes in straits
used for international navigation

1. In conformity with this Part, States bordering straits may designate sea lanes and prescribe traffic separation schemes for navigation in straits where necessary to promote the safe passage of ships.

2. Such States may, when circumstances require, and after giving due publicity thereto, substitute other sea lanes or traffic separation schemes for any sea lanes or traffic separation schemes previously designated or prescribed by them.

3. Such sea lanes and traffic separation schemes shall conform to generally accepted international regulations.

4. Before designating or substituting sea lanes or prescribing or substituting traffic separation schemes, States bordering straits shall refer proposals to the competent international organization with a view to their adoption. The organization may adopt only such sea lanes and traffic separation schemes as may be agreed with the States bordering the straits, after which the States may designate, prescribe or substitute them.

5. In respect of a strait where sea lanes or traffic separation schemes through the waters of two or more States bordering the strait are being proposed, the States concerned shall co-operate in formulating proposals in consultation with the competent international organization.

6. States bordering straits shall clearly indicate all sea lanes and traffic separation schemes designated or prescribed by them on charts to which due publicity shall be given.

7. Ships in transit passage shall respect applicable sea lanes and traffic separation schemes established in accordance with this article.

Article 42
Laws and regulations of States bordering straits relating to transit passage

1. Subject to the provisions of this section, States bordering straits may adopt laws and regulations relating to transit passage through straits, in respect of all or any of the following:

(a) the safety of navigation and the regulation of maritime traffic, as provided in article 41;

(b) the prevention, reduction and control of pollution, by giving effect to applicable international regulations regarding the discharge of oil, oily wastes and other noxious substances in the strait;

(c) with respect to fishing vessels, the prevention of fishing, including the stowage of fishing gear;

(d) the loading or unloading of any commodity, currency or person in contravention of the customs, fiscal, immigration or sanitary laws and regulations of States bordering straits.

2. Such laws and regulations shall not discriminate in form or in fact among foreign ships or in their application have the practical effect of denying, hampering or impairing the right of transit passage as defined in this section.

3. States bordering straits shall give due publicity to all such laws and regulations.

4. Foreign ships exercising the right of transit passage shall comply with such laws and regulations.

5. The flag State of a ship or the State of registry of an aircraft entitled to sovereign immunity which acts in a manner contrary to such laws and regulations or other provisions of this Part shall bear international responsibility for any loss or damage which results to States bordering straits.

Article 43
Navigational and safety aids and other improvements and the prevention, reduction and control of pollution

User States and States bordering a strait should by agreement co-operate:

(a) in the establishment and maintenance in a strait of necessary navigational and safety aids or other improvements in aid of international navigation; and

(b) for the prevention, reduction and control of pollution from ships.

Article 44
Duties of States bordering straits

States bordering straits shall not hamper transit passage and shall give appropriate publicity to any danger to navigation or overflight within or over the strait of which they have knowledge. There shall be no suspension of transit passage.

SECTION 3. INNOCENT PASSAGE
Article 45
Innocent passage

1. The régime of innocent passage, in accordance with Part II, section 3, shall apply in straits used for international navigation:

(a) excluded from the application of the régime of transit passage under article 38, paragraph 1; or

(b) between a part of the high seas or an exclusive economic zone and the territorial sea of a foreign State.

2. There shall be no suspension of innocent passage through such straits.

PART IV
ARCHIPELAGIC STATES
Article 46
Use of terms

For the purposes of this Convention:

(a) "archipelagic State" means a State constituted wholly by one or more archipelagos and may include other islands;

(b) "archipelago" means a group of islands, including parts of islands, interconnecting waters and other natural features which are so closely interrelated that such islands, waters and other natural features form an intrinsic geographical, economic and political entity, or which historically have been regarded as such.

Article 47
Archipelagic baselines

1. An archipelagic State may draw straight archipelagic baselines joining the outermost points of the outermost islands and drying reefs of the archipelago provided that within such baselines are included the main islands and an area in which the ratio of the area of the water to the area of the land, including atolls, is between 1 to 1 and 9 to 1.

2. The length of such baselines shall not exceed 100 nautical miles, except that up to 3 per cent of the total number of baselines enclosing any archipelago may exceed that length, up to a maximum length of 125 nautical miles.

3. The drawing of such baselines shall not depart to any appreciable extent from the general configuration of the archipelago.

4. Such baselines shall not be drawn to and from low-tide elevations, unless lighthouses or similar installations which are permanently above sea level have been built on them or where a low-tide elevation is situated wholly or partly at a distance not exceeding the breadth of the territorial sea from the nearest island.

5. The system of such baselines shall not be applied by an archipelagic State in such a manner as to cut off from the high seas or the exclusive economic zone the territorial sea of another State.

6. If a part of the archipelagic waters of an archipelagic State lies between two parts of an immediately adjacent neighbouring State, existing rights and all other legitimate interests which the latter State has traditionally exercised in such waters and all rights stipulated by agreement between those States shall continue and be respected.

* * *

Article 48

Measurement of the breadth of the territorial sea, the contiguous zone, the exclusive economic zone and the continental shelf

The breadth of the territorial sea, the contiguous zone, the exclusive economic zone and the continental shelf shall be measured from archipelagic baselines drawn in accordance with article 47.

Article 49

Legal status of archipelagic waters, of the air space over archipelagic waters and of their bed and subsoil

1. The sovereignty of an archipelagic State extends to the waters enclosed by the archipelagic baselines drawn in accordance with article 47, described as archipelagic waters, regardless of their depth or distance from the coast.

2. This sovereignty extends to the air space over the archipelagic waters, as well as to their bed and subsoil, and the resources contained therein.

* * *

Article 50

Delimitation of internal waters

Within its archipelagic waters, the archipelagic State may draw closing lines for the delimitation of internal waters, in accordance with articles 9, 10 and 11.

Article 51

Existing agreements, traditional fishing rights and existing submarine cables

1. Without prejudice to article 49, an archipelagic State shall respect existing agreements with other States and shall recognize traditional fishing rights and other legitimate activities of the immediately adjacent neighbouring States in certain areas falling within archipelagic waters. The terms and

conditions for the exercise of such rights and activities, including the nature, the extent and the areas to which they apply, shall, at the request of any of the States concerned, be regulated by bilateral agreements between them. Such rights shall not be transferred to or shared with third States or their nationals.

2. An archipelagic State shall respect existing submarine cables laid by other States and passing through its waters without making a landfall. An archipelagic State shall permit the maintenance and replacement of such cables upon receiving due notice of their location and the intention to repair or replace them.

Article 52

Right of innocent passage

1. Subject to article 53 and without prejudice to article 50, ships of all States enjoy the right of innocent passage through archipelagic waters, in accordance with Part II, section 3.

2. The archipelagic State may, without discrimination in form or in fact among foreign ships, suspend temporarily in specified areas of its archipelagic waters the innocent passage of foreign ships if such suspension is essential for the protection of its security. Such suspension shall take effect only after having been duly published.

Article 53

Right of archipelagic sea lanes passage

1. An archipelagic State may designate sea lanes and air routes thereabove, suitable for the continuous and expeditious passage of foreign ships and aircraft through or over its archipelagic waters and the adjacent territorial sea.

2. All ships and aircraft enjoy the right of archipelagic sea lanes passage in such sea lanes and air routes.

* * *

6. An archipelagic State which designates sea lanes under this article may also prescribe traffic separation schemes for the safe passage of ships through narrow channels in such sea lanes.

* * *

8. Such sea lanes and traffic separation schemes shall conform to generally accepted international regulations.

Article 54

Duties of ships and aircraft during their passage, research and survey activities, duties of the archipelagic State and laws and regulations of the archipelagic State relating to archipelagic sea lanes passage

Articles 39, 40, 42 and 44 apply *mutatis mutandis* to archipelagic sea lanes passage.

PART V
EXCLUSIVE ECONOMIC ZONE

Article 55

Specific legal régime of the exclusive economic zone

The exclusive economic zone is an area beyond and adjacent to the territorial sea, subject to the specific legal régime established in this Part, under which the rights and jurisdiction of the coastal State and the rights and freedoms of other States are governed by the relevant provisions of this Convention.

Article 56

Rights, jurisdiction and duties of the coastal State in the exclusive economic zone

1. In the exclusive economic zone, the coastal State has:

(a) sovereign rights for the purpose of exploring and exploiting, conserving and managing the natural resources, whether living or non-living, of the waters superjacent to the sea-bed and of the sea-bed and its subsoil, and with regard to other activities for the economic exploitation and exploration of the zone, such as the production of energy from the water, currents and winds;

(b) jurisdiction as provided for in the relevant provisions of this Convention with regard to:

(i) the establishment and use of artificial islands, installations and structures;

(ii) marine scientific research;

(iii) the protection and preservation of the marine environment;

(c) other rights and duties provided for in this Convention.

2. In exercising its rights and performing its duties under this Convention in the exclusive economic zone, the coastal State shall have due regard to the rights and duties of other States and shall act in a manner compatible with the provisions of this Convention.

3. The rights set out in this article with respect to the sea-bed and subsoil shall be exercised in accordance with Part VI.

Article 57

Breadth of the exclusive economic zone

The exclusive economic zone shall not extend beyond 200 nautical miles from the baselines from which the breadth of the territorial sea is measured.

Article 58

Rights and duties of other States in the exclusive economic zone

1. In the exclusive economic zone, all States, whether coastal or land-locked, enjoy, subject to the relevant provisions of this Convention, the freedoms referred to in article 87 of navigation and overflight and of the laying of submarine cables and pipelines, and other internationally lawful uses of the sea related to these freedoms, such as those associated with the operation of ships, aircraft and submarine cables and pipelines, and compatible with the other provisions of this Convention.

2. Articles 88 to 115 and other pertinent rules of international law apply to the exclusive economic zone in so far as they are not incompatible with this Part.

3. In exercising their rights and performing their duties under this Convention in the exclusive economic zone, States shall have due regard to the rights and duties of the coastal State and shall comply with the laws and

regulations adopted by the coastal State in accordance with the provisions of this Convention and other rules of international law in so far as they are not incompatible with this Part.

Article 59

Basis for the resolution of conflicts regarding the attribution of rights and jurisdiction in the exclusive economic zone

In cases where this Convention does not attribute rights or jurisdiction to the coastal State or to other States within the exclusive economic zone, and a conflict arises between the interests of the coastal State and any other State or States, the conflict should be resolved on the basis of equity and in the light of all the relevant circumstances, taking into account the respective importance of the interests involved to the parties as well as to the international community as a whole.

Article 60

Artificial islands, installations and structures in the exclusive economic zone

1. In the exclusive economic zone, the coastal State shall have the exclusive right to construct and to authorize and regulate the construction, operation and use of:

(a) artificial islands;

(b) installations and structures for the purposes provided for in article 56 and other economic purposes;

(c) installations and structures which may interfere with the exercise of the rights of the coastal State in the zone.

2. The coastal State shall have exclusive jurisdiction over such artificial islands, installations and structures, including jurisdiction with regard to customs, fiscal, health, safety and immigration laws and regulations.

3. Due notice must be given of the construction of such artificial islands, installations or structures, and permanent means for giving warning of their presence must be maintained. * * *

* * *

7. Artificial islands, installations and structures and the safety zones around them may not be established where interference may be caused to the use of recognized sea lanes essential to international navigation.

8. Artificial islands, installations and structures do not possess the status of islands. They have no territorial sea of their own, and their presence does not affect the delimitation of the territorial sea, the exclusive economic zone or the continental shelf.

Article 61

Conservation of the living resources

1. The coastal State shall determine the allowable catch of the living resources in its exclusive economic zone.

2. The coastal State, taking into account the best scientific evidence available to it, shall ensure through proper conservation and management measures that the maintenance of the living resources in the exclusive economic zone is not endangered by over-exploitation. As appropriate, the

coastal State and competent international organizations, whether subregional, regional or global, shall co-operate to this end.

3. Such measures shall also be designed to maintain or restore populations of harvested species at levels which can produce the maximum sustainable yield, as qualified by relevant environmental and economic factors, including the economic needs of coastal fishing communities and the special requirements of developing States, and taking into account fishing patterns, the interdependence of stocks and any generally recommended international minimum standards, whether subregional, regional or global.

4. In taking such measures the coastal State shall take into consideration the effects on species associated with or dependent upon harvested species with a view to maintaining or restoring populations of such associated or dependent species above levels at which their reproduction may become seriously threatened.

5. Available scientific information, catch and fishing effort statistics, and other data relevant to the conservation of fish stocks shall be contributed and exchanged on a regular basis through competent international organizations, whether subregional, regional or global, where appropriate and with participation by all States concerned, including States whose nationals are allowed to fish in the exclusive economic zone.

Article 62

Utilization of the living resources

1. The coastal State shall promote the objective of optimum utilization of the living resources in the exclusive economic zone without prejudice to article 61.

2. The coastal State shall determine its capacity to harvest the living resources of the exclusive economic zone. Where the coastal State does not have the capacity to harvest the entire allowable catch, it shall, through agreements or other arrangements and pursuant to the terms, conditions, laws and regulations referred to in paragraph 4, give other States access to the surplus of the allowable catch, having particular regard to the provisions of articles 69 and 70, especially in relation to the developing States mentioned therein.

3. In giving access to other States to its exclusive economic zone under this article, the coastal State shall take into account all relevant factors, including, *inter alia,* the significance of the living resources of the area to the economy of the coastal State concerned and its other national interests, the provisions of articles 69 and 70, the requirements of developing States in the subregion or region in harvesting part of the surplus and the need to minimize economic dislocation in States whose nationals have habitually fished in the zone or which have made substantial efforts in research and identification of stocks.

4. Nationals of other States fishing in the exclusive economic zone shall comply with the conservation measures and with the other terms and conditions established in the laws and regulations of the coastal State. These laws and regulations shall be consistent with this Convention. * * *

5. Coastal States shall give due notice of conservation and management laws and regulations.

Article 63

Stocks occurring within the exclusive economic zones of two or more coastal States or both within the exclusive economic zone and in an area beyond and adjacent to it

1. Where the same stock or stocks of associated species occur within the exclusive economic zones of two or more coastal States, these States shall seek, either directly or through appropriate subregional or regional organizations, to agree upon the measures necessary to co-ordinate and ensure the conservation and development of such stocks without prejudice to the other provisions of this Part.

2. Where the same stock or stocks of associated species occur both within the exclusive economic zone and in an area beyond and adjacent to the zone, the coastal State and the States fishing for such stocks in the adjacent area shall seek, either directly or through appropriate subregional or regional organizations, to agree upon the measures necessary for the conservation of these stocks in the adjacent area.

Article 64

Highly migratory species

1. The coastal State and other States whose nationals fish in the region for the highly migratory species listed in Annex I shall co-operate directly or through appropriate international organizations with a view to ensuring conservation and promoting the objective of optimum utilization of such species throughout the region, both within and beyond the exclusive economic zone. In regions for which no appropriate international organization exists, the coastal State and other States whose nationals harvest these species in the region shall co-operate to establish such an organization and participate in its work.

2. The provisions of paragraph 1 apply in addition to the other provisions of this Part.

Article 65

Marine mammals

Nothing in this Part restricts the right of a coastal State or the competence of an international organization, as appropriate, to prohibit, limit or regulate the exploitation of marine mammals more strictly than provided for in this Part. States shall co-operate with a view to the conservation of marine mammals and in the case of cetaceans shall in particular work through the appropriate international organizations for their conservation, management and study.

Article 66

Anadromous stocks

1. States in whose rivers anadromous stocks originate shall have the primary interest in and responsibility for such stocks.

* * *

Article 67
Catadromous species

1. A coastal State in whose waters catadromous species spend the greater part of their life cycle shall have responsibility for the management of these species and shall ensure the ingress and egress of migrating fish.

* * *

Article 68
Sedentary species

This Part does not apply to sedentary species as defined in article 77, paragraph 4.

Article 69
Right of land-locked States

1. Land-locked States shall have the right to participate, on an equitable basis, in the exploitation of an appropriate part of the surplus of the living resources of the exclusive economic zones of coastal States of the same subregion or region, taking into account the relevant economic and geographical circumstances of all the States concerned and in conformity with the provisions of this article and of articles 61 and 62.

2. The terms and modalities of such participation shall be established by the States concerned through bilateral, subregional or regional agreements taking into account, *inter alia:*

(a) the need to avoid effects detrimental to fishing communities or fishing industries of the coastal State;

(b) the extent to which the land-locked State, in accordance with the provisions of this article, is participating or is entitled to participate under existing bilateral, subregional or regional agreements in the exploitation of living resources of the exclusive economic zones of other coastal States;

(c) the extent to which other land-locked States and geographically disadvantaged States are participating in the exploitation of the living resources of the exclusive economic zone of the coastal State and the consequent need to avoid a particular burden for any single coastal State or a part of it;

(d) the nutritional needs of the populations of the respective States.

3. When the harvesting capacity of a coastal State approaches a point which would enable it to harvest the entire allowable catch of the living resources in its exclusive economic zone, the coastal State and other States concerned shall cooperate in the establishment of equitable arrangements on a bilateral, subregional or regional basis to allow for participation of developing land-locked States of the same subregion or region in the exploitation of the living resources of the exclusive economic zones of coastal States of the subregion or region, as may be appropriate in the circumstances and on terms satisfactory to all parties. In the implementation of this provision the factors mentioned in paragraph 2 shall also be taken into account.

4. Developed land-locked States shall, under the provisions of this article, be entitled to participate in the exploitation of living resources only in the exclusive economic zones of developed coastal States of the same subregion or region having regard to the extent to which the coastal State, in giving access to other States to the living resources of its exclusive economic zone, has taken into account the need to minimize detrimental effects on fishing communities and economic dislocation in States whose nationals have habitually fished in the zone.

5. The above provisions are without prejudice to arrangements agreed upon in subregions or regions where the coastal States may grant to land-locked States of the same subregion or region equal or preferential rights for the exploitation of the living resources in the exclusive economic zones.

Article 70
Right of geographically disadvantaged States

[This article is in all essential respects identical to Article 69, supra.]

Article 71
Non-applicability of articles 69 and 70

The provisions of articles 69 and 70 do not apply in the case of a coastal State whose economy is overwhelmingly dependent on the exploitation of the living resources of its exclusive economic zone.

Article 72
Restrictions on transfer of rights

* * *

Article 73
Enforcement of laws and regulations of the coastal State

1. The coastal State may, in the exercise of its sovereign rights to explore, exploit, conserve and manage the living resources in the exclusive economic zone, take such measures, including boarding, inspection, arrest and judicial proceedings, as may be necessary to ensure compliance with the laws and regulations adopted by it in conformity with this Convention.

2. Arrested vessels and their crews shall be promptly released upon the posting of reasonable bond or other security.

3. Coastal State penalties for violations of fisheries laws and regulations in the exclusive economic zone may not include imprisonment, in the absence of agreements to the contrary by the States concerned, or any other form of corporal punishment.

4. In cases of arrest or detention of foreign vessels the coastal State shall promptly notify the flag State, through appropriate channels, of the action taken and of any penalties subsequently imposed.

Article 74
Delimitation of the exclusive economic zone between States with opposite or adjacent coasts

1. The delimitation of the exclusive economic zone between States with opposite or adjacent coasts shall be effected by agreement on the basis of

international law, as referred to in Article 38 of the Statute of the International Court of Justice, in order to achieve an equitable solution.

2. If no agreement can be reached within a reasonable period of time, the States concerned shall resort to the procedures provided for in Part XV.

* * *

Article 75

Charts and lists of geographical co-ordinates

* * *

PART VI
CONTINENTAL SHELF

Article 76

Definition of the continental shelf

1. The continental shelf of a coastal State comprises the sea-bed and subsoil of the submarine areas that extend beyond its territorial sea throughout the natural prolongation of its land territory to the outer edge of the continental margin, or to a distance of 200 nautical miles from the baselines from which the breadth of the territorial sea is measured where the outer edge of the continental margin does not extend up to that distance.

2. The continental shelf of a coastal State shall not extend beyond the limits provided for in paragraphs 4 to 6.

3. The continental margin comprises the submerged prolongation of the land mass of the coastal State, and consists of the sea-bed and subsoil of the shelf, the slope and the rise. It does not include the deep ocean floor with its oceanic ridges or the subsoil thereof.

4. (a) For the purposes of this Convention, the coastal State shall establish the outer edge of the continental margin wherever the margin extends beyond 200 nautical miles from the baselines from which the breadth of the territorial sea is measured, by either:

(i) a line delineated in accordance with paragraph 7 by reference to the outermost fixed points at each of which the thickness of sedimentary rocks is at least 1 per cent of the shortest distance from such point to the foot of the continental slope; or

(ii) a line delineated in accordance with paragraph 7 by reference to fixed points not more than 60 nautical miles from the foot of the continental slope.

(b) In the absence of evidence to the contrary, the foot of the continental slope shall be determined as the point of maximum change in the gradient at its base.

5. The fixed points comprising the line of the outer limits of the continental shelf on the sea-bed, drawn in accordance with paragraph 4(a)(i) and (ii), either shall not exceed 350 nautical miles from the baselines from which the breadth of the territorial sea is measured or shall not exceed 100 nautical miles from the 2,500 metre isobath, which is a line connecting the depths of 2,500 metres.

6. Notwithstanding the provisions of paragraph 5, on submarine ridges, the outer limit of the continental shelf shall not exceed 350 nautical miles from the baselines from which the breadth of the territorial sea is measured. This paragraph does not apply to submarine elevations that are natural components of the continental margin, such as its plateaux, rises, caps, banks and spurs.

7. The coastal State shall delineate the outer limits of its continental shelf, where that shelf extends beyond 200 nautical miles from the baselines from which the breadth of the territorial sea is measured, by straight lines not exceeding 60 nautical miles in length, connecting fixed points, defined by coordinates of latitude and longitude.

* * *

Article 77
Rights of the coastal State over the continental shelf

1. [*See* Basic Document 4.4, Art. 2(1).]

2. The rights referred to in paragraph 1 are exclusive in the sense that if the coastal State does not explore the continental shelf or exploit its natural resources, no one may undertake these activities without the express consent of the coastal State.

3. [*See* Basic Document 4.4, Art. 2(3).]

4. [*See* Basic Document 4.4, Art. 2(4).]

Article 78
Legal status of the superjacent waters and air space and the rights and freedoms of other States

1. The rights of the coastal State over the continental shelf do not affect the legal status of the superjacent waters or of the air space above those waters.

2. The exercise of the rights of the coastal State over the continental shelf must not infringe or result in any unjustifiable interference with navigation and other rights and freedoms of other States as provided for in this Convention.

Article 79
Submarine cables and pipelines on the continental shelf

1. All States are entitled to lay submarine cables and pipelines on the continental shelf, in accordance with the provisions of this article.

2. Subject to its right to take reasonable measures for the exploration of the continental shelf, the exploitation of its natural resources and the prevention, reduction and control of pollution from pipelines, the coastal State may not impede the laying or maintenance of such cables or pipelines.

3. The delineation of the course for the laying of such pipelines on the continental shelf is subject to the consent of the coastal State.

4. Nothing in this Part affects the right of the coastal State to establish conditions for cables or pipelines entering its territory or territorial sea, or its jurisdiction over cables and pipelines constructed or used in connection with the exploration of its continental shelf or exploitation of its resources or the

operations of artificial islands, installations and structures under its jurisdiction.

5. When laying submarine cables or pipelines, States shall have due regard to cables or pipelines already in position. In particular, possibilities of repairing existing cables or pipelines shall not be prejudiced.

Article 80

Artificial islands, installations and structures on the continental shelf

Article 60 applies *mutatis mutandis* to artificial islands, installations and structures on the continental shelf.

Article 81

Drilling on the continental shelf

The coastal State shall have the exclusive right to authorize and regulate drilling on the continental shelf for all purposes.

Article 82

Payments and contributions with respect to the exploitation of the continental shelf beyond 200 nautical miles

1. The coastal State shall make payments or contributions in kind in respect of the exploitation of the non-living resources of the continental shelf beyond 200 nautical miles from the baselines from which the breadth of the territorial sea is measured.

2. The payments and contributions shall be made annually with respect to all production at a site after the first five years of production at that site. For the sixth year, the rate of payment or contribution shall be 1 per cent of the value or volume of production at the site. The rate shall increase by 1 per cent for each subsequent year until the twelfth year and shall remain at 7 per cent thereafter. Production does not include resources used in connection with exploitation.

3. A developing State which is a net importer of a mineral resource produced from its continental shelf is exempt from making such payments or contributions in respect of that mineral resource.

4. The payments or contributions shall be made through the Authority, which shall distribute them to States Parties to this Convention, on the basis of equitable sharing criteria, taking into account the interests and needs of developing States, particularly the least developed and the land-locked among them.

Article 83

Delimitation of the continental shelf between States with opposite or adjacent coasts

1. The delimitation of the continental shelf between States with opposite or adjacent coasts shall be effected by agreement on the basis of international law, as referred to in Article 38 of the Statute of the International Court of Justice, in order to achieve an equitable solution.

2. If no agreement can be reached within a reasonable period of time, the States concerned shall resort to the procedures provided for in Part XV.

Article 84

Charts and lists of geographical co-ordinates

* * *

Article 85

Tunnelling

This Part does not prejudice the right of the coastal State to exploit the subsoil by means of tunnelling, irrespective of the depth of water above the subsoil.

PART VII

HIGH SEAS

SECTION 1.   GENERAL PROVISIONS

Article 86

Application of the provisions of this Part

The provisions of this Part apply to all parts of the sea that are not included in the exclusive economic zone, in the territorial sea or in the internal waters of a State, or in the archipelagic waters of an archipelagic State.   This article does not entail any abridgement of the freedoms enjoyed by all States in the exclusive economic zone in accordance with article 58.

Article 87

Freedom of the high seas

1.   The high seas are open to all States, whether coastal or land-locked. Freedom of the high seas is exercised under the conditions laid down by this Convention and by other rules of international law.   It comprises, *inter alia,* both for coastal and land-locked States:

(a) freedom of navigation;

(b) freedom of overflight;

(c) freedom to lay submarine cables and pipelines, subject to Part VI;

(d) freedom to construct artificial islands and other installations permitted under international law, subject to Part VI;

(e) freedom of fishing, subject to the conditions laid down in section 2;

(f) freedom of scientific research, subject to Parts VI and XIII.

2.   These freedoms shall be exercised by all States with due regard for the interests of other States in their exercise of the freedom of the high seas, and also with due regard for the rights under this Convention with respect to activities in the Area.

Article 88

Reservation of the high seas for peaceful purposes

The high seas shall be reserved for peaceful purposes.

Article 89

Invalidity of claims of sovereignty over the high seas

No State may validly purport to subject any part of the high seas to its sovereignty.

Article 90

Right of navigation

[*See* Basic Document 4.3, Art. 4.]

Article 91

Nationality of ships

[*See* Basic Document 4.3, Art. 5.]

Article 92

Status of ships

[*See* Basic Document 4.3, Art. 6.]

Article 93

Ships flying the flag of the United Nations, its specialized agencies and the International Atomic Energy Agency

The preceding articles do not prejudice the question of ships employed on the official service of the United Nations, its specialized agencies or the International Atomic Energy Agency, flying the flag of the organization.

Article 94

Duties of the flag State

1. Every State shall effectively exercise its jurisdiction and control in administrative, technical and social matters over ships flying its flag.

2. In particular every State shall:

(a) maintain a register of ships containing the names and particulars of ships flying its flag, except those which are excluded from generally accepted international regulations on account of their small size; and

(b) assume jurisdiction under its internal law over each ship flying its flag and its master, officers and crew in respect of administrative, technical and social matters concerning the ship.

3. Every State shall take such measures for ships flying its flag as are necessary to ensure safety at sea with regard, *inter alia,* to:

(a) the construction, equipment and seaworthiness of ships;

(b) the manning of ships, labour conditions and the training of crews, taking into account the applicable international instruments;

(c) the use of signals, the maintenance of communications and the prevention of collisions.

4. Such measures shall include those necessary to ensure:

(a) that each ship, before registration and thereafter at appropriate intervals, is surveyed by a qualified surveyor of ships, and has on board such charts, nautical publications and navigational equipment and instruments as are appropriate for the safe navigation of the ship;

(b) that each ship is in the charge of a master and officers who possess appropriate qualifications, in particular in seamanship, navigation, communications and marine engineering, and that the crew is appropriate in qualification and numbers for the type, size, machinery and equipment of the ship;

(c) that the master, officers and, to the extent appropriate, the crew are fully conversant with and required to observe the applicable international regulations concerning the safety of life at sea, the prevention of collisions, the prevention, reduction and control of marine pollution, and the maintenance of communications by radio.

5. In taking the measures called for in paragraphs 3 and 4 each State is required to conform to generally accepted international regulations, procedures and practices and to take any steps which may be necessary to secure their observance.

6. A State which has clear grounds to believe that proper jurisdiction and control with respect to a ship have not been exercised may report the facts to the flag State. Upon receiving such a report, the flag State shall investigate the matter and, if appropriate, take any action necessary to remedy the situation.

7. Each State shall cause an inquiry to be held by or before a suitably qualified person or persons into every marine casualty or incident of navigation on the high seas involving a ship flying its flag and causing loss of life or serious injury to nationals of another State or serious damage to ships or installations of another State or to the marine environment. The flag State and the other State shall co-operate in the conduct of any inquiry held by that other State into any such marine casualty or incident of navigation.

Article 95

Immunity of warships on the high seas

[*See* Basic Document 4.3, Art. 8(1).]

Article 96

Immunity of ships used only on government non-commercial service

[*See* Basic Document 4.3, Art. 9.]

Article 97

*Penal jurisdiction in matters of collision or
in any other incident of navigation*

[*See* Basic Document 4.3, Art. 11.]

Article 98

Duty to render assistance

[*See* Basic Document 4.3, Art. 12.]

Article 99

Prohibition of the transport of slaves

[*See* Basic Document 4.3, Art. 13.]

Article 100

Duty to co-operate in the repression of piracy

[*See* Basic Document 4.3, Art. 14.]

Article 101

Definition of piracy

[*See* Basic Document 4.3, Art. 15.]

Article 102
Piracy by a warship, government ship or government
aircraft whose crew has mutinied

The acts of piracy, as defined in article 101, committed by a warship, government ship or government aircraft whose crew has mutinied and taken control of the ship or aircraft are assimilated to acts committed by a private ship or aircraft.

Article 103
Definition of a pirate ship or aircraft

A ship or aircraft is considered a pirate ship or aircraft if it is intended by the persons in dominant control to be used for the purpose of committing one of the acts referred to in article 101. The same applies if the ship or aircraft has been used to commit any such act, so long as it remains under the control of the persons guilty of that act.

Article 104
Retention or loss of the nationality of a pirate ship or aircraft

[*See* Basic Document 4.3, Art. 18.]

Article 105
Seizure of a pirate ship or aircraft

[*See* Basic Document 4.3, Art. 19.]

Article 106
Liability for seizure without adequate grounds

[*See* Basic Document 4.3, Art. 20.]

Article 107
Ships and aircraft which are entitled to seize on account of piracy

[*See* Basic Document 4.3, Art. 21.]

Article 108
Illicit traffic in narcotic drugs or psychotropic substances

1. All States shall co-operate in the suppression of illicit traffic in narcotic drugs and psychotropic substances engaged in by ships on the high seas contrary to international conventions.

2. Any State which has reasonable grounds for believing that a ship flying its flag is engaged in illicit traffic in narcotic drugs or psychotropic substances may request the co-operation of other States to suppress such traffic.

Article 109
Unauthorized broadcasting from the high seas

1. All States shall co-operate in the suppression of unauthorized broadcasting from the high seas.

2. For the purposes of this Convention, "unauthorized broadcasting" means the transmission of sound radio or television broadcasts from a ship or installation on the high seas intended for reception by the general public contrary to international regulations, but excluding the transmission of distress calls.

3. Any person engaged in unauthorized broadcasting may be prosecuted before the court of:

(a) the flag State of the ship;

(b) the State of registry of the installation;

(c) the State of which the person is a national;

(d) any State where the transmissions can be received; or

(e) any State where authorized radio communication is suffering interference.

4. On the high seas, a State having jurisdiction in accordance with paragraph 3 may, in conformity with article 110, arrest any person or ship engaged in unauthorized broadcasting and seize the broadcasting apparatus.

Article 110
Right of visit

1. Except where acts of interference derive from powers conferred by treaty, a warship which encounters on the high seas a foreign ship, other than a ship entitled to complete immunity in accordance with articles 95 and 96, is not justified in boarding it unless there is reasonable ground for suspecting that:

(a) the ship is engaged in piracy;

(b) the ship is engaged in the slave trade;

(c) the ship is engaged in unauthorized broadcasting and the flag State of the warship has jurisdiction under article 109;

(d) the ship is without nationality; or

(e) though flying a foreign flag or refusing to show its flag, the ship is, in reality, of the same nationality as the warship.

2. In the cases provided for in paragraph 1, the warship may proceed to verify the ship's right to fly its flag. To this end, it may send a boat under the command of an officer to the suspected ship. If suspicion remains after the documents have been checked, it may proceed to a further examination on board the ship, which must be carried out with all possible consideration.

3. If the suspicions prove to be unfounded, and provided that the ship boarded has not committed any act justifying them, it shall be compensated for any loss or damage that may have been sustained.

4. These provisions apply *mutatis mutandis* to military aircraft.

5. These provisions also apply to any other duly authorized ships or aircraft clearly marked and identifiable as being on government service.

Article 111
Right of hot pursuit

1. The hot pursuit of a foreign ship may be undertaken when the competent authorities of the coastal State have good reason to believe that the ship has violated the laws and regulations of that State. Such pursuit must be commenced when the foreign ship or one of its boats is within the internal waters, the archipelagic waters, the territorial sea or the contiguous zone of the pursuing State, and may only be continued outside the territorial sea or

the contiguous zone if the pursuit has not been interrupted. It is not necessary that, at the time when the foreign ship within the territorial sea or the contiguous zone receives the order to stop, the ship giving the order should likewise be within the territorial sea or the contiguous zone. If the foreign ship is within a contiguous zone, as defined in article 33, the pursuit may only be undertaken if there has been a violation of the rights for the protection of which the zone was established.

2. The right of hot pursuit shall apply *mutatis mutandis* to violations in the exclusive economic zone or on the continental shelf, including safety zones around continental shelf installations, of the laws and regulations of the coastal State applicable in accordance with this Convention to the exclusive economic zone or the continental shelf, including such safety zones.

3. [*See* Basic Document 4.3, Art. 23(2).]

4. Hot pursuit is not deemed to have begun unless the pursuing ship has satisfied itself by such practicable means as may be available that the ship pursued or one of its boats or other craft working as a team and using the ship pursued as a mother ship is within the limits of the territorial sea, or, as the case may be, within the contiguous zone or the exclusive economic zone or above the continental shelf. The pursuit may only be commenced after a visual or auditory signal to stop has been given at a distance which enables it to be seen or heard by the foreign ship.

5. The right of hot pursuit may be exercised only by warships or military aircraft, or other ships or aircraft clearly marked and identifiable as being on government service and authorized to that effect.

6. Where hot pursuit is effected by an aircraft:

(a) the provisions of paragraphs 1 to 4 shall apply *mutatis mutandis;*

(b) [See Basic Document 4.3, Art. 23(5)(b).]

7. The release of a ship arrested within the jurisdiction of a State and escorted to a port of that State for the purposes of an inquiry before the competent authorities may not be claimed solely on the ground that the ship, in the course of its voyage, was escorted across a portion of the exclusive economic zone or the high seas, if the circumstances rendered this necessary.

8. Where a ship has been stopped or arrested outside the territorial sea in circumstances which do not justify the exercise of the right of hot pursuit, it shall be compensated for any loss or damage that may have been thereby sustained.

Article 112
Right to lay submarine cables and pipelines

1. All States are entitled to lay submarine cables and pipelines on the bed of the high seas beyond the continental shelf.

2. Article 79, paragraph 5, applies to such cables and pipelines.

Article 113
Breaking or injury of a submarine cable or pipeline

[*See* Basic Document 4.3, Art. 27.]

Article 114

*Breaking or injury by owners of a submarine cable or
pipeline of another submarine cable or pipeline*

[*See* Basic Document 4.3, Art. 28.]

Article 115

*Indemnity for loss incurred in avoiding injury
to a submarine cable or pipeline*

[*See* Basic Document 4.3, Art. 29.]

SECTION 2. CONSERVATION AND MANAGEMENT OF THE LIVING RESOURCES OF THE HIGH SEAS

Article 116

Right to fish on the high seas

All States have the right for their nationals to engage in fishing on the high seas subject to:

(a) their treaty obligations;

(b) the rights and duties as well as the interests of coastal States provided for, *inter alia,* in article 63, paragraph 2, and articles 64 to 67; and

(c) the provisions of this section.

Article 117

*Duty of States to adopt with respect to their nationals measures
for the conservation of the living resources of the high seas*

[*See* Basic Document 6.3, Art. 1(2).]

Article 118

*Co-operation of States in the conservation
and management of living resources*

States shall co-operate with each other in the conservation and management of living resources in the areas of the high seas. States whose nationals exploit identical living resources, or different living resources in the same area, shall enter into negotiations with a view to taking the measures necessary for the conservation of the living resources concerned. They shall, as appropriate, co-operate to establish subregional or regional fisheries organizations to this end.

Article 119

Conservation of the living resources of the high seas

1. In determining the allowable catch and establishing other conservation measures for the living resources in the high seas, States shall:

(a) take measures which are designed, on the best scientific evidence available to the States concerned, to maintain or restore populations of harvested species at levels which can produce the maximum sustainable yield, as qualified by relevant environmental and economic factors, including the special requirements of developing States, and taking into account fishing patterns, the interdependence of stocks and any generally recommended international minimum standards, whether subregional, regional or global;

(b) take into consideration the effects on species associated with or dependent upon harvested species with a view to maintaining or restoring populations of such associated or dependent species above levels at which their reproduction may become seriously threatened.

2. Available scientific information, catch and fishing effort statistics, and other data relevant to the conservation of fish stocks shall be contributed and exchanged on a regular basis through competent international organizations, whether subregional, regional or global, where appropriate and with participation by all States concerned.

3. States concerned shall ensure that conservation measures and their implementation do not discriminate in form or in fact against the fishermen of any State.

Article 120

Marine mammals

Article 65 also applies to the conservation and management of marine mammals in the high seas.

PART VIII
REGIME OF ISLANDS

Article 121

Régime of islands

1. An island is a naturally formed area of land, surrounded by water, which is above water at high tide.

2. Except as provided for in paragraph 3, the territorial sea, the contiguous zone, the exclusive economic zone and the continental shelf of an island are determined in accordance with the provisions of this Convention applicable to other land territory.

3. Rocks which cannot sustain human habitation or economic life of their own shall have no exclusive economic zone or continental shelf.

PART IX
ENCLOSED OR SEMI–ENCLOSED SEAS

Article 122

Definition

For the purposes of this Convention, "enclosed or semi-enclosed sea" means a gulf, basin or sea surrounded by two or more States and connected to another sea or the ocean by a narrow outlet or consisting entirely or primarily of the territorial seas and exclusive economic zones of two or more coastal States.

Article 123

Co-operation of States bordering enclosed or semi-enclosed seas

States bordering an enclosed or semi-enclosed sea should co-operate with each other in the exercise of their rights and in the performance of their duties under this Convention. * * *

PART X
RIGHT OF ACCESS OF LAND–LOCKED STATES TO AND FROM THE SEA AND FREEDOM OF TRANSIT

Article 124

Use of terms

1. For the purposes of this Convention:

(a) "land-locked State" means a State which has no sea-coast;

(b) "transit State" means a State, with or without a sea-coast, situated between a land-locked State and the sea, through whose territory traffic in transit passes;

(c) "traffic in transit" means transit of persons, baggage, goods and means of transport across the territory of one or more transit States, when the passage across such territory, with or without trans-shipment, warehousing, breaking bulk or change in the mode of transport, is only a portion of a complete journey which begins or terminates within the territory of the land-locked State;

(d) "means of transport" means:

(i) railway rolling stock, sea, lake and river craft and road vehicles;

(ii) where local conditions so require, porters and pack animals.

2. Land-locked States and transit States may, by agreement between them, include as means of transport pipelines and gas lines and means of transport other than those included in paragraph 1.

Article 125

Right of access to and from the sea and freedom of transit

1. Land-locked States shall have the right of access to and from the sea for the purpose of exercising the rights provided for in this Convention including those relating to the freedom of the high seas and the common heritage of mankind. To this end, land-locked States shall enjoy freedom of transit through the territory of transit States by all means of transport.

2. The terms and modalities for exercising freedom of transit shall be agreed between the land-locked States and transit States concerned through bilateral, subregional or regional agreements.

3. Transit States, in the exercise of their full sovereignty over their territory, shall have the right to take all measures necessary to ensure that the rights and facilities provided for in this Part for land-locked States shall in no way infringe their legitimate interests.

Article 126

Exclusion of application of the most-favoured-nation clause

* * *

Article 127

Customs duties, taxes and other charges

1. Traffic in transit shall not be subject to any customs duties, taxes or other charges except charges levied for specific services rendered in connection with such traffic.

2.　Means of transport in transit and other facilities provided for and used by land-locked States shall not be subject to taxes or charges higher than those levied for the use of means of transport of the transit State.

Article 128
Free zones and other customs facilities

* * *

Article 129
Co-operation in the construction and improvement of means of transport

* * *

Article 130
Measures to avoid or eliminate delays or other difficulties of a technical nature in traffic in transit

* * *

Article 131
Equal treatment in maritime ports

* * *

Article 132
Grant of greater transit facilities

* * *

PART XI
THE AREA

SECTION 1.　GENERAL PROVISIONS
Article 133
Use of terms

For the purposes of this Part:

(a) "resources" means all solid, liquid or gaseous mineral resources in situ in the Area at or beneath the sea-bed, including polymetallic nodules;

(b) resources, when recovered from the Area, are referred to as "minerals".

Article 134
Scope of this Part

1.　This Part applies to the Area.

2.　Activities in the Area shall be governed by the provisions of this Part.

3.　The requirements concerning deposit of, and publicity to be given to, the charts or lists of geographical co-ordinates showing the limits referred to in article 1, paragraph 1(1), are set forth in Part VI.

4.　Nothing in this article affects the establishment of the outer limits of the continental shelf in accordance with Part VI or the validity of agreements relating to delimitation between States with opposite or adjacent coasts.

Article 135

Legal status of the superjacent waters and air space

Neither this Part nor any rights granted or exercised pursuant thereto shall affect the legal status of the waters superjacent to the Area or that of the air space above those waters.

SECTION 2. PRINCIPLES GOVERNING THE AREA

Article 136

Common heritage of mankind

The Area and its resources are the common heritage of mankind.

Article 137

Legal status of the Area and its resources

1. No State shall claim or exercise sovereignty or sovereign rights over any part of the Area or its resources, nor shall any State or natural or juridical person appropriate any part thereof. No such claim or exercise of sovereignty or sovereign rights nor such appropriation shall be recognized.

2. All rights in the resources of the Area are vested in mankind as a whole, on whose behalf the Authority shall act. These resources are not subject to alienation. The minerals recovered from the Area, however, may only be alienated in accordance with this Part and the rules, regulations and procedures of the Authority.

3. No State or natural or juridical person shall claim, acquire or exercise rights with respect to the minerals recovered from the Area except in accordance with this Part. Otherwise, no such claim, acquisition or exercise of such rights shall be recognized.

Article 138

General conduct of States in relation to the Area

The general conduct of States in relation to the Area shall be in accordance with the provisions of this Part, the principles embodied in the Charter of the United Nations and other rules of international law in the interests of maintaining peace and security and promoting international co-operation and mutual understanding.

Article 139

Responsibility to ensure compliance and liability for damage

1. States Parties shall have the responsibility to ensure that activities in the Area, whether carried out by States Parties, or state enterprises or natural or juridical persons which possess the nationality of States Parties or are effectively controlled by them or their nationals, shall be carried out in conformity with this Part. The same responsibility applies to international organizations for activities in the Area carried out by such organizations.

* * *

Article 140

Benefit of mankind

1. Activities in the Area shall, as specifically provided for in this Part, be carried out for the benefit of mankind as a whole, irrespective of the

geographical location of States, whether coastal or land-locked, and taking into particular consideration the interests and needs of developing States and of peoples who have not attained full independence or other self-governing status recognized by the United Nations in accordance with General Assembly resolution 1514 (XV) and other relevant General Assembly resolutions.

2. The Authority shall provide for the equitable sharing of financial and other economic benefits derived from activities in the Area through any appropriate mechanism, on a non-discriminatory basis, in accordance with article 160, paragraph 2(f)(i).

Article 141

Use of the Area exclusively for peaceful purposes

The Area shall be open to use exclusively for peaceful purposes by all States, whether coastal or land-locked, without discrimination and without prejudice to the other provisions of this Part.

Article 142

Rights and legitimate interests of coastal States

1. Activities in the Area, with respect to resource deposits in the Area which lie across limits of national jurisdiction, shall be conducted with due regard to the rights and legitimate interests of any coastal State across whose jurisdiction such deposits lie.

* * *

Article 143

Marine scientific research

1. Marine scientific research in the Area shall be carried out exclusively for peaceful purposes and for the benefit of mankind as a whole, in accordance with Part XIII.

2. The Authority may carry out marine scientific research concerning the Area and its resources, and may enter into contracts for that purpose. The Authority shall promote and encourage the conduct of marine scientific research in the Area, and shall co-ordinate and disseminate the results of such research and analysis when available.

3. States Parties may carry out marine scientific research in the Area. States Parties shall promote international co-operation in marine scientific research in the Area by:

(a) participating in international programmes and encouraging co-operation in marine scientific research by personnel of different countries and of the Authority;

(b) ensuring that programmes are developed through the Authority or other international organizations as appropriate for the benefit of developing States and technologically less developed States with a view to:

(i) strengthening their research capabilities;

(ii) training their personnel and the personnel of the Authority in the techniques and applications of research;

(iii) fostering the employment of their qualified personnel in research in the Area;

(c) effectively disseminating the results of research and analysis when available, through the Authority or other international channels when appropriate.

Article 144

Transfer of technology

1. The Authority shall take measures in accordance with this Convention:

(a) to acquire technology and scientific knowledge relating to activities in the Area; and

(b) to promote and encourage the transfer to developing States of such technology and scientific knowledge so that all States Parties benefit therefrom.

2. To this end the Authority and States Parties shall co-operate in promoting the transfer of technology and scientific knowledge relating to activities in the Area so that the Enterprise and all States Parties may benefit therefrom. In particular they shall initiate and promote:

(a) programmes for the transfer of technology to the Enterprise and to developing States with regard to activities in the Area, including, *inter alia,* facilitating the access of the Enterprise and of developing States to the relevant technology, under fair and reasonable terms and conditions;

(b) measures directed towards the advancement of the technology of the Enterprise and the domestic technology of developing States, particularly by providing opportunities to personnel from the Enterprise and from developing States for training in marine science and technology and for their full participation in activities in the Area.

Article 145

Protection of the marine environment

Necessary measures shall be taken in accordance with this Convention with respect to activities in the Area to ensure effective protection for the marine environment from harmful effects which may arise from such activities. To this end the Authority shall adopt appropriate rules, regulations and procedures for *inter alia:*

(a) the prevention, reduction and control of pollution and other hazards to the marine environment, including the coastline, and of interference with the ecological balance of the marine environment, particular attention being paid to the need for protection from harmful effects of such activities as drilling, dredging, excavation, disposal of waste, construction and operation or maintenance of installations, pipelines and other devices related to such activities;

(b) the protection and conservation of the natural resources of the Area and the prevention of damage to the flora and fauna of the marine environment.

Article 146

Protection of human life

With respect to activities in the Area, necessary measures shall be taken to ensure effective protection of human life. * * *

Article 147

Accommodation of activities in the Area and in the marine environment

1. Activities in the Area shall be carried out with reasonable regard for other activities in the marine environment.

2. Installations used for carrying out activities in the Area shall be subject to the following conditions:

(a) such installations shall be erected, emplaced and removed solely in accordance with this Part and subject to the rules, regulations and procedures of the Authority. Due notice must be given of the erection, emplacement and removal of such installations, and permanent means for giving warning of their presence must be maintained;

(b) such installations may not be established where interference may be caused to the use of recognized sea lanes essential to international navigation or in areas of intense fishing activity;

(c) safety zones shall be established around such installations with appropriate markings to ensure the safety of both navigation and the installations. The configuration and location of such safety zones shall not be such as to form a belt impeding the lawful access of shipping to particular maritime zones or navigation along international sea lanes;

(d) such installations shall be used exclusively for peaceful purposes;

(e) such installations do not possess the status of islands. They have no territorial sea of their own, and their presence does not affect the delimitation of the territorial sea, the exclusive economic zone or the continental shelf.

3. Other activities in the marine environment shall be conducted with reasonable regard for activities in the Area.

Article 148

Participation of developing States in activities in the Area

The effective participation of developing States in activities in the Area shall be promoted as specifically provided for in this Part, having due regard to their special interests and needs, and in particular to the special need of the land-locked and geographically disadvantaged among them to overcome obstacles arising from their disadvantaged location, including remoteness from the Area and difficulty of access to and from it.

Article 149

Archaeological and historical objects

All objects of an archaeological and historical nature found in the Area shall be preserved or disposed of for the benefit of mankind as a whole, particular regard being paid to the preferential rights of the State or country of origin, or the State of cultural origin, or the State of historical and archaeological origin.

SECTION 3. DEVELOPMENT OF RESOURCES OF THE AREA

Article 150

Policies relating to activities in the Area

Activities in the Area shall, as specifically provided for in this Part, be carried out in such a manner as to foster healthy development of the world economy and balanced growth of international trade, and to promote international co-operation for the over-all development of all countries, especially developing States, and with a view to ensuring:

(a) the development of the resources of the Area;

(b) orderly, safe and rational management of the resources of the Area, including the efficient conduct of activities in the Area and, in accordance with sound principles of conservation, the avoidance of unnecessary waste;

(c) the expansion of opportunities for participation in such activities consistent in particular with articles 144 and 148;

(d) participation in revenues by the Authority and the transfer of technology to the Enterprise and developing States as provided for in this Convention;

(e) increased availability of the minerals derived from the Area as needed in conjunction with minerals derived from other sources, to ensure supplies to consumers of such minerals;

(f) the promotion of just and stable prices remunerative to producers and fair to consumers for minerals derived both from the Area and from other sources, and the promotion of long-term equilibrium between supply and demand;

(g) the enhancement of opportunities for all States Parties, irrespective of their social and economic systems or geographical location, to participate in the development of the resources of the Area and the prevention of monopolization of activities in the Area;

(h) the protection of developing countries from adverse effects on their economies or on their export earnings resulting from a reduction in the price of an affected mineral, or in the volume of exports of that mineral, to the extent that such reduction is caused by activities in the Area, as provided in article 151;

(i) the development of the common heritage for the benefit of mankind as a whole; and

(j) conditions of access to markets for the imports of minerals produced from the resources of the Area and for imports of commodities produced from such minerals shall not be more favourable than the most favourable applied to imports from other sources.

Article 151

Production policies

1. (a) Without prejudice to the objectives set forth in article 150 and for the purpose of implementing subparagraph (h) of that article, the Authority, acting through existing forums or such new arrangements or agreements as may be appropriate, in which all interested parties, including both producers

and consumers, participate, shall take measures necessary to promote the growth, efficiency and stability of markets for those commodities produced from the minerals derived from the Area, at prices remunerative to producers and fair to consumers. All States Parties shall co-operate to this end.

* * *

2. (a) During the interim period specified in paragraph 3, commercial production shall not be undertaken pursuant to an approved plan of work until the operator has applied for and has been issued a production authorization by the Authority. Such production authorizations may not be applied for or issued more than five years prior to the planned commencement of commercial production under the plan of work unless, having regard to the nature and timing of project development, the rules, regulations and procedures of the Authority prescribe another period.

* * *

3. The interim period shall begin five years prior to 1 January of the year in which the earliest commercial production is planned to commence under an approved plan of work. If the earliest commercial production is delayed beyond the year originally planned, the beginning of the interim period and the production ceiling originally calculated shall be adjusted accordingly. The interim period shall last 25 years or until the end of the Review Conference referred to in article 155 or until the day when such new arrangements or agreements as are referred to in paragraph 1 enter into force, whichever is earliest. The Authority shall resume the power provided in this article for the remainder of the interim period if the said arrangements or agreements should lapse or become ineffective for any reason whatsoever.

4. [This provision establishes the production ceiling for any one year of the interim period and the manner of its calculation.]

5. The Authority shall reserve to the Enterprise for its initial production a quantity of 38,000 metric tonnes of nickel from the available production ceiling calculated pursuant to paragraph 4.

6. [This provision authorizes supplementing production subject to certain conditions.]

7. The levels of production of other metals such as copper, cobalt and manganese extracted from the polymetallic nodules that are recovered pursuant to a production authorization should not be higher than those which would have been produced had the operator produced the maximum level of nickel from those nodules pursuant to this article. The Authority shall establish rules, regulations and procedures pursuant to Annex III, article 17, to implement this paragraph.

8. Rights and obligations relating to unfair economic practices under relevant multilateral trade agreements shall apply to the exploration for and exploitation of minerals from the Area. In the settlement of disputes arising under this provision, States Parties which are Parties to such multilateral trade agreements shall have recourse to the dispute settlement procedures of such agreements.

9. The Authority shall have the power to limit the level of production of minerals from the Area, other than minerals from polymetallic nodules, under

such conditions and applying such methods as may be appropriate by adopting regulations in accordance with article 161, paragraph 8.

10.   Upon the recommendation of the Council on the basis of advice from the Economic Planning Commission, the Assembly shall establish a system of compensation or take other measures of economic adjustment assistance including co-operation with specialized agencies and other international organizations to assist developing countries which suffer serious adverse effects on their export earnings or economies resulting from a reduction in the price of an affected mineral or in the volume of exports of that mineral, to the extent that such reduction is caused by activities in the Area.   The Authority on request shall initiate studies on the problems of those States which are likely to be most seriously affected with a view to minimizing their difficulties and assisting them in their economic adjustment.

Article 152

Exercise of powers and functions by the Authority

1.   The Authority shall avoid discrimination in the exercise of its powers and functions, including the granting of opportunities for activities in the Area.

2.   Nevertheless, special consideration for developing States, including particular consideration for the land-locked and geographically disadvantaged among them, specifically provided for in this Part shall be permitted.

Article 153

System of exploration and exploitation

1.   Activities in the Area shall be organized, carried out and controlled by the Authority on behalf of mankind as a whole in accordance with this article as well as other relevant provisions of this Part and the relevant Annexes, and the rules, regulations and procedures of the Authority.

2.   Activities in the Area shall be carried out as prescribed in paragraph 3:

(a) by the Enterprise, and

(b) in association with the Authority by States Parties, or state enterprises or natural or juridical persons which possess the nationality of States Parties or are effectively controlled by them or their nationals, when sponsored by such States, or any group of the foregoing which meets the requirements provided in this Part and in Annex III.

3.   Activities in the Area shall be carried out in accordance with a formal written plan of work drawn up in accordance with Annex III and approved by the Council after review by the Legal and Technical Commission.   In the case of activities in the Area carried out as authorized by the Authority by the entities specified in paragraph 2(b), the plan of work shall, in accordance with Annex III, article 3, be in the form of a contract.   Such contracts may provide for joint arrangements in accordance with Annex III, article 11.

* * *

Article 154
Periodic review

Every five years from the entry into force of this Convention, the Assembly shall undertake a general and systematic review of the manner in which the international régime of the Area established in this Convention has operated in practice. In the light of this review the Assembly may take, or recommend that other organs take, measures in accordance with the provisions and procedures of this Part and the Annexes relating thereto which will lead to the improvement of the operation of the régime.

Article 155
The Review Conference

1. Fifteen years from 1 January of the year in which the earliest commercial production commences under an approved plan of work, the Assembly shall convene a conference for the review of those provisions of this Part and the relevant Annexes which govern the system of exploration and exploitation of the resources of the Area. * * *

* * *

SECTION 4. THE AUTHORITY
SUBSECTION A. GENERAL PROVISIONS
Article 156
Establishment of the Authority

1. There is hereby established the International Sea–Bed Authority, which shall function in accordance with this Part.

2. All States Parties are ipso facto members of the Authority.

3. Observers at the Third United Nations Conference on the Law of the Sea who have signed the Final Act and who are not referred to in article 305, paragraph 1(c), (d), (e) or (f), shall have the right to participate in the Authority as observers, in accordance with its rules, regulations and procedures.

4. The seat of the Authority shall be in Jamaica.

5. The Authority may establish such regional centres or offices as it deems necessary for the exercise of its functions.

Article 157
Nature and fundamental principles of the Authority

1. The Authority is the organization through which States Parties shall, in accordance with this Part, organize and control activities in the Area, particularly with a view to administering the resources of the Area.

2. The powers and functions of the Authority shall be those expressly conferred upon it by this Convention. The Authority shall have such incidental powers, consistent with this Convention, as are implicit in and necessary for the exercise of those powers and functions with respect to activities in the Area.

3. The Authority is based on the principle of the sovereign equality of all its members.

4. All members of the Authority shall fulfil in good faith the obligations assumed by them in accordance with this Part in order to ensure to all of them the rights and benefits resulting from membership.

Article 158
Organs of the Authority

1. There are hereby established, as the principal organs of the Authority, an Assembly, a Council and a Secretariat.

2. There is hereby established the Enterprise, the organ through which the Authority shall carry out the functions referred to in article 170, paragraph 1.

3. Such subsidiary organs as may be found necessary may be established in accordance with this Part.

4. Each principal organ of the Authority and the Enterprise shall be responsible for exercising those powers and functions which are conferred upon it. In exercising such powers and functions each organ shall avoid taking any action which may derogate from or impede the exercise of specific powers and functions conferred upon another organ.

SUBSECTION B. THE ASSEMBLY
Article 159
Composition, procedure and voting

1. The Assembly shall consist of all the members of the Authority. Each member shall have one representative in the Assembly, who may be accompanied by alternates and advisers.

2. The Assembly shall meet in regular annual sessions and in such special sessions as may be decided by the Assembly, or convened by the Secretary–General at the request of the Council or of a majority of the members of the Authority.

3. Sessions shall take place at the seat of the Authority unless otherwise decided by the Assembly.

4. The Assembly shall adopt its rules of procedure. At the beginning of each regular session, it shall elect its President and such other officers as may be required. They shall hold office until a new President and other officers are elected at the next regular session.

5. A majority of the members of the Assembly shall constitute a quorum.

6. Each member of the Assembly shall have one vote.

* * *

Article 160
Powers and functions

1. The Assembly, as the sole organ of the Authority consisting of all the members, shall be considered the supreme organ of the Authority to which the other principal organs shall be accountable as specifically provided for in this Convention. The Assembly shall have the power to establish general

policies in conformity with the relevant provisions of this Convention on any question or matter within the competence of the Authority.

* * *

SUBSECTION C. THE COUNCIL
Article 161
Composition, procedure and voting

1. The Council shall consist of 36 members of the Authority elected by the Assembly in the following order:

(a) four members from among those States Parties which, during the last five years for which statistics are available, have either consumed more than 2 per cent of total world consumption or have had net imports of more than 2 per cent of total world imports of the commodities produced from the categories of minerals to be derived from the Area, and in any case one State from the Eastern European (Socialist) region, as well as the largest consumer;

(b) four members from among the eight States Parties which have the largest investments in preparation for and in the conduct of activities in the Area, either directly or through their nationals, including at least one State from the Eastern European (Socialist) region;

(c) four members from among States Parties which on the basis of production in areas under their jurisdiction are major net exporters of the categories of minerals to be derived from the Area, including at least two developing States whose exports of such minerals have a substantial bearing upon their economies;

(d) six members from among developing States Parties, representing special interests. The special interests to be represented shall include those of States with large populations, States which are land-locked or geographically disadvantaged, States which are major importers of the categories of minerals to be derived from the Area, States which are potential producers of such minerals, and least developed States;

(e) eighteen members elected according to the principle of ensuring an equitable geographical distribution of seats in the Council as a whole, provided that each geographical region shall have at least one member elected under this subparagraph. For this purpose, the geographical regions shall be Africa, Asia, Eastern European (Socialist), Latin America and Western European and Others.

2. In electing the members of the Council in accordance with paragraph 1, the Assembly shall ensure that:

(a) land-locked and geographically disadvantaged States are represented to a degree which is reasonably proportionate to their representation in the Assembly;

(b) coastal States, especially developing States, which do not qualify under paragraph 1(a), (b), (c) or (d) are represented to a degree which is reasonably proportionate to their representation in the Assembly;

(c) each group of States Parties to be represented on the Council is represented by those members, if any, which are nominated by that group.

3. Elections shall take place at regular sessions of the Assembly. Each member of the Council shall be elected for four years. At the first election, however, the term of one half of the members of each group referred to in paragraph 1 shall be two years.

4. Members of the Council shall be eligible for re-election, but due regard should be paid to the desirability of rotation of membership.

5. The Council shall function at the seat of the Authority, and shall meet as often as the business of the Authority may require, but not less than three times a year.

6. A majority of the members of the Council shall constitute a quorum.

7. Each member of the Council shall have one vote.

* * *

Article 162
Powers and functions

1. The Council is the executive organ of the Authority. The Council shall have the power to establish, in conformity with this Convention and the general policies established by the Assembly, the specific policies to be pursued by the Authority on any question or matter within the competence of the Authority.

* * *

Article 163
Organs of the Council

1. There are hereby established the following organs of the Council:

(a) an Economic Planning Commission;

(b) a Legal and Technical Commission.

2. Each Commission shall be composed of 15 members, elected by the Council from among the candidates nominated by the States Parties. However, if necessary, the Council may decide to increase the size of either Commission having due regard to economy and efficiency.

3. Members of a Commission shall have appropriate qualifications in the area of competence of that Commission. States Parties shall nominate candidates of the highest standards of competence and integrity with qualifications in relevant fields so as to ensure the effective exercise of the functions of the Commissions.

* * *

Article 164
The Economic Planning Commission

1. Members of the Economic Planning Commission shall have appropriate qualifications such as those relevant to mining, management of mineral resource activities, international trade or international economics. The Coun-

cil shall endeavour to ensure that the membership of the Commission reflects all appropriate qualifications. The Commission shall include at least two members from developing States whose exports of the categories of minerals to be derived from the Area have a substantial bearing upon their economies.

* * *

Article 165
The Legal and Technical Commission

1. Members of the Legal and Technical Commission shall have appropriate qualifications such as those relevant to exploration for and exploitation and processing of mineral resources, oceanology, protection of the marine environment, or economic or legal matters relating to ocean mining and related fields of expertise. The Council shall endeavour to ensure that the membership of the Commission reflects all appropriate qualifications.

* * *

SUBSECTION D. THE SECRETARIAT
Article 166
The Secretariat

1. The Secretariat of the Authority shall comprise a Secretary–General and such staff as the Authority may require.

2. The Secretary–General shall be elected for four years by the Assembly from among the candidates proposed by the Council and may be re-elected.

3. The Secretary–General shall be the chief administrative officer of the Authority, and shall act in that capacity in all meetings of the Assembly, of the Council and of any subsidiary organ, and shall perform such other administrative functions as are entrusted to the Secretary–General by these organs.

4. The Secretary–General shall make an annual report to the Assembly on the work of the Authority.

Article 167
The staff of the Authority

* * *

Article 168
International character of the Secretariat

1. In the performance of their duties the Secretary–General and the staff shall not seek or receive instructions from any government or from any other source external to the Authority. They shall refrain from any action which might reflect on their position as international officials responsible only to the Authority. * * *

* * *

Article 169
Consultation and co-operation with international and non-governmental organizations

* * *

SUBSECTION E. THE ENTERPRISE
Article 170
The Enterprise

1.   The Enterprise shall be the organ of the Authority which shall carry out activities in the Area directly, pursuant to article 153, paragraph 2(a), as well as the transporting, processing and marketing of minerals recovered from the Area.

2.   The Enterprise shall, within the framework of the international legal personality of the Authority, have such legal capacity as is provided for in the Statute set forth in Annex IV.   The Enterprise shall act in accordance with this Convention and the rules, regulations and procedures of the Authority, as well as the general policies established by the Assembly, and shall be subject to the directives and control of the Council.

* * *

SUBSECTION F.   FINANCIAL ARRANGEMENTS OF THE AUTHORITY
Article 171
Funds of the Authority

The funds of the Authority shall include:

(a) assessed contributions made by members of the Authority in accordance with article 160, paragraph 2(e);

(b) funds received by the Authority pursuant to Annex III, article 13, in connection with activities in the Area;

(c) funds transferred from the Enterprise in accordance with Annex IV, article 10;

(d) funds borrowed pursuant to article 174;

(e) voluntary contributions made by members or other entities; and

(f) payments to a compensation fund, in accordance with article 151, paragraph 10, whose sources are to be recommended by the Economic Planning Commission.

Article 172
Annual budget of the Authority

* * *

Article 173
Expenses of the Authority

* * *

Article 174
Borrowing power of the Authority

* * *

Article 175
Annual audit

* * *

SUBSECTION G.   LEGAL STATUS, PRIVILEGES AND IMMUNITIES

Article 176

Legal status

The Authority shall have international legal personality and such legal capacity as may be necessary for the exercise of its functions and the fulfilment of its purposes.

Article 177

Privileges and immunities

To enable the Authority to exercise its functions, it shall enjoy in the territory of each State Party the privileges and immunities set forth in this subsection.   The privileges and immunities relating to the Enterprise shall be those set forth in Annex IV, article 13.

Article 178

Immunity from legal process

The Authority, its property and assets, shall enjoy immunity from legal process except to the extent that the Authority expressly waives this immunity in a particular case.

Article 179

Immunity from search and any form of seizure

* * *

Article 180

Exemption from restrictions, regulations, controls and moratoria

* * *

Article 181

Archives and official communications of the Authority

* * *

Article 182

Privileges and immunities of certain persons connected with the Authority

* * *

Article 183

Exemption from taxes and customs duties

* * *

SUBSECTION H.   SUSPENSION OF THE EXERCISE OF RIGHTS AND PRIVILEGES OF MEMBERS

Article 184

Suspension of the exercise of voting rights

A State Party which is in arrears in the payment of its financial contributions to the Authority shall have no vote if the amount of its arrears equals or exceeds the amount of the contribution due from it for the preceding two full years.   The Assembly may, nevertheless, permit such a member to vote if it is satisfied that the failure to pay is due to conditions beyond the control of the member.

Article 185

Suspension of exercise of rights and privileges of membership

1. A State Party which has grossly and persistently violated the provisions of this Part may be suspended from the exercise of the rights and privileges of membership by the Assembly upon the recommendation of the Council.

2. No action may be taken under paragraph 1 until the Sea–Bed Disputes Chamber has found that a State Party has grossly and persistently violated the provisions of this Part.

SECTION 5. SETTLEMENT OF DISPUTES AND ADVISORY OPINIONS

Article 186

Sea–Bed Disputes Chamber of the International Tribunal for the Law of the Sea

The establishment of the Sea–Bed Disputes Chamber and the manner in which it shall exercise its jurisdiction shall be governed by the provisions of this section, of Part XV and of Annex VI.

Article 187

Jurisdiction of the Sea–Bed Disputes Chamber

The Sea–Bed Disputes Chamber shall have jurisdiction under this Part and the Annexes relating thereto in disputes with respect to activities in the Area falling within the following categories:

(a) disputes between States Parties concerning the interpretation or application of this Part and the Annexes relating thereto;

(b) disputes between a State Party and the Authority concerning:

(i) acts or omissions of the Authority or of a State Party alleged to be in violation of this Part or the Annexes relating thereto or of rules, regulations and procedures of the Authority adopted in accordance therewith; or

(ii) acts of the Authority alleged to be in excess of jurisdiction or a misuse of power;

(c) disputes between parties to a contract, being States Parties, the Authority or the Enterprise, state enterprises and natural or juridical persons referred to in article 153, paragraph 2(b), concerning:

(i) the interpretation or application of a relevant contract or a plan of work; or

(ii) acts or omissions of a party to the contract relating to activities in the Area and directed to the other party or directly affecting its legitimate interests;

(d) disputes between the Authority and a prospective contractor who has been sponsored by a State as provided in article 153, paragraph 2(b), and has duly fulfilled the conditions referred to in Annex III, article 4, paragraph 6, and article 13, paragraph 2, concerning the refusal of a contract or a legal issue arising in the negotiation of the contract;

(e) disputes between the Authority and a State Party, a state enterprise or a natural or juridical person sponsored by a State Party as provided for in article 153, paragraph 2(b), where it is alleged that the Authority has incurred liability as provided in Annex III, article 22;

(f) any other disputes for which the jurisdiction of the Chamber is specifically provided in this Convention.

Article 188
Submission of disputes to a special chamber of the International Tribunal for the Law of the Sea or an ad hoc chamber of the Sea–Bed Disputes Chamber or to binding commercial arbitration

* * *

Article 189
Limitation on jurisdiction with regard to decisions of the Authority

* * *

Article 190
Participation and appearance of sponsoring States Parties in proceedings

* * *

Article 191
Advisory opinions

The Sea–Bed Disputes Chamber shall give advisory opinions at the request of the Assembly or the Council on legal questions arising within the scope of their activities. Such opinions shall be given as a matter of urgency.

PART XII
PROTECTION AND PRESERVATION OF THE MARINE ENVIRONMENT
SECTION 1. GENERAL PROVISIONS
Article 192
General obligation

States have the obligation to protect and preserve the marine environment.

Article 193
Sovereign right of States to exploit their natural resources

States have the sovereign right to exploit their natural resources pursuant to their environmental policies and in accordance with their duty to protect and preserve the marine environment.

Article 194
Measures to prevent, reduce and control pollution of the marine environment

1. States shall take, individually or jointly as appropriate, all measures consistent with this Convention that are necessary to prevent, reduce and control pollution of the marine environment from any source, using for this purpose the best practicable means at their disposal and in accordance with

their capabilities, and they shall endeavour to harmonize their policies in this connection.

2. States shall take all measures necessary to ensure that activities under their jurisdiction or control are so conducted as not to cause damage by pollution to other States and their environment, and that pollution arising from incidents or activities under their jurisdiction or control does not spread beyond the areas where they exercise sovereign rights in accordance with this Convention.

3. The measures taken pursuant to this Part shall deal with all sources of pollution of the marine environment. These measures shall include, *inter alia,* those designed to minimize to the fullest possible extent:

(a) the release of toxic, harmful or noxious substances, especially those which are persistent, from land-based sources, from or through the atmosphere or by dumping;

(b) pollution from vessels, in particular measures for preventing accidents and dealing with emergencies, ensuring the safety of operations at sea, preventing intentional and unintentional discharges, and regulating the design, construction, equipment, operation and manning of vessels;

(c) pollution from installations and devices used in exploration or exploitation of the natural resources of the sea-bed and subsoil, in particular measures for preventing accidents and dealing with emergencies, ensuring the safety of operations at sea, and regulating the design, construction, equipment, operation and manning of such installations or devices;

(d) pollution from other installations and devices operating in the marine environment, in particular measures for preventing accidents and dealing with emergencies, ensuring the safety of operations at sea, and regulating the design, construction, equipment, operation and manning of such installations or devices.

4. In taking measures to prevent, reduce or control pollution of the marine environment, States shall refrain from unjustifiable interference with activities carried out by other States in the exercise of their rights and in pursuance of their duties in conformity with this Convention.

5. The measures taken in accordance with this Part shall include those necessary to protect and preserve rare or fragile ecosystems as well as the habitat of depleted, threatened or endangered species and other forms of marine life.

Article 195

Duty not to transfer damage or hazards or transform
one type of pollution into another

* * *

Article 196

Use of technologies or introduction of alien or new species

1. States shall take all measures necessary to prevent, reduce and control pollution of the marine environment resulting from the use of technol-

ogies under their jurisdiction or control, or the intentional or accidental introduction of species, alien or new, to a particular part of the marine environment, which may cause significant and harmful changes thereto.

2. This article does not affect the application of this Convention regarding the prevention, reduction and control of pollution of the marine environment.

SECTION 2.   GLOBAL AND REGIONAL CO–OPERATION

Article 197

Co-operation on a global or regional basis

States shall co-operate on a global basis and, as appropriate, on a regional basis, directly or through competent international organizations, in formulating and elaborating international rules, standards and recommended practices and procedures consistent with this Convention, for the protection and preservation of the marine environment, taking into account characteristic regional features.

Article 198

Notification of imminent or actual damage

When a State becomes aware of cases in which the marine environment is in imminent danger of being damaged or has been damaged by pollution, it shall immediately notify other States it deems likely to be affected by such damage, as well as the competent international organizations.

Article 199

Contingency plans against pollution

In the cases referred to in article 198, States in the area affected, in accordance with their capabilities, and the competent international organizations shall co-operate, to the extent possible, in eliminating the effects of pollution and preventing or minimizing the damage. To this end, States shall jointly develop and promote contingency plans for responding to pollution incidents in the marine environment.

Article 200

Studies, research programmes and exchange of information and data

States shall co-operate, directly or through competent international organizations, for the purpose of promoting studies, undertaking programmes of scientific research and encouraging the exchange of information and data acquired about pollution of the marine environment. They shall endeavour to participate actively in regional and global programmes to acquire knowledge for the assessment of the nature and extent of pollution, exposure to it, and its pathways, risks and remedies.

Article 201

Scientific criteria for regulations

In the light of the information and data acquired pursuant to article 200, States shall co-operate, directly or through competent international organizations, in establishing appropriate scientific criteria for the formulation and elaboration of rules, standards and recommended practices and procedures for the prevention, reduction and control of pollution of the marine environment.

SECTION 3.   TECHNICAL ASSISTANCE
Article 202
Scientific and technical assistance to developing States

States shall, directly or through competent international organizations:

(a) promote programmes of scientific, educational, technical and other assistance to developing States for the protection and preservation of the marine environment and the prevention, reduction and control of marine pollution.   Such assistance shall include, *inter alia:*

(i) training of their scientific and technical personnel;

(ii) facilitating their participation in relevant international programmes;

(iii) supplying them with necessary equipment and facilities;

(iv) enhancing their capacity to manufacture such equipment;

(v) advice on and developing facilities for research, monitoring, educational and other programmes;

(b) provide appropriate assistance, especially to developing States, for the minimization of the effects of major incidents which may cause serious pollution of the marine environment;

(c) provide appropriate assistance, especially to developing States, concerning the preparation of environmental assessments.

Article 203
Preferential treatment for developing States

Developing States shall, for the purposes of prevention, reduction and control of pollution of the marine environment or minimization of its effects, be granted preference by international organizations in:

(a) the allocation of appropriate funds and technical assistance; and

(b) the utilization of their specialized services.

SECTION 4.   MONITORING AND ENVIRONMENTAL ASSESSMENT
Article 204
Monitoring of the risks or effects of pollution

1.   States shall, consistent with the rights of other States, endeavour, as far as practicable, directly or through the competent international organizations, to observe, measure, evaluate and analyse, by recognized scientific methods, the risks or effects of pollution of the marine environment.

2.   In particular, States shall keep under surveillance the effects of any activities which they permit or in which they engage in order to determine whether these activities are likely to pollute the marine environment.

Article 205
Publication of reports

States shall publish reports of the results obtained pursuant to article 204 or provide such reports at appropriate intervals to the competent international organizations, which should make them available to all States.

Article 206

Assessment of potential effects of activities

When States have reasonable grounds for believing that planned activities under their jurisdiction or control may cause substantial pollution of or significant and harmful changes to the marine environment, they shall, as far as practicable, assess the potential effects of such activities on the marine environment and shall communicate reports of the results of such assessments in the manner provided in article 205.

SECTION 5. INTERNATIONAL RULES AND NATIONAL LEGISLATION TO PREVENT, REDUCE AND CONTROL POLLUTION OF THE MARINE ENVIRONMENT

Article 207

Pollution from land-based sources

1. States shall adopt laws and regulations to prevent, reduce and control pollution of the marine environment from land-based sources, including rivers, estuaries, pipelines and outfall structures, taking into account internationally agreed rules, standards and recommended practices and procedures.

2. States shall take other measures as may be necessary to prevent, reduce and control such pollution.

3. States shall endeavour to harmonize their policies in this connection at the appropriate regional level.

4. States, acting especially through competent international organizations or diplomatic conference, shall endeavour to establish global and regional rules, standards and recommended practices and procedures to prevent, reduce and control pollution of the marine environment from land-based sources, taking into account characteristic regional features, the economic capacity of developing States and their need for economic development. Such rules, standards and recommended practices and procedures shall be re-examined from time to time as necessary.

5. Laws, regulations, measures, rules, standards and recommended practices and procedures referred to in paragraphs 1, 2 and 4 shall include those designed to minimize, to the fullest extent possible, the release of toxic, harmful or noxious substances, especially those which are persistent, into the marine environment.

Article 208

Pollution from sea-bed activities subject to national jurisdiction

[This article is in all essential respects identical to article 207, *supra.*]

Article 209

Pollution from activities in the Area

1. International rules, regulations and procedures shall be established in accordance with Part XI to prevent, reduce and control pollution of the marine environment from activities in the Area. Such rules, regulations and procedures shall be re-examined from time to time as necessary.

2. Subject to the relevant provisions of this section, States shall adopt laws and regulations to prevent, reduce and control pollution of the marine environment from activities in the Area undertaken by vessels, installations,

structures and other devices flying their flag or of their registry or operating under their authority, as the case may be. The requirements of such laws and regulations shall be no less effective than the international rules, regulations and procedures referred to in paragraph 1.

Article 210
Pollution by dumping

1. States shall adopt laws and regulations to prevent, reduce and control pollution of the marine environment by dumping.

2. States shall take other measures as may be necessary to prevent, reduce and control such pollution.

3. Such laws, regulations and measures shall ensure that dumping is not carried out without the permission of the competent authorities of States.

4. States, acting especially through competent international organizations or diplomatic conference, shall endeavour to establish global and regional rules, standards and recommended practices and procedures to prevent, reduce and control such pollution. Such rules, standards and recommended practices and procedures shall be re-examined from time to time as necessary.

5. Dumping within the territorial sea and the exclusive economic zone or onto the continental shelf shall not be carried out without the express prior approval of the coastal State, which has the right to permit, regulate and control such dumping after due consideration of the matter with other States which by reason of their geographical situation may be adversely affected thereby.

6. National laws, regulations and measures shall be no less effective in preventing, reducing and controlling such pollution than the global rules and standards.

Article 211
Pollution from vessels

1. States, acting through the competent international organization or general diplomatic conference, shall establish international rules and standards to prevent, reduce and control pollution of the marine environment from vessels and promote the adoption, in the same manner, wherever appropriate, of routing systems designed to minimize the threat of accidents which might cause pollution of the marine environment, including the coastline, and pollution damage to the related interests of coastal States. Such rules and standards shall, in the same manner, be re-examined from time to time as necessary.

2. States shall adopt laws and regulations for the prevention, reduction and control of pollution of the marine environment from vessels flying their flag or of their registry. Such laws and regulations shall at least have the same effect as that of generally accepted international rules and standards established through the competent international organization or general diplomatic conference.

3. States which establish particular requirements for the prevention, reduction and control of pollution of the marine environment as a condition for the entry of foreign vessels into their ports or internal waters or for a call at their off-shore terminals shall give due publicity to such requirements and

shall communicate them to the competent international organization. Whenever such requirements are established in identical form by two or more coastal States in an endeavour to harmonize policy, the communication shall indicate which States are participating in such co-operative arrangements. Every State shall require the master of a vessel flying its flag or of its registry, when navigating within the territorial sea of a State participating in such co-operative arrangements, to furnish, upon the request of that State, information as to whether it is proceeding to a State of the same region participating in such co-operative arrangements and, if so, to indicate whether it complies with the port entry requirements of that State. This article is without prejudice to the continued exercise by a vessel of its right of innocent passage or to the application of article 25, paragraph 2.

4. Coastal States may, in the exercise of their sovereignty within their territorial sea, adopt laws and regulations for the prevention, reduction and control of marine pollution from foreign vessels, including vessels exercising the right of innocent passage. Such laws and regulations shall, in accordance with Part II, section 3, not hamper innocent passage of foreign vessels.

5. Coastal States, for the purpose of enforcement as provided for in section 6, may in respect of their exclusive economic zones adopt laws and regulations for the prevention, reduction and control of pollution from vessels conforming to and giving effect to generally accepted international rules and standards established through the competent international organization or general diplomatic conference.

6. (a) Where the international rules and standards referred to in paragraph 1 are inadequate to meet special circumstances and coastal States have reasonable grounds for believing that a particular, clearly defined area of their respective exclusive economic zones is an area where the adoption of special mandatory measures for the prevention of pollution from vessels is required for recognized technical reasons in relation to its oceanographical and ecological conditions, as well as its utilization or the protection of its resources and the particular character of its traffic, the coastal States, after appropriate consultations through the competent international organization with any other States concerned, may, for that area, direct a communication to that organization, submitting scientific and technical evidence in support and information on necessary reception facilities. Within 12 months after receiving such a communication, the organization shall determine whether the conditions in that area correspond to the requirements set out above. If the organization so determines, the coastal States may, for that area, adopt laws and regulations for the prevention, reduction and control of pollution from vessels implementing such international rules and standards or navigational practices as are made applicable, through the organization, for special areas. These laws and regulations shall not become applicable to foreign vessels until 15 months after the submission of the communication to the organization.

(b) The coastal States shall publish the limits of any such particular, clearly defined area.

(c) If the coastal States intend to adopt additional laws and regulations for the same area for the prevention, reduction and control of pollution from vessels, they shall, when submitting the aforesaid communication, at the same time notify the organization thereof. Such additional laws and regulations may relate to discharges or navigational practices but shall not require foreign vessels to observe design, construction, manning or equipment standards other than generally accepted international rules and standards; they shall become applicable to foreign vessels 15 months after the submission of the communication to the organization, provided that the organization agrees within 12 months after the submission of the communication.

7. The international rules and standards referred to in this article should include *inter alia* those relating to prompt notification to coastal States, whose coastline or related interests may be affected by incidents, including maritime casualties, which involve discharges or probability of discharges.

Article 212

Pollution from or through the atmosphere

1. States shall adopt laws and regulations to prevent, reduce and control pollution of the marine environment from or through the atmosphere, applicable to the air space under their sovereignty and to vessels flying their flag or vessels or aircraft of their registry, taking into account internationally agreed rules, standards and recommended practices and procedures and the safety of air navigation.

2. States shall take other measures as may be necessary to prevent, reduce and control such pollution.

3. States, acting especially through competent international organizations or diplomatic conference, shall endeavour to establish global and regional rules, standards and recommended practices and procedures to prevent, reduce and control such pollution.

SECTION 6. ENFORCEMENT

Article 213

Enforcement with respect to pollution from land-based sources

States shall enforce their laws and regulations adopted in accordance with article 207 and shall adopt laws and regulations and take other measures necessary to implement applicable international rules and standards established through competent international organizations or diplomatic conference to prevent, reduce and control pollution of the marine environment from land-based sources.

Article 214

Enforcement with respect to pollution from sea-bed activities

States shall enforce their laws and regulations adopted in accordance with article 208 and shall adopt laws and regulations and take other measures necessary to implement applicable international rules and standards established through competent international organizations or diplomatic conference to prevent, reduce and control pollution of the marine environment arising from or in connection with sea-bed activities subject to their jurisdiction and from artificial islands, installations and structures under their jurisdiction, pursuant to articles 60 and 80.

Article 215

Enforcement with respect to pollution from activities in the Area

Enforcement of international rules, regulations and procedures established in accordance with Part XI to prevent, reduce and control pollution of the marine environment from activities in the Area shall be governed by that Part.

Article 216

Enforcement with respect to pollution by dumping

1. Laws and regulations adopted in accordance with this Convention and applicable international rules and standards established through competent international organizations or diplomatic conference for the prevention, reduction and control of pollution of the marine environment by dumping shall be enforced:

(a) by the coastal State with regard to dumping within its territorial sea or its exclusive economic zone or onto its continental shelf;

(b) by the flag State with regard to vessels flying its flag or vessels or aircraft of its registry;

(c) by any State with regard to acts of loading of wastes or other matter occurring within its territory or at its off-shore terminals.

2. No State shall be obliged by virtue of this article to institute proceedings when another State has already instituted proceedings in accordance with this article.

Article 217

Enforcement by flag States

1. States shall ensure compliance by vessels flying their flag or of their registry with applicable international rules and standards, established through the competent international organization or general diplomatic conference, and with their laws and regulations adopted in accordance with this Convention for the prevention, reduction and control of pollution of the marine environment from vessels and shall accordingly adopt laws and regulations and take other measures necessary for their implementation. Flag States shall provide for the effective enforcement of such rules, standards, laws and regulations, irrespective of where a violation occurs.

2. States shall, in particular, take appropriate measures in order to ensure that vessels flying their flag or of their registry are prohibited from sailing, until they can proceed to sea in compliance with the requirements of the international rules and standards referred to in paragraph 1, including requirements in respect of design, construction, equipment and manning of vessels.

3. States shall ensure that vessels flying their flag or of their registry carry on board certificates required by and issued pursuant to international rules and standards referred to in paragraph 1. States shall ensure that vessels flying their flag are periodically inspected in order to verify that such certificates are in conformity with the actual condition of the vessels. These certificates shall be accepted by other States as evidence of the condition of the vessels and shall be regarded as having the same force as certificates

issued by them, unless there are clear grounds for believing that the condition of the vessel does not correspond substantially with the particulars of the certificates.

4. If a vessel commits a violation of rules and standards established through the competent international organization or general diplomatic conference, the flag State, without prejudice to articles 218, 220 and 228, shall provide for immediate investigation and where appropriate institute proceedings in respect of the alleged violation irrespective of where the violation occurred or where the pollution caused by such violation has occurred or has been spotted.

5. Flag States conducting an investigation of the violation may request the assistance of any other State whose co-operation could be useful in clarifying the circumstances of the case. States shall endeavour to meet appropriate requests of flag States.

6. States shall, at the written request of any State, investigate any violation alleged to have been committed by vessels flying their flag. If satisfied that sufficient evidence is available to enable proceedings to be brought in respect of the alleged violation, flag States shall without delay institute such proceedings in accordance with their laws.

7. Flag States shall promptly inform the requesting State and the competent international organization of the action taken and its outcome. Such information shall be available to all States.

8. Penalties provided for by the laws and regulations of States for vessels flying their flag shall be adequate in severity to discourage violations wherever they occur.

Article 218

Enforcement by port States

1. When a vessel is voluntarily within a port or at an off-shore terminal of a State, that State may undertake investigations and, where the evidence so warrants, institute proceedings in respect of any discharge from that vessel outside the internal waters, territorial sea or exclusive economic zone of that State in violation of applicable international rules and standards established through the competent international organization or general diplomatic conference.

2. No proceedings pursuant to paragraph 1 shall be instituted in respect of a discharge violation in the internal waters, territorial sea or exclusive economic zone of another State unless requested by that State, the flag State, or a State damaged or threatened by the discharge violation, or unless the violation has caused or is likely to cause pollution in the internal waters, territorial sea or exclusive economic zone of the State instituting the proceedings.

3. When a vessel is voluntarily within a port or at an off-shore terminal of a State, that State shall, as far as practicable, comply with requests from any State for investigation of a discharge violation referred to in paragraph 1, believed to have occurred in, caused, or threatened damage to the internal waters, territorial sea or exclusive economic zone of the requesting State. It shall likewise, as far as practicable, comply with requests from the flag State

for investigation of such a violation, irrespective of where the violation occurred.

4. The records of the investigation carried out by a port State pursuant to this article shall be transmitted upon request to the flag State or to the coastal State. Any proceedings instituted by the port State on the basis of such an investigation may, subject to section 7, be suspended at the request of the coastal State when the violation has occurred within its internal waters, territorial sea or exclusive economic zone. The evidence and records of the case, together with any bond or other financial security posted with the authorities of the port State, shall in that event be transmitted to the coastal State. Such transmittal shall preclude the continuation of proceedings in the port State.

Article 219

Measures relating to seaworthiness of vessels to avoid pollution

Subject to section 7, States which, upon request or on their own initiative, have ascertained that a vessel within one of their ports or at one of their off-shore terminals is in violation of applicable international rules and standards relating to seaworthiness of vessels and thereby threatens damage to the marine environment shall, as far as practicable, take administrative measures to prevent the vessel from sailing. Such States may permit the vessel to proceed only to the nearest appropriate repair yard and, upon removal of the causes of the violation, shall permit the vessel to continue immediately.

Article 220

Enforcement by coastal States

1. When a vessel is voluntarily within a port or at an off-shore terminal of a State, that State may, subject to section 7, institute proceedings in respect of any violation of its laws and regulations adopted in accordance with this Convention or applicable international rules and standards for the prevention, reduction and control of pollution from vessels when the violation has occurred within the territorial sea or the exclusive economic zone of that State.

2. Where there are clear grounds for believing that a vessel navigating in the territorial sea of a State has, during its passage therein, violated laws and regulations of that State adopted in accordance with this Convention or applicable international rules and standards for the prevention, reduction and control of pollution from vessels, that State, without prejudice to the application of the relevant provisions of Part II, section 3, may undertake physical inspection of the vessel relating to the violation and may, where the evidence so warrants, institute proceedings, including detention of the vessel, in accordance with its laws, subject to the provisions of section 7.

3. Where there are clear grounds for believing that a vessel navigating in the exclusive economic zone or the territorial sea of a State has, in the exclusive economic zone, committed a violation of applicable international rules and standards for the prevention, reduction and control of pollution from vessels or laws and regulations of that State conforming and giving effect to such rules and standards, that State may require the vessel to give information regarding its identity and port of registry, its last and its next

port of call and other relevant information required to establish whether a violation has occurred.

4.   States shall adopt laws and regulations and take other measures so that vessels flying their flag comply with requests for information pursuant to paragraph 3.

5.   Where there are clear grounds for believing that a vessel navigating in the exclusive economic zone or the territorial sea of a State has, in the exclusive economic zone, committed a violation referred to in paragraph 3 resulting in a substantial discharge causing or threatening significant pollution of the marine environment, that State may undertake physical inspection of the vessel for matters relating to the violation if the vessel has refused to give information or if the information supplied by the vessel is manifestly at variance with the evident factual situation and if the circumstances of the case justify such inspection.

6.   Where there is clear objective evidence that a vessel navigating in the exclusive economic zone or the territorial sea of a State has, in the exclusive economic zone, committed a violation referred to in paragraph 3 resulting in a discharge causing major damage or threat of major damage to the coastline or related interests of the coastal State, or to any resources of its territorial sea or exclusive economic zone, that State may, subject to section 7, provided that the evidence so warrants, institute proceedings, including detention of the vessel, in accordance with its laws.

7.   Notwithstanding the provisions of paragraph 6, whenever appropriate procedures have been established, either through the competent international organization or as otherwise agreed, whereby compliance with requirements for bonding or other appropriate financial security has been assured, the coastal State if bound by such procedures shall allow the vessel to proceed.

8.   The provisions of paragraphs 3, 4, 5, 6 and 7 also apply in respect of national laws and regulations adopted pursuant to article 211, paragraph 6.

Article 221
Measures to avoid pollution arising from maritime casualties

1.   Nothing in this Part shall prejudice the right of States, pursuant to international law, both customary and conventional, to take and enforce measures beyond the territorial sea proportionate to the actual or threatened damage to protect their coastline or related interests, including fishing, from pollution or threat of pollution following upon a maritime casualty or acts relating to such a casualty, which may reasonably be expected to result in major harmful consequences.

2.   For the purposes of this article, "maritime casualty" means a collision of vessels, stranding or other incident of navigation, or other occurrence on board a vessel or external to it resulting in material damage or imminent threat of material damage to a vessel or cargo.

Article 222
Enforcement with respect to pollution from or through the atmosphere

States shall enforce, within the air space under their sovereignty or with regard to vessels flying their flag or vessels or aircraft of their registry, their laws and regulations adopted in accordance with article 212, paragraph 1, and with other provisions of this Convention and shall adopt laws and regulations and take other measures necessary to implement applicable international rules and standards established through competent international organizations or diplomatic conference to prevent, reduce and control pollution of the marine environment from or through the atmosphere, in conformity with all relevant international rules and standards concerning the safety of air navigation.

SECTION 7. SAFEGUARDS

Article 223

Measures to facilitate proceedings

In proceedings instituted pursuant to this Part, States shall take measures to facilitate the hearing of witnesses and the admission of evidence submitted by authorities of another State, or by the competent international organization, and shall facilitate the attendance at such proceedings of official representatives of the competent international organization, the flag State and any State affected by pollution arising out of any violation. The official representatives attending such proceedings shall have such rights and duties as may be provided under national laws and regulations or international law.

Article 224

Exercise of powers of enforcement

The powers of enforcement against foreign vessels under this Part may only be exercised by officials or by warships, military aircraft, or other ships or aircraft clearly marked and identifiable as being on government service and authorized to that effect.

Article 225

Duty to avoid adverse consequences in the exercise of the powers of enforcement

In the exercise under this Convention of their powers of enforcement against foreign vessels, States shall not endanger the safety of navigation or otherwise create any hazard to a vessel, or bring it to an unsafe port or anchorage, or expose the marine environment to an unreasonable risk.

Article 226

Investigation of foreign vessels

1. (a) States shall not delay a foreign vessel longer than is essential for purposes of the investigations provided for in articles 216, 218 and 220. Any physical inspection of a foreign vessel shall be limited to an examination of such certificates, records or other documents as the vessel is required to carry by generally accepted international rules and standards or of any similar documents which it is carrying; further physical inspection of the vessel may be undertaken only after such an examination and only when:

    (i) there are clear grounds for believing that the condition of the vessel or its equipment does not correspond substantially with the particulars of those documents;

    (ii) the contents of such documents are not sufficient to confirm or verify a suspected violation; or

    (iii) the vessel is not carrying valid certificates and records.

    (b) If the investigation indicates a violation of applicable laws and regulations or international rules and standards for the protection and preservation of the marine environment, release shall be made promptly subject to reasonable procedures such as bonding or other appropriate financial security.

(c) Without prejudice to applicable international rules and standards relating to the seaworthiness of vessels, the release of a vessel may, whenever it would present an unreasonable threat of damage to the marine environment, be refused or made conditional upon proceeding to the nearest appropriate repair yard. Where release has been refused or made conditional, the flag State of the vessel must be promptly notified, and may seek release of the vessel in accordance with Part XV.

2. States shall co-operate to develop procedures for the avoidance of unnecessary physical inspection of vessels at sea.

Article 227
Non-discrimination with respect to foreign vessels

* * *

Article 228
Suspension and restrictions on institution of proceedings

* * *

Article 229
Institution of civil proceedings

* * *

Article 230
Monetary penalties and the observance of recognized rights of the accused

* * *

Article 231
Notification to the flag State and other States concerned

* * *

Article 232
Liability of States arising from enforcement measures

States shall be liable for damage or loss attributable to them arising from measures taken pursuant to section 6 when such measures are unlawful or exceed those reasonably required in the light of available information. States shall provide for recourse in their courts for actions in respect of such damage or loss.

Article 233
Safeguards with respect to straits used for international navigation

* * *

SECTION 8. ICE–COVERED AREAS
Article 234
Ice-covered areas

Coastal States have the right to adopt and enforce non-discriminatory laws and regulations for the prevention, reduction and control of marine pollution from vessels in ice-covered areas within the limits of the exclusive economic zone, where particularly severe climatic conditions and the presence of ice covering such areas for most of the year create obstructions or exceptional hazards to navigation, and pollution of the marine environment could cause major harm to or irreversible disturbance of the ecological balance. Such laws and regulations shall have due regard to navigation and the protection and preservation of the marine environment based on the best available scientific evidence.

SECTION 9. RESPONSIBILITY AND LIABILITY

Article 235

Responsibility and liability

1. States are responsible for the fulfilment of their international obligations concerning the protection and preservation of the marine environment. They shall be liable in accordance with international law.

2. States shall ensure that recourse is available in accordance with their legal systems for prompt and adequate compensation or other relief in respect of damage caused by pollution of the marine environment by natural or juridical persons under their jurisdiction.

3. With the objective of assuring prompt and adequate compensation in respect of all damage caused by pollution of the marine environment, States shall co-operate in the implementation of existing international law and the further development of international law relating to responsibility and liability for the assessment of and compensation for damage and the settlement of related disputes, as well as, where appropriate, development of criteria and procedures for payment of adequate compensation, such as compulsory insurance or compensation funds.

SECTION 10. SOVEREIGN IMMUNITY

Article 236

Sovereign immunity

The provisions of this Convention regarding the protection and preservation of the marine environment do not apply to any warship, naval auxiliary, other vessels or aircraft owned or operated by a State and used, for the time being, only on government non-commercial service. However, each State shall ensure, by the adoption of appropriate measures not impairing operations or operational capabilities of such vessels or aircraft owned or operated by it, that such vessels or aircraft act in a manner consistent, so far as is reasonable and practicable, with this Convention.

SECTION 11. OBLIGATIONS UNDER OTHER CONVENTIONS ON THE PROTECTION AND PRESERVATION OF THE MARINE ENVIRONMENT

Article 237

Obligations under other conventions on the protection and preservation of the marine environment

1. The provisions of this Part are without prejudice to the specific obligations assumed by States under special conventions and agreements

concluded previously which relate to the protection and preservation of the marine environment and to agreements which may be concluded in furtherance of the general principles set forth in this Convention.

2. Specific obligations assumed by States under special conventions, with respect to the protection and preservation of the marine environment, should be carried out in a manner consistent with the general principles and objectives of this Convention.

PART XIII
MARINE SCIENTIFIC RESEARCH
SECTION 1. GENERAL PROVISIONS
Article 238
Right to conduct marine scientific research

All States, irrespective of their geographical location, and competent international organizations have the right to conduct marine scientific research subject to the rights and duties of other States as provided for in this Convention.

Article 239
Right to conduct marine scientific research

States and competent international organizations shall promote and facilitate the development and conduct of marine scientific research in accordance with this Convention.

Article 240
General principles for the conduct of marine scientific research

In the conduct of marine scientific research the following principles shall apply:

(a) marine scientific research shall be conducted exclusively for peaceful purposes;

(b) marine scientific research shall be conducted with appropriate scientific methods and means compatible with this Convention;

(c) marine scientific research shall not unjustifiably interfere with other legitimate uses of the sea compatible with this Convention and shall be duly respected in the course of such uses;

(d) marine scientific research shall be conducted in compliance with all relevant regulations adopted in conformity with this Convention including those for the protection and preservation of the marine environment.

Article 241
Non-recognition of marine scientific research
activities as the legal basis for claims

Marine scientific research activities shall not constitute the legal basis for any claim to any part of the marine environment or its resources.

SECTION 2. INTERNATIONAL CO–OPERATION
Article 242
Promotion of international co-operation

1. States and competent international organizations shall, in accordance with the principle of respect for sovereignty and jurisdiction and on the basis

of mutual benefit, promote international co-operation in marine scientific research for peaceful purposes.

2. In this context, without prejudice to the rights and duties of States under this Convention, a State, in the application of this Part, shall provide, as appropriate, other States with a reasonable opportunity to obtain from it, or with its co-operation, information necessary to prevent and control damage to the health and safety of persons and to the marine environment.

Article 243

Creation of favourable conditions

States and competent international organizations shall co-operate, through the conclusion of bilateral and multilateral agreements, to create favourable conditions for the conduct of marine scientific research in the marine environment and to integrate the efforts of scientists in studying the essence of phenomena and processes occurring in the marine environment and the interrelations between them.

Article 244

Publication and dissemination of information and knowledge

* * *

SECTION 3. CONDUCT AND PROMOTION OF MARINE SCIENTIFIC RESEARCH

Article 245

Marine scientific research in the territorial sea

Coastal States, in the exercise of their sovereignty, have the exclusive right to regulate, authorize and conduct marine scientific research in their territorial sea. Marine scientific research therein shall be conducted only with the express consent of and under the conditions set forth by the coastal State.

Article 246

Marine scientific research in the exclusive economic zone and on the continental shelf

1. Coastal States, in the exercise of their jurisdiction, have the right to regulate, authorize and conduct marine scientific research in their exclusive economic zone and on their continental shelf in accordance with the relevant provisions of this Convention.

2. Marine scientific research in the exclusive economic zone and on the continental shelf shall be conducted with the consent of the coastal State.

3. Coastal States shall, in normal circumstances, grant their consent for marine scientific research projects by other States or competent international organizations in their exclusive economic zone or on their continental shelf to be carried out in accordance with this Convention exclusively for peaceful purposes and in order to increase scientific knowledge of the marine environment for the benefit of all mankind. To this end, coastal States shall establish rules and procedures ensuring that such consent will not be delayed or denied unreasonably.

4. For the purposes of applying paragraph 3, normal circumstances may exist in spite of the absence of diplomatic relations between the coastal State and the researching State.

5. Coastal States may however in their discretion withhold their consent to the conduct of a marine scientific research project of another State or competent international organization in the exclusive economic zone or on the continental shelf of the coastal State if that project:

(a) is of direct significance for the exploration and exploitation of natural resources, whether living or non-living;

(b) involves drilling into the continental shelf, the use of explosives or the introduction of harmful substances into the marine environment;

(c) involves the construction, operation or use of artificial islands, installations and structures referred to in articles 60 and 80;

(d) contains information communicated pursuant to article 248 regarding the nature and objectives of the project which is inaccurate or if the researching State or competent international organization has outstanding obligations to the coastal State from a prior research project.

6. Notwithstanding the provisions of paragraph 5, coastal States may not exercise their discretion to withhold consent under subparagraph (a) of that paragraph in respect of marine scientific research projects to be undertaken in accordance with the provisions of this Part on the continental shelf, beyond 200 nautical miles from the baselines from which the breadth of the territorial sea is measured, outside those specific areas which coastal States may at any time publicly designate as areas in which exploitation or detailed exploratory operations focused on those areas are occurring or will occur within a reasonable period of time. Coastal States shall give reasonable notice of the designation of such areas, as well as any modifications thereto, but shall not be obliged to give details of the operations therein.

7. The provisions of paragraph 6 are without prejudice to the rights of coastal States over the continental shelf as established in article 77.

8. Marine scientific research activities referred to in this article shall not unjustifiably interfere with activities undertaken by coastal States in the exercise of their sovereign rights and jurisdiction provided for in this Convention.

Article 247

*Marine scientific research projects undertaken by or under
the auspices of international organizations*

* * *

Article 248

Duty to provide information to the coastal State

States and competent international organizations which intend to undertake marine scientific research in the exclusive economic zone or on the continental shelf of a coastal State shall, not less than six months in advance of the expected starting date of the marine scientific research project, provide that State with a full description of:

(a) the nature and objectives of the project;

(b) the method and means to be used, including name, tonnage, type and class of vessels and a description of scientific equipment;

(c) the precise geographical areas in which the project is to be conducted;

(d) the expected date of first appearance and final departure of the research vessels, or deployment of the equipment and its removal, as appropriate;

(e) the name of the sponsoring institution, its director, and the person in charge of the project; and

(f) the extent to which it is considered that the coastal State should be able to participate or to be represented in the project.

Article 249

Duty to comply with certain conditions

1. States and competent international organizations when undertaking marine scientific research in the exclusive economic zone or on the continental shelf of a coastal State shall comply with the following conditions:

(a) ensure the right of the coastal State, if it so desires, to participate or be represented in the marine scientific research project, especially on board research vessels and other craft or scientific research installations, when practicable, without payment of any remuneration to the scientists of the coastal State and without obligation to contribute towards the costs of the project;

(b) provide the coastal State, at its request, with preliminary reports, as soon as practicable, and with the final results and conclusions after the completion of the research;

(c) undertake to provide access for the coastal State, at its request, to all data and samples derived from the marine scientific research project and likewise to furnish it with data which may be copied and samples which may be divided without detriment to their scientific value;

(d) if requested, provide the coastal State with an assessment of such data, samples and research results or provide assistance in their assessment or interpretation;

(e) ensure, subject to paragraph 2, that the research results are made internationally available through appropriate national or international channels, as soon as practicable;

(f) inform the coastal State immediately of any major change in the research programme;

(g) unless otherwise agreed, remove the scientific research installations or equipment once the research is completed.

2. This article is without prejudice to the conditions established by the laws and regulations of the coastal State for the exercise of its discretion to grant or withhold consent pursuant to article 246, paragraph 5, including requiring prior agreement for making internationally available the research

results of a project of direct significance for the exploration and exploitation of natural resources.

Article 250

Communications concerning marine scientific research projects

Communications concerning the marine scientific research projects shall be made through appropriate official channels, unless otherwise agreed.

Article 251

General criteria and guidelines

States shall seek to promote through competent international organizations the establishment of general criteria and guidelines to assist States in ascertaining the nature and implications of marine scientific research.

Article 252

Implied consent

States or competent international organizations may proceed with a marine scientific research project six months after the date upon which the information required pursuant to article 248 was provided to the coastal State unless within four months of the receipt of the communication containing such information the coastal State has informed the State or organization conducting the research that:

(a) it has withheld its consent under the provisions of article 246; or

(b) the information given by that State or competent international organization regarding the nature or objectives of the project does not conform to the manifestly evident facts; or

(c) it requires supplementary information relevant to conditions and the information provided for under articles 248 and 249; or

(d) outstanding obligations exist with respect to a previous marine scientific research project carried out by that State or organization, with regard to conditions established in article 249.

Article 253

Suspension or cessation of marine scientific research activities

1. A coastal State shall have the right to require the suspension of any marine scientific research activities in progress within its exclusive economic zone or on its continental shelf if:

(a) the research activities are not being conducted in accordance with the information communicated as provided under article 248 upon which the consent of the coastal State was based; or

(b) the State or competent international organization conducting the research activities fails to comply with the provisions of article 249 concerning the rights of the coastal State with respect to the marine scientific research project.

* * *

Article 254

Rights of neighbouring land-locked and geographically disadvantaged States

1. States and competent international organizations which have submitted to a coastal State a project to undertake marine scientific research referred to in article 246, paragraph 3, shall give notice to the neighbouring land-locked and geographically disadvantaged States of the proposed research project, and shall notify the coastal State thereof.

2. After the consent has been given for the proposed marine scientific research project by the coastal State concerned, in accordance with article 246 and other relevant provisions of this Convention, States and competent international organizations undertaking such a project shall provide to the neighbouring land-locked and geographically disadvantaged States, at their request and when appropriate, relevant information as specified in article 248 and article 249, paragraph 1(f).

3. The neighbouring land-locked and geographically disadvantaged States referred to above shall, at their request, be given the opportunity to participate, whenever feasible, in the proposed marine scientific research project through qualified experts appointed by them and not objected to by the coastal State, in accordance with the conditions agreed for the project, in conformity with the provisions of this Convention, between the coastal State concerned and the State or competent international organizations conducting the marine scientific research.

* * *

Article 255

Measures to facilitate marine scientific research and assist research vessels

States shall endeavour to adopt reasonable rules, regulations and procedures to promote and facilitate marine scientific research conducted in accordance with this Convention beyond their territorial sea and, as appropriate, to facilitate, subject to the provisions of their laws and regulations, access to their harbours and promote assistance for marine scientific research vessels which comply with the relevant provisions of this Part.

Article 256

Marine scientific research in the Area

All States, irrespective of their geographical location, and competent international organizations have the right, in conformity with the provisions of Part XI, to conduct marine scientific research in the Area.

Article 257

Marine scientific research in the water column
beyond the exclusive economic zone

All States, irrespective of their geographical location, and competent international organizations have the right, in conformity with this Convention, to conduct marine scientific research in the water column beyond the limits of the exclusive economic zone.

SECTION 4. SCIENTIFIC RESEARCH INSTALLATIONS OR EQUIPMENT IN THE MARINE ENVIRONMENT

Article 258

Deployment and use

The deployment and use of any type of scientific research installations or equipment in any area of the marine environment shall be subject to the same conditions as are prescribed in this Convention for the conduct of marine scientific research in any such area.

Article 259

Legal status

The installations or equipment referred to in this section do not possess the status of islands. They have no territorial sea of their own, and their presence does not affect the delimitation of the territorial sea, the exclusive economic zone or the continental shelf.

Article 260

Safety zones

Safety zones of a reasonable breadth not exceeding a distance of 500 metres may be created around scientific research installations in accordance with the relevant provisions of this Convention. All States shall ensure that such safety zones are respected by their vessels.

Article 261

Non-interference with shipping routes

The deployment and use of any type of scientific research installations or equipment shall not constitute an obstacle to established international shipping routes.

Article 262

Identification markings and warning signals

Installations or equipment referred to in this section shall bear identification markings indicating the State of registry or the international organization to which they belong and shall have adequate internationally agreed warning signals to ensure safety at sea and the safety of air navigation, taking into account rules and standards established by competent international organizations.

SECTION 5. RESPONSIBILITY AND LIABILITY

Article 263

Responsibility and liability

1. States and competent international organizations shall be responsible for ensuring that marine scientific research, whether undertaken by them or on their behalf, is conducted in accordance with this Convention.

2. States and competent international organizations shall be responsible and liable for the measures they take in contravention of this Convention in respect of marine scientific research conducted by other States, their natural or juridical persons or by competent international organizations, and shall provide compensation for damage resulting from such measures.

3. States and competent international organizations shall be responsible and liable pursuant to article 235 for damage caused by pollution of the marine environment arising out of marine scientific research undertaken by them or on their behalf.

SECTION 6. SETTLEMENT OF DISPUTES AND INTERIM MEASURES

Article 264

Settlement of disputes

Disputes concerning the interpretation or application of the provisions of this Convention with regard to marine scientific research shall be settled in accordance with Part XV, sections 2 and 3.

Article 265

Interim measures

Pending settlement of a dispute in accordance with Part XV, sections 2 and 3, the State or competent international organization authorized to conduct a marine scientific research project shall not allow research activities to commence or continue without the express consent of the coastal State concerned.

PART XIV
DEVELOPMENT AND TRANSFER OF MARINE TECHNOLOGY
SECTION 1. GENERAL PROVISIONS

Article 266

Promotion of the development and transfer of marine technology

1. States, directly or through competent international organizations, shall cooperate in accordance with their capabilities to promote actively the development and transfer of marine science and marine technology on fair and reasonable terms and conditions.

2. States shall promote the development of the marine scientific and technological capacity of States which may need and request technical assistance in this field, particularly developing States, including land-locked and geographically disadvantaged States, with regard to the exploration, exploitation, conservation and management of marine resources, the protection and preservation of the marine environment, marine scientific research and other activities in the marine environment compatible with this Convention, with a view to accelerating the social and economic development of the developing States.

3. States shall endeavour to foster favourable economic and legal conditions for the transfer of marine technology for the benefit of all parties concerned on an equitable basis.

Article 267

Protection of legitimate interests

States, in promoting co-operation pursuant to article 266, shall have due regard for all legitimate interests including, *inter alia,* the rights and duties of holders, suppliers and recipients of marine technology.

Article 268
Basic objectives

States, directly or through competent international organizations, shall promote:

(a) the acquisition, evaluation and dissemination of marine technological knowledge and facilitate access to such information and data;

(b) the development of appropriate marine technology;

(c) the development of the necessary technological infrastructure to facilitate the transfer of marine technology;

(d) the development of human resources through training and education of nationals of developing States and countries and especially the nationals of the least developed among them;

(e) international co-operation at all levels, particularly at the regional, subregional and bilateral levels.

Article 269
Measures to achieve the basic objectives

In order to achieve the objectives referred to in article 268, States, directly or through competent international organizations, shall endeavour, *inter alia,* to:

(a) establish programmes of technical co-operation for the effective transfer of all kinds of marine technology to States which may need and request technical assistance in this field, particularly the developing land-locked and geographically disadvantaged States, as well as other developing States which have not been able either to establish or develop their own technological capacity in marine science and in the exploration and exploitation of marine resources or to develop the infrastructure of such technology;

(b) promote favourable conditions for the conclusion of agreements, contracts and other similar arrangements, under equitable and reasonable conditions;

(c) hold conferences, seminars and symposia on scientific and technological subjects, in particular on policies and methods for the transfer of marine technology;

(d) promote the exchange of scientists and of technological and other experts;

(e) undertake projects and promote joint ventures and other forms of bilateral and multilateral co-operation.

SECTION 2. INTERNATIONAL CO–OPERATION
Article 270
Ways and means of international co-operation

International co-operation for the development and transfer of marine technology shall be carried out, where feasible and appropriate, through existing bilateral, regional or multilateral programmes, and also through expanded and new programmes in order to facilitate marine scientific research, the transfer of marine technology, particularly in new fields, and appropriate international funding for ocean research and development.

Article 271
Guidelines, criteria and standards

States, directly or through competent international organizations, shall promote the establishment of generally accepted guidelines, criteria and standards for the transfer of marine technology on a bilateral basis or within the framework of international organizations and other fora, taking into account, in particular, the interests and needs of developing States.

Article 272
Co-ordination of international programmes

In the field of transfer of marine technology, States shall endeavour to ensure that competent international organizations co-ordinate their activities, including any regional or global programmes, taking into account the interests and needs of developing States, particularly land-locked and geographically disadvantaged States.

Article 273
Co-operation with international organizations and the Authority

States shall co-operate actively with competent international organizations and the Authority to encourage and facilitate the transfer to developing States, their nationals and the Enterprise of skills and marine technology with regard to activities in the Area.

Article 274
Objectives of the Authority

Subject to all legitimate interests including, *inter alia*, the rights and duties of holders, suppliers and recipients of technology, the Authority, with regard to activities in the Area, shall ensure that:

(a) on the basis of the principle of equitable geographical distribution, nationals of developing States, whether coastal, land-locked or geographically disadvantaged, shall be taken on for the purposes of training as members of the managerial, research and technical staff constituted for its undertakings;

(b) the technical documentation on the relevant equipment, machinery, devices and processes is made available to all States, in particular developing States which may need and request technical assistance in this field;

(c) adequate provision is made by the Authority to facilitate the acquisition of technical assistance in the field of marine technology by States which may need and request it, in particular developing States, and the acquisition by their nationals of the necessary skills and know-how, including professional training;

(d) States which may need and request technical assistance in this field, in particular developing States, are assisted in the acquisition of necessary equipment, processes, plant and other technical know-how through any financial arrangements provided for in this Convention.

SECTION 3. NATIONAL AND REGIONAL MARINE SCIENTIFIC AND TECHNOLOGICAL CENTRES

Article 275

Establishment of national centres

1.   States, directly or through competent international organizations and the Authority, shall promote the establishment, particularly in developing coastal States, of national marine scientific and technological research centres and the strengthening of existing national centres, in order to stimulate and advance the conduct of marine scientific research by developing coastal States and to enhance their national capabilities to utilize and preserve their marine resources for their economic benefit.

* * *

Article 276

Establishment of regional centres

* * *

Article 277

Functions of regional centres

* * *

SECTION 4. CO–OPERATION AMONG INTERNATIONAL ORGANIZATIONS

Article 278

Co-operation among international organizations

The competent international organizations referred to in this Part and in Part XIII shall take all appropriate measures to ensure, either directly or in close co-operation among themselves, the effective discharge of their functions and responsibilities under this Part.

PART XV

SETTLEMENT OF DISPUTES

SECTION 1.   GENERAL PROVISIONS

Article 279

Obligation to settle disputes by peaceful means

States Parties shall settle any dispute between them concerning the interpretation or application of this Convention by peaceful means in accordance with Article 2, paragraph 3, of the Charter of the United Nations and, to this end, shall seek a solution by the means indicated in Article 33, paragraph 1, of the Charter.

Article 280

Settlement of disputes by any peaceful means chosen by the parties

Nothing in this Part impairs the right of any States Parties to agree at any time to settle a dispute between them concerning the interpretation or application of this Convention by any peaceful means of their own choice.

Article 281

Procedure where no settlement has been reached by the parties

1. If the States Parties which are parties to a dispute concerning the interpretation or application of this Convention have agreed to seek settlement of the dispute by a peaceful means of their own choice, the procedures provided for in this Part apply only where no settlement has been reached by recourse to such means and the agreement between the parties does not exclude any further procedure.

2. If the parties have also agreed on a time-limit, paragraph 1 applies only upon the expiration of that time-limit.

Article 282

Obligations under general, regional or bilateral agreements

If the States Parties which are parties to a dispute concerning the interpretation or application of this Convention have agreed, through a general, regional or bilateral agreement or otherwise, that such dispute shall, at the request of any party to the dispute, be submitted to a procedure that entails a binding decision, that procedure shall apply in lieu of the procedures provided for in this Part, unless the parties to the dispute otherwise agree.

Article 283

Obligation to exchange views

1. When a dispute arises between States Parties concerning the interpretation or application of this Convention, the parties to the dispute shall proceed expeditiously to an exchange of views regarding its settlement by negotiation or other peaceful means.

2. The parties shall also proceed expeditiously to an exchange of views where a procedure for the settlement of such a dispute has been terminated without a settlement or where a settlement has been reached and the circumstances require consultation regarding the manner of implementing the settlement.

Article 284

Conciliation

1. A State Party which is a party to a dispute concerning the interpretation or application of this Convention may invite the other party or parties to submit the dispute to conciliation in accordance with the procedure under Annex V, section 1, or another conciliation procedure.

2. If the invitation is accepted and if the parties agree upon the conciliation procedure to be applied, any party may submit the dispute to that procedure.

3. If the invitation is not accepted or the parties do not agree upon the procedure, the conciliation proceedings shall be deemed to be terminated.

4. Unless the parties otherwise agree, when a dispute has been submitted to conciliation, the proceedings may be terminated only in accordance with the agreed conciliation procedure.

Article 285

Application of this section to disputes submitted pursuant to Part XI

This section applies to any dispute which pursuant to Part XI, section 5, is to be settled in accordance with procedures provided for in this Part. If an entity other than a State Party is a party to such a dispute, this section applies *mutatis mutandis.*

SECTION 2. COMPULSORY PROCEDURES ENTAILING BINDING DECISIONS

Article 286

Application of procedures under this section

Subject to section 3, any dispute concerning the interpretation or application of this Convention shall, where no settlement has been reached by recourse to section 1, be submitted at the request of any party to the dispute to the court or tribunal having jurisdiction under this section.

Article 287

Choice of procedure

1. When signing, ratifying or acceding to this Convention or at any time thereafter, a State shall be free to choose, by means of a written declaration, one or more of the following means for the settlement of disputes concerning the interpretation or application of this Convention:

(a) the International Tribunal for the Law of the Sea established [in Hamburg, West Germany] in accordance with Annex VI;

(b) the International Court of Justice;

(c) an arbitral tribunal constituted in accordance with Annex VII;

(d) a special arbitral tribunal constituted in accordance with Annex VIII for one or more of the categories of disputes specified therein.

2. A declaration made under paragraph 1 shall not affect or be affected by the obligation of a State Party to accept the jurisdiction of the Sea–Bed Disputes Chamber of the International Tribunal for the Law of the Sea to the extent and in the manner provided for in Part XI, section 5.

3. A State Party, which is a party to a dispute not covered by a declaration in force, shall be deemed to have accepted arbitration in accordance with Annex VII.

4. If the parties to a dispute have accepted the same procedure for the settlement of the dispute, it may be submitted only to that procedure, unless the parties otherwise agree.

5. If the parties to a dispute have not accepted the same procedure for the settlement of the dispute, it may be submitted only to arbitration in accordance with Annex VII, unless the parties otherwise agree.

6. A declaration made under paragraph 1 shall remain in force until three months after notice of revocation has been deposited with the Secretary–General of the United Nations.

7. A new declaration, a notice of revocation or the expiry of a declaration does not in any way affect proceedings pending before a court or tribunal having jurisdiction under this article, unless the parties otherwise agree.

8.   Declarations and notices referred to in this article shall be deposited with the Secretary–General of the United Nations, who shall transmit copies thereof to the States Parties.

Article 288
Jurisdiction

1.   A court or tribunal referred to in article 287 shall have jurisdiction over any dispute concerning the interpretation or application of this Convention which is submitted to it in accordance with this Part.

2.   A court or tribunal referred to in article 287 shall also have jurisdiction over any dispute concerning the interpretation or application of an international agreement related to the purposes of this Convention, which is submitted to it in accordance with the agreement.

3.   The Sea–Bed Disputes Chamber of the International Tribunal for the Law of the Sea established in accordance with Annex VI, and any other chamber or arbitral tribunal referred to in Part XI, section 5, shall have jurisdiction in any matter which is submitted to it in accordance therewith.

4.   In the event of a dispute as to whether a court or tribunal has jurisdiction, the matter shall be settled by decision of that court or tribunal.

Article 289
Experts

In any dispute involving scientific or technical matters, a court or tribunal exercising jurisdiction under this section may, at the request of a party or *proprio motu,* select in consultation with the parties no fewer than two scientific or technical experts chosen preferably from the relevant list prepared in accordance with Annex VII, article 2, to sit with the court or tribunal but without the right to vote.

Article 290
Provisional measures

1.   If a dispute has been duly submitted to a court or tribunal which considers that *prima facie* it has jurisdiction under this Part or Part XI, section 5, the court or tribunal may prescribe any provisional measures which it considers appropriate under the circumstances to preserve the respective rights of the parties to the dispute or to prevent serious harm to the marine environment, pending the final decision.

* * *

6.   The parties to the dispute shall comply promptly with any provisional measures prescribed under this article.

Article 291
Access

1.   All the dispute settlement procedures specified in this Part shall be open to States Parties.

2.   The dispute settlement procedures specified in this Part shall be open to entities other than States Parties only as specifically provided for in this Convention.

Article 292

Prompt release of vessels and crews

1.   Where the authorities of a State Party have detained a vessel flying the flag of another State Party and it is alleged that the detaining State has not complied with the provisions of this Convention for the prompt release of the vessel or its crew upon the posting of a reasonable bond or other financial security, the question of release from detention may be submitted to any court or tribunal agreed upon by the parties or, failing such agreement within 10 days from the time of detention, to a court or tribunal accepted by the detaining State under article 287 or to the International Tribunal for the Law of the Sea, unless the parties otherwise agree.

2.   The application for release may be made only by or on behalf of the flag State of the vessel.

3.   The court or tribunal shall deal without delay with the application for release and shall deal only with the question of release, without prejudice to the merits of any case before the appropriate domestic forum against the vessel, its owner or its crew. The authorities of the detaining State remain competent to release the vessel or its crew at any time.

4.   Upon the posting of the bond or other financial security determined by the court or tribunal, the authorities of the detaining State shall comply promptly with the decision of the court or tribunal concerning the release of the vessel or its crew.

Article 293

Applicable law

1.   A court or tribunal having jurisdiction under this section shall apply this Convention and other rules of international law not incompatible with this Convention.

2.   Paragraph 1 does not prejudice the power of the court or tribunal having jurisdiction under this section to decide a case *ex aequo et bono,* if the parties so agree.

Article 294

Preliminary proceedings

1.   A court or tribunal provided for in article 287 to which an application is made in respect of a dispute referred to in article 297 shall determine at the request of a party, or may determine *proprio motu,* whether the claim constitutes an abuse of legal process or whether *prima facie* it is well founded. If the court or tribunal determines that the claim constitutes an abuse of legal process or is *prima facie* unfounded, it shall take no further action in the case.

* * *

Article 295

Exhaustion of local remedies

Any dispute between States Parties concerning the interpretation or application of this Convention may be submitted to the procedures provided for in this section only after local remedies have been exhausted where this is required by international law.

Article 296

Finality and binding force of decisions

1. Any decision rendered by a court or tribunal having jurisdiction under this section shall be final and shall be complied with by all the parties to the dispute.

2. Any such decision shall have no binding force except between the parties and in respect of that particular dispute.

SECTION 3.   LIMITATIONS AND EXCEPTIONS TO APPLICABILITY OF SECTION 2

Article 297

Limitations on applicability of section 2

1. Disputes concerning the interpretation or application of this Convention with regard to the exercise by a coastal State of its sovereign rights or jurisdiction provided for in this Convention shall be subject to the procedures provided for in section 2 in the following cases:

(a) when it is alleged that a coastal State has acted in contravention of the provisions of this Convention in regard to the freedoms and rights of navigation, overflight or the laying of submarine cables and pipelines, or in regard to other internationally lawful uses of the sea specified in article 58;

(b) when it is alleged that a State in exercising the aforementioned freedoms, rights or uses has acted in contravention of this Convention or of laws or regulations adopted by the coastal State in conformity with this Convention and other rules of international law not incompatible with this Convention; or

(c) when it is alleged that a coastal State has acted in contravention of specified international rules and standards for the protection and preservation of the marine environment which are applicable to the coastal State and which have been established by this Convention or through a competent international organization or diplomatic conference in accordance with this Convention.

2. (a) Disputes concerning the interpretation or application of the provisions of this Convention with regard to marine scientific research shall be settled in accordance with section 2, except that the coastal State shall not be obliged to accept the submission to such settlement of any dispute arising out of:

(i) the exercise by the coastal State of a right or discretion in accordance with article 246; or

(ii) a decision by the coastal State to order suspension or cessation of a research project in accordance with article 253.

(b) A dispute arising from an allegation by the researching State that with respect to a specific project the coastal State is not exercising its rights under articles 246 and 253 in a manner compatible with this Convention shall be submitted, at the request of either party, to conciliation under Annex V, section 2, provided that the conciliation commission shall not call in question the exercise by the coastal State of its discretion to designate specific areas as referred to in article 246, paragraph 6, or of its discretion to withhold consent in accordance with article 246, paragraph 5.

3. (a) Disputes concerning the interpretation or application of the provisions of this Convention with regard to fisheries shall be settled in accordance with section 2, except that the coastal State shall not be obliged to accept the submission to such settlement of any dispute relating to its sovereign rights with respect to the living resources in the exclusive economic zone or their exercise, including its discretionary powers for determining the allowable catch, its harvesting capacity, the allocation of surpluses to other States and the terms and conditions established in its conservation and management laws and regulations.

(b) Where no settlement has been reached by recourse to section 1 of this Part, a dispute shall be submitted to conciliation under Annex V, section 2, at the request of any party to the dispute, when it is alleged that:

(i) a coastal State has manifestly failed to comply with its obligations to ensure through proper conservation and management measures that the maintenance of the living resources in the exclusive economic zone is not seriously endangered;

(ii) a coastal State has arbitrarily refused to determine, at the request of another State, the allowable catch and its capacity to harvest living resources with respect to stocks which that other State is interested in fishing; or

(iii) a coastal State has arbitrarily refused to allocate to any State, under articles 62, 69 and 70 and under the terms and conditions established by the coastal State consistent with this Convention, the whole or part of the surplus it has declared to exist.

(c) In no case shall the conciliation commission substitute its discretion for that of the coastal State.

(d) The report of the conciliation commission shall be communicated to the appropriate international organizations.

(e) In negotiating agreements pursuant to articles 69 and 70, States Parties, unless they otherwise agree, shall include a clause on measures which they shall take in order to minimize the possibility of a disagreement concerning the interpretation or application of the agreement, and on how they should proceed if a disagreement nevertheless arises.

Article 298

Optional exceptions to applicability of section 2

1. When signing, ratifying or acceding to this Convention or at any time thereafter, a State may, without prejudice to the obligations arising under section 1, declare in writing that it does not accept any one or more of the procedures provided for in section 2 with respect to one or more of the following categories of disputes:

(a)(i) disputes concerning the interpretation or application of articles 15, 74 and 83 relating to sea boundary delimitations, or those involving historic bays or titles, provided that a State having made such a declaration shall, when such a dispute arises subsequent to the entry into force of this Convention and where no agreement within a reasonable period of time is reached in negotiations between the parties, at the request of any party to the dispute, accept submission of the matter to conciliation under Annex V, section 2; and provided further that any dispute that necessarily involves the concurrent consideration of any unsettled dispute concerning sovereignty or other rights over continental or insular land territory shall be excluded from such submission;

(ii) after the conciliation commission has presented its report, which shall state the reasons on which it is based, the parties shall negotiate an agreement on the basis of that report; if these negotiations do not result in an agreement, the parties shall, by mutual consent, submit the question to one of the procedures provided for in section 2, unless the parties otherwise agree;

(iii) this subparagraph does not apply to any sea boundary dispute finally settled by an arrangement between the parties, or to any such dispute which is to be settled in accordance with a bilateral or multilateral agreement binding upon those parties;

(b) disputes concerning military activities, including military activities by government vessels and aircraft engaged in non-commercial service, and disputes concerning law enforcement activities in regard to the exercise of sovereign rights or jurisdiction excluded from the jurisdiction of a court or tribunal under article 297, paragraph 2 or 3;

(c) disputes in respect of which the Security Council of the United Nations is exercising the functions assigned to it by the Charter of the United Nations, unless the Security Council decides to remove the matter from its agenda or calls upon the parties to settle it by the means provided for in this Convention.

2. A State Party which has made a declaration under paragraph 1 may at any time withdraw it, or agree to submit a dispute excluded by such declaration to any procedure specified in this Convention.

3. A State Party which has made a declaration under paragraph 1 shall not be entitled to submit any dispute falling within the excepted category of disputes to any procedure in this Convention as against another State Party, without the consent of that party.

4. If one of the States Parties has made a declaration under paragraph 1(a), any other State Party may submit any dispute falling within an excepted category against the declarant party to the procedure specified in such declaration.

5. A new declaration, or the withdrawal of a declaration, does not in any way affect proceedings pending before a court or tribunal in accordance with this article, unless the parties otherwise agree.

6. Declarations and notices of withdrawal of declarations under this article shall be deposited with the Secretary–General of the United Nations, who shall transmit copies thereof to the States Parties.

Article 299

Right of the parties to agree upon a procedure

1.   A dispute excluded under article 297 or excepted by a declaration made under article 298 from the dispute settlement procedures provided for in section 2 may be submitted to such procedures only by agreement of the parties to the dispute.

2.   Nothing in this section impairs the right of the parties to the dispute to agree to some other procedure for the settlement of such dispute or to reach an amicable settlement.

PART XVI
GENERAL PROVISIONS

Article 300

Good faith and abuse of rights

States Parties shall fulfil in good faith the obligations assumed under this Convention and shall exercise the rights, jurisdiction and freedoms recognized in this Convention in a manner which would not constitute an abuse of right.

Article 301

Peaceful uses of the seas

In exercising their rights and performing their duties under this Convention, States Parties shall refrain from any threat or use of force against the territorial integrity or political independence of any State, or in any other manner inconsistent with the principles of international law embodied in the Charter of the United Nations.

Article 302

Disclosure of information

Without prejudice to the right of a State Party to resort to the procedures for the settlement of disputes provided for in this Convention, nothing in this Convention shall be deemed to require a State Party, in the fulfilment of its obligations under this Convention, to supply information the disclosure of which is contrary to the essential interests of its security.

Article 303

Archaeological and historical objects found at sea

1.   States have the duty to protect objects of an archaeological and historical nature found at sea and shall co-operate for this purpose.

2.   In order to control traffic in such objects, the coastal State may, in applying article 33, presume that their removal from the sea-bed in the zone referred to in that article without its approval would result in an infringement within its territory or territorial sea of the laws and regulations referred to in that article.

3.   Nothing in this article affects the rights of identifiable owners, the law of salvage or other rules of admiralty, or laws and practices with respect to cultural exchanges.

4.   This article is without prejudice to other international agreements and rules of international law regarding the protection of objects of an archaeological and historical nature.

Article 304

Responsibility and liability for damage

The provisions of this Convention regarding responsibility and liability for damage are without prejudice to the application of existing rules and the development of further rules regarding responsibility and liability under international law.

PART XVII
FINAL PROVISIONS

* * *

Article 309

Reservations and exceptions

No reservations or exceptions may be made to this Convention unless expressly permitted by other articles of this Convention.

Article 310

Declarations and statements

Article 309 does not preclude a State, when signing, ratifying or acceding to this Convention, from making declarations or statements, however phrased or named, with a view, *inter alia,* to the harmonization of its laws and regulations with the provisions of this Convention, provided that such declarations or statements do not purport to exclude or to modify the legal effect of the provisions of this Convention in their application to that State.

Article 311

Relation to other conventions and international agreements

1. This Convention shall prevail, as between States Parties, over the Geneva Conventions on the Law of the Sea of 29 April 1958.

2. This Convention shall not alter the rights and obligations of States Parties which arise from other agreements compatible with this Convention and which do not affect the enjoyment by other States Parties of their rights or the performance of their obligations under this Convention.

3. Two or more States Parties may conclude agreements modifying or suspending the operation of provisions of this Convention, applicable solely to the relations between them, provided that such agreements do not relate to a provision derogation from which is incompatible with the effective execution of the object and purpose of this Convention, and provided further that such agreements shall not affect the application of the basic principles embodied herein, and that the provisions of such agreements do not affect the enjoyment by other States Parties of their rights or the performance of their obligations under this Convention.

4. States Parties intending to conclude an agreement referred to in paragraph 3 shall notify the other States Parties through the depositary of this Convention of their intention to conclude the agreement and of the modification or suspension for which it provides.

5. This article does not affect international agreements expressly permitted or preserved by other articles of this Convention.

6. State Parties agree that there shall be no amendments to the basic principle relating to the common heritage of mankind set forth in article 136 and that they shall not be party to any agreement in derogation thereof.

* * *

Article 317
Denunciation

1. A State Party may, by written notification addressed to the Secretary–General of the United Nations, denounce this Convention and may indicate its reasons. Failure to indicate reasons shall not affect the validity of the denunciation. The denunciation shall take effect one year after the date of receipt of the notification, unless the notification specifies a later date.

2. A State shall not be discharged by reason of the denunciation from the financial and contractual obligations which accrued while it was a Party to this Convention, nor shall the denunciation affect any right, obligation or legal situation of that State created through the execution of this Convention prior to its termination for that State.

3. The denunciation shall not in any way affect the duty of any State Party to fulfil any obligation embodied in this Convention to which it would be subject under international law independently of this Convention.

Article 318
Status of Annexes

The Annexes form an integral part of this Convention and, unless expressly provided otherwise, a reference to this Convention or to one of its Parts includes a reference to the Annexes relating thereto.

* * *

ANNEX V. CONCILIATION
SECTION 1. CONCILIATION PROCEDURE PURSUANT TO SECTION 1 OF PART XV

Article 1
Institution of proceedings

If the parties to a dispute have agreed, in accordance with article 284, to submit it to conciliation under this section, any such party may institute the proceedings by written notification addressed to the other party or parties to the dispute.

Article 2
List of conciliators

A list of conciliators shall be drawn up and maintained by the Secretary–General of the United Nations. Every State Party shall be entitled to nominate four conciliators, each of whom shall be a person enjoying the highest reputation for fairness, competence and integrity. The names of the persons so nominated shall constitute the list. If at any time the conciliators nominated by a State Party in the list so constituted shall be fewer than four, that State Party shall be entitled to make further nominations as necessary. The name of a conciliator shall remain on the list until withdrawn by the State Party which made the nomination, provided that such conciliator shall continue to serve on any conciliation commission to which that conciliator has been appointed until the completion of the proceedings before that commission.

Article 3
Constitution of conciliation commission

The conciliation commission shall, unless the parties otherwise agree, be constituted as follows:

(a) Subject to subparagraph (g), the conciliation commission shall consist of five members.

(b) The party instituting the proceedings shall appoint two conciliators to be chosen preferably from the list referred to in article 2 of this Annex, one of whom may be its national, unless the parties otherwise agree. Such appointments shall be included in the notification referred to in article 1 of this Annex.

(c) The other party to the dispute shall appoint two conciliators in the manner set forth in subparagraph (b) within 21 days of receipt of the notification referred to in article 1 of this Annex. If the appointments are not made within that period, the party instituting the proceedings may, within one week of the expiration of that period, either terminate the proceedings by notification addressed to the other party or request the Secretary–General of the United Nations to make the appointments in accordance with subparagraph (e).

(d) Within 30 days after all four conciliators have been appointed, they shall appoint a fifth conciliator chosen from the list referred to in article 2 of this Annex, who shall be chairman. If the appointment is not made within that period, either party may, within one week of the expiration of that period, request the Secretary–General of the United Nations to make the appointment in accordance with subparagraph (e).

(e) Within 30 days of the receipt of a request under subparagraph (c) or (d), the Secretary–General of the United Nations shall make the necessary appointments from the list referred to in article 2 of this Annex in consultation with the parties to the dispute.

(f) Any vacancy shall be filled in the manner prescribed for the initial appointment.

(g) Two or more parties which determine by agreement that they are in the same interest shall appoint two conciliators jointly. Where two or more parties have separate interests or there is a disagreement as to whether they are of the same interest, they shall appoint conciliators separately.

(h) In disputes involving more than two parties having separate interests, or where there is disagreement as to whether they are of the same interest, the parties shall apply subparagraphs (a) to (f) in so far as possible.

Article 4
Procedure

The conciliation commission shall, unless the parties otherwise agree, determine its own procedure. The commission may, with the consent of the parties to the dispute, invite any State Party to submit to it its views orally or in writing. Decisions of the commission regarding procedural matters, the report and recommendations shall be made by a majority vote of its members.

Article 5

Amicable settlement

The commission may draw the attention of the parties to any measures which might facilitate an amicable settlement of the dispute.

Article 6

Functions of the commission

The commission shall hear the parties, examine their claims and objections, and make proposals to the parties with a view to reaching an amicable settlement.

Article 7

Report

1. The commission shall report within 12 months of its constitution. Its report shall record any agreements reached and, failing agreement, its conclusions on all questions of fact or law relevant to the matter in dispute and such recommendations as the commission may deem appropriate for an amicable settlement. The report shall be deposited with the Secretary–General of the United Nations and shall immediately be transmitted by him to the parties to the dispute.

2. The report of the commission, including its conclusions or recommendations, shall not be binding upon the parties.

Article 8

Termination

The conciliation proceedings are terminated when a settlement has been reached, when the parties have accepted or one party has rejected the recommendations of the report by written notification addressed to the Secretary–General of the United Nations, or when a period of three months has expired from the date of transmission of the report to the parties.

Article 9

Fees and expenses

The fees and expenses of the commission shall be borne by the parties to the dispute.

Article 10

Right of parties to modify procedure

The parties to the dispute may by agreement applicable solely to that dispute modify any provision of this Annex.

SECTION 2. COMPULSORY SUBMISSION TO CONCILIATION PROCEDURE PURSUANT TO SECTION 3 OF PART XV

Article 11

Institution of proceedings

1. Any party to a dispute which, in accordance with Part XV, section 3, may be submitted to conciliation under this section, may institute the pro-

ceedings by written notification addressed to the other party or parties to the dispute.

2. Any party to the dispute, notified under paragraph 1, shall be obliged to submit to such proceedings.

Article 12

Failure to reply or to submit to conciliation

The failure of a party or parties to the dispute to reply to notification of institution of proceedings or to submit to such proceedings shall not constitute a bar to the proceedings.

Article 13

Competence

A disagreement as to whether a conciliation commission acting under this section has competence shall be decided by the commission.

Article 14

Application of section 1

Articles 2 to 10 of section 1 of this Annex apply subject to this section.

4.27　ECONOMIC COMMISSION FOR EUROPE DECLARATION OF POLICY ON THE RATIONAL USE OF WATER.　Adopted 14 April 1984. ECE/DEC/C(XXXIX)

The Economic Commission for Europe,

Mindful of the importance and urgency of combating wasteful use of water, both in terms of quantity and quality, and of promoting all measures which stimulate rational, economic and efficient water use to enable economic development to take place in a manner compatible with maintaining or improving the quality of life for present and future generations,

Bearing in mind the pertinent provisions of the Final Act of the Conference on Security and Co-operation in Europe by which participating States affirmed that "the protection of nature and the rational utilization of its resources in the interest of present and future generations is one of the tasks of major importance to the well-being of people and the economic development of all countries" and by which they expressed in particular their wish to enhance co-operation with a view to improving fresh water utilization "by developing methods of production which are less polluting and lead to less consumption of fresh water",

Bearing further in mind the relevant provisions of the Concluding Document of the Madrid Meeting of Representatives of the Participating States of the Conference on Security and Co-operation in Europe,

Taking note of the Mar del Plata Action Plan which calls upon countries to intensify national and international efforts "to maximize the economic and social efficiency of all water inputs, including measures to heighten awareness, change attitudes and provide the technological means and incentives to conserve and protect available water",

Recalling General Assembly resolution 35/18 of 17 November 1980 on the Proclamation of the International Drinking Water Supply and Sanitation Decade,

Conscious of the useful role played by the Commission over more than 20 years in assisting countries to share their experience regarding the use of natural resources, including both surface water and ground water, and in promoting the rational use of water through the preparation of guidelines and recommendations,

Bearing in mind the Declaration on Low- and Non-waste Technology and Re-utilization and Recycling of Wastes, by which States participating in the High-level Meeting within the Framework of the ECE on the Protection of the Environment declared, *inter alia,* their intent to use resources rationally,

Underlining the importance of the ECE Declaration of Policy on Prevention and Control of Water Pollution, including Transboundary Pollution which, *inter alia,* stipulates that the rational utilization of water resources, both surface and underground, should be considered "a basic element in the framework of long-term water management and be viewed as an effective support to the policy of prevention and control of water pollution, taking into account the special features of each drainage basin",

Commending the efforts already undertaken by the Committee on Water Problems in paying increased attention to questions related to future-oriented water policies and strategies, to water demand management and to measures and instruments which influence user behaviour, thus bringing about economies in water use,

Noting, in this regard, the results of two seminars, namely Rational Utilization of Water (1979, Leipzig, German Democratic Republic) and Economic Instruments for Rational Utilization of Water Resources (1980, Veldhoven, Netherlands) as well as the reports on long-term perspectives for water use and supply in the ECE region (1981) and on policies and strategies for rational use of water in the ECE region (1983),

Recognizing the vital need for further developing and enhancing international co-operation and for improving co-ordination of efforts in ECE countries to formulate and apply strategies of water demand management for coping with limited water supply and to promote the concept of rational water use in the light of experience acquired during past years,

1. *Decides* to adopt the Principles of Rational Use of Water set forth in the appendix to this Declaration;

2. *Recommends* to ECE Governments that they apply these Principles in formulating, reviewing and implementing their water policies on a national and international level, taking into account their specific administrative structures;

3. *Invites* the member Governments to keep the Commission informed at appropriate intervals, through the Committee on Water Problems, of action taken by them in this regard;

4. *Requests* the Executive Secretary to transmit this decision to the member Governments as a Declaration of Policy on the Rational Use of Water; and

5. *Requests* the Executive Secretary to transmit this decision to international organizations concerned, with a view to extending co-operation in this field.

PRINCIPLES

1. It is recognized that:

(a) with increasing urban concentration, industrial expansion, intensified agricultural exploitation, rising living standards and the accelerated development of touristic and recreational activities, water, being an irreplaceable natural resource, is becoming an important issue in many countries or parts of them and, in some, even a limited factor for socio-economic development;

(b) development and further management of water resources is becoming technically difficult, expensive and may conflict with some economic sectors as well as with environmental concerns; and that

(c) water is being used sometimes irrationally, beyond an economically and socially sensible level and used as an undue recipient of harmful pollution loads.

2. Governments are therefore being called upon to formulate and adopt policies at all appropriate levels which foster measures striving for the efficient utilization of water resources from both supply and disposal aspects, in order to secure that, as far as possible, the wastage of water is prevented

together with that of energy and raw materials required for its abstraction, transportation, storage, proper use and treatment of water and for waste water purification, so that rational use of water contributes to the fullest extent to national welfare. Water use should be considered in the context of efficient utilization of common resources and should therefore be of concern to the entire population.

3. In formulating and adopting a future-oriented national water policy it should be taken into account that water, a common resource, must be used economically in the interest of the public at large. Therefore, special emphasis should be given to:

(a) a unified strategy for water withdrawal, distribution, treatment, use and discharge;

(b) integrated water use, attaching priority to drinking water requirements and to environmental protection;

(c) water demand management and preventive measures so as to avoid water shortages and water pollution; management options should be matched to actual supply; usable supplies should be explored and safeguarded;

(d) non-structural measures, which aim at increasing operation efficiency of existing water schemes; they should be designed to fit into a comprehensive approach to the management of water quantity and quality;

(e) co-ordinated utilization of both surface water and ground water, taking into account their close interrelation; public drinking water supply should be given priority in ground water use; and

(f) measures to combat harmful effects of water: flooding, soil erosion, etc.

4. In the over-all planning process of a country, thorough consideration should be given to the concept of rational use of national water resources and to alternative and multi-purpose uses of water and their impact on other natural resources as well as on the economy as a whole. The methods of systems analysis and mathematical modelling may be applied. In these planning procedures, perspectives and forecasts of future water demand, use, consumption and discharge should not only be an extrapolation of past trends but should also take into account the anticipated effect of applied or foreseen control measures, economic incentives and other stimuli on future water-use practices. Due attention should be paid to long-term planning as one of the most important tools for a comprehensive water policy; planning should in particular:

(a) ensure optimal socio-economic and ecological benefits from rational water use;

(b) facilitate proper decision making at all appropriate levels and within economic sectors;

(c) allow for close co-operation and co-ordination with other economic sectors as well as with regional and local administrative authorities;

(d) permit a sufficient period for the formulation and adjustment of a system of regulatory measures and economic instruments; and

(e) provide guidance for a rational allocation of long-term investments to promote sustainable development of water management.

5. Within the framework of the general principles set forth in this declaration of policy, specific attention should be accorded in national water policies and planning to the protection of ground water from the possibility of pollution and overuse.

6. Priority should be accorded to the co-ordination of land-use planning and water management. This could be restrictions on the use of certain areas, already subject to serious water shortages and/or heavy environmental stress, as well as the separation of areas of water use from those of water abstraction. However, the general principle should be maintained, where possible, that the establishment of new industrial complexes, power plants, intensive livestock farming, the development of new settlements and the expansion of urban areas should be compatible with the availability of water of sufficient quality and quantity at reasonable distances. River basin oriented management, including flow transfer within and between basins and the siting of future reservoirs, should be given appropriate attention in land-use planning and water management planning to achieve a long-term integrated and rational approach to an efficient and sustainable use of water. In planning water management systems, consideration should be given to the creation of integrated water supply and disposal systems which could take advantage of diversities in demand patterns over wider areas—thus providing easier response to peak demands—and of economies that may result from the construction and operation of centralized water supply and sewage systems. Attention should also be given to the efficient operation of drinking water and waste water treatment plants.

7. In conformity with the administrative structure and existing regulations, adequate involvement of water users and those involved in decision-making processes should be encouraged, as they can make significant contributions both to the identification of targets and to the development, adoption and effective implementation of water saving programmes. Education and training should be regarded as an important tool in the implementation of national and regional water policies. It should, therefore, be pursued vigorously so that the public understands and respects the importance of using water rationally and appreciates the socio-economic and ecological advantages that can be achieved by improving water conservation practices; measures taken, however, should not go beyond what is in the public interest. To this end, the Governments are called upon to intensify national efforts with a view to enhancing or, if necessary, creating, as appropriate, frameworks for youth education and training in this field, in the interest of present and future generations.

8. Regulations and ordinances under certain conditions together with economic and financial instruments are considered an important regulatory tool for promoting water policy and for determining the rights and obligations of water users and their mutual relationships. Such regulative instruments may take the form of standards, criteria, rules, norms, limitations, permits or licences, control or stop orders and should be applied to setting strict targets for the use, consumption and discharge of water, especially in the industrial and agricultural sector. Administrative instruments should allow for direct

regulatory control through such practices as permits and licences and should oblige prospective water users, including public water supply and pollution control organizations, to obtain authorization for the withdrawal, use, consumption and discharge of water of a certain quality and for a specific time period. Regulation of contaminants and product standards should be enforced on substances which risk impairing the aquatic environment, in order to allow for safe and economic use and recirculation of water as well as to prevent detrimental effects to scarce available water supplies.

9. Governments should increase their efforts to develop or improve methods for the regular collection, the proper analysis and the timely dissemination of directly comparable data on water abstraction, use, consumption and discharge, both in terms of quantity and quality, in the various economic sectors. These statistics on water use and water quality should be considered along with existing data of available water resources to help to identify water-deficient areas, and those vulnerable and sensitive to future water shortages as well as to foresee possible conflicts between water users. These statistics should also be used in the evaluation of effects of administrative and economic components of long-term strategies. In this respect, relevant experience and information gained in the implementation of water-management measures should be considered an important input in water management planning.

10. In developing an advanced water policy at all appropriate levels, priority should be given to the elaboration of an effective system of economic instruments, stimulating rational water use, deriving socio-economic benefits from the saving of water both in terms of quantity and quality. In the formulation and application of such economic instruments, attention should be paid in particular to:

(a) their optimum combination with the existing patterns of legal, administrative and technical instruments;

(b) their consistency with prevailing economic principles; and

(c) anticipated changes of water-use practices due to measures applied.

11. This well-balanced system should at all stages provide water users with increasing incentives to reduce both wastage and pollution of water. For water fees, a differentiated tariff system may be adopted with a consumption-oriented rate encouraging the rational use of water. Effluent charges, when made, should be based both on the amount of waste water discharged and its pollution load. Appropriate sanctions should be applied if established limits, standards or norms are exceeded.

12. The general principle should be that, as far as possible, the direct or indirect costs attributable to pollution should be borne by the polluter and that water users should pay the costs of abstraction, treatment and distribution. However, under certain conditions, governmental aid in the form of subsidies may be considered as a possible economic instrument to reduce both wastage and pollution of water. Such circumstances include the granting of aid for the development of cleaner technologies; some degree of compensation for the heavy costs which some polluters would be obliged to meet in order to achieve a degree of cleanliness higher than the required standards; contribution to public bodies for the construction and operation of an installation for

the protection of the aquatic environment which could not be wholly covered in the short-term from the charges paid by the polluters using it (the polluters would however be required to meet its running costs). In addition, grants may be paid where the immediate application of very stringent standards is likely to lead to serious disturbances in the economy.

13.   Policies at all appropriate levels should be geared towards promoting the rapid development and sound application of relevant technologies and their optimum operation for more efficient use of water and preventing wastage of water; both in terms of quantity and quality in all sectors. To this end, strong emphasis should be placed on those economic and administrative instruments that stimulate the application of the best available technology, taking into account economic reasonableness and feasibility. In further supporting this water strategy, Governments should encourage the establishment of research and development centres, sponsorship and cost-sharing arrangements for pilot application of technical innovations and dissemination of information on available and new technologies aiding their capability to meet the requirements set forth by the concept of rational water use. In this respect, the effects of new technologies should be comprehensively evaluated, in particular for their effects on socio-economic and environmental conditions. Such technologies could, *inter alia,* ensure:

(a) the reduction of total costs, in particular for water and other factors in the production process, as well as the reduction of water losses and of discharge of polluting effluents;

(b) the utilization of usable substances contained in waste water and sewage sludge;

(c) the application of water recycling systems within the production process, as well as the reuse of successive and concurrent uses of water within the same industry, other industrial complexes or in agriculture;

(d) the reduction or substitution of hazardous substances, in particular with regard to toxicity, bio-degradability and bio-accumulation and the reduction of eutrophication; this also in view of their risk of detrimental effects on actual or potential water supplies; and

(e) the use of automatic control and regulation systems for in-process water use and consumption.

14.   Efforts should be directed to the application of effective measures to obtain water savings in the domestic and municipal sector, and in particular to achieve reduction of losses in water distribution systems. To this effect, increased attention should be paid to the detection and repair of leakage in water distribution networks.

15.   In all cases where drinking water quality is not required, users should be encouraged to use water of a quality no higher than necessary. Where communal treatment of waste water is not appropriate, strong emphasis should be given to the application of pollution control measures as close to the source of pollution as possible. Since the major part of water used by industry, including thermal power plants, serves as cooling water, increased attention should be paid to cooling-water management and, in this respect, to the development and application of industrial processes which allow the reuse of cooling water as process and transport water, the recycling of cooling water

with a minimum of evaporative losses and the utilization of waste heat in the industrial, domestic and agricultural sector.

16. Due to the fact that in some countries high consumption of water is frequently for irrigation in agriculture, priority should be given there to the adoption of various technical and organizational measures to combat waste of water; steps should be taken to minimize water losses during its delivery to the place of use, taking into account all aspects related to climate, soil, crops and the use of irrigation systems. Attention should be given to provide water according to the actual water demand of crops in both quantitative and qualitative terms over the growing season. Priority should be given to efficient irrigation techniques in conjunction with advanced agricultural methods in particular those with low-energy consumption. Provided that appropriate precautions are taken and where sufficient experience exists, purified waste water or brackish water may also be used for irrigation, and sewage sludge for land application. If purified waste water and sewage sludge are used, particular attention must be given to hygienic aspects. In addition, the purified waste water, sewage sludge and the soil must be monitored continually to prevent any detrimental effects due to heavy metals or other pollutants. If brackish water is used, possible adverse impacts due to salination must be considered.

17. The concept of rational water use requires that, in the process of the integrated management of river basins, there should be an attempt to meet the water requirements not only of those types of water use which involve withdrawal of part of the flow, but also of those not involving such withdrawal, namely the fish industry, hydropower plants, water transport and recreation, and to maintain the normal state of health of watercourses.

18. Special consideration should be given to the intensification of those research programmes aimed at developing background knowledge for effective implementation of the principles of this Declaration, and in particular to:

(a) the need for enhanced international scientific co-operation;

(b) the development and improvement of programmes for training managers, maintenance personnel, technological advisers and others in industry and agriculture, with a view to developing, along the lines of relevant national or regional policies and strategies, a more creative approach in the search for practical ways to rationalize water use within their sphere of competence; and

(c) research programmes relating to the use of non-conventional water resources and to an improved control of losses through evaporation.

4.28 PROTOCOL OF 1984 TO AMEND THE INTERNATIONAL CONVENTION ON CIVIL LIABILITY FOR OIL POLLUTION DAMAGE, 1969.[1] Concluded at London, 25 May 1984. Not in force as of 31 December 1992. IMO Doc. LEG/CONF6/66

The States Parties to the present Protocol,

Considering that it is desirable to amend the International Convention on Civil Liability for Oil Pollution Damage, done at Brussels on 29 November 1969, to provide for improved scope and enhanced compensation,

Recognizing that special provisions are necessary in connexion with the introduction of corresponding amendments to the International Convention on the Establishment of an International Fund for Compensation for Oil Pollution Damage, 1971,

Have agreed as follows:

Article 1

The Convention which the provisions of this Protocol amend is the International Convention on Civil Liability for Oil Pollution Damage, 1969, hereinafter referred to as the "1969 Liability Convention". For States Parties to the Protocol of 1976 to the 1969 Liability Convention, such reference shall be deemed to include the 1969 Liability Convention as amended by that Protocol.

Article 2

Article I of the 1969 Liability Convention is amended as follows:

1. Paragraph 1 is replaced by the following text:

1. "Ship" means any sea-going vessel and sea-borne craft of any type whatsoever constructed or adapted for the carriage of oil in bulk as cargo, provided that a ship capable of carrying oil and other cargoes shall be regarded as a ship only when it is actually carrying oil in bulk as cargo and during any voyage following such carriage unless it is proved that it has no residues of such carriage of oil in bulk aboard.

2. Paragraph 5 is replaced by the following text:

5. "Oil" means any persistent hydrocarbon mineral oil such as crude oil, fuel oil, heavy diesel oil and lubricating oil, whether carried on board a ship as cargo or in the bunkers of such a ship.

3. Paragraph 6 is replaced by the following text:

6. "Pollution damage" means:

(a) loss or damage caused outside the ship by contamination resulting from the escape or discharge of oil from the ship, wherever such escape or discharge may occur, provided that compensation for impairment of the environment other than loss of profit from such impairment shall be limited to costs of reasonable measures of reinstatement actually undertaken or to be undertaken;

(b) the costs of preventive measures and further loss or damage caused by preventive measures.

4. Paragraph 8 is replaced by the following text:

1. See also Basic Documents 4.8 and 4.18, supra.

8. "Incident" means any occurrence, or series of occurrences having the same origin, which causes pollution damage or creates a grave and imminent threat of causing such damage.

5. Paragraph 9 is replaced by the following text:

9. "Organization" means the International Maritime Organization.

6. After paragraph 9 a new paragraph is inserted reading as follows:

10. "1969 Liability Convention" means the International Convention on Civil Liability for Oil Pollution Damage, 1969. For States Parties to the Protocol of 1976 to that Convention, the term shall be deemed to include the 1969 Liability Convention as amended by that Protocol.

Article 3

Article II of the 1969 Liability Convention is replaced by the following text:

This Convention shall apply exclusively:

(a) to pollution damage caused:

(i) in the territory, including the territorial sea, of a Contracting State, and

(ii) in the exclusive economic zone of a Contracting State, established in accordance with international law, or, if a Contracting State has not established such a zone, in an area beyond and adjacent to the territorial sea of that State determined by that State in accordance with international law and extending not more than 200 nautical miles from the baselines from which the breadth of its territorial sea is measured;

(b) to preventive measures, wherever taken, to prevent or minimize such damage.

Article 4

Article III of the 1969 Liability Convention is amended as follows:

1. Paragraph 1 is replaced by the following text:

1. Except as provided in paragraphs 2 and 3 of this Article, the owner of a ship at the time of an incident, or where the incident consists of a series of occurrences at the time of the first such occurrence, shall be liable for any pollution damage caused by the ship as a result of the incident.

2. Paragraph 4 is replaced by the following text:

4. No claim for compensation for pollution damage may be made against the owner otherwise than in accordance with this Convention. Subject to paragraph 5 of this Article, no claim for compensation for pollution damage under this Convention or otherwise may be made against:

(a) the servants or agents of the owner or the members of the crew;

(b) the pilot or any other person who, without being a member of the crew, performs services for the ship;

(c) any charterer (howsoever described, including a bareboat charterer), manager or operator of the ship;

(d) any person performing salvage operations with the consent of the owner or on the instructions of a competent public authority;

(e) any person taking preventive measures;

(f) all servants or agents of persons mentioned in subparagraphs (c), (d) and (e);

unless the damage resulted from their personal act or omission, committed with the intent to cause such damage, or recklessly and with knowledge that such damage would probably result.

Article 5

Article IV of the 1969 Liability Convention is replaced by the following text:

When an incident involving two or more ships occurs and pollution damage results therefrom, the owners of all the ships concerned, unless exonerated under Article III, shall be jointly and severally liable for all such damage which is not reasonably separable.

Article 6

Article V of the 1969 Liability Convention is amended as follows:

1. Paragraph 1 is replaced by the following text:

1. The owner of a ship shall be entitled to limit his liability under this Convention in respect of any one incident to an aggregate amount calculated as follows:

(a) 3 million units of account for a ship not exceeding 5,000 units of tonnage;

(b) for a ship with a tonnage in excess thereof, for each additional unit of tonnage, 420 units of account in addition to the amount mentioned in subparagraph (a);

provided, however, that this aggregate amount shall not in any event exceed 59.7 million units of account.

2. Paragraph 2 is replaced by the following text:

2. The owner shall not be entitled to limit his liability under this Convention if it is proved that the pollution damage resulted from his personal act or omission, committed with the intent to cause such damage, or recklessly and with knowledge that such damage would probably result.

3. Paragraph 3 is replaced by the following text:

3. For the purpose of availing himself of the benefit of limitation provided for in paragraph 1 of this Article the owner shall constitute a fund for the total sum representing the limit of his liability with the Court or other competent authority of any one of the Contracting States in which action is brought under Article IX or, if no action is brought, with any Court or other competent authority in any one of the Contracting States in which an action can be brought under Article IX. The fund can be constituted either by depositing the sum or by producing a bank

guarantee or other guarantee, acceptable under the legislation of the Contracting State where the fund is constituted, and considered to be adequate by the Court or other competent authority.

4. Paragraph 9 is replaced by the following text:

9. (a) The "unit of account" referred to in paragraph 1 of this Article is the Special Drawing Right as defined by the International Monetary Fund. The amounts mentioned in paragraph 1 shall be converted into national currency on the basis of the value of that currency by reference to the Special Drawing Right on the date of the constitution of the fund referred to in paragraph 3. The value of the national currency, in terms of the Special Drawing Right, of a Contracting State which is a member of the International Monetary Fund, shall be calculated in accordance with the method of valuation applied by the International Monetary Fund in effect on the date in question for its operations and transactions. The value of the national currency, in terms of the Special Drawing Right, of a Contracting State which is not a member of the International Monetary Fund, shall be calculated in a manner determined by that State.

(b) Nevertheless, a Contracting State which is not a member of the International Monetary Fund and whose law does not permit the application of the provisions of paragraph 9(a) may, at the time of ratification, acceptance, approval of or accession to this Convention or at any time thereafter, declare that the unit of account referred to in paragraph 9(a) shall be equal to 15 gold francs. The gold franc referred to in this paragraph corresponds to sixty-five and a half milligrammes of gold of millesimal fineness nine hundred. The conversion of the gold franc into the national currency shall be made according to the law of the State concerned.

(c) The calculation mentioned in the last sentence of paragraph 9(a) and the conversion mentioned in paragraph 9(b) shall be made in such manner as to express in the national currency of the Contracting State as far as possible the same real value for the amounts in paragraph 1 as would result from the application of the first three sentences of paragraph 9(a). Contracting States shall communicate to the depositary the manner of calculation pursuant to paragraph 9(a), or the result of the conversion in paragraph 9(b) as the case may be, when depositing an instrument of ratification, acceptance, approval of or accession to this Convention and whenever there is a change in either.

5. Paragraph 10 is replaced by the following text:

10. For the purpose of this Article the ship's tonnage shall be the gross tonnage calculated in accordance with the tonnage measurement regulations contained in Annex I of the International Convention on Tonnage Measurement of Ships, 1969.

6. The second sentence of paragraph 11 is replaced by the following text:

Such a fund may be constituted even if, under the provisions of paragraph 2, the owner is not entitled to limit his liability, but its constitution shall in that case not prejudice the rights of any claimant against the owner.

Article 7

Article VII of the 1969 Liability Convention is amended as follows:

1. The first two sentences of paragraph 2 are replaced by the following text:

A certificate attesting that insurance or other financial security is in force in accordance with the provisions of this Convention shall be issued to each ship after the appropriate authority of a Contracting State has determined that the requirements of paragraph 1 have been complied with. With respect to a ship registered in a Contracting State such certificate shall be issued or certified by the appropriate authority of the State of the ship's registry; with respect to a ship not registered in a Contracting State it may be issued or certified by the appropriate authority of any Contracting State.

2. Paragraph 4 is replaced by the following text:

4. The certificate shall be carried on board the ship and a copy shall be deposited with the authorities who keep the record of the ship's registry or, if the ship is not registered in a Contracting State, with the authorities of the State issuing or certifying the certificate.

3. The first sentence of paragraph 7 is replaced by the following text:

Certificates issued or certified under the authority of a Contracting State in accordance with paragraph 2 shall be accepted by other Contracting States for the purposes of this Convention and shall be regarded by other Contracting States as having the same force as certificates issued or certified by them even if issued or certified in respect of a ship not registered in a Contracting State.

4. In the second sentence of paragraph 7 the words "with the State of a ship's registry" are replaced by the words "with the issuing or certifying State".

5. The second sentence of paragraph 8 is replaced by the following text:

In such case the defendant may, even if the owner is not entitled to limit his liability according to Article V, paragraph 2, avail himself of the limits of liability prescribed in Article V, paragraph 1.

Article 8

Article IX of the 1969 Liability Convention is amended as follows:

Paragraph 1 is replaced by the following text:

1. Where an incident has caused pollution damage in the territory, including the territorial sea or an area referred to in Article II, of one or more Contracting States or preventive measures have been taken to prevent or minimize pollution damage in such territory including the territorial sea or area, actions for compensation may only be brought in the Courts of any such Contracting State or States. Reasonable notice of any such action shall be given to the defendant.

Article 9

After Article XII of the 1969 Liability Convention two new Articles are inserted as follows:

*Article XII*bis

Transitional provisions

The following transitional provisions shall apply in the case of a State which at the time of an incident is a Party both to this Convention and to the 1969 Liability Convention:

(a) where an incident has caused pollution damage within the scope of this Convention, liability under this Convention shall be deemed to be discharged if, and to the extent that, it also arises under the 1969 Liability Convention;

(b) where an incident has caused pollution damage within the scope of this Convention, and the State is a Party both to this Convention and to the International Convention on the Establishment of an International Fund for Compensation for Oil Pollution Damage, 1971, liability remaining to be discharged after the application of subparagraph (a) of this Article shall arise under this Convention only to the extent that pollution damage remains uncompensated after application of the said 1971 Convention;

(c) in the application of Article III, paragraph 4, of this Convention the expression "this Convention" shall be interpreted as referring to this Convention or the 1969 Liability Convention, as appropriate;

(d) in the application of Article V, paragraph 3, of this Convention the total sum of the fund to be constituted shall be reduced by the amount by which liability has been deemed to be discharged in accordance with subparagraph (a) of this Article.

*Article XII*ter

Final clauses

The final clauses of this Convention shall be Articles 12 to 18 of the Protocol of 1984 to amend the 1969 Liability Convention. References in this Convention to Contracting States shall be taken to mean references to the Contracting States of that Protocol.

Article 10

The model of a certificate annexed to the 1969 Liability Convention is replaced by the model annexed to this Protocol.

Article 11

1. The 1969 Liability Convention and this Protocol shall, as between the Parties to this Protocol, be read and interpreted together as one single instrument.

2. Articles I to XII, including the model certificate, of the 1969 Liability Convention as amended by this Protocol shall be known as the International Convention on Civil Liability for Oil Pollution Damage, 1984 (1984 Liability Convention).

Final clauses

Article 12

Signature, ratification, etc.

1. This Protocol shall be open for signature at London from 1 December 1984 to 30 November 1985 by all States.

2. Subject to paragraph 4, any State may become a Party to this Protocol by:

(a) signature subject to ratification, acceptance or approval followed by ratification, acceptance or approval; or

(b) accession.

3. Ratification, acceptance, approval or accession shall be effected by the deposit of a formal instrument to that effect with the Secretary–General of the Organization.

4. Any Contracting State to the International Convention on the Establishment of an International Fund for Compensation for Oil Pollution Damage, 1971, hereinafter referred to as the 1971 Fund Convention, may ratify, accept, approve or accede to this Protocol only if it ratifies, accepts, approves or accedes to the Protocol of 1984 to amend that Convention at the same time, unless it denounces the 1971 Fund Convention to take effect on the date when this Protocol enters into force for that State.

5. A State which is a Party to this Protocol but not a Party to the 1969 Liability Convention shall be bound by the provisions of the 1969 Liability Convention as amended by this Protocol in relation to other States Parties hereto, but shall not be bound by the provisions of the 1969 Liability Convention in relation to States Parties thereto.

6. Any instrument of ratification, acceptance, approval or accession deposited after the entry into force of an amendment to the 1969 Liability Convention as amended by this Protocol shall be deemed to apply to the Convention so amended, as modified by such amendment.

Article 13

Entry into force

1. This Protocol shall enter into force twelve months following the date on which ten States including six States each with not less than one million units of gross tanker tonnage have deposited instruments of ratification, acceptance, approval or accession with the Secretary–General of the Organization.

2. However, any Contracting State to the 1971 Fund Convention may, at the time of the deposit of its instrument of ratification, acceptance, approval or accession in respect of this Protocol, declare that such instrument shall be deemed not to be effective for the purposes of this Article until the end of the six-month period in Article 31 of the Protocol of 1984 to amend the 1971 Fund Convention. A State which is not a Contracting State to the 1971 Fund Convention but which deposits an instrument of ratification, acceptance, approval or accession in respect of the Protocol of 1984 to amend the 1971 Fund Convention may also make a declaration in accordance with this paragraph at the same time.

3. Any State which has made a declaration in accordance with the preceding paragraph may withdraw it at any time by means of notification addressed to the Secretary–General of the Organization. Any such withdrawal shall take effect on the date the notification is received, provided that such State shall be deemed to have deposited its instrument of ratification, acceptance, approval or accession in respect of this Protocol on that date.

4. For any State which ratifies, accepts, approves or accedes to it after the conditions in paragraph 1 for entry into force have been met, this Protocol shall enter into force twelve months following the date of deposit by such State of the appropriate instrument.

Article 14

Revision and amendment

1. A Conference for the purpose of revising or amending the 1984 Liability Convention may be convened by the Organization.

2. The Organization shall convene a Conference of Contracting States for the purpose of revising or amending the 1984 Liability Convention at the request of not less than one-third of the Contracting States.

Article 15

Amendments of limitation amounts

1. Upon the request of at least one-quarter of the Contracting States any proposal to amend the limits of liability laid down in Article V, paragraph 1, of the Convention as amended by this Protocol shall be circulated by the Secretary–General to all Members of the Organization and to all Contracting States.

2. Any amendment proposed and circulated as above shall be submitted to the Legal Committee of the Organization for consideration at a date at least six months after the date of its circulation.

3. All Contracting States to the Convention as amended by this Protocol, whether or not Members of the Organization, shall be entitled to participate in the proceedings of the Legal Committee for the consideration and adoption of amendments.

4. Amendments shall be adopted by a two-thirds majority of the Contracting States present and voting in the Legal Committee, expanded as provided for in paragraph 3, on condition that at least one-half of the Contracting States shall be present at the time of voting.

5. When acting on a proposal to amend the limits, the Committee shall take into account the experience of incidents and in particular the amount of damage resulting therefrom, changes in the monetary values and the effect of the proposed amendment on the cost of insurance. It shall also take into account the relationship between the limits in Article V, paragraph 1, of the Convention as amended by this Protocol and those in paragraph 4 of Article 4 of the International Convention on the Establishment of an International Fund for Compensation for Oil Pollution Damage, 1984.

6. (a) No amendment of the limits of liability under this Article may be considered less than five years from the date on which this Protocol was opened for signature nor less than five years from the date of entry into force

of a previous amendment under this Article. No amendment under this Article shall be considered before this Protocol has entered into force.

(b) No limit may be increased so as to exceed an amount which corresponds to the limit laid down in the Convention as amended by this Protocol increased by 6 per cent per year calculated on a compound basis from the date on which this Protocol was opened for signature.

(c) No limit may be increased so as to exceed an amount which corresponds to the limit laid down in the Convention as amended by this Protocol multiplied by 3.

7. Any amendment adopted in accordance with paragraph 4 shall be notified by the Organization to all Contracting States. The amendment shall be deemed to have been accepted at the end of a period of eighteen months after the date of notification, unless within that period not less than one-quarter of the States that were Contracting States at the time of the adoption of the amendment by the Committee have communicated to the Organization that they do not accept the amendment in which case the amendment is rejected and shall have no effect.

8. An amendment deemed to have been accepted in accordance with paragraph 7 shall enter into force eighteen months after its acceptance.

9. All Contracting States shall be bound by the amendment, unless they denounce this Protocol in accordance with Article 16, paragraphs 1 and 2, at least six months before the amendment enters into force. Such denunciation shall take effect when the amendment enters into force.

10. When an amendment has been adopted by the Committee but the eighteen-month period for its acceptance has not yet expired, a State which becomes a Contracting State during that period shall be bound by the amendment if it enters into force. A State which becomes a Contracting State after that period shall be bound by an amendment which has been accepted in accordance with paragraph 7. In the cases referred to in this paragraph, a State becomes bound by an amendment when that amendment enters into force, or when this Protocol enters into force for that State, if later.

Article 16

Denunciation

1. This Protocol may be denounced by any Party at any time after the date on which it enters into force for that Party.

2. Denunciation shall be effected by the deposit of an instrument with the Secretary–General of the Organization.

3. A denunciation shall take effect twelve months, or such longer period as may be specified in the instrument of denunciation, after its deposit with the Secretary–General of the Organization.

4. As between the Parties to this Protocol, denunciation by any of them of the 1969 Liability Convention in accordance with Article XVI thereof shall not be construed in any way as a denunciation of the 1969 Liability Convention as amended by this Protocol.

5. Denunciation of the Protocol of 1984 to amend the 1971 Fund Convention by a State which remains a Party to the 1971 Fund Convention shall be deemed to be a denunciation of this Protocol. Such denunciation shall take effect on the date on which denunciation of the Protocol of 1984 to amend the 1971 Fund Convention takes effect according to Article 34 of that Protocol.

Article 17

Depository

1. This Protocol and any amendments accepted under Article 15 shall be deposited with the Secretary–General of the Organization.

2. The Secretary–General of the Organization shall:

(a) inform all States which have signed or acceded to this Protocol of:

(i) each new signature or deposit of an instrument together with the date thereof;

(ii) each declaration and notification under Article 13 and each declaration and communication under Article V, paragraph 9, of the 1984 Liability Convention;

(iii) the date of entry into force of this Protocol;

(iv) any proposal to amend limits of liability which has been made in accordance with Article 15, paragraph 1;

(v) any amendment which has been adopted in accordance with Article 15, paragraph 4;

(vi) any amendment deemed to have been accepted under Article 15, paragraph 7, together with the date on which that amendment shall enter into force in accordance with paragraphs 8 and 9 of that Article;

(vii) the deposit of any instrument of denunciation of this Protocol together with the date of the deposit and the date on which it takes effect;

(viii) any denunciation deemed to have been made under Article 16, paragraph 5;

(ix) any communication called for by any Article of this Protocol.

(b) transmit certified true copies of this Protocol to all Signatory States and to all States which accede to this Protocol.

3. As soon as this Protocol enters into force, the text shall be transmitted by the Secretary–General of the Organization to the Secretariat of the United Nations for registration and publication in accordance with Article 102 of the Charter of the United Nations.

Article 18

Languages

This Protocol is established in a single original in the Arabic, Chinese, English, French, Russian and Spanish languages, each text being equally authentic.

4.29 PROTOCOL TO AMEND THE INTERNATIONAL CONVENTION ON THE ESTABLISHMENT OF AN INTERNATIONAL FUND FOR COMPENSATION FOR OIL POLLUTION DAMAGE, 1971.[1] Concluded at London, 25 May 1984. Not in force as of 31 December 1992. IMO Doc. LEG/CONF6/67

The States Parties to the present Protocol,

Considering that it is desirable to amend the International Convention on the Establishment of an International Fund for Compensation for Oil Pollution Damage, done at Brussels on 18 December 1971, to provide for improved scope and enhanced compensation,

Recognizing the advantage for the States Parties of arranging for the amended Convention to coexist with and be supplementary to the original Convention for a transitional period,

Convinced that the economic consequences of pollution damage resulting from the carriage of oil in bulk at sea by ships should continue to be shared by the shipping industry and by the oil cargo interests,

Bearing in mind the adoption of the Protocol of 1984 to amend the International Convention on Civil Liability for Oil Pollution Damage, 1969,

Have agreed as follows:

Article 1

The Convention which the provisions of this Protocol amend is the International Convention on the Establishment of an International Fund for Compensation for Oil Pollution Damage, 1971, hereinafter referred to as the "1971 Fund Convention". For States Parties to the Protocol of 1976 to the 1971 Fund Convention, such reference shall be deemed to include the 1971 Fund Convention as amended by that Protocol.

Article 2

Article 1 of the 1971 Fund Convention is amended as follows:

1. Paragraph 1 is replaced by the following text:

1. "1984 Liability Convention" means the International Convention on Civil Liability for Oil Pollution Damage, 1984.

2. After paragraph 1 a new paragraph is inserted as follows:

1. "1971 Fund Convention" means the International Convention on the Establishment of an International Fund for Compensation for Oil Pollution Damage, 1971. For States Parties to the Protocol of 1976 to that Convention, the term shall be deemed to include the 1971 Fund Convention as amended by that Protocol.

3. Paragraph 2 is replaced by the following text:

2. "Ship", "Person", "Owner", "Oil", "Pollution Damage", "Preventive Measures", "Incident", and "Organization" have the same meaning as in Article I of the 1984 Liability Convention.

4. Paragraph 4 is replaced by the following text:

---

1. *See also* Basic Documents 4.12 and 4.19, *supra.*

4. "Unit of account" has the same meaning as in Article V, paragraph 9, of the 1984 Liability Convention.

5. Paragraph 5 is replaced by the following text:

5. "Ship's tonnage" has the same meaning as in Article V, paragraph 10, of the 1984 Liability Convention.

6. Paragraph 7 is replaced by the following text:

7. "Guarantor" means any person providing insurance or other financial security to cover an owner's liability in pursuance of Article VII, paragraph 1, of the 1984 Liability Convention.

Article 3

Article 2 of the 1971 Fund Convention is amended as follows:

Paragraph 1 is replaced by the following text:

1. An International Fund for compensation for pollution damage, to be named "The International Oil Pollution Compensation Fund 1984" and hereinafter referred to as "the Fund", is hereby established with the following aims:

(a) to provide compensation for pollution damage to the extent that the protection afforded by the 1984 Liability Convention is inadequate;

(b) to give effect to the related purposes set out in this Convention.

Article 4

Article 3 of the 1971 Fund Convention is replaced by the following text:

This Convention shall apply exclusively:

(a) to pollution damage caused:

(i) in the territory, including the territorial sea, of a Contracting State, and

(ii) in the exclusive economic zone of a Contracting State, established in accordance with international law, or, if a Contracting State has not established such a zone, in an area beyond and adjacent to the territorial sea of that State determined by that State in accordance with international law and extending not more than 200 nautical miles from the baselines from which the breadth of its territorial sea is measured;

(b) to preventive measures, wherever taken, to prevent or minimize such damage.

Article 5

The heading to Articles 4 to 9 of the 1971 Fund Convention is amended by deleting the words "and indemnification".

Article 6

Article 4 of the 1971 Fund Convention is amended as follows:

1. In paragraph 1 the five references to "the Liability Convention" are replaced by references to "the 1984 Liability Convention".

2. Paragraph 3 is replaced by the following text:

3. If the Fund proves that the pollution damage resulted wholly or partially either from an act or omission done with the intent to cause damage by the person who suffered the damage or from the negligence of that person, the Fund may be exonerated wholly or partially from its obligation to pay compensation to such person. The Fund shall in any event be exonerated to the extent that the shipowner may have been exonerated under Article III, paragraph 3, of the 1984 Liability Convention. However, there shall be no such exoneration of the Fund with regard to preventive measures.

3. Paragraph 4 is replaced by the following text:

4. (a) Except as otherwise provided in subparagraphs (b) and (c) of this paragraph, the aggregate amount of compensation payable by the Fund under this Article shall in respect of any one incident be limited, so that the total sum of that amount and the amount of compensation actually paid under the 1984 Liability Convention for pollution damage within the scope of application of this Convention as defined in Article 3 shall not exceed 135 million units of account.

(b) Except as otherwise provided in subparagraph (c), the aggregate amount of compensation payable by the Fund under this Article for pollution damage resulting from a natural phenomenon of an exceptional, inevitable and irresistible character shall not exceed 135 million units of account.

(c) The maximum amount of compensation referred to in subparagraphs (a) and (b) shall be 200 million units of account with respect to any incident occurring during any period when there are three Parties to this Convention in respect of which the combined relevant quantity of contributing oil received by persons in the territories of such Parties, during the preceding calendar year, equalled or exceeded 600 million tons.

(d) Interest accrued on a Fund constituted in accordance with Article V, paragraph 3, of the 1984 Liability Convention, if any, shall not be taken into account for the computation of the maximum compensation payable by the Fund under this Article.

(e) The amounts mentioned in this Article shall be converted into national currency on the basis of the value of that currency by reference to the Special Drawing Right on the date of the decision of the Assembly of the Fund as to the first date of payment of compensation.

4. Paragraph 5 is replaced by the following text:

5. Where the amount of established claims against the Fund exceeds the aggregate amount of compensation payable under paragraph 4, the amount available shall be distributed in such a manner that the proportion between any established claim and the amount of compensation actually recovered by the claimant under this Convention shall be the same for all claimants.

5. Paragraph 6 is replaced by the following text:

6. The Assembly of the Fund may decide that, in exceptional cases, compensation in accordance with this Convention can be paid even if the owner of the ship has not constituted a fund in accordance with Article V, paragraph 3, of the 1984 Liability Convention. In such case paragraph 4(e) of this Article applies accordingly.

Article 7

Article 5 of the 1971 Fund Convention is deleted.

Article 8

Article 6 of the 1971 Fund Convention is amended as follows:

1. In paragraph 1 the paragraph number and the words "or indemnification under Article 5" are deleted.

2. Paragraph 2 is deleted.

Article 9

Article 7 of the 1971 Fund Convention is amended as follows:

1. In paragraphs 1, 3, 4 and 6 the seven references to "the Liability Convention" are replaced by references to "the 1984 Liability Convention".

2. In paragraph 1 the words "or indemnification under Article 5" are deleted.

3. In the first sentence of paragraph 3 the words "or indemnification" and "or 5" are deleted.

4. In the second sentence of paragraph 3 the words "or under Article 5, paragraph 1," are deleted.

Article 10

In Article 8 of the 1971 Fund Convention the reference to "the Liability Convention" is replaced by a reference to "the 1984 Liability Convention".

Article 11

Article 9 of the 1971 Fund Convention is amended as follows:

1. Paragraph 1 is replaced by the following text:

1. The Fund shall, in respect of any amount of compensation for pollution damage paid by the Fund in accordance with Article 4, paragraph 1, of this Convention, acquire by subrogation the rights that the person so compensated may enjoy under the 1984 Liability Convention against the owner or his guarantor.

2. In paragraph 2 the words "or indemnification" are deleted.

Article 12

Article 10 of the 1971 Fund Convention is amended as follows:

The opening phrase of paragraph 1 is replaced by the following text:

Annual contributions to the Fund shall be made in respect of each Contracting State by any person who, in the calendar year referred to in Article 12, paragraphs 2(a) or (b), has received in total quantities exceeding 150,000 tons.

Article 13

Article 11 of the 1971 Fund Convention is deleted.

Article 14

Article 12 of the 1971 Fund Convention is amended as follows:

1. In the opening phrase of paragraph 1 the words "for each person referred to in Article 10" are deleted.

2. In paragraph 1(i), subparagraphs (b) and (c), the words "or 5" are deleted and the words "15 million francs" are replaced by the words "four million units of account".

3. The opening phrase in paragraph 2 is replaced by the following text:

The Assembly shall decide the total amount of contributions to be levied. On the basis of that decision, the Director shall, in respect of each Contracting State, calculate for each person referred to in Article 10 the amount of his annual contribution.

4. Paragraph 4 is replaced by the following text:

4. The annual contribution shall be due on the date to be laid down in the Internal Regulations of the Fund. The Assembly may decide on a different date of payment.

5. Paragraph 5 is replaced by the following text:

5. The Assembly may decide, under conditions to be laid down in the Financial Regulations of the Fund, to make transfers between funds received in accordance with Article 12.2(a) and funds received in accordance with Article 12.2(b).

6. Paragraph 6 is deleted.

Article 15

Article 13 of the 1971 Fund Convention is amended as follows:

1. Paragraph 1 is replaced by the following text:

1. The amount of any contribution due under Article 12 and which is in arrears shall bear interest at a rate which shall be determined in accordance with the Internal Regulations of the Fund, provided that different rates may be fixed for different circumstances.

2. In paragraph 3 the words "Articles 10 and 11" are replaced by the words "Articles 10 and 12" and the words "for a period exceeding three months" are deleted.

Article 16

A new paragraph 4 is added to Article 15 of the 1971 Fund Convention:

4. Where a Contracting State does not fulfil its obligations to submit to the Director the communication referred to in paragraph 2 and this results in a financial loss for the Fund, that Contracting State shall be liable to compensate the Fund for such loss. The Assembly shall, on the recommendation of the Director, decide whether such compensation shall be payable by a Contracting State.

Article 17

Article 16 of the 1971 Fund Convention is replaced by the following text:

The Fund shall have an Assembly and a Secretariat headed by a Director.

Article 18

Article 18 of the 1971 Fund Convention is amended as follows:

1. Paragraph 8 is deleted.

2. Paragraph 9 is replaced by the following text:

9. to establish any temporary or permanent subsidiary body it may consider to be necessary, to define its terms of reference and to give it the authority needed to perform the functions entrusted to it; when appointing the members of such body, the Assembly shall endeavour to secure an equitable geographical distribution of members and to ensure that the Contracting States, in respect of which the largest quantities of contributing oil are being received, are appropriately represented; the Rules of Procedure of the Assembly may be applied, *mutatis mutandis,* for the work of such subsidiary body.

3. In paragraph 10 the words ", the Executive Committee," are deleted.

4. In paragraph 11 the words ", the Executive Committee" are deleted.

5. Paragraph 12 is deleted.

Article 19

Article 19 of the 1971 Fund Convention is amended as follows:

1. Paragraph 1 is replaced by the following text:

1. Regular sessions of the Assembly shall take place once every calendar year upon convocation by the Director.

2. In paragraph 2 the words "of the Executive Committee or" are deleted.

Article 20

Article 21 to 27 of the 1971 Fund Convention and the heading to these articles are deleted.

Article 21

Article 29 of the 1971 Fund Convention is amended as follows:

1. Paragraph 1 is replaced by the following text:

1. The Director shall be the chief administrative officer of the Fund. Subject to the instructions given to him by the Assembly, he shall perform those functions which are assigned to him by this Convention, the Internal Regulations of the Fund and the Assembly.

2. In paragraph 2(e) the words "or the Executive Committee" are deleted.

3. In paragraph 2(f) the words "or to the Executive Committee, as the case may be," are deleted.

4. Paragraph 2(g) is replaced by the following text:

(g) prepare, in consultation with the Chairman of the Assembly, and publish a report of the activities of the Fund during the previous calendar year;

5. In paragraph 2(h) the words ", the Executive Committee" are deleted.

Article 22

In Article 31, paragraph 1, of the 1971 Fund Convention, the words "on the Executive Committee and" are deleted.

Article 23

Article 32 of the 1971 Fund Convention is amended as follows:

1. In the opening phrase the words "and the Executive Committee" are deleted.

2. In subparagraph (b) the words "and the Executive Committee" are deleted.

Article 24

Article 33 of the 1971 Fund Convention is amended as follows:

1. Paragraph 1 is deleted.

2. In paragraph 2 the paragraph number is deleted.

3. Subparagraph (c) is replaced by the following text:

(c) the establishment of subsidiary bodies, under Article 18, paragraph 9, and matters relating to such establishment.

Article 25

Article 25 of the 1971 Fund Convention is replaced by the following text:

Claims for compensation under Article 4 arising from incidents occurring after the date of entry into force of this Convention may not be brought against the Fund earlier than the one hundred and twentieth day after that date.

Article 26

After Article 36 of the 1971 Fund Convention three new articles are inserted as follows:

Article 36bis

The following transitional provisions shall apply in the period, hereinafter referred to as the transitional period, commencing with the date of entry into force of this Convention and ending with the date on which the denunciations provided for in Article 31 of the Protocol of 1984 to amend the 1971 Fund Convention take effect:

(a) In the application of paragraph 1(a) of Article 2 of this Convention, the reference to the 1984 Liability Convention shall include reference to the International Convention on Civil Liability for Oil Pollution Damage, 1969, either in its original version or as amended by the Protocol thereto of 1976 (referred to in this Article as "the 1969 Liability Convention"), and also the 1971 Fund Convention.

(b) Where an incident has caused pollution damage within the scope of this Convention, the Fund shall pay compensation to any person suffering pollution damage only if, and to the extent that, such person has been unable to obtain full and adequate compensation for the damage under the terms of the 1969 Liability Convention, the 1971 Fund Convention and the 1984 Liability Convention, provided that, in respect of pollution damage within the scope of this Convention in respect of a Party to this Convention but not a Party to the 1971 Fund Convention, the Fund shall pay compensation to any person suffering pollution damage only if, and to the extent that, such person would have been unable to obtain full and adequate compensation had that State been party to each of the above-mentioned Conventions.

(c) In the application of Article 4 of this Convention, the amount to be taken into account in determining the aggregate amount of compensation payable by the Fund shall also include the amount of compensation actually paid under the 1969 Liability Convention, if any, and the amount of compensation actually paid or deemed to have been paid under the 1971 Fund Convention.

(d) Paragraph 1 of Article 9 of this Convention shall also apply to the rights enjoyed under the 1969 Liability Convention.

Article 36ter

Notwithstanding the provisions of this Convention, the following provisions shall apply to the administration of the Fund during the period in which both the 1971 Fund Convention and this Convention are in force:

(a) The Secretariat of the Fund, established by the 1971 Fund Convention (hereinafter referred to as "the 1971 Fund"), headed by the Director, may also function as the Secretariat and the Director of the Fund.

(b) If, in accordance with subparagraph (a), the Secretariat and the Director of the 1971 Fund also perform the function of Secretariat and Director of the Fund, the Fund shall be represented, in cases of conflict of interests between the 1971 Fund and the Fund, by the Chairman of the Assembly of the Fund.

(c) The Director and the staff and experts appointed by him, performing their duties under this Convention and the 1971 Fund Convention, shall not be regarded as contravening the provisions of Article 30 of this Convention in so far as they discharge their duties in accordance with this Article.

(d) The Assembly of the Fund shall endeavour not to take decisions which are incompatible with decisions taken by the Assembly of the 1971 Fund. If differences of opinion with respect to common administrative issues arise, the Assembly of the Fund shall try to reach a consensus with the Assembly of the 1971 Fund, in a spirit of mutual cooperation and with the common aims of both Organizations in mind.

(e) The Fund may succeed to the rights, obligations and assets of the 1971 Fund if the Assembly of the 1971 Fund so decides, in accordance with Article 44, paragraph 2, of the 1971 Fund Convention.

(f) The Fund shall reimburse to the 1971 Fund all costs and expenses arising from administrative services performed by the 1971 Fund on behalf of the Fund.

Article 36[quater]
Final clauses

The final clauses of this Convention shall be Articles 28 to 39 of the Protocol of 1984 to amend the 1971 Fund Convention. References in this Convention to Contracting States shall be taken to mean references to the Contracting States of that Protocol.

Article 27

1. The 1971 Fund Convention and this Protocol shall, as between the Parties to this Protocol, be read and interpreted together as one single instrument.

2. Articles 1 to 36 of the 1971 Fund Convention as amended by this Protocol shall be known as the International Convention on the Establishment of an International Fund for Compensation for Oil Pollution Damage, 1984 (1984 Fund Convention).

Final clauses
Article 28
Signature, ratification, etc.

1. This Protocol shall be open for signature at London from 1 December 1984 to 30 November 1985 by any State which has signed the 1984 Liability Convention.

2. Subject to paragraph 4, this Protocol shall be ratified, accepted or approved by States which have signed it.

3. Subject to paragraph 4, this Protocol is open for accession by States which did not sign it.

4. This Protocol may be ratified, accepted, approved or acceded to, only by States which have ratified, accepted, approved or acceded to the 1984 Liability Convention.

5. Ratification, acceptance, approval or accession shall be effected by the deposit of a formal instrument to that effect with the Secretary–General of the Organization.

6. A State which is a Party to this Protocol but is not a Party to the 1971 Fund Convention shall be bound by the provisions of the 1971 Fund Convention as amended by this Protocol in relation to other Parties hereto, but shall not be bound by the provisions of the 1971 Fund Convention in relation to Parties thereto.

The entry into force of an amendment to the 1971 Fund Convention as amended by this Protocol shall be deemed to apply to the Convention so amended, as modified by such amendment.

Article 29
Information on contributing oil

1. Before this Protocol comes into force for a State, that State shall, when depositing an instrument referred to in Article 28, paragraph 5, and

annually thereafter at a date to be determined by the Secretary–General of the Organization, communicate to him the name and address of any person who in respect of that State would be liable to contribute to the Fund pursuant to Article 10 of the 1971 Fund Convention as amended by this Protocol as well as data on the relevant quantities of contributing oil received by any such person in the territory of that State during the preceding calendar year.

2. During the transitional period, the Director shall, for Parties, communicate annually to the Secretary–General of the Organization data on quantities of contributing oil received by persons liable to contribute to the Fund pursuant to Article 10 of the 1971 Fund Convention as amended by this Protocol.

Article 30

Entry into force

1. This Protocol shall enter into force twelve months following the date on which the following requirements are fulfilled:

(a) at least eight States have deposited instruments of ratification, acceptance, approval or accession with the Secretary–General of the Organization; and

(b) the Secretary–General of the Organization has received information in accordance with Article 29 that those persons who would be liable to contribute pursuant to Article 10 of the 1971 Fund Convention as amended by this Protocol have received during the preceding calendar year a total quantity of at least 600 million tons of contributing oil.

2. However, this Protocol shall not enter into force before the 1984 Liability Convention has entered into force.

3. For each State which ratifies, accepts, approves or accedes to this Protocol after the conditions in paragraph 1 for entry into force have been met, the Protocol shall enter into force twelve months following the date of the deposit by such State of the appropriate instrument.

4. Any State may, at the time of the deposit of its instrument of ratification, acceptance, approval or accession in respect of this Protocol declare that such instrument shall not take effect for the purpose of this Article until the end of the six-month period in Article 31.

5. Any State which has made a declaration in accordance with the preceding paragraph may withdraw it at any time by means of a notification addressed to the Secretary–General of the Organization. Any such withdrawal shall take effect on the date the notification is received, and any State making such a withdrawal shall be deemed to have deposited its instrument of ratification, acceptance, approval or accession in respect of this Protocol on that date.

6. Any State which has made a declaration under Article 13, paragraph 2, of the Protocol of 1984 to amend the 1969 Liability Convention shall be deemed to have also made a declaration under paragraph 4 of this Article. Withdrawal of a declaration under the said Article 13, paragraph 2, shall be deemed to constitute withdrawal also under paragraph 5 of this Article.

Article 31

Denunciation

of 1969 and 1971 Conventions

Subject to Article 30, within six months following the date on which the following requirements are fulfilled:

(a) at least eight States have become Parties to this Protocol or have deposited instruments of ratification, acceptance, approval or accession with the Secretary–General of the Organization, whether or not subject to Article 30, paragraph 4, and

(b) the Secretary–General of the Organization has received information in accordance with Article 29 that those persons who are or would be liable to contribute pursuant to Article 10 of the 1971 Fund Convention as amended by this Protocol have received during the preceding calendar year a total quantity of at least 750 million tons of contributing oil;

Each Party to this Protocol and each State which has deposited an instrument of ratification, acceptance, approval or accession, whether or not subject to Article 30, paragraph 4, shall, if party thereto, denounce the 1971 Fund Convention and the 1969 Liability Convention with effect twelve months after the expiry of the above-mentioned six-month period.

Article 32

Revision and amendment

1. A conference for the purpose of revising or amending the 1984 Fund Convention may be convened by the Organization.

2. The Organization shall convene a Conference of Contracting States for the purpose of revising or amending the 1984 Fund Convention at the request of not less than one-third of all Contracting States.

Article 33

Amendment of compensation limits

1. Upon the request of at least one-quarter of the Contracting States, any proposal to amend the limits of amounts of compensation laid down in Article 4, paragraph 4, of the Convention as amended by this Protocol shall be circulated by the Secretary–General to all Members of the Organization and to all Contracting States.

2. Any amendment proposed and circulated as above shall be submitted to the Legal Committee of the Organization for consideration at a date at least six months after the date of its circulation.

3. All Contracting States to the Convention as amended by this Protocol, whether or not Members of the Organization, shall be entitled to participate in the proceedings of the Legal Committee for the consideration and adoption of amendments.

4. Amendments shall be adopted by a two-thirds majority of the Contracting States present and voting in the Legal Committee, expanded as provided for in paragraph 3, on condition that at least one-half of the Contracting States shall be present at the time of voting.

5. When acting on a proposal to amend the limits, the Committee shall take into account the experience of incidents and in particular the amount of

damage resulting therefrom and changes in the monetary values. It shall also take into account the relationship between the limits in Article 4, paragraph 4, of the Convention as amended by this Protocol and those in Article V, paragraph 1 of the International Convention on Civil Liability for Oil Pollution Damage, 1984.

6. (a) No amendment of the limits under this Article may be considered less than five years from the date on which this Protocol was opened for signature nor less than five years from the date of entry into force of a previous amendment under this Article. No amendment under this Article shall be considered before this Protocol has entered into force.

(b) No limit may be increased so as to exceed an amount which corresponds to the limit laid down in the Convention as amended by this Protocol increased by six per cent per year calculated on a compound basis from the date on which this Protocol was opened for signature.

(c) No limit may be increased so as to exceed an amount which corresponds to the limit laid down in the Convention as amended by this Protocol multiplied by three.

7. Any amendment adopted in accordance with paragraph 4 shall be notified by the Organization to all Contracting States. The amendment shall be deemed to have been accepted at the end of a period of eighteen months after the date of notification unless within that period not less than one-quarter of the States that were Contracting States at the time of the adoption of the amendment by the Committee have communicated to the Organization that they do not accept the amendment in which case the amendment is rejected and shall have no effect.

8. An amendment deemed to have been accepted in accordance with paragraph 7 shall enter into force eighteen months after its acceptance.

9. All Contracting States shall be bound by the amendment, unless they denounce this Protocol in accordance with Article 34, paragraphs 1 and 2, at least six months before the amendment enters into force. Such denunciation shall take effect when the amendment enters into force.

10. When an amendment has been adopted by the Committee, but the eighteen-month period for its acceptance has not yet expired, a State which becomes a Contracting State during that period shall be bound by the amendment if it enters into force. A State which becomes a Contracting State after that period shall be bound by an amendment which has been accepted in accordance with paragraph 7. In the cases referred to in this paragraph, a State becomes bound by an amendment when that amendment enters into force, or when this Protocol enters into force for that State, if later.

Article 34
Denunciation

1. This Protocol may be denounced by any Party at any time after the date on which it enters into force for that Party.

2. Denunciation shall be effected by the deposit of an instrument with the Secretary–General of the Organization.

3. A denunciation shall take effect twelve months, or such longer period as may be specified in the instrument of denunciation, after its deposit with the Secretary–General of the Organization.

4. Denunciation of the 1984 Liability Convention shall be deemed to be a denunciation of this Protocol. Such denunciation shall take effect on the date on which denunciation of the Protocol of 1984 to the 1969 Liability Convention takes effect according to Article 16 of that Protocol.

5. Any Contracting State to this Protocol which has not denounced the 1971 Fund Convention and the 1969 Liability Convention as required by Article 31 shall be deemed to have denounced this Protocol with effect twelve months after the expiry of the six-month period in that Article. As from the date on which the denunciations provided for in Article 31 take effect, any Party to this Protocol which deposits an instrument of ratification, acceptance, approval or accession to the 1969 Liability Convention shall be deemed to have denounced this Protocol with effect from the date on which such instrument takes effect.

6. As between the Parties to this Protocol, denunciation by any of them of the 1971 Fund Convention in accordance with Article 41 thereof shall not be construed in any way as a denunciation of the 1971 Fund Convention as amended by this Protocol.

7. Notwithstanding a denunciation of this Protocol by a Party pursuant to this Article, any provisions of this Protocol relating to the obligations to make contributions under Article 10 of the 1971 Fund Convention as amended by this Protocol with respect to an incident referred to in Article 12, paragraph 2(b), of that amended Convention and occurring before the denunciation takes effect shall continue to apply.

Article 35

Extraordinary sessions of the Assembly

1. Any Contracting State may, within ninety days after the deposit of an instrument of denunciation the result of which it considers will significantly increase the level of contributions for the remaining Contracting States, request the Director to convene an extraordinary session of the Assembly. The Director shall convene the Assembly to meet not later than sixty days after receipt of the request.

2. The Director may convene, on his own initiative, an extraordinary session of the Assembly to meet within sixty days after the deposit of any instrument of denunciation, if he considers that such denunciation will result in a significant increase in the level of contributions of the remaining Contracting States.

3. If the Assembly at an extraordinary session convened in accordance with paragraph 1 or 2 decides that the denunciation will result in a significant increase in the level of contributions for the remaining Contracting States, any such State may, not later than one hundred and twenty days before the date on which the denunciation takes effect, denounce this Protocol with effect from the same date.

Article 36

Cessation

1.   This Protocol shall cease to be in force on the date when the number of Contracting States falls below three.

2.   States which are bound by this Protocol on the day before the date it ceases to be in force shall enable the Fund to exercise its functions as described under Article 37 of this Protocol and shall, for that purpose only, remain bound by this Protocol.

Article 37

Winding up of the Fund

1.   If this Protocol ceases to be in force, the Fund shall nevertheless:

(a) meet its obligations in respect of any incident occurring before the Protocol ceased to be in force;

(b) be entitled to exercise its rights to contributions to the extent that these contributions are necessary to meet the obligations under subparagraph (a), including expenses for the administration of the Fund necessary for this purpose.

2.   The Assembly shall take all appropriate measures to complete the winding up of the Fund including the distribution in an equitable manner of any remaining assets among those persons who have contributed to the Fund.

3.   For the purposes of this Article the Fund shall remain a legal person.

Article 38

Depositary

1.   This Protocol and any amendments accepted under Article 33 shall be deposited with the Secretary–General of the Organization.

2.   The Secretary–General of the Organization shall:

(a) inform all States which have signed or acceded to this Protocol of:

(i) each new signature or deposit of an instrument together with the date thereof;

(ii) each declaration and notification under Article 30 including declarations and withdrawals deemed to have been made in accordance with that Article;

(iii) the date of entry into force of this Protocol;

(iv) the date by which denunciations provided for in Article 31 are required to be made;

(v) any proposal to amend limits of amounts of compensation which has been made in accordance with Article 33, paragraph 1;

(vi) any amendment which has been adopted in accordance with Article 33, paragraph 4;

(vii) any amendment deemed to have been accepted under Article 33, paragraph 7, together with the date on which that amendment shall enter into force in accordance with paragraphs 8 and 9 of that Article;

(viii) the deposit of an instrument of denunciation of this Protocol together with the date of the deposit and the date on which it takes effect;

(ix) any denunciation deemed to have been made under Article 34, paragraph 5;

(x) any communication called for by any Article in this Protocol;

(b) transmit certified true copies of this Protocol to all Signatory States and to all States which accede to the Protocol.

3. As soon as this Protocol enters into force, the text shall be transmitted by the Secretary–General of the Organization to the Secretariat of the United Nations for registration and publication in accordance with Article 102 of the Charter of the United Nations.

Article 39

Languages

This Protocol is established in a single original in the Arabic, Chinese, English, French, Russian and Spanish languages, each text being equally authentic.

4.30 MONTREAL GUIDELINES FOR THE PROTECTION OF THE MARINE ENVIRONMENT AGAINST POLLUTION FROM LAND–BASED SOURCES (WITHOUT ANNEXES). Adopted at Montreal, 24 May 1985. UNEP/GC.13/9/Add.3, UNEP/GC/DEC/13/1811, UNEP ELPG No.7

1. *Definitions*

For the purposes of these guidelines:

(a) "Pollution" means the introduction by man, directly or indirectly, of substances or energy into the marine environment which results or is likely to result in such deleterious effects as harm to living resources and marine ecosystems, hazards to human health, hindrance to marine activities, including fishing and other legitimate uses of the sea, impairment of quality for use of sea water and reduction of amenities;

(b) "Land-based sources" means:

(i) Municipal, industrial or agricultural sources, both fixed and mobile, on land, discharges from which reach the marine environment, in particular:

a. From the coast, including from outfalls discharging directly into the marine environment and through run-off;

b. Through rivers, canals of other watercourses, including underground watercourses; and

c. Via the atmosphere;

(ii) Sources of marine pollution from activities conducted on offshore fixed or mobile facilities within the limits of national jurisdiction, save to the extent that these sources are governed by appropriate international agreements.

(c) "Marine environment" means the maritime area extending, in the case of watercourses, up to the freshwater limit and including intertidal zones and salt-water marshes;

(d) "Freshwater limit" means the place in watercourses where, at low tide and in a period of low freshwater flow, there is an appreciable increase in salinity due to the presence of sea water.

2. *Basic obligation*

States have the obligation to protect and preserve the marine environment. In exercising their sovereign right to exploit their natural resources, all States have the duty to prevent, reduce and control pollution of the marine environment.

3. *Discharges affecting other States or areas beyond the limits of national jurisdiction*

States have the duty to ensure that discharges from land-based sources within their territories do not cause pollution to the marine environment of other States or of areas beyond the limits of national jurisdiction.

4. *Adoption of measures against pollution from land-based sources*

(a) States should adopt, individually or jointly, and in accordance with their capabilities, all measures necessary to prevent, reduce and control pollution from land-based sources, including those designed to minimize to the fullest possible extent the release of toxic, harmful or noxious substances; especially those which are persistent, into the marine environment. States should ensure that such measures take into account internationally agreed rules, criteria, standards and recommended practices and procedures.

(b) In taking measures to prevent, reduce and control pollution from land-based sources, States should refrain, in accordance with international law, from unjustifiable interference with activities carried out by other States in the exercise of their sovereign rights and in pursuance of their duties in conformity with internationally agreed rules, criteria, standards and recommended practices and procedures.

5. *Co-operation on a global, regional or bilateral basis*

(a) States should undertake, as appropriate, to establish internationally agreed rules, criteria, standards and recommended practices and procedures to prevent, reduce and control pollution from land-based sources, with a view to co-ordinating their policies in this connection, particularly at the local and regional level. Such rules, criteria, standards and recommended practices and procedures should take into account local ecological, geographical and physical characteristics, the economic capacity of States and their need for sustainable development and environmental protection, and the assimilative capacity of the marine environment, and should be reviewed from time to time as necessary;

(b) States not bordering on the marine environment should co-operate in preventing, reducing and controlling pollution of the marine environment originating or partially originating from releases within their territory into or reaching water basins or watercourses flowing into the marine environment or via the atmosphere. To this end, States concerned should as far as possible, and, as appropriate, in co-operation with competent international organizations, take necessary measures to prevent, reduce and control pollution of the marine environment from land-based sources;

(c) If discharges from a watercourse which flows through the territories of two or more States or forms a boundary between them are likely to cause pollution of the marine environment, the States concerned should co-operate in taking necessary measures to prevent, reduce and control such pollution.

6. *Duty not to transfer or transform pollution from land-based sources*

In taking measures to prevent, reduce and control pollution from land-based sources, States have the duty to act so as not to transfer directly or indirectly, damage or hazards from one area to another or transform such pollution into another type of pollution.

7. *Specially protected areas*

(a) States should, in a manner consistent with international law, take all appropriate measures, such as the establishment of marine sanctuaries and reserves, to protect certain areas to the fullest possible extent from pollution, including that from land-based sources, taking into account the relevant provisions of annex I;

(b) States should, as practicable, undertake to develop, jointly or individually, environmental quality objectives for specially protected areas, conforming with the intended uses, and strive to maintain or ameliorate existing conditions by comprehensive environmental management practices.

8. *Scientific and technical co-operation*

States should co-operate, directly and/or through competent international organizations, in the field of science and technology related to pollution from land-based sources, and exchange data and other scientific information for the purpose of preventing, reducing and controlling such pollution, taking into account national regulations regarding the protection of confidential information. They should, in particular, undertake to develop and co-ordinate to the fullest possible extent their national research programmes and to co-operate in the establishment and implementation of regional and other international research programmes.

9. *Assistance to developing countries*

(a) States should, directly and/or through competent international organizations, promote programmes of assistance to developing countries in the fields of education, environmental and pollution awareness, training, scientific research and transfer of technology and know-how, for the purpose of improving the capacity of the developing countries to prevent, reduce and control pollution from land-based sources and to assess its effects on the marine environment;

(b) Such assistance should include:

(i) Training of scientific and technical personnel;

(ii) Facilitation of the participation of developing countries in relevant international programmes;

(iii) Acquisition, utilization, maintenance and production by those countries of appropriate equipment; and

(iv) Advice on, and development of, facilities for education, training, research, monitoring and other programmes;

(c) States should, directly and/or through competent international organizations, promote programmes of assistance to developing countries for the establishment, as necessary, of infrastructure for the effective implementation of applicable internationally agreed rules, criteria, standards and recommended practices and procedures related to the protection of the marine environment against pollution from land-based sources, including the provision of expert advice on the development of the necessary legal and administrative measures.

10. *Development of a comprehensive environmental management approach*

States should undertake to develop, as far as practicable, a comprehensive environmental management approach to the prevention, reduction and control of pollution from land-based sources, taking into account relevant existing programmes at the bilateral, regional or global level and the provisions of annex I. Such a comprehensive approach should include the identification of desired and attainable water use objectives for the specific marine environments.

11. *Monitoring and data management*

States should endeavour to establish directly or, whenever necessary, through competent international organizations, complementary or joint programmes for monitoring, storage and exchange of data, based, when possible, on compatible procedures and methods, taking into account relevant existing programmes at the bilateral, regional or global level and the provisions of annex III, in order to:

(a) Collect data on natural conditions in the region concerned as regards its physical, biological and chemical characteristics;

(b) Collect data on inputs of substances or energy that cause or potentially cause pollution emanating from land-based sources, including information on the distribution of sources and the quantities introduced to the region concerned;

(c) Assess systematically the levels of pollution along their coasts emanating from land-based sources and the fates and effects of pollution in the region concerned; and

(d) Evaluate the effectiveness of measures in meeting the environmental objectives for specific marine environments.

12. *Environmental assessment*

States should assess the potential effects/impacts, including possible transboundary effects/impacts, of proposed major projects under their jurisdiction or control, particularly in coastal areas, which may cause pollution from land-based sources, so that appropriate measures may be taken to prevent or mitigate such pollution.

13. *Development of control strategies*

(a) States should develop, adopt and implement programmes and measures for the prevention, reduction and control of pollution from land-based sources. They should employ an appropriate control strategy or combination of control strategies, taking into account relevant international or national experience, as described in annex I;

(b) States should, as appropriate, progressively formulate and adopt, in co-operation with competent international organizations, standards based on marine quality or on emissions, as well as recommended practices and procedures, taking into account the provisions of annex I;

(c) Where appropriate, States should undertake to establish priorities for action, based on lists of substances pollution by which should be eliminated and of substances pollution by which should be strictly limited on the basis of their toxicity, persistence, bioaccumulation and other criteria as elaborated in annex II, or in relevant international agreements.

14. *Pollution emergencies arising from land-based sources*

States and, as appropriate, competent international organizations should take all necessary measures for preventing and dealing with marine pollution emergencies from land-based sources, however caused, and for reducing or eliminating damage or the threat of damage therefrom. To this end States should, as appropriate, individually or jointly, develop and promote national and international contingency plans for responding to incidents of pollution from land-based sources and should co-operate with one another and, whenever necessary, through competent international organizations.

15. *Notification, information exchange and consultation*

Whenever releases originating or likely to originate from land-based sources within the territory of a State are likely to cause pollution to the marine environment of one or more other States or of areas beyond the limits of national jurisdiction, that State should immediately notify such other State or States, as well as competent international organizations, and provide them with timely information that will enable them, where necessary, to take appropriate action to prevent, reduce and control such pollution. Furthermore, consultations deemed appropriate by States concerned should be undertaken with a view to preventing, reducing and controlling such pollution.

16. *National laws and procedures*

(a) Each State should adopt and implement national laws and regulations for the protection and preservation of the marine environment against pollution from land-based sources, taking into account internationally agreed rules, criteria, standards and recommended practices and procedures, and take appropriate measures to ensure compliance with such laws and regulations;

(b) Paragraph (a) above is without prejudice to the right of States to take more stringent measures nationally or in co-operation with each other to prevent, reduce and control pollution from land-based sources under their jurisdiction or control;

(c) Each State should, on a reciprocal basis, grant equal access to and non-discriminatory treatment in its courts, tribunals and administrative proceedings to persons in other States who are or may be affected by pollution from land-based sources under its jurisdiction or control.

17. *Liability and compensation for pollution damage emanating from land-based sources*

(a) States should ensure that recourse is available in accordance with their legal systems for prompt and adequate compensation or other relief in respect of damage caused by pollution of the marine environment by natural or juridical persons under their jurisdiction;

(b) To this end, States should formulate and adopt appropriate procedures for the determination of liability for damage resulting from pollution from land-based sources. Such procedures should include measures for addressing damage caused by releases of a significant scale or by the substances referred to in guideline 13(c).

18. *Implementation reports*

States should report, as appropriate, to other States concerned, directly or through competent international organizations, on measures taken, on results achieved and, if the case arises, on difficulties encountered in the implementation of applicable internationally agreed rules, criteria, standards and recommended practices and procedures. To this end, States should designate national authorities as focal points for the reporting of such measures, results and difficulties.

19. *Institutional arrangements*

(a) States should ensure that adequate institutional arrangements are made at the appropriate regional or global level, for the purpose of achieving the objectives of these guidelines, and in particular for promoting the formulation, adoption and application of international rules, criteria, standards and recommended practices and procedures, and for monitoring the condition of the marine environment;

(b) The functions of such institutional arrangements should include:

(i) Periodic assessment of the state of the specific marine environment concerned;

(ii) Formulation and adoption, as appropriate, of a comprehensive environmental management approach consistent with the provisions of guidelines 7 and 10;

(iii) Adoption, review and revision, as necessary, of the lists referred to in guideline 13;

(iv) Development and adoption, as appropriate, of programmes and measures consistent with the provisions of guidelines 10 and 13;

(v) Consideration, where necessary, of the reports and information submitted in accordance with guidelines 15 and 18;

(vi) Recommendation of appropriate measures to be taken for the prevention, reduction and control of pollution from land-based sources, such as assistance to developing countries, the strengthening of regional co-operation mechanisms, consideration of aspects of transboundary pollution, and the difficulties encountered in the implementation of agreed rules; and

(vii) Review of the implementation of relevant internationally agreed rules, criteria, standards and recommended practices and procedures, and of the efficacy of the measures adopted and the advisability of any other measures.

**4.31　CONVENTION FOR THE PROTECTION OF THE NATURAL RE-
SOURCES AND ENVIRONMENT OF THE SOUTH PACIFIC RE-
GION (SREP CONVENTION) (WITHOUT PROTOCOLS). Concluded at Noumea, 25 November 1986. Entered into force, 22 August
1990. 26 I.L.M. 38 (1987)**

Article 1
GEOGRAPHICAL COVERAGE

1.　This Convention shall apply to the South Pacific Region, hereinafter
referred to as "the Convention Area" as defined in paragraph (a) of article 2.

2.　Except as may be otherwise provided in any Protocol to this Convention, the Convention Area shall not include internal waters or archipelagic
waters of the Parties as defined in accordance with international law.

Article 2
DEFINITIONS

For the purpose of this Convention and its Protocols unless otherwise
defined in any such Protocol:

(a) the "Convention Area" shall comprise:

(i) the 200 nautical mile zones established in accordance with
international law off:

American Samoa	Northern Mariana Islands
Australia (East Coast and Islands to eastward including Macquarie Island)	
Cook Islands	Palau
Federated States of Micronesia	Papua New Guinea
Fiji	Pitcairn Islands
French Polynesia	Solomon Islands
Guam	Tokelau
Kiribati	Tonga
Marshall Islands	Tuvalu
Nauru	Vanuatu
New Caledonia and Dependencies	Wallis and Futuna
New Zealand	Western Samoa
Niue	

(ii) those areas of high seas which are enclosed from all sides by
the 200 nautical mile zones referred to in sub-paragraph (i);

(iii) areas of the Pacific Ocean which have been included in the
Convention Area pursuant to article 3;

(b) "dumping" means:

— any deliberate disposal at sea of wastes or other matter from
vessels, aircraft, platforms or other man-made structures at sea;

— any deliberate disposal at sea of vessels, aircraft, platforms or
other man-made structures at sea;

"dumping" does not include:

— the disposal of wastes or other matter incidental to, or derived
from the normal operations of vessels, aircraft, platforms or other
man-made structures at sea and their equipment, other than wastes
or other matter transported by or to vessels, aircraft, platforms or

other man-made structures at sea, operating for the purpose of disposal of such matter or derived from the treatment of such wastes or other matter on such vessels, aircraft, platforms or structures;

— placement of matter for a purpose other than the mere disposal thereof, provided that such placement is not contrary to the aims of this Convention;

(c) "wastes or other matter" means material and substances of any kind, form or description;

(d) the following wastes or other matter shall be considered to be non-radioactive: sewage sludge, dredge spoil, fly ash, agricultural wastes, construction materials, vessels, artificial reef building materials and other such materials, provided that they have not been contaminated with radio nuclides of anthropogenic origin (except dispersed global fallout from nuclear weapons testing), nor are potential sources of naturally occurring radio nuclides for commercial purposes, nor have been enriched in natural or artificial radio nuclides;

if there is a question as to whether the material to be dumped should be considered non-radioactive, for the purposes of this Convention, such material shall not be dumped unless the appropriate national authority of the proposed dumper confirms that such dumping would not exceed the individual and collective dose limits of the International Atomic Energy Agency general principles for the exemption of radiation sources and practices from regulatory control. The national authority shall also take into account the relevant recommendations, standards and guidelines developed by the International Atomic Energy Agency;

(e) "vessels" and "aircraft" means waterborne or airborne craft of any type whatsoever. This expression includes air cushioned craft and floating craft, whether self-propelled or not;

(f) "pollution" means the introduction by man, directly or indirectly, of substances or energy into the marine environment (including estuaries) which results or is likely to result in such deleterious effects as harm to living resources and marine life, hazards to human health, hindrance to marine activities, including fishing and other legitimate uses of the sea, impairment of quality for use of sea water and reduction of amenities;

in applying this definition to the Convention obligations, the Parties shall use their best endeavours to comply with the appropriate standards and recommendations established by competent international organisations, including the International Atomic Energy Agency;

(g) "Organisation" means the South Pacific Commission;

(h) "Director" means the Director of the South Pacific Bureau for Economic Co-operation.

Article 3
ADDITION TO THE CONVENTION AREA

Any Party may add areas under its jurisdiction within the Pacific Ocean between the Tropic of Cancer and 60 degrees South latitude and between 130 degrees East longitude and 120 degrees West longitude to the Convention Area. Such addition shall be notified to the Depositary who shall promptly notify the other Parties and the Organisation. Such areas shall be incorporated within the Convention Area ninety days after notification to the Parties by the Depositary, provided there has been no objection to the proposal to add new areas by any Party affected by that proposal. If there is any such objection the Parties concerned will consult with a view to resolving the matter.

Article 4
GENERAL PROVISIONS

1.   The Parties shall endeavour to conclude bilateral or multilateral agreements, including regional or sub-regional agreements, for the protection, development and management of the marine and coastal environment of the Convention Area. Such agreements shall be consistent with this Convention and in accordance with international law. Copies of such agreements shall be communicated to the Organisation and through it to all Parties to this Convention.

2.   Nothing in this Convention or its Protocols shall be deemed to affect obligations assumed by a Party under agreements previously concluded.

3.   Nothing in this Convention and its Protocols shall be construed to prejudice or affect the interpretation and application of any provision or term in the Convention on the Prevention of Marine Pollution by Dumping of Wastes and Other Matter, 1972.

4.   This Convention and its Protocols shall be construed in accordance with international law relating to their subject matter.

5.   Nothing in this Convention and its Protocols shall prejudice the present or future claims and legal views of any Party concerning the nature and extent of maritime jurisdiction.

6.   Nothing in this Convention shall affect the sovereign right of States to exploit, develop and manage their own natural resources pursuant to their own policies, taking into account their duty to protect and preserve the environment. Each Party shall ensure that activities within its jurisdiction or control do not cause damage to the environment of other States or of areas beyond the limits of its national jurisdiction.

Article 5
GENERAL OBLIGATIONS

1.   The Parties shall endeavour, either individually or jointly, to take all appropriate measures in conformity with international law and in accordance with this Convention and those Protocols in force to which they are party to prevent, reduce and control pollution of the Convention Area, from any source, and to ensure sound environmental management and development of natural resources, using for this purpose the best practicable means at their disposal, and in accordance with their capabilities. In doing so the Parties shall endeavor to harmonize their policies at the regional level.

2.   The Parties shall use their best endeavors to ensure that the implementation of this Convention shall not result in an increase in pollution in the marine environment outside the Convention Area.

3. In addition to the Protocol for the Prevention of Pollution of the South Pacific Region by Dumping and the Protocol Concerning Co-operation in Combating Pollution Emergencies in the South Pacific Region, the Parties shall co-operate in the formulation and adoption of other Protocols prescribing agreed measures, procedures and standards to prevent, reduce and control pollution from all sources or in promoting environmental management in conformity with the objectives of this Convention.

4. The Parties shall, taking into account existing internationally recognized rules, standards, practices and procedures, co-operate with competent global, regional and sub-regional organisations to establish and adopt recommended practices, procedures and measures to prevent, reduce and control pollution from all sources and to promote sustained resource management and to ensure the sound development of natural resources in conformity with the objectives of this Convention and its Protocols, and to assist each other in fulfilling their obligations under this Convention and its Protocols.

5. The Parties shall endeavor to establish laws and regulations for the effective discharge of the obligations prescribed in this Convention. Such laws and regulations shall be no less effective than international rules, standards and recommended practices and procedures.

Article 6
POLLUTION FROM VESSELS

The Parties shall take all appropriate measures to prevent, reduce and control pollution in the Convention Area caused by discharges from vessels, and to ensure the effective application in the Convention Area of the generally accepted international rules and standards established through the competent international organisation or general diplomatic conference relating to the control of pollution from vessels.

Article 7
POLLUTION FROM LAND–BASED SOURCES

The Parties shall take all appropriate measures to prevent, reduce and control pollution in the Convention Area caused by coastal disposal or by discharges emanating from rivers, estuaries, coastal establishments, outfall structures, or any other sources in their territory.

Article 8
POLLUTION FROM SEA–BED ACTIVITIES

The Parties shall take all appropriate measures to prevent, reduce and control pollution in the Convention Area resulting directly or indirectly from exploration and exploitation of the sea-bed and its subsoil.

Article 9
AIRBORNE POLLUTION

The Parties shall take all appropriate measures to prevent, reduce and control pollution in the Convention Area resulting from discharges into the atmosphere from activities under their jurisdiction.

Article 10
DISPOSAL OF WASTES

1. The Parties shall take all appropriate measures to prevent, reduce and control pollution in the Convention Area caused by dumping from vessels,

aircraft, or man-made structures at sea, including the effective application of the relevant internationally recognized rules and procedures relating to the control of dumping of wastes and other matter. The Parties agree to prohibit the dumping of radioactive wastes or other radioactive matter in the Convention area. Without prejudice to whether or not disposal into the seabed and subsoil of wastes or other matter is "dumping", the Parties agree to prohibit the disposal into the seabed and subsoil of the Convention area of radioactive wastes or other radioactive matter.

2. This article shall also apply to the continental shelf of a Party where it extends, in accordance with international law, outward beyond the Convention Area.

Article 11
STORAGE OF TOXIC AND HAZARDOUS WASTES

The Parties shall take all appropriate measures to prevent, reduce and control pollution in the Convention Area resulting from the storage of toxic and hazardous wastes. In particular, the Parties shall prohibit the storage of radioactive wastes or other radioactive matter in the Convention Area.

Article 12
TESTING OF NUCLEAR DEVICES

The Parties shall take all appropriate measures to prevent, reduce and control pollution in the Convention Area which might result from the testing of nuclear devices.

Article 13
MINING AND COASTAL EROSION

The Parties shall take all appropriate measures to prevent, reduce and control environmental damage in the Convention Area, in particular coastal erosion caused by coastal engineering, mining activities, sand removal, land reclamation and dredging.

Article 14
SPECIALLY PROTECTED AREAS AND PROTECTION OF WILD FLORA AND FAUNA

The Parties shall, individually or jointly, take all appropriate measures to protect and preserve rare or fragile ecosystems and depleted, threatened or endangered flora and fauna as well as their habitat in the Convention Area. To this end, the Parties shall, as appropriate, establish protected areas, such as parks and reserves, and prohibit or regulate any activity likely to have adverse effects on the species, ecosystems or biological processes that such areas are designed to protect. The establishment of such areas shall not affect the rights of other Parties or third States under international law. In addition, the Parties shall exchange information concerning the administration and management of such areas.

Article 15
CO–OPERATION IN COMBATING POLLUTION IN CASES OF EMERGENCY

1. The Parties shall co-operate in taking all necessary measures to deal with pollution emergencies in the Convention Area, whatever the cause of

such emergencies, and to prevent, reduce and control pollution or the threat of pollution resulting therefrom. To this end, the Parties shall develop and promote individual contingency plans and joint contingency plans for responding to incidents involving pollution or the threat thereof in the Convention Area.

2. When a Party becomes aware of a case in which the Convention Area is in imminent danger of being polluted or has been polluted, it shall immediately notify other countries and territories it deems likely to be affected by such pollution, as well as the Organisation. Furthermore it shall inform, as soon as feasible, such other countries and territories and the Organisation of any measures it has itself taken to reduce or control pollution or the threat thereof.

Article 16
ENVIRONMENTAL IMPACT ASSESSMENT

1. The Parties agree to develop and maintain, with the assistance of competent global, regional and sub-regional organisations as requested, technical guidelines and legislation giving adequate emphasis to environmental and social factors to facilitate balanced development of their natural resources and planning of their major projects which might affect the marine environment in such a way as to prevent or minimize harmful impacts on the Convention Area.

2. Each Party shall, within its capabilities, assess the potential effects of such projects on the marine environment, so that appropriate measures can be taken to prevent any substantial pollution of, or significant and harmful changes within, the Convention Area.

3. With respect to the assessment referred to in paragraph 2, each Party shall, where appropriate, invite:

(a) public comment according to its national procedures,

(b) other Parties that may be affected to consult with it and submit comments.

The results of these assessments shall be communicated to the Organisation, which shall make them available to interested Parties.

Article 17
SCIENTIFIC AND TECHNICAL CO–OPERATION

1. The Parties shall co-operate, either directly or with the assistance of competent global, regional and sub-regional organisations, in scientific research, environmental monitoring, and the exchange of data and other scientific and technical information related to the purposes of the Convention.

2. In addition, the Parties shall, for the purposes of this Convention, develop and co-ordinate research and monitoring programmes relating to the Convention Area and co-operate, as far as practicable, in the establishment and implementation of regional, sub-regional and international research programmes.

Article 18
TECHNICAL AND OTHER ASSISTANCE

The Parties undertake to co-operate, directly and when appropriate through the competent global, regional and sub-regional organisations, in the provision to other Parties of technical and other assistance in fields relating to pollution and sound environmental management of the Convention Area, taking into account the special needs of the island developing countries and territories.

Article 19
TRANSMISSION OF INFORMATION

The Parties shall transmit to the Organisation information on the measures adopted by them in the implementation of this Convention and of Protocols to which they are Parties, in such form and at such intervals as the Parties may determine.

Article 20
LIABILITY AND COMPENSATION

The Parties shall co-operate in the formulation and adoption of appropriate rules and procedures in conformity with international law in respect of liability and compensation for damage resulting from pollution of the Convention Area.

Article 21
INSTITUTIONAL ARRANGEMENTS

1. The Organisation shall be responsible for carrying out the following secretariat functions:

(a) to prepare and convene the meetings of Parties;

(b) to transmit to the Parties notifications, reports and other information received in accordance with this Convention and its Protocols;

(c) to perform the functions assigned to it by the Protocols to this Convention;

(d) to consider enquiries by, and information from, the Parties and to consult with them on questions relating to this Convention and the Protocols;

(e) to co-ordinate the implementation of co-operative activities agreed upon by the Parties;

(f) to ensure the necessary co-ordination with other competent global, regional and sub-regional bodies;

(g) to enter into such administrative arrangements as may be required for the effective discharge of the secretariat functions;

(h) to perform such other functions as may be assigned to it by the Parties; and

(i) to transmit to the South Pacific Conference and the South Pacific Forum the reports of ordinary and extraordinary meetings of the Parties.

2. Each Party shall designate an appropriate national authority to serve as the channel of communication with the Organisation for the purposes of this Convention.

Article 22
MEETINGS OF THE PARTIES

1. The Parties shall hold ordinary meetings once every two years. Ordinary meetings shall review the implementation of this Convention and its Protocols and, in particular, shall:

(a) assess periodically the state of the environment in the Convention Area;

(b) consider the information submitted by the Parties under article 19;

(c) adopt, review and amend as required annexes to this Convention and to its Protocols, in accordance with the provisions of article 25;

(d) make recommendations regarding the adoption of any Protocols or any amendments to this Convention or its Protocols in accordance with the provisions of articles 23 and 24;

(e) establish working groups as required to consider any matters concerning this Convention and its Protocols;

(f) consider co-operative activities to be undertaken within the framework of this Convention and its Protocols, including their financial and institutional implications and to adopt decisions relating thereto;

(g) consider and undertake any additional action that may be required for the achievement of the purposes of this Convention and its Protocols; and

(h) adopt by consensus financial rules and budget, prepared in consultation with the Organization, to determine, *inter alia,* the financial participation of the Parties under this Convention and those Protocols to which they are party.

2. The Organisation shall convene the first ordinary meeting of the Parties not later than one year after the date on which the Convention enters into force in accordance with article 31.

3. Extraordinary meetings shall be convened at the request of any Party or upon the request of the Organisation, provided that such requests are supported by at least two-thirds of the Parties. It shall be the function of an extraordinary meeting of the Parties to consider those items proposed in the request for the holding of the extraordinary meeting and any other items agreed to by all the Parties attending the meeting.

4. The Parties shall adopt by consensus at their first ordinary meeting, rules of procedure for their meetings.

Article 23
ADOPTION OF PROTOCOLS

1. The Parties may, at a conference of plenipotentiaries, adopt Protocols to this Convention pursuant to paragraph 3 of article 5.

2. If so requested by a majority of the Parties, the Organisation shall convene a conference of plenipotentiaries for the purpose of adopting Protocols to this Convention.

Article 24
AMENDMENT OF THE CONVENTION AND ITS PROTOCOLS

1. Any Party may propose amendments to this Convention. Amendments shall be adopted by a conference of plenipotentiaries which shall be convened by the Organisation at the request of two-thirds of the Parties.

2. Any Party to this Convention may propose amendments to any Protocol. Such amendments shall be adopted by a conference of plenipotentiaries which shall be convened by the Organisation at the request of two-thirds of the Parties to the Protocol concerned.

3. A proposed amendment to the Convention or any Protocol shall be communicated to the Organisation, which shall promptly transmit such proposal for consideration to all the other Parties.

4. A conference of plenipotentiaries to consider a proposed amendment to the Convention or any Protocol shall be convened not less than ninety days after the requirements for the convening of the Conference have been met pursuant to paragraphs 1 or 2, as the case may be.

5. Any amendment to this Convention shall be adopted by a three-fourths majority vote of the Parties to the Convention which are represented at the conference of plenipotentiaries and shall be submitted by the Depositary for acceptance by all Parties to the Convention. Amendments to any Protocol shall be adopted by a three-fourths majority vote of the Parties to the Protocol which are represented at the conference of plenipotentiaries and shall be submitted by the Depositary for acceptance by all Parties to the Protocol.

6. Instruments of ratification, acceptance or approval of amendments shall be deposited with the Depositary. Amendments shall enter into force between Parties having accepted such amendments on the thirtieth day following the date of receipt by the Depositary of the instruments of at least three-fourths of the Parties to this Convention or to the Protocol concerned, as the case may be. Thereafter the amendments shall enter into force for any other Party on the thirtieth day after the date on which that Party deposits its instrument.

7. After the entry into force of an amendment to this Convention or to a Protocol, any new Party to the Convention or such protocol shall become a Party to the Convention or Protocol as amended.

Article 25

ANNEXES AND AMENDMENT OF ANNEXES

1. Annexes to this Convention or to any Protocol shall form an integral part of the Convention or such Protocol respectively.

2. Except as may be otherwise provided in any Protocol with respect to its annexes, the following procedures shall apply to the adoption and entry into force of any amendments to annexes to this Convention or to annexes to any Protocol:

(a) any Party may propose amendments to the annexes to this Convention or annexes to any Protocol;

(b) any proposed amendment shall be notified by the Organisation to the Parties not less than sixty days before the convening of a meeting of the Parties unless this requirement is waived by the meeting;

(c) such amendments shall be adopted at a meeting of the Parties by a three-fourths majority vote of the Parties to the instrument in question;

(d) the Depositary shall without delay communicate the amendments so adopted to all Parties;

(e) any Party that is unable to approve an amendment to the annexes to this Convention or to annexes to any Protocol shall so notify in writing to the Depositary within one hundred days from the date of the communication of the amendment by the Depositary. A Party may at any time substitute an acceptance for a previous declaration of objection, and the amendment shall thereupon enter into force for that Party;

(f) the Depositary shall without delay notify all Parties of any notification received pursuant to the preceding sub-paragraph; and

(g) on expiry of the period referred to in sub-paragraph (e) above, the amendment to the annex shall become effective for all Parties to this Convention or to the Protocol concerned which have not submitted a notification in accordance with the provisions of that sub-paragraph.

3. The adoption and entry into force of a new annex shall be subject to the same procedure as that for the adoption and entry into force of an amendment to an annex as set out in the provisions of paragraph 2, provided that, if any amendment to the Convention or the Protocol concerned is involved, the new annex shall not enter into force until such time as that amendment enters into force.

4. Amendments to the Annex on Arbitration shall be considered to be amendments to this Convention or its Protocols and shall be proposed and adopted in accordance with the procedures set out in article 24.

Article 26
SETTLEMENT OF DISPUTES

1. In case of a dispute between Parties as to the interpretation or application of this Convention or its Protocols, they shall seek a settlement of the dispute through negotiation or any other peaceful means of their own choice. If the Parties concerned cannot reach agreement, they should seek the good offices of, or jointly request mediation by, a third Party.

2. If the Parties concerned cannot settle their dispute through the means mentioned in paragraph 1, the dispute shall, upon common agreement, except as may be otherwise provided in any Protocol to this Convention, be submitted to arbitration under conditions laid down in the Annex on Arbitration to this Convention. However, failure to reach common agreement on submission of the dispute to arbitration shall not absolve the Parties from the responsibility of continuing to seek to resolve it by means referred to in paragraph 1.

3. A Party may at any time declare that it recognizes as compulsory *ipso facto* and without special agreement, in relation to any other Party accepting the same obligation, the application of the arbitration procedure set out in the Annex on Arbitration. Such declaration shall be notified in writing to the Depositary who shall promptly communicate it to the other Parties.

Article 27
RELATIONSHIP BETWEEN THIS CONVENTION AND ITS PROTOCOLS

1. No State may become a Party to this Convention unless it becomes at the same time a Party to one or more Protocols. No State may become a

Party to a Protocol unless it is, or becomes at the same time, a Party to this Convention.

2. Decisions concerning any Protocol pursuant to articles 22, 24 and 25 of this Convention shall be taken only by the Parties to the Protocol concerned.

Article 28
SIGNATURE

This Convention, the Protocol Concerning Co-operation in Combating Pollution Emergencies in the South Pacific Region, and the Protocol for the Prevention of Pollution of the South Pacific Region by Dumping shall be open for signature at the South Pacific Commission Headquarters in Noumea, New Caledonia on 25 November 1986 and at the South Pacific Bureau for Economic Co-operation Headquarters, Suva, Fiji from 26 November 1986 to 25 November 1987 by States which were invited to participate in the Plenipotentiary Meeting of the High Level Conference on the Protection of the Natural Resources and Environment of the South Pacific Region held at Noumea, New Caledonia from 24 November 1986 to 25 November 1986.

Article 29
RATIFICATION, ACCEPTANCE OR APPROVAL

This Convention and any Protocol thereto shall be subject to ratification, acceptance or approval by States referred to in article 28. Instruments of ratification, acceptance or approval shall be deposited with the Director who shall be the Depositary.

Article 30
ACCESSION

1. This Convention and any Protocol thereto shall be open to accession by the States referred to in article 28 as from the day following the date on which the Convention or Protocol concerned was closed for signature.

2. Any State not referred to in paragraph 1 may accede to the Convention and to any Protocol subject to prior approval by three-fourths of the Parties to the Convention or the Protocol concerned.

3. Instruments of accession shall be deposited with the Depositary.

Article 31
ENTRY INTO FORCE

1. This Convention shall enter into force on the thirtieth day following the date of deposit of at least ten instruments of ratification, acceptance, approval or accession.

2. Any Protocol to this Convention, except as otherwise provided in such Protocol, shall enter into force on the thirtieth day following the date of deposit of at least five instruments of ratification, acceptance or approval of such Protocol, or of accession thereto, provided that no Protocol shall enter into force before the Convention. Should the requirements for entry into force of a Protocol be met prior to those for entry into force of the Convention pursuant to paragraph 1, such Protocol shall enter into force on the same date as the Convention.

3. Thereafter, this Convention and any Protocol shall enter into force with respect to any State referred to in articles 28 or 30 on the thirtieth day following the date of deposit of its instrument of ratification, acceptance, approval or accession.

Article 32
DENUNCIATION

1. At any time after two years from the date of entry into force of this Convention with respect to a Party, that Party may denounce the Convention by giving written notification to the Depositary.

2. Except as may be otherwise provided in any Protocol to this Convention, any Party may, at any time after two years from the date of entry into force of such Protocol with respect to that Party, denounce the Protocol by giving written notification to the Depositary.

3. Denunciation shall take effect ninety days after the date on which notification of denunciation is received by the Depositary.

4. Any Party which denounces this Convention shall be considered as also having denounced any Protocol to which it was a Party.

5. Any Party which, upon its denunciation of a Protocol, is no longer a Party to any Protocol to this Convention, shall be considered as also having denounced this Convention.

Article 33
RESPONSIBILITIES OF THE DEPOSITARY

1. The Depositary shall inform the Parties, as well as the Organisation:

(a) of the signature of this Convention and of any Protocol thereto and of the deposit of instruments of ratification, acceptance, approval, or accession in accordance with articles 29 and 30;

(b) of the date on which the Convention and any Protocol will come into force in accordance with the provisions of article 31;

(c) of notification of denunciation made in accordance with article 32;

(d) of notification of any addition to the Convention Area in accordance with article 3;

(e) of the amendments adopted with respect to the Convention and to any Protocol, their acceptance by the Parties and the date of their entry into force in accordance with the provisions of article 24; and

(f) of the adoption of new annexes and of the amendments of any annex in accordance with article 25.

2. The original of this Convention and of any Protocol thereto shall be deposited with the Depositary who shall send certified copies thereof to the Signatories, the Parties, to the Organisation and to the Secretary–General of the United Nations for registration and publication in accordance with article 102 of the United Nations Charter.

4.32 BELLAGIO DRAFT TREATY CONCERNING THE USE OF TRANS-BOUNDARY GROUNDWATERS, 1989. 1 *Basic Document of International Environmental Law* **42 (H. Hohmann ed. 1992)**

Agreement Concerning the Use of Transboundary Groundwaters

The High Contracting Parties, _____ and _____,

Motivated by the spirit of cordiality and cooperation which characterizes the relations between them;

Desirous of expanding the scope of their concerted actions with respect to the problems confronting their Peoples along their common frontier;

Recognizing the critical importance of their transboundary water resources and the need to enhance the rational use and conservation of the said resources on a long-term basis;

Noting especially the present unsatisfactory state of protection and control of their transboundary groundwaters as well as the prospects of crisis conditions in some areas because of increasing demands upon, and the decreasing quality of, those groundwaters;

Seeking to provide for the utilization, protection and control of those groundwaters on an equitable basis and, to that end, for the creation and maintenance of an adequate data base;

Recognizing that the optimum and efficient use of their transboundary water resources is essential to the interests of both Parties;

Resolving to protect the quality of the transboundary groundwaters for present and future generations;

Wishing to resolve amicably any differences that may arise in connection with the use, protection or control of the said transboundary groundwaters and, for that purpose, to utilize a joint agency; and

Concluding that the best means to achieve the rational management of their transboundary water resources and the protection of the underground environment is to adopt, in principle, an integrated approach including, where appropriate, the conjunctive use of surface water and groundwater in their border region,

Have agreed as follows:

Article I

Definitions

As used in this Agreement:

1. "Aquifer" means a subsurface waterbearing geologic formation from which significant quantities of water may be extracted.

2. "Border region" means the area within approximately _____ kilometers from each side of the mutual boundary as set forth on the annexed map.

3. "The Commission" means the agency designated in Article III, para. 1, of this Agreement.

4. "Conjunctive Use" means the integrated development and management of surface and groundwater as a total water supply system.

5. "Contaminant" means any substance, species or energy which detrimentally affects directly, indirectly, cumulatively or in combination with other substances, human health or safety or agricultural or industrial products or processes, or flora, fauna or an ecosystem.

6. "Contamination" means any detrimental chemical, physical, biological, or temperature change in the content or characteristics of a body of water.

7. "Depletion" means the withdrawal of water from an aquifer at a rate faster than it is recharged, otherwise known as "mining" the water.

8. "Drought" means a condition of abnormal water scarcity in a specific area resulting from natural conditions.

9. "Drought Alert" means the declared condition provided for in Article XII.

10. "Drought Emergency" means the declared emergency provided for in Article XII.

11. "Drought Management Plan" means the plan provided for pursuant to Article XII.

12. "Environmental sensitivity" means vulnerability or susceptibility to changes detrimentally affecting the quality of life or one or more biological or physical systems.

13. "Government(s)" means the governments of the Parties to this Agreement.

14. "Groundwater" means the water in aquifers.

15. "Impairment" means any physical change in an aquifer or its recharge area which significantly reduces or restricts the potential for use of the waters of the aquifer.

16. "Interrelated surface water" means those surface waters in the territory of either Party, the quantity or quality of which is affected by the outflows from, or the inflows to, transboundary groundwater.

17. "Pollution" means the introduction of any contaminant by man, directly or indirectly, into groundwaters or surface waters.

18. "Public Health Emergency" means the declared emergency provided for in Article IX.

19. "Recharge" means the addition of water to an aquifer by infiltration of precipitation through the soil or of water from surface streams, lakes, or reservoirs, by discharges of water to the land surface, or by injection of water into the aquifer through wells.

20. "Transboundary aquifer" means an aquifer intersected by a common boundary.

21. "Transboundary Groundwater Conservation Area" means an area declared by the Commission pursuant to Article VII.

22. "Transboundary groundwaters" means waters in transboundary aquifers.

Article II
General Purposes

1. The Parties recognize their common interest and responsibility in ensuring the reasonable and equitable development and management of groundwaters in the border region for the well being of their Peoples.

2. Accordingly, the Parties have entered into this Agreement in order to attain the optimum utilization and conservation of transboundary groundwaters and to protect the underground environment. It is also the purpose of the Parties to develop and maintain reliable data and information concerning transboundary aquifers and their waters in order to use and protect these waters in a rational and informed manner.

Article III
The Commission Responsible Under this Agreement

1. The _____ Commission is designated as the Parties' agency to carry out the functions and responsibilities provided for by this Agreement.

2. The Commission shall be authorized a technical staff, which, in collaboration with the technical staffs of the Governments, shall assist the Commission in the accomplishment of its functions and responsibilities.

3. The Commission is authorized to declare Transboundary Groundwater Conservation Areas, Drought Alerts, Drought Emergencies and Public Health Emergencies, and to promulgate the corresponding plans and Depletion Plans, in accordance with the provisions of this Agreement.

4. The Commission shall have jurisdiction over such additional matters concerning the border region as are from time to time referred to it by the Governments jointly.

5. The Commission shall prepare and propose to the Governments a budget, conforming insofar as practicable to the budget cycles and procedures of the Governments, covering the projected expenses and capital costs of the Commission's joint operations, plant and staff. The total amount of each budget shall be divided between the Governments in the proportions agreed upon by the Commission and approved by the Governments.

6. The budget for the separate operating costs of each national section shall be the responsibility of the respective Government.

7. The Governments may jointly refer a specific matter relating to transboundary groundwater to the Commission for investigation or action. Individually Governments may request the Commission's advice relating to transboundary groundwaters on matters originating within the requesting Government's portion of the order region.

8. The Commission shall cause each such referral and request to be taken up and investigated, studied or acted upon, as appropriate. The Commission shall render a report to the Governments on every referral and request taken up.

Article IV
Enforcement and Oversight Responsibilities

1. The enforcement of water quality and quantity measures and related land use controls within the territory of each Party shall be the responsibility of that Party or of its political subdivisions, as appropriate.

2. The Commission shall biennially conduct a review of the water quality and quantity control measures taken within each Party's territory affecting the border region and shall issue a Report containing its assessment of the adequacy and effectiveness of programs for the protection and improvement of the transboundary aquifers and their waters and withdrawal and land use controls, including with respect to any Transboundary Groundwater Conservation Areas, Depletion Plans, Drought Emergency Plans and Health Emergencies. To that end, each Government shall furnish the Commission with the relevant data, information, and studies for use by the Commission in preparing its Report, in accordance with the reporting formats provided by the Commission.

3. In addition to facilitating, as needed, the Commission's oversight responsibilities under paragraph 2, each Government shall make a biennial Report to the Commission specifying the water quality and conservation measures taken; quantities withdrawn, transferred and exchanged, and any problems encountered in carrying out the provisions of this Agreement or in implementation of any of the conservation, depletion and drought management plans and health emergency measures adopted.

Article V

Establishment and Maintenance of the Database

1. The Commission is charged with the creation and maintenance of a comprehensive and unified database pertaining to transboundary groundwaters, in the languages of the Parties. The database shall include an inventory of all transboundary groundwater resources taking into account quantity, quality, aquifer geometry, recharge rates, interaction with surface waters, and other pertinent data and shall identify all transboundary aquifers.

2. The Commission shall carry out studies directly, or through research programs conducted by or with other bodies, public or private:

(a) to identify inadequacies in available data and to propose remedial action;

(b) to examine present and potential future uses of said groundwaters, taking into account demographic projections and socio-economic development plans;

(c) to assess the impact of present and potential development on transboundary groundwaters and related resources;

(d) to study possible alternative sources of surface water and groundwater for use in the border region, taking into account the quantity and quality of the waters and the potential for the conjunctive use of the available waters; and

(e) to examine the potential for, and the consequences of, drought, floods, and contamination in the border region.

3. The Parties undertake to facilitate the acquisition of information and data by the Commission on a timely basis in accordance with the Commission's requirements.

4. The Commission shall compile, analyze, and disseminate the data, information and studies and provide the results to the Governments.

Article VI

Water Quality Protection

1.　The Parties undertake cooperatively to protect and to improve, insofar as practicable, the quality of transboundary aquifers and their waters in conjunction with their programs for surface water quality control, and to avoid appreciable harm in or to the territories of the Parties.

2.　The Governments shall promptly inform the Commission of any actual or planned, significantly polluting discharge into transboundary groundwaters or recharge areas, or of other activity with the potential for significant leaching into transboundary groundwaters.

3.　The Commission shall without delay consider the gravity of any situation indicating significant groundwater contamination, or the threat thereof, in any part of the border region in accordance with the provisions of Article VII.

Article VII

Transboundary Groundwater Conservation Areas

1.　The Commission shall determine the desirability of declaring any area within the border region containing transboundary groundwaters to be a Transboundary Groundwater Conservation Area.

2.　In the event that the Commission determines that a Transboundary Groundwater Conservation Area is desirable, such determination shall be reported to the Governments with a draft of the proposed declaration and justification therefore, including the delineation of the area and its aquifer(s)

3.　If no Government files an objection with the Commission within one hundred eighty (180) days, the Commission shall issue the formal declaration. Any objection(s) filed shall specify, with an explanation, the objectionable section(s) of the proposed declaration or justification or both.

4.　Unless an objection requires termination of consideration, the Commission shall within ninety (90) days of receipt of objections, report to the Governments a revised proposed declaration, to be effective within ninety (90) days, unless a Government files a subsequent objection with the Commission. If no subsequent objection is filed within the said ninety (90) day period, the formal declaration shall be issued by the Commission. If a subsequent objection is filed within the ninety (90) day period, the Commission shall refer the matter, together with the entire record, to the Governments for resolution by consultation.

5.　In making its determination, the Commission shall consider whether:

(a) groundwater withdrawals exceed or are likely to exceed recharge so as to endanger yield or water quality or are likely to diminish the quantity or quality of interrelated surface waters;

(b) recharge has been or may become impaired;

(c) the use of the included aquifer(s) as an important source of drinking water has been, or may become impaired;

(d) the aquifer(s) have been or may become contaminated;　and

(e) recurring or persistent drought conditions necessitate management of all or some water supplies in the particular area.

6. In making its determination, the Commission shall take into account the impact of the implementation of the declaration under consideration on the sources and uses of water previously allocated by agreements between the Parties or under the Drought Management Plan.

7. The Commission shall periodically review the appropriateness of continuing or modifying Transboundary Groundwater Conservation Areas.

Article VIII

Comprehensive Management Plans

1. For each declared Transboundary Groundwater Conservation Area, the Commission shall prepare a Comprehensive Management Plan for the rational development, use, protection and control of the waters in the Transboundary Groundwater Conservation Area.

2. A Comprehensive Management Plan may:

(a) prescribe measures to prevent, eliminate or mitigate degradation of transboundary groundwater quality, and for that purpose may:

(1) classify transboundary groundwaters according to use and coordinate the formulation of water quality standards;

(2) identify toxic and hazardous contaminants in the Area and require a continuing record of such substances from origin to disposal;

(3) establish criteria for the safe storage of wastes and maintain an inventory of dumpsites, abandoned as well as active, that have caused or may cause transboundary aquifer pollution;

(4) propose a scheme for monitoring water quality conditions including the placement and operation of test wells and for remedial actions where required, including pretreatment and effluent discharge limitations and charges; and

(5) provide for the establishment, where required, of protective zones in which land use must be regulated.

(b) allocate the uses of groundwaters and interrelated surface waters taking into account any other allocation(s) previously made applicable within the Transboundary Groundwater Conservation Area.

(c) prescribe measures including pumping limitations, criteria for well placement and number of new wells, retirement of existing wells, imposition of extraction fees, planned depletion regimes or reservations of groundwaters for future use.

(d) arrange, where conditions are favorable, programs of transboundary aquifer recharge.

(e) articulate programs of conjunctive use where appropriate.

(f) prescribe the integration and coordination of water quality and quantity control programs.

(g) include other measures and actions as may be deemed appropriate by the Commission.

3. In making any allocations of water uses within a Comprehensive Management Plan, the Commission shall consider all relevant factors such as:

(a) hydrogeology and meteorology;

(b) existing and planned uses;

(c) environmental sensitivity;

(d) quality control requirements;

(e) socio-economic implications (including dependency);

(f) water conservation practices (including efficiency of water use);

(g) artificial recharge potential; and

(h) comparative costs and implications of alternative sources of supply.

The weight to be given to each factor is to be determined by its importance in comparison with that of the other relevant factors.

4. The Commission shall submit proposed Comprehensive Management Plans to the Governments.

(a) If no Government files an objection with the Commission within one hundred eighty (180) days, the Commission shall adopt the Plan and monitor its implementation.

(b) A Government's objections shall specify with an explanation the objectionable portions of the proposed Comprehensive Management Plan.

(c) Within ninety (90) days of receipt of objections, the Commission shall submit to the Governments a revised proposed Comprehensive Management Plan to be effective within ninety (90) days unless a subsequent objection is filed. If no subsequent objection is filed with the ninety (90) day period, the proposed Comprehensive Management Plan shall be adopted and the Commission shall monitor its implementation. If subsequent objections are filed within the ninety (90) day period, the Commission shall refer the matter, together with the entire record, to the Governments for resolution by consultation.

5. The Commission is authorized to approve advances and exchanges of water consistent with the objectives of the applicable Comprehensive Management Plan.

6. The Commission shall monitor and evaluate the measures taken under the Comprehensive Management Plan and shall propose, as appropriate, modifications thereto.

Article IX

Public Health Emergencies

1. Upon a determination by the Commission or any Government that there is an imminent or actual public health hazard involving the contamination of transboundary groundwaters, the Commission shall notify the respective Governments, and may declare a Public Health Emergency for a stated period.

2. In the event that the Public Health Emergency is not mitigated or abated within the initial stated period, the Commission may extend the emergency for such additional period as may be deemed necessary under the circumstances.

3. On the basis of the declaration, the Commission shall have authority to investigate the area of imminent or actual contamination and to prescribe measures to prevent, eliminate or mitigate the public health hazard.

4. The Governments shall provide the indicated information, data, studies and reports concerning public health emergencies as set forth in Paragraphs 2 and 3 of Article IV.

Article X
Planned Depletion

1. The Commission, after evaluation of all relevant considerations, may prepare and, with the consent of the Governments, may approve a plan for the depletion of an aquifer over a calculated period. The plan may apportion the uses and specify the rates and means of extraction of the transboundary groundwaters, and may authorize advances, exchanges and transboundary transfers of water consistent with the objectives of the Depletion Plan.

2. The Governments shall provide the indicated information, data, studies and reports concerning depletion as set forth in Paragraphs 2 and 3 of Article IV.

Article XI
Transboundary Transfers

Nothing in this Agreement shall be so construed as to preclude either short-term or long-term transfers of waters between the Parties under terms and conditions approved by the Commission.

Article XII
Planning for Drought

1. The Commission shall, within two (2) years of the coming into force of this Agreement, complete the preparation of a Drought Management Plan applicable to the border region for activation in the region, or in parts thereof, in the event of drought. The completed Plan shall be submitted to the Governments for standby approval.

2. The Drought Management Plan shall:

(a) specify the hydrometeorological preconditions for the declaration of a Drought Alert and, thereunder, the conservation measures to be observed by all water users within the border region;

(b) specify the hydrometeorological preconditions for the declaration of a Drought Emergency and, thereunder, the specific measures to be observed by all water users within the border region;

(c) provide for the monitoring of the hydrometeorological conditions generally in the border region, and compliance with prescribed conservation or other specific measures under any Drought Alert or Drought Emergency; and

(d) provide for periodic reports to the Governments during any Drought Alert or Drought Emergency, to include any proposed modifications to the Drought Emergency Plan and any modifications made to the prescribed measures under any Drought Alert or Drought Emergency.

3. The Drought Management Plan may:

(a) designate and reserve certain transboundary aquifers or specific well sites for use in times of drought;

(b) provide, for the duration of any declared Drought Emergency:

(1) the conjunctive management of groundwater and surface water supplies within or made available to the border region or part(s) thereof governed by the declaration;

(2) increases and reductions in the normal allowable withdrawals and at variance with allocations made under a Comprehensive Management Plan for a Transboundary Groundwater Conservation Area or by prior agreements between the Parties, maintaining to the extent practicable the established withdrawal ratios between the Parties and an equitable balance of all emergency obligations.

(3) authorization to use designated and reserved groundwaters within the border region.

(c) include other structural and nonstructural measures deemed likely to be needed under various drought conditions.

4. The conservation and other specific measures provided in the Plan for Drought Alert declarations or Drought Emergency declarations may be modified or suspended by the Commission to meet the specific requirements of the situation at the time of such declarations and during the time such declarations remain in force.

5. The authority to determine the existence of the preconditions specified in the approved Drought Management Plan and to declare drought alerts and drought emergencies thereunder, in any portion of the border region, is vested in the Commission.

6. The Commission is authorized to modify or terminate a declaration of Drought alert or of Drought Emergency when the hydrometeorological conditions so warrant.

7. Declarations of Drought Alert and Drought Emergency, and modifications to or termination of the same, shall be immediately communicated to the Governments and published so as to come to the attention of all water users in the border region.

8. The Governments shall provide the indicated information, data, studies and reports concerning drought as set forth in Paragraphs 2 and 3 of Article IV.

Article XIII
Inquiry in the Public Interest

1. The Commission shall by general notice invite written statements and information from all persons professing interest in the groundwater-related conditions and activities in the portion of the border region for which a Transboundary Groundwater Conservation Area declaration, a Comprehensive Management Plan, a Depletion Plan, a transboundary transfer, or a Drought Alert or Emergency declaration is under consideration.

2. All submissions received pursuant to Paragraph 1 shall be taken into account by the Commission.

3. Whenever the Commission deems that public interest warrants, it shall schedule and conduct hearings open to the public in appropriate places and facilities in the border region, and shall make and publish a record of such hearings.

4. Any person professing an interest may also petition the Commission at any time requesting the Commission to schedule a hearing or to invite written statements and information concerning groundwater conditions in the border region, or urging the Commission to take a particular action under this Agreement.

5. When deemed useful by the Commission, technical meetings, workshops and briefings relating to transboundary groundwater matters may be held under the auspices of the Commission or in cooperation with authorities and organizations concerned with the welfare of the border region.

Article XIV

Existing Rights and Obligations

The rights and obligations of the Parties as set forth in prior agreements between the Parties shall not be permanently altered by this Agreement or any measures taken hereunder.

Article XV

Accommodation of Differences

1. The Commission shall expend its best efforts to resolve differences within the Commission with respect to the facts and circumstances of a situation within the purview of this Agreement. Failure to resolve such differences within six (6) months at the technical level of the Commission shall result in the submission of the difference(s), together with the entire record, to the Governments for resolution by consultation.

2. If after good faith consultations during a period of twelve (12) months the Governments are unable to reach an accommodation of a difference or differences between them concerning the facts and circumstances of a situation within the purview of this Agreement, or with respect to which the Commission has been unable to reach agreement,

(a) any Government is entitled to invoke this Article to the effect that a commission of inquiry be appointed and charged with a full and impartial study for the purpose of verification of the facts of the situation;

(b) the Governments shall appoint and instruct the commissioner(s), and defray the expenses of such commissions equally, unless otherwise agreed; and

(c) in the event the Governments fail to agree upon the implementation of this Paragraph within six (6) months from the date of its formal invocation, the _____, at the request of any Government shall, after consultation with each Government, appoint the commissioner(s), instruct the same, and apportion the expenses of the commission, as may be required to render the commission operational.

3. A commission of inquiry appointed under this Article shall render a report to the Governments within the terms of its instructions and on the basis of independent and detailed examination of the data and information made available to it by the Governments and the Commission, and may

request such additional data and information as the commission of inquiry deems significant for its deliberations and findings.

4.   On the basis of the report of a commission of inquiry, the Parties undertake promptly to enter into consultations for the purpose of reaching an agreed accommodation of the difference(s).

5.   The Commission shall expend its best efforts to resolve differences within the Commission with respect to the interpretation of this Agreement, of any declaration, plan or prescribed measure, or of any other relevant document, referral, request or decision.   Failure to resolve such differences within six (6) months by the Commission shall result in the submission of such difference(s), together with the record of deliberations, to the Governments for resolution by consultation.

6.   Should the Governments, after six (6) months of consultations fail to agree upon a questioned interpretation submitted to them by the Commission, pursuant to Paragraph 5, or that has otherwise arisen, including with respect to the validity or interpretation of any binding decision by the Commission, the provisions of Article XVI of this Agreement shall apply.

Article XVI

Resolution of Disputes

1.   If the consultations called for under Article XV do not achieve an agreed accommodation, the Governments shall promptly enter into formal, direct negotiations for the purpose of resolving the disagreement.

2.   Should the Governments not achieve agreement after six (6) months of direct negotiations, the Parties shall refer the matter to mediation, conciliation, arbitration, the International Court of Justice or any other means of peaceful settlement, absent a previously agreed, applicable means of dispute settlement binding upon the Parties.

3.   In resolving differences and questions affecting the implementation of this Agreement and decisions taken thereunder, the Parties undertake to avoid delay and to facilitate the process of resolution as between themselves and, as appropriate, before any mediator, conciliator, tribunal or other settlement forum, taking into account the importance of timely resolution with respect to critical transboundary groundwater situations.

Article XVII

Amendment

This Agreement may be amended by agreement of the Parties.

4.33   DRAFT ARTICLES ON THE LAW OF THE NON–NAVIGATIONAL USES OF INTERNATIONAL WATERCOURSES. Adopted by the UN International Law Commission, 19 July 1991. *Report of the International Law Commission on the Work of its Forty–Third Session,* **U.N. GAOR, 46th Sess., Supp. No. 10 at 161, U.N. Doc. A/46/10 (1991)**

PART I

INTRODUCTION

Article 1

Scope of the present articles

1.   The present articles apply to uses of international watercourses and of their waters for purposes other than navigation and to measures of conservation related to the uses of those watercourses and their waters.

2.   The use of international watercourses for navigation is not within the scope of the present articles except in so far as other uses affect navigation or are affected by navigation.

Article 2

Use of terms

For the purposes of the present articles:

(a) "international watercourse" means a watercourse, parts of which are situated in different States;

(b) "watercourse" means a system of surface and underground waters constituting by virtue of their physical relationship a unitary whole and flowing into a common terminus;

(c) "watercourse State" means a State in whose territory part of an international watercourse is situated.

Article 3

Watercourse agreements

1.   Watercourse States may enter into one or more agreements, hereinafter referred to as "watercourse agreements", which apply and adjust the provisions of the present articles to the characteristics and uses of a particular international watercourse or part thereof.

2.   Where a watercourse agreement is concluded between two or more watercourse States, it shall define the waters to which it applies. Such an agreement may be entered into with respect to an entire international watercourse or with respect to any part thereof or a particular project, programme or use, provided that the agreement does not adversely affect, to an appreciable extent, the use by one or more other watercourse States of the waters of the watercourse.

3.   Where a watercourse State considers that adjustment or application of the provisions of the present articles is required because of the characteristics and uses of a particular international watercourse, watercourse States shall consult with a view to negotiating in good faith for the purpose of concluding a watercourse agreement or agreements.

Article 4

Parties to watercourse agreements

1. Every watercourse State is entitled to participate in the negotiation of and to become a party to any watercourse agreement that applies to the entire international watercourse, as well as to participate in any relevant consultations.

2. A watercourse State whose use of an international watercourse may be affected to an appreciable extent by the implementation of a proposed watercourse agreement that applies only to a part of the watercourse or to a particular project, programme or use is entitled to participate in consultations on, and in the negotiation of, such an agreement, to the extent that its use is thereby affected, and to become a party thereto.

PART II
GENERAL PRINCIPLES

Article 5

Equitable and reasonable utilization and participation

1. Watercourse States shall in their respective territories utilize an international watercourse in an equitable and reasonable manner. In particular, an international watercourse shall be used and developed by watercourse States with a view to attaining optimal utilization thereof and benefits therefrom consistent with adequate protection of the watercourse.

2. Watercourse States shall participate in the use, development and protection of an international watercourse in an equitable and reasonable manner. Such participation includes both the right to utilize the watercourse and the duty to cooperate in the protection and development thereof, as provided in the present articles.

Article 6

Factors relevant to equitable and reasonable utilization

1. Utilization of an international watercourse in an equitable and reasonable manner within the meaning of article 5 requires taking into account all relevant factors and circumstances, including:

   (a) geographic, hydrographic, hydrological, climatic, ecological and other factors of a natural character;

   (b) the social and economic needs of the watercourse States concerned;

   (c) the effects of the use or uses of the watercourse in one watercourse State on other watercourse States;

   (d) existing and potential uses of the watercourse;

   (e) conservation, protection, development and economy of use of the water resources of the watercourse and the costs of measures taken to that effect;

   (f) the availability of alternatives, of corresponding value, to a particular planned or existing use.

2.　In the application of article 5 or paragraph 1 of this article, watercourse States concerned shall, when the need arises, enter into consultations in a spirit of cooperation.

Article 7

Obligation not to cause appreciable harm

Watercourse States shall utilize an international watercourse in such a way as not to cause appreciable harm to other watercourse States.

Article 8

General obligation to cooperate

Watercourse States shall cooperate on the basis of sovereign equality, territorial integrity and mutual benefit in order to attain optimal utilization and adequate protection of an international watercourse.

Article 9

Regular exchange of data and information

1.　Pursuant to article 8, watercourse States shall on a regular basis exchange reasonably available data and information on the condition of the watercourse, in particular that of a hydrological, meteorological, hydrogeological and ecological nature, as well as related forecasts.

2.　If a watercourse State is requested by another watercourse State to provide data or information that is not reasonably available, it shall employ its best efforts to comply with the request but may condition its compliance upon payment by the requesting State of the reasonable costs of collecting and, where appropriate, processing such data or information.

3.　Watercourse States shall employ their best efforts to collect and, where appropriate, to process data and information in a manner which facilitates its utilization by the other watercourse States to which it is communicated.

Article 10

Relationship between uses

1.　In the absence of agreement or custom to the contrary, no use of an international watercourse enjoys inherent priority over other uses.

2.　In the event of a conflict between uses of an international watercourse, it shall be resolved with reference to the principles and factors set out in articles 5 to 7, with special regard being given to the requirements of vital human needs.

PART III

PLANNED MEASURES

Article 11

Information concerning planned measures

Watercourse States shall exchange information and consult each other on the possible effects of planned measures on the condition of an international watercourse.

Article 12

Notification concerning planned measures with possible adverse effects

Before a watercourse State implements or permits the implementation of planned measures which may have an appreciable adverse effect upon other watercourse States, it shall provide those States with timely notification thereof. Such notification shall be accompanied by available technical data and information in order to enable the notified States to evaluate the possible effects of the planned measures.

Article 13

Period for reply to notification

Unless otherwise agreed, a watercourse State providing a notification under article 12 shall allow the notified States a period of six months within which to study and evaluate the possible effects of the planned measures and to communicate their findings to it.

Article 14

Obligations of the notifying State during the period for reply

During the period referred to in article 13, the notifying State shall cooperate with the notified States by providing them, on request, with any additional data and information that is available and necessary for an accurate evaluation, and shall not implement or permit the implementation of the planned measures without the consent of the notified States.

Article 15

Reply to notification

1. The notified States shall communicate their findings to the notifying State as early as possible.

2. If a notified State finds that implementation of the planned measures would be inconsistent with the provisions of articles 5 or 7, it shall communicate this finding to the notifying State within the period referred to in article 13, together with a documented explanation setting forth the reasons for the finding.

Article 16

Absence of reply to notification

If, within the period referred to in article 13, the notifying State receives no communication under paragraph 2 of article 15, it may, subject to its obligations under articles 5 and 7, proceed with the implementation of the planned measures, in accordance with the notification and any other data and information provided to the notified States.

Article 17

Consultations and negotiations concerning planned measures

1. If a communication is made under paragraph 2 of article 15, the notifying State and the State making the communication shall enter into consultations and negotiations with a view to arriving at an equitable resolution of the situation.

2. The consultations and negotiations shall be conducted on the basis that each State must in good faith pay reasonable regard to the rights and legitimate interests of the other State.

3. During the course of the consultations and negotiations, the notifying State shall, if so requested by the notified State at the time it makes the communication, refrain from implementing or permitting the implementation of the planned measures for a period not exceeding six months.

Article 18

Procedures in the absence of notification

1. If a watercourse State has serious reason to believe that another watercourse State is planning measures that may have an appreciable adverse effect upon it, the former State may request the latter to apply the provisions of article 12. The request shall be accompanied by a documented explanation setting forth the reasons for such belief.

2. In the event that the State planning the measures nevertheless finds that it is not under an obligation to provide a notification under article 12, it shall so inform the other State, providing a documented explanation setting forth the reasons for such finding. If this finding does not satisfy the other State, the two States shall, at the request of that other State, promptly enter into consultations and negotiations in the manner indicated in paragraphs 1 and 2 of article 17.

3. During the course of the consultations and negotiations, the State planning the measures shall, if so requested by the other State at the time it requests the initiation of consultations and negotiations, refrain from implementing or permitting the implementation of those measures for a period not exceeding six months.

Article 19

Urgent implementation of planned measures

1. In the event that the implementation of planned measures is of the utmost urgency in order to protect public health, public safety or other equally important interests, the State planning the measures may, subject to articles 5 and 7, immediately proceed to implementation, notwithstanding the provisions of article 14 and paragraph 3 of article 17.

2. In such cases, a formal declaration of the urgency of the measures shall be communicated to the other watercourse States referred to in article 12 together with the relevant data and information.

3. The State planning the measures shall, at the request of the States referred to in paragraph 2, promptly enter into consultations and negotiations with it in the manner indicated in paragraphs 1 and 2 of article 17.

PART IV

PROTECTION AND PRESERVATION

Article 20

Protection and preservation of ecosystems

Watercourse States shall, individually or jointly, protect and preserve the ecosystems of international watercourses.

Article 21

Prevention, reduction and control of pollution

1. For the purposes of this article, "pollution of an international watercourse" means any detrimental alteration in the composition or quality of the waters of an international watercourse which results directly or indirectly from human conduct.

2. Watercourse States shall, individually or jointly, prevent, reduce and control pollution of an international watercourse that may cause appreciable harm to other watercourse States or to their environment, including harm to human health or safety, to the use of the waters for any beneficial purpose or to the living resources of the watercourse. Watercourse States shall take steps to harmonize their policies in this connection.

3. Watercourse States shall, at the request of any of them, consult with a view to establishing lists of substances, the introduction of which into the waters of an international watercourse is to be prohibited, limited, investigated or monitored.

Article 22

Introduction of alien or new species

Watercourse States shall take all measures necessary to prevent the introduction of species, alien or new, into an international watercourse which may have effects detrimental to the ecosystem of the watercourse resulting in appreciable harm to other watercourse States.

Article 23

Protection and preservation of the marine environment

Watercourse States shall, individually or jointly, take all measures with respect to an international watercourse that are necessary to protect and preserve the marine environment, including estuaries, taking into account generally accepted international rules and standards.

PART V
HARMFUL CONDITIONS AND EMERGENCY SITUATIONS

Article 24

Prevention and mitigation of harmful conditions

Watercourse States shall, individually or jointly, take all appropriate measures to prevent or mitigate conditions that may be harmful to other watercourse States, whether resulting from natural causes or human conduct, such as flood or ice conditions, water-borne diseases, siltation, erosion, saltwater intrusion, drought or desertification.

Article 25

Emergency situations

1. For the purposes of this article, "emergency" means a situation that causes, or poses an imminent threat of causing, serious harm to watercourse States or other States and that results suddenly from natural causes, such as floods, the breaking up of ice, landslides or earthquakes, or from human conduct as for example in the case of industrial accidents.

2.   A watercourse State shall, without delay and by the most expeditious means available, notify other potentially affected States and competent international organizations of any emergency originating within its territory.

3.   A watercourse State within whose territory an emergency originates shall, in cooperation with potentially affected States and, where appropriate, competent international organizations, immediately take all practicable measures necessitated by the circumstances to prevent, mitigate and eliminate harmful effects of the emergency.

4.   When necessary, watercourse States shall jointly develop contingency plans for responding to emergencies, in cooperation, where appropriate, with other potentially affected States and competent international organizations.

PART VI
MISCELLANEOUS PROVISIONS
Article 26
Management

1.   Watercourse States shall, at the request of any of them, enter into consultations concerning the management of an international watercourse, which may include the establishment of a joint management mechanism.

2.   For the purposes of this article, "management" refers, in particular, to:

(a) planning the sustainable development of an international watercourse and providing for the implementation of any plans adopted; and

(b) otherwise promoting rational and optimal utilization, protection and control of the watercourse.

Article 27
Regulation

1.   Watercourse States shall cooperate where appropriate to respond to needs or opportunities for regulation of the flow of the waters of an international watercourse.

2.   Unless they have otherwise agreed, watercourse States shall participate on an equitable basis in the construction and maintenance or defrayal of the costs of such regulation works as they may have agreed to undertake.

3.   For the purposes of this article, "regulation" means the use of hydraulic works or any other continuing measure to alter, vary or otherwise control the flow of the waters of an international watercourse.

Article 28
Installations

1.   Watercourse States shall, within their respective territories, employ their best efforts to maintain and protect installations, facilities and other works related to an international watercourse.

2.   Watercourse States shall, at the request of any of them which has serious reason to believe that it may suffer appreciable adverse effects, enter into consultations with regard to:

(a) the safe operation or maintenance of installations, facilities or other works related to an international watercourse; or

(b) the protection of installations, facilities or other works from wilful or negligent acts or the forces of nature.

Article 29

International watercourses and installations in time of armed conflict

International watercourses and related installations, facilities and other works shall enjoy the protection accorded by the principles and rules of international law applicable in international and internal armed conflict and shall not be used in violation of those principles and rules.

Article 30

Indirect procedures

In cases where there are serious obstacles to direct contacts between watercourse States, the States concerned shall fulfil their obligations of cooperation provided for in the present articles, including exchange of data and information, notification, communication, consultations and negotiations, through any indirect procedure accepted by them.

Article 31

Data and information vital to national defence or security

Nothing in the present articles obliges a watercourse State to provide data or information vital to its national defence or security. Nevertheless, that State shall cooperate in good faith with the other watercourse States with a view to providing as much information as possible under the circumstances.

Article 32

Non-discrimination

Watercourse States shall not discriminate on the basis of nationality or residence in granting access to judicial and other procedures, in accordance with their legal systems, to any natural or juridical person who has suffered appreciable harm as a result of an activity related to an international watercourse or is exposed to a threat thereof.

5. LITHOSPHERE

5.1 FAO INTERNATIONAL CODE OF CONDUCT ON THE DISTRIBUTION AND USE OF PESTICIDES (AS AMENDED IN 1989). Adopted 28 November 1985. 23 FAO Conf.Res. 10/85

Article 1.

Objectives of the Code

1.1 The objectives of this Code are to set forth responsibilities and establish voluntary standards of conduct for all public and private entities engaged in or affecting the distribution and use of pesticides, particularly where there is no or an inadequate national law to regulate pesticides.

1.2 The Code describes the shared responsibility of many segments of society, including governments, individually or in regional groupings, industry, trade and international institutions, to work together so that the benefits to be derived from the necessary and acceptable use of pesticides are achieved without significant adverse effects on people or the environment. To this end, all references in this Code to a government or governments shall be deemed to apply equally to regional groupings of governments for matters falling within their areas of competence.

1.3 The Code addresses the need for a cooperative effort between governments of exporting and importing countries to promote practices which ensure efficient and safe use while minimizing health and environmental concerns due to improper handling or use.

1.4 The entities which are addressed by this Code include international organizations; governments of exporting and importing countries; industry, including manufacturers, trade associations, formulators and distributors; users; and public-sector organizations such as environmental groups, consumer groups and trade unions.

1.5 The standards of conduct set forth by this Code:

1.5.1 encourage responsible and generally accepted trade practices;

1.5.2 assist countries which have not yet established controls designed to regulate the quality and suitability of pesticide products needed in that country and to address the safe handling and use of such products;

1.5.3 promote practices which encourage the safe and efficient use of pesticides, including minimizing adverse effects on humans and the environment and preventing accidental poisoning from improper handling;

1.5.4 ensure that pesticides are used effectively for the improvement of agricultural production and of human, animal and plant health.

1.6 The Code is designed to be used, within the context of national law, as a basis whereby government authorities, pesticide manufacturers, those

932

engaged in trade and any citizens concerned may judge whether their proposed actions and the actions of others constitute acceptable practices.

Article 2.

Definitions

For the purpose of this Code:

Active ingredient means the biologically active part of the pesticide present in a formulation.

Advertising means the promotion of the sale and use of pesticides by print and electronic media, signs, displays, gift, demonstration or word of mouth.

Banned means a pesticide for which all registered uses have been prohibited by final government regulatory action, or for which all requests for registration or equivalent action for all uses have, for health or environmental reasons, not been granted.

Common name means the name assigned to a pesticide active ingredient by the International Standards Organization or adopted by national standards authorities to be used as a generic or non proprietary name for that particular active ingredient only.

Distinguishing name means the name under which the pesticide is labelled, registered and promoted by the manufacturer and which, if protected under national legislation, can be used exclusively by the manufacturer to distinguish the product from other pesticides containing the same active ingredient.

Distribution means the process by which pesticides are supplied through trade channels on local or international markets.

Environment means surroundings, including water, air, soil and their interrelationship as well as all relationships between them and any living organisms.

Extension service means those entities in the country concerned responsible for the transfer of information and advice to farmers regarding the improvement of agricultural practices, including production, handling, storage and marketing.

Formulation means the combination of various ingredients designed to render the product useful and effective for the purpose claimed; the form of the pesticide as purchased by users.

Hazard means the likelihood that a pesticide will cause an adverse effect (injury) under the conditions in which it is used.

Integrated pest management means a pest management system that, in the context of the associated environment and the population dynamics of the pest species, utilizes all suitable techniques and methods in as compatible a manner as possible and maintains the pest populations at levels below those causing economically unacceptable damage or loss.

Label means the written, printed or graphic matter on, or attached to, the pesticide; or the immediate container thereof and the outside container or wrapper of the retail package of the pesticide.

Manufacturer means a corporation or other entity in the public or private sector or any individual engaged in the business or function (whether directly or through an agent or through an entity controlled by or under contract with it) of manufacturing a pesticide active ingredient or preparing its formulation or product.

Marketing means the overall process of product promotion, including advertising, product public relations and information services as well as distribution and selling on local or international markets.

Maximum residue limit (MRL) means the maximum concentration of a residue that is legally permitted or recognized as acceptable in or on a food, agricultural commodity or animal feedstuff.

Packaging means the container together with the protective wrapping used to carry pesticide products via wholesale or retail distribution to users.

Pesticide means any substance or mixture of substances intended for preventing, destroying or controlling any pest, including vectors of human or animal disease, unwanted species of plants or animals causing harm during or otherwise interfering with the production, processing, storage, transport, or marketing of food, agricultural commodities, wood and wood products or animal feedstuffs, or which may be administered to animals for the control of insects, arachnids or other pests in or on their bodies. The term includes substances intended for use as a plant growth regulator, defoliant, desiccant, or agent for thinning fruit or preventing the premature fall of fruit, and substances applied to crops either before or after harvest to protect the commodity from deterioration during storage and transport.

Pesticide industry means all those organizations and individuals engaged in manufacturing, formulating or marketing pesticides and pesticide products.

Pesticide legislation means any laws or regulations introduced to regulate the manufacture, marketing, storage, labelling, packaging and use of pesticides in their qualitative, quantitative and environmental aspects.

Poison means a substance that can cause disturbance of structure or function, leading to injury or death when absorbed in relatively small amounts by human beings, plants or animals.

Poisoning means occurrence of damage or disturbance caused by a poison, and includes intoxication.

Prior Information Consent (PIC) refers to the principle that international shipment of a pesticide that is banned or severely restricted in order to protect human health or the environment should not proceed without the agreement, where such agreement exists, or contrary to the decision of the designated national authority in the participating importing country.

Prior Informed Consent Procedure (PIC procedure) means the procedure for formally obtaining and disseminating the decisions of importing countries as to whether they wish to receive further shipments of pesticides that have been banned or severely restricted. A specific procedure was established for selecting pesticides for initial implementation of the PIC procedures. These include pesticides that have been previously banned or severely restricted as well as certain pesticide formulations that are acutely toxic. This procedure is described in the Guidelines on the Operation of Prior Informed Consent.

Product means the pesticide in the form in which it is packaged and sold; it usually contains an active ingredient plus adjuvants and may require dilution prior to use.

Protective clothing means any clothes, materials or devices that are designed to provide protection from pesticides when they are handled or applied.

Public sector groups means (but is not limited to) scientific associations; farmer groups; citizens' organizations; environmental, consumer and health organizations; and labour unions.

Registration means the process whereby the responsible national government authority approves the sale and use of a pesticide following the evaluation of comprehensive scientific data demonstrating that the product is effective for the purposes intended and not unduly hazardous to human or animal health or the environment.

Repackaging means the transfer of pesticide from any commercial package into any other, usually smaller, container for subsequent sale.

Residue means any specified substance in food, agricultural commodities, or animal feed resulting from the use of a pesticide. The term includes any derivatives of a pesticide, such as conversion products, metabolites, reaction products, and impurities considered to be of toxicological significance. The term "pesticide residue" includes residues from unknown or unavoidable sources (e.g., environmental) as well as known uses of the chemical.

Responsible authority means the government agency or agencies responsible for regulating the manufacture, distribution or use of pesticides and more generally for implementing pesticide legislation.

Risk means the expected frequency of undesirable effects of exposure to the pesticide.

Severely restricted—a limited ban—means a pesticide for which virtually all registered uses have been prohibited by final government regulatory action but certain specific registered use or uses remain authorized.

Toxicity means a physiological or biological property which determines the capacity of a chemical to do harm or produce injury to a living organism by other than mechanical means.

Trader means anyone engaged in trade, including export, import, formulation and domestic distribution.

Use pattern embodies the combination of all factors involved in the use of a pesticide, including the concentration of active ingredient in the preparation being applied, rate of application, time of treatment, number of treatments, use of adjuvants and methods and sites of application which determine the quantity applied, timing of treatment and interval before harvest, etc.

Article 3.

Pesticide management

3.1 Governments have the overall responsibility and should take the specific powers to regulate the distribution and use of pesticides in their countries.

3.2   The pesticide industry should adhere to the provisions of this Code as a standard for the manufacture, distribution and advertising of pesticides, particularly in countries lacking appropriate legislation and advisory services.

3.3   Governments of exporting countries should help to the extent possible, directly or through their pesticide industries, to:

3.3.1   provide technical assistance to other countries, especially those with shortages of technical expertise, in the assessment of the relevant data on pesticides, including those provided by industry (see also Article 4);

3.3.2   ensure that good trading practices are followed in the export of pesticides, especially to those countries with no or limited regulatory schemes (see also Articles 8 and 9).

3.4   Manufacturers and traders should observe the following practices in pesticide management, especially in countries without legislation or means of implementing regulations:

3.4.1   supply only pesticides of adequate quality, packaged and labelled as appropriate for each specific market;

3.4.2   pay special attention to formulations, presentation, packaging and labelling in order to reduce hazard to users, to the maximum extent possible consistent with the effective functioning of the pesticide in the particular circumstances in which it is to be used;

3.4.3   provide, with each package of pesticide, information and instructions in a form and language adequate to ensure safe and effective use;

3.4.4   retain an active interest in following their products to the ultimate consumer, keeping track of major uses and the occurrence of any problems arising in the actual use of their products as a basis for determining the need for changes in labelling, directions for use, packaging, formulation or product availability.

3.5   Pesticides whose handling and application require the use of uncomfortable and expensive protective clothing and equipment should be avoided, especially in the case of small scale users in tropical climates.

3.6   National and international organizations, governments, and pesticide industries should take action in coordinated efforts to disseminate educational materials of all types to pesticide users, farmers, farmers' organizations, agricultural workers, unions and other interested parties. Similarly, affected parties should seek and understand educational materials before using pesticides and should follow proper procedures.

3.7   Governments should allocate high priority and adequate resources to the task of effectively managing the availability, distribution and use of pesticides in their countries.

3.8   Concerted efforts should be made by governments and pesticide industries to develop and promote integrated pest management systems and the use of safe, efficient, cost-effective application methods. Public-sector groups and international organizations should actively support such activities.

3.9 International organizations should provide information on specific pesticides and give guidance on methods of analysis through the provision of criteria documents, fact sheets, training sessions, etc.

3.10 It is recognized that the development of resistance of pests to pesticides can be a major problem. Therefore, governments, industry, national institutions, international organizations and public sector groups should collaborate in developing strategies which will prolong the useful life of valuable pesticides and reduce the adverse effects of the development of resistant species.

Article 4.

Testing of Pesticides

4.1 Pesticide manufacturers are expected to:

4.1.1 ensure that each pesticide and pesticide product is adequately and effectively tested by well recognized procedures and test methods so as to fully evaluate its safety, efficacy and fate with regard to the various anticipated conditions in regions or countries of use;

4.1.2 ensure that such tests are conducted in accordance with sound scientific procedures and good laboratory practice—the data produced by such tests, when evaluated by competent experts, must be capable of showing whether the product can be handled and used safely without unacceptable hazard to human health, plants, animals, wildlife and the environment;

4.1.3 make available copies or summaries of the original reports of such tests for assessment by responsible government authorities in all countries where the pesticide is to be offered for sale. Evaluation of the data should be referred to qualified experts;

4.1.4 take care to see that the proposed use pattern, label claims and directions, packages, technical literature and advertising truly reflect the outcome of these scientific tests and assessments;

4.1.5 provide, at the request of a country, advice on methods for the analysis of any active ingredient of formulation that they manufacture, and provide the necessary analytical standards;

4.1.6 provide advice and assistance for training technical staff in relevant analytical work. Formulators should actively support this effort;

4.1.7 conduct residue trials prior to marketing in accordance with FAO guidelines on good analytical practice and on crop residue data in order to provide a basis for establishing appropriate maximum residue limits (MRLs).

4.2 Each country should possess or have access to facilities to verify and exercise control over the quality of pesticides offered for sale, to establish the quantity of the active ingredient or ingredients and the suitability of their formulation.

4.3 International organizations and other interested bodies should, within available resources, consider assisting in the establishment of analytical laboratories in pesticide importing countries, either on a country or on a multilateral regional basis; these laboratories should be capable of carrying out product and residue analysis and should have adequate supplies of analytical standards, solvents and reagents.

4.4 Exporting governments and international organizations must play an active role in assisting developing countries in training personnel in the interpretation and evaluation of test data.

4.5 Industry and governments should collaborate in conducting post-registration surveillance or monitoring studies to determine the fate and environmental effect of pesticides under field conditions.

Article 5.

Reducing health hazards

5.1 Governments which have not already done so should:

5.1.1 implement a pesticide registration and control scheme along the lines set out in Article 6;

5.1.2 decide, and from time to time review, the pesticides to be marketed in their country, their acceptable uses and their availability to each segment of the public;

5.1.3 provide guidance and instructions for the treatment of suspected pesticide poisoning for their basic health workers, physicians and hospital staff;

5.1.4 establish national or regional poisoning information and control centres at strategic locations to provide immediate guidance on first aid and medical treatment, accessible at all times by telephone or radio. Governments should collect reliable information about the health aspects of pesticides. Suitably trained people with adequate resources must be made available to ensure information is collected.

5.1.5 keep extension and advisory services, as well as farmers' organizations, adequately informed about the range of pesticide products available for use in each area;

5.1.6 ensure, with the cooperation of industry, that where pesticides are available through outlets which also deal in food, medicines, other products for internal consumption or topical application, or clothing, they are physically segregated from other merchandise, so as to avoid any possibility of contamination or of mistaken identity. Where appropriate, they should be clearly marked as hazardous materials. Every effort should be made to publicize the dangers of storing foodstuffs and pesticides together.

5.2 Even where a control scheme is in operation, industry should:

5.2.1 cooperate in the periodic reassessment of the pesticides which are marketed and in providing the poison control centres and other medical practitioners with information about hazards;

5.2.2 make every reasonable effort to reduce hazard by:

5.2.2.1 making less toxic formulations available;

5.2.2.2 introducing products in ready-to-use packages and otherwise developing safer and more efficient methods of application;

5.2.2.3   using containers that are not attractive for subsequent reuse and promoting programmes to discourage their reuse;

5.2.2.4   using containers that are safe (e.g., not attractive to or easily opened by children), particularly for the more toxic home use products;

5.2.2.5   using clear and concise labelling;

5.2.3   halt sale, and recall products, when safe use does not seem possible under any use directions or restrictions.

5.3   Government and industry should further reduce hazards by making provision for safe storage and disposal of pesticides and containers at both warehouse and farm level, and through proper siting and control of wastes from formulating plants.

5.4   To avoid unjustified confusion and alarm among the public, public-sector groups should consider all available facts and try to distinguish between major differences in levels of risk among pesticides and uses.

5.5   In establishing production facilities in developing countries, manufacturers and governments should cooperate to:

5.5.1   adopt engineering standards and safe operating practices appropriate to the nature of the manufacturing operations and the hazards involved;

5.5.2   take all necessary precautions to protect the health and safety of operatives, bystanders and the environment;

5.5.3   maintain quality-assurance procedures to ensure that the products manufactured comply to the relevant standards of purity, performance, stability and safety.

Article 6.

Regulatory and technical requirements

6.1   Governments should:

6.1.1   take action to introduce the necessary legislation for the regulation, including registration, of pesticides and make provisions for its effective enforcement, including the establishment of appropriate educational, advisory, extension and health-care services; the FAO guidelines for the registration and control of pesticides should be followed, as far as possible, taking full account of local needs, social and economic conditions, levels of literacy, climatic conditions and availability of pesticide application equipment;

6.1.2   strive to establish pesticide registration schemes and infrastructures under which products can be registered prior to domestic use and, accordingly, ensure that each pesticide product is registered under the laws or regulations of the country of use before it can be made available there:

6.1.3   protect the proprietary rights to use of data;

6.1.4   collect and record data on the actual import, formulation and use of pesticides in each country in order to assess the extent of any possible effects on human health or the environment, and to follow trends in use levels for economic and other purposes.

6.2 The pesticides industry should:

6.2.1 provide an objective appraisal together with the necessary supporting data on each product;

6.2.2 ensure that the active ingredient and other ingredients of pesticide preparations marketed correspond in identity, quality, purity and composition to the substances tested, evaluated and cleared for toxicological and environmental acceptability;

6.2.3 ensure that active ingredients and formulated products for pesticides for which international specifications have been developed conform with the specifications of FAO, where intended for use in agriculture; and with WHO pesticide specifications, where intended for use in public health;

6.2.4 verify the quality and purity of the pesticides offered for sale;

6.2.5 when problems occur, voluntarily take corrective action, and when requested by governments, help find solutions to difficulties.

Article 7.
Availability and Use

7.1 Responsible authorities should give special attention to drafting rules and regulations on the availability of pesticides. These should be compatible with existing levels of training and expertise in handling pesticides on the part of the intended users. The parameters on which such decisions are based vary widely and must be left to the discretion of each government, bearing in mind the situation prevailing in the country.

7.2 In addition, governments should take note of and, where appropriate, follow the WHO classifications of pesticides by hazard and associate the hazard class with well-recognized hazard symbols as the basis for their own regulatory measures. In any event, the type of formulation and method of application should be taken into account in determining the risk and degree of restriction appropriate to the product.

7.3 Two methods of restricting availability can be exercised by the responsible authority: not registering a product; or, as a condition of registration, restricting the availability to certain groups of users in accordance with national assessments of hazards involved in the use of the product in the particular country.

7.4 All pesticides made available to the general public should be packaged and labelled in a manner which is consistent with the FAO guidelines on packaging and labelling and with appropriate national regulations.

7.5 Prohibition of the importation, sale and purchase of an extremely toxic product may be desirable if control measures or good marketing practices are insufficient to ensure that the product can be used safely. However, this is a matter for decision in the light of national circumstances.

Article 8.
Distribution and Trade

8.1 Industry should:

8.1.1 test all pesticide products to evaluate safety with regard to human health and the environment prior to marketing, as provided for in

Article 4, and ensure that all pesticide products are likewise adequately tested for efficacy and stability and crop tolerance, under procedures that will predict performance under the conditions prevailing in the region where the product is to be used, before they are offered there for sale;

8.1.2　submit the results of all such tests to the local responsible authority for independent evaluation and approval before the products enter trade channels in that country;

8.1.3　take all necessary steps to ensure that pesticides entering international trade conform to relevant FAO, WHO or equivalent specifications for composition and quality (where such specifications have been developed) and to the principles embodied in pertinent FAO guidelines, and in rules and regulations on classification and packaging, marketing, labelling and documentation laid down by international organizations concerned with modes of transport (ICAO, IMO, RID and IATA in particular);

8.1.4　undertake to see that pesticides which are manufactured for export are subject to the same quality requirements and standards as those applied by the manufacturer to comparable domestic products;

8.1.5　ensure that pesticides manufactured or formulated by a subsidiary company meet appropriate quality requirements and standards which should be consistent with the requirements of the host country and of the parent company;

8.1.6　encourage importing agencies, national or regional formulators and their respective trade organizations to cooperate in order to achieve fair practices and safe marketing and distribution practices and to collaborate with authorities in stamping out any malpractices within the industry;

8.1.7　recognize that the recall of a pesticide by a manufacturer and distributor may be desirable when faced with a pesticide which represents an unacceptable hazard to human and animal health and the environment when used as recommended, and cooperate accordingly;

8.1.8　endeavour to ensure that pesticides are traded by and purchased from reputable traders, who should preferably be members of a recognized trade organization;

8.1.9　see that persons involved in the sale of any pesticide are trained adequately to ensure that they are capable of providing the buyer with advice on safe and efficient use;

8.1.10　provide a range of pack sizes and types which are appropriate for the needs of small-scale farmers and other local users to avoid handling hazards and the risk that resellers will repackage products into unlabelled or inappropriate containers.

8.2　Governments and responsible authorities should take the necessary regulatory measures to prohibit the repackaging, decanting or dispensing of any pesticide in food or beverage containers and should rigidly enforce punitive measures that effectively deter such practices.

8.3　Governments of countries importing food and agricultural commodities should recognize good agricultural practices in countries with which they trade and, in accordance with recommendations of the Codex Alimentarius Commission, should establish a legal basis for the acceptance of pesticide residues resulting from such good agricultural practices.

Article 9.
Information Exchange and Prior Informed Consent

9.1 The government of any country that takes action to ban or severely restrict the use or handling of a pesticide in order to protect health or the environment should notify FAO as soon a possible of the action it has taken. FAO will notify the designated national authorities in other countries of the action of the notifying government.

9.2 The purpose of notification regarding control action is to give competent authorities in other countries the opportunity to assess the risks associated with the pesticides, and to make timely and informed decisions as to the importation and use of the pesticides concerned, after taking into account local, public health, economic, environmental and administrative conditions. The minimum information to be provided for this purpose should be:

9.2.1 the identity (common name, distinguishing name and chemical name);

9.2.2 a summary of the control action taken and of the reasons for it—if the control action bans or restricts certain uses but allows other uses, such information should be included:

9.2.3 an indication of the additional information that is available, and the name and address of the contact point in the country to which a request for further information should be addressed.

Information Exchange Among Countries

9.3 If export of a pesticide banned or severely restricted in the country of export occurs, the country of export should ensure that necessary steps are taken to provide the designated national authority of the country of import with relevant information.

9.4 The purpose of information regarding exports is to remind the country of import of the original notification regarding control action and to alert it to the fact that an export is expected or is about to occur. The minimum information to be provided for this purpose should be:

9.4.1 a copy of, or reference to, the information provided at the time of the notification of control action;

9.4.2 indication that an export of the chemical concerned is expected or is about to occur.

9.5 Provision of information regarding exports should take place at the time of the first export following the control action, and should recur in the case of any significant development of new information or condition surrounding the control action. It is the intention that the information should be provided prior to export.

9.6 The provision to individual countries of any additional information on the reasons for control actions taken by any country must take into account protection of any proprietary data from unauthorized use.

Prior Informed Consent

9.7 Pesticides that are banned or severely restricted for reasons of health or the environment are subject to the Prior Informed Consent procedure. No pesticide in these categories should be exported to an importing country participating in the PIC procedure contrary to that country's decision made in accordance with the FAO operational procedures for PIC.

9.8 FAO will:

9.8.1 review notifications of control actions to ensure conformity with definitions in Article 2 of the Code, and will develop the relevant guidance documents;

9.8.2 in cooperation with UNEP, develop and maintain a data base of control actions and decisions taken by all Member Governments;

9.8.3 inform all designated national authorities and relevant international organizations of, and publicize in such form as may be appropriate, notifications received under Article 9.1 and decisions communicated to it regarding the use and importation of a pesticide that has been included in the PIC procedure;

9.8.4 FAO will seek advice at regular intervals and review the criteria for inclusion of pesticides in the Prior Informed Consent procedure and the operation of the Prior Informed Consent scheme and will report to Member Governments on its findings.

9.9 Governments of importing countries should establish internal procedures and designate the appropriate authority for the receipt and handling of information.

9.10 Governments of importing countries participating in the PIC procedure, when advised by FAO of control action within this procedure, should:

9.10.1 decide on future acceptability of that pesticide in their country and advise FAO as soon as that decision has been made;

9.10.2 ensure that governmental measures or actions taken with regard to an imported pesticide for which information has been received are not more restrictive than those applied to the same pesticide produced domestically or imported from a country other than the one that supplied the information;

9.10.3 ensure that such a decision is not used inconsistently with the provisions of the General Agreement on Tariffs and Trade (GATT).

9.11 Governments of pesticide exporting countries should:

9.11.1 advise their pesticide exporters and industry of the decisions of participating importing countries;

9.11.2 take appropriate measures, within their authority and legislative competence, designed to ensure that exports do not occur contrary to the decision of participating importing countries.

Article 10.

Labelling, Packaging, Storage and Disposal

10.1 All pesticide containers should be clearly labelled in accordance with applicable international guidelines, such as the FAO guidelines on good labelling practice.

10.2 Industry should use labels that:

10.2.1 include recommendations consistent with those of the recognized research and advisory agencies in the country of sale;

10.2.2 include appropriate symbols and pictograms whenever possible, in addition to written instructions, warnings and precautions;

10.2.3 in international trade, clearly show appropriate WHO hazard classification of the contents or, if this is inappropriate or inconsistent with national regulations, use the relevant classification;

10.2.4 include, in the appropriate language or languages, a warning against the reuse of containers, and instructions for the safe disposal or decontamination of empty containers;

10.2.5 identify each lot or batch of the product in numbers or letters that can be read, transcribed and communicated by anyone without the need for codes or other means of deciphering;

10.2.6 are marked with the date (month and year) of formulation of the lot or batch and with relevant information on the storage stability of the product.

10.3 Industry should ensure that:

10.3.1 packaging, storage and disposal of pesticides conform in principle to the FAO guidelines for packaging and storage, the FAO guidelines for the disposal of waste pesticides and containers, and WHO specifications for pesticides used in public health;

10.3.2 in cooperation with governments, packaging or repackaging is carried out only on licensed premises where the responsible authority is convinced that staff are adequately protected against toxic hazards, that the resulting product will be properly packaged and labelled, and that the content will conform to the relevant quality standards.

10.4 Governments should take the necessary regulatory measures to prohibit the repacking, decanting or dispensing of any pesticide into food or beverage containers in trade channels and rigidly enforce punitive measures that effectively deter such practices.

Article 11.

Advertising

11.1 Industry should ensure that:

11.1.1 all statements used in advertising are capable of technical substantiation;

11.1.2 advertisements do not contain any statement or visual presentation which, directly or by implication, omission, ambiguity or exaggerated claim, is likely to mislead the buyer, in particular with regard to the safety of the product, its nature, composition, or suitability for use, or official recognition or approval;

11.1.3 pesticides which are legally restricted to use by trained or registered operators are not publicly advertised through journals other than those catering for such operations, unless the restricted availability is clearly and prominently shown:

11.1.4 no firm or individual in any one country simultaneously markets different pesticide active ingredients or combinations of ingredients under a single distinguishing name;

11.1.5 advertising does not encourage uses other than those specified on the approved label;

11.1.6 promotional material does not include use recommendations at variance with those of the recognized research and advisory agencies;

11.1.7 advertisements do not misuse research results or quotations from technical and scientific literature; and scientific jargon and irrelevances are not used to make claims appear to have a scientific basis they do not possess;

11.1.8 claims as to safety, including statements such as "safe", "non-poisonous", "harmless", "non-toxic", are not made, with or without a qualifying phrase such as "when used as directed";

11.1.9 statements comparing the safety of different products are not made;

11.1.10 misleading statements are not made concerning the effectiveness of the product;

11.1.11 no guarantees or implied guarantees—e.g. "more profits with * * *", "guarantees high yields"—are given unless definite evidence to substantiate such claims is available;

11.1.12 advertisements do not contain any visual representation of potentially dangerous practices, such as mixing or application without sufficient protective clothing, use near food, or use by or near children;

11.1.13 advertising or promotional material draws attention to the appropriate warning phrases and symbols as laid down in the labeling guidelines;

11.1.14 technical literature provides adequate information on correct practices, including the observance of recommended rates, frequency of applications, and safe pre-harvest intervals;

11.1.15 false or misleading comparisons with other pesticides are not made;

11.1.16 all staff involved in sales promotion are adequately trained and possess sufficient technical knowledge to present complete, accurate and valid information on the products sold;

11.1.17 advertisements encourage purchasers and users to read the label carefully, or have the label read to them if they cannot read.

11.2 International organizations and public-sector groups should call attention to departures from this Article.

11.3 Governments are encouraged to work with manufacturers to take advantage of their marketing skills and infrastructure, in order to provide public-service advertising regarding the safe and effective use of pesticides. This advertising could focus on such factors as proper maintenance and use of equipment, special precautions for children and pregnant women, the danger of reusing containers, and the importance of following label directions.

Article 12.

Monitoring the Observance of the Code

12.1 The Code should be published and should be observed through collaborative action on the part of governments, individually or in regional groupings, appropriate organizations and bodies of the United Nations system, international governmental organizations and the pesticide industry.

12.2 The Code should be brought to the attention of all concerned in the manufacture, marketing and use of pesticides and in the control of such activities, so that governments, individually or in regional groupings, industry and international institutions understand their shared responsibilities in working together to ensure that the objectives of the Code are achieved.

12.3 All parties addressed by this Code should observe this Code and should promote the principles and ethics expressed by the Code, irrespective of other parties' ability to observe the Code. The pesticide industry should cooperate fully in the observance of the Code and promote the principles and ethics expressed by the Code, irrespective of a government's ability to observe the Code.

12.4 Independently of any measures taken with respect to the observance of this Code, all relevant legal rules, whether legislative, administrative, judicial or customary, dealing with liability, consumer protection, conservation, pollution control and other related subjects should be strictly applied.

12.5 FAO and other competent international organizations should give full support to the observance of the Code, as adopted.

12.6 Governments should monitor the observance of the Code and report on progress made to the Director–General of FAO.

12.7 Governing Bodies should periodically review the relevance and effectiveness of the Code. The Code should be considered a dynamic text which must be brought up to date as required, taking into account technical, economic and social progress.

5.2 OECD COUNCIL DECISION/RECOMMENDATION ON EXPORTS OF HAZARDOUS WASTES FROM THE OECD AREA (WITH MEASURES CONCERNING THE CONTROL OF EXPORTS OF HAZARDOUS WASTES AND APPENDED DEFINITIONS). Adopted 5 June 1986. 1986 O.E.C.D. C(86)64 (Final), O.E.C.D. 86

The Council

Having regard to Articles 5(*a*) and 5(*b*) of the Convention on the Organisation for Economic Co-operation and Development of 14th December 1960;

Having regard to the Decision and Recommendation of the Council of 1st February 1984 on Transfrontier Movements of Hazardous Waste [C(83)180(Final)] and without prejudice to that Decision and Recommendation;

Having regard to the Resolution of the Council of 20th June, 1985 on International Co-operation Concerning Transfrontier Movements of Hazardous Wastes [C(85)100], by which it has been decided to develop an international system for effective control of transfrontier movements of hazardous wastes, including an international agreement of a legally binding character;

Considering the European Communities Council Directive of 6th December, 1984 on the Supervision and Control within the European Community of the Transfrontier Shipment of Hazardous Waste [84/631/EEC], supplemented by the Decision of the Council of the European Communities of 6th March, 1986;

Considering the work carried out within the United Nations Environment Programme on the environmentally sound management of hazardous wastes;

Considering the particular nature of wastes and the distinction between wastes and products which are traded internationally;

Convinced that the exports of hazardous wastes may, if not properly monitored and controlled, result in serious risks to health and the environment;

On the proposal of the Environment Committee:

I. *Decides* that Member countries shall:

(*i*) Monitor and control exports of hazardous wastes to a final destination which is outside the OECD area; and for this purpose shall ensure that their competent authorities are empowered to prohibit such exports in appropriate instances;

(*ii*) Apply no less strict controls on transfrontier movements of hazardous wastes involving non-Member countries than they would on movements involving only Member countries;

(*iii*) Prohibit movements of hazardous wastes to a final destination in a non-Member country without the consent of that country and the prior notification to any transit countries of the proposed movements;

(*iv*) Prohibit movements of hazardous wastes to a non-Member country unless the wastes are directed to an adequate disposal facility in that country.

II. *Recommends* that, to implement this Decision, Member countries should:

(*i*) Seek to conclude bilateral or multilateral agreements with non-Member countries to which frequent exports of hazardous wastes are taking place or are foreseen to take place;

(*ii*) Apply the measures set out below concerning the control of exports of hazardous wastes to a final destination outside the OECD area.

III. *Instructs* the Environment Committee to take account of the elements of this Decision–Recommendation in developing the draft international agreement referred to in the resolution of the Council of International Cooperation Concerning Transfrontier Movements of Hazardous Wastes [C(85)100].

MEASURES CONCERNING THE CONTROL OF EXPORTS OF HAZARDOUS WASTES

1. The following measures are designed to facilitate the harmonization of policies concerning transfrontier movements of hazardous wastes to a final destination outside the OECD area. They do not prejudice the implementation of stricter measures which have been or might be adopted at national, regional or world level to reduce the dangers associated with the transport and disposal of hazardous wastes.

2. These measures should apply in the absence of a bilateral or multilateral agreement concerning transfrontier movements of hazardous wastes between the exporting Member country and the importing non-Member country concerned, and should be taken into account in the negotiation of such an agreement.

3. Member countries should require, with respect to any export of hazardous wastes to a final destination outside the OECD area, that the measures set out below be taken by the exporter or by the competent authorities of the exporting country.

4. The exporter should:

(*a*) provide the competent authorities of the importing country (and of any transit countries) with at least the same information that he would provide them if they were Member countries;

(*b*) inform the competent authorities of the importing country of any specific disposal methods legally required or forbidden for such wastes in the exporting country;

(*c*) provide to the competent authorities of the exporting country:

(*i*) the information used by the exporter to assure himself that the proposed disposal operation can be performed in an environmentally sound manner;

(*ii*) certification that the proposed disposal facility may, under the laws and regulations of the importing country, dispose of the kinds of wastes whose export is proposed;

(*iii*) a copy of an undertaking by the operator of the proposed disposal facility that he will dispose of the wastes as foreseen in the disposal contract, and in the facility specified therein;

(*iv*) a copy of the information transmitted to the competent authorities of the importing country to obtain their written consent to the import and disposal of the wastes;

(*v*) a copy of the written consent of the competent authorities of the importing country, and confirmation that the competent authorities of any transit countries have received delivery of notification;

(*d*) demand and receive from the disposer documents confirming that the wastes have been handed over to the disposer and disposed of as foreseen, and put these documents at the disposition of the competent authorities of the exporting country.

5. Member countries may choose to charge their competent authorities instead of the exporter with some of the tasks listed above.

6. The competent authorities of the exporting country should:

(*a*) before any final decision is taken, inform the competent authorities of the importing country when they have specific environmental concerns regarding the proposed disposal operation;

(*b*) prohibit the export of the hazardous wastes whenever:

(*i*) they are not satisfied with the information provided under 4(*c*) above;

(*ii*) an objection is made by any country of transit and no appropriate alternative route can be found by the exporter;

(*iii*) the proposed disposal operation is not in conformity with applicable international law;

(*c*) prohibit additional exports of hazardous waste to a given destination when the documents specified in 4(*d*) above were not provided to the exporter by the disposer after a previous export to the same destination;

(*d*) notify the exporter promptly whether or not they object to the proposed transfrontier movement;

(*e*) notify the competent authorities of the importing country if they have prohibited the export of the wastes.

APPENDIX
DEFINITIONS

For the purpose of this Decision–Recommendation:

(*a*) "Waste" means any material considered as waste or legally defined as waste in the country where it is situated or through or to which it is conveyed;

(*b*) "Hazardous waste" means any waste other than radioactive waste considered as hazardous or legally defined as hazardous in the country where it is situated or through or to which it is conveyed, because of the potential risk to man or the environment likely to result from an accident or from improper transport or disposal;

(*c*) "Transfrontier movement of hazardous wastes" means any shipment of wastes from one country to another, where the wastes are considered as being hazardous wastes in at least one of the countries concerned. Hazardous wastes arising from the normal operation of ships, including slopes and residues, shall not be considered a transfrontier movement covered by this Decision–Recommendation;

(*d*) "Exporting country" means any country from which a transfrontier movement of hazardous wastes is initiated or is envisaged;

(*e*) "Importing country" means any country to which a transfrontier movement of hazardous wastes takes place or is envisaged for purpose of disposal (treatment, landfill, storage, dumping or incineration at sea);

(*f*) "Transit country" means any country other than the exporting or importing country across which a transfrontier movement of hazardous waste takes place or is envisaged;

(*g*) "Exporter" means the generator of the wastes or the person in the exporting country who arranges for exporting the wastes at the request and on behalf of the generator;

(*h*) "OECD area" means all land or marine areas under the national jurisdiction of any OECD Member country.

5.3 UNEP GOVERNING COUNCIL DECISION ON CAIRO GUIDELINES AND PRINCIPLES FOR THE ENVIRONMENTALLY SOUND MANAGEMENT OF HAZARDOUS WASTES (WITHOUT ANNEX). Adopted by the UNEP Governing Council at Cairo, 17 June 1987. UNEP/GC/DEC/14/30, UNEP ELPG No. 8

Introduction

This set of guidelines and principles is addressed to Governments with a view to assisting them in the process of developing policies for the environmentally sound management of hazardous wastes. They have been prepared on the basis of common elements and principles derived from relevant existing bilateral, regional and global agreements and national regulations, drawing upon experience already gained through their preparation and implementation. Special importance is attached to respect for the balance achieved in principle 21 of the Stockholm Declaration on the Human Environment between the rights and duties of States concerning their natural resources and the environment.

These general guidelines cover the management of hazardous wastes from their generation to their final disposal and, in particular, the problem of transfrontier movements of such wastes, which calls for international co-operation between exporting and importing countries in the light of their joint responsibility for the protection of the global environment.

These guidelines are without prejudice to the provisions of particular systems arising from international agreements in the field of hazardous waste management. They have been developed with a view to assisting States in the process of developing appropriate bilateral, regional and multilateral agreements and national legislation for the environmentally sound management of hazardous wastes. The guidelines deal mainly with the administrative aspects of the environmentally sound management of hazardous wastes, and do not claim to give specific guidance on the more technical aspects of dealing with hazardous wastes.

At the present time, waste management differs substantially in different regions of the world, particularly according to their state of economic development. This imbalance necessitates co-operation to improve the management of hazardous wastes in the interest of the environment, especially as regards actual and potential transfrontier movements of such wastes.

Although the guidelines have not been prepared specifically to address the situation of developing countries, they nevertheless provide a framework for effective and environmentally sound hazardous waste management policies in those countries. Implementation of the guidelines should thus help them to avoid serious and costly environmental problems due to mismanagement of hazardous wastes. By implementing the guidelines, countries could incorporate a sound waste management policy into their national economic development policies.

PART 1

GENERAL PROVISIONS

1. *Definitions*

For the purposes of the present guidelines and principles:

(a) "Wastes" means any materials considered as wastes or legally defined as wastes in the State where they are situated or through or to which they are conveyed;

(b) "Hazardous wastes" means wastes other than radioactive wastes which, by reason of their chemical reactivity or toxic, explosive, corrosive or other characteristics causing danger or likely to cause danger to health or the environment, whether alone or when coming into contact with other wastes, are legally defined as hazardous in the State in which they are generated or in which they are disposed of or through which they are transported;

(c) "Management" means the collection, transport (including transfrontier movements), storage (including storage at transfer stations), treatment and disposal of hazardous wastes;

(d) "Transport" means the movement of hazardous wastes from the place at which they are generated until they arrive at an approved site or facility for disposal;

(e) "Disposal" means final disposal;

(f) "Approved site or facility" means a site or facility for the storage, treatment or disposal of hazardous wastes which has been the subject of a prior written authorization or operating permit for this purpose from a competent authority in the State where the site or facility is located.

(g) "Competent authority" means a governmental authority with appropriate qualifications designated or established by a State to be responsible, within such geographical area and with such jurisdiction as the State may think fit, for the planning, organization, authorization and supervision of the management of hazardous wastes;

(h) "Pollution" means the introduction by man, directly or indirectly, of any hazardous wastes into the environment as a result of which there arises any hazard to human health, plant or animal life, harm to living resources or to ecosystems, damage to amenities or interference with other legitimate uses of the environment;

(i) "Contingency" means any accident or other event occurring during the management of hazardous wastes which gives rise to or presents a threat of pollution;

(j) "Territory" means areas over which a State has jurisdiction for the protection of the environment;

(k) "Export" means the movement of hazardous wastes beyond the territory of the State in which they were generated;

(*l*) "State of export" means a State in which hazardous wastes which are the subject of an export are generated;

(m) "State of import" means a State in which hazardous wastes are received for disposal;

(n) "Transit State" means a State, not being the State of export or of import, through the territory of which a movement of hazardous wastes takes place.

2. *General Principles*

    (a) States should take such steps as are necessary, whether by legislation or otherwise, to ensure the protection of health and the environment from damage arising from the generation and management of hazardous wastes. To this end, States should, *inter alia,* ensure that transfrontier movements of hazardous wastes are kept to the minimum compatible with the efficient and environmentally sound management of such wastes.

    (b) States should take all practicable steps to ensure that the management of hazardous wastes is conducted in accordance with international law applicable in matters of environmental protection.

3. *Non–Discriminatory Control of Hazardous Wastes*

Each State should ensure that, within its jurisdiction, hazardous wastes to be exported are controlled no less stringently than those remaining within its territory.

4. *International Co–Operation*

Without prejudice to the other provisions of these guidelines and principles, States should, in a manner appropriate to their needs and capabilities, initiate and co-operate in:

    (a) The achievement and improvement of the environmentally sound management of hazardous wastes;

    (b) The development and implementation of new environmentally sound low-waste technologies and the improvement of existing technologies with a view to reducing the generation of hazardous wastes and achieving more effective and efficient methods of ensuring their management in an environmentally sound manner, including the study of the economic, social and environmental effects of the adoption of such new or improved technologies;

    (c) Monitoring the effects of the management of hazardous wastes on health and the environment;

    (d) Exchanges of information, whether on a bilateral or multilateral basis, with a view to promoting the environmentally sound management of hazardous wastes.

5. *Transfer of Technology*

States should, in a manner appropriate to their needs and capabilities, whether directly or through the appropriate international organizations, promote actively and in accordance with their legitimate interests the transfer of fair and reasonable conditions of technology related to the environmentally sound management of hazardous wastes. They should also promote the technical capacity of States, especially of developing States, which may need and request technical assistance in this field.

6. *Transfer or Transformation of Pollution*

States and persons involved in the management of hazardous wastes should recognize that protection of health and the environment is not achieved by the mere transformation of one form of pollution into another, nor by the mere transfer of the effects of pollution from one location to another, but only by the use of the waste treatment option (which may include transformation or transfer) which minimizes the environmental impact.

PART II
GENERATION AND MANAGEMENT OF HAZARDOUS WASTES

7. *Preventive Measures*

(a) States should take such steps as are appropriate to ensure that the generation of hazardous wastes within their territories is reduced to a minimum.

(b) States should ensure that persons involved in the management of hazardous wastes take such steps as are necessary to prevent pollution arising from such management and, if pollution should occur, to minimize the consequences thereof for health and the environment.

(c) In particular, States should take such steps as are necessary to promote the development and employment of low-waste technologies applicable to activities generating hazardous wastes and the recycling and reuse of hazardous wastes unavoidably produced by such activities.

8. *Establishment of Competent Authorities*

Each State should designate or establish one or more competent authorities as defined in guideline 1.

PART III
CONTROL OVER DISPOSAL OF HAZARDOUS WASTES

9. *Disposal Plans for Hazardous Wastes*

(a) States should ensure that each competent authority prepares, in its area of responsibility, in consultation with the other public authorities concerned and with the participation of the public as appropriate, a plan for the management of hazardous wastes describing the arrangements for implementing that plan.

(b) Such plans should be reviewed by the competent authorities to ensure their continuing adequacy in the light of experience in the operation of the plans and of changes in circumstances, including changes in the state of scientific knowledge.

10. *Separation of Hazardous Wastes*

The competent authorities should ensure that persons concerned in the management of hazardous wastes keep them separate from other wastes where it is necessary to do so for their environmentally sound management.

11. *Collection of Hazardous Wastes*

States should promote the establishment of a system of collection of hazardous wastes, including those that are generated in small quantities.

12. *Duty to Ensure Safe Disposal*

States should ensure that persons engaged in activities in the course of which hazardous wastes are generated are required to make appropriate arrangements for the disposal of those wastes in an environmentally sound manner. In particular, they should satisfy themselves as to the capability and reliability of persons and facilities involved in the management of such wastes.

13. *Use of Best Practicable Means*

States should ensure that persons involved in the management of hazardous wastes employ the best practicable means in all aspects of such management.

14. *Approved Sites and Facilities*

(a) States should take such steps as are necessary to require that the storage, treatment and disposal of hazardous wastes take place only at approved sites or facilities.

(b) An authorization or operating permit for approved sites or facilities should be granted only if:

(i) An assessment undertaken by or at the request of the competent authority has established that no significant adverse effects on health or the environment are to be expected as a result of such storage, treatment or disposal;

(ii) The competent authority is satisfied as to the suitability of the operator of the facility at which such storage, treatment or disposal is to be carried out, including the technical knowledge and financial means of that operator to carry out the operations in respect of which the authorization or operating permit is sought to be granted and to take the appropriate safety measures in respect thereof.

15. *International Listing of Approved Sites and Facilities*

For the guidance of their competent authorities and to ensure the optimal use of their disposal facilities in conformity with guideline 2, States should consider the establishment, on a bilateral or multilateral basis, of lists of approved sites and facilities in their respective territories.

16. *Transfrontier Effects of Approved Sites and Facilities—Pre–Authorization Information*

(a) States should ensure that, where it is proposed to grant an authorization or operating permit under guideline 14 in respect of activities which may have significant effects on health or the environment in another State (hereinafter referred to as "the State concerned"), the State concerned is provided in a timely manner by the State entitled to grant the authorization or operating permit (hereinafter referred to as "the authorizing State") with sufficient information, in conformity with the laws and regulations of the latter State, to enable it to evaluate accurately the likely effects of those activities.

(b) The State concerned should respect the confidentiality of the information transmitted to it under paragraph (a) above.

17. *Transfrontier Effects—Consultation*

In the circumstances described in guideline 16, the authorizing State and the State concerned should, prior to the adoption of any decision in the authorizing State as to the granting of the authorization or operating permit, enter into consultations which shall be conducted in good faith. These consultations should take place promptly and should be concluded within a reasonable time.

18. *Transfrontier Effects—Equal Access and Treatment*

In the circumstances described in guideline 16, the authorizing State should accord to the public authorities and nationals of the State concerned the same rights of participation in the administrative and judicial proceedings related to the granting of authorizations or operating permits and in any appeal or review thereof as those which are accorded to its own public authorities and nationals.

PART IV

MONITORING, REMEDIAL ACTION AND RECORD–KEEPING

19. *Monitoring*

(a) States should ensure that the operators of sites or facilities at which hazardous wastes are managed are required, as appropriate, to monitor the effects of those activities on health and the environment and to supply the competent authorities with the results of such monitoring, either periodically or on demand. States should ensure that the protection of abandoned sites or closed facilities against the subsequent unauthorized disposal of hazardous wastes, and the monitoring of such sites or facilities for effects on health and the environment, continue after their abandonment or closure.

(b) States should ensure that the competent authorities have the power to enter upon the sites or facilities mentioned in paragraph (a) above and upon such other premises as may be necessary for the purposes of monitoring the effects upon health and the environment of the activities carried out at those sites or facilities. States should also ensure that the competent authorities have the power to order the cessation, limitation or modification of those activities if it is determined that adverse effects on health and the environment are taking place, or are likely to take place.

(c) States should ensure that appropriate remedial action is taken in cases where monitoring gives indications that management of hazardous wastes has resulted in adverse effects on health or the environment.

(d) States should ensure that persons involved in the management of hazardous wastes keep accurate and precise records, as appropriate, of the relevant information concerning wastes, including the type, quantity, physical and chemical characteristics, origin and location within the site or facility of such wastes.

20. *Public Access to Information*

States should ensure that competent authorities keep a record of the authorizations or operating permits issued by them under guideline 14, and that the public have access to information concerning the number and types of those authorizations or permits and the conditions attached thereto.

PART V
SAFETY AND CONTINGENCY PLANNING

21. *Instruction of Workers*

States should ensure that persons employed at sites or facilities at which hazardous wastes are managed receive, on a continuing basis, information on the conditions attached to authorizations or permits, and full and appropriate instruction as to the safety precautions necessary to ensure the protection of health and the environment, including the actions to be taken by them in any contingency.

22. *Contingency Plans*

States within whose territories hazardous wastes are managed should recognize the need for studies on the risks of sites or facilities, and contingency plans prepared by operators of sites or facilities, or by the competent authorities, as appropriate, and the application of such plans as and when necessary. These plans should take into account any potential adverse effects on health and the environment in other States.

23. *Contingency Plans—Transfrontier Effects*

(a) If a State has reason to believe that a contingency which has arisen within its territory is likely to have significant adverse effects on health and the environment in another State, that State should as soon as practicable supply the other State with the information necessary to enable it to adopt effective counter-measures.

(b) States should provide such assistance as they can reasonably make available to other States in which a contingency has occurred.

PART VI
TRANSPORT OF HAZARDOUS WASTES

24. *Transport Rules*

States should ensure that the transport of hazardous wastes is conducted in a manner compatible with international conventions and other international instruments governing the transport of hazardous materials or wastes.

25. *Transport Documentation*

To ensure that hazardous wastes are safely transported for disposal, and to maintain records of the transport and disposal of such wastes, States should establish a system by which all transport of such wastes should be accompanied by a hazardous wastes movement document from the point of generation to the point of disposal. This document should be available to the competent authorities and to all parties involved in the management of such wastes.

26. *Notification and Consent Procedure in Respect of Transfrontier Movements of Hazardous Wastes*

(a) States should establish a system which ensures that all States involved in a transfrontier movement of hazardous wastes receive full information sufficiently in advance to enable them to assess the proposed movement properly.

(b) A State of export should take such steps as are necessary to ensure that a request from a State of import or transit State for relevant information concerning the transfrontier movement in question elicits a constructive and timely response.

(c) In the absence of bilateral, regional or multilateral arrangements, States should provide that it shall not be lawful for any person to initiate a transfrontier movement of hazardous wastes until the State of import and any transit State have given their consent to that movement.

(d) The consent of the State of import referred to in paragraph (c) above should take the form of an explicit consent, provided always that States may by bilateral or multilateral arrangements adopt a tacit consent procedure.

(e) Any transit State should be notified in a timely manner of a proposed movement, and may object to it within a reasonable time in accordance with its national laws and regulations. The consent of a transit State referred to in paragraph (c) above may also take the form of a tacit consent.

(f) The State of export should not permit a transfrontier movement of hazardous wastes to be initiated unless it is not satisfied that the wastes in question can be managed in an environmentally sound manner, at an approved site or facility and with the consent of the State of import.

(g) In order to facilitate implementation of this guideline, each State should designate an agency which shall be the focal point to which the notifications and inquiries mentioned in the foregoing paragraphs may be addressed.

(h) Nothing in this guideline shall be so construed as to affect the sovereign right of a State to refuse to accept within its territory hazardous wastes originating elsewhere.

27. *States of Export to Readmit Exports*

Where a State of import or transit State, in conformity with its laws and regulations, opposes a transfrontier movement of hazardous wastes into its territory, and where the hazardous wastes which are the subject of the transfrontier movement have already left the State of export, the latter should not object to reimport any of the wastes.

28. *States to Co–Operate in the Management of Hazardous Wastes*

States should, in pursuance of guideline 2, enter into bilateral, regional or multilateral agreements for the management of their hazardous wastes in order to ensure the optimal use of their treatment and disposal facilities.

PART VII

LIABILITY AND COMPENSATION

29. *Liability, Insurance and Compensation for Damage caused by hazardous wastes*

States should ensure that provision is made in their national laws and regulations for (a) liability, (b) insurance and (c) compensation and/or other remedies for damage arising from the management of hazardous wastes, and they should take such steps as are necessary to ensure the compatibility and, where appropriate, the harmonization of such laws and regulations.

5.4 UNEP GOVERNING COUNCIL DECISION ON LONDON GUIDELINES FOR THE EXCHANGE OF INFORMATION ON CHEMICALS IN INTERNATIONAL TRADE (WITH ANNEXES II & III AND AS AMENDED IN 1989). Adopted by the UNEP Governing Council at London, 19 June 1987. UNEP/PIC/WG.2/2, at 9, UNEP ELPG No. 10, UNEP/GC/DEC/15/30

Introduction to the Guidelines

1.   This set of Guidelines is addressed to Governments with a view to assisting them in the process of increasing chemical safety in all countries through the exchange of information on chemicals in international trade. They have been developed on the basis of common elements and principles derived from relevant existing bilateral, regional and global instruments and national regulations, drawing upon experience already gained through their preparation and implementation.

2.   The Guidelines are general in nature and are aimed at enhancing the sound management of chemicals through the exchange of scientific, technical, economic and legal information.   Special provisions have been included regarding the exchange of information on banned or severely restricted chemicals in international trade, which call for co-operation between exporting and importing countries in the light of their joint responsibility for the protection of human health and the environment at the global level.   To this end, all references in these Guidelines to a Government or Governments shall be deemed to apply equally to regional economic integration organizations for matters falling within their areas of competence.

3.   The Guidelines are without prejudice to the provisions of particular systems or procedures included in existing or future national legislation and bilateral, regional and multilateral instruments for the exchange of information on chemicals; rather, they have been prepared with a view to assisting States in the process of developing such arrangements.

4.   These Guidelines do not preclude States from instituting broader and more frequent information exchange or other systems involving consultation with importing countries on banned or severely restricted chemicals designed to gain experience with alternative procedures.

5.   These Guidelines provide a mechanism for importing countries to formally record and disseminate their decisions regarding the future importation of chemicals which have been banned or severely restricted and outlines the shared responsibilities of importing and exporting countries and exporting industries in ensuring that these decisions are heeded.

6.   The importance of technical and financial assistance to enhance decision-making and training in the safe use of chemicals is recognized by the Guidelines.

7.   These Guidelines are complementary to existing instruments developed by the United Nations and the World Health Organization and to the International Code of Conduct on the Distribution and Use of Pesticides of the Food and Agriculture Organization of the United Nations, which is the primary guidance for the management of pesticides internationally.   These Guidelines should be implemented in a non-duplicative manner for the different classes of chemicals covered by existing instruments.

8. Although the Guidelines have not been prepared specifically to address the situation of developing countries, they nevertheless provide a framework for the establishment of procedures for the effective use of information on chemicals in these countries. Implementation of the Guidelines should thus help them to avoid serious and costly health and environmental problems due to ignorance about the risks associated with the use of chemicals, particularly those that have been banned or severely restricted in other States.

PART I

GENERAL PROVISIONS

1. *Definitions*

For the purposes of the Guidelines:

(a) "Chemical" means a chemical substance whether by itself or in a mixture or preparation, whether manufactured or obtained from nature and includes such substances used as industrial chemicals and pesticides;

(b) "Banned chemical" means a chemical which has, for health or environmental reasons, been prohibited for all uses by final governmental regulatory action;

(c) "Severely restricted chemical" means a chemical for which, for health or environmental reasons, virtually all uses have been prohibited nationally by final government regulatory action, but for which certain specific uses remain authorized;

(d) "International trade" means export or import of chemicals;

(e) "Export" and "import" mean, in their respective connotations, the movement of a chemical from one State to another State, but exclude mere transit operations;

(f) "Management" means the handling, supply, transport, storage, treatment, application, or other use of a chemical subsequent to its initial manufacture or formulation;

(g) "Prior informed consent" (PIC) refers to the *principle* that international shipment of a chemical that is banned or severely restricted in order to protect human health or the environment should not proceed without the agreement, where such agreement exists, or contrary to the decision, of the designated national authority in the importing country;

(h) "Prior informed consent procedure" (PIC procedure) means the *procedure* for formally obtaining and disseminating the decisions of importing countries as to whether they wish to receive future shipments of chemicals which have been banned or severely restricted. A specific procedure was established for selecting chemicals for initial implementation of the PIC procedures. These include chemicals which have been previously banned or severely restricted as well as certain pesticide formulations which are acutely toxic. This is explained in annex II.

2. *General Principles*

(a) Both States of export and States of import should protect human health and the environment against potential harm by exchanging information on chemicals in international trade;

(b) In their activities with regard to chemicals, States should act, in so far as is applicable, in accordance with principle 21 of the Declaration of the United Nations Conference on the Human Environment;

(c) States taking measures to regulate chemicals with a view to protecting human, animal or plant life or health, or the environment, should ensure that regulations and standards for this purpose do not create unnecessary obstacles to international trade;

(d) States should ensure that governmental control measures or actions taken with regard to an imported chemical for which information has been received in implementation of the Guidelines are not more restrictive than those applied to the same chemical produced for domestic use or imported from a State other than the one that supplied the information;

(e) States with more advanced systems for the safe management of chemicals should share their experience with those countries in need of improved systems;

(f) Both States of import and States of export should, as appropriate, strengthen their existing infrastructures and institutions in the following ways:

(i) Establishing and strengthening legislative and regulatory systems and other mechanisms for improving control and management of chemicals. This may include development of model legislation or regulations, in light of these Guidelines and other relevant guidelines prepared by other organizations;

(ii) Creating national registers of toxic chemicals, including both industrial chemicals and pesticides;

(iii) Preparing and updating manuals, directories and documentation for better utilization of facilities for information collection and dissemination at the country level and to on-line facilities at the regional level.

3. *Exemptions*

These Guidelines should not apply to:

(a) Pharmaceuticals, including narcotics, drugs and psychotropic substances;

(b) Radioactive materials;

(c) Chemicals imported for the purpose of research or analysis in quantities not likely to affect the environment or human health;

(d) Chemicals imported as personal or household effects, in quantities reasonable for these uses;

(e) Food additives.

4. *Effects on Other Instruments*

(a) States should take the necessary measures with regard to implementation of these Guidelines;

(b) The provisions of these Guidelines do not affect the obligations of States deriving from any relevant international agreement to which they are or may become party.

5. *Institutional Arrangements*

5.1 UNEP and FAO should develop an information exchange system to ensure that designated national authorities of importing and exporting countries have a single contact point for obtaining information and communicating decisions on chemicals subject to the PIC procedure;

5.2 UNEP should share with FAO the operational responsibility for the implementation of the PIC procedure and jointly manage and implement common elements including the selection of chemicals to be included in the PIC procedure, preparation of the PIC guidance documents, mechanisms for information sharing, and creation of data bases;

5.3 UNEP should collaborate with FAO in reviewing the implementation of the PIC procedure, including participation, responses, and violations of importing country decisions;

5.4 For purposes of international communications, each State should designate a national governmental authority (or authorities) competent to perform the administrative functions related to the exchange of information and decisions regarding importation of chemicals included in the PIC procedure;

5.5 The designated national authority should be authorized to communicate, directly or as provided by national law or regulation, with designated national authorities of other States and with international organizations concerned to exchange information, to make and communicate decisions regarding chemicals included in the PIC procedure and to submit reports at the request of such States or organizations or on its own initiative;

5.6 States should ensure that designated national authorities have sufficient national resources to assume responsibility with regard to implementation of these Guidelines;

5.7 States should as soon as possible make available the name and address of their designated national authority to the International Register of Potentially Toxic Chemicals (IRPTC), as well as subsequent changes;

5.8 A register of designated national authorities should be maintained, regularly updated, and disseminated by IRPTC;

5.9 IRPTC should, in addition:

(a) Co-ordinate the network of designated national authorities;

(b) Develop recommendations on practices and procedures, and such joint programmes and measures as may be required to make the Guidelines effective;

(c) Maintain liaison with other concerned intergovernmental and non-governmental organizations;

(d) Keep under review the implementation of these Guidelines, on the basis of periodic reports from designated national authorities and provide biennial reports on the effectiveness of the Guidelines and suggestions for their improvement.

PART II
NOTIFICATION AND INFORMATION REGARDING BANNED AND SEVERELY RESTRICTED CHEMICALS AND OPERATION OF THE PIC PROCEDURE

6. *Notification of Control Action*

(a) States having taken control action to ban or severely restrict a chemical as defined in these Guidelines should notify IRPTC. IRPTC will disseminate these notifications as provided in these Guidelines;

(b) The purpose of the notification regarding control action is to give competent authorities in other States the opportunity to assess the risks associated with the chemical, and to make timely and informed decisions thereon, taking into account local environmental, public health, economic and administrative conditions, and with regard to existing information on toxicology, safety and regulatory aspects;

(c) The minimum information to be provided for this purpose should be:

(i) The chemical identification/specification of the chemical;

(ii) A summary of the control action taken and of the reasons for it. If the control action bans or restricts certain uses but allows other uses, such information should be included;

(iii) The fact that additional information is available, and the indication of the contact point in the State of export to which a request for further information should be addressed;

(d) To the extent practicable, the designated national authority issuing the notification should provide information concerning alternative measures, such as, for example, integrated pest management procedures, non-chemical alternatives and impact mitigation measures;

(e) Notification of control action should be provided as soon as practicable after the control action is taken. For chemicals banned or severely restricted before the implementation of these Guidelines, an inventory of prior control actions should be provided to IRPTC, unless such information has already been provided and circulated by IRPTC to all designated national authorities.

7. *Operation of the PIC Procedure*

7.1 *Determination of Participation in the PIC Procedure*

PIC is a procedure which operates in addition to information exchange and export notification. Those countries which elect to participate in the PIC procedure will have the opportunity to record their decisions regarding future imports of banned or severely restricted chemicals in a formal way.

(a) Countries may participate in the information exchange procedures under these Guidelines without participating in the PIC procedure;

(b) All exporting countries are expected to participate in the PIC procedure by respecting the decisions of importing countries;

(c) IRPTC should invite countries to participate in the PIC procedure with respect to imports. Designated national authorities should reply indicating whether their country will participate. If there is no reply a follow-up letter should be sent 60 days after the first invitation. If there is no response, IRPTC should take additional steps to obtain a decision. If after that, there is still no response then it will be assumed that the country does not wish to participate in the procedure;

(d) A country may designate one competent body to handle both industrial chemicals and pesticides or may designate separate competent bodies for each;

(e) A country may elect at any time to participate or not participate in the PIC procedure by communicating its decision to IRPTC;

(f) IRPTC should make available on request a list of countries who have elected to participate, countries which have elected not to participate and countries which did not respond.

7.2 *Identification of Chemicals for Inclusion in the PIC Procedure*

(a) As provided in paragraph 9, IRPTC will notify each participating country of each chemical that is the subject of a notification of a final government control action and that meets the definitions as being banned or severely restricted for environmental or human health reasons for a decision under its conditions of use as to whether that country wishes to permit use and importation of the chemical. An informal consultative process may be used to assist IRPTC in determining whether the control action meets the definitions of the Guidelines;

(b) As provided in paragraph 9, IRPTC should send qualifying control actions, along with PIC decision guidance documents, to the appropriate designated national authority or authorities in each participating country for decision.

7.3 *Response to Notification of Control Action for Chemicals Identified for Inclusion in the PIC Procedure*

(a) The designated national authority in each participating importing country shall make an initial response to IRPTC within 90 days. A response may take either of two forms:

(i) A final decision to permit use and importation, to prohibit use and importation or to permit importation only under specified stated conditions;

(ii) An interim response which may be:

a. A statement that importation is under active review but that final decision has not yet been reached;

b. A request for further information; and/or

c. A request for assistance in evaluating the chemical.

An interim response may also contain a statement permitting importation with or without stated specified conditions or prohibiting importation during the interim period until a final decision is made;

(b) The designated national authority shall use the form provided to make such response;

(c) IRPTC should send reminders to countries as necessary to encourage a response and should facilitate the provision of technical assistance where requested;

(d) If a participating importing country does not make a response or responds with an interim decision that does not address importation, the *status quo* with respect to importation of the chemical should continue. This means that the chemical should not be exported without the explicit consent of the importing country, unless it is a pesticide which is registered in the importing country or is a chemical the use or importation of which has been allowed by other governmental action of the importing country;

(e) If a country takes a unilateral action which affects the *status quo* with respect to a chemical, it must so notify IRPTC to make IRPTC aware of the decision. Such a unilateral action will be interpreted as superseding any previous decision it has made with respect to the chemical;

(f) When an importing country takes a final or interim decision which affects the *status quo,* it should also communicate this decision to the national competent authority responsible for controlling imports so that it can take appropriate import control actions under its authority.

7.4 *Dissemination of Information*

(a) IRPTC will inform designated national authorities of decisions taken by participating importing countries in a timely fashion and should also make these available to industry and other interested parties on request, preferably through a computer data base. This information should also be included in the regular updates of the United Nations Consolidated List of Products whose Consumption and/or Sale have been Banned, Withdrawn or Severely Restricted by Governments. Semi-annually, IRPTC will notify all Governments in writing of the status of the decisions by importing countries;

(b) Governments of exporting countries shall, upon receipt of importing countries' decisions, transmit them to their industry.

8. *Information regarding exports*

(a) If an export of a chemical banned or severely restricted in the State of export occurs, the State of export should ensure that necessary steps are taken to provide the designated national authority of the State of import with relevant information;

(b) The purpose of information regarding exports is to remind the State of import of the original notification regarding control action and to alert it to the fact that an export will occur or is occurring;

(c) The minimum information to be provided for this purpose should be:

(i) A copy of, or reference to, the information provided at the time of notification of control action;

(ii) Indication that an export of the chemical concerned will occur or is occurring;

(iii) An estimate of the quantity to be exported annually as well as any shipment-specific information that might be available;

(d) States should endeavor to ensure that, to the extent possible, information regarding exports provided or received in implementation of these guidelines is forwarded to the State of final destination and to IRPTC;

(e) Provision of information regarding exports should take place when the first export following the control action occurs, and should recur periodically or in the case of any significant development of new information or condition surrounding the control action. It is the intention that, in so far as possible, the information should be provided prior to export. Where the chemical has been banned or severely restricted before the adoption of these Guidelines, the "first export following the control action" should be considered to be the first export after adoption of these Guidelines.

9. *Channels of Notification and Information*

(a) Notifications of control actions should be addressed to IRPTC for transmission to designated national authorities;

(b) Participating importing countries should send their response on the prescribed forms to IRPTC for appropriate dissemination;

(c) PIC decision guidance documents will be transmitted by IRPTC to designated national authorities in participating importing countries for their decision and response and to designated national authorities in other countries for their information;

(d) Information on exports should be addressed to the national authority designated for this purpose in the State of import.

10. *Feedback*

Designated national authorities of States of import should provide to IRPTC, for the purpose of periodic review pursuant to paragraph 5.9(d), a summary of action taken as a result of notifications and information received pursuant to paragraphs 6, 7.3 and 8 and information on any difficulties which they have experienced in using these Guidelines.

11. *Confidential Data*

(a) States undertaking information exchange in implementation of these Guidelines should establish internal procedures for the receipt, handling and protection of confidential and proprietary information received from other States;

(b) States receiving notifications and information regarding exports should be responsible for the protection of proprietary rights and the confidentiality of data received under these Guidelines when claimed by the State supplying the information.

12. *Functions of Designated National Authorities*

(a) *Control action.* It should be the function of designated national authorities, with regard to control action taken by States to ban or severely restrict a chemical:

(i) To provide notification to IRPTC, in accordance with these Guidelines, that such control action has been taken;

(ii) To receive from IRPTC notification that such action has been taken in other States, and to ensure its prompt transmittal to all other national authorities concerned;

(iii) To receive from the United Nations the regular updates of the United Nations Consolidated List of Products Whose Consumption and/or Sale have been Banned, Withdrawn or Severely Restricted by Governments;

(iv) To reply to the request for participation in the PIC procedures in accordance with paragraph 7.1 of these Guidelines;

(v) To respond to notifications of control action in accordance with paragraph 7.3 of these Guidelines, including response to the lists to be circulated in accordance with paragraph 7.2 and Annex II;

(b) *Imports.* It should be the function of designated national authorities, with regard to imports of banned or severely restricted chemicals:

(i) To receive from States of export information on exports, and to ensure the prompt transmittal of such information to all other authorities concerned in the State of import;

(ii) To transmit to States of export requests for further information as required;

(iii) To provide feedback information to IRPTC on action taken as a result of notifications and information received and on any difficulties experienced in the exchange of data with States of exports;

(iv) To advise and assist import control authorities so that they can take appropriate import control actions under their authority;

(v) To strengthen national decision-making procedures and import control mechanisms;

(vi) To ensure that decisions apply uniformly to all sources of import and to domestic production of chemicals for domestic use;

(vii) To encourage that chemicals subject to PIC be purchased only from sources in exporting countries which are participants in that procedure;

(c) *Exports.* It should be the function of designated national authorities, with regard to exports of banned or severely restricted chemicals:

(i) To ensure the issuance or transmittal of information on exports;

(ii) To respond to requests for information from other States, especially as regards sources of precautionary information on safe use and handling of the chemicals concerned;

(iii) To communicate PIC decisions to their export industry;

(iv) To implement appropriate procedures, within their authority, designed to ensure that exports do not occur contrary to the PIC decisions of participating importing countries;

(d) *Other functions.* Designated national authorities should also consider the need:

    (i) To provide information regarding applicable national regulations for the management of banned or severely restricted chemicals;

    (ii) To ensure the provision of appropriate precautionary information to persons using or handling the chemicals concerned;

    (iii) To keep records of notifications and information received, issued and transmitted which could be open for public inspection in accordance with national law, except for information classified as confidential or proprietary;

    (iv) To keep records of imports and exports of banned and severely restricted chemicals.

PART III

GENERAL INFORMATION EXCHANGE AND PROVISION OF
TECHNICAL ASSISTANCE REGARDING CHEMICALS

13. *Information, Advice and Assistance*

    (a) For the protection of human health and the environment, States should facilitate:

    (i) The exchange of scientific information (including toxicological and safety data) and technical, economic and legal information concerning the management of chemicals, particularly through designated national governmental authorities and through intergovernmental organizations as appropriate;

    (ii) The provision upon request of technical advice and assistance concerning the management of chemicals to other States, on a bilateral or multilateral basis, taking into account the special needs of developing countries.

    (b) With regard to the export of chemicals, States of export should ensure that, where appropriate, information, advice and assistance is provided to States of import concerned regarding the sound management of such chemicals, including appropriate precautionary information;

    (c) With regard to the use of imported chemicals, States of import should, on the basis of notification and information provided by States of export, take the necessary measures to ensure that users are provided with information, advice and assistance for the sound management of such chemicals, including appropriate precautionary information;

    (d) As far as practicable, precautionary information should be provided in the principal language or languages of the State of import and of the area of intended use, and should be accompanied by suitable pictorial and/or tactile aids and labels.

14. *Classification, Packaging and Labelling*

    (a) States should recognize that classification, packaging and labelling are important elements in information exchange on chemicals in international trade, and that it is desirable that chemicals exported from their territories are subject to no less stringent requirements of classification, packaging and labelling than comparable products destined for use in the State of export;

(b) In the development and implementation of existing and future internationally harmonized procedures for the classification, packaging and labelling of chemicals in international trade, States should take into account the special circumstances surrounding the management of chemicals in developing countries;

(c) In the absence of other standards in the State of import, States should ensure that the classification, packaging and labelling of chemicals exported from their territories conform to recognized and, where appropriate, internationally harmonized procedures and practices for ensuring the protection of human health and the environment during use of these chemicals.

15. *Technical Assistance*

(a) IRPTC should encourage funding agencies, such as the development banks and the United Nations Development Programme, and bilateral donors to provide training, technical assistance and funding for institutional strengthening and should further encourage other United Nations organizations to strengthen their activities related to safe management of chemicals;

(b) States with more advanced chemical regulatory programmes should provide technical assistance to other countries in developing infrastructure and capacity to manage chemicals within their countries, including implementation of the provisions of these Guidelines. Developing countries with more advanced systems should be particularly encouraged to provide technical assistance to other developing countries with no, or less advanced, systems of chemical management. To the extent possible, donor countries and institutions and recipient countries should inform IRPTC of all such technical assistance activities;

(c) Special attention should be devoted by technical assistance and funding authorities to those countries without any regulatory procedures on chemicals in developing a régime for their control;

(d) Essential elements of technical assistance needed by developing countries for the management of chemicals include:

(i) Strengthening existing infrastructure and institutions;

(ii) Provision for the interchange of experts, including short missions, from developed countries to developing countries and vice versa and in particular from one developing country to another for the purposes of:

a. Sharing each other's experience and exchanging ideas;

b. Advising on analysis of information on chemical risks and benefits, conducting environmental impact assessment, and disposing of unusable products safely;

c. Sharing information on new products and alternatives;

d. Ascertaining research and development requirements for local pesticide efficacy studies and development of alternatives;

e. Assisting one another in dealing with practical difficulties in implementing these Guidelines;

(iii) Training to include:

a. Technical workshops on a local, regional and international level;

b. Awareness campaigns on the safe management of chemicals for industrial and agricultural workers, customs officials and doctors;

c. Opportunities for decision makers in developing countries to study systems in countries which have been successfully implementing these Guidelines.

* * *

ANNEX II
PROCEDURE FOR INITIAL IDENTIFICATION OF CHEMICALS FOR INCLUSION IN THE PRIOR INFORMED CONSENT PROCEDURE

1. Control actions have been taken prior to the adoption of the prior informed consent (PIC) procedure in the London Guidelines for the Exchange of Information on Chemicals in International Trade. Some have been notified to the International Register of Potentially Toxic Chemicals (IRPTC) and some have not been submitted. It is necessary to take these into account in starting up the PIC procedures. The following approach will be used to incorporate previous control actions:

(a) Designated national authorities in all States should submit inventories of control actions in accordance with paragraph 6 of these Guidelines, including all information specified in that paragraph, to IRPTC if they have not already done so. Submissions should be made as soon as possible to be available in IRPTC prior to the date of implementation of the PIC procedures;

(b) On the basis of these submissions, IRPTC will identify all chemicals banned or severely restricted by five or more countries. These will be introduced into the PIC process according to the following criteria:

(i) All chemicals banned or severely restricted as defined in these Guidelines by 10 or more countries should be immediately placed on a list and circulated, with PIC decision guidance documents, to countries participating in these Guidelines for determination regarding future use and importation;

(ii) Chemicals banned or severely restricted by 5 or more countries, but by less than 10, should be submitted to an informal consultation to determine whether they meet the definitions of banned and severely restricted for human health or environmental reasons. This determination should be made as expeditiously as possible. Those chemicals that meet the definitions will be circulated as an addition to the list referred to in subparagraph (i) above, with PIC decision guidance documents, for a determination by participating importing countries regarding their future use and importation;

(c) Should additional inventories of past control actions be received by IRPTC subsequent to the implementation date of the PIC procedures, they will be added to the original inventory. This updated inventory should be assessed annually in the same manner as the original inventory under step (b) above and incorporated into the PIC procedure as appropriate. These additional chemicals should be circulated to participating importing countries for their consideration and determinations regarding future use and importation under the PIC procedures. This annual reappraisal of the inventory of past control actions should continue until IRPTC has received adequate information from Governments that these reappraisals are no longer essential to the operation of the PIC procedures.

2. Additionally, an Expert Group will consider the problem of acutely hazardous pesticide formulations to determine if there exists a need for a list of such products to supplement the chemicals already subject to the PIC procedure.

3. This Expert Group should be made up of representatives from the World Health Organization (WHO), the Food and Agriculture Organization of the United Nations (FAO), the United Nations Environment Programme (UNEP) and national pesticide registrars. They may call upon the expertise of industry and non-governmental organizations and other experts as they deem necessary and will review formulations based on the WHO Class 1A compounds.

4. If the Group concludes that there are acutely hazardous pesticide formulations of concern to developing countries which are not already included in the PIC procedure, a supplemental list of such formulations will be recommended for inclusion.

ANNEX III

INFORMATION TO BE INCLUDED IN A PRIOR INFORMED CONSENT (PIC) DECISION GUIDANCE DOCUMENT

A prior informed consent (PIC) decision guidance document will be prepared for each chemical placed into the PIC procedures. The document should consist of three parts, containing the following information to the extent it is available. In the case of the initial list, a summary of all control actions to date will be provided. For subsequent control actions, each national action will be provided as received with appropriate references to previous actions for the second and following notifications by additional countries.

    (a) *A summary of the control action:*

        (i) The common and trade names of the chemical, its specification and numerical identification, using widely recognized chemical numbering systems;

        (ii) Whether a pesticide or industrial chemical, or both;

        (iii) Nature of the control action and date taken;

        (iv) Reasons for the control action;

        (v) Uses banned;

(vi) Uses continued in effect, if any;

(vii) Alternatives considered effective replacements by the country taking the control action, including, e.g., integrated pest management and non-chemical alternatives;

(viii) A contact for further information in the country taking the control action, including telephone, telefax and telex numbers, in addition to a mailing address;

(ix) Relevant references supporting the action;

(b) *Summary information on the chemical, including:*

(i) Description of the chemical;

(ii) Uses and formulations;

(iii) Chemical and physical properties;

(iv) Toxicological characteristics;

(v) Environmental characteristics, including effects on fish and wildlife, mechanisms of transport and fate.

(vi) Exposure potential, including:

    a. Dietary, through food and water;

    b. Occupational, both chronic and acute, including manufacture and use;

    c. Environmental;

    d. Product use, storage, transport and disposal;

    e. Accidental poisoning;

(vii) Protective measures to reduce exposure;

(viii) Packaging and labelling recommendations;

(ix) Storage recommendations;

(x) Waste disposal methods;

(xi) Maximum residue limits assessment (for pesticides);

(xii) References;

(c) *Response form(s)* to provide a convenient way for a participating importing country to register its decision with the International Register of Potentially Toxic Chemicals (IRPTC). (In the case of the initial list one form will be necessary for each chemical.)

**5.5　OAU COUNCIL OF MINISTERS RESOLUTION ON DUMPING OF NU-
CLEAR AND INDUSTRIAL WASTE IN AFRICA.　Adopted at Addis
Ababa, 23 May 1988.　28 I.L.M. 567 (1989)**

The Council of Ministers of the Organization of African Unity, meeting in
its Forty-eighth Ordinary Session, in Addis Ababa, Ethiopia, from 19 to 23
May 1988,

Aware of the growing practice of dumping nuclear and industrial wastes
in African countries by transnational corporations and other enterprises from
industrialized countries, which they cannot dispose of within their territories,

Gravely concerned about the growing tendency of some African countries
to conclude agreements or arrangements with such corporations and enterprises which facilitate the dumping of nuclear and industrial wastes in their
territorial boundaries,

Bearing in mind the harmful effects of radiation from nuclear and other
hazardous industrial wastes to human and marine life as well as to the
ecosystems on which they depend for their existence:

　　1.　DECLARES that the dumping of nuclear and industrial wastes in
Africa is a crime against Africa and the African people;

　　2.　CONDEMNS all transnational corporations and enterprises involved in the introduction, in any form, of nuclear and industrial wastes
in Africa;　and DEMANDS that they clean up the areas that have already
been contaminated by them;

　　3.　CALLS UPON African countries which have concluded or are in
the process of concluding agreements or arrangements for dumping
nuclear and industrial wastes in their territories to put an end to these
transactions;

　　4.　REQUESTS Member States of the OAU to carry out information
campaigns among their people about the danger of Nuclear and Industrial
Wastes;

　　5.　REQUESTS the Secretary–General of the Organization of African Unity (OAU), in close collaboration with the Director–General of the
International Atomic Energy Agency (IAEA), the Executive Secretary of
the United Nations Economic Commission for Africa (ECA), the Executive Director of the United Nations Environment Programme (UNEP),
and other concerned organizations, to assist African countries to establish
appropriate mechanisms for monitoring and control of the movement and
disposal of Nuclear and Industrial Wastes in Africa;

　　6.　REQUESTS ALSO the Secretary–General of the Organization of
African Unity (OAU) to take appropriate steps to ensure the inscription
of The Dumping of Nuclear and Industrial Wastes in Africa as an item on
the Agenda of the Forty-third Session of the U.N. General Assembly;

　　7.　REQUESTS FURTHER the Secretary–General of the Organization of African Unity (OAU) to report to the Council of Ministers at its
Fiftieth Session, on the implementation of this resolution;

　　8.　CALLS UPON Member States to adhere to the guidelines and
principles of Cairo on the dumping of dangerous wastes using ecologically
rational methods;

9. INVITES Member States to participate in the Working Group charged with the drafting of the Convention on the Control of the Movement of Dangerous Wastes across Borders.

5.6 BASEL CONVENTION ON THE CONTROL OF TRANSBOUNDARY MOVEMENTS OF HAZARDOUS WASTES AND THEIR DISPOSAL (WITH ANNEXES). Concluded at Basel, 22 March 1989. Entered into force, 5 May 1992. 28 I.L.M. 657 (1989)

PREAMBLE

The Parties to this Convention,

Aware of the risk of damage to human health and the environment caused by hazardous wastes and other wastes and the transboundary movement thereof,

Mindful of the growing threat to human health and the environment posed by the increased generation and complexity, and transboundary movement of hazardous wastes and other wastes,

Mindful also that the most effective way of protecting human health and the environment from the dangers posed by such wastes is the reduction of their generation to a minimum in terms of quantity and/or hazard potential,

Convinced that States should take necessary measures to ensure that the management of hazardous wastes and other wastes including their transboundary movement and disposal is consistent with the protection of human health and the environment whatever the place of their disposal,

Noting that States should ensure that the generator should carry out duties with regard to the transport and disposal of hazardous wastes and other wastes in a manner that is consistent with the protection of the environment, whatever the place of disposal.

Fully recognizing that any State has the sovereign right to ban the entry or disposal of foreign hazardous wastes and other wastes in its territory.

Recognizing also the increasing desire for the prohibition of transboundary movements of hazardous wastes and their disposal in other States, especially developing countries,

Convinced that hazardous wastes and other wastes should, as far as is compatible with environmentally sound and efficient management, be disposed of in the State where they were generated,

Aware also that transboundary movements of such wastes from the State of their generation to any other State should be permitted only when conducted under conditions which do not endanger human health and the environment, and under conditions in conformity with the provisions of this Convention,

Considering that enhanced control of transboundary movement of hazardous wastes and other wastes will act as an incentive for their environmentally sound management and for the reduction of the volume of such transboundary movement,

Convinced that States should take measures for the proper exchange of information on and control of the transboundary movement of hazardous wastes and other wastes from and to those States,

Noting that a number of international and regional agreements have addressed the issue of protection and preservation of the environment with regard to the transit of dangerous goods.

Taking into account the Declaration of the United Nations Conference on the Human Environment (Stockholm, 1972), the Cairo Guidelines and Principles for the Environmentally Sound Management of Hazardous Wastes adopted by the Governing Council of the United Nations Environment Programme (UNEP) by decision 14/30 of 17 June 1987, the Recommendations of the United Nations Committee of Experts on the Transport of Dangerous Goods (formulated in 1957 and updated biennially), relevant recommendations, declarations, instruments and regulations adopted within the United Nations system and the work and studies done within other international and regional organizations,

Mindful of the spirit, principles, aims and functions of the World Charter for Nature adopted by the General Assembly of the United Nations at its thirty-seventh session (1982) as the rule of ethics in respect of the protection of the human environment and the conservation of natural resources,

Affirming that States are responsible for the fulfilment of their international obligations concerning the protection of human health and protection and preservation of the environment, and are liable in accordance with international law,

Recognizing that in the case of a material breach of the provisions of this Convention or any protocol thereto the relevant international law of treaties shall apply,

Aware of the need to continue the development and implementation of environmentally sound low-waste technologies, recycling options, good housekeeping and management systems with a view to reducing to a minimum the generation of hazardous wastes and other wastes,

Aware also of the growing international concern about the need for stringent control of transboundary movement of hazardous wastes and other wastes, and of the need as far as possible to reduce such movement to a minimum,

Concerned about the problem of illegal transboundary traffic in hazardous wastes and other wastes,

Taking into account also the limited capabilities of the developing countries to manage hazardous wastes and other wastes,

Recognizing the need to promote the transfer of technology for the sound management of hazardous wastes and other wastes produced locally, particularly to the developing countries in accordance with the spirit of the Cairo Guidelines and decision 14/16 of the Governing Council of UNEP on Promotion of the transfer of environmental protection technology,

Recognizing also that hazardous wastes and other wastes should be transported in accordance with relevant international conventions and recommendations,

Convinced also that the transboundary movement of hazardous wastes and other wastes should be permitted only when the transport and the ultimate disposal of such wastes is environmentally sound, and

Determined to protect, by strict control, human health and the environment against the adverse effects which may result from the generation and management of hazardous wastes and other wastes,

HAVE AGREED AS FOLLOWS:

Article 1

Scope of the Convention

1. The following wastes that are subject to transboundary movement shall be "hazardous wastes" for the purposes of this Convention:

(a) Wastes that belong to any category contained in Annex I, unless they do not possess any of the characteristics contained in Annex III; and

(b) Wastes that are not covered under paragraph (a) but are defined as, or are considered to be, hazardous wastes by the domestic legislation of the Party of export, import or transit.

2. Wastes that belong to any category contained in Annex II that are subject to transboundary movement shall be "other wastes" for the purposes of this Convention.

3. Wastes which, as a result of being radioactive, are subject to other international control systems, including international instruments, applying specifically to radioactive materials, are excluded from the scope of this Convention.

4. Wastes which derive from the normal operations of a ship, the discharge of which is covered by another international instrument, are excluded from the scope of this Convention.

Article 2

Definitions

For the purposes of this Convention:

1. "Wastes" are substances or objects which are disposed of or are intended to be disposed of or are required to be disposed of by the provisions of national law;

2. "Management" means the collection, transport and disposal of hazardous wastes or other wastes, including after-care of disposal sites;

3. "Transboundary movement" means any movement of hazardous wastes or other wastes from an area under the national jurisdiction of one State to or through an area under the national jurisdiction of another State or to or through an area not under the national jurisdiction of any State, provided at least two States are involved in the movement;

4. "Disposal" means any operation specified in Annex IV to this Convention;

5. "Approved site or facility" means a site or facility for the disposal of hazardous wastes or other wastes which is authorized or permitted to operate for this purpose by a relevant authority of the State where the site or facility is located;

6. "Competent authority" means one governmental authority designated by a Party to be responsible, within such geographical areas as the Party may think fit, for receiving the notification of a transboundary movement of hazardous wastes or other wastes, and any information related to it, and for responding to such a notification, as provided in Article 6;

7. "Focal point" means the entity of a Party referred to in Article 5 responsible for receiving and submitting information as provided for in Articles 13 and 16;

8. "Environmentally sound management of hazardous wastes or other wastes" means taking all practicable steps to ensure that hazardous wastes or other wastes are managed in a manner which will protect human health and the environment against the adverse effects which may result from such wastes;

9. "Area under the national jurisdiction of a State" means any land, marine area or airspace within which a State exercises administrative and regulatory responsibility in accordance with international law in regard to the protection of human health or the environment;

10. "State of export" means a Party from which a transboundary movement of hazardous wastes or other wastes is planned to be initiated or is initiated;

11. "State of import" means a Party to which a transboundary movement of hazardous wastes or other wastes is planned or takes place for the purpose of disposal therein or for the purpose of loading prior to disposal in an area not under the national jurisdiction of any State;

12. "State of transit" means any State, other than the State of export or import, through which a movement of hazardous wastes or other wastes is planned or takes place;

13. "States concerned" means Parties which are States of export or import, or transit States, whether or not Parties;

14. "Person" means any natural or legal person;

15. "Exporter" means any person under the jurisdiction of the State of export who arranges for hazardous wastes or other wastes to be exported;

16. "Importer" means any person under the jurisdiction of the State of import who arranges for hazardous wastes or other wastes to be imported;

17. "Carrier" means any person who carries out the transport of hazardous wastes or other wastes;

18. "Generator" means any person whose activity produces hazardous wastes or other wastes or, if that person is not known, the person who is in possession and/or control of those wastes;

19. "Disposer" means any person to whom hazardous wastes or other wastes are shipped and who carries out the disposal of such wastes;

20. "Political and/or economic integration organization" means an organization constituted by sovereign States to which its member States have transferred competence in respect of matters governed by this Convention and which has been duly authorized, in accordance with its internal procedures, to sign, ratify, accept, approve, formally confirm or accede to it;

21. "Illegal traffic" means any transboundary movement of hazardous wastes or other wastes as specified in Article 9.

Article 3

National Definitions of Hazardous Wastes

1. Each Party shall, within six months of becoming a Party to this Convention, inform the Secretariat of the Convention of the wastes, other than those listed in Annexes I and II, considered or defined as hazardous under its national legislation and of any requirements concerning transboundary movement procedures applicable to such wastes.

2. Each Party shall subsequently inform the Secretariat of any significant changes to the information it has provided pursuant to paragraph 1.

3. The Secretariat shall forthwith inform all Parties of the information it has received pursuant to paragraphs 1 and 2.

4. Parties shall be responsible for making the information transmitted to them by the Secretariat under paragraph 3 available to their exporters.

Article 4

General Obligations

1. (a) Parties exercising their right to prohibit the import of hazardous wastes or other wastes for disposal shall inform the other Parties of their decision pursuant to Article 13.

(b) Parties shall prohibit or shall not permit the export of hazardous wastes and other wastes to the Parties which have prohibited the import of such wastes, when notified pursuant to subparagraph (a) above.

(c) Parties shall prohibit or shall not permit the export of hazardous wastes and other wastes if the State of import does not consent in writing to the specific import, in the case where that State of import has not prohibited the import of such wastes.

2. Each Party shall take the appropriate measures to:

(a) Ensure that the generation of hazardous wastes and other wastes within it is reduced to a minimum, taking into account social, technological and economic aspects;

(b) Ensure the availability of adequate disposal facilities, for the environmentally sound management of hazardous wastes and other wastes, that shall be located, to the extent possible, within it, whatever the place of their disposal;

(c) Ensure that persons involved in the management of hazardous wastes or other wastes within it take such steps as are necessary to prevent pollution due to hazardous wastes and other wastes arising from such management and, if such pollution occurs, to minimize the consequences thereof for human health and the environment;

(d) Ensure that the transboundary movement of hazardous wastes and other wastes is reduced to the minimum consistent with the environmentally sound and efficient management of such wastes, and is conducted in a manner which will protect human health and the environment against the adverse effects which may result from such movement;

(e) Not allow the export of hazardous wastes or other wastes to a State or group of States belonging to an economic and/or political integration organization that are Parties, particularly developing countries, which have prohibited by their legislation all imports, or if it has reason to believe that the wastes in question will not be managed in an environmentally sound manner, according to criteria to be decided on by the Parties at their first meeting.

(f) Require that information about a proposed transboundary movement of hazardous wastes and other wastes be provided to the States concerned, according to Annex V A, to state clearly the effects of the proposed movement on human health and the environment;

(g) Prevent the import of hazardous wastes and other wastes if it has reason to believe that the wastes in question will not be managed in an environmentally sound manner;

(h) Co-operate in activities with other Parties and interested organizations, directly and through the Secretariat, including the dissemination of information on the transboundary movement of hazardous wastes and other wastes, in order to improve the environmentally sound management of such wastes and to achieve the prevention of illegal traffic;

3. The Parties consider that illegal traffic in hazardous wastes or other wastes is criminal.

4. Each Party shall take appropriate legal, administrative and other measures to implement and enforce the provisions of this Convention, including measures to prevent and punish conduct in contravention of the Convention.

5. A Party shall not permit hazardous wastes or other wastes to be exported to a non-Party or to be imported from a non-Party.

6. The Parties agree not to allow the export of hazardous wastes or other wastes for disposal within the area south of 60° South latitude, whether or not such wastes are subject to transboundary movement.

7. Furthermore, each Party shall:

(a) Prohibit all persons under its national jurisdiction from transporting or disposing of hazardous wastes or other wastes unless such persons are authorized or allowed to perform such types of operations;

(b) Require that hazardous wastes and other wastes that are to be the subject of a transboundary movement be packaged, labelled, and transported in conformity with generally accepted and recognized international rules and standards in the field of packaging, labelling, and transport, and that due account is taken of relevant internationally recognized practices;

(c) Require that hazardous wastes and other wastes be accompanied by a movement document from the point at which a transboundary movement commences to the point of disposal.

8. Each Party shall require that hazardous wastes or other wastes, to be exported, are managed in an environmentally sound manner in the State of import or elsewhere. Technical guidelines for the environmentally sound management of wastes subject to this Convention shall be decided by the Parties at their first meeting.

9. Parties shall take the appropriate measures to ensure that the transboundary movement of hazardous wastes and other wastes only be allowed if:

(a) The State of export does not have the technical capacity and the necessary facilities, capacity or suitable disposal sites in order to dispose of the wastes in question in an environmentally sound and efficient manner; or

(b) The wastes in question are required as a raw material for recycling or recovery industries in the State of import; or

(c) The transboundary movement in question is in accordance with other criteria to be decided by the Parties, provided those criteria do not differ from the objectives of this Convention.

10. The obligation under this Convention of States in which hazardous wastes and other wastes are generated to require that those wastes are managed in an environmentally sound manner may not under any circumstances be transferred to the States of import or transit.

11. Nothing in this Convention shall prevent a Party from imposing additional requirements that are consistent with the provisions of this Convention, and are in accordance with the rules of international law, in order better to protect human health and the environment.

12. Nothing in this Convention shall affect in any way the sovereignty of States over their territorial sea established in accordance with international law, and the sovereign rights and the jurisdiction which States have in their exclusive economic zones and their continental shelves in accordance with international law, and the exercise by ships and aircraft of all States of navigational rights and freedoms as provided for in international law and as reflected in relevant international instruments.

13. Parties shall undertake to review periodically the possibilities for the reduction of the amount and/or the pollution potential of hazardous wastes and other wastes which are exported to other States, in particular to developing countries.

Article 5
Designation of Competent Authorities and Focal Point

To facilitate the implementation of this Convention, the Parties shall:

1. Designate or establish one or more competent authorities and one focal point. One competent authority shall be designated to receive the notification in case of a State of transit.

2. Inform the Secretariat, within three months of the date of the entry into force of this Convention for them, which agencies they have designated as their focal point and their competent authorities.

3. Inform the Secretariat, within one month of the date of decision, of any changes regarding the designation made by them under paragraph 2 above.

Article 6
Transboundary Movement between Parties

1. The State of export shall notify, or shall require the generator or exporter to notify, in writing, through the channel of the competent authority

of the State of export, the competent authority of the States concerned of any proposed transboundary movement of hazardous wastes or other wastes. Such notification shall contain the declarations and information specified in Annex V A, written in a language acceptable to the State of import. Only one notification needs to be sent to each State concerned.

2. The State of import shall respond to the notifier in writing, consenting to the movement with or without conditions, denying permission for the movement, or requesting additional information. A copy of the final response of the State of import shall be sent to the competent authorities of the States concerned which are Parties.

3. The State of export shall not allow the generator or exporter to commence the transboundary movement until it has received written confirmation that:

(a) The notifier has received the written consent of the State of import; and

(b) The notifier has received from the State of import confirmation of the existence of a contract between the exporter and the disposer specifying environmentally sound management of the wastes in question.

4. Each State of transit which is a Party shall promptly acknowledge to the notifier receipt of the notification. It may subsequently respond to the notifier in writing, within 60 days, consenting to the movement with or without conditions, denying permission for the movement, or requesting additional information. The State of export shall not allow the transboundary movement to commence until it has received the written consent of the State of transit. However, if at any time a Party decides not to require prior written consent, either generally or under specific conditions, for transit transboundary movements of hazardous wastes or other wastes, or modifies its requirements in this respect, it shall forthwith inform the other Parties of its decision pursuant to Article 13. In this latter case, if no response is received by the State of export within 60 days of the receipt of a given notification by the State of transit, the State of export may allow the export to proceed through the State of transit.

5. In the case of a transboundary movement of wastes where the wastes are legally defined as or considered to be hazardous wastes only:

(a) By the State of export, the requirements of paragraph 9 of this Article that apply to the importer or disposer and the State of import shall apply *mutatis mutandis* to the exporter and State of export, respectively:

(b) By the State of import, or by the States of import and transit which are Parties, the requirements of paragraphs 1, 3, 4 and 6 of this Article that apply to the exporter and State of export shall apply *mutatis mutandis* to the importer or disposer and State of import, respectively; or

(c) By any State of transit which is a Party, the provisions of paragraph 4 shall apply to such State.

6. The State of export may, subject to the written consent of the States concerned, allow the generator or the exporter to use a general notification where hazardous wastes or other wastes having the same physical and

chemical characteristics are shipped regularly to the same disposer via the same customs office of exit of the State of export via the same customs office of entry of the State of import, and, in the case of transit, via the same customs office of entry and exist of the State or States of transit.

7. The States concerned may make their written consent to the use of the general notification referred to in paragraph 6 subject to the supply of certain information, such as the exact quantities or periodical lists of hazardous wastes or other wastes to be shipped.

8. The general notification and written consent referred to in paragraphs 6 and 7 may cover multiple shipments of hazardous wastes or other wastes during a maximum period of 12 months.

9. The Parties shall require that each person who takes charge of a transboundary movement of hazardous wastes or other wastes sign the movement document either upon delivery or receipt of the wastes in question. They shall also require that the disposer inform both the exporter and the competent authority of the State of export of receipt by the disposer of the wastes in question and, in due course, of the completion of disposal as specified in the notification. If no such information is received within the State of export, the competent authority of the State of export or the exporter shall so notify the State of import.

10. The notification and response required by this Article shall be transmitted to the competent authority of the Parties concerned or to such governmental authority as may be appropriate in the case of non-Parties.

11. Any transboundary movement of hazardous wastes or other wastes shall be covered by insurance, bond or other guarantee as may be required by the State of import or any State of transit which is a Party.

Article 7

Transboundary Movement from a Party through
States which are not Parties

Paragraph 2 of Article 6 of the Convention shall apply *mutatis mutandis* to transboundary movement of hazardous wastes or other wastes from a Party through a State or States which are not Parties.

Article 8

Duty to Re-import

When a transboundary movement of hazardous wastes or other wastes to which the consent of the States concerned has been given, subject to the provisions of this Convention, cannot be completed in accordance with the terms of the contract, the State of export shall ensure that the wastes in question are taken back into the State of export, by the exporter, if alternative arrangements cannot be made for their disposal in an environmentally sound manner, within 90 days from the time that the importing State informed the State of export and the Secretariat, or such other period of time as the States concerned agree. To this end, the State of export and any Party of transit shall not oppose, hinder or prevent the return of those wastes to the State of export.

Article 9

Illegal Traffic

1. For the purpose of this Convention, any transboundary movement of hazardous wastes or other wastes:

(a) without notification pursuant to the provisions of this Convention to all States concerned; or

(b) without the consent pursuant to the provisions of this Convention of a State concerned; or

(c) with consent obtained from States concerned through falsification, misrepresentation or fraud; or

(d) that does not conform in a material may with the documents; or

(e) that results in deliberate disposal (e.g. dumping) of hazardous wastes or other wastes in contravention of this Convention and of general principles of international law, shall be deemed to be illegal traffic.

2. In case of a transboundary movement of hazardous wastes or other wastes deemed to be illegal traffic as the result of conduct on the part of the exporter or generator, the State of export shall ensure that the wastes in question are:

(a) taken back by the exporter or the generator or, if necessary, by itself into the State of export, or, if impracticable,

(b) are otherwise disposed of in accordance with the provisions of this Convention, within 30 days from the time the State of export has been informed about the illegal traffic or such other period of time as States concerned may agree. To this end the Parties concerned shall not oppose, hinder or prevent the return of those wastes to the State of export.

3. In the case of a transboundary movement of hazardous wastes or other wastes deemed to be illegal traffic as the result of conduct on the part of the importer or disposer, the State of import shall ensure that the wastes in question are disposed of in an environmentally sound manner by the importer or disposer or, if necessary, by itself within 30 days from the time the illegal traffic has come to the attention of the State of import or such other period of time as the States concerned may agree. To this end, the Parties concerned shall co-operate, as necessary, in the disposal of the wastes in an environmentally sound manner.

4. In cases where the responsibility for the illegal traffic cannot be assigned either to the exporter or generator or to the importer or disposer, the Parties concerned or other Parties, as appropriate, shall ensure, through co-operation, that the wastes in question are disposed of as soon as possible in an environmentally sound manner either in the State of export or the State of import or elsewhere as appropriate.

5. Each Party shall introduce appropriate national/domestic legislation to prevent and punish illegal traffic. The Parties shall co-operate with a view to achieving the objects of this Article.

Article 10

International Co-operation

1. The Parties shall co-operate with each other in order to improve and achieve environmentally sound management of hazardous wastes and other wastes.

2. To this end, the Parties shall:

(a) Upon request, make available information, whether on a bilateral or multilateral basis, with a view to promoting the environmentally sound management of hazardous wastes and other wastes, including harmonization of technical standards and practices for the adequate management of hazardous wastes and other wastes;

(b) Co-operate in monitoring the effects of the management of hazardous wastes on human health and the environment;

(c) Co-operate, subject to their national laws, regulations and policies, in the development and implementation of new environmentally sound low-waste technologies and the improvement of existing technologies with a view to eliminating, as far as practicable, the generation of hazardous wastes and other wastes and achieving more effective and efficient methods of ensuring their management in an environmentally sound manner, including the study of the economic, social and environmental effects of the adoption of such new or improved technologies;

(d) Co-operate actively, subject to their national laws, regulations and policies, in the transfer of technology and management systems related to the environmentally sound management of hazardous wastes and other wastes. They shall also co-operate in developing the technical capacity among Parties, especially those which may need and request technical assistance in this field;

(e) Co-operate in developing appropriate technical guidelines and/or codes of practice.

3. The Parties shall employ appropriate means to co-operate in order to assist developing countries in the implementation of subparagraphs a, b, c and d of paragraph 2 of Article 4.

4. Taking into account the needs of developing countries, co-operation between Parties and the competent international organizations is encouraged to promote, *inter alia,* public awareness, the development of sound management of hazardous wastes and other wastes and the adoption of new low-waste technologies.

Article 11

Bilateral, Multilateral and Regional Agreements

1. Notwithstanding the provisions of Article 4, paragraph 5, Parties may enter into bilateral, multilateral, or regional agreements or arrangements regarding transboundary movement of hazardous wastes or other wastes with Parties or non-Parties provided that such agreements or arrangements do not derogate from the environmentally sound management of hazardous wastes and other wastes as required by this Convention. These agreements or arrangements shall stipulate provisions which are not less environmentally

sound than those provided for by this Convention in particular taking into account the interests of developing countries.

2. Parties shall notify the Secretariat of any bilateral, multilateral or regional agreements or arrangements referred to in paragraph 1 and those which they have entered into prior to the entry into force of this Convention for them, for the purpose of controlling transboundary movements of hazardous wastes and other wastes which take place entirely among the Parties to such agreements. The provisions of this Convention shall not affect transboundary movements which take place pursuant of such agreements provided that such agreements are compatible with the environmentally sound management of hazardous wastes and other wastes as required by this Convention.

Article 12

Consultations on Liability

The Parties shall co-operate with a view to adopting, as soon as practicable, a protocol setting out appropriate rules and procedures in the field of liability and compensation for damage resulting from the transboundary movement and disposal of hazardous wastes and other wastes.

Article 13

Transmission of Information

1. The Parties shall, whenever it comes to their knowledge, ensure that, in the case of an accident occurring during the transboundary movement of hazardous wastes or other wastes or their disposal, which are likely to present risks to human health and the environment in other States, those states are immediately informed.

2. The Parties shall inform each other, through the Secretariat, of:

(a) Changes regarding the designation of competent authorities and/or focal points, pursuant to Article 5;

(b) Changes in their national definition of hazardous wastes, pursuant to Article 3;

and, as soon as possible,

(c) Decisions made by them not to consent totally or partially to the import of hazardous wastes or other wastes for disposal within the area under their national jurisdiction;

(d) Decisions taken by them to limit or ban the export of hazardous wastes or other wastes;

(e) Any other information required pursuant to paragraph 4 of this Article.

3. The Parties, consistent with national laws and regulations, shall transmit, through the Secretariat, to the Conference of the Parties established under Article 15, before the end of each calendar year, a report on the previous calendar year, containing the following information:

(a) Competent authorities and focal points that have been designated by them pursuant to Article 5;

(b) Information regarding transboundary movements of hazardous wastes or other wastes in which they have been involved, including:

(i) The amount of hazardous wastes and other wastes exported, their category, characteristics, destination, any transit country and disposal method as stated on the response to notification;

(ii) The amount of hazardous wastes and other wastes imported, their category, characteristics, origin, and disposal methods;

(iii) Disposals which did not proceed as intended;

(iv) Efforts to achieve a reduction of the amount of hazardous wastes or other wastes subject to transboundary movement;

(c) Information on the measures adopted by them in implementation of this Convention;

(d) Information on available qualified statistics which have been complied by them on the effects on human health and the environment of the generation, transportation and disposal of hazardous wastes or other wastes;

(e) Information concerning bilateral, multilateral and regional agreements and arrangements entered into pursuant to Article 11 of this Convention;

(f) Information on accidents occurring during the transboundary movement and disposal of hazardous wastes and other wastes and on the measures undertaken to deal with them;

(g) Information on disposal options operated within the area of their national jurisdiction;

(h) Information on measures undertaken for development of technologies for the reduction and/or elimination of production of hazardous wastes and other wastes; and

(i) Such other matters as the Conference of the Parties shall deem relevant.

4. The Parties, consistent with national laws and regulations, shall ensure that copies of each notification concerning any given transboundary movement of hazardous wastes or other wastes, and the response to it, are sent to the Secretariat when a Party considers that its environment may be affected by that transboundary movement has requested that this should be done.

Article 14

Financial Aspects

1. The Parties agree that, according to the specific needs of different regions and subregions, regional or sub-regional centres for training and technology transfers regarding the management of hazardous wastes and other wastes and the minimization of their generation should be established. The Parties shall decide on the establishment of appropriate funding mechanisms of a voluntary nature.

2. The Parties shall consider the establishment of a revolving fund to assist on an interim basis in case of emergency situations to minimize damage

from accidents arising from transboundary movement of hazardous wastes and other wastes or during the disposal of those wastes.

Article 15

Conference of the Parties

1. A Conference of the Parties is hereby established. The first meeting of the Conference of the Parties shall be convened by the Executive Director of UNEP not later than one year after the entry into force of this Convention. Thereafter, ordinary meetings of the Conference of the Parties shall be held at regular intervals to be determined by the Conference at its first meeting.

2. Extraordinary meetings of the Conference of the Parties shall be held at such other times as may be deemed necessary by the Conference, or at the written request of any Party, provided that, within six months of the request being communicated to them by the Secretariat, it is supported by at least one third of the Parties.

3. The Conference of the Parties shall by consensus agree upon and adopt rules of procedure for itself and for any subsidiary body it may establish, as well as financial rules to determine in particular the financial participation of the Parties under this Convention.

4. The Parties at their first meeting shall consider any additional measures needed to assist them in fulfilling their responsibilities with respect to the protection and the preservation of the marine environment in the context of this Convention.

5. The Conference of the Parties shall keep under continuous review and evaluation the effective implementation of this Convention, and, in addition, shall:

(a) Promote the harmonization of appropriate policies, strategies and measures for minimizing harm to human health and the environment by hazardous wastes and other wastes;

(b) Consider and adopt, as required, amendments to this Convention and its annexes, taking into consideration, *inter alia,* available scientific, technical, economic and environmental information;

(c) Consider and undertake any additional action that may be required for the achievement of the purposes of this Convention in the light of experience gained in its operation and in the operation of the agreements and arrangements envisaged in Article 11;

(d) Consider and adopt protocols as required; and

(e) Establish such subsidiary bodies as are deemed necessary for the implementation of this Convention.

6. The United Nations, its specialized agencies, as well as any State not party to this Convention, may be represented as observers at meetings of the Conference of the Parties. Any other body or agency, whether national or international, governmental or non-governmental, qualified in fields relating to hazardous wastes or other wastes which has informed the Secretariat of its wish to be represented as an observer at a meeting of the Conference of the Parties, may be admitted unless at least one third of the Parties present

object. The admission and participation of observers shall be subject to the rules of procedure adopted by the Conference of the Parties.

7. The Conference of the Parties shall undertake three years after the entry into force of this Convention, and at least every six years thereafter, an evaluation of its effectiveness and, if deemed necessary, to consider the adoption of a complete or partial ban of transboundary movements of hazardous wastes and other wastes in light of the latest scientific, environmental, technical and economic information.

Article 16

Secretariat

1. The functions of the Secretariat shall be:

(a) To arrange for and service meetings provided for in Article 15 and 17;

(b) To prepare and transmit reports based upon information received in accordance with Articles 3, 4, 6, 11 and 13 as well as upon information derived from meetings of subsidiary bodies established upon Article 15 as well as upon, as appropriate, information provided by relevant intergovernmental and nongovernmental entities;

(c) To prepare reports on its activities carried out in implementation of its functions under this Convention and present them to the Conference of the Parties;

(d) To ensure the necessary coordination with relevant international bodies, and in particular to enter into such administrative and contractual arrangements as may be required for the effective discharge of its functions;

(e) To communicate with focal points and competent authorities established by the Parties in accordance with Article 5 of this Convention;

(f) To compile information concerning authorized national sites and facilities of Parties available for the disposal of their hazardous wastes and other wastes and to circulate this information among Parties;

(g) To receive and convey information from and to Parties on:

sources of technical assistance and training;

available technical and scientific know-how;

sources of advice and expertise; and

availability of resources

with a view to assisting them, upon request, in such areas as:

the handling of the notification system of this Convention;

the management of hazardous wastes and other wastes;

environmentally sound technologies relating to hazardous wastes and other wastes, such as low- and non-waste technology;

the assessment of disposal capabilities and sites;

the monitoring of hazardous wastes and other wastes; and

emergency responses;

(h) To provide Parties, upon request, with information on consultants or consulting firms having the necessary technical competence in the field, which can assist them to examine a notification for a transboundary movement, the concurrence of a shipment of hazardous wastes or other wastes with the relevant notification, and/or the fact that the proposed disposal facilities for hazardous wastes or other wastes are environmentally sound, when they have reason to believe that the wastes in question will not be managed in an environmentally sound manner. Any such examination would not be at the expense of the Secretariat;

(i) To assist Parties upon request in their identification of cases of illegal traffic and to circulate immediately to the Parties concerned any information it has received regarding illegal traffic;

(j) To co-operate with Parties and with relevant and competent international organizations and agencies in the provision of experts and equipment for the purpose of rapid assistance to States in the event of an emergency situation; and

(k) To perform such other functions relevant to the purposes of this Convention as may be determined by the Conference of the Parties.

2. The Secretariat functions will be carried out on an interim basis by UNEP until the completion of the first meeting of the Conference of the Parties held pursuant to Article 15.

3. At its first meeting, the Conference of the Parties shall designate the Secretariat from among those existing competent intergovernmental organizations which have signified their willingness to carry out the Secretariat functions under this Convention. At this meeting, the Conference of the Parties shall also evaluate the implementation by the interim Secretariat of the functions assigned to it, in particular under paragraph 1 above, and decide upon the structures appropriate for those functions.

Article 17

Amendment of the Convention

1. Any Party may propose amendments to this Convention and any Party to a protocol may propose amendments to that protocol. Such amendments shall take due account, *inter alia,* of relevant scientific and technical considerations.

2. Amendments to this Convention shall be adopted at a meeting of the Conference of the Parties. Amendments to any protocol shall be adopted at a meeting of the Parties to the protocol in question. The text of any proposed amendment to this Convention or to any protocol, except as may otherwise be provided in such protocol, shall be communicated to the Parties by the Secretariat at least six months before the meeting at which it is proposed for adoption. The Secretariat shall also communicate proposed amendments to the Signatories to this Convention for information.

3. The Parties shall make every effort to reach agreement on any proposed amendment to this Convention by consensus. If all efforts at consensus have been exhausted, and no agreement reached, the amendment shall as a last resort be adopted by a three-fourths majority vote of the Parties

present and voting at the meeting, and shall be submitted by the Depositary to all Parties for ratification, approval, formal confirmation or acceptance.

4. The procedure mentioned in paragraph 3 above shall apply to amendments to any protocol, except that a two-thirds majority of the Parties to that protocol present and voting at the meeting shall suffice for their adoption.

5. Instruments of ratification, approval, formal confirmation or acceptance of amendments shall be deposited with the Depositary. Amendments adopted in accordance with paragraphs 3 or 4 above shall enter into force between Parties having accepted them on the ninetieth day after the receipt by the Depositary of their instrument of ratification, approval, formal confirmation or acceptance by at least three-fourths of the Parties who accepted the amendments to the protocol concerned, except as may otherwise be provided in such protocol. The amendments shall enter into force for any other Party on the ninetieth day after that Party deposits its instrument of ratification, approval, formal confirmation or acceptance of the amendments.

6. For the purpose of this Article, "Parties present and voting" means Parties present and casting an affirmative or negative vote.

Article 18

Adoption and Amendment of Annexes

1. The annexes of this Convention or to any protocol shall form an integral part of this Convention or of such protocol, as the case may be and, unless expressly provided otherwise, a reference to this Convention or its protocols constitutes at the same time a reference to any annexes thereto. Such annexes shall be restricted to scientific, technical and administrative matters.

2. Except as may be otherwise provided in any protocol with respect to its annexes, the following procedure shall apply to the proposal, adoption and entry into force of additional annexes to this Convention or of annexes to a protocol:

(a) Annexes to this Convention and its protocols shall be proposed and adopted according to the procedure laid down in Article 17, paragraphs 2, 3 and 4;

(b) Any Party that is unable to accept an additional annex to this Convention or an annex to any protocol to which it is party shall so notify the Depositary, in writing, within six months from the date of the communication of the adoption by the Depositary. The Depositary shall without delay notify all Parties of any such notification received. A Party may at any time substitute an acceptance for a previous declaration of objection and the annexes shall thereupon enter into force for that Party;

(c) On the expiry of six months from the date of the circulation of the communication by the Depositary, the annex shall become effective for all Parties to this Convention or to any protocol concerned, which have not submitted a notification in accordance with the provision of subparagraph (b) above.

3. The proposal, adoption and entry into force of amendments to annexes to this Convention or to any protocol shall be subject to the same procedure as for the proposal, adoption and entry into force of annexes to the Conven-

tion or annexes to a protocol. Annexes and amendments thereto shall take due account, *inter alia*, of relevant scientific and technical considerations.

4. If an additional annex or an amendment to an annex involves an amendment to this Convention or to any protocol, the additional annex or amended annex shall not enter into force until such time as the amendment to this Convention or to the protocol enters into force.

Article 19

Verification

Any Party which has reason to believe that another Party is acting or has acted in breach of its obligations under this Convention may inform the Secretariat thereof, and in such an event, shall simultaneously and immediately inform, directly or through the Secretariat, the Party against whom the allegations are made. All relevant information should be submitted by the Secretariat to the Parties.

Article 20

Settlement of Disputes

1. In case of a dispute between Parties as to the interpretation or application of, or compliance with, this Convention or any protocol thereto, they shall seek a settlement of the dispute through negotiation or any other peaceful means of their own choice.

2. If the Parties concerned cannot settle their dispute through the means mentioned in the preceding paragraph, the dispute, if the parties to the dispute agree, shall be submitted to the International Court of Justice or to arbitration under the conditions set out in Annex VI on Arbitration. However, failure to reach common agreement on submission of the dispute to the International Court of Justice or to arbitration shall not absolve the Parties from the responsibility of continuing to seek to resolve it by the means referred to in paragraph 1.

3. When ratifying, accepting, approving, formally confirming or acceding to this Convention, or at any time thereafter, a State or political and/or economic integration organization may declare that it recognizes as compulsory *ipso facto* and without special agreement, in relation to any Party accepting the same obligation:

   (a) submission of the dispute to the International Court of Justice; and/or

   (b) arbitration in accordance with the procedures set out in Annex VI.

Such declaration shall be notified in writing to the Secretariat which shall communicate it to the Parties.

Article 21

Signature

This Convention shall be open for signature by States, by Namibia, represented by the United Nations Council for Namibia, and by political and/or economic integration organizations, in Basel on 22 March 1989, at the Federal Department of Foreign Affairs of Switzerland in Berne from 23 March

1989 to 30 June 1989 and at United Nations Headquarters in New York from 1 July 1989 to 22 March 1990.

Article 22

Ratification, Acceptance, Formal Confirmation or Approval

1. This Convention shall be subject to ratification, acceptance or approval by States and by Namibia, represented by the United Nations Council for Namibia, and to formal confirmation or approval by political and/or economic integration organizations. Instruments of ratification, acceptance, formal confirmation, or approval shall be deposited with the Depositary.

2. Any organization referred to in paragraph 1 above which becomes a Party to this Convention without any of its member States being a party shall be bound by all the obligations under the Convention. In the case of such organizations, one or more of whose member States is a Party to the Convention, the organization and its member States shall decide on their respective responsibilities for the performance of their obligations under the Convention. In such cases, the organization and the member States shall not be entitled to exercise rights under the Convention concurrently.

3. In their instruments of formal confirmation or approval, the organizations referred to in paragraph 1 above shall declare the extent of their competence with respect to the matters governed by the Convention. These organizations shall also inform the Depositary, who will inform the Parties of any substantial modification in the extent of their competence.

Article 23

Accession

1. This Convention shall be open for accession by States, by Namibia, represented by the United Nations Council for Namibia, and by political and/or economic integration organizations from the day after the date on which the Convention is closed for signature. The instruments of accession shall be deposited with the Depositary.

2. In their instruments of accession, the organizations referred to in paragraph 1 above shall declare the extent of their competence with respect to the matters governed by the Convention. These organizations shall also inform the Depositary of any substantial modification in the extent of their competence.

3. The provisions of Article 22, paragraph 2, shall apply to political and/or economic integration organizations which accede to this Convention.

Article 24

Right to Vote

1. Except as provided for in paragraph 2 below, each Contracting Party to this Convention shall have one vote.

2. Political and/or economic integration organizations, in matters within their competence, in accordance with Article 22, paragraph 3, and Article 23, paragraph 2, shall exercise their right to vote with a number of votes equal to the number of their member States which are Parties to the Convention or the relevant protocol. Such organizations shall not exercise their right to vote if their member States exercise theirs, and vice versa.

Article 25

Entry into Force

1. This Convention shall enter into force on the ninetieth day after the date of deposit of the twentieth instrument of ratification, acceptance, formal confirmation, approval or accession.

2. For each State or political and/or economic integration organization which ratifies, accepts, approves or formally confirms this Convention or accedes thereto after the date of the deposit of the twentieth instrument of ratification, acceptance, approval, formal confirmation or accession, it shall enter into force on the ninetieth day after the date of deposit by such State or political and/or economic integration organization of its instrument of ratification, acceptance, approval, formal confirmation or accession.

3. For the purposes of paragraphs 1 and 2 above, any instrument deposited by a political and/or economic integration organization shall not be counted as additional to those deposited by member States of such organization.

Article 26

Reservations and Declarations

1. No reservation or exception may be made to this Convention.

2. Paragraph 1 of this Article does not preclude a State or political and/or economic integration organization, when signing, ratifying, accepting, approving, formally confirming or acceding to this Convention, from making declarations or statements, however phrased or named, with a view, *inter alia,* to the harmonization of its laws and regulations with the provisions of this Convention, provided that such declarations or statements do not purport to exclude or to modify the legal effects of the provisions of the Convention in their application to that State.

Article 27

Withdrawal

1. At any time after three years from the date on which this Convention has entered into force for a Party, that Party may withdraw from the Convention by giving written notification to the Depositary.

2. Withdrawal shall be effective one year from receipt of notification by the Depositary, or on such later date as may be specified in the notification.

Article 28

Depositary

The Secretary–General of the United Nations shall be the Depository of this Convention and of any protocol thereto.

Article 29

Authentic Texts

The original Arabic, Chinese, English, French, Russian and Spanish texts of this Convention are equally authentic.

* * *

ANNEX I

CATEGORIES OF WASTES TO BE CONTROLLED

Waste Streams
Y1   Clinical wastes from medical care in hospitals, medical centers and clinics
Y2   Wastes from the production and preparation of pharmaceutical products
Y3   Waste pharmaceuticals, drugs and medicines
Y4   Wastes from the production, formulation and use of biocides and phytopharma-
        ceuticals
Y5   Wastes from the manufacture, formulation and use of wood preserving chemicals
Y6   Wastes from the production, formulation and use of organic solvents
Y7   Wastes from heat treatment and tempering operations containing cyanides
Y8   Waste mineral oils unfit for their originally intended use
Y9   Waste oils/water, hydrocarbons/water mixtures, emulsions
Y10 Waste substances and articles containing or contaminated with polychlorinated
        biphenyls (PCBs) and/or polychlorinated terphenyls (PCTs) and/or polybromi-
        nated biphenyls (PBBs)
Y11 Waste tarry residues arising from refining, distillation and any pyrolytic treat-
        ment
Y12 Wastes from production, formulation and use of inks, dyes, pigments, paints,
        lacquers, varnish
Y13 Wastes from production, formulation and use of resins, latex, plasticizers,
        glues/adhesives
Y14 Waste chemical substances arising from research and development or teaching
        activities which are not identified and/or are new and whose effects on man
        and/or the environment are not known
Y15 Wastes of an explosive nature not subject to other legislation
Y16 Wastes from production, formulation and use of photographic chemicals and
        processing materials
Y17 Wastes resulting from surface treatment of metals and plastics
Y18 Residues arising from industrial waste disposal operations

Wastes Having as Constituents:
Y19 Metal carbonyls
Y20 Beryllium; beryllium compounds
Y21 Hexavalent chromium compounds
Y22 Cooper compounds
Y23 Zinc compounds
Y24 Arsenic; arsenic compounds
Y25 Selenium; selenium compounds
Y26 Cadmium; cadmium compounds
Y27 Antimony; antimony compounds
Y28 Tellurium; tellurium compounds
Y29 Mercury; mercury compounds
Y30 Thallium; thallium compounds
Y31 Lead; lead compounds
Y32 Inorganic fluorine compounds excluding calcium fluoride
Y33 Inorganic cyanides
Y34 Acidic solutions or acids in solid form
Y35 Basic solutions or bases in solid form
Y36 Asbestos (dust and fibres)
Y37 Organic phosphorous compounds
Y38 Organic cyanides
Y39 Phenols; phenol compounds including chlorophenols
Y40 Ethers
Y41 Halogenated organic solvents
Y42 Organic solvents excluding halogenated solvents
Y43 Any congenor of polychlorinated dibenzo-furan
Y44 Any congenor of polychlorinated dibenzo-p-dioxin

Y45 Organohalogen compounds other than substances referred to in this Annex (e.g. Y39, Y41, Y42, Y43, Y44).

ANNEX II
CATEGORIES OF WASTES REQUIRING SPECIAL CONSIDERATION

Y46 Wastes collected from households
Y47 Residues arising from the incineration of household wastes

ANNEX III
LIST OF HAZARDOUS CHARACTERISTICS

UN Class [1]	Code	Characteristics
1	H1	**Explosive** An explosive substance or waste is a solid or liquid substance or waste (or mixture of substances or wastes) which is in itself capable by chemical reaction of producing gas at such a temperature and pressure and at such a speed as to cause damage to the surroundings.
3	H3	**Flammable liquids** The word "flammable" has the same meaning as "inflammable". Flammable liquids are liquids, or mixtures of liquids, or liquids containing solids in solution or suspension (for example, paints, varnishes, lacquers, etc., but not including substances or wastes otherwise classified on account of their dangerous characteristics) which give off a flammable vapour at temperatures of not more than 60.5°C, closed-cup test, or not more than 65.6°C, open-cup test. (Since the results of open-cup tests and of closed-cup tests are not strictly comparable and even individual results by the same test are often variable, regulations varying from the above figures to make allowance for such differences would be within the spirit of this definition.)
4.1	H4.1	**Flammable solids** Solids, or waste solids, other than those classed as explosives, which under conditions encountered in transport are readily combustible, or may cause or contribute to fire through friction.
4.2	H4.2	**Substances or wastes liable to spontaneous combustion** Substances or wastes which are liable to spontaneous heating under normal conditions encountered in transport, or to heating upon contact with air, and being then liable to catch fire.
4.3	H4.3	**Substances or wastes which, in contact with water emit flammable gases** Substances or wastes which, by interaction with water, are liable to become spontaneously flammable or to give off flammable gases in dangerous quantities.
5.1	H5.1	**Oxidizing** Substances or wastes which, while in themselves not necessarily combustible, may, generally by yielding oxygen cause, or contribute to, the combustion of other materials.
5.2	H5.2	**Organic Peroxides** Organic substances or wastes which contain the bivalent–O–O– structure are thermally unstable substances which may undergo exothermic self-accelerating decomposition.
6.1	H6.1	**Poisonous (Acute)** Substances or wastes liable either to cause death or serious injury or to harm human health if swallowed or inhaled or by skin contact.

UN Class [1]	Code	Characteristics
6.2	H6.2	**Infectious substances** Substances or wastes containing viable microorganisms or their toxins which are known or suspected to cause disease in animals or humans.
8	H8	**Corrosives** Substances or wastes which, by chemical action, will cause severe damage when in contact with living tissue, or, in the case of leakage, will materially damage, or even destroy, other goods or the means of transport; they may also cause other hazards.
9	H10	**Liberation of toxic gases in contact with air or water** Substances or wastes which, by interaction with air or water, are liable to give off toxic gases in dangerous quantities.
9	H11	**Toxic (Delayed or chronic)** Substances or wastes which, if they are inhaled or ingested or if they penetrate the skin, may involve delayed or chronic effects, including carcinogenicity.
9	H12	**Ecotoxic** Substances or wastes which if released present or may present immediate or delayed adverse impacts to the environment by means of bioaccumulation and/or toxic effects upon biotic systems.
9	H13	**Capable, by any means, after disposal, of yielding another material, e.g., leachate, which possesses any of the characteristics listed above.**

[1] Corresponds to the hazards classification system included in the United Nations Recommendations on the Transport of Dangerous Goods (ST/SG/AC.10/Rev.5, United Nations, New York, 1988).

Tests

The potential hazards posed by certain types of wastes are not yet fully documented; tests to define quantitatively these hazards do not exist. Further research is necessary in order to develop means to characterize potential hazards posed to man and/or the environment by these wastes. Standardized tests have been derived with respect to pure substances and materials. Many countries have developed national tests which can be applied to materials listed in Annex I, in order to decide if these materials exhibit any of the characteristics listed in this Annex.

ANNEX IV
DISPOSAL OPERATIONS

A. *Operations which do not lead to the Possibility of Resource Recovery, Recycling, Reclamation, Direct re-use or Alternative Users*

Section A encompasses all such disposal operations which occur in practice.

D1   Deposit into or onto land, (e.g., landfill, etc.)
D2   Land treatment, (e.g., biodegradation of liquid or sludgy discards in soils, etc.)
D3   Deep injection, (e.g. injection of pumpable discards into wells, salt domes or naturally occurring repositories, etc.)
D4   Surface impoundment, (e.g., placement of liquid or sludge discards into pits, ponds or lagoons, etc.)
D5   Specially engineered landfill, (e.g., placement into lined discrete cells which are capped and isolated from one another and the environment, etc.)
D6   Release into a water body except seas/oceans
D7   Release into seas/oceans including sea-bed insertion

D8 Biological treatment not specified elsewhere in this Annex which results in final compounds or mixtures which are discarded by means of any of the operations in Section A

D9 Physico chemical treatment not specified elsewhere in this Annex which results in final compounds or mixtures which are discarded by means of any of the operations in Section A, (e.g., evaporation, drying, calcination, neutralization, precipitation, etc.)

D10 Incineration on land

D11 Incineration at sea

D12 Permanent storage (e.g., emplacement of containers in a mine, etc.)

D13 Blending or mixing prior to submission to any of the operations in Section A

D14 Repackaging prior to submission to any of the operations in Section A

D15 Storage pending any of the operations in Section A

B. *Operations which may lead to Resource Recovery, Recycling, Reclamation, Direct re-use or Alternative Uses*

Section B encompasses all such operations with respect to materials legally defined as or considered to be hazardous waste and which otherwise would have been destined for operations included in Section A

R1 Use as a fuel (other than in direct incineration) or other means to generate energy

R2 Solvent reclamation/regeneration

R3 Recycling/reclamation of organic substances which are not used as solvents

R4 Recycling/reclamation of metals and metal compounds

R5 Recycling/reclamation of other inorganic materials

R6 Regeneration of acids or bases

R7 Recovery of components used for pollution abatement

R8 Recovery of components from catalysts

R9 Used oil-refining or other uses of previously used oil

R10 Land treatment resulting in benefit to agriculture or ecological improvement

R11 Uses of residual materials obtained from any of the operations numbered R1–R10

R12 Exchange of wastes for submission to any of the operations numbered R1–R11

R13 Accumulation of material intended for any operation in Section B

ANNEX V A

INFORMATION TO BE PROVIDED ON NOTIFICATION

1. Reason for waste export
2. Exporter of the waste
3. Generator(s) of the waste and site of generation
4. Disposer of the waste and actual site of disposal
5. Intended carrier(s) of the waste of their agents, if known
6. Country of export of the waste
   Competent authority
7. Expected countries of transit
   Competent authority
8. Country of import of the waste
   Competent authority
9. General or single notification
10. Projected date(s) of shipment(s) and period of time over which waste is to be exported and proposed itinerary (including point of entry and exit)
11. Means of transport envisaged (road, rail, sea, air, inland waters)
12. Information relating to insurance
13. Designation and physical description of the wastes including Y number and UN number and its composition and information on any special handling requirements including emergency provisions in case of accidents
14. Type of packaging envisaged (e.g. bulk, drummed, tanker)
15. Estimated quantity in weight/volume
16. Process by which the waste is generated

17. For wastes listed in Annex I, classifications from Annex III: hazardous characteristic, H number, and UN class.
18. Method of disposal as per Annex IV
19. Declaration by the generator and exporter that the information is correct
20. Information transmitted (including technical description of the plant) to the exporter or generator from the disposer of the waste upon which the latter has based his assessment that there was no reason to believe that the wastes will not be managed in an environmentally sound manner in accordance with the laws and regulations of the country of import.
21. Information concerning the contract between the exporter and disposer.

ANNEX V B
INFORMATION TO BE PROVIDED ON THE MOVEMENT DOCUMENT

1. Exporter of the waste
2. Generator(s) of the waste and site of generation
3. Disposer of the waste and actual site of disposal
4. Carrier(s) of the waste or his agent(s)
5. Subject of general or single notification
6. The date the transboundary movement started and date(s) and signature on receipt by each person who takes charge of the waste
7. Means of transport (road, rail, inland, waterway, sea, air) including countries of export, transit and import, als point of entry and exit where these have been designated
8. General description of the waste (physical state, proper UN shipping name and class, UN number, Y number and H number as applicable)
9. Information on special handling requirements including emergency provision in case of accidents
10. Type and number of packages
11. Quantity in weight/volume
12. Declaration by the generator or exporter that the information is correct
13. Declaration by the generator or exporter indicating no objection from the component authorities of all States concerned which are Parties
14. Certification by disposer of receipt at designated disposal facility and indication of method of disposal and of the approximate date of disposal

ANNEX VI
ARBITRATION
Article 1

Unless the agreement referred to in Article 20 of the Convention provides otherwise, the arbitration procedure shall be conducted in accordance with Articles 2 to 10 below.

Article 2

The claimant party shall notify the Secretariat that the parties have agreed to submit the dispute to arbitration pursuant to paragraph 2 or paragraph 3 of Article 20 and include, in particular, the Articles of the Convention the interpretation or application of which are at issue. The Secretariat shall forward the information thus received to all Parties to the Convention.

Article 3

The arbitral tribunal shall consist of three members. Each of the Parties to the dispute shall appoint an arbitrator, and the two arbitrators so appointed shall designate by common agreement the third arbitrator, who shall be the chairman of the tribunal. The latter shall not be a national of one of the parties to the dispute, nor have his usual place of residence in the territory of one of these parties, nor be employed by any of them, nor have dealt with the case in any other capacity.

Article 4

1. If the chairman of the arbitral tribunal has not been designated within two months of the appointment of the second arbitrator, the Secretary–General of the United Nations shall, at the request of either party, designate him within a further two months period.

2. If one of the parties to the dispute does not appoint an arbitrator within two months of the receipt of the request, the other party may inform the Secretary–General of the United Nations who shall designate the chairman of the arbitral tribunal within a further two months' period. Upon designation, the chairman of the arbitral shall request the party which has not appointed an arbitration to do so within two months. After such period, he shall inform the Secretary–General of the United Nations, who shall make this appointment within a further two months' period.

Article 5

1. The arbitral tribunal shall render its decision in accordance with international law and in accordance with the provisions of this Convention.

2. Any arbitral tribunal constituted under the provisions of this Annex shall draw up its own rules of procedure.

Article 6

1. The decisions of the arbitral tribunal both on procedure and on substance, shall be taken by majority vote of its members.

2. The tribunal may take all appropriate measures in order to establish the facts. It may, at the request of one of the parties, recommend essential interim measures of protection.

3. The parties to the dispute shall provide all facilities necessary for the effective conduct of the proceedings.

4. The absence or default of a party in the dispute shall not constitute an impediment to the proceedings.

Article 7

The tribunal may hear and determine counter-claims arising directly out of the subject-matter of the dispute.

Article 8

Unless the arbitral tribunal determines otherwise because of the particular circumstances of the case, the expenses of the tribunal, including the remuneration of its members, shall be borne by the parties to the dispute in equal shares. The tribunal shall keep a record of all its expenses, and shall furnish a final statement thereof to the parties.

Article 9

Any Party that has an interest of a legal nature in the subject-matter of the dispute which may be affected by the decision in the case, may intervene in the proceedings with the consent of the tribunal.

Article 10

1. The tribunal shall render its award within five months of the date on which it is established unless it finds it necessary to extend the time-limit for a period which should not exceed five months.

2. The award of the arbitral tribunal shall be accompanied by a statement of reasons. It shall be final and binding upon the parties to the dispute.

3. Any dispute which may arise between the parties concerning the interpretation or execution of the award may be submitted by either party to the arbitral tribunal which made the award or, if the latter cannot be seized thereof, to another tribunal constituted for this purpose in the same manner as the first.

5.7 BAMAKO CONVENTION ON THE BAN OF IMPORT INTO AFRICA AND THE CONTROL OF TRANSBOUNDARY MOVEMENT AND MANAGEMENT OF HAZARDOUS WASTES WITHIN AFRICA (WITH ANNEXES). Concluded at Bamako, 29 January 1991. Not in force as of 31 December 1992. 30 I.L.M. 775 (1991)

PREAMBLE

The Parties to this Convention,

1. Mindful of the growing threat to human health and the environment posed by the increased generation and the complexity of hazardous wastes,

2. Further mindful that the most effective way of protecting human health and the environment from the dangers posed by such wastes is the reduction of their generation to a minimum in terms of quantity and/or hazard potential,

3. Aware of the risk of damage to human health and the environment caused by transboundary movements of hazardous wastes,

4. Reiterating that States should ensure that the generator should carry out his responsibilities with regard to the transport and disposal of hazardous wastes in a manner that is consistent with the protection of human health and environment, whatever the place of disposal,

5. Recalling relevant Chapter of the Charter of the Organization of African Unity (OAU) on environmental protection, the African Charter for Human and Peoples' Rights, chapter IX of the Lagos Plan of Action and other Recommendations adopted by the Organization of African Unity on the environment,

6. Further recognizing the sovereignty of States to ban the importation into, and the transit through, their territory, of hazardous wastes and substances for human health and environmental reasons,

7. Recognizing also the increasing mobilization in Africa for the prohibition of transboundary movements of hazardous wastes and their disposal in African countries,

8. Convinced that hazardous wastes should, as far as is compatible with environmentally sound and efficient management, be disposed in the State where they were generated,

9. Convinced that the effective control and minimization of transboundary movements of hazardous wastes will act as an incentive, in Africa and elsewhere, for the reduction of the volume of the generation of such wastes,

10. Noting that a number of international and regional agreements deal with the problem of the protection and preservation of the environment with regard to the transit of dangerous goods,

11. Taking into account the Declaration of the United Nations Conference on the Human Environment (Stockholm, 1972), the Cairo Guidelines and Principles for the Environmentally Sound Management of Hazardous Wastes adopted by the Governing Council of the United Nations Environment Programme (UNEP) by Decision 14/30 of 17 June, 1987, the Recommendations of the United Nations Committee of Experts on the Transport of Dangerous Goods (formulated in 1957 and updated biennially), the Charter of Human Rights, relevant recommendations, declarations, instruments and regulations

adopted within the United Nations System, the relevant Articles of the 1989 Basel Convention on the Control of Transboundary Movements of Hazardous Wastes and their Disposal, allows for the establishment of regional agreements which may be equal to or stronger than its own provisions, Article 39 of the Lome IV Convention relating to the international movement of hazardous wastes and radioactive wastes, African intergovernmental organizations and the work and studies done within other international and regional organizations,

12.   Mindful of the spirit, principles, aims and functions of the African Convention on the Conservation of Nature and Natural Resources adopted by the African Heads of State and Government in Algiers (1968) and the World Charter for Nature adopted by the General Assembly of the United Nations at its thirty-seventh session (1982) as the rule of ethics in respect of the protection of human environment and the conservation of natural resources,

13.   Concerned by the problems of the transboundary traffic in hazardous wastes,

14.   Recognizing the need to promote the development of clean production methods, including clean technologies, for the sound management of hazardous wastes produced in Africa, in particular, to avoid, minimize and eliminate the generation of such wastes,

15.   Recognizing also that when necessary hazardous wastes should be transported in accordance with relevant international conventions and recommendations,

16.   Determined to protect, by strict control, the human health of the African population and the environment against the adverse effects which may result from the generation of hazardous wastes,

17.   Affirming a commitment also to responsibly address the problem of hazardous wastes originating within the Continent of Africa,

HAVE AGREED AS FOLLOWS:

ARTICLE 1

DEFINITIONS

For the purpose of this Convention:

1.   "Wastes" are substances or materials which are disposed of, or are intended to be disposed of, or are required to be disposed of by the provisions of national law;

2.   "Hazardous wastes" shall mean wastes as specified in Article 2 of this Convention.

3.   "Management" means the prevention and reduction of hazardous wastes and the collection, transport, storage, treatment either for re-use or disposal of hazardous wastes including after-care of disposal sites;

4.   "Transboundary movement" means any movement of hazardous wastes from an area under the national jurisdiction of any state to or through an area under the national jurisdiction of another State, or to or through an area not under the national jurisdiction of another State, provided at least two States are involved in the movement;

5. "Clean production methods" means production or industrial systems which avoid or eliminate the generation of hazardous wastes and hazardous products in conformity with Article 4, Section 3(f) and (g) of this Convention;

6. "Disposal" means any operation specified in Annex III to this Convention;

7. "Approved site or facility" means a site or facility for the disposal of hazardous wastes which is authorised or permitted to operate for this purpose by a relevant authority of the State where the site or facility is located;

8. "Competent authority" means one governmental authority designated by a Party to be responsible, within such geographical areas as the Party may think fit, for receiving the notification of a transboundary movement of hazardous wastes and any information related to it, and for responding to such a notification, as provided in Article 6;

9. "Focal point" means the entity of a Party referred to in Article 5 responsible for receiving and submitting information as provided for in Articles 13 and 16;

10. "Environmentally sound management of hazardous wastes" means taking all practicable steps to ensure that hazardous wastes are managed in a manner which will protect human health and the environment against the adverse effects which may result from such wastes;

11. "Area under the national jurisdiction of a State" means any land, marine area or airspace within which a State exercises administrative and regulatory responsibility in accordance with international law in regard to the protection of human health or the environment;

12. "State of export" means a State from which a transboundary movement of hazardous wastes is planned to be initiated or is initiated;

13. "State of import" means a State to which a transboundary movement is planned or takes place for the purpose of disposal therein or for the purpose of loading prior to disposal in an area not under the national jurisdiction of any State;

14. "State of transit" means any State, other than the State of export or import, through which a movement of hazardous wastes is planned or takes place;

15. "States concerned" means Parties which are States of export or import, or transit States whether or not Parties;

16. "Person" means any natural or legal person;

17. "Exporter" means any person under the jurisdiction of the State of export who arranges for hazardous wastes to be exported;

18. "Importer" means any person under the jurisdiction of the State of import who arranges for hazardous wastes to be imported;

19. "Carrier" means any person who carries out the transport of hazardous wastes;

20. "Generator" means any person whose activity produces hazardous wastes, or, if that person is not known, the person who is in possession and/or control of those wastes;

21. "Disposer" means any person to whom hazardous wastes are shipped and who carries out the disposal of such wastes;

22. "Illegal traffic" means any transboundary movement of hazardous wastes as specified in Article 9;

22. "Dumping at sea" means the deliberate disposal of hazardous wastes at sea from vessels, aircraft, platforms or other man-made structures at sea, and includes ocean incineration and disposal into the seabed and sub-seabed.

ARTICLE 2
SCOPE OF THE CONVENTION

1. The following substances shall be "hazardous wastes" for the purposes of this convention:

(a) Wastes that belong to any category contained in Annex I of this Convention;

(b) Wastes that are not covered under paragraph (a) above but are defined as, or are considered to be, hazardous wastes by the domestic legislation of the State of export, import or transit;

(c) Wastes which possess any of the characteristics contained in Annex II of this Convention;

(d) Hazardous substances which have been banned, cancelled or refused registration by government regulatory action, or voluntarily withdrawn from registration, in the country of manufacture, for human health and environmental reasons.

2. Wastes which, as a result of being radioactive, are subject to any international control systems, including international instruments, applying specifically to radioactive materials, are included in the scope of this Convention.

3. Wastes which derive from the normal operations of a ship, the discharge of which is covered by another international instrument, shall not fall within the scope of this Convention.

ARTICLE 3
NATIONAL DEFINITIONS OF HAZARDOUS WASTES

1. Each State shall, within six months of becoming a Party to this Convention, inform the Secretariat of the Convention of the wastes, other than those listed in Annex 1 of this Convention, considered or defined as hazardous under its national legislation and of any requirements concerning transboundary movement procedures applicable to such wastes.

2. Each Party shall subsequently inform the Secretariat of any significant changes to the information it has provided pursuant to Paragraph 1 of this Convention.

3. The Secretariat shall forthwith inform all Parties of the information it has received pursuant to Paragraphs 1 and 2 of this Article.

4. Parties shall be responsible for making the information transmitted to them by the Secretariat under Paragraph 3 of this Article, available to their exporters and other appropriate bodies.

ARTICLE 4
GENERAL OBLIGATIONS

1. Hazardous Waste Import Ban

All Parties shall take appropriate legal, administrative and other measures within the area under their jurisdiction to prohibit the import of all hazardous wastes, for any reason, into Africa from non-Contracting Parties. Such import shall be deemed illegal and a criminal act. All Parties shall:

(a) Forward as soon as possible, all information relating to such illegal hazardous waste import activity to the Secretariat who shall distribute the information to all Contracting Parties;

(b) Co-operate to ensure that no imports of hazardous wastes from a non-Party enter to this Convention. To this end, the Parties shall, at the Conference of the Contracting Parties consider other enforcement mechanisms.

2. Ban on Dumping of Hazardous Wastes at Sea, Internal Waters and Waterways

(a) Parties in conformity with related international conventions and instruments shall, in the exercise of their jurisdiction within their internal waters, territorial seas, exclusive economic zones and continental shelf, adopt legal, administrative and other appropriate measures to control all carriers from non-Parties, and prohibit the dumping at sea of hazardous wastes, including their incineration at sea and their disposal in the seabed and sub-seabed; any dumping of hazardous wastes at sea, including incineration at sea as well as seabed and sub-seabed disposal, by Contracting Parties, whether in internal waters, territorial seas, exclusive economic zones or high seas shall be deemed to be illegal;

(b) Parties shall forward, as soon as possible, all information relating to dumping of hazardous wastes to the Secretariat which shall distribute the information to all Contracting Parties.

3. Waste Generation in Africa

Each Party shall:

(a) Ensure that hazardous waste generators submit to the Secretariat reports regarding the wastes that they generate in order to enable the Secretariat of the Convention to produce a complete hazardous waste audit;

(b) Impose unlimited liability as well as joint and several liability on hazardous waste generators;

(c) Ensure that the generation of hazardous wastes within the area under its jurisdiction is reduced to a minimum taking into account social, technological and economic aspects;

(d) Ensure the availability of adequate treatment and/or disposal facilities, for the environmentally sound management of hazardous wastes which shall be located, to the extent possible, within its jurisdiction;

(e) Ensure that persons involved in the management of hazardous wastes within its jurisdiction take such steps as are necessary to prevent pollution arising from such wastes and, if such pollution occurs, to minimize the consequence thereof for human health and the environment;

The Adoption of Precautionary Measures:

(f) Each Party shall strive to adopt and implement the preventive, precautionary approach to pollution problems which entails, inter-alia, preventing the release into the environment of substances which may cause harm to humans or the environment without waiting for scientific proof regarding such harm. The Parties shall co-operate with each other in taking the appropriate measures to implement the precautionary principle to pollution prevention through the application of clean production methods, rather than the pursuit of a permissible emissions approach based on assimilative capacity assumptions;

(g) In this respect Parties shall promote clean production methods applicable to entire product life cycles including:

— raw material selection, extraction and processing;

— product conceptualisation, design, manufacture and assemblage;

— materials transport during all phases;

— industrial and household usage;

— reintroduction of the product into industrial systems or nature when it no longer serves a useful function;

Clean production shall not include "end-of-pipe" pollution controls such as filters and scrubbers, or chemical, physical or biological treatment. Measures which reduce the volume of waste by incineration or concentration, mask the hazard by dilution, or transfer pollutants from one environmental medium to another, are also excluded.

(h) The issue of the transfer to Africa of polluting technologies shall be kept under systematic review by the Secretariat of the Conference and periodic reports made to the Conference of the Parties.

Obligations in the Transport and Transboundary Movement of Hazardous Wastes from Contracting Parties:

(i) Each Party shall prevent the export of hazardous wastes to States which have prohibited by their legislation or international agreements all such imports, or if it has reason to believe that the wastes in question will not be managed in an environmentally sound manner, according to criteria to be decided on by the Parties at their first meeting;

(j) A Party shall not permit hazardous wastes to be exported to a State which does not have the facilities for disposing of them in an environmentally sound manner;

(k) Each Party shall ensure that hazardous wastes to be exported are managed in an environmentally sound manner in the State of import and of transit. Technical guidelines for the environmentally sound management of wastes subject to this Convention shall be decided by the Parties at their first meeting;

(*l*) The Parties agree not to allow the export of hazardous wastes for disposal within the area South of 60 degrees South Latitude, whether or not such wastes are subject to transboundary movement;

(m) Furthermore, each Party shall:

(i) prohibit all persons under its national jurisdiction from transporting or disposing of hazardous wastes unless such persons are authorized or allowed to perform such operations;

(ii) ensure that hazardous wastes that are to be the subject of a transboundary movement are packaged, labelled, and transported in conformity with generally accepted and recognized international rules and standards in the field of packaging, labelling and transport, and that due account is taken of relevant internationally recognized practices;

(iii) ensure that hazardous wastes be accompanied by a movement document, containing information specified in Annex IV B, from the point at which a transboundary movement commences to the point of disposal;

(n) Parties shall take the appropriate measures to ensure that the transboundary movements of hazardous wastes only are allowed if:

(i) the State of export does not have the technical capacity and the necessary facilities, capacity or suitable disposal sites in order to dispose of the wastes in question in an environmentally sound and efficient manner, or

(ii) the transboundary movement in question is in accordance with other criteria to be decided by the Parties, provided those criteria do not differ from the objectives of this Convention;

(*o*) Under this Convention, the obligation of States in which hazardous wastes are generated, requiring that those wastes are managed in an environmentally sound manner, may not under any circumstances be transferred to the States of import or transit;

(p) Parties shall undertake to review periodically the possibilities for the reduction of the amount and/or the pollution potential of hazardous wastes which are exported to other States;

(q) Parties exercising their right to prohibit the import of hazardous wastes for disposal shall inform the other Parties of their decision pursuant to Article 13;

(r) Parties shall prohibit or shall not permit the export of hazardous wastes to States which have prohibited the import of such wastes when notified by the Secretariat or any competent authority pursuant to subparagraph (q) above;

(s) Parties shall prohibit or shall not permit the export of hazardous wastes if the State of import does not consent in writing to the specific import, in the case where that State of import has not prohibited the import of such wastes;

(t) Parties shall ensure that the transboundary movement of hazardous wastes is reduced to the minimum consistent with the environmentally sound and efficient management of such wastes, and is conducted in a manner which will protect human health and the environment against the adverse effects which may result from such movements;

(u) Parties shall require that information about a proposed transboundary movement of hazardous wastes be provided to the States concerned, according to Annex IV A, and state clearly the potential effects of the proposed movement on human health and the environment.

4. Furthermore

(a) Parties shall undertake to enforce the obligation of this Convention against offenders and infringements according to relevant national laws and/or order to better protect human health and the environment;

(b) Nothing in this Convention shall prevent a Party from imposing additional requirements that are consistent with the provisions of this Convention, and are in accordance with the rules of international law, in order to better protect human health and the environment;

(c) This Convention recognizes the sovereignty of States over their territorial seas, waterways and air space established in accordance with international law, and jurisdiction which States have in their exclusive economic zone and their continental shelves in accordance with international law, and the exercise by ships and aircraft of all States of navigation rights and freedoms as provided for in international law and as reflected in relevant international instruments.

ARTICLE 5
DESIGNATION OF COMPETENT AUTHORITIES
FOCAL POINT AND DUMPWATCH

To facilitate the implementation of this Convention, the Parties shall:

1. Designate or establish one or more competent authorities and one focal point. One competent authority shall be designated to receive the notification in case of a State of transit.

2. Inform the Secretariat, within three months of the date of the entry into force of this Convention for them, which agencies they have designated as their focal point and their competent authorities.

3. Inform the Secretariat, within one month of the date of decision, of any changes regarding the designations made by them under paragraph 2 above.

4. Appoint a national body to act as a Dumpwatch. In such capacity as a Dumpwatch, the designated national body only will be required to coordinate with the concerned governmental and non-governmental bodies.

ARTICLE 6
TRANSBOUNDARY MOVEMENT AND NOTIFICATION PROCEDURES

1. The State of export shall notify, or shall require the generator or exporter to notify, in writing, through the channel of the competent authority of the State of export, the competent authority of the States concerned of any proposed transboundary movement of hazardous wastes. Such notification shall contain the declaration and information specified in Annex IV A, of this

Convention, written in a language acceptable to the State of import. Only one notification needs to be sent to each State concerned.

2. The State of import shall respond to the notifier in writing consenting to the movement with or without conditions, denying permission for the movement, or requesting additional information. A copy of the final response of the State of import shall be sent to the competent authorities of the States concerned that are Parties to this Convention.

3. The State of export shall not allow the transboundary movement until it has received:

(a) written consent of the State of import, and

(b) from the State of import written confirmation of the existence of a contract between the exporter and the disposer specifying environmentally sound management of the wastes in question.

4. Each State of transit which is a Party to this Convention shall promptly acknowledge to the notifier receipt of the notification. It may subsequently respond to the notifier in writing within 60 days consenting to the movement with or without conditions, denying permission for the movement, or requesting additional information. The State of export shall not allow the transboundary movement to commence until it has received the written consent of the State of transit.

5. In the case of a transboundary movement of hazardous wastes where the wastes are legally defined as or considered to be hazardous wastes only:

(a) by the State of export, the requirements of paragraph 8 of this Article that apply to the importer or disposer and the State of import shall apply *mutatis mutandis* to the exporter and State of export respectively;

(b) by the State of import or by the States of import and transit which are Parties to this Convention, the requirements of paragraphs 1, 3, 4 and 6 of this Article that apply to the exporter and State of export shall apply *mutatis mutandis* to the importer or disposer and State of import, respectively; or

(c) by any State of transit which is Party to this Convention, the provisions of paragraph 4 shall apply to such State.

6. The State shall use a shipment specific notification even where hazardous wastes having the same physical and chemical characteristics are shipped regularly to the same disposer via the same customs office of entry of the State of import, and in the case of transit via the same customs office of entry and exit of the State or States of transit; specific notification of each and every shipment shall be required and contain the information in Annex IV A of this Convention.

7. Each Party to this Convention shall limit their points or ports of entry and notify the Secretariat to this effect for distribution to all Contracting Parties. Such points and ports shall be the only ones permitted for the transboundary movement of hazardous wastes.

8. The Parties to this Convention shall require that each person who takes charge of a transboundary movement of hazardous wastes sign the movement document either upon delivery or receipt of the wastes in question.

They shall also require that the disposer inform both the exporter and the competent authority of the State of export of receipt by the disposer of the wastes in question and, in due course, of the completion of disposal as specified in the notification. If no such information is received within the State of export, the competent authority of the State of export or the exporter shall so notify the State of import.

9. The notification and response by this Article shall be transmitted to the competent authority of the States concerned.

10. Any transboundary movement of hazardous wastes shall be covered by insurance, bond or other guarantee as may be required by the State of import or any State of transit which is a Party of this Convention.

ARTICLE 7
TRANSBOUNDARY MOVEMENT FROM A PARTY THROUGH STATES WHICH ARE NOT PARTIES

Paragraph 2 of Article 6 of the Convention shall apply *mutatis mutandis* to transboundary movements of hazardous wastes from a Party through a State or States which are not Parties.

ARTICLE 8
DUTY TO RE–IMPORT

When a transboundary movement of hazardous wastes to which the consent of the States concerned has been given, subject to the provisions of this Convention, cannot be completed in accordance with the terms of the contract, the State of export shall ensure that the wastes in question are taken back into the State of export, by the exporter, if alternative arrangements cannot be made for their disposal in an environmentally sound manner within a maximum of 90 days from the time that the importing State informed the State of export and the Secretariat. To this end, the State of export and any State of transit shall not oppose, hinder or prevent the return of those wastes to the State of export.

ARTICLE 9
ILLEGAL TRAFFIC

1. For the purpose of this Convention, any transboundary movement of hazardous wastes under the following situations shall be deemed to be illegal traffic:

(a) if carried out without notification, pursuant to the provisions of this Convention, to all States concerned, or

(b) if carried out without the consent, pursuant to the provisions of this Convention, of a State concerned; or

(c) if consent is obtained from States concerned through falsification, misrepresentation or fraud; or

(d) if it does not conform in a material way with the documents; or

(e) if it results in deliberate disposal of hazardous wastes in contravention of this Convention and of general principles of international law.

2. Each State shall introduce appropriate national legislation for imposing criminal penalties on all persons who have planned, carried out, or

assisted in such illegal imports. Such penalties shall be sufficiently high to both punish and deter such conduct.

3. In case of a transboundary movement of hazardous wastes deemed to be illegal traffic as the result of conduct on the part of the exporter or generator the State of export shall ensure that the wastes in question are taken back by the exporter or generator or if necessary by itself into the State of export, within 30 days from the time the State of export has been informed about the illegal traffic. To this end the States concerned shall not oppose, hinder or prevent the return of those wastes to the State of export and appropriate legal action shall be taken against the contravenor(s).

4. In the case of a transboundary movement of hazardous wastes deemed to be illegal traffic as the result of conduct on the part of the importer or disposer, the State of import shall ensure that the wastes in question are returned to the exporter by the importer and that legal proceedings according to the provisions of this Convention are taken against the contravenor(s).

ARTICLE 10
INTRA-AFRICAN CO-OPERATION

1. The Parties to this Convention shall co-operate with one another and with relevant African organizations, to improve and achieve the environmentally sound management of hazardous wastes.

2. To this end, the Parties shall:

(a) Make available information, whether on a bilateral or multilateral basis, with a view to promoting clean production methods and the environmentally sound management of hazardous wastes, including harmonization of technical standards and practices for the adequate management of hazardous wastes;

(b) Co-operate in monitoring the effects of the management of hazardous wastes on human health and the environment;

(c) Co-operate, subject to their national laws, regulations and policies, in the development and implementation of new environmentally sound clean production technologies and the improvement of existing technologies with a view to eliminating, as far as practicable, the generation of hazardous wastes and achieving more effective and efficient methods of ensuring their management in an environmentally sound manner, including the study of the economic, social and environmental effects of the adoption of such new and improved technologies;

(d) Co-operate actively to their national laws, regulations and policies, in the transfer of technology and management systems related to the environmentally sound management of hazardous wastes. They shall also co-operate in developing the technical capacity among Parties, especially those which may need and request technical assistance in this field;

(e) Co-operate in developing appropriate technical guidelines and/or codes of practice;

(f) Co-operate in the exchange and dissemination of information on the movement of hazardous wastes in conformity with Article 13 of this Convention.

ARTICLE 11
INTERNATIONAL CO–OPERATION
BILATERAL, MULTILATERAL AND REGIONAL AGREEMENTS

1. Parties to this Convention may enter into bilateral, multilateral, or regional agreements or arrangements regarding the transboundary movement and management of hazardous wastes generated in Africa with Parties or non-Parties provided that such agreements or arrangements do not derogate from the environmentally sound management of hazardous wastes as required by this Convention. These agreements or arrangements shall stipulate provisions which are no less environmentally sound than those provided for by this Convention.

2. Parties shall notify the Secretariat of any bilateral, multilateral or regional agreements or arrangements referred to in paragraph 1 of this Article and those which they have entered into prior to the entry into force of this Convention for them, for purpose of controlling transboundary movements of hazardous wastes which take place entirely among the Parties to such agreements. The provisions of this Convention shall not affect transboundary movements of hazardous wastes generated in Africa which take place pursuant to such agreements provided that such agreements are compatible with the environmentally sound management of hazardous wastes as required by this Convention.

3. Each Contracting Party shall prohibit vessels flying its flag or aircraft registered in its territory from carrying out activities in contravention of this Convention.

4. Parties shall use appropriate measures to promote South–South cooperation in the implementation of this Convention.

5. Taking into account the needs of developing countries, cooperation between international organizations is encouraged in order to promote, among other things, public awareness, the development of the rational management of hazardous wastes and the adoption of new and less polluting technologies.

ARTICLE 12
LIABILITIES AND COMPENSATION

The Conference of Parties shall set up an Ad Hoc expert organ to prepare a draft protocol setting out appropriate rules and procedures in the field of liabilities and compensation for damage resulting from the transboundary movement of hazardous wastes.

ARTICLE 13
TRANSMISSION OF INFORMATION

1. The Parties shall ensure that in the case of an accident occurring during the transboundary movement of hazardous wastes or their disposal which is likely to present risks to human health and the environment in other States, those States are immediately informed.

2. The States shall inform each other, through the Secretariat, of:

(a) Changes regarding the designation of competent authorities and/or focal points, pursuant to Article 5 of the present Convention.

(b)   Changes in their national definition of hazardous wastes, pursuant to article 3 of the present Convention;

(c)   Decisions made by them to limit or ban the import of hazardous wastes;

(d)   Any other information required pursuant to paragraph 4 of this Article.

3.   The Parties, consistent with national laws and regulations, shall set up information collection and dissemination mechanisms for hazardous wastes.   They shall transmit such information through the Secretariat, to the Conference of the Parties established under Article 15 of the present Convention, before the end of each calendar year, in a report on the previous calendar year, containing the following information:

(a)   Competent authorities, Dumpwatch, and focal points that have been designated by them pursuant to Article 5 of the present Convention.

(b)   Information regarding transboundary movements of hazardous wastes in which they have been involved including:

(i)   The quantity of hazardous wastes exported, their category, characteristics, destination, any transit country and disposal methods as stated in the notification;

(ii)   The amount of hazardous wastes imported, their category, characteristics, origin, and disposal methods;

(iii)   Disposals which did not proceed as intended;

(iv)   Efforts to achieve a reduction of the amount of hazardous wastes subject to transboundary movements.

(c)   Information on the measures adopted by them in the implementation of this Convention;

(d)   Information on available qualified statistics—which have been compiled by them on the effects on human health and the environment of the generation, transportation, and disposal of hazardous wastes—as part of the information required in conformity with Article 4 Section 3(a) of this Convention;

(e)   Information concerning bilateral, multilateral and regional agreements and arrangements entered into pursuant to Article 11 of this Convention;

(f)   Information on accidents occurring during the transboundary movements and disposal of hazardous wastes and on the measures undertaken to deal with them;

(g)   Information on disposal options operated within the area under their national jurisdiction;

(h)   Information on measures undertaken for the development of clean production methods, including clean production technologies, for the reduction and/or elimination of the production of hazardous wastes; and

(i)   Such other matters as the Conference of the Parties shall deem relevant.

4.   The Parties, consistent with national laws and regulations, shall ensure that copies of each notification concerning any given transboundary movement of hazardous wastes, and the response to it, are sent to the Secretariat.

ARTICLE 14
FINANCIAL ASPECTS

1.   The regular budget of the Conference of the Parties, as required in Articles 15 and 16 of this Convention, shall be prepared by the Secretariat and approved by the Conference.

2.   Parties shall, at the first meeting of the Conference of the Parties, agree on a scale of contributions to the recurrent budget of the Secretariat.

3.   The Parties shall also consider the establishment of a revolving fund to assist on an interim basis, in case of emergency situations to minimize damage from disasters or accidents arising from transboundary movements of hazardous wastes or during the disposal of such wastes.

4.   The Parties agree that, according to the specific needs of different regions and sub-regions, regional or sub-regional centres for training and technology transfers regarding the management of hazardous wastes and the minimization of their generation should be established as well as appropriate funding mechanisms of a voluntary nature.

ARTICLE 15
CONFERENCE OF THE PARTIES

1.   A Conference of the Parties, made up of Ministers having the environment as their mandate, is hereby established.   The first meeting of the Conference of the Parties shall be convened by the Secretary–General of the OAU not later than one year after the entry into force of this Convention. Thereafter, ordinary meetings of the Conference of the Parties shall be held at regular intervals to be determined by the Conference at its first meeting.

2.   The Conference of the Parties to this Convention shall adopt Rules of Procedure for itself and for any subsidiary body it may establish, as well as financial rules to determine in particular the financial participation of the Parties under this Convention.

3.   The Parties to this Convention at their first meeting shall consider any additional measures needed to assist them in fulfilling their responsibilities with respect to the protection and the preservation of the marine and inland waters environments in the context of this Convention.

4.   The Conference of the Parties shall keep under continuous review and evaluation the effective implementation of this Convention, and in addition, shall:

(a)   promote the harmonization of appropriate policies, strategies and measures for minimizing harm to human health and the environment by hazardous wastes;

(b)   consider and adopt, as required, amendments to this Convention and its annexes, taking into consideration, inter alia, available scientific, technical, economic and environmental information;

(c) consider and undertake any additional action that may be required for the achievement of the purpose of this Convention in the light of experience gained in its operation and in the operation of the agreements and arrangements envisaged in Article 11 of the present Convention;

(d) consider and adopt protocols as required;

(e) establish such subsidiary bodies as are deemed necessary for the implementation of this Convention; and

(f) make decisions for the peaceful settlement of disputes arising from the transboundary movement of hazardous wastes, if need be, according to international law.

5. Organisations may be represented as observers at meetings of the Conference of the Parties to this Convention. Any body or agency, whether national or international, governmental or non-governmental, qualified in fields relating to hazardous wastes which has informed the Secretariat, may be represented as an observer at a meeting of the Conference of the Parties to this Convention. The admission and participation of observers shall be subject to the rules of procedures adopted by the Conference of the Parties.

ARTICLE 16
SECRETARIAT

1. The functions of the secretariat shall be:

(a) to arrange for, and service, meetings provided for in Articles 15 and 17 of the present Convention.

(b) to prepare and transmit reports based upon information received in accordance with Articles 3, 4, 6, 11, and 13 of the present Convention as well as upon information derived from meetings of subsidiary bodies established under Article 15 of the present Convention as well as upon, as appropriate, information provided by relevant inter-governmental and non-governmental entities;

(c) to prepare reports on its activities carried out in the implementation of its functions under this Convention and present them to the Conference of the Parties;

(d) to ensure the necessary co-ordination with relevant international bodies, and in particular to enter into such administrative and contractual arrangements as may be required for the effective discharge of its functions;

(e) to communicate with focal points, competent authorities and Dumpwatch established by the Parties in accordance with Article 5 of this Convention as well as appropriate inter-governmental and non-governmental organizations which may provide assistance in the implementation of this Convention.

(f) to compile information concerning approved national sites and facilities of Parties to this Convention available for the disposal an treatment of their hazardous wastes and to circulate this information;

(g) to receive and convey information from and to Parties to this Convention on:

— sources of technical assistance and training;

— available technical and scientific know-how;

— sources of advice and expertise; and

— availability of resources.

This information will assist them in:

— the management of the notification system of this Convention;

— environmentally sound clean production methods relating to hazardous wastes, such as clean production technologies;

— the assessment of disposal capabilities and sites;

— the monitoring of hazardous wastes; and

— emergency responses;

(h) to provide the Parties to this Convention with information on consultants or consulting firms having the necessary technical competence in the field, which can assist them with examining a notification for a transboundary movement, the concurrence of a shipment of hazardous wastes with the relevant notification, and/or whether the proposed disposal facilities for hazardous wastes are environmentally sound, when they have reason to believe that the wastes in question will not be managed in an environmentally sound manner. Any such examinations would not be at the expense of the Secretariat;

(i) to assist Parties to this Convention in their identification of cases of illegal traffic and to circulate immediately to the Parties concerned any information it has received regarding illegal traffic;

(j) to co-operate with Parties to this Convention and with relevant and competent international organizations and agencies in the provision of experts and equipment for the purpose of rapid assistance to States in the event of an emergency situation; and

(k) to perform such other functions relevant to the purposes of this Convention as may be determined by the Conference of the Parties to this Convention.

2. The Secretariat's functions shall be carried out on an interim basis by the Organization of African Unity (OAU) jointly with the United Nations Economic Commission for Africa (ECA) until the completion of the first meeting of the Conference of the Parties held pursuant to Article 15 of the present Convention. At this meeting, the Conference of the Parties shall also evaluate the implementation by the interim Secretariat of the functions assigned to it, in particular under paragraph 1 above, and decide upon the structures appropriate for those functions.

ARTICLE 17

AMENDMENT OF THE CONVENTION AND OF PROTOCOLS

1. Any Party may propose amendments to this Convention and any Party to a Protocol may propose amendments to that Protocol. Such amendments shall take due account, *inter alia,* of relevant scientific, technical, environmental and social considerations.

2.   Amendments to this Convention shall be adopted at a meeting of the Conference of the Parties.   Amendments to any Protocol shall be adopted at a meeting of the Parties to the Protocol in question.   The text of any proposed amendment to this Convention or to any Protocol, except as may otherwise be provided in such Protocol, shall be communicated to the Parties by the Secretariat at least six months before the meeting at which it is proposed for adoption.   The Secretariat shall also communicate proposed amendments to the Signatories to this Convention for their information.

3.   The Parties shall make every effort to reach agreement on any proposed amendment to this Convention by consensus.   If all efforts at consensus have been exhausted, and no agreement reached, the amendment shall, as a last resort, be adopted by a two-thirds majority vote of the Parties present and voting at the meeting.   It shall then be submitted by the Depository to all Parties for ratification, approval, formal confirmation or acceptance.

Amendments of Protocols to this Convention

4.   The procedure specified in paragraph 3 above shall apply to amendments to any Protocol, except that a two-thirds majority of the Parties to that Protocol present and voting at the meeting shall suffice for their adoption.

GENERAL PROVISIONS

5.   Instruments of ratification, approval, formal confirmation or acceptance of amendments shall be deposited with the Depository.   Amendments adopted in accordance with paragraph 3 or 4 above shall enter into force between Parties having accepted them, on the ninetieth day after the receipt by the Depository of the instrument of ratification, approval, formal confirmation or acceptance by at least two-thirds of the Parties who accepted the amendments to the Protocol concerned, except as may otherwise be provided in such Protocol.   The amendments shall enter into force for any other Party on the ninetieth day after that Party deposits its instrument of ratification, approval, formal confirmation or acceptance of the amendments.

6.   For the purpose of this Article, "Parties present and voting" means Parties present and casting an affirmative or negative vote.

ARTICLE 18
ADOPTION AND AMENDMENT OF ANNEXES

1.   The annexes to this Convention or to any Protocol shall form an integral part of this Convention or of such Protocol, as the case may be and, unless expressly provided otherwise, a reference to this Convention or its Protocols constitutes at the same time a reference to any annexes thereto. Such annexes shall be restricted to scientific, technical and administrative matters.

2.   Except as may be otherwise provided in any Protocol with respect to its annexes, the following procedures shall apply to the proposal, adoption and entry into force of additional annexes to this Convention or of annexes to a protocol:

(a)   Annexes to this Convention and its Protocols shall be proposed and adopted according to the procedures laid down in Article 17, paragraphs 1, 2, 3, and 4 of the present Convention;

(b) Any Party that is unable to accept an additional annex to this Convention or an annex to any Protocol to which it is Party shall so notify the Depository, in writing, within six months from the date of the communication of the adoption by the Depository. The Depository shall without delay notify all Parties of any such notification received. A Party may at any time substitute an acceptance for a previous declaration of objection and the annexes shall thereupon enter into force for that Party;

(c) Upon the expiration of six months from the date of the circulation of the communication by the Depository, the annex shall become effective for all Parties to this Convention or to any Protocol concerned, which have not submitted a notification in accordance with the provision of subparagraph (b) above.

3. The proposal, adoption and entry into force of amendments to annexes to this Convention or to any Protocol shall be subject to the same procedure as for the proposal, adoption and entry into force of annexes to the Convention or annexes to a Protocol. Annexes and amendments thereto shall take due account, *inter alia,* of relevant scientific and technical considerations.

4. If an additional annex or an amendment to an annex involves an amendment to this Convention or to any Protocol, the additional annex or amended annex shall not enter into force until such time as the amendment to this Convention or to the Protocol enters into force.

ARTICLE 19
VERIFICATION

Any Party which has reason to believe that another Party is acting or has acted in breach of its obligations under this Convention must inform the Secretariat thereof, and in such an event, shall simultaneously and immediately inform, directly or through the Secretariat, the Party against whom the allegations are made. The Secretariat shall carry out a verification of the substance of the allegation and submit a report thereof to all the Parties to this convention.

ARTICLE 20
SETTLEMENT OF DISPUTES

1. In case of dispute between Parties as to the interpretation or application of, or compliance with, this Convention or any Protocol thereto, the Parties shall seek a settlement of the dispute through negotiations or any other peaceful means of their own choice.

2. If the Parties concerned cannot settle their dispute as provided in paragraph 1 of this Article, the dispute shall be submitted either to an Ad Hoc organ set up by the Conference for this purpose or to the International Court of Justice.

3. The conduct of arbitration of disputes between Parties by the Ad Hoc organ provided for in paragraph 2 of this Article shall be as provided in Annex V of this Convention.

ARTICLE 21
SIGNATURE

This Convention shall be open for signature by Member States of the OAU in Bamako and Addis Ababa for a period of six months from 30 January 1991 to 31 July 1991.

ARTICLE 22
RATIFICATION, ACCEPTANCE, FORMAL CONFIRMATION OR APPROVAL

1. This Convention shall be subject to ratification, acceptance, formal confirmation or approval by Member States of the OAU. Instruments of ratification, acceptance, formal confirmation, or approval shall be deposited with the Depository.

2. Parties shall be bound by all obligations of this Convention.

ARTICLE 23
ACCESSION

This Convention shall be open for accession by Member States of the OAU from the date after the day on which the Convention is closed for signature. The instruments of accession shall be deposited with the Depository.

ARTICLE 24
RIGHT TO VOTE

Each Contracting Party to this Convention shall have one vote.

ARTICLE 25
ENTRY INTO FORCE

1. This Convention shall enter into force on the ninetieth day after the date of deposit of the tenth instrument of ratification from Parties signatory to this Convention.

2. For each State which ratifies this Convention or accedes thereto after the date of the deposit of the tenth instrument of ratification, it shall enter into force on the ninetieth day after the date of deposit by such State of its instrument of accession or ratification.

ARTICLE 26
RESERVATIONS AND DECLARATIONS

1. No reservations or exception may be made to this Convention.

2. Paragraph 1 of this Article does not preclude a State when signing, ratifying, or acceding to this Convention, from making declarations or statements, however phrased or named, with a view, inter alia, to the harmonization of its laws and regulations with the provisions of this Convention, provided that such declarations or statements do not purport to exclude or to modify the legal effects of the provisions of the Convention in their application to that State.

ARTICLE 27
WITHDRAWAL

1. At any time after three years from the date on which this Convention has entered into force for a Party, that Party may withdraw from the Convention by giving written notification to the Depository.

2. Withdrawal shall be effective one year after receipt of notification by the Depository, or on such later date as may be specified in the notification.

3. Withdrawal shall not exempt the withdrawing Party from fulfilling any obligations it might have incurred under this Convention.

ARTICLE 28
DEPOSITORY

The Secretary–General of the Organization of African Unity shall be the Depository for this Convention and of any Protocol thereto.

ARTICLE 29
REGISTRATION

This Convention, as soon as it enters into force, shall be registered with the Secretary–General of the United Nations Organization in conformity with Article 102 of the Charter of the United Nations.

ARTICLE 30
AUTHENTIC TEXTS

The Arabic, English, French and Portuguese texts of this Convention are equally authentic.

* * *

ANNEX I
CATEGORIES OF WASTES WHICH ARE HAZARDOUS WASTES

Waste Streams

Y0 All wastes containing or contaminated by radionuclides, the concentration or properties of which result from human activity.

Y1 Clinical wastes from medical care in hospitals, medical centres and clinics.

Y2 Wastes from the production and preparation of pharmaceutical products.

Y3 Wastes pharmaceuticals, drugs and medicines.

Y4 Wastes from the production, formulation and use of biocides and phytopharmaceuticals.

Y5 Wastes from the manufacture, formulation and use of wood preserving chemicals.

Y6 Wastes from the production, formulation and use of organic solvents.

Y7 Wastes from heat treatment and tempering operations containing cyanides.

Y8 Waste mineral oils unfit for their originally intended use.

Y9 Waste oils/water, hydrocarbons/water mixtures, emulsions.

Y10 Waste substances and articles containing or contaminated with polychlorinated biphenyls (PCBs) and/or polychlorinated terphenyls (PCTs) and/or polybrominated biphenyls (PBBs).

Y11 Waste tarry residues arising from refining, distillation and any pyrolytic treatment.

Y12 Wastes from production, formulation and use of inks, dyes, pigments, paints, lacquers, varnish.

Y13 Wastes from production, formulation and use of resins, latex, plasticizers, glues/adhesives.

Y14 Waste chemical substances arising from research and development or teaching activities which are not identified and/or are new and whose effects on man and/or the environment are not known.

Y15 Wastes of an explosive nature not subject to other legislation.

Y16 Wastes from production, formulation and use of photographic chemicals and processing materials.

Y17 Wastes resulting from surface treatment of metals and plastics.

Y18 Residues arising from industrial waste disposal operations.

Y46 Wastes collected from households, including sewage and sewage sludges.

Y47 Residues arising from the incineration of household wastes.

Wastes having as constituents:

Y19   Metal carbonyls.
Y20   Beryllium; beryllium compounds.
Y21   Hexavalant chromium compounds.
Y22   Copper compounds.
Y23   Zinc compounds.
Y24   Arsenic; arsenic compounds.
Y25   Selenium; selenium compounds.
Y26   Cadmium; cadmium compounds.
Y27   Antimony; antimony compounds.
Y28   Tellurium; tellurium compounds.
Y29   Mercury; mercury compounds.
Y30   Thallium; thallium compounds.
Y31   Lead; lead compounds.
Y32   Inorganic fluorine compounds excluding calcium fluoride.
Y33   Inorganic cyanides.
Y34   Acidic solutions or acids in solid form.
Y35   Basic solutions or bases in solid form.
Y36   Asbestos (dust and fibres).
Y37   Organic phosphorous compounds.
Y38   Organic cyanides.
Y39   Phenols; phenol compounds including chlorophenols.
Y40   Ethers.
Y41   Halogenated organic solvents.
Y42   Organic solvents excluding halogenated solvents.
Y43   Any congenor of polychlorinated dibenzo-furan.
Y44   Any congenor of polychlorinated dibenzo-p-dioxin.
Y45   Organohalogen compounds other than substances referred to in this Annex (e.g., Y39, Y41, Y42, Y43, Y44).

ANNEX II
LIST OF HAZARDOUS CHARACTERISTICS

UN Class [1]	Code	Characteristics
1	HI	**Explosive** An explosive substance or waste is a solid or liquid substance or waste (or mixture of substances or wastes) which is in itself capable by chemical reaction or producing gas at such a temperature and pressure and at such a speed as to cause damage to the surroundings.
3	H3	**Flammable liquids** The word "flammable" has the same meaning as "inflammable". Flammable liquids are liquids, or mixtures of liquids, or liquids containing solids in solution or suspension (for example paints, varnishes, lacquers, etc.., but not including substances or wastes otherwise classified on account of their dangerous characteristics) which give off a flammable vapour at temperatures of not more than 60.5 degrees C, closed up test, or not more than 65.6 degrees C, open-cup test. (Since the results of open-cup tests and of closed-up tests are not strictly comparable and even individual results by the same test are often variable, regulations varying from the above figures to make allowance for such difference would be within the spirit of this definition).
4.1	H4.1	**Flammable solids** Solids, or waste solids, other than those classed as explosives, which under conditions encountered in transport are readily combustible, or may cause or contribute to fire through friction.

UN Class [1]	Code	Characteristics
4.2	H4.2	Substances or wastes liable to spontaneous combustion. Substances or wastes which are liable to spontaneous heating under normal conditions encountered in transport, or to heating up on contact with air, and being then liable to catch fire.
4.3	H4.3	Substances or wastes which, in contact with water emit flammable gases. Substances or wastes which, by interaction with water, are liable to become spontaneously flammable or to give off flammable gases in dangerous quantities.
5.1	H5.1	Oxidizing Substances or wastes which, while in themselves not necessarily combustible, may, generally by yielding oxygen, cause or contribute to the combustion of other materials.
5.2	H5.2	Organic peroxides Organic substances or wastes which contain the bivalent -O-O- structure are thermally unstable substances which may undergo exothermic self-accelerating decomposition.
6.1	H6.1	Poisonous (Acute) Substances or wastes liable either to cause death or serious injury or to harm human health if swallowed or inhaled or by skin contact.
6.2	H6.2	Infectious substances. Substances or wastes containing viable micro organisms or their toxins which are known or suspected to cause disease in animals or humans.
8	H8	Corrosives Substances or wastes which, by chemical action, will cause severe damage when in contact with living tissue, or in the case of leakage, will materially damage, or even destroy, other goods or the means of transport; they may also cause other hazards.
9	H10	Liberation of toxic gases in contact with air or water. Substances or wastes which, by interaction with air or water, are liable to give off toxic gases in dangerous quantities.
9	H11	Toxic (Delayed or chronic) Substances or wastes which, if they are inhaled or ingested or if they penetrate the skin, may involve delayed or chronic effects, including carcinogenicity.
9	H12	Ecotoxic Substances or wastes which if released present or may present immediate or delayed adverse impacts to the environment by means of bioaccumulation and/or toxic effects upon biotic systems.
9	H13	Capable, by any means, after disposal, of yielding another material, e.g., leachate, which possesses any of the characteristics listed above.

1. Corresponds to the hazardous classification system included in the United Nations Recommendations on the transport of Dangerous Goods (ST/SG/AC.10/1/Rev. 5, United Nations, New York, 1988).

ANNEX III

DISPOSAL OPERATIONS

D1   Deposit into or onto land, (e.g., landfill, etc..).

D2   Land treatment, (e.g. biodegradation of liquid or sludgy discards in soils, etc..).

D3   Deep injection, (e.g., injection of pumpable discards into wells, salt domes or naturally occurring repositories, etc.).

D4   Surface impoundment, (e.g., placement of liquid into lined discrete cells which are capped and isolated from one another and the environment, etc..).

D6   Release into a water body except seas/oceans.

D7   Release into seas/oceans including sea-bed insertion.

D8   Biological treatment not specified elsewhere in this Annex which results in final compounds or mixtures which are discarded by means of any of the operations in Annex III.

D9   Physico-chemical treatment not specified elsewhere in the Annex which results in final compounds or mixtures which are discarded by means of any of the operations in Annex III (e.g., evaporation, drying, calcination, neutralisation, precipitation, etc..).

D10   Incineration on land.

D11   Incineration at sea.

D12   Permanent storage, (e.g., emplacement of containers in a mine, etc..).

D13   Blending or mixing prior to submission to any of the operations in Annex III.

D14   Repackaging prior to submission to any of the operations in Annex III.

D15   Storage pending any of the operations in Annex III.

D16   Use of a fuel (other than in direct incineration) or other means to generate energy.

D17   Solvent reclamation/regeneration.

D18   Recycling/reclamation of organic substances which are not used as solvents.

D19   Recycling/reclamation of metals and metal compounds.

D20   Recycling/reclamation of other inorganic materials.

D21   Regeneration of acids and bases.

D22   Recovery of components used for pollution abatement.

D23   Recovery of components from catalysts.

D24   Used oil re-refining or other reuses of previously used oil,

D25   Land treatment resulting in benefit to agriculture or ecological improvement.

D26   Uses of residual materials obtained from any of the operations numbered D1–D25.

D27   Exchange of wastes for submission to any of the operations numbered D1–D26.

D28   Accumulation of material intended for any operation in Annex III.

ANNEX IV A

INFORMATION TO BE PROVIDED ON NOTIFICATION

1. Reason for waste export
2. Exporter of the waste
3. Generator(s) of the waste and site of generation
4. Importer and disposer of the waste and actual site of disposal
5. Intended carrier(s) of the waste or their agents, if known
6. Country of export of the waste.
   Competent authority
7. Countries of transit.
   Competent authority
8. [omitted]
9. Projected date of shipment and period of time over which waste is to be exported and proposed itinerary (including point of entry and exit).
10. Means of transport envisaged (road, rail, sea, air, inland waters).
11. Information relating to insurance
12. Designation and physical description of the waste including Y number and UN number and its composition and information on any special handling requirements including emergency provisions in case of accidents.
13. Type of packaging envisaged (e.g., bulk, drummer, tanker).
14. Estimated quantity in weight/volume
15. Process by which the waste is generated

16. Waste classification from Annex II: Hazardous characteristics, H number, and UN class.
17. Method of disposal as per Annex III.
18. Declaration by the generator and exporter that the information is correct.
19. Information transmitted (including technical description of the plant) to the exporter or generator from the disposer of the waste upon which the latter has based his assessment that there was no reason to believe that the wastes will not be managed in an environmentally sound manner in accordance with the laws and regulations of the country of import.
20. Information concerning the contract between the exporter and disposer.

* * *

ANNEX IV B
INFORMATION TO BE PROVIDED ON THE MOVEMENT DOCUMENT

1. Exporter of the waste
2. Generator(s) of the waste and site of generation
3. Importer and disposer of the waste and actual site of disposal
4. Carrier(s) of the waste or his agent(s)
5. The date the transboundary movement started and date(s) and signature on receipt by each person who takes charge of the waste.
6. Means of transport (road, rail, inland waterway, sea, air) including countries of export, transit and import, also point of entry and exit where these have been designated.
7. General description of the waste (physical state, proper UN shipping name and class, UN number, Y number and H number as applicable).
8. Information on special handling requirements including emergency provisions in case of accidents.
9. Type and number of packages.
10. Quantity in weight/volume.
11. Declaration by the generator or exporter that the information is correct.
12. Declaration by disposer or exporter indicating no objection from the competent authorities of all States concerned.
13. Certification by disposer of receipt at designated disposal facility and indication of method of disposal and of the appropriate date of disposal.

* * *

ANNEX V
ARBITRATION
Article 1

Unless the agreement referred to in Article 20 of the Convention provides otherwise, the arbitration procedure shall be conducted in accordance with Articles 2 to 10 below.

Article 2

The claimant Party shall notify the Secretariat that the Parties have agreed to submit the dispute to arbitration pursuant to paragraph 1 or paragraph 2 of Article 20 of the Convention and include, in particular, the Articles of the Convention, and the interpretation or application of which are at issue. The Secretariat shall forward the information thus received to all Parties to the Convention.

Article 3

The arbitral tribunal shall consist of three members. Each of the Parties to the dispute shall appoint an arbitrator, and the two arbitrators so appointed shall designate by common agreement the third arbitrator, who shall be the chairman of the tribunal. The latter shall not be a national of one of the parties to the dispute, nor have his usual place of residence in one of the Parties, nor be employed by any of them, nor have dealt with the case in any other capacity.

Article 4

1. If the Chairman of the arbitral tribunal has not been designated within two months of the appointment of the second arbitrator, the Secretary–General of the OAU shall, at the request of either Party, designate him within a further two months period.

2. If one of the Parties to the dispute does not appoint an arbitrator within two months of the receipt of the request, the other Party may inform the Secretary–General of the OAU who shall designate the chairman of the arbitral tribunal within a further two months period. Upon designation, the chairman of the arbitral tribunal shall request the Party which has not appointed an arbitrator to do so within two months. After such period, he shall inform the Secretary–General of the OAU who shall make this appointment within a further two month's period.

Article 5

1. The arbitral tribunal shall render its decision in accordance with international law and in accordance with the provisions of this Convention.

2. Any arbitral tribunal constituted under the provisions of this Annex shall draw up its own rules of procedure.

Article 6

1. The decision of the arbitral tribunal both on procedure and on substance, shall be taken by majority vote of its members.

2. The tribunal may take all appropriate measures in order to establish the facts. It may, at the request of one of the Parties, recommend essential interim measures of protection.

3. The Parties to the dispute shall provide all facilities necessary for the effective conduct of the proceedings.

4. The absence or default of a Party in the dispute shall not constitute an impediment to the proceedings.

Article 7

The tribunal may hear and determine counter-claims arising directly out of the subject-matter of the dispute.

Article 8

Unless the arbitral tribunal determines otherwise because of the particular circumstances of the case, the expenses of the tribunal, including the remuneration of its members, shall be borne by the Parties to the dispute in equal shares. The tribunal shall keep a record of all its expenses, and shall furnish a final statement thereof to the Parties.

Article 9

Any Party that has an interest of a legal nature in the subject-matter of the dispute which may be affected by the decision in the case, may intervene in the proceedings with the consent of the tribunal.

Article 10

1. The tribunal shall render its award within five months of the date on which it is established unless it finds it necessary to extend the time-limit for a period which should not exceed five months.

2. The award of the arbitral tribunal shall be accompanied by a statement of reasons. It shall be final and binding upon the Parties to the dispute.

3. Any dispute which may arise between the Parties concerning the interpretation or execution of the award may be submitted by either Party to the arbitral tribunal which made the award or, if the latter cannot be seized thereof, to another tribunal constituted for this purpose in the same manner as the first.

6. BIOSPHERE

6.1 CONVENTION ON NATURE PROTECTION AND WILDLIFE PRESERVATION IN THE WESTERN HEMISPHERE (WITHOUT ANNEX). Concluded at Washington, 12 October 1940. Entered into force, 1 May 1942. 161 U.N.T.S. 193, 56 Stat. 1354, T.S. No. 981

PREAMBLE

The Governments of the American Republics, wishing to protect and preserve in their natural habitat representatives of all species and genera of their native flora and fauna, including migratory birds, in sufficient numbers and over areas extensive enough to assure them from becoming extinct through any agency within man's control; and

Wishing to protect and preserve scenery of extraordinary beauty, unusual and striking geologic formations, regions and natural objects of aesthetic, historic or scientific value, and areas characterized by primitive conditions in those cases covered by this Convention; and

Wishing to conclude a convention on the protection of nature and the preservation of flora and fauna to effectuate the foregoing purposes, have agreed upon the following Articles:

Article I

DESCRIPTION OF TERMS USED IN THE WORDING OF THIS CONVENTION

1. The expression NATIONAL PARKS shall denote:

Areas established for the protection and preservation of superlative scenery, flora and fauna of national significance which the general public may enjoy and from which it may benefit when placed under public control.

2. The expression NATIONAL RESERVES shall denote:

Regions established for conservation and utilization of natural resources under government control, on which protection of animal and plant life will be afforded in so far as this may be consistent with the primary purpose of such reserves.

3. The expression NATURE MONUMENTS shall denote:

Regions, objects, or living species of flora or fauna of aesthetic, historic or scientific interest to which strict protection is given. The purpose of nature monuments is the protection of a specific object, or a species of flora or fauna, and setting aside an area, an object, or a single species, as an inviolate nature monument, except for duly authorized scientific investigations or government inspection.

4. The expression STRICT WILDERNESS RESERVES shall denote:

A region under public control characterized by primitive conditions of flora, fauna, transportation and habitation wherein there is no provision for the passage of motorized transportation and all commercial developments are included.

5. The expression MIGRATORY BIRDS shall denote:

Birds of those species, all or some of whose individual members, may in any season cross any of the boundaries between the American countries. Some of the species of the following families are examples of birds characterized as migratory: Charadriidae, Scolopacidae, Caprimulgidae, Hirundinidae.

Article II

1. The Contracting Governments will explore at once the possibility of establishing in their territories national parks, national reserves, nature monuments, and strict wilderness reserves as defined in the preceding article. In cases where such establishment is feasible, the creation thereof shall be begun as soon as possible after the effective date of the present Convention.

2. If in any country the establishment of national parks, national reserves, nature monuments, or strict wilderness reserves is found to be impractical at present, suitable areas, objects or living species of fauna or flora, as the case may be, shall be selected as early as possible to be transformed into national parks, national reserves, nature monuments or strict wilderness reserves as soon as, in the opinion of the authorities concerned, circumstances will permit.

3. The Contracting Governments shall notify the Pan American Union of the establishment of any national parks, national reserves, nature monuments, or strict wilderness reserves, and of the legislation, including the methods of administrative control, adopted in connection therewith.

Article III

The Contracting Governments agree that the boundaries of national parks shall not be altered, or any portion thereof be capable of alienation, except by the competent legislative authority. The resources of these reserves shall not be subject to exploitation for commercial profit.

The Contracting Governments agree to prohibit hunting, killing and capturing of members of the fauna and destruction or collection of representatives of the flora in national parks except by or under the direction or control of the park authorities, or for duly authorized scientific investigations.

The Contracting Governments further agree to provide facilities for public recreation and education in national parks consistent with the purposes of this Convention.

Article IV

The Contracting Governments agree to maintain the strict wilderness reserves inviolate, as far as practicable, except for duly authorized scientific investigations or government inspection, or such uses as are consistent with the purposes for which the area was established.

Article V

1. The Contracting Governments agree to adopt, or to propose such adoption to their respective appropriate law-making bodies, suitable laws and regulations for the protection and preservation of flora and fauna within their national boundaries, but not included in the national parks, national reserves, nature monuments, or strict wilderness reserves referred to in Article II

hereof. Such regulations shall contain proper provisions for the taking of specimens of flora and fauna for scientific study and investigation by properly accredited individuals and agencies.

2. The Contracting Governments agree to adopt, or to recommend that their respective legislatures adopt, laws which will assure the protection and preservation of the natural scenery, striking geological formations, and regions and natural objects of aesthetic interest or historic or scientific value.

Article VI

The Contracting Governments agree to cooperate among themselves in promoting the objectives of the present Convention. To this end they will lend proper assistance, consistent with national laws, to scientists of the American Republics engaged in research and field study; they may, when circumstances warrant, enter into agreements with one another or with scientific institutions of the Americas in order to increase the effectiveness of this collaboration; and they shall make available to all the American Republics equally through publication or otherwise the scientific knowledge resulting from such cooperative effort.

Article VII

The Contracting Governments shall adopt appropriate measures for the protection of migratory birds of economic or aesthetic value or to prevent the threatened extinction of any given species. Adequate measures shall be adopted which will permit, in so far as the respective governments may see fit, a rational utilization of migratory birds for the purpose of sports as well as for food, commerce, and industry, and for scientific study and investigation.

Article VIII

The protection of the species mentioned in the Annex to the present Convention is declared to be of special urgency and importance. Species included therein shall be protected as completely as possible, and their hunting, killing, capturing, or taking, shall be allowed only with the permission of the appropriate government authorities in the country. Such permission shall be granted only under special circumstances, in order to further scientific purposes, or when essential for the administration of the area in which the animal or plant is found.

Article IX

Each Contracting Government shall take the necessary measures to control and regulate the importation, exportation and transit of protected fauna or flora or any part thereof by the following means:

1. The issuing of certificates authorizing the exportation or transit of protected species of flora or fauna, or parts thereof.

2. The prohibition of the importation of any species of fauna or flora or any part thereof protected by the country of origin unless accompanied by a certificate of lawful exportation as provided for in Paragraph 1 of this Article.

Article X

1. The terms of this convention shall in no way be interpreted as replacing international agreements previously entered into by one or more of the High Contracting Powers.

2. The Pan American Union shall notify the Contracting Parties of any information relevant to the purposes of the present Convention communicated to it by any national museums or by any organizations, national or international, established within their jurisdiction and interested in the purposes of the Convention.

Article XI

1. The original of the present Convention in Spanish, English, Portuguese and French shall be deposited with the Pan American Union and opened for signature by the American Governments on October 12, 1940.

2. The present Convention shall remain open for signature by the American Governments. The instruments of ratification shall be deposited with the Pan American Union, which shall notify their receipt and the dates thereof, and the terms of any accompanying declarations or reservations, to all participating Governments.

3. The present Convention shall come into force three months after the deposit of not less than five ratifications with the Pan American Union.

4. Any ratification received after the date of the entry into force of the Convention, shall take effect three months after the date of its deposit with the Pan American Union.

Article XII

1. Any Contracting Government may at any time denounce the present Convention by a notification in writing addressed to the Pan American Union. Such denunciation shall take effect one year after the date of the receipt of the notification by the Pan American Union, provided, however, that no denunciation shall take effect until the expiration of five years from the date of the entry into force of this Convention.

2. If, as the result of simultaneous or successive denunciations, the number of Contracting Governments is reduced to less than three, the Convention shall cease to be in force from the date on which the last of such denunciations takes effect in accordance with the provisions of the preceding Paragraph.

3. The Pan American Union shall notify all of the American Governments of any denunciations and the date on which they take effect.

4. Should the Convention cease to be in force under the provisions of Paragraph 2 of this article, the Pan American Union shall notify all of the American Governments, indicating the date on which this will become effective.

IN WITNESS WHEREOF, the undersigned Plenipotentiaries, having deposited their full powers found to be in due and proper form, sign this Convention at the Pan American Union, Washington, D.C., on behalf of their respective Governments and affix thereto their seals on the dates appearing opposite their signatures.

* * *

6.2 INTERNATIONAL CONVENTION FOR THE REGULATION OF WHAL-ING (WITHOUT SCHEDULE BUT AS AMENDED BY 1956 PROTO-COL). Concluded at Washington, 2 December 1946. Entered into force, 10 November 1948. 161 U.N.T.S. 72, T.I.A.S. No. 1849; 338 U.N.T.S. 366, 10 U.S.T. 952, T.I.A.S. No. 4228

The Governments whose duly authorized representatives have subscribed hereto,

Recognizing the interest of the nations of the world in safeguarding for future generations the great natural resources represented by the whale stocks;

Considering that the history of whaling has seen overfishing of one area after another and of one species of whale after another to such a degree that it is essential to protect all species of whales from further overfishing;

Recognizing that the whale stocks are susceptible of natural increases if whaling is properly regulated, and that increases in the size of whale stocks will permit increases in the numbers of whales which may be captured without endangering these natural resources;

Recognizing that it is in the common interest to achieve the optimum level of whale stocks as rapidly as possible without causing wide-spread economic and nutritional distress;

Recognizing that in the course of achieving these objectives, whaling operations should be confined to those species best able to sustain exploitation in order to give an interval for recovery to certain species of whales now depleted in numbers;

Desiring to establish a system of international regulation for the whale fisheries to ensure proper and effective conservation and development of whale stocks on the basis of the principles embodied in the provisions of the International Agreement for the Regulation of Whaling signed in London on June 8, 1937 and the protocols to that Agreement signed in London on June 24, 1938 and November 26, 1945; and

Having decided to conclude a convention to provide for the proper conservation of whale stocks and thus make possible the orderly development of the whaling industry;

Have agreed as follows:

Article I

1. This Convention includes the Schedule attached thereto which forms an integral part thereof. All references to "Convention" shall be understood as including the said Schedule either in its present terms or as amended in accordance with the provisions of Article V.

2. This Convention applies to factory ships, land stations, and whale catchers under the jurisdiction of the Contracting Governments, and to all waters in which whaling is prosecuted by such factory ships, land stations, and whale catchers.

Article II

As used in this Convention

1. "factory ship" means a ship in which or on which whales are treated whether wholly or in part;

2. "land station" means a factory on the land at which whales are treated whether wholly or in part;

3. "whale catcher" means a helicopter, or other aircraft, or a ship, used for the purpose of hunting, taking, killing, towing, holding on to, or scouting for whales;

4. "Contracting Government" means any Government which has deposited an instrument of ratification or has given notice of adherence to this Convention.

Article III

1. The Contracting Governments agree to establish an International Whaling Commission, hereinafter referred to as the Commission, to be composed of one member of each Contracting Government. Each member shall have one vote and may be accompanied by one or more experts and advisers.

2. The Commission shall elect from its own members a Chairman and Vice Chairman and shall determine its own Rules of Procedure. Decisions of the Commission shall be taken by a simple majority of those members voting except that a three-fourths majority of those members voting shall be required for action in pursuance of Article V. The Rules of Procedure may provide for decisions otherwise than at meetings of the Commission.

3. The Commission may appoint its own Secretary and staff.

4. The Commission may set up, from among its own members and experts or advisers, such committees as it considers desirable to perform such functions as it may authorize.

5. The expenses of each member of the Commission and of his experts and advisers shall be determined and paid by his own Government.

6. Recognizing that specialized agencies related to the United Nations will be concerned with the conservation and development of whale fisheries and the products arising therefrom and desiring to avoid duplication of functions, the Contracting Governments will consult among themselves within two years after the coming into force of this Convention to decide whether the Commission shall be brought within the framework of a specialized agency related to the United Nations.

7. In the meantime the Government of the United Kingdom of Great Britain and Northern Ireland shall arrange, in consultation with the other Contracting Governments, to convene the first meeting of the Commission, and shall initiate the consultation referred to in paragraph 6 above.

8. Subsequent meetings of the Commission shall be convened as the Commission may determine.

Article IV

1. The Commission may either in collaboration with or through independent agencies of the Contracting Governments or other public or private agencies, establishments, or organizations, or independently

(a) encourage, recommend, or if necessary, organize studies and investigations relating to whales and whaling;

(*b*) collect and analyze statistical information concerning the current condition and trend of the whale stocks and the effects of whaling activities thereon;

(*c*) study, appraise, and disseminate information concerning methods of maintaining and increasing the populations of whale stocks.

2. The Commission shall arrange for the publication of reports of its activities, and it may publish independently or in collaboration with the International Bureau for Whaling Statistics at Sandefjord in Norway and other organizations and agencies such reports as it deems appropriate, as well as statistical, scientific, and other pertinent information relating to whales and whaling.

Article V

1. The Commission may amend from time to time the provisions of the Schedule by adopting regulations with respect to the conservation and utilization of whale resources, fixing (*a*) protected and unprotected species; (*b*) open and closed seasons; (*c*) open and closed waters, including the designation of sanctuary areas; (*d*) size limits for each species; (*e*) time, methods, and intensity of whaling (including the maximum catch of whales to be taken in any one season); (*f*) types and specifications of gear and apparatus and appliances which may be used; (*g*) methods of measurement; (*h*) catch returns and other statistical and biological records; and (*i*) methods of inspection.

2. These amendments of the Schedule (*a*) shall be such as are necessary to carry out the objectives and purposes of this Convention and to provide for the conservation, development, and optimum utilization of the whale resources; (*b*) shall be based on scientific findings; (*c*) shall not involve restrictions on the number or nationality of factory ships or land stations, nor allocate specific quotas to any factory ship or land station or to any group of factory ships or land stations; and (*d*) shall take into consideration the interests of the consumers of whale products and the whaling industry.

3. Each of such amendments shall become effective with respect to the Contracting Governments ninety days following notification of the amendment by the Commission to each of the Contracting Governments, except that (*a*) if any Government presents to the Commission objection to any amendment prior to the expiration of this ninety-day period, the amendment shall not become effective with respect to any of the Governments for an additional ninety days; (*b*) thereupon, any other Contracting Government may present objection to the amendment at any time prior to the expiration of the additional ninety-day period, or before the expiration of thirty days from the date of receipt of the last objection received during such additional ninety-day period, whichever date shall be the later; and (*c*) thereafter, the amendment shall become effective with respect to all Contracting Governments which have not presented objection but shall not become effective with respect to any Government which has so objected until such date as the objection is withdrawn. The Commission shall notify each Contracting Government immediately upon receipt of each objection and withdrawal and each Contracting Government shall acknowledge receipt of all notification of amendments, objections, and withdrawals.

4. No amendments shall become effective before July 1, 1949.

Article VI

The Commission may from time to time make recommendations to any or all Contracting Governments on any matters which relate to whales or whaling and to the objectives and purposes of this Convention.

Article VII

The Contracting Governments shall ensure prompt transmission to the International Bureau for Whaling Statistics at Sandefjord in Norway, or to such other body as the Commission may designate, of notifications and statistical and other information required by this Convention in such form and manner as may be prescribed by the Commission.

Article VIII

1. Notwithstanding anything contained in this Convention, any Contracting Government may grant to any of its nationals a special permit authorizing that national to kill, take, and treat whales for purposes of scientific research subject to such restrictions as to number and subject to such other conditions as the Contracting Government thinks fit, and the killing, taking, and treating of whales in accordance with the provisions of this Article shall be exempt from the operation of this Convention. Each Contracting Government shall report at once to the Commission all such authorizations which it has granted. Each Contracting Government may at any time revoke any such special permit which it has granted.

2. Any whales taken under these special permits shall so far as practicable be processed and the proceeds shall be dealt with in accordance with directions issued by the Government by which the permit was granted.

3. Each Contracting Government shall transmit to such body as may be designated by the Commission, in so far as practicable, and at intervals of not more than one year, scientific information available to that Government with respect to whales and whaling, including the results of research conducted pursuant to paragraph 1 of this Article and to Article IV.

4. Recognizing that continuous collection and analysis of biological data in connection with the operations of factory ships and land stations are indispensable to sound and constructive management of the whale fisheries, the Contracting Governments will take all practicable measures to obtain such data.

Article IX

1. Each Contracting Government shall take appropriate measures to ensure the application of the provisions of this Convention and the punishment of infractions against the said provisions in operations carried out by persons or by vessels under its jurisdiction.

2. No bonus or other remuneration calculated with relation to the results of their work shall be paid to the gunners and crews of whale catchers in respect of any whales the taking of which is forbidden by this Convention.

3. Prosecution for infractions against or contraventions of this Convention shall be instituted by the Government having jurisdiction over the offense.

4.   Each Contracting Government shall transmit to the Commission full details of each infraction of the provisions of this Convention by persons or vessels under the jurisdiction of that Government as reported by its inspectors.   This information shall include a statement of measures taken for dealing with the infraction and of penalties imposed.

Article X

1.   This Convention shall be ratified and the instruments of ratification shall be deposited with the Government of the United States of America.

2.   Any Government which has not signed this Convention may adhere thereto after it enters into force by a notification in writing to the Government of the United States of America.

3.   The Government of the United States of America shall inform all other signatory Governments and all adhering Governments of all ratifications deposited and adherences received.

4.   This Convention shall, when instruments of ratification have been deposited by at least six signatory Governments, which shall include the Governments of the Netherlands, Norway, the Union of Soviet Socialist Republics, the United Kingdom of Great Britain and Northern Ireland, and the United States of America, enter into force with respect to those Governments and shall enter into force with respect to each Government which subsequently ratifies or adheres on the date of the deposit of its instrument of ratification or the receipt of its notification of adherence.

5.   The provisions of the Schedule shall not apply prior to July 1, 1948. Amendments to the Schedule adopted pursuant to Article V shall not apply prior to July 1, 1949.

Article XI

Any Contracting Government may withdraw from this Convention on June thirtieth of any year by giving notice on or before January first of the same year to the depositary Government, which upon receipt of such a notice shall at once communicate it to the other Contracting Governments.   Any other Contracting Government may, in like manner, within one month of the receipt of a copy of such notice from the depositary Government, give notice of withdrawal, so that the Convention shall cease to be in force on June thirtieth of the same year with respect to the Government giving notice of withdrawal.

This Convention shall bear the date on which it is opened for signature and shall remain open for signature for a period of fourteen days thereafter.

6.3 CONVENTION ON FISHING AND CONSERVATION OF THE LIVING RESOURCES OF THE HIGH SEAS.[1] Concluded at Geneva, 29 April 1958. Entered into force, 20 March 1966. 559 U.N.T.S. 285, 17 U.S.T. 138, T.I.A.S. No. 5969[2]

Article 1

1. All States have the right for their nationals to engage in fishing on the high seas, subject (a) to their treaty obligations, (b) to the interests and rights of coastal States as provided for in this Convention, and (c) to the provisions contained in the following articles concerning conservation of the living resources of the high seas.

2. All States have the duty to adopt, or to co-operate with other States in adopting, such measures for their respective nationals as may be necessary for the conservation of the living resources of the high seas.

Article 2

As employed in this Convention, the expression "conservation of the living resources of the high seas" means the aggregate of the measures rendering possible the optimum sustainable yield from those resources so as to secure a maximum supply to food and other marine products. Conservation programmes should be formulated with a view to securing in the first place a supply of food for human consumption.

Article 3

A State whose nationals are engaged in fishing any stock or stocks of fish or other living marine resources in any area of the high seas where the nationals of other States are not thus engaged shall adopt, for its own nationals, measures in that area when necessary for the purpose of the conservation of the living resources affected.

Article 4

1. If the nationals of two or more States are engaged in fishing the same stock or stocks of fish or other living marine resources in any area or areas of the high seas, these States shall, at the request of any of them, enter into negotiations with a view to prescribing by agreement for their nationals the necessary measures for the conservation of the living resources affected.

2. If the States concerned do not reach agreement within twelve months, any of the parties may initiate the procedure contemplated by article 9.

Article 5

1. If, subsequent to the adoption of the measures referred to in articles 3 and 4, nationals of other States engage in fishing the same stock or stocks of fish or other living marine resources in any area or areas of the high seas, the other States shall apply the measures, which shall not be discriminatory in form or in fact, to their own nationals not later than seven months after the date on which the measures shall have been notified to the Director–General

---

1. *See also* Basic Documents 4.3, 4.4 and 4.5, *supra*.

2. *See also* Optional Protocol to the 1958 Law of the Sea Conventions Concerning the Compulsory Settlement of Disputes (which provides for reference to the International Court of Justice of disputes arising out of this agreement), concluded 29 April 1958 and entered into force 30 September 1962 (450 UNTS 169).

of the Food and Agriculture Organization of the United Nations. The Director–General shall notify such measures to any State which so requests and, in any case, to any State specified by the State initiating the measure.

2. If these other States do not accept the measures so adopted and if no agreement can be reached within twelve months, any of the interested parties may initiate the procedure contemplated by article 9. Subject to paragraph 2 of article 10, the measures adopted shall remain obligatory pending the decision of the special commission.

Article 6

1. A coastal State has a special interest in the maintenance of the productivity of the living resources in any area of the high seas adjacent to its territorial sea.

2. A coastal State is entitled to take part on an equal footing in any system of research and regulation for purposes of conservation of the living resources of the high seas in that area, even though its nationals do not carry on fishing there.

3. A state whose nationals are engaged in fishing in any area of the high seas adjacent to the territorial sea of a State shall, at the request of that coastal State, enter into negotiations with a view to prescribing by agreement the measures necessary for the conservation of the living resources of the high seas in that area.

4. A State whose nationals are engaged in fishing in any area of the high seas adjacent to the territorial sea of a coastal State shall not enforce conservation measures in that area which are opposed to those which have been adopted by the coastal State, but may enter into negotiations with the coastal State with a view to prescribing by agreement the measures necessary for the conservation of the living resources of the high seas in that area.

5. If the States concerned do not reach agreement with respect to conservation measures within twelve months, any of the parties may initiate the procedure contemplated by article 9.

Article 7

1. Having regard to the provisions of paragraph 1 of article 6, any coastal State may, with a view to the maintenance of the productivity of the living resources of the sea, adopt unilateral measures of conservation appropriate to any stock of fish or other marine resources in any area of the high seas adjacent to its territorial sea, provided that negotiations to that effect with the other States concerned have not led to an agreement within six months.

2. The measures which the coastal State adopts under the previous paragraph shall be valid as to other States only if the following requirements are fulfilled:

(a) That there is a need for urgent application of conservation measures in the light of the existing knowledge of the fishery;

(b) That the measures adopted are based on appropriate scientific findings;

(*c*) That such measures do not discriminate in form or in fact against foreign fishermen.

3. These measures shall remain in force pending the settlement, in accordance with the relevant provisions of this Convention, of any disagreement as to their validity.

4. If the measures are not accepted by the other States concerned, any of the parties may initiate the procedure contemplated by article 9. Subject to paragraph 2 of article 10, the measures adopted shall remain obligatory pending the decision of the special commission.

5. The principles of geographical demarcation as defined in article 12 of the Convention on the Territorial Sea and the Contiguous Zone shall be adopted when coasts of different States are involved.

Article 8

1. Any State which, even if its nationals are not engaged in fishing in an area of the high seas not adjacent to its coast, has a special interest in the conservation of the living resources of the high seas in that area, may request the State or States whose nationals are engaged in fishing there to take the necessary measures of conservation under articles 3 and 4 respectively, at the same time mentioning the scientific reasons which in its opinion make such measures necessary, and indicating its special interest.

2. If no agreement is reached within twelve months, such State may initiate the procedure contemplated by article 9.

Article 9

1. Any dispute which may arise between States under articles 4, 5, 6, 7 and 8 shall, at the request of any of the parties, be submitted for settlement to a special commission of five members, unless the parties agree to seek a solution by another method of peaceful settlement, as provided for in Article 33 of the Charter of the United Nations.

2. The members of the commission, one of whom shall be designated as chairman, shall be named by agreement between the States in dispute within three months of the request for settlement in accordance with the provisions of this article. Failing agreement they shall, upon the request of any State party, be named by the Secretary–General of the United Nations, within a further three-month period, in consultation with the States in dispute and with the President of the International Court of Justice and the Director–General of the Food and Agriculture Organization of the United Nations, from amongst well-qualified persons being nationals of States not involved in the dispute and specializing in legal, administrative or scientific questions relating to fisheries, depending upon the nature of the dispute to be settled. Any vacancy arising after the original appointment shall be filled in the same manner as provided for the initial selection.

3. Any State party to proceedings under these articles shall have the right to name one of its nationals to the special commission, with the right to participate fully in the proceedings on the same footing as a member of the commission, but without the right to vote or to take part in the writing of the commission's decision.

4. The commission shall determine its own procedure, assuring each party to the proceedings a full opportunity to be heard and to present its case. It shall also determine how the costs and expenses shall be divided between the parties to the dispute, failing agreement by the parties on this matter.

5. The special commission shall render its decision within a period of five months from the time it is appointed unless it decides, in case of necessity, to extend the time limit for a period not exceeding three months.

6. The special commission shall, in reaching its decisions, adhere to these articles and to any special agreements between the disputing parties regarding settlement of the dispute.

7. Decisions of the commission shall be by majority vote.

Article 10

1. The special commission shall, in disputes arising under article 7, apply the criteria listed in paragraph 2 of that article. In disputes under articles 4, 5, 6 and 8, the commission shall apply the following criteria, according to the issues involved in the dispute:

(*a*) Common to the determination of disputes arising under articles 4, 5 and 6 are the requirements:

(i) That scientific findings demonstrate the necessity of conservation measures;

(ii) That the specific measures are based on scientific findings and are practicable; and

(iii) That the measures do not discriminate, in form or in fact, against fishermen of other States;

(*b*) Applicable to the determination of disputes arising under article 8 is the requirement that scientific findings demonstrate the necessity for conservation measures, or that the conservation programme is adequate, as the case may be.

2. The special commission may decide that pending its award the measures in dispute shall not be applied, provided that, in the case of disputes under article 7, the measures shall only be suspended when it is apparent to the commission on the basis of *prima facie* evidence that the need for the urgent application of such measures does not exist.

Article 11

The decisions of the special commission shall be binding on the States concerned and the provisions of paragraph 2 of Article 94 of the Charter of the United Nations shall be applicable to those decisions. If the decisions are accompanied by any recommendations, they shall receive the greatest possible consideration.

Article 12

1. If the factual basis of the award of the special commission is altered by substantial changes in the conditions of the stock or stocks of fish or other living marine resources or in methods of fishing, any of the States concerned may request the other States to enter into negotiations with a view to prescribing by agreement the necessary modifications in the measures of conservation.

2. If no agreement is reached within a reasonable period of time, any of the States concerned may again resort to the procedure contemplated by article 9 provided that at least two years have elapsed from the original award.

Article 13

1. The regulation of fisheries conducted by means of equipment embedded in the floor of the sea in areas of the high seas adjacent to the territorial sea of a State may be undertaken by that State where such fisheries have long been maintained and conducted by its nationals, provided that non-nationals are permitted to participate in such activities on an equal footing with nationals except in areas where such fisheries have by long usage been exclusively enjoyed by such nationals. Such regulations will not, however, affect the general status of the areas as high seas.

2. In this article, the expression "fisheries conducted by means of equipment embedded in the floor of the sea" means those fisheries using gear with supporting members embedded in the sea floor, constructed on a site and left there to operate permanently or, if removed, restored each season on the same site.

Article 14

In articles 1, 3, 4, 5, 6 and 8, the term "nationals" means fishing boats or craft of any size having the nationality of the State concerned, according to the law of that State, irrespective of the nationality of the members of their crews.

Article 15

This Convention shall, until 31 October 1958, be open for signature by all States Members of the United Nations or of any of the specialized agencies, and by any other State invited by the General Assembly of the United Nations to become a Party to the Convention.

Article 16

This Convention is subject to ratification. The instruments of ratification shall be deposited with the Secretary–General of the United Nations.

Article 17

This Convention shall be open for accession by any States belonging to any of the categories mentioned in article 15. The instruments of accession shall be deposited with the Secretary–General of the United Nations.

Article 18

1. This Convention shall come into force on the thirtieth day following the date of deposit of the twenty-second instrument of ratification or accession with the Secretary–General of the United Nations.

2. For each State ratifying or acceding to the Convention after the deposit of the twenty-second instrument of ratification or accession, the Convention shall enter into force on the thirtieth day after deposit by such State of its instrument of ratification or accession.

Article 19

1. At the time of signature, ratification or accession, any State may make reservations to articles of the Convention other than to articles 6, 7, 9, 10, 11 and 12.

2. Any contracting State making a reservation in accordance with the preceding paragraph may at any time withdraw the reservation by a communication to that effect addressed to the Secretary–General of the United Nations.

Article 20

1. After the expiration of a period of five years from the date on which this Convention shall enter into force, a request for the revision of this Convention may be made at any time by any contracting party by means of a notification in writing addressed to the Secretary–General of the United Nations.

2. The General Assembly of the United Nations shall decide upon the steps, if any, to be taken in respect of such request.

Article 21

The Secretary–General of the United Nations shall inform all States Members of the United Nations and the other States referred to in article 15:

(a) Of signatures to this Convention and of the deposit of instruments of ratification or accession, in accordance with articles 15, 16 and 17;

(b) Of the date on which this Convention will come into force, in accordance with article 18;

(c) Of requests for revision in accordance with article 20;

(d) Of reservations to this Convention, in accordance with article 19.

Article 22

The original of this Convention, of which the Chinese, English, French, Russian and Spanish texts are equally authentic, shall be deposited with the Secretary–General of the United Nations, who shall send certified copies thereof to all States referred to in article 15.

6.4 AFRICAN CONVENTION ON THE CONSERVATION OF NATURE AND NATURAL RESOURCES (WITH LIST OF PROTECTED SPECIES). Concluded at Algiers, 15 September 1968. Entered into force, 16 June 1969. 1001 U.N.T.S. 3

PREAMBLE

We, the Heads of State and Government of Independent African States,

Fully conscious that soil, water, flora and faunal resources constitute a capital of vital importance to mankind;

Confirming, as we accepted upon declaring our adherence to the Charter of the Organization of African Unity, that we know that it is our duty "to harness the natural and human resources of our continent for the total advancement of our peoples in spheres of human endeavour";

Fully conscious of the ever-growing importance of natural resources from an economic, nutritional, scientific, educational, cultural and aesthetic point of view;

Conscious of the dangers which threaten some of these irreplaceable assets;

Accepting that the utilization of the natural resources must aim at satisfying the needs of man according to the carrying capacity of the environment;

Desirous of undertaking individual and joint action for the conservation, utilization and development of these assets by establishing and maintaining their rational utilization for the present and future welfare of mankind;

Convinced that one of the most appropriate means of achieving this end is to bring into force a convention;

Have agreed as follows:

Article I

The Contracting States hereby establish an African Convention on the Conservation of nature and natural resources.

Article II. FUNDAMENTAL PRINCIPLE

The Contracting States shall undertake to adopt the measures necessary to ensure conservation, utilization and development of soil, water, flora and faunal resources in accordance with scientific principles and with due regard to the best interests of the people.

Article III. DEFINITIONS

For purposes of the present Convention, the meaning of the following expressions shall be as defined below:

1. "Natural Resources" means renewable resources; that is soil, water, flora and fauna.

2. "Specimen" means an individual example of a species of wild animal or wild plant or part of a wild plant.

3. "Trophy" means any dead animal specimen or part thereof whether included in a manufactured or processed object or otherwise dealt with, unless it has lost its original identity; also nests, eggs and eggshells.

4. "Conservation area" means any protected natural resource area, whether it be a strict natural reserve, a national park or a special reserve;

(*a*) "strict nature reserve" means an area:

(1) under State control and the boundaries of which may not be altered nor any portion alienated except by the competent legislative authority,

(2) throughout which any form of hunting or fishing, any undertaking connected with forestry, agriculture or mining, any grazing, any excavation or prospecting, drilling, levelling of the ground or construction, any work tending to alter the configuration of the soil or the character of the vegetation, any water pollution and, generally, any act likely to harm or disturb the fauna or flora, including introduction of zoological or botanical species, whether indigenous or imported, wild or domesticated, are strictly forbidden,

(3) where it shall be forbidden to reside, enter, traverse or camp, and where it shall be forbidden to fly over at low altitude, without a special written permit from the competent authority, and in which scientific investigations (including removal of animals and plants in order to maintain an ecosystem) may only be undertaken by permission of the competent authority;

(*b*) "national park" means an area:

(1) under State control and the boundaries of which may not be altered or any portion alienated except by the competent legislative authority,

(2) exclusively set aside for the propagation, protection, conservation and management of vegetation and wild animals as well as for the protection of sites, land-scapes or geological formations of particular scientific or aesthetic value, for the benefit and enjoyment of the general public, and

(3) in which the killing, hunting and capture of animals and the destruction or collection of plants are prohibited except for scientific and management purposes and on the condition that such measures are taken under the direction or control of the competent authority,

(4) covering any aquatic environment to which all of the provisions of section (*b*)(1–3) above are applicable.

The activities prohibited in strict nature reserve under the provisions of section (*a*)(2) of paragraph 4 of this article are equally prohibited in national parks except in so far as they are necessary to enable the park authorities to implement the provisions of section (2) of this paragraph, by applying, for example, appropriate management practices, and to enable the public to visit these parks; however, sport fishing may be practiced with the authorization and under the control of the competent authority.

(*c*) "special reserve" means other protected areas such as:

(1) "game reserve" which shall denote an area

(*a*) set aside for the conservation, management and propagation of wild animal life and the protection and management of its habitat,

(*b*) within which the hunting, killing or capture of fauna shall be prohibited except by or under the direction or control of the reserve authorities,

(*c*) where settlement and other human activities shall be controlled or prohibited;

(2) "partial reserve" or "sanctuary" which shall denote an area

(*a*) set aside to protect characteristic wildlife and especially bird communities, or to protect particularly threatened animal or plant species and especially those listed in the Annex to this Convention, together with the biotopes essential for their survival,

(*b*) in which all other interests and activities shall be subordinated to this end;

(3) "soil", "water" or "forest" reserve shall denote areas set aside to protect such resources.

Article IV. Soil

The Contracting States shall take effective measures for conservation and improvement of the soil and shall in particular combat erosion and misuse of the soil. To this end:

(*a*) they shall establish land-use plans based on scientific investigations (ecological, pedological, economic, and sociological) and, in particular, classification of land-use capability;

(*b*) they shall, when implementing agricultural practices and agrarian reforms,

(1) improve soil-conservation and introduce improved farming methods, which ensure long-term productivity of the land,

(2) control erosion caused by various forms of land-use which may lead to loss of vegetation cover.

Article V. Water

1. The Contracting States shall establish policies for conservation, utilization and development of underground and surface water, and shall endeavour to guarantee for their populations a sufficient and continuous supply of suitable water, taking appropriate measures with due regard to

(1) the study of water cycles and the investigation of each catchment area,

(2) the co-ordination and planning of water resources development projects,

(3) the administration and control of all water utilization, and

(4) prevention and control of water pollution.

2. Where surface or underground water resources are shared by two or more of the Contracting States, the latter shall act in consultation, and if the

need arises, set up inter-State Commissions to study and resolve problems arising from the joint use of these resources, and for the joint development and conservation thereof.

Article VI. FLORA

1. The Contracting States shall take all necessary measures for the protection of flora and to ensure its best utilization and development. To this end the Contracting States shall:

(*a*) adopt scientifically-based conservation, utilization and management plans of forests and rangeland, taking into account the social and economic needs of the States concerned, the importance of the vegetation cover for the maintenance of the water balance of an area, the productivity of soils and the habitat requirements of the fauna;

(*b*) observe section (*a*) above by paying particular attention to controlling bush fires, forest exploitation, land clearing for cultivation, and over-grazing by domestic and wild animals;

(*c*) set aside areas for forest reserves and carry out afforestation programmes where necessary;

(*d*) limitation of forest grazing to season and intensities that will not prevent forest regeneration; and

(*e*) establish botanical gardens to perpetuate plant species of particular interest.

2. The Contracting States also shall undertake the conservation of plant species or communities, which are threatened and/or of special scientific or aesthetic value by ensuring that they are included in conservation areas.

Article VII. FAUNAL RESOURCES

1. The Contracting States shall ensure conservation, wise use and development of faunal resources and their environment, within the framework of land-use planning and of economic and social development. Management shall be carried out in accordance with plans based on scientific principles, and to that end the Contracting States shall:

(*a*) manage wildlife populations inside designated areas according to the objectives of such areas and also manage exploitable wildlife populations outside such areas for an optimum sustained yield, compatible with and complementary to other land uses; and

(*b*) manage aquatic environments, whether in fresh, brackish or coastal water, with a view to minimize deleterious effects of any water and land use practice which might adversely affect aquatic habitats.

2. The Contracting States shall adopt adequate legislation on hunting, capture and fishing, under which:

(*a*) the issue of permits is properly regulated;

(*b*) unauthorized methods are prohibited;

(*c*) the following methods of hunting, capture and fishing are prohibited:

(1) any methods liable to cause a mass destruction of wild animals,

(2) the use of drugs, poisons, poisoned weapons or poisoned baits,

(3) the use of explosives,

(4) the following methods of hunting and capture are particularly prohibited:

    1 the use of mechanically propelled vehicles,

    2 the use of fire,

    3 the use of fire arms capable of firing more than one round at each pull of the trigger,

    4 hunting or capture at night,

    5 the use of missiles containing detonators;

(*d*) the following methods of hunting or capture are as far as possible prohibited:

(1) the use of nets and stockades,

(2) the use of concealed traps, pits, snares, set-gun traps, deadfalls, and hunting from a blind or hide;

(*e*) with a view to as rational use as possible of game meat the abandonment by hunters of carcasses of animals, which represent a food resource, is prohibited.

Capture of animals with the aid of drugs or mechanically-propelled vehicles, or hunting or capture by night if carried out by, or under the control of, the competent authority shall nevertheless be exempted from the prohibitions under (*c*) above.

Article VIII. PROTECTED SPECIES

1. The Contracting States recognize that it is important and urgent to accord a special protection to those animal and plant species that are threatened with extinction, or which may become so, and to the habitat necessary to their survival. Where such a species is represented only in the territory of one Contracting State, that State has a particular responsibility for its protection. These species which are, or may be listed, according to the degree of protection that shall be given to them are placed in Class A or B of the annex to this Convention, and shall be protected by Contracting States as follows:

(1) species in Class A shall be totally protected throughout the entire territory of the Contracting States; the hunting, killing, capture or collection of specimens shall be permitted only on the authorization in each case of the highest competent authority and only if required in the national interest or for scientific purposes; and

(2) species in Class B shall be totally protected, but may be hunted, killed, captured or collected under special authorization granted by the competent authority.

2. The competent authority of each Contracting State shall examine the necessity of applying the provisions of this article to species not listed in the annex, in order to conserve the indigenous flora and fauna of their respective

countries. Such additional species shall be placed in Class A or B by the State concerned, according to its specific requirements.

Article IX. TRAFFIC IN SPECIMENS AND TROPHIES

1. In the case of animal species to which Article VIII does not apply the Contracting States shall:

(*a*) regulate trade in and transport of specimens and trophies;

(*b*) control the application of these regulations in such a way as to prevent trade in specimens and trophies which have been illegally captured or killed or obtained.

2. In the case of plant and animal species to which Article VIII, paragraph (1), applies, the Contracting States shall:

(*a*) take all measures similar to those in paragraph (1);

(*b*) make the export of such specimens and trophies subject to an authorization:

(1) additional to that required for their capture, killing or collection by Article VIII

(2) which indicates their destination,

(3) which shall not be given unless the specimens or trophies have been obtained legally,

(4) which shall be examined prior to exportation;

(5) which shall be on a standard form, as may be arranged under Article XVI;

(*c*) make the import and transit of such specimens and trophies subject to the presentation of the authorization required under section (*b*) above, with due provision for the confiscation of specimens and trophies exported illegally, without prejudice to the application of other penalties.

Article X. CONSERVATION AREAS

1. The Contracting States shall maintain and extend where appropriate, within their territory and where applicable in their territorial waters, the conservation areas existing at the time of entry into force of the present Convention and, preferably within the framework of land-use planning programmes, assess the necessity of establishing additional conservation areas in order to:

(1) protect those ecosystems which are most representative of and particularly those which are in any respect peculiar to their territories;

(2) ensure conservation of all species and more particularly of those listed or may be listed in the annex to this Convention;

2. The Contracting States shall establish where necessary, around the borders of conservation areas, zones within which the competent authorities shall control activities detrimental to the protected natural resources.

Article XI. CUSTOMARY RIGHTS

The Contracting States shall take all necessary legislative measures to reconcile customary rights with the provisions of this Convention.

Article XII. RESEARCH

The Contracting States shall encourage and promote research in conservation, utilization and management of natural resources and shall pay particular attention to ecological and sociological factors.

Article XIII. CONSERVATION EDUCATION

1. (*a*) The Contracting States shall ensure that their peoples appreciate their close dependence on natural resources and that they understand the need, and rules for, the rational utilization of these resources.

(*b*) For this purpose they shall ensure that the principles indicated in paragraph (1):

(1) are included in educational programmes at all levels,

(2) form the object of information campaigns capable of acquainting the public with, and winning it over to, the idea of conservation.

2. In order to put into effect paragraph (1) above, the Contracting States shall make maximum use of the educational value of conservation areas.

Article XIV. DEVELOPMENT PLANS

1. The Contracting States shall ensure that conservation and management of natural resources are treated as an integral part of national and/or regional development plans.

2. In the formulation of all development plans, full consideration shall be given to ecological, as well as to economic and social factors.

3. Where any development plan is likely to affect the natural resources of another State, the latter shall be consulted.

Article XV. ORGANIZATION OF NATIONAL CONSERVATION SERVICES

Each Contracting State shall establish, if it has not already done so, a single agency empowered to deal with all matters covered by this Convention, but, where this is not possible a co-ordinating machinery shall be established for this purpose.

Article XVI. INTER-STATE CO-OPERATION

1. The Contracting States shall co-operate:

(*a*) whenever such co-operation is necessary to give effect to the provisions of this Convention, and

(*b*) whenever any national measure is likely to affect the natural resources of any other State.

2. The Contracting States shall supply the Organization of African Unity with:

(*a*) the text of laws, decrees, regulations and instructions in force in their territories, which are intended to ensure the implementation of this Convention,

(*b*) reports on the results achieved in applying the provisions of this Convention, and

(*c*) all the information necessary for the complete documentation of matters dealt with by this Convention if requested.

3. If so requested by Contracting States, the Organization of African Unity shall organize any meeting which may be necessary to dispose of any matters covered by this Convention. Requests for such meetings must be made by at least three of the Contracting States and be approved by two thirds of the States which it is proposed should participate in such meetings.

4. Any expenditure arising from this Convention, which devolves upon the Organization of African Unity shall be included in its regular budget, unless shared by the Contracting States or otherwise defrayed.

Article XVII. PROVISION FOR EXCEPTIONS

1. The provisions of this Convention shall not affect the responsibilities of Contracting States concerning:

(1) the paramount interest of the State,

(2) "force majeure",

(3) defence of human life.

2. The provisions of this Convention shall not prevent Contracting States:

(1) in time of famine,

(2) for the protection of public health,

(3) in defence of property,

to enact measures contrary to the provisions of the Convention, provided their application is precisely defined in respect of aim, time and place.

Article XVIII. SETTLEMENT OF DISPUTES

Any dispute between the Contracting States relating to the interpretation or application of this Convention, which cannot be settled by negotiation, shall at the request of any party be submitted to the Commission of Mediation, Conciliation and Arbitration of the Organization of African Unity.

Article XIX. SIGNATURE AND RATIFICATION

1. This Convention shall be open for signature immediately after being approved by the Assembly of Heads of State and Government of the Organization of African Unity.

2. This Convention shall be ratified by each of the Contracting States. The instruments of ratification shall be deposited with the Administrative Secretary–General of the Organization of African Unity.

Article XX. RESERVATIONS

1. At the time of signature, ratification or accession, any State may declare its acceptance of this Convention in part only, provided that such reservation may not apply to the provisions of Articles II–XI.

2. Reservations made in conformity with the preceding paragraph shall be deposited together with the instruments of ratification or accession.

3. Any Contracting State which has formulated a reservation in conformity with the preceding paragraph may at any time withdraw it by notifying the Administrative Secretary–General of the Organization of African Unity.

Article XXI. ENTRY INTO FORCE

1. This Convention shall come into force on the thirtieth day following the date of deposit of the fourth instrument of ratification or accession with the Administrative Secretary–General of the Organization of African Unity, who shall inform participating States accordingly.

2. In the case of a State ratifying or acceding to the Convention after the depositing of the fourth instrument of ratification or accession, the Convention shall come into force on the thirtieth day after the deposit by such State of its instrument of ratification or accession.

3. The London Convention of 1933 or any other Convention on the conservation of flora and fauna in their natural state shall cease to have effect in States in which this Convention has come into force.

Article XXII. ACCESSION

1. After the date of approval specified in Article XIX, paragraph (1), this Convention shall be open to accession by any independent and sovereign African State.

2. The instruments of accession shall be deposited with the Administrative Secretary–General of the Organization of African Unity.

Article XXIII. DENUNCIATION

1. Any Contracting State may denounce this Convention by notification in writing addressed to the Administrative Secretary–General of the Organization of African Unity.

2. Such denunciation shall take effect, for such a State, one year after the date of receipt of its notification by the Administrative Secretary–General of the Organization of African Unity.

3. No denunciation shall, however, be made before the expiry of a period of five years from the date at which for the State concerned this Convention comes into force.

Article XXIV. REVISION

1. After the expiry of a period of five years from the date of entry into force of this Convention, any Contracting State may at any time make a request for the revision of part or the whole of this Convention by notification in writing addressed to the Administrative Secretary–General of the Organization of African Unity.

2. In the event of such a request the appropriate organ of the Organization of African Unity shall deal with the matter in accordance with the provision of sections 3 and 4 of Article XVI of this Convention.

3. (i) At the request of one or more Contracting States and notwithstanding the provisions of paragraphs (1) and (2) of this Article, the annex to this Convention may be revised or added to by the appropriate organ of the Organization of African Unity.

(ii) Such revision or addition shall come into force three months after the approval by the appropriate organ of the Organization of African Unity.

Article XXV. FINAL PROVISIONS

The original of this Convention of which both the English and the French texts are authentic, shall be deposited with the Administrative Secretary–General of the Organization of African Unity.

LIST OF PROTECTED SPECIES

CLASS A

Mammalia	*Mammals*
Primates	Primates
Lemuroidae	All Malagasy lemuroids
Macaca sylvana	Barbary ape
Theropithecus gelada	Gelada baboon
Cercocebus galeritus galeritus	Tana River mangabey
Cercopithecus diana	Diana monkey
Colobus badius kirkii	Zanzibar red colobus
Colobus badius rufomitratus	Tana River red colobus
Colobus badius gordonorum	Uhehe red colobus
Colobus verus	Green colobus
Pan troglodytes	Chimpanzee
Pan paniscus	Pygmy chimpanzee
Gorilla gorilla	Gorilla
Rodentia	Rodentia
Epixerus spp.	African palm squirrels
Carnivora	Carnivora
Canis simensis	Simenian jackal
Osbornictis piscivora	Water civet
Fossa fossa	Malagasy civet
Eupleres spp.	Falanouc
Felis nigripes	Black-footed cat
Felis aurata	African golden cat
Acinonyx jubatus	Cheetah
Pinnipedia	Pennipedia
Monachus monachus	Mediterranean monk seal
Sirenia	Sirenia
Dugong dugon	Dugong
Trichechus senegalensis	West African manatee
Perissodactyla	Perissodactyla
Equus asinus	Wild ass
Equus zebra zebra	Cape mountain zebra
Ceratotherium simum	Square-lipped rhinoceros
Artiodactyla	Artiodactyla
Choeropsis liberiensis	Pygmy hippopotamus
Cervus elaphus barbarus	Barbary stag
Okapia johnstoni	Okapi
Taurotragus derbianus derbianus	Western giant eland
Cephalophus jentinki	Jentink's duiker
Hippotragus niger variani	Giant sable antelope
Alcelaphus buselaphus tora	Tora Hartebeest
Alcelaphus buselaphus swaynei	Swayne's hartebeest
Nesotragus moschatus moschatus	Zanzibar suni
Dorcatragus megalotis	Beira antelope
Gazella dorcas neglecta	Algerian dorcas gazelle
Gazella dorcas massaesyla	Moroccan dorcas gazelle
Gazella gazella cuvieri	Cuvier's gazelle
Gazella leptocerus leptocerus	Slender-horned gazelle
Gazella pelzelni	Pelseln's gazelle
Gazella spekei	Speke's gazelle

Gazella dama mhorr	Mhorr gazelle
Gazella dama lazonoi	Rio de Oro dama gazelle
Gapra walie	Walia ibex
Aves	*Birds*
Pelecanidae	All pelicans
Ciconiidae, Scopidae et Ardeidae	All storks, hammerkops, ibises, spoonbills, herons, egrets and bitters
Phoenicopteridae	All Flamingos
Sagittarius serpentarius	Secretary bird
Aegypius, Gyps, Pseudogyps, Torgos	All vultures [1]
Trigonoceps, Neophron et Necrosyrtes	Lammergeyer
Gypaëtus barbatus	Crowned hawk-eagle
Stephanoaëtus coronatus	Teita falcon
Falco fasciinucha	White-headed guineafowl
Agelastes meleagrides	Congo peacock
Afropavo congensis	All cranes
Gruidae	All ground bornbills
Bucorvus spp.	White-necked rockfowl
Picarthartes oreas	Grey-necked rockfowl
Picarthartes gymnocephalus	Warsangli linnet
Warsanglia johannis	
Reptilia	*Reptiles*
Cheloniidae, Dermochelyidae	All marine turtles
Testudo gigantea	Giant tortoise
Testudo yniphora	Angulated tortoise
Testudo radiata	Testudo radiata
Macroscinous coctei	Cape Verde skink
Gecko uroplates	Leaf-tailed gecko
Casarea dussumieri	Plate Island boa
Bolieria multicarinata	Ronde Island boa
Acrantophis madagascariensi	Acrantophis madagascariensi
Acrantophis dumerili	Acrantophis dumerili
Amphibia	*Amphibians*
Bufo superciliaris	Cameroon toad
Nectophrynoides occidentalis	Viviparous toad
Pisces	*Fishes*
Caecobarbus, Caecomastacembelus	Blind fishes
Eilichthys, Typhleotris	Blind fishes
Phreatichthys, Uegitglanis	Blind fishes
Plantes	*Plants*
Welwitschia bainesii	Welwitschia
Encephalartos laurentanus	Encephalartos
Encephalartos septentrionalis	Encephalartos

CLASS B

Mammalia	*Mammals*
Insectivora	*Insectivora*
	All other shrews of the family Potamogalidae

1. The term "All vultures" has been placed erroneously opposite the first line of the Latin term "*Aegypius, Gyps, Pseudogyps, Torgos Trigonoceps, Neophron et Necrosyrtes*", thus displacing each translation up to and including that corresponding to "*Warsanglia johannis*" by one line.

Primates	*Primates*
Lorisidae	All prosimians of the family Lorisidae
Primates	All monkeys except common baboons
Pholidota	*Pholidota*
Manis gigantea	Giant pangolin
Manis temmincki	Cape pangolin
Manis tricuspis	Tree pangolin
Manis longicaudata	Long-tailed tree pangolin
Carnivora	*Carnivora*
Lutrinae	All otters of the sub family Lutrinae
Proteles cristatus	Aardwolf
Hyaena brunnea	Brown hyaena
Hyaena hyaena barbara	Barbary hyaena
Felis caracal	Caracal lynx
Felis serval	Serval
Felis leo	Lion
Panthera pardus	Leopard
Tenrecidae	Madagascar Tenrecs (all species) Fossa
Cryptoprocta ferox	Foassa
Galidiinae	All Malagasy mongooses of the sub family Galidiinae
Tubulidentata	*Tubulidentata*
Orycteropus afer	Aardvark
Proboscidea	*Proboscidea*
Loxodonta africana	Elephant
Perissodactyla	*Perissodactyla*
Equus zebra bartmannae	Hartmann's mountain zebra
Equus burchelli	Burchell's zebra
Equus grevyi	Grevy's zebra
Diceros bicornis	Black rhinoceros
Hylochoerus meinertzhageni	*Artiodactyla* [2]
Hippopotamus amphibius	Giant forest hog
Hyemoschus aquaticus	Hippopotamus
Giraffa camelopardalis	Water chevrotain
Tragelaphus angasi	Giraffe
Tragelaphus buxtoni	Nyala
Tragelaphus spekei	Mountain nyala
Tragelaphus imberbis	Situtunga
Tragelaphus strepsiceros	Lesser kudu
Taurotragus oryx	Greater kudu
Taurotragus derbianus	Eland
Boocercus eurycerus	Giant eland
Syncerus caffer	Bongo
Cephalophus adorsi	Buffalo
Cephalophus ogilbyi	Zanzibar duiker
Cephalophus silvicultor	Ogilby's duiker
Cephalophus spadix	Yellow-baked duiker
Cephalophus zebra	Abbott's duiker
Kobus ellipsiprymnus	Banded duiker
Kobus defassa	Waterbuck
Kobus leche	Defassa waterbuck
Kobus megaceros	Lechwe
Adenota kob	Nile lechwe
	Kob
Redunca arundinum	Reedbuck

2. The title "*Artiodactyla*" has been placed erroneously opposite the Latin term "hylochoerus meinertzhageni", thus displacing each translation up to and including that corresponding to "Adenota Kob" by one line; "*Artiodactyla*" should also appear as the title for the Latin term list.

Redunca fulvorufula	Mountain reedbuck
Redunca equinus	Bohor reedbuck
Hipptragus equinus	Roan antelope
Hippotragus niger	Sable antelope
Oryx gazella	Oryx
Oryx tao	Scimitar-horned oryx
Adax nasomaculatus	Addax
Damaliscus lunatus	Tsessebe (Sassaby)
Damaliscus korrigum	Topi
Damaliscus dorcas dorcas	Bontebok
Damaliscus dorcas phillipsi	Blesbok
Damaliscus hunteri	Hunter's hartebeest
Alcelaphus buselaphus	Hartebeest
Alcelaphus lichtensteini	Lichtenstein's hartebeest
Connochaetes gnou	Black wildebeest
Connochaetes taurinus	Wildebeest
Oreotragus oreotragus	Klipspringer
Ourebia spp.	Oribis (All species)
Neotragus pygmaeus	Royal antelope
Neotragus batesi	Dwarf antelope
Madoqua kirki	Damara dikdik
Aepyceros melampus	Impala
Ammodorcas clarkei	Dibatag
Litodranius walleri	Gerenuk
Gazella dorcas	Dorcas gazelle
Gazella rufifrons	Korin gazelle
Gazella tilonura	Houglin's gazelle
Gazella dama	Dama gazelle
Gazella soemmerringi	Doemmering's gazelle
Capra ibex nubiana	Nubian ibex
Ammotragus lervia	Barbary sheep (Aoudad)

Aves	*Birds*
Struthio camelus	Ostrich
Falconiformes et strigiformes	All birds of prey and all owls not in [Class A]
Otididae	All bustards

Reptilia	*Reptiles*
Crocodylia	All crocodiles

**6.5 CONVENTION ON INTERNATIONAL TRADE IN ENDANGERED SPE-
CIES OF WILD FAUNA AND FLORA (CITES) (WITH APPENDICES I
AND II, AND AS AMENDED). Concluded at Washington, 3 March
1973. Entered into force, 1 July 1975. 993 U.N.T.S. 243, 27 U.S.T.
1087, T.I.A.S. No. 8249, 12 I.L.M. 1085 (1973)**

The Contracting States,

RECOGNIZING that wild fauna and flora in their many beautiful and
varied forms are an irreplaceable part of the natural systems of the earth
which must be protected for this and the generations to come;

CONSCIOUS of the ever-growing value of wild fauna and flora from
aesthetic, scientific, cultural, recreational and economic points of view;

RECOGNIZING that peoples and States are and should be the best
protectors of their own wild fauna and flora;

RECOGNIZING, in addition, that international cooperation is essential
for the protection of certain species of wild fauna and flora against over-
exploitation through international trade;

CONVINCED of the urgency of taking appropriate measures to this end;

HAVE AGREED as follows:

Article I

Definitions

For the purpose of the present Convention, unless the context otherwise
requires:

(a) "Species" means any species, sub-species, or geographically separate population thereof;

(b) "Specimen" means:

(i) any animal or plant, whether alive or dead;

(ii) in the case of an animal: for species included in Appendices
I and II, any readily recognizable part or derivative thereof; and for
species included in Appendix III, any readily recognizable part or
derivative thereof specified in Appendix III in relation to the species;
and

(iii) in the case of a plant: for species included in Appendix I,
any readily recognizable part or derivative thereof; and for species
included in Appendices II and III, any readily recognizable part or
derivative thereof specified in Appendices II and III in relation to the
species;

(c) "Trade" means export, re-export, import and introduction from
the sea;

(d) "Re-export" means export of any specimen that has previously
been imported;

(e) "Introduction from the sea" means transportation into a State
of specimens of any species which were taken in the marine environment
not under the jurisdiction of any State;

(f) "Scientific Authority" means a national scientific authority designated in accordance with Article IX;

(g) "Management Authority" means a national management authority designated in accordance with Article IX;

(h) "Party" means a State for which the present Convention has entered into force.

Article II

Fundamental Principles

1. Appendix I shall include all species threatened with extinction which are or may be affected by trade. Trade in specimens of these species must be subject to particularly strict regulation in order not to endanger further their survival and must only be authorized in exceptional circumstances.

2. Appendix II shall include:

(a) all species which although not necessarily now threatened with extinction may become so unless trade in specimens of such species is subject to strict regulation in order to avoid utilization incompatible with their survival; and

(b) other species which must be subject to regulation in order that trade in specimens of certain species referred to in sub-paragraph (a) of this paragraph may be brought under effective control.

3. Appendix III shall include all species which any Party identifies as being subject to regulation within its jurisdiction for the purpose of preventing or restricting exploitation, and as needing the cooperation of other parties in the control of trade.

4. The Parties shall not allow trade in specimens of species included in Appendices I, II and III except in accordance with the provisions of the present Convention.

Article III

Regulation of Trade in Specimens of Species included in Appendix I

1. All trade in specimens of species included in Appendix I shall be in accordance with the provisions of this Article.

2. The export of any specimen of a species included in Appendix I shall require the prior grant and presentation of an export permit. An export permit shall only be granted when the following conditions have been met:

(a) a Scientific Authority of the State of export has advised that such export will not be detrimental to the survival of that species;

(b) a Management Authority of the State of export is satisfied that the specimen was not obtained in contravention of the laws of that State for the protection of fauna and flora;

(c) a Management Authority of the State of export is satisfied that any living specimen will be so prepared and shipped as to minimize the risk of injury, damage to health or cruel treatment; and

(d) a Management Authority of the State of export is satisfied that an import permit has been granted for the specimen.

3. The import of any specimen of a species included in Appendix I shall require the prior grant and presentation of an import permit and either an

export permit or a re-export certificate. An import permit shall only be granted when the following conditions have been met:

(a) a Scientific Authority of the State of import has advised that the import will be for purposes which are not detrimental to the survival of the species involved;

(b) a Scientific Authority of the State of import is satisfied that the proposed recipient of a living specimen is suitably equipped to house and care for it; and

(c) a Management Authority of the State of import is satisfied that the specimen is not to be used for primarily commercial purposes.

4. The re-export of any specimen of a species included in Appendix I shall require the prior grant and presentation of a re-export certificate. A re-export certificate shall only be granted when the following conditions have been met:

(a) a Management Authority of the State of re-export is satisfied that the specimen was imported into that State in accordance with the provisions of the present Convention;

(b) a Management Authority of the State of re-export is satisfied that any living specimen will be so prepared and shipped as to minimize the risk of injury, damage to health or cruel treatment; and

(c) a Management Authority of the State of re-export is satisfied that an import permit has been granted for any living specimen.

5. The introduction from the sea of any specimen of a species included in Appendix I shall require the prior grant of a certificate from a Management Authority of the State of introduction. A certificate shall only be granted when the following conditions have been met:

(a) a Scientific Authority of the State of introduction advises that the introduction will not be detrimental to the survival of the species involved;

(b) a Management Authority of the State of introduction is satisfied that the proposed recipient of a living specimen is suitably equipped to house and care for it; and

(c) a Management Authority of the State of introduction is satisfied that the specimen is not to be used for primarily commercial purposes.

Article IV

Regulation of Trade in Specimens of Species included in Appendix II

1. All trade in specimens of species included in Appendix II shall be in accordance with the provisions of this Article.

2. The export of any specimen of a species included in Appendix II shall require the prior grant and presentation of an export permit. An export permit shall only be granted when the following conditions have been met:

(a) a Scientific Authority of the State of export has advised that such export will not be detrimental to the survival of that species;

(b) a Management Authority of the State of export is satisfied that the specimen was not obtained in contravention of the laws of that State for the protection of fauna and flora; and

(c) a Management Authority of the State of export is satisfied that any living specimen will be so prepared and shipped as to minimize the risk of injury, damage to health or cruel treatment.

3. A Scientific Authority in each Party shall monitor both the export permits granted by that State for specimens of species included in Appendix II and the actual exports of such specimens. Whenever a Scientific Authority determines that the export of specimens of any such species should be limited in order to maintain that species throughout its range at a level consistent with its role in the ecosystems in which it occurs and well above the level at which that species might become eligible for inclusion in Appendix I, the Scientific Authority shall advise the appropriate Management Authority of suitable measures to be taken to limit the grant of export permits for specimens of that species.

4. The import of any specimen of a species included in Appendix II shall require the prior presentation of either an export permit or a re-export certificate.

5. The re-export of any specimen of a species included in Appendix II shall require the prior grant and presentation of a re-export certificate. A re-export certificate shall only be granted when the following conditions have been met:

(a) a Management Authority of the State of re-export is satisfied that the specimen was imported into that State in accordance with the provisions of the present Convention; and

(b) a Management Authority of the State of re-export is satisfied that any living specimen will be so prepared and shipped as to minimize the risk of injury, damage to health or cruel treatment.

6. The introduction from the sea of any specimen of a species included in Appendix II shall require the prior grant of a certificate from a Management Authority of the State of introduction. A certificate shall only be granted when the following conditions have been met:

(a) a Scientific Authority of the State of introduction advises that the introduction will not be detrimental to the survival of the species involved; and

(b) a Management Authority of the State of introduction is satisfied that any living specimen will be so handled as to minimize the risk of injury, damage to health or cruel treatment.

7. Certificates referred to in paragraph 6 of this Article may be granted on the advice of a Scientific Authority, in consultation with other national scientific authorities or, when appropriate, international scientific authorities, in respect of periods not exceeding one year for total numbers of specimens to be introduced in such periods.

Article V
Regulation of Trade in Specimens of Species included in Appendix III

1. All trade in specimens of species included in Appendix III shall be in accordance with the provisions of this Article.

2. The export of any specimen of a species included in Appendix III from any State which has included that species in Appendix III shall require the prior grant and presentation of an export permit. An export permit shall only be granted when the following conditions have been met:

(a) a Management Authority of the State of export is satisfied that the specimen was not obtained in contravention of the laws of that State for the protection of fauna and flora; and

(b) a Management Authority of the State of export is satisfied that any living specimen will be so prepared and shipped as to minimize the risk of injury, damage to health or cruel treatment.

3. The import of any specimen of a species included in Appendix III shall require, except in circumstances to which paragraph 4 of this Article applies, the prior presentation of a certificate of origin and, where the import is from a State which has included that species in Appendix III, an export permit.

4. In the case of re-export, a certificate granted by the Management Authority of the State of re-export that the specimen was processed in that State or is being re-exported shall be accepted by the State of import as evidence that the provisions of the present Convention have been complied with in respect of the specimen concerned.

Article VI
Permits and Certificates

1. Permits and certificates granted under the provisions of Articles III, IV, and V shall be in accordance with the provisions of this Article.

2. An export permit shall contain the information specified in the model set forth in Appendix IV, and may only be used for export within a period of six months from the date on which it was granted.

3. Each permit or certificate shall contain the title of the present Convention, the name and any identifying stamp of the Management Authority granting it and a control number assigned by the Management Authority.

4. Any copies of a permit or certificate issued by a Management Authority shall be clearly marked as copies only and no such copy may be used in place of the original, except to the extent endorsed thereon.

5. A separate permit or certificate shall be required for each consignment of specimens.

6. A Management Authority of the State of import of any specimen shall cancel and retain the export permit or re-export certificate and any corresponding import permit presented in respect of the import of that specimen.

7. Where appropriate and feasible a Management Authority may affix a mark upon any specimen to assist in identifying the specimen. For these purposes "mark" means any indelible imprint, lead seal or other suitable means of identifying a specimen, designed in such a way as to render its imitation by unauthorized persons as difficult as possible.

Article VII
Exemptions and Other Special Provisions Relating to Trade

1. The provisions of Articles III, IV and V shall not apply to the transit or trans-shipment of specimens through or in the territory of a Party while the specimens remain in Customs control.

2. Where a Management Authority of the State of export or re-export is satisfied that a specimen was acquired before the provisions of the present Convention applied to that specimen, the provisions of Articles III, IV and V shall not apply to that specimen where the Management Authority issues a certificate to that effect.

3. The provisions of Articles III, IV and V shall not apply to specimens that are personal or household effects. This exemption shall not apply where:

(a) in the case of specimens of a species included in Appendix I, they were acquired by the owner outside his State of usual residence, and are being imported into that State; or

(b) in the case of specimens of species included in Appendix II:

(i) they were acquired by the owner outside his State of usual residence and in a State where removal from the wild occurred;

(ii) they are being imported into the owner's State of usual residence; and

(iii) the State where removal from the wild occurred requires the prior grant of export permits before any export of such specimens;

unless a Management Authority is satisfied that the specimens were acquired before the provisions of the present Convention applied to such specimens.

4. Specimens of an animal species included in Appendix I bred in captivity for commercial purposes, or of a plant species included in Appendix I artificially propagated for commercial purposes, shall be deemed to be specimens of species included in Appendix II.

5. Where a Management Authority of the State of export is satisfied that any specimen of an animal species was bred in captivity or any specimen of a plant species was artificially propagated, or is a part of such an animal or plant or was derived therefrom, a certificate by that Management Authority to that effect shall be accepted in lieu of any of the permits or certificates required under the provisions of Articles III, IV or V.

6. The provisions of Articles III, IV and V shall not apply to the non-commercial loan, donation or exchange between scientists or scientific institutions registered by a Management Authority of their State, of herbarium specimens, other preserved, dried or embedded museum specimens, and live plant material which carry a label issued or approved by a Management Authority.

7. A Management Authority of any State may waive the requirements of Articles III, IV and V and allow the movement without permits or certificates of specimens which form part of a travelling zoo, circus, menagerie, plant exhibition or other travelling exhibition provided that:

(a) the exporter or importer registers full details of such specimens with that Management Authority;

(b) the specimens are in either of the categories specified in paragraphs 2 or 5 of this Article; and

(c) the Management Authority is satisfied that any living specimen will be so transported and cared for as to minimize the risk of injury, damage to health or cruel treatment.

Article VIII

Measures to be Taken by the Parties,

1. The Parties shall take appropriate measures to enforce the provisions of the present Convention and to prohibit trade in specimens in violation thereof. These shall include measures:

(a) to penalize trade in, or possession of, such specimens, or both; and

(b) to provide for the confiscation or return to the State of export of such specimens.

2. In addition to the measures taken under paragraph 1 of this Article a Party may, when it deems it necessary, provide for any method of internal reimbursement for expenses incurred as a result of the confiscation of a specimen traded in violation of the measures taken in the application of the provisions of the present Convention.

3. As far as possible, the Parties shall ensure that specimens shall pass through any formalities required for trade with a minimum of delay. To facilitate such passage, a Party may designate ports of exit and ports of entry at which specimens must be presented for clearance. The Parties shall ensure further that all living specimens, during any period of transit, holding or shipment, are properly cared for so as to minimize the risk of injury, damage to health or cruel treatment.

4. Where a living specimen is confiscated as a result of measures referred to in paragraph 1 of this Article:

(a) the specimen shall be entrusted to a Management Authority of the State of confiscation;

(b) the Management Authority shall, after consultation with the State of export, return the specimen to that State at the expense of that State, or to a rescue centre or such other place as the Management Authority deems appropriate and consistent with the purposes of the present Convention; and

(c) the Management Authority may obtain the advice of a Scientific Authority, or may, whenever it considers it desirable, consult the Secretariat in order to facilitate the decision under sub-paragraph (b) of this paragraph, including the choice of a rescue centre or other place.

5. A rescue centre as referred to in paragraph 4 of this Article means an institution designated by a Management Authority to look after the welfare of living specimens, particularly those that have been confiscated.

6. Each Party shall maintain records of trade in specimens of species included in Appendices I, II and III which shall cover:

(a) the names and addresses of exporters and importers; and

(b) the number and type of permits and certificates granted; the States with which such trade occurred; the numbers or quantities and types of specimens, names of species as included in Appendices I, II and III and, where applicable, the size and sex of the specimens in question.

7. Each Party shall prepare periodic reports on its implementation of the present Convention and shall transmit to the Secretariat:

(a) an annual report containing a summary of the information specified in sub-paragraph (b) of paragraph 6 of this Article; and

(b) a biennial report on legislative, regulatory and administrative measures taken to enforce the provisions of the present Convention.

8. The information referred to in paragraph 7 of this Article shall be available to the public where this is not inconsistent with the law of the Party concerned.

Article IX
Management and Scientific Authorities

1. Each Party shall designate for the purposes of the present Convention:

(a) one or more Management Authorities competent to grant permits or certificates on behalf of that Party; and

(b) one or more Scientific Authorities.

2. A State depositing an instrument of ratification, acceptance, approval or accession shall at that time inform the Depositary Government of the name and address of the Management Authority authorized to communicate with other Parties and with the Secretariat.

3. Any changes in the designations or authorizations under the provisions of this Article shall be communicated by the Party concerned to the Secretariat for transmission to all other Parties.

4. Any Management Authority referred to in paragraph 2 of this Article shall if so requested by the Secretariat or the Management Authority of another Party, communicate to it impression of stamps, seals or other devices used to authenticate permits or certificates.

Article X
Trade with States not Party to the Convention

Where export or re-export is to, or import is from, a State not a Party to the present Convention, comparable documentation issued by the competent authorities in that State which substantially conforms with the requirements of the present Convention for permits and certificates may be accepted in lieu thereof by any Party.

Article XI
Conference of the Parties

1. The Secretariat shall call a meeting of the Conference of the Parties not later than two years after the entry into force of the present Convention.

2. Thereafter the Secretariat shall convene regular meetings at least once every two years, unless the Conference decides otherwise, and extraordinary meetings at any time on the written request of at least one-third of the Parties.

3. At meetings, whether regular or extraordinary, the Parties shall review the implementation of the present Convention and may:

(a) make such provision as may be necessary to enable the Secretariat to carry out its duties and adopt financial provisions;

(b) consider and adopt amendments to Appendices I and II in accordance with Article XV;

(c) review the progress made towards the restoration and conservation of the species included in Appendices I, II and III;

(d) receive and consider any reports presented by the Secretariat or by any Party; and

(e) where appropriate, make recommendations for improving the effectiveness of the present Convention.

4. At each regular meeting, the Parties may determine the time and venue of the next regular meeting to be held in accordance with the provisions of paragraph 2 of this Article.

5. At any meeting, the Parties may determine and adopt rules of procedure for the meeting.

6. The United Nations, its Specialized Agencies and the International Atomic Energy Agency, as well as any State not a Party to the present Convention, may be represented at meetings of the Conference by observers, who shall have the right to participate but not to vote.

7. Any body or agency technically qualified in protection, conservation or management of wild fauna and flora, in the following categories, which has informed the Secretariat of its desire to be represented at meetings of the Conference by observers, shall be admitted unless at least one-third of the Parties present object:

(a) international agencies or bodies, either governmental or non-governmental, and national governmental agencies and bodies; and

(b) national non-governmental agencies or bodies which have been approved for this purpose by the State in which they are located. Once admitted, these observers shall have the right to participate but not to vote.

Article XII

The Secretariat

1. Upon entry into force of the present Convention, a Secretariat shall be provided by the Executive Director of the United Nations Environment Programme. To the extent and in the manner he considers appropriate, he may be assisted by suitable inter-governmental or non-governmental international or national agencies and bodies technically qualified in protection, conservation and management of wild fauna and flora.

2. The functions of the Secretariat shall be:

(a) to arrange for and service meetings of the Parties;

(b) to perform the functions entrusted to it under the provisions of Articles XV and XVI of the present Convention;

(c) to undertake scientific and technical studies in accordance with programmes authorized by the Conference of the parties as will contribute to the implementation of the present Convention, including studies concerning standards for appropriate preparation and shipment of living specimens and the means of identifying specimens;

(d) to study the reports of Parties and to request from Parties such further information with respect thereto as it deems necessary to ensure implementation of the present Convention;

(e) to invite the attention of the Parties to any matter pertaining to the aims of the present Convention;

(f) to publish periodically and distribute to the Parties current editions of Appendices I, II and III together with any information which will facilitate identification of specimens of species included in those Appendices;

(g) to prepare annual reports to the Parties on its work and on the implementation of the present Convention and such other reports as meetings of the Parties may request;

(h) to make recommendations for the implementation of the aims and provisions of the present Convention, including the exchange of information of a scientific or technical nature;

(i) to perform any other function as may be entrusted to it by the Parties.

Article XIII

International Measures

1. When the Secretariat in the light of information received is satisfied that any species included in Appendices I or II is being affected adversely by trade in specimens of that species or that the provisions of the present Convention are not being effectively implemented, it shall communicate such information to the authorized Management Authority of the Party or Parties concerned.

2. When any Party receives a communication as indicated in paragraph 1 of this Article, it shall, as soon as possible, inform the Secretariat of any relevant facts insofar as its laws permit and, where appropriate, propose remedial action. Where the Party considers that an inquiry is desirable, such inquiry may be carried out by one or more persons expressly authorized by the Party.

3. The information provided by the Party or resulting from any inquiry as specified in paragraph 2 of this Article shall be reviewed by the next Conference of the Parties which may make whatever recommendations it deems appropriate.

Article XIV

Effect on Domestic Legislation and International Conventions

1. The provisions of the present Convention shall in no way affect the right of Parties to adopt:

(a)   stricter domestic measures regarding the conditions for trade, taking, possession or transport of specimens of species included in Appendices I, II and III, or the complete prohibition thereof; or

(b)   domestic measures restricting or prohibiting trade, taking, possession, or transport of species not included in Appendices I, II or III.

2.   The provisions of the present Convention shall in no way affect the provisions of any domestic measures or the obligations of Parties deriving from any treaty, convention, or international agreement relating to other aspects of trade, taking, possession, or transport of specimens which is in force or subsequently may enter into force for any Party including any measure pertaining to the Customs, public health, veterinary or plant quarantine fields.

3.   The provisions of the present Convention shall in no way affect the provisions of, or the obligations deriving from, any treaty, convention or international agreement concluded or which may be concluded between States creating a union or regional trade agreement establishing or maintaining a common external customs control and removing customs control between the parties thereto insofar as they relate to trade among the States members of that union or agreement.

4.   A State Party to the present Convention, which is also a Party to any other treaty, convention or international agreement which is in force at the time of the coming into force of the present Convention and under the provisions of which protection is afforded to marine species included in Appendix II, shall be relieved of the obligations imposed on it under the provisions of the present Convention with respect to trade in specimens of species included in Appendix II that are taken by ships registered in that State and in accordance with the provisions of such other treaty, convention or international agreement.

5.   Notwithstanding the provisions of Articles III, IV and V, any export of a specimen taken in accordance with paragraph 4 of this Article shall only require a certificate from a Management Authority of the State of introduction to the effect that the specimen was taken in accordance with the provisions of the other treaty, convention or international agreement in question.

6.   Nothing in the present Convention shall prejudice the codification and development of the law of the sea by the United Nations Conference on the Law of the Sea convened pursuant to Resolution 2750 C(XXV) of the General Assembly of the United Nations nor the present or future claims and legal views of any State concerning the law of the sea and the nature and extent of coastal and flag State jurisdiction.

Article XV

Amendments to Appendices I and II

1.   The following provisions shall apply in relation to amendments to Appendices I and II at meetings of the Conference of the Parties:

(a)   Any Party may propose an amendment to Appendix I or II for consideration at the next meeting.   The text of the proposed amendment shall be communicated to the Secretariat at least 150 days before the meeting. The Secretariat shall consult the other Parties and interested bodies on the amendment in accordance with the provisions of sub-paragraphs (b) and (c) of paragraph 2 of this Article and shall communicate the response to all Parties not later than 30 days before the meeting.

(b) Amendments shall be adopted by a two-thirds majority of Parties present and voting. For these purposes "Parties present and voting" means Parties present and casting an affirmative or negative vote. Parties abstaining from voting shall not be counted among the two-thirds required for adopting an amendment.

(c) Amendments adopted at a meeting shall enter into force 90 days after that meeting for all Parties except those which make a reservation in accordance with paragraph 3 of this Article.

2. The following provisions shall apply in relation to amendments to Appendices I and II between meetings of the Conference of the Parties:

(a) Any Party may propose an amendment to Appendix I or II for consideration between meetings by the postal procedures set forth in this paragraph.

(b) For marine species, the Secretariat shall, upon receiving the text of the proposed amendment, immediately communicate it to the Parties. It shall also consult inter-governmental bodies having a function in relation to those species especially with a view to obtaining scientific data these bodies may be able to provide and to ensuring co-ordination with any conservation measures enforced by such bodies. The Secretariat shall communicate the views expressed and data provided by these bodies and its own findings and recommendations to the Parties as soon as possible.

(c) For species other than marine species, the Secretariat shall, upon receiving the text of the proposed amendment, immediately communicate it to the Parties, and, as soon as possible thereafter, its own recommendations.

(d) Any Party may, within 60 days of the date on which the Secretariat communicated its recommendations to the Parties under sub-paragraphs (b) or (c) of this paragraph, transmit to the Secretariat any comments on the proposed amendment together with any relevant scientific data and information.

(e) The Secretariat shall communicate the replies received together with its own recommendations to the Parties as soon as possible.

(f) If no objection to the proposed amendment is received by the Secretariat within 30 days of the date the replies and recommendations were communicated under the provisions of sub-paragraph (e) of this paragraph, the amendment shall enter into force 90 days later for all Parties except those which make a reservation in accordance with paragraph 3 of this Article.

(g) If an objection by any Party is received by the Secretariat, the proposed amendment shall be submitted to a postal vote in accordance with the provisions of sub-paragraphs (h), (i) and (j) of this paragraph.

(h) The Secretariat shall notify the Parties that notification of objection has been received.

(i) Unless the Secretariat receives the votes for, against or in abstention from at least one-half of the Parties within 60 days of the date of notification under sub-paragraph (h) of this paragraph, the proposed amendment shall be referred to the next meeting of the Conference for further consideration.

(j) Provided that votes are received from one-half of the Parties, the amendment shall be adopted by a two-thirds majority of Parties casting an affirmative or negative vote.

(k) The Secretariat shall notify all Parties of the result of the vote.

(*l*) If the proposed amendment is adopted it shall enter into force 90 days after the date of the notification by the Secretariat of its acceptance for all Parties except those which make a reservation in accordance with paragraph 3 of this Article.

3. During the period of 90 days provided for by sub-paragraph (c) of paragraph 1 or sub-paragraph (*l*) of paragraph 2 of this Article any Party may by notification in writing to the Depositary Government make a reservation with respect to the amendment. Until such reservation is withdrawn the Party shall be treated as a State not a Party to the present Convention with respect to trade in the species concerned.

Article XVI
Appendix III and Amendments thereto

1. Any Party may at any time submit to the Secretariat a list of species which it identifies as being subject to regulation within its jurisdiction for the purpose mentioned in paragraph 3 of Article II. Appendix III shall include the names of the Parties submitting the species for inclusion therein, the scientific names of the species so submitted, and any parts or derivatives of the animals or plants concerned that are specified in relation to the species for the purposes of sub-paragraph (b) of Article I.

2. Each list submitted under the provisions of paragraph 1 of this Article shall be communicated to the Parties by the Secretariat as soon as possible after receiving it. The list shall take effect as part of Appendix III 90 days after the date of such communication. At any time after the communication of such list, any Party may by notification in writing to the Depositary Government enter a reservation with respect to any species or any parts or derivatives, and until such reservation is withdrawn, the State shall be treated as a State not a Party to the present Convention with respect to trade in the species or part or derivative concerned.

3. A Party which has submitted a species for inclusion in Appendix III may withdraw it at any time by notification to the Secretariat which shall communicate the withdrawal to all Parties. The withdrawal shall take effect 30 days after the date of such communication.

4. Any Party submitting a list under the provisions of paragraph 1 of this Article shall submit to the Secretariat a copy of all domestic laws and regulations applicable to the protection of such species, together with any interpretations which the Party may deem appropriate or the Secretariat may

request. The Party shall, for as long as the species in question is included in Appendix III, submit any amendments of such laws and regulations or any new interpretations as they are adopted.

Article XVII
Amendment of the Convention

1. An extraordinary meeting of the Conference of the Parties shall be convened by the Secretariat on the written request of at least one-third of the Parties to consider and adopt amendments to the present Convention. Such amendments shall be adopted by a two-thirds majority of Parties present and voting. For these purposes "Parties present and voting" means Parties present and casting an affirmative or negative vote. Parties abstaining from voting shall not be counted among the two-thirds required for adopting an amendment.

2. The text of any proposed amendment shall be communicated by the Secretariat to all Parties at least 90 days before the meeting.

3. An amendment shall enter into force for the Parties which have accepted it 60 days after two-thirds of the Parties have deposited an instrument of acceptance of the amendment with the Depositary Government. Thereafter, the amendment shall enter into force for any other Party 60 days after that Party deposits its instrument of acceptance of the amendment.

Article XVIII
Resolution of Disputes

1. Any dispute which may arise between two or more Parties with respect to the interpretation or application of the provisions of the present Convention shall be subject to negotiation between the Parties involved in the dispute.

2. If the dispute cannot be resolved in accordance with paragraph 1 of this Article, the Parties may, by mutual consent, submit the dispute to arbitration, in particular that of the Permanent Court of Arbitration at The Hague, and the Parties submitting the dispute shall be bound by the arbitral decision.

Article XIX
Signature

The present Convention shall be open for signature at Washington until 30th April 1973 and thereafter at Berne until 31st December 1974.

Article XX
Ratification, Acceptance, Approval

The present Convention shall be subject to ratification, acceptance or approval. Instruments of ratification, acceptance or approval shall be deposited with the Government of the Swiss Confederation which shall be the Depositary Government.

Article XXI
Accession

The present Convention shall be open indefinitely for accession. Instruments of accession shall be deposited with the Depositary Government.[1]

Article XXII

Entry into Force

1. The present Convention shall enter into force 90 days after the date of deposit of the tenth instrument of ratification, acceptance, approval or accession, with the Depositary Government.

2. For each State which ratifies, accepts or approves the present Convention or accedes thereto after the deposit of the tenth instrument of ratification, acceptance, approval or accession, the present Convention shall enter into force 90 days after the deposit by such State of its instrument of ratification, acceptance, approval or accession.

Article XXIII

Reservations

1. The provisions of the present Convention shall not be subject to general reservations. Specific reservations may be entered in accordance with the provisions of this Article and Articles XV and XVI.

2. Any State may, on depositing its instrument of ratification, acceptance, approval or accession, enter a specific reservation with regard to:

(a) any species included in Appendix I, II or III; or

(b) any parts or derivatives specified in relation to a species included in Appendix III.

3. Until a Party withdraws its reservation entered under the provisions of this Article, it shall be treated as a State not a Party to the present Convention with respect to trade in the particular species or parts or derivatives specified in such reservation.

1. The Amendments to the Convention adopted in Gaborone further adds to Article XXI, after the words "Depositary Government," the following 5 paragraphs:

1. This Convention shall be open for accession by regional economic integration organizations constituted by sovereign States which have competence in respect of the negotiation, conclusion and implementation of international agreements in matters transferred to them by their Member States and covered by this Convention.

2. In their instruments of accession, such organizations shall declare the extent of their competence with respect to the matters governed by the Convention. These organizations shall also inform the Depositary Government of any substantial modification in the extent of their competence. Notifications by regional economic integration organizations concerning their competence with respect to matters governed by this Convention and modifications thereto shall be distributed to the Parties by the Depositary Government.

3. In matters within their competence, such regional economic organizations shall exercise the rights and fulfill the obligations which this Convention attributes to their Member States, which are Parties to the Convention. In such cases the Member States of the organization shall not be entitled to exercise such rights individually.

4. In the fields of their competence, regional economic integration organizations shall exercise their right to vote with a number of votes equal to the number of their Member States which are Parties to the Convention. Such organizations shall not exercise their right to vote if their Member States exercise theirs, and vice versa.

5. Any reference to 'Party' in the sense used in Article 1(h) of this Convention to 'State'/'States' or to 'State Party'/'States Parties' to the Convention shall be construed as including a reference to any regional economic organization having competence in respect of the negotiation, conclusion and application of international agreements in matters covered by this Convention.

Article XXIV

Denunciation

Any Party may denounce the present Convention by written notification to the Depositary Government at any time. The denunciation shall take effect twelve months after the Depositary Government has received the notification.

Article XXV

Depositary

1. The original of the present Convention, in the Chinese, English, French, Russian and Spanish languages, each version being equally authentic, shall be deposited with the Depositary Government, which shall transmit certified copies thereof to all States that have signed it or deposited instruments of accession to it.

2. The Depositary Government shall inform all signatory and acceding States and the Secretariat of signatures, deposit of instruments of ratification, acceptance, approval or accession, entry into force of the present Convention, amendments thereto, entry and withdrawal of reservations and notifications of denunciation.

3. As soon as the present Convention enters into force, a certified copy thereof shall be transmitted by the Depositary Government to the Secretariat of the United Nations for registration and publication in accordance with Article 102 of the Charter of the United Nations.

Appendix I to the Convention*

MAMMALIA

MARSUPIALIA

Macropodidae

Macropus parma—Parma wallaby
Onychogalea frenata—Bridled wallaby
O. lunata—Crescent nail-tailed wallaby
Lagorchestes hirsutus—Western hare-wallaby
Lagostrophus fasciatus—Banded hare-wallaby
Caloprymnus campestris—Desert rat kangaroo
Bettongia penicillata—Brush-tailed rat kangaroo
B. lesueur—Lesuers rat kangaroo
B. tropica—Queensland rat kangaroo

Phalangeridae

Wyulda squamicaudata—Scaly-tailed possum

Burramyidae

Burramys parvus—Mountain pigmy possum

Vombatidae

Lasiorhinus gillespiei—Gillespie's wombat

Peramelidae

Perameles bougainville—Barred bandicoot
Chaeropus ecaudatus—Pig-footed bandicoot
Macrotis lagotis—Rabbit bandicoot
M. leucura—Lesser rabbit bandicoot

Dasyuridae

Planigale tenuirostris—Southern planigale
P. subtilissima—Little planigale
Sminthopsis psammophila—Large desert marsupial mouse
S. longicaudata—Long-tailed marsupial mouse
Antechinomys laniger—Eastern jerboa marsupial
Myrmecobius fasciatus rufus—Rusty numbat

Thylacinidae

Thylacinus cynocephalus—Thylacine

---

* Includes all species threatened with extinction which are or may be affected by trade.

Not printed in the Bulletin. Footnotes appear at the end of the appendices.

PRIMATES

Lemuridae

Lemur spp.[1]—Lemur
Lepilemur spp.—Lemur
Hapalemur spp.—Lemur
Allocebus spp.—Lemur
Cheirogaleus spp.—Lemur
Mirocebus spp.—Lemur
Phaner spp.—Lemur

Indriidae

Indri spp.—Indris, Avahis, Sifakas
Propithecus spp.—Indris, Avahis, Sifakas
Avahi spp.—Indris, Avahis, Sifakas

Daubentoniidae

Daubentonia madagascariensis—Aye-aye

Callithricidae

Leontopithecus (Leontideus) spp.—Golden lion tamarin
Callimico goeldii—Goeldi's marmoset

Cebidae

Saimiri oerstedii—Squirrel monkey
Chiropotes albinasus—White-nosed saki
Cacajao spp.—Uakaris
Alouatta palliata (villosa)—Howler monkey
Ateles geoffroyi frontatus—Spider monkey
A. g. panamensis—Spider monkey
Brachyteles arachnoides—Wooley spider monkey

Cercopithecidae

Cercocebus galeritus galeritus—Tana R. mangabey
Macaca silenus—Lion-tailed macaque
Colobus badius rufomitratus—Red colobus
C. b. kirkii—Zanzibar red colobus
Presbytis geei—Golden langur
P. pileatus—Langur
P. entellus—Langur
Nadalis larvatus—Proboscis monkey
Simias concolor—Pagi Island langur
Pygathrix nemaeus—Douc langur

Hylobatidae

Hylobates spp.—Gibbons
Symphalangus syndactylus—Siamang

Pongidae

Pongo pygmaeus pygmaeus—Orangutans
P. p. abelii—Orangutans
Gorilla gorilla—Gorilla

EDENTATA

Dasypodidae

Priodontes giganteus (= maximus)—Giant armadillo

PHOLIDOTA

Manidae

Manis temmincki—Scaly anteater

LAGOMORPHA

Leporidae

Romerolagus diazi—Volcano rabbit
Caprolagus hispidus—Hispid hare

RODENTIA

Sciuridae

Cynomys mexicanus—Mexican prairie dog

Castoridae

Castor fiber birulaia—Beaver
Castor canadensis mexicanus—Mexican beaver

Muridae

Zyzomys pedunculatus—Australian native mouse
Leporillus conditor—Australian native mouse
Pseudomys novaehollandiae—New Holland mouse
P. praeconis—Shark bay mouse
P. shortridgei—Shortridge's mouse
P. fumeus—Smoky mouse
P. occidentalis—Western mouse
P. fieldi—Field's mouse
Notomys aquilo—Australian native mouse
Xeromys myoides—False water rat

Chinchillidae

Chinchilla brevicaudata boliviana—Chinchilla

CETACEA

Platanistidae

Platanista gangetica—Ganges River dolphin

Eschrichtidae

Eschrichtius robustus (glaucus)[2]—Gray whale

Balaenopteridae

Balaenoptera musculus[2]—Blue whale
Megaptera novaeangliae[2]—Humpback whale

Balaenidae

Balaena mysticetus[2]—Bowhead whale
Eubalaena spp.[2]—Right whale

CARNIVORA

Canidae

Canis lupus monstrabilis—Gray wolf
Vulpes velox hebes—Swift fox

Viverridae

Prionodon pardicolor—Spotted linsang

Ursidae

Ursus americanus emmonsii—Glacier bear

U. arctos pruinosus—Brown bear
U. arctos [3]—Brown bear
U. a. nelsoni—Mexican bear

Mustelidae

Mustela nigripes—Black-footed ferret
Lutra longicaudis [1]—Long-tailed otter
L. felina—Marine otter
L. provocax—Southern River otter
Pteronura brasiliensis—Giant otter
Aonyx microdon—Small-clawed otter
Enhydra lutris nereis—Southern Sea otter

Hyaenidae

Hyaena brunnea—Brown hyaena

Felidae

Felis planiceps—Flat-headed cat
F. nigripes—Black-footed cat
F. concolor coryi—Florida puma
F. c. costaricensis—Costa Rican puma
F. c. cougar—Eastern puma
F. temmincki—Temminck's cat
F. bengalensis bengalensis—Leopard cat
F. yagouaroundi cacomitli—Jaguarundi
F. y. fossata—Jaguarundi
F. y. panamensis—Jaguarundi
F. y. tolteca—Jaguarundi
F. pardalis mearnsi—Ocelot
F. p. mitis—Ocelot
F. wiedii nicaraguae—Margays
F. w. salvinia—Margays
F. tigrina oncilla—Tiger cat
F. marmorata—Marbled cat
F. jacobita—Andean cat
F. (Lynx) rufa escuinapae—Lynx
Neofelis nebulosa—Clouded leopard
Panthera tigris—Tiger
P. pardus—Leopard
P. uncia—Snow leopard
P. onca—Jaguar
Acinonyx jubatus—Cheetah

PINNIPEDIA

Phocidae

Monachus spp.—Monk seals
Mirounga angustirostris—Elephant seal

PROBOSCIDEA

Elephantidae

Elephas maximus—Asian Elephant

SIRENIA

Dugongidae

Dugong dugon [6]—Dugong

Trichechidae

Trichechus manatus—West Indian manatee
T. inunguis—South American manatee

PERISSODACTYLA

Equidae

Equus przewalskii—Przewalski's horse
E. hemionus hemionus—Asian wild ass
E. h. khur—Asian wild ass
E. zebra zebra—Mountain zebra

Tapiridae

Tapirus pinchaque—Mountain tapir
T. bairdii—Central American tapir
T. indicus—Asian tapir

Rhinocerotidae

Rhinoceros unicornis—Great Indian one-horned rhinoceros
R. sondaicus—Javan rhino
Didermocerus sumatrensis—Sumatran rhino
Ceratotherium simum cottoni—Northern white rhino

ARTIODACTYLA

Suidae

Sus salvanius—Pigmy hog
Babyrousa babyrussa—Babiroussa

Camelidae

Vicugna vicugna—Vicugna
Camelus bactrianus—Bactrian camel

Cervidae

Moschus moschiferus moschiferus—Musk deer
Axis (Hyelaphus) porcinus annamiticus—Hog deer
A. (Hyelaphus) calamianensis—Philippine deer
A. (Hyelaphus) kuhlii—Kuhl's deer
Cervus duvauceli—Swamp deer
C. eldi—Eld's Brow-antlered deer
C. elaphus hanglu—Kashmir stag
Hippocamelus bisulcus—South Andean huemal
H. antisiensis—North Andean huemal
Blastoceros dichotomus—Marsh deer
Ozotoceros bezoarticus—Pampas deer
Pudu pudu—Pudu

Antilocapridae

Antilocapra americana sonoriensis—Sonoran pronghorn
A. a. peninsularis—Peninsular pronghorn

Bovidae

Bubalus (Anoa) mindorensis—Tamaraw
B. (Anoa) depressicornis—Lowland anoa
B. (Anoa) quarlesi—Mountain anoa
Bos gaurus—Seladang
B. (grunniens) mutus—Wild yak
Novibos (Bos) sauveli—Kouprey
Bison bison athabascae—Woods bison
Kobus leche—Lechwe
Hippotragus niger variani—Sable antelope

Oryx leucoryx—Arabian oryx
Damaliscus dorcas dorcas—Dorcas gazelle
Saiga tatarica mongolica—Saiga antelope
Nemorhaedus goral—Goral
Capricornis sumatraensis—Sumatran serow
Rupicapra rupicapra ornata—Chamois
Capra falconeri jerdoni—Straight-horned markhor
C. f. megaceros—Kabal markhor
C. f. chiltanensis—Chiltan markhor
Ovis orientalis ophion—Urial (Asiatic mouflon, red sheep)
O. ammon hodgsoni—Argali
O. vignei—Shapo

AVES

TINAMIFORMES
Tinamidae
Tinamus solitarius—Solitary tinamou
PODICIPEDIFORMES
Podicipedidae
Podilymbus gigas—Atitlan grebe
PROCELLARIFORMES
Diomedeidae
Diomedea albatrus—Short-tailed albatross
PELECANIFORMES
Sulidae
Sula abbotti—Abbott's booby
Fregatidae
Fregata andrewsi—Frigate bird
CICONIFORMES
Ciconiidae
Ciconia ciconia boyciana—Oriental white stork
Threskiornithidae
Nipponia nippon—Japanese crested ibis
ANSERIFORMES
Anatidae
Anas aucklandica nesiotis—Campboll Island flightless teal
Anas oustaleti—Marianas mallard
Anas laysanensis—Laysan duck
Anas diazi—Mexican duck
Cairina scutulata—White-winged wood duck
Rhodonessa caryophyllacea—Pink-headed duck
Branta canadensis leucopareia—Aleutian Canada goose

Branta sandvicensis—Hawaiian goose (nene)
FALCONIFORMES
Cathartidae
Vultur gryphus—Andean condor
Gymnogyps californianus—California condor
Accipitridae
Pithecophaga jefferyi—Monkey-eating eagle
Harpia harpyja—Harpy eagle
Haliaeetus l. leucocephalus—Southern bald eagle
Haliaeetus heliaca adalberti—Spanish Imperial eagle
Haliaeetus albicilla green-landicus—Greenland white-tailed eagle
Falconidae
Falco peregrinus anatum—Peregrine falcon
Falco peregrinus tundrius—Peregrine falcon
Falco peregrinus peregrinus—Peregrine falcon
Falco peregrinus babylonicus—Peregrine falcon
GALLIFORMES
Megapodiidae
Macrocephalon maleo—Maleo
Cracidae
Crax blumenbachii—Red-billed curassow
Pipile p. pipile—Trinidad white-headed curassow
Pipile jacutinga—Black-fronted piping-guan
Mitu mitu mitu—Mitu
Oreophasis derbianus—Horned guan
Tetraonidae
Tympanuchus cupido attwateri—Greater prairie chicken
Phasianidae
Colinus virginanus ridgwayi—Masked bobwhite
Tragopan blythii—Blyth's tragopan
Tragopan caboti—Cabot's tragopan
Tragopan melanocephalus—Western tragopan
Lophophorus sclateri—Sclater's monal
Lophophorus lhuysii—Chinese monal
Lophophorus impejanus—Himalayan monal
Crossoptilon mantchuricum—Brown-eared pheasant
Crossoptilon crossoptilon—White-eared pheasant
Lophura swinhoii—Swinhoe's pheasant

Lophura imperialis—Imperial pheasant
Lophura edwardsi—Edward's pheasant
Syrmaticus ellioti—Elliot's pheasant
Syrmaticus humiae—Bar-tailed pheasant
Syrmaticus mikado—Mikado pheasant
Polyplectron emphanum—Palawan peacock pheasant
Tetraogallus tibetanus—Tibetan snowcock
Cyrtonyx montezumae merriami—Montezuma quail

GRUIFORMES

Gruidae

Grus japonensis—Japanese crane
Grus leucogeranus—Siberian white crane
Grus americana—Whooping crane
Grus canadensis pulla—Mississippi sandhill crane
Grus canadensis nesiotes—Cuba sandhill crane
Grus nigricollis—Black-necked crane
Grus vipio—White-naped crane
Grus monacha—Hooded crane

Rallidae

Tricholimnas sylvestris—Lord Howe wood rail

Rhynochetidae

Rhynochetos jubatus—Kagu

Otididae

Eupodotis bengalensis—Bengal floricon

CHARADRIIFORMES

Scolopacidae

Numenius borealis—Eskimo curlew
Tringa guttifer—Nordmann's greenshank

Laridae

Larus relictus—Khar turuut tsakhlai

COLUMBIFORMES

Columbidae

Ducula mindorensis—Mindoro zone-tailed pigeon (or Mindo Imperial Pigeon)

PSITTACIFORMES

Psittacidae

Strigops habroptilus—Owl parrot
Rhynchopsitta pachyrhyncha—Thick-billed parrot
Amazona leucocephala—Bahamas parrot
Amazona vittata—Puerto Rican parrot
Amazona guildingii—St. Vincent parrot
Amazona versicolor—St. Lucia parrot
Amazona imperialis—Imperial parrot
Amazona rhodocorytha—Red-browed parrot
Amazona pretrei pretrei—Red-spectacled parrot

Amazona vinacea—Vinaceous breasted parrot
Pyrrhura cruentata—Ochre-marked parakeet
Anodorhynchus glaucus—Glaucous macaw
Anodorhynchus leari—Indigo macaw
Cyanopsitta spixii—Little blue mac
Pionopsitta pileata—Red-capped parrot
Aratinga guaruba—Golden parakeet
Psattacula krameri echo—Mauritius ring-necked parakeet
Psephotus pulcherrimus—Beautiful parakeet
Psephotus chrysopterygius—Paradise parakeet
Neophema chrysogaster—Orange-bellied parakeet
Neophema splendida—Splendid parakeet
Cyanoramphus novaezelandiae—New Zealand parakeet
Cyanoramphus auriceps forbesi—Forbe's parakeet
Geopsittacus occidentalis—Australian night parrot
Psittacus erithacus princeps—Principe parrot

APODIFORMES

Trochilidae

Ramphodon dohrnii—Hook-billed hermit

TROGONIFORMES

Trogonidae

Pharomachrus mocinno mocinno—Resplendent quetzal
Pharomachrus mocinno costaricensis—Resplendent quetzal

STRIGIFORMES

Strigidae

Otus gurneyi—Giant scops owl

CORACIIFORMES

Bucerotidae

Rhinoplax vigil—Helmeted hornbill

PICIFORMES

Picidae

Dryocopus javensis richardsii—Tristaan's woodpecker
Campephilus imperialis—Imperial woodpecker

PASSERIFORMES

Contingidae

Cotinga maculata—Banded cotinga
Xipholena atro-purpurea—White-winged cotinga

Pittidae

Pitta kochi—Koch's pitta

Atrichornithidae

Atrichornis clamosa—Noisy scrub-bird

Muscicapidae

Picathartes gymnocephalus—White-necked rock-fowl
Picathartes oreas—Gray-necked rock-fowl
Psophodes nigrogularis—Western whip-bird
Amytornis goyderi—Eyrean grass wren
Dasyornis brachypterus longirostris—Western bristlebird
Dasyornis broadbenti littoralis—Western rufous bristlebird

Sturnidae

Leucopsar rothschildi—Rothschild's starling

Meliphagidae

Meliphaga cassidix—Helmeted honeyeater

Zosteropidae

Zosterops albogularis—White-breasted silvereye

Fringillidae

Spinus cucullatus—Red siskin

AMPHIBIA

URODELA

Cryptobranchidae

Andrias (= Megalobatrachus) davidianus japonicus—Japanese giant salamander
Andrias (= Megalobatrachus) davidianus davidianus—Chinese giant salamander

SALIENTIA

Bufonidae

Bufo superciliaris—Cameroon toad
Bufo periglenes—Monteverde toad
Nectophrynoides spp.—African viviparous toads

Atelopodidae

Atelopus varius zeteki—Panamanian golden frog

REPTILIA

CROCODYLIA

Alligatoridae

Alligator mississippiensis—American alligator
Alligator sinensis—Chinese alligator
Melanosuchus niger—Black caiman
Caiman crocodilus apaporiensis—Apaporis River caiman

Caiman latirostris—Broad-snouted caiman

Crocodylidae

Tomistoma schlegelii—Tomistoma
Osteolaemus tetraspis tetraspis—African dwarf crocodile
Osteolaemus tetraspis osborni—Congo dwarf crocodile
Crocodylus cataphractus—African slender-snouted crocodile
Crocodylus siamensis—Siamese crocodile
Crocodylus palustris palustris—Mugger crocodile
Crocodylus palustris kimbula—Ceylon mugger crocodile
Crocodylus novaeguineae mindorensis—Philippine crocodile
Crocodylus intermedius—Orinoco crocodile
Crocodylus rhombifer—Cuban crocodile
Crocodylus moreletii—Morelet's crocodile
Crocodylus niloticus—Nile crocodile

Gavialidae

Gavialis gangeticus—Gavial

TESTUDINATA

Emydidae

Batagur baska—River terrapin
Geoclemmys (= Damonia) hamiltonii—Spotted pond turtle
Geoemyda (= Nicoria) tricarinata—Three-keeled Asian turtle
Kachuga tecta tecta—Indian sawback turtle
Morenia ocellata—Burmese peacock turtle
Terrapene coahuila—Water box turtle

Testudinidae

Geochelone (= Testudo) elephantopus—Galapagos turtle
Geochelone (= Testudo) geometrica—Geometric turtle
Geochelone (= Testudo) radiata—Rayed tortoise
Geochelone (= Testudo) yniphora—Angulated tortoise

Cheloniidae

Eretmochelys imbricata imbricata—Atlantic hawksbill turtle
Lepidochelys kempii—Mexican ridley sea turtle

Trionychidae

Lissemys punctata punctata—Indian flapshell turtle
Trionyx ater—Cuartro Cienegas softshell turtle
Trionyx nigricans—Black softshell turtle

Trionyx gangeticus—Indian softshell turtle

Trionyx hurum—Peacock softshell turtle

Chelidae

Pseudemydura umbrina—Short-necked swamp turtle

LACERTILIA

Varanidae

Varanus komodoensis—Komodo Island monitor

Varanus flavescens—Yellow monitor

Varanus bengalensis—Bengal monitor

Varanus griseus—Desert monitor

SERPENTES

Boidae

Epicrates inornatus inornatus—Puerto Rican boa

Epicrates subflavus—Jamaican boa

Python molurus molurus—Indian python

RHYNCHOCEPHALIA

Sphenodontidae

Sphenodon punctatus—Tuatara

PISCES

ACIPENSERIFORMES

Acipenseridae

Acipenser brevirostrum—Short-nosed sturgeon

Acipenser oxyrhynchus—Atlantic sturgeon

OSTEOGLOSSIFORMES

Osteoglossidae

Scleropages formosus—Asiatic bony-tongue

SALMONIFORMES

Salmonidae

Coregonus alpenae—Longjaw cisco

CYPRINIFORMES

Catostomidae

Chasmistes cujus—Cui-ui

Cyprinidae

Probarbus jullieni—Ikan temolek or pla eesok

SILURIFORMES

Schilbeidae

Pangasianodon gigas—Giant catfish

PERCIFORMES

Percidae

Stizostedion vitreum glaucum—Blue pike

MOLLUSCA

NAIADOIDA

Unionidae

Conradilla caelata—Birdwing pearly mussel

Dromus dromas—Dromedary pearly mussel

Epioblasma (= Dysnomia) florentina curtisi—Curtis' pearly mussel

Epioblasma (= Dysnomia) florentina florentina—Yellow-blossom pearly mussel

Epioblasma (= Dysnomia) sampsoni—Sampson's pearly mussel

Epioblasma (= Dysnomia) sulcata perobliqua—White cat's paw

Epioblasma (= Dysnomia) torulosa gubernaculum—Green-blossom pearly mussel

Epioblasma (= Dysnomia) torulosa torulosa—Tuberculed-blossom pearly mussel

Epioblasma (= Dysnomia) turgidula—Turgid-blossom pearly mussel

Epioblasma (= Dysnomia) walkeri—Brown-blossom pearly mussel

Fusconaia cuneolus—Fine-rayed pigtoe

Fusconaia edgariana—Shiny pigtoe

Lampsilis higginsi—Higgin's eye

Lampsilis orbiculata orbiculata—Pink mucket

Lampsilis satura—Plain pocketbook

Lampsilis virescens—Alabama lamp pearly mussel

Plethobasis cicatricosus—White wartyback

Plethobasis cooperianus—Orange-footed pimpleback

Pleurobema plenum—Rough pigtoe

Potamilus (= Proptera) capax—Fat pocketbook

Quadrula intermedia—Cumberland monkey face

Quadrula sparsa—Appalachian monkey face

Toxolasma (= Carunculina) cylindrella—Pale lilliput pearly mussel

Unio (possibly Megalonaias) nickliniana—Nicklin's pearly mussel

Unio (possibly Lampsilis) tampicoensis tecomatensis—Tampico pearly mussel

Villosa (= Micromya) trabalis—Cumberland bean

Appendix II to the Convention *

MAMMALIA

MARSUPIALIA

Macropodidae

Dendrolagus inustus—Tree kangaroo
Dendrolagus ursinus—Tree kangaroo

INSECTIVORA

Erinaceidae

Erinaceus frontalis—Hedgehog

PRIMATES

Lemuridae

Lemur catta—Ring-tailed lemur

Lorisidae

Nycticebus coucang—Slow loris
Loris tardigradus—Slender loris

Cebidae

Cebus capucinus—Weeper capuchin

Cercopithecidae

Macaca sylvanus—Barbary ape
Colobus badius gordonorum—Uhehe red colobus
Colobus verus—Olive colobus
Rhinopithecus roxellanae—Snub-nosed langur
Presbytis johnii—Nilgiri langur

Pongidae

Pan paniscus—Chimpanzee
Pan troglodytes—Pigmy chimpanzee

EDENTATA

Myrmecophagidae

Myrmecophaga tridactyla—Giant anteater
Tamandua tetradactyla chapadensis—Tamandua

Bradypodidae

Bradypus boliviensis—Three-toed sloth

PHOLIDOTA

Manidae

Manis crassicaudata—Pangolin
Manis pentadactyla—Chinese pangolin
Manis javanica—Malayan pangolin

LAGOMORPHA

Leporidae

Nesolagus netscheri—Sumatra short-eared rabbit

RODENTIA

Heteromyidae

Dipodomys phillipsii phillipsii—Phillips kangaroo rat

Sciuridae

Ratufa spp.—Giant squirrels
Lariscus hosei—Four-striped ground squirrel

Castoridae

Castor canadensis frondator—Beaver
Castor canadensis repentinus—Beaver

Cricetidae

Ondatra zibethicus bernardi—Muskrat

Canidae

Canis lupus pallipes—Gray wolf
Canis lupus irremotus—Gray wolf
Canis lupus crassodon—Gray wolf
Chrysocyon brachyurus—Maned wolf
Cuon alpinus—Dhole

Ursidae

Ursus (Thalarctos) maritimus—Polar bear
Ursus arctos [7]—Brown bear
Helarctos malayanus—Malayan sun bear

Procyonidae

Ailurus fulgens—Lesser panda

Mustelidae

Martes americana atrata—Marten

Viveridae

Prionodon linsang—Linsang
Cynogale bennetti—Otter civet
Helogale derbianus—Dwarf mongoose

Felidae

Felis yagouaroundi [8]—Jaguarundi
Felis colocolo pajeros—Andean cat
Felis colocolo crespoi—Andean cat
Felis colocolo budini—Andean cat
Felis concolor missoulensis—Mountain lion (puma)
Felis concolor mayensis—Mountain lion (puma)
Felis concolor azteca—Mountain lion (puma)
Felis serval—Serval
Felis lynx isabellina—Spanish lynx
Felis wiedit [8]—Margay
Felis pardalis [8]—Ocelot
Felis tigrina [8]—Tiger cat
Felis (= Caracal) caracal—Caracal
Panthera leo persica—Indian lion
Panthera tigris altaica (= amurensis)—Siberian tiger

PINNIPEDIA

Otariidae

Arctocephalus australis—Southern fur seal

* Includes all species which although not necessarily now threatened with extinction may become so unless trade in specimens of such species is subject to strict regulation. Not printed in the Bulletin. Footnotes appear at the end of this appendix.

Arctocephalus galapagoensis—Galapagos fur seal

Arctocephalus philippii—Juan Fernandez fur seal

Arctocephalus townsendi—Guadalupe fur seal

Phocidae

Mirounga leonina—South Atlantic elephant seal

TUBULIDENTATA

Orycteropidae

Orycteropus afer—Aardvark

SIRENIA

Dugongidae

Dugong dugon [8]—Dugong

Trichechidae

Trichechus senegalensis—West African manatee

PERISSODACTYLA

Equidae

Equus hemionus [8]—Asiatic wild ass

Tapiridae

Tapirus terrestris—South American tapir

Rhinocerotidae

Diceros bicornis—Black rhinoceros

ARTIODACTYLA

Hippopotamidae

Choeropus liberiensis—Pigmy hippopotamus

Cervidae

Cervus elaphus bactrianus—Bactrian deer
Pudu mephistophiles—Pudu

Antilocapridae

Antilocapra americana mexicana—Mexican pronghorn

Bovidae

Cephalophus monticola—Duiker
Oryx (tao) dammah—Scimitar-horned oryx
Addax nasomaculatus—Addax
Pantholops hodgsoni—Tibetan antelope
Capra falconeri [8]—Markhor
Ovis ammon [8]—Argali or Marco Polo sheep
Ovis canadensis—Bighorn sheep

AVES

SPENISCIFORMES

Spheniscidae

Spheniscus demersus—Jackass penguin

RHEIFORMES

Rheidae

Rhea americana albescens—Nandu suri
Pterocnemia pennata pennata—Nandu petizo de la patugonia
Pterocnemia pennata garleppi—Nandu cordillerano

TINAMIFORMES

Tinamidae

Rhynchotus rufescens rufescens—Red-winged tinamou
Rhynchotus rufescens pallescens—Red-winged tinamou
Rhynchotus rufescens maculicollis—Red-winged tinamou

CICONIIFORMES

Ciconiidae

Ciconia nigra—Black stork

Threskornithidae

Geronticus calvus—Southern bald ibis
Platalea leucorodia—Spoonbill

Phoenicopteridae

Phoenicopterus ruber chilensis—Chilean flamingo
Phoenicoparrus andinus—Andean flamingo
Phoenicoparrus jamesi—James flamingo

PELECANIFORMES

Pelecanidae

Pelecanus crispus—Dalmatian pelican

ANSERIFORMES

Anatidae

Anas aucklandica aucklandica—Auckland Island flightless teal
Anas aucklandica chlorotis—New Zealand brown teal
Anas bernieri—Madagascar teal
Dendrocygna arborea—Cuban tree duck
Sarkidiornis melanotos—Comb duck
Anser albifrons gambelli—Tule white-fronted goose
Cygnus buccinator—Trumpeter swan
Cygnus bewickii jankowskii—Jankowski's swan
Cygnus melancoryphus—Black-necked swan
Coscoroba coscoroba—Cascoroba swan
Branta ruficollis—Red-breasted goose

FALCONIFORMES

Accipitridae

Gypaetus barbatus meridionalis—African lammergeyer
Aquila chrysaetos—Golden eagle

Falconidae

All species [10]

GALLIFORMES

Megapodiidae

Megapodius freycinet   )
   nicobariensis   )   The
Megapodius freycinet   )   Nicobar
   abbotti   )   megapodes

Tetraonidae

Tympanuchus cupido pinnatus—Northern greater prairie chicken

Phasianidae

Francolinus ochropectus—Tadjoura francolin
Francolinus swierstrai—Swierstra's francolin
Catreus wallichii—Cheer pheasant
Polyplectron malacense—Malaysian peacock pheasant
Polyplectron germaini—Peacock pheasant
Polyplectron bicalcaratum—Peacock pheasant
Gallus sonnerati—Gray jungle fowl
Argusianus argus—Great Argus pheasant
Ithaginus cruentus—Blood-pheasant
Cyrtonyx montezumae montezumae—Montezuma quail
Cyrtonyx montezumae mearnsi—Montezuma quail

GRUIFORMES

Gruidae

Balearica regulorum—Crowned crane
Grus canadensis pratensis—Florida sandhill crane

Rallidae

Gallirallus australis hectori—Eastern weka

Otididae

Chlamydotis undulata—Houbara bustard
Choriotis nigriceps—Great Indian bustard
Otis tarda—Great bustard

CHARADRIIFORMES

Scolopacidae

Numenius tenuirostris—Slender-billed curlew
Numenius minutus—Little whimbrel

Laridae

Larus brunneicephalus—Brown-headed gull

COLUMBIFORMES

Columbidae

Gallicolumba luzonica—Bleeding heart pigeon
Goura cristata—Blue-crowned pigeon
Goura scheepmakeri—Maroon-breasted crowned pigeon
Goura victoria—Victoria crowned pigeon
Caloenas nicobarica pelewensis—Nicobar pigeon

PSITTACIFORMES

Psittacidae

Coracopsis nigra barklyi—Seychelles Vasa parrot
Prosopeia personata—Masked parakeet
Eunymphicus cornutus—Horned parakeet
Cyanoramphus unicolor—Antipodes Island parakeet
Cyanoramphus novaezelandiae—Norfolk Island parakeet
Cyanoramphus malherbi—Orange-fronted parakeet
Poicephalus robustus—Cape parrot
Tanygnathus luzoniensis—Blue-naped parrot
Probosciger aterrimus—Great black cockatoo

CUCULIFORMES

Musophagidae

Turaco corythaix—Knysna loury
Gallirex porphyreolophus—Purple-crested loury

STRIGIFORMES

Strigidae

Otus nudipes newtoni—Virgin Island screech owl

CORACIFORMES

Bucerotidae

Buceros rhinoceros rhinoceros—Rhinoceros hornbill
Buceros bicornis—Great Indian hornbill
Buceros hydrocorax hydrocorax—Rufous hornbill
Aceros narcondami—Narcondam hornbill

PICIFORMES

Picidae

Picus squamatus flavirostris—Scaly-bellied green woodpecker

PASSERIFORMES

Cotingidae

Rupicola rupicolar—Cock-of-the-rock
Rupicola peruviana—Peruvian cock-of-the-rock

Pittidae

Pitta brachyura nympha—Fairy pitta

Hirundinidae

Pseudochelidon sirintarae—White-eyed river martin

Paradisaeidae

All species [10]

Muscicapidae

Muscicapa ruecki—Rueck's blue flycatcher

Fringillidae

Spinus yarrellii—Yellow-faced siskin

AMPHIBIA

URODELA

Ambystomidae

Ambystoma mexicanum—Axolotl
Ambystoma dumerillii—Lake Patzcuaro salamander
Ambystoma lermaensis—Lake Lerma salamander

SALIENTIA

Bufonidae

Bufo retiformis—Sonoran green toad

REPTILIA

CROCODYLIA

Alligatoridae

Caiman crocodilus crocodilus—Common caiman
Caiman crocodilus yacare—Yacare
Caiman crocodilus fuscus [11]—Brown caiman
Paleosuchus palpebrosus—Dwarf caiman
Paleosuchus trigonatus—Smooth-fronted caiman

Crocodylidae

Crocodylus johnsoni—Johnson's crocodile
Crocodylus novaeguineae—New Guinea crocodile
Crocodylus porosus—Salt water crocodile
Crocodylus acutus—American crocodile

TESTUDINATA

Emydidae

Clemmys muhlenbergi—Muhlenberg turtle

Testudinidae

Chersine spp.—Bow-sprit tortoises
Geochelone spp. [12]—Land tortoises
Gopherus spp.—Gopher tortoises
Homopus spp.—African parrot-beaked tortoises
Kinixys spp.—Hinged-back tortoises
Malacochersus spp.—Pancake tortoises
Pyxis spp.—Madagascar spider tortoises
Testudo spp. [13]—Land tortoises

Cheloniidae

Caretta caretta—Loggerhead sea turtle

Chelonia mydas—Green sea turtle
Chelonia depressa—Flat-back sea turtle
Eretmochelys imbricata bissa—Pacific hawksbill sea turtle
Lepidochelys olivacea—Pacific Ridley sea turtle

Dermochelidae

Dermochelys coriacea—Leatherback sea turtle

Pelomedusidae

Podocnemis spp.—South American river turtles

LACERTILIA

Teiidae

Cnemidophorus hyperythrus—Orange-throated whiptail

Iguanidae

Conolophus pallidus—Barrington Island land lizard
Cololophus subcristatus—Galapagos land iguana
Amblyrhynchus cristatus—Galapagos marine iguana
Phrynosoma coronatum blainvillei—San Diego horned lizard

Helodermatidae

Heloderma suspectum—Gila monster
Heloderma horridum—Beaded lizard

Varanidae

Varanus spp. [13]—Monitor lizards

SERPENTES

Boidae

Epicrates cenchris cenchris—Rainbow boa
Eunectes notaeus—Yellow anaconda
Constrictor constrictor—Boa constrictor
Python spp. [13]—Pythons

Colubridae

Cyclagras gigas—South American false cobra
Pseudoboa cloelia—Mussurana
Elachistodon westermanni—Indian egg-eater
Thamnophis elegans hammondi—Two-striped garter snake

PISCES

ACIPENSERIFORMES

Acipenseridae

Acipenser fulvescens—Lake sturgeon
Acipenser sturio—Baltic sturgeon

OSTEOGLOSSIFORMES

Osteoglossidae

Arapaima gigas—Arapaima

SALMONIFORMES
Salmonidae

Stenodus leucichthys leucichthys—Beloribitsa

Salmo chrysogaster—Mexican golden trout

CYPRINIFORMES
Cyprinidae

Plagopterus argentissimus—Woundfin

Ptychocheilus lucius—Colorado squawfish

ATHERINIFORMES
Cyprinodontidae

Cynolebias constanciae—Annual tropical killifish

Cynolebias marmoratus—Annual tropical killifish

Cynolebias minimus—Annual tropical killifish

Cynolebias opalescens—Annual tropical killifish

Cynolebias splendens—Annual tropical killifish

Poeciliidae

Xiphophorus couchianus—Monterey platyfish

COELACANTHIFORMES
Coelacanthidae

Latimeria chalumnae—Coelacanth

CERATODIFORMES
Ceratodidae

Neoceratodus forsteri—Australian lungfish

MOLLUSCA

NAIADOIDA
Unionidae

Cyprogenia aberti—Edible pearly mussel

Epioblasma (=Dysnomia) torulosa rangiana—Tan-blossom pearly mussel

Fusconaia subrotunda—Long solid

Lampsilis brevicula—Ozark lamp pearly mussel

Lexingtonia dolabelloides—Slab-sided pearly mussel

Pleorobema clava—Club pearly mussel

STYLOMMATOPHORA
Camaenidae

Papustyla (=Papuina) pulcherrima—Manus Island tree snail

Paraphantidae

Paraphanta spp.[13]—New Zealand amber snails

PROSOBRANCHIA
Hydrobiidae

Coahuilix hubbsi—Coahuilix de Hubbs snail

Cochliopina milleri—Cochliopina de Miller snail

Durangonella coahuilae—Durangonella de Coahuila snail

Mexipyrgus carranzae—Mexipyrgus de Carranza snail

Mexipyrgus churinceanus—Mexipyrgus de Churince snail

Mexipyrgus escobedae—Mexipyrgus de Escobeda snail

Mexipyrgus lugoi—Mexipyrgus de lugo snail

Mexipyrgus mojarralis—Mexipyrgus de West El Mojarral snail

Mexipyrgus multilineatus—Mexipyrgus de East El Mojarral snail

Mexithauma quadripaludium—Mexithauma de Cuatro Cienegas snail

Nymphophilus minckleyi—Nymphophilus de Minckley snail

Paludiscala caramba—Paludiscala de oro snail

INSECTA

LEPIDOPTERA

Parnassius apollo apollo—Mountain apollo

NOTES FOR APPENDICES I AND II:

1. Except species listed in Appendix II.
2. Pursuant to the 1972 International Whaling Commission Moratorium.
3. Distinct Italian population only.
4. Includes *Lutra platensis* and *L. annectens*.
5. Except subspecies listed in Appendix II.
6. Except distinct Australian population.
7. All North American subspecies, except those in Appendix I.
8. Except subspecies listed in Appendix I.
9. Distinct Australian population only.
10. Except those species or subspecies in Appendix I.
11. Includes *chiapaisus*.
12. Except those species in Appendix I.
13. New Zealand species only.

6.6 ENDANGERED SPECIES ACT OF 1973, AS AMENDED. 16 U.S.C. §§ 1531 & 1537 (1976 & Supp. V 1981)

§ 1531. Congressional findings and declaration of purposes and policy

(a). Findings

The Congress finds and declares that—

(1). various species of fish, wildlife, and plants in the United States have been rendered extinct as a consequence of economic growth and development untempered by adequate concern and conservation;

(2). other species of fish, wildlife, and plants have been so depleted in numbers that they are in danger of or threatened with extinction;

(3). these species of fish, wildlife, and plants are of esthetic, ecological, educational, historical, recreational, and scientific value to the Nation and its people;

(4). the United States has pledged itself as a sovereign state in the international community to conserve to the extent practicable the various species of fish or wildlife and plants facing extinction, pursuant to—

(A) migratory bird treaties with Canada and Mexico;

(B) the Migratory and Endangered Bird Treaty with Japan;

(C) the Convention on Nature Protection and Wildlife Preservation in the Western Hemisphere;

(D) the International Convention for the Northwest Atlantic Fisheries;

(E) the International Convention for the High Seas Fisheries of the North Pacific Ocean;

(F) the Convention on International Trade in Endangered Species of Wild Fauna and Flora; and

(G) other international agreements.

(5). encouraging the States and other interested parties, through Federal financial assistance and a system of incentives, to develop and maintain conservation programs which meet national and international standards is a key to meeting the Nation's international commitments and to better safeguarding, for the benefit of all citizens, the Nation's heritage in fish and wildlife.

(b). Purposes

The purposes of this chapter are to provide a means whereby the ecosystems upon which endangered species and threatened species depend may be conserved, to provide a program for the conservation of such endangered species and threatened species, and to take such steps as may be appropriate to achieve the purposes of the treaties and conventions set forth in subsection (a) of this section.

(c). Policy

It is further declared to be the policy of Congress that all Federal departments and agencies shall seek to conserve endangered species and threatened species and shall utilize their authorities in furtherance of the purposes of this chapter.

(Pub.L. 93–205, § 2, Dec. 28, 1973, 87 Stat. 884.)

* * *

§ 1537. International cooperation

(a). Financial assistance

As a demonstration of the commitment of the United States to the worldwide protection of endangered species and threatened species, the President may, subject to the provisions of section 724 of title 31, use foreign currencies accruing to the United States Government under the Agricultural Trade Development and Assistance Act of 1954 [7 U.S.C. 1691 et seq.] or any other law to provide to any foreign country (with its consent) assistance in the development and management of programs in that country which the Secretary determines to be necessary or useful for the conservation of any endangered species or threatened species listed by the Secretary pursuant to section 1533 of this title. The President shall provide assistance (which includes, but is not limited to, the acquisition, by lease or otherwise, of lands, waters, or interests therein) to foreign countries under this section under such terms and conditions as he deems appropriate. Whenever foreign currencies are available for the provision of assistance under this section, such currencies shall be used in preference to funds appropriated under the authority of section 1542 of this title.

(b). Encouragement of foreign programs

In order to carry out further the provisions of this chapter, the Secretary, through the Secretary of State, shall encourage—

    (1) foreign countries to provide for the conservation of fish or wildlife including endangered species and threatened species listed pursuant to section 1533 of this title;

    (2) the entering into of bilateral or multilateral agreements with foreign countries to provide for such conservation; and

    (3) foreign persons who directly or indirectly take fish or wildlife in foreign countries or on the high seas for importation into the United States for commercial or other purposes to develop and carry out with such assistance as he may provide, conservation practices designed to enhance such fish or wildlife and their habitat.

(c). Personnel

After consultation with the Secretary of State, the Secretary may—

    (1) assign or otherwise make available any officer or employee of his department for the purpose of cooperating with foreign countries and international organizations in developing personnel resources and programs which promote the conservation of fish or wildlife; and

    (2) conduct or provide financial assistance for the educational training of foreign personnel, in this country or abroad, in fish, wildlife, or plant management, research and law enforcement and to render professional assistance abroad in such matters.

(d). Investigations

After consultation with the Secretary of State and the Secretary of the Treasury, as appropriate, the Secretary may conduct or cause to be conducted such law enforcement investigations and research abroad as he deems necessary to carry out the purposes of this chapter.

(e). Convention implementation

The President is authorized and directed to designate agencies to act as the Management Authority or Authorities and the Scientific Authority or Authorities pursuant to the Convention. The agencies so designated shall thereafter be authorized to do all things assigned to them under the Convention, including the issuance of permits and certificates. The agency designated by the President to communicate with other parties to the Convention and with the Secretariat shall also be empowered, where appropriate, in consultation with the State Department, to act on behalf of and represent the United States in all regards as required by the Convention. The President shall also designate those agencies which shall act on behalf of and represent the United States in all regards as required by the Convention on Nature Protection and Wildlife Preservation in the Western Hemisphere.

(Pub.L. 93–205, § 8, Dec. 28, 1973, 87 Stat. 892.)

6.7 CONVENTION FOR THE PROHIBITION OF FISHING WITH LONG DRIFTNETS IN THE SOUTH PACIFIC (WITHOUT PROTOCOLS). Concluded at Wellington, 23 November 1989. Entered into force, 17 May 1991. 29 I.L.M. 1454 (1990)

The Parties to this Convention,

RECOGNISING the importance of marine living resources to the people of the South Pacific region;

PROFOUNDLY CONCERNED at the damage now being done by pelagic drift-net fishing to the albacore tuna resource and to the environment and economy of the South Pacific region;

CONCERNED ALSO for the navigational threat posed by drift-net fishing;

NOTING that the increasing fishing capacity induced by large scale drift-net fishing threatens the fish stocks in the South Pacific;

MINDFUL OF the relevant rules of international law, including the provisions of the United Nations Convention on the Law of the Sea, done at Montego Bay on 10 December 1982, in particular Parts V, VII and XVI;

RECALLING the Declaration of the South Pacific Forum at Tarawa, 11 July 1989, that a Convention should be adopted to ban the use of drift nets in the South Pacific region;

RECALLING ALSO the Resolution of the 29th South Pacific Conference at Guam, which called for an immediate ban on the practice of drift-net fishing in the South Pacific Commission region;

HAVE AGREED as follows:

Article 1

DEFINITIONS

For the purpose of this Convention and its Protocols:

(a) The "Convention Area",

(i) Subject to subparagraph (ii) of this paragraph, shall be the area lying within 10 degrees North latitude and 50 degrees South latitude and 130 degrees East longitude and 120 degrees West longitude, and shall also include all waters under the fisheries jurisdiction of any Party to this Convention;

(ii) In the case of a State or Territory which is Party to the Convention by virtue of paragraph 1(b) or 1(c) of article 10, it shall include only waters under the fisheries jurisdiction of that Party, adjacent to the Territory referred to in paragraph 1(b) or 1(c) of article 10.

(b) "drift net" means a gillnet or other net or a combination of nets which is more than 2.5 kilometres in length the purpose of which is to enmesh, entrap or entangle fish by drifting on the surface of or in the water;

(c) "drift net fishing activities" means:

(i) catching, taking or harvesting fish with the use of a drift net;

(ii) attempting to catch, take or harvest fish with the use of a drift net;

(iii) engaging in any other activity which can reasonably be expected to result in the catching, taking or harvesting of fish with the use of a drift net, including searching for and locating fish to be taken by that method;

(iv) any operations at sea in support of, or in preparation for, any activity described in this paragraph, including operations of placing, searching for or recovering fish aggregating devices or associated electronic equipment such as radio beacons;

(v) aircraft use, relating to the activities described in this paragraph, except for flights in emergencies involving the health or safety of crew members or the safety of a vessel; or

(vi) transporting, transshipping and processing any drift-net catch, and cooperation in the provision of food, fuel and other supplies for vessels equipped for or engaged in drift-net fishing.

(d) the "FFA" means the South Pacific Forum Fisheries Agency; and

(e) "fishing vessel" means any vessel or boat equipped for or engaged in searching for, catching, processing or transporting fish or other marine organisms.

Article 2
MEASURES REGARDING NATIONALS AND VESSELS

Each Party undertakes to prohibit its nationals and vessels documented under its laws from engaging in drift-net fishing activities within the Convention Area.

Article 3
MEASURES AGAINST DRIFT–NET FISHING ACTIVITIES

1. Each Party undertakes:

(a) not to assist or encourage the use of driftnets within the Convention Area; and

(b) to take measures consistent with international law to restrict drift-net fishing activities within the Convention Area, including but not limited to:

(i) prohibiting the use of driftnets within areas under its fisheries jurisdiction; and

(ii) prohibiting the transshipment of drift-net catches within areas under its jurisdiction.

2. Each Party may also take measures consistent with international law to:

(a) prohibit the landing of drift-net catches within its territory;

(b) prohibit the processing of drift-net catches in facilities under its jurisdiction;

(c) prohibit the importation of any fish or fish product, whether processed or not, which was caught using a driftnet.

(d) restrict port access and port servicing facilities for drift-net fishing vessels; and

(e) prohibit the possession of drift nets on board any fishing vessel within areas under its fisheries jurisdiction.

3. Nothing in this Convention shall prevent a Party from taking measures against drift-net fishing activities which are stricter than those required by the Convention.

Article 4
ENFORCEMENT

1. Each Party shall take appropriate measures to ensure the application of the provisions of this Convention.

2. The Parties undertake to collaborate to facilitate surveillance and enforcement of measures taken by Parties pursuant to this Convention.

3. The Parties undertake measures leading to the withdrawal of good standing on the Regional Register of Foreign Fishing Vessels maintained by the FFA against any vessel engaging in drift-net fishing activities.

Article 5
CONSULTATION WITH NON–PARTIES

1. The Parties shall seek to consult with any State which is eligible to become a Party to this Convention on any matter relating to drift-net fishing activities which appear to affect adversely the conservation of marine living resources within the Convention Area or the implementation of the Convention and its protocols.

2. The Parties shall seek to reach agreement with any State referred to in paragraph 1 of this article, concerning the prohibitions established pursuant to articles 2 and 3.

Article 6
INSTITUTIONAL ARRANGEMENTS

1. The FFA shall be responsible for carrying out the following functions:

(a) the collection, preparation and dissemination of information on drift-net fishing activities within the Convention Area;

(b) the facilitation of scientific analyses on the effects of drift-net fishing activities within the Convention Area, including consultations with appropriate regional and international organizations; and

(c) the preparation and transmission to the Parties of the annual report on any drift-net fishing activities within the Convention Area and the measures taken to implement this Convention or its Protocols.

2. Each Party shall expeditiously convey to the FFA:

(a) information on the measures adopted by it pursuant to the implementation of the Convention; and

(b) information on, and scientific analyses on the effects of, drift-net fishing activities relevant to the Convention Area.

3. All Parties, including States or Territories not members of the FFA, and the FFA shall cooperate to promote the effective implementation of this article.

Article 7

REVIEW AND CONSULTATION AMONG PARTIES

1. Without prejudice to the conduct of consultations among Parties by other means, the FFA, at the request of three Parties, shall convene meetings of the Parties to review the implementation of this Convention and its Protocols.

2. Parties to the Protocols shall be invited to any such meeting and to participate in a manner to be determined by the Parties to the Convention.

Article 8

CONSERVATION AND MANAGEMENT MEASURES

Parties to this Convention shall co-operate with each other and with appropriate distant water fishing nations and other entities or organizations in the development of conservation and management measures for South Pacific albacore tuna within the Convention Area.

Article 9

PROTOCOLS

This Convention may be supplemented by Protocols or associated instruments to further its objectives.

Article 10

SIGNATURE, RATIFICATION AND ACCESSION

1. This Convention shall be open for signature by:

(a) any member of the FFA; and

(b) any State in respect of any Territory situated within the Convention Area for which it is internationally responsible; or

(c) any Territory situated within the Convention Area which has been authorized to sign the Convention and to assume rights and obligations under it by the Government of the State which is internationally responsible for it.

2. This Convention is subject to ratification by members of the FFA and the other States and Territories referred to in paragraph 1 of this article. The instruments of ratification shall be deposited with the Government of New Zealand which shall be the depositary.

3. This Convention shall remain open for accession by the members of the FFA and the other States and Territories referred to in paragraph 1 of this article. The instruments of accession shall be deposited with the Depositary.

Article 11

RESERVATIONS

This Convention shall not be subject to reservations.

Article 12
AMENDMENTS

1. Any Party may propose amendments to this Convention.

2. Amendments shall be adopted by consensus among the Parties.

3. Any amendments adopted shall be submitted by the Depositary to all Parties for ratification, approval or acceptance.

4. An amendment shall enter into force thirty days after receipt by the Depositary of instruments of ratification, approval or acceptance from all Parties.

Article 13
ENTRY INTO FORCE

1. This Convention shall enter into force on the date of deposit of the fourth instrument of ratification or accession.

2. For any member of the FFA or a State or Territory which ratifies or accedes to this Convention after the date of deposit of the fourth instrument of ratification or accession, the Convention shall enter into force on the date of deposit of its instruments of ratification or accession.

Article 14
CERTIFICATION AND REGISTRATION

1. The original of this Convention and its Protocols shall be deposited with the Depositary, which shall transmit certified copies to all States and Territories eligible to become Party to Convention and to all States eligible to become Party to a Protocol to the Convention.

2. The Depositary shall register this Convention and its Protocols in accordance with Article 102 of the Charter of the United Nations.

6.8 RESOLUTION ON LARGE–SCALE PELAGIC DRIFTNET FISHING AND ITS IMPACT ON THE LIVING MARINE RESOURCES OF THE WORLD'S OCEANS AND SEAS.[1] Adopted by the U.N. General Assembly, 22 December 1989. U.N. Doc. A/RES/44/225, 29 I.L.M. 1555 (1990)

The General Assembly,

Noting that many countries are disturbed by the increase in the use of large-scale pelagic driftnets, which can reach or exceed 30 miles (48 kilometres) in total length, to catch living marine resources on the high seas of the world's oceans and seas,

Mindful that large-scale pelagic driftnet fishing, a method of fishing with a net or a combination of nets intended to be held in a more or less vertical position by floats and weights, the purpose of which is to enmesh fish by drifting on the surface of or in the water, can be a highly indiscriminate and wasteful fishing method that is widely considered to threaten the effective conservation of living marine resources, such as highly migratory and anadromous species of fish, birds and marine mammals,

Drawing attention to the fact that the present resolution does not address the question of small-scale driftnet fishing traditionally conducted in coastal waters, especially by developing countries, which provides an important contribution to their subsistence and economic development,

Expressing concern that, in addition to targeted species of fish, non-targeted fish, marine mammals, seabirds and other living marine resources of the world's oceans and seas can become entangled in large-scale pelagic driftnets, either in those in active use or in those that are lost or discarded, and as a result of such entanglement are often either injured or killed,

Recognizing that more than one thousand fishing vessels use large-scale pelagic driftnets in the Pacific, Atlantic and Indian Oceans and in other areas of the high seas,

Recognizing also that any regulatory measure to be taken for the conservation and management of living marine resources should take account of the best available scientific data and analysis,

Recalling the relevant principles elaborated in the United Nations Convention on the Law of the Sea,

Affirming that, in accordance with the relevant articles of the Convention, all members of the international community have a duty to co-operate globally and regionally in the conservation and management of living resources on the high seas, and a duty to take, or to co-operate with others in taking, such measures for their nationals as may be necessary for the conservation of those resources,

Recalling that, in accordance with the relevant articles of the Convention, it is the responsibility of all members of the international community to ensure the conservation and management of living marine resources and the protection and preservation of the living marine environment within their exclusive economic zones,

1. *See also* Basic Document 6.9.

Noting the serious concern, particularly among coastal States and States with fishing interests, that the overexploitation of living marine resources of the high seas adjacent to the exclusive economic zones of coastal States is likely to have an adverse impact on the same resources within such zones, and noting also, in this regard, the responsibility for co-operation in accordance with the relevant articles of the Convention,

Noting further that the countries of the South Pacific Forum and the South Pacific Commission, in recognition of the importance of living marine resources to the people of the South Pacific region, have called for a cessation of such fishing in the South Pacific and the implementation of effective management programmes,

Taking note of the adoption of the Tarawa Declaration on this subject by the Twentieth South Pacific Forum at Tarawa, Kiribati, on 11 July 1989 and the adoption by South Pacific States and territories of the Convention on the Prohibition of Driftnet Fishing in the South Pacific, at Wellington on 24 November 1989,

Noting that some members of the international community have entered into co-operative enforcement and monitoring programmes for the immediate evaluation of the impact of large-scale pelagic driftnet fishing,

Recognizing that some members of the international community have taken steps to reduce their driftnet operations in some regions in response to regional concerns,

1. *Calls upon* all members of the international community, particularly those with fishing interests, to strengthen their co-operation in the conservation and management of living marine resources;

2. *Calls upon* all those involved in large-scale pelagic driftnet fishing to co-operate fully with the international community, and especially with coastal States and the relevant international and regional organizations, in the enhanced collection and sharing of statistically sound scientific data in order to continue to assess the impact of such fishing methods and to secure conservation of the world's living marine resources;

3. *Recommends* that all interested members of the international community, particularly within regional organizations, continue to consider and, by 30 June 1991, review the best available scientific data on the impact of large-scale pelagic driftnet fishing and agree upon further co-operative regulation and monitoring measures, as needed;

4. *Also recommends* that all members of the international community, bearing in mind the special role of regional organizations and regional and bilateral co-operation in the conservation and management of living marine resources as reflected in the relevant articles of the United Nations Convention on the Law of the Sea, agree to the following measures:

(*a*) Moratoria should be imposed on all large-scale pelagic driftnet fishing by 30 June 1992, with the understanding that such a measure will not be imposed in a region or, if implemented, can be lifted, should effective conservation and management measures be taken based upon statistically sound analysis to be jointly made by concerned parties of the international community with an interest in the fishery resources of the region, to prevent unacceptable impact of such fishing practices on that

region and to ensure the conservation of the living marine resources of
that region;

(*b*) Immediate action should be taken to reduce progressively large-
scale pelagic driftnet fishing activities in the South Pacific region with a
view to the cessation of such activities by 1 July 1991, as an interim
measure, until appropriate conservation and management arrangements
for South Pacific albacore tuna resources are entered into by the parties
concerned;

(*c*) Further expansion of large-scale pelagic driftnet fishing on the
high seas of the North Pacific and all the other high seas outside the
Pacific Ocean should cease immediately, with the understanding that this
measure will be reviewed subject to the conditions in paragraph 4(*a*) of
the present resolution;

5. *Encourages* those coastal countries which have exclusive economic
zones adjacent to the high seas to take appropriate measures and to co-
operate in the collection and submission of scientific information on driftnet
fishing in their own exclusive economic zones, taking into account the
measures taken for the conservation of living marine resources of the high
seas;

6. *Requests* specialized agencies, particularly the Food and Agriculture
Organization of the United Nations, and other appropriate organs, organizations and programmes of the United Nations system, as well as the various
regional and subregional fisheries organizations, urgently to study large-scale
pelagic driftnet fishing and its impact on living marine resources and to report
their views to the Secretary–General;

7. *Requests* the Secretary–General to bring the present resolution to the
attention of all members of the international community, intergovernmental
organizations, non-governmental organizations in consultative status with the
Economic and Social Council, and well-established scientific institutions with
expertise in relation to living marine resources;

8. *Requests* the Secretary–General to submit to the General Assembly at
its forty-fifth session a report on the implementation of the present resolution.

6.9   RESOLUTION ON LARGE–SCALE PELAGIC DRIFTNET FISHING AND ITS IMPACT ON THE LIVING MARINE RESOURCES OF THE WORLD'S OCEANS AND SEAS.[1]   Adopted by the UN General Assembly, 20 December 1991.   U.N.Doc. A/RES/46/215, 30 I.L.M. 241 (1991)

The General Assembly,

Recalling its resolutions 44/225 and 45/197, concerning large-scale pelagic drift-net fishing and its impact on the living marine resources of the world's oceans and seas, including enclosed and semi-enclosed seas, which took into account the concerns of the developing countries and were adopted by consensus on 22 December 1989 and 21 December 1990, respectively,

Also recalling, in particular, that the General Assembly recommended that all members of the international community agree to certain measures specified in the operative paragraphs of resolution 44/225,

Further recalling the relevant principles elaborated in the United Nations Convention on the Law of the Sea, which are referred to in the seventh to tenth preambular paragraphs of resolution 44/225,

Expressing deep concern about reports of expansion of large-scale pelagic drift-net fishing activities on the high seas in contravention of resolutions 44/225 and 45/197, including attempts to expand large-scale pelagic drift-net fishing in the high seas areas of the Indian Ocean,

Commending the unilateral, regional and international efforts that have been undertaken by members of the international community and international organizations to implement and support the objectives of resolutions 44/225 and 45/197,

Noting that at the Twenty-second South Pacific Forum, held at Palikir on 29 and 30 July 1991, the heads of Government reaffirmed their opposition to large-scale pelagic drift-net fishing, and in this regard, *inter alia,* welcomed the entry into force on 17 May 1991 of the Convention for the Prohibition of Fishing with Long Drift-nets in the South Pacific,

Recalling the Castries Declaration, in which the Authority of the Organization of Eastern Caribbean States resolved to establish a regional regime for the regulation and management of the pelagic resources in the Lesser Antilles region that would outlaw the use of drift-nets and called upon other States in the region to cooperate in this regard,

Welcoming the actions taken that have resulted in the cessation of all large-scale pelagic drift-net fishing activities in the South Pacific in advance of the date stipulated in paragraph 4(*b*) of resolution 44/225 for the termination of such activities,

Also welcoming the decision of other members of the international community to cease large-scale pelagic drift-net fishing on the high seas,

Commending the efforts of many members of the international community to compile data on large-scale pelagic drift-net fishing and to submit their findings to the Secretary–General,

---

1.   *See also* Basic Document 6.8.

Noting the contributions to the report of the Secretary–General made by some members of the international community and by intergovernmental and non-governmental organizations,

Noting also the significant concerns expressed by members of the international community and competent regional fisheries bodies regarding the impact of large-scale pelagic drift-net fishing on the marine environment,

Noting further that, in accordance with paragraph 3 of resolution 44/225, some members of the international community have reviewed the best available scientific data on the impact of large-scale pelagic drift-net fishing and have failed to conclude that this practice has no adverse impact which threatens the conservation and sustainable management of living marine resources,

Noting that the grounds for concerns expressed about the unacceptable impact of large-scale pelagic drift-net fishing in resolutions 44/225 and 45/197 have been confirmed and that evidence has not demonstrated that the impact can be fully prevented,

Recognizing that a moratorium on large-scale pelagic drift-net fishing is required, notwithstanding that it will have adverse socio-economic effects on the communities involved in high seas pelagic drift-net fishing operations,

1. *Recalls* its resolutions 44/225 and 45/197;

2. *Commends* the efforts jointly to collect statistically sound data regarding large-scale pelagic drift-net fishing in the North Pacific Ocean, which were reviewed at the meeting of scientists held at Sidney, Canada, in June 1991, and presented at the symposium on the high seas drift-net fisheries in the North Pacific Ocean, held at Tokyo in November 1991 under the auspices of the International North Pacific Fisheries Commission;

3. *Calls upon* all members of the international community to implement resolutions 44/225 and 45/197 by, *inter alia,* taking the following actions:

(*a*) Beginning on 1 January 1992, reduce fishing effort in existing large-scale pelagic high seas drift-net fisheries by, *inter alia,* reducing the number of vessels involved, the length of the nets and the area of operation, so as to achieve, by 30 June 1992, a 50 per cent reduction in fishing effort;

(*b*) Continue to ensure that the areas of operation of large-scale pelagic high seas drift-net fishing are not expanded and, beginning on 1 January 1992, are further reduced in accordance with paragraph 3(*a*) of the present resolution;

(*c*) Ensure that a global moratorium on all large-scale pelagic drift-net fishing is fully implemented on the high seas of the world's oceans and seas, including enclosed seas and semi-enclosed seas, by 31 December 1992;

4. *Reaffirms* the importance it attaches to compliance with the present resolution and encourages all members of the international community to take measures, individually and collectively, to prevent large-scale pelagic drift-net fishing operations on the high seas of the world's oceans and seas, including enclosed seas and semi-enclosed seas;

5. *Requests* the Secretary–General to bring the present resolution to the attention of all members of the international community, intergovernmental and non-governmental organizations and well-established scientific institutions with expertise in relation to living marine resources;

6. *Requests* the members and organizations referred to above to submit to the Secretary–General information concerning activities or conduct inconsistent with the terms of the present resolution;

7. *Also requests* the Secretary–General to submit to the General Assembly at its forty-seventh session a report on the implementation of the present resolution.

6.10 CONVENTION ON BIOLOGICAL DIVERSITY (WITH ANNEXES). Concluded at Rio de Janeiro, 5 June 1992. Entered into force, 29 December 1993. 31 I.L.M. 818 (1992)

Preamble

The Contracting Parties,

Conscious of the intrinsic value of biological diversity and of the ecological, genetic, social, economic, scientific, educational, cultural, recreational and aesthetic values of biological diversity and its components,

Conscious also of the importance of biological diversity for evolution and for maintaining life sustaining systems of the biosphere,

Affirming that the conservation of biological diversity is a common concern of humankind,

Reaffirming that States have sovereign rights over their own biological resources,

Reaffirming also that States are responsible for conserving their biological diversity and for using their biological resources in a sustainable manner,

Concerned that biological diversity is being significantly reduced by certain human activities,

Aware of the general lack of information and knowledge regarding biological diversity and of the urgent need to develop scientific, technical and institutional capacities to provide the basic understanding upon which to plan and implement appropriate measures,

Noting that it is vital to anticipate, prevent and attack the causes of significant reduction or loss of biological diversity at source,

Noting also that where there is a threat of significant reduction or loss of biological diversity, lack of full scientific certainty should not be used as a reason for postponing measures to avoid or minimize such a threat,

Noting further that the fundamental requirement for the conservation of biological diversity is the *in-situ* conservation of ecosystems and natural habitats and the maintenance and recovery of viable populations of species in their natural surroundings,

Noting further that *ex-situ* measures, preferably in the country of origin, also have an important role to play,

Recognizing the close and traditional dependence of many indigenous and local communities embodying traditional lifestyles on biological resources, and the desirability of sharing equitably benefits arising from the use of traditional knowledge, innovations and practices relevant to the conservation of biological diversity and the sustainable use of its components,

Recognizing also the vital role that women play in the conservation and sustainable use of biological diversity and affirming the need for the full participation of women at all levels of policy-making and implementation for biological diversity conservation,

Stressing the importance of, and the need to promote, international, regional and global cooperation among States and intergovernmental organizations and the non-governmental sector for the conservation of biological diversity and the sustainable use of its components,

Acknowledging that the provision of new and additional financial resources and appropriate access to relevant technologies can be expected to make a substantial difference in the world's ability to address the loss of biological diversity,

Acknowledging further that special provision is required to meet the needs of developing countries, including the provision of new and additional financial resources and appropriate access to relevant technologies,

Noting in this regard the special conditions of the least developed countries and small island States,

Acknowledging that substantial investments are required to conserve biological diversity and that there is the expectation of a broad range of environmental, economic and social benefits from those investments,

Recognizing that economic and social development and poverty eradication are the first and overriding priorities of developing countries,

Aware that conservation and sustainable use of biological diversity is of critical importance for meeting the food, health and other needs of the growing world population, for which purpose access to and sharing of both genetic resources and technologies are essential,

Noting that, ultimately, the conservation and sustainable use of biological diversity will strengthen friendly relations among States and contribute to peace for humankind,

Desiring to enhance and complement existing international arrangements for the conservation of biological diversity and sustainable use of its components, and

Determined to conserve and sustainably use biological diversity for the benefit of present and future generations.

Have agreed as follows:

Article 1.   Objectives

The objectives of this Convention, to be pursued in accordance with its relevant provisions, are the conservation of biological diversity, the sustainable use of its components and the fair and equitable sharing of the benefits arising out of the utilization of genetic resources, including by appropriate access to genetic resources and by appropriate transfer of relevant technologies, taking into account all rights over those resources and to technologies, and by appropriate funding.

Article 2.   Use of Terms

For the purposes of this Convention:

"Biological diversity" means the variability among living organisms from all sources including, *inter alia,* terrestrial, marine and other aquatic ecosystems and the ecological complexes of which they are part; this includes diversity within species, between species and of ecosystems.

"Biological resources" includes genetic resources, organisms or parts thereof, populations, or any other biotic component of ecosystems with actual or potential use or value for humanity.

"Biotechnology" means any technological application that uses biological systems, living organisms, or derivatives thereof, to make or modify products or processes for specific use.

"Country of origin of genetic resources" means the country which possesses those genetic resources in *in-situ* conditions.

"Country providing genetic resources" means the country supplying genetic resources collected from *in-situ* sources, including populations of both wild and domesticated species, or taken from *ex-situ* sources, which may or may not have originated in that country.

"Domesticated or cultivated species" means species in which the evolutionary process has been influenced by humans to meet their needs.

"Ecosystem" means a dynamic complex of plant, animal and microorganism communities and their non-living environment interacting as a functional unit.

"Ex-situ conservation" means the conservation of components of biological diversity outside their natural habitats.

"Genetic material" means any material of plant, animal, microbial or other origin containing functional units of heredity.

"Genetic resources" means genetic material of actual or potential value.

"Habitat" means the place or type of site where an organism or population naturally occurs.

"In-situ conditions" means conditions where genetic resources exist within ecosystems and natural habitats, and, in the case of domesticated or cultivated species, in the surroundings where they have developed their distinctive properties.

"In-situ conservation" means the conservation of ecosystems and natural habitats and the maintenance and recovery of viable populations of species in their natural surroundings and, in the case of domesticated or cultivated species, in the surroundings where they have developed their distinctive properties.

"Protected area" means a geographically defined area which is designated or regulated and managed to achieve specific conservation objectives.

"Regional economic integration organization" means an organization constituted by sovereign States of a given region, to which its member States have transferred competence in respect of matters governed by this Convention and which has been duly authorized, in accordance with its internal procedures, to sign, ratify, accept, approve or accede to it.

"Sustainable use" means the use of components of biological diversity in a way and at a rate that does not lead to the long-term decline of biological diversity, thereby maintaining its potential to meet the needs and aspirations of present and future generations.

"Technology" includes biotechnology.

Article 3. Principle

States have, in accordance with the Charter of the United Nations and the principles of international law, the sovereign right to exploit their own resources pursuant to their own environmental policies, and the responsibility to ensure that activities within their jurisdiction or control do not cause damage to the environment of other States or of areas beyond the limits of national jurisdiction.

Article 4. Jurisdictional Scope

Subject to the rights of other States, and except as otherwise expressly provided in this Convention, the provisions of this Convention apply, in relation to each Contracting Party:

(a) In the case of components of biological diversity, in areas within the limits of its national jurisdiction; and

(b) In the case of processes and activities, regardless of where their effects occur, carried out under its jurisdiction or control, within the area of its national jurisdiction or beyond the limits of national jurisdiction.

Article 5. Cooperation

Each Contracting Party shall, as far as possible and as appropriate, cooperate with other Contracting Parties, directly or, where appropriate, through competent international organizations, in respect of areas beyond national jurisdiction and on other matters of mutual interest, for the conservation and sustainable use of biological diversity.

Article 6. General Measures for Conservation and Sustainable Use

Each Contracting Party shall, in accordance with its particular conditions and capabilities:

(a) Develop national strategies, plans or programmes for the conservation and sustainable use of biological diversity or adapt for this purpose existing strategies, plans or programmes which shall reflect, inter alia, the measures set out in this Convention relevant to the Contracting Party concerned; and

(b) Integrate, as far as possible and as appropriate, the conservation and sustainable use of biological diversity into relevant sectoral or cross-sectoral plans, programmes and policies.

Article 7. Identification and Monitoring

Each Contracting Party shall, as far as possible and as appropriate, in particular for the purposes of Articles 8 to 10:

(a) Identify components of biological diversity important for its conservation and sustainable use having regard to the indicative list of categories set down in Annex I;

(b) Monitor, through sampling and other techniques, the components of biological diversity identified pursuant to subparagraph (a) above, paying particular attention to those requiring urgent conservation measures and those which offer the greatest potential for sustainable use;

(c) Identify processes and categories of activities which have or are likely to have significant adverse impacts on the conservation and sustainable use of biological diversity, and monitor their effects through sampling and other techniques; and

(d) Maintain and organize, by any mechanism data, derived from identification and monitoring activities pursuant to subparagraphs (a), (b) and (c) above.

Article 8. In-situ Conservation

Each Contracting Party shall, as far as possible and as appropriate:

(a) Establish a system of protected areas or areas where special measures need to be taken to conserve biological diversity;

(b) Develop, where necessary, guidelines for the selection, establishment and management of protected areas or areas where special measures need to be taken to conserve biological diversity;

(c) Regulate or manage biological resources important for the conservation of biological diversity whether within or outside protected areas, with a view to ensuring their conservation and sustainable use;

(d) Promote the protection of ecosystems, natural habitats and the maintenance of viable populations of species in natural surroundings;

(e) Promote environmentally sound and sustainable development in areas adjacent to protected areas with a view to furthering protection of these areas;

(f) Rehabilitate and restore degraded ecosystems and promote the recovery of threatened species, *inter alia,* through the development and implementation of plans or other management strategies;

(g) Establish or maintain means to regulate, manage or control the risks associated with the use and release of living modified organisms resulting from biotechnology which are likely to have adverse environmental impacts that could affect the conservation and sustainable use of biological diversity, taking also into account the risks to human health;

(h) Prevent the introduction of, control or eradicate those alien species which threaten ecosystems, habitats or species;

(i) Endeavour to provide the conditions needed for compatibility between present uses and the conservation of biological diversity and the sustainable use of its components;

(j) Subject to its national legislation, respect, preserve and maintain knowledge, innovations and practices of indigenous and local communities embodying traditional lifestyles relevant for the conservation and sustainable use of biological diversity and promote their wider application with the approval and involvement of the holders of such knowledge, innovations and practices and encourage the equitable sharing of the benefits arising from the utilization of such knowledge, innovations and practices;

(k) Develop or maintain necessary legislation and/or other regulatory provisions for the protection of threatened species and populations;

(*l*) Where a significant adverse effect on biological diversity has been determined pursuant to Article 7, regulate or manage the relevant processes and categories of activities; and

(m) Cooperate in providing financial and other support for *in-situ* conservation outlined in subparagraphs (a) to (*l*) above, particularly to developing countries.

Article 9. Ex-situ Conservation

Each Contracting Party shall, as far as possible and as appropriate, and predominantly for the purpose of complementing *in-situ* measures:

(a) Adopt measures for the *ex-situ* conservation of components of biological diversity, preferably in the country of origin of such components;

(b) Establish and maintain facilities for *ex-situ* conservation of and research on plants, animals and micro-organisms, preferably in the country of origin of genetic resources;

(c) Adopt measures for the recovery and rehabilitation of threatened species and for their reintroduction into their natural habitats under appropriate conditions;

(d) Regulate and manage collection of biological resources from natural habitats for *ex-situ* conservation purposes so as not to threaten ecosystems and *in-situ* populations of species, except where special temporary *ex-situ* measures are required under subparagraph (c) above; and

(e) Cooperate in providing financial and other support for *ex-situ* conservation outlined in subparagraphs (a) to (d) above and in the establishment and maintenance of *ex-situ* conservation facilities in developing countries.

Article 10. Sustainable Use of Components of Biological Diversity

Each Contracting Party shall, as far as possible and as appropriate:

(a) Integrate consideration of the conservation and sustainable use of biological resources into national decision-making;

(b) Adopt measures relating to the use of biological resources to avoid or minimize adverse impacts on biological diversity;

(c) Protect and encourage customary use of biological resources in accordance with traditional cultural practices that are compatible with conservation or sustainable use requirements;

(d) Support local populations to develop and implement remedial action in degraded areas where biological diversity has been reduced; and

(e) Encourage cooperation between its governmental authorities and its private sector in developing methods for sustainable use of biological resources.

Article 11. Incentive Measures

Each Contracting Party shall, as far as possible and as appropriate, adopt economically and socially sound measures that act as incentives for the conservation and sustainable use of components of biological diversity.

Article 12. Research and Training

The Contracting Parties, taking into account the special needs of developing countries, shall:

(a)   Establish and maintain programmes for scientific and technical education and training in measures for the identification, conservation and sustainable use of biological diversity and its components and provide support for such education and training for the specific needs of developing countries;

(b)   Promote and encourage research which contributes to the conservation and sustainable use of biological diversity, particularly in developing countries, *inter alia,* in accordance with decisions of the Conference of the Parties taken in consequence of recommendations of the Subsidiary Body on Scientific, Technical and Technological Advice; and

(c)   In keeping with the provisions of Articles 16, 18 and 20, promote and cooperate in the use of scientific advances in biological diversity research in developing methods for conservation and sustainable use of biological resources.

Article 13.   Public Education and Awareness

The Contracting Parties shall:

(a)   Promote and encourage understanding of the importance of, and the measures required for, the conservation of biological diversity, as well as its propagation through media, and the inclusion of these topics in educational programmes; and

(b)   Cooperate, as appropriate, with other States and international organizations in developing educational and public awareness programmes, with respect to conservation and sustainable use of biological diversity.

Article 14.   Impact Assessment and Minimizing Adverse Impacts

1.   Each Contracting Party, as far as possible and as appropriate, shall:

(a)   Introduce appropriate procedures requiring environmental impact assessment of its proposed projects that are likely to have significant adverse effects on biological diversity with a view to avoiding or minimizing such effects and, where appropriate, allow for public participation in such procedures;

(b)   Introduce appropriate arrangements to ensure that the environmental consequences of its programmes and policies that are likely to have significant adverse impacts on biological diversity are duly taken into account;

(c)   Promote, on the basis of reciprocity, notification, exchange of information and consultation on activities under their jurisdiction or control which are likely to significantly affect adversely the biological diversity of other States or areas beyond the limits of national jurisdiction, by encouraging the conclusion of bilateral, regional or multilateral arrangements, as appropriate;

(d)   In the case of imminent or grave danger or damage, originating under its jurisdiction or control, to biological diversity within the area under jurisdiction of other States or in areas beyond the limits of national jurisdiction, notify immediately the potentially affected States of such danger or damage, as well as initiate action to prevent or minimize such danger or damage; and

(e) Promote national arrangements for emergency responses to activities or events, whether caused naturally or otherwise, which present a grave and imminent danger to biological diversity and encourage international cooperation to supplement such national efforts and, where appropriate and agreed by the States or regional economic integration organizations concerned, to establish joint contingency plans.

2. The Conference of the Parties shall examine, on the basis of studies to be carried out, the issue of liability and redress, including restoration and compensation, for damage to biological diversity, except where such liability is a purely internal matter.

Article 15. Access to Genetic Resources

1. Recognizing the sovereign rights of States over their natural resources, the authority to determine access to genetic resources rests with the national governments and is subject to national legislation.

2. Each Contracting Party shall endeavour to create conditions to facilitate access to genetic resources for environmentally sound uses by other Contracting Parties and not to impose restrictions that run counter to the objectives of this Convention.

3. For the purpose of this Convention, the genetic resources being provided by a Contracting Party, as referred to in this Article and Articles 16 and 19, are only those that are provided by Contracting Parties that are countries of origin of such resources or by the Parties that have acquired the genetic resources in accordance with this Convention.

4. Access, where granted, shall be on mutually agreed terms and subject to the provisions of this Article.

5. Access to genetic resources shall be subject to prior informed consent of the Contracting Party providing such resources, unless otherwise determined by that Party.

6. Each Contracting Party shall endeavour to develop and carry out scientific research based on genetic resources provided by other Contracting Parties with the full participation of, and where possible in, such Contracting Parties.

7. Each Contracting Party shall take legislative, administrative or policy measures, as appropriate, and in accordance with Articles 16 and 19 and, where necessary, through the financial mechanism established by Articles 20 and 21 with the aim of sharing in a fair and equitable way the results of research and development and the benefits arising from the commercial and other utilization of genetic resources with the Contracting Party providing such resources. Such sharing shall be upon mutually agreed terms.

Article 16. Access to and Transfer of Technology

1. Each Contracting Party, recognizing that technology includes biotechnology, and that both access to and transfer of technology among Contracting Parties are essential elements for the attainment of the objectives of this Convention, undertakes subject to the provisions of this Article to provide and/or facilitate access for and transfer to other Contracting Parties of technologies that are relevant to the conservation and sustainable use of

biological diversity or make use of genetic resources and do not cause significant damage to the environment.

2. Access to and transfer of technology referred to in paragraph 1 above to developing countries shall be provided and/or facilitated under fair and most favourable terms, including on concessional and preferential terms where mutually agreed, and, where necessary, in accordance with the financial mechanism established by Articles 20 and 21. In the case of technology subject to patents and other intellectual property rights, such access and transfer shall be provided on terms which recognize and are consistent with the adequate and effective protection of intellectual property rights. The application of this paragraph shall be consistent with paragraphs 3, 4 and 5 below.

3. Each Contracting Party shall take legislative, administrative or policy measures, as appropriate, with the aim that Contracting Parties, in particular those that are developing countries, which provide genetic resources are provided access to and transfer of technology which makes use of those resources, on mutually agreed terms, including technology protected by patents and other intellectual property rights, where necessary, through the provisions of Articles 20 and 21 and in accordance with international law and consistent with paragraphs 4 and 5 below.

4. Each Contracting Party shall take legislative, administrative or policy measures, as appropriate, with the aim that the private sector facilitates access to, joint development and transfer of technology referred to in paragraph 1 above for the benefit of both governmental institutions and the private sector of developing countries and in this regard shall abide by the obligations included in paragraphs 1, 2 and 3 above.

5. The Contracting Parties, recognizing that patents and other intellectual property rights may have an influence on the implementation of this Convention, shall cooperate in this regard subject to national legislation and international law in order to ensure that such rights are supportive of and do not run counter to its objectives.

Article 17. *Exchange of Information*

1. The Contracting Parties shall facilitate the exchange of information, from all publicly available sources, relevant to the conservation and sustainable use of biological diversity, taking into account the special needs of developing countries.

2. Such exchange of information shall include exchange of results of technical, scientific and socio-economic research, as well as information on training and surveying programmes, specialized knowledge, indigenous and traditional knowledge as such and in combination with the technologies referred to in Article 16, paragraph 1. It shall also, where feasible, include repatriation of information.

Article 18. *Technical and Scientific Cooperation*

1. The Contracting Parties shall promote international technical and scientific cooperation in the field of conservation and sustainable use of biological diversity, where necessary, through the appropriate international and national institutions.

2.   Each Contracting Party shall promote technical and scientific cooperation with other Contracting Parties, in particular developing countries, in implementing this Convention, inter alia, through the development and implementation of national policies. In promoting such cooperation, special attention should be given to the development and strengthening of national capabilities, by means of human resources development and institution building.

3.   The Conference of the Parties, at its first meeting, shall determine how to establish a clearing-house mechanism to promote and facilitate technical and scientific cooperation.

4.   The Contracting Parties shall, in accordance with national legislation and policies, encourage and develop methods of cooperation for the development and use of technologies, including indigenous and traditional technologies, in pursuance of the objectives of this Convention. For this purpose, the Contracting Parties shall also promote cooperation in the training of personnel and exchange of experts.

5.   The Contracting Parties shall, subject to mutual agreement, promote the establishment of joint research programmes and joint ventures for the development of technologies relevant to the objectives of this Convention.

Article 19.   Handling of Biotechnology and Distribution of its Benefits

1.   Each Contracting Party shall take legislative, administrative or policy measures, as appropriate, to provide for the effective participation in biotechnological research activities by those Contracting Parties, especially developing countries, which provide the genetic resources for such research, and where feasible in such Contracting Parties.

2.   Each Contracting Party shall take all practicable measures to promote and advance priority access on a fair and equitable basis by Contracting Parties, especially developing countries, to the results and benefits arising from biotechnologies based upon genetic resources provided by those Contracting Parties. Such access shall be on mutually agreed terms.

3.   The Parties shall consider the need for and modalities of a protocol setting out appropriate procedures, including, in particular, advance informed agreement, in the field of the safe transfer, handling and use of any living modified organism resulting from biotechnology that may have adverse effect on the conservation and sustainable use of biological diversity.

4.   Each Contracting Party shall, directly or by requiring any natural or legal person under its jurisdiction providing the organisms referred to in paragraph 3 above, provide any available information about the use and safety regulations required by that Contracting Party in handling such organisms, as well as any available information on the potential adverse impact of the specific organisms concerned to the Contracting Party into which those organisms are to be introduced.

Article 20.   Financial Resources

1.   Each Contracting Party undertakes to provide, in accordance with its capabilities, financial support and incentives in respect of those national activities which are intended to achieve the objectives of this Convention, in accordance with its national plans, priorities and programmes.

2. The developed country Parties shall provide new and additional financial resources to enable developing country Parties to meet the agreed full incremental costs to them of implementing measures which fulfil the obligations of this Convention and to benefit from its provisions and which costs are agreed between a developing country Party and the institutional structure referred to in Article 21, in accordance with policy, strategy, programme priorities and eligibility criteria and an indicative list of incremental costs established by the Conference of the Parties. Other Parties, including countries undergoing the process of transition to a market economy, may voluntarily assume the obligations of the developed country Parties. For the purpose of this Article, the Conference of the Parties, shall at its first meeting establish a list of developed country Parties and other Parties which voluntarily assume the obligations of the developed country Parties. The Conference of the Parties shall periodically review and if necessary amend the list. Contributions from other countries and sources on a voluntary basis would also be encouraged. The implementation of these commitments shall take into account the need for adequacy, predictability and timely flow of funds and the importance of burden-sharing among the contributing Parties included in the list.

3. The developed country Parties may also provide, and developing country Parties avail themselves of, financial resources related to the implementation of this Convention through bilateral, regional and other multilateral channels.

4. The extent to which developing country Parties will effectively implement their commitments under this Convention will depend on the effective implementation by developed country Parties of their commitments under this Convention related to financial resources and transfer of technology and will take fully into account the fact that economic and social development and eradication of poverty are the first and overriding priorities of the developing country Parties.

5. The Parties shall take full account of the specific needs and special situation of least developed countries in their actions with regard to funding and transfer of technology.

6. The Contracting Parties shall also take into consideration the special conditions resulting from the dependence on, distribution and location of, biological diversity within developing country Parties, in particular small island States.

7. Consideration shall also be given to the special situation of developing countries, including those that are most environmentally vulnerable, such as those with arid and semi-arid zones, coastal and mountainous areas.

Article 21. *Financial Mechanism*

1. There shall be a mechanism for the provision of financial resources to developing country Parties for purposes of this Convention on a grant or concessional basis the essential elements of which are described in this Article. The mechanism shall function under the authority and guidance of, and be accountable to, the Conference of the Parties for purposes of this Convention. The operations of the mechanism shall be carried out by such institutional structure as may be decided upon by the Conference of the

Parties at its first meeting. For purposes of this Convention, the Conference of the Parties shall determine the policy, strategy, programme priorities and eligibility criteria relating to the access to and utilization of such resources. The contributions shall be such as to take into account the need for predictability, adequacy and timely flow of funds referred to in Article 20 in accordance with the amount of resources needed to be decided periodically by the Conference of the Parties and the importance of burden-sharing among the contributing Parties included in the list referred to in Article 20, paragraph 2. Voluntary contributions may also be made by the developed country Parties and by other countries and sources. The mechanism shall operate within a democratic and transparent system of governance.

2.   Pursuant to the objectives of this Convention, the Conference of the Parties shall at its first meeting determine the policy, strategy and programme priorities, as well as detailed criteria and guidelines for eligibility for access to and utilization of the financial resources including monitoring and evaluation on a regular basis of such utilization. The Conference of the Parties shall decide on the arrangements to give effect to paragraph 1 above after consultation with the institutional structure entrusted with the operation of the financial mechanism.

3.   The Conference of the Parties shall review the effectiveness of the mechanism established under this Article, including the criteria and guidelines referred to in paragraph 2 above, not less than two years after the entry into force of this Convention and thereafter on a regular basis. Based on such review, it shall take appropriate action to improve the effectiveness of the mechanism if necessary.

4.   The Contracting Parties shall consider strengthening existing financial institutions to provide financial resources for the conservation and sustainable use of biological diversity.

Article 22.   Relationship with Other International Conventions

1.   The provisions of this Convention shall not affect the rights and obligations of any Contracting Party deriving from any existing international agreement, except where the exercise of those rights and obligations would cause a serious damage or threat to biological diversity.

2.   Contracting Parties shall implement this Convention with respect to the marine environment consistently with the rights and obligations of States under the law of the sea.

Article 23.   Conference of the Parties

1.   A Conference of the Parties is hereby established. The first meeting of the Conference of the Parties shall be convened by the Executive Director of the United Nations Environment Programme not later than one year after the entry into force of this Convention. Thereafter, ordinary meetings of the Conference of the Parties shall be held at regular intervals to be determined by the Conference at its first meeting.

2.   Extraordinary meetings of the Conference of the Parties shall be held at such other times as may be deemed necessary by the Conference, or at the written request of any Party, provided that, within six months of the request being communicated to them by the Secretariat, it is supported by at least one third of the Parties.

3. The Conference of the Parties shall by consensus agree upon and adopt rules of procedure for itself and for any subsidiary body it may establish, as well as financial rules governing the funding of the Secretariat. At each ordinary meeting, it shall adopt a budget for the financial period until the next ordinary meeting.

4. The Conference of the Parties shall keep under review the implementation of this Convention, and, for this purpose, shall:

(a) Establish the form and the intervals for transmitting the information to be submitted in accordance with Article 26 and consider such information as well as reports submitted by any subsidiary body;

(b) Review scientific, technical and technological advice on biological diversity provided in accordance with Article 25;

(c) Consider and adopt, as required, protocols in accordance with Article 28;

(d) Consider and adopt, as required, in accordance with Articles 29 and 30, amendments to this Convention and its annexes;

(e) Consider amendments to any protocol, as well as to any annexes thereto, and, if so decided, recommend their adoption to the Parties to the protocol concerned;

(f) Consider and adopt, as required, in accordance with Article 30, additional annexes to this Convention;

(g) Establish such subsidiary bodies, particularly to provide scientific and technical advice, as are deemed necessary for the implementation of this Convention;

(h) Contact, through the Secretariat, the executive bodies of conventions dealing with matters covered by this Convention with a view to establishing appropriate forms of cooperation with them; and

(i) Consider and undertake any additional action that may be required for the achievement of the purposes of this Convention in the light of experience gained in its operation.

5. The United Nations, its specialized agencies and the International Atomic Energy Agency, as well as any State not Party to this Convention, may be represented as observers at meetings of the Conference of the Parties. Any other body or agency, whether governmental or nongovernmental, qualified in fields relating to conservation and sustainable use of biological diversity, which has informed the Secretariat of its wish to be represented as an observer at a meeting of the Conference of the Parties, may be admitted unless at least one third of the Parties present object. The admission and participation of observers shall be subject to the rules of procedure adopted by the Conference of the Parties.

Article 24. Secretariat

1. A secretariat is hereby established. Its functions shall be:

(a) To arrange for and service meetings of the Conference of the Parties provided for in Article 23;

(b) To perform the functions assigned to it by any protocol;

(c) To prepare reports on the execution of its functions under this Convention and present them to the Conference of the Parties;

(d) To coordinate with other relevant international bodies and, in particular to enter into such administrative and contractual arrangements as may be required for the effective discharge of its functions; and

(e) To perform such other functions as may be determined by the Conference of the Parties.

2. At its first ordinary meeting, the Conference of the Parties shall designate the secretariat from amongst those existing competent international organizations which have signified their willingness to carry out the secretariat functions under this Convention.

Article 25. Subsidiary Body on Scientific, Technical and Technological Advice

1. A subsidiary body for the provision of scientific, technical and technological advice is hereby established to provide the Conference of the Parties and, as appropriate, its other subsidiary bodies with timely advice relating to the implementation of this Convention. This body shall be open to participation by all Parties and shall be multidisciplinary. It shall comprise government representatives competent in the relevant field of expertise. It shall report regularly to the Conference of the Parties on all aspects of its work.

2. Under the authority of and in accordance with guidelines laid down by the Conference of the Parties, and upon its request, this body shall:

(a) Provide scientific and technical assessments of the status of biological diversity;

(b) Prepare scientific and technical assessments of the effects of types of measures taken in accordance with the provisions of this Convention;

(c) Identify innovative, efficient and state-of-the-art technologies and know-how relating to the conservation and sustainable use of biological diversity and advise on the ways and means of promoting development and/or transferring such technologies;

(d) Provide advice on scientific programmes and international cooperation in research and development related to conservation and sustainable use of biological diversity; and

(e) Respond to scientific, technical, technological and methodological questions that the Conference of the Parties and its subsidiary bodies may put to the body.

3. The functions, terms of reference, organization and operation of this body may be further elaborated by the Conference of the Parties.

Article 26. Reports

Each Contracting Party shall, at intervals to be determined by the Conference of the Parties, present to the Conference of the Parties, reports on measures which it has taken for the implementation of the provisions of this Convention and their effectiveness in meeting the objectives of this Convention.

Article 27. Settlement of Disputes

1. In the event of a dispute between Contracting Parties concerning the interpretation or application of this Convention, the parties concerned shall seek solution by negotiation.

2. If the parties concerned cannot reach agreement by negotiation, they may jointly seek the good offices of, or request mediation by, a third party.

3. When ratifying, accepting, approving or acceding to this Convention, or at any time thereafter, a State or regional economic integration organization may declare in writing to the Depositary that for a dispute not resolved in accordance with paragraph 1 or paragraph 2 above, it accepts one or both of the following means of dispute settlement as compulsory:

(a) Arbitration in accordance with the procedure laid down in Part 1 of Annex II;

(b) Submission of the dispute to the International Court of Justice.

4. If the parties to the dispute have not, in accordance with paragraph 3 above, accepted the same or any procedure, the dispute shall be submitted to conciliation in accordance with Part 2 of Annex II unless the parties otherwise agree.

5. The provisions of this Article shall apply with respect to any protocol except as otherwise provided in the protocol concerned.

Article 28. Adoption of Protocols

1. The Contracting Parties shall cooperate in the formulation and adoption of protocols to this Convention.

2. Protocols shall be adopted at a meeting of the Conference of the Parties.

3. The text of any proposed protocol shall be communicated to the Contracting Parties by the Secretariat at least six months before such a meeting.

Article 29. Amendment of the Convention or Protocols

1. Amendments to this Convention may be proposed by any Contracting Party. Amendments to any protocol may be proposed by any Party to that protocol.

2. Amendments to this Convention shall be adopted at a meeting of the Conference of the Parties. Amendments to any protocol shall be adopted at a meeting of the Parties to the Protocol in question. The text of any proposed amendment to this Convention or to any protocol, except as may otherwise be provided in such protocol, shall be communicated to the Parties to the instrument in question by the Secretariat at least six months before the meeting at which it is proposed for adoption. The Secretariat shall also communicate proposed amendments to the signatories to this Convention for information.

3. The Parties shall make every effort to reach agreement on any proposed amendment to this Convention or to any protocol by consensus. If all efforts at consensus have been exhausted, and no agreement reached, the amendment shall as a last resort be adopted by a two-thirds majority vote of the Parties to the instrument in question present and voting at the meeting,

and shall be submitted by the Depositary to all Parties for ratification, acceptance or approval.

4. Ratification, acceptance or approval of amendments shall be notified to the Depositary in writing. Amendments adopted in accordance with paragraph 3 above shall enter into force among Parties having accepted them on the ninetieth day after the deposit of instruments of ratification, acceptance or approval by at least two thirds of the Contracting Parties to this Convention or of the Parties to the protocol concerned, except as may otherwise be provided in such protocol. Thereafter the amendments shall enter into force for any other Party on the ninetieth day after that Party deposits its instrument of ratification, acceptance or approval of the amendments.

5. For the purposes of this Article, "Parties present and voting" means Parties present and casting an affirmative or negative vote.

Article 30. Adoption and Amendment of Annexes

1. The annexes to this Convention or to any protocol shall form an integral part of the Convention or of such protocol, as the case may be, and, unless expressly provided otherwise, a reference to this Convention or its protocols constitutes at the same time a reference to any annexes thereto. Such annexes shall be restricted to procedural, scientific, technical and administrative matters.

2. Except as may be otherwise provided in any protocol with respect to its annexes, the following procedure shall apply to the proposal, adoption and entry into force of additional annexes to this Convention or of annexes to any protocol:

(a) Annexes to this Convention or to any protocol shall be proposed and adopted according to the procedure laid down in Article 29;

(b) Any Party that is unable to approve an additional annex to this Convention or an annex to any protocol to which it is Party shall so notify the Depositary, in writing, within one year from the date of the communication of the adoption by the Depositary. The Depositary shall without delay notify all Parties of any such notification received. A Party may at any time withdraw a previous declaration of objection and the annexes shall thereupon enter into force for that Party subject to subparagraph (c) below;

(c) On the expiry of one year from the date of the communication of the adoption by the Depositary, the annex shall enter into force for all Parties to this Convention or to any protocol concerned which have not submitted a notification in accordance with the provisions of subparagraph (b) above.

3. The proposal, adoption and entry into force of amendments to annexes to this Convention or to any protocol shall be subject to the same procedure as for the proposal, adoption and entry into force of annexes to the Convention or annexes to any protocol.

4. If an additional annex or an amendment to an annex is related to an amendment to this Convention or to any protocol, the additional annex or

amendment shall not enter into force until such time as the amendment to the Convention or to the protocol concerned enters into force.

Article 31. *Right to Vote*

1. Except as provided for in paragraph 2 below, each Contracting Party to this Convention or to any protocol shall have one vote.

2. Regional economic integration organizations, in matters within their competence, shall exercise their right to vote with a number of votes equal to the number of their member States which are Contracting Parties to this Convention or the relevant protocol. Such organizations shall not exercise their right to vote if their member States exercise theirs, and vice versa.

Article 32. *Relationship between this Convention and Its Protocols*

1. A State or a regional economic integration organization may not become a Party to a protocol unless it is, or becomes at the same time, a Contracting Party to this Convention.

2. Decisions under any protocol shall be taken only by the Parties to the protocol concerned. Any Contracting Party that has not ratified, accepted or approved a protocol may participate as an observer in any meeting of the parties to that protocol.

Article 33. *Signature*

This Convention shall be open for signature at Rio de Janeiro by all States and any regional economic integration organization from 5 June 1992 until 14 June 1992, and at the United Nations Headquarters in New York from 15 June 1992 to 4 June 1993.

Article 34. *Ratification, Acceptance or Approval*

1. This Convention and any protocol shall be subject to ratification, acceptance or approval by States and by regional economic integration organizations. Instruments of ratification, acceptance or approval shall be deposited with the Depositary.

2. Any organization referred to in paragraph 1 above which becomes a Contracting Party to this Convention or any protocol without any of its member States being a Contracting Party shall be bound by all the obligations under the Convention or the protocol, as the case may be. In the case of such organizations, one or more of whose member States is a Contracting Party to this Convention or relevant protocol, the organization and its member States shall decide on their respective responsibilities for the performance of their obligations under the Convention or protocol, as the case may be. In such cases, the organization and the member States shall not be entitled to exercise rights under the Convention or relevant protocol concurrently.

3. In their instruments of ratification, acceptance or approval, the organizations referred to in paragraph 1 above shall declare the extent of their competence with respect to the matters governed by the Convention or the relevant protocol. These organizations shall also inform the Depositary of any relevant modification in the extent of their competence.

Article 35. *Accession*

1. This Convention and any protocol shall be open for accession by States and by regional economic integration organizations from the date on

which the Convention or the protocol concerned is closed for signature. The instruments of accession shall be deposited with the Depositary.

2. In their instruments of accession, the organizations referred to in paragraph 1 above shall declare the extent of their competence with respect to the matters governed by the Convention or the relevant protocol. These organizations shall also inform the Depositary of any relevant modification in the extent of their competence.

3. The provisions of Article 34, paragraph 2, shall apply to regional economic integration organizations which accede to this Convention or any protocol.

Article 36. Entry Into Force

1. This Convention shall enter into force on the ninetieth day after the date of deposit of the thirtieth instrument of ratification, acceptance, approval or accession.

2. Any protocol shall enter into force on the ninetieth day after the date of deposit of the number of instruments of ratification, acceptance, approval or accession, specified in that protocol, has been deposited.

3. For each Contracting Party which ratifies, accepts or approves this Convention or accedes thereto after the deposit of the thirtieth instrument of ratification, acceptance, approval or accession, it shall enter into force on the ninetieth day after the date of deposit by such Contracting Party of its instrument of ratification, acceptance, approval or accession.

4. Any protocol, except as otherwise provided in such protocol, shall enter into force for a Contracting Party that ratifies, accepts or approves that protocol or accedes thereto after its entry into force pursuant to paragraph 2 above, on the ninetieth day after the date on which that Contracting Party deposits its instrument of ratification, acceptance, approval or accession, or on the date on which this Convention enters into force for that Contracting Party, whichever shall be the later.

5. For the purposes of paragraphs 1 and 2 above, any instrument deposited by a regional economic integration organization shall not be counted as additional to those deposited by member States of such organization.

Article 37. Reservations

No reservations may be made to this Convention.

Article 38. Withdrawals

1. At any time after two years from the date on which this Convention has entered into force for a Contracting Party, that Contracting Party may withdraw from the Convention by giving written notification to the Depositary.

2. Any such withdrawal shall take place upon expiry of one year after the date of its receipt by the Depositary, or on such later date as may be specified in the notification of the withdrawal.

3. Any Contracting Party which withdraws from this Convention shall be considered as also having withdrawn from any protocol to which it is party.

Article 39. *Financial Interim Arrangements*

Provided that it has been fully restructured in accordance with the requirements of Article 21, the Global Environment Facility of the United Nations Development Programme, the United Nations Environment Programme and the International Bank for Reconstruction and Development shall be the institutional structure referred to in Article 21 on an interim basis, for the period between the entry into force of this Convention and the first meeting of the Conference of the Parties or until the Conference of the Parties decides which institutional structure will be designated in accordance with Article 21.

Article 40. *Secretariat Interim Arrangements*

The secretariat to be provided by the Executive Director of the United Nations Environment Programme shall be the secretariat referred to in Article 24, paragraph 2, on an interim basis for the period between the entry into force of this Convention and the first meeting of the Conference of the Parties.

Article 41. *Depositary*

The Secretary–General of the United Nations shall assume the functions of Depositary of this Convention and any protocols.

Article 42. *Authentic Texts*

The original of this Convention, of which the Arabic, Chinese, English, French, Russian and Spanish texts are equally authentic, shall be deposited with the Secretary–General of the United Nations.

Annex I

IDENTIFICATION AND MONITORING

1. Ecosystems and habitats: containing high diversity, large numbers of endemic or threatened species, or wilderness; required by migratory species; of social, economic, cultural or scientific importance; or, which are representative, unique or associated with key evolutionary or other biological processes;

2. Species and communities which are: threatened; wild relatives of domesticated or cultivated species; of medicinal, agricultural or other economic value; or social, scientific or cultural importance; or importance for research into the conservation and sustainable use of biological diversity, such as indicator species; and

3. Described genomes and genes of social, scientific or economic importance.

Annex II

Part 1

ARBITRATION

Article 1

The claimant party shall notify the Secretariat that the parties are referring a dispute to arbitration pursuant to Article 27. The notification shall state the subject-matter of arbitration and include, in particular, the articles of the Convention or the protocol, the interpretation or application of which are at issue. If the parties do not agree on the subject matter of the dispute before the President of the tribunal is designated, the arbitral tribunal shall determine the subject matter. The Secretariat shall forward the information thus received to all Contracting Parties to this Convention or to the protocol concerned.

Article 2

1. In disputes between two parties, the arbitral tribunal shall consist of three members. Each of the parties to the dispute shall appoint an arbitrator and the two arbitrators so appointed shall designate by common agreement the third arbitrator who shall be the President of the tribunal. The latter shall not be a national of one of the parties to the dispute, nor have his or her usual place of residence in the territory of one of these parties, nor be employed by any of them, nor have dealt with the case in any other capacity.

2. In disputes between more than two parties, parties in the same interest shall appoint one arbitrator jointly by agreement.

3. Any vacancy shall be filled in the manner prescribed for the initial appointment.

Article 3

1. If the President of the arbitral tribunal has not been designated within two months of the appointment of the second arbitrator, the Secretary–General of the United Nations shall, at the request of a party, designate the President within a further two-month period.

2. If one of the parties to the dispute does not appoint an arbitrator within two months of receipt of the request, the other party may inform the Secretary–General who shall make the designation within a further two-month period.

Article 4

The arbitral tribunal shall render its decisions in accordance with the provisions of this Convention, any protocols concerned, and international law.

Article 5

Unless the parties to the dispute otherwise agree, the arbitral tribunal shall determine its own rules of procedure.

Article 6

The arbitral tribunal may, at the request of one of the parties, recommend essential interim measures of protection.

Article 7

The parties to the dispute shall facilitate the work of the arbitral tribunal and, in particular, using all means at their disposal, shall:

    (a) Provide it with all relevant documents, information and facilities; and

    (b) Enable it, when necessary, to call witnesses or experts and receive their evidence.

Article 8

The parties and the arbitrators are under an obligation to protect the confidentiality of any information they receive in confidence during the proceedings of the arbitral tribunal.

Article 9

Unless the arbitral tribunal determines otherwise because of the particular circumstances of the case, the costs of the tribunal shall be borne by the parties to the dispute in equal shares. The tribunal shall keep a record of all its costs, and shall furnish a final statement thereof to the parties.

Article 10

Any Contracting Party that has an interest of a legal nature in the subject-matter of the dispute which may be affected by the decision in the case, may intervene in the proceedings with the consent of the tribunal.

Article 11

The tribunal may hear and determine counterclaims arising directly out of the subject-matter of the dispute.

Article 12

Decisions both on procedure and substance of the arbitral tribunal shall be taken by a majority vote of its members.

Article 13

If one of the parties to the dispute does not appear before the arbitral tribunal or fails to defend its case, the other party may request the tribunal to continue the proceedings and to make its award. Absence of a party or a failure of a party to defend its case shall not constitute a bar to the proceedings. Before rendering its final decision, the arbitral tribunal must satisfy itself that the claim is well founded in fact and law.

Article 14

The tribunal shall render its final decision within five months of the date on which it is fully constituted unless it finds it necessary to extend the time-limit for a period which should not exceed five more months.

Article 15

The final decision of the arbitral tribunal shall be confined to the subject-matter of the dispute and shall state the reasons on which it is based. It shall contain the names of the members who have participated and the date of the final decision. Any member of the tribunal may attach a separate or dissenting opinion to the final decision.

Article 16

The award shall be binding on the parties to the dispute. It shall be without appeal unless the parties to the dispute have agreed in advance to an appellate procedure.

Article 17

Any controversy which may arise between the parties to the dispute as regards the interpretation or manner of implementation of the final decision may be submitted by either party for decision to the arbitral tribunal which rendered it.

Part 2
CONCILIATION
Article 1

A conciliation commission shall be created upon the request of one of the parties to the dispute. The commission shall, unless the parties otherwise agree, be composed of five members, two appointed by each Party concerned and a President chosen jointly by those members.

Article 2

In disputes between more than two parties, parties in the same interest shall appoint their members of the commission jointly by agreement. Where two or more parties have separate interests or there is a disagreement as to whether they are of the same interest, they shall appoint their members separately.

Article 3

If any appointments by the parties are not made within two months of the date of the request to create a conciliation commission, the Secretary–General of the United Nations shall, if asked to do so by the party that made the request, make those appointments within a further two-month period.

Article 4

If a President of the conciliation commission has not been chosen within two months of the last of the members of the commission being appointed, the Secretary–General of the United Nations shall, if asked to do so by a party, designate a President within a further two-month period.

Article 5

The conciliation commission shall take its decisions by majority vote of its members. It shall, unless the parties to the dispute otherwise agree, determine its own procedure. It shall render a proposal for resolution of the dispute, which the parties shall consider in good faith.

Article 6

A disagreement as to whether the conciliation commission has competence shall be decided by the commission.

6.11 NON–LEGALLY BINDING AUTHORITATIVE STATEMENT OF PRIN-CIPLES FOR A GLOBAL CONSENSUS ON THE MANAGEMENT, CONSERVATION AND SUSTAINABLE DEVELOPMENT OF ALL TYPES OF FORESTS. Adopted by the UN Conference on Environment and Development at Rio de Janeiro, 13 June 1992. U.N. Doc. A/CONF. 151/26 (Vol. III) (1992), 31 I.L.M. 881 (1992)

PREAMBLE

(a) The subject of forests is related to the entire range of environmental and development issues and opportunities, including the right to socio-economic development on a sustainable basis.

(b) The guiding objective of these principles is to contribute to the management, conservation and sustainable development of forests and to provide for their multiple and complementary functions and uses.

(c) Forestry issues and opportunities should be examined in a holistic and balanced manner within the overall context of environment and development, taking into consideration the multiple functions and uses of forests, including traditional uses, and the likely economic and social stress when these uses are constrained or restricted, as well as the potential for development that sustainable forest management can offer.

(d) These principles reflect a first global consensus on forests. In committing themselves to the prompt implementation of these principles, countries also decide to keep them under assessment for their adequacy with regard to further international cooperation on forest issues.

(e) These principles should apply to all types of forests, both natural and planted, in all geographic regions and climatic zones, including austral, boreal, subtemperate, temperate, subtropical and tropical.

(f) All types of forests embody complex and unique ecological processes which are the basis for their present and potential capacity to provide resources to satisfy human needs as well as environmental values, and as such their sound management and conservation is of concern to the Governments of the countries to which they belong and are of value to local communities and to the environment as a whole.

(g) Forests are essential to economic development and the maintenance of all forms of life.

(h) Recognizing that the responsibility for forest management, conservation and sustainable development is in many States allocated among federal/national, state/provincial and local levels of government, each State, in accordance with its constitution and/or national legislation, should pursue these principles at the appropriate level of government.

PRINCIPLES/ELEMENTS

1. (a) States have, in accordance with the Charter of the United Nations and the principles of international law, the sovereign right to exploit their own resources pursuant to their own environmental policies and have the responsibility to ensure that activities within their jurisdiction or control do not cause damage to the environment of other States or of areas beyond the limits of national jurisdiction.

(b) The agreed full incremental cost of achieving benefits associated with forest conservation and sustainable development requires increased international cooperation and should be equitably shared by the international community.

2. (a) States have the sovereign and inalienable right to utilize, manage and develop their forests in accordance with their development needs and level of socio-economic development and on the basis of national policies consistent with sustainable development and legislation, including the conversion of such areas for other uses within the overall socio-economic development plan and based on rational land-use policies.

(b) Forest resources and forest lands should be sustainably managed to meet the social, economic, ecological, cultural and spiritual human needs of present and future generations. These needs are for forest products and services, such as wood and wood products, water, food, fodder, medicine, fuel, shelter, employment, recreation, habitats for wildlife, landscape diversity, carbon sinks and reservoirs, and for other forest products. Appropriate measures should be taken to protect forests against harmful effects of pollution, including air-borne pollution, fires, pests and diseases in order to maintain their full multiple value.

(c) The provision of timely, reliable and accurate information on forests and forest ecosystems is essential for public understanding and informed decision-making and should be ensured.

(d) Governments should promote and provide opportunities for the participation of interested parties, including local communities and indigenous people, industries, labour, non-governmental organizations and individuals, forest dwellers and women, in the development, implementation and planning of national forest policies.

3. (a) National policies and strategies should provide a framework for increased efforts, including the development and strengthening of institutions and programmes for the management, conservation and sustainable development of forests and forest lands.

(b) International institutional arrangements, building on those organizations and mechanisms already in existence, as appropriate, should facilitate international cooperation in the field of forests.

(c) All aspects of environmental protection and social and economic development as they relate to forests and forest lands should be integrated and comprehensive.

4. The vital role of all types of forests in maintaining the ecological processes and balance at the local, national, regional and global levels through, *inter alia,* their role in protecting fragile ecosystems, watersheds and freshwater resources and as rich storehouses of biodiversity and biological resources and sources of genetic material for biotechnology products, as well as photosynthesis, should be recognized.

5. (a) National forest policies should recognize and duly support the identity, culture and the rights of indigenous people, their communities and other communities and forest dwellers. Appropriate conditions should be promoted for these groups to enable them to have an economic stake in forest use, perform economic activities, and achieve and maintain cultural identity

and social organization, as well as adequate levels of livelihood and well-being, through, *inter alia,* those land tenure arrangements which serve as incentives for the sustainable management of forests.

(b) The full participation of women in all aspects of the management, conservation and sustainable development of forests should be actively promoted.

6. (a) All types of forests play an important role in meeting energy requirements through the provision of a renewable source of bio-energy, particularly in developing countries, and the demands for fuelwood for household and industrial needs should be met through sustainable forest management, afforestation and reforestation. To this end, the potential contribution of plantations of both indigenous and introduced species for the provision of both fuel and industrial wood should be recognized.

(b) National policies and programmes should take into account the relationship, where it exists, between the conservation, management and sustainable development of forests and all aspects related to the production, consumption, recycling and/or final disposal of forest products.

(c) Decisions taken on the management, conservation and sustainable development of forest resources should benefit, to the extent practicable, from a comprehensive assessment of economic and non-economic values of forest goods and services and of the environmental costs and benefits. The development and improvement of methodologies for such evaluations should be promoted.

(d) The role of planted forests and permanent agricultural crops as sustainable and environmentally sound sources of renewable energy and industrial raw material should be recognized, enhanced and promoted. Their contribution to the maintenance of ecological processes, to offsetting pressure on primary/old-growth forest and to providing regional employment and development with the adequate involvement of local inhabitants should be recognized and enhanced.

(e) Natural forests also constitute a source of goods and services, and their conservation, sustainable management and use should be promoted.

7. (a) Efforts should be made to promote a supportive international economic climate conducive to sustained and environmentally sound development of forests in all countries, which include, *inter alia,* the promotion of sustainable patterns of production and consumption, the eradication of poverty and the promotion of food security.

(b) Specific financial resources should be provided to developing countries with significant forest areas which establish programmes for the conservation of forests including protected natural forest areas. These resources should be directed notably to economic sectors which would stimulate economic and social substitution activities.

8. (a) Efforts should be undertaken towards the greening of the world. All countries, notably developed countries, should take positive and transparent action towards reforestation, afforestation and forest conservation, as appropriate.

(b) Efforts to maintain and increase forest cover and forest productivity should be undertaken in ecologically, economically and socially sound ways through the rehabilitation, reforestation and re-establishment of trees and forests on unproductive, degraded and deforested lands, as well as through the management of existing forest resources.

(c) The implementation of national policies and programmes aimed at forest management, conservation and sustainable development, particularly in developing countries, should be supported by international financial and technical cooperation, including through the private sector, where appropriate.

(d) Sustainable forest management and use should be carried out in accordance with national development policies and priorities and on the basis of environmentally sound national guidelines. In the formulation of such guidelines, account should be taken, as appropriate and if applicable, of relevant internationally agreed methodologies and criteria.

(e) Forest management should be integrated with management of adjacent areas so as to maintain ecological balance and sustainable productivity.

(f) National policies and/or legislation aimed at management, conservation and sustainable development of forests should include the protection of ecologically viable representative or unique examples of forests, including primary/old-growth forests, cultural, spiritual, historical, religious and other unique and valued forests of national importance.

(g) Access to biological resources, including genetic material, shall be with due regard to the sovereign rights of the countries where the forests are located and to the sharing on mutually agreed terms of technology and profits from biotechnology products that are derived from these resources.

(h) National policies should ensure that environmental impact assessments should be carried out where actions are likely to have significant adverse impacts on important forest resources, and where such actions are subject to a decision of a competent national authority.

9. (a) The efforts of developing countries to strengthen the management, conservation and sustainable development of their forest resources should be supported by the international community, taking into account the importance of redressing external indebtedness, particularly where aggravated by the net transfer of resources to developed countries, as well as the problem of achieving at least the replacement value of forests through improved market access for forest products, especially processed products. In this respect, special attention should also be given to the countries undergoing the process of transition to market economies.

(b) The problems that hinder efforts to attain the conservation and sustainable use of forest resources and that stem from the lack of alternative options available to local communities, in particular the urban poor and poor rural populations who are economically and socially dependent on forests and forest resources, should be addressed by Governments and the international community.

(c) National policy formulation with respect to all types of forests should take account of the pressures and demands imposed on forest ecosystems and resources from influencing factors outside the forest sector, and intersectoral means of dealing with these pressures and demands should be sought.

10.   New and additional financial resources should be provided to developing countries to enable them to sustainably manage, conserve and develop their forest resources, including through afforestation, reforestation and combating deforestation and forest and land degradation.

11.   In order to enable, in particular, developing countries to enhance their endogenous capacity and to better manage, conserve and develop their forest resources, the access to and transfer of environmentally sound technologies and corresponding know-how on favourable terms, including on concessional and preferential terms, as mutually agreed, in accordance with the relevant provisions of Agenda 21, should be promoted, facilitated and financed, as appropriate.

12.   (a) Scientific research, forest inventories and assessments carried out by national institutions which take into account, where relevant, biological, physical, social and economic variables, as well as technological development and its application in the field of sustainable forest management, conservation and development, should be strengthened through effective modalities, including international cooperation.   In this context, attention should also be given to research and development of sustainably harvested non-wood products.

(b) National and, where appropriate, regional and international institutional capabilities in education, training, science, technology, economics, anthropology and social aspects of forests and forest management are essential to the conservation and sustainable development of forests and should be strengthened.

(c) International exchange of information on the results of forest and forest management research and development should be enhanced and broadened, as appropriate, making full use of education and training institutions, including those in the private sector.

(d) Appropriate indigenous capacity and local knowledge regarding the conservation and sustainable development of forests should, through institutional and financial support, and in collaboration with the people in local communities concerned, be recognized, respected, recorded, developed and, as appropriate, introduced in the implementation of programmes.   Benefits arising from the utilization of indigenous knowledge should therefore be equitably shared with such people.

13.   (a) Trade in forest products should be based on non-discriminatory and multilaterally agreed rules and procedures consistent with international trade law and practices.   In this context, open and free international trade in forest products should be facilitated.

(b) Reduction or removal of tariff barriers and impediments to the provision of better market access and better prices for higher value-added forest products and their local processing should be encouraged to enable producer countries to better conserve and manage their renewable forest resources.

(c) Incorporation of environmental costs and benefits into market forces and mechanisms, in order to achieve forest conservation and sustainable development, should be encouraged both domestically and internationally.

(d) Forest conservation and sustainable development policies should be integrated with economic, trade and other relevant policies.

(e) Fiscal, trade, industrial, transportation and other policies and practices that may lead to forest degradation should be avoided. Adequate policies, aimed at management, conservation and sustainable development of forests, including where appropriate, incentives, should be encouraged.

14. Unilateral measures, incompatible with international obligations or agreements, to restrict and/or ban international trade in timber or other forest products should be removed or avoided, in order to attain long-term sustainable forest management.

15. Pollutants, particularly air-borne pollutants, including those responsible for acidic deposition, that are harmful to the health of forest ecosystems at the local, national, regional and global levels should be controlled.

7. MISCELLANEOUS

A ECONOMIC TRADE/DEVELOPMENT

7.1 GENERAL AGREEMENT ON TARIFFS AND TRADE (GATT) (WITHOUT ANNEXES, PROTOCOLS AND SCHEDULES BUT AS REVISED TO 1986).[1] Concluded at Geneva, 30 October 1947. Not in force as of 31 December 1991. 55 U.N.T.S. 187, T.I.A.S. No. 1700, 61–V Stat. All: *Arts. I, III, IX, XI and XX*

ARTICLE I

General Most–Favoured–Nation Treatment

1. With respect to customs duties and charges of any kind imposed on or in connection with importation or exportation or imposed on the international transfer of payments for imports or exports, and with respect to the method of levying such duties and charges, and with respect to all rules and formalities in connection with importation and exportation, and with respect to all matters referred to in paragraphs 2 and 4 of Article III, any advantage, favour, privilege or immunity granted by any contracting party to any product originating in or destined for any other country shall be accorded immediately and unconditionally to the like product originating in or destined for the territories of all other contracting parties.

2. The provisions of paragraph 1 of this Article shall not require the elimination of any preference in respect of import duties or charges which do not exceed the levels provided for in paragraph 4 of this Article and which fall within the following descriptions:

(a) Preferences in force exclusively between two or more of the territories listed in Annex A, subject to the conditions set forth therein;

(b) Preferences in force exclusively between two or more territories which on July 1, 1939, were connected by common sovereignty or relations of protection or suzerainty and which are listed in Annexes B, C and D, subject to the conditions set forth therein;

(c) Preferences in force exclusively between the United States of America and the Republic of Cuba;

(d) Preferences in force exclusively between neighbouring countries listed in Annexes E and F.

3. The provisions of paragraph 1 shall not apply to preferences between the countries formerly a part of the Ottoman Empire and detached from it on July 24, 1923, provided such preferences are approved under paragraph 5 of Article XXV, which shall be applied in this respect in the light of paragraph 1 of Article XXIX.

4. The margin of preference on any product in respect of which a preference is permitted under paragraph 2 of this Article but is not specifical-

---

1. See also Basic Document 7.4.

ly set forth as a maximum margin of preference in the appropriate Schedule annexed to this Agreement shall not exceed:

(a) in respect of duties or charges on any product described in such schedule, the difference between the most-favoured-nation and preferential rates provided for therein; if no preferential rate is provided for, the preferential rate shall for the purposes of this paragraph be taken to be that in force on April 10, 1947, and, if no most-favoured-nation rate is provided for, the margin shall not exceed the difference between the most-favoured-nation and preferential rates existing on April 10, 1947;

(b) in respect of duties or charges on any product not described in the appropriate Schedule, the difference between the most-favoured-nation and preferential rates existing on April 10, 1947.

In the case of the contracting parties named in Annex G, the date of April 10, 1947, referred to in sub-paragraph (a) and (b) of this paragraph shall be replaced by the respective dates set forth in that Annex.

* * *

ARTICLE III
National Treatment on Internal Taxation and Regulation

1. The contracting parties recognize that internal taxes and other internal charges, and laws, regulations and requirements affecting the internal sale, offering for sale, purchase, transportation, distribution or use of products, and internal quantitative regulations requiring the mixture processing or use of products in specified amounts or proportions, should not be applied to imported or domestic products so as to afford protection to domestic production.

2. The products of the territory of any contracting party imported into the territory of any other contracting party shall not be subject, directly or indirectly, to internal taxes or other internal charges of any kind in excess of those applied, directly or indirectly, to like domestic products. Moreover, no contracting party shall otherwise apply internal taxes or other internal charges to imported or domestic products in a manner contrary to the principles set forth in paragraph 1.

3. With respect to any existing internal tax which is inconsistent with the provisions of paragraph 2, but which is specifically authorized under a trade agreement, in force on April 10, 1947, in which the import duty on the taxed product is bound against increase, the contracting party imposing the tax shall be free to postpone the application of the provisions of paragraph 2 to such tax until such time as it can obtain release from the obligations of such trade agreement in order to permit the increase of such duty to the extent necessary to compensate for the elimination of the protective element of the tax.

4. The products of the territory of any contracting party imported into the territory of any other contracting party shall be accorded treatment no less favourable than that accorded to like products of national origin in respect of all laws, regulations and requirements affecting their internal sale, offering for sale, purchase, transportation, distribution or use. The provisions of this paragraph shall not prevent the applications of differential

internal transportation charges which are based exclusively on the economic operation of the means of transport and not on the nationality of the product.

5.   No contracting party shall establish or maintain any internal quantitative regulation relating to the mixture, processing or use of products in specified amounts or proportions which requires, directly or indirectly, that any specified amount or proportion of any product which is the subject of the regulation must be supplied from domestic sources. Moreover, no contracting party shall otherwise apply internal quantitative regulations in an manner contrary to the principles set forth in paragraph 1.

6.   The provisions of paragraph 5 shall not apply to any internal quantitative regulation in force in the territory of any contracting party on July 1, 1939, April 10, 1947, or March 24, 1948, at the option of that contracting party; *Provided* that any such regulation which is contrary to the provisions of paragraph 5 shall not be modified to the detriment of imports and shall be treated as a customs duty for the purpose of negotiation.

7.   No internal quantitative regulation relating to the mixture, processing or use of products in specified amounts or proportions shall be applied in such a manner as to allocate any such amount or proportion among external sources of supply.

8.   (a) The provisions of this Article shall not apply to laws, regulations or requirements governing the procurement by governmental agencies of products purchased for governmental purposes and not with a view to commercial resale or with a view to use in the production of goods for commercial sale.

(b) The provisions of this Article shall not prevent the payment of subsidies exclusively to domestic producers, including payments to domestic producers derived from the proceeds of internal taxes or charges applied consistently with the provisions of this Article and subsidies effected through governmental purchases of domestic products.

9.   The contracting parties recognize that internal maximum price control measures, even though conforming to the other provisions of this Article, can have effects prejudicial to the interests of contracting parties supplying imported products. Accordingly, contracting parties applying such measures shall take account of the interests of exporting contracting parties with a view to avoiding to the fullest practicable extent such prejudicial effects.

10.   The provisions of this Article shall not prevent any contracting party from establishing or maintaining internal quantitative regulations relating to exposed cinematograph films and meeting the requirements of Article IV.

* * *

ARTICLE IX

Marks of Origin

1.   Each contracting party shall accord to the products of the territories of their contracting parties treatment with regard to marking requirements no less favourable than the treatment accorded to like products of any third country.

2. The contracting parties recognize that, in adopting and enforcing laws and regulations relating to marks of origin, the difficulties and inconveniences which such measures may cause to the commerce and industry of exporting countries should be reduced to a minimum, due regard being had to the necessity of protecting consumers against fraudulent or misleading indications.

3. Whenever it is administratively practicable to do so, contracting parties should permit required marks of origin to be affixed at the time of importation.

4. The laws and regulations of contracting parties relating to the marking of imported products shall be such as to permit compliance without seriously damaging the products, or materially reducing their value, or unreasonably increasing their cost.

5. As a general rule, no special duty or penalty should be imposed by any contracting party for failure to comply with marking requirements prior to importation unless corrective marking is unreasonably delayed or deceptive marks have been affixed or the required marking has been intentionally omitted.

6. The contracting parties shall co-operate with each other with a view to preventing the use of trade names in such manner as to misrepresent the true origin of a product, to the detriment of such distinctive regional or geographical names of products of the territory of a contracting party as are protected by its legislation. Each contracting party shall accord full and sympathetic consideration to such requests or representations as may be made by any other contracting party regarding the application of the undertaking set forth in the preceding sentence to names of products which have been communicated to it by the other contracting party.

* * *

ARTICLE XI

General Elimination of Quantitative Restrictions

1. No prohibitions or restrictions other than duties, taxes or other charges, whether made effective through quotas, import or export licences or other measures, shall be instituted or maintained by any contracting party on the importation of any product of the territory of any other contracting party or on the exportation or sale for export of any product destined for the territory of any other contracting party.

2. The provisions of paragraph 1 of this Article shall not extend to the following:

(a) Export prohibitions or restrictions temporarily applied to prevent or relieve critical shortages of foodstuffs or other products essential to the exporting contracting party;

(b) Import and export prohibitions or restrictions necessary to the application of standards or regulations for the classification, grading or marketing of commodities in international trade;

(c) Import restrictions on any agricultural or fisheries product, imported in any form, necessary to the enforcement of governmental measures which operate:

(i) to restrict the quantities of the like domestic product permitted to be marketed or produced, or, if there is no substantial domestic production of the like product, of a domestic product for which the imported product can be directly substituted; or

(ii) to remove a temporary surplus of the like domestic product or, if there is no substantial domestic production of the like product, of a domestic product for which the imported product can be directly substituted, by making the surplus available to certain groups of domestic consumers free of charge or at prices below the current market level; or

(iii) to restrict the quantities permitted to be produced of any animal product the production of which is directly dependent, wholly or mainly, on the imported commodity, if the domestic production of that commodity is relatively negligible.

Any contracting party applying restrictions on the importation of any product pursuant to sub-paragraph (c) of this paragraph shall give public notice of the total quantity or value of the product permitted to be imported during a specified future period and of any change in such quantity or value. Moreover, any restrictions applied under (i) above shall not be such as will reduce the total of imports relative to the total of domestic production, as compared with the proportion which might reasonably be expected to rule between the two in the absence of restrictions. In determining this proportion, the contracting party shall pay due regard to the proportion prevailing during a previous representative period and to any special factors which may have affected or may be affecting the trade in the product concerned.

* * *

ARTICLE XX
General Exceptions

Subject to the requirement that such measures are not applied in a manner which would constitute a means of arbitrary or unjustifiable discrimination between countries where the same conditions prevail, or a disguised restriction on international trade, nothing in this Agreement shall be construed to prevent the adoption or enforcement by any contracting party of measures:

(a) necessary to protect public morals;

(b) necessary to protect human, animal or plant life or health;

(c) relating to the importation or exportation of gold or silver;

(d) necessary to secure compliance with laws or regulations which are not inconsistent with the provisions of this Agreement, including those relating to customs enforcement, the enforcement of monopolies operated under paragraph 4 of Article II and Article XVII, the protection of patents, trade marks and copyrights, and the prevention of deceptive practices;

(e) relating to the products of prison labour;

(f) imposed for the protection of national treasures of artistic, historic or archaeological value;

(g) relating to the conservation of exhaustible natural resources if such measures are made effective in conjunction with restrictions on domestic production or consumption;

(h) undertaken in pursuance of obligations under any intergovernmental commodity agreement which conforms to criteria submitted to the contracting parties and not disapproved by them or which is itself so submitted and not so disapproved;

(i) involving restrictions on exports of domestic materials necessary to ensure essential quantities of such materials to a domestic processing industry during periods when the domestic price of such materials is held below the world price as part of a governmental stabilization plan; *Provided* that such restrictions shall not operate to increase the exports of or the protection afforded to such domestic industry, and shall not depart from the provisions of this Agreement relating to nondiscrimination;

(j) essential to the acquisition or distribution of products in general or local short supply; *Provided* that any such measures shall be consistent with the principle that all contracting parties are entitled to an equitable share of the international supply of such products, and that any such measures which are inconsistent with the other provisions of this Agreement shall be discontinued as soon as the conditions giving rise to them have ceased to exist. The contracting parties shall review the need for this sub-paragraph not later than 30 June 1960.

7.2 CHARTER OF ECONOMIC RIGHTS AND DUTIES OF STATES. Adopted by the U.N. General Assembly, 12 December 1974. G.A. Res. 3281, U.N. GAOR, 29th Sess., Supp. No. 31, at 50, UN Doc. A/9631 (1975), 14 I.L.M. 251 (1975): *Arts. 3, 30*

Article 3. In the exploitation of natural resources shared by two or more countries, each State must co-operate on the basis of a system of information and prior consultations in order to achieve optimum use of such resources without causing damage to the legitimate interest of others.

* * *

Article 30. The protection, preservation and enhancement of the environment for the present and future generations is the responsibility of all States. All States shall endeavour to establish their own environmental and developmental policies in conformity with such responsibility. The environmental policies of all States shall enhance and not adversely affect the present and future development potential of developing countries. All States have the responsibility to ensure that activities within their jurisdiction or control do not cause damage to the environment of other States or of areas beyond the limits of national jurisdiction. All States should co-operate in evolving international norms and regulations in the field of the environment.

**7.3 DRAFT CODE OF CONDUCT ON TRANSNATIONAL CORPORATIONS.
Adopted by the U.N. Economic and Social Council, 1 February 1988.
U.N. Doc. E/1988/39/Add. 1 (1988): *Paras. 43–45***

Environmental protection

43.   Transnational corporations shall carry out their activities in accordance with national laws, regulations, established administrative practices and policies relating to the preservation of the environment of the countries in which they operate and with due regard to relevant international standards. Transnational corporations should, in performing their activities, take steps to protect the environment and where damaged to rehabilitate it and should make efforts to develop and apply adequate technologies for this purpose.

44.   Transnational corporations shall, in respect of the products, processes and services they have introduced or propose to introduce in any country, supply to the competent authorities of that country on request or on a regular basis, as specified by these authorities, all relevant information concerning:

Characteristics of these products, processes and other activities including experimental uses and related aspects which may harm the environment and the measures and costs necessary to avoid or at least to mitigate their harmful effects;

Prohibitions, restrictions, warnings and other public regulatory measures imposed in other countries on grounds of protection of the environment on these products, processes and services.

45.   Transnational corporations should be responsive to requests from Governments of the countries in which they operate and be prepared where appropriate to co-operate with international organizations in their efforts to develop and promote national and international standards for the protection of the environment.

7.4 FINAL ACT EMBODYING THE RESULTS OF THE URUGUAY ROUND OF MULTILATERAL TRADE NEGOTIATIONS: UNDERSTANDING ON RULES AND PROCEDURES GOVERNING THE SETTLEMENT OF DISPUTES (VERSION OF 13 DECEMBER 1993).[1] Available from the Office of the U.S. Trade Representative, Executive Office of the President, Washington, D.C.: *Paras. 2.1, 11.1, 16.4, 17.1, 17.14, 21.1*

* * *

2.1. The Dispute Settlement Body (DSB) established pursuant to the Agreement Establishing the MTO shall administer these rules and procedures and, except as otherwise provided in a covered agreement, the consultation and dispute settlement provisions of the covered agreements. Accordingly, the DSB shall have the authority to establish panels, adopt panel and Appellate Body reports, maintain surveillance of implementation of rulings and recommendations, and authorize suspension of concessions and other obligations under the covered agreements. With respect to disputes arising under covered agreements contained in Annex 4 to the MTO Agreement, the term "Member" as used herein shall refer only to those Members that are parties to the relevant Annex 4 Agreements. Where the DSB administers the dispute settlement provisions of a covered agreement contained in Annex 4, only those Members that are parties to that agreement may participate in decisions or actions taken by the DSB with respect to that dispute.

* * *

11.1. The function of panels is to assist the DSB in discharging its responsibilities under this Understanding and the covered agreements. Accordingly, a panel should make an objective assessment of the matter before it, including an objective assessment of the facts of the case and the applicability of and conformity with the relevant covered agreements, and make such other findings as will assist the DSB in making the recommendations or in giving the rulings provided for in the covered agreements. Panels should consult regularly with the parties to the dispute and give them adequate opportunity to develop a mutually satisfactory solution.

* * *

16.4. Within sixty days of the issuance of a panel report to the Members, the report shall be adopted at a DSB meeting unless one of the parties to the dispute formally notifies the DSB of its decision to appeal or the DSB decides by consensus not to adopt the report. If a party has notified its intention to appeal, the report by the panel shall not be considered for adoption by the DSB until after completion of the appeal. This adoption procedure is without prejudice to the right of Members to express their views on a panel report.

* * *

17.1. A standing Appellate Body shall be established by the DSB. The Appellate Body shall hear appeals from panel cases. It shall be composed of seven persons, three of whom shall serve on any one case.

* * *

---

1. *See also* Basic Document 7.1.

17.14.   An appellate report shall be adopted by the DSB and unconditionally accepted by the parties to the dispute unless the DSB decides by consensus not to adopt the appellate report within thirty days following its issuance to the Members.   This adoption procedure is without prejudice to the right of Members to express their views on an appellate report.

* * *

21.1.   Prompt compliance with recommendations or rulings of the DSB is essential in order to ensure effective resolution of disputes to the benefit of all Members.

* * *

B.   HUMAN RIGHTS/SOCIAL JUSTICE

7.5   CONVENTION ON THE PREVENTION AND PUNISHMENT OF THE CRIME OF GENOCIDE.   Concluded at New York, 9 December 1948. Entered into force, 12 January 1951.   78 U.N.T.S. 277: *Arts. II–IV*

Article II.   In the present Convention, genocide means any of the following acts committed with intent to destroy, in whole or in part, a national, ethnical, racial or religious group, as such:

(a) Killing members of the group;

(b) Causing serious bodily or mental harm to members of the group;

(c) Deliberately inflicting on the group conditions of life calculated to bring about its physical destruction in whole or in part;

(d) Imposing measures intended to prevent births within the group;

(e) Forcibly transferring children of the group to another group.

Article III.   The following acts shall be punishable:

(a) Genocide;

(b) Conspiracy to commit genocide;

(c) Direct and public incitement to commit genocide;

(d) Attempt to commit genocide;

(e) Complicity in genocide.

Article IV.   Persons committing genocide or any of the other acts enumerated in Article III shall be punished, whether they are constitutionally responsible rulers, public officials or private individuals.

7.6 UNIVERSAL DECLARATION OF HUMAN RIGHTS. Adopted by the U.N. General Assembly, 10 December 1948. G.A.Res. 217A, U.N. GAOR, 3rd Sess., Pt. I, Resolutions, at 71, U.N. Doc. A/810 (1948)

PREAMBLE

Whereas recognition of the inherent dignity and of the equal and inalienable rights of all members of the human family is the foundation of freedom, justice and peace in the world,

Whereas disregard and contempt for human rights have resulted in barbarous acts which have outraged the conscience of mankind, and the advent of a world in which human beings shall enjoy freedom of speech and belief and freedom from fear and want has been proclaimed as the highest aspiration of the common people,

Whereas it is essential, if man is not to be compelled to have recourse, as a last resort, to rebellion against tyranny and oppression, that human rights should be protected by the rule of law,

Whereas it is essential to promote the development of friendly relations between nations,

Whereas the peoples of the United Nations have in the Charter reaffirmed their faith in fundamental human rights, in the dignity and worth of the human person and in the equal rights of men and women and have determined to promote social progress and better standards of life in larger freedom,

Whereas Member States have pledged themselves to achieve, in cooperation with the United Nations, the promotion of universal respect for and observance of human rights and fundamental freedoms,

Whereas a common understanding of these rights and freedoms is of the greatest importance for the full realization of this pledge,

Now, therefore,

The General Assembly

Proclaims this Universal Declaration of Human Rights as a common standard of achievement for all peoples and all nations, to the end that every individual and every organ of society, keeping this Declaration constantly in mind, shall strive by teaching and education to promote respect for these rights and freedoms and by progressive measures, national and international, to secure their universal and effective recognition and observance, both among the peoples of Member States themselves and among the peoples of territories under their jurisdiction.

Article 1. All human beings are born free and equal in dignity and rights. They are endowed with reason and conscience and should act towards one another in a spirit of brotherhood.

Article 2. Everyone is entitled to all the rights and freedoms set forth in this Declaration, without distinction of any kind, such as race, colour, sex, language, religion, political or other opinion, national or social origin, property, birth or other status.

Furthermore, no distinction shall be made on the basis of the political, jurisdictional or international status of the country or territory to which a person belongs, whether it be independent, trust, non-self-governing or under any other limitation of sovereignty.

Article 3. Everyone has the right to life, liberty and the security of person.

Article 4. No one shall be held in slavery or servitude; slavery and the slave trade shall be prohibited in all their forms.

Article 5. No one shall be subjected to torture or to cruel, inhuman or degrading treatment or punishment.

Article 6. Everyone has the right to recognition everywhere as a person before the law.

Article 7. All are equal before the law and are entitled without any discrimination to equal protection of the law. All are entitled to equal protection against any discrimination in violation of this Declaration and against any incitement to such discrimination.

Article 8. Everyone has the right to an effective remedy by the competent national tribunals for acts violating the fundamental rights granted him by the constitution or by law.

Article 9. No one shall be subjected to arbitrary arrest, detention or exile.

Article 10. Everyone is entitled in full equality to a fair and public hearing by an independent and impartial tribunal, in the determination of his rights and obligations and of any criminal charge against him.

Article 11. (1) Everyone charged with a penal offence has the right to be presumed innocent until proved guilty according to law in a public trial at which he has had all the guarantees necessary for his defence.

(2) No one shall be held guilty of any penal offence on account of any act or omission which did not constitute a penal offence, under national or international law, at the time when it was committed. Nor shall a heavier penalty be imposed than the one that was applicable at the time the penal offence was committed.

Article 12. No one shall be subjected to arbitrary interference with his privacy, family, home or correspondence, nor to attacks upon his honour and reputation. Everyone has the right to the protection of the law against such interference or attacks.

Article 13. (1) Everyone has the right to freedom of movement and residence within the borders of each State.

(2) Everyone has the right to leave any country, including his own, and to return to his country.

Article 14. (1) Everyone has the right to seek and to enjoy in other countries asylum from persecution.

(2) This right may not be invoked in the case of prosecutions genuinely arising from nonpolitical crimes or from acts contrary to the purposes and principles of the United Nations.

Article 15. (1) Everyone has the right to a nationality.

(2) No one shall be arbitrarily deprived of his nationality nor denied the right to change his nationality.

Article 16. (1) Men and women of full age, without any limitation due to race, nationality or religion, have the right to marry and to found a family. They are entitled to equal rights as to marriage, during marriage and at its dissolution.

(2) Marriage shall be entered into only with the free and full consent of the intending spouses.

(3) The family is the natural and fundamental group unit of society and is entitled to protection by society and the State.

Article 17. (1) Everyone has the right to own property alone as well as in association with others.

(2) No one shall be arbitrarily deprived of his property.

Article 18. Everyone has the right to freedom of thought, conscience and religion; this right includes freedom to change his religion or belief, and freedom, either alone or in community with others and in public or private, to manifest his religion or belief in teaching, practice, worship and observance.

Article 19. Everyone has the right to freedom of opinion and expression; this right includes freedom to hold opinions without interference and to seek, receive and impart information and ideas through any media and regardless of frontiers.

Article 20. (1) Everyone has the right to freedom of peaceful assembly and association.

(2) No one may be compelled to belong to an association.

Article 21. (1) Everyone has the right to take part in the government of his country, directly or through freely chosen representatives.

(2) Everyone has the right of equal access to public service in his country.

(3) The will of the people shall be the basis of the authority of government; this will shall be expressed in periodic and genuine elections which shall be by universal and equal suffrage and shall be held by secret vote or by equivalent free voting procedures.

Article 22. Everyone, as a member of society, has the right to social security and is entitled to realization, through national effort and international co-operation and in accordance with the organization and resources of each State, of the economic, social and cultural rights indispensable for his dignity and the free development of his personality.

Article 23. (1) Everyone has the right to work, to free choice of employment, to just and favourable conditions of work and to protection against unemployment.

(2) Everyone, without any discrimination, has the right to equal pay for equal work.

(3) Everyone who works has the right to just and favourable remuneration ensuring for himself and his family an existence worthy of

human dignity, and supplemented, if necessary, by other means of social protection.

(4) Everyone has the right to form and to join trade unions for the protection of his interests.

Article 24. Everyone has the right to rest and leisure, including reasonable limitation of working hours and periodic holidays with pay.

Article 25. (1) Everyone has the right to a standard of living adequate for the health and well-being of himself and of his family, including food, clothing, housing and medical care and necessary social services, and the right to security in the event of unemployment, sickness, disability, widowhood, old age or other lack of livelihood in circumstances beyond his control.

(2) Motherhood and childhood are entitled to special care and assistance. All children, whether born in or out of wedlock, shall enjoy the same social protection.

Article 26. (1) Everyone has the right to education. Education shall be free, at least in the elementary and fundamental stages. Elementary education shall be compulsory. Technical and professional education shall be made generally available and higher education shall be equally accessible to all on the basis of merit.

(2) Education shall be directed to the full development of the human personality and to the strengthening of respect for human rights and fundamental freedoms. It shall promote understanding, tolerance and friendship among all nations, racial or religious groups, and shall further the activities of the United Nations for the maintenance of peace.

(3) Parents have a prior right to choose the kind of education that shall be given to their children.

Article 27. (1) Everyone has the right freely to participate in the cultural life of the community, to enjoy the arts and to share in scientific advancement and its benefits.

(2) Everyone has the right to the protection of the moral and material interests resulting from any scientific, literary or artistic production of which he is the author.

Article 28. Everyone is entitled to a social and international order in which the rights and freedoms set forth in this Declaration can be fully realized.

Article 29. (1) Everyone has duties to the community in which alone the free and full development of his personality is possible.

(2) In the exercise of his rights and freedoms, everyone shall be subject only to such limitations as are determined by law solely for the purpose of securing due recognition and respect for the rights and freedoms of others and of meeting the just requirements of morality, public order and the general welfare in a democratic society.

(3) These rights and freedoms may in no case be exercised contrary to the purposes and principles of the United Nations.

Article 30. Nothing in this Declaration may be interpreted as implying for any State, group or person any right to engage in any activity or to perform any act aimed at the destruction of any of the rights and freedoms set forth herein.

7.7 INTERNATIONAL COVENANT ON ECONOMIC, SOCIAL AND CULTUR-AL RIGHTS. Concluded at New York, 16 December 1966. Entered into force, 3 January 1976. 993 U.N.T.S. 3: *Arts. 1, 2, 10, 15, 25*

* * *

Article 1. (1) All peoples have the right of self-determination. By virtue of that right they freely determine their political status and freely pursue their economic, social and cultural development.

(2) All peoples may, for their own ends, freely dispose of their natural wealth and resources without prejudice to any obligations arising out of international economic co-operation, based upon the principle of mutual benefit, and international law. In no case may a people be deprived of its own means of subsistence.

(3) The States Parties to the present Covenant, including those having responsibility for the administration of Non–Self–Governing and Trust Territories, shall promote the realization of the right of self-determination, and shall respect that right, in conformity with the provisions of the Charter of the United Nations.

* * *

Article 2. (1) Each State Party to the present Covenant undertakes to take steps, individually and through international assistance and co-operation, especially economic and technical, to the maximum of its available resources, with a view to achieving progressively the full realization of the rights recognized in the present Covenant by all appropriate means, including particularly the adoption of legislative measures.

(2) The States Parties to the present Covenant undertake to guarantee that the rights enunciated in the present Covenant will be exercised without discrimination of any kind as to race, colour, sex, language, religion, political or other opinion, national or social origin, property, birth or other status.

(3) Developing countries, with due regard to human rights and their national economy, may determine to what extent they would guarantee the economic rights recognized in the present Covenant to non-nationals.

* * *

Article 10. The States Parties to the present Covenant recognize that:

(1) The widest possible protection and assistance should be accorded to the family, which is the natural and fundamental group unit of society, particularly for its establishment and while it is responsible for the care and education of dependent children. Marriage must be entered into with the free consent of the intending spouses.

(2) Special protection should be accorded to mothers during a reasonable period before and after childbirth. During such period working mothers should be accorded paid leave or leave with adequate social security benefits.

(3) Special measures of protection and assistance should be taken on behalf of all children and young persons without any discrimination for reasons of parentage or other conditions. Children and young persons

should be protected from economic and social exploitation. Their employment in work harmful to their morals or health or dangerous to life or likely to hamper their normal development should be punishable by law. States should also set age limits below which the paid employment of child labour should be prohibited and punishable by law.

* * *

Article 15. (1) The States Parties to the present Covenant recognize the right of everyone:

(a) To take part in cultural life;

(b) To enjoy the benefits of scientific progress and its applications;

(c) To benefit from the protection of the moral and material interests resulting from any scientific, literary or artistic production of which he is the author.

(2) The steps to be taken by the States Parties to the present Covenant to achieve the full realization of this right shall include those necessary for the conservation, the development and the diffusion of science and culture.

(3) The States Parties to the present Covenant undertake to respect the freedom indispensable for scientific research and creative activity.

(4) The States Parties to the present Covenant recognize the benefits to be derived from the encouragement and development of international contacts and co-operation in the scientific and cultural fields.

* * *

Article 25. Nothing in the present Covenant shall be interpreted as impairing the inherent right of all peoples to enjoy and utilize fully and freely their natural wealth and resources.

7.8 INTERNATIONAL COVENANT ON CIVIL AND POLITICAL RIGHTS.
Concluded at New York, 16 December 1966. Entered into force, 23
March 1976. 999 U.N.T.S. 171: *Arts. 1, 2, 6, 14, 23, 24, 27, 47*

* * *

Article 1. (1) All peoples have the right of self-determination. By virtue
of that right they freely determine their political status and freely pursue
their economic, social and cultural development.

(2) All peoples may, for their own ends, freely dispose of their
natural wealth and resources without prejudice to any obligations arising
out of international economic co-operation, based upon the principle of
mutual benefit, and international law. In no case may a people be
deprived of its own means of subsistence.

(3) The States Parties to the present Covenant, including those
having responsibility for the administration of Non–Self–Governing and
Trust Territories, shall promote the realization of the right of self-
determination, and shall respect that right, in conformity with the
provisions of the Charter of the United Nations.

* * *

Article 2. (1) Each State Party to the present Covenant undertakes to
respect and to ensure to all individuals within its territory and subject to its
jurisdiction the rights recognized in the present Covenant, without distinction
of any kind, such as race, colour, sex, language, religion, political or other
opinion, national or social origin, property, birth or other status.

(2) Where not already provided for by existing legislative or other
measures, each State Party to the present Covenant undertakes to take
the necessary steps, in accordance with its constitutional processes and
with the provisions of the present Covenant, to adopt such legislative or
other measures as may be necessary to give effect to the rights recognized
in the present Covenant.

(3) Each State Party to the present Covenant undertakes:

(a) To ensure that any person whose rights or freedoms as
herein recognized are violated shall have an effective remedy, notwithstanding that the violation has been committed by persons
acting in an official capacity;

(b) To ensure that any person claiming such a remedy shall have
his right thereto determined by competent judicial, administrative or
legislative authorities, or by any other competent authority provided
for by the legal system of the State, and to develop the possibilities of
judicial remedy;

(c) To ensure that the competent authorities shall enforce such
remedies when granted.

* * *

Article 6. (1) Every human being has the inherent right to life. This
right shall be protected by law. No one shall be arbitrarily deprived of his
life.

(2) In countries which have not abolished the death penalty, sentence of death may be imposed only for the most serious crimes in accordance with the law in force at the time of the commission of the crime and not contrary to the provisions of the present Covenant and to the Convention on the Prevention and Punishment of the Crime of Genocide. This penalty can only be carried out pursuant to a final judgment rendered by a competent court.

(3) When deprivation of life constitutes the crime of genocide, it is understood that nothing in this article shall authorize any State Party to the present Covenant to derogate in any way from any obligation assumed under the provisions of the Convention on the Prevention and Punishment of the Crime of Genocide.

(4) Anyone sentenced to death shall have the right to seek pardon or commutation of the sentence. Amnesty, pardon or commutation of the sentence of death may be granted in all cases.

(5) Sentence of death shall not be imposed for crimes committed by persons below eighteen years of age and shall not be carried out on pregnant women.

(6) Nothing in this article shall be invoked to delay or to prevent the abolition of capital punishment by any State Party to the present Covenant.

* * *

Article 14. (1) All persons shall be equal before the courts and tribunals. In the determination of any criminal charge against him, or of his rights and obligations in a suit at law, everyone shall be entitled to a fair and public hearing by a competent, independent and impartial tribunal established by law. The Press and the public may be excluded from all or part of a trial for reasons of morals, public order (*ordre public*) or national security in a democratic society, or when the interest of the private lives of the parties so requires, or to the extent strictly necessary in the opinion of the court in special circumstances where publicity would prejudice the interests of justice; but any judgment rendered in a criminal case or in a suit at law shall be made public except where the interest of juvenile persons otherwise requires or the proceedings concern matrimonial disputes or the guardianship of children.

(2) Everyone charged with a criminal offence shall have the right to be presumed innocent until proved guilty according to law.

(3) In the determination of any criminal charge against him, everyone shall be entitled to the following minimum guarantees, in full equality:

(a) To be informed promptly and in detail in a language which he understands of the nature and cause of the charge against him;

(b) To have adequate time and facilities for the preparation of his defence and to communicate with counsel of his own choosing;

(c) To be tried without undue delay;

(d) To be tried in his presence, and to defend himself in person or through legal assistance of his own choosing; to be informed, if he does not have legal assistance, of this right; and to have legal assistance assigned to him, in any case where the interests of justice so require, and without payment by him in any such case if he does not have sufficient means to pay for it;

(e) To examine, or have examined, the witnesses against him and to obtain the attendance and examination of witnesses on his behalf under the same conditions as witnesses against him;

(f) To have the free assistance of an interpreter if he cannot understand or speak the language used in court;

(g) Not to be compelled to testify against himself or to confess guilt.

(4) In the case of juvenile persons, the procedure shall be such as will take account of their age and the desirability of promoting their rehabilitation.

(5) Everyone convicted of a crime shall have the right to his conviction and sentence being reviewed by a higher tribunal according to law.

(6) When a person has by a final decision been convicted of a criminal offense and when subsequently his conviction has been reversed or he has been pardoned on the ground that a new or newly discovered fact shows conclusively that there has been a miscarriage of justice, the person who has suffered punishment as a result of such conviction shall be compensated according to law, unless it is proved that the non-disclosure of the unknown fact in time is wholly or partly attributable to him.

(7) No one shall be liable to be tried or punished again for an offence for which he has already been finally convicted or acquitted in accordance with the law and penal procedure of each country.

* * *

Article 23.   (1) The family is the natural and fundamental group unit of society and is entitled to protection by society and the State.

(2) The right of men and women of marriageable age to marry and to found a family shall be recognized.

(3) No marriage shall be entered into without the free and full consent of the intending spouses.

(4) States Parties to the present Covenant shall take appropriate steps to ensure equality of rights and responsibilities of spouses as to marriage, during marriage and at its dissolution.   In the case of dissolution, provision shall be made for the necessary protection of any children.

Article 24.   (1) Every child shall have, without any discrimination as to race, colour, sex, language, religion, national or social origin, property or birth, the right to such measures of protection as are required by his status as a minor, on the part of his family, society and the State.

(2) Every child shall be registered immediately after birth and shall have a name.

(3) Every child has the right to acquire a nationality.

* * *

Article 27.   In those States in which ethnic, religious or linguistic minorities exist, persons belonging to such minorities shall not be denied the right, in community with the other members of their group, to enjoy their own culture, to profess and practise their own religion, or to use their own language.

* * *

Article 47.   Nothing in the present Covenant shall be interpreted as impairing the inherent right of all peoples to enjoy and utilize fully and freely their natural wealth and resources.

7.9 FINAL ACT OF THE UNITED NATIONS INTERNATIONAL CONFER-ENCE ON HUMAN RIGHTS AT TEHERAN, 13 MAY 1968. *United Nations, Human Rights: A Compilation of International Instruments* **43 (1988)**

The International Conference on Human Rights,

Having met at Teheran from April 22 to May 13, 1968 to review the progress made in the twenty years since the adoption of the Universal Declaration of Human Rights and to formulate a programme for the future,

Having considered the problems relating to the activities of the United Nations for the promotion and encouragement of respect for human rights and fundamental freedoms,

Bearing in mind the resolutions adopted by the Conference,

Noting that the observance of the International Year for Human Rights takes place at a time when the world is undergoing a process of unprecedented change,

Having regard to the new opportunities made available by the rapid progress of science and technology,

Believing that, in an age when conflict and violence prevail in many parts of the world, the fact of human interdependence and the need for human solidarity are more evident than ever before,

Recognizing that peace is the universal aspiration of mankind and that peace and justice are indispensable to the full realization of human rights and fundamental freedoms,

Solemnly proclaims that:

1. It is imperative that the members of the international community fulfil their solemn obligations to promote and encourage respect for human rights and fundamental freedoms for all without distinctions of any kind such as race, colour, sex, language, religion, political or other opinions;

2. The Universal Declaration of Human Rights states a common understanding of the peoples of the world concerning the inalienable and inviolable rights of all members of the human family and constitutes an obligation for the members of the international community;

3. The International Covenant on Civil and Political Rights, the International Covenant on Economic, Social and Cultural Rights, the Declaration on the Granting of Independence to Colonial Countries and Peoples, the International Convention on the Elimination of All Forms of Racial Discrimination as well as other conventions and declarations in the field of human rights adopted under the auspices of the United Nations, the specialized agencies and the regional intergovernmental organizations, have created new standards and obligations to which States should conform;

4. Since the adoption of the Universal Declaration of Human Rights the United Nations has made substantial progress in defining standards for the enjoyment and protection of human rights and fundamental freedoms. During this period many important international instruments

were adopted but much remains to be done in regard to the implementation of those rights and freedoms;

5. The primary aim of the United Nations in the sphere of human rights is the achievement by each individual of the maximum freedom and dignity. For the realization of this objective, the laws of every country should grant each individual, irrespective of race, language, religion or political belief, freedom of expression, of information, of conscience and of religion, as well as the right to participate in the political, economic, cultural and social life of his country;

6. States should reaffirm their determination effectively to enforce the principles enshrined in the Charter of the United Nations and in other international instruments that concern human rights and fundamental freedoms;

7. Gross denials of human rights under the repugnant policy of *apartheid* is a matter of the gravest concern to the international community. This policy of *apartheid,* condemned as a crime against humanity, continues seriously to disturb international peace and security. It is therefore imperative for the international community to use every possible means to eradicate this evil. The struggle against *apartheid* is recognized as legitimate;

8. The peoples of the world must be made fully aware of the evils of racial discrimination and must join in combating them. The implementation of this principle of non-discrimination, embodied in the Charter of the United Nations, the Universal Declaration of Human Rights, and other international instruments in the field of human rights, constitutes a most urgent task of mankind at the international as well as at the national level. All ideologies based on racial superiority and intolerance must be condemned and resisted;

9. Eight years after the General Assembly's Declaration on the Granting of Independence to Colonial Countries and Peoples the problems of colonialism continue to preoccupy the international community. It is a matter of urgency that all Member States should co-operate with the appropriate organs of the United Nations so that effective measures can be taken to ensure that the Declaration is fully implemented;

10. Massive denials of human rights, arising out of aggression or any armed conflict with their tragic consequences, and resulting in untold human misery, engender reactions which could engulf the world in ever growing hostilities. It is the obligation of the international community to co-operate in eradicating such scourges;

11. Gross denials of human rights arising from discrimination on grounds of race, religion, belief or expressions of opinion outrage the conscience of mankind and endanger the foundations of freedom, justice and peace in the world;

12. The widening gap between the economically developed and developing countries impedes the realization of human rights in the international community. The failure of the Development Decade to reach its modest objectives makes it all the more imperative for every

nation, according to its capacities, to make the maximum possible effort to close this gap;

13. Since human rights and fundamental freedoms are indivisible, the full realization of civil and political rights without the enjoyment of economic, social and cultural rights is impossible. The achievement of lasting progress in the implementation of human rights is dependent upon sound and effective national and international policies of economic and social development;

14. The existence of over seven hundred million illiterates throughout the world is an enormous obstacle to all efforts at realizing the aims and purposes of the Charter of the United Nations and the provisions of the Universal Declaration of Human Rights. International action aimed at eradicating illiteracy from the face of the earth and promoting education at all levels requires urgent attention;

15. The discrimination of which women are still victims in various regions of the world must be eliminated. An inferior status for women is contrary to the Charter of the United Nations as well as the provisions of the Universal Declaration of Human Rights. The full implementation of the Declaration on the Elimination of Discrimination against Women is a necessity for the progress of mankind;

16. The protection of the family and of the child remains the concern of the international community. Parents have a basic human right to determine freely and responsibly the number and the spacing of their children;

17. The aspirations of the younger generation for a better world, in which human rights and fundamental freedoms are fully implemented, must be given the highest encouragement. It is imperative that youth participate in shaping the future of mankind;

18. While recent scientific discoveries and technological advances have opened vast prospects for economic, social and cultural progress, such developments may nevertheless endanger the rights and freedoms of individuals and will require continuing attention;

19. Disarmament would release immense human and material resources now devoted to military purposes. These resources should be used for the promotion of human rights and fundamental freedoms. General and complete disarmament is one of the highest aspirations of all peoples;

Therefore,

The International Conference on Human Rights,

1. *Affirming* its faith in the principles of the Universal Declaration of Human Rights and other international instruments in this field,

2. *Urges* all peoples and governments to dedicate themselves to the principles enshrined in the Universal Declaration of Human Rights and to redouble their efforts to provide for all human beings a life consonant with freedom and dignity and conducive to physical, mental, social and spiritual welfare.

7.10　AMERICAN CONVENTION ON HUMAN RIGHTS.　Concluded at San José, 22 November 1969.　Entered into force, 18 July 1978. O.A.S.T.S. No. 36, O.A.S. Off.Rec. O.E.A./Ser. L/V/II.23 doc. 21 rev. 6 (1979), 9 I.L.M. 673 (1970): *Arts. 1, 4, 16, 21, 27*

* * *

Article 1.　Obligation to Respect Rights

1.　The States Parties to this Convention undertake to respect the rights and freedoms recognized herein and to ensure to all persons subject to their jurisdiction the free and full exercise of those rights and freedoms, without any discrimination for reasons of race, color, sex, language, religion, political or other opinion, national or social origin, economic status, birth, or any other social condition.

2.　For the purposes of this Convention, "person" means every human being.

* * *

Article 4.　Right to Life

1.　Every person has the right to have his life respected.　This right shall be protected by law and, in general, from the moment of conception.　No one shall be arbitrarily deprived of his life.

2.　In countries that have not abolished the death penalty, it may be imposed only for the most serious crimes and pursuant to a final judgment rendered by a competent court and in accordance with a law establishing such punishment, enacted prior to the commission of the crime.　The application of such punishment shall not be extended to crimes to which it does not presently apply.

3.　The death penalty shall not be reestablished in states that have abolished it.

4.　In no case shall capital punishment be inflicted for political offenses or related common crimes.

5.　Capital punishment shall not be imposed upon persons who, at the time the crime was committed, were under 18 years of age or over 70 years of age;　nor shall it be applied to pregnant women.

6.　Every person condemned to death shall have the right to apply for amnesty, pardon, or commutation of sentence, which may be granted in all cases.　Capital punishment shall not be imposed while such a petition is a pending decision by the competent authority.

* * *

Article 16.　Freedom of Association

1.　Everyone has the right to associate freely for ideological, religious, political, economic, labor, social, cultural, sports, or other purposes.

2.　The exercise of this right shall be subject only to such restrictions established by law as may be necessary in a democratic society, in the interest of national security, public safety or public order, or to protect public health or morals or the rights and freedoms of others.

3. The provisions of this article do not bar the imposition of legal restrictions, including even deprivation of the exercise of the right of association, on members of the armed forces and the police.

* * *

Article 21. Right to Property

1. Everyone has the right to the use and enjoyment of his property. The law may subordinate such use and enjoyment to the interest of society.

2. No one shall be deprived of his property except upon payment of just compensation, for reasons of public utility or social interest, and in the cases and according to the forms established by law.

3. Usury and any other form of exploitation of man by man shall be prohibited by law.

* * *

Article 27. Suspension of Guarantees

1. In time of war, public danger, or other emergency that threatens the independence or security of a State Party, it may take measures derogating from its obligations under the present Convention to the extent and for the period of time strictly required by the exigencies of the situation, provided that such measures are not inconsistent with its other obligations under international law and do not involve discrimination on the ground of race, color, sex, language, religion, or social origin.

2. The foregoing provision does not authorize any suspension of the following articles: Article 3 (Right to Juridical Personality), Article 4 (Right to Life), Article 5 (Right to Humane Treatment), Article 6 (Freedom from Slavery), Article 9 (Freedom from Ex Post Facto Laws), Article 12 (Freedom of Conscience and Religion), Article 17 (Rights of the Family), Article 18 (Right to a Name), Article 19 (Rights of the Child), Article 20 (Right to Nationality), and Article 23 (Right to Participate in Government), or of the judicial guarantees essential for the protection of such rights.

3. Any State Party availing itself of the right of suspension shall immediately inform the other States Parties, through the Secretary General of the Organization of American States, of the provisions the application of which it has suspended, the reasons that gave rise to the suspension, and the date set for the termination of such suspension.

* * *

**7.11 DECLARATION ON SOCIAL PROGRESS AND DEVELOPMENT.
Adopted by the U.N. General Assembly, 11 December 1969. G.A.
Res. 2542, U.N. GAOR, 24th Sess., Supp. No. 30, at 49, U.N. Doc.
A/7630 (1970)**

The General Assembly,

Mindful of the pledge of Members of the United Nations under the
Charter to take joint and separate action in co-operation with the Organization to promote higher standards of living, full employment and conditions of
economic and social progress and development,

Reaffirming faith in human rights and fundamental freedoms and in the
principles of peace, of the dignity and worth of the human person, and of
social justice proclaimed in the Charter,

Recalling the principles of the Universal Declaration of Human Rights,
the International Covenants on Human Rights, the Declaration of the Rights
of the Child, the Declaration on the Granting of Independence to Colonial
Countries and Peoples, the International Convention on the Elimination of All
Forms of Racial Discrimination, the United Nations Declaration on the
Elimination of All Forms of Racial Discrimination, the Declaration on the
Promotion among Youth of the Ideals of Peace, Mutual Respect and Understanding between Peoples, the Declaration on the Elimination of Discrimina-
tion against Women and of resolutions of the United Nations,

Bearing in mind the standards already set for social progress in the
constitutions, conventions, recommendations and resolutions of the Interna-
tional Labour Organisation, the Food and Agriculture Organization of the
United Nations, the United Nations Educational, Scientific and Cultural
Organization, the World Health Organization, the United Nations Children's
Fund and of other organizations concerned,

Convinced that man can achieve complete fulfilment of his aspirations
only within a just social order and that it is consequently of cardinal
importance to accelerate social and economic progress everywhere, thus
contributing to international peace and solidarity,

Convinced that international peace and security on the one hand, and
social progress and economic development on the other, are closely interdependent and influence each other,

Persuaded that social development can be promoted by peaceful coexistence, friendly relations and co-operation among States with different social,
economic or political systems,

Emphasizing the interdependence of economic and social development in
the wider process of growth and change, as well as the importance of a
strategy of integrated development which takes full account at all stages of its
social aspects,

Regretting the inadequate progress achieved in the world social situation
despite the efforts of States and the international community,

Recognizing that the primary responsibility for the development of the
developing countries rests on those countries themselves and acknowledging
the pressing need to narrow and eventually close the gap in the standards of
living between economically more advanced and developing countries and, to

that end, that Member States shall have the responsibility to pursue internal and external policies designed to promote social development throughout the world, and in particular to assist developing countries to accelerate their economic growth,

Recognizing the urgency of devoting to works of peace and social progress resources being expended on armaments and wasted on conflict and destruction,

Conscious of the contribution that science and technology can render towards meeting the needs common to all humanity,

Believing that the primary task of all States and international organizations is to eliminate from the life of society all evils and obstacles to social progress, particularly such evils as inequality, exploitation, war, colonialism and racism,

Desirous of promoting the progress of all mankind towards these goals and of overcoming all obstacles to their realization,

Solemnly proclaims this Declaration on Social Progress and Development and calls for national and international action for its use as a common basis for social development policies:

PART I

PRINCIPLES

Article 1

All peoples and all human beings, without distinction as to race, colour, sex, language, religion, nationality, ethnic origin, family or social status, or political or other conviction, shall have the right to live in dignity and freedom and to enjoy the fruits of social progress and should, on their part, contribute to it.

Article 2

Social progress and development shall be founded on respect for the dignity and value of the human person and shall ensure the promotion of human rights and social justice, which requires:

(*a*) The immediate and final elimination of all forms of inequality, exploitation of peoples and individuals, colonialism and racism, including nazism and *apartheid,* and all other policies and ideologies opposed to the purposes and principles of the United Nations;

(*b*) The recognition and effective implementation of civil and political rights as well as of economic, social and cultural rights without any discrimination.

Article 3

The following are considered primary conditions of social progress and development:

(*a*) National independence based on the right of peoples to self-determination;

(*b*) The principle of non-interference in the internal affairs of States;

(*c*) Respect for the sovereignty and territorial integrity of States;

(*d*) Permanent sovereignty of each nation over its natural wealth and resources;

(*e*) The right and responsibility of each State and, as far as they are concerned, each nation and people to determine freely its own objectives of social development, to set its own priorities and to decide in conformity with the principles of the Charter of the United Nations the means and methods of their achievement without any external interference;

(*f*) Peaceful coexistence, peace, friendly relations and co-operation among States irrespective of differences in their social, economic or political systems.

Article 4

The family as a basic unit of society and the natural environment for the growth and well-being of all its members, particularly children and youth, should be assisted and protected so that it may fully assume its responsibilities within the community. Parents have the exclusive right to determine freely and responsibly the number and spacing of their children.

Article 5

Social progress and development require the full utilization of human resources, including, in particular:

(*a*) The encouragement of creative initiative under conditions of enlightened public opinion;

(*b*) The dissemination of national and international information for the purpose of making individuals aware of changes occurring in society as a whole;

(*c*) The active participation of all elements of society, individually or through associations, in defining and in achieving the common goals of development with full respect for the fundamental freedoms embodied in the Universal Declaration of Human Rights;

(*d*) The assurance to disadvantaged or marginal sectors of the population of equal opportunities for social and economic advancement in order to achieve an effectively integrated society.

Article 6

Social development requires the assurance to everyone of the right to work and the free choice of employment.

Social progress and development require the participation of all members of society in productive and socially useful labour and the establishment, in conformity with human rights and fundamental freedoms and with the principles of justice and the social function of property, of forms of ownership of land and of the means of production which preclude any kind of exploitation of man, ensure equal rights to property for all and create conditions leading to genuine equality among people.

Article 7

The rapid expansion of national income and wealth and their equitable distribution among all members of society are fundamental to all social progress, and they should therefore be in the forefront of the preoccupations of every State and Government.

The improvement in the position of the developing countries in international trade resulting, among other things, from the achievement of favourable terms of trade and of equitable and remunerative prices at which developing countries market their products is necessary in order to make it possible to increase national income and in order to advance social development.

Article 8

Each Government has the primary role and ultimate responsibility of ensuring the social progress and well-being of its people, of planning social development measures as part of comprehensive development plans, of encouraging and co-ordinating or integrating all national efforts towards this end and of introducing necessary changes in the social structure. In planning social development measures, the diversity of the needs of developing and developed areas, and of urban and rural areas, within each country, shall be taken into due account.

Article 9

Social progress and development are the common concerns of the international community, which shall supplement, by concerted international action, national efforts to raise the living standards of peoples.

Social progress and economic growth require recognition of the common interest of all nations in the exploration, conservation, use and exploitation, exclusively for peaceful purposes and in the interests of all mankind, of those areas of the environment such as outer space and the sea-bed and ocean floor and the subsoil thereof, beyond the limits of national jurisdiction, in accordance with the purposes and principles of the Charter of the United Nations.

PART II

OBJECTIVES

Social progress and development shall aim at the continuous raising of the material and spiritual standards of living of all members of society, with respect for and in compliance with human rights and fundamental freedoms, through the attainment of the following main goals:

Article 10

(*a*) The assurance at all levels of the right to work and the right of everyone to form trade unions and workers' associations and to bargain collectively; promotion of full productive employment and elimination of unemployment and under-employment; establishment of equitable and favourable conditions of work for all, including the improvement of health and safety conditions; assurance of just remuneration for labour without any discrimination as well as a sufficiently high minimum wage to ensure a decent standard of living; the protection of the consumer;

(*b*) The elimination of hunger and malnutrition and the guarantee of the right to proper nutrition;

(*c*) The elimination of poverty; the assurance of a steady improvement in levels of living and of a just and equitable distribution of income;

(*d*) The achievement of the highest standards of health and the provision of health protection for the entire population, if possible free of charge;

(*e*) The eradication of illiteracy and the assurance of the right to universal access to culture, to free compulsory education at the elementary level and to free education at all levels; the raising of the general level of life-long education;

(*f*) The provision for all, particularly persons in low-income groups and large families, of adequate housing and community services.

Social progress and development shall aim equally at the progressive attainment of the following main goals:

Article 11

(*a*) The provision of comprehensive social security schemes and social welfare services; the establishment and improvement of social security and insurance schemes for all persons who, because of illness, disability or old age, are temporarily or permanently unable to earn a living, with a view to ensuring a proper standard of living for such persons and for their families and dependents;

(*b*) The protection of the rights of the mother and child; concern for the upbringing and health of children; the provision of measures to safeguard the health and welfare of women and particularly of working mothers during pregnancy and the infancy of their children, as well as of mothers whose earnings are the sole source of livelihood for the family; the granting to women of pregnancy and maternity leave and allowances without loss of employment or wages;

(*c*) The protection of the rights and the assuring of the welfare of children, the aged and the disabled; the provision of protection for the physically or mentally disadvantaged;

(*d*) The education of youth in, and promotion among them of, the ideals of justice and peace, mutual respect and understanding among peoples; the promotion of full participation of youth in the process of national development;

(*e*) The provision of social defence measures and the elimination of conditions leading to crime and delinquency, especially juvenile delinquency;

(*f*) The guarantee that all individuals, without discrimination of any kind, are made aware of their rights and obligations and receive the necessary aid in the exercise and safeguarding of their rights.

Social progress and development shall further aim at achieving the following main objectives:

Article 12

(*a*) The creation of conditions for rapid and sustained social and economic development, particularly in the developing countries; change in international economic relations; new and effective methods of international cooperation in which equality of opportunity should be as much a prerogative of nations as of individuals within a nation;

(*b*) The elimination of all forms of discrimination and exploitation and all other practices and ideologies contrary to the purposes and principles of the Charter of the United Nations;

(*c*) The elimination of all forms of foreign economic exploitation, particularly that practiced by international monopolies, in order to enable the people of every country to enjoy in full the benefits of their national resources.

Social progress and development shall finally aim at the attainment of the following main goals:

Article 13

(*a*) Equitable sharing of scientific and technological advances by developed and developing countries, and a steady increase in the use of science and technology for the benefit of the social development of society;

(*b*) The establishment of a harmonious balance between scientific, technological and material progress and the intellectual, spiritual, cultural and moral advancement of humanity;

(*c*) The protection and improvement of the human environment.

PART III

MEANS AND METHODS

On the basis of the principles set forth in this Declaration, the achievement of the objectives of social progress and development requires the mobilization of the necessary resources by national and international action, with particular attention to such means and methods as:

Article 14

(*a*) Planning for social progress and development, as an integrated part of balanced over-all development planning;

(*b*) The establishment, where necessary, of national systems for framing and carrying out social policies and programmes, and the promotion by the countries concerned of planned regional development, taking into account differing regional conditions and needs, particularly the development of regions which are less favoured or under-developed by comparison with the rest of the country;

(*c*) The promotion of basic and applied social research, particularly comparative international research applied to the planning and execution of social development programmes.

Article 15

(*a*) The adoption of measures to ensure the effective participation, as appropriate, of all the elements of society in the preparation and execution of national plans and programmes of economic and social development;

(*b*) The adoption of measures for an increasing rate of popular participation in the economic, social, cultural and political life of countries through national governmental bodies, non-governmental organizations, co-operatives, rural associations, workers' and employers' organizations and women's and youth organizations, by such methods as national and regional plans for social and economic progress and community development, with a view to achieving a fully integrated national society, accelerating the process of social mobility and consolidating the democratic system;

(*c*) Mobilization of public opinion, at both national and international levels, in support of the principles and objectives of social progress and development;

(*d*) The dissemination of social information, at the national and the international level, to make people aware of changing circumstances in society as a whole, and to educate the consumer.

Article 16

(*a*) Maximum mobilization of all national resources and their rational and efficient utilization; promotion of increased and accelerated productive investment in social and economic fields and of employment; orientation of society towards the development process;

(*b*) Progressively increasing provision of the necessary budgetary and other resources required for financing the social aspects of development;

(*c*) Achievement of equitable distribution of national income, utilizing, *inter alia,* the fiscal system and government spending as an instrument for the equitable distribution and redistribution of income in order to promote social progress;

(*d*) The adoption of measures aimed at prevention of such an outflow of capital from developing countries as would be detrimental to their economic and social development.

Article 17

(*a*) The adoption of measures to accelerate the process of industrialization, especially in developing countries, with due regard for its social aspects, in the interests of the entire population; development of an adequate organizational and legal framework conducive to an uninterrupted and diversified growth of the industrial sector; measures to overcome the adverse social effects which may result from urban development and industrialization, including automation; maintenance of a proper balance between rural and urban development, and in particular, measures designed to ensure healthier living conditions, especially in large industrial centres;

(*b*) Integrated planning to meet the problems of urbanization and urban development;

(*c*) Comprehensive rural development schemes to raise the levels of living of the rural populations and to facilitate such urban-rural relationships and population distribution as will promote balanced national development and social progress;

(*d*) Measures for appropriate supervision of the utilization of land in the interests of society.

The achievement of the objectives of social progress and development equally requires the implementation of the following means and methods:

Article 18

(*a*) The adoption of appropriate legislative, administrative and other measures ensuring to everyone not only political and civil rights, but also the full realization of economic, social and cultural rights without any discrimination;

(*b*) The promotion of democratically based social and institutional reforms and motivation for change basic to the elimination of all forms of discrimination and exploitation and conducive to high rates of economic and social progress, to include land reform, in which the ownership and use of land will be made to serve best the objectives of social justice and economic development;

(*c*) The adoption of measures to boost and diversify agricultural production through, *inter alia,* the implementation of democratic agrarian reforms, to ensure an adequate and well-balanced supply of food, its equitable distribution among the whole population and the improvement of nutritional standards;

(*d*) The adoption of measures to introduce, with the participation of the Government, low-cost housing programmes in both rural and urban areas;

(*e*) Development and expansion of the system of transportation and communications, particularly in developing countries.

Article 19

(*a*) The provision of free health services to the whole population and of adequate preventive and curative facilities and welfare medical services accessible to all;

(*b*) The enactment and establishment of legislative measures and administrative regulations with a view to the implementation of comprehensive programmes of social security schemes and social welfare services and to the improvement and co-ordination of existing services;

(*c*) The adoption of measures and the provision of social welfare services to migrant workers and their families, in conformity with the provisions of Convention No. 97 of the International Labour Organisation and other international instruments relating to migrant workers;

(*d*) The institution of appropriate measures for the rehabilitation of mentally or physically disabled persons, especially children and youth, so as to enable them to the fullest possible extent to be useful members of society—these measures shall include the provision of treatment and technical appliances, education, vocational and social guidance, training and selective placement, and other assistance required—and the creation of social conditions in which the handicapped are not discriminated against because of their disabilities.

Article 20

(*a*) The provision of full democratic freedoms to trade unions; freedom of association for all workers, including the right to bargain collectively and to strike, recognition of the right to form other organizations of working people; the provision for the growing participation of trade unions in economic and social development; effective participation of all members of trade unions in the deciding of economic and social issues which affect their interests;

(*b*) The improvement of health and safety conditions for workers, by means of appropriate technological and legislative measures and the provision of the material prerequisites for the implementation of those measures, including the limitation of working hours;

(*c*) The adoption of appropriate measures for the development of harmonious industrial relations.

Article 21

(*a*) The training of national personnel and cadres, including administrative, executive, professional and technical personnel needed for social development and for over-all development plans and policies;

(*b*) The adoption of measures to accelerate the extension and improvement of general, vocational and technical education and of training and retraining, which should be provided free at all levels;

(*c*) Raising the general level of education; development and expansion of national information media, and their rational and full use towards continuing education of the whole population and towards encouraging its participation in social development activities; the constructive use of leisure, particularly that of children and adolescents;

(*d*) The formulation of national and international policies and measures to avoid the "brain drain" and obviate its adverse effects.

Article 22

(*a*) The development and co-ordination of policies and measures designed to strengthen the essential functions of the family as a basic unit of society;

(*b*) The formulation and establishment, as needed, of programmes in the field of population, within the framework of national demographic policies and as part of the welfare medical services, including education, training of personnel and the provision to families of the knowledge and means necessary to enable them to exercise their right to determine freely and responsibly the number and spacing of their children;

(*c*) The establishment of appropriate child-care facilities in the interest of children and working parents.

The achievement of the objectives of social progress and development finally requires the implementation of the following means and methods:

Article 23

(*a*) The laying down of economic growth rate targets for the developing countries within the United Nations policy for development, high enough to lead to a substantial acceleration of their rates of growth;

(*b*) The provision of greater assistance on better terms; the implementation of the aid volume target of a minimum of 1 per cent of the gross national product at market prices of economically advanced countries; the general easing of the terms of lending to the developing countries through low interest rates on loans and long grace periods for the repayment of loans, and the assurance that the allocation of such loans will be based strictly on socio-economic criteria free of any political considerations;

(*c*) The provision of technical, financial and material assistance, both bilateral and multilateral, to the fullest possible extent and on favourable terms, and improved co-ordination of international assistance for the achievement of the social objectives of national development plans;

(*d*) The provision to the developing countries of technical, financial and material assistance and of favourable conditions to facilitate the direct exploitation of their national resources and natural wealth by those countries with a view to enabling the peoples of those countries to benefit fully from their national resources;

(*e*) The expansion of international trade based on principles of equality and non-discrimination, the rectification of the position of developing countries in international trade by equitable terms of trade, a general non-reciprocal and non-discriminatory system of preferences for the exports of developing countries to the developed countries, the establishment and implementation of general and comprehensive commodity agreements, and the financing of reasonable buffer stocks by international institutions.

Article 24

(*a*) Intensification of international co-operation with a view to ensuring the international exchange of information, knowledge and experience concerning social progress and development;

(*b*) The broadest possible international technical, scientific and cultural co-operation and reciprocal utilization of the experience of countries with different economic and social systems and different levels of development, on the basis of mutual advantage and strict observance of and respect for national sovereignty;

7.12 CONVENTION ON THE ELIMINATION OF ALL FORMS OF DISCRIMINATION AGAINST WOMEN. Concluded at New York, 18 December 1979. Entered into force, 3 September 1981. 1249 U.N.T.S. 13, 19 I.L.M. 33 (1980): *Art. 12*

Article 12. (1) States Parties shall take all appropriate measures to eliminate discrimination against women in the field of health care in order to ensure, on a basis of equality of men and women, access to health care services, including those related to family planning.

(2) Notwithstanding the provisions of paragraph 1 above, States Parties shall ensure to women appropriate services in connexion with pregnancy, confinement and the post-natal period, granting free services where necessary, as well as adequate nutrition during pregnancy and lactation.

7.13 DECLARATION ON THE RIGHT TO DEVELOPMENT. Adopted by the U.N. General Assembly, 4 December 1986. G.A. Res. 41/128 (Annex), U.N. GAOR, 41st Sess., Supp. No. 53, at 186, U.N. Doc. A/41/53 (1987)

The General Assembly,

Bearing in mind the purposes and principles of the Charter of the United Nations relating to the achievement of international co-operation in solving international problems of an economic, social, cultural or humanitarian nature, and in promoting and encouraging respect for human rights and fundamental freedoms for all without distinction as to race, sex, language or religion,

Recognizing that development is a comprehensive economic, social, cultural and political process, which aims at the constant improvement of the well-being of the entire population and of all individuals on the basis of their active, free and meaningful participation in development and in the fair distribution of benefits resulting therefrom,

Considering that under the provisions of the Universal Declaration of Human Rights everyone is entitled to a social and international order in which the rights and freedoms set forth in that Declaration can be fully realized,

Recalling the provisions of the International Covenant on Economic, Social and Cultural Rights and the International Covenant on Civil and Political Rights,

Recalling further the relevant agreements, conventions, resolutions, recommendations and other instruments of the United Nations and its specialized agencies concerning the integral development of the human being, economic and social progress and development of all peoples, including those instruments concerning decolonization, the prevention of discrimination, respect for, and observance of, human rights and fundamental freedoms, the maintenance of international peace and security and the further promotion of friendly relations and co-operation among States in accordance with the Charter,

Recalling the right of peoples to self-determination, by virtue of which they have the right freely to determine their political status and to pursue their economic, social and cultural development,

Recalling further the right of peoples to exercise, subject to relevant provisions of both International Covenants on Human Rights, their full and complete sovereignty over all their natural wealth and resources,

Mindful of the obligation of States under the Charter to promote universal respect for and observance of human rights and fundamental freedoms for all without distinction of any kind such as race, colour, sex, language, religion, political or other opinion, national or social origin, property, birth or other status,

Considering that the elimination of the massive and flagrant violations of the human rights of the peoples and individuals affected by situations such as those resulting from colonialism, neo-colonialism, *apartheid,* all forms of racism and racial discrimination, foreign domination and occupation, aggression and threats against national sovereignty, national unity and territorial integrity and threats of war would contribute to the establishment of circumstances propitious to the development of a great part of mankind,

Concerned at the existence of serious obstacles to development, as well as to the complete fulfilment of human beings and of peoples, constituted, *inter alia,* by the denial of civil, political, economic, social and cultural rights, and considering that all human rights and fundamental freedoms are indivisible and interdependent and that, in order to promote development, equal attention and urgent consideration should be given to the implementation, promotion and protection of civil, political, economic, social and cultural rights and that, accordingly, the promotion of, respect for, and enjoyment of certain human rights and fundamental freedoms cannot justify the denial of other human rights and fundamental freedoms,

Considering that international peace and security are essential elements for the realization of the right to development,

Reaffirming that there is a close relationship between disarmament and development and that progress in the field of disarmament would considerably promote progress in the field of development and that resources released through disarmament measures should be devoted to the economic and social development and well-being of all peoples and, in particular, those of the developing countries,

Recognizing that the human person is the central subject of the development process and that development policy should therefore make the human being the main participant and beneficiary of development,

Recognizing that the creation of conditions favourable to the development of peoples and individuals is the primary responsibility of their States,

Aware that efforts to promote and protect human rights at the international level should be accompanied by efforts to establish a new international economic order,

Confirming that the right to development is an inalienable human right and that equality of opportunity for development is a prerogative both of nations and of individuals who make up nations,

Proclaims the following Declaration on the right to development:

Article 1

1. The right to development is an inalienable human right by virtue of which every human person and all peoples are entitled to participate in, contribute to, and enjoy economic, social, cultural and political development, in which all human rights and fundamental freedoms can be fully realized.

2. The human right to development also implies the full realization of the right of peoples to self-determination, which includes, subject to relevant provisions of both International Covenants on Human Rights, the exercise of their inalienable right to full sovereignty over all their natural wealth and resources.

Article 2

1. The human person is the central subject of development and should be the active participant and beneficiary of the right to development.

2. All human beings have a responsibility for development, individually and collectively, taking into account the need for full respect of their human rights and fundamental freedoms as well as their duties to the community, which alone can ensure the free and complete fulfilment of the human being, and they should therefore promote and protect an appropriate political, social and economic order for development.

3. States have the right and the duty to formulate appropriate national development policies that aim at the constant improvement of the well-being of the entire population and of all individuals, on the basis of their active, free and meaningful participation in development and in the fair distribution of the benefits resulting therefrom.

Article 3

1. States have the primary responsibility for the creation of national and international conditions favourable to the realization of the right to development.

2. The realization of the right to development requires full respect for the principles of international law concerning friendly relations and co-operation among States in accordance with the Charter of the United Nations.

3. States have the duty to co-operate with each other in ensuring development and eliminating obstacles to development. States should fulfil their rights and duties in such a manner as to promote a new international economic order based on sovereign equality, interdependence, mutual interest and co-operation among all States, as well as to encourage the observance and realization of human rights.

Article 4

1. States have the duty to take steps, individually and collectively, to formulate international development policies with a view to facilitating the full realization of the right to development.

2. Sustained action is required to promote more rapid development of developing countries. As a complement to the efforts of developing countries effective international co-operation is essential in providing these countries with appropriate means and facilities to foster their comprehensive development.

Article 5

States shall take resolute steps to eliminate the massive and flagrant violations of the human rights of peoples and human beings affected by situations such as those resulting from *apartheid,* all forms of racism and racial discrimination, colonialism, foreign domination and occupation, aggression, foreign interference and threats against national sovereignty, national unity and territorial integrity, threats of war and refusal to recognize the fundamental right of peoples to self-determination.

Article 6

1. All States should co-operate with a view to promoting, encouraging and strengthening universal respect for and observance of all human rights and fundamental freedoms for all without any distinction as to race, sex, language and religion.

2. All human rights and fundamental freedoms are indivisible and interdependent, equal attention and urgent consideration should be given to the implementation, promotion and protection of civil, political, economic, social and cultural rights.

3. States should take steps to eliminate obstacles to development resulting from failure to observe civil and political rights as well as economic, social and cultural rights.

Article 7

All States should promote the establishment, maintenance and strengthening of international peace and security and, to that end, should do their utmost to achieve general and complete disarmament under effective international control as well as to ensure that the resources released by effective disarmament measures are used for comprehensive development, in particular that of the developing countries.

Article 8

1. States should undertake, at the national level, all necessary measures for the realization of the right to development and shall ensure, *inter alia,* equality of opportunity for all in their access to basic resources, education, health services, food, housing, employment and the fair distribution of income. Effective measures should be undertaken to ensure that women have an active role in the development process. Appropriate economic and social reforms should be made with a view to eradicating all social injustices.

2. States should encourage popular participation in all spheres as an important factor in development and in the full realization of all human rights.

Article 9

1. All the aspects of the right to development set forth in this Declaration are indivisible and interdependent and each of them should be considered in the context of the whole.

2. Nothing in this Declaration shall be construed as being contrary to the purposes and principles of the United Nations, or as implying that any State, group or person has a right to engage in any activity or to perform any act aimed at the violation of the rights set forth in the Universal Declaration of Human Rights and in the International Covenants on Human Rights.

Article 10

Steps should be taken to ensure the full exercise and progressive enhancement of the right to development, including the formulation, adoption and implementation of policy, legislative and other measures at the national and international levels.

7.14　UNESCO DECLARATION ON THE PRINCIPLES OF INTERNATIONAL CULTURAL CO-OPERATION. *United Nations, Human Rights: A Compilation of International Instruments* **409 (1988)**

The General Conference of the United Nations Educational, Scientific and Cultural Organization, met in Paris for its fourteenth session, this fourth day of November 1966, being the twentieth anniversary of the foundation of the Organization,

Recalling that the Constitution of the Organization declares that "since wars begin in the minds of men, it is in the minds of men that the defences of peace must be constructed" and that the peace must be founded, if it is not to fail, upon the intellectual and moral solidarity of mankind,

Recalling that the Constitution also states that the wide diffusion of culture and the education of humanity for justice and liberty and peace are indispensable to the dignity of man and constitute a sacred duty which all the nations must fulfil in a spirit of mutual assistance and concern,

Considering that the Organization's Member States, believing in the pursuit of truth and the free exchange of ideas and knowledge, have agreed and determined to develop and to increase the means of communication between their peoples,

Considering that, despite the technical advances which facilitate the development and dissemination of knowledge and ideas, ignorance of the way of life and customs of peoples still presents an obstacle to friendship among the nations, to peaceful co-operation and to the progress of mankind,

Taking account of the Universal Declaration of Human Rights, the Declaration of the Rights of the Child, the Declaration on the Granting of Independence to Colonial Countries and Peoples, the United Nations Declaration on the Elimination of All Forms of Racial Discrimination, the Declaration on the Promotion among Youth of the Ideals of Peace, Mutual Respect and Understanding between Peoples, and the Declaration on the Inadmissibility of Intervention in the Domestic Affairs of States and the Protection of their Independence and Sovereignty, proclaimed successively by the General Assembly of the United Nations,

Convinced by the experience of the Organization's first twenty years that, if international cultural co-operation is to be strengthened, its principles require to be affirmed,

Proclaims this Declaration of the principles of international cultural co-operation, to the end that governments, authorities, organizations, associations and institutions responsible for cultural activities may constantly be guided by these principles; and for the purpose, as set out in the Constitution of the Organization, of advancing, through the educational, scientific and cultural relations of the peoples of the world, the objectives of peace and welfare that are defined in the Charter of the United Nations:

Article 1

1.　Each culture has a dignity and value which must be respected and preserved.

2.　Every people has the right and the duty to develop its culture.

3. In their rich variety and diversity, and in the reciprocal influences they exert on one another, all cultures form part of the common heritage belonging to all mankind.

Article II

Nations shall endeavour to develop the various branches of culture side by side and, as far as possible, simultaneously, so as to establish a harmonious balance between technical progress and the intellectual and moral advancement of mankind.

Article III

International cultural co-operation shall cover all aspects of intellectual and creative activities relating to education, science and culture.

Article IV

The aims of international cultural co-operation in its various forms, bilateral or multilateral, regional or universal, shall be:

1. To spread knowledge, to stimulate talent and to enrich cultures;

2. To develop peaceful relations and friendship among the peoples and bring about a better understanding of each other's way of life;

3. To contribute to the application of the principles set out in the United Nations Declarations that are recalled in the Preamble to this Declaration;

4. To enable everyone to have access to knowledge, to enjoy the arts and literature of all peoples, to share in advances made in science in all parts of the world and in the resulting benefits, and to contribute to the enrichment of cultural life;

5. To raise the level of the spiritual and material life of man in all parts of the world.

Article V

Cultural co-operation is a right and a duty for all peoples and all nations, which should share with one another their knowledge and skills.

Article VI

International co-operation, while promoting the enrichment of all cultures through its beneficent action, shall respect the distinctive character of each.

Article VII

1. Broad dissemination of ideas and knowledge, based on the freest exchange and discussion, is essential to creative activity, the pursuit of truth and the development of the personality.

2. In cultural co-operation, stress shall be laid on ideas and values conducive to the creation of a climate of friendship and peace. Any mark of hostility in attitudes and in expression of opinion shall be avoided. Every effort shall be made, in presenting and disseminating information, to ensure its authenticity.

Article VIII

Cultural co-operation shall be carried on for the mutual benefit of all the nations practising it. Exchanges to which it gives rise shall be arranged in a spirit of broad reciprocity.

Article IX

Cultural co-operation shall contribute to the establishment of stable, long-term relations between peoples, which should be subjected as little as possible to the strains which may arise in international life.

Article X

Cultural co-operation shall be specially concerned with the moral and intellectual education of young people in a spirit of friendship, international understanding and peace and shall foster awareness among States of the need to stimulate talent and promote the training of the rising generations in the most varied sectors.

Article XI

1. In their cultural relations, States shall bear in mind the principles of the United Nations. In seeking to achieve international co-operation, they shall respect the sovereign equality of States and shall refrain from intervention in matters which are essentially within the domestic jurisdiction of any State.

2. The principles of this Declaration shall be applied with due regard for human rights and fundamental freedoms.

7.15 INTERNATIONAL LABOUR ORGANIZATION CONVENTION (NO. 169) CONCERNING INDIGENOUS AND TRIBAL PEOPLES IN INDEPENDENT COUNTRIES. Concluded at Geneva, 27 June 1989. Not in force as of 31 December 1992. International Labor Conference, Draft Report of the Committee on Convention No. 107, Appendix I, C.C. 107/D. 303 (June 1989), 28 I.L.M. 1382 (1989)

The General Conference of the International Labour Organization,

Having been convened at Geneva by the Governing Body of the International Labour Office, and having met in its 76th Session on 7 June 1989, and

Noting the international standards contained in the Indigenous and Tribal Populations Convention and Recommendation, 1957, and

Recalling the terms of the Universal Declaration of Human Rights, the International Covenant on Economic, Social and Cultural Rights, the International Covenant on Civil and Political Rights, and the many international instruments on the prevention of discrimination, and

Considering that the developments which have taken place in international law since 1957, as well as developments in the situation of indigenous and tribal peoples in all regions of the world, have made it appropriate to adopt new international standards on the subject with a view to removing the assimilationist orientation of the earlier standards, and

Recognising the aspirations of these peoples to exercise control over their own institutions, ways of life and economic development and to maintain and develop their identities, languages and religions, within the framework of the States in which they live, and

Noting that in many parts of the world these peoples are unable to enjoy their fundamental human rights to the same degree as the rest of the population of the States within which they live, and that their laws, values, customs and perspectives have often been eroded, and

Calling attention to the distinctive contributions of indigenous and tribal peoples to the cultural diversity and social and ecological harmony of humankind and to international co-operation and understanding, and

Noting that the following provisions have been framed with the co-operation of the United Nations, the Food and Agriculture Organisation of the United Nations, the United Nations Educational, Scientific and Cultural Organisation and the World Health Organisation, as well as of the Inter–American Indian Institute, at appropriate levels and in their respective fields, and that it is proposed to continue this co-operation in promoting and securing the application of these provisions, and

Having decided upon the adoption of certain proposals with regard to the partial revision of the Indigenous and Tribal Populations Convention, 1957 (No. 107), which is the fourth item on the agenda of the session, and

Having determined that these proposals shall take the form of an international Convention revising the Indigenous and Tribal Populations Convention, 1957;

adopts this twenty-seventh day of June of the year one thousand nine hundred and eighty-nine the following Convention, which may be cited as the Indigenous and Tribal Peoples Convention, 1989:

PART I. GENERAL POLICY

Article 1

1. This Convention applies to:

(*a*) tribal peoples in independent countries whose social, cultural and economic conditions distinguish them from other sections of the national community, and whose status is regulated wholly or partially by their own customs or traditions or by special laws or regulations;

(*b*) peoples in independent countries who are regarded as indigenous on account of their descent from the populations which inhabited the country, or a geographical region to which the country belongs, at the time of conquest or colonisation or the establishment of present state boundaries and who, irrespective of their legal status, retain some or all of their own social, economic, cultural and political institutions.

2. Self-identification as indigenous or tribal shall be regarded as a fundamental criterion for determining the groups to which the provisions of this Convention apply.

3. The use of the term "peoples" in this Convention shall not be construed as having any implications as regards the rights which may attach to the term under international law.

Article 2

1. Governments shall have the responsibility for developing, with the participation of the peoples concerned, co-ordinated and systematic action to protect the rights of these peoples and to guarantee respect for their integrity.

2. Such action shall include measures for:

(*a*) ensuring that members of these peoples benefit on an equal footing from the rights and opportunities which national laws and regulations grant to other members of the population;

(*b*) promoting the full realisation of the social, economic and cultural rights of these peoples with respect for their social and cultural identity, their customs and traditions and their institutions;

(*c*) assisting the members of the peoples concerned to eliminate socio-economic gaps that may exist between indigenous and other members of the national community, in a manner compatible with their aspirations and ways of life.

Article 3

1. Indigenous and tribal peoples shall enjoy the full measure of human rights and fundamental freedoms without hindrance or discrimination. The provisions of the Convention shall be applied without discrimination to male and female members of these peoples.

2. No form of force or coercion shall be used in violation of the human rights and fundamental freedoms of the peoples concerned, including the rights contained in this Convention.

Article 4

1. Special measures shall be adopted as appropriate for safeguarding the persons, institutions, property, labour, cultures and environment of the peoples concerned.

2. Such special measures shall not be contrary to the freely-expressed wishes of the peoples concerned.

3. Enjoyment of the general rights of citizenship, without discrimination, shall not be prejudiced in any way by such special measures.

Article 5

In applying the provisions of this Convention:

(a) the social, cultural, religious and spiritual values and practices of these peoples shall be recognised and protected, and due account shall be taken of the nature of the problems which face them both as groups and as individuals;

(b) the integrity of the values, practices and institutions of these peoples shall be respected;

(c) policies aimed at mitigating the difficulties experienced by these peoples in facing new conditions of life and work shall be adopted, with the participation and co-operation of the peoples affected.

Article 6

1. In applying the provisions of this Convention, governments shall:

(a) consult the peoples concerned, through appropriate procedures and in particular through their representative institutions, whenever consideration is being given to legislative or administrative measures which may affect them directly;

(b) establish means by which these peoples can freely participate, to at least the same extent as other sectors of the population, at all levels of decision-making in elective institutions and administrative and other bodies responsible for policies and programmes which concern them;

(c) establish means for the full development of these peoples' own institutions and initiatives, and in appropriate cases provide the resources necessary for this purpose.

2. The consultations carried out in application of this Convention shall be undertaken, in good faith and in a form appropriate to the circumstances, with the objective of achieving agreement or consent to the proposed measures.

Article 7

1. The peoples concerned shall have the right to decide their own priorities for the process of development as it affects their lives, beliefs, institutions and spiritual well-being and the lands they occupy or otherwise use, and to exercise control, to the extent possible, over their own economic, social and cultural development. In addition, they shall participate in the formulation, implementation and evaluation of plans and programmes for national and regional development which may affect them directly.

2. The improvement of the conditions of life and work and levels of health and education of the peoples concerned, with their participation and co-operation, shall be a matter of priority in plans for the overall economic development of areas they inhabit. Special projects for development of the areas in question shall also be so designed as to promote such improvement.

3. Governments shall ensure that, whenever appropriate, studies are carried out, in co-operation with the peoples concerned, to assess the social, spiritual, cultural and environmental impact on them of planned development activities. The results of these studies shall be considered as fundamental criteria for the implementation of these activities.

4. Governments shall take measures, in co-operation with the peoples concerned, to protect and preserve the environment of the territories they inhabit.

Article 8

1. In applying national laws and regulations to the peoples concerned, due regard shall be had to their customs or customary laws.

2. These peoples shall have the right to retain their own customs and institutions, where these are not incompatible with fundamental rights defined by the national legal system and with internationally recognised human rights. Procedures shall be established, whenever necessary, to resolve conflicts which may arise in the application of this principle.

3. The application of paragraphs 1 and 2 of this Article shall not prevent members of these peoples from exercising the rights granted to all citizens and from assuming the corresponding duties.

Article 9

1. To the extent compatible with the national legal system and internationally recognised human rights, the methods customarily practised by the peoples concerned for dealing with offences committed by their members shall be respected.

2. The customs of these peoples in regard to penal matters shall be taken into consideration by the authorities and courts dealing with such cases.

Article 10

1. In imposing penalties laid down by general law on members of these peoples account shall be taken of their economic, social and cultural characteristics.

2. Preference shall be given to methods of punishment other than confinement in prison.

Article 11

The exaction from members of the peoples concerned of compulsory personal services in any form, whether paid or unpaid, shall be prohibited and punishable by law, except in cases prescribed by law for all citizens.

Article 12

The peoples concerned shall be safeguarded against the abuse of their rights and shall be able to take legal proceedings, either individually or through their representative bodies, for the effective protection of these rights. Measures shall be taken to ensure that members of these peoples can understand and be understood in legal proceedings, where necessary through the provision of interpretation or by other effective means.

PART II. LAND

Article 13

1. In applying the provisions of this Part of the Convention governments shall respect the special importance for the cultures and spiritual values of the peoples concerned of their relationship with the lands or territories, or both as applicable, which they occupy or otherwise use, and in particular the collective aspects of this relationship.

2. The use of the term "lands" in Articles 15 and 16 shall include the concept of territories, which covers the total environment of the areas which the peoples concerned occupy or otherwise use.

Article 14

1. The rights of ownership and possession of the peoples concerned over the lands which they traditionally occupy shall be recognised. In addition, measures shall be taken in appropriate cases to safeguard the right of the peoples concerned to use lands not exclusively occupied by them, but to which they have traditionally had access for their subsistence and traditional activities. Particular attention shall be paid to the situation of nomadic peoples and shifting cultivators in this respect.

2. Governments shall take steps as necessary to identify the lands which the peoples concerned traditionally occupy, and to guarantee effective protection of their rights of ownership and possession.

3. Adequate procedures shall be established within the national legal system to resolve land claims by the peoples concerned.

Article 15

1. The rights of the peoples concerned to the natural resources pertaining to their lands shall be specially safeguarded. These rights include the right of these peoples to participate in the use, management and conservation of these resources.

2. In cases in which the State retains the ownership of mineral or subsurface resources or rights to other resources pertaining to lands, governments shall establish or maintain procedures through which they shall consult these peoples, with a view to ascertaining whether and to what degree their interests would be prejudiced, before undertaking or permitting any programmes for the exploration or exploitation of such resources pertaining to their lands. The peoples concerned shall wherever possible participate in the benefits of such activities, and shall receive fair compensation for any damages which they may sustain as a result of such activities.

Article 16

1. Subject to the following paragraphs of this Article, the peoples concerned shall not be removed from the lands which they occupy.

2. Where the relocation of these peoples is considered necessary as an exceptional measure, such relocation shall take place only with their free and informed consent. Where their consent cannot be obtained, such relocation shall take place only following appropriate procedures established by national laws and regulations, including public inquiries where appropriate, which provide the opportunity for effective representation of the peoples concerned.

3. Whenever possible, these peoples shall have the right to return to their traditional lands, as soon as the grounds for relocation cease to exist.

4. When such return is not possible, as determined by agreement or, in the absence of such agreement, through appropriate procedures, these peoples shall be provided in all possible cases with lands of quality and legal status at least equal to that of the lands previously occupied by them, suitable to provide for their present needs and future development. Where the peoples concerned express a preference for compensation in money or in kind, they shall be so compensated under appropriate guarantees.

5. Persons thus relocated shall be fully compensated for any resulting loss or injury.

Article 17

1. Procedures established by the peoples concerned for the transmission of land rights among members of these peoples shall be respected.

2. The peoples concerned shall be consulted whenever consideration is being given to their capacity to alienate their lands or otherwise transmit their rights outside their own community.

3. Persons not belonging to these peoples shall be prevented from taking advantage of their customs or of lack of understanding of the laws on the part of their members to secure the ownership, possession or use of land belonging to them.

Article 18

Adequate penalties shall be established by law for unauthorised intrusion upon, or use of, the lands of the peoples concerned, and governments shall take measures to prevent such offences.

Article 19

National agrarian programmes shall secure to the peoples concerned treatment equivalent to that accorded to other sectors of the population with regard to:

(a) the provision of more land for these peoples when they have not the area necessary for providing the essentials of a normal existence, or for any possible increase in their numbers;

(b) the provision of the means required to promote the development of the lands which these peoples already possess.

PART III. RECRUITMENT AND CONDITIONS OF EMPLOYMENT

Article 20

1. Governments shall, within the framework of national laws and regulations, and in co-operation with the peoples concerned, adopt special measures to ensure the effective protection with regard to recruitment and conditions of employment of workers belonging to these peoples, to the extent that they are not effectively protected by laws applicable to workers in general.

2. Governments shall do everything possible to prevent any discrimination between workers belonging to the peoples concerned and other workers, in particular as regards:

(a) admission to employment, including skilled employment, as well as measures for promotion and advancement;

(b) equal remuneration for work of equal value;

(c) medical and social assistance, occupational safety and health, all social security benefits and any other occupationally related benefits, and housing;

(d) the right of association and freedom for all lawful trade union activities, and the right to conclude collective agreements with employers or employers' organisations.

3. The measures taken shall include measures to ensure:

(a) that workers belonging to the peoples concerned, including seasonal, casual and migrant workers in agricultural and other employment, as well as those employed by labour contractors, enjoy the protection afforded by national law and practice to other such workers in the same sectors, and that they are fully informed of their rights under labour legislation and of the means of redress available to them;

(b) that workers belonging to these peoples are not subjected to working conditions hazardous to their health, in particular through exposure to pesticides or other toxic substances;

(c) that workers belonging to these peoples are not subjected to coercive recruitment systems, including bonded labour and other forms of debt servitude;

(d) that workers belonging to these peoples enjoy equal opportunities and equal treatment in employment for men and women, and protection from sexual harassment.

4. Particular attention shall be paid to the establishment of adequate labour inspection services in areas where workers belonging to the peoples concerned undertake wage employment, in order to ensure compliance with the provisions of this Part of this Convention.

PART IV. VOCATIONAL TRAINING, HANDICRAFTS AND RURAL INDUSTRIES

Article 21

Members of the peoples concerned shall enjoy opportunities at least equal to those of other citizens in respect of vocational training measures.

Article 22

1. Measures shall be taken to promote the voluntary participation of members of the peoples concerned in vocational training programmes of general application.

2. Whenever existing programmes of vocational training of general application do not meet the special needs of the peoples concerned, governments shall, with the participation of these peoples, ensure the provision of special training programmes and facilities.

3. Any special training programmes shall be based on the economic environment, social and cultural conditions and practical needs of the peoples concerned. Any studies made in this connection shall be carried out in co-operation with these peoples, who shall be consulted on the organisation and

operation of such programmes. Where feasible, these peoples shall progressively assume responsibility for the organisation and operation of such special training programmes, if they so decide.

Article 23

1. Handicrafts, rural and community-based industries, and subsistence economy and traditional activities of the peoples concerned, such as hunting, fishing, trapping and gathering, shall be recognised as important factors in the maintenance of their cultures and in their economic self-reliance and development. Governments shall, with the participation of these people and whenever appropriate, ensure that these activities are strengthened and promoted.

2. Upon the request of the peoples concerned, appropriate technical and financial assistance shall be provided wherever possible, taking into account the traditional technologies and cultural characteristics of these peoples, as well as the importance of sustainable and equitable development.

PART V. SOCIAL SECURITY AND HEALTH

Article 24

Social security schemes shall be extended progressively to cover the peoples concerned, and applied without discrimination against them.

Article 25

1. Governments shall ensure that adequate health services are made available to the peoples concerned, or shall provide them with resources to allow them to design and deliver such services under their own responsibility and control, so that they may enjoy the highest attainable standard of physical and mental health.

2. Health services shall, to the extent possible, be community-based. These services shall be planned and administered in co-operation with the peoples concerned and take into account their economic, geographic, social and cultural conditions as well as their traditional preventive care, healing practices and medicines.

3. The health care system shall give preference to the training and employment of local community health workers, and focus on primary health care while maintaining strong links with other levels of health care services.

4. The provision of such health services shall be co-ordinated with other social, economic and cultural measures in the country.

PART VI. EDUCATION AND MEANS OF COMMUNICATION

Article 26

Measures shall be taken to ensure that members of the peoples concerned have the opportunity to acquire education at all levels on at least an equal footing with the rest of the national community.

Article 27

1. Education programmes and services for the peoples concerned shall be developed and implemented in co-operation with them to address their special needs, and shall incorporate their histories, their knowledge and

technologies, their value systems and their further social, economic and cultural aspirations.

2. The competent authority shall ensure the training of members of these peoples and their involvement in the formulation and implementation of education programmes, with a view to the progressive transfer of responsibility for the conduct of these programmes to these peoples as appropriate.

3. In addition, governments shall recognise the right of these peoples to establish their own educational institutions and facilities, provided that such institutions meet minimum standards established by the competent authority in consultation with these peoples. Appropriate resources shall be provided for this purpose.

Article 28

1. Children belonging to the peoples concerned shall, wherever practicable, be taught to read and write in their own indigenous language or in the language most commonly used by the group to which they belong. When this is not practicable, the competent authorities shall undertake consultations with these peoples with a view to the adoption of measures to achieve this objective.

2. Adequate measures shall be taken to ensure that these peoples have the opportunity to attain fluency in the national language or in one of the official languages of the country.

3. Measures shall be taken to preserve and promote the development and practice of the indigenous languages of the peoples concerned.

Article 29

The imparting of general knowledge and skills that will help children belonging to the peoples concerned to participate fully and on an equal footing in their own community and in the national community shall be an aim of education for these peoples.

Article 30

1. Governments shall adopt measures appropriate to the traditions and cultures of the peoples concerned, to make known to them their rights and duties, especially in regard to labour, economic opportunities, education and health matters, social welfare and their rights deriving from this Convention.

2. If necessary, this shall be done by means of written translations and through the use of mass communications in the languages of these peoples.

Article 31

Educational measures shall be taken among all sections of the national community, and particularly among those that are in most direct contact with the peoples concerned, with the object of eliminating prejudices that they may harbour in respect of these peoples. To this end, efforts shall be made to ensure that history textbooks and other educational materials provide a fair, accurate and informative portrayal of the societies and cultures of these peoples.

PART VII. CONTACTS AND CO-OPERATION ACROSS BORDERS

Article 32

Governments shall take appropriate measures, including by means of international agreements, to facilitate contacts and co-operation between indigenous and tribal peoples across borders, including activities in the economic, social, cultural, spiritual and environmental fields.

PART VIII. ADMINISTRATION

Article 33

1. The governmental authority responsible for the matters covered in this Convention shall ensure that agencies or other appropriate mechanisms exist to administer the programmes affecting the peoples concerned, and shall ensure that they have the means necessary for the proper fulfilment of the functions assigned to them.

2. These programmes shall include:

(a) the planning, co-ordination, execution and evaluation, in co-operation with the peoples concerned, of the measures provided for in this Convention;

(b) the proposing of legislative and other measures to the competent authorities and supervision of the application of the measures taken, in co-operation with the peoples concerned.

PART IX. GENERAL PROVISIONS

Article 34

The nature and scope of the measures to be taken to give effect to this Convention shall be determined in a flexible manner, having regard to the conditions characteristic of each country.

Article 35

The application of the provisions of this Convention shall not adversely affect rights and benefits of the peoples concerned pursuant to other Conventions and Recommendations, international instruments, treaties, or national laws, awards, custom or agreements.

PART X. FINAL PROVISIONS

Article 36

This Convention revises the Indigenous and Tribal Populations Convention, 1957.

Article 37

The formal ratifications of this Convention shall be communicated to the Director–General of the International Labour Office for registration.

7.16 CONVENTION ON THE RIGHTS OF THE CHILD. Concluded at New York, 20 November 1989. Not in force as of 31 December 1992. G.A.Res. 44/25 (Annex), U.N. GAOR, 44th Sess., Supp. No. 49, at 166, U.N.Doc. A/RES/44/49 (1990), 30 I.L.M. 1448 (1989); Art. 2

Article 2

1. States Parties shall respect and ensure the rights set forth in the present Convention to each child within their jurisdiction without discrimination of any kind, irrespective of the child's or his or her parent's or legal guardian's race, colour, sex, language, religion, political or other opinion, national, ethnic or social origin, property, disability, birth or other status.

2. States Parties shall take all appropriate measures to ensure that the child is protected against all forms of discrimination or punishment on the basis of the status, activities, expressed opinions, or beliefs of the child's parents, legal guardians, or family members.

7.17 DRAFT DECLARATION ON THE RIGHTS OF INDIGENOUS PEOPLES AS AGREED UPON BY THE MEMBERS OF THE WORKING GROUP ON INDIGENOUS PEOPLES AT ITS ELEVENTH SESSION. 23 August 1993. UN Doc. E/CN. 4/Sub. 2/1993/29

Affirming that indigenous peoples are equal in dignity and rights to all other peoples, while recognizing the right of all peoples to be different, to consider themselves different, and to be respected as such,

Affirming also that all peoples contribute to the diversity and richness of civilizations and cultures, which constitute the common heritage of humankind,

Affirming further that all doctrines, policies and practices based on or advocating superiority of peoples or individuals on the basis of national origin, racial, religious, ethnic or cultural differences are racist, scientifically false, legally invalid, morally condemnable and socially unjust,

Reaffirming also that indigenous peoples, in the exercise of their rights, should be free from discrimination of any kind,

Concerned that indigenous peoples have been deprived of their human rights and fundamental freedoms, resulting, *inter alia,* in their colonization and dispossession of their lands, territories and resources, thus preventing them from exercising, in particular, their right to development in accordance with their own needs and interests,

Recognizing the urgent need to respect and promote the inherent rights and characteristics of indigenous peoples, especially their rights to their lands, territories and resources, which derive from their political, economic and social structures, and from their cultures, spiritual traditions, histories and philosophies,

Welcoming the fact that indigenous peoples are organizing themselves for political, economic, social and cultural enhancement and in order to bring an end to all forms of discrimination and oppression wherever they occur,

Convinced that control by indigenous peoples over developments affecting them and their lands, territories and resources will enable them to maintain and strengthen their institutions, cultures and traditions, and to promote their development in accordance with their institutions, cultures and traditions, and to promote their development in accordance with their aspirations and needs,

Recognizing also that respect for indigenous knowledge, cultures and traditional practices contributes to sustainable and equitable development and proper management of the environment,

Emphasizing the need for demilitarization of the lands and territories of indigenous peoples, which will contribute to peace, economic and social progress and development, understanding and friendly relations among nations and peoples of the world,

Recognizing in particular the right of indigenous families and communities to retain shared responsibility for the upbringing, training, education and well-being of their children,

Recognizing also that indigenous peoples have the right freely to determine their relationships with States in a spirit of coexistence, mutual benefit and full respect,

Considering that treaties, agreements and other arrangements between States and indigenous peoples are properly matters of international concern and responsibility,

Acknowledging that the Charter of the United Nations, the International Covenant on Economic, Social and Cultural Rights and the International Covenant on Civil and Political Rights affirm the fundamental importance of the right of self-determination of all peoples, by virtue of which they freely determine their political status and freely pursue their economic, social and cultural development,

Bearing in mind that nothing in this Declaration may be used to deny any peoples their right of self-determination,

Encouraging States to comply with and effectively implement all international instruments, in particular those related to human rights, as they apply to indigenous peoples, in consultation and cooperation with the peoples concerned,

Emphasizing that the United Nations has an important and continuing role to play in promoting and protecting the rights of indigenous peoples,

Believing that this Declaration is a further important step forward for the recognition, promotion and protection of the rights and freedoms of indigenous peoples United Nations system in this field,

Solemnly proclaims the following United Nations Declaration on the Rights of Indigenous Peoples:

ARTICLES

PART I

1. Indigenous peoples have the right to the full and effective enjoyment of all human rights and fundamental freedoms recognized in the Charter of the United Nations, the Universal Declaration of Human Rights and international human rights law.

2. Indigenous individuals and peoples are free and equal to all other individuals and peoples in dignity and rights, and have the right to be free from any kind of adverse discrimination, in particular that based on their indigenous origin or identity.

3. Indigenous peoples have the right of self-determination. By virtue of that right they freely determine their political status and freely pursue their economic, social and cultural development.

4. Indigenous peoples have the right to maintain and strengthen their distinct political, economic, social and cultural characteristics, as well as their legal systems, while retaining their rights to participate fully, if they so choose, in the political, economic, social and cultural life of the State.

5. Every indigenous individual has the right to a nationality.

PART II

6. Indigenous peoples have the collective right to live in freedom, peace and security as distinct peoples and to full guarantees against genocide or any other act of violence, including the removal of indigenous children from their families and communities under any pretext.

In addition, they have the individual rights to life, physical and mental integrity, liberty and security of person.

7. Indigenous peoples have the collective and individual right not to be subjected to ethnocide and cultural genocide, including prevention of and redress for:

(a) Any action which has the aim or effect of depriving them of their integrity as distinct peoples, or of their cultural values or ethnic identities;

(b) Any action which has the aim or effect of dispossessing them of their lands, territories or resources;

(c) Any form of population transfer which has the aim or effect of violating or undermining any of their rights;

(d) Any form of assimilation or integration by other cultures or ways of life imposed on them by legislative, administrative or other measures;

(e) Any form of propaganda directed against them.

8. Indigenous peoples have the collective and individual right to maintain and develop their distinct identities and characteristics, including the right to identify themselves as indigenous and to be recognized as such.

9. Indigenous peoples and individuals have the right to belong to an indigenous community or nation, in accordance with the traditions and customs of the community or nation concerned. No disadvantage of any kind may arise from the exercise of such a right.

10. Indigenous peoples shall not be forcibly removed from their lands or territories. No relocation shall take place without the free and informed consent of the indigenous peoples concerned and after agreement on just and fair compensation and, where possible, with the option of return.

11. Indigenous peoples have the right to special protection and security in periods of armed conflict.

States shall observe international standards, in particular the Fourth Geneva Convention of 1949, for the protection of civilian populations in circumstances of emergency and armed conflict, and shall not:

(a) Recruit indigenous individuals against their will into the armed forces and, in particular, for use against other indigenous peoples;

(b) Recruit indigenous children into the armed forces under any circumstances;

(c) Force indigenous individuals to abandon their lands, territories or means of subsistence, or relocate them in special centres for military purposes;

(d) Force indigenous individuals to work for military purposes under any discriminatory conditions.

PART III

12. Indigenous peoples have the right to practise and revitalize their cultural traditions and customs. This includes the right to maintain, protect and develop the past, present and future manifestations of their cultures, such as archaeological and historical sites, artifacts, designs, ceremonies, technologies and visual and performing arts and literature, as well as the right to the restitution of cultural, intellectual, religious and spiritual property taken without their free and informed consent or in violation of their laws, traditions and customs.

13. Indigenous peoples have the right to manifest, practise, develop and teach their spiritual and religious traditions, customs and ceremonies; the right to maintain, protect, and have access in privacy to their religious and cultural sites; the right to the use and control of ceremonial objects; and the right to the repatriation of human remains.

States shall take effective measures, in conjunction with the indigenous peoples concerned, to ensure that indigenous sacred places, including burial sites, be preserved, respected and protected.

14. Indigenous peoples have the right to revitalize, use, develop and transmit to future generations their histories, languages, oral traditions, philosophies, writing systems and literatures, and to designate and retain their own names for communities, places and persons.

States shall take effective measures, whenever any right of indigenous peoples may be threatened, to ensure this right is protected and also to ensure that they can understand and be understood in political, legal and administrative proceedings, where necessary through the provision of interpretation or by other appropriate means.

PART IV

15. Indigenous children have the right to all levels and forms of education of the State. All indigenous peoples also have this right and the right to establish and control their educational systems and institutions providing education in their own languages, in a manner appropriate to their cultural methods of teaching and learning.

Indigenous children living outside their communities have the right to be provided access to education in their own culture and language.

States shall take effective measures to provide appropriate resources for these purposes.

16. Indigenous peoples have the right to have the dignity and diversity of their cultures, traditions, histories and aspirations appropriately reflected in all forms of education and public information.

States shall take effective measures, in consultation with the indigenous peoples concerned, to eliminate prejudice and discrimination and to promote tolerance, understanding and good relations among indigenous peoples and all segments of society.

17. Indigenous peoples have the right to establish their own media in their own languages. They also have the right to equal access to all forms of non-indigenous media.

States shall take effective measures to ensure that State-owned media duly reflect indigenous cultural diversity.

18. Indigenous peoples have the right to enjoy fully all rights established under international labour law and national labour legislation.

Indigenous individuals have the right not to be subjected to any discriminatory conditions of labour, employment or salary.

PART V

19. Indigenous peoples have the right to participate fully, if they so choose, at all levels of decision-making in matters which may affect their rights, lives and destinies through representatives chosen by themselves in accordance with their own procedures, as well as to maintain and develop their own indigenous decision-making institutions.

20. Indigenous peoples have the right to participate fully, if they so choose, through procedures determined by them, in devising legislative or administrative measures that may affect them.

States shall obtain the free and informed consent of the peoples concerned before adopting and implementing such measures.

21. Indigenous peoples have the right to maintain and develop their political, economic and social systems, to be secure in the enjoyment of their own means of subsistence and development, and to engage freely in all their traditional and other economic activities. Indigenous peoples who have been deprived of their means of subsistence and development are entitled to just and fair compensation.

22. Indigenous peoples have the right to special measures for the immediate, effective and continuing improvement of their economic and social conditions, including in the areas of employment, vocational training and retraining, housing, sanitation, health and social security.

Particular attention shall be paid to the rights and special needs of indigenous elders, women, youth, children and disabled persons.

23. Indigenous peoples have the right to determine and develop priorities and strategies for exercising their right to development. In particular, indigenous peoples have the right to determine and develop all health, housing and other economic and social programmes affecting them and, as far as possible, to administer such programmes through their own institutions.

24. Indigenous peoples have the right to their traditional medicines and health practices, including the right to the protection of vital medicinal plants, animals and minerals.

They also have the right to access, without any discrimination, to all medical institutions, health services and medical care.

PART VI

25. Indigenous peoples have the right to maintain and strengthen their distinctive spiritual and material relationship with the lands, territories, waters and coastal seas and other resources which they have traditionally owned or otherwise occupied or used, and to uphold their responsibilities to future generations in this regard.

26. Indigenous peoples have the right to own, develop, control and use the lands and territories, including the total environment of the lands, air, waters, coastal seas, sea-ice, flora and fauna and other resources which they have traditionally owned or otherwise occupied or used. This includes the right to the full recognition of their laws, traditions and customs, land-tenure systems and institutions for the development and management of resources, and the right to effective measures by States to prevent any interference with, alienation of or encroachment upon these rights.

27. Indigenous peoples have the right to the restitution of the lands, territories and resources which they have traditionally owned or otherwise occupied or used; and which have been confiscated, occupied, used or damaged without their free and informed consent. Where this is not possible, they have the right to just and fair compensation. Unless otherwise freely agreed upon by the peoples concerned, compensation shall take the form of lands, territories and resources equal in quality, size and legal status.

28. Indigenous peoples have the right to the conservation, restoration and protection of the total environment and the productive capacity of their lands, territories and resources, as well as to assistance for this purpose from States and through international cooperation. Military activities shall not take place in the lands and territories of indigenous peoples, unless otherwise freely agreed upon by the peoples concerned.

States shall take effective measures to ensure that no storage or disposal of hazardous materials shall take place in the lands and territories of indigenous peoples.

States shall also take effective measures to ensure, as needed, that programmes for monitoring, maintaining and restoring the health of indigenous peoples, as developed and implemented by the peoples affected by such materials, are duly implemented.

29. Indigenous peoples are entitled to the recognition of the full ownership, control and protection of their cultural and intellectual property.

They have the right to special measures to control, develop and protect their sciences, technologies and cultural manifestations, including human and other genetic resources, seeds, medicines, knowledge of the properties of fauna and flora, oral traditions, literatures, designs and visual and performing arts.

30. Indigenous peoples have the right to determine and develop priorities and strategies for the development or use of their lands, territories and other resources, including the right to require that States obtain their free and informed consent prior to the approval of any project affecting their lands, territories and other resources, particularly in connection with the development, utilization or exploitation of mineral, water or other resources. Pursuant to agreement with the indigenous peoples concerned, just and fair compensation shall be provided for any such activities and measures taken to mitigate adverse environmental, economic, social, cultural or spiritual impact.

PART VII

31. Indigenous peoples, as a specific form of exercising their right to self-determination, have the right to autonomy or self-government in matters relating to their internal and local affairs, including culture, religion, edu-

cation, information, media, health, housing, employment, social welfare, economic activities, land and resources management, environment and entry by non-members, as well as ways and means for financing these autonomous functions.

32. Indigenous peoples have the collective right to determine their own citizenship in accordance with their customs and traditions. Indigenous citizenship does not impair the right of indigenous individuals to obtain citizenship of the States in which they live.

Indigenous peoples have the right to determine the structures and to select the membership of their institutions in accordance with their own procedures.

33. Indigenous peoples have the right to promote, develop and maintain their institutional structures and their distinctive juridical customs, traditions, procedures and practices, in accordance with internationally recognized human rights standards.

34. Indigenous peoples have the collective right to determine the responsibilities of individuals to their communities.

35. Indigenous peoples, in particular those divided by international borders, have the right to maintain and develop contracts, relations and cooperation, including activities for spiritual, cultural, political, economic and social purposes, with other peoples across borders.

States shall take effective measures to ensure the exercise and implementation of this right.

36. Indigenous peoples have the right to the recognition, observance and enforcement of treaties, agreements and other constructive arrangements concluded with States or their successors, according to their original spirit and intent, and to have States honour and respect such treaties, agreements and other constructive arrangements. Conflicts and disputes which cannot otherwise be settled should be submitted to competent international bodies agreed to by all parties concerned.

PART VIII

37. States shall take effective and appropriate measures, in consultation with the indigenous peoples concerned, to give full effect to the provisions of this Declaration. The rights recognized herein shall be adopted and included in national legislation in such a manner that indigenous peoples can avail themselves of such rights in practice.

38. Indigenous peoples have the right to have access to adequate financial and technical assistance, from States and through international cooperation, to pursue freely their political, economic, social, cultural and spiritual development and for the enjoyment of the rights and freedoms recognized in this Declaration.

39. Indigenous peoples have the right to have access to and prompt decision through mutually acceptable and fair procedures for the resolution of conflicts and disputes with States, as well as to effective remedies for all infringements of their individual and collective rights. Such a decision shall take into consideration the customs, traditions, rules and legal systems of the indigenous peoples concerned.

40. The organs and specialized agencies of the United Nations system and other intergovernmental organizations shall contribute to the full realization of the provisions of this Declaration through the mobilization, *inter alia,* of financial cooperation and technical assistance. Ways and means of ensuring participation of indigenous peoples on issues affecting them shall be established.

41. The United Nations shall take the necessary steps to ensure the implementation of this Declaration including the creation of a body at the highest level with special competence in this field and with the direct participation of indigenous peoples. All United Nations bodies shall promote respect for and full application of the provisions of this Declaration.

PART IX

42. The rights recognized herein constitute the minimum standards for the survival, dignity and well-being of the indigenous peoples of the world.

43. All the rights and freedoms recognized herein are equally guaranteed to male and female indigenous individuals.

44. Nothing in this Declaration may be construed as diminishing or extinguishing existing or future rights indigenous peoples may have or acquire.

45. Nothing in this Declaration may be interpreted as implying for any State, group or person any right to engage in any activity or to perform any act contrary to the Charter of the United Nations.

C. WAR/PEACE

7.18 CONVENTION (NO. IV) RESPECTING THE LAWS AND CUSTOMS OF WAR ON LAND, WITH ANNEX OF REGULATIONS.[1] Concluded at The Hague, 18 October 1907. Entered into force, 26 January 1910. 36 Stat. 2277, T.S. No. 539

* * *

ARTICLE 1

The Contracting Powers shall issue instructions to their armed land forces which shall be in conformity with the Regulations respecting the Laws and Customs of War on Land, annexed to the present Convention.

ARTICLE 2

The provisions contained in the Regulations referred to in Article 1, as well as in the present Convention, do not apply except between Contracting Powers, and then only if all the belligerents are parties to the Convention.

ARTICLE 3

A belligerent party which violates the provisions of the said Regulations shall, if the case demands, be liable to pay compensation. It shall be responsible for all acts committed by persons forming part of its armed forces.

ARTICLE 4

The present Convention, duly ratified, shall as between the Contracting Powers, be substituted for the Convention of the 29th July, 1899, respecting the Laws and Customs of War on Land.

The Convention of 1899 remains in force as between the Powers which signed it, and which do not also ratify the present Convention.

ARTICLE 5

The present Convention shall be ratified as soon as possible.

The ratifications shall be deposited at The Hague.

The first deposit of ratifications shall be recorded in a procès-verbal signed by the Representatives of the Powers which take part therein and by the Netherlands Minister for Foreign Affairs.

The subsequent deposits of ratifications shall be made by means of a written notification, addressed to the Netherlands Government and accompanied by the instrument of ratification.

A duly certified copy of the procès-verbal relative to the first deposit of ratifications, of the notifications mentioned in the preceding paragraph, as well as of the instruments of ratifications, shall be immediately sent by the Netherlands Government, through the diplomatic channel, to the Powers

---

1. The Preamble to this Convention (No. IV) which contains the famous "De Martens clause," after its author Feodor de Martens, the principle Russian delegate to the First and Second Hague Peace Conferences of 1899 and 1907 has been omitted. The "De Martens Clause" provides:

Until a more complete code of the laws of war has been issued, the High Contracting Parties deem it expedient to declare that, in cases not included in the Regulations adopted by them, the inhabitants and the belligerents remain under the protection and the rule of the principles of the law of nations, as they result from the usages established among civilized peoples, from the laws of humanity, and from the dictates of the public conscience.

invited to the Second Peace Conference, as well as to the other Powers which have adhered to the Convention. In the cases contemplated in the preceding paragraph the said Government shall at the same time inform them of the date on which it received the notification.

ARTICLE 6

Non–Signatory Powers may adhere to the present Convention.

The Power which desires to adhere notifies in writing its intention to the Netherlands Government, forwarding to it the act of adhesion, which shall be deposited in the archives of the said Government.

This Government shall at once transmit to all the other Powers a duly certified copy of the notification as well as the act of adhesion, mentioning the date on which it received the notification.

ARTICLE 7

The present Convention shall come into force, in the case of the Powers which were a party to the first deposit of ratifications, sixty days after the date of the procès-verbal of this deposit, and, in the case of the Powers which ratify subsequently or which adhere, sixty days after the notification of their ratification or of their adhesion has been received by the Netherlands Government.

ARTICLE 8

In the event of one of the Contracting Powers wishing to denounce the present Convention, the denunciation shall be notified in writing to the Netherlands Government, which shall at once communicate a duly certified copy of the notification to all the other Powers, informing them of the date on which it was received.

The denunciation shall only have effect in regard to the notifying Power, and one year after the notification has reached the Netherlands Government.

ARTICLE 9

A register kept by the Netherlands Ministry for Foreign Affairs shall give the date of the deposit of ratifications made in virtue of Article 5, paragraphs 3 and 4, as well as the date on which the notifications of adhesion (Article 6, paragraph 2) or of denunciation (Article 8, paragraph 1) were received.

Each Contracting Power is entitled to have access to this register and to be supplied with duly certified extracts.

ANNEX TO THE CONVENTION
REGULATIONS RESPECTING THE LAWS AND CUSTOMS OF WAR ON LAND
SECTION 1.   ON BELLIGERENTS
CHAPTER I.   *The Qualifications of Belligerents*
ARTICLE 1

The laws, rights, and duties of war apply not only to armies, but also to militia and volunteer corps fulfilling the following conditions:

    1.   To be commanded by a person responsible for his subordinates;

    2.   To have a fixed distinctive emblem recognizable at a distance;

    3.   To carry arms openly; and

4. To conduct their operations in accordance with the laws and customs of war.

In countries where militia or volunteer corps constitute the army, or form part of it, they are included under the denomination "army".

* * *

SECTION II. HOSTILITIES

CHAPTER I. *Means of Injuring the Enemy, Sieges, and Bombardments*

ARTICLE 22

The right of belligerents to adopt means of injuring the enemy is not unlimited.

ARTICLE 23

In addition to the prohibitions provided by special Conventions, it is especially forbidden:

(a) To employ poison or poisoned weapons;

(b) To kill or wound treacherously individuals belonging to the hostile nation or army;

(c) To kill or wound an enemy who, having laid down his arms, or having no longer means of defence, has surrendered at discretion;

(d) To declare that no quarter will be given;

(e) To employ arms, projectiles, or material calculated to cause unnecessary suffering;

(f) To make improper use of a flag of truce, of the national flag, or of the military insignia and uniform of the enemy, as well as the distinctive badges of the Geneva Convention;

(g) To destroy or seize the enemy's property, unless such destruction or seizure be imperatively demanded by the necessities of war;

(h) To declare abolished, suspended, or inadmissible in a Court of law the rights and actions of the nationals of the hostile party.

A belligerent is likewise forbidden to compel the nationals of the hostile party to take part in the operations of war directed against their own country, even if they were in the belligerent's service before the commencement of the war.

ARTICLE 24

Ruses of war and the employment of measures necessary for obtaining information about the enemy and the country are considered permissible.

ARTICLE 25

The attack or bombardment, by whatever means, of towns, villages, dwellings, or buildings which are undefended is prohibited.

ARTICLE 26

The officer in command of an attacking force must, before commencing a bombardment, except in cases of assault, do all in his power to warn the authorities.

ARTICLE 27

In sieges and bombardments all necessary steps must be taken to spare, as far as possible, buildings dedicated to religion, art, science, or charitable purposes, historic monuments, hospitals, and places where the sick and wounded are collected, provided they are not being used at the time for military purposes.

It is the duty of the besieged to indicate the presence of such buildings or places by distinctive and visible signs, which shall be notified to the enemy beforehand.

ARTICLE 28

The pillage of a town or place, even when taken by assault, is prohibited.

* * *

7.19 GENEVA CONVENTION (NO. IV) RELATIVE TO THE PROTECTION OF CIVILIAN PERSONS IN TIME OF WAR (WITHOUT ANNEXES).[1] Concluded at Geneva, 12 August 1949. Entered into force, 21 October 1950. 75 U.N.T.S. 287, 6 T.S. 3114, T.I.A.S. No. 3362: *Arts. 2, 53, 146, 147, 158*

* * *

ARTICLE 2

In addition to the provisions which shall be implemented in peacetime, the present Convention shall apply to all cases of declared war or of any other armed conflict which may arise between two or more of the High Contracting Parties, even if the state of war is not recognized by one of them.

The Convention shall also apply to all cases of partial or total occupation of the territory of a High Contracting Party, even if the said occupation meets with no armed resistance.

Although one of the Powers in conflict may not be a party to the present Convention, the Powers who are parties thereto shall remain bound by it in their mutual relations. They shall furthermore be bound by the Convention in relation to the said Power, if the latter accepts and applies the provisions thereof.

* * *

ARTICLE 53

Any destruction by the Occupying Power of real or personal property belonging individually or collectively to private persons, or to the State, or to other public authorities, or to social or cooperative organizations, is prohibited, except where such destruction is rendered absolutely necessary by military operations.

* * *

ARTICLE 146

The High Contracting Parties undertake to enact any legislation necessary to provide effective penal sanctions for persons committing, or ordering to be committed, any of the grave breaches of the present Convention defined in the following Article.

Each High Contracting Party shall be under the obligation to search for persons alleged to have committed, or to have ordered to be committed, such grave breaches, and shall bring such persons, regardless of their nationality, before its own courts. It may also, if it prefers, and in accordance with the provisions of its own legislation, hand such persons over for trial to another High Contracting Party concerned, provided such High Contracting Party has made out a prima facie case.

Each High Contracting Party shall take measures necessary for the suppression of all acts contrary to the provisions of the present Convention other than the grave breaches defined in the following Article.

In all circumstances, the accused persons shall benefit by safeguards of proper trial and defence, which shall not be less favourable than those

1. *See also* Basic Document 7.23, *infra.*

provided by Article 105 and those following of the Geneva Convention relative to the Treatment of Prisoners of War of August 12, 1949.

ARTICLE 147

Grave breaches to which the preceding Article relates shall be those involving any of the following acts, if committed against persons or property protected by the present Convention: wilful killing, torture or inhuman treatment, including biological experiments, wilfully causing great suffering or serious injury to body or health, unlawful deportation or transfer or unlawful confinement of a protected person, compelling a protected person to serve in the forces of a hostile Power, or wilfully depriving a protected person of the right of fair and regular trial prescribed in the present Convention, taking of hostages and extensive destruction and appropriation of property, not justified by military necessity and carried out unlawfully and wantonly.

* * *

ARTICLE 158

Each of the High Contracting Parties shall be at liberty to denounce the present Convention.

The denunciation shall be notified in writing to the Swiss Federal Council, which shall transmit it to the Governments of all the High Contracting Parties.

The denunciation shall take effect one year after the notification thereof has been made to the Swiss Federal Council. However, a denunciation of which notification has been made at a time when the denouncing Power is involved in a conflict shall not take effect until peace has been concluded, and until after operations connected with the release, repatriation and re-establishment of the person protected by the present Convention have been terminated.

The denunciation shall have effect only in respect of the denouncing Power. It shall in no way impair the obligations which the Parties to the conflict shall remain bound to fulfil by virtue of the principles of the law of nations, as they result from the usages established among civilized peoples, from the laws of humanity and the dictates of the public conscience.

7.20 PRINCIPLES OF INTERNATIONAL LAW RECOGNIZED IN THE CHARTER OF THE NUREMBERG TRIBUNAL AND IN THE JUDGMENT OF THE TRIBUNAL.[1] Adopted by the U.N. International Law Commission, 2 August 1950. 2 Y.B.I.L.C. 374 (1950)

PRINCIPLE I

Any person who commits an act which constitutes a crime under international law is responsible therefor and liable to punishment.

98.   This principle is based on the first paragraph of article 6 of the Charter of the Nuremberg Tribunal which established the competence of the Tribunal to try and punish persons who, acting in the interests of the European Axis countries, whether as individuals or as members of organizations, committed any of the crimes defined in sub-paragraphs (a), (b) and (c) of article 6.   The text of the Charter declared punishable only persons "acting in the interests of the European Axis countries" but, as a matter of course, Principle I is now formulated in general terms.

99.   The general rule underlying Principle I is that international law may impose duties on individuals directly without any interposition of internal law.   The findings of the Tribunal were very definite on the question whether rules of international law may apply to individuals.   "That international law imposes duties and liabilities upon individuals as well as upon States", said the judgment of the Tribunal, "has long been recognized".   It added: "Crimes against international law are committed by men, not by abstract entities, and only by punishing individuals who commit such crimes can the provision of international law be enforced."

PRINCIPLE II

The fact that internal law does not impose a penalty for an act which constitutes a crime under international law does not relieve the person who committed the act from responsibility under international law.

100.   This principle is a corollary to Principle I.   Once it is admitted that individuals are responsible for crimes under international law, it is obvious that they are not relieved from their international responsibility by the fact that their acts are not held to be crimes under the law of any particular country.

101.   The Charter of the Nurnberg Tribunal referred, in express terms, to this relation between international and national responsibility only with respect to crimes against humanity.   Sub-paragraph (c) of article 6 of the Charter defined as crimes against humanity certain acts "whether or not [committed] in violation of the domestic law of the country where perpetrated".   The Commission has formulated Principle II in general terms.

102.   The principle that a person who has committed an international crime is responsible therefore and liable to punishment under international law, independently of the provisions of internal law, implies what is commonly called the "supremacy" of international law over national law.   The Tribunal considered that international law can bind individuals even if national law does not direct them to observe the rules of international law, as shown by

---

1.   *See also* Affirmation of the Principles of International Law Recognized by the Charter of the Nuremberg Tribunal, GA Res. 95, 1st Sess., Supp. for 23 Oct.–15 Dec. 1946, at 188, UN Doc. A/236 (1946).

the following statement of the judgment: "* * * the very essence of the Charter is that individuals have international duties which transcend the national obligations of obedience imposed by the individual State".

PRINCIPLE III

The fact that a person who committed an act which constitutes a crime under international law acted as Head of State or responsible Government official does not relieve him from responsibility under international law.

103. This principle is based on article 7 of the Charter of the Nurnberg Tribunal. According to the Charter and the judgment, the act that an individual acted as Head of State or responsible government official did not relieve him from international responsibility. "The principle of international law which, under certain circumstances, protects the representatives of a State", said the Tribunal, "cannot be applied to acts which are condemned as criminal by international law. The authors of these acts cannot shelter themselves behind their official position in order to be freed from punishment...." The same idea was also expressed in the following passage of the findings: "He who violates the laws of war cannot obtain immunity while acting in pursuance of the authority of the State if the State in authorizing action moves outside its competence under international law."

104. The last phrase of article 7 of the Charter, "or mitigating punishment", has not been retained in the formulation of Principle III. The Commission considers that the question of mitigating punishment is a matter for the competent court to decide.

PRINCIPLE IV

The fact that a person acted pursuant to order of his Government or of a superior does not relieve him from responsibility under international law, provided a moral choice was in fact possible to him.

105. This text is based on the principle contained in article 88 of the Charter of the Nurnberg Tribunal as interpreted in the judgment. The idea expressed in Principle IV is that superior orders are not a defence provided a moral choice was possible to the accused. In conformity with this conception, the Tribunal rejected the argument of the defence that there could not be any responsibility since most of the defendants acted under the orders of Hitler. The Tribunal declared: "The provisions of this article [article 8] are in conformity with the law of all nations. That a soldier was ordered to kill or torture in violation of the international law of war has never been recognized as a defence to such acts of brutality, though, as the Charter here provides, the order may be urged in mitigation of the punishment. The true test, which is found in varying degrees in the criminal law of most nations, is not the existence of the order but whether moral choice was in fact possible."

106. The last phrase of article 88 of the Charter "but may be considered in mitigation of punishment, if the Tribunal determines that justice so requires", has not been retained for the reason stated under Principle III, in paragraph 104 above.

PRINCIPLE V

Any person charged with a crime under international law has the right to a fair trial on the facts and law.

107. The principle that a defendant charged with a crime under international law must have the right to a fair trial was expressly recognized and

carefully developed by the Charter of the Nurnberg Tribunal. The Charter contained a chapter entitled: "Fair Trial for Defendants," which for the purpose of ensuring such fair trial provided the following procedure:

"a   The indictment shall include full particulars specifying in details the charges against the defendants. A copy of the indictment and of all the documents lodged with the indictment, translated into a language which he understands, shall be furnished to the defendant at a reasonable time before the trial.

"b   During any preliminary examination or trial of a defendant he shall have the right to give any explanation relevant to the charges made against him.

"c   A preliminary examination of a defendant and his trial shall be conducted in, or translated into, a language which the defendant understands.

"d   A defendant shall have the right to conduct his own defence before the Tribunal or to have the assistance of counsel.

"e   A defendant shall have the right through himself or through his counsel to present evidence at the trial in support of his defence, and to cross-examine any witness called by the prosecution."

108.   The right to a fair trial was also referred to in the judgment itself. The Tribunal said in this respect: "With regard to the constitution of the Court all that the defendants are entitled to ask is to receive a fair trial on the facts and law."

109.   In the view of the Commission, the expression "fair trial" should be understood in the light of the above-quoted provisions of the Charter of the Nurnberg Tribunal.

PRINCIPLE VI

The crimes hereinafter set out are punishable as crimes under international law:

a   *Crimes against peace:*

(i) *Planning, preparation, initiation or waging of a war of aggression or a war in violation of international treaties, agreements or assurances;*

(ii) *Participation in a common plan or conspiracy for the accomplishment of any of the acts mentioned under (i).*

110.   Both categories of crimes are characterized by the fact that they are connected with "war of aggression or war in violation of international treaties, agreements or assurances".

111.   The Tribunal made a general statement to the effect that its Charter was "the expression of international law existing at the time to its creation". It, in particular, refuted the argument of the defence that aggressive war was not an international crime. For this refutation the Tribunal relied primarily on the General Treaty for the Renunciation of War of 27 August 1928 (Kellogg–Briand Pact) which in 1939 was in force between sixty-three States. "The nations who signed the Pact or adhered to it uncondition-

ally", said the Tribunal, "condemned recourse to war for the future as an instrument of policy, and expressly renounced it. After the signing of the Pact, any nation resorting to war as an instrument of national policy breaks the Pact. In the opinion of the Tribunal, the solemn renunciation of war as an instrument of national policy necessarily involves the proposition that such a war is illegal in international law; and that those who planned and waged such a war, with its inevitable and terrible consequences, are committing a crime in so doing. War for the solution of international controversies undertaken as an instrument of national policy certainly includes a war of aggression, and such a war is therefore outlawed by the Pact".

112. In support of its interpretation of the Kellogg–Briand Pact, the Tribunal cited some other international instruments which condemned war of aggression as an international crime. The draft of a Treaty of Mutual Assistance sponsored by the League of Nations in 1923 declared, in its article 1, "that aggressive war is an international crime". The Preamble to the League of Nations Protocol for the Pacific Settlement of International disputes (Geneva Protocol), of 1924, "recognizing the solidarity of the members of the International Community", stated that "a war of aggression constitutes a violation of this solidarity, and is an international crime", and that the contracting parties were "desirous of facilitating the complete application of the system provided in the Covenant of the League of Nations for the pacific settlement of disputes between the States and of ensuring the repression of international crimes". The declaration concerning wars of aggression adopted on 24 September 1927 by the Assembly of the League of Nations declared, in its preamble, that war was an "international crime". The resolution unanimously adopted on 18 February 1928 by twenty-one American Republics at the Sixth (Havana) International Conference of American States, provided that "war of aggression constitutes an international crime against the human species".

113. The Charter of the Nurnberg Tribunal did not contain any definition of "war of aggression", nor was there any such definition in the judgment of the Tribunal. It was by reviewing the historical events before and during the war that it found that certain of the defendants planned and waged aggressive wars against twelve nations and were therefore guilty of a series of crimes.

114. According to the Tribunal, this made it unnecessary to discuss the subject in further detail, or to consider at any length the extent to which these aggressive wars were also "wars in violation of international treaties, agreements, or assurances".

115. The term "assurances" is understood by the Commission as including any pledge or guarantee of peace given by a State, even unilaterally.

116. The terms "planning" and "preparation" of a war of aggression were considered by the Tribunal as comprising all the stages in the bringing about of a war of aggression from the planning to the actual initiation of the war. In view of that, the Tribunal did not make any clear distinction between planning and preparation. As stated in the judgment, "planning and preparation are essential to the making of war".

117. The meaning of the expression "waging of a war of aggression" was discussed in the Commission during the consideration of the definition of

"crimes against peace". Some members of the Commission feared that everyone in uniform who fought in a war of aggression might be charged with the "waging" of such a war. The Commission understands the expression to refer only to high ranking military personnel and high State officials, and believes that this was also the view of the Tribunal.

118. A legal notion of the Charter to which the defence objected was the one concerning "conspiracy". The Tribunal recognized that "conspiracy is not defined in the Charter". However, it stated the meaning of the term, though only in a restricted way. "But in the opinion of the Tribunal", it was said in the judgment, "the conspiracy must be clearly outlined in its criminal purpose. It must not be too far removed from the time of decision and of action. The planning, to be criminal, must not rest merely on the declarations of a party programme such as are found in the twenty-five points of the Nazi Party, announced in 1920, or the political affirmations expressed in *Mein Kampf* in later years. The Tribunal must examine whether a concrete plan to wage war existed, and determine the participants in that concrete plan".

b *War crimes:*

Violations of the laws or customs of war which include, but are not limited to, murder, ill-treatment or deportation to slave-labour or for any other purpose of civilian population of or in occupied territory, murder or ill-treatment of prisoners of war, of persons on the seas, killing of hostages, plunder of public or private property, wanton destruction of cities, towns, or villages, or devastation not justified by military necessity.

119. The Tribunal emphasized that before the last war the crimes defined by article 6(b) of its Charter were already recognized as crimes under international law. The Tribunal stated that such crimes were covered by specific provisions of the Regulations annexed to The Hague Convention of 1907 respecting the Laws and Customs of War on Land and of the Geneva Convention of 1929 on the Treatment of Prisoners of War. After enumerating the said provisions, the Tribunal stated: "That violation of these provisions constituted crimes for which the guilty individuals were punishable is too well settled to admit or argument."

c *Crimes against humanity:*

Murder, extermination, enslavement, deportation and other inhuman acts done against any civilian population, or persecutions on political, racial or religious grounds, when such acts are done or such persecutions are carried on in execution of or in connexion with any crime against peace or any war crime.

120. Article 6(c) of the Charter of the Nurnberg Tribunal distinguished two categories of punishable acts, to wit: first, murder, extermination, enslavement, deportation and other inhuman acts committed against any civilian population, before or during the war, and second, persecution on political, racial or religious grounds. Acts within these categories, according to the Charter, constituted international crimes only when committed "in execution of or in connexion with any crimes within the jurisdiction of the Tribunal". The crimes referred to as falling, within the jurisdiction of the Tribunal were crimes against peace and war crimes.

121. Though it found that "political opponents were murdered in Germany before the war, and that many of them were kept in concentration camps in circumstances of great horror and cruelty", that "the policy of

persecution, repression and murder of civilians in Germany before the war of 1939, who were likely to be hostile to the Government, was most ruthlessly carried out", and that "the persecution of Jews during the same period is established beyond all doubt", the Tribunal considered that it had not been satisfactorily proved that before the outbreak of war these acts had been committed in execution of, or in connexion with, any crime within the jurisdiction of the Tribunal. For this reason the Tribunal declared itself unable to "make a general declaration that the acts before 1939 were crimes against humanity within the meaning of the Charter".

122. The Tribunal did not, however, thereby exclude the possibility that crimes against humanity might be committed also before a war.

123. In its definition of crimes against humanity the Commission has omitted the phrase "before or during the war" contained in article 6(c) of the Charter of the Nurnberg Tribunal because this phrase referred to a particular war, the war of 1939. The omission of the phrase does not mean that the Commission considers that crimes against humanity can be committed only during a War. On the contrary, the Commission is of the opinion that such crimes may take place also before a war in connexion with crimes against peace.

124. In accordance with article 6(c) of the Charter, the above formulation characterizes as crimes against humanity murder, extermination, enslavement, etc., committed against "any" civilian population. This means that these acts may be crimes against humanity even if they are committed by the perpetrator against his own population.

PRINCIPLE VII

Complicity in the commission of a crime against peace, a war crime, or a crime against humanity as set forth in Principle VI is a crime under international law.

125. The only provision in the Charter of the Nurnberg Tribunal regarding responsibility for complicity was that of the last paragraph of article 6 which reads as follows: "Leaders, organizers, instigators and accomplices participating in the formulation or execution of a common plan or conspiracy to commit any of the foregoing crimes are responsible for all acts performed by any persons in execution of such a plan."

126. The Tribunal, commenting on this provision in connexion with its discussion of count one of the indictment, which charged certain defendants with conspiracy to commit aggressive war, war crimes and crimes against humanity, said that, in its opinion, the provision did not "add a new and separate crime to those already listed". In the view of the Tribunal, the provision was designed to "establish the responsibility of persons participating in a common plan" to prepare, initiate and wage aggressive war. Interpreted literally, this statement would seem to imply that the complicity rule did not apply to crimes perpetrated by individual action.

127. On the other hand, the Tribunal convicted several of the defendants of war crimes and crimes against humanity because they gave orders resulting in atrocious and criminal acts which they did not commit themselves. In practice, therefore, the Tribunal seems to have applied general principles of criminal law regarding complicity. This view is corroborated by expressions used by the Tribunal in assessing the guilt of particular defendants.

7.21 DRAFT ARTICLES ON THE DRAFT CODE OF CRIMES AGAINST THE PEACE AND SECURITY OF MANKIND (AS REVISED THROUGH 1991). First adopted by the U.N. International Law Commission, 4 December 1954. G.A. Res. 46/405, U.N. GAOR, 46th Sess., Supp. No. 10, at 198, U.N. Doc. A/46/405 (1991), 30 I.L.M. 1554 (1991)

PART I

CHAPTER 1. DEFINITION AND CHARACTERIZATION

Article 1

Definition

The crimes [under international law] defined in this Code constitute crimes against the peace and security of mankind.

Article 2

Characterization

The characterization of an act or omission as a crime against the peace and security of mankind is independent of internal law. The fact that an act or omission is or is not punishable under internal law does not affect this characterization.

CHAPTER 2. GENERAL PRINCIPLES

Article 3

Responsibility and punishment

1. An individual who commits a crime against the peace and security of mankind is responsible therefore and is liable to punishment.

2. An individual who aids, abets or provides the means for the commission of a crime against the peace and security of mankind or conspires in or directly incites the commission of such a crime is responsible therefore and is liable to punishment.

3. An individual who commits an act constituting an attempt to commit a crime against the peace and security of mankind [as set out in articles * * *] is responsible therefore and is liable to punishment. Attempt means any commencement of execution of a crime that failed or was halted only because of circumstances independent of the perpetrator's intention.

Article 4

Motives

Responsibility for a crime against the peace and security of mankind is not affected by any motives invoked by the accused which are not covered by the definition of the crime.

Article 5

Responsibility of States

Prosecution of an individual for a crime against the peace and security of mankind does not relieve a State of any responsibility under international law for an act or omission attributable to it.

Article 6

Obligation to try or extradite

1. A State in whose territory an individual alleged to have committed a crime against the peace and security of mankind is present shall either try or extradite him.

2. If extradition is requested by several States, special consideration shall be given to the request of the State in whose territory the crime was committed.

3. The provisions of paragraphs 1 and 2 do not prejudge the establishment and the jurisdiction of an international criminal court.

Article 7

Non-applicability of statutory limitations

No statutory limitation shall apply to crimes against the peace and security of mankind.

Article 8

Judicial guarantees

An individual charged with a crime against the peace and security of mankind shall be entitled without discrimination to the minimum guarantees due to all human beings with regard to the law and the facts. In particular, he shall have the right to be presumed innocent until proved guilty and have the rights:

(a) in the determination of any charge against him, to have a fair and public hearing by a competent, independent and impartial tribunal duly established by law or by treaty;

(b) to be informed promptly and in detail in a language which he understands of the nature and cause of the charge against him;

(c) to have adequate time and facilities for the preparation of his defence and to communicate with counsel of his own choosing;

(d) to be tried without undue delay;

(e) to be tried in his presence, and to defend himself in person or through legal assistance of his own choosing; to be informed, if he does not have legal assistance, of this right; and to have legal assistance assigned to him and without payment by him in any such case if he does not have sufficient means to pay for it;

(f) to examine, or have examined, the witnesses against him and to obtain the attendance and examination of witnesses on his behalf under the same conditions as witnesses against him;

(g) to have the free assistance of an interpreter if he cannot understand or speak the language used in court;

(h) not to be compelled to testify against himself or to confess guilt.

Article 9

Non bis in idem

1. No one shall be tried or punished for a crime under this Code for which he has already been finally convicted or acquitted by an international criminal court.

2. Subject to paragraphs 3, 4 and 5, no one shall be tried or punished for a crime under this Code in respect of an act for which he has already been finally convicted or acquitted by a national court, provided that, if a punishment was imposed, it has been enforced or is in the process of being.

3. Notwithstanding the provisions of paragraph 2, an individual may be tried and punished by an international criminal court or by a national court for a crime under this Code if the act which was the subject of a trial and judgement as an ordinary crime corresponds to one of the crimes characterized in this Code.

4. Notwithstanding the provisions of paragraph 2, an individual may be tried and punished by a national court of another State for a crime under the Code:

(a) if the act which was the subject of the previous judgement took place in the territory of that State; or

(b) if that State has been the main victim of the crime.

5. In the case of a subsequent conviction under this Code, the court, in passing sentence, shall deduct any penalty imposed and implemented as a result of a previous conviction for the same act.

Article 10
Non-retroactivity

1. No one shall be convicted under this Code for acts committed before its entry into force.

2. Nothing in this article shall preclude the trial and punishment of anyone for any act which, at the time when it was committed, was criminal in accordance with international law or domestic law applicable in conformity with international law.

Article 11
Order of a Government or a superior

The fact that an individual charged with a crime against the peace and security of mankind acted pursuant to an order of a Government or a superior does not relieve him of criminal responsibility if, in the circumstances at the time, it was possible for him not to comply with that order.

Article 12
Responsibility of the superior

The fact that a crime against the peace and security of mankind was committed by a subordinate does not relieve his superiors of criminal responsibility, if they knew or had information enabling them to conclude, in the circumstances at the time, that the subordinate was committing or was going to commit such a crime and if they did not take all feasible measures within their power to prevent or repress the crime.

Article 13
Official position and responsibility

The official position of an individual who commits a crime against the peace and security of mankind, and particularly the fact that he acts as head of State or Government, does not relieve him of criminal responsibility.

Article 14
Defences and extenuating circumstances

1. The competent court shall determine the admissibility of defences under the general principles of law, in the light of the character of each crime.

2. In passing sentence, the court shall, where appropriate, take into account extenuating circumstances.

PART II
CRIMES AGAINST THE PEACE AND SECURITY OF MANKIND
Article 15
Aggression

1. An individual who as leader or organizer plans, commits, or orders the commission of an act of aggression shall, on conviction thereof, be sentenced [to * * *].

2. Aggression is the use of armed force by a State against the sovereignty, territorial integrity or political independence of another State, or in any other manner inconsistent with the Charter of the United Nations.

3. The first use of armed force by a State in contravention of the Charter shall constitute prima facie evidence of an act of aggression, although the Security Council may, in conformity with the Charter, conclude that a determination that an act of aggression has been committed would not be justified in the light of other relevant circumstances, including the fact that the acts concerned or their consequences are not of sufficient gravity.

4. Any of the following acts, regardless of a declaration of war, constitutes an act of aggression, due regard being paid to paragraphs 2 and 3:

(a) the invasion or attack by the armed forces of a State of the territory of another State, or any military occupation, however temporary, resulting from such invasion or attack, or any annexation by the use of force of the territory of another State or part thereof;

(b) bombardment by the armed forces of a State against the territory of another State or the use of any weapons by a State against the territory of another State;

(c) the blockade of the port or coasts of a State by the armed forces of another State;

(d) an attack by the armed forces of a State on the land, sea or air forces, or marine and air fleets of another State;

(e) the use of armed forces of one State which are within the territory of another State with the agreement of the receiving State, in contravention of the conditions provided for in the agreement, or any extension of their presence in such territory beyond the termination of the agreement;

(f) the action of a State in allowing its territory, which it has placed at the disposal of another State, to be used by that other State for perpetrating an act of aggression against a third State;

(g) the sending by or on behalf of a State of armed bands, groups, irregulars or mercenaries, which carry out acts of armed force against another State of such gravity as to amount to the acts listed above, or its substantial involvement therein;

(h) any other acts determination by the Security Council as constituting acts of aggression under the provisions of the Charter;

[5. Any determination by the Security Council as to the existence of an act of aggression is binding on national courts.]

6. Nothing in this article shall be interpreted as in any way enlarging or diminishing the scope of the Charter of the United Nations including its provisions concerning cases in which the use of force is lawful.

7. Nothing in this article could in any way prejudice the right to self-determination, freedom and independence, as derived from the Charter, of peoples forcibly deprived of that right and referred to in the Declaration on Principles of International Law concerning Friendly Relations and Cooperation among States in accordance with the Charter of the United Nations, particularly peoples under colonial and racist regimes or other forms of alien domination, nor the right of these peoples to struggle to that end and to seek and receive support, in accordance with the principles of the Charter and in conformity with the above-mentioned Declaration.

Article 16
Threat of aggression

1. An individual who as leader or organizer commits or orders the commission of a threat of aggression shall, on conviction thereof, be sentenced [to * * *].

2. Threat of aggression consists of declarations, communications, demonstrations of force or any other measures which would give good reason to the Government of a State to believe that aggression is being seriously contemplated against that State.

Article 17
Intervention

1. An individual who as leader or organizer commits or orders the commission of an act of intervention in the internal or external affairs of a State shall, on conviction thereof, be sentenced [to * * *].

2. Intervention in the internal or external affairs of a State consists of fomenting [armed] subversive or terrorist activities or by organizing, assisting or financing such activities, or supplying arms for the purpose of such activities, thereby [seriously] undermining the free exercise by that State of its sovereign rights.

3. Nothing in this article shall in any way prejudice the right of peoples to self-determination as enshrined in the Charter of the United Nations.

Article 18
Colonial domination and other forms of alien domination

An individual who as leader or organizer establishes or maintains by force or orders the establishment or maintenance by force of colonial domination or any other form of alien domination contrary to the right of peoples to self-determination as enshrined in the Charter of the United Nations, shall, on conviction thereof, be sentenced [to * * *].

Article 19
Genocide

1. An individual who commits or orders the commission of an act of genocide shall, on conviction thereof, be sentenced [to * * *].

2. Genocide means any of the following acts committed with intent to destroy, in whole or in part, a national, ethnic, racial or religious group as such:

(a) killing members of the group;

(b) causing serious bodily or mental harm to members of the group;

(c) deliberately inflicting on the group conditions of life calculated to bring about its physical destruction in whole or in part;

(d) imposing measures intended to prevent births within the group.

Article 20

Apartheid

1. An individual who as leader or organizer commits or orders the commission of the crime of apartheid shall, on conviction thereof, be sentenced [to * * *].

2. Apartheid consists of any of the following acts based on policies and practices of racial segregation and discrimination committed for the purpose of establishing or maintaining domination by one racial group over any other racial group and systematically oppressing it:

(a) denial to a member or members of a racial group of the right to life and liberty of person;

(b) deliberate imposition on a racial group of living conditions calculated to cause its physical destruction in whole or in part;

(c) any legislative measures and other measures calculated to prevent a racial group from participating in the political, social, economic and cultural life of the country and the deliberate creation of conditions preventing the full development of such a group;

(d) any measures, including legislative measures, designated to divide the population along racial lines, in particular by the creation of separate reserves and ghettos for the members of a racial group, the prohibition of marriages among members of various racial groups or the expropriation of landed property belonging to a racial group or to members thereof;

(e) exploitation of the labour of the members of a racial group, in particular by submitting them to forced labour;

(f) persecution of organizations and persons, by depriving them of fundamental rights and freedoms, because they oppose apartheid.

Article 21

Systematic or mass violations of human rights

An individual who commits or orders the commission of any of the following violations of human rights:

— murder

— torture

— establishing or maintaining over persons a status of slavery, servitude or forced labour

— persecution on social, political, racial, religious or cultural grounds in a systematic manner or on a mass scale; or

— deportation or forcible transfer of population shall, on conviction thereof, be sentenced [to * * *].

Article 22
Exceptionally serious war crimes

1. An individual who commits or orders the commission of an exceptionally serious war crime shall, on conviction thereof, be sentenced [to * * *].

2. For the purposes of this Code, an exceptionally serious war crime is an exceptionally serious violation of principles and rules of international law applicable in armed conflict consisting of any of the following acts:

(a) acts of inhumanity, cruelty or barbarity directed against the life, dignity or physical or mental integrity of persons[, in particular wilful killing, torture, mutilation, biological experiments, taking of hostages, compelling a protected person to serve in the forces of a hostile Power, unjustifiable delay in the repatriation of prisoners of war after the cessation of active hostilities, deportation or transfer of the civilian population and collective punishment];

(b) establishment of settlers in an occupied territory and changes to the demographic composition of an occupied territory;

(c) use of unlawful weapons;

(d) employing methods or means of warfare which are intended or may be expected to cause widespread, long-term and severe damage to the natural environment;

(e) large-scale destruction of civilian property;

(f) wilful attacks on property of exceptional religious, historical or cultural value.

Article 23
Recruitment, use, financing and training of mercenaries

1. An individual who as an agent or representative of a State commits or orders the commission of any of the following acts:

— recruitment, use, financing or training of mercenaries for activities directed against another State or for the purpose of opposing the legitimate exercise of the inalienable right of peoples to self-determination as recognized under international law

shall, on conviction thereof, be sentenced [to * * *].

2. A mercenary is any individual who:

(a) is specially recruited locally or abroad in order to fight in an armed conflict;

(b) is motivated to take part in the hostilities essentially by the desire for private gain and, in fact, is promised, by or on behalf of a party to the conflict, material compensation substantially in excess of that promised or paid to combatants of similar rank and functions in the armed forces of that party;

(c) is neither a national or a party to the conflict nor a resident of territory controlled by a party to the conflict;

(d) is not a member of the armed forces of a party to the conflict; and

(e) has not been sent by a State which is not a party to the conflict on official duty as a member of its armed forces.

3. A mercenary is also any individual who, in any other situation:

(a) is specially recruited locally or abroad for the purpose of participating in a concerted act of violence aimed at:

(i) overthrowing a Government or otherwise undermining the constitution order of a State; or

(ii) undermining the territorial integrity of a State;

(b) is motivated to take part therein essentially by the desire for significant private gain and is prompted by the promise or payment of material compensation;

(c) is neither a national nor a resident of the State against which such an act is directed;

(d) has not been sent by a State on official duty; and

(e) is not a member of the armed forces of the State is whose territory the act is undertaken.

Article 24
International terrorism

An individual who as an agent or representative of a State commits or orders the commission of any of the following acts:

— undertaking, organizing, assisting, financing, encouraging or tolerating act against another State directed at persons or property and of such a nature as to create a state of terror in the minds of public figures, groups of persons or the general public

shall, on conviction thereof, be sentenced [to * * *].

Article 25
Illicit traffic in narcotic drugs

1. An individual who commits or orders the commission of any of the following acts:

— undertaking, organizing, facilitating, financing or encouraging illicit traffic in narcotic drugs on a large scale, whether within the confines of a State or in a transboundary context

shall, on conviction thereof, be sentenced [to * * *].

2. For the purposes of paragraph 1, facilitating or encouraging illicit traffic in narcotic drugs includes the acquisition, holding, conversion or transfer of property by an individual who knows that such property is derived from the crime described in this article in order to conceal or disguise the illicit origin of the property.

3. Illicit traffic in narcotic drugs means any production, manufacture, extraction, preparation, offering, offering for sale, distribution, sale, delivery

on any terms whatsoever, brokerage, dispatch, dispatch in transit, transport, importation or exportation of any narcotic drug or any psychotropic substance contrary to international law.

Article 26
Wilful and severe damage to the environment

An individual who wilfully causes or orders the causing of widespread, long-term and severe damage to the natural environment shall, on conviction thereof, be sentenced [to * * *].

7.22   TREATY ON THE NON–PROLIFERATION OF NUCLEAR WEAPONS. Concluded at London, Moscow, and Washington, 1 July 1968. Entered into force, 5 March 1970. 729 U.N.T.S. 161, 21 T.S. 483, T.I.A.S. No. 6839, 7 I.L.M. 809 (1968): *Arts. III, VI*

Article III

1.   Each non-nuclear-weapon State Party to the Treaty undertakes to accept safeguards, as set forth in an agreement to be negotiated and concluded with the International Atomic Energy Agency in accordance with the Statute of the International Atomic Energy Agency and the Agency's safeguards system, for the exclusive purpose of verification of the fulfilment of its obligations assumed under this Treaty with a view to preventing diversion of nuclear energy from peaceful uses to nuclear weapons or other nuclear explosive devices. Procedures for the safeguards required by this Article shall be followed with respect to source or special fissionable material whether it is being produced, processed or used in any principal nuclear facility or is outside any such facility. The safeguards required by this Article shall be applied on all source or special fissionable material in all peaceful nuclear activities within the territory of such State, under its jurisdiction, or carried out under its control anywhere.

2.   Each State Party to the Treaty undertakes not to provide: (a) source or special fissionable material, or (b) equipment or material especially designed or prepared for the processing, use or production of special fissionable material, to any non-nuclear-weapon State for peaceful purposes, unless the source or special fissionable material shall be subject to the safeguards required by this Article.

3.   The safeguards required by this Article shall be implemented in a manner designed to comply with Article IV of this Treaty, and to avoid hampering the economic or technological development of the Parties or international co-operation in the field of peaceful nuclear activities, including the international exchange of nuclear material and equipment for the processing, use or production of nuclear material for peaceful purposes in accordance with the provisions of this Article and the principle of safeguarding set forth in the Preamble of the Treaty.

4.   Non-nuclear-weapon States Party to the Treaty shall conclude agreements with the International Atomic Energy Agency to meet the requirements of this Article either individually or together with other States in accordance with the Statute of the International Atomic Energy Agency. Negotiation of such agreements shall commence within 180 days from the original entry into force of this Treaty. For States depositing their instruments of ratification or accession after the 180–day period, negotiation of such agreements shall commence not later than the date of such deposit. Such agreements shall enter into force not later than eighteen months after the date of initiation of negotiations.

* * *

Article VI

Each of the Parties to the Treaty undertakes to pursue negotiations in good faith on effective measures relating to cessation of the nuclear arms race at an early date and to nuclear disarmament, and on a treaty on general and complete disarmament under strict and effective international control.

7.23 CONVENTION ON THE PROHIBITION OF MILITARY OR ANY OTHER HOSTILE USE OF ENVIRONMENTAL MODIFICATION TECHNIQUES (ENMOD) (WITHOUT ANNEX). Adopted by the U.N. General Assembly, 10 December 1976. Entered into force, 5 October 1978. 1108 U.N.T.S. 151, 31 T.S. 333, T.I.A.S. No. 9614, 16 I.L.M. 88 (1977)

The States Parties to this Convention,

Guided by the interest of consolidating peace, and wishing to contribute to the cause of halting the arms race, and of bringing about general and complete disarmament under strict and effective international control, and of saving mankind from the danger of using new means of warfare,

Determined to continue negotiations with a view to achieving effective progress towards further measures in the field of disarmament,

Recognizing that scientific and technical advances may open new possibilities with respect to modification of the environment,

Recalling the Declaration of the United Nations Conference on the Human Environment, adopted at Stockholm on 16 June 1972,

Realizing that the use of environmental modification techniques for peaceful purposes could improve the interrelationship of man and nature and contribute to the preservation and improvement of the environment for the benefit of present and future generations,

Recognizing, however, that military or any other hostile use of such techniques could have effects extremely harmful to human welfare,

Desiring to prohibit effectively military or any other hostile use of environmental modification techniques in order to eliminate the dangers to mankind from such use, and affirming their willingness to work towards the achievement of this objective,

Desiring also to contribute to the strengthening of trust among nations and to the further improvement of the international situation in accordance with the purposes and principles of the Charter of the United Nations,

Have agreed on the following:

Article I

1. Each State Party to this Convention undertakes not to engage in military or any other hostile use of environmental modification techniques having widespread, long-lasting or severe effects as the means of destruction, damage or injury to any other State Party.

2. Each State Party to this Convention undertakes not to assist, encourage or induce any State, group of States or international organization to engage in activities contrary to the provisions of paragraph 1 of this article.

Article II

As used in article I, the term "environmental modification techniques" refers to any technique for changing—through the deliberate manipulation of natural processes—the dynamics, composition or structure of the earth, including its biota, lithosphere, hydrosphere and atmosphere, or of outer space.

Article III

1. The provisions of this Convention shall not hinder the use of environmental modification techniques for peaceful purposes and shall be without prejudice to the generally recognized principles and applicable rules of international law concerning such use.

2. The States Parties to this Convention undertake to facilitate, and have the right to participate in, the fullest possible exchange of scientific and technological information on the use of environmental modification techniques for peaceful purposes. States Parties in a position to do so shall contribute, alone or together with other States or international organizations, to international economic and scientific co-operation in the preservation, improvement and peaceful utilization of the environment, with due consideration for the needs of the developing areas of the world.

Article IV

Each State Party to this Convention undertakes to take any measures it considers necessary in accordance with its constitutional processes to prohibit and prevent any activity in violation of the provisions of the Convention anywhere under its jurisdiction or control.

Article V

1. The States Parties to this Convention undertake to consult one another and to co-operate in solving any problems which may arise in relation to the objectives of, or in the application of the provisions of, the Convention. Consultation and co-operation pursuant to this article may also be undertaken through appropriate international procedures within the framework of the United Nations and in accordance with its Charter. These international procedures may include the services of appropriate international organizations, as well as of a Consultative Committee of Experts as provided for in paragraph 2 of this article.

2. For the purposes set forth in paragraph 1 of this article, the Depositary shall, within one month of the receipt of a request from any State Party to this Convention, convene a Consultative Committee of Experts. Any State Party may appoint an expert to this Committee whose functions and rules of procedure are set out in the annex, which constitutes an integral part of the Convention. The committee shall transmit to the Depositary a summary of its findings of fact, incorporating all views and information presented to the Committee during its proceedings. The Depositary shall distribute the summary to all States Parties.

3. Any State Party to this Convention which has reasons to believe that any other State Party is acting in breach of obligations deriving from the provisions of the Convention may lodge a complaint with the Security Council of the United Nations. Such a complaint should include all relevant information as well as all possible evidence supporting its validity.

4. Each State Party to this Convention undertakes to co-operate in carrying out any investigation which the Security Council may initiate, in accordance with the provisions of the Charter of the United Nations, on the basis of the complaint received by the Council. The Security Council shall inform the States Parties of the results of the investigation.

5. Each State Party to this Convention undertakes to provide or support assistance, in accordance with the provisions of the Charter of the United Nations, to any State Party which so requests, if the Security Council decides that such Party has been harmed or is likely to be harmed as a result of violation of the Convention.

Article VI

1. Any State Party may propose amendments to this Convention. The text of any proposed amendment shall be submitted to the Depositary, who shall promptly circulate it to all States Parties.

2. An amendment shall enter into force for all States Parties which have accepted it, upon the deposit with the Depositary of instruments of acceptance by a majority of States Parties. Thereafter it shall enter into force for any remaining State Party on the date of deposit of its instrument of acceptance.

Article VII

This Convention shall be of unlimited duration.

Article VIII

1. Five years after the entry into force of this Convention, a conference of the States Parties to the Convention shall be convened by the Depositary at Geneva. The conference shall review the operation of the Convention with a view to ensuring that its purposes and provisions are being realized, and shall in particular examine the effectiveness of the provisions of article I, paragraph 1, in eliminating the dangers of military or any other hostile use of environmental modification techniques.

2. At intervals of not less than five years thereafter, a majority of the States Parties to this Convention may obtain, by submitting a proposal to this effect to the Depositary, the convening of a conference with the same objectives.

3. If no review conference has been convened pursuant to paragraph 2 of this article within ten years following the conclusion of a previous review conference, the Depositary shall solicit the views of all States Parties to this Convention on the holding of such a conference. If one third or ten of the States Parties, whichever number is less, respond affirmatively, the Depositary shall take immediate steps to convene the conference.

Article IX

1. This Convention shall be open to all States for signature. Any State which does not sign the Convention before its entry into force in accordance with paragraph 3 of this article may accede to it at any time.

2. This Convention shall be subject to ratification by signatory States. Instruments of ratification and of accession shall be deposited with the Secretary–General of the United Nations.

3. This Convention shall enter into force upon the deposit with the Depositary of instruments of ratification by twenty Governments in accordance with paragraph 2 of this article.

4. For those States whose instruments of ratification or accession are deposited after the entry into force of this Convention, it shall enter into force on the date of the deposit of their instruments of ratification or accession.

5. The Depositary shall promptly inform all signatory and acceding States of the date of each signature, the date of deposit of each instrument of ratification or accession and the date of the entry into force of this Convention and of any amendments thereto, as well as of the receipt of other notices.

6. This Convention shall be registered by the Depositary in accordance with Article 102 of the Charter of the United Nations.

Article X

This Convention, of which the Arabic, Chinese, English, French, Russian and Spanish texts are equally authentic, shall be deposited with the Secretary–General of the United Nations who shall send certified copies thereof to the Governments of the signatory and acceding States.

7.24 PROTOCOL ADDITIONAL (NO. I) TO THE GENEVA CONVENTIONS OF AUGUST 12, 1949, AND RELATING TO THE PROTECTION OF VICTIMS OF INTERNATIONAL ARMED CONFLICTS.[1] Concluded at Geneva, 8 June 1977. Entered into force, 7 December 1978. 1125 U.N.T.S. 3, 16 I.L.M. 1391 (1977): *Arts. 1, 35, 36, 51, 54–58, 85*

Article 1—General principles and scope of application

1.   The High Contracting Parties undertake to respect and to ensure respect for this Protocol in all circumstances.

2.   In cases not covered by this Protocol or by other internation agreements, civilians and combatants remain under the protection and authority of the principles of international law derived from established custom, from the principles of humanity and from dictates of public conscience.

3.   This Protocol, which supplements the Geneva Conventions of 12 August 1949 for the protection of war victims, shall apply in the situations referred to in Article 2 common to those Conventions.

4.   The situations referred to in the preceding paragraph include armed conflicts in which peoples are fighting against colonial domination and alien occupation and against racist regimes in the exercise of their right of self-determination, as enshrined in the Charter of the United Nations and Declaration of Principles of International Law concerning Friendly Relations and Co-operation among States in accordance with the Charter of the United Nations.

* * *

Article 35—Basic rules

1.   In any armed conflict, the right of the Parties to the conflict to choose methods or means of warfare is not unlimited.

2.   It is prohibited to employ weapons, projectiles and material and methods of warfare of a nature to cause superfluous injury or unnecessary suffering.

3.   It is prohibited to employ methods or means of warfare which are intended, or may be expected, to cause widespread, long-term and severe damage to the natural environment.

Article 36—New weapons

In the study, development, acquisition or adoption of a new weapon, means or method of warfare, a High Contracting Party is under an obligation to determine whether its employment would, in some or all circumstances, be prohibited by this Protocol or by any other rule of international law applicable to the High Contracting Party.

* * *

Article 51—Protection of the civilian population

1.   The civilian population and individual civilians shall enjoy general protection against dangers arising from military operations. To give effect to

1. *See Basic* Document 7.18, *supra.*

this protection, the following rules, which are additional to other applicable rules of international law, shall be observed in all circumstances.

2. The civilian population as such, as well as individual civilians, shall not be the object of attack.

Acts or threats of violence the primary purpose of which is to spread terror among the civilian population are prohibited.

3. Civilians shall enjoy the protection afforded by this section, unless and for such time as they take a direct part in hostilities.

4. Indiscriminate attacks are prohibited. Indiscriminate attacks are:

(a) those which are not directed at a specific military objective;

(b) those which employ a method or means of combat which cannot be directed at a specific military objective; or

(c) those which employ a method or means of combat the effects of which cannot be limited as required by this Protocol;

and consequently, in each such case, are of a nature to strike military objectives and civilians or civilian objects without distinction.

5. Among others, the following types of attacks are to be considered as indiscriminate:

(a) an attack by bombardment by any methods or means which treats as a single military objective a number of clearly separated and distinct military objectives located in a city, town, village or other area containing a similar concentration of civilians or civilian objects; and

(b) an attack which may be expected to cause incidental loss of civilian life, injury to civilians, damage to civilian objects, or a combination thereof, which would be excessive in relation to the concrete and direct military advantage anticipated.

6. Attacks against the civilian population or civilians by way of reprisals are prohibited.

7. The presence or movements of the civilian population or individual civilians shall not be used to render certain points or areas immune from military operations, in particular in attempts to shield military objectives from attacks or to shield, favour or impede military operations. The Parties to the conflict shall not direct the movement of the civilian population or individual civilians in order to attempt to shield military objectives from attacks or to shield military operations.

8. Any violation of these prohibitions shall not release the Parties to the conflict from their legal obligations with respect to the civilian population and civilians, including the obligation to take the precautionary measures provided for in Article 57.

* * *

Article 54—Protection of objects indispensable to the survival of the civilian population

1. Starvation of civilians as a method of warfare is prohibited.

2. It is prohibited to attack, destroy, remove or render useless objects indispensable to the survival of the civilian population, such as food-stuffs, agricultural areas for the production of food-stuffs, crops, livestock, drinking water installations and supplies and irrigation works, for the specific purpose of denying them for their sustenance value to the civilian population or to the adverse Party, whatever the motive, whether in order to starve out civilians, to cause them to move away, or for any other motive.

3. The prohibitions in paragraph 2 shall not apply to such of the objects covered by it as are used by an adverse Party:

(a) as sustenance solely for the members of its armed forces; or

(b) if not as sustenance, then in direct support of military action, provided, however, that in no event shall actions against these objects be taken which may be expected to leave the civilian population with such inadequate food or water as to cause its starvation or force its movement.

4. These objects shall not be made the object of reprisals.

5. In recognition of the vital requirements of any Party to the conflict in the deference of its national territory against invasion, derogation from the prohibitions contained in paragraph 2 may be made by a Party to the conflict within such territory under its own control where required by imperative military necessity.

Article 55—Protection of the natural environment

1. Care shall be taken in warfare to protect the natural environment against widespread, long-term and severe damage. This protection includes a prohibition of the use of methods or means of warfare which are intended or may be expected to cause such damage to the natural environment and thereby to prejudice the health or survival of the population.

2. Attacks against the natural environment by way of reprisals are prohibited.

Article 56—Protection of works and installations containing dangerous forces

1. Works or installations containing dangerous forces, namely dams, dykes and nuclear electrical generating stations, shall not be made the object of attack, even where these objects are military objectives, if such attack may cause the release of dangerous forces and consequent severe losses among the civilian population. Other military objectives located at or in the vicinity of these works or installations shall not be made the object of attack if such attack may cause the release of dangerous forces from the works or installations and consequent severe losses among the civilian population.

2. The special protection against attack provided by paragraph 1 shall cease:

(a) for a dam or a dyke only if it is used for other than its normal function and in regular, significant and direct support of military operations and if such attack is the only feasible way to terminate such support;

(b) for a nuclear electrical generating station only if it provides electric power in regular, significant and direct support of military operations and if such attack is the only feasible way to terminate such support;

(c) for other military objectives located at or in the vicinity of these works or installations only if they are used in regular, significant and direct support of military operations and if such attack is the only feasible way to terminate such support.

3. In all cases, the civilian population and individual civilians shall remain entitled to all the protection accorded them by international law, including the protection of the precautionary measures provided for in Article 57. If the protection ceases and any of the works, installations or military objectives mentioned in paragraph 1 is attacked, all practical precautions shall be taken to avoid the release of dangerous forces.

4. It is prohibited to make any of the works, installations or military objectives mentioned in paragraph 1 the object of reprisals.

5. The Parties to the conflict shall endeavour to avoid locating any military objectives in the vicinity of the works or installations mentioned in paragraph 1. Nevertheless, installations erected for the sole purpose of defending the protected works or installations from attack are permissible and shall not themselves be made the object of attack, provided that they are not used in hostilities except for defensive actions necessary to respond to attacks against the protected works or installations and that their armament is limited to weapons capable only of repelling hostile action against the protected works or installations.

6. The High Contracting Parties and the Parties to the conflict are urged to conclude further agreements among themselves to provide additional protection for objects containing dangerous forces.

7. In order to facilitate the identification of the objects protected by this article, the Parties to the conflict may mark them with a special sign consisting of a group of three bright orange circles placed on the same axis, as specified in Article 16 of Annex I to this Protocol. The absence of such marking in no way relieves any Party to the conflict of its obligations under this Article.

CHAPTER IV
PRECAUTIONARY MEASURES

Article 57—Precautions in attack

1. In the conduct of military operations, constant care shall be taken to spare the civilian population, civilians and civilian objects.

2. With respect to attacks, the following precautions shall be taken:

(a) those who plan or decide upon an attack shall:

(i) do everything feasible to verify that the objectives to be attacked are neither civilians nor civilian objects and are not subject to special protection but are military objectives within the meaning of paragraph 2 of Article 52 and that it is not prohibited by the provisions of this Protocol to attack them;

(ii) take all feasible precautions in the choice of means and methods of attack with a view to avoiding, and in any event to minimizing, incidental loss of civilian life, injury to civilians and damage to civilian objects;

(iii) refrain from deciding to launch any attack which may be expected to cause incidental loss of civilian life, injury to civilians, damage to civilian objects, or a combination thereof, which would be excessive in relation to the concrete and direct military advantage anticipated.

(b) an attack shall be cancelled or suspended if it becomes apparent that the objective is not a military one or is subject to special protection or that the attack may be expected to cause incidental loss of civilian life, injury to civilians, damage to civilian objects, or a combination thereof, which would be excessive in relation to the concrete and direct military advantage anticipated;

(c) effective advance warning shall be given of attacks which may affect the civilian population, unless circumstances do not permit.

3. When a choice is possible between several military objectives for obtaining a similar military advantage; the objective to be selected shall be that the attack on which may be expected to cause the least danger to civilian lives and to civilian objects.

4. In the conduct of military operations at sea or in the air, each Party to the conflict shall, in conformity with its rights and duties under the rules of international law applicable in armed conflict, take all reasonable precautions to avoid losses of civilian lives and damage to civilian objects.

5. No provision of this article may be constructed as authorizing any attacks against the civilian population, civilians or civilian objects.

Article 58—Precautions against the effects of attacks

The Parties to the conflict shall, to the maximum extent feasible:

(a) without prejudice to Article 49 of the Fourth Convention, endeavour to remove the civilian population, individual civilians and civilian objects under their control from the vicinity of military objectives;

(b) avoid locating military objectives within or near densely populated areas;

(c) take the other necessary precautions to protect the civilian population, individual civilians and civilian objects under their control against the dangers resulting from military operations.

* * *

Article 85—Repression of breaches of this protocol

1. The provisions of the Conventions relating to the repression of breaches and grave breaches, supplemented by this Section, shall apply to the repression of breaches and grave breaches of this Protocol.

2. Acts described as grave breaches in the Conventions are grave breaches of this Protocol if committed against persons in the power of an adverse Party protected by Articles 44, 45 and 73 of this Protocol, or against the wounded, sick and shipwrecked of the adverse Party who are protected by this Protocol, or against those medical or religious personnel, medical units or

medical transports which are under the control of the adverse Party and are protected by this Protocol.

3. In addition to the grave breaches defined in Article 11, the following acts shall be regarded as grave breaches of this Protocol, when committed wilfully, in violation of the relevant provisions of this Protocol, and causing death or serious injury to body or health:

(a) making the civilian population or individual civilians the object of attack;

(b) launching an indiscriminate attack affecting the civilian population or civilian objects in the knowledge that such attack will cause excessive loss of life, injury to civilians or damage to civilian objects, as defined in Article 57, paragraph 2(a)(iii);

(c) launching an attack against works or installations containing dangerous forces in the knowledge that such attack will cause excessive loss of life, injury to civilians or damage to civilian objects, as defined in Article 57, paragraph 2(a)(iii);

(d) making non-defended localities and demilitarized zones the object of attack;

(e) making a person the object of attack in the knowledge that he is *hors de combat;*

(f) the perfidious use, in violation of Article 37, of the distinctive emblem of the red cross, red crescent or red lion and sun or of other protective signs recognized by the Conventions or this Protocol.

4. In addition to the grave breaches defined in the preceding paragraphs and in the Conventions, the following shall be regarded as grave breaches of this Protocol, when committed wilfully and in violation of the Conventions or the Protocol.

(a) the transfer by the occupying Power of parts of its own civilian populations into the territory it occupies, or the deportation or transfer of all or parts of the population of the occupied territory within or outside this territory, in violation of Article 49 of the Fourth Convention;

(b) unjustifiable delay in the repatriation of prisoners of war or civilians;

(c) practices of *apartheid* and other inhuman and degrading practices involving outrages upon personal dignity, based on racial discrimination.

(d) making the clearly-recognized historic monuments, works of art or places of worship which constitute the cultural or spiritual heritage of peoples and to which special protection has been given by special arrangement, for example, within the framework of a competent international organization, the object of attack, causing as a result extensive destruction thereof, where there is no evidence of the violation by the adverse Party of Article 53, subparagraph (b), and when such historic monuments, works of art and places of worship are not located in the immediate proximity of military objectives;

(e) depriving a person protected by the Conventions or referred to in paragraph 2 of this Article of the rights of fair and regular trial.

5. Without prejudice to the application of the Conventions and of this Protocol, grave breaches of these instruments shall be regarded as war crimes.

7.25 SOUTH PACIFIC NUCLEAR FREE ZONE TREATY (WITHOUT ANNEXES AND PROTOCOLS).[1] Concluded at Rarotonga, 6 August 1985. Entered into force, 11 December 1986. U.N.Doc. CD/633 (1985), U.N.Doc. CD/633/Corr. 2 (1985), and U.N.Doc. CD/633/Annex 4/Rev. 1 (1987), 24 I.L.M. 1442 (1985)

ARTICLE 1
USAGE OF TERMS

For the purposes of this Treaty and its Protocols:

(a) "South Pacific Nuclear Free Zone" means the areas described in Annex I as illustrated by the map attached to that Annex;

(b) "territory" means internal waters, territorial sea and archipelagic waters, the seabed and subsoil beneath, the land territory and the airspace above them;

(c) "nuclear explosive device" means any nuclear weapon or other explosive device capable of releasing nuclear energy, irrespective of the purpose for which it could be used. The term includes such a weapon or device in unassembled and partly assembled forms, but does not include the means of transport or delivery of such a weapon or device if separable from and not an indivisible part of it;

(d) "stationing" means emplantation, emplacement, transportation on land or inland waters, stockpiling, storage, installation and deployment.

ARTICLE 2
APPLICATION OF THE TREATY

1. Except where otherwise specified, this Treaty and its Protocols shall apply to territory within the South Pacific Nuclear Free Zone.

2. Nothing in this Treaty shall prejudice or in any way affect the rights, or the exercise of the rights, of any State under international law with regard to freedom of the seas.

ARTICLE 3
RENUNCIATION OF NUCLEAR EXPLOSIVE DEVICES

Each Party undertakes:

(a) not to manufacture or otherwise acquire, possess or have control over any nuclear explosive device by any means anywhere inside or outside the South Pacific Nuclear Free Zone;

(b) not to seek or receive any assistance in the manufacture or acquisition of any nuclear explosive device;

---

1. This Treaty, also known as "the Treaty of Rarotonga," incorporates two annexes and three protocols, none of which are included here. All three protocols are in force. *Protocol 1* (open to France, the U.K., and the U.S.) requires parties with dependent territories within the zone to comply with the relevant provisions of the Treaty. *Protocol 2* (open to China, France, the U.K., the U.S., and the U.S.S.R.) requires the parties not to assist a violation of the Treaty or its protocols and not to use or threaten to use nuclear weapons against parties to the Treaty or territories within the zone for which Protocol 1 parties are responsible. *Protocol 3* (open to China, France, the U.K., the U.S., and the U.S.S.R.) requires the parties not to test nuclear weapons within the zone.

(c) not to take any action to assist or encourage the manufacture or acquisition of any nuclear explosive device by any State.

ARTICLE 4
PEACEFUL NUCLEAR ACTIVITIES

Each Party undertakes:

(a) not to provide source or special fissionable material, or equipment or material especially designed or prepared for the processing, use or production of special fissionable material for peaceful purposes to:

(i) any non-nuclear-weapon State unless subject to the safeguards required by Article III.1 of the NPT, or

(ii) any nuclear-weapon State unless subject to applicable safeguards agreements with the International Atomic Energy Agency (IAFA).

Any such provision shall be in accordance with strict non-proliferation measures to provide assurance of exclusively peaceful non-explosive use;

(b) to support the continued effectiveness of the international non-proliferation system based on the NPT and the LAEA safeguards system.

ARTICLE 5
PREVENTION OF STATIONING OF NUCLEAR EXPLOSIVE DEVICES

1. Each Party undertakes to prevent in its territory the stationing of any nuclear explosive device.

2. Each Party in the exercise of its sovereign rights remains free to decide for itself whether to allow visits by foreign ships and aircraft to its ports and airfields, transit of its airspace by foreign aircraft, and navigation by foreign ships in its territorial sea or archipelagic waters in a manner not covered by the rights of innocent passage, archipelagic sea lane passage or transit passage of straits.

ARTICLE 6
PREVENTION OF TESTING OF NUCLEAR EXPLOSIVE DEVICES

Each Party undertakes:

(a) to prevent in its territory the testing of any nuclear explosive device;

(b) not to take any action to assist or encourage the testing of any nuclear explosive device by any State.

ARTICLE 7
PREVENTION OF DUMPING

1. Each Party undertakes:

(a) not to dump radioactive wastes and other radioactive matter at sea anywhere within the South Pacific Nuclear Free Zone;

(b) to prevent the dumping of radioactive wastes and other radioactive matter by anyone in its territorial sea;

(c) not to take any action to assist or encourage the dumping by anyone of radioactive wastes and other radioactive matter at sea anywhere within the South Pacific Nuclear Free Zone;

(d) to support the conclusion as soon as possible of the proposed Convention relating to the protection of the natural resources and environment of the South Pacific region and its Protocol for the prevention of pollution of the South Pacific region by dumping, with the aim of precluding dumping at sea of radioactive wastes and other radioactive matter by anyone anywhere in the region.

2. Paragraphs 1(a) and 1(b) of this Article shall not apply to areas of the South Pacific Nuclear Free Zone in respect of which such a Convention and Protocol have entered into force.

ARTICLE 8
CONTROL SYSTEM

1. The Parties hereby establish a control system for the purpose of verifying compliance with their obligations under this Treaty.

2. The control system shall comprise:

(a) reports and exchange of information as provided for in Article 9;

(b) consultations as provided for in Article 10 and Annex 4(1);

(c) the application to peaceful nuclear activities of safeguards by the IAEA as provided for in Annex 2;

(d) a complaints procedure as provided for in Annex 4.

ARTICLE 9
REPORTS AND EXCHANGE OF INFORMATION

1. Each Party shall report to the Director of the South Pacific Bureau for Economic Co-operation (the Director) as soon as possible any significant event within its jurisdiction affecting the implementation of this Treaty. The Director shall circulate such reports promptly to all Parties.

2. The Parties shall endeavour to keep each other informed on matters arising under or in relation to this Treaty. They may exchange information by communicating it to the Director, who shall circulate it to all Parties.

3. The Director shall report annually to the South Pacific Forum on the status of this Treaty and matters arising under or in relation to it, incorporating reports and communications made under paragraphs 1 and 2 of this Article and matters arising under Articles 8(2)(d) and 10 and Annex 2(4).

ARTICLE 10
CONSULTATIONS AND REVIEW

Without prejudice to the conduct of consultations among Parties by other means, the Director, at the request of any Party, shall convene a meeting of the Consultative Committee established by Annex 3 for consultation and co-operation on any matter arising in relation to this Treaty or for reviewing its operation.

ARTICLE 11
AMENDMENT

The Consultative Committee shall consider proposals for amendment of the provisions of this Treaty proposed by any Party and circulated by the Director to all Parties not less than three months prior to the convening of the Consultative Committee for this purpose. Any proposal agreed upon by consensus by the Consultative Committee shall be communicated to the Director who shall circulate it for acceptance to all Parties. An amendment shall enter into force thirty days after receipt by the depositary of acceptances from all Parties.

ARTICLE 12
SIGNATURE AND RATIFICATION

1. This Treaty shall be open for signature by any Member of the South Pacific Forum.

2. This Treaty shall be subject to ratification. Instruments of ratification shall be deposited with the Director who is hereby designated depositary of this Treaty and its Protocols.

3. If a Member of the South Pacific Forum whose territory is outside the South Pacific Nuclear Free Zone becomes a Party to this Treaty, Annex 1 shall be deemed to be amended so far as is required to enclose at least the territory of that Party within the boundaries of the South Pacific Nuclear Free Zone. The delineation of any area added pursuant to this paragraph shall be approved by the South Pacific Forum.

7.26 UNITED NATIONS SECURITY COUNCIL RESOLUTION 687 (CONCERNING THE RESTORATION OF PEACE AND SECURITY IN IRAQ AND KUWAIT). Adopted at the 2981st mtg., 3 April 1991. U.N. Doc. S/RES/687 (1991), 30 I.L.M. 846 (1991)

The Security Council.

Recalling its resolutions 660 (1990) of 2 August 1990, 661 (1990) of 6 August 1990, 662 (1990) of 9 August 1990, 664 (1990) of 18 August 1990, 665 (1990) of 25 August 1990, 666 (1990) of 13 September 1990, 667 (1990) of 16 September 1990, 669 (1990) of 24 September 1990, 670 (1990) of 25 September 1990, 674 (1990) of 29 October 1990, 677 (1990) of 28 November 1990, 678 (1990) of 29 November 1990 and 686 (1991) of 2 March 1991,

Welcoming the restoration to Kuwait of its sovereignty, independence and territorial integrity and the return of its legitimate Government,

Affirming the commitment of all Member States to the sovereignty, territorial integrity and political independence of Kuwait and Iraq, and noting the intention expressed by the Member States cooperating with Kuwait under paragraph 2 of resolution 678 (1990) to bring their military presence in Iraq to an end as soon as possible consistent with paragraph 8 of resolution 686 (1991),

Reaffirming the need to be assured to Iraq's peaceful intentions in the light of its unlawful invasion and occupation of Kuwait,

Taking note of the letter sent by the Minister for Foreign Affairs of Iraq on 27 February 1991 and those sent pursuant to resolution 686 (1991),

Noting that Iraq and Kuwait, as independent sovereign States, signed at Baghdad on 4 October 1963 "Agreed Minutes Between the State of Kuwait and the Republic of Iraq Regarding the Restoration of Friendly Relations, Recognition and Related Matters", thereby recognizing formally the boundary between Iraq and Kuwait and the allocation of islands, which were registered with the United Nations in accordance with Article 102 of the Charter of the United Nations and in which Iraq recognized the independence and complete sovereignty of the State of Kuwait within its borders as specified and accepted in the letter of the Prime Minister of Iraq dated 21 July 1932, and as accepted by the Ruler of Kuwait in his letter dated 10 August 1932,

Conscious of the need for demarcation of the said boundary,

Conscious also of the statements by Iraq threatening to use weapons in violation of its obligations under the Geneva Protocol for the Prohibition of the Use of War of Asphyxiating, Poisonous or Other Gases, and of Bacteriological Methods of Warfare, signed at Geneva on 17 June 1925, and of its prior use of chemical weapons and affirming that grave consequences would follow any further use by Iraq of such weapons,

Recalling that Iraq has subscribed to the Declaration adopted by all States participating in the Conference of States Parties to the 1925 Geneva Protocol and Other Interested States, held in Paris from 7 to 11 January 1989, establishing the objective of universal elimination of chemical and biological weapons,

Recalling also that Iraq has signed the Convention on the Prohibition of the Development, Production and Stockpiling of Bacteriological (Biological) and Toxin Weapons and on Their Destruction, of 10 April 1972,

Noting the importance of Iraq ratifying this Convention,

Noting moreover the importance of all States adhering to this Convention and encouraging its forthcoming Review Conference to reinforce the authority, efficiency and universal scope of the convention,

Stressing the importance of an early conclusion by the Conference on Disarmament of its work on a Convention on the Universal Prohibition of Chemical Weapons and of universal adherence thereto,

Aware of the use by Iraq of ballistic missiles in unprovoked attacks and therefore of the need to take specific measures in regard to such missiles located in Iraq,

Concerned by the reports in the hands of Member States that Iraq has attempted to acquire materials for a nuclear-weapons programme contrary to its obligations under the Treaty on the Non–Proliferation of Nuclear Weapons of 1 July 1968,

Recalling the objective of the establishment of a nuclear-weapons-free zone in the region of the Middle East,

Conscious of the threat that all weapons of mass destruction pose to peace and security in the area and of the need to work towards the establishment in the Middle East of a zone free of such weapons,

Conscious also of the objective of achieving balanced and comprehensive control of armaments in the region,

Conscious further of the importance of achieving the objectives noted above using all available means, including a dialogue among the States of the region,

Noting that resolution 686 (1991) marked the lifting of the measures imposed by resolution 661 (1990) in so far as they applied to Kuwait,

Noting that despite the progress being made in fulfilling the obligations of resolution 686 (1991), many Kuwait and third country nations are still not accounted for and property remains unreturned,

Recalling the International Convention against the Taking of Hostages, opened for signature at New York on 18 December 1979, which categorizes all acts of taking hostages as manifestations of international terrorism,

Deploring threats made by Iraq during the recent conflict to make use of terrorism against targets outside Iraq and the taking of hostages by Iraq,

Taking note with grave concern of the reports of the Secretary–General of 20 March 1991 and 28 March 1991, and conscious of the necessity to meet urgently the humanitarian needs in Kuwait and Iraq,

Bearing in mind its objective of restoring international peace and security in the area as set out in recent resolutions of the Security Council,

Conscious of the need to take the following measures acting under Chapter VII of the Charter,

1. *Affirms* all thirteen resolutions noted above, except as expressly changed below to achieve the goals of this resolution, including a formal cease-fire;

A

2. *Demands* that Iraq and Kuwait respect the inviolability of the international boundary and the allocation of islands set out in the "Agreed Minutes Between the State of Kuwait and the Republic of Iraq Regarding the Restoration of Friendly Relations, Recognition and Related Matters", signed by them in the exercise of their sovereignty at Baghdad on 4 October 1963 and registered with the United Nations and published by the United Nations in document 7063, United Nations, Treaty Series, 1964;

3. *Calls upon* the Secretary–General to lend his assistance to make arrangements with Iraq and Kuwait to demarcate the boundary between Iraq and Kuwait, drawing on appropriate material, including the map transmitted by Security Council document S/22412 and to report back to the Security Council within one month;

4. *Decides* to guarantee the inviolability of the above-mentioned international boundary and to take as appropriate all necessary measures to that end in accordance with the Charter of the United Nations;

B

5. *Requests* the Secretary–General, after consulting with Iraq and Kuwait, to submit within three days to the Security Council for its approval a plan for the immediate deployment of a United Nations observer unit to monitor the Khor Abdullah and a demilitarized zone, which is hereby established, extending ten kilometres into Iraq and five kilometres into Kuwait from the boundary referred to in the "Agreed Minutes Between the State of Kuwait and the Republic of Iraq Regarding the Restoration of Friendly Relations, Recognition and Related Matters" of 4 October 1963; to deter violations of the boundary through its presence in and surveillance of the demilitarized zone; to observe any hostile or potentially hostile action mounted from the territory of one State to the other; and for the Secretary–General to report regularly to the Security Council on the operations of the unit, and immediately if there are serious violations of the zone or potential threats to peace;

6. *Notes* that as soon as the Secretary–General notifies the Security Council of the completion of the deployment of the United Nations observer unit, the conditions will be established for the Member States cooperating with Kuwait in accordance with resolution 678 (1990) to bring their military presence in Iraq to an end consistent with resolution 686 (1991);

C

7. *Invites* Iraq to reaffirm unconditionally its obligations under the Geneva Protocol for the Prohibition of the Use in War of Asphyxiating, Poisonous or Other Gases, and of Bacteriological Methods of Warfare, signed at Geneva on 17 June 1925, and to ratify the Convention on the Prohibition of the Development, Production and Stockpiling of Bacteriological (Biological) and Toxin Weapons and on Their Destruction, of 10 April 1972;

8. *Decides* that Iraq shall unconditionally accept the destruction, removal, or rendering harmless, under international supervision, of:

(a) All chemical and biological weapons and all stocks of agents and all related subsystems and components and all research, development, support and manufacturing facilities;

(b) All ballistic missiles with range greater than 150 kilometres and related major parts, and repair and production facilities;

9. *Decides,* for the implementation of paragraph 8 above, the following:

(a) Iraq shall submit to the Secretary–General, within fifteen days of the adoption of the present resolution, a declaration of the locations, amounts and types of all items specified in paragraph 8 and agree to urgent, on-site inspection as specified below;

(b) The Secretary–General, in consultation with the appropriate Governments and, where appropriate, with the Director–General of the World Health Organization, within forty-five days of the passage of the present resolution, shall develop, and submit to the Council for approval, a plan calling for the completion of the following acts within forty-five days of such approval:

(i) The forming of a Special Commission, which shall carry out immediate on-site inspection of Iraq's biological, chemical and missile capabilities, based on Iraq's declarations and the designation of any additional locations by the Special Commission itself;

(ii) The yielding by Iraq of possession to the Special Commission for destruction, removal or rendering harmless, taking into account the requirements of public safety, of all items specified under paragraph 8(a) above, including items at the additional locations designated by the Special Commission under paragraph 9(b)(i) above and the destruction by Iraq, under the supervision of the Special Commission, of all its missile capabilities, including launchers, as specified under paragraph 8(b) above;

(iii) The provision by the Special Commission of the assistance and cooperation to the Director–General of the International Atomic Energy Agency required in paragraphs 12 and 13 below;

10. *Decides* that Iraq shall unconditionally undertake not to use, develop, construct or acquire any of the items specified in paragraphs 8 and 9 above and requests the Secretary–General, in consultation with the Special Commission, to develop a plan for the future ongoing monitoring and verification of Iraq's compliance with this paragraph, to be submitted to the Security Council for approval within one hundred and twenty days of the passage of this resolution;

11. *Invites* Iraq to reaffirm unconditionally its obligations under the Treaty on the Non–Proliferation of Nuclear Weapons of 1 July 1968;

12. *Decides* that Iraq shall unconditionally agree not to acquire or develop nuclear weapons or nuclear-weapons-usable material or any subsystems or components or any research, development, support or manufacturing facilities related to the above; to submit to the Secretary–General and the Director–General of the International Atomic Energy Agency within fifteen

days of the adoption of the present resolution a declaration of the locations, amounts, and types of all items specified above; to place all of its nuclear-weapons-usable materials under the exclusive control, for custody and removal, of the International Atomic Energy Agency, with the assistance and cooperation of the Special Commission as provided for in the plan of the Secretary–General discussed in paragraph 9(b) above; to accept, in accordance with the arrangements provided for in paragraph 13 below, urgent on-site inspection and the destruction, removal or rendering harmless as appropriate of all items specified above; and to accept the plan discussed in paragraph 13 below for the future ongoing monitoring and verification of its compliance with these undertakings;

13. *Requests* the Director–General of the International Atomic Energy Agency, through the Secretary–General, with the assistance and cooperation of the Special Commission as provided for in the plan of the Secretary–General in paragraph 9(b) above, to carry out immediate on-site inspection of Iraq's nuclear capabilities based on Iraq's declarations and the designation of any additional locations by the Special Commission; to develop a plan for submission to the Security Council within forty-five days calling for the destruction, removal, or rendering harmless as appropriate of all items listed in paragraph 12 above; to carry out the plan within forty-five days following approval by the Security Council; and to develop a plan, taking into account the rights and obligations of Iraq under the Treaty on the Non–Proliferation of Nuclear Weapons of 1 July 1968, for the future ongoing monitoring and verification of Iraq's compliance with paragraph 12 above, including an inventory of all nuclear material in Iraq subject to the Agency's verification and inspections to confirm that Agency safeguards cover all relevant nuclear activities in Iraq, to be submitted to the Security Council for approval within one hundred and twenty days of the passage of the present resolution;

14. *Takes note* that the actions to be taken by Iraq in paragraphs 8, 9, 10, 11, 12 and 13 of the present resolution represent steps towards the goal of establishing in the Middle East a zone free from weapons of mass destruction and all missiles for their delivery and the objective of a global ban on chemical weapons;

D

15. *Requests* the Secretary–General to report to the Security Council on the steps taken to facilitate the return of all Kuwait property seized by Iraq, including a list of any property that Kuwait claims has not been returned or which has not been returned intact;

E

16. *Reaffirms* that Iraq, without prejudice to the debts and obligations of Iraq arising prior to 2 August 1990, which will be addressed through the normal mechanisms, is liable under international law for any direct loss, damage, including environmental damage and the depletion of natural resources, or injury to foreign Governments, nationals and corporations, as a result of Iraq's unlawful invasion and occupation of Kuwait;

17. *Decides* that all Iraqi statements made since 2 August 1990 repudiating its foreign debt are null and void, and demands that Iraq adhere

scrupulously to all of its obligations concerning servicing and repayment of its foreign debt;

18. *Decides* also to create a fund to pay compensation for claims that fall within paragraph 16 above and to establish a Commission that will administer the fund;

19. *Directs* the Secretary–General to develop and present to the Security Council for decision, no later than thirty days following the adoption of the present resolution, recommendations for the fund to meet the requirement for the payment of claims established in accordance with paragraph 18 above and for a programme to implement the decisions in paragraphs 16, 17 and 18 above, including: administration of the fund; mechanisms for determining the appropriate level of Iraq's contribution to the fund based on a percentage of the value of the exports of petroleum and petroleum products from Iraq not to exceed a figure to be suggested to the Council by the Secretary–General, taking into account the requirements of the people of Iraq, Iraq's payment capacity as assessed in conjunction with the international financial institutions taking into consideration external debt service, and the needs of the Iraqi economy; arrangements for ensuring that payments are made to the fund; the process by which funds will be allocated and claims paid; appropriate procedures for evaluating losses, listing claims and verifying their validity and resolving disputed claims in respect of Iraq's liability as specified in paragraph 16 above; and the composition of the Commission designated above;

F

20. *Decides,* effective immediately, that the prohibition against the sale or supply to Iraq of commodities or products, other than medicine and health supplies, and prohibitions against financial transactions related thereto contained in resolution 661 (1990) shall not apply to foodstuffs notified to the Security Council Committee established by resolution 661 (1990) concerning the situations between Iraq and Kuwait or, with the approval of that Committee, under the simplified and accelerated "no-objection" procedure, to materials and supplies for essential civilian needs as identified in the report of the Secretary–General dated essential civilian needs as identified in the report of the Secretary–General dated 20 March 1991, and in any further findings of humanitarian need by the Committee;

21. *Decides* that the Security Council shall review the provisions of paragraph 20 above every sixty days in the light of the policies and practices of the Government of Iraq, including the implementation of all relevant resolutions of the Security Council, for the purpose of determining whether to reduce or lift the prohibitions referred to therein;

22. *Decides* that upon the approval by the Security Council of the programme called for in paragraph 19 above and upon Council agreement that Iraq has completed all actions contemplated in paragraphs 8, 9, 10, 11, 12 and 13 above, the prohibitions against the import of commodities and products originating in Iraq and the prohibitions against financial transactions related thereto contained in resolution 661 (1990) shall have no further force or effect;

23. *Decides* that, pending action by the Security Council under paragraph 22 above, the Security Council Committee established by resolution 661 (1990) shall be empowered to approve, when required to assure adequate financial resources on the part of Iraq to carry out the activities under paragraph 20 above, exceptions to the prohibition against the import of commodities and products originating in Iraq;

24. *Decides* that, in accordance with resolution 661 (1990) and subsequent related resolutions and until a further decision is taken by the Security Council, all States shall continue to prevent the sale or supply, or the promotion or facilitation of such sale or supply, to Iraq by their nationals, or from their territories or using their flag vessels or aircraft, of:

(a) Arms and related *materiel* of all types, specifically including the sale or transfer through other means of all forms of conventional military equipment, including for paramilitary forces, and spare parts and components and their means of production, for such equipment;

(b) Items specified and defined in paragraphs 8 and 12 above not otherwise covered above;

(c) Technology under licensing or other transfer arrangements used in the production, utilization or stockpiling of items specified in subparagraphs (a) and (b) above;

(d) Personnel or materials for training or technical support services relating to the design, development, manufacture, use, maintenance or support of items specified in subparagraphs (a) and (b) above;

25. *Calls upon* all States and international organizations to act strictly in accordance with paragraph 24 above, notwithstanding the existence of any contracts, agreements, licences or any other arrangements;

26. *Requests* the Secretary–General, in consultation with appropriate Governments, to develop within sixty days, for the approval of the Security Council, guidelines to facilitate full international implementation of paragraphs 24 and 25 above and paragraph 27 below, and to make them available to all States and to establish procedure for updating these guidelines periodically;

27. *Calls upon* all states to maintain such national controls and procedures and to take such other actions consistent with the guidelines to be established by the Security Council under paragraph 26 above as may be necessary to ensure compliance with the terms of paragraph 24 above, and calls upon international organizations to take all appropriate steps to assist in ensuring such full compliance;

28. *Agrees* to review its decisions in paragraphs 22, 23, 24 and 25 above, except for the items specified and defined in paragraphs 8 and 12 above, on a regular basis and in any case one hundred and twenty days following passage of the present resolution, taking into account Iraq's compliance with the resolution and general progress towards the control of armaments in the region;

29. *Decides* that all States, including Iraq, shall take the necessary measures to ensure that no claim shall lie at the instance of the Government of Iraq, or of any person or body in Iraq, or of any person claiming through or

for the benefit of any such person or body, in connection with any contract or other transaction where its performance was affected by reason of the measures taken by the Security Council in resolution 661 (1990) and related resolutions;

G

30. *Decides* that, in furtherance of its commitment to facilitate the repatriation of all Kuwaiti and third country national, Iraq shall extend all necessary cooperation to the International Committee of the Red Cross, providing lists of such persons, facilitating the access of the International Committee of the Red Cross to all such persons wherever located or detained and facilitating the search by the International Committee of the Red Cross for those Kuwaiti and third country nationals still unaccounted for;

31. *Invites* the International Committee of the Red Cross to keep the Secretary–General apprised as appropriate of all activities undertaken in connection with facilitating the repatriation or return of all Kuwaiti and third country nationals or their remains present in Iraq on or after 2 August 1990;

H

32. Requires Iraq to inform the Security Council that it will not commit or support any act of international terrorism or allow any organization directed towards commission of such acts to operate within its territory and to condemn unequivocally and renounce all acts, methods and practices of terrorism;

I

33. *Declares* that, upon official notification by Iraq to the Secretary–General and to the Security Council of its acceptance of the provisions above, a formal cease-fire is effective between Iraq and Kuwait and the Member States cooperating with Kuwait in accordance with resolution 678 (1990);

34. *Decides* to remain seized of the matter and to take such further steps as may be required for the implementation of the present resolution and to secure peace and security in the area.

8. ARBITRAL/JUDICIAL DECISIONS

8.1 SUMMARY OF CASE RELATING TO THE TERRITORIAL JURISDICTION OF THE INTERNATIONAL COMMISSION OF THE RIVER ORDER (Czech., Den., Fr., Ger., Swed., U.K./Pol.), 1929 P.C.I.J. (ser. A) No. 23, at 5

In this case, the Permanent Court of International Justice was called upon to decide whether the jurisdiction of the International Commission of the River Oder, established under the Versailles Peace Treaty of June 28, 1919 to facilitate the internationalization of the navigable sections of the Oder, extended as well to the navigable sections of the Warta and Noteć rivers, tributaries of the Oder situated in Polish territory. The Court held that the Oder Commission's jurisdiction was defined in Article 331 of the Versailles Treaty. To reach this conclusion, however, the P.C.I.J. was obliged to interpret Article 331, and in so doing it invoked two clusters of customary international law principles: first, the canons of treaty interpretation, in particular the canon that insists upon an interpretation "which is most favourable to the freedom of States" when, as in this instance, the intentions of the Parties are in doubt; and second, "the principles governing international fluvial law in general". The Court reasoned, at 27–28:

> * * * [W]hen consideration is given to the manner in which States have regarded the concrete situations arising out of the fact that a single waterway traverses or separates the territory of more than one State, and the possibility of fulfilling the requirements of justice and the considerations of utility which this fact places in relief, it is at once seen that a solution of the problem has been sought not in the idea of a right of passage in favour of upstream States, but in that of a community of interest of riparian States. This community of interest in a navigable river becomes the basis of a common legal right, the essential features of which are the perfect equality of all riparian States in the user of the whole course of the river and the exclusion of any preferential privilege of any one riparian State in relation to the others.

> It is on this conception that international river law * * * is undoubtedly based. * * * If the common legal right is based on the existence of a navigable waterway separating or traversing several States, it is evident that this common right extends to the whole navigable course of the river and does not stop short at the last frontier; no instance of a treaty in which the upstream limit of an internationalization of a river is determined by such frontier rather than by certain conditions of navigability has been brought to the attention of the Court.

8.2 SUMMARY OF DIVERSION OF WATER FROM THE MEUSE CASE (Neth. v. Belg.), 1937 P.C.I.J. (ser. A/B) No. 70, at 4

In this case, pitting The Netherlands against Belgium for diversions of canal and irrigation water from the River Meuse allegedly in violation of Belgium's international obligations, the Permanent Court of International

Justice had to interpret an 1863 treaty between the two countries, the purpose of which was to prevent the excessive speed of the current of the Zuid–Willemsvaart, a canal running from Maastrich in The Netherlands to Bois-le-Duc in Belgium. Finding no violation of the 1863 treaty but faced with the taking of water not regulated by the treaty, the Court was forced to look to customary State practice and general principles of law. In so doing, it announced the following rule:

> As regards [canals which are situated entirely in Dutch or Belgian territory], each of the two States is at liberty, in its own territory, to modify them, to enlarge them, to transform them, to fill them in and even to increase the volume of water in them from new sources, provided that the diversion of water at the treaty feeder and the volume of water to be discharged therefrom to maintain the normal level and flow in the Zuid–Willemsvaart is not affected.

Thus the P.C.I.J. invoked and formalized the customary rule that a State is at liberty to do what it wants in its own territory as long as it does not endanger the physical well-being of its neighbors.

8.3 SUMMARY OF LAKE LANOUX ARBITRATION (Spain v. Fr.), 12 U.N.R.I.A.A. 281 (1957)

In this dispute, wherein Spain unsuccessfully objected to a French hydro-electric power plan on the grounds that, if effectuated, it would alter the natural flow of a river crossing from France into Spain, the decision turned, as noted above, on the interpretation of an 1866 treaty. However, because Spain claimed, beyond the treaty, that customary international law requires prior agreement among co-riparians whenever a substantial alteration of a transboundary system of waters is contemplated, the Tribunal considered itself obliged to take "international common law" into account. It did so, at 308 and 316, echoing all the above-summarized cases, as follows:

> International practice reflects the conviction that States ought to strive to conclude * * * agreements [regarding the industrial use of international rivers] * * *. But international practice does not so far permit more than the following conclusion: the rule that States may utilize the hydraulic power of international watercourses only on condition of a *prior* agreement between the interested States cannot be established as a custom, even less a general principle of law * * *.
>
> * * *
>
> As a matter of form, the upstream State has, procedurally, a right of initiative; it is not obliged to associate the downstream State in the elaboration of its schemes. If, in the course of discussions, the downstream State submits schemes to it, the upstream State must examine them, but it has the right to give preference to the solution contained in its own scheme provided that it takes into consideration in a reasonable manner the interests of the downstream State.

The Tribunal then held that, although the State Parties had failed to reach agreement, France had sufficiently involved Spain in the preparation of its hydroelectric scheme.

8.4 TRAIL SMELTER ARBITRATION (U.S. V. CAN.) (1941), 3 U.N.R.I.A.A. 1938 (1949)

[*Eds.*—This case resulted from sulphur dioxide (SO_2) fumes emitted into the atmosphere by a smelter plant owned by a Canadian corporation (the Consolidated Mining and Smelting Company of Canada, Limited), located on the Columbia River at Trail, British Columbia, seven miles from the State of Washington. The Trail smelter plant was alleged to have caused environmental damage in that United States jurisdiction (Washington). It was decided by a special Arbitral Tribunal composed of one American chosen by the United States, one Canadian chosen by Canada, and a Belgian chosen by the United States and Canada jointly. The convention establishing the Tribunal called for the application of the "law and practice followed in dealing with cognate questions in the United States of America as well as international law and practice." 3 U.N.R.I.A.A. 1905, 1908 (1949). In a prior decision, the Tribunal had determined that the air pollution created by the smelter had caused damage in the State of Washington over a 12–year period, from 1925 to 1937. In the instant decision, reported on March 11, 1941, the Tribunal held Canada responsible and directed injunctive relief and payment of an indemnity, as follows:]

[1]. This Tribunal is constituted under, and its powers are derived from and limited by, the Convention between the United States of America and the Dominion of Canada signed at Ottawa, April, 15, 1935, duly ratified by the two parties, and ratifications exchanged at Ottawa, August 3, 1935 (hereinafter termed "the Convention").

* * *

[4]. The Tribunal herewith reports its final decisions.

[5]. The controversy is between two Governments involving damage occurring, or having occurred, in the territory of one of them (the United States of America) and alleged to be due to an agency situated in the territory of the other (the Dominion of Canada). In this controversy, the Tribunal did not sit and is not sitting to pass upon claims presented by individuals or on behalf of one or more individuals by their Government, although individuals may come within the meaning of "parties concerned", in Article IV and of "interested parties", in Article VIII of the Convention and although the damage suffered by individuals did, in part, "afford a convenient scale for the calculation of the reparation due to the State" * * *

[6]. As between the two countries involved, each has an equal interest that if a nuisance is proved, the indemnity to damaged parties for proven damage shall be just and adequate and each has also an equal interest that unproven or unwarranted claims shall not be allowed. For, while the United States' interests may now be claimed to be injured by the operations of a Canadian corporation, it is equally possible that at some time in the future Canadian interests might be claimed to be injured by an American corporation. As has well been said: "It would not be to the advantage of the two countries concerned that industrial effort should be prevented by exaggerating the interests of the agricultural community. Equally, it would not be to the advantage of the two countries that the agricultural community should be oppressed to advance the interest of industry."

[7]. Considerations like the above are reflected in the provisions of the Convention in Article IV, that "the desire of the high contracting parties" is "to reach a solution just to all parties concerned". And the phraseology of the questions submitted to the Tribunal clearly evinces a desire and an intention that, to some extent, in making its answers to the questions, the Tribunal should endeavor to adjust the conflicting interests by some "just solution" which would allow the continuance of the operation of the Trail Smelter but under such restrictions and limitations as would, as far as foreseeable, prevent damage in the United States, and as would enable indemnity to be obtained, if in spite of such restrictions and limitations, damage should occur in the future in the United States.

[8]. In arriving at its decision, the Tribunal has had always to bear in mind the further fact that in the preamble to the Convention, it is stated that it is concluded with the recognition of "the desirability and necessity of effecting a permanent settlement".

[9]. The duty imposed upon the Tribunal by the Convention was to "finally decide" the following questions:

(1) Whether damage caused by the Trail Smelter in the State of Washington has occurred since the first day of January, 1932, and, if so, what indemnity should be paid therefor?

(2) In the event of the answer to the first part of the preceding question being in the affirmative, whether the Trail Smelter should be required to refrain from causing damage in the State of Washington in the future and, if so, to what extent?

(3) In the light of the answer to the preceding question, what measures or régime, if any, should be adopted or maintained by the Trail Smelter?

(4) What indemnity or compensation, if any, should be paid on account of any decision or decisions rendered by the Tribunal pursuant to the next two preceding questions?

* * *

[13]. On April 16, 1938, the Tribunal reported its "final decision" on Question No. 1, as well as its temporary decisions on Questions No. 2 and No. 3, and provided for a temporary régime thereunder. The decision reported on April 16, 1938, will be referred to hereinafter as the "previous decision".

[14]. Concerning Question No. 1, in the statement presented by the Agent for the Government of the United States, claims for damages of $1,849,156.16 with interest of $250,855.01—total $2,100,011.17—were presented, divided into seven categories, in respect of (a) cleared land and improvements; (b) of uncleared land and improvements; (c) live stock; (d) property in the town of Northport; (e) wrong done the United States in violation of sovereignty, measured by cost of investigation from January 1, 1932, to June 30, 1936; (f) interest on $350,000 accepted in satisfaction of damage to January 1, 1932, but not paid on that date; (g) business enterprises. The area claimed to be damaged contained "more than 140,000 acres", including the town of Northport.

[15]. The Tribunal disallowed the claims of the United States with reference to items (c), (d), (e), (f) and (g) but allowed them, in part, with respect to the remaining items (a) and (b).

[16]. In conclusion (end of Part Two of the previous decision), the Tribunal answered Question No. 1 as follows:

> Damage caused by the Trail Smelter in the State of Washington has occurred since the first day of January, 1932, and up to October 1, 1937, and the indemnity to be paid therefor is seventy-eight thousand dollars ($78,000), and is to be complete and final indemnity and compensation for all damage which occurred between such dates. Interest at the rate of six per centum per year will be allowed on the above sum of seventy-eight thousand dollars ($78,000) from the date of the filing of this report and decision until date of payment. This decision is not subject to alteration or modification by the Tribunal hereafter. The fact of existence of damage, if any, occurring after October 1, 1937, and the indemnity to be paid therefor, if any, the Tribunal will determine in its final decision.

[17]. Answering Questions No. 2 and No. 3, the Tribunal decided that, until a final decision should be made, the Trail Smelter should be subject to a temporary régime (described more in detail in Part Four of the present decision) and a trial period was established to a date not later than October 1, 1940, in order to enable the Tribunal to establish a permanent régime based on a "more adequate and intensive study", since the Tribunal felt that the information that had been placed before it did not enable it to determine at that time with sufficient certainty upon a permanent régime.

* * *

[19]. It had been provided in the previous decision that a final decision on the outstanding questions would be rendered within three months from the termination of the trial period therein prescribed, i.e., from October 1, 1940, unless the trial period was ended sooner. The trial period was not terminated before October 1, 1940, * * *.

* * *

[21]. The period within which the Tribunal shall report its final decisions was extended by agreement of the two Governments until March 12, 1941.

* * *

[57]. The first question under Article III of the Convention is: "(1) Whether damage caused by the Trail Smelter in the State of Washington has occurred since the first day of January, 1932, and, if so, what indemnity should be paid therefor."

[58]. This question has been answered by the Tribunal in its previous decision, as to the period from January 1, 1932 to October 1, 1937, as set forth above.

* * *

[113]. The Tribunal is requested to say that damage has occurred in the State of Washington since October 1, 1937, as a consequence of the emission

of sulphur dioxide by the smelters of the Consolidated Mining and Smelting Company at Trail, B.C., and that an indemnity in the sum of $34,807 should be paid therefor.

* * *

[137]. Since the Tribunal has, in its previous decision, answered Question No. 1 with respect to the period from the first day of January, 1932, to the first day of October, 1937, it now answers Question No. 1 with respect to the period from the first day of October, 1937, to the first day of October, 1940, as follows:

> (1) No damage caused by the Trail Smelter in the State of Washington has occurred since the first day of October, 1937, and prior to the first day of October, 1940, and hence no indemnity shall be paid therefor.

* * *

[138]. The second question under Article III of the Convention is as follows:

> In the event of the answer to the first part of the preceding question being in the affirmative, whether the Trail Smelter should be required to refrain from causing damage in the State of Washington in the future and, if so, to what extent?

[139]. Damage has occurred since January 1, 1932, as fully set forth in the previous decision. To that extent, the first part of the preceding question has thus been answered in the affirmative.

* * *

[142]. The first problem which arises is whether the question should be answered on the basis of the law followed in the United States or on the basis of international law. The Tribunal, however, finds that this problem need not be solved here as the law followed in the United States in dealing with the quasi-sovereign rights of the States of the Union, in the matter of air pollution, whilst more definite, is in conformity with the general rules of international law.

[143]. Particularly in reaching its conclusions as regards this question as well as the next, the Tribunal has given consideration to the desire of the high contracting parties "to reach a solution just to all parties concerned".

[144]. As Professor Eagleton puts in (*Responsibility of States in International Law,* 1928, p. 80): "A State owes at all times a duty to protect other States against injurious acts by individuals from within its jurisdiction." A great number of such general pronouncements by leading authorities concerning the duty of a State to respect other States and their territory have been presented to the Tribunal. These and many others have been carefully examined. International decisions, in various matters, from the Alabama case onward, and also earlier ones, are based on the same general principle, and, indeed, this principle, as such, has not been questioned by Canada. But the real difficulty often arises rather when it comes to determine what, *pro subjecta materie,* is deemed to constitute an injurious act.

* * *

[146]. No case of air pollution dealt with by an international tribunal has been brought to the attention of the Tribunal nor does the Tribunal know of any such case. The nearest analogy is that of water pollution. But, here also, no decision of an international tribunal has been cited or has been found.

[147]. There are, however, as regards both air pollution and water pollution, certain decisions of the Supreme Court of the United States which may legitimately be taken as a guide in this field of international law, for it is reasonable to follow by analogy, in international cases, precedents established by that court in dealing with controversies between States of the Union or with other controversies concerning the quasi-sovereign rights of such States, where no contrary rule prevails in international law and no reason for rejecting such precedents can be adduced from the limitations of sovereignty inherent in the Constitution of the United States.

[148]. In the suit of the *State of Missouri v. the State of Illinois* (200 U.S. 496, 521) concerning the pollution, within the boundaries of Illinois, of the Illinois River, an affluent of the Mississippi flowing into the latter where it forms the boundary between that State and Missouri, an injunction was refused. "Before this court ought to intervene", said the court, "the case should be of serious magnitude, clearly and fully proved, and the principle to be applied should be one which the court is prepared deliberately to maintain against all considerations on the other side. (See *Kansas v. Colorado,* 185 U.S. 125.)" The court found that the practice complained of was general along the shores of the Mississippi River at that time, that it was followed by Missouri itself and that thus a standard was set up by the defendant which the claimant was entitled to invoke.

[149]. As the claims of public health became more exacting and methods for removing impurities from the water were perfected, complaints ceased. It is significant that Missouri sided with Illinois when the other riparians of the Great Lakes' system sought to enjoin it to desist from diverting the waters of that system into that of the Illinois and Mississippi for the very purpose of disposing of the Chicago sewage.

[150]. In the more recent suit of the State of New York against the State of New Jersey (256 U.S. 296, 309), concerning the pollution of New York Bay, the injunction was also refused for lack of proof, some experts believing that the plans which were in dispute would result in the presence of "offensive odors and unsightly deposits", other equally reliable experts testifying that they were confidently of the opinion that the waters would be sufficiently purified. The court, referring to *Missouri v. Illinois,* said: " * * * the burden upon the State of New York of sustaining the allegations of its bill is much greater than that imposed upon a complainant in an ordinary suit between private parties. Before this court can be moved to exercise its extraordinary power under the Constitution to control the conduct of one State at the suit of another, the threatened invasion of rights must be of serious magnitude and it must be established by clear and convincing evidence."

[151]. What the Supreme Court says there of its power under the Constitution equally applies to the extraordinary power granted this Tribunal under the Convention. What is true between States of the Union is, at least, equally true concerning the relations between the United States and the Dominion of Canada.

[152]. In another recent case concerning water pollution (283 U.S. 473), the complainant was successful. The City of New York was enjoined, at the request of the State of New Jersey, to desist, within a reasonable time limit, from the practice of disposing of sewage by dumping it into the sea, a practice which was injurious to the coastal waters of New Jersey in the vicinity of her bathing resorts.

[153]. In the matter of air pollution itself, the leading decisions are those of the Supreme Court in the *State of Georgia v. Tennessee Copper Company and Ducktown Sulphur, Copper and Iron Company, Limited.* Although dealing with a suit against private companies, the decisions were on questions cognate to those here at issue. Georgia stated that it had in vain sought relief from the State of Tennessee, on whose territory the smelters were located, and the court defined the nature of the suit by saying: "This is a suit by a State for an injury to it in its capacity of quasi-sovereign. In that capacity, the State has an interest independent of and behind the titles of its citizens, in all the earth and air within its domain."

[154]. On the question whether an injunction should be granted or not, the court said (206 U.S. 230):

> It (the State) has the last word as to whether its mountains shall be stripped of their forests and its inhabitants shall breathe pure air * * *. It is not lightly to be presumed to give up quasi-sovereign rights for pay and * * * if that be its choice, it may insist that an infraction of them shall be stopped. This court has not quite the same freedom to balance the harm that will be done by an injunction against that of which the plaintiff complains, that it would have in deciding between two subjects of a single political power. Without excluding the considerations that equity always takes into account * * * it is a fair and reasonable demand on the part of a sovereign that the air over its territory should not be polluted on a great scale by sulphurous acid gas, that the forests on its mountains, be they better or worse, and whatever domestic destruction they may have suffered, should not be further destroyed or threatened by the act of persons beyond its control, that the crops and orchards on its hills should not be endangered from the same source * * *. Whether Georgia, by insisting upon this claim, is doing more harm than good to her own citizens, is for her to determine. The possible disaster to those outside the State must be accepted as a consequence of her standing upon her extreme rights.

[155]. Later on, however, when the court actually framed an injunction, in the case of the *Ducktown Company* (237 U.S. 474, 477) (an agreement on the basis of an annual compensation was reached with the most important of the two smelters, the Tennessee Copper Company), they did not go beyond a decree "adequate to diminish materially the present probability of damage to its (Georgia's) citizens".

[156]. Great progress in the control of fumes has been made by science in the last few years and this progress should be taken into account.

[157]. The Tribunal, therefore, finds that the above decisions, taken as a whole, constitute an adequate basis for its conclusions, namely, that, under the principles of international law, as well as of the law of the United States, no State has the right to use or permit the use of its territory in such a

manner as to cause injury by fumes in or to the territory of another or the properties or persons therein, when the case is of serious consequence and the injury is established by clear and convincing evidence.

[158]. The decisions of the Supreme Court of the United States which are the basis of these conclusions are decisions in equity and a solution inspired by them, together with the régime hereinafter prescribed, will, in the opinion of the Tribunal, be "just to all parties concerned", as long, at least, as the present conditions in the Columbia River Valley continue to prevail.

[159]. Considering the circumstances of the case, the Tribunal holds that the Dominion of Canada is responsible in international law for the conduct of the Trail Smelter. Apart from the undertakings in the Convention, it is, therefore, the duty of the Government of the Dominion of Canada to see to it that this conduct should be in conformity with the obligation of the Dominion under international law as herein determined.

[160]. The Tribunal, therefore, answers Question No. 2 as follows: (2) So long as the present conditions in the Columbia River Valley prevail, the Trail Smelter shall be required to refrain from causing any damage through fumes in the State of Washington; the damage herein referred to and its extent being such as would be recoverable under the decisions of the courts of the United States in suits between private individuals. The indemnity for such damage should be fixed in such manner as the Governments, acting under Article XI of the Convention, should agree upon.

PART FOUR

[161]. The third question under Article III of the Convention is as follows: "In the light of the answer to the preceding question, what measures or régime, if any, should be adopted and maintained by the Trail Smelter?"

[162]. Answering this question in the light of the preceding one, since the Tribunal has, in its previous decision, found that damage caused by the Trail Smelter has occurred in the State of Washington since January 1, 1932, and since the Tribunal is of opinion that damage may occur in the future unless the operations of the Smelter shall be subject to some control, in order to avoid damage occurring, the Tribunal now decides that a régime or measure of control shall be applied to the operations of the Smelter and shall remain in full force unless and until modified in accordance with the provisions hereinafter set forth in Section 3, Paragraph VI of the present part of this decision.

* * *

PART FIVE

[227]. The fourth question under Article III of the Convention is as follows:

What indemnity or compensation, if any, should be paid on account of any decision or decisions rendered by the Tribunal pursuant to the next two preceding Questions?

[228]. The Tribunal is of opinion that the prescribed régime will probably remove the causes of the present controversy and, as said before, will probably result in preventing any damage of a material nature occurring in the State of Washington in the future.

[229]. But since the desirable and expected result of the régime or measure of control hereby required to be adopted and maintained by the Smelter may not occur, and since in its answer to Question No. 2, the Tribunal has required the Smelter to refrain from causing damage in the State of Washington in the future, as set forth therein, the Tribunal answers Question No. 4 and decides that on account of decisions rendered by the Tribunal in its answers to Question No. 2 and Question No. 3 there shall be paid as follows: (*a*) if any damage as defined under Question No. 2 shall have occurred since October 1, 1940, or shall occur in the future, whether through failure on the part of the Smelter to comply with the regulations herein prescribed or notwithstanding the maintenance of the régime, an indemnity shall be paid for such damage but only when and if the two Governments shall make arrangements for the disposition of claims for indemnity under the provisions of Article XI of the Convention; (*b*) if as a consequence of the decision of the Tribunal in its answers to Question No. 2 and Question No. 3, the United States shall find it necessary to maintain in the future an agent or agents in the area in order to ascertain whether damage shall have occurred in spite of the régime prescribed herein, the reasonable cost of such investigations not in excess of $7,500 in any one year shall be paid to the United States as a compensation, but only if and when the two Governments determine under Article XI of the Convention that damage has occurred in the year in question, due to the operation of the Smelter, and "disposition of claims for indemnity for damage" has been made by the two Governments; but in no case shall the aforesaid compensation be payable in excess of the indemnity for damage; and further it is understood that such payment is hereby directed by the Tribunal only as a compensation to be paid on account of the answers of the Tribunal to Question No. 2 and Question No. 3 (as provided for in Question No. 4) and *not* as any part of indemnity for the damage to be ascertained and to be determined upon by the two Governments under Article XI of the Convention.

PART SIX

[230]. Since further investigations in the future may be possible under the provisions of Part Four and of Part Five of this decision, the Tribunal finds it necessary to include in its report, the following provision:

[231]. Investigators appointed by or on behalf of either Government, whether jointly or severally, and the members of the Commission provided for in Paragraph VI of Section 3 of Part Four of this decision, shall be permitted at all reasonable times to inspect the operations of the Smelter and to enter upon and inspect any of the properties in the State of Washington which may be claimed to be affected by fumes. This provision shall also apply to any localities where instruments are operated under the present régime or under any amended régime. Wherever under the present régime or any amended régime, instruments have to be maintained and operated by the Smelter on the territory of the United States, the Government of the United States shall undertake to secure for the Government of the Dominion of Canada the facilities reasonably required to that effect.

[232]. The Tribunal expresses the strong hope that any investigations which the Governments may undertake in the future, in connection with the matters dealt with in this decision, shall be conducted jointly.

8.5 CORFU CHANNEL CASE (U.K. V. ALB.), 1949 I.C.J. 4

[*Eds.*—On May 15, 1946, British warships passing through the Corfu Channel, in Albanian territorial waters, were fired upon by Albanian coastal batteries; and on October 22, 1946, two British warships passing through that Channel struck mines, which caused damage to the vessels and loss of lives among the crews. On November 12–13, 1946, without Albanian consent, units of the Royal British Navy swept for mines that part of the Corfu Channel that was situated in Albanian waters. The United Kingdom raised the issue in the Security Council, which recommended that the two Parties refer the matter to the International Court of Justice. When the case first came up for hearing, Albania unsuccessfully raised a Preliminary Objection to the Court's jurisdiction (1948 I.C.J. 4, 15). At the hearing on the merits, pursuant to a Special Agreement between the State parties, the Court had to consider the following two questions:

"(1) Is Albania responsible under international law for the explosions which occurred on the 22nd October 1946 in Albanian waters and for the damage and loss of human life which resulted from them and is there any duty to pay compensation?"

"(2) Has the United Kingdom under international law violated the sovereignty of the Albanian People's Republic by reason of the acts of the Royal Navy in Albanian waters on the 22nd October and on the 12th and 13th November 1946 and is there any duty to give satisfaction?"

On April 9, 1949, by 11 votes to 5, the Court held that Albania was responsible for the explosions and the ensuing damage, and, unanimously, that the United Kingdom had violated Albanian sovereignty in November. In so holding, the Court reasoned as follows:]

[16]. By the first part of the Special Agreement, the following question is submitted to the Court:

"(1) Is Albania responsible under international law for the explosions which occurred on the 22nd October 1946 in Albanian waters and for the damage and loss of·human life which resulted from them and is there any duty to pay compensation?"

[17]. On October 22nd, 1946, a squadron of British warships, the cruisers *Mauritius* and *Leander* and the destroyers *Saumarez* and *Volage,* left the port of Corfu and proceeded northward through a channel previously swept for mines in the North Corfu Strait. The cruiser *Mauritius* was leading, followed by the destroyer *Saumarez;* at a certain distance thereafter came the cruiser *Leander* followed by the destroyer *Volage.* Outside the Bay of Saranda, *Saumarez* struck a mine and was heavily damaged. *Volage* was ordered to give her assistance and to take her in tow. Whilst towing the damaged ship, *Volage* struck a mine and was much damaged. Nevertheless, she succeeded in towing the other ship back to Corfu.

[18]. Three weeks later, on November 13th, the North Corfu Channel was swept by British minesweepers and twenty-two moored mines were cut. Two mines were taken to Malta for expert examination. During the mine-sweeping operation it was thought that the mines were of the German GR

type, but it was subsequently established that they were of the German GY type.

* * *

[28]. The Court consequently finds that the following facts are established. The two ships were mined in Albanian territorial waters in a previously swept and check-swept channel just at the place where a newly laid minefield consisting of moored contact German GY mines was discovered three weeks later. The damage sustained by the ships was inconsistent with damage which could have been caused by floating mines, magnetic ground mines, magnetic moored mines, or German GR mines, but its nature and extent were such as would be caused by mines of the type found in the minefield. In such circumstances the Court arrives at the conclusion that the explosions were due to mines belonging to that minefield.

[29]. Such are the facts upon which the Court must, in order to reply to the first question of the Special Agreement, give judgment as to Albania's responsibility for the explosions on October 22nd, 1946, and for the damage and loss of human life which resulted, and for the compensation, if any, due in respect of such damage and loss.

[30]. To begin with, the foundation for Albania's responsibility, as alleged by the United Kingdom, must be considered. On this subject, the main position of the United Kingdom is to be found in its submission No. 2: that the minefield which caused the explosions was laid between May 15th, 1946, and October 22nd, 1946, by or with the connivance or knowledge of the Albanian Government.

[31]. The Court considered first the various grounds for responsibility alleged in this submission.

[32]. In fact, although the United Kingdom Government never abandoned its contention that Albania herself laid the mines, very little attempt was made by the Government to demonstrate this point. In the written Reply, the United Kingdom Government takes note of the Albanian Government's formal statement that it did not lay the mines, and was not in a position to do so, as Albania possessed no navy; and that, on the whole Albanian littoral, the Albanian authorities only had a few launches and motor boats. In the light of these statements, the Albanian Government was called upon, in the Reply, to disclose the circumstances in which two Yugoslav war vessels, the *Mljet* and the *Meljine,* carrying contact mines of the GY type, sailed southward from the port of Sibenik on or about October 18th, and proceeded to the Corfu Channel. The United Kingdom Government, having thus indicated the argument upon which it was thenceforth to concentrate, stated that it proposed to show that the said warships, with the knowledge and connivance of the Albanian Government, laid mines in the Corfu Channel just before October 22nd, 1946. The facts were presented in the same light and in the same language in the oral reply by Counsel for the United Kingdom Government at the sittings on January 17th and 18th, 1949.

[33]. Although the suggestion that the minefield was laid by Albania was repeated in the United Kingdom statement in Court on January 18th, 1949, and in the final submissions read in Court on the same day, this

suggestion was in fact hardly put forward at that time except *pro memoria,* and no evidence in support was furnished.

[34].   In these circumstances, the Court need pay no further attention to this matter.

[35].   The Court now comes to the second alternative argument of the United Kingdom Government, namely, that the minefield was laid with the connivance of the Albanian Government.   According to this argument, the minelaying operation was carried out by two Yugoslav warships at a date prior to October 22nd, but very near that date.   This would imply collusion between the Albanian and the Yugoslav Governments, consisting either of a request by the Albanian Government to the Yugoslav Government for assistance, or of acquiescence by the Albanian authorities in the laying of the mines.

* * *

[42].   In the light of the information now available to the Court, the authors of the minelaying remain unknown.   In any case, the task of the Court, as defined by the Special Agreement, is to decide whether Albania is responsible, under international law, for the explosions which occurred on October 22nd, 1946, and to give judgment as to the compensation, if any.

[43].   Finally, the United Kingdom Government put forward the argument that, whoever the authors of the minelaying were, it could not have been done without the Albanian Government's knowledge.

[44].   It is clear that knowledge of the minelaying cannot be imputed to the Albanian Government by reason merely of the fact that a minefield discovered in Albanian territorial waters caused the explosions of which the British warships were the victims.   It is true, as international practice shows, that a State on whose territory or in whose waters an act contrary to international law has occurred, may be called upon to give an explanation.   It is also true that that State cannot evade such a request by limiting itself to a reply that it is ignorant of the circumstances of the act and of its authors. The State may, up to a certain point, be bound to supply particulars of the use made by it of the means of information and inquiry at its disposal.   But it cannot be concluded from the mere fact of the control exercised by a State over its territory and waters that that State necessarily knew, or ought to have known, of any unlawful act perpetrated therein, nor yet that it necessarily knew, or should have known, the authors.   This fact, by itself and apart from other circumstances, neither involves *prima facie* responsibility nor shifts the burden of proof.

[45].   On the other hand, the fact of this exclusive territorial control exercised by a State within its frontiers has a bearing upon the methods of proof available to establish the knowledge of that State as to such events.   By reason of this exclusive control, the other State, the victim of a breach of international law, is often unable to furnish direct proof of facts giving rise to responsibility.   Such a State should be allowed a more liberal recourse to inferences of fact and circumstantial evidence.   This indirect evidence is admitted in all systems of law, and its use is recognized by international decisions.   It must be regarded as of special weight when it is based on a series of facts linked together and leading logically to a single conclusion.

[46]. The Court must examine therefore whether it has been established by means of indirect evidence that Albania has knowledge of minelaying in her territorial waters independently of any connivance on her part in this operation. The proof may be drawn from inferences of fact, provided that they leave *no room* for reasonable doubt. The elements of fact on which these inferences can be based may differ from those which are relevant to the question of connivance.

[47]. In the present case, two series of facts, which corroborate one another, have to be considered: the first relates to Albania's attitude before and after the disaster of October 22nd, 1946; the other concerns the feasibility of observing minelaying from the Albanian coast.

[48]. 1. It is clearly established that the Albanian Government constantly kept a close watch over the waters of the North Corfu Channel, at any rate after May 1946.... This vigilance sometimes went so far as to involve the use of force....

* * *

[53]. Another indication of the Albanian Government's knowledge consists in the fact that that Government did not notify the presence of mines in its waters, at the moment when it must have known this, at the latest after the sweep on November 13th, and further, whereas the Greek Government immediately appointed a Commission to inquire into the events of October 22nd, the Albanian Government took no decision of such a nature, nor did it proceed to the judicial investigation incumbent, in such a case, on the territorial sovereign.

[54]. This attitude does not seem reconcilable with the alleged ignorance of the Albanian authorities that the minefield had been laid in Albanian territorial waters. It could be explained if the Albanian Government, while knowing of the minelaying, desired the circumstances of the operation to remain secret.

[55]. 2. As regards the possibility of observing minelaying from the Albanian coast, the Court regards the following facts, relating to the technical conditions of a secret minelaying and to the Albanian surveillance, as particularly important.

[56]. The Bay of Saranda and the channel used by shipping through the Strait are, from their geographical configuration, easily watched; the entrance of the bay is dominated by heights offering excellent observation points, both over the bay and over the Strait; whilst the channel throughout is close to the Albanian coast. The laying of a minefield in these waters could hardly fail to have been observed by the Albanian coastal defences.

[57]. On this subject, it must first be said that the minelaying operation itself must have required a certain time. The method adopted required, according to the Experts of the Court, the methodical and well thought-out laying of two rows of mines that had clearly a combined offensive and defensive purpose: offensive, to prevent the passage, through the Channel, of vessels drawing ten feet of water or more; defensive, to prevent vessels of the same draught from entering the Bay of Saranda. The report of the Experts reckons the time that the minelayers would have been in the waters, between Cape Kiephali and St. George's Monastery, at between two and two and a half

hours. This is sufficient time to attract the attention of the observation posts, placed, as the Albanian Government stated, at Cape Kiephali and St. George's Monastery.

* * *

[62]. The Court cannot fail to give great weight to the opinion of the Experts who examined the locality in a manner giving every guarantee of correct and impartial information. Apart from the existence of a look-out post at Cape Denta, which has not been proved, the Court, basing itself on the declarations of the Albanian Government that look-out posts were stationed at Cape Kiephali and St. George's Monastery, refers to the following conclusions in the Experts' Report: (1) that in the case of minelaying from the North towards the South, the minelayers would have been seen from Cape Kiephali; (2) in the case of minelaying from the South, the minelayers would have been seen from Cape Kiephali and St. George's Monastery.

[63]. From all the facts and observations mentioned above, the Court draws the conclusion that the laying of the minefield which caused the explosions on October 22nd, 1946, could not have been accomplished without the knowledge of the Albanian Government.

[64]. The obligations resulting for Albania from this knowledge are not disputed between the Parties. Counsel for the Albanian Government expressly recognized that [*translation*] "if Albania had been informed of the operation before the incidents of October 22nd, and in time to warn the British vessels and shipping in general of the existence of mines in the Corfu Channel, her responsibility would be involved * * *.".

[65]. The obligations incumbent upon the Albanian authorities consisted in notifying, for the benefit of shipping in general, the existence of a minefield in Albanian territorial waters and in warning the approaching British warships of the imminent danger to which the minefield exposed them. Such obligations are based, not on the Hague Convention of 1907, No. VIII, which is applicable in time of war, but on certain general and well-recognized principles, namely: elementary considerations of humanity, even more exacting in peace than in war; the principle of the freedom of maritime communication; and every State's obligation not to allow knowingly its territory to be used for acts contrary to the rights of other States.

[66]. In fact, Albania neither notified the existence of the minefield, nor warned the British warships of the danger they were approaching.

[67]. But Albania's obligation to notify shipping of the existence of mines in her waters depends on her having obtained knowledge of that fact in sufficient time before October 22nd; and the duty of the Albanian coastal authorities to warn the British ships depends on the time that elapsed between the moment that these ships were reported and the moment of the first explosion.

[68]. On this subject, the Court makes the following observations. As has already been stated, the Parties agree that the mines were recently laid. It must be concluded that the minelaying, whatever may have been its exact date, was done at a time when there was a close Albanian surveillance over the Strait. If it be supposed that it took place at the last possible moment, i.e., in the night of October 21st–22nd, the only conclusion to be drawn would

be that a general notification to the shipping of all States before the time of the explosions would have been difficult, perhaps even impossible. But this would certainly not have prevented the Albanian authorities from taking, as they should have done, all necessary steps immediately to warn ships near the danger zone, more especially those that were approaching that zone. When on October 22nd about 13.00 hours the British warships were reported by the look-out post at St. George's Monastery to the Commander of the Coastal Defences as approaching Cape Long, it was perfectly possible for the Albanian authorities to use the interval of almost two hours that elapsed before the explosion affecting *Saumarez* (14.53 hours or 14.55 hours) to warn the vessels of the danger into which they were running.

[69]. In fact, nothing was attempted by the Albanian authorities to prevent the disaster. These grave omissions involve the international responsibility of Albania.

[70]. The Court therefore reaches the conclusion that Albania is responsible under international law for the explosions which occurred on October 22nd, 1946, in Albanian waters, and for the damage and loss of human life which resulted from them, and that there is a duty upon Albania to pay compensation to the United Kingdom.

* * *

[84]. In the second part of the Special Agreement, the following question is submitted to the Court:

"(2). Has the United Kingdom under international law violated the sovereignty of the Albanian People's Republic by reason of the acts of the Royal Navy in Albanian waters on the 22nd October and on the 12th and 13th November 1946 and is there any duty to give satisfaction?"

[85]. The Court will first consider whether the sovereignty of Albania was violated by reason of the acts of the British Navy in Albanian waters on October 22nd, 1946.

* * *

[91]. It is, in the opinion of the Court, generally recognized and in accordance with international custom that States in time of peace have a right to send their warships through straits used for international navigation between two parts of the high seas without the previous authorization of a coastal State, provided that the passage is *innocent*. Unless otherwise prescribed in an international convention, there is no right for a coastal State to prohibit such passage through straits in time of peace.

[92]. The Albanian Government does not dispute that the North Corfu Channel is a strait in the geographical sense; but it denies that this Channel belongs to the class of international highways through which a right of passage exists, on the grounds that it is only of secondary importance and not even a necessary route between two parts of the high seas, and that it is used almost exclusively for local traffic to and from the ports of Corfu and Saranda.

* * *

[94]. One fact of particular importance is that the North Corfu Channel constitutes a frontier between Albania and Greece, that a part of it is wholly

within the territorial waters of these States, and that the Strait is of special importance to Greece by reason of the traffic to and from the port of Corfu.

[95]. Having regard to these various considerations, the Court has arrived at the conclusion that the North Corfu Channel should be considered as belonging to the class of international highways through which passage cannot be prohibited by a coastal State in time of peace.

[96]. On the other hand, it is a fact that the two coastal States did not maintain normal relations, that Greece had made territorial claims precisely with regard to a part of Albanian territory bordering on the Channel, that Greece had declared that she considered herself technically in a state of war with Albania, and that Albania, invoking the danger of Greek incursions, had considered it necessary to take certain measures of vigilance in this region. The Court is of opinion that Albania, in view of these exceptional circumstances, would have been justified in issuing regulations in respect of the passage of warships through the Strait, but not in prohibiting such passage or in subjecting it to the requirement of special authorization.

[97]. For these reasons the Court is unable to accept the Albanian contention that the Government of the United Kingdom has violated Albanian sovereignty by sending the warships through the Strait without having obtained the previous authorization of the Albanian Government.

[98]. In these circumstances, it is unnecessary to consider the more general question, much debated by the Parties, whether States under international law have a right to send warships in time of peace through territorial waters not included in a strait.

* * *

[101]. It remains, therefore, to consider whether the *manner* in which the passage was carried out was consistent with the principle of innocent passage and to examine the various contentions of the Albanian Government in so far as they appear to be relevant.

* * *

[108]. Having examined the various contentions of the Albanian Government in so far as they appear to be relevant, the Court has arrived at the conclusion that the United Kingdom did not violate the sovereignty of Albania by reason of the acts of the British Navy in Albanian waters on October 22nd, 1946.

[109]. In addition to the passage of the United Kingdom warships on October 22nd, 1946, the second question in the Special Agreement relates to the acts of the Royal Navy in Albanian waters on November 12th and 13th, 1946. This is the minesweeping operation called "Operation Retail" by the Parties during the proceedings. This name will be used in the present Judgment.

* * *

[112]. The United Kingdom Government does not dispute that "Operation Retail" was carried out against the clearly expressed wish of the Albanian Government. It recognizes that the operation had not the consent of the international mine clearance organizations, that it could not be justified as

the exercise of a right of innocent passage, and lastly that, in principle, international law does not allow a State to assemble a large number of warships in the territorial waters of another State and to carry out minesweeping in those waters. The United Kingdom Government states that the operation was one of extreme urgency, and that it considered itself entitled to carry it out without anybody's consent.

* * *

[118]. The Court cannot accept such a line of defence. The Court can only regard the alleged right of intervention as the manifestation of a policy of force, such as has, in the past, given rise to most serious abuses and such as cannot, whatever be the present defects in international organization, find a place in international law. Intervention is perhaps still less admissible in the particular form it would take here; for, from the nature of things, it would be reserved for the most powerful States, and might easily lead to perverting the administration of international justice itself.

8.6 NUCLEAR TESTS CASES (N.Z. V. FR.), 1974 I.C.J. 253.[1]

[*Eds.*—In 1973, both Australia and New Zealand protested announced French atmospheric nuclear tests to be held in the South Pacific at France's Mururoa atoll. Additionally, they instituted proceedings before the International Court of Justice, by unilateral application in accordance with the General Act for the Pacific Settlement of International Disputes [2] as well as Article 36 of the Court's Statute **(Basic Document 1.4, supra)**. France denied the Court's competence and refused to appear. Australia and New Zealand also requested the Court to indicate interim measures of protection, on the ground that radioactive fallout from any tests held before the final judgment of the Court on the legality of such tests would prejudice the interests of the two countries concerned. In 1973, the Court, by 8 votes to 6, issued the requested order (1973 I.C.J. 99, 135). France ignored the Order and announced a further series of tests. Australia and New Zealand then asked the Court to declare such atmospheric tests to be illegal and to order France to abstain in the future. The Court considered the present hearing as related to preliminary matters and stated that it would avoid decisions on the substance. After the institution of proceedings, the French Government issued a number of statements intimating that no further tests would be held, and the Court decided, by 9 votes to 6, that the claims no longer had any object and that it was therefore not called upon to give a decision. The Court reasoned as follows:]

15. It is to be regretted that the French Government has failed to appear in order to put forward its arguments on the issues arising in the present phase of the proceedings, and the Court has thus not had the assistance it might have derived from such arguments or from any evidence adduced in support of them. The Court nevertheless has to proceed and reach a conclusion, and in doing so must have regard not only to the evidence brought before it and the arguments addressed to it by the Applicant, but also to any documentary or other evidence which may be relevant. It must on this basis satisfy itself, first that there exists no bar to the exercise of its judicial function, and secondly, if no such bar exists, that the Application is well founded in fact and in law.

16. The present case relates to a dispute between the Government of New Zealand and the French Government concerning the legality of atmospheric nuclear tests conducted by the latter Government in the South Pacific region. Since in the present phase of the proceedings the Court has to deal only with preliminary matters, it is appropriate to recall that its approach to a phase of this kind must be, as it was expressed in the *Fisheries Jurisdiction* cases, as follows:

"The issue being thus limited, the Court will avoid not only all expressions of opinion on matters of substance, but also any pronounce-

---

1. The case of Australia v. France, identical in all essential respects, is omitted due to space limitations.

2. Concluded 26 September 1928, entered into force 16 August 1929, 93 L.N.T.S. 343. The General Act was superseded in 1949 by the Revised General Act for the Pacific Settlement of International Disputes, concluded 28 April 1949, entered into force 20 September 1950, 71 UNTS 101, *reprinted as* Basic Document I.H.4 in 1 *International Law and World Order: Basic Documents* (B. Weston ed.1994).

ment which might prejudge or appear to prejudge any eventual decision on the merits." (*I.C.J. Reports 1973,* pp. 7 and 54.)

It will however be necessary to give a summary of the principal facts underlying the case.

17.   Prior to the filing of the Application instituting proceedings in this case, the French Government had carried out atmospheric tests of nuclear devices at its Centre d'expérimentations du Pacifique in the territory of French Polynesia, in the years 1966, 1967, 1968, 1970, 1971 and 1972.   The main firing site used has been Mururoa atoll, some 2,500 nautical miles from the nearest point of the North Island of New Zealand and approximately 1,050 nautical miles from the nearest point of the Cook Islands, a self-governing State linked in free association with New Zealand.   The French Government has created "Prohibited Zones" for aircraft and "Dangerous Zones" for aircraft and shipping, in order to exclude aircraft and shipping from the area of the tests centre;   these "zones" have been put into effect during the period of testing in each year in which tests have been carried out.

18.   As the United Nations Scientific Committee on the Effects of Atomic Radiation has recorded in its successive reports to the General Assembly, the testing of nuclear devices in the atmosphere has entailed the release into the atmosphere and the consequent dissipation, in varying degrees throughout the world, of measurable quantities of radio-active matter.   It is asserted by New Zealand that the French atmospheric tests have caused some fall-out of this kind to be deposited, *inter alia,* on New Zealand territory;   France has maintained, in particular, that the radio-active matter produced by its tests has been so infinitesimal that it may be regarded as negligible and that any fall-out on New Zealand territory has never involved any danger to the health of the population of New Zealand.   These disputed points are clearly matters going to the merits of the case, and the Court must therefore refrain, for the reasons given above, from expressing any view on them.

19.   By letters of 21 September 1973 and 1 November 1974, the Government of New Zealand informed the Court that subsequent to the Court's Order of 22 June 1973 indicating, as interim measures under Article 41 of the Statute, *(inter alia)* that the French Government should avoid nuclear tests causing the deposit of radio-active fall-out on New Zealand territory, two further series of atmospheric tests, in the months of July and August 1973 and June to September 1974, had been carried out at the Centre d'expérimentations du Pacifique.   The letters also stated that fall-out had been recorded on New Zealand territory, analysis of samples of which, according to the New Zealand Government, established conclusively the presence of fall-out from these tests, and that it was "the view of the New Zealand Government that there has been a clear breach by the French Government of the Court's Order of 22 June 1973".

20.   Recently a number of authoritative statements have been made on behalf of the French Government concerning its intentions as to future nuclear testing in the South Pacific region.   The significance of these statements, and their effect for the purposes of the present proceedings, will be examined in detail later in the present Judgment.

* * *

33. At the hearing of 10 July 1974 the Court was presented by counsel for New Zealand with an interpretation of certain expressions of intention communicated to the New Zealand Government by the French Government and the French President. In particular he referred to a communiqué of 8 June 1974 (paragraph 35 below) and a diplomatic Note of 10 June 1974 (paragraph 36 below), and after quoting from that Note, he said:

> "I emphasize two points: first, the most France is offering is that in her own time she will cease to disregard an existing Order of the Court; and second, even that offer is qualified by the phrase 'in the normal course of events'. New Zealand has not been given anything in the nature of an unqualified assurance that 1974 will see the end of atmospheric nuclear testing in the South Pacific."

Since that time, certain French authorities have made a number of consistent public statements concerning future tests which provide material facilitating the Court's task of assessing the Applicant's interpretation of the earlier documents, and which indeed require to be examined in order to discern whether they embody any modification of intention as to France's future conduct. It is true that these statements have not been made before the Court, but they are in the public domain, are known to the New Zealand Government, and were commented on by its Prime Minister in his statement of 1 November 1974. It will clearly be necessary to consider all these statements, both those drawn to the Court's attention in July 1974 and those subsequently made.

* * *

35. It will be convenient to take the statements referred to above in chronological order. The first statement is contained in the communiqué issued by the Office of the President of the French Republic on 8 June 1974, shortly before the commencement of the 1974 series of French nuclear tests:

> "The Decree reintroducing the security measures in the South Pacific nuclear test zone has been published in the Official Journal of 8 June 1974.
>
> The Office of the President of the Republic takes this opportunity of stating that in view of the stage reached in carrying out the French nuclear defence programme France will be in a position to pass on to the stage of underground explosions as soon as the series of tests planned for this summer is completed."

36. The second is contained in a Note of 10 June 1974 from the French Embassy in Wellington to the New Zealand Ministry of Foreign Affairs:

> "It should * * * be pointed out that the decision taken by the Office of the President of the French Republic to have the opening of the nuclear test series preceded by a press communiqué represents a departure from the practice of previous years. This procedure has been chosen in view of the fact that a new element has intervened in the development of the programme for perfecting the French deterrent force. This new element is as follows: France, at the point which has been reached in the execution of its programme of defence by nuclear means, will be in a position to move to the stage of underground firings as soon as the test series planned for this summer is completed.

Thus the atmospheric tests which will be carried out shortly will, in the normal course of events, be the last of this type.

The French authorities express the hope that the New Zealand Government will find this information of some interest and will wish to take it into consideration."

37.   As indicated by counsel for the Applicant at the hearing of 10 July 1974, the reaction of the New Zealand Prime Minister to this second statement was expressed in a letter to the President of the French Republic dated 11 June 1974, from which the following are two extracts:

" * * * I have noted that the terms of the announcement do not represent an unqualified renunciation of atmospheric testing for the future."

"I would hope that even at this stage you would be prepared to weigh the implications of any further atmospheric testing in the Pacific and resolve to put an end to this activity which has been the source of grave anxiety to the people in the Pacific region for more than a decade."

Thus the phrase "in the normal course of events" was regarded by New Zealand as qualifying the statement made, so that it did not meet the expectations of the Applicant, which evidently regarded those words as a form of escape clause.   This is clear from the observations of counsel for New Zealand at the hearing of 10 July 1974.   In a Note of 17 June 1974, the New Zealand Embassy in Paris stated that it had good reason to believe that France had carried out an atmospheric nuclear test on 16 June and made this further comment:

"The announcement that France will proceed to underground tests in 1975, while presenting a new development, does not affect New Zealand's fundamental opposition to all nuclear testing, nor does it in any way reduce New Zealand's opposition to the atmospheric tests set down for this year: the more so since the French Government is unable to give firm assurances that no atmospheric testing will be undertaken after 1974."

38.   The third French statement is contained in a reply made on 1 July 1974 by the President of the Republic to the New Zealand Prime Minister's letter of 11 June:

"In present circumstances, it is at least gratifying for me to note the positive reaction in your letter to the announcement in the communiqué of 8 June 1974 that we are going over to underground tests.   There is in this a new element whose importance will not, I trust, escape the New Zealand Government."

39.   These three statements were all drawn to the notice of the Court by the Applicant at the time of the oral proceedings.   As already indicated, the Court will also have to consider the relevant statements subsequently made by the French authorities: on 25 July 1974 by the President of the Republic; on 16 August 1974 by the Minister of Defence; on 25 September 1974 by the Minister for Foreign Affairs in the United Nations General Assembly; and on 11 October 1974 by the Minister of Defence.

40.   The next statement to be considered, therefore, will be that made on 25 July at a press conference given by the President of the Republic, when he said:

"* * * on this question of nuclear tests, you know that the Prime Minister had publicly expressed himself in the National Assembly in his speech introducing the Government's programme. He had indicated that French nuclear testing would continue. I had myself made it clear that this round of atmospheric tests would be the last, and so the members of the Government were completely informed of our intentions in this respect * * *"

41.   On 16 August 1974, in the course of an interview on French television, the Minister of Defence said that the French Government had done its best to ensure that the 1974 nuclear tests would be the last atmospheric tests.

42.   On 25 September 1974, the French Minister for Foreign Affairs, addressing the United Nations General Assembly, said:

"We have now reached a stage in our nuclear technology that makes it possible for us to continue our programme by underground testing, and we have taken steps to do so as early as next year."

43.   On 11 October 1974, the Minister of Defence held a press conference during which he stated twice, in almost identical terms, that there would not be any atmospheric tests in 1975 and that France was ready to proceed to underground tests. When the comment was made that he had not added "in the normal course of events", he agreed that he had not. This latter point is relevant in view of the Note of 10 June 1974 from the French Embassy in Wellington to the Ministry of Foreign Affairs of New Zealand (paragraph 36 above), to the effect that the atmospheric tests contemplated "will, in the normal course of events, be the last of this type". The Minister also mentioned that, whether or not other governments had been officially advised of the decision, they could become aware of it through the press and by reading the communiqués issued by the Office of the President of the Republic.

44.   In view of the foregoing, the Court finds that the communiqué issued on 8 June 1974 (paragraph 35 above), the French Embassy's Note of 10 June 1974 (paragraph 36 above) and the President's letter of 1 July 1974 (paragraph 38) conveyed to New Zealand the announcement that France, following the conclusion of the 1974 series of tests, would cease the conduct of atmospheric nuclear tests. Special attention is drawn to the hope expressed in the Note of 10 June 1974 "that the New Zealand Government will find this information of some interest and will wish to take it into consideration", and the reference in that Note and in the letter of 1 July 1974 to "a new element" whose importance is urged upon the New Zealand Government. The Court must consider in particular the President's statement of 25 July 1974 (paragraph 40 above) followed by the Defence Minister's statement of 11 October 1974 (paragraph 43). These reveal that the official statements made on behalf of France concerning future nuclear testing are not subject to whatever proviso, if any, was implied by the expression "in the normal course of events [*normalement*]".

45. Before considering whether the declarations made by the French authorities meet the object of the claim by the Applicant that no further atmospheric nuclear tests should be carried out in the South Pacific, it is first necessary to determine the status and scope on the international plane of these declarations.

46. It is well recognized that declarations made by way of unilateral acts, concerning legal or factual situations, may have the effect of creating legal obligations. Declarations of this kind may be, and often are, very specific. When it is the intention of the State making the declaration that it should become bound according to its terms, that intention confers on the declaration the character of a legal undertaking, the State being thenceforth legally required to follow a course of conduct consistent with the declaration. An undertaking of this kind, if given publicly, and with an intent to be bound, even though not made within the context of international negotiations, is binding. In these circumstances, nothing in the nature of a *quid pro quo,* nor any subsequent acceptance of the declaration, nor even any reply or reaction from other States, is required for the declaration to take effect, since such a requirement would be inconsistent with the strictly unilateral nature of the juridical act by which the pronouncement by the State was made.

47. Of course, not all unilateral acts imply obligation; but a State may choose to take up a certain position in relation to a particular matter with the intention of being bound—the intention is to be ascertained by interpretation of the act. When States make statements by which their freedom of action is to be limited, a restrictive interpretation is called for.

48. With regard to the question of form, it should be observed that this is not a domain in which international law imposes any special or strict requirements. Whether a statement is made orally or in writing makes no essential difference, for such statements made in particular circumstances may create commitments in international law, which does not require that they should be couched in written form. Thus the question of form is not decisive. As the Court said in its Judgment on the preliminary objections in the case concerning the *Temple of Preah Vihear:*

"Where * * * as is generally the case in international law, which places the principal emphasis on the intention of the parties, the law prescribes no particular form, parties are free to choose what form they please provided their intention clearly results from it." (*I.C.J. Reports 1961,* p. 31.)

The Court further stated in the same case: " * * * the sole relevant question is whether the language employed in any given declaration does reveal a clear intention * * * " (*ibid.,* p. 32).

49. One of the basic principles governing the creation and performance of legal obligations, whatever their source, is the principle of good faith. Trust and confidence are inherent in international co-operation, in particular in an age when this co-operation in many fields is becoming increasingly essential. Just as the very rule of *pacta sunt servanda* in the law of treaties is based on good faith, so also is the binding character of an international obligation assumed by unilateral declaration. Thus interested States may take cognizance of unilateral declarations and place confidence in them, and are entitled to require that the obligation thus created be respected.

50. Having examined the legal principles involved, the Court will now turn to the particular statements made by the French Government. The Government of New Zealand has made known to the Court its own interpretation of some of these statements at the oral proceedings (paragraph 27 above). As to subsequent statements, reference may be made to what was said by the Prime Minister of New Zealand on 1 November 1974 (paragraph 28 above). It will be observed that New Zealand has recognized the possibility of the dispute being resolved by a unilateral declaration, of the kind specified above, on the part of France. In the public statement of 1 November 1974, it is stated that "Until we have an assurance that nuclear testing of this kind is finished for good, the dispute between New Zealand and France persists". This is based on the view that "the option of further atmospheric tests have been left open". The Court must however form its own view of the meaning and scope intended by the author of a unilateral declaration which may create a legal obligation, and cannot in this respect be bound by the view expressed by another State which is in no way a party to the text.

51. Of the statements by the French Government now before the Court, the most essential are clearly those made by the President of the Republic. There can be no doubt, in view of his functions, that his public communications or statements, oral or written, as Head of State, are in international relations acts of the French State. His statements, and those of members of the French Government acting under his authority, up to the last statement made by the Minister of Defence (of 11 October 1974), constitute a whole. Thus, in whatever form these statements were expressed, they must be held to constitute an engagement of the State, having regard to their intention and to the circumstances in which they were made.

52. The unilateral statements of the French authorities were made outside the Court, publicly and *erga omnes,* even if some of them were communicated to the Government of New Zealand. As was observed above, to have legal effect, there was no need for these statements to be addressed to a particular State, nor was acceptance by any other State required. The general nature and characteristics of these statements are decisive for the evaluation of the legal implications, and it is to the interpretation of the statements that the Court must now proceed. The Court is entitled to presume, at the outset, that these statements were made *in vacuo,* but in relation to the tests which constitute the very object of the present proceedings, although France has not appeared in the case.

53. In announcing that the 1974 series of atmospheric tests would be the last, the French Government conveyed to the world at large, including the Applicant, its intention effectively to terminate these tests. It was bound to assume that other States might take note of these statements and rely on their being effective. The validity of these statements and their legal consequences must be considered within the general framework of the security of international intercourse, and the confidence and trust which are so essential in the relations among States. It is from the actual substance of these statements and from the circumstances attending their making, that the legal implications of the unilateral act must be deduced. The objects of these statements are clear and they were addressed to the international community as a whole, and the Court holds that they constitute an undertaking possessing legal effect. The Court considers that the President of the Republic, in

deciding upon the effective cessation of atmospheric tests, gave an undertaking to the international community to which his words were addressed. It is true that the French Government has consistently maintained that its nuclear experiments do not contravene any subsisting provision of international law, nor did France recognize that it was bound by any rule of international law to terminate its tests, but this does not affect the legal consequences of the statements examined above. The Court finds that the unilateral undertaking resulting from these statements cannot be interpreted as having been made in implicit reliance on an arbitrary power of reconsideration. The Court finds further that the French Government has undertaken an obligation the precise nature and limits of which must be understood in accordance with the actual terms in which they have been publicly expressed.

54. The Court will now confront the commitment entered into by France with the claim advanced by the Applicant. Though the latter has formally requested from the Court a finding on the rights and obligations of the Parties, it has throughout the dispute maintained as its final objective the termination of the tests. It has sought from France an assurance that the French programme of atmospheric nuclear testing would come to an end. While expressing its opposition to the 1974 tests, the Government of New Zealand made specific reference to an assurance that "1974 will see the end of atmospheric nuclear testing in the South Pacific" (paragraph 33 above). On more than one occasion it has indicated that it would be ready to accept such an assurance. Since the Court now finds that a commitment in this respect has been entered into by France, there is no occasion for a pronouncement in respect of rights and obligations of the Parties concerning the past—which in other circumstances the Court would be entitled and even obliged to make—whatever the date by reference to which such pronouncement might be made.

55. Thus the Court faces a situation in which the objective of the Applicant has in effect been accomplished, inasmuch as the Court finds that France has undertaken the obligation to hold no further nuclear tests in the atmosphere in the South Pacific.

* * *

58. The Court, as a court of law, is called upon to resolve existing disputes between States. Thus the existence of a dispute is the primary condition for the Court to exercise its judicial function; it is not sufficient for one party to assert that there is a dispute, since "whether there exists an international dispute is a matter for objective determination" by the Court (*Interpretation of Peace Treaties with Bulgaria, Hungary and Romania (First Phase), Advisory Opinion, I.C.J. Reports 1950,* p. 74). The dispute brought before it must therefore continue to exist at the time when the Court makes its decision. It must not fail to take cognizance of a situation in which the dispute has disappeared because the final objective which the Applicant has maintained throughout has been achieved by other means. If the declarations of France concerning the effective cessation of the nuclear tests have the significance described by the Court, that is to say if they have caused the dispute to disappear, all the necessary consequences must be drawn from this finding.

59. It may be argued that although France may have undertaken such an obligation, by a unilateral declaration, not to carry out atmospheric

nuclear tests in the South Pacific region, a judgment of the Court on this subject might still be of value because, if the Judgment upheld the Applicant's contentions, it would reinforce the position of the Applicant by affirming the obligation of the Respondent. However, the Court having found that the Respondent has assumed an obligation as to conduct, concerning the effective cessation of nuclear tests, no further judicial action is required. The Applicant has repeatedly sought from the Respondent an assurance that the tests would cease, and the Respondent has, on its own initiative, made a series of statements to the effect that they will cease. Thus the Court concludes that, the dispute having disappeared, the claim advanced by New Zealand no longer has any object. It follows that any further finding would have no *raison d'être*.

* * *

62. Thus the Court finds that no further pronouncement is required in the present case. It does not enter into the adjudicatory functions of the Court to deal with issues *in abstracto*, once it has reached the conclusion that the merits of the case no longer fall to be determined. The object of the claim having clearly disappeared, there is nothing on which to give judgment.

APPENDIX

STATUS OF BASIC DOCUMENTS IN INTERNATIONAL ENVIRONMENTAL LAW AND WORLD ORDER (AS OF 31 DECEMBER 1992)

*For the texts of reservations, declarations, and statements of understanding qualifying the ratification of, or accession or succession to, the multilateral treaties listed herein, see **United Nations Multilateral Treaties Deposited with the Secretary General**, published each year.*

1. CONSTITUTIVE/ORGANIC

General

1.1 CONSTITUTION OF THE UNITED STATES

1.2 CONSTITUTION OF THE INTERNATIONAL LABOUR ORGANISATION

Entered into force: 10 January 1920

> Note: The ILO Constitution was an integral part of, and came into force with, the Treaty of Peace between the Allied and Associated Powers and Germany (Treaty of Versailles) which was concluded 28 June 1919 and entered into force 10 January 20. Membership in the League of Nations carried with it automatic membership in the ILO.

Members: 165

Afghanistan (27 Sep 34), Algeria (19 Oct 62), Angola (4 Jun 76), Antigua and Barbuda (16 Feb 82), Argentina (1919), Armenia (1992), Austria (24 Jun 47), Azerbaijan (1992), Bahamas (25 May 76), Bahrain (18 Apr 77), Bangladesh (22 Jun 72), Barbados (8 May 67), Belarus (Byelorussian SSR) (12 May 54), Belgium (1919), Belize (17 Nov 81), Benin (12 Dec 60), Bolivia (1919), Bosnia and Herzegovina (1991), Botswana (27 Feb 78), Brazil (1919), Bulgaria (16 Dec 20), Burma (18 May 48), Burundi (11 Mar 63), Cameroon (7 Jun 60), Canada (1919), Cape Verde (3 Apr 79), Central African Republic (27 Oct 60), Chad (10 Nov 60), Chile (1919), China (1919), Colombia (1919), Comoros (23 Oct 78), Congo 10 Nov 60), Costa Rica (21 Apr 44), Côte d'Ivoire (21 Nov 60), (21 Nov 60), Croatia (1992), Cuba (1919), Cyprus (23 Sep 60), Czechoslovakia (1919), Denmark (1919), Djibouti (3 May 78), Dominica (17 Jun 82), Dominican Republic (29 Sep 24), Ecuador (28 Sep 34), Egypt (19 Jun 36), El Salvador (21 Jun 48), Equatorial Guinea (30 Jan 81), Estonia (1991), Ethiopia (28 Sep 23), Fiji (19 Apr 74), Finland (16 Dec 20), France (1919), Gabon (14 Oct 60), Germany (12 Jun 51), Ghana (20 May 57), Georgia (1992), Greece (1919), Guyana (8 Jun 66), Haiti (1919), Honduras (1 Jan 55), Hungary (18 Sep 22), Iceland (19 Oct 45), India (1919), Indonesia (12 Jun 50), Iran (1919), Iraq (3 Oct 32), Ireland (10 Sep 23), Israel (13 May 49), Italy (19 Oct 45), Jamaica (26 Dec 62), Japan (26 Nov 51), Jordan (26 Jan 56), Kampuchea (24 Feb 69), Kazakhstan (1992), Korea (South) (1991), Kyrgyzstan (1992), Kenya (13 Jan 64), Kuwait (13 Jun 61), Latvia (1991), Lithuania (1991), Luxembourg (16 Dec 20), Madagascar (1 Nov 60), Malawi (22 Mar 65), Malaysia (11 Nov 57), Mali (22 Sep 31), Mexico (12 Sep 31), Moldova (1992), Mongolia (24 May 68), Morocco (13 Jun 56), Mozambique (28 May 76), Namibia (3 Oct 78), Nepal (30 Aug 66), Netherlands (1919), New Zealand (1919), Nicaragua (9 Apr 57), Niger (27 Feb 61), Nigeria (17 Oct 60), Norway (1919), Pakistan (31 Oct 47), Panama (1919), Papua New Guinea (1 May 76), Paraguay (5 Sep 56), Peru (1919), Philippines (15 Jun 48), Poland (1919), Portugal (1919), Qatar (25 Apr 72), Romania (11 May 56), Russia (USSR) (26 Apr 54), Rwanda (18 Sep 62), St. Lucia (9 Apr 80), San Marino (18 Jun 82), São Tomé and Príncipe (1 Jun 82), Saudi Arabia (12 Jan 76), Senegal (4 Nov 60), Seychelles (25 Apr 77), Sierra Leone (13 Jun 61), Singapore (25 Oct 65), Slovenia (1992), Solomon Islands (28 May 84), Somalia (18 Nov 60), Spain (28 May 56), Sri Lanka (28 Jun 48), Sudan (12 Jun 56), Suriname (24 Feb 76), Swaziland (20 May 75), Sweden (1919), Switzerland (1919), Syria (4 Dec 47), Tanzania (30 Jan 62), Thailand (1919), Togo (7 Jun 60), Trinidad and Tobago (24 May 63), Tunisia (12 Jun 56), Turkey (18 Jul 32), Turkmenistan (1992), Uganda (25 Mar 63), Ukraine (Ukrainian SSR) (12 May 54), United Arab Emirates (25 Apr 72), United Kingdom (1919), United States (18 Feb 80), Upper Volta (21 Nov 60), Uruguay (1919), Uzbekistan (1992), Venezuela (16 mar 58), Yemen (20 May 65), Yemen (Democratic) (14 Apr 69), Yugoslavia (23 May 51), Zaire (20 Sep 60), Zambia (2 Dec 64), Zimbabwe (6 Jun 80)

Denunciations: 1
Vietnam (17 Jan 80)

1.3　**CHARTER OF THE UNITED NATIONS**

Entered into force: 24 October 1945

Parties: 166

Original members: 51
Argentina (24 Sep 45), Australia (1 Nov 45), Belarus (Byelorussian SSR) (24 Oct 45), Belgium (27 Dec 45), Bolivia (14 Nov 45), Brazil (21 Sep 45), Canada (9 Nov 45), Chile (11 Oct 45), China* (28 Sep 45), Colombia (5 Nov 45), Costa Rica (2 Nov 45), Cuba (15 Oct 45), Czechoslovakia (19 Oct 45), Denmark (9 Oct 45), Dominican Republic (4 Sep 45), Ecuador (21 Dec 45), Egypt (22 Oct 45), El Salvador (26 Sep 45), Ethiopia (13 Nov 45), France (31 Aug 45), Greece (25 Oct 45), Guatemala (21 Nov 45), Haiti (27 Sep 45), Honduras (17 Dec 45), India (30 Oct 45), Iran (16 Oct 45), Iraq (21 Dec 45), Lebanon (17 Oct 45), Liberia (15 Oct 45), Luxembourg (2 Nov 45), Mexico (7 Nov 45), Netherlands (10 Dec 45), New Zealand (10 Sep 45), Nicaragua (6 Sep 45), Norway (27 Nov 45), Panama (13 Nov 45), Paraguay (12 Oct 45), Peru (31 Oct 45), Philippines (11 Oct 45), Poland (24 Oct 45), Russia (USSR) (24 Oct 45), Saudi Arabia (18 Oct 45), South Africa (7 Nov 45), Syria (19 Oct 45), Turkey (28 Sep 45), Ukraine (Ukrainian SSR) (24 Oct 45), United Kingdom (20 Oct 45), United States (8 Aug 45), Uruguay (18 Dec 45), Venezuela (15 Nov 45), Yugoslavia (19 Oct 45)

　　*　China was originally represented in the UN by the Government of the Republic of China (R.O.C.) on Taiwan until 25 October 1971. Since then, China has been represented by the Government of the People's Republic of China. The R.O.C. is not a member of the UN and has no representation.

Non-signatories admitted under Article 4: 128

Afghanistan (9 Nov 46), Albania (14 Dec 55), Algeria (8 Oct 62), Angola (1 Dec 76), Antigua and Barbuda (11 Nov 81), Armenia (2 Mar 92), Austria (14 Dec 55), Azerbaijan (2 Mar 92), Bahamas (18 Sep 73), Bahrain (21 Sep 71), Bangladesh (17 Sep 74), Barbados (9 Dec 66), Belize (25 Sep 81), Benin (20 Sep 60), Bhutan (21 Sep 71), Botswana (17 Oct 66), Bosnia and Herzegovina (22 May 92), Brunei (21 Sep 84), Bulgaria (14 Dec 55), Burkina Faso (20 Sep 60), Burundi (18 Sep 62), Cambodia (14 Dec 55), Cameroon (20 Sep 60), Cape Verde (16 Sep 75), Central African Republic (20 Sep 60), Chad (20 Sep 60), Comoros (12 Nov 75), Congo (20 Sep 60), Côte d'Ivoire (20 Sep 60), Croatia (22 May 92), Cyprus (20 Sep 60), Djibouti (20 Sep 77), Dominica (18 Dec 78), Equatorial Guinea (12 Nov 68), Estonia (17 Sep 91), Fiji (13 Oct 70), Finland (14 Dec 55), Gabon (20 Sep 60), Gambia (21 Sep 65), Georgia (31 Jul 92), Germany (18 Sep 73), Ghana (8 Mar 57), Grenada (17 Sep 74), Guinea (12 Dec 58), Guinea–Bissau (17 Sep 74), Guyana (20 Sep 66), Hungary (14 Dec 55), Iceland (19 Nov 46), Indonesia (28 Sep 50), Ireland (14 Dec 55), Israel (11 May 49), Italy (14 Dec 55), Jamaica (18 Sep 62), Japan (18 Dec 56), Jordan (14 Dec 55), Kazakhstan (2 Mar 92), Kenya (16 Dec 63), Korea (North) (17 Sep 91), Korea (South) (17 Sep 91), Kuwait (14 May 63), Kyrgyzstan (2 Mar 92), Lao People's Democratic Republic (14 Dec 55), Latvia (17 Sep 91), Lesotho (17 Oct 66), Libya (14 Dec 55), Liechtenstein (18 Sep 90), Lithuania (17 Sep 91), Madagascar (20 Sep 60), Malawi (1 Dec 64), Malaysia (17 Sep 57), Maldives (21 Sep 65), Mali (28 Sep 60), Malta (1 Dec 64), Marshall Islands (17 Sep 91), Mauritania (27 Oct 61), Mauritius (24 Apr 68), Micronesia (17 Sep 91), Republic of Moldova (2 Mar 92), Mongolia (27 Oct 61), Morocco (12 Nov 56), Mozambique (16 Sep 75), Myanmar (19 Apr 48), Namibia (23 Apr 90), Nepal (14 Dec 55), Niger (20 Sep 60), Nigeria (7 Oct 60), Oman (7 Oct 71), Pakistan (30 Sep 47), Papua New Guinea (10 Oct 75), Portugal (14 Dec 55), Qatar (21 Sep 71), Romania (14 Dec 55), Rwanda (18 Sep 62), St. Kitts and Nevis (23 Sep 83), St. Lucia (18 Sep 79), St. Vincent and the Grenadines (18 Sep 80), Samoa (15 Dec 76), San Marino (2 Mar 92), São Tomé and Príncipe (16 Sep 75), Senegal (28 Sep 60), Seychelles (21 Sep 76), Sierra Leone (27 Sep 61), Singapore (21 Sep 65), Solomon Islands (19 Sep 78), Slovenia (22 May 92), Somalia (20 Sep 60), Spain (14 Dec 55), Sri Lanka (14 Dec 55), Sudan (12 Nov 56), Suriname (4 Dec 75), Swaziland (24 Sep 68), Sweden (19 Nov 46), Tajikistan (2 Mar 92), Tanzania (26 Apr 61), Thailand (15 Dec 46), Togo (20 Sep 60), Trinidad and Tobago (18 Sep 62), Tunisia (12 Nov 56), Turkmenistan (2 Mar 92), Uganda (25 Oct 62), United Arab Emirates (9 Dec 71), Uzbekistan (2 Mar 92), Vanuatu (15 Sep 81), Vietnam (20 Sep 77), Yemen (30 Sep 47), Zaire (20 Sep 60), Zambia (1 Dec 64), Zimbabwe (25 Aug 80)

1.4   STATUTE OF THE INTERNATIONAL COURT OF JUSTICE

Entered into force: 24 October 1945

Note: The Statute is part of the UN Charter. All members of the UN are parties to the Statute. Non-members may become parties to the Statute on conditions set in each case by the General Assembly on the recommendation of the Security Council. (Art. 93, Charter)

Non-members who are parties to the Statute: 4

Nauru (29 Jan 88), Switzerland (28 Jun 48), San Marino (18 Feb 54)

1.5   STATUTE OF THE INTERNATIONAL ATOMIC AGENCY (IAEA)

Entered into force: 29 July 1957

Ratified/accepted/approved without qualification: 100
Afghanistan (31 May 57), Algeria (24 Dec 63), Australia (29 Jul 57),
Austria (10 May 57), Bangladesh (27 Sep 72), Belgium (29 Apr 58),
Bolivia (15 Mar 63), Brazil (29 Jul 57), Bulgaria (17 Aug 57), Cambodia
(6 Feb 58), Cameroon (13 Jul 64), Canada (29 Jul 57), Chile (19 Sep 60),
China (1 Jan 84), Colombia (30 Sep 60), Costa Rica (25 Mar 65), Côte
d'Ivoire (19 Nov 63), Cuba (1 Oct 57), Cyprus (7 Jun 65), Denmark (16
Jul 57), Dominican Republic (11 Jul 57), Ecuador (3 Mar 58), Egypt (4
Sep 57), El Salvador (22 Nov 57), Estonia (31 Jan 92), Ethiopia (30 Sep
57), Finland (7 Jan 58), France (29 Jul 57), Gabon (21 Jan 64),
Germany (1 Oct 57), Ghana (28 Sep 60), Greece (30 Sep 57), Guatemala
(29 Mar 57), Haiti (7 Oct 57), Holy See (29 Aug 57), Iceland (6 Aug 57),
Indonesia (7 Aug 57), Iran (16 Sep 58), Iraq (4 Mar 59), Ireland (6 Jan
70), Israel (12 Jul 57), Italy (30 Sep 57), Jamaica (29 Dec 65), Japan (16
Jul 57), Jordan (18 Apr 66), Kenya (12 Jul 65), Korea (North) (18 Sep
74), Korea (South) (8 Aug 57), Kuwait (1 Dec 64), Lebanon (29 Jun 61),
Liberia (5 Oct 62), Libya (9 Sep 63), Liechtenstein (13 Dec 68), Luxembourg (29 Jan 58), Madagascar (22 Mar 65), Malaysia (15 Jan 69), Mali
(10 Aug 61), Mauritius (31 Dec 74), Mexico (7 Apr 58), Monaco (19 Sep
57), Mongolia (20 Sep 73), Morocco (17 Sep 57), Myanmar (18 Oct 57),
Namibia (17 Feb 83), Netherlands (30 Jul 57), New Zealand (13 Sep 57),
Nicaragua (25 Mar 77), Niger (27 Mar 69), Nigeria (25 Mar 64), Norway
(10 Jun 57), Pakistan (2 May 57), Panama (2 Mar 66), Paraguay (30 Sep
57), Peru (30 Sep 57), Philippines (2 Sep 58), Portugal (12 Jul 57),
Qatar (27 Feb 76), Saudi Arabia (13 Dec 62), Senegal (1 Nov 60), Sierra
Leone (4 Jun 67), Singapore (5 Jan 67), South Africa (6 Jun 57),
Slovenia (1992), Spain (26 Aug 57), Sri Lanka (22 Aug 57), Sudan (17
Jul 58), Sweden (19 Jun 57), Syria (6 Jun 53), Tanzania (6 Jan 76),
Thailand (15 Oct 57), Tunisia (14 Oct 57), Turkey (19 Jul 57), Uganda
(30 Aug 67), United Arab Emirates (15 Jan 76), Uruguay (22 Jan 63),
Vietnam (24 Sep 57), Yugoslavia (17 Sep 57), Zaire (10 Oct 61), Zambia
(8 Jan 69), Zimbabwe (1 Aug 86)

Ratified/accepted/approved with qualification: 15
Albania (23 Aug 57), Argentina (3 Oct 57), Belarus (Byelorussian SSR)
(8 Apr 57), Czechoslovakia (5 Jul 57), German Democratic Republic (18
Sep 73), Hungary (8 Aug 57), India (16 Jul 57), Poland (31 Jul 57),
Romania (12 Apr 57), Russia (USSR) (8 Apr 57), Switzerland (5 Apr 57),
Ukraine (Ukrainian SSR) (31 Jul 57), United Kingdom (29 Jul 57),
United States (29 Jul 57), Venezuela (19 Aug 57)

1.6   TREATY ESTABLISHING THE EUROPEAN ECONOMIC COMMUNITY

Entered into force: 1 January 1958

Parties: 12
Belgium (13 Dec 57), Denmark (18 Oct 72), France (25 Nov 57),
German Federal Republic (9 Dec 57), Greece (24 Jan 80), Ireland (16
Dec 72), Italy (23 Nov 57), Luxembourg (13 Dec 57), Netherlands (13
Dec 57), Portugal (1 Jan 86), Spain (1 Jan 86), United Kingdom (18 Oct
72)

1.7   VIENNA CONVENTION ON THE LAW OF TREATIES

Entered into force: 27 January 1980

Signed but not ratified: 23
Afghanistan (23 May 69), Bolivia (23 May 69), Brazil (23 May 69), Cambodia (23 May 69), Costa Rica (23 May 69), Côte d'Ivoire (23 Jul 69), Ecuador (23 May 69), El Salvador (16 Feb 70), Ethiopia (30 Apr 70), Ghana (23 May 69), Guatemala (23 May 69), Guyana (23 May 69), Iran (23 May 69), Kenya (23 May 69), Luxembourg (4 Sep 69), Madagascar (23 May 69), Nepal (23 May 69), Pakistan (29 Apr 70), Peru (23 May 69), Sudan (23 May 69), Trinidad and Tobago (23 May 69), United States (24 Apr 70), Zambia (23 May 69)

Ratified/accepted/approved without qualification: 45
Australia (13 Jun 74), Austria (30 Apr 79), Barbados (24 Jun 71), Belgium (1 Sep 92), Cameroon (23 Oct 91), Central African Republic (10 Dec 71), Congo (12 Apr 82), Croatia (12 Oct 92), Cyprus (28 Dec 76), Czechoslovakia (29 Jul 87), Estonia (21 Oct 91), Greece (30 Oct 74), Haiti (25 Aug 80), Holy See (25 Feb 77), Honduras (20 Sep 79), Hungary (19 Jun 87), Italy (25 Jul 74), Jamaica (28 Jul 70), Korea (South) (27 Apr 77), Lesotho (3 Mar 72), Liberia (29 Aug 85), Liechtenstein (8 Feb 90), Lithuania (15 Jan 92), Malawi (23 Aug 83), Mauritius (18 Jan 73), Mexico (25 Sep 74), Nauru (5 May 78), New Zealand (4 Aug 71), Niger (27 Oct 71), Nigeria (31 Jul 69), Panama (28 Jul 80), Paraguay (3 Feb 72), Philippines (15 Nov 72), Poland (2 Jul 90), Rwanda (3 Jan 80), Senegal (11 Apr 86), Slovenia (6 Jul 92), Solomon Islands (9 Aug 89), Spain (16 May 72), Suriname (31 Jan 91), Switzerland (7 May 90), Togo (28 Dec 79), Uruguay (5 Mar 82), Yugoslavia (27 Aug 70), Zaire (25 Jul 77)

Ratified/accepted/approved with qualification: 25
Algeria (8 Nov 88), Argentina (5 Dec 72), Belarus (Byelorussian SSR) * (1 May 86), Bulgaria (21 Apr 87), Canada (14 Oct 70), Chile (9 Apr 81), Columbia (10 Apr 85), Denmark (1 Jun 76), Egypt (11 Feb 82), Finland (19 Aug 77), Germany (21 Jul 87), Japan (2 Jul 81), Kuwait (11 Nov 75), Mongolia (16 May 88), Morocco * (26 Sep 72), Netherlands (9 Apr 85), Oman (18 Oct 90), Russia (USSR) ** (29 Apr 86), Sweden (4 Feb 75), Syria *** (2 Oct 70), Tanzania (12 Apr 76), Tunisia ** (23 Jun 71), Ukraine (Ukrainian SSR) ** (14 May 86), United Kingdom (25 Jun 71)

    *   Reservation not accepted by Algeria, Israel
   **   Reservation not accepted by German Federal Republic, Japan, New Zealand, Sweden, United Kingdom, United States
 *** Reservation not accepted by Israel, Japan, Netherlands, New Zealand, Sweden, United Kingdom, United States

1.8   **DECLARATION ON PRINCIPLES OF INTERNATIONAL LAW CONCERNING FRIENDLY RELATIONS AND CO-OPERATION AMONG STATES IN ACCORDANCE WITH THE CHARTER OF THE UNITED NATIONS**

Adopted without recorded vote: 24 October 1970

1.9   **INTERNATIONAL LAW COMMISSION DRAFT ARTICLES ON STATE RESPONSIBILITY**

Adopted: 25 July 1980

1.10 **SINGLE EUROPEAN ACT**

Entered into force: 1 July 1987

Parties: 12

Belgium (25 Aug 86), Denmark (13 Jun 86), France (29 Dec 87), German Federal Republic (29 Dec 86), Greece (31 Dec 86), Ireland (24 Jun 87), Italy (30 Dec 86), Luxembourg (17 Dec 86), Netherlands (24 Dec 86), Portugal (31 Dec 86), Spain (18 Dec 86), United Kingdom (19 Nov 86)

1.11 INTERNATIONAL LAW COMMISSION DRAFT ARTICLES ON INTERNATIONAL LIABILITY FOR INJURIOUS CONSEQUENCES ARISING OUT OF ACTS NOT PROHIBITED BY INTERNATIONAL LAW

Adopted: 30 May 1989

1.12 TREATY ON EUROPEAN UNION

Entered into force: 1 November 1993

Parties: 12
Belgium (10 Dec 92), Denmark (6 Jun 93), France (4 Nov 92), Germany (13 Oct 93), Greece (3 Nov 93), Ireland (23 Nov 92), Italy (5 Dec 92), Luxembourg (28 Aug 92), Netherlands (28 Dec 92), Portugal (16 Feb 93), Spain (31 Dec 92), United Kingdom (8 Aug 93)

Environmental

1.13 **UNGA** RESOLUTION **1803** ON PERMANENT SOVEREIGNTY OVER NATURAL RESOURCES

Adopted: 14 December 1962

For: 87
Afghanistan, Algeria, Argentina, Australia, Austria, Belgium, Benin, Bolivia, Brazil, Burkina Faso, Burundi, Cambodia, Cameroon, Canada, Central African Republic, Chad, Chile, China, Colombia, Congo (Leopoldville), Costa Rica, Côte d'Ivoire, Cyprus, Dominican Republic, El Salvador, Ethiopia, Finland, Greece, Guatemala, Guinea, Haiti, Honduras, Iceland, India, Indonesia, Iran, Iraq, Ireland, Israel, Italy, Jamaica, Japan, Jordan, Lebanon, Liberia, Libya, Luxembourg, Madagascar, Malaysia, Mali, Mauritania, Mexico, Morocco, Netherlands, New Zealand, Nicaragua, Niger, Nigeria, Norway, Pakistan, Panama, Paraguay, Peru, Philippines, Rwanda, Saudi Arabia, Senegal, Sierra Leone, Spain, Sri Lanka, Sweden, Syria, Tanzania, Thailand, Togo, Trinidad and Tobago, Tunisia, Turkey, Uganda, United Arab Emirates, United Kingdom, United States, Uruguay, Venezuela, Yemen, Yugoslavia

Against: 2
France, South Africa

Abstaining: 12
Belarus (Byelorussian SSR), Bulgaria, Cuba, Czechoslovakia, Ghana, Hungary, Mongolia, Myanmar, Poland, Romania, Ukraine (Ukrainian SSR), Union of Soviet Socialist Republics

1.14 STOCKHOLM DECLARATION OF THE UNITED NATIONS CONFERENCE ON THE HUMAN ENVIRONMENT

Adopted: 16 June 1972

For: 103 *

Against: 0

Abstaining: 12

   * Adopted with no roll call vote recorded

1.15 **UNGA** RESOLUTION ON THE INSTITUTIONAL AND FINANCIAL ARRANGEMENT FOR INTERNATIONAL ENVIRONMENT COOPERATION

Adopted: 15 December 1972

For: 116 *

Against: 0

Abstaining: 10

   * Adopted with no roll call vote recorded

1.16 **UNGA** RESOLUTION ON CO-OPERATION IN THE FIELD OF THE ENVIRONMENT CONCERNING NATURAL RESOURCES SHARED BY TWO OR MORE STATES

Adopted: 13 December 1973

For: 77

Algeria, Argentina, Australia, Bahrain, Botswana, Burundi, Cameroon, Canada, Central African Republic, Chad, Congo, Cyprus, Dahomey, Egypt, El Salvador, Fiji, Gabon, Gambia, Ghana, Greece, Guatemala, Guinea, Indonesia, Iran, Iraq, Ireland, Jamaica, Jordan, Kenya, Kuwait, Laos, Lesotho, Liberia, Libya, Madagascar, Malawi, Malaysia, Mali, Mauritania, Mexico, Morocco, Nepal, Netherlands, New Zealand, Niger, Nigeria, Norway, Oman, Pakistan, Peru, Qatar, Romania, Rwanda, Saudi Arabia, Senegal, Sierra Leone, Singapore, Somalia, Sri Lanka, Sudan, Swaziland, Syria, Thailand, Togo, Tunisia, Uganda, United Arab Emirates, Upper Volta, Yemen, Yemen (Democratic), Yugoslavia, Zaire, Zambia

Against: 5

Bolivia, Brazil, Nicaragua, Paraguay, Portugal

Abstaining: 43

Afghanistan, Austria, Barbados, Belgium, Bhutan, Bulgaria, Burma, Belarus (Byelorussian SSR), Chile, China, Colombia, Côte d'Ivoire, Costa Rica, Czechoslovakia, Denmark, Ecuador, Ethiopia, Finland, France, Germany (East), Germany (West), Guyana, Hungary, Iceland, India, Israel, Italy, Japan, Lebanon, Luxembourg, Mongolia, Poland, Russia (USSR), South Africa, Spain, Sweden, Trinidad and Tobago, Turkey, Ukraine (Ukrainian SSR), United Kingdom, United States, Uruguay, Venezuela

1.17 **UNGA** RESOLUTION 3171 ON PERMANENT SOVEREIGNTY OVER NATURAL RESOURCES

Adopted: 17 December 1973

For: 108

Afghanistan, Albania, Algeria, Argentina, Australia, Austria, Bahrain, Barbados, Belarus (Byelorussian SSR), Benin, Bhutan, Bolivia, Botswana, Brazil, Bulgaria, Burundi, Cambodia, Cameroon, Canada, Chad, Chile, China, Congo, Costa Rica, Côte d'Ivoire, Cuba, Cyprus, Czechoslovakia, Dominican Republic, Ecuador, Egypt, El Salvador, Equatorial Guinea, Ethiopia, Fiji, Finland, Gabon, Germany (East), Ghana, Guatemala, Guinea, Guyana, Haiti, Honduras, Hungary, Iceland, India, Indonesia, Iran, Iraq, Jamaica, Jordan, Kenya, Kuwait, Lebanon, Lesotho, Liberia, Libya, Madagascar, Malawi, Malaysia, Mali, Malta, Mexico, Mongolia, Morocco, Myanmar, Nepal, New Zealand, Niger, Nigeria, Oman, Pakistan, Panama, Paraguay, Peru, Philippines, Poland, Qatar, Romania, Russia (USSR), Rwanda, Saudi Arabia, Senegal, Sierra Leone,

Singapore, Somalia, Spain, Sri Lanka, Sudan, Sweden, Syria, Tanzania, Thailand, Togo, Trinidad and Tobago, Tunisia, Turkey, Uganda, Ukraine (Ukrainian SSR), United Arab Emirates, Uruguay, Venezuela, Yemen, Yemen (Democratic), Yugoslavia, Zaire, Zambia

Against: 1
United Kingdom

Abstaining: 16
Belgium, Denmark, France, German Federal Republic, Greece, Ireland, Israel, Italy, Japan, Luxembourg, Netherlands, Nicaragua, Norway, Portugal, South Africa, United States

1.18   CONVENTION ON THE PROTECTION OF THE ENVIRONMENT BETWEEN DENMARK, FINLAND, NORWAY, AND SWEDEN

Entered into force: 5 October 1976

Ratified/accepted/approved without qualification: 4
Denmark (9 Sep 74), Finland (5 Apr 76), Norway (26 Mar 75), Sweden (10 May 74)

1.19   FINAL ACT OF THE CONFERENCE ON SECURITY AND CO-OPERATION IN EUROPE

Adopted: 1 August 1975

Conferees: 35
Austria, Belgium, Bulgaria, Canada, Cyprus, Czechoslovakia, Denmark, Finland, France, German Democratic Republic, German Federal Republic, Greece, Holy See, Hungary, Iceland, Ireland, Italy, Liechtenstein, Luxembourg, Malta, Monaco, Netherlands, Norway, Poland, Portugal, Romania, Russia (USSR), San Marino, Spain, Sweden, Switzerland, Turkey, United Kingdom, United States, Yugoslavia

Signed: 35
Austria, Belgium, Bulgaria, Canada, Cyprus, Czechoslovakia, Denmark, Finland, France, German Democratic Republic, German Federal Republic, Greece, Holy See, Hungary, Iceland, Ireland, Italy, Liechtenstein, Luxembourg, Malta, Monaco, Netherlands, Norway, Poland, Portugal, Romania, Russia (USSR), San Marino, Spain, Sweden, Switzerland, Turkey, United Kingdom, United States, Yugoslavia

1.20   DRAFT PRINCIPLES OF CONDUCT IN THE FIELD OF THE ENVIRONMENT FOR GUIDANCE OF STATES IN THE CONSERVATION AND HARMONIOUS UTILIZATION OF NATURAL RESOURCES SHARED BY TWO OR MORE STATES

Adopted: 7 February 1978

1.21   UNGA RESOLUTION ON HISTORICAL RESPONSIBILITY OF STATES FOR THE PRESERVATION OF NATURE FOR BENEFIT OF PRESENT AND FUTURE GENERATION

Adopted: 30 October 1980

For: 68 *

Against: 0

Abstaining: 47

   * Adopted with no roll call vote recorded

1.22   ILA RULES ON INTERNATIONAL LAW APPLICABLE TO TRANSFRONTIER POLLUTION

Adopted: 4 September 1982

1.23 WORLD CHARTER FOR NATURE

Adopted: 28 October 1982

For: 111
Afghanistan, Angola, Australia, Austria, Bahrain, Bangladesh, Barbados, Belarus (Byelorussian SSR), Belgium, Benin, Bulgaria, Burkina Faso, Burundi, Cambodia, Canada, Cape Verde, Central African Republic, Chad, China, Cameroon, Comoros, Congo, Costa Rica, Cuba, Cyprus, Czechoslovakia, Denmark, Djibouti, Egypt, El Salvador, Equatorial Guinea, Ethiopia, Finland, France, Gabon, Gambia, Germany (East), Germany (West), Greece, Guinea, Guinea—Bissau, Honduras, Hungary, Iceland, India, Indonesia, Iran, Iraq, Ireland, Italy, Côte d'Ivoire, Jamaica, Japan, Kenya, Kuwait, Lao People's Democratic Republic, Libya, Luxembourg, Madagascar, Malawi, Malaysia, Maldives, Mali, Malta, Mauitania, Mongolia, Morocco, Mozambique, Nepal, Netherlands, New Zealand, Nicaragua, Niger, Nigeria, Norway, Oman, Pakistan, Papua New Guinea, Poland, Portugal, Qatar, Romania, Russia (USSR), Rwanda, Samoa, São Tomé and Príncipe, Saudi Arabia, Senegal, Seychelles, Singapore, Solomon Islands, Somalia, Spain, Sri Lanka, Sudan, Swaziland, Sweden, Tanzania, Thailand, Togo, Tunisia, Turkey, Uganda, Ukraine (Ukrainian SSR), United Arab Emirates, United Kingdom, Uruguay, Yemen, Yugoslavia, Zaire, Zambia

Against: 1
United States

Abstaining: 18
Algeria, Argentina, Bolivia, Brazil, Chile, Colombia, Dominican Republic, Ecuador, Ghana, Guyana, Lebanon, Mexico, Paraguay, Peru, Philippines, Suriname, Trinidad and Tobago, Venezuela

1.24 RESTATEMENT (THIRD) OF THE FOREIGN RELATIONS LAW OF THE UNITED STATES

Adopted: 14 May 1987

1.25 EXPERTS GROUP ON ENVIRONMENTAL LAW OF THE WORLD COMMISSION ON ENVIRONMENT AND DEVELOPMENT, LEGAL PRINCIPLES FOR ENVIRONMENTAL PROTECTION AND SUSTAINABLE DEVELOPMENT

Adopted: 18–20 June 1986

1.26 DECLARATION OF THE HAGUE

Adopted: 11 March 1989

Conferees: 24
Australia, Brazil, Canada, Côte d'Ivoire, Egypt, France, Germany (West), Hungary, India, Indonesia, Italy, Japan, Jordan, Kenya, Malta, Norway, New Zealand, Netherlands, Senegal, Spain, Sweden, Tunisia, Venezuela, Zimbabwe

1.27 THE LANGKAWI COMMONWEALTH HEADS OF GOVERNMENT DECLARATION ON ENVIRONMENT

Unanimously adopted by the heads of the Commonwealth nations (49 at the time): 21 October 1989

1.28   AFRICAN, CARIBBEAN, AND PACIFIC STATES–EUROPEAN ECONOMIC COMMUNITY CONVENTION (LOMÉ IV)

Entered into force: 1 September 1991

Signatories: 4
Iceland, São Tomé and Príncipe, Somalia, Tuvalu

Parties: 81
Angola (15 Oct 90), Antigua and Barbuda (19 Jun 91), Bahamas (28 Sep 90), Barbados (2 Oct 90), Belgium (12 Jul 91), Belize (17 Jan 91), Benin (2 Sep 91), Botswana (7 Sep 90), Burkina Faso (10 Apr 91), Burundi (21 Sep 90), Cameroon (4 Apr 91), Cape Verde (4 Nov 91), Central African Republic (4 Oct 91), Chad (13 May 91), Comoros (24 Jun 91), Congo (20 Nov 91), Côte d'Ivoire (23 Nov 90), Denmark (4 Jul 91), Djibouti (2 May 91), Dominica (31 Aug 90), Dominican Republic (14 Nov 90), Equatorial Guinea (2 Sep 91), Ethiopia (15 Mar 91), Fiji (29 Jun 90), France (1 Feb 91), Gabon (5 Feb 92), Gambia (26 Oct 90), Germany (31 Jan 91), Ghana (8 Mar 91), Greece (28 May 91), Grenada (6 Jul 90), Guinea (4 Sep 90), Guinea–Bissau (3 Oct 90), Guyana (23 Aug 90), Haiti (16 May 90), Ireland (7 May 91), Italy (29 May 91), Jamaica (10 Jan 91), Kenya (21 Dec 90), Kiribati (18 Mar 92), Lesotho (7 Dec 90), Liberia (20 May 92), Luxembourg (20 Jan 91), Madagascar (27 Feb 91), Malawi (5 Feb 91), Mali (14 Sep 90), Mauritania (29 Apr 91), Mauritius (1 Oct 90), Mozambique (3 Dec 90), Namibia (31 Oct 91), Netherlands (31 May 91), Niger (7 May 91), Nigeria (31 Oct 91), Papua New Guinea (8 Oct 90), Portugal (24 Jul 91), Rwanda (14 May 91), St. Kitts and Nevis (18 Jan 91), St. Lucia (5 Dec 90), St. Vincent (6 Nov 90), Samoa (19 Nov 90), Senegal (21 Nov 90), Seychelles (3 Oct 90), Sierra Leone (7 May 91), Solomon Islands (16 Jul 91), Spain (31 May 91), Sudan (25 Apr 90), Suriname (15 Jan 91), Swaziland (25 Mar 91), Tanzania (13 Mar 91), Togo (2 Jul 91), Trinidad and Tobago (31 May 90), Uganda (17 Sep 90), United Kingdom (30 May 91), Vanuatu (7 Feb 92), Western Samoa, Zaire (11 Jan 91), Zambia (4 Apr 91), Zimbabwe (15 Oct 90)

1.29   CONVENTION ON ENVIRONMENTAL IMPACT ASSESSMENT IN A TRANSBOUNDARY CONTEXT

Entered into force: Not in force as of 31 December 1991

Signed but not ratified: 28
Austria (26 Feb 91), Belarus (Byelorussian SSR) (26 Feb 91), Belgium (26 Feb 91), Bulgaria (26 Feb 91), Canada (26 Feb 91), Czechoslovakia (26 Feb 91), Denmark (26 Feb 91), European Economic Community (26 Feb 91), Finland (26 Feb 91), France (26 Feb 91), Germany (26 Feb 91), Greece (26 Feb 91), Hungary (26 Feb 91), Iceland (26 Feb 91), Ireland (26 Feb 91), Italy (26 Feb 91), Luxembourg (26 Feb 91), Netherlands (26 Feb 91), Norway (26 Feb 91), Poland (26 Feb 91), Portugal (26 Feb 91), Romania (26 Feb 91), Russia (USSR) (26 Feb 91), Spain (26 Feb 91), Sweden (26 Feb 91), Ukraine (Ukrainian SSR) (26 Feb 91), United Kingdom (26 Feb 91), United States (26 Feb 91)

Ratified/accepted/approved without qualification: 1
Albania (4 Oct 91)

1.30   RIO DECLARATION ON ENVIRONMENT AND DEVELOPMENT

Adopted by consensus by the U.N. Conference on Environment and Development: 13 June 1992

1.31 AGENDA 21

Approved by the U.N. Conference on Environment and Development: 13 June 1992

1.32 UNGA RESOLUTION ON INSTITUTIONAL ARRANGEMENT TO FOLLOW UP THE UNITED NATIONS CONFERENCE ON ENVIRONMENT AND DEVELOPMENT

Adopted without recorded vote: 22 December 1992

2. GLOBAL COMMONS: ANTARCTICA

2.1 ANTARCTIC TREATY

Entered into force: 23 June 1961

Ratified/accepted/approved without qualification: 37
Argentina (23 Jun 61), Australia (23 Jun 61), Austria (25 Aug 87), Belgium (26 Jun 60), Brazil (16 May 75), Bulgaria (11 Sep 78), Canada (4 May 88), Chile (23 Jun 61), China (8 Jun 83), Colombia (31 Jan 89), Cuba (16 Aug 84), Czechoslovakia (14 Jun 62), Denmark (20 May 65), Ecuador (15 Sep 87), Finland (15 May 84), France (16 Sep 60), Germany (5 Feb 79), Greece (8 Jan 87), Guatemala (31 Jul 91), Hungary (27 Jan 84), Italy (18 Mar 81), Japan (8 Aug 60), Korea (North) (21 Jan 87), Korea (South) (28 Nov 86), Netherlands (30 Mar 67), New Zealand (1 Nov 60), Norway (24 Aug 60), Papua New Guinea (16 Mar 81), Peru (10 Apr 81), Poland (8 Jun 61), Russia (USSR) (2 Nov 60), South Africa (21 Jun 60), Spain (31 Mar 82), Sweden (25 Apr 84), Switzerland (15 Nov 90), United Kingdom (31 May 60), United States (18 Aug 60)

Ratified/accepted/approved with qualification: 4
German Democratic Republic (19 Nov 74), India (19 Aug 83), Romania (15 Sep 71), Uruguay (11 Jan 80)

2.2 CERTAIN RECOMMENDATIONS OF THIRD ANTARCTIC TREATY CONSULTATIVE MEETING, ANNEX: AGREED MEASURES FOR THE CONSERVATION OF ANTARCTIC FAUNA AND FLORA

Adopted: 13 June 1964

2.3 CONVENTION FOR THE CONSERVATION OF ANTARCTIC SEALS

Entered into force: 11 March 1978

Signed but not ratified: 1
New Zealand (9 Jun 72)

Ratified/accepted/approved without qualification: 13
Australia (1 Jul 87), Belgium (9 Feb 78), Brazil (2 Nov 91), Canada (4 Oct 90), Germany (30 Sep 87), France (19 Feb 75), Italy (4 Feb 87), Japan (28 Aug 80), Norway (10 Dec 73), Poland (15 Aug 80), South Africa (15 Aug 72), United Kingdom (10 Sep 74), United States (19 Jan 77)

Ratified/accepted/approved with qualification: 3
Argentina (7 Mar 78), Chile (7 Feb 80), Russia (USSR) (8 Feb 78)

2.4 CONVENTION ON THE CONSERVATION OF ANTARCTIC MARINE LIVING RESOURCES (CCAMLR)

Entered into force: 7 April 1982

Ratified/accepted/approved without qualification: 26
Australia (6 May 81), Belgium (22 Feb 84), Brazil (28 Jan 86), Canada (1 Jul 88), Chile (22 Jul 81), European Economic Community (21 Apr

82), Germany (23 Apr 82), Finland (6 Sep 89), German Democratic Republic (30 Mar 82), Greece (12 Feb 87), India (17 Jun 85), Italy (29 Mar 89), Japan (26 May 81), Korea (South) (29 Mar 85), Netherlands (23 Feb 90), New Zealand (8 Mar 82), Norway (6 Dec 83), Peru (23 Jun 89), Poland (28 Mar 84), Russia (USSR) (26 May 81), South Africa (23 Jul 81), Spain (9 Apr 84), Sweden (6 Jun 84), United Kingdom (31 Aug 81), United States (19 Feb 82), Uruguay (22 Mar 85)

Ratified/accepted/approved with qualification: 2
Argentina (28 May 82), France (16 Sep 82)

2.5   **UNGA** RESOLUTION **38/77** ON THE QUESTION OF ANTARCTICA
Adopted without recorded vote: 15 December 1983

2.6   **UNGA** RESOLUTION **39/152** ON THE QUESTION OF ANTARCTICA
Adopted without recorded vote: 17 December 1984

2.7   CONVENTION ON THE REGULATION OF ANTARCTIC MINERAL RESOURCE ACTIVITIES **(CRAMRA)**
Entered into force: Not in force as of 31 December 1992

Signed but not ratified: 19
Argentina (17 Mar 89), Brazil (25 Nov 88), Chile (17 Mar 89), China (28 Jun 89), Czechoslovakia (21 Nov 89), Denmark (25 Feb 89), Finland (25 Nov 88), German Democratic Republic (21 Nov 89), Japan (22 Nov 89, Korea (South) (25 Nov 88), New Zealand (25 Nov 88), Norway (25 Nov 88), Poland (25 Feb 89), Russia (USSR) (25 Nov 88), South Africa (25 Nov 88), Sweden (25 Nov 88), United Kingdom (22 Mar 89), United States (30 Nov 88), Uruguay (25 Nov 88)

2.8   **UNGA** RESOLUTION **46/41** ON THE QUESTION OF ANTARCTICA
Adopted: 6 December 1991

For Part A: 109
Algeria, Angola, Antigua and Barbuda, Bahamas, Bahrain, Bangladesh, Barbados, Belize, Benin, Bhutan, Bolivia, Botswana, Brunei Darussalam, Burkina Faso, Burundi, Cameroon, Cape Verde, Central African Republic, Chad, Comoros, Costa Rica, Côte d'Ivoire, Cyprus, Djibouti, Dominica, Egypt, El Salvador, Ethiopia, Gabon, Gambia, Ghana, Grenada, Guatemala, Guinea, Guinea–Bissau, Guyana, Honduras, Indonesia, Iran, Iraq, Jamaica, Jordan, Kenya, Kuwait, Lebanon, Lesotho, Liberia, Libya, Madagascar, Malawi, Malaysia, Maldives, Mali, Mauritania, Mauritius, Mexico, Mongolia, Morocco, Mozambique, Myanmar, Namibia, Nepal, Nicaragua, Niger, Nigeria, Oman, Pakistan, Panama, Paraguay, Philippines, Qatar, Saint Kitts and Nevis, Saint Lucia, Saint Vincent and the Grenadines, São Tomé and Príncipe, Saudi Arabia, Senegal, Seychelles, Sierra Leone, Singapore, Somalia, Sri Lanka, Sudan, Suriname, Swaziland, Syria, Thailand, Togo, Trinidad and Tobago, Tunisia, Uganda, United Arab Emirates, Tanzania, Vanuatu, Venezuela, Viet Nam, Yemen, Yugoslavia, Zaire, Zambia, Zimbabwe

Against Part A: 0

Abstaining Part A: 0

For Part B: 108
Afghanistan, Algeria, Angola, Antigua and Barbuda, Bahamas, Bahrain, Bangladesh, Barbados, Belize, Benin, Bhutan, Bolivia, Brazil, Brunei

Darussalam, Burkina Faso, Burundi, Cameroon, Cape Verde, Central African Republic, Chad, China, Colombia, Comoros, Costa Rica, Cuba, Cyprus, Djibouti, Dominica, Dominican Republic, Ecuador, Egypt, El Salvador, Ethiopia, Fiji, Gabon, Gambia, Ghana, Grenada, Guatemala, Guinea, Guinea–Bissau, Guyana, Haiti, Honduras, India, Indonesia, Iran, Iraq, Jamaica, Jordan, Kenya, Korea (North), Kuwait, Lao People's Democratic Republic, Lebanon, Liberia, Libya, Malaysia, Maldives, Mali, Mauritainia, Mexico, Mongolia, Morocco, Mozambique, Myanmar, Namibia, Nepal, Nicaragua, Niger, Nigeria, Oman, Pakistan, Panama, Paraguay, Peru, Philippines, Qatar, Saint Kitts and Nevis, Saint Lucia, Saint Vincent and the Grenadines, São Tomé and Príncipe, Saudi Arabia, Senegal, Seychelles, Sierra Leone, Singapore, Somalia, Sri Lanka, Sudan, Suriname, Syria, Thailand, Togo, Trinidad and Tobago, Tunisia, Uganda, United Arab Emirates, Tanzania, Vanuatu, Venezuela, Viet Nam, Yemen, Yugoslavia, Zaire, Zambia, Zimbabwe

Against Part B: 0

Abstaining Part B: 6
Ireland, Liechtenstein, Malta, Mauritius, Portugal, Ukraine

2.9   **PROTOCOL ON ENVIRONMENTAL PROTECTION TO THE ANTARCTIC TREATY**

Entered into force: Not in force as of 31 December 1992

Signed but not ratified: 30
Argentina, Australia, Austria, Belgium, Brazil, Canada, Chile, China, Ecuador, Finland, France, Germany, Greece, Hungary, Italy, Korea (North), Norway, New Zealand, Netherlands, Peru, Poland, Romania, Russia (USSR), South Africa, Sweden, Switzerland, United Kingdom, United States, Uruguay

Ratified/accepted/approved without qualification: 1
Spain

3. ATMOSPHERE/SPACE

3.1   **CONVENTION ON THIRD PARTY LIABILITY IN THE FIELD OF NUCLEAR ENERGY**

Entered into force: 1 April 1968

Signed but not ratified: 3
Austria (29 Jul 60), Luxembourg (29 Jul 60), Switzerland (29 Jul 60)

Ratified/accepted/approved without qualification: 10
Belgium (3 Aug 66), Denmark (4 Sep 74), Finland (8 Jun 62), France (9 Mar 66), Italy (17 Sep 75), Netherlands (28 Dec 79), Portugal (29 Sep 77), Spain (31 Oct 61), Turkey (10 Oct 61), United Kingdom (23 Feb 66)

Ratified/accepted/approved with qualification: 4
Germany (30 Sep 75), Greece (12 May 70), Norway (2 Jul 73), Sweden (1 Apr 68)

3.2   **CONVENTION SUPPLEMENTARY TO THE 1960 CONVENTION ON THIRD PARTY LIABILITY IN THE FIELD OF NUCLEAR ENERGY**

Entered into force: 4 December 1974

Signed but not ratified: 3
Austria, Luxembourg, Switzerland

Ratified/accepted/approved without qualification: 7
Belgium (20 Aug 85), Denmark (4 Sep 74), France (30 Mar 66), Italy (3 Feb 76), Spain (27 Jul 66), Sweden (3 Apr 68), United Kingdom (24 Mar 66)

Ratified/accepted/approved with qualification: 4
Finland (14 Jan 77), Germany (1 Oct 75), Netherlands (28 Sep 79),
Norway (9 Jul 73)

3.3   **VIENNA CONVENTION ON CIVIL LIABILITY FOR NUCLEAR DAMAGE**
Entered into force: 11 November 1977
Signed but not ratified: 4
Colombia (21 May 63), Morocco (30 Nov 84), Spain (6 Sep 63), United
Kingdom (11 Nov 64)
Ratified/accepted/approved without qualification: 14
Argentina (25 Apr 67), Bolivia (10 Apr 68), Cameroon (6 Mar 64), Chile
(23 Nov 89), Cuba (25 Oct 65), Egypt (5 Nov 65), Hungary (28 Jul 89),
Mexico (25 Apr 89), Niger (24 Jul 79), Philippines (15 Nov 65), Peru (26
Aug 80), Poland (23 Jan 90), Trinidad and Tobago (31 Jan 66), Yugo-
slavia (12 Aug 77)

3.4   **TREATY ON PRINCIPLES GOVERNING THE ACTIVITIES OF STATES IN THE
EXPLORATION AND USE OF OUTER SPACE, INCLUDING THE MOON AND OTHER
CELESTIAL BODIES**
Entered into force: 10 October 1967
Signed but not ratified: 28
Bolivia (27 Jan 67), Botswana (27 Jan 67), Burundi (27 Jan 67),
Cameroon (27 Jan 67), Central African Republic (27 Jan 67), Colombia
(27 Jan 67), Ethiopia (27 Jan 67), Gambia (2 Jun 67), Ghana (27 Jan
67), Guyana (3 Feb 67), Haiti (27 Jan 67), Holy See (5 Apr 67),
Honduras (27 Jan 67), Indonesia (27 Jan 67), Iran (27 Jan 67), Jordan
(2 Feb 67), Lesotho (27 Jan 67), Luxembourg (27 Jan 67), Malaysia (20
Feb 67), Nicaragua (27 Jan 67), Panama (27 Jan 67), Philippines (27
Jan 67), Rwanda (27 Jan 67), Somalia (2 Feb 67), Togo (27 Jan 67),
Trinidad and Tobago (24 Jul 67), Yugoslavia (27 Jan 67), Zaire (27 Jan
67)
Ratified/accepted/approved without qualifications: 89
Afghanistan (17 Mar 88), Algeria (27 Jan 92), Antigua and Barbuda (26
Jan 89), Argentina (26 Mar 69), Australia (10 Oct 67), Austria (26 Feb
68), Bahamas (11 Aug 76), Bangladesh (14 Jan 86), Barbados (12 Sep
68), Belgium (30 Mar 73), Benin (19 Jun 86), Bulgaria (28 Mar 67),
Burma (18 Mar 70), Belarus (Byelorussian SSR) (31 Oct 67), Canada (10
Oct 67), Chile (8 Oct 81), Cuba (3 Jun 77), Cyprus (5 Jul 72), Czechoslo-
vakia (11 May 67), Denmark (10 Oct 67), Dominican Republic (21 Nov
68), Ecuador (7 Mar 69), Egypt (10 Oct 67), El Salvador (15 Jan 69),
Equatorial Guinea (16 Jan 89), Fiji (18 Jul 72), Finland (12 Jul 67),
France (5 Aug 70), Germany (10 Dec 71), Greece (19 Jan 71), Guinea–
Bissau (20 Aug 76), Hungary (26 Jun 67), Iceland (5 Feb 68), India (18
Jan 82),Iraq (4 Dec 68), Ireland (17 Jul 68), Israel (18 Feb 77), Italy (4
May 72), Jamaica (6 Aug 70), Japan (10 Oct 67), Kenya (19 Jan 84),
Korea (South) (13 Oct 67), Laos (27 Nov 72), Lebanon (31 Mar 69),
Libya (3 Jul 68), Mali (11 Jun 68), Mauritius (7 Apr 69), Mexico (31 Jan
68), Mongolia (10 Oct 67), Morocco (21 Dec 67), Nepal (10 Oct 67),
Netherlands (10 Oct 69), New Zealand (31 May 68), Niger (17 Apr 67),
Nigeria (14 Nov 67), Norway (1 Jul 69), Pakistan (8 Apr 68), Papua
New Guinea (27 Oct 80), Peru (26 Feb 79), Poland (30 Jan 68),
Romania (9 Apr 68), Russia (USSR) (10 Oct 67), San Marino (29 Oct
68), Saudi Arabia (17 Dec 68), Seychelles (5 Jan 78), Sierra Leone (13

Jul 67), Singapore (10 Sep 76), South Africa (30 Sep 68), Spain (27 Nov 68), Sri Lanka (18 Nov 86), Sweden (11 Oct 67), Switzerland (18 Dec 69), Syria (14 Nov 68),Thailand (5 Sep 68), Tonga (7 Jul 71), Togo (26 Jun 89), Tunisia (28 Mar 68), Turkey (27 Mar 68), Uganda (24 Apr 68), Ukraine (Ukrainian SSR) (31 Oct 67), United Kingdom (10 Oct 67), United States (10 Oct 67), Burkina Faso (18 Jun 68), Uruguay (31 Aug 70), Venezuela (3 Mar 70), Vietnam (20 Jun 80), Yemen (Democratic) (1 Jul 79), Zambia (20 Aug 73)

Ratified/accepted/approved with qualification: 4
Brazil (5 Mar 69), China (30 Dec 83), Kuwait (7 Jun 72), Madagascar (22 Aug 68)

3.5 **COUNCIL OF EUROPE COMMITTEE OF MINISTERS RESOLUTION ON AIR POLLUTION IN FRONTIER AREAS**
Adopted: 26 March 1971

3.6 **CONVENTION ON THE INTERNATIONAL LIABILITY FOR DAMAGE CAUSED BY SPACE OBJECTS**
Entered into force: 1 September 1972
Signed but not ratified: 27
Algeria (20 Apr 72), Burundi (29 Mar 72), Central African Republic (27 Apr 72), Colombia (29 Mar 72), Costa Rica (29 Mar 72), Egypt (19 Apr 72), El Salvador (29 Mar 72), Gambia (2 Jun 72), Ghana (29 Mar 72), Guatemala (29 Mar 72), Haiti (29 Mar 72), Honduras (29 Mar 72), Iceland (29 Mar 72), Jordan (25 May 72), Kampuchea (29 Mar 72), Lebanon (29 Mar 72), Nepal (29 Mar 72), Nicaragua (29 Mar 72), Norway (29 Mar 72), Oman (23 Jun 72), Peru (10 Apr 72), Philippines (22 Aug 72), Rwanda (29 Mar 72), Sierra Leone (14 Jul 72), South Africa (29 Mar 72), Tanzania (31 May 72), Zaire (29 Mar 72)

Ratified/accepted/approved without qualification: 63
Antigua and Barbuda (16 Nov 88), Argentina (14 Nov 86), Australia (20 Jan 75), Belgium (13 Aug 76), Benin (25 Apr 75), Botswana (14 Mar 74), Brazil (9 Mar 73), Bulgaria (14 May 73), Belarus (Byelorussian SSR) (27 Dec 73), Chile (1 Dec 76), Cuba (25 Nov 82), Cyprus (15 May 73), Czechoslovakia (8 Sep 76), Dominican Republic (23 Feb 73), Ecuador (17 Aug 72), Fiji (4 Apr 73), Finland (1 Feb 77), France (31 Dec 75), Gabon (5 Feb 82), Germany (18 Dec 75), Hungary (27 Dec 72), India (9 Jul 79), Iran (13 Feb 74), Iraq (4 Oct 72), Israel (21 Jun 77), Italy (22 Feb 83), Japan (20 Jun 83), Kenya (25 Sep 75), Laos (20 Mar 73), Liechtenstein (24 Dec 79), Luxembourg (18 Oct 83), Mali (9 Jun 72), Malta (13 Jan 78), Mexico (8 Apr 74), Mongolia (5 Sep 72), Morocco (15 Mar 83), Niger (1 Sep 72), Pakistan (4 Apr 73), Panama (5 Jun 74), Papua New Guinea (27 Oct 80), Poland (25 Jan 73), Qatar (11 Jan 74), Romania (5 Mar 80), Russia (USSR) (9 Oct 73), Saudi Arabia (17 Dec 76), Senegal (26 Mar 75), Seychelles (5 May 78), Singapore (19 Aug 75), Spain (2 Jan 80), Sri Lanka (9 Apr 73), Switzerland (22 Jan 74), Syria (6 Feb 80), Togo (26 Apr 76), Trinidad and Tobago (8 Feb 80), Tunisia (18 May 73), Ukraine (Ukrainian SSR) (16 Oct 73), United Kingdom (9 Oct 73), United States (9 Oct 73), Uruguay (7 Jan 77), Venezuela (1 Aug 78), Yugoslavia (20 Oct 75), Zambia (20 Aug 73)

Ratified/accepted/approved with qualification: 12
Austria (10 Jan 80), Canada (20 Feb 75), China (19 Dec 88), Denmark (1 Apr 77), Eutelsat (30 Nov 87), Greece (27 Apr 77), Ireland (29 Jun

72), Korea (South) (14 Jan 80), Kuwait (30 Oct 72), Netherlands (17 Feb 81), New Zealand (30 Oct 74), Sweden (15 Jun 76)

3.7   **OECD COUNCIL RECOMMENDATION ON PRINCIPLES CONCERNING TRANS-FRONTIER POLLUTION**

Adopted: 14 November 1974

3.8   **OECD COUNCIL RECOMMENDATION FOR THE IMPLEMENTATION OF A REGIME OF EQUAL RIGHT OF ACCESS AND NON-DISCRIMINATION IN RELATION TO TRANSFRONTIER POLLUTION**

Adopted: 17 May 1977

3.9   **CONVENTION ON LONG-RANGE TRANSBOUNDARY AIR POLLUTION**

Entered into force: 16 March 1983

Signed but not ratified: 2
Holy See (14 Nov 79), San Marino (14 Nov 79)

Ratified/accepted/approved without qualification: 33
Austria (16 Dec 82), Belarus (Byelorussian SSR) (13 Jun 80), Belgium (15 Jul 82), Bulgaria (9 Jun 81), Canada (15 Dec 81), Cyprus (20 Nov 91), Czechoslovakia (23 Dec 83), Denmark (18 Jun 82), European Economic Community (15 Jul 82), Finland (15 Apr 81), France (3 Nov 81), Germany (15 Jul 82), Greece (30 Aug 83), Hungary (22 Sep 80), Iceland (5 May 83), Ireland (15 Jul 82), Italy (15 Jul 82), Liechtenstein (22 Nov 83), Luxembourg (15 Jul 82), Netherlands (15 Jul 82), Norway (13 Feb 81), Poland (19 Jul 85), Portugal (29 Sep 80), Russia (USSR) (22 May 80), Slovenia (6 Jul 92), Spain (15 Jun 82), Sweden (12 Feb 81), Switzerland (6 May 83), Turkey (18 Apr 83), Ukraine (Ukrainian SSR) (5 Jun 80), United Kingdom (15 Jul 82), United States (30 Nov 81), Yugoslavia (18 Mar 87)

Ratified/accepted/approved with qualification: 1
Romania (27 Feb 91)

3.10 **AGREEMENT GOVERNING THE ACTIVITIES OF STATES ON THE MOON AND OTHER CELESTIAL BODIES**

Entered into force: 11 June 1984

Signed but not ratified: 6
France (29 Jan 80), Guatemala (20 Nov 80), India (18 Jan 82), Morocco (25 Jul 80), Peru (23 Jun 81), Romania (17 Apr 80)

Ratified/accepted/approved without qualification: 8
Australia (7 Jul 86), Austria (11 Jun 84), Chile (12 Nov 81), Mexico (11 Oct 91), Netherlands (17 Feb 83), Pakistan (27 Feb 86), Philippines (26 May 81), Uruguay (9 Nov 81)

3.11 **EUROPEAN COMMUNITIES COUNCIL DIRECTIVE NO 80/779 ON AIR QUALITY LIMIT VALUES**

Adopted: 15 July 1980

3.12 **MEMORANDUM OF INTENT BETWEEN CANADA AND THE UNITED STATES CONCERNING TRANSBOUNDARY AIR POLLUTION**

Entered into force: 5 August 1980

3.13 MEXICO-UNITED STATES AGREEMENT TO CO-OPERATE IN THE SOLUTION OF ENVIRONMENTAL PROBLEMS IN THE BORDER AREA
Entered into force: 16 February 1984

3.14 EUROPEAN COMMUNITIES COUNCIL DIRECTIVE No. 85/203 ON AIR QUALITY STANDARDS FOR NITROGEN DIOXIDE
Adopted: 7 March 1985

3.15 VIENNA CONVENTION FOR THE PROTECTION OF THE OZONE LAYER
Entered into force: 22 September 1988
Signed but not ratified: 1
Morocco (7 Feb 86)

Ratified/accepted/approved without qualification: 95
Algeria (22 Oct 92), Antigua and Barbuda (3 Dec 92), Argentina (18 Jan 90), Australia (16 Sep 87), Austria (19 Aug 87), Bahrain (27 Apr 90), Bangladesh (2 Aug 90), Barbados (16 Oct 92), Belarus (Byelorussian SSR) (20 Jun 86), Belgium (17 Oct 88), Botswana (4 Dec 91), Brazil (19 Mar 90), Brunei (26 Jul 90), Bulgaria (20 Nov 90), Burkina Faso (30 Mar 89), Cameroon (30 Aug 89), Canada (4 Jun 86), Chad (18 May 89), Chile (6 Mar 90), China (11 Sep 89), Colombia (16 Jul 90), Costa Rica (30 Jul 91), Croatia (21 Sep 92), Cuba (14 Jul 92), Cyprus (28 May 92), Czechoslovakia (1 Oct 90), Denmark (29 Sep 88), Ecuador (10 Apr 90), Egypt (9 May 88), Equatorial Guinea (17 Aug 88), Fiji (23 Oct 89), France (4 Dec 87), Gambia (25 Jul 90), Germany (30 Sep 88), Ghana (24 Jul 89), Greece (29 Dec 88), Guatemala (11 Sep 87), Guinea (25 Jun 92), Hungary (4 May 88), Iceland (29 Aug 89), India (18 Mar 91), Indonesia (26 Jun 92), Iran (3 Oct 90), Ireland (15 Sep 88), Israel (30 Jun 92), Italy (19 Sep 88), Japan (30 Sep 88), Jordan (31 May 89), Kenya (9 Nov 88), Korea (South) (27 Feb 92), Kuwait (23 Nov 92), Liechtenstein (8 Feb 89), Luxembourg (17 Oct 88), Libya (11 Jul 90), Malawi (9 Jan 91), Malaysia (29 Aug 89), Maldives (26 Apr 88), Malta (15 Sep 88), Mauritius (18 Aug 92), Mexico (14 Sep 87), Niger (9 Oct 92), Nigeria (31 Oct 88), Panama (13 Feb 89), Pakistan (18 Dec 92), Papua New Guinea (27 Oct 92), Paraguay (3 Dec 92), Peru (7 Apr 89), Philippines (17 Jul 91), Poland (13 Jul 90), Portugal (17 Oct 88), Russia (USSR) (18 Jun 86), St. Kitts and St. Nevis (10 Aug 92), Samoa (21 Dec 92), Singapore (5 Jan 89), Slovenia (6 Jul 92), South Africa (15 Jan 90), Spain (25 Jul 88), Sri Lanka (15 Dec 89), Swaziland (10 Nov 92), Switzerland (17 Dec 87), Syria (12 Dec 89), Thailand (7 Jul 89), Togo (25 Feb 91), Trinidad and Tobago (28 Aug 89), Tunisia (25 Sep 89), Turkey (20 Sep 91), Uganda (24 Jun 88), Ukraine (Ukrainian SSR) (18 Jun 86), United Arab Emirates (22 Dec 89), United States (27 Aug 86), Uruguay (27 Feb 89), Venezuela (1 Sep 88), Yugoslavia (16 Apr 90), Zambia (24 Jan 90), Zimbabwe (3 Nov 92)

Ratified/accepted/approved with qualification: 7
European Economic Community (17 Oct 88), Finland (26 Sep 86), Netherlands (28 Sep 88), New Zealand (2 Jun 87), Norway (23 Sep 86), Sweden (26 Nov 86), United Kingdom (15 May 87)

3.16 CONVENTION ON EARLY NOTIFICATION OF A NUCLEAR ACCIDENT
Entered into force: 27 October 1986
Signed but not ratified: 25

Afghanistan (26 Sep 86), Algeria (24 Sep 87), Belgium (26 Sep 86), Cameroon (25 Sep 87), Chile (26 Sep 86), Côte d'Ivoire (26 Sep 86), Cuba (26 Sep 86), Greece (26 Sep 86), Holy See (26 Sep 86), Indonesia (26 Sep 86), Iran (26 Sep 86), Korea (North) (26 Sep 86), Lebanon (26 Sep 86), Liechtenstein (26 Sep 86), Luxembourg (29 Sep 86), Mali (2 Oct 86), Morocco (26 Sep 86), Niger (26 Sep 86), Panama (26 Sep 86), Paraguay (2 Oct 86), Portugal (26 Sep 86), Senegal (15 Jun 87), Sierra Leone (25 Mar 87), Sudan (26 Sep 86), Syria (2 Jul 87), Zaire (30 Sep 86), Zimbabwe (26 Sep 86)

Ratified/accepted/approved without qualification: 29
Austria (18 Feb 88), Bangladesh (7 Jan 88), Brazil (4 Dec 90), Costa Rica (16 Sep 91), Cuba (8 Jan 91), Cyprus (4 Jan 89), Denmark (26 Sep 86), Finland (11 Dec 86), Greece (6 Jun 91), Guatemala (8 Aug 88), Hungary (10 Mar 87), Ireland (13 Sep 91), Iceland (27 Sep 89), Japan (9 Jun 87), Jordan (11 Dec 87), Korea (South) (8 Jun 90), Mexico (10 May 88), Netherlands (23 Sep 91), New Zealand (11 Mar 87), Nigeria (10 Aug 90), Norway (26 Sep 86), Sri Lanka (11 Jan 91), Sweden (27 Feb 87), Switzerland (31 May 88), Tunisia (24 Feb 89), Turkey (3 Jan 91), Uruguay (21 Dec 89), Vietnam (29 Sep 87), Yugoslavia (8 Feb 89)

Ratified/accepted/approved with qualification: 31
Argentina (17 Jan 90), Australia (22 Sep 87), Bulgaria (24 Feb 88), Belarus (Byelorussian SSR) (26 Jan 87), Canada (18 Jan 90), China (10 Sep 87), Czechoslovakia (26 Sep 86), Egypt (6 Jul 88), Food and Agricultural Organisation (19 Oct 90), France (6 Mar 89), Germany (14 Sep 89), India (28 Jan 88), Iraq (21 Jul 88), Israel (25 May 89), Italy (8 Feb 90), Malaysia (1 Sep 87), Monaco (19 Jul 89), Mongolia (11 Jun 87), Pakistan (11 Sep 89), Poland (24 Mar 88), Romania (12 Jun 90), Russia (USSR) (23 Dec 86), Saudi Arabia (3 Nov 89), South Africa (10 Aug 87), Spain (13 Sep 89), Thailand (2 Mar 89), Ukraine (Ukrainian SSR) (26 Jan 87), United Arab Emirates (2 Oct 87), United States (19 Sep 88), World Health Organisation (10 Aug 88), World Meteorological Organisation (17 Apr 90)

3.17 **IAEA** CONVENTION ON ASSISTANCE IN THE CASE OF A NUCLEAR ACCIDENT OR RADIOLOGICAL EMERGENCY

Entered into force: 26 February 1987

Signed but not ratified: 31
Afghanistan (26 Sep 86), Algeria (24 Sep 87), Belgium (26 Sep 86), Cameroon (25 Sep 87), Canada (26 Sep 86), Chile (26 Sep 86), Côte d'Ivoire (26 Sep 86), Denmark (26 Sep 86), Greece (26 Sep 86), Holy See (26 Sep 86), Iceland (26 Sep 86), Indonesia (26 Sep 86), Iran (26 Sep 86), Jordan (2 Oct 86), Korea (North) (26 Sep 86), Lebanon (26 Sep 86), Liechtenstein (26 Sep 86), Mali (2 Oct 86), Morocco (26 Sep 86), Niger (26 Sep 86), Panama (26 Sep 86), Paraguay (2 Oct 86), Portugal (26 Sep 86), Senegal (15 Jun 87), Sierra Leone (25 Mar 87), Sudan (26 Sep 86), Sweden (26 Sep 86), Syria (2 Jul 87), Zaire (30 Sep 86), Zimbabwe (26 Sep 86)

Ratified/accepted/approved without qualification: 22
Bangladesh (7 Jan 88), Brazil (4 Dec 90), Costa Rica (16 Sep 91), Cuba (8 Jan 91), Cyprus (4 Jan 89), FAO (19 Oct 90), Germany (14 Sep 89), Guatemala (8 Aug 88), Hungary (10 Mar 87), Ireland (13 Sep 91), Jordan (11 Dec 87), Libya (27 Jun 90), Mexico (10 May 88), Netherlands (23 Sep 91), Nigeria (10 Aug 90), Sri Lanka (11 Jan 91), Switzerland (31

May 88), Tunisia (24 Feb 89), Turkey (3 Jan 91), Uruguay (21 Dec 89), Vietnam (29 Sep 87), Yugoslavia (9 Apr 91)

Ratified/accepted/approved with qualification: 34
Argentina (17 Jan 90), Australia (22 Sep 87), Austria (21 Nov 89), Belarus (Byelorussian SSR) (26 Jan 87), Bulgaria (24 Feb 88), China (10 Sep 87), Czechoslovakia (4 Aug 88), Egypt (17 Oct 88), Finland (27 Nov 90), France (6 Mar 89), India (28 Jan 88), Iraq (21 Jul 88), Israel (25 May 89), Italy (2 Oct 90), Japan (9 Jun 87), Korea (South) (8 Jun 90), Malaysia (1 Sep 87), Monaco (19 Jul 89), Mongolia (11 Jun 87), New Zealand (11 Mar 87), Norway (26 Sep 86), Poland (24 Mar 88), Romania (12 Jun 90), Russia (USSR) (23 Dec 86), Saudi Arabia (3 Nov 89), South Africa (10 Aug 87), Spain (13 Sep 89), Thailand (21 Mar 89), Ukraine (Ukrainian SSR) (26 Jan 87), United Arab Emirates (2 Oct 87), United Kingdom (9 Feb 90), United States (19 Sep 88), World Health Organisation (10 Aug 88), World Meteorological Organisation (17 Apr 90)

3.18 **MONTREAL PROTOCOL ON SUBSTANCES THAT DEPLETE THE OZONE LAYER**
Entered into force: 1 January 1989

Signed but not ratified: 5
Congo (15 Sep 88), Indonesia (21 Jul 88), Israel (14 Jan 88), Morocco (7 Jan 88), Senegal (16 Sep 87)

Ratified/accepted/approved without qualification: 70
Argentina (18 Sep 90), Australia (19 May 89), Austria (3 May 89), Bahrain (27 Apr 90), Bangladesh (2 Aug 90), Belarus (Byelorussian SSR) (31 Oct 88), Belgium (30 Dec 88), Botswana (4 Dec 91), Brazil (19 Mar 90), Bulgaria (20 Nov 90), Burkina Faso (20 Jul 89), Cameroon (30 Aug 89), Canada (30 Jun 88), Chile (26 Mar 90), China (14 Jun 91), Costa Rica (30 Jul 91), Czechoslovakia (1 Oct 90), Ecuador (30 Apr 90), Egypt (2 Aug 88), Fiji (23 Oct 89), Finland (23 Dec 88), France (28 Dec 88), Gambia (25 Jul 90), Germany (16 Dec 88), Ghana (24 Jul 89), Greece (29 Dec 88), Guatemala (7 Nov 89), Hungary (20 Apr 89), Iceland (29 Aug 89), Iran (3 Oct 90), Ireland (16 Dec 88), Italy (16 Dec 88), Japan (30 Sep 88), Jordan (31 May 89), Kenya (9 Nov 88), Liechtenstein (8 Feb 89), Luxembourg (17 Oct 88), Libya (11 Jul 90), Malawi (9 Jan 91), Malaysia (29 Aug 89), Maldives (16 May 89), Malta (29 Dec 88), Mexico (31 Mar 88), Nigeria (31 Oct 88), Norway (24 Jun 88), Panama (3 Mar 89), Philippines (17 Jul 91), Poland (13 Jul 90), Portugal (17 Oct 88), Russia (USSR) (10 Nov 88), Singapore (5 Jan 89), South Africa (15 Jan 90), Spain (16 Dec 88), Sri Lanka (15 Dec 89), Sweden (29 Jun 88), Switzerland (28 Dec 88), Syria (12 Dec 89), Thailand (7 Jul 89), Togo (25 Feb 91), Trinidad and Tobago (28 Aug 89), Tunisia (25 Sep 89), Turkey (20 Sep 91), Uganda (15 Sep 88), Ukraine (Ukrainian SSR) (20 Sep 88), United Arab Emirates (22 Dec 89), United States (21 Apr 88), Uruguay (8 Jan 91), Venezuela (6 Feb 89), Yugoslavia (3 Jan 91), Zambia (24 Jan 90)

Ratified/accepted/approved with qualification: 5
Denmark (16 Dec 88), European Economic Community (16 Dec 88), Netherlands (16 Dec 88), New Zealand (21 Jul 88), United Kingdom (16 Dec 88)

3.19 **PROTOCOL TO THE 1979 LONG-RANGE TRANSBOUNDARY AIR POLLUTION CONCERNING THE CONTROL OF EMISSIONS OF NITROGEN OXIDES OR THEIR TRANSBOUNDARY FLUXES**
Entered into force: 14 February 1991

Signed but not ratified: 8

Belgium (1 Nov 88), Denmark (1 Nov 88), Greece (1 Nov 88), Ireland (1 May 89), Italy (1 Nov 88), Liechtenstein (1 Nov 88), Poland (1 Nov 88), Spain (1 Nov 88)

Ratified/accepted/approved without qualification: 18

Austria (15 Jan 90), Bulgaria (30 Mar 89), Belarus (Byelorussia SSR) (8 Jun 89), Canada (25 Jan 91), Czechoslovakia (17 Aug 90), Finland (1 Feb 90), France (20 Jul 89), Germany (16 Nov 90), Hungary (12 Nov 91), Netherlands (11 Oct 89), Norway (11 Oct 89), Russia (USSR) (21 Jun 89), Sweden (27 Jul 90), Switzerland (18 Sep 90), Ukraine (Ukrainian SSR) (24 Jul 89), United Kingdom (15 Oct 90), United States (13 Jul 89)

3.20 **HELSINKI DECLARATION ON THE PROTECTION OF THE OZONE LAYER**

Adopted: 2 May 1989

3.21 **AMENDMENT TO THE MONTREAL PROTOCOL ON SUBSTANCES THAT DEPLETE THE OZONE LAYER**

Entered into force: 8 October 1992

Ratified/accepted/approved without qualification: 40

Argentina (4 Dec 92), Australia (11 Aug 92), Austria (11 Dec 92), Brazil (1 Oct 92), Cameroon (8 Jun 92), Canada (5 Jul 91), Chile (9n Apr 92), China (14 Jun 91), Denmark (20 Dec 91), European Economic Community (20 Dec 91), Finland (20 Dec 91), France (12 Feb 92), Germany (27 Dec 91), Ghana (24 Jul 92), India (19 Jun 92), Indonesia (26 Jun 92), Ireland (20 Dec 91), Israel (30 Jun 92), Italy (21 Feb 92), Japan (4 Sep 91), Korea (South) (10 Dec 92), Luxembourg (20 May 92), Maldives (31 Jul 91), Mexico (11 Oct 91), Netherlands (20 Dec 91), New Zealand (1 Oct 90), Norway (18 Nov 91), Pakistan (18 Dec 92), Paraguay (3 Dec 92), Portugal (24 Nov 92), Russia (13 Jan 92), Slovenia (8 Dec 92), South Africa (12 May 92), Sweden (2 Aug 91), Switzerland (16 Sep 91), Thailand (25 Jun 92), United Kingdom (20 Dec 91), United States (18 Dec 91)

3.22 **UNITED NATIONS FRAMEWORK CONVENTION ON CLIMATE CHANGE**

Entered into force: Entered into force: 21 March 1994

Signed but not ratified: 148

Afghanistan (12 Jun 92), Algeria (13 Jun 92), Angola (14 Jun 92), Argentina (12 Jun 92), Armenia (13 Jun 92), Austria (8 Jun 92), Azerbaijan (12 Jun 92), Bahamas (12 Jun 92), Bahrain (8 Jun 92), Bangladesh (9 Jun 92), Barbudos (12 Jun 92), Belarus (13 Jun 92), Belgium (4 Jun 92), Belize (13 Jun 92), Benin (13 Jun 92), Bhutan (11 Jun 92), Bolivia (10 Jun 92), Botswana (12 Jun 92), Brazil (4 Jun 92), Bulgaria (5 Jun 92), Burkina Faso (12 Jun 92), Burundi (11 Jun 92), Cameroon (14 Jun 92), Canada (12 Jun 92), Cape Verde (12 Jun 92), Central African Republic (13 Jun 92), Chad (12 Jun 92), Chile (13 Jun 93), China (11 Jun 92), Colombia (13 Jun 92), Comoros (11 Jun 92), Congo (12 Jun 92), Cook Islands (12 Jun 92), Costa Rica (13 Jun 92), Côte d'Ivoire (10 Jun 92), Croatia (11 Jun 92), Cuba (13 Jun 92), Cyprus (12 Jun 92), Korea (North) (11 Jun 92), Denmark (9 Jun 92), European Economic Community (13 Jun 92), Ecuador (9 Jun 92), Egypt (9 Jun 92), El Salvador (13 Jun 92), Estonia (12 Jun 92), Ethiopia (10 Jun 92), Fiji (9 Jun 92), Finland (4 Jun 92), France (13 Jun 92), Gabon

(12 Jun 92), Gambia (12 Jun 92), Germany (12 Jun 92), Ghana (12 Jun 92), Greece (12 Jun 92), Grenada (3 Dec 92), Guatemala (13 Jun 92), Guinea (12 Jun 92), Guinea–Bissau (12 Jun 92), Guyana (13 Jun 92), Haiti (13 Jun 92), Honduras (13 Jun 92), Hungary (13 Jun 92), Iceland (4 Jun 92), India (10 Jun 92), Indonesia (5 Jun 92), Iran (14 Jun 92), Ireland (13 Jun 92), Israel (4 Jun 92), Italy (5 Jun 92), Jamaica (12 Jun 92), Japan (13 Jun 92), Kazakhstan (8 Jun 92), Kenya (12 Jun 92), Kiribati (13 Jun 92), Latvia (11 Jun 92), Lebanon (12 Jun 92), Lesotho (11 Jun 92), Liberia (12 Jun 92), Libya (29 Jun 92), Liechtenstein (4 Jun 92), Lithuania (11 Jun 92), Luxembourg (9 Jun 92), Madagascar (10 Jun 92), Malawi (10 Jun 92), Malta (12 Jun 92), Mauritania (12 Jun 92), Moldova (12 Jun 92), Mongolia (12 Jun 92), Morocco (13 Jun 92), Mozambique (12 Jun 92), Myanmar (11 Jun 92), Namibia (12 Jun 92), Nauru (8 Jun 92), Nepal (12 Jun 92), Netherlands (4 Jun 92), New Zealand (4 Jun 92), Nicaragua (13 Jun 92), Niger (11 Jun 92), Nigeria (13 Jun 92), Norway (4 Jun 92), Oman (11 Jun 92), Pakistan (13 Jun 92), Paraguay (12 Jun 92), Peru (12 Jun 92), Philippines (12 Jun 92), Poland (5 Jun 92), Portugal (13 Jun 92), Korea (South) (13 Jun 93), Romania (5 Jun 92), Russia (13 Jun 92), Rwanda (10 Jun 92), St. Kitts and St. Nevis (12 Jun 92), Samoa (12 Jun 92), San Marino (10 Jun 92), São Tomé and Príncipe (12 Jun 92), Senegal (13 Jun 92), Singapore (13 Jun 92), Slovenia (13 Jun 92), Soloman Islands (13 Jun 92), Spain (13 Jun 92), Sri Lanka (10 Jun 92), Sudan (9 Jun 92), Suriname (13 Jun 92), Swaziland (12 Jun 92), Sweden (8 Jun 92), Switzerland (12 Jun 92), Tanzania (12 Jun 92), Thailand (12 Jun 92), Togo (12 Jun 92), Trinidad and Tobago (4 Jun 92), Tunisia (13 Jun 92), Tuvalu (8 Jun 92), Uganda (13 Jun 92), Ukraine (11 Jun 92), United Kingdom (12 Jun 92), Uruguay (4 Jun 92), Nanatu (9 Jun 92), Venezuela (12 Jun 92), Vietnam (11 Jun 92), Yemen (12 Jun 92), Zaire (11 Jun 92), Zambia (11 Jun 92)

Ratified/accepted/approved without qualification: 8
Canada (4 Dec 92), Maldives (9 Nov 92), Marshall Islands (8 Oct 92), Mauritius (4 Sep 92), Monaco (20 Nov 92), Seychelles (22 Sep 92), United States (15 Oct 92), Zimbabwe (3 Nov 92)

3.23 **MONTREAL PROTOCOL PARTIES: ADJUSTMENTS AND AMENDMENTS TO THE MONTREAL PROTOCOL ON SUBSTANCES THAT DEPLETE THE OZONE LAYER**
Adopted : 23–25 November 1992

4. HYDROSPHERE

4.1 **TREATY BETWEEN CANADA AND THE UNITED STATES RELATING TO BOUNDARY WATERS AND QUESTIONS ARISING ALONG THE BOUNDARY BETWEEN THE UNITED STATES AND CANADA**
Entered into force: 5 May 1910

4.2 **INTERNATIONAL CONVENTION FOR THE PREVENTION OF POLLUTION OF THE SEA BY OIL (OILPOL)**
Entered into force: 26 July 1958

Ratified/accepted/approved without qualification: 54
Algeria (20 Jan 64), Austria (19 May 75), Bahrain (21 Oct 85), Bangladesh (28 Sep 81), Belgium (16 Apr 57), Canada (19 Dec 56), Congo (10 Sep 85), Cyprus (10 Jun 80), Denmark (26 Nov 56), Djibouti (1 Mar 84),

Dominican Republic (29 May 63), Egypt (22 Apr 63), Finland (30 Dec 58), Ghana (17 May 62), Greece (28 Mar 67), Guinea (19 Jan 81), Iceland (23 Feb 62), India (4 Mar 74), Ireland (13 Feb 57), Israel (11 Nov 65), Côte d'Ivoire (17 Mar 67), Japan (21 Aug 67), Jordan (8 May 63), Kenya (12 Sep 75), Korea (South) (31 Jul 78), Kuwait (27 Nov 61), Lebanon (31 May 67), Libya (18 Feb 72), Madagascar (1 Feb 65), Maldives (17 May 82), Malta (10 Jan 75), Mexico (10 May 56), Monaco (25 Mar 70), Morocco (29 Feb 68), New Zealand (1 Jun 71), Nigeria (22 Jan 68), Papua New Guinea (12 Mar 80), Philippines (19 Nov 63), Poland (28 Feb 61), Qatar (31 Jan 80), Senegal (27 Mar 72), Spain (22 Jan 64), Sri Lanka (30 Aug 83), Suriname (1 Dec 76), Sweden (24 May 56), Switzerland (12 Jan 66), Syria (24 Dec 68), United Arab Emirates (15 Dec 83), Uruguay (9 Dec 75), Vanuatu (2 Feb 83), Venezuela (12 Dec 63), Yemen (6 Mar 79), Yemen (Democratic) (20 May 69), Yugoslavia (11 Mar 74)

Ratified/accepted/approved with qualification: 14
Argentina (30 Dec 76), Bahamas (22 Jul 76), Chile (2 Aug 77), Fiji (15 Aug 72), France (26 Jul 57), Italy (25 May 64), Liberia (28 Mar 62), Norway (26 Jan 57), Panama (25 Sep 63), Portugal (28 Mar 67), Saudi Arabia (30 Dec 71), Tunisia (11 Jun 73), United Kingdom (6 May 55), United States (8 Sep 61), Russia (USSR) (3 Sep 69)

Denunciations: 4
Australia (14 Oct 88), Bulgaria (12 Dec 85), Netherlands and the Netherland Antilles (1 Jun 84)

4.3 **CONVENTION ON THE HIGH SEAS**

Entered into force: 30 September 1962

Signed but not ratified: 19
Argentina (29 Apr 58), Bolivia (17 Oct 58), Canada (29 Apr 58), Colombia (29 Apr 58), Cuba (29 Apr 58), France (30 Oct 58), Ghana (29 Apr 58), Holy See (30 Apr 58), Iceland (29 Apr 58), Iran (28 May 58), Ireland (2 Oct 58), Lebanon (29 May 58), Liberia (27 May 58), New Zealand (29 Oct 58), Pakistan (31 Oct 58), Panama (2 May 58), Sri Lanka (30 Oct 58), Tunisia (30 Oct 58), Uruguay (29 Apr 58)

Ratified/accepted/approved without qualification: 45
Afghanistan (28 Apr 59), Australia (14 May 63), Austria (10 Jan 74), Belgium (6 Jan 72), Burkina Faso (4 Oct 65), Cambodia (18 Mar 60), Central African Republic (15 Oct 62), Costa Rica (16 Feb 72), Croatia (3 Aug 92), Cyprus (23 May 88), Denmark (26 Sep 68), Dominican Republic (11 Aug 64), Fiji (25 Mar 71), Finland (16 Feb 65), Germany (26 Jul 73), Guatemala (27 Nov 61), Haiti (29 Mar 60), Israel (6 Sep 61), Italy (17 Dec 64), Jamaica (8 Oct 65), Japan (10 Jun 68), Kenya (20 Jun 69), Latvia (12 Nov 92), Lesotho (23 Oct 73), Madagascar (31 Jul 62), Malawi (3 Nov 65), Malaysia (21 Dec 60), Mauritius (5 Oct 70), Nepal (28 Dec 62), Netherlands (18 Feb 66), Nigeria (26 Jun 61), Portugal (8 Jan 63), Senegal (25 Apr 61), Sierra Leone (13 Mar 62), Solomon Islands (3 Sep 81), South Africa (9 Apr 63), Swaziland (16 Oct 70), Switzerland (18 May 66), Thailand (2 Jul 68), Tonga (29 Jun 71), Trinidad and Tobago (11 Apr 66), Uganda (14 Sep 64), United States (12 Apr 61), Venezuela (15 Aug 61), Yugoslavia (28 Jan 66)

Ratified/accepted/approved with qualification: 14
Albania (7 Dec 64), Belarus (Byelorussian SSR) (27 Feb 61), Bulgaria (31 Aug 62), Czechoslovakia (31 Aug 61), Hungary (6 Dec 61), Indonesia (10 Aug 61), Mexico (2 Aug 66), Mongolia (15 Oct 76), Poland (29 Jun

62), Romania (12 Dec 61), Russia (USSR) (22 Nov 60), Spain (25 Feb 71), Ukraine (Ukrainian SSR) (12 Jan 61), United Kingdom (14 Mar 60)

4.4 CONVENTION ON THE CONTINENTAL SHELF

Entered into force: 10 June 1964

Signed but not ratified: 21
Afghanistan (30 Oct 58), Argentina (29 Apr 58), Bolivia (17 Oct 58), Chile (31 Oct 58), Cuba (29 Apr 58), Ecuador (31 Oct 58), Germany (30 Oct 58), Ghana (29 Apr 58), Iceland (29 Apr 58), Indonesia (8 May 58), Iran (28 May 58), Ireland (2 Oct 58), Lebanon (29 May 58), Liberia (27 May 58), Nepal (29 Apr 58), Pakistan (31 Oct 58), Panama (2 May 58), Peru (31 Oct 58), Sri Lanka (30 Oct 58), Tunisia (30 Oct 58), Uruguay (29 Apr 58)

Ratified/accepted/approved without qualification: 48
Albania (17 Feb 64), Australia (14 May 63), Belarus (Byelorussian SSR) (27 Feb 61), Bulgaria (31 Aug 62), Cambodia (18 Mar 60), Colombia (8 Jan 62), Costa Rica (16 Feb 72), Croatia (3 Aug 92), Cyprus (11 Apr 74), Czechoslovakia (31 Aug 61), Denmark (12 Jun 63), Dominican Republic (11 Aug 64), Fiji (25 Mar 71), Finland (16 Feb 65), Guatemala (27 Nov 61), Haiti (29 Mar 60), Israel (6 Sep 61), Jamaica (8 Oct 65), Kenya (20 Jun 69), Latvia (2 Dec 92), Lesotho (23 Oct 73), Madagascar (31 Jul 62), Malawi (3 Nov 65), Malaysia (21 Dec 60), Malta (19 May 66), Mauritius (5 Oct 70), Mexico (2 Aug 66), Netherlands (18 Feb 66), New Zealand (18 Jan 65), Nigeria (28 Apr 71), Norway (9 Sep 71), Poland (29 Jun 62), Portugal (8 Jan 63), Romania (12 Dec 61), Russia (USSR) (22 Nov 60), Senegal (25 Apr 61), Sierra Leone (25 Nov 66), Solomon Islands (3 Sep 81), South Africa (9 Apr 63), Swaziland (16 Oct 70), Sweden (1 Jun 66), Switzerland (18 May 66), Thailand (2 Jul 68), Tonga (29 Jun 71), Trinidad and Tobago (11 Jul 68), Uganda (14 Sep 64), Ukraine (Ukrainian SSR) (12 Jan 61), United Kingdom (11 May 64), United States (12 Apr 61)

Ratified/accepted/approved with qualification: 7
Canada (6 Feb 70), France (14 Jun 65), Germany (27 Dec 73), Greece (6 Nov 72), Spain (25 Feb 71), Venezuela (15 Aug 61), Yugoslavia (28 Jan 66)

Denunciation: Senegal (30 Mar 76) *

> * Denunciation objected by United Kingdom. Senegal still listed as a party by depository.

4.5 CONVENTION ON THE TERRITORIAL SEA AND CONTIGUOUS ZONE

Entered into force: 10 September 1964

Signed but not ratified: 22
Afghanistan (30 Oct 58), Argentina (29 Apr 58), Austria (27 Oct 58), Bolivia (17 Oct 58), Canada (29 Apr 58), Colombia (29 Apr 58), Costa Rica (29 Apr 58), Cuba (29 Apr 58), Ghana (29 Apr 58), Guatemala (29 Apr 58), Holy See (30 Apr 58), Iceland (29 Apr 58), Iran (28 May 58), Ireland (2 Oct 58), Liberia (27 May 58), Nepal (29 Apr 58), New Zealand (29 Oct 58), Pakistan (31 Oct 58), Panama (2 May 58), Sri Lanka (30 Oct 58), Tunisia (30 Oct 58), Uruguay (29 Apr 58)

Ratified/accepted/approved without qualification: 33
Australia (14 May 63), Belgium (6 Jan 72), Cambodia (18 Mar 60), Croatia (3 Aug 92), Dominican Republic (11 Aug 64), Finland (16 Feb 65), Haiti (29 Mar 60), Israel (6 Sep 61), Jamaica (8 Oct 65), Japan (10

Jun 68), Kenya (20 Jun 69), Latvia (17 Nov 92), Lesotho (23 Oct 73), Madagascar (31 Jul 62), Malawi (3 Nov 65), Malaysia (21 Dec 60), Malta (19 May 66), Mauritius (5 Oct 70), Mexico (2 Aug 66), Netherlands (18 Feb 66), Nigeria (26 Jun 61), Portugal (8 Jan 63), Senegal (25 Apr 61), Sierra Leone (13 Mar 62), South Africa (9 Apr 63), Swaziland (16 Oct 70), Switzerland (18 May 66), Thailand (2 Jul 68), Tonga (29 Jun 71), Trinidad and Tobago (11 Apr 66), Uganda (14 Sep 64), United States (12 Apr 61), Yugoslavia (28 Jan 66)

Ratified/accepted/approved with qualification: 14
Bulgaria (31 Aug 62), Belarus (Byelorussian SSR) (27 Feb 61), Czecho-slovakia (31 Aug 61), Denmark (26 Sep 68), Fiji (25 Mar 71), Hungary (6 Dec 61), Italy (17 Dec 64), Romania (12 Dec 61), Russia (USSR) (22 Nov 60), Solomon Islands (3 Sep 81), Spain (25 Feb 71), Ukraine (Ukrainian SSR) (12 Jan 61), United Kingdom (14 Mar 60), Venezuela (15 Aug 61)

Denunciation: Senegal (9 Jul 71) *

* Denunciation objected by United Kingdom. Senegal still listed as a party by depository.

4.6 **CONVENTION ON THE LIABILITY OF OPERATORS OF NUCLEAR SHIPS**

Entered into force: 15 July 1975

Signed but not ratified: 13
Belgium (25 May 62), China (25 May 62), Germany (25 Oct 74), India (25 May 62), Indonesia (25 May 62), Ireland (25 May 62), Liberia (25 May 62), Malaysia (25 May 62), Monaco (25 May 62), Panama (25 May 62), Philippines (25 May 62), United Arab Emirates (25 May 62), Yugoslavia (25 May 62)

Ratified/accepted/approved without qualification: 5
Lebanon (3 Jun 75), Madagascar (13 Jul 65), Portugal (31 Jun 68), Syria (1 Aug 74), Zaire (17 Jul 67)

Ratified/accepted/approved with qualification: 2
Netherlands (20 Mar 74), Suriname (20 Mar 74)

4.7 **HELSINKI RULES ON THE USES OF THE WATERS OF INTERNATIONAL RIVERS**

Adopted: 20 August 1966

4.8 **INTERNATIONAL CONVENTION ON CIVIL LIABILITY FOR OIL POLLUTION DAMAGE**

Entered into force: 19 June 1975

Signed but not ratified: 5
China (29 Nov 69), Ireland (18 Dec 70), Madagascar (29 Nov 69), Romania (30 Dec 70), United States (29 Nov 69)

Ratified/accepted/approved without qualification: 53
Algeria (14 Jun 74), Bahamas (22 Jul 76), Belize (2 Apr 91), Benin (1 Nov 85), Brazil (17 Dec 76), Cameroon (14 May 84), Canada (24 Jan 89), Chile (2 Aug 77), Colombia (26 Mar 90), Côte d'Ivoire (21 Jun 73), Cyprus (19 Jun 89), Djibouti (1 Mar 90), Dominican Republic (2 Apr 75), Ecuador (23 Dec 76), Egypt (3 Feb 89), Fiji (15 Aug 72), Finland (10 Oct 80), Gabon (21 Jan 82), Gambia (1 Nov 91), Ghana (20 Apr 78), Greece (29 Jun 76), Iceland (17 Jul 80), India (1 May 87), Indonesia (1 Sep 78), Korea (South) (18 Dec 78), Kuwait (2 Apr 81), Lebanon (9 Apr 74), Liberia (25 Sep 72), Luxembourg (14 Feb 91), Maldives (16 Mar

81), Malta (27 Sep 91), Monaco (21 Aug 75), Morocco (11 Apr 74), Nigeria (7 May 81), Oman (24 Jan 85), Panama (7 Jan 76), Papua New Guinea (12 Mar 80), Poland (18 Mar 76), Portugal (26 Nov 76), Qatar (2 Jun 88), Senegal (27 Mar 72), Seychelles (12 Apr 88), Singapore (16 Sep 81), South Africa (17 Mar 76), Spain (8 Dec 75), Sri Lanka (12 Apr 83), St. Vincent (19 Apr 89), Switzerland (15 Dec 87), Tunisia (4 May 76), United Arab Emirates (15 Dec 83), Vanuatu (2 Feb 83), Yemen (6 Mar 79), Yugoslavia (18 Jun 76)

Ratified/accepted/approved with qualification: 17
Australia (7 Nov 83), Belgium (12 Jan 77), China (30 Jan 80), Denmark (2 Apr 75), France (17 Mar 75), German Democratic Republic (13 Mar 78), Germany (20 May 75), Guatemala (20 Oct 82), Italy (27 Feb 79), Japan (3 Jun 76), Netherlands (9 Sep 75), New Zealand (27 Apr 76), Norway (21 Mar 75), Russia (USSR) (24 Jun 75), Sweden (17 Mar 75), Syria (6 Feb 75), United Kingdom (17 Mar 75)

4.9 **INTERNATIONAL CONVENTION RELATING TO INTERVENTION ON THE HIGH SEAS IN CASES OF OIL POLLUTION CASUALTIES**

Entered into force: 6 May 1975

Signed but not ratified: 6
Brazil (30 Dec 69), Greece (14 Apr 70), Guatemala (29 Nov 69), Korea (South) (29 Nov 69), Madagascar (29 Nov 69), Romania (30 Dec 69)

Ratified/accepted/approved without qualification: 45
Argentina (21 Apr 87), Bahamas (22 Jul 76), Bangladesh (6 Nov 81), Belgium (21 Oct 71), Benin (11 Nov 85), Cameroon (14 May 84), China (23 Feb 90), Denmark (18 Dec 70), Djibouti (1 Mar 90), Dominican Republic (5 Feb 75), Ecuador (23 Dec 76), Egypt (3 Feb 89), Fiji (15 Aug 72), Finland (6 Sep 76), Gabon (21 Jan 82), Ghana (20 Apr 78), Iceland (17 Jul 80), Ireland (21 Aug 80), Italy (27 Feb 79), Côte d'Ivoire (8 Jan 88), Jamaica (13 Mar 91), Kuwait (2 Apr 81), Lebanon (5 Jun 75), Liberia (25 Sep 72), Mexico (8 Apr 76), Monaco (24 Feb 75), Morocco (11 Apr 74), Netherlands (19 Sep 75), New Zealand (26 Mar 75), Norway (12 Jul 72), Oman (24 Jan 85), Panama (7 Jan 76), Papua New Guinea (12 Mar 80), Poland (1 Jun 76), Portugal (15 Feb 80), Qatar (2 Jun 88), Senegal (27 Mar 72), South Africa (1 Jul 86), Spain (8 Nov 73), Sri Lanka (12 Apr 83), Suriname (25 Nov 75), Sweden (8 Feb 73), Switzerland (15 Dec 87), Tunisia (4 May 76), United Arab Emirates (15 Dec 83), United States (21 Feb 74), Yemen (6 Mar 79), Yugoslavia (3 Feb 76)

Ratified/accepted/approved with qualification: 10
Australia (7 Nov 83), Bulgaria (2 Nov 83), Cuba * (5 May 76), France (10 May 72), Germany (7 May 75), Japan (6 Apr 71), Russia (USSR) (30 Dec 74), Syria (6 Feb 75), United Kingdom (12 Jan 71)

* Reservation not accepted by France and Japan

4.10 **DECLARATION OF PRINCIPLES GOVERNING THE SEA-BED AND THE OCEAN FLOOR, AND THE SUBSOIL THEREOF, BEYOND THE LIMITS OF NATIONAL JURISDICTION**

Adopted: 17 December 1970

For: 108 *

Against: 0

Abstaining: 14

* Adopted with no roll call vote recorded

4.11   CONVENTION RELATING TO CIVIL LIABILITY IN THE FIELD OF MARITIME
       CARRIAGE OF NUCLEAR MATERIAL

Entered into force: 15 July 1975

Signed but not ratified: 4
Brazil (17 Dec 71), Portugal (17 Dec 71), United Kingdom (17 Dec 71),
Yugoslavia (17 Dec 71)

Ratified/accepted/approved without qualification: 14
Argentina (18 May 81), Belgium (15 Jun 89), Denmark (4 Sep 74),
Finland (4 Sep 91), France (2 Feb 73), Gabon (21 Jan 82), Germany (1
Oct 75), Italy (21 Jul 80), Liberia (17 Feb 81), Netherlands (1 Aug 91),
Norway (16 Apr 75), Spain (21 May 74), Sweden (22 Nov 74), Yemen (6
Mar 79)

4.12   INTERNATIONAL CONVENTION ON THE ESTABLISHMENT OF AN INTERNATIONAL
       FUND FOR COMPENSATION FOR OIL POLLUTION DAMAGE

Entered into force: 16 October 1978

Signed but not ratified: 5
Belgium (18 Dec 71), Brazil (18 Dec 71), Ireland (21 Dec 72), Switzerland (18 Dec 71), United States (18 Dec 71)

Ratified/accepted/approved without qualification: 41
Algeria (2 Jun 75), Bahamas (22 Jul 76), Benin (1 Nov 85), Cameroon
(14 May 84), Côte d'Ivoire (5 Oct 87), Cyprus (26 Jul 89), Denmark (2
Apr 75), Djibouti (1 Mar 90), Fiji (4 Mar 83), Finland (10 Oct 80),
France (11 May 78), Gabon (21 Jan 82), Germany (30 Dec 76), Ghana
(20 Apr 78), Greece (16 Dec 86), Iceland (17 Jul 80), India (10 Jul 90),
Indonesia (1 Sep 78), Italy (27 Feb 79), Japan (7 Jul 76), Kuwait (2 Apr
81), Liberia (25 Sep 72), Maldives (16 Mar 81), Monaco (23 Aug 79),
Netherlands (3 Aug 82), Nigeria (11 Sep 87), Norway (21 Mar 76),
Oman (10 May 85), Papua New Guinea (12 Mar 80), Poland (16 Sep 85),
Portugal (11 Sep 85), Qatar (2 Jun 88), Russia (USSR) (17 Jun 87),
Seychelles (12 Apr 88), Sri Lanka (12 Apr 83), Spain (8 Oct 81), Sweden
(17 Mar 75), Tunisia (4 May 76), United Arab Emirates (15 Dec 83),
Vanuatu (13 Jan 89), Yugoslavia (16 Mar 78)

Ratified/accepted/approved with qualification: 3
Canada (24 Jan 89), Syria (6 Feb 75), United Kingdom (2 Apr 76)

4.13   **ILA DRAFT ARTICLES ON MARINE POLLUTION OF CONTINENTAL ORIGIN**

Adopted: 26 August 1972

4.14   CONVENTION ON THE PREVENTION OF MARINE POLLUTION BY DUMPING OF
       WASTES AND OTHER MATTER

Entered into force: 30 August 1975

Signed but not ratified: 13
Bolivia (29 Dec 72), Chad (29 Dec 72), Colombia (29 Dec 72), Costa Rica
(29 Dec 72), Kuwait (1 Mar 73), Lebanon (29 Dec 72), Lesotho (8 Jan
73), Liberia (29 Dec 72), Senegal (29 Dec 72), Somalia (16 Apr 73), Togo
(21 Nov 73), Uruguay (29 Dec 72), Venezuela (30 May 73)

Ratified/accepted/approved without qualification: 61
Afghanistan (2 Apr 75), Antigua and Barbuda (6 Jan 89), Argentina (11
Sep 79), Australia (21 Aug 85), Belgium (12 Jun 85), Brazil (26 Jul 82),

Belarus (Byelorussian SSR) (29 Jan 76), Canada (13 Nov 75), Cape
Verde (26 May 77), Chile (4 Aug 77), Côte d'Ivoire (9 Oct 87), Cuba (1
Dec 75), Cyprus (7 Jun 90), Denmark (23 Oct 74), Dominican Republic
(17 Feb 74), Finland (3 May 79), Gabon (5 Feb 82), Greece (10 Aug 81),
Guatemala (14 Jul 75), Haiti (28 Aug 75), Honduras (2 May 80),
Hungary (5 Feb 76), Iceland (24 May 73), Ireland (17 Feb 82), Jamaica
(22 Mar 91), Japan (15 Oct 75), Jordan (11 Nov 74), Kenya (7 Jan 76),
Kiribati (3 Jun 82), Libya (22 Nov 76), Luxembourg (21 Feb 91), Malta
(28 Dec 89), Mexico (7 Apr 75), Monaco (16 May 77), Morocco (18 Feb
77), Nauru (26 Jul 82), Netherlands (2 Dec 77), Nigeria (19 Mar 76),
Norway (4 Apr 74), Oman (13 Mar 84), Panama (31 Jul 75), Papua New
Guinea (10 Mar 80), Philippines (10 Aug 73), Poland (23 Jan 79),
Portugal (14 Apr 78), Russia (USSR) (30 Dec 75), Seychelles (29 Oct
84), Solomon Islands (6 Mar 84), South Africa (7 Aug 78), Spain (31 Jul
74), St. Lucia (23 Aug 85), Suriname (21 Oct 80), Sweden (21 Feb 74),
Switzerland (31 Jul 79), Tunisia (13 Apr 76), Ukraine (Ukrainian SSR)
(5 Feb 76), United Arab Emirates (9 Aug 74), United States (29 Apr 74),
Yugoslavia (25 Jun 76), Zaire (16 Sep 75)

Ratified/accepted/approved with qualification: 6
China (5 Nov 85), France (3 Feb 77), Germany (8 Nov 77), Italy (30 Apr
84), New Zealand (30 Apr 75), United Kingdom (17 Nov 75)

4.15 INTERNATIONAL CONVENTION FOR THE PREVENTION OF POLLUTION FROM SHIPS (MARPOL)

Entered into force: Not in force as of 31 December 1992

Signed but not ratified: 11
Australia (24 Dec 74), Brazil (12 Dec 74), Denmark (15 Jan 74), France
(27 Aug 74), Ireland (30 Dec 74), Netherlands (30 Dec 74), Poland (2
Oct 74), Russia (USSR) (10 Jul 74), Spain (20 Sep 74), Sweden (31 May
74), United States (7 Mar 74)

Ratified/accepted/approved without qualification: 17
Antigua and Barbuda (9 Feb 87), Belgium (6 Mar 84), Benin (1 Jan 85),
Brunei (23 Oct 86), Bulgaria (12 Dec 84), Colombia (27 Jul 81),
Germany (21 Jan 82), Hungary (16 Dec 83), Italy (1 Oct 82), Jordan (17
Mar 75), Kenya (12 Sep 75), Peru (25 Apr 80), Tunisia (4 May 76),
United Kingdom (22 May 80), Uruguay (30 Apr 79), Yemen (6 Mar 79),
Yugoslavia (31 Oct 80)

Ratified/accepted/approved with qualification: 1
Norway (15 Jul 80)

4.16 CONVENTION ON THE PROTECTION OF THE MARINE ENVIRONMENT OF THE BALTIC SEA AREA

Entered into force: 3 May 1980

Ratified/accepted/approved without qualification: 6
Denmark (20 Jul 77), Finland (27 Jun 75), Germany (3 Mar 80), Poland
(19 Nov 79), Sweden (30 Jul 76), Russia (USSR) (2 Nov 78)

4.17 CONVENTION FOR THE PREVENTION OF MARINE POLLUTION FROM LAND-BASED SOURCES

Entered into force: 6 May 1978

Signed but not ratified: 1
Luxembourg (11 Jun 74)

Ratified/accepted/approved without qualification: 13
Belgium (12 Jan 84), Denmark (1 Mar 76), European Economic Community (23 Jun 75), France (19 Jan 77), Germany (2 Mar 82), Iceland (19 Jun 81), Ireland (29 Aug 84), Netherlands (10 Nov 77), Norway (6 Apr 77), Portugal (10 May 78), Spain (17 Apr 80), Sweden (30 Jul 76), United Kingdom (6 Apr 78)

4.18 PROTOCOL TO THE **1969** INTERNATIONAL CONVENTION ON CIVIL LIABILITY FOR OIL POLLUTION DAMAGE
Entered into force: 8 April 1981

Ratified/accepted/approved without qualification: 36
Australia (7 Nov 83), Bahamas (3 Mar 80), Belgium (15 Jun 89), Belize (2 Apr 91), Cameroon (14 May 84), Canada (24 Jan 89), China (29 Sep 86), Colombia (26 Mar 90), Cyprus (15 Jun 89), Denmark (3 Jun 81), Egypt (3 Jan 89), Finland (8 Jan 81), France (7 Nov 80), India (1 May 87), Italy (3 Jun 83), Kuwait (1 Jul 81), Liberia (8 Apr 81), Luxembourg (14 Feb 91), Maldives (14 Jun 81), Malta (27 Sep 91), Netherlands (3 Aug 82), Norway (17 Jul 78), Oman (24 Jan 85), Peru (24 Feb 87), Poland (30 Oct 85), Portugal (2 Jan 86), Qatar (2 Jun 88), Russia (USSR) (2 Dec 88), Singapore (15 Dec 81), Spain (22 Oct 81), Sweden (7 Jul 76), Switzerland (15 Dec 87), United Arab Emirates (14 Mar 84), United Kingdom (31 Jan 80), Vanuatu (13 Jan 89), Yemen (4 Jun 79)

Ratified/accepted/approved with qualification: 2
Germany (28 Aug 80), Greece (10 May 89)

4.19 PROTOCOL TO THE **1971** INTERNATIONAL CONVENTION ON THE ESTABLISHMENT OF AN INTERNATIONAL FUND FOR COMPENSATION FOR OIL POLLUTION DAMAGE
Entered into force: 8 April 1981

Ratified/accepted/approved without qualification: 19
Bahamas (3 Mar 80), Cyprus (26 Jul 89), Denmark (3 Jun 81), Finland (8 Jan 81), France (7 Nov 80), Germany (28 Aug 80), India (10 Jul 90), Italy (21 Sep 83), Liberia (17 Feb 81), Malta (27 Sep 91), Netherlands (1 Nov 82), Norway (17 Jul 78), Poland (30 Oct 85), Portugal (11 Sep 85), Russia (USSR) (30 Jan 89), Spain (5 Apr 82), Sweden (7 Jul 78), United Kingdom (31 Jan 80), Vanuatu (13 Jan 89)

4.20 CONVENTION FOR THE PROTECTION OF THE MEDITERRANEAN SEA AGAINST POLLUTION
Entered into force: 12 February 1978

Ratified/accepted/approved without qualification: 15
Albania (30 May 90), Algeria (16 Feb 81), Cyprus (19 Nov 79), European Economic Community (16 Mar 78), Greece (3 Jan 79), Italy (3 Feb 79), Lebanon (8 Nov 77), Libya (31 Jan 79), Malta (30 dec 77), Monaco (20 Sep 77), Morocco (15 Jan 80), Spain (17 Dec 76), Tunisia (30 Jul 77), Turkey (6 Apr 81), Yugoslavia (13 Jan 78)

Ratified/accepted/approved with qualification: 4
Egypt (24 Aug 78), France (11 Mar 78), Israel (3 Mar 78), Syria (26 Dec 78)

4.21 CONVENTION FOR THE PROTECTION OF THE RHINE RIVER AGAINST POLLUTION BY CHEMICAL POLLUTION
Entered into force: 1 February 1979

Ratified/accepted/approved without qualification: 6
European Economic Community (26 Sep 78), France (28 Dec 77),
Germany (7 Dec 78), Luxembourg (3 May 78), Netherlands (18 Sep 78),
Switzerland (28 Nov 77)

4.22 CONVENTION FOR THE PROTECTION OF THE RHINE RIVER AGAINST POLLUTION
BY CHLORIDES

Entered into force: 5 July 1985

Ratified/accepted/approved without qualification: 5
France (2 Feb 84), Germany (7 Dec 78), Luxembourg (3 May 78),
Netherlands (18 Sep 78), Switzerland (28 Nov 77)

4.23 PROTOCOL OF **1978** RELATING TO THE INTERNATIONAL CONVENTION FOR THE
PREVENTION OF POLLUTION FROM SHIPS, **1973** (MARPOL)

Entered into force: 2 October 1983

Signed but not ratified: 2
Mexico (1 Jun 78), Uruguay (30 Apr 79)

Ratified/accepted/approved without qualification: 40
Algeria (31 Jan 89), Antigua and Barbuda (29 Jan 88), Austria (27 May
88), Colombia (27 Feb 81), Côte d'Ivoire (5 Oct 87), Cyprus (22 Jun 89),
Czechoslovakia (2 Jul 84), Djibouti (1 Mar 80), Ecuador (18 May 90),
Egypt (7 Aug 86), Estonia (16 Dec 91), Finland (20 Sep 83), Gabon (26
Apr 83), Gambia (1 Nov 91), Ghana (3 Jun 91), Greece (23 Sep 82),
Hungary (14 Jan 85), Italy (1 Oct 82), Jamaica (13 Mar 91), Lebanon
(18 Jul 83), Lithuania (4 Dec 91), Luxembourg (14 Feb 91), Malta (12
Jun 91), Marshall Islands (26 Apr 88), Panama (20 Feb 85), Peru (25
Apr 80), Poland (1 Apr 86), Portugal (22 Oct 87), St. Vincent and the
Grenadines (28 Oct 83), Seychelles (28 Nov 90), Singapore (1 Nov 90),
Suriname (4 Nov 88), Sweden (9 Jun 80), Togo (9 Feb 90), Tunisia (10
Oct 80), Turkey (10 Oct 90), Tuvalu (22 Aug 85), Vanuatu (13 Apr 89),
Vietnam (29 May 91), Yugoslavia (31 Oct 80)

Ratified/accepted/approved with qualification: 27
Australia (14 Oct 87), Bahamas (7 Jun 83), Belgium (6 Mar 84), Brazil
(29 Jan 88), Brunei (23 Oct 86), Bulgaria (12 Dec 84), China (1 Jul 83),
Denmark (27 Nov 80), France (25 Sep 81), Germany (21 Jan 82),
Iceland (25 Jun 85), India (24 Sep 86), Indonesia (21 Oct 86), Israel (31
Aug 83), Japan (9 Jun 83), Korea (South) (23 Jul 84), Liberia (28 Oct
80), Myanmar (4 May 88), Netherlands (30 Jun 83), Norway (15 Jul 80),
Oman (13 Mar 84), Russia (USSR) (3 Nov 83), South Africa (28 Nov 84),
Spain (6 Jul 84), Syria (9 Nov 88), United Kingdom (22 May 80), United
States (12 Aug 80)

4.24 KUWAIT REGIONAL CONVENTION FOR CO-OPERATION ON THE PROTECTION OF
THE MARINE ENVIRONMENT FROM POLLUTION

Entered into force: 30 June 1979

Ratified/accepted/approved without qualification: 8
Bahrain (1 Jul 79), Iran (1 Jun 80), Iraq (1 Jul 79), Kuwait (1 Jul 79),
Oman (1 Jul 79), Qatar (1 Jul 79), Saudi Arabia (26 Mar 82), United
Arab Emirates (1 Mar 80)

4.25 PROTOCOL FOR THE PROTECTION OF THE MEDITERRANEAN SEA AGAINST
POLLUTION FROM LAND-BASED SOURCES

Entered into force: 17 June 1983

Signed but not ratified: 1
Lebanon (17 May 80)

Ratified/accepted/approved without qualification: 16
Albania (30 Mar 90), Algeria (2 May 83), Cyprus (28 Jun 88), Egypt (18 May 83), European Economic Community (7 Oct 83), Greece (26 Jan 87), Israel (21 Feb 91), Italy (4 Jul 85), Libya (6 Jun 89), Malta (2 Mar 89), Monaco (12 Jan 83), Morocco (9 Feb 87), Spain (6 Jan 84), Tunisia (29 Oct 81), Turkey (21 Feb 83), Yugoslavia (16 Apr 90)

Ratified/accepted/approved with qualification: 1
France (13 Jul 82)

4.26 UNITED NATIONS CONVENTION ON THE LAW OF THE SEA

Enters into force: 16 November 94

Signed but not ratified: 99
Afghanistan (18 Mar 83), Algeria (10 Dec 82), Argentina (5 Oct 84), Australia (10 Dec 82), Austria (10 Dec 82), Bangladesh (10 Dec 82), Belarus (Byelorussian SSR) (10 Dec 82), Belgium (5 Dec 84), Benin (30 Aug 83), Bhutan (10 Dec 82), Bolivia (27 Nov 84), Brunei (5 Dec 84), Bulgaria (10 Dec 82), Burkina Faso (10 Dec 82), Burundi (10 Dec 82), Cambodia (1 Jul 83), Canada (10 Dec 82), Central African Republic (4 Dec 84), Chad (10 Dec 82), Chile (10 Dec 82), China (10 Dec 82), Colombia (10 Dec 82), Comoros (6 Dec 84), Congo (10 Dec 82), Cook Islands (10 Dec 82), Czechoslovakia (10 Dec 82), Denmark (10 Dec 82), Dominican Republic (10 Dec 82), El Salvador (5 Dec 84), Equatorial Guinea (30 Jan 84), Ethiopia (10 Dec 82), European Economic Community (7 Dec 84), Finland (10 Dec 82), France (10 Dec 82), Gabon (10 Dec 82), Greece (10 Dec 82), Guatemala (8 Jul 83), Haiti (10 Dec 82), Hungary (10 Dec 82), India (10 Dec 82), Iran (10 Dec 82), Ireland (10 Dec 82), Italy (7 Dec 84), Japan (7 Feb 83), Korea (North) (10 Dec 82), Korea (South) (14 Mar 83), Lao People's Democratic Republic (10 Dec 82), Lebanon (7 Dec 84), Lesotho (10 Dec 82), Liberia (10 Dec 82), Libya (3 Dec 84), Liechtenstein (30 Nov 84), Luxembourg (5 Dec 84), Madagascar (25 Feb 83), Malawi (7 Dec 84), Malaysia (10 Dec 82), Maldives (10 Dec 82), Mauritania (10 Dec 92), Mauritius (10 Dec 82), Monaco (10 Dec 82), Mongolia (10 Dec 82), Morocco (10 Dec 82), Mozambique (10 Dec 82), Myanmar (10 Dec 82), Nauru (10 Dec 82), Nepal (10 Dec 82), Netherlands (10 Dec 82), New Zealand (10 Dec 82), Nicaragua (9 Dec 84), Niger (10 Dec 82), Niue (5 Dec 84), Norway (10 Dec 82), Pakistan (10 Dec 82), Panama (10 Dec 82), Papua New Guinea (10 Dec 82), Poland (10 Dec 82), Portugal (10 Dec 82), Qatar (27 Nov 84), Romania (10 Dec 82), Russia (USSR) (10 Dec 82), Rwanda (10 Dec 82), Samoa (28 Sep 84), Saudi Arabia (7 Dec 84), Sierra Leone (10 Dec 82), Singapore (10 Dec 82), Solomon Islands (10 Dec 82), South Africa (5 Dec 84), Spain (4 Dec 84), Sri Lanka (10 Dec 82), Suriname (10 Dec 82), Swaziland (18 Jan 84), Sweden (10 Dec 82), Switzerland (17 Oct 84), Thailand (10 Dec 82), Tuvalu (10 Dec 82), Ukraine (Ukrainian SSR) (10 Dec 82), United Arab Emirates (10 Dec 82), Vanuatu (10 Dec 82), Vietnam (10 Dec 82)

Ratified/accepted/approved without qualification: 40
Antigua and Barbuda (2 Feb 89), Bahamas (29 Jul 83), Bahrain (30 May 85), Barbados (12 Oct 93), Belize (13 Aug 83), Bosnia–Herzegovina (12 Jan 94), Botswana (2 May 90), Cameroon (19 Nov 85), Côte d'Ivoire (26 Mar 84), Cyprus (12 Dec 88), Djibouti (8 Oct 91), Dominica (24 Oct 91),

Fiji (10 Dec 82), Gambia (22 May 84), Ghana (7 Jun 83), Grenada (25 Apr 91), Guyana (16 Nov 93), Honduras (5 Oct 93), Indonesia (3 Feb 86), Jamaica (21 Mar 83), Kenya (2 Mar 89), Malta (20 May 93), Marshall Islands (9 Aug 91), Mexico (18 Mar 83), Micronesia (29 Apr 91), Namibia (18 Apr 83), Nigeria (14 Aug 86), Paraguay (26 Sep 86), St. Kitts and Nevis (7 Jan 93), St. Lucia (27 Mar 85), St. Vincent and the Grenadines (1 Oct 93), Senegal (25 Oct 84), Seychelles (16 Sep 91), Somalia (24 Jul 89), Togo (16 Apr 85), Trinidad and Tobago (25 Apr 86), Uganda (9 Nov 90), Zaire (17 Feb 89), Zambia (7 Mar 83), Zimbabwe (24 Feb 93)

Ratified/accepted/approved with qualification: 21
Angola (5 Dec 90), Brazil (22 Dec 88), Cape Verde (10 Aug 87), Costa Rica (29 Sep 92), Cuba (15 Aug 84), Egypt (26 Aug 83), Guinea (6 Sep 85), Guinea–Bissau (25 Aug 86), Iceland (21 Jun 85), Iraq (30 Jul 85), Kuwait (2 May 86), Mali (16 Jul 85), Oman (17 Aug 89), Philippines (8 May 84), São Tomé and Príncipe (3 Nov 87), Sudan (23 Jan 85), Tanzania (30 Sep 85), Tunisia (24 Apr 85), Uruguay (10 Dec 92), Yemen (21 Jul 87), Yugoslavia (5 May 86)

4.27 **ECE D**ECLARATION OF **P**OLICY ON THE **R**ATIONAL **U**SE OF **W**ATER
Adopted: 14 April 1984

4.28 **P**ROTOCOL OF **1984** TO **A**MEND THE **I**NTERNATIONAL **C**ONVENTION ON **C**IVIL **L**IABILITY FOR **O**IL **P**OLLUTION **D**AMAGE
Entered into force: Not in force as of 31 December 1992
Signed but not ratified: 11
China (25 May 84), Denmark (25 May 84), Finland (25 May 84), Morocco (25 May 84), Netherlands (25 May 84), Norway (25 May 84), Poland (25 May 84), Portugal (25 May 84), Sweden (25 May 84), United Kingdom (25 May 84), United States (25 May 84)
Ratified/accepted/approved without qualification: 6
Australia (22 Jun 88), France (8 Sep 87), Luxembourg (14 Feb 91), Peru (26 Aug 87), St. Vincent and the Grenadines (19 Apr 89), South Africa (31 Jan 86)
Ratified/accepted/approved with qualification: 1
Germany (18 Oct 88)

4.29 **P**ROTOCOL TO **A**MEND THE **I**NTERNATIONAL **C**ONVENTION ON THE **E**STABLISH-MENT OF AN **I**NTERNATIONAL **F**UND FOR **C**OMPENSATION FOR **O**IL **P**OLLUTION **D**AMAGE
Entered into force: Not in force as of 31 December 1992
Signed but not ratified: 10
Denmark (25 May 84), Finland (25 May 84), Morocco (25 May 84), Netherlands (25 May 84), Norway (25 May 84), Poland (25 May 84), Portugal (25 May 84), Sweden (25 May 84)
Ratified/accepted/approved without qualification: 2
France (8 Sep 87), Germany (18 Oct 88)

4.30 **M**ONTREAL **G**UIDELINES FOR THE **P**ROTECTION OF THE **M**ARINE **E**NVIRONMENT **A**GAINST **P**OLLUTION FROM **L**AND-**B**ASED **S**OURCES
Adopted: 24 May 1985

4.31 CONVENTION FOR THE PROTECTION OF THE NATURAL RESOURCES AND ENVIRONMENT OF THE SOUTH PACIFIC REGION

Entered into force: 22 August 1990

Signed but not ratified: 4
Nauru (15 Apr 87), Palau (25 Nov 86), Tuvalu (14 Aug 87), United Kingdom (16 Jul 87)

Ratified/accepted/approved without qualification: 11
Australia (19 Jun 89), Cook Islands (9 Sep 87), Fiji (18 Sep 89), France (25 Nov 86), Marshall Islands (4 May 87), Micronesia (9 Apr 87), New Zealand (25 Nov 86), Papau New Guinea (15 Sep 89), Samoa (24 Jul 90), Solomon Islands (10 Aug 89), United States (25 Nov 86)

4.32 BELLAGIO DRAFT TREATY CONCERNING THE USE OF TRANSBOUNDARY GROUNDWATERS, 1989

Entered into force: Not in force as of 31 December 1992

4.33 ILC DRAFT ARTICLES ON THE NON-NAVIGATIONAL USES OF INTERNATIONAL WATERCOURSES

Adopted: 19 July 1991

5. LITHOSPHERE

5.1 FAO INTERNATIONAL CODE OF CONDUCT ON THE DISTRIBUTION AND USE OF PESTICIDES

Adopted: 28 November 1985

5.2 OECD COUNCIL DECISION/RECOMMENDATION ON EXPORTS OF HAZARDOUS WASTES FROM THE OECD AREA

Adopted: 5 June 1986

5.3 CAIRO GUIDELINES AND PRINCIPLES FOR THE ENVIRONMENTALLY SOUND MANAGEMENT OF HAZARDOUS WASTES

Adopted: 17 June 1987

5.4 LONDON GUIDELINES FOR THE EXCHANGE OF INFORMATION ON CHEMICALS IN INTERNATIONAL TRADE

Adopted: 19 June 1987

5.5 OAU COUNCIL OF MINISTERS RESOLUTION ON DUMPING OF NUCLEAR AND INDUSTRIAL WASTE IN AFRICA

Adopted: 23 May 1988

5.6 BASEL CONVENTION ON THE CONTROL OF TRANSBOUNDARY MOVEMENTS OF HAZARDOUS WASTES AND THEIR DISPOSAL

Entered into force: 5 May 1992

Signed but not ratified: 30
Afghanistan (22 Mar 89), Austria (19 Mar 90), Belgium (22 Mar 89), Bolivia (22 Mar 89), Colombia (22 Mar 89), Denmark (22 Mar 89), Ecuador (22 Mar 89), European Economic Community (22 Mar 89), Germany (23 Oct 89), Greece (22 Mar 89), Guatemala (22 Mar 89), Haiti (22 Mar 89), India (15 Mar 90), Ireland (31 Jan 90), Israel (22 Mar 89), Italy (22 Mar 89), Kuwait (22 Mar 89), Lebanon (22 Mar 89),

Luxembourg (22 Mar 89), Netherlands (22 Mar 89), New Zealand (18 Dec 89), Philippines (22 Mar 89), Portugal (26 Jun 89), Russia (USSR) (22 Mar 90), Spain (22 Mar 89), Thailand (22 Mar 90), Turkey (22 Mar 89), United Kingdom (6 Oct 89), United States (22 Mar 90), Venezuela (22 Mar 89)

Ratified/accepted/approved without qualification: 33
Argentina (27 Jun 91), Australia (5 Feb 92), Bahamas (12 Aug 92), Bahrain (15 Oct 92), Brazil (1)ct 92), Canada (28 Aug 92), Chile (11 Aug 92), China (17 Dec 91), Cyprus (17 Sep 92), Czechoslovakia (24 Jul 91), El Salvador (13 Dec 91), Estonia (21 Jul 92), Finland (19 Nov 91), France (7 Jan 91), Hungary (21 May 90), Jordan (22 Jun 89), Latvia (14 Apr 92), Liechtenstein (77 Jan 92), Mauritius (24 Nov 92), Mexico (22 Feb 91), Monaco (31 Aug 92), Nigeria (13 Mar 91), Norway (2 Jul 90), Panama (22 Feb 91), Poland (20 Mar 92), Romania (27 Feb 91), Saudi Arabia (7 Mar 90), Sri Lanka (28 Aug 92), Sweden (2 Aug 91), Switzerland (31 Jan 90), Syria (22 Jan 92), United Arab Emirates (17 Nov 92), Uruguay (20 Dec 91)

5.7 **BAMAKO CONVENTION ON THE BAN OF IMPORT INTO AFRICA AND THE CONTROL OF TRANSBOUNDARY MOVEMENT AND MANAGEMENT OF HAZARDOUS WASTES WITHIN AFRICA**

Entered into force: Not in force as of 31 December 1992

Signed but not ratified : 20
Benin (30 Jan 91), Burkina Faso (30 Jan 91), Burundi (30 Jan 91), Cameroon (1 Mar 91), Central African Republic (30 Jan 91), Chad (27 Jan 92), Côte d'Ivoire (30 Jan 91), Djibouti (20 Dec 91), Egypt (30 Jan 91), Guinea (30 Nov 91), Guinea–Bissau (1 Mar 91), Lesotho (1 Jun 91), Libya (30 Jan 91), Mali (30 Jan 91), Niger (30 Jan 91), Rwanda (26 Aug 91), Senegal (30 Jan 91), Somalia (1 Jun 91), Tanzania (26 Nov 91), Togo (30 Jan 91)

6. BIOSPHERE

6.1 **CONVENTION ON NATURE PROTECTION AND WILDLIFE PRESERVATION IN THE WESTERN HEMISPHERE**

Entered into force: 1 May 1942

Signed but not ratified: 3
Bolivia (12 Oct 40), Colombia (12 Oct 40), Cuba (12 Oct 40)

Ratified/accepted/approved without qualification: 18
Brazil (26 Aug 65), Chile (4 Dec 67), Costa Rica (12 Jan 67), Dominican Republic (3 Mar 42), Ecuador (20 Oct 44), El Salvador (2 Dec 41), Guatemala (14 Aug 41), Haiti (31 Jan 42), Mexico (27 Mar 42), Nicaragua (22 May 46), Panama (16 Mar 72), Paraguay (30 Jan 81), Peru (26 Nov 46), Suriname (30 Apr 85), Trinidad and Tobago (24 Apr 69), United States (28 Apr 41), Uruguay (9 Apr 70), Venezuela (3 Nov 41)

Ratified/accepted/approved with qualification: 1
Argentina (27 Jun 46)

6.2 **INTERNATIONAL CONVENTION FOR THE REGULATION OF WHALING**

Entered into force: 10 November 1948

Ratified/accepted/approved without qualification: 25
Antigua and Barbuda (21 Jul 82), Australia (1 Dec 47), Brazil (4 Jan 74), Costa Rica (24 Jul 81), Denmark (23 May 50), Finland (23 Feb 83),

India (9 Mar 81), Ireland (2 Jan 85), Japan (21 Apr 51), Kenya (2 Dec 81), Korea (South) (29 Dec 78), Mexico (30 Jun 49), Monaco (15 Mar 82), Netherlands (14 Jun 77), New Zealand (15 Jun 76), Oman (15 Jul 80), Senegal (15 Jul 82), Seychelles (19 Mar 79), South Africa (5 May 48), Spain (6 Jul 79), St. Lucia (29 Jun 81), St. Vincent and the Grenadines (22 Jul 81), Sweden (15 Jun 79), Switzerland (29 May 80), Venezuela (11 Jul 91)

Ratified/accepted/approved with qualification: 11
Argentina (18 May 60), Chile (6 Jul 79), China (24 Sep 80), Ecuador (2 May 91), France (3 Dec 48), Germany (2 Jul 82), Norway (23 Sep 60), Peru (18 Jun 76), Russia (USSR) (11 Sep 48), United Kingdom (17 Jun 47), United States (18 Jul 47)

Denunciations: 9
Belize (30 Jun 88), Canada (30 Jun 82), Dominica (30 Jun 83), Egypt (30 Jun 89), Iceland (30 Jun 92), Jamaica (30 Jun 84), Mauitius (30 Jun 88), Solomon Islands (30 Jun 90), Uruguay (30 Jun 91)

6.3   CONVENTION ON FISHING AND CONSERVATION OF LIVING RESOURCES OF THE HIGH SEAS

Entered into force: 20 March 1966

Signed but not ratified: 21
Afghanistan (30 Oct 58), Argentina (29 Apr 58), Bolivia (17 Oct 58), Canada (29 Apr 58), Costa Rica (29 Apr 58), Cuba (29 Apr 58), Ghana (29 Apr 58), Iceland (29 Apr 58), Indonesia (8 May 58), Iran (28 May 58), Ireland (2 Oct 58), Israel (29 Apr 58), Lebanon (29 May 58), Liberia (27 May 58), Nepal (29 Apr 58), New Zealand (29 Oct 58), Pakistan (31 Oct 58), Panama (2 May 58), Sri Lanka (30 Oct 58), Tunisia (30 Oct 58), Uruguay (29 Apr 58)

Ratified/accepted/approved without qualification: 32
Australia (14 May 63), Belgium (6 Jan 72), Burkina Faso (4 Oct 65), Cambodia (18 Mar 60), Colombia (3 Jan 63), Dominican Republic (11 Aug 64), Fiji (25 Mar 71), Finland (16 Feb 65), France (18 Sep 70), Haiti (29 Mar 60), Jamaica (16 Apr 64), Kenya (20 Jun 69), Lesotho (23 Oct 73), Madagascar (31 Jul 62), Malawi (3 Nov 65), Malaysia (21 Dec 60), Mauritius (5 Oct 70), Mexico (2 Aug 66), Netherlands (18 Feb 66), Nigeria (26 Jun 61), Portugal (8 Jan 63), Senegal (25 Apr 61), Sierra Leone (13 Mar 62), Solomon Islands (3 Sep 81), South Africa (9 Apr 63), Switzerland (18 May 66), Thailand (2 Jul 68), Tonga (29 Jun 71), Trinidad and Tobago (11 Apr 66), Uganda (14 Sep 64), Venezuela (10 Jul 63), Yugoslavia (28 Jan 66)

Ratified/accepted/approved with qualification: 4
Denmark (26 Sep 68), Spain (25 Feb 71), United Kingdom (14 Mar 60), United States (12 Apr 61)

6.4   AFRICAN CONVENTION ON THE CONSERVATION OF NATURE AND NATURAL RESOURCES

Entered into force: 16 June 1969

Signed but not ratified: 12
Benin (15 Sep 68), Botswana (15 Sep 68), Chad (15 Sep 68), Ethiopia (15 Sep 68), Gambia (15 Sep 68), Guinea (15 Sep 68), Lesotho (15 Sep 68), Libya (15 Sep 68), Mauritania (15 Sep 68), Mauritiua (15 Sep 68), Sierra Leone (15 Sep 68), Somalia (15 Sep 68)

Ratified/accepted/approved without qualification: 30

Algeria (25 May 83), Burkina Faso (29 Aug 69), Cameroon (29 Sep 78), Central African Republic (16 Mar 70), Côte d'Ivoire (15 Jan 69), Djibouti (17 Apr 78), Egypt (12 Apr 72), Gabon (18 Nov 88), Ghana (17 May 69), Kenya (12 May 69), Liberia (22 Nov 78), Madagascar (23 Sep 71), Malawi (6 Mar 73), Malawi (6 Mar 73), Mali (2 Jul 74), Morocco (14 Nov 77), Mozambique (1 Apr 81), Niger (27 Jan 70), Nigeria (7 May 74), Rwanda (4 Feb 80), Senegal (24 Feb 72), Seychelles (14 Oct 77), Sudan (30 Oct 73), Swaziland (7 Apr 69), Tanzania (22 Nov 74), Togo (20 Nov 79), Tunisia (4 Feb 79), Uganda (30 Nov 77), Zaire (14 Oct 76), Zambia (1 May 72)

6.5   **INTERNATIONAL CONVENTION ON INTERNATIONAL TRADE IN ENDANGERED SPECIES OF WILD FAUNA AND FLORA (CITES)**

Entered into force: 1 July 1975

Signed but not ratified: 4

Cambodia (17 Feb 73), Kuwait (9 Apr 74), Lesotho (17 Jul 74), Vietnam (3 Mar 73)

Ratified/accepted/approved without qualification: 90

Afghanistan (30 Oct 85), Algeria (23 Nov 83), Argentina (8 Jan 81), Austria (27 Jan 82), Bahamas (20 Jun 79), Bangladesh (20 Nov 81), Barbados (12 Dec 92), Belgium (3 Oct 83), Belize (19 Aug 86), Benin (28 Feb 84), Bolivia (6 Jul 79), Brazil (6 Aug 75), Burkina Faso (13 Oct 89), Burundi (8 Aug 88), Chad (2 Feb 89), Cameroon (5 Jun 81), Central African Republic (27 Aug 80), China (8 Jan 81), Colombia (31 Aug 81), Congo (31 Jan 83), Costa Rica (30 Jun 75), Cuba (20 Apr 90), Cyprus (18 Oct 74), Djibouti (7 Feb 92), Dominican Republic (17 Dec 86), Ecuador (11 Feb 75), Egypt (4 Jan 78), El Salvador (30 Apr 87), Equatorial Guinea (10 Mar 92), Estonia (22 Jul 92), Ethiopia (5 Apr 89), Finland (10 May 76), Gabon (13 Feb 89), Gambia (26 Aug 77), Ghana (14 Nov 75), Greece (8 Oct 92), Guatemala (7 Nov 79), Guinea (21 Sep 81), Guinea–Bissau (16 May 90), Guyana (27 May 77), Honduras (15 Mar 85), Hungary (29 May 85), India (20 Jul 76), Indonesia (28 Dec 78), Iran (3 Aug 76), Israel (18 Dec 79), Jordan (14 Dec 78), Kenya (13 Dec 78), Liberia (11 Mar 81), Luxembourg (13 Dec 83), Madagascar (20 Aug 75), Malawi (5 Feb 82), Malaysia (20 Oct 77), Mauritius (28 Apr 75), Mexico (2 Jul 91), Monaco (19 Apr 78), Morocco (16 Oct 75), Mozambique (25 Mar 81), Namibia (18 Dec 90), Nepal (18 Jun 75), Netherlands (19 Apr 84), New Zealand (10 May 89), Nicaragua (6 Aug 77), Niger (8 Sep 75), Nigeria (9 May 74), Pakistan (20 Apr 76), Panama (17 Aug 78), Papua New Guinea (12 Dec 75), Paraguay (15 Nov 76), Peru (27 Jun 75), Philippines (18 Aug 81), Poland (12 Dec 89), Portugal (111 Feb 80), Rwanda (20 Oct 80), Senegal (5 Aug 77), Seychelles (8 Feb 77), Somolia (2 Dec 85), Sri Lanka (4 May 82), St. Lucia (15 Dec 82), Sweden (20 Aug 74), Tanzania (29 Nov 79), Togo (23 Oct 78), Trinidad and Tobago (19 Jan 84), Tunisia (10 Jul 74), Uganda (18 Jul 91), United Kingdom (2 Aug 76), Uruguay (2 Apr 75), Vanuatu (12 Jul 89) Venezuela (24 Oct 77), Zaire (20 Jul 76)

Ratified/accepted/approved with qualification: 24

Australia (29 Jul 76), Botswana (14 Nov 77), Canada (10 Apr 75), Chile (14 Feb 75), Denmark (26 Jul 77), France (11 May 78), Germany (22 Mar 76), Japan (6 Aug 80), Liechtenstein (30 Nov 79), Norway (27 Feb 76), Russia (USSR) (9 Sep 76), Singapore (30 Nov 86), South Africa (15 Jul 75), Spain (30 May 86), Sudan (26 Nov 82), Suriname (17 Nov 80), Switzerland (9 Jul 74), Thailand (21 Jan 83), United Arab Emirates (8

Feb 90), United States (14 Jan 74), Zambia (24 Nov 80), Zimbabwe (19 May 81)

6.6 **ENDANGERED SPECIES ACT OF 1973, AS AMENDED**
Enacted: 28 December 1973 (amended 10 November 1978)

6.7 **CONVENTION FOR THE PROHIBITION OF FISHING WITH LONG DRIFTNETS IN THE SOUTH PACIFIC**
Entered into force: 17 May 1991
Signed but not ratified: 10
Australia (2 Feb 90), France (30 Apr 90), Marshall Islands (29 Nov 89), Nauru (13 Feb 90), Niue (29 Nov 89), Palau (29 Nov 89), Solomon Islands (7 Mar 91), Tuvalu (13 Feb 90), United States (14 Nov 90), Vanuatu (13 Feb 90)
Ratified/accepted/approved without qualification: 5
Cook Islands (24 Jan 90), Kiribati (10 Jan 92), Micronesia (20 Dec 90), New Zealand (17 May 91), Tokelau (17 May 91)

6.8 **UNGA RESOLUTION 44/225 ON LARGE-SCALE PELAGIC DRIFTNET FISHING AND ITS IMPACT ON THE LIVING MARINE RESOURCES OF THE WORLD'S OCEANS AND SEAS**
Adopted unanimously: 22 December 1989

6.9 **UNGA RESOLUTION 46/215 ON LARGE-SCALE PELAGIC DRIFTNET FISHING AND ITS IMPACT ON THE LIVING MARINE RESOURCES OF THE WORLD'S OCEANS AND SEAS**
Adopted without recorded vote: 20 December 1991

6.10 **CONVENTION ON BIOLOGICAL DIVERSITY**
Entered into force: Entered into force 29 December 1993
Signed but not ratified: 152
Afghanistan (12 Jun 92), Algeria (13 Jun 92), Angola (12 Jun 92), Antigua and Barbuda (5 Jun 92), Argentina (12 Jun 92), Armenia (13 Jun 92), Australia (5 Jun 92), Austria (13 Jun 92), Azerbaijan (12 Jun 92), Bahamas (12 Jun 92), Bahrain (9 Jun 92), Bangladesh (5 Jun 92), Barbados (12 Jun 92), Belarus (11 Jun 92), Belgium (5 Jun 92), Belize (13 Jun 92), Benin (13 Jun 92), Bhutan (11 Jun 92), Bolivia (13 Jun 92), Botswana (9 Jun 92), Brazil (5 Jun 92), Bulgaria (12 Jun 92), Burkina Faso (12 Jun 92), Burundi (11 Jun 92), Cameroon (14 Jun 92), Cape Verde (12 Jun 92), Central African Republic (12 Jun 92), Chad (12 Jun 92), Chile (13 Jun 92), Colombia (12 Jun 92), Comoros (11 Jun 92), Congo (11 Jun 92), Cook Islands (12 Jun 92), Costa Rica (13 Jun 92), Côte d'Ivoire (10 Jun 92), Croatia (11 Jun 92), Cuba (12 Jun 92), Cyprus (12 Jun 92), Denmark (12 Jun 92), Djibouti (13 Jun 92), Dominican Republic (13 Jun 92), European Economic Community (13 Jun 92), Ecuador (9 Jun 92), Egypt (9 Jun 92), El Salvador (13 Jun 92), Estonia (12 Jun 92), Ethiopia (10 Jun 92), Fiji (9 Oct 92), Finland (5 Jun 92), France (13 Jun 92), Gabon (12 Jun 92), Gambia (12 Jun 92), Germany (12 Jun 92), Ghana (12 Jun 92), Greece (12 Jun 92), Grenada (3 Dec 92), Guatemala (13 Jun 92), Guinea (12 Jun 92), Guinea–Bissau (12 Jun 92), Guyana (13 Jun 92), Haiti (13 Jun 92), Honduras (13 Jun 92), Hungary (13 Jun 92), Iceland (10 Jun 92), India (5 Jun 92), Indonesia (5 Jun 92), Iran (14 Jun 92), Ireland (13 Jun 92), Israel (13

Jun 92), Italy (5 Jun 92), Jamaica (11 Jun 92), Japan (13 Jun 92), Jordan (11 Jun 92), Kazakhstan (9 Jun 92), Kenya (11 Jun 92), Korea (North) (11 Jun 92), Korea (South) (13 Jun 92), Kuwait (9 Jun 92), Latvia (11 Jun 92), Lebanon (12 Jun 92), Lesotho (11 Jun 92), Liberia (12 Jun 92), Libya (29 Jun 92), Liechtenstein (5 Jun 92), Lithuania (11 Jun 92), Luxembourg (9 Jun 92), Madagascar (9 Jun 92), Malawi (10 Jun 92), Malaysia (12 Jun 92), Malta (12 Jun 92), Mauritania (12 Jun 92), Mexico (13 Jun 92), Micronesia (12 Jun 92), Moldova (5 Jun 92), Mongolia (12 Jun 92), Morocco (13 Jun 92), Mozambique (12 Jun 92), Myanmar (11 Jun 92), Namibia (12 Jun 92), Nauru (5 Jun 92), Nepal (12 Jun 92), Netherlands (5 Jun 92), New Zealand (12 Jun 92), Nicaragua (13 Jun 92), Niger (11 Jun 92), Nigeria (13 Jun 92), Norway (9 Jun 92), Oman (10 Jun 92), Pakistan (5 Jun 92), Panama (13 Jun 92), Papua New Guinea (13 Jun 92), Paraguay (12 Jun 92), Peru (12 Jun 92), Philippines (12 Jun 92), Poland (5 Jun 92), Portugal (13 Jun 92), Qatar (11 Jun 92), Romania (5 Jun 92), Russia (13 Jun 92), Rwanda (10 Jun 92), St. Kitts and St. Nevis (12 Jun 92), Samoa (12 Jun 92), San Marino (10 Jun 920, São Tomé and Príncipe (12 Jun 92), Senegal (13 Jun 92), Slovenia (13 Jun 92), Solomon Islands (13 Jun 92), Spain (13 Jun 92), Sudan (9 Jun 92), Suriname (13 Jun 92), Swaziland (12 Jun 92), Sweden (9 Jun 92), Switzerland (12 Jun 92), Thailand (12 Jun 92), Togo (12 Jun 92), Trinidad and Tobago (11 Jun 92), Tunisia (13 Jun 92), Turkey (11 Jun 92), Tuvalu (9 Jun 92), Uganda (12 Jun 92), Ukraine (11 Jun 92), United Arab Emirates (11 Jun 92), United Kingdom (12 Jun 92), Tanzania (12 Jun 92), Uruguay (9 Jun 92), Vanatu (9 Jun 92), Venezuela (12 Jun 92), Yemen (12 Jun 92), Yugoslavia (9 Jun 92), Zaire (11 Jun 92), Zambia (11 Jun 92), Zimbabwe (12 Jun 92)

Ratified/accepted/approved without qualification: 6
Canada (4 Dec 92), Maldives (9 Nov 92), Marshall islands (8 Oct 92), Mauritius (4 Sep 92), Moldova (20 Nov 92), Seychelles (22 Sep 92)

6.11 NON-LEGALLY BINDING AUTHORITATIVE STATEMENT OF PRINCIPLES FOR A GLOBAL CONSENSUS ON THE MANAGEMENT, CONSERVATION AND SUSTAINABLE DEVELOPMENT OF ALL TYPES OF FORESTS
Adopted: 13 June 1992

7. MISCELLANEOUS
Economic Trade/Development

7.1 GENERAL AGREEMENT ON TARIFFS AND TRADE AND PROTOCOL OF PROVISIONAL APPLICATION OF THE GATT
Agreement not entered into force as of 31 December 1992
Protocol entered into force: 1 January 1948
GATT Parties: 103
Antigua (30 Mar 87), Argentina (11 Oct 67), Australia (1 Jan 48), Austria (19 Oct 51), Bangladesh (16 Dec 72), Barbados (15 Feb 67), Belgium (1 Jan 48), Belize (21 Sep 81), Benin (12 Sep 63), Bolivia (8 Sep 90), Botswana (28 Aug 87), Brazil (30 Jul 48), Burkina Faso (3 May 63), Burundi (13 Mar 65), Cameroon (3 May 63), Canada (1 Jan 48), Central African Republic (3 May 63), Chad (12 Jul 63), Chile (16 Mar 49), Colombia (3 Oct 81), Congo (3 May 63), Costa Rica (24 Nov 90), Côte d'Ivoire (31 Dec 63), Cuba (1 Jan 48), Cyprus (15 Jul 63), Czechoslo-

vakia (20 Apr 48), Denmark (28 May 50), Dominican Republic (19 May 50), Egypt (9 May 70), El Salvador (22 Apr 91), Finland (25 May 50), France (1 Jan 48), Gabon (3 May 63), Gambia (22 Feb 65), Germany (1 Oct 51), Ghana (17 Oct 57), Greece (1 Mar 50), Guatemala (10 Sep 91), Guyana (5 Jul 66), Haiti (1 Jan 50), Hong Kong (23 Apr 86), Hungary (9 Sep 73), Iceland (21 Apr 68), India (8 Jul 48), Indonesia (24 Feb 50, Ireland (22 Dec 67), Israel (5 Jul 62), Italy (30 May 50), Jamaica (31 Dec 63), Japan (10 Sep 55), Kenya (5 Feb 64), Korea (North) (14 Apr 67), Kuwait (3 May 63), Lesotho (8 Jan 88), Luxembourg (1 Jan 48), Macao (11 Jan 91), Madagascar (30 Sep 63), Malawi (28 Aug 64), Malaysia (24 Oct 57), Maldives (19 Apr 83), Malta (17 Nov 64), Mauritania (30 Sep 63), Mauritius (2 Sep 70), Mexico (24 Aug 86), Morocco (17 Jun 87), Myanmar (29 Jul 48), Netherlands (1 Jan 48), New Zealand (30 Jul 48), Nicaragua (28 May 50), Niger (31 Dec 63), Nigeria (18 Nov 60), Norway (10 Jul 48), Pakistan (30 Jul 48), Peru (7 Oct 51), Philippines (27 Dec 79), Poland (18 Oct 67), Portugal (6 May 62), Romania (14 Nov 71), Rwanda (1 Jan 66), Senegal (27 Sep 63), Sierra Leone (19 May 61), Singapore (20 Aug 73), South Africa (13 Jun 48), Spain (29 Aug 63), Sri Lanka (29 Jul 48), Suriname (22 Mar 78), Sweden (30 Apr 50), Switzerland (1 Aug 66), Tanzania (9 Dec 61), Thailand (20 Nov 82), Togo (20 Mar 64), Trinidad and Tobago (23 Oct 62), Tunisia (19 Aug 90), Turkey (17 Oct 51), Uganda (23 Oct 62), United Kingdom (1 Jan 48), United States (1 Jan 48), Uruguay (16 Dec 53), Yugoslavia (25 Aug 66), Venezuela (31 Aug 90), Zaire (11 Sep 71), Zambia (10 Feb 82), Zimbabwe (11 Jul 48)

7.2 CHARTER OF ECONOMIC RIGHTS AND DUTIES OF STATES

Adopted: 12 December 1974

For: 120
Afghanistan, Albania, Algeria, Argentina, Australia, Bahamas, Bahrain, Bangladesh, Barbados, Belarus (Byelorussian SSR), Benin, Bhutan, Bolivia, Botswana, Brazil, Bulgaria, Burkina Faso, Burundi, Cambodia, Cameroon, Central African Republic, Chad, Chile, China, Colombia, Congo, Costa Rica, Cuba, Cyprus, Czechoslovakia, Dominican Republic, Ecuador, Egypt, El Salvador, Equatorial Guinea, Ethiopia, Fiji, Finland, Gabon, Gambia, Germany (East), Ghana, Greece, Grenada, Guatemala, Guinea, Guinea–Bissau, Guyana, Haiti, Honduras, Hungary, Iceland, India, Indonesia, Iran, Iraq, Ivory Coast, Jamaica, Jordan, Kenya, Kuwait, Laos, Lebanon, Lesotho, Liberia, Libya, Madagascar, Malawi, Malaysia, Mali, Malta, Mauritania, Mauritius, Mozambique, Mexico, Mongolia, Morocco, Myanmar, Nepal, New Zealand, Nicaragua, Niger, Nigeria, Oman, Pakistan, Panama, Paraguay, Peru, Philippines, Poland, Portugal, Qatar, Romania, Russia (USSR), Rwanda, Saudi Arabia, Senegal, Sierra Leone, Singapore, Somalia, Sri Lanka, Sudan, Swaziland, Sweden, Syria, Tanzania, Thailand, Togo, Trinidad and Tobago, Tunisia, Turkey, Uganda, Ukraine (Ukrainian SSR), United Arab Emirates, Uruguay, Venezuela, Yemen, Yugoslavia, Zaire, Zambia

Against: 6
Belgium, Denmark, Germany (West), Luxembourg, Norway, United Kingdom, United States

Abstaining: 10
Austria, Canada, France, Ireland, Israel, Italy, Japan, Netherlands, Norway, Spain

7.3   **DRAFT CODE OF CONDUCT ON TRANSNATIONAL CORPORATIONS**
      Adopted: 1 February 1988

7.4   **FINAL ACT EMBODYING THE RESULTS OF THE URUGUAY ROUND OF MULTILAT-
      ERAL TRADE NEGOTIATIONS: UNDERSTANDING ON RULES AND PROCEDURES
      GOVERNING THE SETTLEMENT OF DISPUTES**
      Adopted: 13 December 1993

Human Rights/Social Justice

7.5   **CONVENTION ON THE PREVENTION AND PUNISHMENT OF THE CRIME OF
      GENOCIDE**
      Entered into force: 12 January 1951
      Signed but not ratified: 3
      Bolivia (11 Feb 48), Dominican Republic (11 Feb 48), Paraguay (11 Feb
      48)
      Ratified/accepted/approved without qualification: 76
      Afghanistan (22 Mar 56), Antigua and Barbuda (25 Oct 88), Australia (8
      Jul 49), Austria (19 Mar 58), Bahamas (5 Aug 75), Barbados (14 Jan
      80), Belgium (5 Sep 51), Bosnia and Herzegovina (29 Dec 92), Brazil (15
      Apr 52), Burkina Faso (14 Sep 65), Cambodia (14 Oct 50), Canada (3
      Sep 52), Chile (3 Jun 53), Colombia (27 Oct 59), Costa Rica (14 Oct 50),
      Croatia (12 Oct 92), Cuba (4 Mar 53), Cyprus (29 Mar 82), Ecuador (21
      Dec 49), Egypt (8 Feb 52), El Salvador (28 Sep 50), Ethiopia (1 Jul 49),
      Fiji (11 Jan 73), France (14 Oct 50), Gabon (21 Jan 83), Gambia (29 Dec
      78), Germany (24 Nov 54), Ghana (24 Dec 58), Greece (8 Dec 54),
      Guatemala (13 Jan 50), Haiti (14 Oct 50), Honduras (5 Mar 52), Iceland
      (29 Aug 49), Iran (14 Aug 56), Iraq (20 Jan 59), Ireland (22 Jun 76),
      Jamaica (23 Sep 68), Jordan (3 Mar 50), Korea (North) (31 Jan 89),
      Korea (South) (14 Oct 50), Lao People's Democratic Republic (8 Dec
      50), Lebanon (17 Dec 53), Lesotho (29 Nov 74), Liberia (9 Jun 50),
      Libya (16 May 89), Luxembourg (7 Oct 81), Maldives (24 Apr 84), Mali
      (16 Jul 79), Monaco (30 Mar 50), Mozambique (18 Apr 83), Nepal (17
      Jan 69), Netherlands (20 Jun 66), New Zealand (28 Dec 78), Nicaragua
      (29 Jan 52), Norway (22 Jul 49), Pakistan (12 Oct 57), Panama (11 Jan
      50), Papua New Guinea (27 Jan 82), Peru (24 Feb 60), St. Vincent and
      the Grenadines (9 Nov 81), Saudi Arabia (13 Jul 50), Senegal (4 Aug
      83), Seychelles (5 May 92), Slovenia (6 Jul 92), Sri Lanka (12 Oct 50),
      Syria (25 Jun 55), Tanzania (5 Apr 84), Togo (24 May 84), Tonga (16
      Feb 72), Tunisia (29 Nov 56), Turkey (31 Jul 50), Uruguay (11 Jul 67),
      Yugoslavia (29 Aug 50), Zaire (31 May 62), Zimbabwe (3 May 91)

      *   Ratification by Cambodia by the "Government of Kampuchea"
          not accepted by Belarus (Byelorussian SSR), Czechoslovakia, Ethi-
          opia, France, Mongolia, Russia (USSR), Ukraine (Ukrainian SSR),
          Vietnam

      Ratified/accepted/approved with qualification: 31
      Albania (12 May 55), Algeria (31 Oct 63), Argentina (5 Jun 56), Bahrain
      (27 Mar 90), Belarus (Byelorussian SSR) (11 Aug 54), Bulgaria (21 Jul
      50), China (18 Apr 83), Czechoslovakia (21 Dec 50), Denmark (15 Jun
      51), Estonia (21 Oct 91), Finland (18 Dec 59), Hungary (7 Jan 52), India
      (27 Aug 49), Israel (9 Mar 50), Italy (4 Jun 52), Mexico (22 Jul 52),
      Mongolia (5 Jan 67), Morocco (24 Jan 58), Myanmar 14 Mar 56),
      Philippines (7 Jul 50), Poland (14 Nov 50), Romania (2 Nov 50), Russia

(USSR) (3 May 54), Rwanda (16 Apr 75), Spain (13 Sep 68), Sweden (27 May 52), Ukraine (Ukrainian SSR) (15 Nov 54), United Kingdom (30 Jan 70), United States (25 Nov 88), Venezuela (12 Jul 60), Vietnam (9 Jun 81), Yemen* (9 Feb 87)

> * Reservation not accepted by Australia, Belgium, Canada, Denmark, Finland, France, Germany (West), Italy, Mexico, Netherlands, New Zealand, Norway, Sweden, United Kingdom

7.6   **UNIVERSAL DECLARATION OF HUMAN RIGHTS**

Adopted: 10 December 1948

For: 48

Afghanistan, Argentina, Australia, Belgium, Bolivia, Brazil, Canada, Chile, China, Colombia, Costa Rica, Cuba, Denmark, Dominican Republic, Ecuador, Egypt, El Salvador, Ethiopia, France, Greece, Guatemala, Haiti, Iceland, India, Iran, Iraq, Lebanon, Liberia, Luxembourg, Mexico, Myanmar, Netherlands, New Zealand, Nicaragua, Norway, Pakistan, Panama, Paraguay, Peru, Philippines, Siam (Thailand), Sweden, Syria, Turkey, United Kingdom, United States, Uruguay, Venezuela

Against: 0

Abstaining: 8

Belarus (Byelorussian SSR), Czechoslovakia, Poland, Russia (USSR), Saudi Arabia, South Africa, Ukraine (Ukrainian SSR), Yugoslavia

7.7   **INTERNATIONAL COVENANT ON ECONOMIC, SOCIAL AND CULTURAL RIGHTS**

Entered into force: 3 January 1976

Signed but not ratified: 3

Israel (19 Feb 66), Liberia (18 Apr 67), United States (5 Oct 77)

Ratified/accepted/approved without qualification: 82

Albania (4 Oct 91), Angola (10 Jan 92), Argentina (8 Aug 86), Australia (10 Dec 75), Austria (10 Sep 78), Azerbaijan (13 Aug 92), Benin (12 Mar 92), Bolivia (12 Aug 82), Brazil (24 Jun 92), Burundi (9 May 90), Cambodia (26 May 92), Cameroon (27 Jun 84), Canada (19 May 76), Central African Republic (8 May 81), Chile (10 Dec 72), Colombia (29 Oct 69), Costa Rica (29 Nov 68), Côte d'Ivoire (26 Mar 92), Croatia (12 Oct 92), Cyprus (2 Apr 69), Dominican Republic (4 Jan 78), Ecuador (6 Mar 69), Egypt (14 Jan 82), El Salvador (30 Nov 79), Equatorial Guinea (25 Sep 87), Estonia (21 Oct 91), Finland (19 Aug 75), Gabon (21 Jan 83), Gambia (29 Dec 78), Germany (17 Dec 73), Greece (16 May 85), Grenada (6 Sep 91), Guatemala (19 May 88), Guinea Bissau (2 Jul 92), Guyana (15 Feb 77), Haiti (6 Feb 91), Honduras (17 Feb 81), Iceland (22 Aug 79), Iran (24 Jun 75), Israel (3 Oct 91), Italy (15 Sep 78), Jamaica (3 Oct 75), Jordan (28 May 75), Korea (North) (14 Sep 81), Korea (South) (10 Apr 90), Latvia (14 Apr 92), Lebanon (13 Jan 72), Lesotho (9 Sep 92), Lithuania (20 Nov 91), Luxembourg (18 Aug 83), Mali (16 Jul 74), Mauritius (12 Dec 73), Morocco (3 May 79), Nepal (14 May 91), Nicaragua (12 Mar 80), Niger (7 Mar 86), Panama (8 Mar 77), Paraguay (10 Jun 92), Peru (28 Apr 78), Philippines (7 Jun 74), Poland (18 Mar 77), San Marino (18 Oct 85), Senegal (13 Feb 78), Seychelles (5 May 92), Slovenia (6 Jul 92), Solomon Islands (17 Mar 82), Somalia (24 Jan 90), Spain (27 Apr 77), Sri Lanka (11 Jun 80), St. Vincent and the Grenadines (9 Nov 81), Sudan (18 Mar 86), Suriname (28 Dec 76), Switzerland (18 Jun 92), Tanzania (11 Jun 76), Togo (24 May 84), Tunisia (18

Mar 69), Uganda (21 Jan 87), Uruguay (1 Apr 70), Venezuela (10 May 78), Yugoslavia (2 Jun 71), Zaire (11 Nov 76), Zimbabwe (13 May 91)

Ratified/accepted/approved with qualification: 38

Afghanistan (24 Jan 83), Algeria * (12 Sep 89), Barbados (5 Jan 73), Belarus (Byelorussian SSR) (12 Nov 73), Belgium (21 Apr 83), Bulgaria (21 Sep 70), Burundi (9 May 90), Congo (5 Oct 83), Czechoslovakia (23 Dec 75), Denmark (6 Jan 72), France (4 Nov 80), Guinea (24 Jan 78), Hungary (17 Jan 74), India ** (10 Apr 79), Iraq (25 Jan 71), Ireland (8 Dec 89), Japan (21 Jun 79), Kenya (1 May 75), Libya (15 May 70), Madagascar (22 Sep 71), Malta (13 Sep 90), Mexico (23 Mar 81), Mongolia (18 Nov 74), Netherlands (11 Feb 78), New Zealand (28 Dec 78), Norway (13 Sep 72), Portugal (31 Jul 78), Romania (9 Dec 74), Russia (USSR) (16 Oct 73), Rwanda (16 Apr 75), Sweden (6 Dec 71), Syria (21 Apr 69), Trinidad and Tobago (8 Dec 78), Ukraine (Ukrainian SSR) (12 Nov 73), United Kingdom (20 May 76), Vietnam (24 Sep 82), Yemen (9 Feb 87), Zambia (10 Apr 84)

   *   Reservation not accepted by Netherlands, Portugal
  **   Reservation not accepted by France, Germany, Netherlands

7.8   **INTERNATIONAL COVENANT ON CIVIL AND POLITICAL RIGHTS**

Entered into force: 23 March 1976

Signed but not ratified: 3

Cambodia (17 Oct 80), Honduras (19 Dec 66), Liberia (18 Apr 67)

Ratified/accepted/approved without qualification: 66

Angola (10 Jan 92), Azerbaijan (13 Aug 92), Benin (12 Mar 92), Bolivia (12 Aug 82), Brazil (24 Jan 92), Burundi (9 May 90), Cambodia (26 May 92), Cameroon (27 Jun 84), Canada (19 May 76), Central African Republic (8 May 81), Chile (10 Dec 72), Colombia (29 Oct 69), Costa Rica (29 Nov 68), Côte d'Ivoire (26 Mar 92), Croatia (12 Oct 92), Cyprus (2 Apr 69), Dominican Republic (4 Jan 78), Ecuador (6 Mar 69), Egypt (14 Jan 82), El Salvador (30 Nov 79), Equatorial Guinea (25 Sep 87), Estonia (21 Oct 91), Gabon (21 Jan 83), Guatemala (5 May 92), Haiti (6 Feb 91), Iran (24 Jun 75), Jamaica (3 Oct 75), Jordan (28 May 75), Kenya (1 May 72), Korea (North) (14 Sep 81), Latvia (14 Apr 92), Lebanon (13 Jan 72), Lesotho (9 Sep 92), Lithuania (20 Nov 91), Madagascar (21 Jun 71), Mali (16 Jul 74), Mauritius (12 Dec 73), Morocco (3 May 79), Netherlands (11 Feb 78), Nicaragua (12 Mar 80), Niger (7 Mar 86), Panama (8 Mar 77), Paraguay (10 Jun 92), Peru (28 Apr 78), Philippines (23 Oct 86), Poland (18 Mar 77), Portugal (15 Jun 78), Rwanda (16 Apr 75), St. Vincent and the Grenadines (9 Nov 81), San Marino (18 Oct 85), Senegal (13 Feb 78), Seychelles (5 May 92), Slovenia (6 Jul 92), Somalia (24 Jan 90), Spain (27 Apr 77), Sri Lanka (11 Jun 80), Sudan (18 Mar 86), Suriname (28 Dec 76), Tanzania (11 Jun 76), Togo (24 May 84), Tunisia (18 Mar 69), Uruguay (1 Apr 70), Yugoslavia (2 Jun 71), Zaire (11 Nov 76), Zambia (10 Apr 84), Zimbabwe (13 May 91)

Ratified/accepted/approved with qualification: 48

Afghanistan (24 Jan 83), Albania (4 Oct 91), Algeria * (12 Sep 89), Argentina (8 Aug 86), Australia (13 Aug 80), Austria (10 Sep 78), Barbados (5 Jan 73), Belarus (Byelorussian SSR) (12 Nov 73), Belgium (21 Apr 83), Bulgaria (21 Sep 70), Congo ** (5 Oct 83), Czechoslovakia (23 Dec 75), Denmark (6 Jan 72), Finland (19 Aug 75), France (4 Nov 80), Gambia (22 Mar 79), Germany (17 Dec 73), Guinea (24 Jan 78), Guyana (15 Feb 77), Hungary (17 Jan 74), Iceland (22 Aug 79),

India *** (10 Apr 79), Iraq (25 Jan 71), Ireland (8 Dec 89), Israel (3 Oct 91), Italy (15 Sep 78), Japan (21 Jun 79), Korea (South) **** (10 Apr 90), Libya (15 May 70), Luxembourg (18 Aug 83), Malta (13 Sep 90), Mexico (23 Mar 81), Mongolia (18 Nov 74), New Zealand (28 Dec 78), Norway (13 Sep 72), Romania (9 Dec 74), Russia (USSR) (16 Oct 73), Sweden (6 Dec 71), Switzerland (18 Jun 92), Syria (21 Apr 69), Trinidad and Tobago ***** (21 Dec 78), Ukraine (Ukrainian SSR) (12 Nov 73), United Kingdom (20 May 76), United States (8 Jun 92), Uruguay (1 Apr 70), Venezuela (10 May 78), Vietnam (24 Sep 82), Yemen (9 Feb 87)

*	Reservation not accepted by Portugal
**	Reservation not accepted by Belgium
***	Reservation not accepted by France
****	Reservation not accepted by Czechoslovakia, Netherlands, United Kingdom
*****	Reservation not accepted by Germany, Netherlands

7.9   FINAL ACT OF THE UNITED NATIONS INTERNATIONAL CONFERENCE ON HUMAN RIGHTS AT TEHERAN

Adopted: 13 May 1968

7.10   AMERICAN CONVENTION ON HUMAN RIGHTS

Entered into force: 18 July 1978

Signed but not ratified: 1
United States (1 Jun 77)

Ratified/accepted/approved without qualification: 13
Bolivia (19 Jul 79), Brazil (25 Sep 92), Colombia (31 Jul 73), Costa Rica (8 Apr 70), Grenada (18 Jul 78), Guatemala (25 May 78), Haiti (27 Sep 77), Honduras (8 Sep 77), Nicaragua (25 Sep 79), Panama (22 Jun 78), Peru (28 Jul 78), Suriname (12 Nov 87), Trinidad (29 May 91)

Ratified/accepted/approved with qualification: 11
Argentina (5 Sep 84), Barbados (5 Nov 81), Chile (21 Aug 90), Dominican Republic (19 Apr 78), Ecuador (28 Dec 77), El Salvador (23 Jun 78), Jamaica (7 Aug 78), Mexico (24 Mar 81), Paraguay (24 Aug 89), Uruguay (19 Apr 85), Venezuela (9 Aug 77)

7.11   DECLARATION ON SOCIAL PROGRESS AND DEVELOPMENT

Adopted: 11 December 1969

For: 119 *

Against: 0

Abstaining: 2

   * Adopted with no roll call vote recorded

7.12   CONVENTION ON THE ELIMINATION OF ALL FORMS OF DISCRIMINATION AGAINST WOMEN

Entered into force: 3 September 1981

Signed but not ratified: 10
Afghanistan (14 Aug 80), Cameroon (6 Jun 83), Côte d'Ivoire (17 Jul 80), Gambia (29 Jul 80), India (30 Jul 80), Lesotho (17 Jul 80), Switzerland (23 Jan 87), United States (17 Jul 80)

Ratified/accepted/approved without qualification: 76

Angola (17 Sep 86), Antigua and Barbuda (1 Aug 89), Barbados (16 Oct 80), Belarus (Byelorussian SSR) (4 Feb 81), Belize (16 May 90), Benin (12 Mar 92), Bhutan (31 Aug 81), Bolivia (30 May 80), Burkina Faso (14 Oct 87), Burundi (8 Jan 92), Cambodia (15 Oct 92), Cape Verde (5 Dec 80), Central African Republic (21 Jun 91), Czechoslovakia (16 Feb 82), Colombia (19 Jan 82), Congo (26 Jul 82), Costa Rica (4 Apr 86), Croatia (9 Sep 92), Denmark (21 Apr 83), Dominica (15 Sep 80), Dominican Republic (2 Sep 82), Ecuador (9 Nov 81), Equatorial Guinea (23 Oct 84), Estonia (21 Oct 91), Finland (4 Sep 86), Gabon (21 Jan 83), Ghana (2 Jan 86), Greece (7 Jun 83), Grenada (30 Aug 90), Guatemala (12 Aug 82), Guinea (9 Aug 82), Guinea–Bissau (23 Aug 85), Guyana (17 Jul 80), Haiti (20 Jul 81), Honduras (3 Mar 83), Iceland (18 Jun 85), Japan (25 Jun 85), Kenya (9 Mar 84), Lao People's Democratic Republic (14 Aug 81), Latvia (14 Apr 92), Liberia (17 Jul 84), Madagascar (17 Mar 89), Malawi (12 Mar 87), Mali (10 Sep 85), Mongolia (20 Jul 81), Namibia (23 Nov 92), Nepal (22 Apr 91), Nicaragua (27 Oct 81), Nigeria (13 Jun 85), Norway (21 May 81), Panama (29 Oct 81), Paraguay (6 Apr 87), Peru (13 Sep 82), Philippines (5 Aug 81), Portugal (30 Jul 80), Russia (USSR) (23 Jan 81),Rwanda (2 Mar 81), Samoa (25 Sep 92), St. Kitts and Nevis (25 Apr 85), St. Lucia (8 Oct 82), St. Vincent and the Grenadines (4 Aug 81), Senegal (5 Feb 85), Seychelles (5 May 92), Sierra Leone (11 Nov 88), Slovenia (6 Jul 92), Sri Lanka (5 Oct 81), Sweden (2 Jul 80), Tanzania (20 Aug 85), Togo (26 Sep 83), Uganda (22 Jul 85), Ukraine (Ukrainian SSR) (12 Mar 81), Uruguay (9 Oct 81), Yugoslavia (26 Feb 82), Zaire (17 Oct 86), Zambia (21 Jun 85), Zimbabwe (13 May 91)

Ratified/accepted/approved with qualification: 47
Argentina (15 Jul 85), Australia (28 Jul 83), Austria (31 Mar 82), Bangladesh * (6 Nov 84), Belgium (10 Jul 85), Brazil * (1 Feb 84), Bulgaria (8 Feb 82), Canada (10 Dec 81), Chile (7 Dec 89), China (4 Nov 80), Cuba (17 Jul 80), Cyprus ****** (23 Jul 85), Egypt * (18 Sep 81), El Salvador (19 Aug 81), Ethiopia (10 Sep 81), France (14 Dec 83), Germany (10 Jul 85), Hungary (22 Dec 80), Indonesia (13 Sep 84), Iraq * 13 Aug 86), Ireland (23 Dec 85), Israel (3 Oct 91), Italy (10 Jun 85), Jamaica * (19 Oct 84), Jordan (1 Jul 92), Korea (South) * (27 Dec 84), Lao People's Democratic Republic (14 Aug 81), Libya ***** (16 May 89), Luxembourg (2 Feb 89), Malawi ** (12 Mar 87), Malta (8 Mar 91), Mauritius * (9 Jul 84), Mexico (23 Mar 81), Netherlands (23 Jul 91), New Zealand **** (10 Jan 85), Poland (30 Jul 80), Romania (7 Jan 82), Spain (5 Jan 84), Sweden (2 Jul 80), Thailand * (9 Aug 85), Trinidad and Tobago (12 Jan 90), Tunisia ** (20 Sep 85), Turkey *** (12 Feb 85), United Kingdom (7 Apr 86), Venezuela (2 May 83), Vietnam (17 Feb 82), Yemen (Democratic) (30 May 84)

*	Reservation not accepted by Germany, Mexico, Netherlands, Sweden
**	Reservation not accepted by Germany, Netherlands, Sweden
***	Reservation not accepted by Mexico, Netherlands
****	Reservation not accepted by Mexico, Sweden
*****	Reservation not accepted by Denmark, Finland, Germany, Mexico, Norway, Netherlands, Sweden
******	Reservation not accepted by Mexico

7.13 DECLARATION ON THE RIGHT TO DEVELOPMENT
Adopted: 4 December 1986

For: 146

Afghanistan, Algeria, Angola, Antigua and Barbuda, Argentina, Australia, Austria, Bahamas, Bahrain, Bangladesh, Barbados, Belarus (Byelorussian SSR), Belgium, Belize, Benin, Bhutan, Bolivia, Botswana, Brazil, Brunei, Bulgaria, Burkina Faso, Burundi, Cambodia, Cameroon, Canada, Cape Verde, Central African Republic, Chad, Chile, China, Colombia, Comoros, Congo, Costa Rica, Côte d'Ivoire, Cuba, Cyprus, Czechoslovakia, Djibouti, Dominican Republic, Ecuador, Egypt, El Salvador, Equatorial Guinea, Ethiopia, Fiji, France, Gabon, Gambia, German Democratic Republic, Ghana, Greece, Grenada, Guatemala, Guinea, Guinea–Bissau, Guyana, Haiti, Honduras, Hungary, India, Indonesia, Iran, Iraq, Ireland, Italy, Jamaica, Jordan, Kenya, Kuwait, Lao People's Democratic Republic, Lebanon, Lesotho, Liberia, Libya, Luxembourg, Madagascar, Malawi, Malaysia, Maldives, Mali, Mauritania, Mauritius, Mexico, Mongolia, Morocco, Mozambique, Myanmar, Nepal, Netherlands, New Zealand, Nicaragua, Niger, Nigeria, Norway, Oman, Pakistan, Panama, Papua New Guinea, Paraguay, Peru, Philippines, Poland, Portugal, Qatar, Romania, Russia (USSR), Rwanda, Samoa, São Tomé and Príncipe, Saudi Arabia, Senegal, Seychelles, Sierra Leone, Singapore, Solomon Islands, Somalia, Spain, Sri Lanka, St. Kitts and Nevis, St. Lucia, St. Vincent and the Grenadines, Sudan, Suriname, Swaziland, Syria, Tanzania, Thailand, Togo, Trinidad and Tobago, Tunisia, Turkey, Uganda, Ukraine (Ukrainian SSR), United Arab Emirates, Uruguay, Vanuatu, Venezuela, Vietnam, Yemen, Yemen (Democratic), Yugoslavia, Zaire, Zambia, Zimbabwe

Against: 1

United States

Abstaining: 8

Denmark, Finland, Germany (West), Iceland, Israel, Japan, Sweden, United Kingdom

7.14 DECLARATION ON THE PRINCIPLES OF INTERNATIONAL CULTURAL CO-OPERATION

Adopted: 4 November 1966

7.15 INTERNATIONAL LABOR ORGANIZATION CONVENTION (No. 169) CONCERNING INDIGENOUS AND TRIBAL PEOPLES IN INDEPENDENT COUNTRIES

Entered into force: 5 September 1991

Ratified/accepted/approved without qualification: 4

Bolivia (11 Dec 91), Colombia (7 Aug 91), Mexico (5 Sep 90), Norway (19 Jun 90)

7.16 CONVENTION ON THE RIGHTS OF THE CHILD

Entered into force: 2 September 1990

Signed but not ratified: 28

Afghanistan (27 Sep 90), Albania (26 Jan 90), Algeria (26 Jan 90), Antigua and Barbuda (21 Mar 91), Austria (26 Jan 90), Cameroon (25 Sep 90), Comoros (30 Sep 90), Gabon (26 Jan 90),Greece (26 Jan 90), Haiti (26 Jan 90), Iran (5 Sep 91), Japan (21 Sep 90), Liberia (26 Apr 90), Liechtenstein (30 Sep 90), Luxembourg (21 Mar 90), Morocco (26 Jan 90), Mozambique (30 Sep 90), Netherlands (26 Jan 90), New Zealand (1 Oct 90), Papua New Guinea (30 Sep 90), St. Lucia (30 Sep 90), Samoa (30 Sep 90), Suriname (26 Jan 90), Swaziland (22 Aug 90),

Switzerland (1 May 91), Syria (18 Sep 90), Turkey (14 Sep 90), Vanuatu (30 Sep 90)

Ratified/accepted/approved without qualification: 86
Angola (5 Dec 90), Azerbaijan (13 Aug 92), Bahrain (13 Feb 92), Barbados (9 Oct 90), Belarus (Byelorussian SSR) (1 Oct 90), Belize (2 May 90), Benin (3 Aug 90), Bhutan (1 Aug 90), Bolivia (26 Jun 90), Brazil (24 Sep 90), Bulgaria (3 Jun 91), Burkina Faso (31 Aug 90), Burundi (19 Oct 90), Cambodia (15 Oct 92), Cape Verde (4 Jun 92), Central African Republic (23 Apr 92), Chad (2 Oct 90), Chile (13 Aug 90), China (2 Mar 92), Costa Rica (21 Aug 90), Côte d'Ivoire (4 Feb 91), Cyprus (7 Feb 91), Dominica (13 Mar 91), Dominican Republic (11 Jun 91), El Salvador (10 Jul 90), Equatorial Guinea (15 Jul 92), Estonia (21 Oct 91), Ethiopia (14 May 91), Finland (20 Jun 91), Gambia (8 Aug 90), Ghana (5 Feb 90), Grenada (5 Nov 90), Guinea (13 Jul 90), Guinea–Bissau (20 Jul 90), Guyana (14 Jan 91), Honduras (10 Aug 90), Hungary (7 Oct 91), Ireland (28 Sep 92), Israel (3 Oct 91), Italy (5 Sep 91), Jamaica (14 May 91), Kenya (30 Jul 90), Korea (North) (21 Sep 90), Lao People's Democratic Republic (8 May 91), Latvia (14 Apr 92), Lebanon (14 May 91), Lesotho (10 Mar 92), Lithuania (31 Jan 92), Madagascar (19 Mar 91), Malawi (2 Jan 91), Mexico (21 Sep 90), Mongolia (5 Jul 90), Namibia (30 Sep 90), Nepal (14 Sep 90), Nicaragua (5 Oct 90), Niger (30 Sep 90), Nigeria (19 Apr 91), Panama (12 Dec 90), Paraguay (25 Sep 90), Peru (4 Sep 90), Philippines (21 Aug 90), Portugal (21 Sep 90), Romania (28 Sep 90), Russia (USSR) (16 Aug 90), Rwanda (28 Sep 90), St. Kitts and Nevis (24 Jul 90), San Marino (25 Nov 91), São Tomé and Príncipe (14 May 91), Senegal (30 Jul 90), Seychelles (7 Sep 90), Sierra Leone (18 Jun 90), Slovenia (6 Jul 92), Sri Lanka (12 Jul 91), Sudan (3 Aug 90), Sweden (29 Jun 90), Thailand (27 Mar 92), Togo (1 Aug 90), Trinidad and Tobago (5 Dec 91), Uganda (17 Aug 90), Ukraine (28 Aug 91), Tanzania (10 Jun 91), Vietnam (28 Feb 90), Yemen (1 May 91), Zaire (27 Sep 90), Zambia (6 Dec 91), Zimbabwe (11 Sep 90)

Ratified/accepted/approved with qualification: 37
Argentina (4 Dec 90), Australia (17 Dec 90), Bahamas (20 Feb 91), Bangladesh (3 Aug 90), Belgium (16 Dec 91), Canada (13 Dec 91), Colombia (28 Jan 91), Croatia (12 Oct 92), Cuba (21 Aug 91), Czechoslovakia (7 Jan 91), Denmark (19 Jul 91), Djibouti ** (6 Dec 90), Ecuador (23 Mar 90), Egypt (6 Jul 90), France (7 Aug 90), Germany (6 Mar 92), Guatemala (6 Jun 90), Holy See (20 Apr 90), Iceland (28 Oct 92), Indonesia (5 Sep 90), Jordan (24 May 91), Korea (South) (21 Sep 90), Kuwait *** (21 Oct 91), Maldives (11 Feb 91), Mali (20 Sep 90), Malta (30 Sep 90), Mauritius (26 Jul 90), Myanmar (15 Jul 91), Norway (8 Jan 91), Pakistan * (12 Nov 90), Poland (7 Jun 91), Spain (6 Dec 90), Tunisia (30 Jan 92), United Kingdom (16 Dec 91), Uruguay (20 Nov 90), Venezuela (13 Sep 90), Yugoslavia (3 Jan 91)

   *   Reservation not accepted by Finland, Norway, Sweden
   **   Reservation not accepted by Norway
   ***   Reservation not accepted by Czechoslovakia

7.17 **DRAFT DECLARATION ON THE RIGHTS OF INDIGENOUS PEOPLES AS AGREED UPON BY THE MEMBERS OF THE WORKING GROUP ON INDIGENOUS PEOPLES AT ITS ELEVENTH SESSION**

Adopted: 23 August 1993

War/Peace

7.18 CONVENTION (NO. IV) RESPECTING THE LAWS AND CUSTOMS OF WAR ON LAND, WITH ANNEX OF REGULATIONS

Entered into force: 26 January 1910

Signed but not ratified: 15

Argentina (18 Oct 07), Bulgaria (18 Oct 07), Chile (18 Oct 07), Colombia (18 Oct 07), Ecuador (18 Oct 07), Greece (18 Oct 07), Italy (18 Oct 07), Montenegro (18 Oct 07), Paraguay (18 Oct 07), Persia (Iran) (18 Oct 07), Peru (18 Oct 07), Serbia (18 Oct 07), Turkey (18 Oct 07), Uruguay (18 Oct 07), Venezuela (18 Oct 07)

Ratified/accepted/approved without qualification: 33

Belgium (8 Aug 10), Bolivia (27 Nov 09), Brazil (5 Jan 14), Belarus (Byelorussian SSR) (4 Jun 62), China (10 May 17), Cuba (22 Feb 12), Denmark (27 Nov 09), Dominican Republic (16 May 58), El Salvador (27 Nov 09), Ethiopia (5 Aug 35), Fiji (2 Apr 73), Finland (30 Dec 18), France (7 Oct 10) German Democratic Republic (9 Feb 59), Guatemala (15 May 11), Haiti (2 Feb 10), Liberia (4 Feb 14), Luxembourg (5 Sep 12), Mexico (27 Nov 09), Netherlands (27 Nov 09), Nicaragua (16 Dec 09), Norway (19 Sep 10), Panama (11 Sep 11), Poland (9 May 25), Portugal (13 Apr 11), Romania (1 Mar 12), Russia (USSR) (7 Mar 55), Siam (Thailand) (12 Mar 10), South Africa (10 Mar 78), Sweden (27 Oct 09), Switzerland (12 May 10), United Kingdom (27 Nov 09), United States (27 Nov 09)

Ratified/accepted/approved with qualification: 4

Austria–Hungary (27 Nov 09), Germany (27 Nov 09), Japan (13 Dec 11), Russia (27 Nov 09)

7.19 GENEVA CONVENTION (NO. IV) RELATIVE TO THE PROTECTION OF CIVILIAN PERSONS IN TIME OF WAR

Entered into force: 21 October 1950

Ratified/accepted/approved without qualification: 138

Afghanistan (26 Sep 56), Algeria (20 Jun 60), Antigua and Barbuda (6 Oct 86), Austria (27 Aug 53), Bahamas (11 Jul 75), Bahrain (30 Nov 71), Bangladesh (4 Apr 72), Belgium (3 Sep 52), Belize (29 Jun 84), Benin (14 Dec 61), Bhutan, Bolivia (10 Dec 76), Bosnia and Herzegovina (92), Botswana (29 Mar 68), Burkina Faso (7 Nov 61), Burundi (27 Dec 71), Cambodia (8 Dec 58), Cameroon (16 Sep 63), Cape Verde (11 May 84), Central African Republic (1 Aug 66), Chad (5 Aug 70), Chile (12 Oct 50), Colombia (8 Nov 61), Comoros (21 Nov 85), Congo (30 Jan 67), Costa Rica (15 Oct 69), Côte d'Ivoire (28 Dec 61), Croatia (92), Cuba (15 Apr 54), Cyprus (23 May 62), Denmark (27 Jun 51), Djibouti (26 Jan 78), Dominica (28 Sep 81), Dominican Republic (22 Jan 58), Ecuador (11 Aug 54), Egypt (10 Nov 52), El Salvador (17 Jun 53), Equatorial Guinea (24 Jun 86), Ethiopia (2 Oct 69), Fiji (9 Aug 71), Finland (22 Feb 55), France (28 Jun 51), Gabon (20 Feb 65), Gambia (11 Oct 66), Ghana (2 Aug 58), Greece (5 Jun 56), Grenada (13 Apr 81), Guatemala (14 May 52), Guinea (11 Jul 84), Guyana (22 Jul 68), Haiti (11 Apr 57), Holy See (22 Feb 51), Honduras (31 Dec 65), Iceland (10 Aug 65), India (9 Nov 50), Indonesia (30 Sep 58), Iraq (14 Feb 56), Ireland (27 Sep 62), Jamaica (17 Jul 64), Japan (21 Apr 53), Jordan (29 May 51), Kazakhstan (5 May 92), Kenya (20 Sep 66), Kiribati (5 Jan 89), Kyrgyzstan (18 Sep 92), Lao People's Democratic Republic (29 Oct 56), Latvia (92), Lebanon (10 Apr 51), Lesotho (20 May 68), Liberia (29 Mar 54), Libya

(22 May 56), Liechtenstein (21 Sep 50), Madagascar (13 Jul 63), Malawi
(5 Jan 68), Malaysia (24 Aug 62), Mali (24 May 65), Malta (22 Aug 68),
Mauritania (27 Oct 62), Mauritius (18 Aug 70), Mexico (29 Oct 52),
Monaco (5 Jul 50), Mongolia (12 Feb 58), Morocco (26 Jul 56), Mozam-
bique (14 Mar 83), Myanmar (25 Aug 92), Namibia * (18 Oct 83), Nepal
(7 Feb 64), Nicaragua (17 Dec 53), Niger (16 Apr 64), Nigeria (9 Jun
61), Norway (3 Aug 51), Oman (31 Jan 74), Panama (10 Feb 56), Papua
New Guinea (26 May 76), Paraguay (23 Oct 61), Peru (15 Feb 56),
Philippines (7 Mar 51), Qatar (15 Oct 75), Rwanda (21 Mar 64), St.
Kitts and Nevis (14 Feb 86), St. Lucia (18 Sep 81), St. Vincent and the
Grenadines (1 Apr 81), Samoa (23 Aug 84), San Marino (29 Aug 53),
São Tomé and Príncipe (21 May 76), Saudi Arabia (18 May 63), Senegal
(23 Apr 63), Seychelles (8 Nov 84), Sierra Leone (31 May 65), Singapore
(27 Apr 73), Slovenia (92), Solomon Islands (6 Jul 81), Somalia (12 Jul
62), South Africa (31 Mar 52), Sri Lanka (28 Feb 59), Sudan (23 Sep
57), Swaziland (28 Jun 73), Sweden (28 Dec 53), Switzerland (31 Mar
50), Syria (2 Nov 53), Tanzania (12 Dec 62), Thailand (29 Dec 54), Togo
(6 Jan 62), Tonga (13 Apr 78), Trinidad and Tobago (17 May 63),
Tunisia (4 May 57), Turkey (10 Feb 54), Turkmenistan (10 Apr 92),
Tuvalu (19 Feb 81), Uganda (18 May 64), United Arab Emirates (10
May 72), Vanuatu (27 Oct 82), Venezuela (13 Feb 56), Yemen (16 Jul
70), Zaire (20 Feb 61), Zambia (19 Oct 66), Zimbabwe (7 Mar 83)

    *   The acceptance by Namibia was by the UN Council for Namibia.
South Africa does not recognize Namibia's acceptance as having
any legal effect.

Ratified/accepted/approved with qualification: 36
Albania (27 May 57), Angola (20 Sep 84), Argentina (18 Sep 56),
Australia (14 Oct 58), Barbados (10 Sep 68), Belarus (Byelorussian SSR)
(3 Aug 54), Brazil (29 Jun 57), Bulgaria (22 Jul 54), Canada (14 May
65), China (28 Dec 56), Czechoslovakia (19 Dec 50), German Democratic
Republic (30 Nov 56), Germany (3 Sep 54), Guinea–Bissau (2 Feb 74),
Hungary (3 Aug 54), Iran (20 Feb 57), Israel (6 Jul 51), Italy (17 Dec
51), Korea (North) (27 Aug 57), Korea (South) (16 Aug 66), Kuwait (2
Sep 67), Luxembourg (1 Jul 53), Netherlands (3 Aug 54), New Zealand
(2 May 59), Pakistan (12 Jun 51), Poland (26 Nov 54), Portugal (14 Mar
61), Romania (1 Jun 54), Russia (USSR) (10 May 54), Spain (4 Aug 52),
Suriname (13 Oct 76), Ukraine (Ukrainian SSR) (3 Aug 54), United
Kingdom (23 Sep 57), United States (2 Aug 55), Uruguay (5 Mar 69),
Vietnam (28 Jun 57), Yemen (Democratic) (25 May 77), Yugoslavia (21
Apr 50)

7.20   **PRINCIPLES OF INTERNATIONAL LAW RECOGNIZED IN THE CHARTER OF THE
NUREMBERG TRIBUNAL AND IN THE JUDGMENT OF THE TRIBUNAL**
     Adopted: 2 August 1950

7.21   **DRAFT ARTICLES ON THE DRAFT CODE OF CRIMES AGAINST THE PEACE AND
SECURITY OF MANKIND**
     First adopted: 4 December 1954

7.22   **TREATY ON THE NON-PROLIFERATION OF NUCLEAR WEAPONS**
     Entered into force: 5 March 1970
     Ratified/accepted/approved without qualification: 148 *
Afghanistan (4 Feb 70), Albania (12 Sep 90), Antigua and Barbuda (4
Nov 81), Australia (23 Jan 73), Austria (27 Jun 69), Bahamas (11 Aug

76), Bangladesh (31 Aug 79), Barbados (21 Feb 80), Belgium (2 May 75), Belize (9 Sep 82), Benin (31 Oct 72), Bhutan (23 May 85), Bolivia (26 May 70), Botswana (28 Apr 69), Brunei (26 Mar 85), Bulgaria (5 Sep 69), Burkina Faso (3 Mar 70), Burundi (19 Mar 71), Cambodia (2 Jun 72), Cameroon (8 Jan 69), Canada (8 Jan 69), Cape Verde (24 Oct 79), Central African Republic (25 Oct 70), Chad (10 Mar 71), China (9 Mar 92), Colombia (8 Apr 86), Congo (23 Oct 78), Costa Rica (3 Mar 70), Côte d'Ivoire (6 Mar 73), Cyprus (10 Feb 70), Czechoslovakia (22 Jul 69), Denmark (3 Jan 69), Dominica (10 Aug 84), Dominican Republic (24 Jul 71), Ecuador (7 Mar 69), Egypt (26 Feb 81), El Salvador (11 Jul 72), Equatorial Guinea (1 Nov 84), Estonia (7 Jan 92), Ethiopia (5 Feb 70), Fiji (14 Jul 72), Finland (5 Feb 69), Gabon (19 Feb 74), Gambia (12 May 75), Germany (2 May 75), Ghana (4 May 70), Greece (11 Mar 70), Grenada (9 Sep 75), Guatemala (22 Sep 70), Guinea (29 Apr 85), Guinea–Bissau (20 Aug 76), Haiti (2 Jun 70), Holy See (25 Feb 71), Honduras (16 May 73), Hungary (27 May 69), Iceland (18 Jul 69), Indonesia (12 Jul 79), Iran (2 Feb 70), Iraq (29 Oct 69), Ireland (1 Jul 68), Italy (2 May 75), Jamaica (5 Mar 70), Japan (8 Jun 76), Jordan (11 Feb 70), Kenya (11 Jun 70), Kiribati (18 Apr 85), Korea (North) (12 Dec 85), Korea (South) (23 Apr 75), Lao People's Democratic Republic (20 Feb 70), Latvia (31 Jan 92), Lebanon (15 Jul 70), Lesotho (20 May 70), Liberia (5 Mar 70), Libya (26 May 75), Liechtenstein (20 Apr 78), Lithuania (23 Sep 91), Luxembourg (2 May 75), Madagascar (8 Oct 70), Malawi (18 Feb 86), Malaysia (5 Mar 70), Maldive Islands (7 Apr 70), Mali (10 Feb 70), Malta (6 Feb 70), Mauritius (8 Apr 69), Mexico (21 Jan 69), Mongolia (14 May 69), Morocco (27 Nov 70), Mozambique (12 Sep 90), Myanmar (2 Dec 92), Nauru (7 Jun 82), Nepal (5 Jan 70), Netherlands (2 May 75), New Zealand (10 Sep 69), Nicaragua (6 Mar 73), Nigeria (27 Sep 68), Norway (5 Feb 69), Panama (13 Jul 77), Papua New Guinea (13 Jan 82), Paraguay (4 Feb 70), Peru (3 Mar 70), Philippines (5 Oct 72), Poland (12 Jun 69), Portugal (15 Dec 77), Qatar (3 Apr 89), Romania (4 Feb 70), Russia (USSR) (5 Mar 70), Rwanda (20 May 75), St. Lucia (28 Dec 79), St. Vincent and the Grenadines (6 Nov 84), Samoa (17 Mar 75), San Marino (10 Aug 70), São Tomé and Príncipe (20 Jul 83), Saudi Arabia (3 Oct 88), Senegal (17 Dec 70), Seychelles (8 Apr 85), Sierra Leone (26 Feb 75), Singapore (10 Mar 76), Solomon Islands (17 Jun 81), Somalia (5 Mar 70), South Africa (10 Jul 91), Spain (5 Nov 87), Sri Lanka (5 Mar 79), Sudan (31 Oct 73), Suriname (30 Jun 76), Swaziland (11 Dec 69), Sweden (9 Jan 70), Switzerland (9 Mar 77), Syria (24 Sep 69), Tanzania (7 Jul 91), Thailand (7 Dec 72), Taiwan (27 Jan 70), Togo (26 Feb 70), Tonga (14 Jul 71), Trinidad and Tobago (30 Oct 86), Tunisia (26 Feb 70), Turkey (17 Apr 80), Tuvalu (11 Jan 79), Uganda (20 Oct 82), United Kingdom (27 Nov 68), United States (5 Mar 70), Uruguay (31 Aug 70), Venezuela (25 Sep 75), Vietnam (14 Jun 72), Yemen (1 Jun 79), Yugoslavia (5 Mar 70), Zaire (4 Aug 70), Zambia (14 May 91)

Ratified/accepted/approved with qualification: 2
Bahrain (13 Jan 88), Kuwait (17 Nov 89)

* The United States considers St. Kitts and Nevis as being "bound by the obligations in the treaty" on the basis of a general declaration of succession deposited with the United Nations Secretary General

7.23 CONVENTION ON THE PROHIBITION OF MILITARY OR ANY OTHER HOSTILE USE OF ENVIRONMENTAL MODIFICATION TECHNIQUES (ENMOD)

Entered into force: 5 October 1978

Signed but not ratified: 17

Bolivia (18 May 77), Ethiopia (18 May 77), Holy See (27 May 77), Iceland (18 May 77), Iran (18 May 77), Iraq (15 Aug 77), Lebanon (18 May 77), Liberia (18 May 77), Luxembourg (18 May 77), Morocco (18 May 77), Nicaragua (11 Aug 77), Portugal (18 May 77), Sierra Leone (12 Apr 78), Syria (4 Aug 77), Turkey (18 May 77), Uganda (18 May 77), Zaire (28 Feb 78)

Ratified/accepted/approved without qualification: 45

Afghanistan (22 Oct 85), Algeria (19 Dec 91), Antigua and Barbuda (25 Oct 88), Australia (7 Sep 84), Bangladesh (3 Oct 79), Belarus (Byelorussian SSR) (7 Jun 88), Belgium (12 Jul 82), Benin (30 Jun 86), Brazil (12 Oct 84), Bulgaria (31 May 78), Canada (11 Jun 81), Cape Verde (3 Oct 79), Cuba (10 Apr 78), Cyprus (12 Apr 78), Czechoslovakia (12 May 78), Denmark (19 Apr 78), Dominica (9 Nov 92), Egypt (1 Apr 82), Finland (12 May 78), Germany (24 May 83), Ghana (22 Jun 78), Greece (23 Aug 83), Hungary (19 Apr 78), India (15 Dec 78), Ireland (16 Dec 82), Italy (27 Nov 81), Japan (9 Jun 82), Korea (North) (8 Nov 84), Lao People's Democratic Republic (5 Oct 78), Malawi (5 Oct 78), Mongolia (19 May 78), Norway (15 Feb 79), Pakistan (27 Feb 86), Papua New Guinea (28 Oct 80), Poland (8 Jun 78), Romania (6 May 83), São Tomé and Príncipe (5 Oct 79), Solomon Islands (19 Jun 81), Spain (19 Jul 78), Sri Lanka (25 Apr 78), Sweden (27 Apr 84), Tunisia (11 May 78), Ukraine (Ukrainian SSR) (13 Jun 78), Vietnam (26 Aug 80), Yemen (20 Jul 77)

Ratified/accepted/approved with qualification: 12

Argentina (20 Mar 87), Austria (17 Jan 90), Guatemala (21 Mar 88), Korea (South) (2 Dec 86), Kuwait (2 Jan 80) *, Netherlands (15 Apr 83), New Zealand (7 Sep 84), Russia (USSR) (30 May 78), Switzerland (5 Aug 88), United Kingdom (16 May 78), United States (17 Jan 80)

    *   Reservation not accepted by Israel

7.24   PROTOCOL ADDITIONAL TO THE GENEVA CONVENTIONS OF AUGUST **12, 1949,** AND RELATING TO THE PROTECTION OF VICTIMS OF INTERNATIONAL ARMED CONFLICTS

Entered into force: 7 December 1978

Signed but not ratified: 16

Egypt (12 Dec 77), Honduras (12 Dec 77), Iran (12 Dec 77), Ireland (12 Dec 77), Madagascar (13 Oct 78), Mongolia (12 Dec 77), Morocco (12 Dec 77), Nicaragua (12 Dec 77), Pakistan (12 Dec 77), Panama (12 Dec 77), Philippines (12 Dec 77), Poland (12 Dec 77), Portugal (12 Dec 77), San Marino (22 Jun 78), United Kingdom (12 Dec 77), United States (12 Dec 77)

Ratified/accepted/approved without qualification: 80

Antigua and Barbuda (5 Oct 86), Bahamas (10 Apr 80), Bahrain (30 Oct 86), Bangladesh (8 Sep 80), Barbados (19 Feb 90), Belarus (Byelorussian SSR) (23 Oct 89), Belize (29 Jun 84), Benin (28 May 86), Bolivia (8 Dec 83), Botswana (23 May 79), Brunei (14 Oct 91), Bulgaria (26 Sep 89), Burkina Faso (20 Oct 87), Cameroon (16 Mar 84), Central African Republic (17 Jul 84), Chile (24 Apr 91), Comoros (21 Nov 85), Congo (10 Nov 83), Costa Rica (15 Dec 83), Côte d'Ivoire (20 Sep 89), Cuba (25 Nov 82), Cyprus (1 Jun 79), Czechoslovakia (14 Feb 90), Djibouti (8 Apr 91), Ecuador (10 Apr 79), El Salvador (23 Nov 78), Equatorial Guinea (24 Jul 86), Gabon (8 Apr 80), Gambia (12 Jan 89), Ghana (28 Feb 78),

Greece (31 Mar 89), Guatemala (19 Oct 87), Guinea (11 Jul 84), Guinea–Bissau (21 Oct 86), Guyana (18 Jan 88), Hungary (12 Apr 89), Iceland (10 Apr 87), Jamaica (29 Jul 86), Jordan (1 May 79), Korea (North) (9 Mar 88), Kuwait (17 Jan 85), Lao People's Democratic Republic (18 Nov 80), Liberia (30 Jun 88), Libya (7 Jun 78), Luxembourg (29 Aug 89), Malawi (7 Oct 91), Maldives (3 Sep 91), Mali (8 Feb 89), Mauritania (14 Mar 80), Mauritius (22 Mar 82), Mexico (10 Mar 83), Mozambique (14 Mar 83), Namibia (18 Oct 83), Netherlands (26 Jun 87), Niger (8 Jun 79), Nigeria (10 Oct 88), Paraguay (30 Nov 90), Peru (14 Jul 89), Romania (21 Jun 90), Rwanda (19 Nov 84), St. Kitts and Nevis (14 Feb 86), St. Lucia (7 Oct 82), St. Vincent and the Grenadines (8 Apr 83), Samoa (23 Aug 84), Senegal (7 May 85), Seychelles (8 Nov 84), Sierra Leone (21 Oct 86), Solomon Islands (19 Sep 88), Spain (7 Nov 78), Suriname (16 Dec 85), Tanzania (15 Feb 83), Togo (21 Jun 84), Tunisia (9 Aug 79), Uganda (13 Mar 91), Ukraine (Ukrainian SSR) (25 Jan 90), Uruguay (13 Dec 85), Vanuatu (28 Feb 85), Vietnam (19 Oct 81), Yemen (12 Apr 90), Zaire (3 Jun 82)

Ratified/accepted/approved with qualification: 28
Algeria (16 Aug 89), Angola (20 Sep 84), Argentina (26 Nov 86), Australia (21 Jun 91), Austria (13 Aug 82), Belgium (20 May 86), Canada (20 Nov 90), China (14 Sep 83), Denmark (17 Jun 82), Finland (7 Aug 80), Germany (14 Feb 91), Holy See (21 Nov 85), Italy (27 Feb 86), Korea (South) (15 Jan 82), Liechtenstein (10 Aug 89), Malta (17 Apr 89), New Zealand (8 Feb 88), Norway (14 Dec 81), Oman (29 Mar 84), Qatar (5 Apr 88), Russia (USSR) (29 Sep 89), Saudi Arabia (21 Aug 87), Spain (21 Apr 89), Sweden (31 Aug 79), Switzerland (17 Feb 82), Syria (14 Nov 83), United Arab Emirates (9 Mar 83), Yugoslavia (11 Jun 79)

7.25 **SOUTH PACIFIC NUCLEAR FREE ZONE TREATY**

Entered into force: 11 December 1986

Ratified/accepted/approved without qualification: 11
Australia (11 Feb 86), Cook Islands (28 Oct 85), Fiji (4 Oct 85), Kiribati (28 Oct 86), Nauru (13 Apr 87), New Zealand (13 Nov 86), Niue (12 May 86), Papua New Guinea (89), Samoa (20 Oct 86), Solomon Islands (27 Jan 89), Tuvalu (16 Jan 86)

7.26 **UNSC RESOLUTION 687 (CONCERNING THE RESTORATION OF PEACE AND SECURITY IN IRAQ AND KUWAIT)**

Adopted: 3 April 1991

For: 12
Austria, Belgium, China, Côte d'Ivoire, France, India, Romania, Russia (USSR), United Kingdom, United States, Zaire, Zimbabwe

Against: 1
Cuba

Abstaining: 2
Ecuador, Yemen

†